American Casebook Series
Hornbook Series and Basic Legal Texts
Nutshell Series

of

WEST PUBLISHING COMPANY
P.O. Box 3526
St. Paul, Minnesota 55165
June, 1982

ACCOUNTING

Fiflis and Kripke's Teaching Materials on Accounting for Business Lawyers, 2nd Ed., 684 pages, 1977 (Casebook)

ADMINISTRATIVE LAW

Davis' Cases, Text and Problems on Administrative Law, 6th Ed., 683 pages, 1977 (Casebook)

Davis' Basic Text on Administrative Law, 3rd Ed., 617 pages, 1972 (Text)

Davis' Police Discretion, 176 pages, 1975 (Text)

Gellhorn and Boyer's Administrative Law and Process in a Nutshell, 2nd Ed., 445 pages, 1981 (Text)

Mashaw and Merrill's Introduction to the American Public Law System, 1095 pages, 1975, with 1980 Supplement (Casebook)

Robinson, Gellhorn and Bruff's The Administrative Process, 2nd Ed., 959 pages, 1980 (Casebook)

ADMIRALTY

Healy and Sharpe's Cases and Materials on Admiralty, 875 pages, 1974 (Casebook)

AGENCY—PARTNERSHIP

Fessler's Alternatives to Incorporation for Persons in Quest of Profit, 258 pages, 1980 (Casebook)

Henn's Cases and Materials on Agency, Partnership and Other Unincorporated Business Enterprises, 396 pages, 1972 (Casebook)

Reuschlein and Gregory's Hornbook on the Law of Agency and Partnership, 625 pages, 1979, with 1981 pocket part (Text)

AGENCY—PARTNERSHIP—Continued

Seavey's Hornbook on Agency, 329 pages, 1964 (Text)

Seavey and Hall's Cases on Agency, 431 pages, 1956 (Casebook)

Seavey, Reuschlein and Hall's Cases on Agency and Partnership, 599 pages, 1962 (Casebook)

Selected Corporation and Partnership Statutes and Forms, approximately 775 pages, 1982

Steffen and Kerr's Cases and Materials on Agency-Partnership, 4th Ed., 859 pages, 1980 (Casebook)

Steffen's Agency-Partnership in a Nutshell, 364 pages, 1977 (Text)

AMERICAN INDIAN LAW

Canby's American Indian Law in a Nutshell, 288 pages, 1981 (Text)

Getches, Rosenfelt and Wilkinson's Cases on Federal Indian Law, 660 pages, 1979 (Casebook)

ANTITRUST LAW

Gellhorn's Antitrust Law and Economics in a Nutshell, 2nd Ed., 425 pages, 1981 (Text)

Oppenheim, Weston and McCarthy's Cases and Comments on Federal Antitrust Laws, 4th Ed., 1168 pages, 1981 (Casebook)

Posner and Easterbrook's Cases and Economic Notes on Antitrust, 2nd Ed., 1077 pages, 1981 (Casebook)

Sullivan's Hornbook of the Law of Antitrust, 886 pages, 1977 (Text)

See also Regulated Industries, Trade Regulation

LAW SCHOOL PUBLICATIONS—Continued

BANKING LAW

See Regulated Industries

BUSINESS PLANNING

Epstein and Scheinfeld's Teaching Materials on Business Reorganization Under the Bankruptcy Code, 216 pages, 1980 (Casebook)

Painter's Problems and Materials in Business Planning, 791 pages, 1975, with 1982 Supplement (Casebook)

Selected Securities and Business Planning Statutes, Rules and Forms, approximately 490 pages, 1982

CIVIL PROCEDURE

Casad's Res Judicata in a Nutshell, 310 pages, 1976 (text)

Cound, Friedenthal and Miller's Cases and Materials on Civil Procedure, 3rd Ed., 1147 pages, 1980 with 1982 Supplement (Casebook)

Cound, Friedenthal and Miller's Cases on Pleading, Joinder and Discovery, 643 pages, 1968 (Casebook)

Ehrenzweig, Louisell and Hazard's Jurisdiction in a Nutshell, 4th Ed., 232 pages, 1980 (Text)

Federal Rules of Civil-Appellate-Criminal Procedure—West Law School Edition, approximately 350 pages, 1982

Hodges, Jones and Elliott's Cases and Materials on Texas Trial and Appellate Procedure, 2nd Ed., 745 pages, 1974 (Casebook)

Hodges, Jones and Elliott's Cases and Materials on the Judicial Process Prior to Trial in Texas, 2nd Ed., 871 pages, 1977 (Casebook)

Kane's Civil Procedure in a Nutshell, 271 pages, 1979 (Text)

Karlen's Procedure Before Trial in a Nutshell, 258 pages, 1972 (Text)

Karlen and Joiner's Cases and Materials on Trials and Appeals, 536 pages, 1971 (Casebook)

Karlen, Meisenholder, Stevens and Vestal's Cases on Civil Procedure, 923 pages, 1975 (Casebook)

Koffler and Reppy's Hornbook on Common Law Pleading, 663 pages, 1969 (Text)

McBaine's Cases on Introduction to Civil Procedure, 399 pages, 1950 (Casebook)

McCoid's Cases on Civil Procedure, 823 pages, 1974 (Casebook)

Park's Computer-Aided Exercises on Civil Procedure, 118 pages, 1976 (Coursebook)

Shipman's Hornbook on Common-Law Pleading, 3rd Ed., 644 pages, 1923 (Text)

CIVIL PROCEDURE—Continued

Siegel's Hornbook on New York Practice, 1011 pages, 1978 with 1981–82 Pocket Part (Text)

See also Federal Jurisdiction and Procedure

CIVIL RIGHTS

Abernathy's Cases and Materials on Civil Rights, 660 pages, 1980 (Casebook)

Cohen's Cases on the Law of Deprivation of Liberty: A Study in Social Control, 755 pages, 1980 (Casebook)

Lockhart, Kamisar and Choper's Cases on Constitutional Rights and Liberties, 5th Ed., 1298 pages plus Appendix, 1981, with 1982 Supplement (Casebook)—reprint from Lockhart, et al. Cases on Constitutional Law, 5th Ed., 1980

Vieira's Civil Rights in a Nutshell, 279 pages, 1978 (Text)

COMMERCIAL LAW

Bailey's Secured Transactions in a Nutshell, 2nd Ed., 391 pages, 1981 (Text)

Epstein and Martin's Basic Uniform Commercial Code Teaching Materials, 599 pages, 1977 (Casebook)

Henson's Hornbook on Secured Transactions Under the U.C.C., 2nd Ed., 504 pages, 1979 with 1979 P.P. (Text)

Murray's Commercial Law, Problems and Materials, 366 pages, 1975 (Coursebook)

Nordstrom and Clovis' Problems and Materials on Commercial Paper, 458 pages, 1972 (Casebook)

Nordstrom and Lattin's Problems and Materials on Sales and Secured Transactions, 809 pages, 1968 (Casebook)

Nordstrom, Murray and Clovis' Problems and Materials on Sales, 515 pages, 1982 (Casebook)

Nordstrom's Hornbook on Sales, 600 pages, 1970 (Text)

Selected Commercial Statutes, 1367 pages, 1981

Speidel, Summers and White's Teaching Materials on Commercial and Consumer Law, 3rd Ed., 1490 pages, 1981 (Casebook)

Stockton's Sales in a Nutshell, 2nd Ed., 370 pages, 1981 (Text)

Stone's Uniform Commercial Code in a Nutshell, 507 pages, 1975 (Text)

Uniform Commercial Code, Official Text with Comments, 994 pages, 1978

UCC Article 8, 1977 Amendments, 249 pages, 1978

UCC Article 9, Reprint from 1962 Code, 128 pages, 1976

UCC Article 9, 1972 Amendments, 304 pages, 1978

LAW SCHOOL PUBLICATIONS—Continued

COMMERCIAL LAW—Continued

Weber and Speidel's Commercial Paper in a Nutshell, 3rd Ed., 404 pages, 1982 (Text)

White and Summers' Hornbook on the Uniform Commercial Code, 2nd Ed., 1250 pages, 1980 (Text)

COMMUNITY PROPERTY

Huie's Texas Cases and Materials on Marital Property Rights, 681 pages, 1966 (Casebook)

Mennell's Community Property in a Nutshell, approximately 410 pages, 1982 (Text)

Verrall's Cases and Materials on California Community Property, 3rd Ed., 547 pages, 1977 (Casebook)

COMPARATIVE LAW

Glendon, Gordon, and Osakwe's Comparative Legal Traditions in a Nutshell, 402 pages, 1982 (Text)

Langbein's Comparative Criminal Procedure: Germany, 172 pages, 1977 (Casebook)

CONFLICT OF LAWS

Cramton, Currie and Kay's Cases-Comments-Questions on Conflict of Laws, 3rd Ed., 1026 pages, 1981 (Casebook)

Ehrenzweig's Conflicts in a Nutshell, 3rd Ed., 432 pages, 1974 (Text)

Scoles and Hay's Hornbook on Conflict of Laws, approximately 950 pages, 1982 (Text)

Scoles and Weintraub's Cases and Materials on Conflict of Laws, 2nd Ed., 966 pages, 1972, with 1978 Supplement (Casebook)

Siegel's Conflicts in a Nutshell, 469 pages, 1982 (Text)

CONSTITUTIONAL LAW

Engdahl's Constitutional Power in a Nutshell: Federal and State, 411 pages, 1974 (Text)

Lockhart, Kamisar and Choper's Cases-Comments-Questions on Constitutional Law, 5th Ed., 1705 pages plus Appendix, 1980, with 1982 Supplement (Casebook)

Lockhart, Kamisar and Choper's Cases-Comments-Questions on the American Constitution, 5th Ed., 1185 pages plus Appendix, 1981, with 1982 Supplement (Casebook)—reprint from Lockhart, et al. Cases on Constitutional Law, 5th Ed., 1980

Manning's The Law of Church-State Relations in a Nutshell, 305 pages, 1981 (Text)

Miller's Presidential Power in a Nutshell, 328 pages, 1977 (Text)

CONSTITUTIONAL LAW—Continued

Nowak, Rotunda and Young's Handbook on Constitutional Law, 974 pages, 1978, with 1982 pocket part (Text)

Rotunda's Modern Constitutional Law: Cases and Notes, 1034 pages, 1981, with 1982 Supplement (Casebook)

Williams' Constitutional Analysis in a Nutshell, 388 pages, 1979 (Text)

See also Civil Rights

CONSUMER LAW

Epstein and Nickles' Consumer Law in a Nutshell, 2nd Ed., 418 pages, 1981 (Text)

McCall's Consumer Protection, Cases, Notes and Materials, 594 pages, 1977, with 1977 Statutory Supplement (Casebook)

Schrag's Cases and Materials on Consumer Protection, 2nd Ed., 197 pages, 1973 (Casebook)—reprint from Cooper, et al. Cases on Law and Poverty, 2nd Ed., 1973

Selected Commercial Statutes, 1367 pages, 1981

Spanogle and Rohner's Cases and Materials on Consumer Law, 693 pages, 1979, with 1982 Supplement (Casebook)

See also Commercial Law

CONTRACTS

Calamari & Perillo's Cases and Problems on Contracts, 1061 pages, 1978 (Casebook)

Calamari and Perillo's Hornbook on Contracts, 2nd Ed., 878 pages, 1977 (Text)

Corbin's Text on Contracts, One Volume Student Edition, 1224 pages, 1952 (Text)

Fessler and Loiseaux's Cases and Materials on Contracts, approximately 960 pages, 1982 (Casebook)

Freedman's Cases and Materials on Contracts, 658 pages, 1973 (Casebook)

Friedman's Contract Remedies in a Nutshell, 323 pages, 1981 (Text)

Fuller and Eisenberg's Cases on Basic Contract Law, 4th Ed., 1203 pages, 1981 (Casebook)

Jackson and Bollinger's Cases on Contract Law in Modern Society, 2nd Ed., 1329 pages, 1980 (Casebook)

Keyes' Government Contracts in a Nutshell, 423 pages, 1979 (Text)

Reitz's Cases on Contracts as Basic Commercial Law, 763 pages, 1975 (Casebook)

Schaber and Rohwer's Contracts in a Nutshell, 307 pages, 1975 (Text)

Simpson's Hornbook on Contracts, 2nd Ed., 510 pages, 1965 (Text)

COPYRIGHT

Nimmer's Cases and Materials on Copyright and Other Aspects of Law Pertaining to Literary, Musical and Artistic Works, Illustrated, 2nd Ed., 1023 pages, 1979 (Casebook)

See also Patent Law

CORPORATIONS

Hamilton's Cases on Corporations—Including Partnerships and Limited Partnerships, 2nd Ed., 1108 pages, 1981, with 1981 Statutory Supplement (Casebook)

Hamilton's Law of Corporations in a Nutshell, 379 pages, 1980 (Text)

Henn's Cases on Corporations, 1279 pages, 1974, with 1980 Supplement (Casebook)

Henn's Hornbook on Corporations, 2nd Ed., 956 pages, 1970 (Text)

Jennings and Buxbaum's Cases and Materials on Corporations, 5th Ed., 1180 pages, 1979 (Casebook)

Selected Corporation and Partnership Statutes, Regulations and Forms, approximately 775 pages, 1982

Solomon, Stevenson and Schwartz' Materials and Problems on the Law and Policies on Corporations, approximately 1160 pages, 1982 (Casebook)

CORRECTIONS

Krantz's Cases and Materials on the Law of Corrections and Prisoners' Rights, 2nd Ed., 735 pages, 1981, with 1982 Supplement (Casebook)

Krantz's Law of Corrections and Prisoners' Rights in a Nutshell, 353 pages, 1976 (Text)

Model Rules and Regulations on Prisoners' Rights and Responsibilities, 212 pages, 1973

Popper's Post-Conviction Remedies in a Nutshell, 360 pages, 1978 (Text)

Robbins' Cases and Materials on Post Conviction Remedies, 506 pages, 1982 (Casebook)

Rubin's Law of Criminal Corrections, 2nd Ed., 873 pages, 1973, with 1978 Supplement (Text)

CREDITOR'S RIGHTS

Epstein's Debtor-Creditor Law in a Nutshell, 2nd Ed., 324 pages, 1980 (Text)

Epstein and Landers' Debtors and Creditors: Cases and Materials, 2nd Ed., approximately 725 pages, 1982 (Casebook)

Epstein and Sheinfeld's Teaching Materials on Business Reorganization Under the Bankruptcy Code, 216 pages, 1980 (Casebook)

CREDITOR'S RIGHTS—Continued

Riesenfeld's Cases and Materials on Creditors' Remedies and Debtors' Protection, 3rd Ed., 810 pages, 1979 with 1979 Statutory Supplement and 1981 Case Supplement (Casebook)

Selected Bankruptcy Statutes, 351 pages, 1979

CRIMINAL LAW AND CRIMINAL PROCEDURE

Cohen and Gobert's Problems in Criminal Law, 297 pages, 1976 (Problem book)

Davis' Police Discretion, 176 pages, 1975 (Text)

Dix and Sharlot's Cases and Materials on Criminal Law, 2nd Ed., 771 pages, 1979 (Casebook)

Federal Rules of Civil-Appellate-Criminal Procedure—West Law School Edition, approximately 350 pages, 1982

Grano's Problems in Criminal Procedure, 2nd Ed., 176 pages, 1981 (Problem book)

Heymann and Kenety's The Murder Trial of Wilbur Jackson: A Homicide in the Family, 340 pages, 1975 (Case Study)

Israel and LaFave's Criminal Procedure in a Nutshell, 3rd Ed., 438 pages, 1980 (Text)

Johnson's Cases, Materials and Text on Substantive Criminal Law in its Procedural Context, 2nd Ed., 956 pages, 1980 (Casebook)

Kamisar, LaFave and Israel's Cases, Comments and Questions on Modern Criminal Procedure, 5th ed., 1635 pages plus Appendix, 1980 with 1982 Supplement (Casebook)

Kamisar, LaFave and Israel's Cases, Comments and Questions on Basic Criminal Procedure, 5th Ed., 869 pages, 1980 with 1982 Supplement (Casebook)—reprint from Kamisar, et al. Modern Criminal Procedure, 5th ed., 1980

LaFave's Modern Criminal Law: Cases, Comments and Questions, 789 pages, 1978 (Casebook)

LaFave and Scott's Hornbook on Criminal Law, 763 pages, 1972 (Text)

Langbein's Comparative Criminal Procedure: Germany, 172 pages, 1977 (Casebook)

Loewy's Criminal Law in a Nutshell, 302 pages, 1975 (Text)

Saltzburg's American Criminal Procedure, Cases and Commentary, 1253 pages, 1980 with 1982 Supplement (Casebook)

LAW SCHOOL PUBLICATIONS—Continued

CRIMINAL LAW AND CRIMINAL PROCEDURE—Continued

Saltzburg's Introduction to American Criminal Procedure, 702 pages, 1980 with 1982 Supplement (Casebook)—reprint from Saltzburg's American Criminal Procedure, 1980

Uviller's The Processes of Criminal Justice: Investigation and Adjudication, 2nd Ed., 1384 pages, 1979 with 1979 Statutory Supplement and 1980 Update (Casebook)

Uviller's The Processes of Criminal Justice: Adjudication, 2nd Ed., 730 pages, 1979. Soft-cover reprint from Uviller's The Processes of Criminal Justice: Investigation and Adjudication, 2nd Ed. (Casebook)

Uviller's The Processes of Criminal Justice: Investigation, 2nd Ed., 655 pages, 1979. Soft-cover reprint from Uviller's The Processes of Criminal Justice: Investigation and Adjudication, 2nd Ed. (Casebook)

Vorenberg's Cases on Criminal Law and Procedure, 2nd Ed., 1088 pages, 1981 (Casebook)

See also Corrections, Juvenile Justice

DECEDENTS ESTATES

See Trusts and Estates

DOMESTIC RELATIONS

Clark's Cases and Problems on Domestic Relations, 3rd Ed., 1153 pages, 1980 (Casebook)

Clark's Hornbook on Domestic Relations, 754 pages, 1968 (Text)

Krause's Cases and Materials on Family Law, 1132 pages, 1976, with 1978 Supplement (Casebook)

Krause's Family Law in a Nutshell, 400 pages, 1977 (Text)

EDUCATION LAW

Morris' The Constitution and American Education, 2nd Ed., 992 pages, 1980 (Casebook)

EMPLOYMENT DISCRIMINATION

Cooper, Rabb and Rubin's Fair Employment Litigation: Text and Materials for Student and Practitioner, 590 pages, 1975 (Coursebook)

Player's Cases and Materials on Employment Discrimination Law, 878 pages, 1980 with 1982 Supplement (Casebook)

Player's Federal Law of Employment Discrimination in a Nutshell, 2nd Ed., 402 pages, 1981 (Text)

EMPLOYMENT DISCRIMINATION—Continued

Sovern's Cases and Materials on Racial Discrimination in Employment, 2nd Ed., 167 pages, 1973 (Casebook)—reprint from Cooper et al. Cases on Law and Poverty, 2nd Ed., 1973

See also Women and the Law

ENERGY AND NATURAL RESOURCES LAW

Rodgers' Cases and Materials on Energy and Natural Resources Law, 995 pages, 1979 (Casebook)

Selected Environmental Law Statutes, 681 pages, 1981

Tomain's Energy Law in a Nutshell, 338 pages, 1981 (Text)

See also Environmental Law, Oil and Gas, Water Law

ENVIRONMENTAL LAW

Currie's Cases and Materials on Pollution, 715 pages, 1975 (Casebook)

Federal Environmental Law, 1600 pages, 1974 (Text)

Findley and Farber's Cases and Materials on Environmental Law, 738 pages, 1981 (Casebook)

Hanks, Tarlock and Hanks' Cases on Environmental Law and Policy, 1242 pages, 1974, with 1976 Supplement (Casebook)

Rodgers' Hornbook on Environmental Law, 956 pages, 1977 (Text)

Selected Environmental Law Statutes, 681 pages, 1981

See also Energy and Natural Resources Law, Water Law

EQUITY

See Remedies

ESTATES

See Trusts and Estates

ESTATE PLANNING

Casner and Stein's Estate Planning under the Tax Reform Act of 1976, 2nd Ed., 456 pages, 1978 (Coursebook)

Kurtz' Cases, Materials and Problems on Family Estate Planning, approximately 850 pages, 1982 (Casebook)

Lynn's Introduction to Estate Planning, in a Nutshell, 2nd Ed., 378 pages, 1978 (Text)

See also Taxation

EVIDENCE

Broun and Meisenholder's Problems in Evidence, 2nd Ed., 304 pages, 1981 (Problem book)

T7202—5g

V

LAW SCHOOL PUBLICATIONS—Continued

EVIDENCE—Continued

Cleary and Strong's Cases, Materials and Problems on Evidence, 3rd Ed., 1143 pages, 1981 (Casebook)

Federal Rules of Evidence for United States Courts and Magistrates, 325 pages, 1979

Graham's Federal Rules of Evidence in a Nutshell, 429 pages, 1981 (Text)

Kimball's Programmed Materials on Problems in Evidence, 380 pages, 1978 (Problem book)

Lempert and Saltzburg's A Modern Approach to Evidence: Text, Problems, Transcripts and Cases, 2nd Ed., approximately 1240 pages, 1982 (Casebook)

Lilly's Introduction to the Law of Evidence, 486 pages, 1978 (Text)

McCormick, Elliott and Sutton's Cases and Materials on Evidence, 5th Ed., 1212 pages, 1981 (Casebook)

McCormick's Hornbook on Evidence, 2nd Ed., 938 pages, 1972, with 1978 pocket part (Text)

Rothstein's Evidence, State and Federal Rules in a Nutshell, 2nd Ed., 514 pages, 1981 (Text)

Saltzburg's Evidence Supplement: Rules, Statutes, Commentary, 245 pages, 1980 (Casebook Supplement)

FEDERAL JURISDICTION AND PROCEDURE

Currie's Cases and Materials on Federal Courts, 3rd Ed., approximately 1050 pages, 1982 (Casebook)

Currie's Federal Jurisdiction in a Nutshell, 2nd Ed., 258 pages, 1981 (Text)

Federal Rules of Civil-Appellate-Criminal Procedure—West Law School Edition, approximately 350 pages, 1982

Forrester and Moye's Cases and Materials on Federal Jurisdiction and Procedure, 3rd Ed., 917 pages, 1977 with 1981 Supplement (Casebook)

Merrill and Vetri's Problems on Federal Courts and Civil Procedure, 460 pages, 1974 (Problem book)

Wright's Hornbook on Federal Courts, 3rd Ed., 818 pages, 1976 (Text)

FUTURE INTERESTS

See Trusts and Estates

HOUSING AND URBAN DEVELOPMENT

Berger's Cases and Materials on Housing, 2nd Ed., 254 pages, 1973 (Casebook)—reprint from Cooper et al. Cases on Law and Poverty, 2nd Ed., 1973

See also Land Use

INDIAN LAW

See American Indian Law

INSURANCE

Dobbyn's Insurance Law in a Nutshell, 281 pages, 1981 (Text)

Keeton's Cases on Basic Insurance Law, 2nd Ed., 1086 pages, 1977

Keeton's Basic Text on Insurance Law, 712 pages, 1971 (Text)

Keeton's Case Supplement to Keeton's Basic Text on Insurance Law, 334 pages, 1978 (Casebook)

Keeton's Programmed Problems in Insurance Law, 243 pages, 1972 (Text Supplement)

York and Whelan's Cases, Materials and Problems on Insurance Law, aproximately 780 pages, 1982 (Casebook)

INTERNATIONAL LAW

Henkin, Pugh, Schachter and Smit's Cases and Materials on International Law, 2nd Ed., 1152 pages, 1980, with Documents Supplement (Casebook)

Jackson's Legal Problems of International Economic Relations, 1097 pages, 1977, with Documents Supplement (Casebook)

Kirgis' International Organizations in Their Legal Setting, 1016 pages, 1977, with 1981 Supplement (Casebook)

Weston, Falk and D'Amato's International Law and World Order—A Problem Oriented Coursebook 1195 pages, 1980, with Documents Supplement (Casebook)

Wilson's International Business Transactions in a Nutshell, 393 pages, 1981 (Text)

INTRODUCTION TO LAW

Dobbyn's So You Want to go to Law School, Revised First Edition, 206 pages, 1976 (Text)

Kinyon's Introduction to Law Study and Law Examinations in a Nutshell, 389 pages, 1971 (Text)

See also Legal Method and Legal System

JUDICIAL ADMINISTRATION

Carrington, Meador and Rosenberg's Justice on Appeal, 263 pages, 1976 (Casebook)

Leflar's Appellate Judicial Opinions, 343 pages, 1974 (Text)

Nelson's Cases and Materials on Judicial Administration and the Administration of Justice, 1032 pages, 1974 (Casebook)

JURISPRUDENCE

Christie's Text and Readings on Jurisprudence—The Philosophy of Law, 1056 pages, 1973 (Casebook)

LAW SCHOOL PUBLICATIONS—Continued

JUVENILE JUSTICE

Fox's Cases and Materials on Modern Juvenile Justice, 2nd Ed., 960 pages, 1981 (Casebook)

Fox's Juvenile Courts in a Nutshell, 2nd Ed., 275 pages, 1977 (Text)

LABOR LAW

Gorman's Basic Text on Labor Law-Unionization and Collective Bargaining, 914 pages, 1976 (Text)

Leslie's Labor Law in a Nutshell, 403 pages, 1979 (Text)

Nolan's Labor Arbitration Law and Practice in a Nutshell, 358 pages, 1979 (Text)

Oberer, Hanslowe and Andersen's Cases and Materials on Labor Law—Collective Bargaining in a Free Society, 2nd Ed., 1168 pages, 1979, with 1979 Statutory Supplement and 1982 Case Supplement (Casebook)

See also Employment Discrimination, Social Legislation

LAND FINANCE

See Real Estate Transactions

LAND USE

Hagman's Cases on Public Planning and Control of Urban and Land Development, 2nd Ed., 1301 pages, 1980 (Casebook)

Hagman's Hornbook on Urban Planning and Land Development Control Law, 706 pages, 1971 (Text)

Wright and Gitelman's Cases and Materials on Land Use, 3rd Ed., 1300 pages, 1982 (Casebook)

Wright and Webber's Land Use in a Nutshell, 316 pages, 1978 (Text)

See also Housing and Urban Development

LAW AND ECONOMICS

Manne's The Economics of Legal Relationships—Readings in the Theory of Property Rights, 660 pages, 1975 (Text)

See also Antitrust, Regulated Industries

LAW AND MEDICINE—PSYCHIATRY

Cohen's Cases and Materials on the Law of Deprivation of Liberty: A Study in Social Control, 755 pages, 1980 (Casebook)

King's The Law of Medical Malpractice in a Nutshell, 340 pages, 1977 (Text)

Shapiro and Spece's Problems, Cases and Materials on Bioethics and Law, 892 pages, 1981 (Casebook)

Sharpe, Fiscina and Head's Cases on Law and Medicine, 882 pages, 1978 (Casebook)

LEGAL CLINICS

See Office Practice

LEGAL HISTORY

Presser and Zainaldin's Cases on Law and American History, 855 pages, 1980 (Casebook)

See also Legal Method and Legal System

LEGAL METHOD AND LEGAL SYSTEM

Aldisert's Readings, Materials and Cases in the Judicial Process, 948 pages, 1976 (Casebook)

Bodenheimer, Oakley and Love's Readings and Cases on an Introduction to the Anglo-American Legal System, 161 pages, 1980 (Casebook)

Davies and Lawry's Institutions and Methods of the Law—Introductory Teaching Materials, 547 pages, 1982 (Casebook)

Dvorkin, Himmelstein and Lesnick's Becoming a Lawyer: A Humanistic Perspective on Legal Education and Professionalism, 211 pages, 1981 (Text)

Fryer and Orentlicher's Cases and Materials on Legal Method and Legal System, 1043 pages, 1967 (Casebook)

Greenberg's Judicial Process and Social Change, 666 pages, 1977 (Coursebook)

Kempin's Historical Introduction to Anglo-American Law in a Nutshell, 2nd Ed., 280 pages, 1973 (Text)

Kimball's Historical Introduction to the Legal System, 610 pages, 1966 (Casebook)

Mashaw and Merrill's Introduction to the American Public Law System, 1095 pages, 1975, with 1980 Supplement (Casebook)

Murphy's Cases and Materials on Introduction to Law—Legal Process and Procedure, 772 pages, 1977 (Casebook)

Reynolds' Judicial Process in a Nutshell, 292 pages, 1980 (Text)

See also Legal Research and Writing

LEGAL PROFESSION

Aronson's Problems in Professional Responsibility, 280 pages, 1978 (Problem book)

Aronson and Weckstein's Professional Responsibility in a Nutshell, 399 pages, 1980 (Text)

Mellinkoff's The Conscience of a Lawyer, 304 pages, 1973 (Text)

Mellinkoff's Lawyers and the System of Justice, 983 pages, 1976 (Casebook)

Pirsig and Kirwin's Cases and Materials on Professional Responsibility, 3rd Ed., 667 pages, 1976, with 1981 Supplement (Casebook)

LAW SCHOOL PUBLICATIONS—Continued

LEGAL PROFESSION—Continued

Smith's Preventing Legal Malpractice, 142 pages, 1981 (Text)

LEGAL RESEARCH AND WRITING

Cohen's Legal Research in a Nutshell, 3rd Ed., 415 pages, 1978 (Text)

Dickerson's Materials on Legal Drafting, 425 pages, 1981 (Casebook)

Felsenfeld and Siegel's Writing Contracts in Plain English, 290 pages, 1981 (Text)

Gopen's Writing From a Legal Perspective, 225 pages, 1981 (Text)

How to Find the Law With Special Chapters on Legal Writing, 7th Ed., 542 pages, 1976. Problem book available (Coursebook)

Mellinkoff's Legal Writing Sense and Nonsense, 242 pages, 1982 (Text)

Rombauer's Legal Problem Solving—Analysis, Research and Writing, 3rd Ed., 352 pages, 1978 (Coursebook)

Squires and Rombauer's Legal Writing in a Nutshell, 294 pages, 1982 (Text)

Statsky's Legal Research, Writing and Analysis, 2nd Ed., 167 pages, 1982 (Coursebook)

Statsky's Legislative Analysis: How to Use Statutes and Regulations, 216 pages, 1975 (Text)

Statsky and Wernet's Case Analysis and Fundamentals of Legal Writing, 576 pages, 1977 (Text)

Teply's Programmed Materials on Legal Research and Citation, 334 pages, 1982. Student Library Exercises available (Coursebook)

Weihofen's Legal Writing Style, 2nd Ed., 332 pages, 1980 (Text)

LEGISLATION

Davies' Legislative Law and Process in a Nutshell, 279 pages, 1975 (Text)

Nutting and Dickerson's Cases and Materials on Legislation, 5th Ed., 744 pages, 1978 (Casebook)

Statsky's Legislative Analysis: How to Use Statutes and Regulations, 216 pages, 1975 (Text)

LOCAL GOVERNMENT

McCarthy's Local Government Law in a Nutshell, 386 pages, 1975 (Text)

Michelman and Sandalow's Cases-Comments-Questions on Government in Urban Areas, 1216 pages, 1970, with 1972 Supplement (Casebook)

Reynolds' Hornbook on Local Government Law, approximately 780 pages, 1982 (Text)

Stason and Kauper's Cases and Materials on Municipal Corporations, 3rd Ed., 692 pages, 1959 (Casebook)

LOCAL GOVERNMENT—Continued

Valente's Cases and Materials on Local Government Law, 2nd Ed., 980 pages, 1980 with 1982 Supplement (Casebook)

MASS COMMUNICATION LAW

Gillmor and Barron's Cases and Comment on Mass Communication Law, 3rd Ed., 1008 pages, 1979 (Casebook)

Ginsburg's Regulation of Broadcasting: Law and Policy Towards Radio, Television and Cable Communications, 741 pages, 1979 (Casebook)

Zuckman and Gayne's Mass Communications Law in a Nutshell, 431 pages, 1977 (Text)

MILITARY LAW

Shanor and Terrell's Military Law in a Nutshell, 378 pages, 1980 (Text)

MORTGAGES

See Real Estate Transactions

NATURAL RESOURCES LAW

See Energy and Natural Resources Law, Environmental Law, Oil and Gas, Water Law

OFFICE PRACTICE

Binder and Price's Legal Interviewing and Counseling: A Client-Centered Approach, 232 pages, 1977 (Text)

Edwards and White's Problems, Readings and Materials on the Lawyer as a Negotiator, 484 pages, 1977 (Casebook)

Hegland's Trial and Practice Skills in a Nutshell, 346 pages, 1978 (Text)

Shaffer's Legal Interviewing and Counseling in a Nutshell, 353 pages, 1976 (Text)

Strong and Clark's Law Office Management, 424 pages, 1974 (Casebook)

Williams' Legal Negotiation and Settlement, approximately 207 pages, 1982 (Coursebook)

OIL AND GAS

Hemingway's Hornbook on Oil and Gas, 486 pages, 1971, with 1979 pocket part (Text)

Huie, Woodward and Smith's Cases and Materials on Oil and Gas, 2nd Ed., 955 pages, 1972 (Casebook)

See also Energy and Natural Resources Law

PARTNERSHIP

See Agency—Partnership

LAW SCHOOL PUBLICATIONS—Continued

PATENT LAW

Choate and Francis' Cases and Materials on Patent Law, 2nd Ed., 1110 pages, 1981 (Casebook)

See also Copyright

POVERTY LAW

Brudno's Poverty, Inequality, and the Law: Cases-Commentary-Analysis, 934 pages, 1976 (Casebook)

Cooper, Dodyk, Berger, Paulsen, Schrag and Sovern's Cases and Materials on Law and Poverty, 2nd Ed., 1208 pages, 1973 (Casebook)

LaFrance, Schroeder, Bennett and Boyd's Hornbook on Law of the Poor, 558 pages, 1973 (Text)

See also Social Legislation

PRODUCTS LIABILITY

Noel and Phillips' Cases on Products Liability, 2nd Ed., 821 pages, 1982 (Casebook)

Noel and Phillips' Products Liability in a Nutshell, 2nd Ed., 341 pages, 1981 (Text)

PROPERTY

Aigler, Smith and Tefft's Cases on Property, 2 volumes, 1339 pages, 1960 (Casebook)

Bernhardt's Real Property in a Nutshell, 2nd Ed., 448 pages, 1981 (Text)

Boyer's Survey of the Law of Property, 766 pages, 1981 (Text)

Browder, Cunningham, Julin and Smith's Cases on Basic Property Law, 3rd Ed., 1447 pages, 1979 (Casebook)

Burby's Hornbook on Real Property, 3rd Ed., 490 pages, 1965 (Text)

Chused's A Modern Approach to Property: Cases-Notes-Materials, 1069 pages, 1978 with 1980 Supplement (Casebook)

Cohen's Materials for a Basic Course in Property, 526 pages, 1978 (Casebook)

Donahue, Kauper and Martin's Cases on Property, 1501 pages, 1974 (Casebook)

Hill's Landlord and Tenant Law in a Nutshell, 319 pages, 1979 (Text)

Moynihan's Introduction to Real Property, 254 pages, 1962 (Text)

Phipps' Titles in a Nutshell, 277 pages, 1968 (Text)

Uniform Land Transactions Act, Uniform Simplification of Land Transfers Act, Uniform Condominium Act, 1977 Official Text with Comments, 462 pages, 1978

See also Housing and Urban Development, Real Estate Transactions, Land Use

REAL ESTATE TRANSACTIONS

Bruce's Real Estate Finance in a Nutshell, 292 pages, 1979 (Text)

Maxwell, Riesenfeld, Hetland and Warren's Cases on California Security Transactions in Land, 2nd Ed., 584 pages, 1975 (Casebook)

Nelson and Whitman's Cases on Real Estate Transfer, Finance and Development, 2nd Ed., 1114 pages, 1981 (Casebook)

Osborne's Cases and Materials on Secured Transactions, 559 pages, 1967 (Casebook)

Osborne, Nelson and Whitman's Hornbook on Real Estate Finance Law, 3rd Ed., 885 pages, 1979 (Text)

REGULATED INDUSTRIES

Gellhorn and Pierce's Regulated Industries in a Nutshell, 394 pages, 1982 (Text)

Morgan's Cases and Materials on Economic Regulation of Business, 830 pages, 1976, with 1978 Supplement (Casebook)

Pozen's Financial Institutions: Cases, Materials and Problems on Investment Management, 844 pages, 1978 (Casebook)

White's Teaching Materials on Banking Law, 1058 pages, 1976, with 1980 Case and Statutory Supplement (Casebook)

See also Mass Communication Law

REMEDIES

Cribbet's Cases and Materials on Judicial Remedies, 762 pages, 1954 (Casebook)

Dobbs' Hornbook on Remedies, 1067 pages, 1973 (Text)

Dobbs' Problems in Remedies, 137 pages, 1974 (Problem book)

Dobbyn's Injunctions in a Nutshell, 264 pages, 1974 (Text)

Friedman's Contract Remedies in a Nutshell, 323 pages, 1981 (Text)

Leavell, Love and Nelson's Cases and Materials on Equitable Remedies and Restitution, 3rd Ed., 704 pages, 1980 (Casebook)

McCormick's Hornbook on Damages, 811 pages, 1935 (Text)

O'Connell's Remedies in a Nutshell, 364 pages, 1977 (Text)

York and Bauman's Cases and Materials on Remedies, 3rd Ed., 1250 pages, 1979 (Casebook)

REVIEW MATERIALS

Ballantine's Problems

Black Letter Series

LAW SCHOOL PUBLICATIONS—Continued

REVIEW MATERIALS—Continued

Smith's Review Series

West's Review Covering Multistate Subjects

SECURITIES REGULATION

Ratner's Securities Regulation: Materials for a Basic Course, 2nd Ed., 1050 pages, 1980 with 1982 Supplement (Casebook)

Ratner's Securities Regulation in a Nutshell, 300 pages, 1978 (Text)

Selected Securities and Business Planning Statutes, Rules and Forms, approximately 490 pages, 1982

SOCIAL LEGISLATION

Brudno's Income Redistribution Theories and Programs: Cases-Commentary-Analyses, 480 pages, 1977 (Casebook)—reprint from Brudno's Poverty, Inequality and the Law, 1976

LaFrance's Welfare Law: Structure and Entitlement in a Nutshell, 455 pages, 1979 (Text)

Malone, Plant and Little's Cases on Workers' Compensation and Employment Rights, 2nd Ed., 951 pages, 1980 (Casebook)

See also Poverty Law

TAXATION

Chommie's Hornbook on Federal Income Taxation, 2nd Ed., 1051 pages, 1973 (Text)

Dodge's Federal Taxation of Estates, Trusts and Gifts: Principles and Planning, 771 pages, 1981 with 1982 Supplement (Casebook)

Garbis and Struntz' Cases and Materials on Tax Procedure and Tax Fraud, 829 pages, 1982 (Casebook)

Gunn's Cases and Materials on Federal Income Taxation of Individuals, 785 pages, 1981 (Casebook)

Hellerstein and Hellerstein's Cases on State and Local Taxation, 4th Ed., 1041 pages, 1978 with 1982 Supplement (Casebook)

Kahn's Handbook on Basic Corporate Taxation, 3rd Ed., Student Ed., 614 pages, 1981 with 1982 Supplement (Text)

Kahn and Gann's Corporate Taxation and Taxation of Partnerships and Partners, 1107 pages, 1979, with 1981 Supplement (Casebook)

Kragen and McNulty's Cases and Materials on Federal Income Taxation, Vol. I: Taxation of Individuals, 3rd Ed., 1283 pages, 1979 with 1982 Supplement (Casebook)

TAXATION—Continued

Kragen and McNulty's Cases and Materials on Federal Income Taxation, Vol. II: Taxation of Corporations, Shareholders, Partnerships and Partners, 3rd Ed., 989 pages, 1981 with 1982 Supplement (Casebook)

Kramer and McCord's Problems for Federal Estate and Gift Taxes, 206 pages, 1976 (Problem book)

Lowndes, Kramer and McCord's Hornbook on Federal Estate and Gift Taxes, 3rd Ed., 1099 pages, 1974 (Text)

McCord's 1976 Estate and Gift Tax Reform-Analysis, Explanation and Commentary, 377 pages, 1977 (Text)

McNulty's Federal Estate and Gift Taxation in a Nutshell, 2nd Ed., 488 pages, 1979 (Text)

McNulty's Federal Income Taxation of Individuals in a Nutshell, 2nd Ed., 422 pages, 1978 (Text)

Rice's Problems and Materials in Federal Estate and Gift Taxation, 3rd Ed., 474 pages, 1978 (Casebook)

Rice and Solomon's Problems and Materials in Federal Income Taxation, 3rd Ed., 670 pages, 1979 (Casebook)

Rose and Raskind's Advanced Federal Income Taxation: Corporate Transactions—Cases, Materials and Problems, 955 pages, 1978 (Casebook)

Selected Federal Taxation Statutes and Regulations, approximately 1350 pages, 1982

Soboleff and Weidenbruch's Federal Income Taxation of Corporations and Stockholders in a Nutshell, 362 pages, 1981 (Text)

TORTS

Green, Pedrick, Rahl, Thode, Hawkins, Smith and Treece's Cases and Materials on Torts, 2nd Ed., 1360 pages, 1977 (Casebook)

Green, Pedrick, Rahl, Thode, Hawkins, Smith, and Treece's Advanced Torts: Injuries to Business, Political and Family Interests, 2nd Ed., 544 pages, 1977 (Casebook)—reprint from Green, et al. Cases and Materials on Torts, 2nd Ed., 1977

Keeton's Computer-Aided and Workbook Exercises on Tort Law, 164 pages, 1976 (Coursebook)

Keeton and Keeton's Cases and Materials on Torts, 2nd Ed., 1200 pages, 1977, with 1981 Supplement (Casebook)

Kionka's Torts in a Nutshell: Injuries to Persons and Property, 434 pages, 1977 (Text)

Malone's Torts in a Nutshell: Injuries to Family, Social and Trade Relations, 358 pages, 1979 (Text)

TORTS—Continued

Prosser's Hornbook on Torts, 4th Ed., 1208 pages, 1971 (Text)

Shapo's Cases on Tort and Compensation Law, 1244 pages, 1976 (Casebook)

See also Products Liability

TRADE REGULATION

McManis' Unfair Trade Practices in a Nutshell, approximately 400 pages, 1982 (Text)

Oppenheim and Weston's Cases and Materials on Unfair Trade Practices and Consumer Protection, 3rd Ed., 1065 pages, 1974, with 1981 Supplement (Casebook)

See also Antitrust, Regulated Industries

TRIAL AND APPELLATE ADVOCACY

Appellate Advocacy, Handbook of, 249 pages, 1980 (Text)

Bergman's Trial Advocacy in a Nutshell, 402 pages, 1979 (Text)

Goldberg's The First Trial (Where Do I Sit?) (What Do I Say?) in a Nutshell, 396 pages, 1982 (Text)

Hegland's Trial and Practice Skills in a Nutshell, 346 pages, 1978 (Text)

Jeans' Handbook on Trial Advocacy, Student Ed., 473 pages, 1975 (Text)

McElhaney's Effective Litigation, 457 pages, 1974 (Casebook)

Nolan's Cases and Materials on Trial Practice, 518 pages, 1981 (Casebook)

Parnell and Shellhaas' Cases, Exercises and Problems for Trial Advocacy, 171 pages, 1982 (Coursebook)

TRUSTS AND ESTATES

Atkinson's Hornbook on Wills, 2nd Ed., 975 pages, 1953 (Text)

Averill's Uniform Probate Code in a Nutshell, 425 pages, 1978 (Text)

Bogert's Hornbook on Trusts, 5th Ed., 726 pages, 1973 (Text)

Clark, Lusky and Murphy's Cases and Materials on Gratuitous Transfers, 2nd Ed., 1102 pages, 1977 (Casebook)

Gulliver's Cases and Materials on Future Interests, 624 pages, 1959 (Casebook)

TRUSTS AND ESTATES—Continued

Gulliver's Introduction to the Law of Future Interests, 87 pages, 1959 (Casebook)—reprint from Gulliver's Cases and Materials on Future Interests, 1959

Halbach (Editor)—Death, Taxes, and Family Property: Essays and American Assembly Report, 189 pages, 1977 (Text)

McGovern's Cases and Materials on Wills, Trusts and Future Interests: An Introduction to Estate Planning, approximately 750 pages, 1982 (Casebook)

Mennell's Cases and Materials on California Decedent's Estates, 566 pages, 1973 (Casebook)

Mennell's Wills and Trusts in a Nutshell, 392 pages, 1979 (Text)

Powell's The Law of Future Interests in California, 91 pages, 1980 (Text)

Simes' Hornbook on Future Interests, 2nd Ed., 355 pages, 1966 (Text)

Turrentine's Cases and Text on Wills and Administration, 2nd Ed., 483 pages, 1962 (Casebook)

Uniform Probate Code, 5th Ed., Official Text With Comments, 384 pages, 1977

Waggoner's Future Interests in a Nutshell, 361 pages, 1981 (Text)

WATER LAW

Trelease's Cases and Materials on Water Law, 3rd Ed., 833 pages, 1979 (Casebook)

See also Energy and Natural Resources Law, Environmental Law

WILLS

See Trusts and Estates

WOMEN AND THE LAW

Kay's Text, Cases and Materials on Sex-Based Discrimination, 2nd Ed., 1045 pages, 1981 (Casebook)

Thomas' Sex Discrimination in a Nutshell, 399 pages, 1982 (Text)

See also Employment Discrimination

WORKMEN'S COMPENSATION

See Social Legislation

A MODERN APPROACH TO EVIDENCE

TEXT, PROBLEMS, TRANSCRIPTS AND CASES

SECOND EDITION

By

RICHARD O. LEMPERT
Professor of Law, University of Michigan

and

STEPHEN A. SALTZBURG
Professor of Law, University of Virginia

AMERICAN CASEBOOK SERIES

ST. PAUL, MINN.
WEST PUBLISHING CO.
1982

COPYRIGHT © 1977 By Richard O. Lempert & Stephen A. Saltzburg
COPYRIGHT © 1983 By Richard O. Lempert & Stephen A. Saltzburg
50 West Kellogg Boulevard
P.O. Box 3526
St.Paul, Minnesota 55165

Library of Congress Cataloging in Publication Data

Lempert, Richard O.
    A modern approach to evidence.

    (American casebook series)
    Includes index.
    1.   Evidence (Law)—United States—Cases.
I. Saltzburg, Stephen A.   II. Title.   III. Series.
KF8934.L45   1982   347.73'6   82-13578
                         347.3076

ISBN 0-314-67594-9

PREFACE TO THE SECOND EDITION

We published the first edition of *A Modern Approach to Evidence* shortly after the Federal Rules of Evidence had been enacted. Since the first edition appeared, Congress has replaced FRE 410 dealing with offers to plead guilty and has written a new rule, FRE 412, to take account of the special plight of rape victims. Numerous decisions interpreting the Federal Rules have raised issues not clearly identified when the first edition went to press. Also, the Supreme Court has handed down important decisions dealing with presumptions, privileges and the confrontation clause. We deal with these developments in this, the second edition.

The most significant changes in this edition are not, however, those that keep the book current. Rather they stem from the many areas in which we saw opportunities to improve our treatment of evidentiary matters. No chapter is untouched and many have been changed substantially. In particular, we took special pains to re-evaluate our problem material. We have eliminated some, rewritten others and introduced a number of new problems, many of which are based on recent cases. In the process we may have eliminated a few problems that are particular favorites of those who used the first edition. Anyone who adopts and teaches from this edition of our book has our permission to reproduce for classroom use any problems that have been eliminated in the revising process.

In revising this book we have benefited substantially from the comments of students and colleagues. We are particularly grateful to those using the first edition who shared both critical and praising comments with us. We cannot acknowledge the many people who aided us with unsolicited comments or returned a questionnaire we circulated, but two individuals deserve special mention. Professor Edward Kimball of Brigham Young Law School read the first printing of the first edition with a marvelously keen proofreader's eye. He raised a number of substantive questions and pointed out numerous flaws of typography and style, many of which we were able to correct in subsequent printings of the first edition. Professor J. Alexander Tanford of the Indiana University Law School wrote a book review length commentary on the first edition entirely for our benefit. We were guided at many points in revising by his comments. He also gave us permission to reproduce several problems that he had prepared for his classes. They will be recognized by their central characters, members of the Gebippe family.

In the research for and writing of this book, we received help from a number of people. Professor Lempert would like to thank Helen Foster, Douglas Greenswag and Bonny Hendricksmeyer, who worked as student research assistants and Dorothy Blair and Fran Swanson who were his secretaries during the period he was working on the second edition. He is also grateful to the University of Iowa Law School which provided a congenial and supportive setting during much of the time he was working on this edition and to Professor Ronald Allen for his helpful comments on certain portions of the manuscript. The contributions of the Cook Funds of the University of Michigan Law School are also gratefully acknowledged.

Professor Saltzburg would like to thank Lane Kneedler, Graham Lilly, Richard Pierce, Glen Robinson and Calvin Sharpe, each of whom taught from the book and provided an almost daily critique of its strengths and weaknesses. Their suggestions and criticisms prompted changes in almost every part of the book. Their willingness to talk about how various problems worked and why some failed was tremendously helpful in the preparation of the second edition. And their collegiality made teaching evidence a great deal of fun during the five years between the publication of the first edition and this one. Professor Saltzburg also thanks Charles Goetz and John Monahan, who each sat in on an entire evidence course and whose insights from the perspectives of an economist and a psychologist have been invaluable.

We are grateful for permissions to reprint granted by many sources. Special thanks are extended to three publishers: West Publishing Company, for allowing us to quote from the McCormick treatise; Little, Brown & Company, for allowing us to quote from the Wigmore treatise; and to The Michie Co., for allowing us to quote from the Federal Rules of Evidence Manual. Other sources from whom we have borrowed include the following:

Bermant & Jacoubovitch, Fish Out of Water: A Brief Overview of Social and Psychological Concerns About Videotaped Trials, 26 Hastings L.J. 999 (1975). Reprinted with the permission of the authors and the Hastings Law Journal.

Blasi, The Newsman's Privilege: An Empirical Study, 70 Mich.L.Rev. 229 (1971). Reprinted with the permission of the Michigan Law Review.

Buckhout, Eyewitness Testimony, 231 Scientific American 23 (Dec. 1974). Copyright © 1974 by Scientific American. All rights reserved. Reprinted with permission.

Cady, Objections to Demonstrative Evidence, 32 Mo.L.Rev. 333 (1967). Copyright 1967 by The Curators of the University of Missouri. Reprinted with the permission of the Missouri Law Review.

Cleary, Presuming and Pleading: An Essay on Juristic Immaturity, 12 Stan.L.Rev. 5 (1959). Reprinted with the permission of the Stanford Law Review.

Diamond, The Fallacy of the Impartial Expert, 3 Archives of Criminal Psychodynamics 221 (1959). Reprinted with the permission of the author.

Doret, Trial By Videotape—Can Justice Be Seen To Be Done? 47 Temp.L.Q. 228 (1974). Reprinted with the permission of the Temple Law Quarterly.

PREFACE TO THE SECOND EDITION

Examining the Medical Expert: Lectures and Trial Demonstrations, Volume 2, Legal-Medical Library, Michigan Institute of Continuing Legal Education (1969). Reprinted with the permission of the Institute of Continuing Legal Education, Ann Arbor, Michigan.

Freed, Fenwick & McGonigal, Mock Trial: Admissibility of Computerized Business Records, 15 Jurimetrics Journal 206 (Spring 1975). Reprinted with the permission of the authors.

Freedman, Professional Responsibility of the Criminal Defense Lawyer: The Three Hardest Questions, 64 Mich.L.Rev. 1469 (1966). Reprinted with the permission of the Michigan Law Review.

Gardner, A Re-Evaluation of the Attorney-Client Privilege, 8 Vill.L.Rev. 279 (1963). Copyright 1963 by Villanova University. Reprinted with the permission of the Villanova Law Review.

Goldstein & Lane, Trial Technique (1966). Reprinted with the permission of Goldstein Trial Technique, published by Callaghan and Company, 6141 North Cicero Avenue, Chicago, Illinois 60646.

Hornaday, Some Suggestions on the Investigation of Facts, 15 Ind.L.J. 498 (1940). Reprinted with the permission of the Indiana Law Journal and Fred B. Rothman & Co.

Jones, Danger—Voiceprints Ahead, 11 Am.Crim.L.Rev. 549 (1973). Reprinted with the permission of the American Bar Association, Section of Criminal Justice.

Karjala, The Evidentiary Uses of Neutron Activation Analysis, 59 Cal.L.Rev. 997 (1971). Reprinted with the permission of the California Law Review and Fred B. Rothman & Co.

Levin & Cohen, The Exclusionary Rules in Nonjury Criminal Cases, 119 U.Pa.L.Rev. 905 (1971). Reprinted with the permission of the University of Pennsylvania Law Review and Fred B. Rothman & Co.

Louisell, Confidentiality, Conformity and Confusion: Privileges in Federal Court Today, 31 Tulane L.Rev. 101 (1956). Reprinted with the permission of the Tulane Law Review.

McCormick & Ray, Texas Law of Evidence (1937). Reprinted with the permission of West Publishing Company.

Michigan Standard Jury Instructions—Civil 21.01 & 21.04. Reprinted with the permission of the Institute of Continuing Legal Education, Ann Arbor, Michigan.

Mitchell, The Proposed Federal Rules of Evidence: How They Affect Product Liability Practice, 12 Duquesne L.Rev. 551 (1974). Reprinted with the permission of the Duquesne Law Review.

Moenssens, Moses & Inbau, Scientific Evidence in Criminal Cases (1973). Reprinted with the permission of The Foundation Press, Inc.

Morgan, Further Observations on Presumptions, 16 So.Cal.L.Rev. 245 (1943). Reprinted with the permission of the Southern California Law Review.

Morgan, Presumptions, 12 Wash.L.Rev. 255 (1937). Reprinted with the permission of the Washington Law Review and Fred B. Rothman & Co.

PREFACE TO THE SECOND EDITION

Morgan, Some Observations Concerning A Model Code of Evidence, 89 U.Pa.L.Rev. 145 (1940). Reprinted with the permission of the University of Pennsylvania Law Review and Fred B. Rothman & Co.

Saltzburg, The Harm of Harmless Error, 59 Va.L.Rev. 988 (1973). Reprinted with the permission of the Virginia Law Review and Fred B. Rothman & Co.

Schwartz, A Suggestion for the Demise of Judicial Notice of "Judicial Facts," 45 Tex.L.Rev. 1212 (1967). Reprinted with the permission of the Texas Law Review and Fred B. Rothman & Co.

Stewart, Perception, Memory, and Hearsay: A Criticism of Present Law and the Proposed Federal Rules of Evidence, 1970 Utah L.Rev. 1. Reprinted with the permission of the Utah Law Review.

Symposium: The Use of Videotape in the Courtroom, 1975 Brig.Y.U.L.Rev. 327. Reprinted with the permission of the Brigham Young University Law Review.

Weinstein, Probative Force of Hearsay, 46 Iowa L.Rev. 331 (1961). Reprinted with the permission of the author and the Iowa Law Review.

Westen, The Compulsory Process Clause, 73 Mich.L.Rev. 71 (1974). Reprinted with the permission of the Michigan Law Review.

Wellman, The Art of Cross-Examination (4th ed. 1936). Copyright 1936 by MacMillan Publishing Co., Inc.; renewed 1964 by Ethel Wellman. Reprinted with the permission of the MacMillian Publishing Co., Inc.

Finally, in the course of writing both editions of this book we have become acutely aware that what we thought, when reading other books, were perfunctory acknowledgments of the support of spouses are by no means perfunctory. We are indeed grateful for the support of our spouses, Cynthia Lempert and Linda Saltzburg, and the way in which they bore up under the pressure which this book placed on us and them.

RICHARD O. LEMPERT
STEPHEN A. SALTZBURG

September, 1982

INTRODUCTION

I. AN APPROACH TO EVIDENCE

This is not a casebook. It bears little resemblance to the materials used in most law school courses. This book consists largely of text, problems and transcripts. The cases we include are used primarily to raise policy issues, not to teach substantive points of law. This book is a product of our disappointment with the materials currently available for the teaching of evidence. We have found that teaching the substantive law of evidence through case analysis makes little sense. Great amounts of time are devoted to reading and analyzing cases in order to extract principles that can be stated in a paragraph or less. Often little time is left for serious policy analysis. Codifications of evidence law, increasingly important to the modern practitioner, are inevitably slighted. The case approach also creates malaise among students who correctly sense that appellate courts are far removed from the setting in which most evidentiary battles are resolved. There are many good evidence teachers in this country, but from talking to the students of some of them, we sense that evidence courses succeed despite the materials used rather than because of them.

We both find evidence to be one of the most interesting and, indeed, exciting courses in the law school curriculum. It is at once eminently practical and highly intellectual. There are rules to be learned and concepts to be pondered. The rules of evidence may be examined from historical, logical and psychological perspectives. They may also be examined as tools that lawyers use to win cases. Ethical issues are close to the surface in this course and are important to a full understanding of what it is to be a lawyer. Underlying everything is the often unexplored relationship between rules of evidence and the quality of justice that a legal system delivers. We have found that by using textual material and problems we can explore each of these aspects of evidence law in greater depth than we could by using the case method.

We recognize that most students taking evidence are concerned primarily with the practicalities of litigation, but we believe that even the most practically oriented will benefit from serious reflection on the policies behind the rules. In evidence, as in much of law, practical and philosophic concerns complement each other. We hope our book demonstrates this to those using it, and we like to think that future Thayers, Wigmores, McCormicks and Morgans will benefit from considering some of the issues raised herein.

The strength of our approach lies in the responsibility it places on students. Students are expected to learn the rudiments of evidence law from the text. The problems offered for discussion in class are a test of the students' mastery of the subject, not an introduction to the rules of evidence. To facilitate independent learning, we try to be as straightforward as possible in our explication of the rules. Our experience has been that students take their responsibility well, enjoying the change from a steady diet of cases. This is not to say that those adopting these materials need never concern themselves with teaching basics. Class discussion will at times reveal confusion which the instructor must remove.

When we began writing this book, we were unsure whether we should take positions on controversial issues of evidence policy. We hesitated to do so because of the danger that beginning students would misread statements of preference as statements about the way the law in fact is, and because of the greater danger that students would accept our analyses without giving sufficient weight to competing considerations. Eventually, we decided that the book would be more interesting and valuable if, in our attempt to grapple with difficult policy questions, we took specific positions and stated our reasons for them. Where we have taken controversial positions we try to alert our readers, at least in the footnotes, to the fact that controversy exists. On more important issues we discuss positions opposing ours at some length. Our views are often unorthodox, contrary to the received truths that have guided generations of evidence scholars. In fact, we have created some controversies that have not heretofore existed. Frequently, we disagree ourselves as to the best answer to hard questions. Undoubtedly, other instructors will have great fun in taking positions contrary to ours and in emphasizing what they see as flaws in our analyses. We encourage them to do so. We are more concerned with exposing students to the debate than we are with obtaining converts to our positions.

In this book we use the Federal Rules of Evidence in two ways. First, they are presented with the specific goal of teaching them. We believe that any modern evidence course should teach the federal rules. They are used in federal courts in all states and are the model on which a number of state evidence codes have been and will be based. Second, we use them heuristically, as a modern counterpart to the rules of the common law. We believe that both the federal rules and the common law are more easily understood when they are presented in conjunction with each other. Comparative presentation also highlights modern trends and raises interesting questions about which of two approaches is preferable. Our heuristic use of the federal rules does not depend on the precise wording of these rules. Indeed, the Uniform Rules of Evidence, the California Evidence Code or any other modern codification would have had the same heuristic value. So future changes in the Federal Rules of Evidence will not render our textual discussion irrelevant. However, the precise wording of the federal rules is obviously important when the goal is to learn them. For this reason and because we do not present the text of every federal rule, users of this book are advised to acquire a current copy of the Federal Rules of Evidence.

This book is designed to be a self-contained teaching device. It is written so that students will not have to resort to hornbooks, nutshells, texts or other works in order to understand these materials or to answer the problems. Nevertheless, we recognize that some students find two treatments of an issue more helpful than one. For them, we recommend McCormick's excellent hornbook, although there is considerable redundancy between that work and this one.

INTRODUCTION

Those who have not taught from problems before may find that teaching problems takes considerably more time than they anticipated. A problem only a paragraph in length may present all the salient facts of an actual case. In writing this book we faced a choice: either to include only those problems that we liked best and that we thought could be taught in a three hour course, or to include many more problems than could ever be covered in a three hour course, with the expectation that instructors would pick those problems that they found most interesting or most relevant to the special needs of their students. We have opted for the latter course. In the interest of time, instructors may also want to eliminate certain textual material. In some chapters, such as the chapter on real and scientific evidence, we offer several detailed examples of what we are discussing, knowing that many instructors will not want to explore every example in the detail provided. In other chapters, instructors may not want to discuss every evidence rule or subrule that we choose to analyze. The book was written with the expectation that instructors would feel no compulsion to assign everything that is in it or to discuss everything that is assigned. We wrote with this expectation because we wished to include enough material to allow instructors to emphasize what they believe is most important.

Our goals are many and ambitious, but we think our expectations are realistic. A book that attempts several different things may disappoint people who are looking at the book for a specific purpose. Those who want only a treatise may find too many problems. Those who want only problems may find there is more text than they care to teach. We do not claim that this book is perfect; nor that it will achieve perfectly the goals we have set. We have found that it teaches well. We offer it in the hope that it will serve others as it has served us. It is an innovative effort, with the weaknesses as well as the strengths of innovation. We welcome comments from students and instructors which will enable us to eliminate weaknesses and improve the book in future editions.

II. NOTES ON STYLE

In Chapter One the reader will quickly notice something that will be repeated in other chapters: some footnotes are printed in boldface and others are not. Where the footnotes to transcripts are designed to explain points of law to the students or to get them to focus on other important ideas, we wish the footnote to stand out. This explains the use of boldface. Where transcripts are particularly lengthy and the comments in footnotes particularly important, we use large type for further emphasis. We also use boldface in footnotes to textual material when we wish to draw special attention to the footnotes.

To avoid lengthy citations and to make our text read more smoothly, we have adopted certain conventions. We cite Wigmore's Treatise on Evidence, as "Wigmore." We cite to the most recent edition, although we do not otherwise note this. For most volumes of Wigmore, this is the third edition published in 1940, and updated at various times. We cite McCormick's Hornbook on Evidence as "McCormick." All cites are to the second edition, revised under the general editorship of Professor Edward W. Cleary.

INTRODUCTION

We save space and make judicial opinions read more easily by eliminating most internal citations. These deletions are not noted. Deletions of textual material in opinions and articles are noted by three asterisks. We also delete footnotes found in opinions and articles without otherwise noting this. Where we choose to keep footnotes appearing in the material we reproduce, we identify these footnotes by lower case letters. Our own footnotes appear in Arabic numerals.

We have given names to the characters that appear in most problems in order to make them seem more human. Except in some instances where names are drawn from actual cases, the names bear no relationship to real people. We hope that if we have inadvertently given your name to an axe murderer, you are not offended by the coincidence.

We have prepared three appendices to help you in your studies: a short appendix tracing the development of the Federal Rules of Evidence; a longer appendix outlining the entire evidence course with specific notations to the federal rules that are applicable on the various points; and a complex problem that affords you an opportunity to test your knowledge of most evidence rules in one factual setting.

III. BIBLIOGRAPHY

Many sources are cited in the footnotes. In addition, each chapter ends with a suggested list of additional readings. These should be of special interest to those who wish to pursue particular topics in greater depth and to those who believe that we have treated some familiar doctrines too harshly.

For general reading on the law of evidence, one cannot go wrong by reading widely in Wigmore's treatise, the single most respected source. The historically minded may wish to inspect Thayer's Preliminary Treatise on Evidence, a superb work of scholarship, published in 1898 but still cited for certain propositions. For quick reference we recommend McCormick's hornbook. Students interested in shorter books may like Maguire's Evidence —Common Sense and Common Law (1947) and Morgan's Basic Problems of Evidence (1962).

For those interested in the codification process, a Review of the Model Code of Evidence and of the Uniform Rules of Evidence, discussed in Appendix I, should be helpful. Comparing the 1969, 1971, 1972 (Supreme Court approved) drafts and the final version of the Federal Rules of Evidence with each other and with state-approved versions should highlight both general and specific problems of codifying evidence rules. For further discussion of the Federal Rules of Evidence, you might investigate several multivolume works: Weinstein and Berger's "Weinstein's Evidence;" Wright and Graham's "Federal Practice and Procedure" § 5000 et seq.; and Louisell and Mueller's "Federal Evidence." An instructive one volume work is Saltzburg & Redden's Federal Rules of Evidence Manual (3d ed. 1982), co-authored by one of the authors of this book.

SUMMARY OF CONTENTS

SUMMARY OF CONTENTS

SUMMARY OF CONTENTS

*

TABLE OF CONTENTS

TABLE OF CONTENTS

TABLE OF CONTENTS

TABLE OF CONTENTS

TABLE OF CONTENTS

TABLE OF CONTENTS

TABLE OF CONTENTS

TABLE OF CONTENTS

TABLE OF CONTENTS

TABLE OF CONTENTS

TABLE OF CASES

The principal cases are in Italic type. Cases cited or discussed are in Roman type. References are to Pages.

TABLE OF CASES

TABLE OF CASES

XL

TABLE OF RULES, STATUTES AND STANDARDS

TABLE OF RULES, STATUTES AND STANDARDS

TABLE OF RULES, STATUTES AND STANDARDS

TABLE OF RULES, STATUTES AND STANDARDS

TABLE OF RULES, STATUTES AND STANDARDS

TABLE OF RULES, STATUTES AND STANDARDS

TABLE OF AUTHORITIES

TABLE OF AUTHORITIES

TABLE OF AUTHORITIES

TABLE OF AUTHORITIES

TABLE OF AUTHORITIES

TABLE OF AUTHORITIES

TABLE OF AUTHORITIES

TABLE OF AUTHORITIES

A MODERN APPROACH TO EVIDENCE

SECOND EDITION

*

Chapter One

SOME BASICS

SECTION I. INTRODUCTION TO EVIDENCE

A. THE "TRIAL GAME"

Do you remember when you first decided to become a lawyer? If you are one of those who decided for law in childhood, the chances are that in your earliest fantasies you saw yourself before a jury, arguing eloquently to save your (most assuredly innocent) client from undeserved punishment. Perry Mason was your model, if not your idol, and the prosecutor was an adversary, the opposition in a fateful game. In form, the trial has many features characteristic of two-sided games. The goals of the players are clear and generally of a zero-sum form; that is, to the extent one side wins the other side loses. The roles of the players are well-defined. Rules exist defining permissible moves, and a judge sits to ensure that the most important rules are followed. The stakes may be enormous: millions of dollars, years in prison, or even life itself. It is a strange game in that the most active players, the opposing attorneys, have less at risk than those they represent, individuals sitting "on the sidelines" as it were. But in the long run careers are made on how well one performs at trial, and the satisfactions which make any profession worthwhile may turn on courtroom performance. To be given the opportunity to stave off injustice and to fail is painful, whatever the prior odds against success. An attorney must be prepared to do his or her best.

It is here that knowledge of the rules of evidence is crucial. The rules of evidence are among the most important rules which govern the trial game. They determine the information which will reach the fact finder, that is, the judge or jury.* You may have the strongest possible case, but unless the fact finder can hear the facts you wish to present, these facts cannot influence the decision. Conversely your opponent's case may appeal to base prejudice or impermissible sentiment, but if the fact finder hears the appeal its decision may respond to prejudice or sentiment.

Like many of the rules in active games, it is often unclear how the rules of evidence should apply to particular fact situations. It is the lawyer's task to convince the judge through rational argument that his or her preferred interpretation of the rules should be adopted. The lawyer's arguments will usually draw on familiar sources, statutes and prior court decisions; but, particularly when arguing at the appellate level, scientific data and a sensitive appreciation of policy may be important. Though this is not a trial

---

* Throughout this book we will generally assume that the trier of fact is a jury, but almost everything we say applies, at least in theory, whether the trier of fact is the judge or a jury. In later chapters we shall consider what, if any, modifications of evidence rules should be permitted or encouraged when the judge is the ultimate arbiter.

1

practice book, we hope in this text to thoroughly familiarize you with the rules of evidence so that you may perform as well as you possibly can in your trial work.   We hope also to sensitize you to some of the ways in which knowledge of evidence law is integrated into a well thought-out litigation strategy.   Finally, we intend to pose many of the policy questions which must be faced in any honest attempt to evaluate the implications which our system of evidence law holds for the quality of justice in this country.

We intend shortly to leave the metaphor of the trial as game, but before we do two further points should be made.   First, to the extent that rulings on evidence law determine the outcome of the game, the game is almost always won or lost at the trial rather than the appellate level.   This statement may seem strange to advanced law students who have thus far been fed an almost steady diet of appellate opinions, and it must seem stranger still to any of you familiar with the more traditional evidence casebooks, filled almost entirely with the reports of appellate court opinions.   The reason for this is that appellate judges in reviewing cases seek generally to ensure that justice was done below;   they are less concerned with upholding the letter of the law.   Consequently, except to some extent when constitutional values are implicated, appellate courts will rarely reverse trial courts for mistaken rulings of evidence law unless they have some reason to suspect the substantive justice of the trial result.   This is so even if a correct ruling on the evidence matter below might conceivably have led the fact finder to render a different verdict.   If you are skeptical of this claim (or even if you are not) perform a simple test.   Go to the Federal Reporter or the appropriate reporter of appellate decisions for your state.   Look at the number of criminal appeals in which questions of evidence are raised.   Note the propensity of the courts to dispose of evidence issues without discussion in a catch-all paragraph, to rationalize rulings below as correct, or to conclude, without reasons, that possible errors below could not have affected the trial results. Are you as confident as the court that the alleged errors might not have influenced the fact finder's verdict?   Now look at those few cases which are reversed on non-constitutional evidentiary grounds.   Is it obvious to you that the errors cited are more substantial than errors for which the same court has refused to reverse?   Is the defendant's case generally sympathetic?   Does there appear a greater possibility that—totally apart from the evidentiary point at issue—an injustice has been done?   The criminal defendant who wins an evidence point below always wins if the jury is thereby led to favor him, since the prosecution will be unable to appeal.   The prosecutor or civil litigant who wins an argument about evidence is in a more ambiguous position. It is possible that the information which is thereby given or kept from the jury may in no way affect the verdict, yet it may provide an appellate court with a convenient peg on which to hang a reversal.   The sophisticated trial lawyer knows when to refrain from pressing an evidence point too hard.

Finally, as in all games, the quality of refereeing may be spotty.   Judges, like attorneys, vary in the skill and knowledge which they bring to their task.   Judges, like referees, almost always have the last word.   In this book you will be taught the rules of evidence in a relatively precise form and you will learn nice distinctions between particular aspects of various rules.   In court the rules may be fuzzy and the distinctions may disappear, or, worse still, they may disappear in one judge's court and reappear in another's. Phrases like "res gestae" may serve to summarily dispose of matters which you will learn to treat as a series of separate and distinct exceptions to the hearsay rule. You will, no doubt, learn to adapt your arguments to the judges you are appearing before. But the distinctions you learn in this course should still serve you in good stead. They should help you appreciate what is behind some of the fuzzy distinctions which prevail in certain courtrooms. When you have an appealable case they should suggest arguments which justify a decision in your favor. And, if you should someday ascend the bench, you might be one of those judges to whom this paragraph does not apply.

The chances are that by this time in law school you have left all dreams of being Perry Mason incarnate behind you. You probably realize that the overwhelming majority of cases commenced, both civil and criminal, never go to trial and you are no doubt aware that many lawyers pass fruitful careers without once standing before a jury. If you do not see yourself as a litigator of what use is a course in evidence to you? Knowledge of evidence law has many uses. First, though you may never appear in court, the possibility of litigation may be present in many of the things you do. You may have to draft instruments or advise clients with an eye to possible court tests. To do this effectively you must know what kinds of information the court would be willing to admit in reaching a decision. Second, as a negotiator you must be aware that the value of a case may turn on the probability that particular kinds of evidence will be admitted or excluded if the matter were to reach trial. Third, as an appellate specialist you obviously must be able to evaluate a trial transcript for evidentiary errors as well as for grander errors of law. Fourth, no matter what your practice you will find that one of the most interesting features of evidence law is that many of these supposedly neutral procedural rules in fact disproportionately advantage either plaintiffs or defendants. When issues of evidence law revision are before your legislature, you may have a significant stake in the way the matter is finally resolved. Finally, you will be a lawyer. You will be expected by your non-lawyer associates to possess some of the basic knowledge which, in the popular mind, characterizes your chosen profession. Evidence, you will find, is one of those fields which you will be expected to know something about. Your life will be happier if you do.

B. A TRIAL: AN INTRODUCTION TO BASIC RULES

We have chosen to begin with an annotated transcript because we have found that this format is an understandable and interesting way of introducing a number of the basic rules that apply at trials. In addition, most people, including many law students, have never seen a complete trial or read through a trial transcript. We believe you will find it helpful at the outset of your evidence course to see how a trial may look. You should, however, be aware that all trials are different and some will look very different from the run-of-the-mill trial we reproduce in this chapter.

As you read through the transcript you should take time to study the footnotes. The footnotes are essential, for they introduce some of the most basic principles of the American trial process.   Most of those principles are taught only in this chapter.

Perhaps the most basic rule of the trial is that the decision maker, be it judge or jury, must decide the case on the basis of what is presented in court.   This does not mean that the decision maker may not use common sense or the kind of general information that one culls from experience.   It does mean that no information pertaining to the parties or to the specific incident giving rise to the litigation may be considered by the decision maker unless the law permits the information to be received by a court.   The law which governs what courts can receive is, of course, the law of evidence.

Parties can attempt to establish their cases in several ways.   The most common is through the testimony of witnesses.   People familiar with an event answer questions designed to elicit what they know—we call this direct examination.   Then they answer questions designed to test the accuracy of their original account—we call this cross-examination.

There are today few restrictions on the kinds of people who may be asked to testify.   All that is important is that a person knows something that might help in the resolution of the case.   The kinds of biases that would disqualify a judge or juror do not affect the admissibility of a witness' evidence although they may be considered by the fact finder in deciding how much weight to give the witness' testimony.   Chapter Five discusses ways in which the accuracy of testimony can be challenged, but the basic rules of cross-examination are introduced in the footnotes to this opening chapter.

Because the judge or jury has the responsibility for resolving factual disputes, the details of what a witness knows are usually preferred to the conclusions the witness has reached.   Indeed, courts sometimes say that the opinions of non-expert witnesses are not allowed; their testimony must be confined to facts.   But, as you shall see in the footnotes accompanying this chapter and the problems that follow it, the line between facts, on the one hand, and opinions or conclusions, on the other, is not easily drawn, and what are analytically opinions may be more helpful to the trier of fact than the perceptions they summarize.

Where fixed lines cannot be drawn or where rigidity would interfere with accurate fact finding, rules tend to be tempered by judicial discretion.   You shall see that this is the case with the rules regarding the opinions of lay witnesses.   We return to aspects of the opinion rules when we discuss expert testimony, but we do not again treat the subject of lay opinion.

People without personal knowledge of events or conditions may have heard things that might be of interest to a fact finder.   When a witness relates information provided by another, problems of hearsay may arise.   Chapter Six is devoted to the hearsay rule and its exceptions. You are well advised not to worry about what is or is not hearsay until you reach this chapter.

Not all evidence at a trial is oral.   Documents and other tangible objects may be given to a fact finder for examination.   We call such objects "exhibits."   Sometimes witnesses will be needed to explain how an exhibit relates to a case while on other occasions an exhibit, once identified, will "speak" for itself.   Special rules exist to ensure that documents are genuine and that other tangible exhibits are what they purport to be.   We discuss these rules in Chapter Eleven.   In this chapter, we discuss only the basic requirements for using exhibits at trial.

In the transcript you will see that the parties stipulate to certain facts. Stipulations are one way of establishing facts without requiring a party to introduce evidence that bears on the issue.   Stipulations require an agreement between the parties.   Other methods do not require agreement.   In Chapter Nine you will learn that where a fact is indisputable, a court can instruct a jury that it may or must accept that fact as true even though the jury has heard no testimony relating to the fact in question.   When a court treats a fact as established on the basis of its indisputability, it is engaging in judicial notice.   Chapter Nine also discusses presumptions.   When a party benefits from a presumption, the party may by establishing one fact require the decision maker to presume another fact to be true unless the opposing party offers evidence that suggests or proves the nonexistence of the presumed fact.

In addition to introducing certain basic concepts, this chapter illustrates how dependent our adversary system of litigation is on the parties.   It is the parties who must discover the facts and bring them to the court's attention;   it is the parties who call the witnesses;   and it is the parties, usually through their lawyers, who ask the questions.   If a party believes that evidence is inadmissible, that party must object to the evidence and tell the court why it should be excluded.   The proponent of the evidence must respond with an explanation of why the objection is unsound.   If the parties ignore evidentiary problems, the trial court is likely to ignore them as well and, except where error is plain and egregious, an appellate court will not consider the matter on appeal.   The transcript is a continuous illustration of the process of offering and objecting to evidence.   However, the transcript we have chosen is not a model in this respect.   You will see some things that are missed and much that could be better done.

The transcript also provides an introduction to the respective roles of the trial judge and the jury, a subject examined at greater length in Chapter Twelve.   You will see from the transcript that it is the trial judge who decides whether to admit or to exclude evidence and the jury which decides whether to believe the evidence that is admitted.   The judge also instructs the jury as to how it must or may use certain information, and at the close of the trial the judge may summarize, and in some jurisdictions comment on, the evidence.   In addition, the judge's attitude toward the parties and the case may suggest to the jurors how the judge wishes the matter to be resolved.   The ideal judge will try not to convey an attitude toward the case and will use other modes of influence to enhance the fairness and rationality of the trial process.   As you read the transcript you can compare the presiding judge to this ideal.

A transcript is written, but litigation is largely oral.   Like an appellate court, you will not be able to see the lawyers and witnesses or hear intonations of voice that might be important, but you can learn who said what at what times during the trial.   You will also see the order in which a trial proceeds: opening statements, the presentation of the state's case, the presentation of the defendant's case, rebuttal evidence if any, closing arguments, instructions to the jury, and the return of the jury verdict.

A transcript is an important part of the record that is made of a trial, but it is only a part. The full record should capture everything of consequence that happens in the course of the litigation. This includes pre-trial motions and objections that are made in the judge's chambers rather than in open court. It also includes the exhibits that are offered at the trial whether or not they are admitted. Often counsel will wish to offer a written statement in support of a legal point. These statements may also become part of the record.

It is counsel's responsibility to "make the record." There are few responsibilities that are more important to the litigator. Generally speaking information that is not in the record will not be considered on appeal and misinformation that has been recorded without objection may be taken by an appellate court to be true. Ambiguity can be almost as damaging as the failure to include information in the first instance. Counsel must be articulate and clear. The record can only reflect what counsel says. Neither judges nor stenographers can read minds.

As a lawyer you should always be conscious of the way a trial is being recorded. If an audio tape is used be sure that your statements and those of the witnesses are audible. If a stenographer is present speak distinctly at a rate that is easy to follow. In either case, you must make a special effort to be sure that some things are not missed. Names of people, places and important objects may have to be spelled to be sure that they are correctly recorded. Exhibits should be referred to by their identifying numbers to avoid ambiguity. Assertive gestures like nods and pointing will be lost entirely unless counsel describes the gesture for the record. ("Let the record show that the witness pointed to the defendant.") What occurs at the bench may be missed if the stenographer is not present or if voices are too hushed to be captured on tape. Finally, it is almost impossible to reproduce simultaneous speech. If you find that you are speaking simultaneously with a witness or opposing counsel, restate your position if you want it to be preserved.

As you shall see in the transcript, a lawyer will not always have an adequate opportunity to explain an offer of, or objection to, evidence at the time the offer or objection is made. Counsel can ask for, and is entitled to, a later opportunity to complete the record. To facilitate thorough discussion lawyers may request rulings on difficult points of law prior to trial. The *motion in limine* which is the principal device by which this is accomplished also helps one plan for trial since one learns what portion of any questionable evidence is likely to be admitted. Because the admissibility of evidence often depends on the context in which it is offered, a ruling *in limine* is typically discretionary with the judge.

Chapter One concludes with problems that test your understanding of the principles set out in these introductory materials. By the end of the chapter you should be familiar with Federal Rules of Evidence 101–105; 601–604; 611; 615; 701–702; 704; and 901–902. You may want to read these rules before you begin the transcript and you should read them carefully before turning to the problems. You will find that you use Rules 103 and 104 throughout the course. Rules 601–603 are relevant every time a witness testifies, although their application raises few problems. Rule 611 is particularly important since it controls the mode and order of witness interrogation. Lay opinion, the subject of Rule 701, is discussed only in this chapter, but we shall return to aspects of expert opinion in Chapter Ten. Authentication, the subject of rules 901 and 902, is discussed in detail in Chapter Eleven. The teacher may wish to postpone discussion of these rules until that point.

In order to preserve the anonymity of the parties we have changed the names of people and places in the transcript that follows. But you should know that at the time of this trial in the state where it occurred the crime of possessing marihuana was a serious felony punishable by a substantial term in the state penitentiary. The trial of Nelson Whale is in many ways typical of the quality of criminal litigation in the crowded felony courts of large urban areas. This does not mean that it is like all other trials. Some are handled better and others even less well. Whale's trial is somewhat unusual in that Whale, who is not a wealthy man, is represented by his own counsel rather than by a public defender or an appointed counsel. It is also unusual in that Whale's defense includes an attack on the validity of the statute he has allegedly violated. Except when laws are recent and controversial, such attacks are rare. We suggest that you read this transcript twice. First, read the text quickly but completely to get some feel for what is occurring. Then read the transcript more slowly, paying close attention to the footnotes. Try to answer the questions posed in the footnotes as you read. You will find that even if you know little about evidence or trial tactics at this point, your common sense will often serve you well.

PEOPLE v. WHALE

THE COURT:[1] Ladies and Gentlemen of the Panel: As I have indicated previously, and I think some of you have heard this before, I ask that the entire panel rise and be sworn at the same time so that if any replacements are made on the temporary jury panel, it won't be necessary to swear them in separately.

1. The trial is about to begin. Yet much has happened already, and the final outcome of the trial may by this point have been determined. Consider how the jury has been chosen, how this judge has been assigned the case, how the prosecutor has gathered information to build the state's case, how the defense counsel has prepared the defense, and how the law has apportioned the burden of proof. What is left may have less influence on the final outcome than what has gone before. What are the different advantages enjoyed by the two sides?

The judge's opening remarks indicate that at least some jurors are not hearing their first case. Later in the judge's remarks to the jury, this is confirmed. Lawyers thinking about the kind of case they wish to present may be influenced by the jurors' exposure to other cases, and in deciding whether to challenge a juror lawyers will sometimes know and be influenced by how the juror voted in other cases.

(Whereupon the entire panel of temporary jurors was sworn by the clerk of the Court.)

THE COURT:[2]   Ladies and Gentlemen of the Panel: This is a criminal case, the People versus Nelson Whale.   Mr. Nelson Whale is charged as follows:

"In the Name of the People of the State of _____, William J. Carlyle, Prosecuting Attorney in and for said County of Boone, who prosecutes for and on behalf of the People of said State in said Court, comes now here in said Court in the March term thereof A.D.1967, and gives the said Court to understand and be informed that Nelson Whale, late of the City of Hamster in said County, heretofore, to wit on the 25th day of January, A.D.1967, at the said City of Hamster in said County, did then and there unlawfully and feloniously sell a certain "narcotic drug, to wit, 23.53 grains of marihuana, without first obtaining a license so to do, under the provisions of Act 343, P.A.1937, as amended, being Sections 335.51 to 335.78, inclusive, of the Compiled Laws of 1948, contrary to the forms of the Statute in such case made and provided, and against the peace and dignity of the People of the State of _____"

(Whereupon a Jury was duly impaneled and sworn.)

———

THE COURT: You may proceed with your opening statement, Mr. Bryers.

OPENING STATEMENT BY MR. BRYERS:[3]

Ladies and Gentlemen: My name is Leonard Bryers, and I am an Assistant Prosecuting Attorney of Boone County.

2. Note the mystique of the trial: the swearing in of the jury, the reading of the information, the oaths taken by witnesses.   Why do these elements exist? For purely historical reasons?   What effect, if any, would you expect these mystical elements to have on the jury? On the defendant?   On the parties if this were a civil suit?   Would you expect the jury to react differently if this were the tenth case they had heard rather than the first?   Would you expect a first offender to react differently than a fifth offender? Why is the information read to the jury? Does the fact that it is read by the presiding judge in the name of the people put the defendant at a disadvantage before any testimony has been introduced?   Who is "the Court"?   Whom does the Court represent?   The prosecutor?   The defense counsel?

3. The opening statements allow the opposing parties to present their theories of the case to the jury.   The prosecutor (or plaintiff in a civil case) speaks first. This may be a significant advantage. There is a body of social psychological literature which suggests that the party speaking first has the opportunity to prepare a neutral audience so that it will not be fully receptive to the arguments of a second speaker.   What is crucial is that the first party expose the audience to some of the arguments of the other party and provide a framework in which these arguments may be rejected.   [See, e.g. Lawson, Experimental Research on the Organization of Persuasive Arguments: An Application to Courtroom Communications, 1970 L. & Soc.Order 579].   The defendant's opening statement may, as in this case, immediately follow the prosecution's statement, or the right to make

The defendant in this case is charged with violating the laws of the State in that he " * * * did then and there unlawfully and feloniously sell a certain narcotic drug, to wit, 23.53 grains of marihuana, without first obtaining a license so to do   * * *." as required under the statutes and laws of this State.

The prosecution in this case will offer evidence proving beyond a reasonable doubt that this defendant, Nelson Whale, is guilty of this crime. We will show you that on the evening of January 25, 1967, Darrell Norton, a

an opening statement may be reserved until the presentation of the defendant's case-in-chief. Note that the defense counsel begins his opening statement by warning the jury that they are likely to hear him object to evidence at various points in the trial. Why does counsel do this? What is he afraid of? Suppose that counsel has reason to believe that the opposing party will attempt to introduce certain evidence of questionable admissibility? What can a lawyer do so that it does not appear that he is trying to keep important information from the jury? What would you try to do in these circumstances? One solution is to seek some pre-trial resolution of the matter. The exact procedure will vary depending on the kind of determination which is sought. Where one seeks a pre-trial ruling on a non-constitutional evidentiary issue, the device generally used is known as a motion in limine. What advantages, apart from that suggested above, exist for deciding evidentiary matters before testimony is taken? What effect does such a procedure have on plea bargaining or settlement decisions? Most evidentiary issues which arise at trial are not amenable to settlement at the pre-trial stage because the judge must know the context in which they will arise in order to determine how they should be resolved.

Defense counsel in this case makes a serious mistake in his opening statement by promising the jury more than he can later deliver. He suggests that he will present a defense of entrapment (and note what he gives away in making such a suggestion) and then presents his case in such a way that an entrapment instruction is later ruled inappropriate. Was the jury influenced by this lapse? It is impossible to say. But this possibility does emphasize the extent to which an attorney must

be familiar with both the available evidence and relevant legal principles before the start of a case. Typically, counsel's opening statement does not harm his own client.

An opening statement is not supposed to provide an opportunity to argue a case. It is an occasion for the lawyer to outline the facts that he expects to present so that the jury will understand the evidence that is to be introduced. It is permissible to object to improper argument in an opening statement, although many lawyers are reluctant to interrupt their adversary and prefer to argue back in turn. Not all courts allow the defendant to reserve the opportunity for opening statement until the end of the government's case; some require defense counsel to make an opening statement at the beginning of the trial or to forego it entirely. The argument for allowing the opening statement to be reserved is that the defense counsel should not have to commit himself to a defense until the government's case is introduced. This argument has some force, especially in the light of the limited discovery that often characterizes criminal cases. The opposing argument is that if the defense counsel is required to state at the outset what the defense is expected to be, the opportunity for manufacturing a false defense following the presentation of the government's case is limited. The argument presumes that at least some defense counsel will act unethically if given the opportunity.

Some very interesting suggestions concerning how to make powerful opening statements and how to be more impressive in jury trials generally are made by an anthropologist in Givens, Posture is Power, 8 Barrister 14 (Spring 1981).

police officer not in uniform, employed by the City of Hamster, went to the home of the defendant, Nelson Whale, in the evening, and while there engaged in a transaction with the defendant whereby he paid the defendant $22.50 and received from the defendant a can, which was a Prince Albert tobacco can, and in that can was marihuana.

He then took that can and turned that can over to his superior, Richard Barrott, another police officer—this was done about a half hour later—at which time in the presence of Officer Barrott, Darrell Norton marked his initials on this can; and also Richard Barrott, the other officer, marked his initials on this can.

The can was then taken by Richard Barrott to the Police Department property room and placed in a locker by Richard Barrott. Richard Barrott is the only one that has a key to that locker.

The next morning Richard Barrott went to the locker, opened it up and removed this Prince Albert can with its contents. He then proceeded downtown and turned these contents over to the chief chemist of the United States Government here. At that time, Stanley Wall, who is the chief chemist, made an analysis of the contents of this Prince Albert can, and after analyzing it, he determined that the analysis showed that there was 23.53 grains of marihuana.

And Ladies and Gentlemen, that is the case that the People will present to you.

Thank you.

THE COURT: Mr. Evert, you may proceed with your opening statement.

OPENING STATEMENT BY MR. EVERT:

Ladies and Gentlemen of the Jury, I am counsel for the defendant, and I will have this and another opportunity to address you.

During the course of the trial, I may well have occasion to make frequent objections, but it will be my purpose at that time to see to it that you get all of the facts, and I will start right now with a development of the facts other than those that the Prosecutor just told you about that are going to be important in your determination of this case.

The evidence will show principally through the witnesses that the prosecution will present to you that there was not one contact by a certain ex-police sergeant at the defendant's home on the 25th of January; there were four contacts.

The evidence will show that throughout all of those contacts, the incentive, the motivation, the provocation for the transaction about which you will hear evidence, came from that police officer and not from this defendant.

The evidence will show that at approximately 7 o'clock that afternoon, this police officer went over to this defendant's house and asked him to sell him two cans of marihuana, and the defendant had none.

The evidence will show that the same police officer came back a half hour later, this time with two empty Prince Albert cans from where he bought the tobacco and emptied them out, and this time he presented the cans to the defendant and requested a sale, and the defendant had none.

The evidence will show that the police officer came back a third time. Then the police officer will testify that that's when the sale of not two cans, but one can, all he could get from the defendant, was received by him.

The evidence will show that then the police officer came back a fourth time, this time to have a special accounting with the defendant as to the quantity of the alleged sale.

The evidence will show that there was a fifth contact with the defendant, this time as the result of a search warrant to search his house for non-existent marihuana.

I am going to ask the judge at the close of this case to instruct you jurors on the elements of entrapment, that principle of law which says the police shall not by their own actions create a crime in order to prevent the defendant from doing it.

The conduct of this police officer in order to get this case into the court will be further viewed by you in connection with some of his other activities since he became a police officer in the City of Hamster, which is of recent date. He will tell you, for example, that in order to get to this defendant, in order to get him charged with this crime, he had to get somebody that he had to buy whiskey for. He will tell you that he bought—that he bought—that he gave two sticks of marihuana, the same substance that this defendant is being charged with, to another person in order to get an introduction to the defendant.

At the close of all the proofs, you will have to evaluate not only the objective facts here but whether or not the transaction, as the prosecution gives it to you, and as the witnesses give it to you, was consummated as he said it was, but whether or not under the circumstances and under the law of entrapment, as this judge gives it to you, whether or not the crime here was totally motivated and induced by this police officer.

The proofs will show you why he was there doing what he was doing; what the motives were; and the only thing that the defendant asks you to do is to be fair to him.

*   *   *

THE COURT: You may call your first witness.

At 12:10 p. m.

DARRELL NORTON, called as a witness in behalf of the People, and having been first duly sworn, testified as follows:

DIRECT EXAMINATION

BY MR. BRYERS: [4]

Q. What is your name, witness? A. Darrell D. Norton.

Q. And by whom are you employed? A. I'm employed by the Hamster Police Department.

4. **The assistant prosecutor is beginning the presentation of the state's case.**

Read the first page or so of officer Norton's testimony. Why doesn't the prose-

Q. Were you so employed on January 25, 1967?   **A.**   I was, sir.

Q. And what was the nature of your duties on that particular evening?
A. The nature of our duties was to—

MR. EVERT:[5] He's saying "ours".

Q. (By Mr. Bryers, continuing): Of your duties?   **A.**   The nature of my duties was to primarily suppress narcotics in the City of Hamster.

cutor simply say, "Officer Norton, will you please give the court a complete account of your association with Nelson Whale?" This would not necessarily be impermissible. Witnesses may testify in a narrative form with the permission of the court, and, of course, the responses to particular questions may be narrations of several paragraphs in length. See Federal Rule 611 of the Federal Rules of Evidence (FRE 611). If you were the defense attorney in this case what objections would you have to a request to allow officer Norton to relate his story in narrative form? If you were the prosecutor would you wish to have your witnesses testify in narrative form or in response to your questions? On cross-examination attorneys are particularly wary of asking open-ended questions. Indeed, a general rule of thumb is that an attorney should never ask a question on cross-examination unless he has a good idea of what the answer is likely to be. What dangers exist for the attorney who asks vague or general questions on cross-examination?

At one time people were not allowed to testify, regardless of what they knew, if they occupied certain statuses. Agnostics, convicted felons, and parties to the litigation were among those kept from the stand. Most common law incompetencies have long since disappeared, and today witnesses are presumed competent. Witnesses must, however, unless they are experts, have personal knowledge of the facts they describe (FRE 602) and all witnesses must by oath or affirmation promise to tell the truth (FRE 603). Some state rules of evidence do not allow people to testify unless they can express themselves in ways that can be understood and unless they understand the duty to tell the truth. The federal rules do not explicitly estab-

lish mental qualifications, but an appreciation of the duty to tell the truth is arguably an implicit requirement of FRE 603 while the testimony of a person who cannot adequately communicate might be irrelevant and thus inadmissible under FRE 402 or excludable under FRE 403 if the judge believes it is likely to be more prejudicial than probative or unduly time-consuming.

5. Why is Mr. Evert objecting here? Is he making an important evidentiary point on behalf of his client? What is the impression he is afraid Officer Norton's testimony will make on the jury? What other reasons exist for making objections of a relatively insubstantial sort? Is it proper (ethical) to object in order to break up the jury's involvement in the opposition's story? In order to give your own witness time to stop and think before responding to a tricky question asked on cross-examination? To impress your client that you are actively working on his behalf and so deserve your fat fee even if the case is lost on the merits? There is a danger in objecting too often on insubstantial points. It may appear to the jury that you are being picky, that you are trying to win the case on technicalities, or that you are trying to keep information from them. In addition, if you object too often to trivial matters you are likely to generate a string of adverse judicial rulings. To the extent that the jury takes clues from the judge as to their proper behavior such a set of adverse rulings may put you at a disadvantage when the jury begins deliberating.

Some grounds for objection are based more on common sense and traditional beliefs as to what are unfair practice in the examination of a witness than on spe-

Q. All right. Now, did you see the defendant, Nelson Whale, on that evening? **A.** Yes, I did, sir.

Q. Can you identify the defendant, Nelson Whale? **A.** Yes, I can, sir.

Q. Will you please identify him? **A.** Sitting right next to his counsel, in the white shirt, sir.

cific rules. For example, the question, "Did you see Whale or did you not go to his house?" is objectionable because it has two parts that should be separated. Questions that are flawed in this way are called "compound." If there is no evidence that a witness has a drug habit the question, "When did you stop taking daily doses of narcotics?" is objectionable because it assumes facts that are not in evidence. Such questions are often called "misleading." Another familiar objection is that a question has been asked and answered. This may be used when opposing counsel is repeating, perhaps in different words, a question that has been fully answered. It is useful for curbing opponents who are attempting to emphasize favorable points or to browbeat witnesses into changing stories. Other objectionable behavior by examining attorneys includes badgering witnesses, arguing with witnesses, and putting assertions in the guise of questions.

FRE 103 codifies the common law rule that to preserve error attorneys must object in a timely fashion. If an objection is not made or is not timely appellate courts will only reverse for plain errors affecting substantial rights. An objection to the form of a question should be made, if possible, before the answer is given. An objection to the answer should be made immediately after the grounds for objection become clear. If the objection is sound, the answer should be stricken and the jury should be instructed to ignore both the question and answer.

FRE 103 requires that specific grounds for objection be stated, meaning that one should not object by simply saying, "I object" or by using catchall phrases like "incompetent, immaterial and irrelevant," but should instead specify precisely the basis

for the objection. Many judges tolerate general objections because they are a quick way of alerting a court to an obvious source of error. The danger of a general objection is that if it is overruled an appellate court is likely to hold that it did not preserve error because it did not sufficiently alert the trial judge to defects in the proffered evidence. Thus, the objecting party is held responsible for the judge's failure to spot the specific basis on which the evidence should have been excluded. When a general objection is sustained the party offering the evidence may reasonably argue that FRE 103, or its state equivalent, implies a right to know the specific grounds for an opponent's objection and the specific basis on which the judge sustains it. By pinpointing the specific grounds for decisions at trial, counsel increases the likelihood that an appellate court will spot errors below. This is particularly important where trial judges have considerable discretion. When discretionary decisions are unexplained they are likely to be sustained. When they are explained, the explanation may reveal that impermissible factors were considered or that important factors were not weighed in the balance. Recognizing this, some appellate courts are beginning to demand explanations of trial court decisions made under rules that require a balancing of probative value against prejudicial effect.

If there is more than one basis for an objection, judges often take the clearest ground and rule on it without mentioning the others. For general discussion on the wisdom of ruling on all grounds for objection, see Saltzburg, Another Ground for Decision—Harmless Trial Court Errors, 47 Temp.L.Q. 193 (1974).

MR. BRYERS:[6]   Let the record show that the witness identifies the defendant, Nelson Whale.

Q.   (By Mr. Bryers, continuing): What time did you see him that evening?   A.   I saw the defendant about, around approximately 8 o'clock.

Q.   About 8 o'clock?   A.   8, 8:10, around that.

Q.   And where did you see him?   A.   I first saw the defendant at his home.

Q.   And with whom did you go to his home?   A.   I went to his home with a Mr. Earl Stible.

Q.   And did you enter the house?   A.   Yes, I did, sir.

Q.   And did you have a conversation with the defendant at that time? A.   Yes, I did, sir.

Q.   And what did you say to him?   A.   I asked the defendant for a can or cans of marihuana.

Q.   How were you dressed that night?   A.   I was dressed in civilian clothes.

Q.   And what did he say?   A.   He said that he didn't have that large a quantity on hand.

Q.   All right.   A.   And would have to get it.

Q.   And what did you do then?   A.   I informed him that I wanted it, but I wanted it in a Prince Albert can.   I didn't want it in the packets; a half would be the denominations in these boxes, and so I informed him I would go get a Prince Albert can.

Q.   You informed him that you would go get a Prince Albert can?   A. Yes, sir.

Q.   And what did you do then?   A.   I left the place and went to the corner of Alandale and Morrison Avenue to the People's Drug Store.

Q.   And when you got to this drug store, what did you do?   A.   I bought a can of Prince Albert tobacco, two cans.

Q.   And what did you do then?   A.   I emptied the contents of the cans out and took it back to the defendant's home.

Q.   You went back to the defendant's home?   A.   Yes, I did.

Q.   And who was with you when you went back?   A.   Mr. Stible.

---

6. In some courts a reporter is present solely to monitor a tape recorder. It may be important in such courtrooms for counsel to repeat clearly for the benefit of the recording machine any statements made at a time in which more than one person was talking. If a stenographer is present and cannot understand testimony, the stenographer often will say so. But where everything is being recorded, the person monitoring the machine may not be as careful to make sure that all statements can be heard clearly on the tape.

Q. And was he in the house when you got there? **A.** No, he—Who was in the house?

Q. The defendant? **A.** Yes, he was.

Q. He was there. All right. Then did you have a conversation with him at that time? **A.** Yes, I gave him the cans.

Q. You gave him the can? **A.** Yes, I did.

Q. And what did he do? **A.** He said for me to come back in about a half hour, he would have it.

Q. What did you do then? **A.** I left, and I don't remember exactly what I did after I left the place.

Q. And did you come back later? **A.** Yes, I did.

Q. And did you go into the defendant's house again? **A.** Yes, I did. The defendant was not home so I went back to my car which was parked outside.

Q. Your car was parked in front of the defendant's home, right? **A.** Right—across from his home.

Q. And when did you see the defendant? **A.** The defendant came up in a 1962 or '63 Dodge, I think it was; I can't remember.

Q. And what happened then? **A.** The defendant got out of the car and went into the house.

Q. And did you go along with him? **A.** Yes, we went in behind him.

Q. He was with you when you went in? **A.** More or less. He walked in and we walked in right behind him.

Q. What happened then? **A.** We were in a room, and Mr. Stible, he left or something—I don't remember exactly. And the defendant handed me a can, a Prince Albert can, and there was a can sitting up on a shelf, and I took that can, also.

Q. You took both cans? **A.** Yes, sir.

Q. And what did you do then? **A.** I gave the defendant $45.

Q. And what did you do then? **A.** And then, feeling one of the cans, I noticed it was empty. I said, "Wait a minute, we got things mixed up," so the defendant gave me back $22.50 out of the $45.

Q. And you paid him $22.50 for this can? **A.** Yes, I did, sir.

Q. What did you do then? **A.** After then, I left, me and Mr. Stible left the defendant's home.

Q. And then what did you do? **A.** We drove down the street out Murane onto Green where I stopped and inspected the contents of the can.

Q. You stopped and inspected the contents, you say? **A.** Yes, sir.

Q. What did you observe? **A.** After inspecting the contents of the can, the can had some dents. When I opened the can, it appeared to have been shorted.

Q. What did you do then?

THE COURT (to witness): What do you mean by "shorted"?

THE WITNESS: There wasn't the quantity. The can was not full. The can was short. A—I looked at the cans and a—

Q. (By Mr. Bryers, continuing): What did you do then? **A.** I said to the defendant—not to the defendant, correction. I said to the subject in the car—

MR. EVERT: Object to what he said to the subject in the car.

THE COURT:[7] Sustained, because it was not in the presence of the defendant.

Q. (By Mr. Bryers, continuing): You had a conversation then with Mr. Stible, is that right? **A.** Yes, I did.

Q. And as a result of that conversation, what did you do? **A.** I returned the can back to the defendant, back to his home.

Q. You went back to the defendant's home? **A.** Yes.

Q. And did you see the defendant at that time? **A.** Yes, I did.

7. Here we have what may be a rather important objection, for it is possible that officer Norton, if allowed to testify to what he said, might further incriminate Whale or strengthen his (Norton's) own credibility as a witness. You should first note the form of this objection. It does not use the neat categories which students learn in evidence courses, but it appears obvious that the objection is on the ground of hearsay.

The court's ruling on this point is an interesting example of the way in which nice analytical distinctions taught in classrooms may be overlooked in courtrooms. The court sustains the objection because the statement was not made in the presence of the defendant, thereby implying that had the statement been made in the presence of the defendant it would have been admissible. There is a class of statements which are admissible in evidence despite their hearsay character if they are made in the presence of a defendant who does not respond [they are called "admissions by silence"], and it is also possible that if the statements were part of a conversation with the defendant they would be admissible for some non-hearsay purpose. However, there is no general rule that all statements made in the presence of the defendant are admissible in evidence, nor is there an absolute rule that statements made outside the presence of the defendant are inadmissible. The presiding judge in this trial may have adopted the "presence of defendant" test as an easy talisman for determining which out-of-court statements to admit. If so, you would do well to know this when litigating before this judge. You would also do well to be prepared with a more detailed analysis of the intricacies of the hearsay rule in case this judge's rule of thumb leads to mistaken rulings which are harmful to your client.

At this point, of course, you have not encountered the hearsay rule and need not know exactly what it excludes. Suffice it to say that here the judge applied the rule erroneously, although his ruling nevertheless is correct.

Q. And did you go into his house? **A.** Yes, I did.

Q. And what did you say to him? **A.** Well, I asked him—I can't remember the exact conversation, word, you know, for word—but in general I asked him what was wrong. "You're trying to short me. I gave you a fair shake." And the defendant took a piece of newspaper and spread it out on a small counter which was in this foyer-like room and dumped the contents out of the can into the—on the paper, and I went over. He said, "See, man, this is choice smoke."

Q. Who said that? **A.** The defendant. "And you can roll a hundred right from here on now." And he took the contents—the spread of marihuana that was on the paper—and emptied it back into the can, I mean, you know, returned it back to the can.

Q. It was put back in the can by the defendant? **A.** Yes, sir.

Q. And what happened then? **A.** I told him that I was satisfied and I was sorry, and I took the can and left.

Q. You left his house? **A.** That's right.

Q. What did you do then after you left his home? **A.** I dropped Mr. Stible off.

Q. Then what did you do? **A.** I went to the rear of Cherry Tree High School, which is in the City of Hamster to meet with Officer Barrott.

Q. And was Officer Barrott there? **A.** Yes, sir.

Q. And then what did you do? **A.** I showed Officer Barrott the can. I signed it, I mean, initialed the can, and I dated it.

Q. Do you recall what initials you put on the can? **A.** D.D.N., sir.

Q. Did Officer Barrott do anything? **A.** I believe he signed the can, also, or initialed the can.[8]

Q. Are you sure or you are not sure? **A.** I'm pretty sure he did.

Q. And did you turn the can over to Officer Barrott? **A.** Yes, I did, sir.

Q. And then what did you do? **A.** From there we went to Judge McCarthey's home.

MR. BRYERS:[9] You may cross-examine.

8. Why did officer Norton sign the can which allegedly contained marihuana before turning it over to officer Barrott? Why did officer Barrott sign the can? What kinds of arguments would opposing counsel make had the can not been signed by both officers? Note how evidence law affects the behavior of police officers far from the courtroom, indeed before an arrest has taken place.

9. The direct examination of officer Norton is over and the cross-examination will begin. You should consider the kinds of questions which are asked on direct examination. Generally they are questions of the type, "What happened then?" or "And then what did you do?" Norton is not asked, "Did you tell him you were satisfied and then leave the can?" or "Did you then go to Judge McCarthey's home?"

THE COURT: It's ten minutes before lunch, and I have another jury out whom I have to send to lunch. You will not conclude in the few minutes that are left, I am sure.

The latter kinds of questions suggest the desired answer. They are known as "leading questions" and are generally inappropriate on direct examination. In the cross-examination which follows you will find many questions which are leading— e.g., "The defendant Nelson Whale is not the only person from whom you claim you purchased narcotics. Is that statement correct?" On cross-examination such questions are appropriate. Why does the judicial attitude toward leading questions differ, depending on whether they are asked on direct or cross-examination? What is the purpose of direct examination? What is the purpose of cross-examination? Who is testifying when the witness is fed a succession of leading questions, the witness or the attorney? The right to use leading questions on cross-examination helps an attorney keep control of the witness and helps to avoid damaging surprises. Why isn't such control needed on direct examination? How does an attorney know what to expect from his client on direct?

Do you note any leading questions asked officer Norton on direct examination? Why are no objections made? Although officer Norton is not introduced through a series of leading questions, leading questions are generally a proper means of dealing quickly with undisputed preliminary matters such as a witness' name, address, and occupation. Questions which seek a "yes" or "no" answer often come close to being leading because much of the information sought is conveyed in the question; only the crucial point as to whether the specified situation exists depends on the answer. If it is clear that an attorney is leading a witness through a series of "yes-no" questions in order to describe the witness' experience, the questions are probably objectionable as leading. Yet in other situations one or more "yes-no" questions may be the most economical and least awkward way of asking for certain details of a witness' story. Here

it may be unclear whether the attorney is leading his witness. Most attorneys will not object to isolated questions of this sort and will be unlikely to object generally to leading questions unless they deal with matters which are in dispute. What benefits may accrue to an attorney who does not object when a witness is given leading question after leading question? At what point in the string might an attorney object?

FRE 611(c) provides:

Leading questions. Leading questions should not be used on the direct examination of a witness except as may be necessary to develop his testimony. Ordinarily leading questions should be permitted on cross-examination. When a party calls a hostile witness, an adverse party, or a witness identified with an adverse party, interrogation may be by leading questions.

Allowing hostile and adverse witnesses to be interrogated through leading questions is supported by the same rationales which support the use of leading questions on cross-examination. What are they? Can you think of any reasons why the courts should be somewhat more protective of hostile witnesses called by an adverse party than they are of witnesses on cross-examination? If P calls W as a hostile witness and questions him by leading questions, should D be forced to examine W on cross-examination by non-leading questions? Can you think of reasons why D should also be allowed to use leading questions?

A problem does arise in some states as to when a witness is hostile. Generally speaking there is a presumption, which in some courts may be close to irrebuttable, that a witness, other than an adverse party, is not hostile to the party calling that witness. This is an echo of the now discredited common law rule that one "vouched for credibility" of one's witnesses. Consider, e.g., Chambers v. Mississippi, 410 U.S. 284 (1973), discussed in Chapter Seven,

(To jury) I will admonish the jury not to discuss this matter with anybody and not among themselves. Remember, now, as I indicated before, until such time as I charge you as to the law and you go to your jury room and elect your foreman in the secrecy of the jury room, you are not to begin your deliberations at all.

With that admonition, I shall adjourn this case until 2 o'clock, and you will report back here at that time.

At 2:10 p. m.

(The trial was continued.)

THE COURT: Mr. Norton, will you resume the stand? You are still under oath and are about to be cross-examined. You may proceed, Mr. Evert.

(Whereupon Darrell D. Norton, having been previously sworn, resumed the stand and testified as follows:)

CROSS-EXAMINATION

BY MR. EVERT:

Q. Mr. Norton, when did you first become a member of the Hamster Police force? A. That would be December 12, 1966.

Q. What did you do before that time? A. I was a police officer in the Township of Lussinia.

Q. You attained the rank of sergeant there, is that right? A. That is correct, sir.

---

infra. Other courts refuse to declare witnesses hostile unless they give testimony which actually harms the party calling the witness. The problem with this approach is that where the testimony of a hostile witness is needed one's case may be undermined without that witness ever saying anything positively harmful.

A basic objection to leading questions is that they are likely to be suggestive. The fear is that a witness may acquiesce in the lawyer's version of events without interposing an independent view as to what occurred. This danger might appear particularly great in the case of small children, the mentally retarded, or individuals who do not know the language well. Yet leading questions are typically allowed when examining witnesses who would otherwise have trouble relating an intelligible story. Leading questions may also be allowed to refresh the memory of individuals who claim they have forgotten important events. The rationale for allowing leading questions in such circumstances is that the need for the witness' information outweighs any infirmities in the mode of extracting it. The jury is trusted to discount stories elicited by leading questions in some appropriate manner. They may well do so, but individuals have been imprisoned and civil judgments awarded on the basis of stories told by lawyers with only occasional pauses for the perfunctory assent of the witness being questioned. If you were in federal court, where in the federal rules would you find a justification for examining a six-year-old child by leading questions?

Q. You gave us a statement of your purpose and your duties to suppress the narcotic traffic in Hamster. You didn't exactly say that, but I take it that is what you said.

THE COURT: I think that's exactly what he said.

Q. (By Mr. Evert, continuing): Now, who indicated to you when you were hired that that was your purpose? **A.** I was informed by the city manager and Officer Barrott.

Q. All right. And who made the decision that you were to work in plain clothes? **A.** The decision was made by the city manager.

Q. All right. And did the city manager give you any particular instructions or leads which you should follow in your work? **A.** No, sir.

Q. All right. Did he tell you anything about the methods you should use as a police officer in obtaining evidence of a crime? **A.** No, sir.

Q. Who was your immediate superior? With whom did you have your contact? **A.** Officer Barrott.

Q. Have you made any reports to the city manager in connection with this case? **A.** Yes and no, sir.

Q. Would you explain what you mean by "yes"? **A.** The reports were made directly to the officer in charge of the unit, which was Officer Richard Barrott. He, in turn, made the report to the city manager.

Q. The defendant, Nelson Whale, is not the only person from whom you claim you purchased narcotics. Is that statement correct? **A.** Yes, sir.

Q. All right. Is this the first of the cases that you investigated that have reached Circuit Court for trial? **A.** No, sir.

Q. Some of the other cases have been tried, is that right? **A.** Yes, sir.

Q. Some of the cases that you investigated have been dismissed, have they not?

MR. BRYERS: I'll object to that, your Honor.

THE COURT:[10] Objection sustained.

10. Why did the prosecutor object when Norton was asked whether other cases he had investigated had been dismissed? How would Norton's answer to this question be helpful to this case? Would the prosecutor have objected if none of the other cases which Norton had investigated had been dismissed? Would Evert have asked the question if this had been the case? Why did Evert ask this question? Could he lose anything by asking it? If Norton had admitted that other investigations he had conducted had been dismissed might that not cast doubt on his credibility and competence? If, as is the case here, the objection is made and sustained, what impression do you think the jury is left with? Do you think the judge's instruction to the jury will eliminate any advantage which may have accrued to the defendant? Is it ethical to ask a question which one knows to be almost certainly

Sec. 1

(To jury) You may strike that from your minds, ignore it. It has
~~hing~~ to do with this case. When I sustain an objection and ask you to
~~egard~~ it, you must do just that.[11]

~~).~~ (By Mr. Evert, continuing): How long was Nelson Whale a target
~~r~~ investigation? A. You have to explain the word "target", sir.

Well, let me put it differently. You testified that on January 25th
~~ere~~ with a person named Earl Stible, is that correct? A. Yes, sir.

Q. All right. Did Earl Stible introduce you to the defendant? A.
~~Yes~~, sir.

Q. Now, how long did you know Earl Stible? A. Ever since about
the 30th of December. I'm not exactly sure on that.

Q. The 30th of December is your answer? A. Right along in that
period.

Q. Was Earl Stible assisting you generally in your investigation of narcotics in Hamster? A. No, sir.

Q. Did he introduce you to any defendants in your investigation other
than this defendant? A. Yes, sir.

Q. All right. Now, you offered Earl Stible certain inducements for
his work with you, did you not? A. No, sir.

Q. You have bought him drinks, is that correct? A. Yes, sir.

Q. And you have supplied him with marihuana, is that right? A. No,
sir.

Q. Have you ever testified in open court that you have given marihuana to Earl Stible? A. I don't recall, sir.

Q. Will you state whether or not you ever gave Earl Stible two marihuana cigarettes? A. No, sir, they weren't given to him.[12]

objectionable? Does the fact that the opposing attorney might choose not to object have any bearing on the ethical question? Where an attorney does not move
to exclude objectionable evidence, the jury
may treat that evidence in the same way
it treats other evidence in the case.

11. Should the judge do more than
this? Should he, for example, explain the
theory of his ruling to the jury?

12. Individuals such as police officers
and forensic scientists who regularly appear in court may become very adept at
the art of responding to cross-examination. It is important that the lawyer be
particularly careful in questioning such
witnesses; a careless question may give
the experienced witness an opportunity to
make a fool of the interrogator. In one
case, for example, a noted academic physician made it a point to personally conduct his first autopsy in several years before testifying at trial on a cause of death
issue. When the cross-examiner attempting to disparage his qualifications asked
him when he had last conducted an autopsy, the expert was able to reply, "This
morning!", thus making it appear that his
testimony was backed by more practical
experience than he actually had. In another well-known case, a lawyer thought
it necessary to discount the testimony of
a mild-mannered foreigner who had conducted a crucial autopsy in the case.
When the witness appeared to be count-

Q. All right, You said "they". You are then referring to, at some point you gave somebody some marihuana cigarettes, is that correct?

MR. BRYERS: Your Honor, I will object to that as being immaterial.

MR. EVERT: Oh, I think it's very material.

THE COURT: Sustained. It has nothing to do with this case whether he gave anybody else anything.

MR. EVERT: I would like to make a legal argument, Your Honor.

THE COURT: [13] You may proceed to trial. I have already ruled on this. You may make it at a later time.

(To jury) Disregard that question, Members of the Jury.

ing on his fingers before responding affirmatively to the lawyer's question of whether he had conducted as many as ten autopsies, the lawyer thought he could demonstrate inexperience. He pressed the witness for the exact number of autopsies he had conducted, only to find out that the witness had been the coroner of the city of Berlin before emigrating to the United States, and so had conducted tens of thousands of autopsies. This fact would never have been brought out had the attorney not explored the matter on cross-examination. Finally there is the Clarence Darrow story about the man accused of mayhem for biting off the ear of another. Having asked the only eyewitness whether he saw the defendant bite off the ear, defense counsel received a favorable reply—"No!" Unfortunately he went further and asked how the witness knew the defendant bit off the ear. The reply, "I saw him spit it out."

Careless questioning on cross-examination may, of course, do more than embarrass the interrogator or strengthen the credentials of opposing witnesses. Witnesses may respond to questions on cross-examination with information that they could not have offered on direct examination. As long as a witness responds to the question that is put, the lawyer may be held to have "opened the door" to whatever the witness says.

If the witness answers a question in a way that is not responsive—i.e., volunteers information that the lawyer has not requested—the cross-examiner may be able to have the answer stricken. This cannot

guarantee that jurors will forget it. In most courts, non-responsive answers can only be objected to by the person who has asked the question, not by the other side. The reason is that if the answer is not objectionable on any other ground except that it is not responsive, the lawyer could simply ask another question and get the same answer. Thus, the law saves time by allowing the questioner to accept the answer as given.

Officer Norton appears to have the kind of experience which should make a cross-examiner wary. Note how at an earlier point he changed the tempo and the mood of the cross-examination by asking for an explanation of the word "target" when Evert asked him how long Whale was a target of the investigation. At the point noted here, Norton is responding to the literal language of the question, though at a later point it becomes clear that he did give two marihuana cigarettes to a companion of Stible, apparently with the knowledge that at least one was to be given to Stible. Clearly Norton is not a witness who is going to volunteer information.

Why, incidentally, is Evert asking Norton about this incident? How does this relate to the case against Whale?

13. It is relatively common for a court to postpone extended argument on an issue to a later point in the trial. Where argument on an issue is postponed it is very unlikely that the judge's ruling will later be changed. However, this device does

Q. (By Mr. Evert, continuing): All right. Now, Nelson Whale was in the company of Earl Stible on the 25th of January, is that correct? **A.** No, sir.

Q. Well, were Nelson Whale and Earl Stible ever together in the same room on January 25th? **A.** Yes, sir.

Q. Now, you had been with Earl Stible earlier that day, is that right? **A.** Yes, sir.

Q. And you had had a drink with him that day, had you not? **A.** Yes, sir.

Q. And you had given him a marihuana cigarette on that day, had you not? **A.** No, sir.

Q. Earl Stible suggested that you go to the defendant's house to purchase marihuana, is that correct? **A.** No, sir.

Q. It was your idea to go to the defendant's house to purchase marihuana, is that correct? **A.** No, sir.

Q. Was there any discussion prior to the time you went to the defendant's house the first time on the 25th? **A.** Yes, sir.

Q. (By Mr. Evert, continuing): Did the discussion include a plan to go over to Nelson Whale's house? **A.** Yes, sir.

Q. Who suggested that? **A.** It was suggested by another party, sir.

Q. Neither you nor Earl Stible? **A.** Correct, sir.

Q. Who was the third party that made the suggestion? **A.** A Mr. Pumplin, sir.

Q. Was Mr. Pumplin ever present on the 25th of January when—was he ever present with Mr. Stible? **A.** No, sir.

Q. Was it after you talked to Mr. Pumplin that you met Mr. Stible? **A.** Yes, sir.

Q. All right. Now, did you discuss going over to the defendant Nelson Whale's house with Mr. Stible? **A.** Yes, sir.

give the attorney a chance to particularize the objection for the record and avoids the need to interrupt the flow of the trial to argue a matter about which the judge feels confident. You should note that Evert might have had a chance to make whatever legal argument he wanted to make immediately following Bryers' objection, but instead of presenting reasons why he thought the objection inappropriate he responded simply, "Oh, I think it's very material." This is not the kind of argument which is likely to influence a judge.

A lawyer who expects a legal point to arise and who knows that it may be a difficult one can help his cause by preparing a memorandum of law on the point and having it ready at trial. If it is a point that the other side has not anticipated, the judge may give a recess so that other side can research the law. Often, however, the recess is short and the party that is well prepared has a substantial advantage.

Q. Did you tell him about your conversation with Mr. Pumplin? **A.** Yes, sir.

Q. Did you promise to give Mr. Stible any marihuana for going over there with you? **A.** No, sir.

Q. Did you offer him any inducements whatsoever to go over there with you? **A.** No, sir.

Q. You and Mr. Stible were alone when you got to Mr. Whale's house, is that correct? **A.** Yes, sir.

Q. Now, did Mr. Stible go in with you? **A.** Yes, sir.

Q. And was he present during the time there was a conversation between you and the defendant? **A.** I don't exactly remember, sir.

Q. Let's go back a bit. Did Mr. Whale open the door? **A.** No, sir.

Q. All right. Where did you talk to the defendant, Mr. Whale? **A.** In the foyer.

Q. All right. And Mr. Stible, did he go in before or after you? **A.** He went in before I did.

Q. Did he stay there with you or did he go into another room? **A.** He went into another room, sir.

Q. All right. Did he leave with you after that first conversation? **A.** Yes, sir.

Q. But in any event, you had told him what you were going to do over at Mr. Whale's house, is that right? **A.** No, sir.

Q. Well, there was some discussion? **A.** Yes, sir.

Q. And that discussion included the fact that you were going to try to buy some cans of marihuana from the defendant, is that right? **A.** Yes and no, sir.

Q. In what sense do you mean "yes"? **A.** We discussed the purchase of marihuana.

Q. From the defendant? **A.** Yes, sir.

Q. But you didn't tell him the quantity, is that right? **A.** That is correct.

Q. That's the sense in which you mean "no"? **A.** Yes, sir.

Q. So you and Mr. Whale are alone in the foyer now. And who spoke first? **A.** The initial—the start of the conversation—Mr. Stible made the start of the conversation.

Q. What did Mr. Stible say? **A.** That—he told Mr. Whale that I wanted to see him about something.

Q. And what did Mr. Whale then say? **A.** Mr. Whale said, "Okay, maybe we can talk in here". And Mr. Stible left the room.

Q. And then you and he went there together. **A.** Yes.

Q. Who spoke next? **A.** I did, sir.

Q. What did you say? **A.** I told the defendant that I wanted to purchase a can or two of marihuana.

Q. All right. And what did he say to that? **A.** He said he didn't have that much on hand right now.

Q. What's the next thing you said? **A.** "When can I get it"?

Q. What did he say? **A.** He told me to come back in about half an hour.

Q. And it was his suggestion that you produce some cans or tins to contain the marihuana, is that correct? **A.** No, sir.

Q. You wanted it in one can? **A.** I bought two cans, sir.

Q. Yes, sir. **A.** So I left—when I came back the second time I left two cans, not knowing if I would get one can or two cans.

Q. But you knew it was one or the other. **A.** Yes, sir.

Q. Is that because of what he said to you? **A.** It was the agreement we made.

Q. He told you, did he not, what was the quantity he had? **A.** No sir, he didn't say what quantity he did have.

Q. All right. And you had a discussion about money? **A.** Yes, sir.

Q. All right. Tell me about that. He asked you about money? **A.** Correction, counselor. I'm sorry. I asked him what it would cost.

Q. You asked him what it would cost? **A.** Yes, sir.

Q. And what did he say it would cost per can? **A.** $25.

Q. When you left then, there was no agreement as to what the quantity would be, is that right? **A.** Not really.

Q. All right. You didn't leave any money, did you? **A.** No, sir.

Q. Now, did Mr. Stible go with you when you got the Prince Albert cans? **A.** Yes, sir.

Q. And he was there when you dumped it out, is that right? **A.** Yes, sir.

Q. And did you have any conversation with Mr. Stible then about what you were doing? **A.** Just that I was going to take the cans up to Tweedie's [14] house.

Q. He never asked you why, and you never told him, is that right? **A.** No.

---

14. **Who is Tweedie? Should a confused juror be able to ask for clarification?** In a few courts they can, for judges have discretion to allow jurors to question wit-

Q. Now, when you got back the second time, who let you in? **A.** I really don't remember who let us in. Mr. Stible went into the door first.

Q. Now, eventually you talked with the defendant on the second occasion. **A.** Yes, sir.

Q. And you handed him the two cans? **A.** Yes, sir.

Q. And you had a conversation at the time you were doing that, is that right? **A.** I can't remember, sir.

Q. Did you ask him whether or not he had the narcotics then? **A.** No, sir.

Q. Should I understand that you just handed him the two cans and left? **A.** More or less.

Q. What do you mean "more"? **A.** There could have been a conversation, but if there was, I don't recall it.

Q. It is certainly true you had no more conversation about price or quantity, is that right? Can you state that as a fact? **A.** Correct, sir.

Q. And there certainly wasn't any discussion as to when you should get this marihuana, is that right? **A.** I don't really know. He told me to come back in a half hour the first time I came there.

Q. And you left? **A.** Right, sir.

Q. All right. Now, when you left, you came back a half hour later? **A.** Yes, sir.

Q. This time, did you have any discussion about the transaction? **A.** I told him I would have to go back in a half hour.

Q. Still no discussion about what you were going to do? **A.** No, sir, because he knew.[15]

Q. Had you ever told him? **A.** In the Capri Lounge.

Q. You told him in the Capri Lounge that you were going to purchase two cans of marihuana from the defendant? **A.** No. I told him in the Capri Lounge that I was sent there by Mr. Pumplin to find him to talk to Mr. Whale to purchase marihuana.

Q. And was it then that you gave him marihuana cigarettes? **A.** I didn't give him any, sir.

nesses. Where this is allowed, jurors typically write down their questions following the conclusion of the cross-examination. The judge screens the questions to eliminate those that are objectionable or not worth the time they require. The remaining questions are put to the witnesses, either as the jurors have written them or in the judge's own words. See Saltzburg, The Unnecessarily Expanding Role of the American Trial Judge, 64 Va.L.Rev. 1, 63–64 (1978). What are the advantages and disadvantages of such a procedure?

15. Who is "he"? Once again, couldn't this be much clearer? How might the lawyer know the jury is confused? What should counsel do?

Q. Was it then that you promised him some marihuana? **A.** No, sir.

Q. All right. You came back in a half hour. Who let you in then? **A.** We walked in behind Mr. Whale.

Q. So Mr. Whale wasn't in the house the third time you came over? **A.** No, sir.

Q. All right. You saw him doing what outside? **A.** He had pulled up in a vehicle and just as we had pulled up, we went to the door and they said he wasn't home, so we said we would sit and wait a bit.

Q. Mr. Whale wasn't there, is that right? **A.** No, sir.

Q. And the defendant came up in a car, is that right? **A.** Yes, sir.

Q. Was he alone? **A.** No, sir.

Q. Was the person a man or woman? **A.** There were some men in the car.

Q. The two of you walked in behind Mr. Whale, is that right? **A.** Yes, sir.

Q. The people in the car didn't come in? **A.** No, sir.

Q. The car drove off, is that right? **A.** That's correct.

Q. And for the purpose of this case, the car was never seen again. The car has no significance in this case, is that right? **A.** Yes.

THE COURT: The fact that it wasn't seen by him is all he can testify to.

MR. EVERT: No, except he has not testified to that.

THE COURT: You asked him a question: It was never seen again by anybody. Ask him if he ever saw it again.

MR. EVERT: I will withdraw the question.

THE COURT: You may withdraw it.

Q. (By Mr. Evert, continuing): In any event, the three of you were in the house, is that right? **A.** Yes, sir.

Q. Again, you had some conversation with the defendant, Mr. Whale, is that right? **A.** Yes, sir.

Q. What about Mr. Stible? Did he leave the room again? **A.** Yes, sir, he did.

Q. Now, at any point did he come back in the room before you left? **A.** During our talk.

Q. All right. What were you doing, if you remember, when he came back? **A.** I was in the process of picking up the cans, the cans of suspected marihuana, or paying Mr. Whale. I can't remember.

Q. Eventually, you testified, you got two Prince Albert cans from the defendant, is that right? **A.** Right.

Q. Did he hand them to you? **A.** He handed me one of them, sir.

Q. He handed you one of them? **A.** Yes, sir.

Q. And you got the second can, is that right? **A.** I picked up the second can myself, sir, off the shelf.

Q. All right. And during the time that you were receiving the can and picking up the other can off the shelf, you had some conversations with the defendant, is that right? **A.** Yes, sir.

Q. And what was that conversation? First of all, what did he say to you? **A.** I can't remember, sir.

Q. Do you remember any of the conversation? **A.** Yes, sir.

Q. Will you tell me as much of it as you can remember? **A.** At what point, sir?

Q. At the time that you were receiving a can from the defendant and picking the other one up off the shelf. **A.** The defendant gave me the can and I picked the other one off the shelf, and I believe—I mean, I'm really not certain. In generalities—

Q. Let me ask you a more specific question. Did you say anything about money? **A.** Yes, sir.

Q. Who said what to whom about money? **A.** The defendant told me it would be $22.50.

Q. And you gave him $22.50? **A.** Yes—no, sir.

Q. You gave him how much? **A.** I gave him $45, sir.

Q. He told you that it would be $22.50? **A.** Per can.

Q. Wait a minute, wait a minute. He told you it would be $22.50 and you gave him $45, is that right?

THE COURT: He said "per can".

MR. EVERT: Is that what he said, your Honor?

THE COURT: That's right.

Q. (By Mr. Evert, continuing): Is that right? **A.** Yes, sir, per can.

THE COURT: He just said that to you—"per can".

Q. (By Mr. Evert, continuing): And you gave him $45? **A.** Right, sir.

Q. And then what did he say? **A.** He didn't say anything. I made the next statement.

Q. What did you say next? **A.** The can that I picked up off the shelf was empty, and I said, "Wait a minute. This can is empty". He said, "Yes, I thought you only wanted one can".

Q. Now, did the defendant still have the $45 in his hand at the time of this discussion of one can or two cans? **A.** Yes.

Q. So you asked him for your $22.50 back? **A.** No, he gave me back $22.50.

Q. All right. Now, eventually, you marked one of the cans with your initials. What did you do with the second can? **A.** Threw it away.

Q. Where? **A.** I don't remember.

Q. When? **A.** When I got out of the house.

Q. Now, who started the conversation between yourself and Mr. Whale when you came back that third time? **A.** I don't know which one of us started it. One of us started it. I can't remember exactly. I may have started it. This is something the defendant may have started.

Q. It is correct to state that you don't remember one way or the other, is that right? **A.** Not who started the exact conversation.

Q. Have you told us all you can about the third conversation you had with the defendant, the third time you came to his house that evening? Is there anything else that you can remember that you haven't told us? **A.** No, there is nothing else I can remember.

Q. Will you state whether or not any person other than Mr. Stible was at the house? The first time you said some young man opened the door. Is that the thrust of your testimony? **A.** Yes, sir.

Q. And you never saw him any more that day, is that right? **A.** No, sir.

Q. Now, did any other person come over to the house that day while you were there? **A.** Somebody walked in.

Q. Was that a man or woman? **A.** I believe it was a woman. I'm not sure. I mean, I didn't pay any attention, really.

Q. Well, did you speak to whomever came in? **A.** I might have, sir.

Q. But you still don't remember whether it was a woman or man? **A.** Not really, sir.

Q. All right. As soon as you walked in the door, Mr. Whale handed you the can of marihuana, is that right? **A.** More or less, sir.

Q. And in what sense do you mean "more"? **A.** There was a discussion, a brief conversation.

Q. But you don't remember what that conversation was? **A.** No, sir, I can't, not verbatim, word for word.

Q. In any event, you left the house again with Mr. Stible, is that right? **A.** Yes, sir.

Q. All right. That's when you told Mr. Stible that you had made a purchase, is that right? **A.** Not in those exact words.

Q. What were the words? **A.** He asked me, did I take care of my business, and I told him yes.

Q. And that's when you gave him marihuana? **A.** I didn't give him any marihuana.

Q. Now, when you went back the fourth time, was Mr. Stible with you? **A.** Yes, he was.

Q. And I think you testified that you went back and either you or the defendant dumped this marihuana on a piece of paper? **A.** The defendant did.

Q. The defendant did? And Mr. Stible was there, wasn't he? **A.** I don't remember whether he was in the room or not.

Q. Do you remember whether or not he was there when Mr. Whale dumped the marihuana on a piece of paper? **A.** No, sir.

Q. Definitely not there? **A.** I can't remember him being there, sir.

Q. Now, when you left the fourth time, did you give Mr. Stible any marihuana? **A.** No, sir.

Q. And then you left him to meet Mr. Barrott, is that right? **A.** Correct, sir.

Q. And upon leaving the fourth time, you had this can of marihuana, is that right, with you? **A.** Yes, sir.

Q. At some point you went before the judge to get a search warrant, is that right? **A.** To sign one.

Q. Yes. And did the judge sign it while you were there? **A.** I believe so, sir.

Q. And were you there when the search warrant was executed? **A.** Yes, sir.

Q. All right. And was the search warrant executed at 4051 or 4061 Murane at Hamster? **A.** Yes, sir.

Q. And you were searching for narcotics, is that right? **A.** Yes, sir.

Q. Did you find any? **A.** No, sir.

Q. Will you state whether or not the search warrant was ever executed on January 27th? I don't mean signed. I mean when you took the search warrant to the defendant's house. **A.** It was executed on the day of our initial raid, sir.

Q. And was that on January 27th? **A.** No, sir.

Q. What date was it? **A.** January 28th.

Q. Do you recall there was a day or two between the time the search warrant was signed and it was executed? Is that what you say? **A.** Yes, the date the search warrant was executed, sir.

Q. Did you find any marihuana? **A.** No, sir.

Q. Now, in order to have the warrant issued to search the defendant's house, you signed a statement as to what happened on January 25th, is that right? **A.** Yes, sir.

Q. Do you recall if the statement specifically dealt with January 25th? **A.** I can't answer that question, sir.

(Whereupon a document was handed to the witness.)

Q. I will show you a document and ask you if your signature appears thereon. **A.** Yes, sir.

Q. Do you recognize any other signatures on the document? **A.** The signature of Judge McCarthey.

Q. Were you present when he signed it? **A.** I can't recall. We signed so many papers on that term.

Q. It is for that reason that you don't recall? **A.** I can't recall that specific.

Q. On any of the trips to the defendant's house on January 25th, did he state whether or not he was going to have to leave the house to get this marihuana? **A.** Yes, sir.

Q. All right. What did he say about that? **A.** He said he didn't have it here, he had to get it.

Q. All right. Now, you signed this sworn affidavit that said, "Deponent further states that he believes that marihuana is stored and sold at 4061 Murane." You didn't mean it was stored there, did you? **A.** It could have been, sir.

Q. Did you believe it was stored there? **A.** I didn't know. It could have been.

MR. BRYERS: Your Honor, I will object to the marihuana because I think it's immaterial to this particular case.

THE COURT: I think what he is doing is testing the credibility of the witness, and while there is great latitude given on cross-examination, at some point or other it probably should be disposed of. But I think I will let him answer that question. It goes to the credibility of the witness. This is not material, however, as to the case itself that is before us, but you can ask that question.

MR. EVERT: Should I restrict myself to the 25th? There was an analysis after that.

THE COURT: I just ruled in your favor. I overruled his objection. You are not restricted.

Q. (By Mr. Evert, continuing): Did you believe the defendant stored marihuana on Murane Street? **A.** I did believe it was around that area.

Q. And you believe it, based on your contact with the defendant on January 25, 1967, at about 10 o'clock, is that right? **A.** There was no contact made with the defendant at that time.

Q. Well, now, you signed a sworn affidavit that that's what happened? **A.** It was an error, sir, apparently.

Q. Well, did you read the document before you signed it? **A.** Yes, sir.

Q. Beginning at "Deponent states", that paragraph, would you read that, please? **A.** "Deponent states that on January 25th, 1967, at 10:10 p. m. he purchased a quantity of marihuana". This is an error, sir.

Q. What should it be? **A.** 8:10.

Q. Now, this is a statement that you swore to in order to get the judge to issue a warrant to kick open the door at 4061 Murane Court, is that right? **A.** No, sir.

Q. This is the statement you swore to in order to get a search warrant, isn't it? **A.** Yes, sir.

Q. And how many persons went to that house on the occasion that it was searched? **A.** A group of officers.

Q. Give me your best estimate. **A.** Oh, I would say 15.

Q. All right. And they all went through that house, is that right? **A.** I'm not saying all of them went through it.

THE COURT: I think at this juncture that we are going far afield. I will restrict your cross-examination now, other than testimony testing his credibility, on what happened on the 25th. The 27th is not at issue here.

Q. (By Mr. Evert, continuing): Were you with Mr. Barrott when he got the narcotics analyzed? **A.** No, I was not.

Q. You don't know when he took it down or if he took it down for analysis, do you? **A.** I turned it over to him.

Q. That wasn't the question. The question was: You don't know if or when he took it down for analysis, do you? **A.** No.

Q. But you imagine that was on the 25th, the day we were talking about.

THE COURT: [16] I don't think he should answer a question that contains the words "you imagine".

16. The judge is interfering here not because the word "imagine" is taboo in the courtroom but because it appears that Norton has no personal knowledge of the facts. Non-expert witnesses may only testify to facts that they know firsthand. This limitation should not be confused with witness incompetence. An incompetent witness cannot testify at all, or on a particular topic or against a particular per-

Q. (By Mr. Evert, continuing): Well, was it on the 25th? **A.** What was on the 25th?

Q. When Mr. Barrott took the narcotics down—

MR. BRYERS: He said he didn't know.

THE COURT: He said he didn't know. I will strike that question.

MR. EVERT: I would like to have a recess, your Honor.

THE COURT: If you want to conclude with this gentleman, you will have to do it by 4 o'clock. We have a meeting at 4 o'clock. I'm going to excuse everybody a little earlier, so I would like you to conclude with this witness.

MR. EVERT: Can't I have any time, then?

THE COURT: I thought maybe you had a lot of time before we tried the case. I can't interrupt the trial of a case now. If I give you a recess, we will have only 15 minutes of testimony.

MR. EVERT: Very well.

Q. (By Mr. Evert, continuing): On February 3, 1967, you were present at a preliminary examination held in connection with this case in the Hamster Municipal Court where Judge John L. Komersky was presiding, is that correct? **A.** Correct, sir.

Q. Do you recall on that occasion that I asked you certain questions concerning this matter that is now before the Court? **A.** Yes, sir.

Q. You gave written reports to Mr. Barrott in connection with your investigation of this case, is that right? **A.** That is correct, sir.

Q. Do you have those reports in the court with you? **A.** No, sir.

Q. Have you ever seen them since you gave them to Mr. Barrott? **A.** No, sir.

son, regardless of what he or she knows. Norton is clearly competent for he has been allowed to give valuable testimony. Today the common law incompetencies have all but disappeared, but the firsthand knowledge limitation is still important.

The judge is generally in charge of the trial and may, as he has done several times during the cross-examination of Norton, interrupt the questioning either to ask questions of his own or to keep the testimony focused on the matters at issue. A judge should, however, be careful not to appear to take over any of the burden of examination which appropriately falls on one party, since the jury may be swayed if it appears that the court favors one party. In addition, except where matters are clearly irrelevant, the judge should not interpose evidentiary objections for a party, since otherwise objectionable evidence, such as hearsay or privileged information, is admissible if the party having the right to exclude the evidence does not make a timely objection. Nonetheless, judges have been known to make such objections on behalf of those before them. In pro se cases, judges may become more active and may seek to protect the rights of parties without counsel. It is not easy, however, for the judge to be surrogate counsel while ruling on evidence questions.

Q. Was there an arrangement to make them at any stated times? **A.** Yes, sir.

Q. What was the arrangement? **A.** Any day that there was any activity, we were to turn in a report concerning such.

Q. Now, do you know whether or not Mr. Barrott prepared a memorandum of the material that you turned in to him? Did he, in turn, prepare a report? **A.** I don't know.

Q. You don't know whether he did or not? Is it correct to state that you have never seen any memoranda prepared by Mr. Barrott concerning your investigation in this matter? **A.** There was a record book prepared by Mr. Barrott.

Q. Do you have that record book here in court? **A.** Yes, sir.

Q. Is Mr. Earl Stible in the courtroom? **A.** No, sir.

Q. Would you recognize him? **A.** Yes, sir.

MR. EVERT: That's all.

THE COURT: Is there any redirect examination?

MR. BRYERS: No questions, your Honor.

THE COURT (to witness): You may stand down.

THE COURT: Call your next witness.

RICHARD DEE BARROTT, called as a witness on behalf of the People, and having been first duly sworn, testified as follows:

DIRECT EXAMINATION

BY MR. BRYERS:

Q. Witness, what is your full name? **A.** Richard Dee Barrott.

Q. And by whom are you employed? **A.** I am employed by the City of Hamster as a police officer.

Q. And what rank do you hold? **A.** Patrolman.

Q. And were you so employed on January 25, 1967? **A.** I was.

Q. Now, are you the officer in charge of this case? **A.** I am.

Q. Now, calling your attention to January 25, 1967, did you see your fellow officer, Darrell Norton, on that evening? **A.** I did.

Q. What time did you see him? **A.** Approximately 8:30 p. m.

Q. And where did you see him? **A.** At the parking lot of the Cherry Tree High School located at Alandale and Morrison in the City of Hamster.

Q. Did you have a conversation with him at this time? **A.** I did.

Q. And what did he tell you?

MR. EVERT:[17] I will object to that, your Honor.

THE COURT: Sustained.

Q. (By Mr. Bryers, continuing): You had a conversation with him? A. I did.

Q. All right. And did he give you anything? A. He did.

Q. What did he give you? A. He gave me a Prince Albert tobacco can.

Q. All right. And had he told you where he had obtained this? A. He did.

Q. And was anything done? Was anything done to this can? A. It was marked by Officer Norton and by myself with our initials.

Q. And did he turn the can over to you? A. He did.

Q. And what did you do? A. I placed the can in my pocket and approximately an hour and a half later I transported the can to the Hamster Police Department where I placed it into a locker with a padlock.

Q. You put a lock on it? A. Yes, sir.

Q. Does anybody else have a key to this lock? A. No, sir. I'm the only one with a key.

Q. What time was it that you put this in the locker? A. This would be approximately 10:20, 10:30 that evening.

Q. Prior to putting that in the locker, had that can been out of your possession at any time? A. No, sir, it hadn't.

Q. When did you next see this can? A. At approximately 10 o'clock the following morning.

Q. That would be on January 26th? A. Yes, sir.

Q. And where did you see the can at that time? A. I went back to the locker and unlocked it and took the can out of the locker.

Q. All right. And what did you do with the can? A. I transported it to the City of Boonton to the Federal Building.

Q. The Federal Building? A. Yes, sir.

Q. And when you got to the Federal Building, what did you do? A. I turned the can over to the chief chemist there at the Federal Building, Mr. Stanley Wall, for analysis.

Q. And after he received the can, what did you do? A. I observed him seal the can after analysis.

Q. Did you observe him making the analysis? A. I was present in the room.

17. Why did Evert object to Bryers' question? What would Barrott have answered? How would this have hurt the defendant's case?

Q. And the can or contents—did they leave your sight at any time? **A.** I observed him pour the contents of the can and conduct an analysis.

Q. All right. And after he finished his analysis, what did he do? **A.** He placed the contents back in the can, placed the can back into the original envelope which I had placed it in, and put the package into a brown envelope which he sealed.

MR. BRYERS (to court reporter): Would you mark this "People's Proposed Exhibit 1"?

Q. (By Mr. Bryers, continuing): Now, witness, I will show you People's Proposed Exhibit 1 and ask you if you can identify this. **A.** Yes, I can.

Q. Will you tell the jury and the Court what that is? **A.** This is a brown envelope which I received from Mr. Stanley Wall, which contained the can of—the Prince Albert can of marihuana.

Q. How do you know that's the same envelope? **A.** My name is written on the envelope here.

Q. Your name is written? **A.** Yes, sir.

Q. And do you have a statement in your handwriting there? **A.** I do.

Q. What does that statement say?

MR. EVERT: Objection.

THE COURT: At this juncture, I think it's premature. Are you going to offer that in evidence?

MR. BRYERS: No, not right now. I want him to identify the envelope.

THE COURT:[18] If it's identified and he is going to read the writing on the envelope, it has to be in evidence first.

MR. EVERT: Yes, he will have to lay a proper foundation.

18. Consider the careful way in which the progress of the can which allegedly contained marihuana was traced from officer Norton to officer Barrott to Stanley Wall the chemist who analyzed the substance. Why was this necessary? By this point the prosecutor has gone through the preliminary steps which are necessary if the can in the envelope is to be offered into evidence. He has shown the connection of the item with a matter at issue in the case and has marked the envelope containing the can as People's Proposed Exhibit 1. If Bryers decides that he does want to introduce the envelope containing the can into evidence, it will be given to Mr. Evert for examination and Evert will be allowed to raise any objections he has to admitting the exhibit. If the item is admitted into evidence it may later be given to the jury for their examination. What do you think Evert's objection will be to admitting the can and the envelope? Will he have the same objection if the prosecution seeks to introduce only the can and its contents? When both can and envelope are offered into evidence at a later point in the trial Evert does not object.

BY MR. BRYERS:

Q. Now, witness, after you received People's Proposed Exhibit 1 from Mr. Stanley Wall, chief chemist, what did you do with it? **A.** I transported the envelope back to the Hamster Police Department and placed it back in the same locker in the same padlock.

Q. And you are still the only one that has a key to that lock? **A.** That's correct, sir.

CROSS-EXAMINATION

BY MR. EVERT:

Q. How long have you known Officer Norton? **A.** Since December of 1966.

Q. You worked with him on this and other cases, is that right? **A.** Since that time, yes, sir.

Q. Other than transporting the Prince Albert can down to the government chemist, Mr. Wall, and other than being custodian of the can, have you done any work in connection with this case, done any investigating? **A.** The one other thing I did in connection with this case was conducting the party that searched the premises of the defendant at 4061 Murane.

Q. In any event, though, in your capacity as officer in charge of this case, you received certain written reports from Mr. Norton, is that right? **A.** I did.

Q. And do you have those reports with you in court? **A.** No, sir.

Q. Do you know where those reports are? **A.** They have been destroyed, sir.

Q. Who destroyed them? **A.** I did.

Q. When did you destroy them? **A.** I usually destroyed them a day or so after they were submitted to me.

Q. Is that your recollection of what you did in this case, that you destroyed them as you received them a day or so afterwards? **A.** Yes, sir.

Q. Now, prior to your destruction of these reports, did you make a memorandum for yourself? **A.** On some of them, yes.

Q. You went through them and decided what was important. Is that the idea? **A.** Yes, sir.

Q. Do you have your own memorandum here? **A.** Yes, sir.

Q. I see. May I see it? (Whereupon a book was handed to the witness.) **A.** There is no entry as to January the 25th.

Q. Did Mr. Norton give you a report as to his activities on January 25th? **A.** If I recall correctly, I believe he did, sir.

Q. Let me ask you this. When you got reports from Mr. Norton that didn't get into the book, were there any reasons other than the fact of their importance? **A.** No, sir.

Q. Do you have a specific recollection of a report given to you by Mr. Norton as to the transaction on the 25th of January about which he testified? Do you recall such a report? **A.** I do recall him giving such a report, yes.

Q. What day do you claim that you took the can, the Prince Albert can, to Stanley Wall? **A.** The 26th of January.

Q. Would you examine your records and tell me whether or not there is anything in your report as to that day, any transaction? **A.** No, sir, there is not.

Q. Are some of your own activities placed in this book in connection with your investigation? **A.** Yes, sir.

Q. And is the reason why your memorandum doesn't contain a record of your transportation of the Prince Albert can to Stanley Wall that you didn't consider that important? **A.** As far as transportation of evidence, I never enter any of that in the book.

Q. Now, Mr. Santiago is the City Manager, is that right? **A.** That's Ralph Santiago.

Q. The activities of Mr. Norton were part of a special investigation, is that correct? **A.** Yes, sir.

Q. The propriety of this investigation was discussed with you prior to the time Mr. Norton was hired, is that correct? **A.** No, sir.

Q. You first learned of the special investigation of Norton at some point—when Mr. Santiago informed you that was what he was going to do? **A.** That's correct.

Q. And he assigned you to work with Mr. Norton, is that correct? **A.** That's correct.

Q. Now, did he request a written report as you progressed in the investigation? **A.** No, sir.

Q. He did not request your records, the record that I hold in my hand here, being your own memorandum that you showed to him voluntarily, is that right? **A.** He did not request that record, no, sir.

Q. You took it to him of your own volition? **A.** That's correct, sir.

Q. And were you there when he read or perused it? **A.** For a short period of time, not when he went through the whole record book.

Q. While you were there, you discussed the contents of this memorandum, is that right? **A.** Yes, sir.

Q. And did you discuss anything that wasn't in the book here? **A.** Possibly. I don't recall.

Q. What particularly? Did you discuss the transaction with Mr. Nelson Whale of January 25th with him? **A.** I don't recall if I did or not.

Q. Now, you had discussions with the Chief of Police about your investigation, also. Is that right? **A.** Yes, sir.

Q. And you gave the Chief of Police this book to read, to peruse, is that right? **A.** Yes, sir.

Q. And did you discuss things with the Chief of Police that weren't made a part of your record? **A.** Yes, sir.

Q. And did you have any discussions as to why certain things were not a written part of your record? **A.** No, sir.

Q. And did you have any specific discussion with the Chief of Police prior to the time that Mr. Whale was arrested as to the transaction of January 25th? **A.** No, sir.

Q. You know the witness, Earl Stible, don't you? **A.** Yes, sir.

Q. Since the 25th of January, have you had occasion to discuss the transaction of January 25th with him? **A.** No, sir.

Q. Not one time? **A.** No, sir.

Q. Have any members of the Hamster Police Department had discussions with Earl Stible concerning the transaction of January 25th?

MR. BRYERS: I'll object.

Q. In your presence.

THE COURT: Do you object?

MR. BRYERS: I'll object, but he said "in your presence", so I will withdraw my objection. **A.** No, sir.

Q. You heard the testimony of Mr. Norton in court today, is that right? [19] **A.** Yes, sir.

---

19. Had the parties wished, they could have had all witnesses (except the defendant) excluded while other witnesses were testifying. This is designed to insure that one witness for a party doesn't conform his or her story to the testimony of other witnesses for the same party. The right to exclude non-party witnesses exists at the court's discretion in civil as well as criminal cases. For this reason, an exclusion or sequestration order may include an instruction to the sequestered witnesses to refrain from talking to anyone, including counsel, about evidence that has been presented. FRE 615 requires sequestration of most witnesses (with the exception of parties and witnesses whose presence is necessary to assist a party) upon request of a party, and also provides for judicial discretion to order sequestration sua sponte.

FRE 615 follows the general practice when it exempts from sequestration parties, an officer or representative of a non-natural party and persons whose presence is essential to the presentation of a case. The most controversial aspect of the rule is that which allows a governmental or corporate party to designate a representative who may not be sequestered. Most courts that have addressed the question have allowed the government to designate an investigative officer to be present in a

Q. Is there anything he has testified to here today that is different from that which you might have written in the memorandum? **A.** No, sir.

Q. You don't know of your own knowledge what he did about any of these trips over to Mr. Whale's house. **A.** No, sir.

Q. Did you as officer in charge of the case give him any instructions as to what methods he should employ in making the arrest here, making the arrest or conducting his investigation? **A.** No, sir, not any specific instructions.

Q. Did you authorize Mr. Norton to give Mr. Stible any marihuana? **A.** No, sir.

Q. Did you ever have any discussion with him as to the means with which he should purchase marihuana from the defendant? **A.** No, sir.

Q. Did you give him any instructions as to what he should pay for the marihuana? **A.** No, sir.

Q. Did you give him any instructions as to how much he should buy? **A.** Yes, sir.

Q. All right. How much did you tell him to buy? **A.** His instructions were to purchase as much in bulk as possible.

Q. You supplied him the funds that he used, also, did you not? **A.** Yes, sir.

Q. And were these marked in any way? **A.** No, sir.

Q. Will you state whether or not on January 25th, Mr. Norton gave you other narcotics other than that which is People's Proposed Exhibit No. 1? **A.** He did not.

Q. Will you state whether or not when you transported People's Proposed Exhibit No. 1 to Stanley Wall, you had other narcotics on that occasion? **A.** I did not.

MR. EVERT: That's all.

THE COURT: Is there anything further from this witness?

MR. BRYERS: I have nothing further.

criminal case even if the officer is a crucial witness whose presence throughout the trial does not obviously aid the government's attorney. The court does have the power under FRE 611(a) to make such witnesses testify at the start of the government's case. However, the Supreme Court has held that a court may not force a defendant who wishes to testify on his own behalf to choose betwen testifying at the outset of his case or not at all. Brooks v. Tennessee, 406 U.S. 605 (1972).

In this case counsel for the defendant apparently wanted Barrott to hear Norton's story in order to facilitate questioning Barrott on the substance of Norton's testimony. Does this make sense? Might he have been able to question Barrott more effectively had Barrott not heard Norton's story? Would Barrott have been unaware of Norton's basic story had he not heard Norton recite the details in court?

THE COURT (to witness): You may stand down.

STANLEY G. WALL, called as a witness in behalf of the People, and having been first duly sworn, testified as follows:

DIRECT EXAMINATION

BY MR. BRYERS:

Q. Witness, what is your full name? **A.** Stanley G. Wall.

Q. And by whom are you employed? **A.** The federal government.

Q. In what capacity? **A.** Chemist.

Q. And for how long have you been employed as a chemist? **A.** Over 25 years.

Q. And where did you obtain your degree? **A.** I have a master of science degree in chemistry from the University of Michigan.

Q. For how many years have you been assigned to your present assignment? **A.** I have been assigned as a chemist in the Alcohol and Tobacco Tax Division over 25 years.

Q. All right. And in the course of your duties, how many times have you made analyses of various substances? **A.** If you're referring to narcotics—

Q. Yes. **A.** Well over 5,000 samples.

Q. I see. Now, Mr. Wall, I'm going to show you People's Proposed Exhibit 1(a)—excuse me, Exhibit (1), and ask you if you can identify that. **A.** I can identify the envelope.

Q. What is that envelope? **A.** It is an envelope in which I placed some evidence after analysis on the 26th day of January, 1967.

Q. And will you open that up, please? (Document handed to witness.) Now, the contents of that envelope is marked "People's Proposed Exhibit 1(a), and can you identify that? **A.** Yes, I can.

Q. Will you tell the jury and the Court what that is? **A.** This is the Prince Albert tobacco can which contained the substance that I analyzed on January 26, 1967.

Q. Are there any initials on that can? **A.** There are.

Q. Can you tell what initials are on that can? **A.** I can recognize my own.

Q. Any other initials that you can see there? **A.** I don't readily see any others. Perhaps it's under the labels.

Q. All right. Now, from whom did you receive this exhibit? **A.** Officer Barrott of the Hamster Police Department.

Q. And when did you receive it from him? **A.** On January 26, 1967.

Q.   All right.   Now, did you make an analysis of the contents of that Prince Albert can?   A.   I did, while he was there.

Q.   And what are the results of your analysis?   A.   I found the sample to contain 23 and 53 hundredths grams of marihuana before analysis.

Q.   Now, are you familiar with the designations made as to narcotics by the United States Treasury Department?   A.   I am.

Q.   And can you tell the jury and the Court whether or not marihuana has been designated as a narcotic?   A.   Yes, it has.

MR. BRYERS: You may cross-examine.

THE COURT: Wait a minute.   Are you offering the exhibit in evidence?

MR. BRYERS: Oh, yes, excuse me.

At this time the People offer in evidence People's Proposed Exhibit 1 and 1(a).

MR. EVERT: No objections, your Honor.

CROSS-EXAMINATION

BY MR. EVERT:

Q.   In addition to your familiarity with the Treasury Department's designation, you're also familiar with the state statute under which this case is brought, are you not?   A.   No, sir.

Q.   These 5,000 samples, in excess of 5,000, that you examined, have they all been marihuana samples?   A.   No, sir.

Q.   What else have you anaylzed in these 5,000 samples?   A.   Especially heroin.

Q.   Heroin?   A.   Especially heroin.

Q.   Of these 5,000 samples, what portion has been marihuana, to the best of your estimate?   A.   Oh, I would estimate one-third.

Q.   And you found, did you not, Mr. Wall, in your analysis that the contents of People's Exhibit 1 was like the marihuana that you have been examining over 25 years, is that right?

THE COURT: You mean 1(a), do you not?

MR. EVERT: 1(a), that's correct.

Q.   (By Mr. Evert, continuing): 1(a) is like the other marihuana?   A.   I found it to be marihuana.

Q.   Was this marihuana, then People's Exhibit 1(a), habit-forming?

MR. BRYERS: Just a moment, your Honor.   I object to that as being immaterial.[20]

20. In addition to the relevance objection, counsel might have considered mak- ing two other objections: 1) that the chemist would be guessing as to the prop-

Note 20—Continued

erties of the marihuana, and 2) that the testimony was opinion, not fact. Neither objection would have been availing.

Federal Rule 602 states the general rule regarding the knowledge of a witness, a principle applicable in every jurisdiction:

A witness may not testify to a matter unless evidence is introduced sufficient to support a finding that he has personal knowledge of the matter. Evidence to prove personal knowledge may, but need not, consist of the testimony of the witness himself. * * *

Personal knowledge is usually implicit in the story the witness tells. For this reason, the party offering the evidence does not have to prove personal knowledge unless an objection is made. If, however, it appears that the witness did not observe the events to which he testified or is otherwise lacking in personal knowledge, his testimony will be stricken. While this may appear to support objection 1, an expert is permitted to speculate on the basis of data or theories generally relied upon by experts in his field. Objection 2 is also unavailing as to experts; they may give opinions. But later in the transcript, the judge indicates that he does not view the chemist as an expert on addictive drugs. He would require a doctor.

Witness who are not experts cannot ordinarily give opinions; they only may relate facts.

Originally the doctrine barring opinion testimony was confined to testimony not based on the witness' personal knowledge—i.e., the ban overlapped the ban discussed in the preceding paragraph. Today the ban on opinion testimony extends further. Witnesses are told to give the "facts" and not conclusions drawn from the facts or opinions about the facts.

But can anyone find the line that separates fact from opinion? More than one hundred years ago the New Hampshire Supreme Court said:

A constant observer of the trial of cases, examining the testimony for the purpose of ascertaining how many opinions are received and how many rejected, will find ten of the former as often as he finds one of the latter; and, if he is very critical, he will find the ratio much greater than that. Opinions are constantly given. A case can hardly be tried without them. Their number is so vast, and their use so habitual, that they are not noticed as opinions distinguished from other evidence. (State v. Pike, 49 N.H. 399, (1870) at 423).

Federal Rule 701 dealing with opinion testimony by lay witnesses provides:

If the witness is not testifying as an expert, his testimony in the form of opinions or inferences is limited to those opinions or inferences which are (a) rationally based on the perception of the witness and (b) helpful to a clear understanding of his testimony or the determination of a fact in issue.

Generally lay witnesses are allowed to give what are analytically opinions if they summarize a set of commonly observed facts which it would be difficult to describe in terms of concrete underlying facts. Thus, the opinion that an individual was drunk or that a car was travelling at about a certain speed is allowed in most jurisdictions.

Even where witnesses, whether experts or non-experts, are permitted to give opinions some jurisdictions follow the common law rule that opinions are not allowed on ultimate issues. This approach is more or less restrictive depending on what the court sees as ultimate. Federal Rule 704 abandons any restrictions on testimony on the ultimate issue in a case.

In large measure the opinion rule is a rule of preference. Where specificity is possible, it is preferred to less descriptive conclusions. Where specificity is not possible, more conclusory statements will be allowed so long as they promise to aid the trier of fact. Thus opinions in out-of-court declarations may be received in circumstances where the opinions of testifying witnesses would not be allowed. This is because the testifying witness can usually describe the more concrete facts that underlie his opinion. An out-of-court statement cannot be rephrased, so a court must choose between receiving the opinion or doing without whatever the declarant had to offer.

THE COURT: Objection sustained.

MR. EVERT: Your Honor, I certainly don't know what the basis of the objection is, and I would like to get at the provisions as set up in the state statutes.

THE COURT: The objection is sustained because it is not important to inquire of this man anything further than (1) that it is marihuana, and (2) that it is a narcotic in accordance with the United States Code or Treasury Department rules, and that's it. I assume this is what the Assistant Prosecutor was going to say.[21]

MR. BRYERS: That's right, your Honor.

Q. (By Mr. Evert, continuing): Well, do you know whether or not the United States Code is the same as the state statutes under which this case is brought. A. No, I don't.

Q. Are there any differences in the quality of heroin and those of marihuana? A. If you're talking about physical or chemical qualities—

Q. Yes, sir. A. They aren't the same.

Q. What are those differences? A. Well, one is a plant material, and the other is a chemical that has been prepared from an alkaloid derived from a plant.

Q. Now, which is which? A. Marihuana is a plant material.

Q. Material from what plant? A. Well, if you want a common name, a hemp plant; a chemical name, Cannabis Sativa (C-a-n-n-a-b-i-s S-a-t-i-v-a).

Q. What are the properties that you look for in your analysis? A. To see if it tests for marihuana.

Q. And what are those tests, sir? A. Well, in this case I ran two tests. One was a Duquenois test; the other was a Beam's test.

Q. This U. S. Treasury Department classification—where is this found? A. Well, I'm not a lawyer, but I have read the classifications in a handbook

Note 20—Continued

Witnesses, as we have noted, must testify from personal knowledge. If a witness is not positive as to what he observed, he may say, "I think this is what happened". This is not an opinion of the kind precluded by the opinion rule. It is an honest expression of doubt as to the validity and accuracy of the testimony.

21. Is the court acting appropriately here? Is any harm done?

Certain questions that arise in a case will be decided as matters of law by the trial judge. One such question is whether marihuana is a narcotic within the meaning of a statute. It turns on an analysis of language and legislative history rather than on the facts of the case being tried. When a judge on his own initiative or at the initiative of a party determines the applicable law in a case, the judge is taking judicial notice of the law. The topic of judicial notice is discussed in detail in Chapter Nine. For the moment it is sufficient to note that the judge is acting appropriately when he states the law. There was no need to pretend that this is what the prosecutor would have said.

put out by the Narcotics Bureau listing the drugs that are considered to be narcotics under the law.

Q. And what's the name of this book? A. It's a handbook. I can't tell you the exact title or the year it was published or—

Q. Can you tell me the time that you read it? A. Well, I've read it several times in the last 25 years.

Q. No particular time that you can remember this? A. Not the date, no.

Q. And have there been changes in the classifications of narcotics over the past 25 years? A. Yes.

Q. And has the status of marihuana been consistent in the past 25 years in the U. S. Treasury Department handbook? A. To my recollection, yes.

THE COURT: Counsel, will you both approach the bench, please?

(Whereupon a conference was held between the Court and counsel outside the hearing of the jury and the court reporter.)

MR. BRYERS: [22] Your Honor. I will object to all the testimony regarding the last four or five questions as being immaterial to this matter, and ask that they be stricken from the record.

THE COURT: You say this Cannabis Sativa is a plant. I will sustain the objection and strike any cross-examination concerning the nature of the drug to satisfy the statute. Cannabis Sativa is a plant from which this drug is derived.

MR. EVERT: I have no further questions of this witness.

At 10:15 a. m.

DAMON LORD, called as a witness in behalf of the People, and having been first duly sworn, testified as follows:

DIRECT EXAMINATION

BY MR. BRYERS

Q. What is your name, please? A. Damon Lord.

THE COURT: Before you get to this, when I sustained the objection, I also call attention to State Statutes Annotated 18.1121, Section (2)(g).

Q. (By Mr. Bryers, continuing): Your name is Damon Lord? A. That's right.

22. What occurred during the conference at the bench? Was the judge acting appropriately in taking the initiative he did? Was Mr. Evert's cross-examination of Wall proper? What was Evert trying to establish? It is unlikely that a lower court judge would rule that marihuana was not a narcotic within the meaning of the state statute, but it is important that this issue be preserved for appeal. How else might the matter have been preserved for appeal? Should arguments on this issue be made in the presence of the jury?

Q. How old are you? **A.** 19.

Q. Where are you employed? **A.** I'm not working.

Q. Do you attend school? **A.** No.

Q. And where do you live? **A.** 4061 Murane.

Q. Where is that located? **A.** In Hamster.

Q. Does defendant Nelson Whale live at that same address? **A.** No, he don't.

Q. And how long have you known Nelson Whale? **A.** For about six months now.

MR. BRYERS: [23] you may cross-examine.

CROSS-EXAMINATION

BY MR. EVERT:

Q. Do you know a Hamster police officer by the name of Darrell Norton? **A.** No.

Q. Darrell Norton? **A.** I seen him last time I was in court.

Q. You were in court before? **A.** Yes.

Q. How long ago was that? **A.** It was in April.

Q. And you saw a person that you believe to be Darrell Norton, is that right? **Q.** That's right.

Q. And did you see that same person on the 25th of January at 4061 Murane Court? **A.** I did.

Q. What was he doing when you saw him? **A.** I opened the door for him.

THE COURT (to witness): A little louder, please.

Q. (By Mr. Evert, continuing): And was he alone at that time? **A.** Yes.

23. **Did Lord's testimony in any way advance the state's case?** The reason why Lord was called is that the state in which this trial occurred has a rule that the state is obligated to call all "res gestae" witnesses, that is all witnesses who were present at the commission of the offense. If the state does not call a "res gestae" witness and cannot explain its failure to call the witness, the defendant is entitled to have the jury instructed that had the witness been present in court it is likely that the witness' testimony would have favored the defendant. Where one party has peculiar access to a witness and does not call that witness, the opposing party will in some states be entitled to a similar instruction. The Fifth Amendment prevents such comment on the accused's failure to testify.

Many jurisdictions have done away with res gestae rules on the ground that witnesses are equally available to both parties. They take the view that a party concerned about the absence of a witness should not depend upon a presumption about what a witness would say, but should see to it that the witness is subpoenaed to testify at the trial.

Q. Did you have any conversation with him? **A.** No.

Q. Did he have any conversation with any person in your presence? **A.** Not as I know.

Q. Do you recall specifically whether he had any conversation with the defendant, Nelson Whale, in your presence? **A.** I was in the kitchen. Him and Nelson was talking.

Q. And did you hear any of that conversation? **A.** I know he asked him for some stuff, you know, and Nelson, he said, "Man, what are you talking about?"

Q. Did you hear any other portion of the conversation? **A.** No, I didn't.

MR. EVERT: That's all.

THE COURT: Is there any redirect examination?

MR. BRYERS: No, your Honor.

THE COURT: Then this witness may be excused.

RICHARD DEE BARROTT, recalled as a witness in behalf of the People, was duly sworn to testify.

DIRECT EXAMINATION

BY MR. BRYERS:

Q. Mr. Barrott, did you attempt to serve a subpoena on Earl Stible after you left court here yesterday? **A.** I did.

Q. And where did you go with this subpoena? **A.** I went to 4385 Ridgeland Court in Hamster.

Q. Why did you go there? **A.** That is the residence of Willis Stible.

Q. And when you got to that address, what did you do? **A.** I went to that address on five different occasions during the evening, yesterday. I didn't make contact with Mr. Stible on either occasion. I left a subpoena for him with a Ronald Stible who is the brother of Willis Earl Stible.

Q. Do you know how old Ronald Stible is? **A.** Ronald Stible is approximately 16 years of age.

Q. And did you give him any instructions? **A.** I instructed him to give this to his brother, Willis Earl Stible. He informed me that Willis Earl would be in some time that night. He didn't know when.

MR BRYERS: [24] You may cross-examine.

24. Bryers has recalled Barrott in an attempt to establish the state's inability to serve Stible with a subpoena. Bryers feels that this is important because he wishes to avoid a "missing witness" instruction.

Stible had been subpoenaed to appear on the original trial date and had in fact shown up in court. What might the defense have done after the postponement to ensure that Stible was in court on the cor-

CROSS-EXAMINATION

BY MR. EVERT:

    Q. Is this the first notice that you ever tried to give Earl Stible? **A.** I served Mr. Stible with another subpoena earlier this month.

    Q. Last Wednesday at the municipal court while he was a witness that day? **A.** That's correct.

    Q. And it was directed that he appear when? **A.** On the 22nd of May.

    Q. All right. And did he attend court on the 22nd day of May as far as you know? **A.** I don't know whether he did or not.

    (NOTE: Earlier testimony which has been omitted established that Stible was in court on the 22nd but the judge postponed the case.)

    Q. Was this case scheduled for trial on the 22nd of May? **A.** That's correct, sir.

    Q. And was it adjourned for some reason or other on that day to the 23rd? **A.** That's correct.

    Q. Did you notify him when you found out about the adjourned date? **A.** I was unable to make contact with him, sir.

    Q. Did you come down to court or did you expect by reason of subpoena to tell him? **A.** No, I did not.

    Q. Did you send somebody down to tell him? **A.** I did not.

    Q. And since then you haven't been able to find Mr. Stible, have you? **A.** That's correct.

    Q. Have you ever seen him at 4385 Ridgeland Court? **A.** No, I have not.

    Q. How do you know he lives there? **A.** Mrs. Ernestine Stible, the mother of Willis Earl Stible, told me that he resided at that address.

    Q. When did she tell you that? Yesterday? **A.** No, sir, I didn't see Mrs. Stible yesterday.

    Q. When did she tell you that, sir? **A.** The same Wednesday that you made reference to.

    Q. All right. Now, his father doesn't live at the same place, does he? **A.** I don't know where his father lives.

    Q. You know his father, though, don't you? **A.** I wouldn't know him by sight.

rect day? Does the fact that Stible is not in court suggest that he is not as important to the defense's case as the testimony thus far might indicate, or does it just suggest that the defense counsel was limited in the time and resources he could devote to this case?

Q. You don't know Willis Stible's father? **A.** Not by sight.

Q. You don't know whether or not he lives on Saddlebelt Road in Hamster? **A.** No, sir.

MR. EVERT: I have no further questions.

THE COURT: No further questions?

MR. BRYERS: No further questions.

THE COURT (to witness): You may stand down.

MR. BRYERS: If the Court please, there has been a stipulation between the People and counsel for the defendant as to two witnesses and what their testimony would be if they were here.

THE COURT: Would you approach the rostrum so that we can make sure that we have unanimity?

MR. EVERT: May it please the Court, perhaps I should make a statement then.

THE COURT: Go ahead.

MR. EVERT: The defendant offers to stipulate that if the two other witnesses who are not here were here, they—

THE COURT: Specifically, who are these witnesses?

MR. EVERT: Ambrose M. Choepler.

THE COURT: And Lorenzo Capolito?

MR. EVERT: Mr. Capolito is from the State Board of Pharmacy, and Mr. Choepler is District Director of the Internal Revenue. These witnesses would testify that the defendant herein does not have a license to sell narcotics.

THE COURT: Neither State nor Federal License. Is that what you're saying?

MR. EVERT: That's right.

THE COURT: You waive the necessity of their being here, is this correct, counsel?

MR. EVERT:[25] Yes, your Honor.

---

25. Where both parties agree as to the testimony which a witness will give, they may so stipulate for the record. Stipulations are common in situations such as this where witnesses would be testifying to undisputed matters largely of a technical nature. What advantages does the prosecution gain by agreeing to this stipulation? Who else gains? When do you not want to agree to a stipulation which advances your case? Suppose your client had a back injury in which she strained several vertebrae. Would you agree to the defendant's kind offer to stipulate that your physician witness was an expert, thus avoiding the need to specify the doctor's credentials in court?

MR. BRYERS:[26] The People rest, your Honor.[27]

THE COURT: Defense?

26. The People's case has come to a close. Notice the way in which it has been structured. An opening statement specifying the essence of the prosecution's proposed testimony, an opening witness who laid out the basic case against the defendant, and subsequent witnesses to fill in the details necessary to make out the statutory crime of felonious sale of a narcotic drug. There are various theories about the order in which evidence should be presented with the general view being that it is wise to both begin and end with strong witnesses. However, in many cases, as in this one, the nature of the case will largely control the order in which the evidence is presented. Here there was only one strong witness, Officer Norton, and his testimony was needed at the outset to lay a framework into which supporting testimony would fit.

Did Evert shake any of the prosecution's witnesses? Did he make out the elements of an entrapment defense? Was any of Evert's cross-examination unnecessary? Was any of it positively harmful to the defendant?

27. Now that the prosecutor has rested, we should consider the order of examination at trial.

Usually the plaintiff or prosecutor has the right to present his evidence to the trier of fact first. This is thought to be related to the fact that it is the plaintiff who normally bears the burdens of proof at trial. Plaintiff may call witnesses and offer properly authenticated real evidence (discussed in Chapter Eleven in depth and briefly described in note 34 infra).

After the witnesses testify on direct examination—i.e. the plaintiff's attorney questions the plaintiff's witnesses—the opposing party or parties may cross-examine the witnesses. Jurisdictions differ on the extent to which cross-examination may probe areas not touched upon on direct examination. (See note 29 infra.) After cross-examination, the plaintiff may be permitted redirect examination, which

may be followed by recross-examination. After all examination of a witness has been completed, the witness leaves the stand. When all of the witnesses have been presented, the plaintiff signifies that he has completed his case by announcing that he rests. Then the defendant presents witnesses and tangible evidence. Plaintiff has the same right of cross-examination that defendant had when plaintiff presented his "case-in-chief". When the defendant finishes his proof he rests. If the plaintiff wishes to rebut the defendant's case, he may offer rebuttal evidence. With the permission of the court, plaintiff may also introduce additional evidence which does not technically amount to rebuttal. Witnesses offered for rebuttal may include those who testified as part of the case-in-chief. Rebuttal witnesses, whether or not they have testified before, are subject to cross-examination. In the Whale case no witnesses are taken on redirect examination, nor is there any rebuttal evidence after the close of defendant's case-in-chief. Note, however, that Barrott has been called to testify twice and that Norton is called once by the prosecutor and once by the defense.

In what circumstances should an attorney question a witness on redirect examination? In what circumstances would an attorney want to present rebuttal evidence? Since evidence brought out under an opponent's questioning may appear more devastating than the same evidence brought out on direct examination, an attorney might toy with the idea of holding back part of his case hoping that the opposing counsel will inadvertently ask for it. Totally apart from any ethical considerations, this is a very dangerous procedure. If the attorney's case is insufficient to get to the jury, opposing counsel may refrain from cross-examining or presenting a case and may simply move for a directed verdict. Even if opposing counsel cross-examines or presents an affirmative case, the right of redirect examination and the right to offer rebuttal

MR. EVERT: May counsel and I approach the bench, your Honor?

THE COURT: Yes.

(Whereupon a conference was had between the Court and counsel out of the hearing of the jury and the court reporter.)

THE COURT: We will take a short recess. There is a legal argument which is completely the responsibility of the Court and not the jury. So you will not discuss this matter among yourselves or with anybody else.

(Whereupon at 10:25 a. m. the jury was excused for a recess and the following discussion between the Court and counsel was had in the courtroom.)

MR. EVERT: May it please the Court, I have heretofore requested the opportunity, which the Court granted me, though deferring it, to make a legal argument concerning one of the objections I made before it was sustained, where I was going into the details of Mr. Norton's activities in connection with other arrests, and I have made no statement as to that.

And in addition, and the purpose for this interruption in the proceeding is to request that Darrell Norton, who first testified here, be recalled to the stand for the purpose of cross-examination.

The Court may recall that during yesterday's proceedings I requested a recess in order to complete my preparation and review my notes for the purpose of cross-examination, and the Court was of the opinion that we were close to 4 o'clock and that we should not interrupt the proceedings.

Some five or six or seven minutes later there was an interruption and we did take a recess, but by that time the witness had gotten off the witness stand, and, of course, there was no further opportunity to request that he be recalled until this time.

THE COURT: [28] Why wasn't there further opportunity then more so than now? He stepped off the stand. The People had not yet rested. If

evidence are shaky safety valves at best. Redirect examination is typically limited to the clarification of or elaboration on matters brought out in cross-examination and rebuttal evidence must respond to elements of the opponent's case. If counsel admits that evidence was withheld for tactical reasons, the court is unlikely to allow these losses to be recouped at the rebuttal stage.

Generally a party offers non-testimonial evidence (exhibits) on direct examination, although they are sometimes allowed in on cross-examinations.

28. By waiting until the prosecution formally rested to approach the bench, Evert has created a problem where none would otherwise have existed. He prob-

ably should have advised Bryers that before the state rested he would like an opportunity to approach the bench. The request was, however, made immediately after the close of the state's case. Is there any good reason why the court should not grant the motion? Indeed, should the prosecutor object to recalling Officer Norton? It is a Pyrrhic victory indeed when one wins an argument on a relatively inconsequential point of evidence law only to lose the case on appeal because the ruling was mistaken. Would Norton qualify as a hostile witness at this point? The court does not think so, but the better view is that Norton is so identified with the state's case that he may now be said to be hostile to the defense.

you had made that request at that time, it would have been granted without question. Also I might refute some of the statements that—

MR. EVERT: I'm not trying to be unfair.

THE COURT: I want you to be fair, and I want to be fair to you, too. You had a transcript in your hand when you asked for time to look through that transcript which was not the transcript you have in your hand now.

MR. EVERT: That's correct, your Honor.

THE COURT: All right. So that one has nothing to do with the other. You knew as much yesterday as you did today, except you did not have the transcript. You also had an opportunity this morning to ask that he be recalled for cross-examination before the People rested.

MR. EVERT: The request was made two minutes later, your Honor.

THE COURT: After the resting was done. Now I find myself in this position. The People have rested. This is all that concerns me. Obviously, you can put him on the stand now as your witness until he becomes a hostile witness, if he does. If he does not, then, of course, you're bound by his testimony.[29]

---

29. At best the judge uses words loosely in stating the evidence situation; at worst he is mistaken. If the defendant is bound by Norton's testimony because he is not declared hostile, it is only in the sense that Evert will be unable to impeach Norton's testimony through such devices as the use of prior inconsistent statements. The defense will be able to present witnesses whose testimony contradicts Norton's and will be able to argue to the jury that Norton's responses after being recalled were mistaken and should be ignored. In this case, however, the matter is important because the defense wants to recall Norton to impeach his earlier testimony. Also the defense wants to examine Norton through leading questions. If they must call Norton as their own witness and he is not declared hostile, leading questions will not be allowed.

This reflects the assumption that witnesses are honest and the traditional view that an honest witness can be helpful to both sides.

In the United States, the dominant rule has been that a cross-examination is limited to the scope of the direct examination. The cross-examiner may go beyond the scope of direct only with the court's permission, and even with permission new matters must usually be probed by non-leading questions. In England and in a minority of American jurisdictions, the cross-examiner may cross-examine on any subject relevant to the issues in the case. He is not limited by the facts, issues, or testimony adduced on direct examination. This is known as the wide-open rule of cross-examination.

It is not clear from the opinions of the courts that adopt the restrictive view exactly what they mean by confining cross-examination to the scope of the direct. Sometimes the courts speak as if the cross-examiner may ask questions about any part of the case of the opposing party. In other words, even if testimony on direct does not go to a specific po'nt, so long as the opposing party must prove that point, the cross-examiner may ask questions. Other opinions talk about the same transaction or the same fact or facts elicited on direct examination. Despite the confusion, it is clear that the trial judge is given great discretion in setting the scope of cross-examination. In all of the restrictive rules, there is what McCormick calls an "escape valve"—where part of the transaction, contract, or conversation has been revealed on direct, the remainder may be brought out on cross-examination.

I understand your problem, so why don't we take another five or ten minutes, and if you find me some law where I can do this, I will do it, because I certainly want the ends of justice to be served.

(Whereupon a recess was had at 10:35 a. m.)

At 11:20 a. m.

(The following discussion was had in the courtroom between the Court and counsel out of the presence of the jury.)

MR. EVERT: May it please the Court, while your sheriff is absent to get the particular volume, and still while in the absence of the jury, I would like to complete the record as to another objection that I made at the time the jury wasn't present.

THE COURT: Go ahead.

MR. EVERT: Defendant offers to show by witnesses of his own and offered to show by testimony of Mr. Stanley Wall, that the narcotic drug

FRE 106 exemplifies this principle. Where a party offers a portion of a writing or recording the other party may offer such other portions as ought to in fairness be considered along with it. The rule is limited to writings and recordings because it gives the opposing party the right to offer evidence in the midst of the direct examiner's case. If the rule extended to conversations or descriptions of transactions, the direct examination would be often interrupted for cross-examination, the direct examiner's case would be disrupted and the jury might well be confused.

You should also note that regardless of what was testified to on direct examination, cross-examination always may raise matters which test a witness' credibility or otherwise impeach his testimony.

See Chapter Five, infra.

It may appear that there is really not much difference between the wide-open and the restrictive forms of cross-examination. It seems that under either approach, all witnesses may be examined and the only question is in what order. But as McCormick (§ 23) points out the differences may be important. First, getting concessions from a witness while his story is fresh may be much more effective than similar concessions once the

basic story is stale. Indeed, concessions may not be forthcoming if the witness has time to prepare for cross-examination. Moreover, if cross-examination is not permitted to go beyond the scope of the direct, and a witness cannot be called hostile, a party may never be able to cross-examine on certain issues because the party will have to call the witness as his own, precluding leading questions and impeachment. This is the position that Evert may be in if he cannot call Norton for additional cross-examination.

FRE 611 limits cross-examination "to the subject matter of the direct examination and the matters affecting the credibility of the witness." The rule does provide, however, that the court has discretion to "permit inquiry into additional matters as if on direct examination." This means that the court can permit the cross-examiner to go beyond the scope of direct examination, but if it does leading questions should not be asked unless the cross-examiner could have asked leading questions on direct examination. The advantage of the traditional rule is that it gives a party a chance to present through its witnesses a coherent view of a case without having the other side's alternative or conflicting theories interjected in a way that may confuse a trier of fact.

here in question, and I say "narcotic" ony because it's classified under 335.35 of the Compiled Laws of '48 as a narcotic drug, was not habit-forming.

The defendant contends and would contend if the Court allowed the defendant to offer appropriate proof, medical testimony, testimony of a pharmacologist whom I have now on call—those men are named, Berkley Brite, a pharmacologist, and Dr. William B. Gile, who is a physician—that marihuana, the substance in question in this particular case, is not habit-forming.[30]

The defendant contends that the issue of whether or not marihuana is habit-forming is legitimate because the statute itself refers to the substance of marihuana, makes a distinction as to whether or not it is or is not a habit-forming drug.

At the time Mr. Wall was on the witness stand, I sought to ask him questions concerning the nature and property of the drug, and more particularly whether or not it was habit-forming. This Court first sustained an objection of Mr. Bryers as to the specific questions as to whether or not it was habit-forming. And then when I sought to get it in a round-about manner—and that's precisely what I was doing—the Court after four or five questions, upon the objection of Mr. Bryers, struck that testimony from the consideration of the jury.

The defendant would like to have the Court consider the issue of whether or not the narcotic or the substance, I should say, that Mr. Wall examined, was habit-forming.

30. When an objection is sustained, the party offering evidence must make clear what evidence would be adduced but for the objection. This is called an *offer of proof*. Asking a witness questions and receiving answers outside the presence of the jury and including any admissible documents in the record of the case are normal ways of making the offer of proof on direct examination. It is also common for trial courts to accept good faith representations of counsel as to the expected testimony of a witness, especially when there are several witnesses who would testify similarly but for an objection.

If the offered proof is not plainly relevant, as that term is defined in Chapter Three infra, offering counsel must explain the relationship of the evidence to the case. Similarly, if evidence appears to be barred by a specific evidence rule—e.g., the opinion rule, the personal knowledge rule, the competency of witnesses requirement, or any other rule—counsel must explain the propriety of the evidence. An appellate court is not likely to consider grounds supporting offers of evidence not presented to the trial judge.

A cross-examiner is usually not required to show what a witness would have testified to had an objection not been sustained because the cross-examiner is not expected to know the answer that an opposing witness would give. An appellate court will look to the nature of the question to determine whether relevant information was demanded of a sort that might have been helpful to the cross-examiner's case. Since questions on cross-examination are typically leading, the appellate court will often have a good idea of what the cross-examiner hoped to prove. Nevertheless, if you believe you would have been able to prove some specific fact on cross-examination had a question not been disallowed, you should state for the record what you would have hoped to show. This is particularly important when an entire line of cross-examination has been foreclosed. As with offers of proof on direct examination, the matter should not be raised within the hearing of the jury.

THE COURT: I deny you that motion for the following reasons: (1) State Statutes Annotated 18.1121, Section 2, subsection (g): "Any substance or synthetic narcotic drug which the bureau of narcotics of the United States Treasury Department has heretofore designated as 'narcotic'". That was testified to by Mr. Wall that it was so classified, and you are not entitled to proceed as you indicate, so that I foreclose that for the reasons I gave you. Secondly, he was not a doctor and he could not testify—he indicated that.

In addition to this, section 2(f), "All parts of the plant Cannabis Sativa * * *", and this is what he testified this was, is also listed as a narcotic.

MR. EVERT: Should I understand then that if it was illegitimate or not material, and if testimony from Mr. Wall as to the nature of marihuana, as to whether or not it was habit-forming was excluded during that testimony, that testimony from a physician as to the same subject is also excluded?

THE COURT: Yes, I would exclude it because I don't think it's necessary to establish that because subsection (g) of section 2 indicates a coverall paragraph which I read twice. It is listed by the United States Bureau of Narcotics as a narcotic, and that is all that is necessary.[31]

(Whereupon there was a recess at 11:30 a. m.)

———

At 11:50 a. m.

(The discussion between the Court and counsel in the courtroom out of the presence of the jury continued.)

MR. EVERT: Regarding the argument, People v. Pedderson, 327 State 213—the volume is on the bench, your Honor.

MR. BRYERS: What page is that?

MR. EVERT: 213. In that particular case, on page 220, the Supreme Court advances the proposition that recalling the witnesses rests in the sound discretion of the Court.

THE COURT: What about you, Mr. Prosecutor?

MR. BRYERS: I beg your pardon, sir?

THE COURT: Don't you want to answer the argument?

MR. BRYERS: Well, my argument is that we still make the same objection, and we leave it to the Court to make its decision.

THE COURT: That's a very peculiar type of objection. Of course, the Court is going to make the decision. But what are you urging? Do you have any law to back up what you're urging?

MR. BRYERS: I have no law because I have had no opportunity to check it.

31. How does the judge know this?

THE COURT: You have had opportunity. I just checked some law when you were gone.

Are you telling me I have a right to make a decision? I knew that before you told me. Don't you have anything you want to tell the Court? He has argued his side of it and you have no argument against it.

MR. BRYERS: My argument is that the People have rested their case, and he had an opportunity to cross-examine this witness; he has cross-examined him; and I feel he no longer has a right to cross-examine him.

THE COURT: Do you have any law to back that up?

MR. BRYERS: No, sir, I don't.

THE COURT: Recall for cross-examination—no law on that?

MR. BRYERS: [32] No, sir.

THE COURT: What you are quoting to me is that the extent and control of cross-examination is left largely to the sound discretion of the Court, is that right?

MR. EVERT: The case stands for that proposition, your Honor.

THE COURT: I checked some law in your absence, gentlemen. I refer to State Criminal Law and Procedure, Hearnpipe, Second Series, Chapter 401, on page 486:

The discretion of a trial judge controls the nature and extent of the introduction of collateral matters upon cross-examination and will never be reviewed except in cases of abuse.

I find that the defendant might suffer as a result of my refusal to permit you to recall this man for cross-examination, and the citations I have are here in Hearnpipe, and, therefore, although the People have rested, I will permit you to recall him for cross-examination on this one point only.

MR. EVERT: Yes, your Honor.

THE COURT: Call the jury.

(Whereupon the discussion between the Court and counsel was concluded at 11:55 a. m., the jury returned to the courtroom, and the trial was continued.)

THE COURT: (to the jury) As I told you before, Members of the Jury, when any legal question has to be passed upon, it must be done by the Court.

---

32. This is simply bad (lazy?) lawyering on the part of the assistant prosecutor. He made no effort to do any research in support of his argument and consequently has both annoyed the judge and lost the decision. It may be that Bryers, like many prosecutors, is substantially overworked and that he had to use the recess to attend to more pressing business. Might the prosecutor's performance affect the decision of an appellate court? If so, would the prosecutor have been better off explaining his inept performance? If no sympathetic explanation is available, would an apology be useful?

It is the Court's own responsibility, and sometimes it takes a little longer than other times.

The People have rested.

Defendant?

MR. EVERT: I would like to recall Officer Norton, your Honor, for the purposes of cross-examination.

THE COURT: For the purpose of a limited cross-examination, as you said previously.

Very well.

At 11:55 a. m.

DARRELL NORTON, having been previously sworn, resumed the stand for the purpose of a limited cross-examination by Mr. Evert, and testified as follows:

CROSS-EXAMINATION [33]

BY MR. EVERT:

Q. Officer Norton, yesterday you gave testimony in this case, is that correct? A. It is correct, sir.

Q. And do you recall generally that testimony? A. Yes, I do, sir.

Q. And do you recall that I repeatedly asked you whether or not you had given any narcotics to Earl Stible, a witness about whom there has been testimony? A. Yes, sir.

Q. Do you recall what your answers were yesterday? A. That Earl Stible did not receive any narcotics from me.

Q. And this is another day. Do you still say that that statement is true? A. Yes, sir.

Q. Now, you were present in this court on April 6, 1967, wherein I asked you certain questions concerning the same subject, were you not? A. I was, sir.

Q. Do you recall what your answers to those questions were then?

THE COURT: I think, counsel, if you have a transcript of it, the proper way to do this would be to ask him if he remembers being asked the following questions and making the following answers. I think this is the proper way to do it.

MR. EVERT: Yes, sir.

THE COURT: You may proceed in that fashion.

33. Is this really cross-examination? If so, why does the court later afford the prosecutor an opportunity for cross-examination? What should be the rule on leading questions here?

Q. (By Mr. Evert, continuing): Do you recall the following questions by me and your answers?

"**Q.** All right. And then you left and you and Mr. Stible joined Officer Barrott, is that right? **A.** No, sir, we did not.

"**Q.** What did you do with Mr. Stible? **A.** I dropped Mr. Stible off.

"**Q.** Where? **A.** I think it was up on Harrison or down at the Capri. It was on Harrison or at the Capri Lounge.

"**Q.** What did you pay him? **A.** Nothing.

"**Q.** Had you already paid him in advance? **A.** No, sir.

"**Q.** What did you promise him? **A.** Nothing.

"**Q.** Ever give him anything before or after this transaction—money, narcotics? What did you do? What did you give Mr. Stible to induce him to assist you in this? **A.** I didn't induce him to assist me.

"**Q.** All right. Did you ever give him any money—ever in life? **A.** Bought him a drink. We were in a bar together.

"**Q.** Bought him a drink before you went over to Mr. Whale's house that day? **A.** I can't remember that. I don't remember whether I bought him a drink in a bar that day or not. I was always buying him drinks, more or less.

"**Q.** Does Mr. Stible smoke marihuana, if you know? **A.** Not to my knowledge he doesn't, sir.

"**Q.** You never gave him any, did you? **A.** No, sir.

"**Q.** He never asked for any either. Did he? **A.** Did he ever ask any from me?

"**Q.** Yes, sir. **A.** No.

"**Q.** No? **A.** Correct.

"**Q.** Oh, yes? **A.** On one particular case in hand I did give Mr. Stible and another subject who was in the car with me—they rolled two sticks of marihuana.

"**Q.** And you gave it to them? **A.** Yes, sir.

"**Q.** Were you the only Hamster police officer there at the time of this transaction where you gave him some marihuana to smoke? **A.** Was I the only officer there?

"**Q.** Yes, sir. **A.** Yes, sir.

"**Q.** All right. Did they smoke it in your presence, by the way? **A.** No, sir.

"**Q.** You just saw them roll it, is that right? **A.** Yes, sir. This subject's name is—

"**Q.** I didn't ask you his name. You gave them this marihuana and they rolled it, and what did they do with it? **A.** I don't know what they did with it. They gave me what they rolled from the pack that I had bought—they rolled—you know, they gave it back to me.

"**Q.** Was this before or after the 25th of January? **A.** This was before.

"**Q.** All right."

Q. Do you remember those questions and answers? **A.** I remember the questions. I don't remember the answers.

Q. You don't? **A.** I can't remember the specific answers. I can't remember all the questions, frankly.

Q. All right.

MR. EVERT: Nothing further, except that I would like to have the court reporter sworn as to her testimony regarding preparing the transcript.

THE COURT: Who was going to take testimony while she is being sworn?

MR. EVERT: I want her to be sworn as to the accuracy of the transcript.

THE COURT: Will you concede that this is a transcript prepared by my court reporter if she tells you that?

MR. BRYERS: I will so concede.

THE COURT: I am addressing my remarks to Mrs. Gorman. Maybe you had better stand up and be sworn.

————

HANAH P. GORMAN, was duly sworn by the Court to testify.

THE COURT: You may examine her, but not too quickly, because she has to mark it down.

MR. BRYERS: May I proceed with mine?

THE COURT: You are now conceding that this transcript was typed by Mrs. Gorman, is that correct?

MR. BRYERS: That's right.

THE COURT: You must offer it in evidence. This will be your exhibit.

MR. EVERT: I have no objections to doing that. I simply wanted to ask her whether or not this is an accurate transcript of the witness's statements on April 6, 1967.

THE COURT: (to witness) Is that an accurate transcript?

THE WITNESS: Yes, sir.

THE COURT: The usual accurate transcriptions that you make?

THE WITNESS: Yes, sir.[34]

EXAMINATION

BY MR. EVERT:

Q. And you prepared it for me at my request, is that correct? A. Yes, sir.

Q. Thank you.

THE COURT: Mark it as an exhibit.

(Whereupon Defendant's Exhibit A was marked for identification by the court reporter.)

THE COURT: Are there any objections?

MR. BRYERS: No objections.

---

34. The requirement of authentication or identification of tangible nontestimonial evidence means that before evidence is admitted, the person offering the evidence must show that it is what it purports to be. For example, in this case it was necessary to show that the transcript offered was the accurate transcribed account of testimony which officer Norton had given at the preliminary hearing. In a case where a document prepared by X is relevant, one has to offer evidence tending to show that the document really was prepared by X before introducing the document. If the document were signed, this could be done through the testimony of one who recognized X's signature. If the document were handwritten, a handwriting expert or a lay witness familiar with X's penmanship could authenticate it. The chain of custody that was laid for the tobacco can and marihuana in this case is another form of identification. It is designed to guarantee that the substance that was analyzed by Wall and later introduced at trial is the same substance that was taken from Whale. If it were not, the identification of the substance in the can as marihuana would not be relevant to Whale's guilt, for Whale can only be held responsible for what he possessed. Thus rules of authentication are rules whose fundamental purpose is to enhance the likely probative value of evidence.

If there is a dispute as to whether evidence really is what it is supposed to be, the judge makes a preliminary determination that there is enough evidence for the jury to so find. The judge in such circumstances does not decide whether he accepts the claims of the proponent of the evidence, but instead asks whether a reasonable jury could accept those claims. If this minimum threshold is met the jury may determine in the course of its deliberations whether or not the evidence is what it purports to be. See FRE 104(b) and 901(a). See also McCormick § 227.

When a party seeks to introduce the testimony of an expert witness or the results of a scientific test, the party faces a requirement that is similar to authentication. The basis of the witness' expertise or the validity of the scientific test must be shown before the testimony or the evidence will be allowed. This showing is called "laying a foundation." It is like authentication because it provides special reason to believe that the forthcoming testimony or evidence will be relevant to a matter at issue. In doing so, the judge may have to resolve conflicting issues of fact. This is typically done out of the presence of the jury.

THE COURT: There being no objections, Defendant's Exhibit A is admitted in evidence.

Now I think he has a right to cross-examine Officer Norton.

CROSS-EXAMINATION (OF OFFICER NORTON)

BY MR. BRYERS:

Q. Mr. Norton, this day in question that you were in the car with Mr. Stible and another subject, that's what you were testifying to? **A.** Yes, sir.

Q. On the stand. And you say that marihuana was given to these men?

THE COURT: Why don't you use the transcript? It's in evidence now. You may have the exact verbiage.

Q. (By Mr. Bryers, continuing): You gave an answer:

"**A.** On one particular case in hand I did give Mr. Stible and another subject who was in the car with me—they rolled two sticks of marihuana.

Q. And you gave it to them?

A. Yes, sir."

Q. Now, to whom did you actually give on that particular occasion the marihuana? **A.** The marihuana—I was asked for marihuana by a Mr. Pumplin.

Q. That was the other subject in the car? **A.** Yes, sir.

Q. And you were asked by him? **A.** Yes, sir.

Q. In the presence of Mr. Stible? **A.** Yes, sir.

Q. For what? **A.** He said he took me to make my connections; he wanted to get a couple of sticks.

Q. A couple of sticks? **A.** Right.

Q. Who said that? **A.** Mr. Pumplin.

Q. What did you do then? **A.** I gave it to him.

Q. Whom did you give it to? **A.** I gave it to Mr. Pumplin.

Q. Did you or did you not give it to Mr. Stible? **A.** I did not.

Q. You gave it to Mr. Pumplin? **A.** That is correct.

MR. BRYERS: That's all.

THE COURT (to witness): This was prior to January 25th?

THE WITNESS: Yes, sir.

At 12:05 p. m.

THE COURT: You may proceed to call your next witness.

MR. EVERT: I call the defendant to the stand.

THE COURT: Defendant, come forward, please.

NELSON LILTON WHALE, called as a witness in his own behalf, and having been first duly sworn, testified as follows: [35]

DIRECT EXAMINATION

BY MR. EVERT:

Q. Mr. Whale, do you recall the day of January 25, is that correct? **A.** Yes, I do.

Q. Now, you were arrested some time after the 25th of January. What date was that? **A.** I think it was a couple of days after the 25th.

Q. Who arrested you? **A.** I couldn't be sure. It was at least twenty officers.

Q. You were arrested at home, is that right? **A.** No, I was arrested at my son's house.

Q. That would be at 4061 Murane Court, is that right? **A.** Yes.

Q. And the twenty officers there, were they searching the house at the same time? **A.** They were completely tearing the house up.

---

35. The fifth amendment to the constitution gives the defendant in a criminal case the right not to take the stand. Furthermore, neither the prosecutor nor the judge may comment on the defendant's failure to testify. Nevertheless, the jury cannot help but notice the defendant's silence and may be influenced by this in the jury room. Thus, it is dangerous for defense counsel to keep a client off the stand. However, it may also be dangerous to allow one's client to testify. Once the defendant takes the stand he is treated more or less like any other witness. This means that he is subject to cross-examination and that aspects of his past which arguably bear on his veracity may be brought out to impeach him. In the case of Nelson Whale this means, as you shall see, that the jury will learn of his prior drug involvement. They would not have known of this had Whale chosen not to testify.

The defendant also possesses the right to testify in his own behalf. This was not always the case. At one time defendants in criminal cases, both parties in civil cases, and other persons having a direct interest of a pecuniary or proprietary nature in the outcome of litigation were precluded from testifying. These were among the common law incompetencies which, as we point out in note 4 supra, have long since been abolished. However, in civil cases the effects of the disqualification for interest linger. In abolishing the rules prohibiting interested parties from testifying, most jurisdictions enacted a compromise known as the Dead Man's Statute. Such statutes provide that interested persons are not barred from testifying except concerning a transaction or communication with a deceased person in a suit prosecuted or defended by the executor or administrator of the deceased. If the interested party is called by the executor or administrator, most jurisdictions provide that the party may testify. Dead Man's Statutes have been severely criticized. Some states have liberalized them by permitting interested survivors to testify, but requiring some sort of corroboration to support a judgment. Others provide that the trial judge has discretion to permit such testimony to avoid injustice.

Q. Now, after your arrest, you were taken in custody, is that right? **A.** Yes, I was.

Q. And have you been in custody continuously since that time? **A.** Yes, I have.

Q. Prior to your arrest, were you employed? **A.** Yes, I was.

Q. Where did you work? **A.** At General Motors.

Q. What was your job there? **A.** I was a welder.

Q. All right. Were you working there on the day before your arrest? **A.** Yes, I was, the 25th.

Q. As far as you can remember. **A.** Yes. Yes, I was.

Q. All right. Now, you recall the day of the 25th of January, do you not? **A.** Yes, I do.

Q. Now, could you state whether or not you saw Officer Norton on that day? **A.** Yes, I did.

Q. Where did you see him? **A.** I can't specifically give a correct time, but when I seen him, he was in the parlor of the house.

Q. All right. Would that be the house at 4061 Murane Court? **A.** Yes.

Q. About which he has testified, is that right? **A.** That is true.

Q. Was he alone when you saw him? **A.** No, he was with Earl Stible.

Q. All right. He and Earl Stible came in together, is that right? **A.** Yes, it is.

Q. Did you have a conversation with him when he came in? **A.** Yes, I did.

Q. And who was present at the time of the conversation? **A.** Well, as the conversation began—

Q. No. Who was present? **A.** Earl Stible and Damon Lord.

Q. Damon Lord, Earl Stible and you and Mr. Norton were there together, is that right? **A.** Yes.

Q. All right. Now, did Damon Lord remain in the room? **A.** Briefly.

Q. And then he left, is that right? **A.** That's correct.

Q. Did Earl Stible remain in the room? **A.** Briefly.

Q. And then he left, is that right? **A.** Yes, that's true.

Q. Eventually you and Mr. Norton were alone. **A.** Correct.

Q. All right, Now, do you know the precise—strike that. From the time you walked into the house, I want you to tell me everything that you recall Mr. Norton said to you and what you said to him. **A.** Well, I come downstairs—I was upstairs—and I come downstairs from a call from Damon.

He said that there was somebody that wanted me at the door, so as I entered this intersection of the house which is from the kitchen, sort of a utility room—as I entered this part, here's Earl and here's Norton here. So, Earl had presently just left. So, then Norton.

THE COURT (to witness): When you say "presently", just what do you mean?

THE WITNESS: As I entered the room, your Honor, he just left; he comes out. So then Norton asks me what did I have. And I said, what did he mean. And he said he wanted to get a can from me, a can or half a can. I told him that I didn't know what he was talking about. At this particular time, Damon had left the room during the statement.

THE COURT: That's Damon Lord.

THE WITNESS: Yes.

Q. (By Mr. Evert, continuing): All right. And what happened after that? A. He—actually—he—his exact words were, "You sure you don't have nothing, man?" And I said, "No, I don't have anything. I don't mess with none—in fact, I don't know what you're talking about." I thought the man was crazy. I don't know him.

Q. Did you know him? A. I don't know him from Adam and Eve. This was the first time I had ever seen him.

Q. All right. Now, did he thereupon leave? He left your house then? A. Yes, at that point.

Q. Now, did you see him any more that day? A. Yes, I did; yes, I did.

Q. Give me an approximate time. Well, how long was it before he came back? A. I'll say close to two hours, a little after an hour.

Q. Was he alone then? A. No, I don't—Earl was with him then.

Q. All right. And do you recall who let him in on that occasion? A. I think it was Damon's brother.

Q. Damon's brother? A. Yes.

Q. What is his brother's name? A. Robert.

Q. Robert Lord? A. Yes.

Q. All right. In any event, were you downstairs when he came, or did you have to be called?

THE COURT: I think you had better stay with the direct question. "Were you downstairs?" is all right. This is direct examination.

MR. EVERT: Yes, sir.

THE COURT: I can't have leading questions.[36]

36. Why not? Counsel has not objected. Should the judge be raising this issue of his own accord? Assuming he should not, would such judicial interference ever be grounds for reversal on appeal?

MR. EVERT: All right.

Q. (By Mr. Evert, continuing): You had a conversation with him when he came in the second time? **A.** Yes, I did.

Q. Who was present during that conversation? **A.** Earl was; Earl was present.

Q. Earl Stible? **A.** Yes, he was.

Q. All right. Do you recall whether anybody else was there the second time you had a conversation with him? **A.** Linda, Linda Foss had intervened during the second conversation.

Q. Now, you say "Linda Foss". Who is she? **A.** That is Mildred's sister.

Q. And who is Mildred? **A.** Mildred is the mother of my son.

Q. All right. And Linda Foss came in and intervened, you say? **A.** Yes.

Q. And did she stay in and participate in this conversation? **A.** Well, she hesitated because of what was taking place. I haven't got to this yet.

Q. Now, in any event, Earl was there during the second time you talked to him that day, and you say Linda was there for a moment, she intervened. All right. Now, I want you to tell me on this occasion what conversation you had with Mr. Norton from the time he got there until the time he left. **A.** Well, he come into the—when I come downstairs, he was in the same compartment of the house. This time he went in his pockets and he come out with cans of tobacco, pipe cans. And he asked me, "I want you to tell me,"—they call me "Tweedie"—"I want you to tell me, Tweedie, if this is the stuff". So he takes that—one of the cans, and he hands one of the cans to me. He reached in his pocket and pulls out—I think it was a paper bag or a piece of paper—anyway, he rips it and lays the paper down on the counter—I have a table right there. He lays it down on the counter indicating for me to pour this out. I pours this out, and he says, "Man, I can't roll. Will you?" In other words, twist them up into paper. In other words, "Will you roll a couple and see how it is? Roll a couple and put them in the can". And I say, "Man, I don't bother with it. In fact, what's your name?" At that moment I was looking for something actually to—I thought he was a nut. I was looking for something I could hit him with, to tell you the truth.

Q. What happened after that? **A.** After that he left.

Q. All right. Now, I show you People's Exhibit 1(a), and ask you whether or not, as far as you can recall, this is the can that you saw at your house that day. **A.** That's exactly.

Q. What happened to this can? What happened to the can after you saw it? **A.** He—I took the portion that he had in the can—he had two cans. He handed me the can that was full, and set the empty can on the counter. He had tore open a bag. I poured this out on the bag. He was indicating to me, "I want you to see if this is good stuff. Roll up a couple."

Q. All right. But after the conversation, what happened to the can?
A. Oh, he took the can.

Q. All right. What happened to it? Did he take both cans, or just that can? **A.** He took both cans.

Q. All right. And when was the next time you saw that can? **A.** At my examination in—it was at my examination.

THE COURT (to witness): Well, for the purpose of the jury, you mean a preliminary examination by a judge?

THE WITNESS: Yes, it was.

THE COURT: Do you remember the name of the judge? Was it Judge McCarthey?

THE WITNESS: Yes.

THE COURT: In Hamster?

THE WITNESS: Yes.

MR. EVERT: [37] Your witness.

CROSS-EXAMINATION

BY MR. BRYERS:

Q. Mr. Whale, you say you saw this can again at the preliminary examination? **A.** Yes, I think it was at the preliminary examination.

Q. As a matter of fact, wasn't that can in an envelope that was sealed? **A.** I'm not sure whether—the can was brought up in proof. It had to be brought up to be proved at my examination.

Q. Did you see the envelope opened at the preliminary examination? **A.** No, I don't think I did, come to think of it. I seen it here.

Q. In other words, you really didn't see the can at the preliminary examination, is that right? **A.** I seen it after my preliminary examination.

Q. Where? **A.** Right here.

Q. Here, I see. Do you know Earl Stible? **A.** Yes, I do.

37. What has happened to the defense of entrapment after Nelson Whale's testimony? Can one argue that he was entrapped into selling marihuana if he testifies that he never sold marihuana? It is important that an attorney develop a theory of the case which fits the available facts. It appears that Evert did not do this, though it is possible that Whale surprised Evert with his statements on direct examination. What has this done to the case for the defense? What does the defendant's case turn on now?

Why do you suppose that Evert's plan to raise an entrapment defense has been frustrated by Whale's testimony? Has Evert helped Whale prepare his testimony? Has he talked to him extensively about the case? In thinking about this, consider whether Evert knew where Whale lived before Whale took the stand to testify. Did you notice that the address at which the sale of marihuana allegedly took place was not Whale's home, although Bryers and Evert both indicated it was?

Q. How long have you known him? **A.** I went to school with him; about maybe 15 years.

Q. Fifteen years? And how often do you see him a week? **A.** It varies up. On weekends I see him once in a while.

Q. You just see him on weekends now? **A.** Yes, it varies. I'm liable to see him—you know, Hamster is very small. I might have seen him coming out of the supermarket or at the car wash. He works at the car wash, and I get my car washed there.

Q. Can you tell us how many times a week you see him? **A.** Sometimes once a week, sometimes twice a week, sometimes none at all in a week's period of time.

Q. Have you ever been in his home? **A.** No, I haven't.

Q. Has he ever been in your home? **A.** Yes, he has.

Q. Are you married? [38] **A.** No, I'm not.

Q. Is Mr. Stible married? **A.** Not to my knowledge.

Q. But he's a good friend of yours, is that right? **A.** No, I wouldn't say he's a good friend of mine.

Q. You know him very well. **A.** No, I don't know him very well.

Q. You have known him for 15 years. **A.** Yes, we went to school together.

Q. How old are you? **A.** I'm 26.

Q. Are you single or divorced? **A.** Neither one. I'm single, rather.

Q. Single. Had you ever seen Darrel Norton before the night of January 25, 1967? **A.** No.

Q. Are you sure? **A.** Positive.

Q. Now, you say you never saw Darrell Norton before. You also testified on direct examination that you poured some stuff into a bag at his request. **A.** No, I didn't pour it into a bag. The bag was laid out on a table, you know. The bag was ripped open and laid out on a table.

Q. Who put it out there? **A.** Darrell Norton.

Q. I see. What happened then? **A.** He had handed me this can of marihuana and in return I poured it out on top of the bag. In the process, this—he was indicating for me to—actually he wanted me to see, take a glance and see if this was the stuff he was asking my knowledge of.

---

38. **One may usually establish the basic identity of a witness by asking for the witness's name, age, occupation, place of residence, marital status, etc. On their face such questions are neutral and non-prejudicial. Is that the case here? Should defense counsel have brought up Mildred's** name on direct examination? Had defense counsel objected to this question on the grounds that Whale's marital status was irrelevant, it might have flagged the matter for the jury, so defense counsel is probably wise in refraining from objecting.

Q. You say he had never seen you before and you had never seen him before, is that right? **A.** That's correct.

Q. And he was emptying this stuff out to show you what he had in his bag, is that right? **A.** Not in the bag. In the can.

Q. In the can? **A.** Yes.

Q. And what did he ask you? **A.** He asked me to see if this—he wanted my opinion to know whether or not this was good stuff. Then he wanted me to roll him up a couple of what you—"sticks".

Q. I see. **A.** Actually, what it was he wanted me to sample it. I don't know what it was.

Q. But you had never seen him before? **A.** Yes, I seen him when he had come back that day earlier.

Q. But you had never seen him before this night of January 25th? **A.** No.

Q. Now, how many times have you been convicted of a crime?

MR. EVERT:[39] I object to the form of the question, your Honor.

39. What is the objection to the form of the previous question? How should it have been asked? Of what relevance is this question to the prosecution's case? The theory is that the question is relevant in that it sheds light on the credibility of the witness. Conviction for a felony is thought to reflect a moral stain which means that an ex-convict is more likely to lie from the stand than one never before convicted of a crime. Does this justification seem reasonable to you? Can you think of any other justifications for this rule? The jury is supposed to treat this evidence as bearing only on the probability that the defendant is perjuring him or herself; it is not to be treated as bearing on the probability that the defendant committed the offense in question. How likely is it that the jury can treat this information for only the proper purpose? Would the evidence of a past conviction be as devastating to Whale if the conviction were for a non-drug-related offense? How might a non-drug-related conviction hurt the defendant's chances for an acquittal? Consider Whale's dilemma. If he does not take the stand the jury wonders why he didn't tell his story himself. If he does take the stand the jury learns that he was once convicted of possession of mari-

huana, and they may believe that this means he is particularly likely to have been using and selling marihuana on subsequent occasions. Because of the danger that impeachment by reference to past crimes will cause undue prejudice, FRE 609 allows impeachment by evidence of conviction of crime only if the crime involved dishonesty or false statement or if the crime was punishable by imprisonment in excess of one year and the judge determines that the probative value of admitting the evidence outweighs its prejudicial effect on defendant. It would appear that the formulation of the federal rule is designed to reverse the usual presumption that impeachment by evidence of past crimes is generally proper. A few states have gone farther and decided that defendants should not be impeachable by reference to their past crimes. This matter is discussed in more detail in Chapter Five on impeachment.

FRE 105 gives a party against whom evidence is properly offered for only one of a number of possible purposes, the right to have the judge instruct the jury on the proper, limited use of the evidence. Thus, in a case like this the attorney has a right to have the jury told that the evidence is

THE COURT (to witness): Have you ever been arrested and convicted before?

THE WITNESS: I have been arrested; I wouldn't say I have been convicted.

Q. (By Mr. Bryers, continuing): You say you have never been convicted? A. Yes, I would say I have never been convicted.

Q. You have never been convicted of a crime?

MR. EVERT: He didn't say that.

MR. BRYERS: That's what he said.

THE COURT: Wait a minute. (to witness) Have you ever been arrested and convicted? You know what "convicted" means, don't you?

THE WITNESS: Yes. "Convicted" means found guilty of a crime.

THE COURT: Or pleaded guilty?

THE WITNESS: I have pleaded guilty to a crime.

Q. (By Mr. Bryers, continuing): You have pleaded guilty to a crime? A. Yes, I have.

Q. What crime was that? A. This was possession.

Q. Possession of what? A. Of marihuana.

Q. Possession of marihuana? A. Possession of marihuana.

Q. And when was this that you pleaded guilty to such a crime? A. This was in May of '65.

Q. Are you sure of the date? A. No, I'm not positive. It was in May.

Q. And what was your sentence?

MR. EVERT: I'll object to that as being immaterial, your Honor.

THE COURT: The sentence?

MR. EVERT: Yes.

THE COURT: What crime was he convicted of before a judge?

admissible to test Whale's credibility, but not to establish that Whale is a marihuana user.

It might seem odd that a witness would be confused about a word like "convicted." But remember that lay witnesses are not always familiar with the language that lawyers and judges use every day. For example, in those jurisdictions that allow witnesses to be impeached only by convictions involving moral turpitude, consider how confused a witness might be by the question "Have you been convicted of a crime involving moral turpitude?" A good attorney will always discuss with each witness the meaning of legal terms likely to be used in the course of direct and cross-examination. If counsel doubts a witness' understanding of the terms used in a question, counsel may object to the question or suggest that it be clarified.

MR. BRYERS: Pardon?

THE COURT: Before what judge? Is that what you're going to ask him?

MR. BRYERS: No, I was just going to ask him if he was sentenced.

MR. EVERT: He didn't deny it. He said he was arrested and convicted.

THE COURT: I overrule your objection. This is cross-examination. He is testing his credibility. He may answer the question.

Q. (By Mr. Bryers, continuing): What were you sentenced to on this crime? [40] A. I was sentenced to two years to ten in the Parkson Penitentiary.

Q. All right. Now, what is your present status?

MR. EVERT: I will object to that, your Honor.

THE COURT: Wait a minute. Present status—he's sitting on the stand testifying.

Q. (By Mr. Bryers): Have you ever been convicted of any other crimes?

THE COURT: [41] You had better ask him whether he pleaded guilty or was convicted. He draws a distinction.

Q. (By Mr. Bryers, continuing): Have you ever pleaded guilty to any other crimes?

THE COURT: Or been convicted of any, either way? A. Yes, I have.

Q. What crime was that? A. Attempted robbery.

Q. When was that? A. This was also in '65.

Q. All right. Have you pleaded guilty to any other crimes? A. No, I haven't.

THE COURT (to witness): Have you been convicted of any other crimes?

THE WITNESS: No, I have not.

MR. BRYERS: I have no other questions.

THE COURT: Is there any redirect examination?

REDIRECT EXAMINATION

BY MR. EVERT:

Q. Is it correct that the only time—

40. Why was this question asked? How is the length of the sentence which Whale received for his previous offense relevant to his credibility? To what extent, if any, do you think the information that Whale had received a previous sentence of two to ten years would influence the jurors in this case?

41. What is happening here to the appearance of fairness? The judge is human. Is he by this point a tired human?

THE COURT: Wait a minute.

MR. EVERT: Yes, sir. I'll rephrase it.

THE COURT: This is redirect examination, not cross-examination.

MR. EVERT: I have nothing further.

THE COURT: If there is nothing further, he may stand down.

MR. BRYERS: Nothing further, your Honor.

(Whereupon the witness was excused at 12:15 p. m.)

———

2:35 p. m.

(The following discussion was had in chambers with the Court, counsel and the court reporter present.)

THE COURT: For the record, we are now out of the earshot of the jury and in my private chambers. Both counsel for the prosecution and defense are here.

Requests for charges have been submitted by the defense counsel. Have you approved his requests to charge, Mr. Prosecutor?

MR. BRYERS: I have approved these two.

MR. EVERT: Everything except the entrapment?

MR. BRYERS: I have not approved the entrapment.

MR. EVERT: Now, we get to the matter of the supplemental instructions as to "Entrapment". You object to that request. May I ask why?

MR. BRYERS: Because there has been no testimony in this case about entrapment. The man denies he even sold anything to Darrell Norton.

THE COURT: That's right. I'm afraid I will have to agree with him.

MR. EVERT: Well, now—

THE COURT: How was he entrapped if he denies he ever sold anything? He said he never even had it.

MR. EVERT: I wonder if that's the status of the law. I think the problem here is that Damon Lord testified that when he came into the house, Mr. Norton was trying to get Mr. Whale, the defendant, to sell him some stuff, and the defendant said, "I don't know what you're talking about."

There is testimony in the record from the police officer which would tend to show that a sale was made, and the only thing I want to argue to the jury, and want the Court to instruct, is that if they believe the police officer's version of the testimony, they should further consider whether or not the sale was voluntarily made.

THE COURT: No, sir. There is no sale; your man denied the sale. If he hadn't taken the stand, there is a possibility. Having taken the stand, I will deny that charge. I will not give it because there is nothing that the defendant or defense said to indicate a sale was made, so all they did was take issue with what the People proved.

MR. EVERT: [42]   I said something about it in the opening statement.

THE COURT: I don't care whether you said something in the opening statement.   You didn't prove it.   If your testimony had been, "Yes, I did, but he forced me to do it or 'sucked' me into a play. I wasn't going to commit the act but he talked me into it," that's one thing. But there is no entrapment.   The man said he didn't sell it.

(Whereupon there was an off-the-record discussion.)   So I will not give it, over your objections.

MR. EVERT: Yes, of course, your Honor.

So that it won't be necessary to interrupt the proceedings during my closing argument, at this point should I understand that I am foreclosed to argue that to the jury?

THE COURT: Yes.   This is the purpose of going over your instructions to the jury in advance, because it would be an inconsistent position. I think I have covered everything here.

Now we get to yours.   Yours is innocuous.

MR. BRYERS: I will withdraw it.

THE COURT: It's an innocuous one.   "Criminal convictions of any witness who takes the stand may be taken into consideration by the jury for the purpose of evaluating his credibility."   If you want it or not, I don't care.

MR. EVERT: That is not satisfactory as far as I am concerned.   I think if you are going to say that, you should take the next logical step and indicate that it may not be for the purpose of committing the acts in this instant case.

MR. BRYERS: I think so.

MR. EVERT: That's half a thought.

THE COURT: Do you want to withdraw it or not?

MR. BRYERS: I would just as soon have it in.

THE COURT: Then write the rest of it in.   This goes into the record. You don't have the thing labeled.   The Court of Appeals is going to cut you to ribbons for giving a piece of paper.

MR. BRYERS: Let me withdraw it.

THE COURT: I don't want you to withdraw it.

42. The court rejects a request for an instruction on entrapment because the defense has introduced no evidence which would justify an acquittal on entrapment grounds.   Evert responds that he mentioned the matter in his opening statement.   Why isn't this sufficient to support the requested instruction?   The opening and closing statements of counsel are not evidence.   Why is this?   What is the evidence in this case?   In addition to testimony, what kinds of evidence may an attorney present at trial?

MR. EVERT: If you do, I want to request it about the rest of it.

THE COURT: You have to make up your mind.

The defense has a second supplemental request here, "Failure to Call Res Gestae Witnesses". Do you agree to that?

MR. BRYERS: Yes.

THE COURT: And you agreed to the second one; that's only one. Do you agree to that?

MR. BRYERS: Yes.

THE COURT: I'll decide whether I give it. You're going to argue it anyway.

MR. EVERT: I was going to argue that.

THE COURT: You can argue that; there's no question.

I might tell you that the next time you present a request to charge, you must have a citation.

MR. EVERT: There is a citation with the "Entrapment".

THE COURT: [43] I'm talking about that which I disallowed. It is the rule of the Supreme Court that I don't have to consider it. The obvious reason is that if I do, I have to start checking to find out whether this is the law. If you give me a citation that this is the law cited in such a case, we examine the case and decide whether it is or not.

You ought to have that thing typed, too, before I file it.

MR. EVERT: I will have to call my office. If he's withdrawing it, I'll call my secretary on the telephone.

THE COURT: We don't have time.

Criminal convictions of any witness who takes the stand may be taken into consideration by the jury for the purpose of evaluating his credibility, and it may not be considered that by virtue of his past record that he actually committed this particular crime.

That is what you're talking about.

MR. EVERT: Or " * * * you may not consider the commission of other crimes for the purpose of determining that it is more likely that he may have committed this offense."

THE COURT: I'm not going to say that.

---

43. **The need for preparation should be obvious. An attorney should know what legal theories he or she expects to draw on at trial and should come prepared with supporting arguments which are spelled out and appropriately documented. In litigation as in most other aspects of the lawyer's professional career, hard work is a** key to success. **Unfortunately many of the regular participants in the criminal justice system, prosecutors, public defenders, and appointed counsel, are either so overworked or so underpaid that they cannot afford to put in the time necessary to mount a well thought out, carefully researched case.**

MR. EVERT: That's what *State Criminal Law and Procedure*, Vol. 1, Sec. 446 says.

THE COURT: I'm not going to give that.

You had better type that out because I will deny it.

(Whereupon the discussion in chambers was concluded at 3 p. m.)

———

At 3 p. m.

(The trial was continued in the courtroom, with the jury and all parties present.)

THE COURT: The defense?

MR. EVERT: The defense rests, your Honor.[44]

THE COURT: You may proceed to argument, opening argument by the Prosecutor.

FIRST ARGUMENT BY MR. BRYERS:

MR. BRYERS: Ladies and Gentlemen, the People have rested their case, and the defense has also rested. Shortly, you will be asked to deliberate and to come to a verdict in this case, to decide whether or not the defendant is guilty.

Now, I want to caution you that when you deliberate, the only evidence that you should consider is that evidence which comes in the form of testimony from the stand, as contrasted with what myself or opposing counsel may say in our arguments. We may be wrong in our arguments as to facts. You have heard the facts, and only those facts, only that testimony that comes from the witness stand or exhibits that have been offered and admitted in evidence are to be considered by you in coming to a decision.

Now, what have the People produced in this case? We have shown you through the testimony of Darrell Norton, the police officer, that he went to this address in Hamster where he saw the defendant, Nelson Whale, on January 25, 1967. He stated at that time he asked the defendant if he had any marihuana. There was a discussion, and it was decided that the officer would then go and obtain some Prince Albert cans, so he left this address on Murane in Hamster and proceeded to this drug store, and he obtained two Prince Albert cans of tobacco, emptied the tobacco, and returned to where the defendant was.

He again saw the defendant, Mr. Whale, and Mr. Whale told him that he would have to go and get the "stuff"; he would be back later.

44. At this point the defense is indicating that no more evidence will be offered. Has the defense answered the questions you have about the case? If you were able to ask any possible witness any question you wished, what questions would you ask? Of whom? Has the defense adequately explained to the judge in chambers why the judge's instruction on prior convictions was not adequate? Review the justification for admitting this evidence discussed in note 39 supra.

So, Mr. Norton left and came back for the third time. At this time he met the defendant, Mr. Whale, again; was in the house with him; and made a transaction; paid him $22.50; and received suspected marihuana from him.

He then testified that he left the house, looked over the can of tobacco—tobacco can—and felt that he was shorted, so he came back again for the fourth time, at which time the substance was emptied on the table, looked over and put back in the can.

So there were four trips that he made on that particular day, and Mr. Norton has told you that he was on duty as a police officer, and he has specifically stated what happened on each of these four trips to visit the defendant.

He also said that when he went to the defendant's house, he was in the company of Earl Stible, a man whom the defendant testified that he knew for about 15 years. Mr. Stible was an acquaintance for 15 years with the defendant, Nelson Whale.

Now, Darrell Norton then testified that they took this can with the suspected marihuana, and about a half hour later turned it over to the officer in charge of this case, Richard Barrott. Before turning it over to him, he marked his initials on this can, and Officer Barrott testified he marked his initials on this can, and the can was taken immediately to the Hamster Police Department and placed in a locker, and the locker was locked by Officer Barrott, and he testified that he is the only one that has a key to that locker.

The next morning, Officer Barrott testified, he went to police headquarters, opened this locker, and took out the Prince Albert can, and then proceeded downtown to the Federal Building where he turned this over to the United States chemist, Stanley Wall. Stanley Wall testified that he received this from Mr. Barrott, that he made an analysis, and that this contained 23.53 grains of marihuana. And then Mr. Barrott testified that he took this marihuana back and put it in the police locker and locked it again.

Now, Nelson Whale took the stand. What did he say? He denies that he made a sale. He does admit that he saw Darrell Norton on this evening in question. He admits that he saw him at this particular address on Murane in Hamster. He says he never saw Darrell Norton before, yet he says in his presence Darrell Norton opened up on a table the contents of this Prince Albert can, and they discussed what it was.

Now, does this story seem credible to you? Never saw this man before, yet he is talking to him and he is examining what is supposed to be marihuana.

Now, in determining the facts of this case, you have to decide who is telling the truth, and in this particular case, it appears there is a question of Darrell Norton versus the defendant, Nelson Whale. Now, in deciding who is telling the truth, you must, by your observations of these witnesses on the stand, determine: How did they testify? What did they look like? What is their motivation? What do they have to gain or lose by the truthfulness or untruthfulness of their testimony? This is the thing that is important.

Now, the prosecution feels strongly that we have proven this case beyond a reasonable doubt, and we ask that you return a verdict of guilty.

Thank you.

ARGUMENT OF MR. EVERT:

You may recall, Ladies and Gentlemen of the Jury, at the outset of this case, that I indicated to you that I would have two opportunities to address you—the first at the outset, and now, as the case, in terms of the testimony, comes to a conclusion. The Prosecutor who has just made a statement will have, under the rules of our court system, a second opportunity to rebut what I say to you here now, but this is the only argument that I will have under the rules.

The thing that happens after the arguments and prior to your deliberations will be that the Judge is going to give you certain instructions as to the principles of law that you promised at the outset of this case to apply fairly in the determination of this conflict. He will tell you things about "presumption of innocence" and he will tell you things about "reasonable doubt" and many of the other matters that we have discussed in chambers and which are the principles of law.

In much less detail than perhaps the Prosecutor has just done, I want at this point to review the testimony you have heard in this case with you, both in terms of what you have heard, and in terms of what you haven't heard to the extent that that has been made an issue in this court.

And I want you to take both a negative and positive approach with me as we seek to determine whether or not the People have really satisfied their burden of proof as to the guilt of this defendant beyond a reasonable doubt. I say "reasonable doubt" intentionally, because, as you may recall, Judge Burdick told you at the outset of this case that no defendant has to prove himself innocent, but that it was the burden of the Prosecutor to prove his guilt beyond a reasonable doubt. He even told you that you should not just consider the evidence in terms of what you have heard from the defendant on the witness stand, which we will touch on, but also the nature of the case as shown by the prosecution as this case has proceeded.

There is one important consideration, an observation that the Prosecutor has made, that I am constrained almost to agree with, and that is that much of your decision in this case is a matter of weighing the testimony of the defendant against that offered by the chief witness for the prosecution, or at least a witness for the prosecution, the police officer, Darrell Norton. Upon his testimony, Mr. Norton's testimony, and the credibility you give it, may well rest your decision.

You may recall, however, some of the other things that may have appeared to you as overtones as this case progressed. It may well have had an effect on the presentation of the People and the prosecution and which you may well be called upon to make a decision about.

This is the first negative aspect—that aspect of the absence of any, and I say "any", corroborating testimony of that of the police officer, Darrell

Norton. Let's strip it and look at it for what it is. There have been several instances when you might have, as jurors, not been placed in a position of either believing Darrell Norton and thus convicting this man, or not believing it.

There was an opportunity, for example, that we argued before you for you to have had corroboration of Earl Stible, whose name you have heard batted around this courtroom since this case began. He was the man who, according to the Police Department's testimony, was over on all four occasions. He primarily heard part of the conversations—at least he was in a position to hear part of the conversations. He was there when the cans of Prince Albert tobacco were purchased, and he was there, if the testimony of Mr. Norton is to be completely believed by you, at the time of a sales transaction, or if that is your recollection of the testimony, please consider it as you heard it from the witness stand.

Now, we haven't seen Earl Stible, and I made as much of a point of it as I could within the rules of evidence, to point up to you the unreasonable approach the Police Department made in producing that witness here before you. And I say that Earl Stible is an important witness, and I say that he should have been produced for you so that you could have heard someone other than this police officer, so that you could have considered whether or not this was corroboration of the testimony of this police officer.

What have you heard in regard to the absence of Earl Stible? You have heard he was served a subpoena last Wednesday; you heard that he appeared in this court on Monday; and that's where it stopped, except that you have heard last night one of the other officers, Mr. Barrott, left messages at his house for him to appear. What you didn't hear, though, is that anybody bothered to come here on Monday and inform Earl Stible that he should return here the next day when this case was to be tried. Nobody did, except the Police Department knew about the adjournment on the 20th.

Now, I tell you, and I have requested that the Judge instruct you, that if you should find in your deliberations and in your consideration of this case, that the Police Department or the prosecution have not made a reasonable effort to produce this witness, this witness that we call in law a "res gestae witness" because he was there at the time, then I ask the Court to instruct you that you are entitled to presume that that witness would have testified favorably for the defendant.

This other important area in this case that should bother you when you consider it, is not whether the defendant has proved himself innocent, but whether or not the prosecution has proved the defendant guilty beyond a reasonable doubt.

There have been certain records that the Police Department in their course of investigation of this case have shown to have been produced, and none of which you have been able to see or none of which have been brought to this court so I could examine the police officer on them.

You will recall, for example, the testimony of Mr. Norton who testified under some duty, or as you remember the testimony, that he had to prepare memoranda on the days that he had activities in connection with this case;

that he gave those memoranda without reproducing or keeping a copy for himself or Officer Barrott, which may or may not appear to be unusual to you.

And what did Officer Barrott do with them? He destroyed them. But before he destroyed them, Officer Barrott testified that it was his custom to excerpt—not to quote him, but as you remember the testimony again—to excerpt from them that portion of the activity that seemed to be important.

Do you recall that during the course of this trial that book that Officer Barrott produced was produced in court? And you recall his testimony was that not one word of this transaction in this case that was pretty important to this defendant was in that daily log, although Officer Norton claimed that during the course of these proceedings he made records of what he was doing in regard to defendant Nelson Whale. The name "Nelson Whale" does not appear.

Now, I don't argue, and please understand that I don't argue that the mere fact that there is no record of these things makes the defendant guilty or not one way or the other. But I do say this: That you jurors are entitled to a better case in terms of deciding a "reasonable doubt" question than to have to be placed in the position to believe or not to believe one person that has come into this court.

Let's take another example. I asked Officer Barrott how long he had known Mr. Norton, and if I recall his testimony—again I don't want to mislead you—he said, "Since December," and I asked him whether or not as far as he could remember, he had been reliable, and he said as far as he knew, he had been reliable. Again, I don't want to misquote him—that's my recollection of the testimony.

Now, he testified, also, that he had given him no instructions. Officer Barrott testified that at not one time during the course of this investigation did he have Mr. Norton under surveillance or did he personally check any of the facts about which he testified in this all-important case to defendant Nelson Whale—any of the facts that have been presented to you, other than the fact that Officer Barrott testified that he transported the narcotic drug that he got from Mr. Norton down to Stanley Wall.

I'm talking here, Ladies and Gentlemen of the Jury, about "reasonable doubt" and "lack of corroboration", because again I say to you that if this defendant were required to prove himself innocent while in jail since this offense was committed, then we would have an impossible burden upon the defendant.

So I ask you again to consider whether or not in any of the areas where there could have been corroboration of the testimony of this police officer there has been any.

There was a Prince Albert can, a second can that I asked about, as we talk about destruction of records. Where is the can—some little piece of evidence that would have perhaps further corroborated the testimony of Mr. Norton as to the transaction. The can is not here.

There are other things that may well be conventional things as you may understand in your usual experience, not because you're narcotic experts, but things that could have helped make you a little bit less concerned about "reasonable doubt" and having to rely wholly on the testimony of this officer when there was corroboration possible.

I asked about things like "marked money". There was no marked money. And then there was the matter of a warrant that bothered me, and I don't know whether it bothered you or not. I produced a document that was signed by Mr. Norton, presumably in the presence of the judge, which gave facts concerning the same transaction about which there has been testimony here in court, that Mr. Norton immediately denied the accuracy of.

Here was a sworn document saying, for example, that at 10:10 p. m. on January 25, certain things happened. And what did Mr. Norton say when I confronted him on the witness stand with a document he signed before a judge and swore to? His first reaction, or a reaction—perhaps it was his first, to be fair—his reaction was that this was an error, because it was inconsistent with what he was testifying to. That document should be available to you.

Let's look beyond the question of "corroboration" and "reasonable doubt". Let's look then a little bit at some of the things that Mr. Norton said, removing the fact just for a moment that he's a police officer, that may make you want to consider whether or not they were true.

He said he took four trips to the defendant's house. Four. Now, this is a police officer whose duty and job it is to suppress narcotics in Hamster or whatever he said his job was—words to that effect. And he said that he went over to the defendant's house and there was some conversation about a quantity of marihuana, however you remember the testimony. And the defendant had no marihuana, or didn't have a quantity of marihuana, or whatever the testimony was to that effect. And he left and he did a very unusual thing. Perhaps it will occur to you. He went and he got a container. Then he came back a second time and still there was no marihuana. And on the third occasion he saw the defendant getting out of a car. And now, if you believe his testimony just as it stood from this witness stand— now he has his marihuana. Now this police officer has his evidence which could be the basis of his making an arrest and legitimately bringing this defendant into court to prosecute him for a sale or for whatever crime he was going to be prosecuted for.

And now this police officer does the most unusual thing and incredible thing—a most unusual and incredible thing. He turns around and comes back. Why? Why would a police officer, seeking evidence to convict this defendant, turn around and come back for the fourth time?

Now, Ladies and Gentlemen of the Jury, I don't know, but I can suggest one reason why he turned around and came back. You see, during this entire transaction, this officer had one little disadvantage. He had a witness. The witness that hasn't been produced here. At no point has there been any testimony that Mr. Stible had seen any transaction involving the defendant, Nelson Whale, and this police officer.

He gave him that transaction, didn't he? He gave him that transaction, and the guys are saying, even if you believe the police officer, that he was inspecting the marihuana to see whether or not it was a full measure.

But for whatever reason you decide he came back for the fourth time, is it credible to you that he came back to complain, he being a police officer whose job it was to buy as much marihuana as possible—to complain because he didn't have a full can? There was no arrest made at that time. That should bother you.

Now, this police officer has made a sale, hasn't he? He has gotten this defendant, if you believe him, to sell him some marihuana, and he has passed some money. Why doesn't he arrest him at that time? You say because he wanted to get a search warrant issued. If when he went over to the judge's house that same evening—he had gone over to the judge's house to give the judge some information about his crimes that night—or if he had gotten a search warrant that he had executed in a reasonable time, not two or three days later, perhaps that would be a reasonable conclusion.

But that isn't what he did. He told you and me, as I recall it and I hope you recall it the same way, that their request for a search warrant was made at a different time, and that the search was executed two or three days later.

I know that it's extremely difficult for you, as jurors, as it is for any citizen, to believe that any police officer would come here and intentionally tell you an untruth, and I know that despite the fact that Judge Burdick will instruct you that you should not give more credibility to the testimony of a police officer because he is a police officer than a private citizen, still it's going to bother you. It bothered me, too.

So, all during the trial we looked at the police officer's testimony for any inconsistencies in his testimony that may give you some cause to doubt him.

You know, the interest of the defendant in this case is obvious. He doesn't want to get convicted, does he? The police officers have an interest in the work that they do too, and that interest is not always the glowing law and enforcement symbolism that maybe sometimes you are led to believe. Perhaps you, in your own experience with law enforcement officers, have had situations where police officers tell stories different from your own.

Then, again, the fact that this is a police officer telling a story is not the most important factor, and I ask you to weigh something else in terms of this officer's credibility in your deliberations, and that is the problem of whether or not he supplied Earl Stible, the missing witness again, Earl Stible with marihuana cigarettes.

If I recall, I must have asked that officer twenty-five times yesterday about supplying Earl Stible with marihuana, and every time he told me, "No". Now, today I asked him again, and he told you, "No". And in the face of reading a statement to him taken by this reporter and in this courtroom on April 6, the answer was still negative. Oh, the answer was that he didn't remember, and it was necessary for me to do a highly unusual thing, and that was to swear this reporter as a witness.

Now, what's the importance of that? The crime charged here isn't whether or not this officer supplied Earl Stible with marihuana cigarettes. The importance is two things. First of all, you may recall in my opening statement that I indicated to you that in his zealousness to get this conviction, this officer even went so far as to supply a private citizen—words to that effect—with some marihuana. And the first time we touched upon it, this officer denied it categorically.

Now, he has had to, during the course of this trial, make other statements that you're going to have to believe or not believe, and I say to you that it is very fair for you to consider if he told an untruth about supplying marihuana to Earl Stible, that he may not be telling you the truth about his transaction with the defendant.

You see, Ladies and Gentlemen of the Jury, at some place you will have to decide the question of "reasonable doubt" in terms of the credibility of this officer. And I say to you that an important test of that credibility is what he said about the transaction of supplying some marihuana to Earl Stible. I say that it should be difficult for you to determine that he was lying, mistaken about that, but that he was telling the truth about everything else.

Now, what happened at that point? Mr. Bryers put him back on the witness stand and sought and did elicit some more testimony as to what he meant when he said that he had supplied some marihuana to Earl Stible. And he sought, if I can recall the testimony, to attribute the reason—the most important thing, to excuse his lack of memory or his misstatement by whatever you remember he said—giving it to a second party or not supplying it. But the exhibit, the transcript of the testimony at the prior hearing is in evidence, and you, under the rules are permitted to take it into the jury room and read it for yourself—read it against the twenty-five times a day I asked him the day before about the same thing, and it seems to me at that point you have to worry about the officer's credibility.

Ladies and Gentlemen, beyond the consideration of whether or not the People have proved its case beyond a reasonable doubt, you have to also, I think, concern yourself with the question of the defendant's testimony since he took the witness stand.

And what's the most important thing that you heard about the defendant. You heard this about the defendant—that he was convicted in 1964 or 1965. I guess you remember the testimony of possession of marihuana. And I have also asked the judge to instruct you that you are not to take an inference from that conviction that it's more likely so than not that he committed this crime.

That's a difficult thing for you to do, too, and I tell you it's very difficult for a defense attorney to decide to put his client on the witness stand because that's the only way you're going to hear about it, by my putting him on the witness stand. But I felt that after two days, or a day and a half, you were entitled to hear from the defendant's own lips what happened that day of January 25.

Ladies and Gentlemen of the Jury, this is an important crime to the People of this State. The case is of great importance. It is an important case, also, to this defendant. That which leaves in your own mind an abiding conviction to a certainty of the truth of the testimony that you have heard from this witness stand is a standard of reasonable doubt that this judge is going to charge you on.

Again, I remind you that the defendant, especially one who has been in jail since this offense is charged, is not obligated to prove himself innocent. And if you evaluate the testimony, not only of what you hear but what you couldn't hear because of what the police brought or didn't bring here, I only ask you to be fair and ask yourselves whether or not you are satisfied beyond a reasonable doubt that the defendant is guilty of the crime charged in the information.

Thank you.

THE COURT: You may conclude your argument, Mr. Bryers.

CLOSING ARGUMENT OF MR. BRYERS:

MR. BRYERS: Ladies and Gentlemen, I have just a few remarks to make in rebuttal to counsel for the defendant's argument.

Now, as to proving this case beyond a reasonable doubt, we have the testimony of Nelson Whale in contradiction thereof. And I want to point out to you that when Nelson Whale took the stand, if you recall, as to testing his credibility, believing what he said, he said that he saw this Prince Albert can of tobacco at the preliminary examination. I questioned him a little further on that, and he finally admitted that probably he didn't see it there and that he didn't see it until today. It was brought out that this was in a locked, sealed envelope; it was not even opened.

Now, as far as Earl Stible is concerned, you have heard sufficient testimony by Officer Barrott, the officer in charge of this case, as to what he has done to bring Earl Stible before this Court. And he testified that he served him with a subpoena last week to appear in court on the 22nd day of May, 1967, which was Monday, and that was the day this case was scheduled to be heard.

When the case was adjourned through the fault of nobody, Richard Barrott testified that he made efforts again by going to the home of Earl Stible last night, that he was not there, it was getting late now. In fact, he said he made several trips to the home last night in an effort to get hold of Earl Stible, and on the last trip, thinking there would be no chance of finding him, he left a subpoena with a 16-year old relative of Earl Stible, with instructions that he be here in court today. I don't think there is any more effort he could have shown in order to bring Mr. Stible here before the Court.

Now, as far as the search warrant having a time, 10 o'clock or 10:10, instead of 8:10, a search warrant contains a lot of writing on it. There is a lot of writing, reading, to look over, and these things are usually done in a rush in order to get this thing signed and go out and make a search. It's quite possible that Darrell Norton may have overlooked the actual time on there. He testified that that was a mistake; it should have been 8:10 instead of 10:10. I think this is fly-specking.

Now, it was brought up: Why would an officer who has made a buy, as Darrell Norton testified to, examine this can and then come back on a pretense of being shorted? Why would he do that? Well, the control and the suppression of narcotics is a big operation, and perhaps he was trying to keep the confidence of the defendant so that later they could trace the source of this marihuana. The big source—where does it come from? We don't know exactly what their plan is. We must keep that in mind.

Now, as far as Officer Norton not being supervised by the officer in charge, Richard Barrott, remember that Officer Norton testified that he had been a police officer for two and a half years prior to becoming a member of the Hamster police force, and I would think that two and a half years' experience would indicate that he doesn't have to be closely supervised every move that he makes.

Now, Ladies and Gentlemen, that is the end of my remarks, and I feel that the People have proved this case of a sale of marihuana by the defendant, Nelson Whale, beyond a reasonable doubt, and ask you to bring back a verdict of guilty.

Thank you.[45]

At 10:10 a. m.

(The trial before the jury was continued in the courtroom.)

THE COURT: Good morning, everybody.

Ladies and Gentlemen of the Jury, may I thank you first, and I am sure I am speaking for all of the litigants and counsel for the litigants, for the

---

45. Consider the amount of time devoted to the closing arguments. What the attorneys say may not be "evidence", but it can greatly influence the jury's thinking. In most jurisdictions the prosecution has the right to speak both first and last at the close of the trial. However, a few jurisdictions restrict the prosecutor to one closing argument and do not allow the prosecutor to speak after defense counsel argues. The psychological literature on persuasion suggests that the ability to speak both first and last on an issue should be a substantial advantage, but there is no good empirical evidence which indicates the degree to which this is in fact the case. The justification for giving the prosecution this advantage is that the prosecution begins at a substantial disadvantage because of the need to prove the state's case beyond a reasonable doubt. Yet, the plaintiff in a civil case usually has a similar advantage though the plaintiff may prevail upon a mere preponderance of the evidence. As defense counsel what techniques might you employ to minimize the advantage of the prosecutor?

There are some rare situations in which the usual order of argument may be reversed. The nominal defendant whose counterclaim is the only triable issue, for example, may be able to present his case-in-chief first and have the privilege of arguing last to the jury at the conclusion of the trial. See, e.g., Carmody v. Kolocheski, 181 Wis. 394, 396, 194 N.W. 584, 585 (1923).

In some jurisdictions the attorneys make their closing arguments after the jury has been instructed on the law. The advantage to this procedure is that the jury is familiar with the law as well as the facts before hearing finally from the lawyers. It has the disadvantage of further separating the arguments from the evidence. Even in the more typical case where the instructions follow the arguments, it is important for the lawyers to know how the judge will instruct the jury on the law because the lawyers will want to cast their arguments in terms of the applicable law. For this reason judges commonly review proposed instructions with lawyers before the closing arguments in a case.

courtesy, kindness and patience you have exhibited and for the work that you and they have done.

In the trial of every case, there are important responsibilities to be discharged by counsel for the respective parties; by you as jurors, the exclusive triers of the facts in the case; and by the trial judge, as well, when it comes to the law.

It has been a real pleasure working with you, and while you have only one more day after today, it doesn't appear that I am going to have the pleasure of having you in my courtroom again, but I know that this is going to rate in your minds as one of the most pleasant experiences you have had in your lifetime. Do come back to see us.

It is the right, if not the responsibility, of counsel for all the parties to make motions from time to time and to make objections to the reception of certain evidence. You should not draw any inferences against any attorney because he does so, and even less so should you draw any unfavorable inferences against the client whom he represents. This, again, is part of the responsibility of counsel in this case, for alert and vigorous advocacy is very much a part of the administration of justice. Similarly, it is the right, if not the responsibility, of counsel for both parties to make comments upon the evidence at the close of the case, that is, to make the argument which they concluded Wednesday.

But you are the exclusive triers of the facts in the case, and you, and you alone, are to determine what the facts of the case are, and you should make such determination only from the evidence which was duly received here in open court, under oath, or from the exhibits duly entered.

I do tell you that it is the law of this State that every finding of fact must rest upon evidence. You cannot conjecture, you cannot speculate. You may draw reasonable inferences from those facts you find to be established, including physical facts.[46]

Counsel, in their arguments, saw fit to comment upon the law in this case. This, again, is their right and responsibility. It would be almost impossible for counsel to argue their case in closing argument without referring to and commenting upon some law, and that they have done to some extent in this case.

However, under the delicate separation of the duties and functions in our systems, you must accept—whether the Court likes it or not or whether you like it or not, this is the law and we must accept it, not as counsel gives it to you, but as the Court does. It is my sworn duty to accept it as such and it is your sworn duty to accept it, as well.[47]

At this juncture let me read what the defendant is charged with, and I am reading from the Criminal Information:

46. Can any jury decide any case without engaging in conjecture and speculation? What does the judge mean?

47. At this point why is the judge making such a statement? Has either lawyer exceeded the bounds of proper argument? Is the case the kind of case where the judge wishes he didn't have the assignment of instructing the jury? Who is most likely to be damaged by the comment?

In the Name of the People of the State of _____ , William L. Carlyle, Prosecuting Attorney in and for said County of Boone, who prosecutes for and on behalf of the People of said State in said Court, comes now here in said Court in the March term thereof, A.D. 1967, and gives the said Court to understand and be informed that Nelson Whale, late of the City of Hamster in said County, heretofore, to wit, on the 25th day of January, A.D. 1967, at the said City of Hamster in said County, did then and there unlawfully and feloniously sell a certain narcotic drug, to wit, 23.53 grains of marihuana, without first obtaining a license so to do, under the provisions of Act 343, P.A. 1937, as amended, being Sections 335.51 to 335.78, inclusive, of the Compiled Laws of 1958; contrary to the form of the Statute in such case made and provided, and against the peace and dignity of the People of the State of _____ .

Let me read to you at this time, also, the matter of the statute, and I will read such sections that are material to this rather than read the whole statute, and that is Volume 13, State Statutes Annotated 18.1121, Section 1:

Definitions: The following words and phrases, as used in this act, shall have the following meanings, unless the context otherwise requires:

"Person" includes any corporation, association, partnership, or 1 or more individuals.

"Narcotic" includes the following: Cocaine, opium, morphine, codeine, heroin, all parts of the plant Cannabis Sativa. The term "Cannabis" as used in this act shall include all parts of the plant Cannabis Sativa L., whether growing or not, the seeds thereof * * * etc.

And then we proceed to subsection (i):

Any substance or synthetic narcotic drug which the bureau of narcotics of the United States Treasury Department has heretofore designated as "narcotic".

We have had testimony here by the Federal chemist that marihuana is designated by the Bureau of Narcotics of the United States Treasury Department as a narcotic. This you will remember.[48]

I charge you that the issuance of an information as I have read to you in this case against the defendant, Nelson Whale, is only a formal method of accusing him of having committed the offense charged therein.

You must determine the true facts in this cause without any bias, without any sympathy, without any prejudice, without any regard to race, color, creed or financial standing of the parties.

The essential elements of this crime, and the People must prove this beyond a reasonable doubt, are that the sale took place on or about January 25, 1967—I believe that is the date, is it not?—that the defendant Whale made the sale to Officer Norton; that the sale was made in Hamster, Boone County, of this state; that the item sold was marihuana as charged in the information; and that the defendant had no license to sell narcotics, either

48. Is this an instruction or a command? In either case, is it proper?

Should anything be added to ensure that the jury is certain of its role in the case?

state or federal.   And that is in evidence here by virtue of both counsel indicating that a couple of witnesses who, if they were present, would testify that the defendant did not have such a license.   So that is admitted.

You are the sole judges of the weight of the evidence and the credibility of the witnesses, which means the believability of the witnesses.   You have a right to, and you should, take into consideration the manner in which the various witnesses gave their testimony; the apparent frankness, or want of frankness, with which questions put to them were answered; the knowledge they had about the matter on which they were testifying to, or the lack of knowledge, as the case may be; or the interest of the witness in the outcome of the case, or the lack of interest, as the case may be.

I charge you that it is the law of this State that if you are satisfied that any witness knowingly or willfully testified to that which is false on a material matter, it is within your province to disregard the whole of the testimony of that witness.   It is within your province to give no credit to the testimony of that witness whatsoever, but I might warn you that minor discrepancies do appear in the testimony of many witnesses in many cases for many reasons.   These minor discrepancies often are not based upon a willful intent to misrepresent the facts of the case, so you should not disprove or discount the testimony wholly of any witness because of minor discrepancies. But if you do find there are serious breaches of the truth, and if you find that there has been a failure to testify truthfully, it is within your province to disregard the whole of the testimony of that witness unless it be corroborated by the competent testimony of another witness whom you do believe.

Under the Constitution of this State, a defendant is under no obligation to take the stand and testify.   However, he has the right to take the stand and testify, if he so desires.   In this case the defendant did take the stand and gave you his testimony.   In weighing his testimony, it is your duty to give him and his testimony the same treatment that you give the testimony of any other witness or witnesses in this case, applying the same rules and tests as I have just instructed you to apply to the testimony of all witnesses in this case.

I further charge you that you should give no greater credibility to the testimony of police officers merely because they are police officers than you do to the testimony of any other witnesses in this case, applying the same standards of credibility as I have instructed you concerning the testimony of all witnesses.   Thus, you should consider the testimony of each witness independently of his occupation, and drawing upon your own common sense, give it such weight as you consider proper under the tests and instructions as to credibility as I have given them to you just a short few seconds ago.

The defendant testified that upon two previous occasions he had been convicted or pleaded guilty, once to the crime of possession of marihuana and the other to unarmed robbery.

I charge you that no person shall be disqualified as a witness in any civil or criminal case or proceeding by reason of his interest in the event of the same as a party or otherwise or by reason of his having been convicted of any crime; but such interest or conviction may be shown for the purpose of affecting his credibility. However, the defendant is here upon trial for the offense only that is charged in the information in this case, and is not to be prejudiced in this, or convicted in this case by reason of the commission of any other offenses by him.[49]

Under our system of administration of justice, there are no unimportant cases. Every case in this or any other court of this land is an important case. This is an important case to the litigants here and to every one of them. It is an important case to counsel for the respective parties.

It is your solemn duty and responsibility and privilege to consider the evidence in this case, to apply the facts as you find them to the charge of the Court as to the law, and bring in your verdict without fear or favor to any person. When you have done that, you have done your full duty. When you have done less than that, you have not done your full duty. Of course, counsel for the prosecution and counsel for the defendant and the Court expect you to do only your full duty—no more and no less.

In considering this case, you must remember that what lawyers say in their arguments is not evidence. Evidence comes from the testimony of witnesses under oath from the stand, and the exhibits and the facts that have been agreed upon. If the lawyer's argument is not supported by evidence or is contrary to the evidence, you must disregard it.

It is your responsibility to consider all of the evidence in the case and from the conflicting evidence to decide what the true facts are regarding matters in dispute. It is my responsibility to tell you what the law is and you must accept my instructions as binding upon you. When you commence to deliberate, you are not to consider whether or not the law conforms to your own concept of what it should be, or mine for that matter. Your task is to find out the true facts and apply the law as I am giving it to you.

I charge you that the prosecution has a duty to call to the stand for testimony each and every person known to have been a witness at the time of the crime alleged in the information. The law does not allow the police and the Prosecutor to select only the testimony favorable to their side of the story. They must produce witnesses to the crime, whether they are going to testify in favor of the prosecution or against the prosecution.

Now, this rule is not without exception. Thus, in the event the Prosecutor fails to call all witnesses, he can only be excused upon a showing of a reasonable and diligent effort to present such witnesses that fail to attend through no fault of his own. In other words, the effort must be genuine on the part of the prosecution to produce these witnesses, and in this case there has been testimony concerning the effort made by the Police Department to obtain witness Earl Stible who is a res gestae witness to the crime.

Thus, if you are satisfied that the Prosecutor and police have made a reasonable, diligent and genuine effort to locate and produce Earl Stible for testimony in this cause, but have unavoidably failed, you will attach no significance whatsoever to their failure to produce him.

49. Would the defendant be better or worse off if this instruction were not given? Was the instruction requested by the defendant preferable to this one?

On the other hand, if you find that the prosecution and police have failed, by design or negligence, to take reasonable measures to obtain the witness, Earl Stible, then the defendant is entitled to the presumption that this witness, had he been here, would have testified favorably to the defendant.

As I have told you previously, before you were selected, or while you were being selected, in this particular case, this being a criminal case, under our law every defendant in a criminal case is presumed to be innocent until his guilt is established by competent testimony beyond a reasonable doubt. This presumption of innocence starts at the very inception of the case and it continues until such time as the People, the prosecution, has satisfied you and each of you that the defendant is guilty of the offense beyond a reasonable doubt.

A reasonable doubt is a doubt based upon reason and common sense. It is a fair doubt and not a vague, captious or imaginary doubt, but a doubt growing out of the evidence, or lack of evidence, or the unsatisfactory nature of the evidence in the case. Proof beyond a reasonable doubt is not proof beyond all imaginary doubt but such proof as satisfies the judgment and conscience of the jury as reasonable men and women applying their reason to the evidence before them that the crime charged was committed by the defendant, so satisfies them as to leave no other conclusion possible.[50]

If from all the evidence in the case you have a reasonable doubt because of the lack of proof of any of the essential elements of this crime, it will be your duty to give to the defendant the benefit of that doubt and to acquit him. On the other hand, if you have no such reasonable doubt about the guilt of the accused, it is equally your duty, under your oath, to convict him.

I further charge you that in all criminal cases the burden of proof is upon the State—the Prosecuting Attorney—to prove the defendant's guilt beyond a reasonable doubt. This burden never shifts. At no time is it incumbent upon the defendant to prove his innocence. At the very outset of this trial, the burden is upon the State to establish in the minds of you jurors that the defendant is guilty of the offense charged in the information beyond a reasonable doubt.

I further charge you that the evidence comes from the testimony of the witnesses that you have heard here on the stand, and you are to consider only that which was admitted in evidence. Anything that was excluded or stricken out after it was received, you will not consider.

Ladies and Gentlemen of the Jury, you must bring in one of the following verdicts: (1) Guilty as charged, or (2) Not guilty. I charge you that this being a criminal case, your verdict must be a unanimous one. It is different from a civil case wherein a verdict of ten of the twelve jurors is sufficient. Here, in a criminal case, all twelve of you must agree upon the verdict.

Ladies and Gentlemen of the Jury, it is the practice of this Court, and under the rules of law here, that you may have in your deliberations the use of the several exhibits that were duly received in evidence in this case upon

50. Do you think the jury understands this explanation of the burden of proof? Do you understand it?

special request.　We do not volunteer these to you, but if, after you have picked your foreman in the secrecy of your jury room, you feel the need of any one or more of these exhibits, they may be received by you upon special request.　What you do is rap on the door and hand a slip of paper to the bailiff.　He will bring it to the Court, and the Court, in the presence of counsel, will read it and then send the exhibits over to you.

I am now going to declare a short recess—just sit where you are—and I will ask the Prosecutor and defense counsel and my court reporter to join me in chambers.[51]

––––––––

(The following discussion was held in chambers between the Court, the Prosecutor and defense counsel.)

THE COURT:　Let the record indicate that I have just charged the jury, and the Assistant Prosecutor, defense counsel, the court reporter, and myself are in chambers outside the earshot of the jury.

Gentlemen, do you have any remarks to make concerning the charge that I have just made to the jury?

MR. BRYERS:　The prosecution is satisfied with the charge.

THE COURT:　Defense?

MR. EVERT:　The defense is satisfied.

THE COURT:　Thank you very much.

(Whereupon the proceedings in chambers were concluded, and the Court, counsel and the court reporter returned to the courtroom.)

––––––––

(Whereupon at 10:35 a. m. the jury, accompanied by the bailiff, proceeded to the jury room to commence their deliberations.)

THE COURT:　Counsel, do you intend to remain here?　Mr. Bryers, you are in the building, is this right?

MR. BRYERS:　Yes, your Honor.

THE COURT:　What about you, Mr. Evert?

MR. EVERT:　I will be circulating.

THE COURT:　In the event you should leave, will you please give your telephone number to the clerk so that he may call you and give you 15 or 20 minutes in which to get here to obtain the verdict?

At 12:30 p. m.

(At this time the jury reassembled in the courtroom.)

51.　How did the judge develop this charge to the jury?　What role did counsel play?　Why did the judge decide to phrase the various sections of the charge as he did?　Is this the first time this phraseology has been used by this judge? In this state?

THE COURT: You may be seated.

I assume you have not yet arrived at a verdict.

At this time it is around the lunch hour, so we will excuse you for lunch.

You haven't arrived at a verdict, have you?

(Response in the negative.)

You are not to discuss this matter, incidentally, while you are at lunch, with anybody else or among yourselves. You don't resume your deliberations until you get back to your jury room. You are excused for lunch until 2 o'clock, and you are to report right back to your jury room.

Rise, please.

(Whereupon the proceedings were adjourned until 2 o'clock.)

———

At 2:35 p. m.

(The jury returned to the courtroom, and the proceedings were continued.)

THE COURT: The defendant is here, counsel for both sides are here, and the jury has returned to the courtroom.

Ladies and Gentlemen of the Jury, have you arrived at a verdict, and, if so, who shall speak for you?

THE FOREMAN: I shall.

THE COURT: Mr. Foreman, what is your verdict?

THE FOREMAN: Guilty as charged.

THE COURT: Guilty as charged.

(Whereupon the jury was sworn by the clerk as to their verdict.)

THE COURT: You may be seated. Poll the jury.

(Whereupon the clerk polled the jury, and each juror responded in the affirmative as to their verdict.

THE COURT: A unanimous verdict.

(To clerk) Call the Probation Department, please.

THE COURT: A representative from the Probation Department is here now.

What date do you want to set for sentencing?

PROBATION OFFICER: Is he in custody?

THE COURT: Yes, he is in custody.

PROBATION OFFICER: Three weeks from today, 6–19.

THE COURT: Is that all right with you, counsel?

MR. EVERT: Yes, your Honor, it is.

THE COURT: Is there any bond set for him?

MR. EVERT: Under $5,000 bond.

THE COURT: I think I will have to just remand him to custody until the date of his sentence now that he has been found guilty.

MR. EVERT: Thank you, your Honor.[52]

(Whereupon at 2:45 p. m. the trial was concluded.)

SECTION II. PROBLEMS

Problem I–1. Hamilton Jones placed title to all of his real property in the name of his son Tom. Jones placed the title in Tom's name for the purpose of holding title for Tom's brothers and sisters. After the death of Hamilton Jones, Tom conveyed the title to the property to himself in fee simple. Tom died leaving all his property to Joyce and naming her sole executor of his estate. Joyce refused to convey the property to Tom's brothers and sisters, whereupon they sued her as executor asking the court to impose a constructive trust on the property held by the estate. At trial, plaintiffs wished to testify to conversations between Tom and themselves in which Tom allegedly acknowledged that he held title as their trustee. Joyce objected to the admission of this testimony, contending that none of the plaintiffs was competent to testify. **What is the basis of Joyce's argument? Should she prevail?**

52. The defendant was, of course, convicted and an appeal taken. This should be no surprise because the availability of the transcript tells us as much. In this case the state supreme court overturned Whale's conviction. The court, after ruling that the refusal to give the entrapment instruction was proper, decided that the question about the length of Whale's sentence flagged in Note 40, supra, was improper and justified reversal. Given the court's definitive ruling that the question on sentence length was improper, do you agree that it was so serious an impropriety as to justify reversing the judgment? Would it influence your judgment if you knew that questions about length of sentence are considered a proper part of the process of impeaching by past convictions in some jurisdictions? See Annot. 67 A.L.R.3d 775 (1975). Do you think the justices on the state supreme court were influenced by other factors in deciding this case? Do you think counsel on appeal would have been as successful had he only raised the impeachment issue and not tried to develop the argument that entrapment had occurred?

As a student of evidence you should try to familiarize yourself with trials, both civil and criminal. If you are not involved in legal aid work or a clinical law program, you should try to find some time to go down to the local courthouse and sit in on several trials. Or if you haven't the time to audit trials, borrow trial transcripts from your lawyer friends. They generally make interesting reading. For transcripts of ten trials, all involving criminal cases, see Norris, A Casebook of Complete Criminal Trials (1965). You also should be aware that your local law library may well have the transcripts of some of the most famous trials of the century in their collection. They make particularly interesting reading, but many unfortunately run to thousands of pages. Such "great trials" are, of course, not typical of the everyday litigation which passes through our criminal and civil courts.

Problem I–2. Defendant is indicted for knowingly damaging the dwelling house of X by fire. The house is in New York City. At trial, defendant's son wishes to testify as follows: "About an hour before X's house began to burn, I called my father long distance at a number he had given me in Cleveland, Ohio. My Uncle Sid answered and told me that my father was with him but could not come to the phone because he had just left to walk the dog." The prosecution objects, saying, "This witness lacks personal knowledge of that about which he testifies." **Assuming the son knows his uncle well and recognized his voice, is this a valid objection?** Assume that the son had never before talked with his uncle but when he called the number a man answered, saying, "Son, this is Uncle Sid. We've never met but it's nice to talk with you and have your father here." **Would the objection to the testimony described in the first part of this problem be availing?**

Problem I–3. Defendant was driving his car when it crashed into and broke the show window of plaintiff's jewelry store. The accident imperiled plaintiff's life, as he was pinned beneath defendant's car. Plaintiff sued defendant in tort. Plaintiff contended that the accident was caused by defendant's driving at an excessive rate of speed. At the trial plaintiff called witness A, a merchant who owns a bakery three doors down from plaintiff's store. The merchant testifies, "I first saw defendant's car whiz by the bakery window. It was then going 75 miles per hour." Defendant objects to his testimony. **What is the basis of the objection? What is the proper result?** Defendant calls witness B who was standing on the street corner, and B testifies that defendant's car was going 35 m.p.h. Plaintiff objects. **On what grounds? What is the result?**

Problem I–4. Martha Chamallas brought an action to recover damages for personal injuries allegedly caused by the negligence of Acme's employee, Shane. Chamallas claims that Shane, while driving one of Acme's trucks, plowed into her car as she was stopped for a red light. In order to establish *respondeat superior* liability, Chamallas calls Shane as her first witness. She asks him only whether at the time of the collision he was in the employ of the Acme and engaged in Acme's business, and to identify an accident report he had filled out. On cross-examination, Acme seeks to elicit Shane's description of the collision and of the events preceding and following it. **On what ground might objection be made? What should the ruling be? If the cross-examination is allowed, should the defense counsel be allowed to use leading questions?**

Problem I–5. Plaintiff was driving his car when he was struck by a truck owned by defendant and operated by a third party. In his suit against the defendant, plaintiff's attorney moves to call both the third-party and the defendant as hostile witnesses. **Is this permissible? If a direct action could be brought against the insurance company that insures both the defendant and the third-party, should both of them be treated as hostile witnesses?**

Problem I–6. Plaintiff brings a negligence action against defendant after an automobile accident. Plaintiff was riding in the car of X at the time of the accident. Two of the issues that go to trial are whether the defendant drove at a negligently high rate of speed, and if so, whether this proximately caused plaintiff's injuries. One of the witnesses called by plaintiff was X. On direct examination, X testified only to his own driving up to the moment of the accident. On cross-examination, defendant sought to obtain from X testimony to the effect that X had left the scene of the accident (while plaintiff was unconscious in a drug store to which she had been carried) without notifying anyone of his, X's, identity. **Should this line of inquiry be permitted? What is the objection?**

Problem I–7. Defendant was responsible for a metal filler lid in the sidewalk in front of his store on which pedestrians were accustomed and expected to walk. Plaintiff Jones sued for injuries he sustained in a fall which he said was caused by the fact that the lid in question was old and rusted and that it slipped as he put his weight on it. Defendant contended that Jones fell because he was so intoxicated that he could not maintain his balance. At trial, defendant offers a witness named Smith to testify that he was following Jones about twenty feet to the rear prior to the accident; that in his opinion, from what he observed, Jones was grossly intoxicated; that he saw him fall and that it was his impression that he fell because he was so intoxicated that he could not maintain his equilibrium. Jones objects to his entire testimony. **Should the court allow any of it to be admitted?** Assume that Smith had not seen Jones fall but had heard a noise and rushed up while Jones was on the ground. **If Smith smelled alcohol on Jones' breath, could he so testify? Could Smith testify that Jones was intoxicated? Why or why not?**

Problem I–8. Dibbs endorses in blank his weekly payroll check in the amount of $250 and decides to take the check to the bank at which he maintains a checking account in order to deposit $50. Dibbs presents the check with these instructions to Hill, an experienced teller, who misreads the check. She believes that the date (9-11-74) represents the amount payable and after deducting the $50 deposit pays over the counter the sum of $861.74. Dibbs realizes the teller has made a mistake but takes the money and departs. Subsequently, Dibbs is charged with grand larceny. During the jury trial, Hill is shown a microfilm of the check through an illuminated viewer. Although she admits that she has seen Dibbs sign his name on only one previous occasion, she is, over objection, allowed to identify the endorsement of the payee, Dibbs, as his genuine signature. **Is this a correct ruling? Would the situation be different if the check had been cashed at a grocery store and Hill was a clerk there on her first day on the job? Would you be more or less likely to accept this evidence if the case were a civil action to recover damages, or is the nature of the suit unimportant? As a general proposition, should rules of evidence differ in civil and criminal cases?**

Problem I–9. The guest in an automobile brings an action against the owner and driver. The guest calls as a witness a third party who had been sitting on her front porch about 75 yards from where the defendant's automobile left the road. Although she could not see the car, the witness heard tires squealing and heard the automobile strike some trees on the side of the road immediately before it plunged into a ravine.   Plaintiff asks the witness to give her estimate of the speed of the automobile based upon the sound which she heard.   **An objection is made.   What result?**

Problem I–10.   Smith is tried on an indictment charging him with bribery.   The evidence of the state tends to show that Smith is engaged in the operation of what is generally known as a "numbers racket" and that he paid protection money to 20–30 officers of the local police force to avoid the arrest of his men.   The state seeks to introduce the testimony of a former police officer who will testify that he obtained from some person, whose name he does not remember, a telephone number which he was told was that of the defendant Smith;   that he is unable to remember the telephone number he called;   that he called the number and asked to speak with Smith;   that the person answering the call said he was Smith;   that he (the officer) then inquired as to whether he was entitled to a pay-off;   that the person on the phone said, "yes";   and that in reply to the question from the officer as to why he was so entitled, the party said, "You are supposed to know why, and you will get $10 per month from the pay-off man at headquarters."   The officer never was introduced to the defendant at any time either before or after the phone call.   **Should the trial judge admit the officer's testimony?**

Problem I–11.   In a will contest, one side calls a psychiatrist, the superintendent of a mental institution who examined the testator shortly before his death and near the time when the will was executed.   The psychiatrist testifies that in her opinion the deceased was not sane when he made the will.   The other side in rebuttal calls a nephew aged 23, who testifies that he lived with the deceased for a year prior to his death.   He is then asked, "From your observation of him, in your opinion was the decedent of sound mind at the time of execution?"   The contestant objects.   **How should the court rule?   Assuming the jury believes the nephew, not the doctor, should the court permit a jury verdict based on this belief to stand?**   Suppose there is testimony that the deceased engaged in erratic behavior before his death.   **Can the psychiatrist testify that this behavior together with the information she gained from her examination is symptomatic of acute delusions** (in which case the will would be invalid)?   **Could the nephew testify that this behavior together with what he knows from living with the deceased is at most symptomatic of chronic manic-depression** (in which case the will would be valid)?

Problem I–12.   Clyde Frader sent his fur winter coat to the Knickerbocker Cleaners.   When Clyde arrived to pick up the coat, the proprietor of the cleaners discovered that the coat was missing.   Further investigation failed to produce the coat, and the proprietor concluded that the coat had either been lost or stolen.   She informed her insurance carrier of the missing coat.   The company contacted Clyde and offered $1,000 for the coat.   Clyde refused to accept what in his view was a paltry sum and filed suit against the cleaners for $10,000, claiming that the fur coat was in excellent condition, that similar coats sell for anywhere between $8,000 and $10,000 and that his coat had special significance to him since when he had worn it his luck was exceptional.   At trial Clyde is called to testify by his own counsel.

DIRECT EXAMINATION

Q. When did you take your coat to the cleaners?

A. I am not certain, but I guess it must have been Wednesday or Thursday, January 2 or 3, 1980.

[The defendant objects, citing FRE 602. **What is the proper ruling?**]

Q. What condition was your coat in when you took it to the cleaners?

A. Excellent condition. I mean superb, first-rate, almost mint, perfect condition. Naturally, it was a little dirty so I was taking it to the cleaners. But, other than that, no one, I mean no one, could have been able to tell that the coat was not just off the rack—the high priced rack!

[The defendant objects to all of the answer, citing FRE 701 and also FRE 602. **What is the proper ruling?**]

Q. What did the cleaners look like when you arrived?

A. Well, the place was disheveled, if you know what I mean. There were a lot of clothes laying about, and I was a little bit concerned about the care with which they handled clothes. But then the proprietor said how much she admired my coat, and I figured she would take good care of it.

[The defendant objects. **What is the most likely ground for an objection? What is the proper ruling?**]

Q. How did you come to have such a coat?

A. I bought it a year ago for $6,000.

Q. From whom did you buy it?

A. From Harry Callahan. When I bought it Harry told me it was a steal for $6,000. Harry died shortly thereafter.

[The defense objects, citing FRE 601, 701, and 702. **What is the proper ruling?**]

Q. Do you know what it is worth when you took it to the cleaners?

A. I would say $10,000.

Q. What is the basis for your valuation?

A. I like furs. I look at them in stores all the time. I know what they cost. Also, I have been studying the financial news for several years. I know all about inflation and its effect on the value of money.

[The defendant objects, citing FRE 701, 704. **What is the proper ruling?**]

Q. Does this coat have any special meaning for you?

A. Oh, yes, this coat is not only my favorite coat; it also is my lucky coat. Many of my luckiest moments in the past year occurred while I was wearing the coat.

[The defendant objects, citing FRE 701. **What is the proper ruling?**]

CROSS-EXAMINATION

Q. You sell drugs. You poison little kids to earn money, don't you, you well-dressed drug peddler?
[The plaintiff objects, citing FRE 611. **What is the proper ruling?**]

Q. How many animals died to make that coat anyway?
[The plaintiff objects. **What is the proper ruling?**]

Q. I am going to show you five coats that I have marked as Defendant's exhibits A through E respectively. I want you to tell me how much each is worth?
[The plaintiff objects, citing FRE 611. **What is the proper ruling?**]

Problem I–13. This is a libel suit in which plaintiff, a State Senator, sues a local newspaper alleging that she was libeled by an article suggesting that she had accepted improper funds. Defendant contends that its story was true, that if it was false it was printed in the good faith belief that it was true, and that even if it was false, and recklessly so, plaintiff suffered no real harm. Plaintiff calls citizen X as a witness. The following is a transcript of the direct and cross-examination of the witness. **What objections should have been made?**

Q. You are Mr. X are you not? **A.** Yes, I am.

Q. Where do you live? **A.** 102 South Seventh Street.

Q. That's in the 14th Senatorial District, is it not? **A.** Yes it is.

Q. Maggie Smith was the State Senator there, was she not? **A.** Yes, until this last election.

Q. Are you familiar with Sen. Smith's reputation for honesty in the community? **A.** Yes I am.

Q. And you've been familiar with her reputation for some time? **A.** Yes I have. I've lived in the 14th district for twelve years.

Q. Will you please read this. [Counsel hands a xeroxed sheet of paper to the witness.] This is a copy of a story which appeared in the *Daily Planet* on October 12, 1974, headlined "Smith on Take". Have you read it now? **A.** Yes, I have.

Q. What do you think a story like that would do to a person's reputation? **A.** It would wreck it.

Q. Are you familiar with Smith's reputation in the community before October 12, 1974? **A.** Yes, I am.

Q. It was excellent, wasn't it? **A.** Absolutely first rate.

Q. And do you know what her reputation was after October 12, 1974? **A.** It deteriorated to terrible.

Q. Did this article affect your personal opinion of Sen. Smith? **A.** Yes.

Q. Please describe your opinion of Smith before and after the article. **A.** It was the same as everybody's. I thought she had a pure reputation before the article and a tarnished reputation thereafter.

Q. Do you know whether the 1974 election was a close one or not? **A.** Yes, it was very close.

Q. How many votes did Sen. Smith lose by? **A.** She lost by fifty votes.

Q. In your opinion would Senator Smith have won the election if not for the article? **A.** Absolutely.

Q. Did you vote for Sen. Smith at the last election? **A.** I don't remember.

Q. You don't remember? **A.** It's been so long now.

Q. Do you remember sitting in my office in December of 1974 and telling me how upset you were by the rumor that the story in the Planet was false? **A.** Yes, now that you mention it, I do.

Q. Do you remember why you were upset? **A.** I'm not certain, I guess it's because Smith was a good Senator.

Q. Don't you remember telling me that you felt hoodwinked because you voted against Smith? **A.** "Hoodwinked", that's right. I did use that word. I remember now, I felt hoodwinked because I had voted against Smith.

Q. And you voted against Senator Smith because of the article? **A.** Yes, that's right. I voted against Smith because of the article.

CROSS-EXAMINATION

[After some preliminary questions]

Q. You say you were upset that Smith lost because you thought she was a good senator; isn't that true? **A.** That and because I'm tired of seeing the Planet draw people's reputations in the mud; why, when they ran that smear on Schwartz his mother tried to kill herself.

Q. But there was another reason why Smith's loss upset you, isn't there? **A.** No.

Q. Had you stopped paying bribes to Smith before she lost? **A.** What, I never paid no bribes.

Q. You did want a liquor license for your restaurant, did you not? **A.** Why yes, it would be helpful.

Q. And Smith was helping you get one, was she not? **A.** Well, I had written to her. It didn't do much good.

Q. She was trying to get that license for you, wasn't she? **A.** She wasn't doing anything special.

Q. Nothing special? She was trying to pass a special bill for you, wasn't she? **A.** Not to my knowledge.

Q. She was doing a great deal to get you a liquor license, wasn't she?
A. No. All she did was write one letter to the liquor commissioner saying she thought I had good character, but that was back in '71.

Q. You don't call writing a letter to the liquor commissioner something very special? **A.** No.

Q. You don't think that going out of her way to write to the commissioner on senatorial stationery was putting on special pressure, asking for special favors for you, trying to get you to the top of the heap ahead of those who had been waiting longer? Isn't this the kind of special effort which might lead someone to lie on her behalf from the stand? Come now, speak up. **A.** I don't know what to say.

Problem I–14. Defendant is charged with bank robbery. At the trial the teller who paid over the money is called and testifies that the culprit was wearing a bandanna over his face. Asked if he can identify the bandit, the teller says, "I'm not sure, but I think so." Asked if he sees anyone resembling the bandit in the courtroom, he replies, "That man, sitting at the table there, I think he is the robber." [Indicating the defendant]. Asked by the prosecutor whether he is certain, the teller replies, "No, I can't be certain, but I think he looks like the robber." Defendant moves to strike. **Should the motion be granted?**

Problem I–15. The defendant is being tried for murder. The star witness for the prosecution, Sam Peabody, has testified that he heard two shots coming from around a corner at which point he ran to the corner to see what had happened. The prosecutor's next question was, "What did you see next?" Sam responded, "I saw the defendant about twenty yards from the house running as fast as he could away from that house because he had just shot the murder victim." **Is Peabody's answer objectionable? All of it? Some of it?**

Problem I–16. Plaintiff brought an action to recover rent claimed to be due from the defendant under certain leases. The leases in question covered an entire business block. Plaintiff leased the premises to one Littlefield who assigned the leases to defendant on June 25, 1973. Littlefield then fled the jurisdiction. On the day of Littlefield's departure, defendant paid to plaintiff the rent then in arrears and occupied the premises. Thereafter defendant sublet parts of the building, paid for repairs, and, from rents collected from the subtenants, paid to the plaintiff the rents due under the leases except for $300, which was owed when the lease expired. The issue was whether defendant was Littlefield's agent or whether he was the beneficiary of an outright assignment and liable for the outstanding balance. Defendant took the stand and testified as follows: "Littlefield made me his agent. There was no absolute assignment at all. It is true that Littlefield owed me money and that the assignment was collateral security for his debt, but both of us intended an agency arrangement only." Plaintiff introduces no direct evidence rebutting defendant's testimony, nor does plaintiff cross-examine or object to the evidence. **Is there any possible ground for objection? Assuming an objection might have prevailed but was not raised,**

what weight should the trial judge accord the evidence? (If the assignment was only as security for a debt, and not absolute, then the defendant was operating the leased premises in his capacity as agent and not assignee and would not be liable for the balance. Whether an assignment is absolute where given as collateral for a debt depends in this jurisdiction on the value of the assignment, the amount of the debt, and the powers the assignee is given with respect to the assigned leasehold.)

Problem I–17. Mrs. Combs, the testatrix, died leaving a contested will. The main issue in the will contest was her competency to make a will. George T. Manley, the principal beneficiary under the will, sought to sustain it against attack. During the trial a document signed by Manley, reciting a number of instances in which Mrs. Combs had behaved erratically was introduced over objection to impeach Manley's testimony on direct, which included the following statement:

> I never at any time heard her say or do anything that indicated that her mind was not right or that she didn't understand the things she was talking about, never in my life.

Manley claimed that he had signed the document at the request of his mother and his aunt and that the document contained no information reflecting his personal knowledge or opinion. When the document was admitted, it came in without any restriction as to the issues on which it could be used. Then a Dr. Garrard testified, based in part upon the document, that Mrs. Combs was mentally abnormal. Later, the court, concerned it had made a mistake, decided the document was inadmissible. It charged the jury as follows:

> Gentlemen of the jury, give me your attention for just a moment. Yesterday I admitted into evidence what was termed in speaking of it as a history, that was used in connection with an inquisition of lunacy, the trial in the court of ordinary of Mrs. Combs. This history blank that I am speaking of is the one that the propounder, Mr. Manley, stated here on the stand that he signed. I am withdrawing that, gentlemen, from evidence and from your consideration. I am likewise withdrawing any statements made on direct or cross-examination by Dr. Garrard—you will remember the physician that came over here from the Georgia State Hospital at Milledgeville and was on the stand—where he made any reference to that history blank or quoted from it or read from it or made any statements about the contents of it, gentlemen, now these pieces of evidence that were introduced here and admitted at the time by the court, are now excluded and are not in evidence—you will not let them have any weight upon you whatsoever in arriving at a verdict in this case. You will consider them or this evidence as if it had not been introduced at all.

* * *

Did these instructions effectively withdraw from the jury any opinion that the witness had given which was based on the contents of this document?

Problem I–18. Defendant was charged with forcible rape and assault. The defense at trial was consent, and the case turned on whether the jury

believed the victim or the defendant.   Defendant produced a witness who
testified that he saw the victim at the home of the defendant at the time of
the alleged crime.   After stating that he heard no crying or hysteria, the
witness was about to relate the conversations he had overheard when an objection by the prosecution was sustained.   Defense counsel stated at the time:
"Your Honor, the conversations shed light on who is telling the truth and
who is lying in this case.   Either there was a rape committed or there was
consent.   Let's find out."   The evidence remained excluded, defendant was
convicted, and he appealed.   **Assuming arguendo it was error to exclude
the evidence, is the offer of proof adequate to justify an appellate court's
reversing the conviction?**

Problem I–19.   Sarah Brand left her husband John and their five children to live with Noah Webster.   Soon thereafter, Sarah filed suit demanding custody of the children, but the court ruled that the three youngest children would be in the custody of John and the two oldest children would be
placed in the custody of the State Department of Social Services.   Subsequently, Sarah divorced John and married Noah.   She then sought to modify
the court decree to obtain custody of the two oldest children.   At the hearing on her request for modification, Sarah presented evidence about her new
marriage and her ability to provide for the children.   The judge took the
two children into chambers and privately interviewed them.   One preferred
to live with Sarah, and one preferred to stay in the custody of the Department.   John presented to the judge a series of typewritten exhibits prepared by his counsel which purported to contain the expected testimony of
several witnesses.   The testimony related a series of abuses allegedly committed on one of the younger children, Erika, when she visited Sarah and
Noah.   One statement related what the young child, herself, would say.   The
judge refused to accept the statement, and when John tried to call the child
to testify, the judge barred her from taking the stand, saying:

> I have never talked with Erika, but I have seen her and in my judg-
> ment, she is not competent to testify.   *   *   *

> The court believes it is in its sound discretion to exclude the testi-
> mony of a child of under six years of age on the basis that such testimony
> is essentially unreliable.   The court has never talked with the child di-
> rectly, but the court has observed the child and seen the type of child
> she is, and I believe I have the discretion to exclude her testimony with-
> out going further.

The judge awarded custody of the children to Sarah.   **Is the judge's ruling
on Erika's testimony correct under the Federal Rules?   Should a judge
have the right to reject the testimony of a child?   Should the judge have
talked to Erika before deciding on her competence?**

Problem I–20.   Mary Denhable is indicted for assault with a deadly
weapon and for the attempted murder of the supervisor at the law firm where
she worked.   The supervisor testifies that he fired Mary two days before
the alleged assault.   He then describes the assault.   A portion of his testimony follows:

Q. Okay. Now, after she stabbed you and backed off with the knife, started coming at you again, were you scared at that point?

A. Sure, yes.

Q. What were you afraid she was going to do to you?

A. She was going to kill me. Thought she was going to stab me again.

Q. So you—at that time you were in fear for your life?

A. Yes, sir.

Q. And this particular knife, did you feel that it was a deadly weapon?

A. Yes, sir.

Q. Did you feel that it could kill you?

A. Yes, sir.

Q. How long was the blade again, about how long?

A. (Indicating)

Q. About like that, about what—seven, eight inches?

A. About seven or eight inches.

Q. It's a butcher knife, is that right?

A. Butcher, yes, sir.

Mary's attorney vigorously protests this line of questioning and asks that the answers be stricken. **What is the most likely basis for the lawyer's objections and motion to strike? Should the motion be granted in federal court? In a common law jurisdiction?**

Problem I–21. Francis Speedy is charged with operating an automobile at 60 miles per hour in a 45 mile per hour zone. The speed was determined by radar. In laying the foundation for testimony based upon radar readings, state trooper X testifies that he is familiar with the operation of radar; that he, while working with Trooper Y, set up at the location in question a radar machine used by the state police; that the state police follow a regular procedure to test the accuracy of radar machines both before and after they are put in operation at a particular point; that the procedure is to set up the equipment and allow a short time for it to "warm-up", after which one officer drives his automobile through the zone of operation at speeds of 70, 60 and 50 miles per hour while the second officer reads the radar meter on the ground. Trooper Y is in the hospital on the day of the trial, but Trooper X offers to testify that the standard procedure was followed immediately prior to Speedy's arrest; that after the radar machine was set up and allowed to "warm-up", he drove his automobile through the operation zones at speeds of 70, 60 and 50 miles per hour while Trooper Y read the radar meter. Speedy objects to this evidence. **Is it admissible? Does it**

**matter if Trooper Y is in the hospital with a bullet wound?   On vacation?
Too busy to show up in court?**

BIBLIOGRAPHY

McCormick § 6 (leading questions), §§ 10–12 (personal knowledge and opinion), Ch. 4 (cross-examination), Ch. 6 (admitting and excluding evidence), Ch. 7 (competency), Ch. 16 (relevance), Ch. 22 (authentication).

Morgan, Basic Problems of Evidence 57–58 (leading questions), 65–67 (cross-examination) (1942).

1 Weinstein's Evidence ¶ 401[01] et seq., (relevance); 3 Weinstein's Evidence ¶¶ 601[02]–[04] (competency), 602[03] et seq. (personal knowledge), 611 [02]–[04] (cross-examination), 611[05] (leading questions), 701[01]–[04] (opinion); 5 Weinstein's Evidence ¶ 901(a)[01] et seq. (authentication).

2 Wigmore, Chs. 19–26 (competency), §§ 650–670 (personal knowledge); 3 Wigmore §§ 769-780 (leading questions); 3, 3A Wigmore, Chs. 29–35 (cross-examination), 5 Wigmore §§ 1390–1394; 4 Wigmore §§ 1179–1183, 7 Wigmore §§ 2128–2135 (authentication) 7 Wigmore §§ 1917–1985 (opinion).

Blume, Problem of Preserving Excluded Evidence in the Appellate Record, 13 Minn.L.Rev. 169 (1929).

Carlson, Cross-Examination of the Accused, 52 Cornell L.Q. 705 (1967).

Carlson, Scope of Cross-Examination and the Proposed Federal Rules, 32 Fed. B.J. 244 (1973).

Cleary, Evidence as a Problem in Communicating, 5 Vand.L.Rev. 277 (1951).

Conley, O'Barr & Lind, The Power of Language: Presentational Style in the Courtroom, 1978 Duke L.J. 1375.

Degnan, Non-Rules Evidence Law: Cross-Examination, 6 Utah L.Rev. 323 (1959).

Denbaux & Risinger, Questioning Questions: Objections to Form in the Interrogation of Witnesses, 33 Ark.L.Rev. 439 (1980).

Gardner, The Perception and Memory of Witnesses, 18 Corn.L.Q. 390, 401 (1933).

Ladd, Impeachment of One's Own Witness—New Developments, 4 U.Chi.L.Rev. 69 (1936).

Ladd, Objections, Motions and Foundation Testimony, 43 Corn. L.Q. 543 (1958).

Maguire & Quick, Testimony, Memory and Memoranda, 3 How.L.J. 1 (1957).

McCormick, The Procedure of Admitting and Excluding Evidence, 31 Tex.L.Rev. 128 (1952).

McCormick, The Scope and Art of Cross Examination, 47 Nw.U.L.Rev. 177 (1952).

Pope & Hamilton, Presenting and Excluding Evidence, 9 Tex.Tech.L.Rev. 403 (1978).

Saltzburg, Another Ground for Decision—Harmless Trial Court Errors, 47 Temp.L.Q. 193 (1974).

Saltzburg, The Federal Rules of Evidence and the Quality of Practice in Federal Courts, 27 Cle.St.L.Rev. 173 (1978).

Saltzburg, The Unnecessarily Expanding Role of the American Trial Judge, 64 Va.L.Rev. 1 (1978).

Thomas, The Rule Against Impeaching One's Own Witness, A Reconsideration, 31 Mo.L.Rev. 364 (1961).

Vestal, Sua Sponte Consideration in Appellate Review, 27 Ford. L.Rev. 477 (1919).

Weihofen, Testimonial Competence and Credibility, 34 Geo.Wash.L.Rev. 53 (1965).

Chapter Two

THE GENERATION OF EVIDENCE

SECTION I. GENERALIZATIONS ON THE NEED TO PREPARE

A spectator watching an advocate perform, or a student reading the record in a case like the Whale case might well underestimate the difficulty of the lawyer's job. Direct examination may appear simple and natural to one watching the parties' chosen witnesses parade their knowledge in their own words before the trier of fact. One may wonder what accounts for the high hourly rates of counsel who appear to do little more than ask "What happened then?", and "After that?", or perhaps "What did you do next?" Cross-examination, while more obviously dependent on the examining counsel, often seems to be little more than an effort to rephrase what the witness has said in a way which emphasizes its least favorable side, though one also sees attempts to tease, chastise, and cajole witnesses into adding to, subtracting from, or modifying what has been said, as well as attacks on credibility ranging from the reluctant suggestion that even good and honest people may err to the gleeful demolition of a witness' story and sometimes the witness' character as well.[1]

No one who has tried even a single case would minimize the skill and effort which lie behind the careful examination of witnesses. As in great tennis or a Robert Frost poem, apparent simplicity is the result of training and hard work; it is not in the nature of things. Preparing a case is often difficult, time-consuming and expensive, but preparation is likely to be more important to success at trial than fine oratorical skills or the best tactical sense.

The noted trial lawyer, Louis Nizer, made the point this way:

[I]n a certain sense there is no right or wrong way to try a case, any more than there is a right or wrong way to paint a painting or to write a poem. That is the right way to try a case which expresses your personality and your talents to the full * * *

* * *

There is only one thing that I shall be didactic about * * * I shall brook no disagreement on this subject * * * [T]he most important qualification for an able trial lawyer is *thorough preparation, hard work and industry.*[2]

Investigation, preparation and cogitation are not only prerequisites for effective trial advocacy; they are also essential in settling civil suits and negotiating guilty pleas. The American Bar Association quotes one experienced defense lawyer as follows:

As lawyers we know we plead more defendants guilty than we try. But I always like to think that I know more, or at least as much, about every case in which my client pleads guilty as when I go to trial. Investigation, research, developing a theory of the case legally and factually— the work has been cut out for you and

---

1. We examined the limitations placed upon counsel on direct examination in Chapter One. Cross-examination is fully examined in Chapter Five.

2. Nizer, The Art of Jury Trial, 32 Cornell L.Q. 59, 59–60 (1946) (emphasis in original).

the decision to enter a plea of guilty involves a tremendous amount of work.[3]

The testimony, documents, expert opinions, and exhibits which comprise the evidence that forms a lawyer's case are not always available when the decision to accept a client is made. They must be discovered, compiled, and interpreted. The ethical attorney does not make up evidence in the sense of creating appearances with no basis in reality, but in a very real sense he or she must generate the evidence later presented in negotiations or in court. This chapter discusses some of the ways in which lawyers generate this evidence. Our inquiry focuses on the biography of a typical lawsuit. We will briefly discuss procedures before suit is filed, and we will scrutinize the devices and techniques which attorneys use to enhance their clients' chances in litigation or settlement negotiations.

SECTION II.   BEFORE DISCOVERY

At one time the lawyer, like the doctor, was almost always a generalist. Although specialization has not proceeded as far in the legal profession as it has in medicine, there is today considerable specialization in the discipline, even among those who began practice by accepting all cases that came their way. Some attorneys only take civil cases, while others specialize in criminal litigation. Within these groups there is further specialization by area and side of case. Thus there are well-known "plaintiff's" and "defendant's" attorneys (and even firms) in labor law and personal injury litigation, and, of course, there are government and defense attorneys in the criminal area.

Differences among lawyers are important for many reasons; the one which concerns us here is that they, in part, determine the interests which lawyers bring to cases and the way in which they approach them. Consider such a crass item as the fee. In this country, it is relatively common for the personal injury lawyer to take a case on a contingent fee basis. In the criminal area contingent remuneration is not permitted.[4]   Class action lawyers are often attracted to multi-plaintiff cases by the prospect of receiving large fees from the proceeds of successful litigation,[5] or occasionally from settlement funds.[6] Government lawyers and corporate "house counsel" are both salaried and unaffected by the need to bring in business. Lawyers whose income is dependent upon winning may have views on the kinds of risks they should take that are different from those of lawyers who operate on a fixed fee schedule. And within the class of lawyers whose payment is not contingent on success, those who work for an hourly wage without a ceiling or with a high ceiling may have different incentives to expend time and effort than lawyers whose fee is a flat sum. Lawyers differ in other ways also. Elected prosecutors may respond differently to the public's attitude toward law enforcement activities than appointed prosecutors. Prosecutors appointed specially for one or a series of related cases may exhibit messianic impulses rarely found among careerists.

Our purpose in calling your attention to some of the characteristics that distinguish one group of lawyers from another is not

3.   ABA Standards for Criminal Justice, The Prosecution Function and the Defense Function, Introductory Note to Part IV, The Defense Function (App. Draft 1971).

4.   ABA Code of Professional Responsibility, D.R. 2–106(c).   Why should this be the case?

5.   See, e.g., J. Cound, J. Friedenthal and A. Miller, Civil Procedure 600–601 (3d ed. 1980).

6.   See, e.g., id.   But see Alyeska Pipeline Service Co. v. Wilderness Society, 421, U.S. 240 (1975).

to place the entire bar into occupational pigeonholes. Nor is it to suggest that once a distinguishing characteristic is identified, it should be assumed that the groups separated by the distinction have nothing in common.[7] Our purpose is to make you aware that the discussion that follows on the investigation of a case is a general discussion, as it must be if this book on evidence is not to become a book on lawyers. We discuss, for instance, the initial interview with the client and the information the lawyer will seek to elicit without reference to the particular interests or needs that differently situated lawyers might have. Take a familiar situation, the arrest of a client who is taken to jail to await the first appearance before a magistrate. In these circumstances, the lawyer will focus attention on the facts needed immediately for the bail hearing. After having made appropriate introductions, advised the client to talk to no one about the case and obtained facts bearing on bail, the attorney is likely to seek no further information until a second interview is arranged.[8] A prosecutor may find himself in the opposite situation. He may find that the police have completed an investigation of a crime before he learns of it. Even if they have not, there may be key individuals, like the suspect, whom he cannot interview.

The comments that follow are most relevant to lawyers who take clients from the time when the clients first realize they may be involved in legal action through the denouement of a settlement or trial. The principles we mention are general and should serve most lawyers well in most cases. Some of the problems point up special concerns in specific factual settings. This section, unlike Section III of this chapter, applies equally to both civil and criminal cases. We discuss here interviewing and investigation procedures which may be and often are utilized prior to those legal steps that formally initiate litigation. Early investigation allows a lawyer to decide whether to take a case, may turn up facts which will convince the opposition to drop its case before it has really begun, and can uncover or preserve evidence which would otherwise be lost forever. Later investigation is necessary for counsel to maximize the benefits of available discovery. It enables the persistent review of evidence and legal theory which characterizes the work of the most able attorneys. Before going further we should alert you to the fact that, although interviewing and investigation are among the most basic ways in which lawyers generate evidence, we can barely touch the surface of the topic in a book devoted primarily to the law of evidence. Books on trial practice go into the matter more deeply,[9] and clinical or other practical experience is necessary if you are to acquire confidence in your mastery of these arts.

A. INTERVIEWING THE CLIENT

Assume that the trial presented in Chapter One resulted in an acquittal rather than a conviction. Sometime after this trial Nelson Whale enters your office to inquire

---

7. **Any such suggestion would be nonsense given the common training of lawyers, the fact that some lawyers serve in several different capacities throughout a lifetime with no apparent difficulty, and perhaps most importantly the fact that for the most part the rules of the game—e.g., the rules of civil and criminal procedure, the rules of evidence, and the rules governing appeals—do not change because a lawyer is a specialist.**

8. See generally, Stein, Your First Criminal Case Appointment, 39 D.C.Bar J. 56 (May–June 1972).

9. See, e.g., H. Bodin, Marshalling the Evidence (1946); L. Moore, Motion Practice and Strategy (1953); Institute of Continuing Legal Education, Examining the Medical Expert: Lectures and Trial Demonstrations Vol. 2 (1969); PLI, Investigating and Preparing the Medical Aspects of Personal Injury Actions (1957); PLI, Trial Tactics in Personal Injury Actions (1956).

about the possibility of bringing suit against Officer Norton. Among Whale's complaints the most important are: (1) the entire prosecution for sale of narcotics was maliciously brought, being based upon false charges and perjured testimony; (2) the search of Whale's house was baseless and made unnecessarily offensive by the large number of officers participating; and (3) Norton's false statements on the witness stand which he repeated for the local press after testifying injured Whale's reputation among his friends and in the community. Having never heard of Whale or the trial, you patiently listen to Whale's angry and somewhat rambling discourse. On the assumption that Whale is telling the truth as he knows it, five possible causes of action suggest themselves to you: malicious prosecution, trespass, a federal action for invasion of constitutionally protected rights, slander and the tort of false arrest.

Does Whale's story and the fact that it suggests several different causes of action warrant filing suit? Plainly the answer is no. Before you become involved you want to know more about Whale's case. The easiest way to learn more is to question your prospective client.

It might appear that a client who trusts his lawyer and is informed that everything he says to his attorney will be held in the strictest confidence will voluntarily disclose everything he knows bearing on his legal problems. But few clients, even those who desire to tell everything, are able to spontaneously provide all the information which the lawyer will think relevant. There are several reasons for this. First, the client is often unaware of the way information is relevant to a legal case. Facts which a layperson thinks inconsequential may nonetheless be of substantive or evidential importance. Second, memory is

selective. Without intending to deceive, a client may convince himself that the particular version of the facts which most favors his case is the accurate one. Incongruent information or interpretations are forgotten or ignored. Third, the client may lack the ability to communicate everything he has seen, heard and learned. Finally, not every client wants to tell the lawyer all. Despite assurances of confidentiality, the client may not trust the lawyer with particularly damaging facts; the client may fear a personal loss of esteem if the lawyer learns certain information; the client, particularly one with prior legal contact, may be trying to shape a case which the fully-informed lawyer would refuse to present, or the client may feel that any facts which can be hidden from the attorney may also be hidden successfully from the court. Such intentional concealment of fact is particularly common in criminal cases where experienced defense attorneys call it, in its most extreme form, the "innocence pitch". The attorney should be wary of those factors which lead clients to conceal facts, because a case is most vulnerable when the other side has important information which counsel lacks.

Thus, the conscientious attorney often must *extract* from his client the details of the event which brought the client in. In the process the attorney may force the client to repeat his story several times, he may be openly skeptical, and he may ask penetrating, difficult and embarrassing questions in order to better learn what the client knows. There are no *Miranda* warnings in an attorney's office.[10] In the course of learning the client's version of events the lawyer is likely to learn also about other sources of information. What, for example, would you expect to learn in interviewing Whale?

10. **Indeed some very successful criminal lawyers insist that their clients verify their stories in a "lie detector" examination. They are aware that unless they can have complete faith in their clients' stories** **they cannot continue to get the kinds of results on which they have built their reputations. Only the very successful can afford to be so demanding.**

One client interview will rarely be enough. In the Whale case, you would probably find it necessary to speak with Whale at least once after researching the law that governs the legal theories available to you and again after interviewing the various witnesses to the matters complained of. Since you are searching for information which might eventually have to be presented in court you will need, in all but the most routine cases, to explore the relevant law while you search for useful facts.

Although the Whale hypothetical puts you in the position of plaintiff's attorney, you would probably not proceed in a radically different manner if Officer Norton came to you and indicated that he had heard rumors that Whale was about to sue and he wanted legal help in case a suit was filed. You would, of course, be somewhat less sure of what was relevant, since you would be anticipating possible claims rather than preparing them yourself.

Problem II–1. This problem is designed to communicate some of the difficulty you may encounter in interviewing a client, prospective client or witness. Smiley, an affable chap, came to see Mason, an attorney, about an automobile accident in which he was involved. Despite his usually generous nature, Smiley wanted to sue the driver of the other car for the back injuries he suffered as a result of the accident. Mason refused the case after discovering the following facts, which are contained in this reproduction of Mason's notes. **What questions would Mason have had to ask to elicit this information? Would you have thought to ask such questions? What other facts do you think Smiley might know which you would want to learn?**

Notes of June 3, 1982 interview

a. Smiley injured in accident at Broad and Main Streets on June 1, 1982. Traffic light controls intersection. Smiley claims he had a clear green light and the other driver must have disregarded a red light.

b. Smiley was driving a '72 Dart and the other driver had a '78 or '79 Ford.

c. Accident took place at 11:30 P.M.

d. Smiley had just been to a graduation party—he just graduated from business school at the age of 23.

e. Smiley had one glass of beer at the graduation party at approximately 10:00 P.M.

f. Earlier that evening, at approximately 7:00 or 7:30, Smiley had 3 or 4 martinis at a dinner with some fellow graduates. He says it all wore off in an hour or so.

g. At the time of the accident Smiley was trying to get to another graduation party before it ended at sometime around midnight.

h. Smiley, although married, was alone in his car, because he and his wife had a horrible fight earlier in the evening, and she had refused to go to the graduation party with him.

    i.   Smiley has received two previous tickets for driving under the influence of alcohol; both tickets were issued more than three years ago.

    j.   Smiley says he's seen a doctor who told him he suffered an injury that probably resulted from a sudden impact; the doctor said the injury could have been produced by an automobile accident.

    k.   Smiley is an amateur ice hockey player and plays every winter.

    l.   Smiley is absolutely sure the other guy ran a red light.

Have a friend write down ten other facts concerning Smiley's accident. Interview your friend. How long does it take you to uncover these facts?

B. INTERVIEWING WITNESSES

"The lawyer who would have a success in advocacy must see and talk to his witnesses."[11] Or he must be sure that someone he trusts interviews witnesses for him. There are advantages in the lawyer conducting his own interviews.[12] He gets to know the witnesses, their strengths, weaknesses, and temperaments, and he gets an idea of their credibility. But there are also costs. The time of a senior lawyer may be prohibitively expensive and he may not be as good an interviewer as someone associated with him or those he can hire. Professional investigators may be particularly valuable since they often have law enforcement experience and law enforcement friends.

Discussing the advantages of an investigator, John Flinn, who worked as a private investigator in the State of Virginia, and who had prior experience in an FBI lab, as a Virginia State Trooper, and as a United States Treasury agent, made the following observations:

Just to say that any police officer is going to cooperate with any investigator, or any police officer is not going to cooperate with any attorney would be wrong. But some attorneys can do wonders with *some* policemen and some investigators can do wonders with *most*

policemen. We've got a sort of relationship there—being a policeman is something like I guess being a fraternity brother—once you've been there you've got a lot of things to share with the guys who are out there now and they'll open up to you, so to speak, or rap with you. But attorneys have about two strikes against them every time they contact a police officer, and so I think a good, effective investigator can really help an attorney in getting information from the police.

* * *

Police officers make mistakes, and I think any really good police officer knows his own limitations and the limitations of the people he works with. And whereas the one case you're working on may be the most important thing in your life, for the moment anyway, and for the people you represent it may be the most important thing, for this police officer it's just one of several cases. He knows when he comes to court there are some areas he is weak in and he also knows that if we have been working on the case, or any good investigator has, that that investigator has been working just on that one case probably and may

11. F. Busch, Law and Tactics in Jury Trials § 204, at 294 (1949).

12. We are talking here about early interviews to gather information. The litigator

will always want to talk to those who will testify for his client at least once before trial.

be in a position to trip him up on some things that he may have overlooked. But as far as impeaching a dishonest police officer I don't think any good investigator would have any hesitancy about doing that. Nor would any good police officer regret to see it done.

* * *

What may happen to prospective plaintiffs and their counsel is that they will wait several months before deciding that an investigation in addition to the government's investigation should be conducted. By that time everything is going to be working against us, I'm afraid, because things will have quieted down and people will have been advised what to say and what not to say and they will have gotten all their stories straight. If I was an attorney, * * * and I had a client whose child was involved in an automobile accident or whose family was in any way involved in some type of an episode that might end up in court, I would have an independent investigation conducted just as soon as possible after the thing happened. I think that would be Number 1, because to rely upon a government agency to investigate anything and think that that's going to benefit everybody involved is wrong. I know that from experience, because most government agencies from the * * * Sheriff's Office on up to the FBI conduct sort of an assembly line process, and it's not a real in depth study of any specific occurrence. There are always areas that the investigator wishes he had had time to dig into, but doesn't. A private investigator is able to concentrate on one case at a time if he has the resources coming in and he can cover everything right down the line. And we've found a lot of police officers are

real happy to see us come around because they wish, as I did when I was on the force, that they could have spent more time on a particular case. Thus, they will steer us to things that they would have checked into if they had had more time. And they know that we understand why they don't have more time.

* * *

I don't know if things have changed or what. When I was a police officer I always thought everything was stacked on the side of the defense. Now that I am on the other side, I begin to think everything is stacked on the side of the police. Overall I think everything works out well many times. But both sides must be prepared. The investigation for both sides must be thorough, the lawyers must be prepared, and the adversaries must be evenly matched.[13]

—————

Contrary to what one may learn from television, investigation is not easy. Witnesses are not all cooperative, they are certainly not all accurate, and, sadly enough, not all are honest.

Even the task of locating persons who observed a crime or who have information concerning it may be difficult because of a general distaste for becoming "involved". After witnesses are located, their cooperation must be secured. It may be necessary to interview a witness several times to compare his version of the events with the version gleaned from others and to reconcile conflicting versions.[14]

Some years ago a lawyer and ex-FBI agent offered some practical tips on investigating facts, tips he thought would "appeal most to the young or beginning attorney."

13. Talk given at the University of Virginia Law School, Sept. 7, 1973.

14. ABA Standards for Criminal Justice, The Prosecution Function and the Defense Function, Introductory Note to Part IV of the Defense Function (App. Draft, 1971).

Like the comments of the Charlottesville investigator, the tips emphasize a thorough and prompt investigation. Specific guidance was provided for handling witnesses:

> [I]t is well to remember that if a witness is contacted by the investigator who has learned that the witness actually does or may know something of the matter, or was in a position at the time the event in question occurred which ordinarily would have enabled him to know something about it, and the witness maintains he knows nothing about it, a written signed statement should always be taken from him stating that he knows nothing. If that man later turns up in court as a hostile witness, giving testimony helpful to the opposition, the value of such a written statement for purposes of discrediting the witness or impeaching him is obvious. It frequently is an important to obtain the witness' signature to a statement that he knows nothing as it is to obtain his signature on an otherwise informative statement.

* * *

> Witnesses should always be asked if they can give the names or identities of other witnesses.

* * *

> For a successful interview with witnesses, always observe all courtesies. Never get in an argument with a witness.
> * * *[15]

More specifically, the following recommendation is made:

> Go over the entire subject matter with the witness verbally, if he talks readily. Try to bring out a chronological story; this saves much confusion. Lay witnesses who have had past court experience, or who have had some bad advice from neighbors, sometimes make a flat initial announcement that they do not intend to say a word until they are on the stand in court, or, on some other excuse, will refuse to discuss the matter in hand. Don't accept this as final. A dodge which frequently works is to appear to accept such a pronouncement as the last word in the matter, but then start in passing the time of day on some trivial subject, finally working the conversation around to the matter in hand, asking a few innocent appearing or immaterial questions on it, and then begin asking more pertinent questions. Usually, by being persistent in a manner along this line everything the witness knows can be dragged out of him.

* * *

> After the matter in question has been gone over thoroughly once verbally with the witness, writing materials should then be produced. It frequently is found to be effective to remark to the witness something about as follows: "Well, I guess I'd better make a memorandum of what you have told me." If the witness seems perturbed at this, it may be well to point [out] that when you have made a written memorandum of the conversation at that time when the witness himself can determine its accuracy, there is then no danger that in the future you will misquote him.[16]

Among the other tips are to have the witness sign the statement and initial any changes.[17]

Other sources suggest that it is better to demonstrate that a written statement is preferred at the outset of the interview by beginning to slowly write down the particulars of what the witness says.[18] Still oth-

---

15. Hornaday, Some Suggestions on the Investigation of Facts, 15 Ind.L.J. 498, 500 (1940).

16. Id. at 501–02.

17. Id. at 503–04.

18. See, e. g., Bowman, How to Make an Investigation, 21 Okl.B.A.J. 1346 (1950).

ers praise the question and answer method of eliciting information with both questions and answers transcribed. In fact some techniques probably work better with some witnesses and some with other witnesses. It is a mark of skill to know how to adapt different techniques to different witnesses.

Problem II–2. Ethical Consideration ¶ 19 of the ABA Code of Professional Responsibility (Canon 2) provides in part that "[a]s soon as feasible after a lawyer has been employed, it is desirable that he reach a clear agreement with his client as to the basis of the fee charges to be made." The first part of Ethical Consideration ¶ 26 (Canon 2) states that "[i]n furtherance of the objective of the bar to make legal services fully available, a lawyer should not lightly decline proffered employment." Ethical Consideration ¶ 30 (Canon 2) begins with the warning that "[e]mployment should not be accepted by a lawyer when he is unable to render competent service. * * *" Assume that from your knowledge of the law you believe that even if Nelson Whale's story is true it is likely that he will recover at most a nominal sum—e.g., $100—and that because he is suing a police officer he might well recover nothing. You also know that Whale hasn't enough money to pay the expenses which would be involved in presenting an effective case. **Which of the following statements do you make to Whale?**

a) I cannot handle your case because there is not enough money in it to justify the expenditure of my time.

b) My assessment of the facts, in view of the applicable law, is that you will be lucky to win $100. My hourly rate is $100. I suggest that I put in one hour's time, no more, and you take your chances on that basis. You win or lose based on one hour's work.

c) Your case is so important as a matter of principle that I will personally finance it even though it will require me to turn down $10,000 worth of business and to invest $10,000 of my own funds.

d) Something else. **If so, what?**

If you were a legal aid lawyer earning $13,500 a year for 50 weeks work, 40 hours per week, would you spend more time than a private lawyer on Whale's case? How much more? Would you assign a staff investigator to the case? How would you value the case? Is the expenditure of more funds than a private lawyer would expend fair to Officer Norton who may have to spend substantially more than $100 to present an adequate defense?

Problem II–3. Make the same assumptions as in the previous problem with one change: assume that Whale is very wealthy. **Which of the following statements do you make to Whale?**

a) I cannot handle your case because it is really not significant enough to warrant expending my time, your money, the potential defendant's time and money, and the resources of the judicial system.

b) Every wrong should be righted.   It may cost you $5,000 to win this suit. And if you win you may only recover a nominal amount.   But if you are willing to pay my fee, I am willing to vindicate your principles.

c) Something else.   **If so, what?**

Problem II–4.   Assuming you decide to represent Whale, you proceed to conduct your own investigation.   **When you go to talk with Officer Barrott, would it be improper for you to represent that you are a news reporter and not a lawyer?   Would the situation be different if you hire an investigator who makes the misrepresentation?**

C.   EXAMINING PLACES, INSTRUMENTS AND DOCUMENTS

No matter how lucid a client's or witness' description of a place or an item of tangible evidence, it would be folly to rely upon the description and fail to look for yourself.   In some circumstances your own impressions will suffice, but often you will need the help of others to preserve or appreciate what is there.   You may wish to photograph a scene or xerox documents for use in interviewing witnesses and at trial.   You may also need expert help to analyze blood, verify questioned documents, conduct ballistics tests or engage in the countless other scientific analyses which make or break many a modern case.   The details of such analyses are quite technical, and we can not go into them here, but it may be essential that you have access to those who have mastered them.[19]

Problem II–5.   Passenger in car 1 is thinking of suing driver of car 2 for damages arising from injuries suffered in an accident involving the two cars.   As the lawyer for passenger, you wish to see car 2 and request permission of the driver (also the owner) to do so.   **If permission is refused, might you still obtain an advantage from having made the request?   Would it make any difference if the request were made by telephone or by registered letter?   If the owner refuses permission to examine the vehicle, would it be ethical for you to take pictures of the car while it is parked in front of the owner's house?   To question the local garage mechanic about repairs he has done on the car?   To pay the mechanic to give you certain parts which he replaced when repairing the car and to subject these parts to your own laboratory analysis?   To enter the car at night when the owner is sleeping and then conduct a detailed examination?**

D.   MISCELLANEOUS SOURCES OF INFORMATION

Since many government agencies, both state and federal, investigate a host of subjects and often compile reports on their investigation, a diligent lawyer will always

---

19.   See, e.g., A. Moenssens, R. Moses, F. Inbau, Scientific Evidence in Criminal Cases (1973).

seek to ascertain whether a report of any governmental inquiry is available in a given case. In an automobile accident case, for example, a police officer may appear promptly at the scene and attempt to reconstruct what happened. The officer's report may contain the names of potential witnesses, statements made by witnesses and parties, and some indication of the physical characteristics of the scene such as the type of damage done to the vehicles or the length of skid marks, if any. If an airplane crashes, there is likely to be a study by the regulatory authorities which, if available, may be of tremendous help in litigation. The resources and expertise which a federal agency can put into such an investigation far exceed those available

to private attorneys. The apparent disinterest of the government will also enhance the credibility of the report if there is some way of using it at trial.[20]

Another way of generating information that may be helpful in developing a case is the obvious, but underrated, method of perusing the technical or scientific literature in areas relevant to your case. Many diligent lawyers spend considerable time researching the history, the purpose and the competing interpretations of the law upon which they rely or against which they must labor; yet if they are unable to convey clearly the factual basis of their case or to cross-examine their opponent's experts intelligently, they are likely to lose the

20. It will often be difficult to actually use such a report at trial. What is written is likely to be inadmissible hearsay. But see FRE 803(8), discussed in Chapter Six. Where cooperation with government investigators is mandated by law, information given to satisfy the statute will often be protected by a privilege. Indeed, some such reports are required to be or are by custom kept confidential, so the attorney may find that he is unable to get access to such reports even for the purpose of a pretrial investigation.

The Freedom of Information Act, 5 U.S.C. § 552, and similar state laws, may serve as discovery substitutes. The federal statute provides that governmental agencies must make agency records promptly available to any person, regardless of his identity or need for disclosure, unless the records are exempted from the compulsory disclosure requirements of the Act. The federal exemptions cover the following matters: 1) national security information; 2) records relating solely to internal personnel rules and practices; 3) information protected against disclosure by other federal statutes; 4) trade secrets and commercial or financial information; 5) pre-decisional internal communications; 6) information which would constitute a clearly unwarranted invasion of personal privacy; 7) investigatory records compiled for "law enforcement purposes"; 8) reports prepared by an agency responsible for the regulation or supervision of financial institutions; and

9) geological and geophysical information and data.

The Supreme Court has indicated that "discovery for litigation purposes is not an expressly indicated purpose of the Act." Renegotiation Board v. Bannercraft Clothing Co., 415 U.S. 1, 24 (1974). Several circuit courts have held that the FOIA is not to enlarge the scope of discovery beyond that already provided by the Federal Rules of Civil and Criminal Procedure. See, e.g., United States v. Murdock, 548 F.2d 599, 602 (5th Cir. 1977); Fruehauf Corp. v. Thornton, 507 F.2d 1253 (6th Cir. 1974). Thus, it may be difficult to use the FOIA for discovery, especially in light of Exemption Three, but the Act has nevertheless been used for this purpose. Procedurally, it has certain advantages. Under the Act, an agency has ten days in which to reply to an initial request for information, and 20 days to make a determination with respect to an appeal (§ 552(a)(6)(A)). Thus, obtaining covered information can greatly expedite a proceeding. An adverse FOIA decision is immediately appealable as a final decision (5 U.S.C. § 552(a)(6)(C)). A discovery motion under the Federal Rules of Civil Procedure is reviewable only by obtaining a writ of mandamus or upon appeal after an adverse decision on the merits. A court in an FOIA action may also assess costs and reasonable attorney fees against the government when the complainant substantially prevails (§ 552(a)(4)(E)).

benefits of their legal learning.[21] Skilled lawyers will tell you that the facts and not the law most often decide the outcome of their cases.[22]

SECTION III. FORMAL DISCOVERY

In this section we examine the standard discovery procedures available to litigants once an action commences—i.e., after a complaint is filed in a civil case and after a suspect is arrested or charged by information or indictment in a criminal case. Because discovery is radically different in the two kinds of cases, they are treated separately.

A. CIVIL DISCOVERY

The focus of our inquiry will be on the Federal Rules of Civil Procedure. Since their adoption in 1938, the Federal Rules have been widely praised, and they have been copied in many states. Even if you practice in a state that has not yet adopted the Federal Rules you should still find this discussion useful.

It is not our intention to duplicate a course in civil procedure in this section. Rather, we hope to raise questions that are best understood in the context of an evidence course. In lieu of the procedural emphasis on what can be discovered, we shall consider the harder evidentiary question of what should be discovered.

1. SOME GENERAL PRINCIPLES

Parties to a civil action are entitled under Rule 26 to obtain discovery of any matter that is not privileged[23] as long as the matter is relevant to the issues in the pending lawsuit.[24] The information that is sought need not be admissible in evidence; it need only be helpful in understanding or preparing a case. Plaintiffs are entitled to seek not only information that helps to prove their claims but also information that helps to undercut potential defenses. Defendants are similarly permitted to obtain non-privileged information which aids any aspect of their case.

If a party or any other person from whom information is sought claims that discovery is unduly annoying, burdensome, embar-rassing, expensive, or otherwise oppressive, or that discovery is being used for an illegitimate purpose such as harassment, a protective order can be sought from the court to inhibit or control discovery attempts.

Five general categories of discovery exist: depositions, of which there are two kinds, those taken upon oral examination and those taken upon written questions; written interrogatories; requests for production of documents or things, or permission to view places, documents, or other items; physical and mental examinations; and requests for admissions. Only depositions can be used to secure information held by non-parties, but a subpoena duces

---

21. Expert witnesses may also be used for the same purpose. One of the most valuable services the expert performs is educating the attorney about the technical background of the case and helping him prepare for direct and cross-examination.

22. See, e.g., L. Stryker, The Art of Advocacy (1954).

23. Privilege generally refers to the evidentiary privileges that are discussed in

Chapter Eight. It is not necessary for you to worry about privileges yet. However, we shall examine one form of privilege—work product—later in this section.

24. Relevancy is the subject of Chapter Three. For purposes of this chapter, assume that the next sentence in the text adequately defines relevancy for purposes of discovery.

tecum may be used to require the non-party witness to bring physical evidence to the deposition hearing. Unless a protective order is issued, there is no judicial control of or formal limit on the use of the various methods of obtaining discovery. Of course, a witness can refuse to answer questions, leaving the examiner the choice of seeking an order compelling discovery or doing without.

The suggestion has been made that discovery may serve three distinct goals: 1) to narrow the issues, 2) to obtain evidence for use at trial, and 3) to learn about evidence that might be useful at trial and how to obtain it.[25] But this suggestion reflects more fully the views of those responsible for drafting the discovery rules than it does the aims of lawyers who use the rules. Lawyers may have different purposes in utilizing discovery. As we turn to an examination of depositions, this point becomes clearer.

2. DEPOSITIONS

Rule 30 provides the governing standards for depositions. Any party may take the testimony of any person, including another party. Notice to opposing parties is required, but in most instances the permission of the court is not. Except in special circumstances, a plaintiff cannot notice depositions until either 30 days have expired after service of the summons and the complaint upon defendant, or defendant first notices a deposition. This is to allow the defendant time to secure counsel. Examination and cross-examination proceed as if the testimony were being elicited at trial, with objections noted. A motion to terminate or to limit the examination can be made to prevent harassment or undue annoyance.

To understand the full complexity of the tactical decision whether or not to depose, consider a familiar factual setting: the automobile accident. Plaintiff is driving down Main Street. Defendant is driving down Cross Street. Witness I, plaintiff's husband, is riding in the front passenger seat of plaintiff's auto. Witness II, an employee of defendant, is riding in defendant's passenger seat. Witness III, a stranger to both plaintiff and defendant, sees them collide at the intersection of Main and Cross. Based on the diverse citizenship of the parties, plaintiff sues for damages in federal court. Defendant counterclaims for his damages.

In the hypothetical lawsuit under consideration, plaintiff and her husband take the position that defendant ran a red light. Preliminary investigation of the kind discussed in section II has indicated that the employee will support the employer's allegation that plaintiff disregarded a traffic signal. However, the employee is moving from the East Coast to the West Coast. Defendant, having obtained full cooperation from the employee, feels no need to engage in discovery. Is this wise? Plaintiff's attorney, fearing his client might lose valuable information, schedules a deposition of the employee before the move. Is this necessarily wise? Witness III, truly neutral, agrees to cooperate with both sides. At separate interviews conducted informally by the parties' attorneys, the witness substantiates plaintiff's story. Because of his cooperation, no deposition is taken by either side. Is somebody making a mistake? Who? To answer these questions you must understand that lawyers take depositions for several different reasons, and that the very reason one lawyer wants a deposition may be the reason another does not.

One reason a lawyer takes a deposition is to perpetuate testimony.[26] Ordinarily a

---

25. See 8 C. Wright & A. Miller, Federal Practice and Procedure § 2001, at 15.

26. Rule 27 of the FRCP permits a person to perpetuate by deposition his own or

lawyer will wish only to preserve the testimony of favorable witnesses, not unfavorable ones:

> For although counsel for the party in whose behalf the deposition of a hostile[27] witness is taken is not obligated, at the trial, to read the deposition into evidence if he does not like it, and although he may read such parts of the deposition as he likes, the opposing party may introduce the entire deposition into evidence or such parts of it as he wishes to read, provided, of course, that the witness is then unavailable. Thus, while examining counsel will not be bound by the answers of the witness unless he chooses to read the answers into evidence in court, he has nevertheless placed himself in an unenviable position because he has perpetuated the testimony of a hostile witness. If the witness subsequently does not attend the trial, and statutory grounds exist for the reading of the testimony, the examining counsel will have lost the benefit of cross-examining that witness in court. Even if in taking the deposition counsel asked leading questions because of the hostility of the witness, cross-examination in court is usually far more effective. Furthermore, since the opposing party is entitled to cross-examine persons whose depositions are taken at the instance of the other party, a deponent hostile to the examiner and friendly to the cross-examiner may be interrogated on cross-examination by leading questions. At the trial, counsel for the opposing party could read not only the unfavorable answers which the examiner received on direct examination of the hostile witness but also the answers which the opposing counsel elicited in the so-called "cross-examination". It is therefore of the utmost importance not to take the deposition of a witness for the purpose of perpetuating testimony unless counsel knows that the answers he will receive will be favorable.[28]

Does one automatically depose favorable witnesses? Probably not. Such a procedure often would be prohibitively expensive and might have undesirable side effects. The suggestion has been made that a deposition to perpetuate testimony should not be taken unless absolutely necessary:

> No lawyer should voluntarily and without adequate reason thus lay his case open to his opponent, or disclose the testimony of his own client or that of a

some other witness' testimony prior to filing an action or, with the court's permission, pending appeal, by indicating (in the pre-action situation) the likelihood an action will be filed, the nature of the action, and the reason why the testimony sought to be perpetuated is important to the action. Notice must be given to the actual or likely adverse party and the scope of the deposition is subject to judicial control. In addition, courts, including the federal courts, have historically been open to and continue to be open to independent actions for the purpose of perpetuating testimony. Such actions occasionally provide a prospective party with a more convenient means of preserving testimony than Rule 27 procedures. We are discussing in the text Rule 30 depositions taken after a claim has been filed. These involve less judicial control than Rule 27 depositions. However, the discussion of the strategy of when to depose applies to depositions at both stages of the action.

This section also does not discuss the particular problems of deposing expert witnesses. Nor does this section devote space to a separate discussion of oral and written depositions. We consider only the more common and more useful oral depositions.

The Federal Rules of Civil Procedure (Rule 32) and the Rules of Evidence (FRE 801 and FRE 804(b)(1)) permit depositions to be used as affirmative proof in certain circumstances. In addition FRE 607 and FRE 613 would permit depositions to be used for impeachment of witnesses.

27. Most of the time the author of this excerpt is not using the word "hostile" in a technical sense. He means simply unfavorable witnesses.

28. H. Bodin, Strategy and Technique of Depositions 28–29 (1946).

friendly witness in advance of trial. The advantage to one party of knowing in advance of trial the precise testimony of the opposing party and his witnesses is too great to make such depositions desirable to the examiner except when he has no alternative. His opponent will have the invaluable benefit of being able to prepare in advance to meet all the testimony with precision.[29]

Do you agree that depositions for purposes of preserving testimony should be taken only rarely? Can you see possible advantages in negotiation stemming from the frequent use of such depositions? Are there other advantages to using depositions to preserve testimony? Is it wise, for instance, to have a favorable witness recite his story in a formal proceeding while the event is fresh in his mind? Will the existence of the deposition enable opposing counsel to more effectively cross-examine your witness at trial (when memory has begun to fade)? If this is indeed a danger, is there a countervailing advantage in your ability to choose the time for deposing a witness?

Assuming that you want to perpetuate testimony, how should you do it?

    *   *   *   Since the purpose of perpetuating testimony is to use the examination at the time of the trial in the event that the witness is at that time out of the jurisdiction or otherwise unavailable, the examination should be conducted in all respects as if the witness were then testifying in court. His full story should be elicited from him by examining counsel. In fact, it may be necessary to examine in even greater detail than if that witness were being examined at the trial. If a witness is present in court and available for rebuttal, it is not necessary to elicit all of his information on the case-in-chief. In court it is sometimes advisable to ask the witness only certain es-

sential questions without anticipating a rebuttal of the defense. There is time enough to call that witness in rebuttal if evidence subsequently adduced by the opposing side calls for rebuttal. Not so, however, with a deposition taken to perpetuate testimony. If the witness will not be present at the trial, it will be impossible for him to rebut any testimony that will be offered by the other side. Counsel must therefore anticipate the probable testimony of the opposing party and his witnesses, and should, as far as possible, ask the necessary questions to obtain from the witness all the testimony which he is able to give and which may counteract any evidence that may be offered by the other side at the trial.[30]

Counsel for the opposition has a similar task:

In addition, counsel for the opposing party will also have the opportunity to prepare a more effective cross-examination of the deponent, should the latter thereafter take the stand as a witness at the trial, and to attack the witness in case he deviates at the trial from his prior testimony in the deposition. If, on the other hand, deponent is absent and his testimony is presented by deposition, there may be no opportunity to rebut evidence adduced by the adverse party specially to meet the testimony given by deposition.[31]

Thus, preserving testimony is one important reason to take depositions. Evidence useful at trial or in pre-trial negotiation is generated and preserved.

A second basic reason for deposing witnesses is more familiar to students of civil procedure—i.e., for discovery. Discovery aids counsel in evaluating the strength of the opposition's case and suggests ways in which one's own case may be shored up or the opponent's case undermined. Depositions for discovery are directed to-

---

29. Id. at 29.
30. Id. at 29–30.

31. H. Bodin, supra note 28, at 29.

ward unfriendly or neutral witnesses, since friendly witnesses usually cooperate with counsel. Discovery depositions produce information for the discovering side, give counsel a sense of how firmly set an opponent's theories are, allow early identification of documents and exhibits, and identify issues not in dispute, thus saving much time for both sides.

At trial, depositions taken primarily for discovery can be used to impeach unfavorable witnesses,[32] and under the Federal Rules of Evidence statements in depositions inconsistent with the deponent's statements at trial can be treated by the jury like courtroom testimony despite their common law hearsay status.

There are dangers in taking discovery depositions. Counsel may obtain no useful information but may through questioning disclose adverse facts that the other party had not perceived. More importantly, the witness who has not been helpful may become unavailable, and a discovery deposition may be transformed into a preserved testimony deposition, with the other party reaping the benefits. And the deposition is a dry run for cross-examination. The opposing party or unfriendly witnesses may be better prepared for counsel's questions when they again meet at trial.

Here lies a dilemma for the trial lawyer. The goals of preserving evidence and discovering evidence are often contradictory. In preserving testimony the lawyer enables the other side to learn more about his case. The converse is equally true. This explains why we say that knowing whether to take a deposition is probably more important than knowing when you can take one.

If you are not yet convinced, consider other reasons why depositions might be taken. First, assume that a lawyer knows what an unfriendly witness will say. He does not need discovery and does not want to perpetuate adverse testimony. Yet, if he believes the witness is almost certain to be available for trial, isn't there an obvious advantage in deposing? Isn't the prospect of two chances to test the witness attractive? On the other hand, the difficulty of asking leading questions where the witness is not technically hostile must be taken into account.

Second, assume a lawyer has a very favorable witness who almost certainly will be available for trial. Is it wasteful to take a deposition? Perhaps not, at least not if the lawyer wants to demonstrate that even under oath and cross-examination, the witness' testimony is unshakable. This might provide the key to a pretrial settlement.

Third, noticing a number of depositions may scare the opposition by raising the spectre of unreasonably high litigation costs and considerable pretrial delay.

Fourth, depositions may be used as devices by the side that is first prepared in order to "freeze" the testimony of the side not yet prepared.

Finally, messages are conveyed by how one conducts litigation. Counsel's technique in requesting or conducting depositions may suggest a willingness to settle or symbolically show that the case will be fought to the hilt.

Lawyers must decide whether to pursue one or more of these goals in view of the associated risks. In many cases they must determine how to allocate limited discovery budgets among competing goals. Hard choices must be made. At times, as with the third and fourth factors mentioned above, there are substantial ethical problems raised by the ready availability of pretrial discovery. The more one learns about depositions, the easier it is to see that

32. See Chapter Five for an extended discussion of impeachment by the use of prior inconsistent statements.

much of the sporting theory of justice allegedly dead at the trial level has been reincarnated in the discovery stage of litigation.

———

Problem II–6. Return once more to the lawsuit Whale is bringing against Norton. Assume that Whale has sufficient wealth to be able to afford to depose not only the fifteen officers who participated in the search complained of, but also Officer Barrott, Damon Lord, Lord's brother, Earl Stible, and several people in the community who allegedly talked to Officer Norton about the case. Whale notices more than 20 depositions over a six-month period. You represent Norton and you file the following request for a protective order:

> Mr. Norton has only $363 in the bank. He earns only $190 per week. It is simply impossible for him to have counsel at the requested depositions. Hence, the Court should not permit the taking of the depositions.

Is your motion likely to be granted? Is there any other remedy available that might be more appropriate?

Problem II–7. Officer Barrott asks the Court to prohibit the taking of his deposition on the ground that everything he knows is contained in the transcript of the criminal proceeding, that Whale has not indicated what purpose would be served by taking a deposition and that he cannot afford to miss a day of work. **Should the request be granted?**

———

3. INTERROGATORIES

Rule 33 provides that any party may serve upon any other *party* written interrogatories to be answered by the party served. Interrogatories may seek facts known by the opposing party or they may inquire into the opposing party's theory of how law applies to certain facts. The latter inquiry, however, can be deferred by the court if it could more appropriately be answered later in the pretrial proceedings. The party served with interrogatories has the option of providing the other party with raw business records sufficient to answer the questions, or with summaries of the data, provided that the burden of analyzing the data for the purpose requested would not be significantly greater for the interrogating party than for the party supplying the information.

"The obvious advantage which interrogatories have over depositions is that they are much less expensive. There is no significant expense for the party sending the interrogatories except for the time in preparing the questions."[33] Another advantage is the simplicity of interrogatories. No reporter is necessary, no oath must be administered, and no special place must be reserved for the questioning. Disadvantages include the impossibility of immediately following up an answer with another question and the inability to pose a question that must be answered without time

———

33. 8 C. Wright & A. Miller, Federal Practice and Procedure § 2163, at 486.

for reflection or aid in formulating the answer.

Interrogatories may be especially useful for searching out information such as the names and addresses of witnesses or the location of physical evidence which then provides a basis for the utilization of other discovery devices. They also may be of particular value in probing the kinds of detailed or complicated facts that an opposing party cannot carry in his head, but can easily determine. (See Fed.R.Civ.P. 30(b)(6) for deposing organizations.) Counsel may assist a party in answering interrogatories, and it is not uncommon for answers to interrogatories to be evasive, stilted and unhelpful. But evasion may backfire when answers to interrogatories can be used to impeach a witness at trial.

Problem II–8. You are a United States Representative faced with this proposed amendment to Rule 33:

Interrogatories, like depositions, may be used to elicit relevant information from any person, not just a party.

Would you support the change? Why?

Problem II–9. In representing a client in an automobile accident case you submit ten short, clear interrogatories to the other side. The answer to each is evasive. **Can you think of some way to use the evasive answers to your advantage? How else might you respond in this situation?**

---

4. EXAMINING PHYSICAL EVIDENCE AND PLACES

Any party may, pursuant to Rule 34, examine physical evidence or places in the possession, custody or control of another party by requesting to do so and specifying a reasonable time and place for the examination. Parties can examine physical evidence of non-party witnesses by deposing them and issuing subpoenas duces tecum pursuant to Rule 45. It must be remembered that a protective order can be obtained pursuant to Rule 26 to prevent a party from being unduly burdened by requests to produce evidence. At one time good cause had to be shown before discovery could be obtained under Rule 34, but good cause proved to be an ephemeral and apparently unnecessary restriction. This Rule provides legal means for obtaining access, once litigation commences, to items and areas that careful lawyers will want to examine personally.

5. PHYSICAL AND MENTAL EXAMINATIONS

Under Rule 35, one party can compel the physical or mental examination of another party or person in the custody or control of a party upon a showing that physical or mental condition is in controversy, after making a proper motion to the court premised on a showing of good cause. Because of the delicate nature of these examinations, this is the principal point in the Rules where judicial permission is a prerequisite to discovery. The Supreme Court has sustained Rule 35 against constitutional and statutory challenge.[34] We leave to your course in civil procedure the

---

34. Sibbach v. Wilson & Co., 312 U.S. 1 (1941) (examination of plaintiff); Schlagenhauf v. Holder, 379 U.S. 104 (1964) (examination of defendant).

tricky questions of what good cause is, when physical or mental condition is in controversy, and when a party has legal control over another person.

Of interest to us is the often overlooked section (b) of Rule 35. Paragraph (1) of section (b) provides that if the party or the person within the legal control of a party so requests, he can obtain a detailed written report of the examination setting forth findings and test results. There is a price to be paid for this request, however. The price is disclosure upon request of the reports of any other examination of the same condition and waiver of any doctor-patient privilege in the action with respect to the same condition. Under what circumstances do you suppose it is not advantageous to pay this price in order to know what the other side has learned about a client's physical or mental condition?[35]

6. REQUESTS FOR ADMISSIONS

Rule 36 provides that one party may ask any other party to admit for purposes of their litigation the truth of any relevant matters. Requests can be made to admit facts, to admit that the law applies to facts in a certain way, and to admit the genuineness of documents. Unless a written answer denying the matter or stating that no admission or denial can be made at this time or an objection to a request is timely made, the matter that is the subject of the request is taken as admitted, and once admitted, it cannot be disputed except with the permission of the court. Lack of information is not a sufficient ground for objection unless the party served with the request for admission states that reasonable inquiry has been made and has not provided a sufficient basis for admitting or denying.

Consideration of Rule 36 may appear out of place in a discussion of discovery. It usually provides no new information for the party using it. But Rule 36 is a powerful addition to the arsenal of weapons available to generate evidence. It is powerful because unlike depositions and interrogatories, which rely on an answer from an opposing party or a witness to provide evidence, Rule 36 offers a party the chance to frame factual statements and to demand that they be either admitted or denied, not evaded. What is generated is a favorable statement of a matter.[36]

7. WORK PRODUCT

Most of the privileges examined in Chapter Eight, infra, are designed to encourage personal relationships and to establish zones of privacy between individuals which the government and others may not invade. But another type of privilege, called "work product", exists. It is directly related to discovery in that it may insulate information gathered by one litigant from all other litigants.

The United States Supreme Court placed its imprimatur on the doctrine of work product in Hickman v. Taylor.[37] In that case a tugboat sank in an unusual accident and five of nine crew members died. Three days after the accident the tug owners and underwriters employed a law firm to defend them against potential suits by representatives of the deceased crew members. Less than a month after the ac-

---

35. If the party who is examined under Rule 35 tries to depose the examining physician rather than requesting a copy of the report, the same price is exacted.

36. Rule 37 provides sanctions against unwarranted refusals to comply with proper discovery requests. Many doubt whether it works effectively, despite a presumption in favor of discovery.

37. 329 U.S. 495 (1947).

cident a public hearing was held at which the four surviving crew members were examined. The lawyer for the potential defendants privately interviewed the surviving crew members not long after the hearing. Other interviews with different persons were also conducted. A representative of one of the deceased crewmen filed suit and sought to discover the statements obtained by the lawyer from the survivors and any oral reports or memoranda prepared by defendants relating to the tugboat's operations before sinking, its sinking, and its salvage and repair.

While stating "that the deposition-discovery rules are to be accorded a broad and liberal treatment," the Court held that the requests for discovery were improper. "We are * * * dealing with an attempt to secure the production of written statements and mental impressions contained in the files and mind of the attorney * * * without any showing of necessity or claim that denial of such production would unduly prejudice the preparation of [plaintiff's] case or cause him any hardship or injustice." The Court added that "[n]ot even the most liberal of discovery theories can justify unwarranted inquiries into the files and the mental impressions of an attorney." Why? Because, "[P]roper preparation of a client's case demands that he assemble information, sift what he considers to be the relevant from the irrelevant facts, prepare his legal theories and plan his strategy without undue and needless interference."

Rule 26(b)(3) expands the work product doctrine,[38] answers some of the questions raised by Hickman v. Taylor, and transforms the work product doctrine into a rule for trial preparation materials:

[A] party may obtain discovery of documents and tangible things otherwise discoverable [i.e., relevant and not privileged] * * * and prepared in

anticipation of litigation or for trial by or for another party or by or for that other party's representative (including his attorney, consultant, surety, indemnitor, insurer, or agent) only upon a showing that the party seeking discovery has substantial need of the materials in the preparation of his case and that he is unable without undue hardship to obtain the substantial equivalent of the materials by other means. In ordering discovery * * * the court shall protect against disclosure of the mental impressions, conclusions, opinions, or legal theories of an attorney or other representative of a party. * * *

A party may obtain without the required showing a statement concerning the action or its subject matter previously made by that party. Upon request, a person not a party may obtain without the required showing a statement concerning the action or its subject matter previously made by that person. * * *

———

In Upjohn Co. v. United States, 449 U.S. 383 (1981), the Court said that Fed.R.Crim.P. 26 "accords special protection to work product revealing the attorney's mental processes. * * * As Rule 26 and Hickman make clear, such work product cannot be disclosed simply on a showing of substantial need and inability to obtain the equivalent without undue hardship."

The significance of the work product doctrine should be obvious. If an attorney wants to interview witnesses without disclosing what he learns to the other side, he must interview them informally. Should the interviews produce such favorable evidence that the preservation of testimony is desired, the attorney can later make a formal record—i.e., take depositions.

---

38. Some commentators object to calling the work product doctrine a privilege. Ac-

tually, Rule 26(b)(3) establishes only a qualified immunity from discovery.

One might wonder why one party should be permitted to obtain an advantage at trial or in negotiation because of superior mobility at the outset of litigation. If an avowed purpose of discovery is to share facts and to minimize the sporting aspects of justice, does a trial preparation doctrine make sense? Is the same doctrine that applies to lawyers inherently applicable to all other agents of a party? Note that Rule 26(b)(3) excludes from the coverage of the doctrine a party's own statement. Why is this the case? Does the same reason also explain why a nonparty witness can obtain a copy of his statement upon request? Does the exclusion from protection of nonparty witnesses' statements cast doubt on the wisdom of the general protection of Rule 26(b)(3)?

Problem II–10. As a member of the House of Representatives, you are called upon to examine the following proposal to revise Rule 26(b)(3):

> Any party or prospective party has a right to proceed to discover facts that are relevant to litigation or potential litigation by informal as well as formal discovery. Informal investigation may include interviewing witnesses, photographing places or things, and examining documents, places, or things; but each party or prospective party who desires to proceed by informal investigation must inform other parties or potential parties and arrange to interview witnesses, take photographs, or examine documents, places, or things at a mutually satisfactory time and place. Failure to so inform other parties or potential parties shall result in automatic discovery by those parties not informed of written statements or summaries of oral statements of witnesses, photographs, and reports of any examination of any physical evidence. If given adequate notice, no party shall be able to discover the fruits of informal investigation, unless the failure to perform an informal investigation is excused in the interests of justice by the trial judge.

Would you support this revision? Cf. IBM v. Edelstein, 526 F.2d 37 (2d Cir. 1975).

8. POSTSCRIPT ON CIVIL DISCOVERY

The American legal system is characterized by tension between the adversary system and the search for truth. Lawyers and clients want to win, not to be told that they lost because the truth was against them. Winning may involve presenting a one-sided view of facts, impeaching credible witnesses, and using evidentiary objections to exclude evidence which might contribute to an abstractly correct decision.

To justify this system, in which clients do legal battle with lawyers as champions, it is argued that the contentiousness of opposing sides assists the fact finder in discerning ultimate truth, or in coming as close to truth as possible. Like the philosophical arguments underpinning the First Amendment, the arguments for adversariness rest on a belief that truth can only be known if conflicting ideas are pitted against each other. Logic and experience are the crucibles in which ideas must be tested. Eventually the truth, or the truer idea, wins out.

Assuming (as we do) the validity of such arguments when the issue is freedom of speech, we question whether the arguments hold in the litigation context. Ideas cast adrift may for long periods of time find no agreeable harbor in which to anchor.

Established ideas may be replaced by new conceptions which over time gain the allegiance of large numbers of individuals. Litigation, on the other hand, is a one-time thing, conducted pursuant to a schedule, and posing issues which must be definitively resolved by human beings with relatively little time for reflection. Cases must be decided; the world must go on.

Discovery is an attempt to soften the blows adversaries impose upon each other. It is designed to require both sides of a controversy to pool all of their private knowledge regarding a dispute and only then to fight over the factual and legal significance of pieces of that knowledge. Thus, it is felt, the adversary system works to best advantage. But like other aspects of the adversary system, discovery itself is adversarial. The attitude with which lawyers and clients approach litigation limits the degree to which modern discovery can control the potential excesses of the adversary system.[39]

B. CRIMINAL DISCOVERY

1. GENERAL COMMENTS ON DISCOVERY BY THE DEFENSE

Attitudes toward discovery in criminal cases differ markedly from attitudes toward discovery in civil litigation. Today almost everyone supports broad discovery in civil litigation, but there is a wide divergence of opinion on the wisdom of criminal discovery. Since criminal litigation is in the same adversary tradition as civil litigation, there is no obvious reason why the need for discovery is weaker in criminal than in civil cases. Indeed most opponents of extensive criminal discovery are willing to concede that substantial benefits could be expected were discovery extended.

Arguments against criminal discovery focus on its cost or dangers. The debate has focused for the most part on the implications of the defendant's access to prosecutorial information. Chief Justice Vanderbilt described the dangers he perceived in this way:

In criminal proceedings long experience has taught the courts that often discovery will not lead to honest fact-finding, but on the contrary to perjury and the suppression of evidence. Thus the criminal who is aware of the whole case against him will often procure perjured testimony in order to set up a false defense. * * * Another result of full discovery would be that the criminal defendant who is informed of the names of all the State's witnesses may take steps to bribe or frighten them into giving perjured testimony or into absenting themselves so that they are unavailable to testify. Moreover, many witnesses, if they know that the defendant will have knowledge of their names prior to trial, will be reluctant to come forward with information during the investigation of the crime. * * * All these dangers are more inherent in criminal proceed-

39. We recommend to anyone interested in discovery the excellent empirical study of discovery in certain federal districts in 1962 and 1963: William A. Glaser, Pretrial Discovery and the Adversary System (1968). Mr. Glaser's statistics suggest that discovery often does increase the pool of information available to the parties. But they also suggest that discovery may not reduce claims of surprise in most cases. Factual surprises may be reduced, but lawyers possessed of many facts can develop surprising legal theories. Glaser's data also refute the common notion that discovery produces more efficient trials. Also worthy of mention is the study's conclusion that discovery is not necessarily an aid to settlements and that discovery may impair more settlements than it encourages. Apparently, both sides tend to overestimate the strength of their cases as they add facts to their arsenals. For a discussion of when cases are likely to be settled, see Posner, An Economic Approach to Legal Procedure and Judicial Administration, 2 J. Legal Studies 399 (1973).

ings where the defendant has much more at stake, often his own life, than in civil proceedings. The presence of perjury in criminal proceedings today is extensive despite the efforts of the courts to eradicate it and constitutes a very serious threat to the administration of criminal justice and thus to the welfare of the country as a whole. * * * To permit unqualified disclosure of all statements and information in the hands of the State would go far beyond what is required in civil cases; it would defeat the very ends of justice.[40]

Opponents of criminal discovery have also argued that discovery in criminal cases is one-sided and unfair to the prosecution because of the defendant's privilege against self-incrimination; that prosecutors who fear fabrication by the defense will rely on memories rather than records; and that prosecutors need the edge of pretrial secrecy to satisfy their heavy burden of proof.

Thus far, arguments against discovery have prevailed in most jurisdictions:

Most of the states have * * * limited a defendant's discovery by a variety of doctrines that had their origins in the halting and cautious growth of discovery. The most common of these doctrines holds that the question of whether to grant discovery is in the discretion of the trial court. A second limiting doctrine confines discovery to evidence that would be admissible in court. Another such doctrine requires the defendant to establish a foundation for discovery by demonstrating a particularized need for

the information he requests. Some states surprisingly refuse discovery of evidence about which the defendant already knows on the ground that he has no need of it * * *. In addition many states deny discovery of particular categories of information—for example, the defendant's confession, the confessions of co-defendants, the statements of prospective witnesses, and the transcript of minutes of grand jury testimony.[41]

In recent years arguments in favor of opening up criminal discovery have become increasingly common. Indeed, the weight of critical comment now favors more extensive discovery. Supreme Court Justice William J. Brennan, for example, has argued that most defendants, being indigent, are unable to adequately prepare a case without the benefits of discovery; that the privilege against self-incrimination has not prevented prosecutors from securing confessions and incriminating non-testimonial evidence from accused persons; that perjury is best prevented by early exposure of facts and an emphasis on the ethical responsibilities of defense counsel; that witnesses shown to be in danger can be protected by the trial judge; and that discovery has worked both in this country and in others.[42] Others have made similar arguments.[43]

The change in the general attitude toward criminal discovery is evident in the discovery standards recommended by the American Bar Association. The Advisory Committee that drafted the standards explained its position:

40. State v. Tune, 13 N.J. 203, 210–211; 98 A.2d 881, 884 (1953). See also, Kaufman, Discovery in Criminal Cases, 44 F.R.D. 481 (1968); Flannery, The Prosecutor's Case Against Liberal Discovery, 33 F.R.D. 74 (1963).

41. Nakell, Criminal Discovery for the Defense and the Prosecution—The Developing Constitutional Considerations, 50 N.Car. L.Rev. 437, 474–75 (1972).

42. Brennan, The Criminal Prosecution: Sporting Event or Quest for Truth? 1963 Wash.U.L.Q. 279.

43. See, e.g., Fletcher, Pretrial Discovery in State Criminal Cases, 12 Stan.L.Rev. 293 (1960), Goldstein, The State and the Accused: Balance of Advantage in Criminal Procedure, 69 Yale L.J. 1149 (1960); Louisell, Criminal Discovery: Dilemma Real or Apparent, 49 Cal.L.Rev. 56 (1961); Pye, The Defendant's Case for More Liberal Discovery, 33 F.R.D. 82 (1963).

This report proposes more permissive discovery practices for criminal cases than is provided by applicable law in any jurisdiction in the United States * * *.

What united the Advisory Committee was the view that broad pretrial disclosure of the prosecution's case was the key to satisfying procedural objectives of overriding significance to criminal justice. This view developed as the Committee, simultaneously to [sic] its study of discovery, sought to develop standards for improved procedures in criminal cases prior to trial. The need for changes in procedures appeared manifest in order to lend more finality to criminal dispositions, to speed up and simplify the process, and to make more economical use of resources. Among recent developments which suggested new procedural goals have been the expansion of post-conviction remedies (see generally ABA STANDARDS, POST-CONVICTION REMEDIES [Approved Draft 1968]) and recognition of the validity and public interest in plea discussions and agreements preceding entry of guilty pleas, which account for the great majority of dispositions (see generally ABA STANDARDS, PLEAS OF GUILTY [Approved Draft, 1968]). In order to bring potential constitutional issues to the fore at the earliest practical time and to make for appropriate and enduring dispositions, it seemed essential that defense counsel receive as much information about the case as feasible before trial or other disposition.

In the face of these considerations, traditional grounds of opposition to broad discovery were reappraised. One, the advantages to the prosecution of surprise in the relatively few cases going to trial, was deemed an inappropriate consideration. Another, the fear of subversion of law enforcement by perjury, tampering with or intimidation of witnesses, or by premature disclosure of the identity of informants or details of ongoing investigations, was seen as a matter which occurred in only a minority of prosecutions and thus to be dealt with under the circumstances of particular cases, rather than serving as a barrier to discovery in all cases. Finally, the argument that some defense counsel are untrustworthy was viewed as exaggerated or anachronistic, and in any event as a matter more appropriately treated as a bar disciplinary problem than as a basis for deprivation of the values of discovery to the system.

The Advisory Committee reached these conclusions against a background of knowledge that, for many years and in many places, conscientious—and successful—prosecutors have made the kinds of disclosures here recommended in the traditional exercise of their discretion, motivated in many cases by the considerations which persuaded the Advisory Committee. It has been argued that, with these standards as a guideline, discretion to make or withhold disclosures should be left entirely to the prosecutor, not subject to court intervention except where disclosure is a constitutional requirement. As will be observed in the standards, improved pretrial processes will in large measure depend upon the prosecutor's initiative in complying with the standards. But ultimate responsibility for the validity of convictions and the fairness and efficiency of the judicial process lies with the court, as does responsibility for the exercise of judgment as to the merit of the grounds for withholding disclosure in a particular case. Thus, one of the central features of this report is the articulation of this responsibility of the court for what transpires in a criminal case prior to (as well as at the time of) disposition.[44]

44. ABA Standards for Criminal Justice, Discovery and Procedure Before Trial, Introduction (App.Draft, 1970). Experiments with the ABA standards leave one doubtful that

Professor Wright has summarized the current state of the debate:

This is plainly an issue on which highly responsible and experienced people disagree. Two observations may be made. First, those who favor broad discovery are plainly winning the fight, regardless of the merits of the argument. The trend to free disclosure is unmistakable. Second, the debate over this issue has produced much stirring rhetoric—but very few facts.[45]

In line with the current trend, a few years ago the Supreme Court proposed amendments to Rules 15 and 16, the basic discovery provisions in the Federal Rules of Criminal Procedure. These amendments would have substantially increased available discovery in federal criminal cases. Congress delayed implementation of the amendments following complaints by federal prosecutors and the expressions of concern by some members of Congress. Hearings were held on the amendments, and the familiar arguments pro and con were rehashed. Ultimately, Congress enacted legislation that expanded discovery far less than some proponents had hoped, and less than the Supreme Court's proposed rules. Public Law 94–64, 88 Stat. 370 et seq. (1975).

2. ASPECTS OF CRIMINAL DISCOVERY

Before examining the availability of specific items of information, it is important to emphasize a point noted in the ABA report: in many jurisdictions, there is considerable discovery by grace—i. e., discovery provided by the prosecutor although not compelled by statute, rule, or decision. This fact is often ignored in judicial decisions and law review commentaries. While it is dangerous to generalize too much about the form and scope of this informal discovery in view of the differing attitudes of individual prosecutors, the differing relationships a prosecutor has with individual defense counsel, and the attitudes a prosecutor may have toward a particular case, it seems that the sine qua non of defense discovery is defense cooperation. If the defense attorney is willing to provide information, he may usually obtain access to information[46] in return.

Some might think such discovery by grace adequately protects the legitimate interests of criminal defendants. But clearly any system which relies wholly on discretion entrusted to one side is open to abuse and unfairness. The ability to withhold or grant information is one form of control which prosecutors hold over the defense bar. Information may be given selectively to encourage a guilty plea; a defense counsel who has "unreasonably" refused to plead certain clients guilty may find that his access to information has been shut off, and in the "big case" normal channels of communication may close. It is, of course, the client who suffers when an attorney falls from grace, or when the prosecutor, for other reasons, disregards usual procedures for trading information.

Wholly aside from these worries which imply equal protection and fundamental fairness concerns, there are other problems with informal discovery. There is the question of prosecutorial integrity when prosecutors oppose explicit recognition of discovery in criminal cases for the reasons previously examined, only to ignore their

prosecutors want them to work. See Note, Criminal Discovery and Omnibus Procedure in a Federal Court: A Defense View, 49 So. Cal. L. Rev. 514 (1976). In 1978, the ABA approved a new draft on Discovery and Procedure Before Trial. In the Commentary to Standard 11-1.1, the drafters state "that the need for reform has been aggravated, rather than alleviated, during the intervening years."

45. Wright, Federal Practice and Procedure: Criminal § 252.

46. See, e.g., J. Collins, Discovery in Criminal Cases, in PLI, The Prosecutor's Sourcebook, § 17.1, at 379 (1969); Newman, Discovery in Criminal Cases, 44 F.R.D. 481 (1968); Discovery in Criminal Cases, 33 F.R.D. 51 (1963).

own arguments in their day to day behavior. While prosecutors might claim that an informal discretionary system promotes such important purposes as the protection of witnesses, discovery rules can be drafted so that judges are required to consider such interests in appropriate cases. Reliance on informal discovery is also disturbing in that the public is kept ignorant of the prosecutor's discovery standards, thus eliminating any prosecutorial accountability in this area. Finally, prosecutorial objections lose force because many jurisdictions already allow specific kinds of discovery in certain circumstances and some permit extensive discovery. Let us look at the situations in which discovery is and is not permitted.

a. Names and Statements of Witnesses

Some states mandate disclosure of the names and/or the relevant written or recorded statements of certain potential trial witnesses, but few go as far as Florida does in providing that the prosecutor shall provide within 15 days of a demand by one charged with an offense "[t]he names and addresses of all persons known to the prosecutor to have information which may be relevant to the offense charged, and to any defense with respect thereto."[47] Approximately a dozen states hold that disclosure of statements rests within the discretion of the trial judge, and most require a significant showing of special need to justify discovery.[48] Some states by statute ban disclosure of witnesses' statements, and most states do not affirmatively permit it.

Federal courts have traditionally refused such discovery, relying on the Jencks Act, 18 U.S.C. § 3500. This statute followed the Supreme Court's decision in Jencks v. United States, 353 U.S. 657 (1957), in which the Court exercised its supervisory power to hold that a trial court erred in denying a defense request to examine during the trial statements of two undercover FBI agents. The Court rejected the notion that pretrial statements should only be made available where the defense could show a probable inconsistency between the witness' pretrial statements and his in-court testimony. Without the earlier statements the task of proving probable inconsistency would be difficult indeed. Adverse reaction to the *Jencks* decision was immediate and strong, but the eventual legislative resolution of the dispute, the "Jencks Act", affirmed the Court's basic requirement that the government disclose pretrial statements made by its witnesses. Subsections (b) and (e) of the Act provide that *after* a witness called by the United States has testified on direct examination, the defendant may move for and receive statements of the witness in the government's possession. Statements within the meaning of the act include only written statements approved by the witness, stenographic or mechanical transcripts that purport to be almost verbatim accounts of oral statements, and any statements, however recorded, made to a grand jury. The Court's ruling is modified in that *in camera* review is required for the purpose of separating portions of statements relating to the witness' trial testimony from unrelated portions. Most states have followed the federal lead and patterned statutes upon the Jencks Act, but some states still require a showing of probable conflict between testimony and statement before requiring production.[49] The Supreme Court has affirmed the limitations in the Act, making clear that its decision in *Jencks* was not constitutionally based.[50] In the case of Goldberg v. United States, 425 U.S. 94 (1976), the Court interpreted the Act to mean that statements

---

47. Fla.R.Crim.P. 3.720. Most states do provide that names of witnesses will be turned over to defendants prior to trial. 1 Criminal Defense Techniques ¶ 11.02[2]. But rules are hard to classify and often not as helpful as they would seem on their face. Id.

48. Y. Kamisar, W. LaFave & J. Israel, Modern Criminal Procedure 1158 (5th ed. 1980).

49. Id. at 1235.

50. United States v. Augenblick, 393 U.S. 348 (1969).

made to government lawyers otherwise producible under the Act are not barred from production by the work product doctrine.

Some jurisdictions provide the defendant with a list of prospective witnesses who have made statements, and some require the prosecution to endorse on the indictment the names of grand jury witnesses. This latter requirement provides less disclosure than one might think since an indictment can be secured on the testimony of only a few witnesses. A few jurisdictions require the prosecution to list the names of the witnesses it intends to call at trial.

The ABA Standards would require the prosecutor to disclose "the names and addresses of persons whom the prosecuting attorney intends to call as witnesses at the hearing or trial, together with their relevant written or recorded statements"; and "any record of prior criminal convictions of persons whom the prosecuting attorney intends to call as witnesses at the hearing or trial." (Original Standards 2.1 (a)(i) and (vi); Second Draft, Standards 11-2.1(a)(i) and (vi)). But amended Federal Rule of Criminal Procedure 16, as enacted by the Congress, requires no disclosure of the names of prospective witnesses. The Supreme Court had approved an amendment that would have provided such discovery, but it fell before the complaints of federal prosecutors.

Problem II–11. You are a member of the United States Congress called upon to review yet another proposed amendment to the Rules of Criminal Procedure:

If defense counsel can demonstrate bona fide efforts to interview prospective prosecution witnesses prior to trial, and a showing can be made that a witness has been uncooperative, the prosecutor must disclose pretrial statements of the uncooperative witness to defense counsel. If a prospective witness is cooperative, no disclosure is required.

Would you support this amendment?

---

b. Depositions

In view of the reluctance of legislatures and courts to mandate the disclosure of witnesses' statements and the refusal of some to mandate disclosure of identity,[51] it is not surprising that most jurisdictions do not permit the defense to take discovery depositions. However, depositions to preserve testimony are permitted and may be constitutionally based in the defendant's Sixth Amendment right to compulsory process to produce witnesses in his defense. Some commentators have suggested that pretrial depositions in criminal cases would not be unduly burdensome.[52] But consider the following problem.

---

51. See, e.g., Nakell, Criminal Discovery for the Defense and the Prosecution—The Developing Constitutional Considerations, 50 N.Car.L.Rev. 437, 473 (1972). But see Zagel & Carr, State Criminal Discovery and the New Illinois Rules, 1971 U.Ill.L. Forum 557, 590.

52. About 40 states now regulate discovery by court rule and/or legislation. Courts still may develop discovery rules on a case-by-case adjudicative basis in areas not covered by rules and statutes.

Problem II–12. Defendant is indicted for the offense of rape. The indictment indicates that the alleged victim was the only witness before the grand jury. **Should defense counsel be permitted to take the victim's deposition? Is it likely the defendant would want to take such a deposition? Do we want assistant prosecutors to have to spend their valuable time sitting in on deposition hearings? Could a statute provide that as a quid pro quo for deposing the prosecutor's witnesses the defendant must allow his witnesses to be deposed? Must allow himself to be deposed? How would a liberal system of allowing discovery depositions in criminal cases affect the cost of defending a criminal case? Where should the victim's deposition be taken? The defendant's? Witnesses'?**

The ABA Standards omit any provision authorizing depositions as a matter of right. Instead the trial judge is given authority to grant permission for depositions in particular cases. Fed.R.Crim.P. 15(a) provides:

Whenever due to exceptional circumstances of the case it is in the interest of justice that the testimony of a prospective witness of a party be taken and preserved for use at trial, the court may upon motion of such party and notice to the parties order that testimony of such witness be taken by deposition and that any designated book, paper, document, record, recording, or other material not privileged, be produced at the same time and place. If a witness is committed for failure to give bail to appear to testify at a trial or hearing, the court on written motion of the witness and upon notice to the parties may direct that his deposition be taken. After the deposition has been subscribed the court may discharge the witness.

This is a limited provision authorizing depositions to preserve testimony.

A few states have provided for discovery depositions, and there have been suggestions that they work well.[53]

c. Interrogatories

Currently no jurisdiction allows the defense to discover what the prosecutor knows about a case through written interrogatories. The closest approximation to this is a request for a bill of particulars, but such requests are generally denied when made for purposes of discovery.[54]

d. Physical and Scientific Evidence

In federal courts it has traditionally been easier for a defendant to obtain access to physical and scientific evidence than to witnesses' statements. In fact, defendants have for many years had a right to examine physical evidence and reports of scientific or expert witnesses. Most states bestow no absolute right to such discovery, leaving the trial judge with great discretion to grant or deny discovery. What reasons are there for allowing broader discovery of such evidence than of witnesses' statements? Might it violate due process to refuse to allow discovery of such evidence?

e. Grand Jury Testimony

In a jurisdiction in which a witness' prior statements are not disclosed prior to trial, it is obvious that grand jury testimony is

53. E.g., Langrock, Vermont's Experiment in Criminal Discovery, 53 A.B.A.J. 732 (1967).

54. Y. Kamisar, W. LaFave & J. Israel, Modern Criminal Procedure 1250 (4th ed. 1974).

not discoverable. It is somewhat surprising, however, that some jurisdictions that provide witnesses' statements generally do not provide grand jury testimony along with the statements. A few jurisdictions grant the defendant an opportunity to review a transcript of the grand jury proceedings shortly after an indictment is issued. Many jurisdictions include grand jury testimony as part of the material that is turned over to the defense in the state equivalent of the Jencks Act procedures, but some states require more of a showing for disclosure of this evidence than for other witness statements. Why should this be the case?

f. Preliminary Hearings

Preliminary hearings vary in scope and form throughout the country. We shall not attempt to examine these procedures in detail here. According to one respected authority, screening is the primary function of the preliminary hearing, and most courts do not recognize a discovery purpose.[55] In some jurisdictions prosecutors attempt to present as few witnesses as possible at a preliminary hearing and to rely on evidence, such as hearsay, which is easy to produce but likely to be inadmissible at trial.[56] In other states, a fairly complete case is presented.[57]

If the prosecutor presents a complete case at the preliminary hearing, the potential for discovery at the hearing is great.[58] Cross-examination will generally be permitted, and the hearing may serve as a

substitute for deposition procedures.[59] Even if the prosecutor presents a minimal amount of evidence and cross-examination is restricted, the defense learns something of the prosecutor's case. The type of preliminary hearing, the burden imposed on the prosecutor, the types of evidence accepted, and the attitude of the prosecutor will determine the amount of information conveyed to the defense.

Like depositions, the transcripts of preliminary hearings can be used at trial if witnesses are unavailable. In some jurisdictions, including the federal courts under FRE 801, the transcript is also admissible affirmatively when the witness' testimony at trial is inconsistent with the preliminary hearing evidence.[60] In all jurisdictions statements made at preliminary hearings can be used to impeach a witness' credibility.[61] Hence, the prosecutor may have conflicting incentives in deciding what kind of case to present at the preliminary hearing. He wishes to preserve evidence and, to the extent he will later be allowed to impeach his own witnesses, he wants a story favorable to the state's case in the record, but he doesn't want to preserve testimony which will later give defense counsel a means of impeachment and he may not want to alert defense counsel to certain information or witnesses he intends to use at trial. Recall the Whale case. Defense counsel was able to use Officer Norton's statements about supplying marihuana to informants as a means of impeaching Norton's later trial testimony.

55. Y. Kamisar, W. LaFave & J. Israel, Modern Criminal Procedure 963 (5th ed. 1980).

56. See F. Miller, Prosecution: The Decision to Charge a Suspect with a Crime (1969).

57. See Graham & Letwin, The Preliminary Hearing in Los Angeles: Some Field Findings and Legal-Policy Observations, 18 U.C.L.A. L.Rev. 635 (1971).

58. Most courts attempt to draw a line between cross-examination for purposes of discovery and cross-examination for purposes of attacking the case presented by the prosecutor, allowing only the latter. Some courts limit cross-examination once they find probable cause. Having made such a finding, they may bar defense witnesses from testifying.

59. Motions ostensibly directed toward other ends, such as motions to suppress evidence, may also serve as discovery devices.

60. This subject is discussed at length in Chapters Five and Six, infra.

61. The distinction between impeachment and substantive evidence is complex, and as the previous note indicates is discussed later.

Problem II–13. One of America's famous attorneys describes his approach to preliminary hearings as follows:

The author deems it good criminal law procedure, unless it fairly appears a defendant charged in a criminal case on preliminary hearing will not be held to answer, to expand the preliminary hearing into a searching deposition. Thus, when counsel for defendant charged with crime believes his client will be held to answer regardless of the testimony adduced, the committing magistrate not being held to the same quantum of proof that the triers of fact in the subsequent "main trial" must adhere to, he should force the prosecution to call all the witnesses, or call them himself. In this situation immediately above, when representing a criminal defendant, I use the complete process of the criminal court to call every witness upon whom the prosecution may likely depend for their [sic] case in chief in the higher court. Thus, even though the prosecution puts on only one witness to make out a prima facie case for a holding to the higher court in the lower court, I subpoena all the police officers, all of the defendant witnesses with all of their statements, and fully depose every witness "milking" the prosecution's case in a manner I would not be privileged to do by deposition.[62]

Are there dangers in this approach?

Problem II–14. As a state legislator, you are assigned the task of drafting new provisions for criminal discovery for a state that previously has had no discovery to speak of. Two schools of thought are popular among your fellow legislators. One favors a full-scale preliminary hearing where the defense can present witnesses and affirmative defenses. The other favors pretrial disclosure of witnesses' names and procedures to depose witnesses. **If the legislators view these alternatives as mutually exclusive, which would you prefer? If either approach is adopted, is there still a need for the disclosure of pretrial statements made by witnesses prior to trial?**

g. Expert Non-Legal Help

In 1964, Congress enacted the Federal Criminal Justice Act, which provided that

Counsel for a defendant who is financially unable to obtain investigative, expert, or other services necessary to an adequate defense in his case may request them. * * * [A]fter appropriate inquiry * * * the court shall authorize counsel to obtain the services on behalf of the defendant. * * * The compensation to be paid to a person for such services rendered by him to a defendant * * * shall not exceed $300, exclusive of reimbursement for expenses reasonably incurred.[63]

A 1970 amendment provided that more than $300 could be provided in exceptional circumstances, but that no more than $150 could be paid if no court authorization was sought prior to retention of the special services. One limitation in the statute is the language "necessary to an adequate

---

62. 1 M. Belli, Modern Trials § 16, at 82 (1954).

63. 18 U.S.C. § 3006A(e).

defense", which may not provide help in discovering whether a defense exists.[64] Several recent cases suggest that investi- gative aid may be constitutionally required under some circumstances.[65]

Problem II–15. As a member of Congress, you are asked once again to amend the statute on investigative aid to defendants. **Would you support a change that permitted investigators to take employment on a contingent fee basis—i.e., the court would pay them on the basis of the amount of useful information transmitted to the defendant? Would you prefer a change that required payment on a contingent fee basis?**

---

h. Work Product

ABA Standard 2.6(a) provides that work product is not subject to disclosure:

> Disclosure shall not be required of legal research or of records, correspondence, reports or memoranda to the extent that they contain the opinions, theories or conclusions of the prosecuting attorney or members of his legal staff.[66]

Federal Rule of Criminal Procedure 16(a)(2) provides that unless specifically required by another section of the rule, the prosecutor need not allow discovery of "reports, memoranda, or other internal government documents made by the attorney for the government or other government agents in connection with the investigation or prosecution of the case." Many states have similar provisions, and states that permit discovery of witness statements may exclude discovery of other information gathered by the prosecutor.[67] Note that the federal and many state standards exempt police investigatory reports as well as prosecutorial reports, whereas the ABA Standard is much more limited. The ABA recognizes the need of the defense to know about the product of investigatory efforts:

> The prosecutor and law enforcement agencies are an important source of information needed by the lawyer for the

---

64. See Note, The Indigent's Right to an Adequate Defense: Expert and Investigational Assistance in Criminal Proceedings, 55 Cornell L.Rev. 632 (1970). Most states give trial judges the discretion to grant or deny aid, although several have statutes similar to the federal statute.

65. See, e.g., Mason v. State of Arizona, 504 F.2d 1345 (9th Cir. 1974), affirming 360 F.Supp. 56 (D.Ariz. 1973); United States v. Dolack, 484 F.2d 528 (10th Cir. 1973).

66. Identical language is used in the 1978 Second Draft, Standard 11–2.6(a). Also not subject to disclosure are the following kinds of information which are discussed in Chapter Eight.

* * *

(b) Informants. Disclosure of an informant's identity shall not be required where his identity is a prosecution secret and a failure to disclose will not infringe the constitutional right of the accused. Disclosure shall not be denied hereunder of the identity of witnesses to be produced at a hearing or trial.

(c) National security. Disclosure shall not be required where it involves a substantial risk of grave prejudice to national security and a failure to disclose will not infringe the constitutional rights of the accused. Disclosure shall not thus be denied hereunder regarding witnesses or material to be produced at a hearing or trial.

These are identical also in Standard 11–2.6(b), (c) in the 1978 Second Draft.

67. See Y. Kamisar, W. LaFave & J. Israel, Modern Criminal Procedure 1166 (5th ed. 1980).

defense.   Apart from any formal processes of discovery which are available,
prosecutors and law enforcement officers
have in their possession facts which defense counsel must know.[68]

———

**Problem II–16.   Do the same reasons for work product protection
exist in criminal as in civil cases?   For whom do the police and the prosecutor work?   Once police have gathered information, what justification
is there for confining access to such information to the prosecution?
Would excision of certain specific categories of information by either the
prosecutor or trial judge provide the necessary protections?   If reports
of prosecutors and police were available, would they be helpful?   Consider the following police reports.   Is there anything that the defense
should not be allowed to see?   What aid might the defense get from examining these reports?**

68.   ABA Standards for Criminal Justice,
The Defense Function and the Prosecution
Function, Commentary to § 4.1, The Defense
Function (App. Draft 1971).

P.D. 251 Rev. 1/76

1. TYPE OF REPORT	METROPOLITAN POLICE DEPARTMENT WASHINGTON, D.C. EVENT REPORT	2. COMPLAINT NUMBER
☒ OFFENSE ☐ INCIDENT		597-456

3. EVENT CLASSIFICATION	4. EVENT LOCATION	5. BEAT	6. DIST	7. RA
ADW, Burg.	4950 Marin Ave.		2D	

8. DATE/TIME OF EVENT	9. DATE/TIME OF REPORT	10. RADIO RUN RECEIVED	11. ☐ PUBLIC PROPERTY ☒ PRIVATE PROPERTY
4/7/74 2050	4/7/74 2250	☐ NO ☒ YES TIME 2300	

12. DESCRIBE LOCATION	13. WHERE ENTERED	14. TOOLS, WEAPONS USED	15. METHOD
Apt.	Frt. Door	Gun	

16. COMPLAINANT/MISSING PERSON/FIRM	SEX/RACE/DOB	16. COMPLAINANT/MISSING PERSON	SEX/RACE/DOB
1. Sidney Green	M/W/7/5/33	2.	

Narrative: Complainant reports that at about 2050 hours on 4/7/74 the above suspect entered his apartment through an unlocked front door and drew a gun, which he used to frighten complainant into turning over almost $1000 in cash. Suspect was wearing a white bandanna covering his face and a blue jacket. Complainant did not get good look at suspect, as complainant was facing away from door when suspect entered and suspect stuck gun in back of complainants neck. Suspect locked complainant in closet and fled.

SAMPLE

METROPOLITAN POLICE DEPARTMENT WASH., D.C.	1. PROSECUTOR'S CHARGES	2. COMPLAINT NO. ▶ 597-456
PROSECUTION REPORT		3. I.D. NUMBER ▶ 285764
PD FORM 163 REVISED 3/70	Lem Saltz 6/4/74	4. ARREST NO. ▶ 477756
	Pros's. Name Date	

8. DEFENDANT'S TRUE NAME. *Last, First, Middle* ID ONLY		
Charles, Edgar John		5. T. T. NO.

9. DEFENDANT'S NAME *(Last, First, Middle)*	12. SEX	13. RACE	14. DATE OF BIRTH	
same	M	W	2/20/37	

10. ALIASES OR NICKNAME	15. CITY AND STATE OF BIRTH	6. CID NUMBER
Lefty	Phila. Pa.	

11. ADDRESS ZIP CODE	16. TIME IN THE DISTRICT OF COLUMBIA	7. SOC. SEC. NO.
▶ No.2, Constitution Ave	15 years	147-56-9004

17. ▶ CO-DEFENDANTS: NUMBER_____ IF MORE THAN 4 CO-DEFENDANTS, LIST NAME & ADDRESSES OF OTHERS IN STATEMENT OF FACTS SEC.	
18. NAME, ADDRESS AND ZIP CODE	NAME, ADDRESS AND ZIP CODE
1	2
3	4

19. POLICE CHARGE(S)
ADW, Burg.

20. LOCATION OF OFFENSE	DATE	TIME
▶ 4950 Marin Ave. Wash. D.C.	▶ 4/7/74	▶ 2050

21. LOCATION OF ARREST	DATE	TIME
No.2, Constitution Ave.	6/2/74	1250

22. ARRESTING OFFICER'S NAME, RANK, BADGE NO. & UNIT OR AGENCY	23. ASSISTING OFFICER'S NAME, RANK, BADGE NO. & UNIT OR AGENCY
▶ Rick Stepeh, Lt. 714 2D	▶ Norval Roger, Ptl. 54 2D

24. DEFENDANT ADVISED OF RIGHTS

DATE	TIME	LOCATION	ADVISING OFFICER'S NAME	RANK	BADGE NO.	UNIT

25. WITNESSES: FOR ADDITIONAL WITNESSES SEE STATEMENT OF FACTS SECTION

NAME *(Last, First & M.I.)*	ADDRESS	AGE	HOME PHONE	BUSINESS PHONE
1 ▶ Eric Harold		39	988-0654	
2 ▶ Murray Jones		23	786-9888	
3 ▶				
4 ▶				

26. ▶ PROPERTY STOLEN (✓ IF YES ☐) AND RECOVERED (✓ IF YES ☒) OR ITEMS OF EVIDENCE

	(a) IDENTIFICATION	*(b)* HOW, WHERE, WHEN RECOVERED	*(c)* FROM WHOM	*(d)* ✓ IF STOLEN
1	.45 Cal. Revolv.	Recovered at arrest	Defendant	
2	650 dollars	Recovered at arrest	Defendant	✓
3	White bandanna	Obt. in Search of House	Defendant's House	
4	Blue jacket	Obt. in Search of House	Defendant's House	

27. WORK HISTORY (INCLUDE PRESENT JOB, IF ANY ON LINE 1)

	FROM - DATES - TO	EMPLOYER	ADDRESS	BUS. PHONE	OCCUPATION
1	6/3/72-8/4/73	Pottager Apts.	4950 Marin Ave.	677-8992	Gardener
2					
3					

28. ARREST RECORD SUMMARY		29. M.O. (Weapons or instruments used, Hangouts and Habits)	30. RIGHT THUMB PRINT
1 disorderly 8/63	2 simple assault 8/73	Left-handed carries gun	
3 drunk 9/64	4 traffic 12/71		
5	6		

PAGE 1 TO I.D. - PAGE 2 & 3 TO PROSECUTOR:IF JUVENILE TO Y.D. - PAGE 4 OFFICER - PAGE 5 (YELLOW) DISTRICT COPY.

REVERSE CARBON AND FILL IN REVERSE SIDE OF THIS FORM

PAGE 1   **CHECK LAST COPY FOR LEGIBILITY BEFORE TURNING IN REPORT** [B3675]

REVERSE CARBON

31. FAMILY AND RELATIVES

RELATIONSHIP	AGE	NAME (Last, First & M.I.)	ADDRESS	ZIP CODE	PHONE NUMBER
Wife	36	Charles, Marie	465 Hopt St.		988-7632
Son	7	Charles, Edgar J. Jr.	465 Hopt St.		"

32. FRIENDS AND ASSOCIATES

NAME (Last, First & M.I.)	AGE	ADDRESS	ZIP CODE	PHONE NUMBER

33. ATTACHMENTS BROUGHT TO PROSECUTOR: (Check)

[ ] CONTINUATION REPORT	[x] LOCAL RECORD	
[x] ARREST REPORT	[ ] F B I RECORD	
[x] OFFENSE REPORT	[ ] STATEMENTS	
[ ] SUPPLEMENT REPORT	[ ] CERTIFICATE OF NO	
[ ] SEARCH WARRANT		
[ ] ARREST WARRANT	[ ] CITATION	

34. DRAFT STATUS: NO. & ADDRESS OF LOCAL DRAFT BOARD

35. SELECTIVE SERVICE NO. OR ARMED FORCES SERIAL NUMBER

36. MILITARY EXPERIENCE: BRANCH OF SERVICE & DATES FROM - TO

37. DATE OF INDUCTION   **38. DATE TYPE OF DISCHARGE**

39. STATEMENT OF FACTS Give a brief statement in your own words, of the facts surrounding the offence and the arrest. Indicate oral or written statements made by the defendant(s). Use Continuation Form PD-XXX for additional space. Note present condition of any injured person(s).   TELEPHONE CALL MADE   [ ] YES   [ ] NO

40. FOR PROSECUTORS USE

Defendant was arrested by two officerson 6/2/74 at 1250 hours at his home. He was taken to the stationhouse where he confessed to the crimes for which he was arrested. Shortly thereafter a search of his premises produced a bandanna and a jacket similar to those described by the complainant.

Complainant, Sidney Green, 35 years old, white male, 4950 Marin Ave., reports on 4/7/74, while in his apartment and talking on the phone, a white subject entered the apartment through an unlocked doer. The subject produced a small handgun, made Green hang up the phone, and took approx. 900 dollars cash from the apartment. Subject locked green in closet and fled. Subject was wearing a white bandanna over the lower part of his face and a blue jacket. Green was unable to identify subject. On 4/9/74 Green was shown a photo sample and was unable to identify a suspect. The exact same photos were shown Green the next day and he identified defendant.

41. FINAL DISPOSITION

42. SIG. OF OFFICER MAKING STATEMENT	BADGE	RANK	UNIT	DATE	43. SIGNATURE OF REVIEWING OFFICIAL	DATE

PAGE 1   [B3676]

i. Constitutional Duty to Disclose

Several Supreme Court decisions require the prosecutor to disclose favorable evidence to an accused [69] and to correct trial information known to be false.[70] One court described the prosecutor's duty in the following way:

> The duty of the prosecutor is a broad one and its extent is acknowledged by the government, but the prosecutor properly points out that the law does not require the immediate production of all exculpatory material, nor does it permit the defense to engage in a fishing expedition through all of the government's files. It seems true, * * * that if disclosure of some types of exculpatory evidence were delayed until trial it would not be early enough to enable defendants to make effective use of it, and in this situation it is likely that the late disclosure would violate due process. * * * It is also true that defendants cannot be expected to be specific in advance in asking for exculpatory evidence that might not be known to them. On the other hand, the government cannot be held to strict accountability in advance for each bit of possible exculpatory evidence in its files, some of which might only become of an exculpatory nature after defendants have revealed their defense. The need for full disclosure to insure fairness to the defendants and that due process is observed must be weighed against an insuperable burden on the prosecution in advance of trial. At least, exculpatory information having a material bearing on defense *preparation* should be disclosed well in advance of trial, * * * especially if such information is not Jencks Act material.[71]

Is this satisfactory?

Consider this comment by Jon O. Newman, United States Attorney for Connecticut (now Circuit Judge), delivered in a panel discussion before the Judicial Conference of the Second Judicial Circuit on September 8, 1967:

> I recently had occasion to discuss this problem at a PLI Conference in New York City before a large group of State prosecutors—some of them were very inexperienced—but some of them had considerable experience. I put to them this case: You are prosecuting a bank robbery. You have talked to two or three of the tellers and one or two of the customers at the time of the robbery. They have all taken a look at your defendant in a line-up, and they have said, "This is the man." In the course of your investigation you also have found another customer who was in the bank that day, who viewed the suspect, and came back and said, "That is *not* the man."
>
> The question I put to these prosecutors was, do you believe you should disclose to the defense the name of the witness who, when he viewed the suspect, said "that is not the man"? In a room of prosecutors not quite as large as this group but almost as large, only two hands went up. There were only two prosecutors in that group who felt they should disclose or would disclose that information. Yet I was putting to them what I thought was the easiest case—the clearest case for disclosure of exculpatory information! Indeed, there is a decision of this very Circuit that reverses a State conviction for the failure to disclose just that information. So I dare say I can conclude from that that

---

69. Brady v. State of Maryland, 373 U.S. 83 (1963); Giles v. State of Maryland, 386 U.S. 66 (1967) (opinion of Fortas, J.); Giglio v. United States, 405 U.S. 150 (1972). But see Moore v. Illinois, 408 U.S. 786 (1972).

70. Mooney v. Holohan, 294 U.S. 103 (1935); Napue v. People of State of Illinois, 360 U.S. 264 (1959); Giles v. Maryland, 386 U.S. 66 (1967) (plurality opinion).

71. United States v. Ahmad, 53 F.R.D. 186, 194, 195 (M.D.Pa.1971).

the obligation to disclose favorable evidence is not one fully appreciated by all prosecutors.[72]

While this may not be descriptive of all prosecutors' offices, it does raise the question of whether the prosecutor *can* be sensitive to the needs of the defense.

In Alderman v. United States [73] the Court held that defendants who are victims of illegal electronic surveillance must be given an opportunity to examine transcripts of their own conversations and those that took place on their premises. The Court thought *in camera* review by the trial judge was unsatisfactory. Its opinion suggests that only adversary procedures, and not interested prosecutors and busy judges, are capable of providing the scrutiny that the Fourth Amendment requires.[74]

There also is some question whether the prosecutor has an adequate incentive to bring forth all exculpatory evidence. In United States v. Agurs, 427 U.S. 97 (1976), the Supreme Court discussed the standards to be used in measuring prosecutors' conduct.

"In Brady the request was specific. It gave the prosecutor notice of exactly what the defense desired. Although there is, of course, no duty to provide defense counsel with unlimited discovery of everything known by the prosecutor, if the subject matter of such a request is material, or indeed if a substantial basis for claiming materiality exists, it is reasonable to require the prosecutor to respond either by furnishing the information or by submitting the problem to the trial judge. When the prosecutor receives a specific and rele-

vant request, the failure to make any response is seldom, if ever, excusable.

"In many cases, however, exculpatory information in the possession of the prosecutor may be unknown to defense counsel. In such a situation he may make no request at all, or possibly ask for 'all Brady material' or for 'anything exculpatory.' Such a request really gives the prosecutor no better notice than if no request is made. If there is a duty to respond to a general request of that kind, it must derive from the obviously exculpatory character of certain evidence in the hands of the prosecutor. But if the evidence is so clearly supportive of a claim of innocence that it gives the prosecution notice of a duty to produce, that duty should equally arise even if no request is made. Whether we focus on the desirability of a precise definition of the prosecutor's duty or on the potential harm to the defendant, we conclude that there is no significant difference between cases in which there has been merely a general request for exculpatory matter and cases * * * in which there has been no request at all. * * *

"We now consider whether the prosecutor has any constitutional duty to volunteer exculpatory matter to the defense, and if so, what standard of materiality gives rise to that duty.

* * *

"The problem arises in two principal contexts. First, in advance of trial, and perhaps during the course of a trial as well, the prosecutor must decide what,

---

72. Discovery in Criminal Cases, 44 F.R.D. 481, 500–01 (1968).

73. 394 U.S. 165 (1969).

74. In the dispute between President Nixon and the grand jury investigating the events surrounding the Watergate burglary and its coverup, the courts required the President to turn over certain tapes of White House conversations to the grand jury. Counsel for the President argued that if the tapes were ultimately turned over to the grand jury, all persons charged with criminal offenses arguably related to conversations on the tapes had a right to see them. Given what you know about criminal discovery is such access likely to be given?

if anything, he should voluntarily submit to defense counsel. Second, after trial a judge may be required to decide whether a nondisclosure deprived the defendant of his right to due process. Logically the same standard must apply at both times. For unless the omission deprived the defendant of a fair trial, there was no constitutional violation requiring that the verdict be set aside; and absent a constitutional violation, there was no breach of the prosecutor's constitutional duty to disclose.

"Nevertheless, there is a significant practical difference between the pretrial decision of the prosecutor and the post-trial decision of the judge. Because we are dealing with an inevitably imprecise standard, and because the significance of an item of evidence can seldom be predicted accurately until the entire record is complete, the prudent prosecutor will resolve doubtful questions in favor of disclosure. But to reiterate a critical point, the prosecutor will not have violated his constitutional duty of disclosure unless his omission is of sufficient significance to result in the denial of the defendant's right to a fair trial.

"The Court of Appeals appears to have assumed that the prosecutor has a constitutional obligation to disclose any information that might affect the jury's verdict. That statement of a constitutional standard of materiality approaches the 'sporting theory of justice' which the Court expressly rejected in Brady. For a jury's appraisal of a case 'might' be affected by an improper or trivial consideration as well as by evidence giving rise to a legitimate doubt on the issue of guilt. If everything that might influence a jury must be disclosed, the only way a prosecutor could discharge his constitutional duty would be to allow complete discovery of his files as a matter of routine practice.

"Whether or not procedural rules authorizing such broad discovery might be desirable, the Constitution surely does not demand that much. * * * The mere possibility that an item of undisclosed information might have helped the defense, or might have affected the outcome of the trial, does not establish 'materiality' in the constitutional sense.

"Nor do we believe the constitutional obligation is measured by the moral culpability, or the willfulness, of the prosecutor. If evidence highly probative of innocence is in his file, he should be presumed to recognize its significance even if he has actually overlooked it. Conversely, if evidence actually has no probative significance at all, no purpose would be served by requiring a new trial simply because an inept prosecutor incorrectly believed he was suppressing a fact that would be vital to the defense. If the suppression of evidence results in constitutional error, it is because of the character of the evidence, not the character of the prosecutor.

* * *

"On the one hand, the fact that such evidence was available to the prosecutor and not submitted to the defense places it in a different category than if it had simply been discovered from a neutral source after trial. For that reason the defendant should not have to satisfy the severe burden of demonstrating that newly discovered evidence probably would have resulted in acquittal. If the standard applied to the usual motion for a new trial based on newly discovered evidence were the same when the evidence was in the State's possession as when it was found in a neutral source, there would be no special significance to the prosecutor's obligation to serve the cause of justice.

"On the other hand, since we have rejected the suggestion that the prosecutor has a constitutional duty routinely to deliver his entire file to defense counsel, we cannot consistently treat every nondisclosure as though it were error. It necessarily follows that the judge should not order a new trial every time he is unable to characterize a nondisclosure as harmless under the customary harmless-error standard. Under that standard when error is present in the record, the reviewing judge must set aside the verdict and judgment unless his 'conviction is sure that the error did not influence the jury, or had but very slight effect.' Kotteakos v. United States, 328 U.S. 750. Unless every nondisclosure is regarded as automatic error, the constitutional standard of materiality must impose a higher burden on the defendant.

"The proper standard of materiality must reflect our overriding concern with the justice of the finding of guilt. Such a finding is permissible only if supported by evidence establishing guilt beyond a reasonable doubt. It necessarily follows that if the omitted evidence creates a reasonable doubt that did not otherwise exist, constitutional error has been committed. This means that the omission must be evaluated in the context of the entire record. If there is no reasonable doubt about guilt whether or not the additional evidence is considered, there is no justification for a new trial. On the other hand, if the verdict is already of questionable validity, additional evidence of relatively minor importance might be sufficient to create a reasonable doubt."

————

Do you find this to be a satisfactory test?

One subject that is only beginning to receive attention is whether the prosecutor may have a duty to assist the defense in obtaining possibly exculpatory information. Should the prosecutor, for example, be required to join the defense in requesting immunity for a defense witness who is reluctant to testify because of self-incrimination problems?[75]

3. DISCOVERY BY THE PROSECUTION

Many of the prosecutor's discovery devices are virtually unregulated by rule or statute. The prosecutor's ability to utilize grand juries, to expand the scope of preliminary hearings, to obtain search warrants, to bargain for discovery with potential defendants, to utilize the police, and to call upon the public for assistance in preserving law and order provide many avenues for discovery. The most important limits on the prosecutor's ability to gather information are the defendant's Fifth Amendment right to refuse to answer all questions and the ability of the defendant and defense counsel to keep their trial plans and any information they have gathered secret. But as support for defense discovery grows, arguments for formal

75. Most courts have been reluctant to attempt to force prosecutors to seek immunity for defense witnesses. See, e.g., United States v. Turkish, 623 F.2d 769 (2d Cir. 1980), certiorari denied, 449 U.S. 1077 (1981). But see Government of Virgin Islands v. Smith, 615 F.2d 964 (3d Cir. 1980). See also, Code of Virginia § 19.1–267:

In a criminal prosecution, other than for perjury, or in an action on a penal statute, evidence shall not be given against the accused of any statement made by him as a witness upon a legal examination, unless such statement was made when examined as a witness in his own behalf.

This is discussed at greater length in Chapter Seven, infra.

prosecutorial discovery are made. These arguments, which typically rest on the ground of mutuality, are winning in much the same way as the arguments for defense discovery.

In Williams v. Florida, 399 U.S. 78 (1970), the Supreme Court upheld the constitutionality of Florida's notice of alibi rule which required criminal defendants intending to rely on an alibi defense to notify the prosecution of the place where they claimed to be during the time in question and of the names and addresses of witnesses they intended to call in support of the alibi. But in Wardius v. Oregon, 412 U.S. 470 (1973), the Court struck down a notice of alibi provision that was not reciprocal—i.e., that did not require the prosecution to disclose in advance its rebuttal evidence. The Court said:

> Notice of alibi rules, now in use in a large and growing number of States, are based on the proposition that the ends of justice will best be served by a system of liberal discovery which gives both parties the maximum possible amount of information with which to prepare their cases and thereby reduces the possibility of surprise at trial. * * * The growth of such discovery devices is a salutary development which, by increasing the evidence available to both parties, enhances the fairness of the adversary system. * * *
>
> * * *.

We do not suggest that the Due Process Clause of its own force requires Oregon to adopt such [discovery] provisions. * * * But we do hold that in the absence of any strong showing of state interests to the contrary, discovery must be a two-way street. The State may not insist that trials be run as a "search for truth" so far as defense witnesses are concerned, while maintaining "poker game" secrecy for its own witnesses. * * *

There is an important footnote in the Court's opinion—footnote number 9. The first sentence states the thrust: "Indeed, the State's inherent information-gathering advantages suggest that if there is to be any imbalance in discovery rights, it should work in the defendant's favor."

Unlike a prosecutor, a defendant ordinarily cannot be compelled to disclose evidence that is unfavorable to his case. The privilege against self-incrimination protects against such disclosure. Hence, most statutes providing for prosecutorial discovery require only discovery of evidence or claims that a defendant plans to introduce or make at trial. Federal Rules of Criminal Procedure 12.1 and 16 are examples. A defendant is required to disclose in advance certain defenses that will be made at trial, and, upon request by the government following a defense discovery request, names of witnesses to be called at trial and reports or documents to be offered at trial.[76]

Problem II–17. Defendant is required by statute to provide notice in advance of trial of an alibi defense and to list the witnesses expected to be called to prove the defense. **If there is a possibility that the witnesses might provide evidence that would help the prosecutor's case-in-chief, should discovery be barred?**

76. In jurisdictions like Florida and New York, the defense can obtain the names of prosecution witnesses in exchange for the names of defense witnesses. Are such provisions valid when they go beyond affirmative defenses like alibi or insanity?

How can witnesses be protected by the prosecutor under such a system?

Left open in the *Williams* opinion was the question of the validity of the threatened sanction, refusal to permit a defense or to permit undisclosed witnesses to testify. The issue remains open after *Wardius,* where the Court did not have occasion to reach the issue since the state procedure was declared invalid on another ground.

Fed.R.Crim.P. 16 has traditionally provided that pre-trial discovery by the prosecutor is reciprocal only—i.e., the prosecutor can obtain discovery only after the defendant does. Proposed amendments by the Supreme Court would have given the prosecutor an independent right of discovery but Congress adhered to the reciprocity limitation.[77] Is a system of reciprocal discovery that provides the defendant with the sole opportunity to make the first move preferable to a system in which both sides are given specified discovery rights?

The trend toward increasing the prosecutor's access to defense information is also seen in a more recent Supreme Court decision, United States v. Nobles, 422 U.S. 225 (1975). In this case, the trial court, in effect, applied Jencks Act procedures to an investigator's statements in the hands of the defense.

Nobles had allegedly robbed a federally insured bank. The most significant evidence linking him to the crime was the identification testimony of a bank teller and a bank customer. Prior to trial both witnesses had been interviewed by a defense investigator who had taken notes of the interviews. On cross-examination by defense counsel, the teller denied telling the investigator that he only saw the back of the robber's head.[78] The customer on cross-examination denied stating twice that "all blacks looked alike" to him.[79] The defense, as part of its case, sought to have the investigator testify that the witnesses made these statements, whereupon the judge ordered the defense to produce the investigator's report, so that it might, after irrelevant portions had been edited out, be turned over to the prosecutor.

Citing, *inter alia,* United States v. Nixon, 418 U.S. 683 (1974), discussed in Chapter Eight, infra, the Supreme Court affirmed the trial court's action since "[t]he very integrity of the judicial system and public confidence in the system depend on full disclosure of all the facts, within the framework of the rules of evidence.[80] To

---

77. Rule 16(b)(1)(A):

   DOCUMENTS AND TANGIBLE OBJECTS.—If the defendant requests disclosure under * * * this rule, upon compliance with such request by the government, the defendant, on request of the government, shall permit the government to inspect and copy or photograph books, papers, documents, photographs, tangible objects, or copies or portions thereof, which are within the possession, custody, or control of the defendant and which the defendant intends to introduce as evidence in chief at the trial.

   Rule 16(b)(1)(B):

   REPORTS OF EXAMINATIONS AND TESTS.—If the defendant requests disclosure under * * * this rule, upon compliance with such request by the government, the defendant, on request of the government shall permit the government to inspect and copy or photograph any results or reports of physical or mental examinations and of scientific tests or experiments made in connection with the particular case, or copies thereof, within the possession or control of the defendant, which the defendant intends to introduce as evidence in chief at the trial or which were prepared by a witness whom the defendant intends to call at the trial when the results or reports relate to his testimony.

78. The prosecutor was shown the relevant portion of the investigative report but could not read the handwriting although the witness who was shown part of the statement had no apparent difficulty in this respect.

79. No access was permitted to the portion of the report relating to this statement during cross-examination of the customer.

80. Why is this the proper framework for discovery? Isn't this inconsistent with Fed.R.Civ.P. 26 and Fed.R.Crim.P. 16?

ensure that justice is done, it is imperative to the function of courts that compulsory process be available for the production of evidence needed *either by the prosecution or*[81] by the defense."[82]

The Court dismissed the defendant's Fifth Amendment claims on the ground that the report in question consisted of an investigator's statements and not the defendant's.[83]   The Court also held that Rule 16 of the Federal Rules of Criminal Procedure applied only to pretrial discovery and did not limit discovery once a trial began.   Finally, the Court held that although the work product doctrine "applies to criminal litigation as well as civil," it offered no protection to Nobles because "the defense waived such right as may have existed" by seeking "to adduce the testimony of the investigator and contrast his recollection of the contested statements with that of the prosecution's witnesses."[84]

When the defense refused to turn over the investigator's report, the district court refused to allow him to testify to the statements in question.   The Supreme Court upheld this sanction.   Does it follow that the court will uphold Florida's sanction in *Williams* for failure to give notice of an alibi?

Justice White, joined by Justice Rehnquist, took a slightly different approach to the question of work product privilege. He wrote: "I don't believe the work product doctrine of Hickman v. Taylor   *   *   *

can be extended wholesale from its historic role as a limitation on the nonevidentiary material which may be the subject of pretrial discovery to an unprecedented role as a limitation on the trial judge's power to compel production of evidentiary matter at trial."

Justice White concluded that Fed.R.Civ.P. 26 and Fed.R.Crim.P. 16 are confined to pretrial discovery, as is the general notion of work product.   He reasoned as follows:

> First of all, the injury to the fact finding process is far greater where a rule keeps evidence from the factfinder than when it simply keeps advance disclosure of evidence from a party or keeps from him *leads* to evidence developed by his adversary and which he is just as well able to find by himself.   *   *   *   [T]he danger   *   *   *   that each party to a case will decline to prepare in the hopes of eventually using his adversary's preparation is absent when disclosure will take place at trial.   Indeed, it is very difficult to articulate a reason why statements on the same subject matter as a witness' testimony should not be turned over to an adversary after the witness has testified.

Justice White added that he would be much less sympathetic to attempts by one side to call an attorney for the other side to testify about oral statements of a witness made prior to trial, but he did not find it necessary to fully address this problem.

Following the lead of *Nobles*, the Court approved Fed.R.Crim.P.26.2, and it became effective December 1, 1980.   It read as follows:

Rule 26.2.   Production of statements of witnesses

(a) **Motion for production.**—After a witness other than the defendant has testified on direct examination, the court, on motion of a party

---

81.   Is this necessarily an either-or proposition?   See Westen, The Compulsory Process Clause, 73 Mich.L.Rev. 71, 123–127 (1975).

82.   418 U.S. at 709 (emphasis added).

83.   Justice Powell's majority opinion was fully concurred in by five other Justices.

Justices White and Rehnquist disagreed with the discussion of work product.   Justice Douglas did not participate.

84.   **It is interesting that the Court took pains to note in its footnote 14 that most non-testimonial uses of work product would not constitute waiver.   Thus, asking ques-**

who did not call the witness, shall order the attorney for the government or the defendant and his attorney, as the case may be, to produce, for the examination and use of the moving party, any statement of the witness that is in their possession and that relates to the subject matter concerning which the witness has testified.

(b) **Production of entire statement.**—If the entire contents of the statement relate to the subject matter concerning which the witness has testified, the court shall order that the statement be delivered to the moving party.

(c) **Production of excised statement.**—If the other party claims that the statement contains matter that does not relate to the subject matter concerning which the witness has testified, the court shall order that it be delivered to the court in camera. Upon inspection, the court shall excise the portions of the statement that do not relate to the subject matter concerning which the witness has testified, and shall order that the statement, with such material excised, be delivered to the moving party. Any portion of the statement that is withheld from the defendant over his objection shall be preserved by the attorney for the government, and, in the event of a conviction and an appeal by the defendant, shall be made available to the appellate court for the purpose of determining the correctness of the decision to excise the portion of the statement.

(d) **Recess for examination of statement.**—Upon delivery of the statement to the moving party, the court, upon application of that party, may recess proceedings in the trial for the examination of such statement and for preparation for its use in the trial.

(e) **Sanction for failure to produce statement.**—If the other party elects not to comply with an order to deliver a statement to the moving party, the court shall order that the testimony of the witness be stricken from the record and that the trial proceed, or, if it is the attorney for the government who elects not to comply, shall declare a mistrial if required by the interest of justice.

(f) **Definition.**—As used in this rule a "statement" of a witness means:

(1) a written statement made by the witness that is signed or otherwise adopted or approved by him;

(2) a substantially verbatim recital of an oral statement made by the witness that is recorded contemporaneously with the making of the oral statement and that is contained in a stenographic, mechanical, electrical, or other recording or a transcription thereof; or

(3) a statement, however taken or recorded, or a transcription thereof, made by the witness to a grand jury.

Does this rule go far enough? Too far?

tions on cross-examination based on an investigative report would probably not amount to waiver. Does this make sense? The Court also noted there was no Sixth Amendment violation since any invasion of the defense's theories was prompted by the "testimonial use" of the report.

Problem II–18.   Assume the same facts exist as in United States v. Nobles, supra, except the investigator is never called to testify.   **Should the prosecutor still have access to the investigative report?   Is there access under the new federal rule?   If not, why not?   Is access to the report necessary to the fair assessment of the prosecution witnesses' testimony once cross-examination suggests inconsistencies?   Does your answer depend on the questions which are asked on cross-examination?**

Problem II–19.   Note that the work product rule is not an absolute privilege.   If evidence gathered by one party is clearly unavailable to the other, the work product doctrine will not necessarily bar production in a civil case.   **What would happen in a criminal case if the evidence gathered by the defense investigator was positively incriminating?**   Suppose the investigator had reached a witness before the police and had taken a statement positively identifying Nobles as the robber.   **If the statement was given shortly before the witness died and was admissible under an exception to the hearsay rule, would the prosecution be able to discover and introduce it at trial under the new rule?**   At this point you may want to rethink Problem II–10.

Problem II–20.   Powell is appointed by a state trial court to represent Jarv in a criminal case.   Jarv is charged with robbing a convenience store and with unlawful possession of a firearm.   Knowing he will receive a maximum of $100 compensation, Powell talks with Sharp, the store clerk and only eyewitness.   Powell makes an accurate written record of everything Sharp has to say.   Trial is delayed a year and a half due to the illness of Jarv.   At trial Sharp has difficulty recalling details of the crime.   The prosecution is worried because of Sharp's problems on the stand and defense evidence that Sharp is reputed to be a liar.   At a recess Sharp tells the prosecutor that defense counsel has a written record of a statement made by Sharp shortly after Jarv's arrest.   Sharp and the prosecutor believe the statement will bolster Sharp's testimony.   The prosecutor demands its production.   **Should the Court accede to the demand?   In answering this question, is it important that Powell is appointed, not retained by Jarv?   Is it important that Powell made the record, or would your answer be the same if Sharp gave a written statement in his own hand?   Is there any force to a contention by Powell that the posture of the case required that he seek a statement and that it is unfair to use the statement against the defense?   Do you agree with Justice White that discovery of evidence is more important than discovery of leads?**

Problem II–21.   Powell is appointed to represent two co-defendants, Cary and Fisher, who are charged with robbing a federally insured bank. Since both claim to have been somewhere else together at the time of the robbery, Powell believes he can ethically represent both.[85]   In discussions with Cary and Fisher, Powell learns the two were at the bank at the time of the robbery, although they profess their innocence of the charge.   Fisher decides to plead guilty, a decision that Powell views as requiring a new law-

---

85.   See ABA Standards for Criminal Justice, The Prosecution Function and the Defense Function, Standard 3.5, The Defense Function (App. Draft 1971).

yer for him.[86]   Counsel is appointed separately for Fisher, and Powell continues to represent Cary.   At trial, Cary takes the stand to testify and relates an alibi.   On cross-examination he is asked whether he admitted his presence in the bank to Fisher.   Cary's denial causes the prosecutor to call Fisher to testify about statements made in Powell's office when Cary and Fisher were both represented by Powell.   **Cary objects, but the prosecutor relies on United States v. Nobles and Rule 26.2.   Does Nobles mean that Fisher's testimony must be allowed?   Does the rule require that it be allowed?**

BIBLIOGRAPHY

ABA Standards—Discovery and Procedure Before Trial (App. Draft 1970; Second Draft, 1978).

Bodin, Marshalling the Evidence (1946).

Glaser, Pretrial Discovery and the Adversary System (1968).

Stryker, The Art of Advocacy (1957).

Wright & Miller, Federal Practice and Procedure §§ 2001–2300.

Brennan, The Criminal Prosecution: Sporting Event or Quest for Truth, 1963 Wash.U.L.Q. 279 (1963).

Developments in the Law—Discovery, 74 Harv.L.Rev. 940 (1961).

Flannery, The Prosecutor's Case Against Liberal Discovery, 33 F.R.D. 74 (1963).

Fletcher, Pretrial Discovery in State Criminal Cases, 12 Stan.L.Rev. 293 (1960).

Goldstein, The State and the Accused: Balance of Advantage in Criminal Procedure, 69 Yale L.J. 1149 (1960).

Kaufman, Discovery in Criminal Cases, 44 F.R.D. 481 (1968).

Louisell, Criminal Discovery: Dilemma Real or Apparent?, 49 Cal.L.Rev. 56 (1961).

Nakell, Criminal Discovery for the Defense and Prosecution, 50 N.Car.L.Rev. 437 (1972).

Newman, Discovery in Criminal Cases, 44 F.R.D. 481 (1968).

Nizer, The Art of Jury Trial, 32 Cornell L.Rev. 39 (1946).

Pye, The Defendant's Case for More Liberal Discovery, 33 F.R.D. 82 (1963).

Tolman, Discovery Under the Federal Rules: Production of Documents and the Work Product of the Lawyer, 58 Colum.L.Rev. 498 (1958).

86.   Id.

Chapter Three

RELEVANCE

SECTION I.   BASIC PRINCIPLES

A.   PERSPECTIVES ON THE TRIAL

One may conceive of a trial in a variety of ways. It may be seen as a battle between two "champions", the less bloody descendant of a medieval method of resolving disputes. From this perspective there is an aesthetic element in watching lawyers joust, and involvement when the battle pits "our side" against "theirs" may rise to a fever pitch. Our discussion of discovery in Chapter Two suggests the extent to which this conception has fallen into official disrepute and some areas in which it still retains life. So long as lawyers remain dependent on clients for their livelihood and so long as clients prefer decisions in their favor to abstractly fair decisions, it is unlikely that the modern trial will ever shed entirely its ancestral trappings. From another perspective the trial may be seen as an elaborate ritual designed to reconcile losing litigants to their fate. The attorney's role here is to convince the client that the undesirable outcome was inevitable. From this perspective it is the *appearance* of fairness which is essential and attorneys are well-advised to collect their fees in advance. But only cynical sociologists and losers take this view.[1] A third perspective sees the trial as a mode of dispute settlement. This perspective holds that ultimately it is more important that a dispute be resolved than that it be resolved correctly. This view justifies limited rights of collateral and direct appeal, rules of res judicata and statutes of limitations. Finally, a trial may be seen as a way of finding the truth, a way of correctly resolving a dispute. Procedures for discovery and penalties for perjury respond to concerns of this kind.

B.   RELEVANCE: THE BASIC POLICY

Now these perspectives on the trial are not mutually exclusive; the litigation process reflects elements of all of them. But in modern evidence law the "truth-finding" model dominates. Generally speaking, rules of evidence are to be judged by whether or not they increase the chance that the jury will reach a correct verdict.[2] The law is too practical to concern itself with the nice epistemological question of whether the truth can ever be known. It assumes that it can, and it assumes that the way to find truth is to present the jury, except when there is *good reason* to do otherwise, with the entire body of evidence which bears on the issue to be decided. This basic policy permeates the law of evidence. As we saw when we dis-

1. Cf., Goffman, On Cooling the Mark Out, 15 Psychiatry 451 (1952); and Blumberg, The Practice of Law as a Confidence Game, 1 L. & Soc. Rev. 15 (1967).

2. **The law, including evidence law, may and does respond to other values; but where these values conflict with truth-finding there is sure to be strain and it is likely that at least some individuals will make the case that the value of truth-finding should predominate. The controversy surrounding the Fourth Amendment exclusionary rule, especially as applied to the states in Mapp v. Ohio, 367 U.S. 643 (1961), provides a good example of both these points. The discussion of privileges in Chapter Eight of these materials provides other examples of policies which override truth-finding.**

cussed competency in the first chapter, and as we shall see in our discussion of other rules, the tendency over the past century has been to increase the range of evidence available to the jury.[3]

This basic policy is expressed in Federal Rules 402 and 403.[4]

[Rule 402]　All relevant evidence is admissible, except as otherwise provided by the Constitution of the United States, by Act of Congress, by these rules, or by other rules prescribed by the Supreme Court pursuant to statutory authority.　Evidence which is not relevant is not admissible.

[Rule 403]　Although relevant, evidence may be excluded if its probative value is substantially outweighed by the danger of unfair prejudice, confusion of the issues, or misleading the jury, or by considerations of undue delay, waste of time, or needless presentation of cumulative evidence.

But what evidence is relevant?　FRE 401 provides an acceptable definition: *"Relevant evidence" means evidence having any tendency to make the existence of any fact that is of consequence to the determination of the action more probable or less probable than it would be without the evidence.*

C. MATERIALITY

Let us take this definition apart.　First, evidence may bear on a fact that is of no consequence to the litigation in question because the fact does not relate to any matter in issue.　Where this is the case the evidence is referred to technically as *immaterial* regardless of how probative the evidence is of the fact on which it bears. Immateriality is one kind of irrelevance. Where defendant, the owner of a truck, is being sued under the doctrine of *respondeat superior,* evidence that he is a careful driver is immaterial because it is the care of the truck driver which is in issue not the care of the owner.　Where a seaman is suing a shipowner for maintenance and cure, evidence that the seaman's injury was caused by his own negligence is immaterial.　The owner has a duty to provide maintenance and cure whether or not the injury was caused by the victim's negligence.

The term "materiality" is usually reserved for the relationship between the evidence offered and those legal issues which are raised by the pleadings in the case, but evidence may be material in the sense that it is properly of consequence to the litigation in question even where it does not bear directly on purely legal issues. Evidence affecting the credibility of any witness or the value of any item of demonstrative or real evidence is always material.　This includes basic information about the identity of witnesses, their age,

3.　The history of privileges is somewhat anomalous, but generally speaking the tendency holds in this area as well.　The matter will be discussed more fully in Chapter Eight.

4.　**These rules are in an intellectual tradition which may be traced back to Thayer, who wrote:**

There is a principle—not so much a rule of evidence as a presupposition involved in the very conception of a rational system of evidence, as contrasted with the old formal and mechanical systems—which forbids receiving anything irrelevant, not logically probative.

J. Thayer, Preliminary Treatise on Evidence 264 (1898).

The two leading principles should be brought into conspicuous relief, (1) that nothing is to be received which is not logically probative of some matter requiring (sic) to be proved; and (2) that everything which is thus probative should come in, unless a clear ground of policy or law excludes it.　[Id. at 530.]

Thayer's view on this matter has been generally accepted by the courts and by scholars dealing with evidence problems.

occupation, place of residence and so forth. Information which aids in the understanding of other material evidence is also considered material. Thus, maps, diagrams and graphs are not irrelevant even if there is no dispute about what they portray.

At one time, when pleadings were strictly construed and only limited amendment allowed, a lawyer might find that evidence which seemed highly probative of the general matter in question was excluded as immaterial due to improvidently drafted pleadings. Under liberalized modern rules

of procedure, this difficulty has almost disappeared. As the art of pleading has diminished in importance so has the importance of nice distinctions between materiality and relevance. Today the concept of materiality is treated generally as we treat it, as a subcategory of relevance. The term itself is not mentioned in the federal rules and may eventually linger only as part of the ritualistic objection "incompetent, immaterial, and irrelevant" used by some lawyers to touch the maximum number of bases with the least amount of thought.[5]

D. THE LOGICAL SENSE: CIRCUMSTANTIAL AND DIRECT EVIDENCE

Evidence which is offered for its bearing on a fact of consequence to the determination of the action is irrelevant if, after receipt of the evidence, the existence of that fact appears no more or less probable than it did before the evidence was offered. Thus evidence that a driver involved in an Oklahoma accident was a fanatical supporter of the University of Texas football team would be irrelevant on the issue of whether that driver was speeding because there is no reason to believe that "Longhorn" fans as a class drive faster than non-fans, "Sooner" fans, or fans of other football teams.

Evidence may be irrelevant in this second sense only if it is *circumstantial* rather than *direct* evidence. Direct evidence is testimonial evidence which, if believed, resolves a matter in issue. Circumstantial evidence serves as a basis from which the trier of fact may make reasonable infer-

ences about a matter in issue. It, too, is often testimonial in nature.[6] For example, testimony by a witness, Walters, that he saw the defendant, Clark, pull a gun out and shoot the victim Hill is direct evidence on the issue of who shot Hill. If believed, we know that Clark is the one. Testimony by Walters that he saw Clark standing over Hill's body with a smoking gun is only circumstantial evidence that Clark shot Hill. Even if believed it only justifies the inference that Clark did the shooting. Other inferences are possible: Clark, for example, might have heard the shot, rushed to the scene, and picked up the gun just as Walters approached.

When we say that evidence is irrelevant in this second logical sense, we are saying that knowing the item of circumstantial evidence does not allow the trier of fact to *reasonably* infer anything about the likely existence of a fact in issue.[7] Thus, if an

---

5. This objection is a dangerous one— standing alone an appellate court might not find it specific enough to preserve an evidentiary matter for appeal. See Saltzburg, Another Ground for Decision—Harmless Trial Court Errors, 47 Temp.L.Q. 193, 197 n. 15 (1974).

The concept of materiality is carried forward in the language "of consequence to the determination of the action" in FRE 401.

Although some judges still use the term "material," in federal courts it should be clear by now that an objection on relevance grounds may include objections to both the logical relevance and the materiality of opposing evidence.

6. But see 1 Wigmore § 25.

7. **Different facts may be in issue at different points in the trial so certain testimony may be direct evidence as to some**

Oklahoma jury knew the defendant in tort was a Texas Longhorn fan they could not from this information alone reasonably infer anything about the probability that the defendant was speeding.

The difference between direct and circumstantial evidence does not mean that the former is always, or even presumptively, accorded more weight than the latter. The difference is that direct evidence, if believed, requires no further inference for its bearing on a fact in issue.

However, direct evidence need not be believed or it may be believed in only a tentative or partial fashion, as where an eyewitness admits to poor eyesight. Circumstantial evidence, like the fact that the suspect was seen running from the scene of a murder holding a smoking gun, may be every bit as weighty as direct evidence. Direct and circumstantial evidence pose different inferential problems, but the differences do not mean that one type will necessarily be more valuable than the other.

E. CONNECTING UP

In a trial the evidence can only unfold gradually; obviously it cannot all be presented at once. This may cause difficulties because the relevance of one item of circumstantial evidence may be apparent only when other items are known. Consider the Texas speeder again. If it could be shown that at the time of the accident he had two tickets to the Texas-Oklahoma game in his pocket and that from the point of the accident one would have to travel at 90 m.p.h. in order to reach the stadium by kickoff time, the fact that the driver was absolutely fanatical in his support for the University of Texas would become relevant. A fanatic might be expected to take the risks involved in driving at 90 m.p.h. to reach a key game on time, while a non-fan or one less dedicated to his team would be more likely to drive slowly and arrive late.

Where the relevance of one item of evidence is dependent on the receipt of another item to place it in context, the first item may be received in evidence over objection with the understanding that later, evidence will "connect it up" to matters at issue in the case. In the literature, problems involving evidence which must be connected up are often referred to as problems of "conditional relevance". The notion is the same: one fact standing alone may not appear relevant, but two facts taken together may establish a relevant proposition. Typically the attorney's word that evidence will be connected up is accepted, but where the matter is likely to be prejudicial or excessively time-consuming the attorney may be asked to briefly describe the way in which the matter relates to the ultimate case.

It is, of course, a serious breach of ethics to offer evidence subject to connecting up when one knows the connecting evidence is unavailable. Yet occasionally evidence will not be connected up because crucial testimony proves inadmissible on non-relevance grounds, because witnesses change their stories or don't show up, or through sheer inadvertence. When for any reason there is a failure of connecting evidence, the earlier evidence will, upon request, be stricken from the record and the jury instructed to disregard it. If the stricken evidence is particularly prejudicial, a mistrial might be appropriate.

The converse of the connecting up problem, the situation in which apparently relevant evidence appears irrelevant when

point and circumstantial evidence as to some other. In the hypothetical example used in the text, if there were a question about whether Clark had stood over Hill with a smoking gun, Walters' testimony would be direct evidence on this point, but it would still be circumstantial evidence on the issue of who shot Hill.

placed in context, has received little attention from courts or commentators. Consider, for example, a suspect who attempts
to escape from custody while being transported to jail. In a later trial evidence of
the attempt will be considered relevant, for
flight from pre-trial custody may be reasonably interpreted as an attempt to avoid
conviction and it is reasonable to suppose
that suspects conscious of their guilt will
be more likely to fear conviction than those
who believe themselves innocent. But if
it could be shown that the suspect had read
a recent newspaper story which pictured
the local jail as overcrowded, unsanitary and
a hotbed of sexual assaults and if it could
also be shown that the jailor had threatened to kill the suspect if the suspect came
within his clutches, the escape attempt
might be seen as something which would

be equally likely whether the suspect were
guilty or innocent. Nonetheless, a court
would probably admit evidence of the escape attempt on the issue of the suspect's
consciousness of guilt. There is a good
reason for this. The jury which is responsible for judging the credibility of witnesses might not believe that the defendant had read of the jail conditions or been
threatened by the jailor; if not, the tie between the escape attempt and consciousness of guilt remains logically plausible.
Nevertheless, if you are confident that an
opponent's evidence is irrelevant when
taken in context, you might object on this
ground. But first be sure there are not
significant tactical advantages to be gained
from presenting the jury with the facts from
which they can make their own determination of irrelevance.

F. RELEVANT AND IRRELEVANT

Evidence is often relevant for one purpose and irrelevant for others. In the example of the escape attempt, evidence of
the story on jail conditions would be relevant on the issue of whether the attempt
evinced consciousness of guilt, but the story
would probably be found logically irrelevant on the issue of whether the suspect
committed the crime charged and be held
immaterial if offered in a criminal trial as
an indictment of the local penal system.
In situations like this, where evidence is
relevant for only one purpose, the evidence will almost always be admitted for

that purpose. The opponent's only consolation will be the right to have the jury
instructed that the evidence is to be used
only for the permitted purpose. This may
be a small sop. It is not clear that the jury
can or does follow such instructions; indeed on some occasions attorneys will
waive their right to limiting instructions for
fear they will only call the jury's attention
to the impermissible inferences.[8]

The situation which gives the most
difficulty is the situation in which the
offered evidence is relevant to a periph-

8. Attorneys sometimes seek bench trials
where they fear the opposition will attempt
to introduce evidence on one point which
has its most devastating impact in another
area. They apparently believe that judges,
unlike juries, can separate permissible inferences from the impermissible in resolving legal matters. This might well be so;
but it is unlikely that even judges can make
this separation complete. Indeed, Kalven
and Zeisel in their major study, The American Jury, found a number of judges willing to admit that they would have decided
cases differently from the jury because they

were aware of certain facts which had not
been entered into evidence.
A few judges, e.g., three federal district
court judges in Chicago, have devised systems whereby in any case in which a jury
is waived the litigants can have some other
judge than the one before whom the case is
to be tried rule on evidence questions that
are raised in limine. These judges are
concerned about the possibility that they
will be unable to disregard evidence that is
excluded.

eral point or to a point on which other evidence is available and is either highly prejudicial to an opposing party or probative of a more central point on which it cannot be introduced. Even here courts have been reluctant to interfere with counsel's preferred method of proving the case. Thus, the condition of a corpse may be shown in a series of inflammatory pictures rather than through the colorless testimony of an autopsy surgeon, and plaintiffs in tort actions are given great leeway in the way they prove the extent of their injuries.[9] In the Whale case we see evidence of past crimes admitted only on the credibility issue although the jury may have used this information in evaluating the probability that Whale was selling marihuana. Chapter Four, on matters which are relevant but inadmissible, will provide further examples.

The principle at work here is one which is general to the nonconstitutional areas of evidence law. *Evidence which is admissible for one purpose will not be excluded simply because it is inadmissible for other purposes. Instead, the jury will be instructed, if opposing counsel so requests or if the judge decides to act sua sponte, to consider the evidence only for the proper purpose.* Think of the jury as sitting in a house with many doors. To reach the jury you need only go through one door. It does not matter if the rest are barred. The key to finding the open door is to know your evidence law and to know the substantive law on which theories of admission can be based. *No matter how well you know the rules of evidence, you cannot use them well unless you also master the substantive law which bears on your case.*

G.   LOGICAL OR LEGAL RELEVANCE?

Thayer in his *Preliminary Treatise on Evidence* asserted, "The law furnishes no test of relevance. For this, it tacitly refers to logic and general experience * * *"; and this is the position taken in the federal rules. All that is necessary for evidence to be relevant and hence presumptively admissible is that it tends logically to prove or disprove some fact in issue. There is another view which has been expressed by some courts and given weight by some commentators;[10] this is the view that a mere logical relationship between proffered evidence and a fact in issue is not enough to justify admissibility. There must be something more, some "plus value". Evidence lacking such plus value might be

logically relevant but it would not be legally so. Now this concept of plus value is confusing; it is not clear what it would be. In fact it is probably a less precise way of acknowledging, as modern courts do, that even relevant evidence may be excluded if it seems likely to be prejudicial, misleading or unduly time-consuming. Of course, the less probative the evidence and the less need for it in a party's case, the more likely is exclusion on one of the above grounds despite some relevance. The judge's task is to balance the probative value of and need for the evidence against the harm likely to result from admission.

---

9. **However, if the opposition is willing to stipulate to all the facts which the evidence would show, a party may be required by the judge to accept the stipulation and forego the presentation of more prejudicial proofs. See, e.g., Solomon, Techniques for Shortening Trials, 65 F.R.D. 485, 490 (1975). Under these circumstances an offer to stipulate is treated as a judicial admission.**

10. Most notably Wigmore. Without his support this approach might have died out long ago. Wigmore writes, "[L]egal relevancy denotes * * * *something more than a minimum of probative value.*" 1 Wigmore § 28, at 409–10. Wigmore suggests that "plus value" is necessary "to prevent the jury from being satisfied by matters of slight value, capable of being exaggerated by prejudice and hasty reasoning." Id. at 409.

Consider the example of evidence of jail conditions on the probability that defendant committed a crime. It was suggested above that on this issue the evidence would probably be regarded as irrelevant. But counsel might argue: "My client knew of these conditions and consequently was terrified at the prospect of going to jail. Surely this knowledge makes it very unlikely that he would engage in activity which would lead him to be arrested and thrown in jail." The argument is not completely unreasonable. Some courts might dispose of it without analysis by saying that it lacked plus value; it was not legally relevant. A more thoughtful court would state that in view of the large number of crimes committed despite widespread knowledge of prison conditions the evidence was only slightly relevant. Any value it had in the truth-finding process was clearly outweighed by the interjection of collateral issues confusing to the jury, the possibility the jury would find for a guilty defendant because they didn't want to send him back to jail, and the time which would be expended if the prosecutor chose to dispute the defendant's contentions.

The prime danger of the "legal relevance" approach is that it invites the court to confuse the question of whether evidence is relevant with the question of whether it is sufficient to support a verdict. *Evidence is relevant if alone or in context it tends to prove or disprove a fact in issue; evidence is sufficient if a reasonable jury could conclude from the evidence introduced that the plaintiff or prosecution has met the appropriate burden of proof.*[11] Yet the New York Court of Appeals in Engel v. United Traction Co.[12] once proposed the following standard of relevance: "A fact is admissible as the basis of an inference only when the desired inference is a probable or natural explanation of the fact and a more probable or natural one than the other explanations, if any." The court in its concern for something more than a mere logical relationship has confused relevancy with sufficiency. An example should make this clear. Suppose Smathers takes out a $150,000 fire insurance policy on his new furniture store and three months later the store burns down. If Smathers is tried for arson the existence of the policy is relevant, for it suggests a reason why Smathers might burn his own store. But just as surely the most probable explanation of Smathers' decision to buy fire insurance is not that he intended later to burn the store. Under the *Engel* test evidence of the policy would not be admitted; but while courts may become confused in reviewing specific cases, this test is not systematically applied today in New York or anywhere else.

Legal relevance may be used in a sense other than a requirement that minimally relevant evidence have some "plus value". There are certain *recurring situations* in which various courts have declared evidence to be irrelevant despite some logical relationship between the evidence and facts in issue. By using the language of relevance these courts have obscured the fact that the decision to exclude the evidence is based on considerations of legal policy rather than pure logic. We treat this evidence in Chapter Four as what it is: logically relevant evidence declared inadmissible on policy grounds. However, most treatments and codifications of evidence law discuss these principles under the rubric of relevance because the evidence excluded is often of low relevance. You should remember that these principles, which we will call "the relevance

---

11. For example, evidence that defendant attempted to escape is relevant on the issue of whether the defendant is guilty of the crime with which he is charged, but if this were the only evidence connecting the defendant to the crime it would hardly be sufficient to support a conviction.

12. 203 N.Y. 321, 323, 96 N.E. 731, 732 (1911).

rules", exclude evidence for a variety of different policy reasons, each of which must be evaluated on its own merits. You may think of such evidence as "legally irrelevant" if it helps you remember that such evidence is excluded because numerous courts have so held, and not because there is no logical connection between the evidence and facts in issue. If you can remember this without the concept of "legal irrelevance", so much the better. By clearly distinguishing between evidence that is excluded as irrelevant and relevant evidence that is excluded for other reasons, you may be able to avoid having your evidence excluded under precedents written in sweeping relevance language.

There are a number of other principles of evidence law which at their root reflect a concern for relevance. The need for authentication mentioned in footnote 34 in the Whale case and discussed further in Chapter Eleven, the requirement of a chain of custody for certain real evidence, and some of the requirements pertaining to the competency of witnesses fall into this category. If, for example, an I.O.U. offered by the plaintiff is signed by a Jane Doe other than defendant Jane Doe, its exis-

tence has no bearing on the issue of whether this Ms. Doe owes plaintiff money.[13] Special bodies of rules discussed in other portions of these materials have been formulated to resolve questions in these areas and ensure that offered materials are relevant. These rules as a body generally go beyond the requirement of minimal relevance which is discussed in this section. To again use authentication as the example, consider a situation where there is some reason to believe that an offered note is in fact the note of the defendant in debt. Lingering doubt about the authenticity of the note does not make the note irrelevant in a logical sense since even after the note's value as evidence has been discounted because of this doubt its existence should still affect the calculations of a reasonable trier of fact. However, if the specific requirements for authenticating a note cannot be complied with, the note will be kept from the jury whatever its probative value. In considering principles like authentication, which are based fundamentally on a concern for relevance, ask yourself whether it makes sense for rules to require more than minimal logical relevance.

H. JUDGE OR JURY

Ultimately the jury decides the evidentiary value of all evidence submitted to it; indeed, this weighing of the facts is its principal function. In any given case it is possible that the jury ultimately decides that much of the evidence introduced is irrelevant to the questions it must resolve. However, when evidence is objected to on the ground that it is irrelevant, the judge must decide whether the jury should receive the information in the first place. Where the only issue is logical relevance, the judge's sole task is to determine the logical relationship of the evidence to matters in issue. If the evidence might

influence a reasonable trier of fact it should be admitted regardless of the value which the judge personally would place on it. Where relevance is disputable, the judge is likely to admit the evidence "for what it's worth", since the jury is trusted to discount the evidence if it is not in fact relevant.

The judge's task, however, is usually not this easy. Problems arise when the evidence clearly bears some logical relationship to a matter in issue but threatens to confuse the jury or to be unduly repetitious or time-consuming or, most impor-

13. Though the I.O.U. is irrelevant to the plaintiff's case, it might be relevant to the defendant's. How? What theory would defendant present to the jury?

tantly, to impermissibly bias the jury in its evaluation of the case. In these circumstances the judge cannot escape the chore assigned him by FRE 403. He must weigh the probative value of the evidence and balance it against the detrimental effects of admission. The availability of other evidence on the same point will be an important influence on the judge's decision as will opposing counsel's willingness to stipulate to everything that the evidence might legitimately be used to prove. Where evidence is unique and important and no stipulation is forthcoming, the need for information will almost always outweigh associated detrimental effects.

Where the tradeoff between probative value and prejudicial effect is a close one, FRE 403 mandates admissibility since it allows relevant evidence to be excluded only if its probative value is *"substantially outweighed"* by threats to fair and efficient factfinding. However, the difference between merely "outweighing" and "sub-stantially outweighing" is not yet clear from the case law. What is clear is that appellate courts regard decisions under FRE 403 as committed largely to the discretion of the trial judge. Whatever the decision at trial, the result is unlikely to be overturned on appeal. Trial judges should, however, explain why they reach particular decisions. Some appellate courts have disapproved of trial judges who strike an FRE 403 balance but refuse counsel's request to state a reason for their ruling.

The import of FRE 403 and the discretion it accords trial judges cannot be overstated. Although it codifies what the law was in most jurisdictions before 1975, its explicit recognition of the broad balancing power accorded trial judges has resulted in its being the most frequent ground of objection in most federal and some state courts. A quick glance at reported decisions will reveal the number and variety of occasions in which FRE 403 balancing is invoked.

I. THE MEANING OF PREJUDICE

In casual conversation the word "prejudice" is often used as if it were synonymous with "harm." We say we were prejudiced by something when what we mean is that we were harmed by it. When the law speaks of prejudice, it is not speaking so casually. Prejudice refers to a specific kind of harm: harm which results when evidence is inappropriately influential because it appeals to the biases or emotions of the fact finder.

Evidence may destroy a party's case without being prejudicial. For example, consider a driver arrested for exceeding a 20 mile an hour school zone speed limit. If the arresting officer testifies that the driver was clocked by radar at 35 miles per hour within a block of the school, the driver's case may be destroyed, for unless the officer's testimony is discredited, conviction is almost certain. Yet the testimony is not prejudicial in the sense of being unfairly influential, nor is the driver prejudiced by it. If the driver's protestations of innocence are overwhelmed by the officer's testimony it is because of the probative force of that evidence, its tendency to convince a *rational* fact finder of the existence of a fact in issue.

Conversely, although prejudice may not exist without harm, even slight harm may be prejudicial. Thus, in the case of the speeding driver, evidence that the driver is a registered Democrat would probably not cause great harm even before a jury of Republicans since political differences are unlikely to affect verdicts in matters so mundane as speeding. Yet so long as any harm was attributable to the partisan identification, evidence of the driver's political affiliation is prejudicial. It is prejudicial because so long as political affiliation bears no relationship to the probability that one would speed, evidence of political affiliation can only affect the verdict by an appeal to the fact finder's emotions. It is this appeal that the law regards as impermissible. Testimony about the driver's political affiliation does not mean, however, that any subsequent conviction will be overturned on appeal. The prejudicial potential of evidence may appear so slight and other evidence in a case may be so overwhelming that the admission of prejudicial evidence is harmless error. This is likely to be the case in the example we have pursued. But harmless error is error even if it does not justify overturning decisions below, and evidence that bears no rational relation to the existence of a fact in issue should not be admitted in the first instance.

Often evidence has both probative value and the potential to prejudice a fact finder. In our speeding case, evidence that the arresting officer had been threatened with dismissal if he did not ticket a certain number of drivers each day would be relevant because it might rationally lead a jury to question the officer's testimony. At the same time it might prejudice the state's case because a jury might be so incensed by the existence of rigid ticket quotas that it would acquit a driver it deemed guilty in order to express its disapproval. Where probative value and prejudicial potential are mixed in this way the judge must, as is explained in section H, balance one against the other. Where prejudicial potential is obvious the judge may issue a limiting instruction directing the jury to consider the evidence only for its proper purposes.

J. A MATHEMATICAL RESTATEMENT

We hope that what is written above is clear, but we now intend to restate some of what is written and to extend our remarks in another more precise language, the language of mathematics. While some of you may have chosen a career in law in part because of your preference for verbal as opposed to mathematical reasoning, it is our experience that working through two simple mathematical models can clarify one's thinking about questions of relevance.

The discussion that follows is taken from an article entitled *Modeling Relevance* written by one of the authors (Lempert). Editorial changes are not noted in this excerpt. The original article may be found in Volume 75 of the Michigan Law Review at page 1021.

Mathematics as a language can help clarify those legal rules that involve weighing evidence in an essentially probabilistic

fashion. We have found that two simple models, Bayes' Theorem and regret matrices, are helpful in thinking about the meaning of relevance and in analyzing certain of the rules generally associated with this topic. The discussion assumes that the fact finder is a jury and, unless otherwise noted, that the issue to be resolved is the defendant's guilt. However, the analysis may be readily generalized to the situation where the fact finder is a judge and/or a question other than guilt is at issue. The two models are here applied to a simplified situation where the fact finder must evaluate only one item of indisputably accurate testimony.[14]

1. *Bayes' Theorem*

First we must attend to Bayes' Theorem. This theorem follows directly from two elementary formulas of probability theory: if A and B are any two propositions, then:

14. See the second portion of Lempert's *Modeling Relevance*, cited in the text, for an exploration of complexities that can arise when

a case involves two or more items of possibly unreliable evidence.

$$P(A \& B) = P(A|B) \cdot P(B)^{15} \quad (1)$$
$$P(A) = P(A \& B) + P(A \& \text{not-}B)^{16} \quad (2)$$

From these rather basic equations the following formula may be derived:

$$O(G|E) = \frac{P(E|G)}{P(E|\text{not-}G)} \cdot O(G) \quad (3)$$

This formula describes the way knowledge of a new item of evidence (E) would influence a completely rational decision maker's evaluation of the odds that a defendant is guilty (G). Since the law assumes that a fact finder *should* be rational, this is a normative model; that is, the Bayesian equation describes the way the law's ideal juror evaluates new items of evidence. What this equation says is that the odds (O) that a defendant is guilty, given the introduction of a new item of evidence, is equal to (1) the probability that the evidence would be presented to the jury if the defendant is in fact guilty, (2) divided by the probability that that evidence would be presented to the jury if the defendant is in fact not guilty, (3) times the prior odds [17] on the defendant's guilt. The prior odds are the odds that would have been given of the defendant's guilt before receipt of the item of evidence in question.

For example, suppose at some point in a criminal trial the fact finder believes that the odds are fifty-fifty, or 1:1, that the defendant is guilty. A more familiar way of stating this is that the fact finder believes that the probability of the defendant's guilt is .50. The evidence next received proves the following: that the perpetrator's blood, shed at the scene of the crime, was type A; that the defendant's blood is type A; and that fifty per cent of the suspect population [18] has type A blood. Thus, if the defendant were the perpetrator the probability that the blood found at the scene would be type A is 1.0.[19] The probability that the blood would be type A if someone else committed the crime is .50, or ½, since half of the other possible suspects have type A blood. Plugging these figures into the formula indicates that after receiving the evidence on the blood a rational decision maker would evaluate the odds of guilt as:

$$O(G|E) = \frac{1}{.5} \cdot \frac{1}{1} = \frac{1}{.5} = 2:1.$$

The new evidence has raised the odds in favor of the defendant's guilt to 2:1. Another way of stating this result is that the factfinder's best estimate of the probability that the defendant is guilty is now .67.

---

15. These symbols mean that the probability that events A and B will both occur is equal to the probability that A will occur if B has occurred times the probability that B will occur. For example, if A = a warm day and B = a sunny day, the probability that it will be both warm and sunny equals the probability that it will be warm if it is in fact sunny times the probability that it will be sunny.

16. These symbols mean that the probability that an event A will occur equals the probability that event A will occur with event B plus the probability that event A will occur with any event that is not B. If A = a warm day and B = a sunny day, the probability that it will be a warm day equals the probability that it will be warm and sunny plus the probability that it will be warm and not sunny.

17. The figure for these odds is not important to the following analysis, though it might be very important in analyzing other problems such as harmless error. It seems unlikely that jurors consciously think in terms of the odds of guilt after each item of evi-

dence is received. Yet it may well be that, without stopping to quantify, they are influenced to make incremental changes in their perception of the parties' chances after hearing items of evidence in much the way Bayes' Theorem suggest, and, if asked, they may be able to express these odds in mathematical terms.

18. The suspect populations could be people in the United States, people in a particular locality, males in a locality, black people, white people, etc., based upon what already has been proved about the characteristics of the perpetrator. The textual example assumes that the suspect population is relatively large.

19. At this point some might object that it can never be completely clear that the blood found was the perpetrator's. The point is well taken, but the fact that absolute certainty may never exist with respect to an item of evidence does not affect the basic argument.

Evidence that changes an estimated probability of guilt in this fashion is clearly relevant in a criminal trial.

Consider another case. Assume that the range of possible suspects has been limited to voters in a community so conservative that only one out of ten voters supports the liberal candidate. While a group of conservative jurors drawn from this community might be angered by evidence that the defendant supports the liberal candidate, such a showing would not influence the judgment of an ideal juror. Absent some reason to believe that liberals are more prone to commit the crime in question, the probability that the defendant could have been shown to be a liberal were he guilty is .1, the same as the probability that he could have been shown to be a liberal were he not guilty. Solving the Bayesian equation we find:

$$O(G|E) = \frac{.1}{.1} O(G) = O(G)$$

The odds on the defendant's guilt remains $O(G)$; the same as they were before the jury learned of the defendant's political affiliation. In these circumstances evidence of the defendant's political affiliation is not relevant.

a. Logical Relevance

In both examples the effect of the evidence on the decision maker's final judgment as to guilt turns entirely on the ratio $\frac{P(E|G)}{P(E|\text{not-}G)}$, conventionally called the *likelihood ratio*. In the first example $P(E|G)$ was twice $P(E|\text{not-}G)$, and the fact finder doubled his prior odds of the defendant's guilt. In the second example $P(E|G)$ and $P(E|\text{not-}G)$ were the same, so the likelihood ratio was one and the fact finder's prior estimate of the defendant's guilt remained unchanged. In terms of the Bayesian model, it will always be the case that the impact of new evidence on prior odds on guilt, or on any other disputed hypothesis, will be solely a function of the like-

lihood ratio for that evidence. Where the likelihood ratio for an item of evidence differs from one, that evidence is *logically relevant*. This is the mathematical equivalent of the statement in FRE 401 that "relevant evidence" is "evidence having *any* tendency to make the existence of any fact that is of consequence to the determination of the action more probable or less probable than it would be without the evidence." (Emphasis added) Hence, evidence is logically relevant only when the probability of finding that evidence given the truth of some hypothesis at issue in the case differs from the probability of finding the same evidence given the falsity of the hypothesis at issue. In a criminal trial, if a particular item of evidence is as likely to be found if the defendant is guilty as it is if he is innocent, the evidence is logically irrelevant on the issue of the defendant's guilt.

As a practical matter courts may be justified in rejecting evidence as logically irrelevant when the likelihood ratio is only *slightly* different from one, since such evidence will have little effect on the odds that the disputed hypothesis is true. A slight difference in this context must be very small indeed, since a likelihood ratio of 1.5 would lead a fact finder to increase by fifty per cent the estimate of the odds in question and a likelihood ratio of 2.0 would result in a doubling of the prior odds.

It is clear from the model that the likelihood ratio depends entirely on the relative magnitudes of $P(E|G)$ and $P(E|\text{not-}G)$ and not on the absolute magnitude of either. Thus evidence that is very unlikely to be associated with a guilty defendant will nevertheless be probative of guilt so long as the evidence is more (or less) likely to be associated with an individual who is not guilty. Suppose, for example, that in an assault case it can be shown both that the defendant is a heroin addict and that one out of 500 criminal assailants are heroin addicts. The latter information means that it is very unlikely that any given criminal assailant is a heroin addict. However, if it can also be shown that of the people who never engage in criminal assault only one in 1000 are heroin addicts, knowledge that the defendant is an addict should result in a doubling of the prior odds that the defendant was the assailant. Conversely, if it could be proved that for every 250 nonassailants there is one heroin addict, evidence of the defendant's addiction and the rate of criminal assault among addicts should lead to a halving of the prior odds that the defendant is guilty of assault. In either of these supposed cases there may be good reason to keep evidence of the defendant's addiction from the jury, but the reason is not that the information standing alone is logically irrelevant.

b. Estimation Problems

Courts declare evidence irrelevant for several reasons. Sometimes they are concerned that the likelihood ratio may be one or very close to it. This problem, examined above, is properly called the problem of "logical relevance." On other occasions courts are concerned with the possibility that the fact finder will misestimate the probabilities that make up the likelihood ratio; i.e., $P(E|G)$ and/or $P(E|not\text{-}G)$. Overestimating the numerator or underestimating the denominator makes the conclusion sought by the proponent of the evidence appear more probable than it actually is; underestimating the numerator or overestimating the denominator has the opposite result. In the assault hypothetical presented above, if the fact finder thought that the probability that a nonassailant would be a heroin addict was one in 10,000 rather than one in 1,000, this misestimation would lead to a twentyfold increase in the odds that the defendant was the assailant rather than the twofold in-

crease that was in fact justified. We call such problems "estimation problems."

Estimation problems take several forms. The most obvious is that evidence may be given more weight than it deserves. The jurors may exaggerate the probative value of the evidence because they believe that the association between evidence and hypothesis is more powerful than it in fact is or because they are not estimating probative worth in the context that is proper given the facts of the case. The heroin example of the preceding paragraph is a situation in which the jurors misestimate the strength of a crucial association, throwing the denominator of the likelihood ratio off by a factor of ten. When courts reject evidence because of this type of estimation problem, they often categorize the problem as one of prejudice, a term we prefer to reserve for another situation,[20] or they may speak of the danger of confusing or misleading the jury.

An estimation problem also exists when there is so little information about the relationship of certain evidence to the hypothesis in question that the implications of the evidence are unclear. In these circumstances courts often exclude evidence as irrelevant rather than let the jurors speculate on its import. Since such evidence might well relate to the probability of guilt or innocence if its true implications were known, a more precise justification for exclusion is "relevance unknown." If the textual example that posited a relationship between heroin addiction and assault did not ring true, it is probably because we lack the base rate information needed to evaluate the relationship between heroin addiction and the likelihood of engaging in an assault. Although the image of the "dope fiend" is that of a violent personality, effects associated with addiction suggest that addicts are less likely than nonaddicts to engage in

---

20. See section I of this chapter and subsection 2, infra.

physical violence for its own sake.[21] With no good evidence of appropriate base rates and conflicting images of the violent propensities of heroin addicts, it makes sense to keep evidence of heroin addiction from a jury in assault cases because its relevance is unknown.

Under FRE 403 and at common law, courts have discretion to exclude logically relevant evidence likely to pose estimation problems if the probative value of the evidence is substantially outweighed by the danger that it will mislead the jury. The Bayesian model suggests that in exercising this discretion the more the court's estimate of the proper likelihood ratio for an item of evidence deviates from 1:1 the less willing the court should be to exclude that evidence. If the likelihood ratio for an item of evidence is 2:1 and the fact finder perceives it as 20:1 the misevaluation might well be of critical importance. However, if the likelihood ratio for the evidence is 100:1 and the fact finder misperceives it as 1000:1, the error is less likely to be critical because the evidence whether properly weighed or overweighed usually leads to the same conclusion: that the favored hypothesis is established by the appropriate standard of proof. Furthermore, excluding evidence where the likelihood ratio deviates substantially from 1:1 deprives the fact finder of information that might aid considerably in the rational resolution of disputed factual claims and may prevent a party from making what is, on a *fair* reading of all the evidence, a powerful case. This analysis supports the judicial practice of rarely, if ever, excluding evidence of substantial probative value simply because the jury appears likely to give the evidence even more weight than it deserves or be-

cause the precise weight to be given is unclear.[22] The preferred solution is to provide the jury with the information needed to assess accurately the probative value of the offered evidence.

A similar analysis applies where a court is called on to weigh the probative value of evidence against such factors as confusion of the issues, delay, and waste of time. Where the likelihood ratio for the evidence is far from 1:1, exclusion on these grounds is almost never justified except in the special case where, after considering all other admissible evidence, the court is convinced that the prior odds in favor of the disputed hypothesis are so high or so low that even highly probative evidence is unlikely to change the jury's judgment. This means that courts should be more reluctant in close cases than in clear ones to exclude probative evidence on such grounds as threatened delay, confusion, or waste of time. Appellate courts are certainly influenced by the closeness of cases in reviewing claims that the exclusion of evidence on such grounds was erroneous.

The Bayesian model that has been presented thus far aids in understanding the following aspects of the law relating to relevance: (1) the meaning of logical relevance, (2) the principle that only logically relevant evidence is admissible, (3) the discretion that courts have to exclude relevant evidence when the jury is likely to give it undue weight, and (4) the reluctance of courts to exclude highly probative evidence even though the jury is likely to give it undue weight.

The Bayesian model does not, however, indicate why in some cases it might be desirable to exclude probative evidence not likely to raise estimation problems nor why

21. Since there is good reason to believe that addicts often find it necessary to resort to crime in order to support their habits, if the assault were with an intent to rob the probative value of the evidence of addiction would, no doubt, be higher and the likely direction of the relationship would be clearer.

22. There are other values that may justify the exclusion of highly probative evidence, e.g., the rules of privilege and the rules regarding illegally seized evidence.

it should be reversible error for a court to admit logically irrelevant evidence. However, another model drawn from decision theory helps clarify these aspects of the law of relevance. This model, called a *regret matrix,* aids in thinking about prejudice.

2. *Prejudice and the Regret Matrix*

A regret matrix[23] is not a normative model since it is not clear that the law expects the ideal decision maker to act in a manner consistent with it. It may, however, be a good descriptive model of the way decision makers, be they jurors or judges, actually behave, and values may be inserted into the model that are, arguably, normative. The model assumes that individuals wish to minimize the expected regret felt in the long run as a result of their decisions. In law, for example, a decision maker might wish to find for plaintiffs only when defendants were negligent. In terms of this model, the decision maker would have no regret in finding for plaintiffs when defendants were negligent and no regret in finding for defendants when they were not negligent.[24] Since in the uncertain world of litigation the decision maker can never be absolutely sure that a particular defendant was or was not negligent, the decision maker can never be absolutely sure of avoiding outcomes that would be regretted if the truth were known.

Although absolute certainty is impossible, the decision maker might be able to estimate a probability that the defendant was negligent, e.g., .6 or .7. If this can be done and if the decision maker can articulate the *relative* regret associated with different possible outcomes, a regret matrix can be constructed that indicates which decision—given the probabilities—leads to the least total regret in the long run. Consider the situation portrayed in Figure One.

FIGURE 1

VERDICT	DECISION MAKER'S REGRET MATRIX TRUE STATE OF AFFAIRS		DECISION MAKER'S ESTIMATED PROBABILITY THAT D WAS:		DECISION MAKER'S EXPECTED REGRET IF VERDICT IS FOR:	
	D Negligent	D Not Negligent				
For P	0	1	Negligent	.6	P	.4
For D	1	0	Not Negligent	.4	D	.6

In this matrix no regret is associated with a decision for P when D was negligent or with a decision for D when D was not negligent. One unit of regret is associated with each mistake, that of finding for P when D was not negligent and that of finding for D when D was negligent. How should a decision maker with these values decide? That depends on his estimate of the probability that D was negligent. In the above example this probability is estimated at .6, making the estimated proba-

bility that D was not negligent (1 − .6) or .4. Knowing these probabilities, the expected regret for each verdict can be calculated by multiplying the regret associated with the verdict, given the defendant's actual negligence or non-negligence, times the probability that the defendant actually was negligent or not negligent. The sum of these products for a given verdict equals the total regret to be expected (in the long run) if that verdict were reached in all cases having the same regret matrix and proba-

23. What we refer to as a "regret" matrix is a form of what is generally called a "utility" matrix in the decision theory literature.

24. The example assumes that defenses such as contributory negligence are unavailable in this case, so liability turns solely on the issue of the defendant's negligence.

bility of negligence. In the example, there is a .6 probability that D was negligent. Hence there is a .6 probability the decision maker who decides for P will feel no regret [.6 × 0 = 0]. Conversely, there is a .4 probability that D was not negligent and that a decision for P will result in one unit of regret [.4 × 1 = .4]. Thus, the regret expected from deciding for P given these probabilities of D's negligence will, in the long run, average .4 of whatever unit regret is measured in [0 + .4 = .4]. The situation is reversed when the decision is for D. There is a .6 probability that the decision maker will feel one unit of regret and a .4 probability that the decision maker will feel no regret. Consequently, the average expected regret from deciding for D is .6 units in the long run. An individual concerned with minimizing expected regret will decide for P in these circumstances.

The regret matrix used in this example is normative for most civil cases. A judge or juror *should* feel the same regret in reaching a mistaken decision for P that is felt in reaching a mistaken decision for D. If this is in fact the case (i.e., if this particular regret matrix actually models the decision maker's values), one can show algebraically that regret is minimized by deciding for P whenever the probability of negligence is greater than .5 and deciding for D whenever the probability of negligence is less than .5.[25]

There are many civil cases in which a fact finder might feel uncomfortable with a norm that ascribes equal regret to the two kinds of mistakes. If this norm is rejected and if the fact finder seeks to minimize regret, he may strain to reach decisions that run counter to the weight of the evidence. For example, a juror whose insurance company connections make him sympathetic to tort defendants and hostile to injured plaintiffs might regret mistakenly deciding for P when D was not negligent twice as much as the opposite mistake. (This may be portrayed by changing the value in the upper right-hand cell of the matrix in Figure One to 2 while leaving the value in the lower left-hand cell at 1.) With this relative regret and the same probability that D is negligent as in the earlier example, .6 units of regret would be associated with a decision for D (the same as before) and .8 units of regret [0 × .6 + 2 × .4] with a decision for P. Hence a decision for D could be expected, although the decision maker's estimated probability of D's negligence is sixty per cent.[26]

At law the burden of proof needed to sustain a conviction is the same for all defendants: good or evil, young or old, attractive or unattractive, dangerous or non-threatening. Yet it is likely that jurors regret the mistake of convicting basically good people more than the mistake of convicting the basically evil. These feelings are reversed if the mistake is acquitting. The situation is undoubtedly similar with respect to other characteristics that affect people's attitudes toward their fellow human beings. If most jurors cannot avoid being influenced by such preferences in reaching their verdicts, the burden of proof is effectively changed by any information that affects these preferences.

The law's ideal juror estimates only the probabilities pertaining to the defendant's guilt and does not independently judge the regret associated with possible mistakes. This information is provided, in theory, by the court's instructions on the burden of proof. The requirement that guilt be proved beyond a reasonable doubt may mean that an accused should not be convicted unless the probability of guilt is

25. This is what is meant by a burden of proof by the preponderance of the evidence. Regret is equal when the probability of negligence is exactly .5. Here the law has decided that the defendant should prevail.

26. This assumes that a fact finder with the hypothesized regret schedule would be unwilling to accept the court's instruction that P should prevail if he establishes his case by a preponderance of the evidence.

judged to be at least .91, which is equivalent to saying that the law regards a wrongful conviction as being ten times more regrettable than a wrongful acquittal, or it may mean that conviction should not follow unless some other minimum probability of guilt is obtained; but whatever the degree of certainty associated with proof beyond a reasonable doubt, the law does not contemplate that the standard of proof will vary with the defendant's personal characteristics or with the sordid details of the defendant's criminal activity.

In practice, the ideal of an unvarying standard is not achieved. Instructions on burden of proof, particularly in criminal cases, are so ambiguous that jurors necessarily exercise discretion in determining the degree of certainty needed to support a particular verdict. Furthermore, there is considerable evidence that jury verdicts are influenced by the personal characteristics of victims and defendants and by aspects of criminal activity that do not logically relate to the issue of guilt or innocence. Where this occurs one may properly speak of prejudice, *for prejudicial evidence is any evidence that influences jury verdicts without relating logically to the issue of guilt or innocence.* Evidence that does relate logically to a disputed issue may also have a prejudicial effect, since the probative value of evidence may not fully determine its impact in the case. In terms of the regret model, one can conceptualize the prejudicial *potential* of evidence as the degree to which it affects the regret matrix of a juror viewing the case. The prejudicial *impact* of evidence depends upon prejudicial potential discounted by the juror's ability to ignore personal preferences in interpreting and applying the court's charge on burden of proof. Often the law fictively assumes that this ability is complete so long as the juror is instructed not to use evidence inappropriately, but practicing lawyers know that limiting instructions are no cure-all.

Much of the law relating to relevance reflects an awareness of the way in which

prejudicial information can influence jury decision making. The danger of prejudice justifies the exclusion of some logically relevant evidence that does not pose estimation problems, and the same danger explains why the admission of logically irrelevant evidence may be reversible error. As we shall see in Chapter Four, a number of the relevance rules are justified in part because the evidence they exclude is fraught with prejudicial potential. We shall conclude this discussion by looking briefly at two rules by way of example.

FRE 411 provides that evidence of liability insurance may not be introduced to show negligence. The possession of liability insurance appears so unrelated to carefulness that a jury is not likely to treat the fact that a defendant was insured as tending to prove the defendant's negligence. Thinking solely in terms of Bayes' Theorem, evidence of the defendant's insurance coverage might be objectionable on the ground that its introduction wastes the court's time, but there is no reason to believe that such evidence will hurt either party. However, the regret matrix suggests a more substantial reason for excluding evidence of insurance. Knowledge that the defendant was insured may inappropriately affect the verdict whenever the fact finder's relative regret at mistakenly finding for or against an insured defendant will differ from the regret that would be felt if the fact finder thought the defendant would pay personally for the damages. Such a difference appears likely. Interestingly enough, some have argued that jurors should be informed of the existence of insurance because today's jurors assume insurance exists in all cases and construct their regret matrices accordingly. Insurance companies are not worse off when their interest in the case is revealed, so the argument goes, but uninsured defendants are harmed if jurors are not aware of their status.

Consider finally the rule to be discussed in the next chapter that evidence of other crimes may not generally be admitted for the substantive purpose of showing that the defendant is guilty of the crime in question. There are at least three reasons which may be given for this. First, regardless of the association between a past criminal record and current criminal activity, it may be an important social value that no individual be considered officially more likely to engage in current crime because of past convictions. Even though such a conclusion might be correct in a probabilistic sense, it would increase the detriment which the deviant label brings to those who in fact lead blameless lives after having been convicted. Second, the fact finder in criminal cases might be particularly likely to overestimate the relationship between past convictions and subsequent behavior and thus overestimate the probability that the defendant is guilty of the crime in question. Third, and probably most important, knowledge that an individual has been guilty of past crimes may change the regret which the fact finder associates with mistakenly finding that that person is guilty. The fact finder might well think it absolutely terrible that an individual who has led a blameless life be sent to prison by mistake, but she may think it merely unfortunate that one who has spent a lifetime in and out of prison be sent away by mistake.

These models should tell you not only something about the purposes behind the rules of relevance, they should also tell you something about the tasks you must achieve as a trial lawyer. They indicate the reasons why lawyers have been so adept at circumventing those general rules which prohibit the mention of such things as the presence of insurance or the criminal history of the defendant. They also pose in a clear way the interesting question of whether it is ethical to attempt to introduce evidence solely for the purpose of changing the regret matrix of the fact finders. (Does it matter which side is making the attempt?) If you find this a helpful way to think about relevance problems, you will probably want to experiment a bit with different hypothetical values in the Bayesian equation or the regret matrix. If you are interested in pursuing the matter further, two good articles which deal with Bayesian statistics (for somewhat different purposes) are: Finkelstein and Fairley, "A Bayesian Approach to Identification Evidence" 83 Harv.L.Rev. 489 (1970), and Tribe, "Trial by Mathematics: Precision and Ritual in the Legal Process" 84 Harv.L.Rev. 1329 (1971). Either of these will present you with a derivation of Bayes Theorem from the two basic propositions of probability theory presented above. An article you might want to consult on decision theory and regret matrices is: Kaplan, "Decision Theory and the Factfinding Process" 20 Stan.L.Rev. 1065 (1968).

K. RELEVANCE AND OPINION

The principles expressed by Federal Rules 401, 402 and 403 are at the core of the law of evidence. Most of the evidence rules that you shall study sound variations on the theme that all relevant evidence should be admitted unless its probative value is outweighed by a tendency to prejudice, mislead or otherwise confuse the trier of fact. The hearsay rule, for example, seeks to specify situations where the probative value of evidence is likely to be so low or so indeterminate that it makes sense to keep information from the jury. The rules regarding authentication require special guarantees of relevance where it seems feasible to demand such guarantees and where the class of evidence involved is likely to be of particular importance. Indeed, of those rules commonly used to exclude evidence only the rules of privilege are justified by values that have little to do with the themes of this chapter.

Perhaps no rules come closer to restating the basic relevance theme than FRE 701 and FRE 702, which define the occasions when opinion testimony will be received from lay witnesses and experts respectively. In both cases the key to admissibility is that opinion will help the trier of fact understand evidence or determine a fact in issue. This is the subjective side of FRE 401. If evidence has the objective tendency to make the existence of a consequential fact more or less probable than it otherwise would be, it should aid the fact finder in understanding the evidence or determining facts in issue.

In the case of lay witnesses, disputes over the admissibility of opinion are, as you have seen in Chapter One, disputes about when a preference for concrete description should preclude more conclusory testimony. Lay witnesses are presumed to know no more about the implications of facts than the average juror. Thus, lay testimony that only interprets facts that could be given to the jury is at best redundant since if the witness' interpretation is accurate the jury would presumably reach the same conclusion. If the witness' conclusion is inaccurate, the jury may be misled if the supporting facts have not been sufficiently specified to allow an independent judgment or if the jury mistakenly credits the witness with particular insight into the matter in question. Without an

opinion rule, testimony by a lay witness that does no more than reveal the witness' interpretation of facts in evidence would be properly excluded as irrelevant.[27]

The situation is different with expert witnesses. Where facts in evidence cannot be understood except in the light of scientific, technical or other specialized knowledge the expert is allowed to tell the jury how the facts should be interpreted.[28] If relevance were only an objective phenomenon, the expert's testimony should be excludable as irrelevant (except where the expert reports an investigation of factual matters), for expert interpretations do not make the existence of consequential facts more or less probable than they otherwise would be. What expert interpretation does do is make consequential facts *appear to the jury* as more or less probable because the jury learns what esoteric facts imply to one who is used to dealing with such facts, and may, if the expert testimony is well presented, come to understand the reasons why the facts justify particular conclusions. Evidence which aids the jury in understanding the import of other evidence is properly considered relevant, for fact finding is a subjective process and better understanding of the evidence should lead to more rational judgments.[29]

27. The lay opinions we do allow tell us more than the witness' views of given facts. Typically they imply observations that could not be easily described in more concrete terms, either because the English language does not readily allow more concrete description (as is the case when we estimate the speed of a car) or because the opinion captures a gestalt which is based on facts that we may not consciously attend to or which we would not remember well enough to describe (as is the case when we say someone is drunk).

28. Expert testimony is not limited to interpretations and opinions. An expert may present facts to the jury that are every bit as concrete as the facts lay people testify to. In the Whale case, for example, only an expert could have chemically analyzed the contents of the Prince Albert can, but Wall's report of the results of his analysis falls on the

factual side of the fuzzy line between fact and opinion.

29. **Attention to the subjective dimension also explains how maps, diagrams, charts and the like are relevant. Obviously, they do not make facts in issue more or less probable than they otherwise would be. However, to the extent they aid the jury in understanding other evidence, they make facts in issue appear more or less probable than would otherwise be the case. The admissibility of such aids turns largely on their accuracy, for if they are inaccurate they are more likely to mislead the jury than to aid it. Because such aids do not change objective probabilities, trial judges have considerable discretion in deciding whether to allow them. Judicial authority for controlling modes of proof is given by FRE 611(a).**

Courts welcome expert opinions so long as the experts are interpreting facts of a kind that lay people are not ordinarily called upon to evaluate. They are much less hospitable to experts who seek to apply a body of specialized knowledge to problems that lay people are accustomed to dealing with or to testimony that seeks to sharpen the jury's common sense by acquainting jurors with the way an expert would approach their evaluation problem and telling them what aspects of the evidence an expert would deem important. Thus, despite years of campaigning by Wigmore, few courts have allowed psychiatrists to testify to the credibility of rape victims, and in a celebrated case that forms the basis for one of the problems that follows, a guilty verdict was reversed because the trial judge allowed a statistician to describe how a mathematical decision theorist might evaluate the implications of certain items of circumstantial evidence.[30]

In excluding expert testimony of this kind, courts sometimes speak of "invading the province of the jury." Behind this rhetoric is the idea that the expert's testimony will not aid the jury because it deals with matters that an unassisted group of lay people can intelligently evaluate. There is also the notion that the jurors, as the law's chosen fact finders, should not be told how to view evidence unless their unaided judgment is likely to be deficient in some respect. If it is indeed the case that expert testimony will not assist the jury in evaluating some fact because the jury needs no assistance, the expert testimony does not qualify under FRE 702 and is properly barred under FRE 403 for its tendency to waste time and the possibility it might mislead or confuse the jury.

However, just because we have always trusted juries to make certain kinds of evaluations does not mean that expert instruction will not aid the jury in its task. For example, consider Robert Buckhout's article on eyewitness testimony that we reproduce below. Is the jury in a case that rests largely on an identification by an eyewitness likely to be aided by expert testimony that makes the points Buckhout makes in his article? Exactly how would such testimony be relevant? If experts like Buckhout are allowed to testify, should they be able to express judgments about the accuracy of the particular identifications that are at issue in the case?

These questions are more than just academic. Courts are, with increasing frequency, confronting the issue of whether to allow expert testimony on the foibles of memory and perception. Reading just the appellate cases one might think that the defense, the side that is invariably plumping for admissibility, never wins. As of this writing, it appears that no appellate court has reversed a trial court for excluding such testimony. But the rule is not that experts cannot testify on eyewitness identifications. Rather, it is that trial judges have discretion and their decisions will be respected no matter how they decide. The authors have been told by an acknowledged expert in this area that about half the time her testimony is allowed and they have discovered judges, both federal and state, who favor the use of such experts. Given the basic relevance rules, the centrality of eyewitness identifications in criminal cases and growing psychological learning one wonders how long the rule of discretion will be maintained.[31]

30. People v. Collins, 68 Cal.2d 319, 66 Cal.Rptr. 497, 438 P.2d 33 (1968).

31. **Expert testimony is not the only way to alert juries to the problematic aspects of eyewitness identification. Careful jury instructions based on the scientific literature may be developed, or, in jurisdictions that permit judicial comment on the evidence, the judge may caution the jury about aspects of eyewitness testimony. These possibilities should remind you of a more important point: the jury can and does receive information from sources other than testimony.**

BUCKHOUT, EYEWITNESS TESTIMONY

231 Scientific American 23–31 (Dec. 1974).[32]

The woman in the witness box stares at the defendant, points an accusing finger and says, loudly and firmly, "That's the man! That's him! I could never forget his face!" It is impressive testimony. The only eyewitness to a murder has identified the murderer. Or has she?

Perhaps she has, but she may be wrong. Eyewitness testimony is unreliable. Research and courtroom experience provide ample evidence that an eyewitness to a crime is being asked to be something and do something that a normal human being was not created to be or do. Human perception is sloppy and uneven, albeit remarkably effective in serving our need to create structure out of experience. In an investigation or in court, however, a witness is often asked to play the role of a kind of tape recorder on whose tape the events of the crime have left an impression. The prosecution probes for stored facts and scenes and tries to establish that the witness's recording equipment was and still is in perfect running order. The defense cross-examines the witness to show that there are defects in the recorder and gaps in the tape. Both sides, and usually the witness too, succumb to the fallacy that everything was recorded and can be played back later through questioning.

Those of us who have done research in eyewitness identification reject that fallacy. It reflects a 19th-century view of man as perceiver, which asserted a parallel between the mechanisms of the physical world and those of the brain. Human perception is a more complex information-processing mechanism. So is memory. The person who sees an accident or witnesses a crime and is then asked to describe what he saw cannot call up an "in-stant replay." He must depend on his memory, with all its limitations. The limitations may be unimportant in ordinary daily activities. If someone is a little unreliable, if he trims the truth a bit in describing what he has seen, it ordinarily does not matter too much. When he is a witness, the inaccuracy escalates in importance.

Human perception and memory function effectively by being selective and constuctive. As Ulric Neisser of Cornell University has pointed out, "Neither perception nor memory is a copying process." Perception and memory are decision-making processes affected by the totality of a person's abilities, background, attitudes, motives and beliefs, by the environment and by the way his recollection is eventually tested. The observer is an active rather than a passive perceiver and recorder; he reaches conclusions on what he has seen by evaluating fragments of information and reconstructing them. He is motivated by a desire to be accurate as he imposes meaning on the overabundance of information that impinges on his senses, but also by a desire to live up to the expectations of other people and to stay in their good graces. The eye, the ear and other sense organs are therefore social organs as well as physical ones.

Psychologists studying the capabilities of the sense organs speak of an "ideal observer," one who would respond to lights or tones with unbiased eyes and ears, but we know that the ideal observer does not exist. We speak of an "ideal physical environment," free of distractions and distortions, but we know that such an environment can only be approached, and then only in the laboratory. My colleagues and I at the Brooklyn College of the City University of New York distinguish a number of factors that we believe inherently limit a person's ability to give a complete account of events he once saw or to identify with complete accuracy the people who were involved.

The first sources of unreliability are implicit in the original situation. One is the insignificance—at the time and to the witness—of the events that were observed. In placing someone at or near the scene of a crime, for example, witnesses are often being asked to recall seeing the accused at a time when they were not attaching importance to the event, which was observed in passing, as a part of the normal routine of an ordinary day. As long ago as 1895 J. McKeen Cattell wrote about an experiment in which he asked students to describe the people, places and events they had encountered walking to school over familiar paths. The reports were incomplete and unreliable; some individuals were very sure of details that had no basis in fact. Insignificant events do not motivate a person to bring fully into play the selective process of attention.

The length of the period of observation obviously limits the number of features a person can attend to. When the tachistoscope, a projector with a variable-speed shutter that controls the length of an image's appearance on a screen, is used in controlled research to test recall, the shorter times produce less reliable identification and recall. Yet fleeting glimpses are common in eyewitness accounts, particularly in fast-moving, threatening situations. In the Sacco-Vanzetti case in the 1920's a witness gave a detailed description of one defendant on the basis of a fraction-of-a-second glance. The description must have been a fabrication.

Less then ideal observation conditions usually apply; crimes seldom occur in a well-controlled laboratory. Often distance, poor lighting, fast movement or the presence of a crowd interferes with the efficient working of the attention process. Well-established thresholds for the eye and the other senses have been established by

research, and as those limits are approached eyewitness accounts become quite unreliable. In one case in my experience a police officer testified that he saw the defendant, a black man, shoot a victim as both stood in a doorway 120 feet away. Checking for the defense, we found the scene so poorly lit that we could hardly see a person's silhouette, let alone a face; instrument measurements revealed that the light falling on the eye amounted to less than a fifth of the light from a candle. The defense presented photographs and light readings to demonstrate that a positive identification was not very probable. The members of the jury went to the scene of the crime, had the one black juror stand in the doorway, found they could not identify his features and acquitted the defendant.

The witness himself is a major source of unreliability. To begin with, he may have been observing under stress. When a person's life or well-being is threatened, there is a response that includes an increased heart rate, breathing rate and blood pressure and a dramatic increase in the flow of adrenalin and of available energy, making the person capable of running fast, fighting, lifting enormous weight—taking the steps necessary to ensure his safety or survival. The point is, however, that a person under extreme stress is also a less than normally reliable witness. In experimental situations an observer is less capable of remembering details, less accurate in reading dials and less accurate in detecting signals when under stress; he is quite naturally paying more attention to his own well-being and safety than to non-essential elements in environment. Research I have done with Air Force flight-crew members confirms that even highly trained people become poorer observers under stress. The actual threat that brought on the stress response, having been highly significant at the time, can be remembered; but memory for other details such as clothing and colors is not as clear;

time estimates are particularly exaggerated.

The observer's physical condition is often a factor. A person may be too old or too sick or too tired to perceive clearly, or he may simply lack the necessary faculty. In one case I learned that a witness who had testified about shades of red had admitted to the grand jury that he was color-blind. I testified at the trial that he was apparently dichromatic, or red-green color-blind, and that his testimony was probably fabricated on the basis of information other than visual evidence. The prosecution brought on his ophthalmologist, presumably as a rebuttal witness, but the ophthalmologist testified that the witness was actually monochromatic, which meant he could perceive no colors at all. Clearly the witness was "filling in" his testimony. That, after all, is how color-blind people function in daily life, by making inferences about colors they cannot distinguish.

Psychologists have done extensive research on how "set," or expectancy, is used by the observer to make judgments more efficiently. In a classic experiment done in the 1930's by Jerome S. Bruner and Leo Postman at Harvard University observers were shown a display of playing cards for a few seconds and asked to report the number of aces of spades in the display. After a brief glance most observers reported seeing three aces of spades. Actually there were five; two of them were colored red instead of the more familiar black. People are so familiar with black aces of spades that they do not waste time looking at the display carefully. The prior conditioning of the witness may cause him similarly to report facts or events that were not present but that he thinks should have been present.

Expectancy is seen in its least attractive form in the case of biases or prejudices. A victim of a mugging may initially report being attacked by "niggers" and may, because of prejudice or limited experience

(or both), be unable to tell one black man from another. ("They all look alike to me.") In a classic study of this phenomenon Gordon W. Allport of Harvard had his subjects take a brief look at a drawing of several people on a subway train, including a seated black man and a white man standing with a razor in his hand. Fifty percent of the observers later reported that the razor was in the hand of the black man. Most people file away some stereotypes on the basis of which they make perceptual judgments; such stereotypes not only lead to prejudice but are also tools for making decisions more efficiently. A witness to an automobile accident may report not what he saw but his ingrained stereotype about women drivers. Such short-cuts to thinking may be erroneously reported and expanded on by an eyewitness without his being aware that he is describing his stereotype rather than actual events. If the witness's biases are shared by the investigator taking a statement, the report may reflect their mutual biases rather than what was actually seen.

The tendency to see what we want or need to see has been demonstrated by numerous experiments in which people report seeing things that in fact are not present. R. Levine, Isador Chein and Gardner Murphy had volunteers go without food for 24 hours and report what they "saw" in a series of blurred slides presented on a screen. The longer they were deprived of food the more frequently they reported seeing "food" in the blurred pictures. An analysis of the motives of the eyewitness at the time of a crime can be very valuable in determining whether or not the witness is reporting what he wanted to see. In one study I conducted at Washington University a student dressed in a black bag that covered him completely visited a number of classes. Later the students in those classes were asked to describe the nature of the person in the bag. Most of their reports went far beyond the meager evidence: the bag-covered figure was said to be a black man, "a nut," a symbol of alienation and so on. Further tests showed that the descriptions were related to the needs and motives of the individual witness.

Journalists and psychologists have noted a tendency for people to maintain they were present when a significant historical event took place near where they live even though they were not there at all; such people want to sound interesting, to be a ⟨ ⟩ of history. A journalist once ⟨ ⟩ a charming human interest story ⟨ ⟩aked woman stuck to a newly ⟨ ⟩ilet seat in a small town and got ⟨ ⟩ed by newspaper wire services. ⟨ ⟩ the town and interviewed citi⟨ ⟩claimed to have witnessed and ⟨ ⟩ave played a part in the totally ⟨ ⟩event. In criminal cases with ⟨ ⟩nd a controversial defendant it ⟨ ⟩ommon for volunteer witnesses ⟨ ⟩rward with spurious testimony.

⟨ ⟩ility stemming from the original ⟨ ⟩nd from the observer's fallibility ⟨ ⟩ed by the circumstances attend⟨ ⟩ntual attempt at information re⟨ ⟩rst of all there is the obvious fact, ⟨ ⟩by a considerable amount of re⟨ ⟩t people forget verbal and pic⟨ ⟩mation with the passage of time. ⟨ ⟩imply too busy coping with daily life to keep paying attention to what they heard or saw; perfect recall of information is basically unnecessary and is rarely if ever displayed. The testing of recognition in a police "lineup" or a set of identification photographs is consequently less reliable the longer the time from the event to the test. With time, for example, there is often a filling in of spurious details: an incomplete or fragmentary image is "cleaned up" by the observer when he is tested later. Allport used to have students draw a rough geometric shape right after such a shape was shown to them. Then they were tested on their ability to reproduce the drawing 30 days later and again three months later. The observers

tended first to make the figure more symmetrical than it really was and later to render it as a neat equilateral triangle. This finding was repeated with many objects, the tendency being for people to "improve" their recollection by making it seem more logical.

In analyses of eyewitness reports in criminal cases we have seen the reports get more accurate, more complete and less ambiguous as the witness moves from the initial police report through grand jury questioning to testimony at the trial. The process of filling in is an efficient way to remember but it can lead to unreliable recognition testing: the witness may adjust his memory to fit the available suspects or pictures. The witness need not be lying; he may be unaware he is distorting or reconstructing his memory. In his very effort to be conscientious he may fabricate parts of his recall to make a chaotic memory seem more plausible to the people asking questions. The questions themselves may encourage such fabrication. Beth Loftus of the University of Washington has demonstrated how altering the semantic value of the words in questions about a filmed auto accident causes witnesses to distort their reports. When witnesses were asked a question using the word "smashed" as opposed to "bumped" they gave higher estimates of speed and were more likely to report having seen broken glass—although there was no broken glass.

Unfair test construction often encourages error. The lineup or the array of photographs for testing the eyewitness's ability to identify a suspect can be analyzed as fair or unfair on the basis of criteria most psychologists can agree on. A fair test is designed carefully so that all faces have an equal chance of being selected by someone who did not see the suspect; the faces are similar enough to one another and to the original description of the suspect to be confusing to a person who is merely guessing; the test is conducted without leading questions or suggestions. All too frequently lineups or photograph arrays are carelessly assembled or even rigged. If, for example, there are five pictures, the chance should be only one in five that any one picture will be chosen on the basis of guessing.

Frequently, however, one picture—the picture of the suspect—may stand out. In the case of the black activist Angela Davis one set of nine photographs used to check identification included three pictures of the defendant taken at an outdoor rally, two police "mug shots" of other women with their names displayed, a picture of a 55-year-old woman and so on. It was so easy for a witness to rule out five of the pictures as ridiculous choices that the test was reduced to four photographs, including three of Miss Davis. The probability was therefore 75 percent that a witness would pick out her picture whether he had seen her or not. Such a "test" is meaningless to a psychologist and is probably tainted as evidence in court.

Research on memory has also shown that if one item in the array of photographs is uniquely different—say in dress, race, height, sex or photographic quality—it is more likely to be picked out. Such an array is simply not confusing enough for it to be called a test. A teacher who makes up a multiple-choice test includes several answers that sound or look alike to make it difficult for a person who does not know the right answer to succeed. Police lineups and picture layouts are multiple-choice tests; if the rules for designing tests are ignored, the tests are unreliable.

No test, with photographs or a lineup, can be completely free of suggestion. When a witness is brought in by the police to attempt an identification, he can safely assume that there is some reason: that the authorities have a suspect in mind or even in custody. He is therefore under pressure to pick someone even if the officer

showing the photographs is properly careful not to force the issue. The basic books on eyewitness identification all recommend that no suggestions, hints or pressure be transmitted to the witness, but my experience with criminal investigation reveals frequent abuse by zealous police officers. Such abuses include making remarks about which pictures to skip, saying, "Are you sure?" when the witness makes an error, giving hints, showing enthusiasm when the "right" picture is picked and so on. There is one version of the lineup in which five police officers in civilian clothes stand in the line, glancing obviously at the one real suspect. Suggestion can be subtler. In some experiments the test giver was merely instructed to smile and be very approving when a certain kind of photograph or statement was picked; such social approval led to an increase in the choosing of just those photographs even though there was no "correct" answer. A test that measures a need for social approval has shown that people who are high in that need (particularly those who enthusiastically volunteer information) are particularly strongly influenced by suggestion and approval coming from the test giver.

Conformity is another troublesome influence. One might expect that two eyewitnesses—or 10 or 100—who agree are better than one. Similarity of judgment is a two-edged sword, however: people can agree in error as easily as in truth. A large body of research results demonstrates that an observer can be persuaded to conform to the majority opinion even when the majority is completely wrong. In one celebrated experiment, first performed in the 1950's by Solomon E. Asch at Swarthmore College, seven observers are shown two lines and asked to say which is the shorter. Six of the people are in the pay of the experimenter; they all say that the objectively longer line is the shorter one. After hearing six people say this, the naïve subject is on the spot. Astonishingly the majority of the naïve subjects say that the long line is short—in the face of reality and in spite of the fact that alone they would have no trouble giving the correct answer [see "Opinions and Social Pressure," by Solomon E. Asch; Scientific American, November, 1955].

To test the effect of conformity a group of my students at Brooklyn College, led by Andrea Alper, staged a "crime" in a classroom, asked for individual descriptions and then put the witnesses into groups so as to produce composite descriptions of the suspect. The group descriptions were more complete than the individual reports but gave rise to significantly more errors of commission: an assortment of incorrect and stereotyped details. For example, the groups (but not the individuals) reported incorrectly that the suspect was wearing the standard student attire, blue jeans.

The effects of suggestion increase when figures in obvious authority do the testing. In laboratory research we find more suggestibility and changing of attitudes when the tester is older or of apparently higher status, better dressed or wearing a uniform or a white coat—or is a pretty woman. In court I have noticed that witnesses who work together under a supervisor are hard put to disagree with their boss in testifying or in picking a photograph. The process of filling in details can be exaggerated when the boss and his employee compare their information and the employee feels obligated to back up his boss to remain in his good graces. Legal history is not lacking in anecdotes about convict witnesses who were rewarded by the authorities for their cooperation in making an identification.

In criminal investigations, as in scientific investigations, a theory can be a powerful tool for clarifying confusion, but it can also lead to distortion and unreliability if people attempt, perhaps unconsciously, to make fact fit theory and close their minds to the real meanings of facts. The eye-

witness who feels pressed to say something may shape his memory to fit a theory, particularly a highly publicized and seemingly reasonable one. Robert Rosenthal of Harvard studied this effect. He devised a test in which people were supposed to pick out a "successful" face from a set of photographs. There was actually no correct answer, but the experimenter dropped hints to his assistants as to what he thought the results should be. When they subsequently administered the test the assistants unconsciously signaled the subjects as to which photograph to pick, thus producing results that supported their boss's theory. Any test is a social interaction as well as a test.

There is a nagging gap between data on basic perceptual processes in controlled research settings and important questions about perception in the less well-controlled real world. Inspired by the new approach to perception research exemplified in the work of Neisser and of Ralph Norman Haber of the University of Rochester, my colleagues and I have felt that this gap can only be bridged by conducting empirical research on eyewitness identification in a somewhat real world. In one such experiment we staged an assault on the campus of the California State University at Hayward: a student "attacked" a professor in front of 141 witnesses; another outsider of the same age was on the scene as a bystander. We recorded the entire incident on videotape so that we could compare the true event with the eyewitness reports. After the attack we took sworn statements from each witness, asking them to describe the suspect, his clothes and whatever they could remember about the incident. We also asked each witness to rate his own confidence in the accuracy of his description.

As we expected, the descriptions were quite inaccurate, as is usually the case in such situations. The passage of time was overestimated by a factor of almost two and a half to one. The average weight estimate for the attacker was 14 percent too high, and his age was underestimated by more than two years. The total accuracy score, with points given for those judgments and for others on appearance and dress, was only 25 percent of the maximum possible score. (Only the height estimate was close. This may be because the suspect was of average height; people often cite known facts about the "average" man when they are uncertain.)

We then waited seven weeks and presented a set of six photographs to each witness individually under four different experimental conditions. There were two kinds of instructions: low-bias, in which witnesses were asked only if they recognized anybody in the photographs and high-bias, in which witnesses were reminded of the attack incident, told that we had an idea who the suspect was and asked to find the attacker in one of two arrangements of photographs, all well-lit frontal views of young men including the attacker and the bystander. In the unbiased picture spread all six portraits were neatly set out with about the same expression on all the faces and with similar clothing. In the biased spread the attacker was shown with a distinctive expression and his portrait was positioned at an angle.

Only 40 percent of the witnesses identified the suspect correctly; 25 percent of them identified the innocent bystander instead; even the professor who was attacked picked out the innocent man. The highest proportion of correct identifications, 61 percent, was achieved with a combination of a biased set of photographs and biased instructions. The degree of confidence in picking suspect No. 5, the attacker, was also significantly higher in that condition. We have subsequently tested the same picture spreads with groups that never saw the original incident. We describe the assault and ask people to pick the most likely perpetrator. Under the biased conditions they too pick No. 5.

In another study undertaken at Brooklyn College a student team, led by Miriam Slomovits, staged a live purse-snatching incident in a classroom. We gave the witnesses the usual questionnaire and got the usual bad scores. This time, however, we were concerned with a specific dilemma: Why is recognition so much better than recall? In private most lawyers and judges agree that the recall of a crime by a witness is very bad, but they still believe people can successfully identify a suspect. What we had to do was to break away from our demonstrations of how bad witnesses are at recalling details and search for what makes a witness good at recognizing a face. To do so we took the witnesses who had predictably given poor recall data and gave them a difficult recognition test. Our witnesses got not only a lineup with the actual purse-snatcher in the group but also a second lineup that included only a person who looked like the purse-snatcher. The question was: Would the witnesses pick only the real culprit and avoid making a mistaken identification of the person who looked like him?

We videotaped two lineups of five persons each and showed them in counterbalanced order to 52 witnesses of the purse-snatching. Very few witnesses were completely successful in making a positive identification without ambiguity. An equal number of witnesses impeached themselves by picking the man who resembled the culprit after having correctly picked the culprit. Most people simply made a mistaken identification. Our best witnesses had also been among the best performers in the recall test, that is, they had made significantly fewer errors of commission (adding incorrect details). They had not given particularly complete reports, but at least they had not filled in. The good witnesses also expressed less confidence than witnesses who impeached themselves. Finally, when we referred to the earlier written descriptions of the suspect we found our successful witnesses had given significantly higher, and hence more accurate, estimates of weight. People guessing someone's weight often invoke a mental chart of ideal weight for height and err substantially if the person is fat. Our purse-snatcher was unusually heavy, something the successful witnesses managed to observe in spite of his loose-fitting clothing. The others were guessing.

Once again we noted that witnesses tend not to say, "I don't know." Eighty percent of our witnesses tried to pick the suspect even though most of them were mistaken. The social influence of the lineup itself seems to encourage a "yes" response. This effect presented a disturbing problem that actually drove us back from these rather realistically enacted crimes to the more controlled, emotionally neutral environment of the laboratory. We hoped to design a test for eyewitnesses that could distinguish a good witness from a poor one, under circumstances in which we knew what the true facts were.

Pure measures of accuracy would not be adequate, since there are many different kinds of error, some of which come from the witness's desire to please the questioner with an abundance of details. Eventually we settled on adapting signal-detection theory, espoused by John A. Swets of the Massachusetts Institute of Technology, to the eyewitness situation. Signal-detection theory evolved in psychophysics as a means of coping with the fact that an observer's attitude "interferes" with his detection, processing and reporting of sensory stimuli. Limited to saying "yes" or "no" (I hear or see or smell it, or whatever), the observer applies criteria that vary with personality, experience, anticipated cost or reward, motivation to please the tester or to frustrate him and other factors. What the experimenter does, therefore, is usually to present noise about half of the time and signals plus noise about half of the time and to count correct "yes" answers (hits) and incorrect "yes" answers (false alarms), combining the scores statis-tically into a single measure of observer sensitivity. This quantifies an estimate of the observer's criteria for judging his immediate experience. A very cautious person might have very few false alarms and a high proportion of hits, indicating that he says "yes" sparingly; a less than cautious person might say "yes" most of the time, scoring a large number of hits but only at the price of a large number of false alarms.

In our research at Brooklyn College Lynne Williams and I now show a film of a supposed crime and then present to the observers 20 true statements about the incident and the same number of false statements. The witness indicates "yes" or "no" as to the truth of each statement. We end up with a record of hits and false alarms which, after some complicated statistical processing, yields a curve called a receiver-operating-characteristic (ROC) curve. A person whose hits and false alarms were equal, indicating that the answers had no relation to the true facts would generate a straight diagonal ROC curve. A perfect witness would have all hits and no false alarms. Real people fall somewhere in between. We have found so far that witnesses with the better (which is to say higher) ROC curves go on to do better than other people at recognizing the suspect in a lineup. We are using the ROC function to test various hypotheses about how environmental conditions, stress, mental set, bias in interrogation, age, sex, and social, ethnic and economic group affect the accuracy and reliability of eyewitnesses.

Psychological research on human perception has advanced from the 19th-century recording-machine analogy to a more complex understanding of selective decision-making processes that are more human and hence more useful. My colleagues and I feel that psychologists can make a needed contribution to the judicial system by directing contemporary research methods to real-world problems and by speaking out in court (as George A. Miller of Rockefeller University puts it, by "giving psychology away").

It is discouraging to note that the essential findings on the unreliability of eyewitness testimony were made by Hugo Münsterberg nearly 80 years ago, and yet the practice of basing a case on eyewitness testimony and trying to persuade a jury that such testimony is superior to circumstantial evidence continues to this day. The fact is that both types of evidence involve areas of doubt. Circumstantial evidence is tied together with a theory, which is subject to questioning. Eyewitness testimony is also based on a theory, constructed by a human being (often with help from others), about what reality was like in the past; since that theory can be adjusted or changed in accordance with personality, with the situation or with social pressure, it is unwise to accept such testimony without question. It is up to a jury to determine if the doubts about an eyewitness's testimony are reasonable enough for the testimony to be rejected as untrue. Jurors should be reminded that there can be doubt about eyewitness testimony, just as there is about any other kind of evidence.

Problem III–1. Todd Goodwin, a newspaper columnist, is charged with attempted extortion. He allegedly called Hazel Banks, a single woman running for Congress, and told her that unless she paid him $50,000 he would in his column reveal that she had had an affair some two years before which resulted in an aborted pregnancy. Banks, instead of paying the money, called the police. At trial, Goodwin wants to introduce his informants who will testify that they told him about Banks' affair and that what they told him was true. **Should the trial judge allow this testimony?** Suppose Goodwin had never threatened Banks but had published a column describing her affair. **Should the judge admit the testimony of Goodwin's informants in civil suit for libel brought by Banks against Goodwin?**

Problem III–2. Ruth Smith, a Michigan resident, sues the Buckeye Bus Company, an Ohio corporation, for the wrongful death of her husband. Since her husband's death Ms. Smith has married a millionaire and is financially much better off than she was or ever expected to be while married to her first husband. Nevertheless, she seeks to recover that portion of her first husband's future earnings that would have accrued to her. Buckeye wants to introduce evidence of Smith's remarriage to show that she has not been harmed financially by her first husband's death. It is clear that under Michigan law defendants in wrongful death actions may not introduce evidence of remarriage to mitigate claims for lost spousal earnings. **Should Buckeye be allowed to introduce this evidence in a diversity action brought in the Federal District Court for the Eastern District of Michigan?**

Problem III–3. Hank Jones is on trial for killing a bartender who had accused him of not paying for his drinks. As part of his defense Jones calls Dr. Jacobs, an experienced psychiatrist. Dr. Jacobs testifies over the prosecution's objection that Jones has a personality disorder which when coupled with the use of alcohol causes him to lose all control and lash out at those who threaten him. Dr. Jacobs also testifies that in his opinion it was Jones' personality disorder which led him to stab the bartender when the bartender threatened to call the police unless Jones paid his bar bill. On cross-examination the doctor admits that despite his personality disorder Jones knows right from wrong and that the impulse to lash out is not irresistable unless Jones is very drunk. At the conclusion of her cross-examination the prosecutor renews her objection and moves to strike the doctor's testimony. **Does the judge's ruling depend on whether Jones is charged with first degree murder, second degree murder or manslaughter?** Suppose Dr. Jacobs had testified that he was 80% certain that Jones had stabbed the bartender under the impulse of his personality disorder, but there was a 20% chance that he was mistaken in his diagnosis and that Jones knew exactly what he was doing. **Would this testimony have been admissible in the first instance?**

Problem III–4. Defendant is indicted for knowingly damaging the dwelling house of X by fire. At the trial, the prosecution offers into evidence a large, authenticated photograph showing a portion of the smoldering remains of X's house in the background and the anguished faces of X and her husband prominently featured in the foreground. **Is the photo relevant? How might defendant protect against its admission?**

Problem III–5. Plaintiff was injured in an industrial accident, losing a leg and a hand. In the resulting lawsuit Plaintiff seeks to introduce a film which shows him engaged in a series of activities around his house. The film was taken by a professional photographer over a period of three hours. Plaintiff's activities were not rehearsed, no special camera effects were used, and the film was not edited. However, only 25 minutes of activity were filmed during the time the photographer was in the house. The film depicts the Plaintiff doing normal household activities or attempting to do them. These include such things as raking leaves in his yard, setting the dinner table, moving furniture, getting out of bed and strapping on his prosthetic devices, driving a car, loading a gun (although he was not actually hunting), and operating a fishing reel (although he was not actually fishing). In addition it shows him hugging his daughter and placing a cigarette in the mouth of his quadriplegic brother. The Plaintiff is clearly handicapped in all these activities, although the degree of handicap varies. He manages to do all of them in some way. Plaintiff would like to introduce this film as part of his effort to prove damages at the trial. Defendant objects saying the film is redundant and irrelevant as well as prejudicial. **How should the trial court rule? Should it rule differently with respect to some of the behaviors depicted than with respect to the others? If so, why?**

Problem III–6. Carrie Miles is charged with mail fraud in connection with the advertisement and sale of her "Magnificent Magnetic Oil Detector." The crux of the charge is that she circulated through the mails advertisements which claimed that the machine was an effective way of detecting oil up to seven thousand feet below the earth's surface when in fact it was useless. At trial Miles persists in her claim that the device is effective and as proof of this she offers to testify that before marketing the device she tested it on 60 different occasions, and in each test the device correctly indicated the presence or absence of oil. The prosecutor convinces the judge that the tests were not sufficiently accurate to warrant relying on them as proof that the device worked. **Should the judge nevertheless admit the testimony on Miles' theory? Is there any other theory on which the testimony might be allowed? If you were the prosecutor and had convincing evidence that Miles' tests were scientifically unsound would you have wanted her testimony to be excluded?**

Problem III–7. Defendant is a gynecologist-obstetrician. She is accused of performing an illegal abortion. The prosecution seeks to introduce into evidence cervical dilators found in her office. Cervical dilators are equipment used in performing abortions. **Is the evidence relevant? Can you answer this without knowing anything about gynecology? Could you conduct a proper defense without knowing anything about this field?**

Problem III–8. Assume that in the Whale case officer Barrott had taken the can alleged to contain marihuana from Norton and placed it on his desk in plain sight in the police station. He then was called away for an hour during which time about 20 police officers and 10 civilian employees of the police department could have tampered with the can. Upon his return, Barrott noticed the can and locked it away, later transferring it, as related, to the chemist Wall for analysis. **In these circumstances would Wall's testimony that the substance in the can was marihuana have been irrelevant? Would this testimony have been admissible? Assuming that the facts are as sketched above, what is the likelihood that this version of the facts would be presented to the court?**

Problem III–9. Plaintiff sued to recover the purchase price from the defendant for a drum of paint. Plaintiff had purchased another drum of paint from the defendant at an earlier time—6 months earlier—and after the purchase of the second drum, plaintiff found that the first was defective. As a result of using the defective paint, plaintiff's barn roof rotted. Thus, plaintiff returned the second drum unopened and unexamined to the defendant and asked for the return of the purchase price. Defendant refused. At trial, plaintiff sought to introduce evidence tending to show the defective nature of the first batch of paint. **Should the evidence be admitted on the issue of whether the paint in the second drum was defective? On some other issue? Is it important that the case on which this problem is based arose in the 1920's and not the 1980's?**

Problem III–10. Peggy Pender sues Daphne Defoe, alleging she was injured when Defoe's car in which she, Peggy, was a passenger went off the road because Defoe was driving far over the speed limit. At trial, Pender offers evidence that two years before Defoe had been arrested three times in the space of eight months for drunk driving. Defoe objects to this evidence because there is no allegation that she was drunk at the time of the accident. The judge overrules the objection and admits the evidence, "for what it's worth". **Is this decision correct? May Defoe in her case-inchief introduce evidence proving any of the following:**

  (a) That for sixteen months she has been attending Alcoholics Anonymous meetings on a regular basis and that during that time she hasn't touched a drop of alcohol?

(b) That for a year she has been working as a truckdriver and that she has been recently cited as her company's "safe driver of the year", the first time a "rookie" has won that honor?

(c) That Pender was riding in her car because Pender had recently lost her license after being convicted for the fourth time for drunk driving?

Would your ruling on any of these items of evidence be different if Pender did not succeed in introducing evidence of Defoe's history of drunk driving?

Problem III–11. Seller sues to recover $500 from Buyer, allegedly owing from the sale of an automobile by Seller to Buyer. Seller contends that the parties agreed that the car would be transferred from Seller to Buyer in exchange for Buyer's paying $2,000. The money was to be paid in three installments: first, there would be $500 down; next, there would be a payment of $1,000 one month after the down-payment; and finally, there would be a payment of $500 one month after the second installment. Alleging that only $1,500 was paid, Seller claims that he is entitled to recover the remaining $500. Buyer alleges that the contract called for a total sales price of only $1,500. Seller offers to introduce the testimony of Offeree, who will testify that two days before the sale was consummated between Seller and Buyer, Seller offered him the car for $2,000. Buyer objects to this testimony. **Should it be admitted? Would it make any difference if Seller offered the testimony of Offeree 1, Offeree 2, Offeree 3, and Offeree 4, who will all testify that within a short time before the sale was made between Buyer and Seller, Seller offered each of them the car for $2,000. Is this additional testimony likely to make the probability greater that the testimony of Offeree 1 will be admitted? Is it likely that all four witnesses will be permitted to testify, or will their testimony be deemed cumulative? Would your conclusion be the same if the other sales offers had been made in early August and the sale occurred in late October?**

Problem III–12. Defendant is charged with burglary of a home. He pleads not guilty. The prosecution seeks to introduce into evidence the fact that on the night of the burglary defendant was arrested three houses away for selling narcotics. **Is the evidence relevant? Is it admissible? Assume the judge thinks it is both relevant and admissible, what steps might counsel for defendant take to minimize the prejudicial effect of the evidence?**

Problem III–13. A is charged with killing his wife. One of the pieces of evidence offered by the prosecution is the fact that A is the beneficiary of a $25,000 insurance policy issued on the life of A's wife. A objects on the ground that there is absolutely no evidence indicating that he needed money and that, on the contrary, he has $100,000 in the bank and is free of all debts. **Is the evidence of the insurance policy admissible? Would you answer differently if the policy were in the amount of $250,000?**

Problem III–14. At about 6:00 P.M. on a cold winter's night in Boston two experienced policemen stopped a car that resembled a get-away car that had been used in the armed robbery of a supermarket at about 2:30 that afternoon. What happened next is unclear, but what is clear is that Sam Brown, the driver, ended up dead.   He was shot by the police officers, who fired through the windows from both sides of the car.   Plaintiff, Brown's widow, sued the officers for wrongful death.   The defendant officers claimed that when they ordered Brown to get out of his car he responded by driving into one of them, knocking him down, backing up, trying to run him over, and then shooting at him.   However, no gun had been found on Brown or in the car after Brown's death.   Defendants sought to introduce testimony from two grocery store employees that Brown was one of two people who had robbed them at 2:30 the afternoon of the killing.   The trial judge excluded the employees' testimony, noting that the witnesses' credibility was questionable and that the probative force of their testimony was outweighed by its tendency to prejudice the jury.   **Should the trial judge's ruling be overturned on appeal? On what theory is the defendant's evidence relevant?**   Ms. Brown, knowing the police would say they stopped her husband's car because it resembled one used in a robbery, presented in her case-in-chief a witness who testified that Sam was seen at the hospital where he worked at about 2:30 on the afternoon of the robbery.   **Does this change the way the appellate court should deal with the decision below?**   Suppose that in her closing argument to the jury, Brown's lawyer said "Sam Brown never did anything wrong in his life.   Defendants never brought anybody to the stand to say that Sam Brown robbed them."   Defendants did not object to this closing argument but had given a sufficient offer of proof when the employees' testimony was excluded.   **Should the plaintiff's closing argument affect the decision on appeal?**

Problem III–15.   Plaintiff's wife was killed when her car failed to negotiate a mountain turn and skidded off the road over a cliff.   The accident occurred in mid-afternoon, the wife had not been drinking or taking drugs, the road surface was dry and the car was apparently in good condition. Plaintiff seeks to recover on a life insurance policy which provides that the beneficiary will receive double indemnity should the insured die by accidental means.   The insurance company claims that only the face amount is owing because the wife in fact committed suicide.   As part of its defense the company seeks to introduce evidence that, five years before, the wife had taken an overdose of sleeping pills and almost died.   It also wants to introduce evidence that the wife had changed jobs three times in the past year, that three months before she died she had signed a "living will" (a document which provides that "heroic" measures should not be used to sustain life in the case of terminal illness or irreversible brain damage), and that twice within the preceding eighteen months she had sued her husband for divorce, alleging marital infidelity, but had each time withdrawn the action.   **Should the judge admit any of this evidence over the husband's objection?**

Problem III–16.   Wanda Wiley is charged with bank robbery.   Two witnesses to the robbery, a passerby and a bank teller, have identified Wanda as the robber, but both admit they are somewhat uncertain.   Another teller who witnessed the robbery has said that Wanda may have been the robber, but she is unable to make a positive identification.   Perhaps the most important evidence in the case are photographs that were taken during the robbery by the bank's hidden cameras.   The photographs show the robber to be a young woman with long blond hair and a ponytail. At trial Wanda has short brown hair. At the time of the robbery Wanda was on parole following a conviction for grand larceny. The prosecutor wants to introduce Wanda's parole officer who has known Wanda for two years to testify that about the time of the robbery she had long blond hair which she wore in a ponytail. He would also testify that he recognizes her to be the person pictured in the surveillance photographs. The defendant points out that numbers of people have seen Wanda at least as regularly as the parole officer during the preceding two years. These include Wanda's friends and relatives, patrons of the diner where she worked, her fellow employees, and several shopkeepers in the neighborhood where she lived. **In these circumstances should the parole officer be allowed to testify? If you were representing Wanda, would you be satisfied if the prosecutor agreed that he would not ask the parole officer how it was that she knew Wanda but instead would allude to the basis of their acquaintance as a "business relationship"? If Wanda's appearance had not changed between the time of the robbery and the time of the trial, could a witness who knew Wanda identify her as the woman depicted in the bank surveillance photographs? Should the trial judge grant the defendant's request to instruct the jury that, "it is natural for people to want to change their hair styles, so the fact that Wanda cut and dyed her hair sometime after the robbery may not be taken as evidence that she participated in the robbery"?**

Problem III–17. Sam Park is on trial for assaulting and robbing Kim Lee, a young Korean woman who had come to this country some four months before the attack. The case against Park turned on the accuracy of Lee's eyewitness identification. Both before and at trial Lee described her assailant as a clean-shaven man. Park on the other hand produced several witnesses who testified that on the date of the crime he wore a mustache. Park also wanted to call Rev. Kim who was born in Korea and lived there for 40 years before emigrating to the United States some 10 years ago. Kim was familiar with Korean culture and would have testified that facial hair is culturally significant as a mark of dignity, age, and respect in Korea; that it is a "folkway" in Korea, and that Ms. Lee, as a Korean, would have paid particular attention to a mustache had one been worn by her assailant. Ms. Lee also testified that her assailant was sloppily dressed at the time she was attacked. The defendant wanted to put on several witnesses to testify that he was normally neat and clean in his dress. The trial judge excluded all the proffered evidence. **Did she commit reversible error?**

Problem III–18. On June 18, 1964 Mrs. Juanita Brooks was the victim of a purse snatching while walking down an alley in the San Pedro area of Los Angeles. She neither heard nor saw her assailant as she was pushed from behind, but as she got to her feet she observed a young blond woman with a ponytail running from the scene. Another witness, who heard her scream, saw a blond woman with a ponytail run out of the alley in which Mrs. Brooks had been attacked and dash into a yellow automobile. The car started immediately. It was driven by a black man who had a beard and a mustache. Neither witness saw enough to be able to identify the participants in the crime. The police arrested Janet and Malcolm Collins for the crime.

Janet had dark blonde hair which she wore in a ponytail.   Malcolm was a black man who at the time of his arrest on June 22 had a mustache but no beard.   The couple owned a yellow Lincoln automobile with an off-white top. In addition to the testimony of the witnesses described above, the prosecution introduced the following evidence:

  a. Testimony that when the police came to arrest the Collinses, Malcolm was seen streaking from the back door of the house.

  b. Testimony that Malcolm had a beard when he paid fines on two traffic tickets on June 19.   There is other testimony in the case that Malcolm shaved his beard on June 2 when he married Janet.

  c. Testimony that Malcolm paid $35.00 for fines on two traffic tickets on June 18, testimony that between $35.00 and $40.00 was in Mrs. Brooks' purse when it was stolen, and testimony that the couple had only $12.00 when they were married on June 2, that Malcolm had not worked since that time and that Janet's earnings were not much more than $12.00 a week.

  d. Testimony from a mathematician describing the "product rule"; i.e. a mathematical rule which holds that the probability that a number of independent events will occur together is equal to the product of the probabilities that the individual events will occur.   (e.g. the probability that one die will come up six is $1/6$.   The probability that two dice will each come up six is $1/36$ or $1/6 \times 1/6$.)   The prosecutor then asked the witness to assume that the following probabilities were associated with the characteristics that had been established by the testimony of the other witnesses in the case:

Characteristic	Individual Probability
A. Partly yellow automobile	1/10
B. Man with mustache	1/4
C. Girl with ponytail	1/10
D. Girl with blond hair	1/3
E. Negro man with beard	1/10
F. Interracial couple in car	1/1000

The prosecutor then asked the mathematician to illustrate how the product rule would work if the probabilities of the different events were as assumed. The mathematician responded that applying the product rule to the assumed factors yielded a probability that there was about one chance in twelve million that any couple possessed the distinctive characteristics of the defendants.   **Should any of the evidence described above have been admitted in this case?   How is it relevant?   Should its admission constitute reversible error?   Do you see any special problems with the mathematician's testimony?**

  Problem III–19.   Mission Incorporated is a company owned by a small group of priests who write, produce, and publish musical compositions and recordings.   Music Corporation is a corporation that distributes and promotes music.   In 1980 Mission signed an agreement with Music regarding a rock opera VIRGIN which the priests had composed.   Music agreed to promote the record as well as at least four singles taken from the album in exchange for exclusive rights to distribute the album in the United States. One single taken from the record, "Fear No Evil," had reached #80 on the "Hot Soul Singles" chart of Billboard Magazine when Music breached its agreement, ceased promoting the single, and started withdrawing it from record stores. Even so the record's momentum carried it to an additional 10,000 sales, which placed it at #61 on the Billboard chart. Mission sued Music for the damages it suffered from the breach of contract, one item of which was lost royalties. In support of this they offered a statistical analysis of every one of the 324 songs that had reached #61 on the chart during 1980. This analysis showed that 76% ultimately reached the top 40, 65% the top 30, 51% the top 20, 34% the top 10, 21% the top 5, and 10% #1. Mission had an expert available who would have converted this information concerning other singles into projected sales figures for "Fear No Evil" and the sales figures into lost royalties. They also had an expert available who would have testified about the possibility that a hit single taken from the album would have led to concert tours, substantially more sales of the two-record VIRGIN album, and to a decision to produce VIRGIN on Broadway. The trial judge did not admit any of this evidence. **Was the trial judge's decision correct with regard to any or all of this evidence?**

Problem III–20. X brings suit against National Airlines, alleging that airline noise produced by its airplanes caused extensive damage to X's home. X lives 2 miles from the airport. Sixty percent of the flights over X's home are National's. **Can the plaintiff introduce statistics to show the total number of flights over his house and the number of National flights in order to argue that the probability is 6 out of ten that National planes caused the damage?** Assume that X is complaining about specific noise damage that allegedly occurred between about 10:30 and 11:00 p. m. on Friday, September 28, 1973. The flight records show the following flights, all of which go over X's house: [Arrival times at airport] 10:20 p. m. [National], 10:35 p. m. [National], 10:48 p. m. [National], 10:56 p. m. [National], 11:02 p. m. [Eastern]. **Can X argue that the probability of National being the tortfeasor is 80%? Would you permit this?**

If X later testified that he was confident that the damage occurred at 10:58, and if the flight pattern record was also introduced, would this be enough to support a verdict for X? What if X sues both National and Eastern, and Eastern wants to introduce the statistical evidence?

Problem III–21. You are the trier-of-fact in a civil case. The plaintiff is suing on an insurance policy to recover the loss of her building by fire. The insurance company raises a defense of arson. After most of the evidence relating to the defense is presented, you remain skeptical. You think there is only a one in three chance the plaintiff was the "torch". In fact you believe it is twice as likely that there was no arson. The insurance company presents testimony that nine months before the fire the plaintiff insured her building for a figure more than 25% above its fair market value. The insurance company then introduces an industry-wide survey reporting that in two of every five fires shown to be arson the burned buildings were insured within the year preceding the fire for a figure that was 25% or more above their fair market value. The survey also reports that in only one of a thousand fires not shown to be arson were the burned buildings insured for a figure 25% or more above their fair market value. Would you be willing to multiply your prior odds on arson of 1:2 by $\dfrac{2/5}{1/1000}$ to arrive at odds of 200 to 1 that arson has been committed by the plaintiff? Probably not. **Why do you think you refuse to use the probabilities in the manner suggested? Is the evidence the insurance company wishes to offer not relevant? Do your answers to these questions suggest reasons why the Bayesian model is only a heuristic device and not a technique which should be urged on trial courts as a means of resolving factual disputes?**

   Problem III–22. Sally Zanger, an attorney, is representing a white man accused of robbing a black woman. She knows that the prosecution's case consists largely of an eyewitness identification by the woman who was robbed. In a pretrial motion, Zanger asks the court to rule that at the trial the prosecution may not ask the victim to point out the person who robbed her. Zanger argues that because the defendant will be the only person sitting at the counsel table with her, any courtroom identification of the defendant will have little probative value but, because of its dramatic aspect, will have substantial prejudicial effect. She is willing to stipulate that two weeks after the robbery the victim identified the defendant, from a photograph, as the person who robbed her. Zanger says she will not object to testimony describing that identification. (There was a lineup identification two days after the photo identification, but it did not meet the requisite constitutional standards for admissibility.) **Has Zanger acted wisely in making her motion coupled with the stipulation? Should the court grant Zanger's motion?**

   Zanger is thinking about asking the judge to place her client in a lineup in court along with nine other men and requesting that any identification by the witness be made from this lineup. Coincidentally, the prosecutor is thinking about making a similar request. (He would like the lineup to include only three other men.) **Is the request a wise one for either party to make? If one party makes such a request and the other does not object, should the judge allow the courtroom lineup? Should the judge allow a courtroom lineup at the defendant's motion if the prosecution objects? At the prosecution's motion if the defendant objects?**

   Zanger makes her motion to bar courtroom identification or, in the alternative, to have any courtroom identification made in a lineup. The judge denies the motion in both respects. Zanger then decides to seat the defendant, who is out on bail, in the spectator section of the courtroom and have the defendant's brother sit at counsel's table. **Is it proper for an attorney to take such action without the permission of the court?** The victim points to the defendant's brother sitting at counsel table as the one who robbed her. At the close of the prosecution's case, Zanger reveals her subterfuge and, as there is insufficient evidence to convict the defendant without the eyewitness identification, moves for a directed acquittal. The prosecutor at this point is allowed to reopen his case. He asks the defendant to sit at counsel table where he belongs. Then he puts the robbery victim back on the stand and asks her to point out the person who robbed her. This time the woman points to the defendant.   Zanger renews her motion for a directed verdict of acquittal.   **Should the court grant it?**   Assume that the woman, when asked if she recognizes the one who robbed her, points not to the defendant but to one of the male jurors.   After some minutes of confusion and further questioning by the prosecutor, she changes her mind and points to the defendant.   **Would the defendant be entitled to a directed verdict of acquittal or a mistrial?**

BIBLIOGRAPHY

McCormick, Ch. 16 (1954).

1 Weinstein's Evidence ¶ 401[01]–403[06] (1979).

1 Wigmore §§ 27–36 (3d ed. 1940).

22 Wright & Graham, Federal Practice and Procedure, Evidence §§ 5161–5224 (1978).

Ball, The Moment of Truth: Probability Theory and the Standards of Proof, 14 Vand.L.Rev. 807 (1961).

Fairley & Mosteller, A Conversation About *Collins*, 41 U.Chi.L.Rev. 242 (1974).

Finkelstein & Fairley, A Comment on "Trial by Mathematics," 84 Harv.L.Rev. 1801 (1971).

James, Relevancy, Probability and the Law, 29 Calif.L.Rev. 689 (1941).

Morgan & Maguire, Looking Backward and Forward at Evidence 1886–1936, 50 Harv.L.Rev. 909 (1937).

Saltzburg, A Special Aspect of Relevance: Countering Negative Inferences Associated With the Absence of Evidence, 66 Calif.L.Rev. 1011 (1978).

Slough, Relevancy Unraveled, 5 Kan.L.Rev. 1 (1956).

Trautman, Logical or Legal Relevancy—A Conflict in Theory, 5 Vand.L.Rev. 385 (1952).

Travers, An Essay on the Determination of Relevancy Under the Federal Rules of Evidence, 1977 Ariz.St.L.J. 327.

Tribe, Trial by Mathematics: Precision and Ritual in the Legal Process, 84 Harv.L.Rev. 1329 (1971).

Weyrauch, Law as Mask—Legal Ritual and Relevance, 66 Calif.L.Rev. 699 (1978).

Chapter Four

RELEVANT BUT INADMISSIBLE: THE "RELEVANCE RULES"

SECTION I.   AN OVERVIEW

There is a group of exclusionary rules which are almost always discussed under the general rubric of relevance. Although commentators and thoughtful judges have long been aware that the evidence these rules declare inadmissible is not irrelevant in the logical sense of the term, enough courts have dismissed such behavior as irrelevant that the categorization is likely to stick. Simplifying greatly, the general rules are as follows: (1) Evidence of a defendant's bad character may not be introduced in criminal cases to show a propensity to commit the crime charged. It is even less likely to be admissible for substantive reasons in civil cases.[1] (2) Evidence of other crimes committed by the defendant may not be introduced to sup-

1. Evidence introduced for substantive reasons or as part of a party's affirmative case is introduced for the purpose of proving one or more of the elements that a party is legally required to prove in making or defeating a case. Such evidence, which tends to make one or more elements of a party's case more or less likely, is to be distinguished from evidence introduced for the purpose of testing a witness' credibility, impeaching a witness, or questioning the authority or validity of an exhibit offered as evidence. Of course, impeaching witnesses and attacking the validity of nontestimonial evidence may help prove or disprove a case, but the help comes when the weight of substantive evidence, as defined above, is appropriately discounted.

Often it will be unimportant to the lawyer how the evidence reaches the jury. The jury is likely to be influenced by evidence admissible only for impeachment purposes in deciding aspects of the case which do not relate to credibility or the discounting of evidence. This appears true despite the fact that the opposing party has the right to have the jury instructed on the limited effect which the evidence should have in their deliberations. The distinction does become important when the issue is whether a particular body of evidence is sufficient to support a party's claim. Both trial and appellate courts only look at evidence admissible for substantive purposes when they resolve the sufficiency question. Whether an appellate court will find sufficient evidence to support a judgment may, of course, depend on whether some trial evidence was impeached and, if so, to what extent.

In this chapter we will frequently talk about kinds of evidence which are admissible for one purpose but not another. It appears that attorneys often seek to find a purpose for which evidence is properly admissible in the hope and belief that juries will use that evidence for some other purpose. The analysis suggested with respect to impeachment evidence applies in these circumstances as well. Juries are indeed likely to use the evidence for an impermissible purpose; courts are much less likely to be influenced by the improper aspect of the evidence in deciding whether there is sufficient evidence respecting a particular element of a party's case to avoid a directed verdict.

But, even judges may be swayed in their evaluation of close questions by other things they know about the parties. Some may be surprised by this assertion. Let us call your attention to H. Kalven and H. Zeisel's The American Jury (1966). The authors report that in 2% of the cases where juries acquit defendants whom judges say they would have convicted, a reason given by the judges for the difference is that they knew facts which the jury did not. In other words, these judges would have convicted on the basis of evidence which was either inadvertently not presented by counsel, or, and far more likely, evidence which the judges were required by law to keep from the jury.

port the state's contention that he committed the crime charged. (3) Evidence that remedial measures were taken or neglected after an accident may not be introduced to show that the person responsible for remedial measures was negligent in maintaining the pre-accident state of affairs. (4) Evidence that one party paid the medical expenses of a second party may not be introduced in order to prove that the donor of medical expense payments negligently caused the injuries of the donee. (5) Evidence of an offer to compromise a claim or an offer to plead guilty to a lesser charge may not be introduced to show the strength of the offeree's claim or the offeror's consciousness of guilt. (6) Evidence that a party had liability insurance may not be introduced on the issue of whether the insured party was negligent. (7) Evidence that a party had a certain habit will often not be admissible to show that the party acted in accord with that habit on a specific occasion. It is particularly unlikely to be admissible if eyewitnesses are available to describe the event. And (8) evidence of similar events, offered to support the inference that a particular event occurred in a particular way, will be scrutinized closely for similarity before a court will allow it to be introduced. Such evidence is unlikely to be admitted if it relates to events involving neither party before the court, numerous similarities notwithstanding.

These rules have at least one thing in common: they all resolve questions which arise frequently in the adjudication of cases. It is only because substantial numbers of appellate decisions relate to the subject matter of these rules that commentators, codifiers and appellate judges have been able to extract a set of more or less coherent principles to guide lower courts and trial attorneys. Rationalization of these

cases has led courts to resolve these recurring problems by reference to the set of extracted rules rather than by a case by case balancing of relevance against prejudice, confusion, surprise and waste of time.

Too often trial and appellate courts have ignored the fact that this balancing procedure (codified in FRE 403) is always appropriate to keep out evidence otherwise admissible. Even when an exception to one of the "relevance rules" discussed in this chapter exists, the trial court has discretion to exclude the information if the judge thinks that the probative value of the evidence is outweighed by the usual counterweights to relevance. Admission is not required simply because the conditions for an exception have been met.[2] But the converse is not true. Ad hoc balancing is not appropriate when the conditions for an exception have not been met. The judge should not admit evidence in the face of the rule simply because the evidence promises, in the context of the cases, not to be prejudicial, confusing, surprising, or a waste of time. Can you see why this is so?

These "relevance rules" may be justified in a variety of ways. One feature shared by most, if not all, of them helps explain the continuing tendency to treat these rules as an aspect of relevance. This is that evidence excluded under these rules is in the logical sense generally not very probative of the issues on which introduction is forbidden. Furthermore, the more probable the inference such evidence is introduced to support, the more likely it is that the proponent of the evidence is able to introduce other stronger evidence. Consider an example involving subsequent repairs. Assume the defendant has added a railing to a stairway after the plaintiff has fallen off. If the defendant were indeed negligent in maintaining a stairway without a

---

2. FRE 609 may or may not reflect congressional intent to forbid this kind of balancing when evidence of other crimes is offered for impeachment. On its face, it appears to strike a balance for allowing impeachment by certain prior convictions.

railing, the plaintiff ought to be able to produce expert witnesses who would explain why the stairway was unsafe without a railing, or the very description of the unguarded stairway might suffice to convince the jury that there was negligence in maintaining it. If, on the other hand, the subsequent repair were the plaintiff's only evidence of negligence, the absence of other reasons to believe the stairway unsafe probably means that an inference of negligence is unjustified.[3] Of course, low logical relevance or lack of strategic significance do not by themselves justify the decision to exclude. Items of low relevance may, in combination with each other, make a very strong case which cannot otherwise be made. But the combination of low relevance and low importance in most cases does justify a receptive attitude toward other values which rules of exclusion might promote.

One such value is the value of avoiding extended litigation on collateral issues. Consider the situation where the defendant is accused of robbing B. If the prosecutor could routinely introduce evidence that the defendant robbed A as some evidence that he may have robbed B, the trial might be transformed into a dispute about whether A was indeed robbed by the defendant. The defendant might feel compelled to contest the charge that he robbed A, fearing that if he fails to answer the charge he will be found guilty of robbing B simply because he is a "bad man." Such a dispute might well distract the jury's attention from evidence bearing more directly on the identity of B's robber and

---

3. In terms of the Bayesian model presented in Chapter Three one would argue this way: If the defendant were negligent, the probability that the only evidence of negligence would be those inferences which could be drawn from a subsequent repair is less than the probability that this would be the only evidence suggesting negligence if the defendant were not negligent. Thus the likelihood ratio would be less than one and any prior estimate of the odds of the defendant's negligence would have to be revised downward. The fact of the later repair might still be an indication of negligence, because the downward revision of the prior odds would not be as great as if there were no evidence of negligence at all. But clearly in these circumstances the existence of a subsequent repair would not suggest that negligence was likely.

On the other hand if the defendant were negligent, it is much more likely that the unguarded stairway would appear dangerous to the lay person, that an expert would testify it was dangerous, and that there would be a subsequent repair than that this confluence of evidence would exist if the defendant were not negligent. This evidence might, for example, increase our estimate of the likelihood that the defendant was negligent one hundred fold. However, absent the subsequent repair, the combination of an apparently dangerous situation and expert testimony that the situation is dangerous would still be so much more probable if the defendant were negligent than if he were not that our estimate of the prior odds that the defendant was negligent would be increased perhaps fifty times over.

Thus, the evidence of the subsequent repair, though logically relevant, is not very important to the jury's consideration of the negligence issue. One can of course construct situations where based on all other evidence the odds of the defendant's being negligent are close to fifty-fifty. Here evidence of subsequent repair, to the extent it has probative value, would be crucial. We are suggesting that, as an empirical matter, this situation is unlikely to arise. If the defendant is negligent, stronger evidence of negligence is almost certain to be available; if other evidence of negligence is so weak that evidence of subsequent repairs is an important item in the plaintiff's case, then it is very unlikely that the defendant was negligent. Of course, the same kind of analysis can be made of many kinds of evidence which are admitted. (It is also quite important, for reasons we shall not consider, that the failure to carry out a subsequent repair carries no inference of non-negligence. This will not always be the case with evidence which has low affirmative relevance.) The important implication of the analysis with respect to the "relevance rules" is that it frees the court to pay attention to considerations other than logical relevance.

might suggest to the jury that the incident should be given more weight than it merits. Also, admission of such other crimes evidence might well surprise the defendant, since it is not an integral part of the prosecution's case. This could result in fundamental unfairness to the defendant. Without time to prepare an adequate defense even a mistaken charge of other crimes might be irrefutable. An extended continuance, the proper remedy in such circumstances, lies within the discretion of the judge, but is costly to all involved.

Courts have also been motivated in formulating these relevance rules by their sensitivity to the estimation problems and problems of prejudice that inhere in some of the categories of excluded evidence. Other crimes evidence, discussed above, is a good example of evidence which might prejudice the jury. A jury could convict the defendant not because it was convinced he committed the crime charged, but rather because it was convinced he was a bad person. In terms of the model presented in Chapter Three, evidence of other crimes would substantially decrease the jury's regret at convicting the defendant if he were innocent of the crime charged and would increase its regret at acquitting if the defendant were in fact guilty.

An offer to plead guilty to a lesser offense provides an example of an estimation problem. There may be some probative value to an offer to plead guilty; an innocent person may be less likely to consider pleading than a guilty one. But there are many factors which might lead an innocent person to offer a plea: he might be unable to make bail while waiting for trial and the likely sentence on the lesser charge might be less than the expected period of pretrial detention; the likely penalty if convicted on the greater charge might be so severe that the innocent defendant does not wish to take the risk; or the defendant might feel that ultimately the trial will come down to his word against a police officer's (as in the Whale case) and he may be advised that in these circumstances the jury almost always convicts. Jury members may be unaware of those factors which might lead an innocent person to offer a plea. This ignorance would lead them to substantially underestimate the probability that an innocent defendant would offer to plead guilty and so overestimate the degree to which the evidence suggests the defendant's guilt.[4]

Finally, a court may justify exclusion under these relevance rules for policy reasons which have nothing at all to do with relevance or its usual counterweights: prejudice, confusion of the issues, surprise, and waste of time. To give just one example, the rule concerning subsequent remedial measures is often justified on the ground that society should not discourage repairs after accidents by admitting evidence of such repairs on the issue of negligence.

Not all of these justifications apply to each relevance rule, but each rule is supported by two or more of these reasons. Some courts, proceeding from the mistaken notion that they must find a single justification for a rule of exclusion, may write opinions that don't make a convincing case for exclusion. But generally speaking, if one considers all factors, these exclusionary rules are reasonable.[5]

If you paid close attention to our simplified presentation of the relevance rules, you noted that each of them classified

---

4. Even if the jury knew of situations that can pressure innocent defendants to plead guilty, the fact that they have not been in and do not anticipate being in such situations might lead them to take an exaggerated view of the extent to which they themselves would stand on principle if falsely accused, a view which would lead them to underestimate the probability that an innocent defendant would offer to plead.

5. Ultimately, if one wants to argue that a set of exclusionary rules is justified, one must evaluate the rules vis-a-vis the alternative of resting discretion with the trial

types of evidence as inadmissible on certain specific issues. Perhaps you caught the implication that where evidence of an excluded type is offered for other than the specifically prohibited inference, the evidence is not automatically excluded. There is a good reason for this. Assuming we are correct in our judgment that the kinds of evidence we have described are often of little probative value and not very necessary to the proof of one issue,[6] there is no reason to believe that the same evidence may not be probative and important on another. Hence, courts wisely have refused to extend these rules of exclusion beyond their certain, narrow range.

Consider again the example of subsequent remedial measures. We have already suggested that such evidence is unlikely to be crucial on the issue of whether or not the defendant was negligent. But suppose instead that the issue were one of control. An accident has occurred in a hallway. The defendant landlord claims the hallway was under the control of the tenant, the tenant claims the hallway was the responsibility of the landlord, and the lease is unclear on this critical point. The fact that after the accident the landlord undertook to repair a defective railing is not only relevant to the question of who is responsible for the stairway; it might be the most convincing evidence which the plaintiff can offer on the matter. We are not saying that the relevance or necessity of certain kinds of evidence will always be less with respect to prohibited inferences than it is with respect to permitted ones, but we

do feel that this will be the case sufficiently often so that the lines drawn by the rules are not unreasonable.

The difficulty with admitting for permitted inferences the kinds of evidence we are discussing is that the jury, even if instructed otherwise, might use the evidence for improper purposes. This suggests that courts should be careful in admitting such evidence. They should look closely at the extent to which the evidence is, in context, relevant and necessary to prove the point on which it is properly offered. The better courts do just this. They hold that evidence ostensibly offered for a permitted purpose should be excluded if it has only limited value as support for permitted inferences. Other courts are misled by the existence of rules in the area. They treat commonly permitted purposes as rules of exception and argue, though it is a logical *non sequitur,* that evidence which appears to fall within an exception is admissible for the permitted purpose regardless of its actual probative value or the fact that it is fraught with extrinsic danger. This is a particularly serious problem in the area of character evidence.

An attorney who is worried that the jury may misuse evidence introduced for a permitted purpose can usually keep the evidence out by stipulating to *everything* the evidence might be used to prove. A major problem is that the attorney might lose more by such a stipulation than would be gained from exclusion. Even where an attorney is willing to stipulate, courts sometimes hold that a party is entitled to

---

judge to decide admissibility on an ad hoc basis. This raises questions about the capabilities of trial judges and juries and difficult empirical questions about the actual relevance of excluded evidence. The issue of whether a system of evidence rules is preferable to a system of ad hoc judicial discretion is a very complicated one which we do not wish to address here. Our argument concerning the relevance rules is in its weakest form: if we are going to have a system of evidence rules, these rules make

about as much sense as a number of other rules which exist to guide the judge on the decision of whether or not to admit certain evidence.

6. It can be shown that low logical relevance and redundancy are very closely related. We have treated these aspects separately in order to emphasize the different ways in which evidence may be of low logical relevance.

prove the elements of his case by any competent evidence.

A closely related technique that may be used by a party wishing to concede facts to avoid prejudicial proof by an opponent is the "judicial admission." Judicial admissions are binding concessions that remove some issues from the class of disputed fact questions. If a fact is not in dispute proof of that fact is irrelevant under FRE 401 and thus inadmissible under FRE 402. To preclude evidence of a certain type, a judicial admission must give the opposing party every legitimate advantage that he would obtain from proving the point with the evidence in question. If a judicial admission does this, the concept of relevance under both the federal rules and the common law should preclude an opponent from introducing evidence to secure an illegitimate advantage.

SECTION II. THE RULES IN DETAIL

A. SUBSEQUENT REMEDIAL MEASURES

FRE 407 provides: [7]

When, after an event, measures are taken which, if taken previously, would have made the event less likely to occur, evidence of the subsequent measures is not admissible to prove negligence or culpable conduct in connection with the event. This rule does not require the exclusion of evidence of subsequent measures when offered for another purpose, such as proving ownership, control, or feasibility of precautionary measures, if controverted, or impeachment.

The federal rule is declaratory of the common law, although in its broad definition of subsequent remedial measures the rule uses more inclusive language than the common law courts, which typically refer to "subsequent repairs." However, since courts have been able to find that lowered speed limits, new chemical formulas, and the discharge of employees all constitute subsequent repairs, the broader language should make little difference. Clearly the rationale of the rule regarding subsequent repairs applies to subsequent remedial measures generally.

FRE 407 also accords with the common law in that it excludes evidence of subsequent remedial measures only when the evidence is offered to prove negligence or culpable conduct in connection with some event. The purposes mentioned in the final sentence are the purposes for which evidence of subsequent remedial measures has been most commonly admitted. They appear in FRE 407 as examples and not as an exclusive list of permitted purposes. In providing that evidence of subsequent remedial measures is admissible on an issue only if that issue is controverted, the federal rule codifies the better practice among the states. This limitation is particularly important with respect to feasibility. Since negligence rarely exists in situations where an activity cannot be conducted in any safer fashion, a general exception to show the feasibility of safer conduct would create a loophole which would almost swallow the rule. Even with the rule as it stands, it has been said that

---

7. **We reiterate that throughout this book we use the Federal Rules of Evidence as a heuristic aid to explain basic principles of evidence law. It is impossible as we write to know what changes will be made in the rules over the years; but any changes which are made will not undercut the heuristic** value of the rules as presented here. To learn the current version of the federal rules, you should secure a copy of the current version and check the rules as they appear in it against the rules as they appear in this book.

an adept lawyer is almost always able to show a subsequent repair for some permitted purpose. Consider the kinds of statements concerning the safety of a pre-accident situation which might be elicited from an opposing party on cross-examination and the way in which evidence of a subsequent repair might then be used for impeachment. Consider also a picture of the scene of an accident and the need which might arise to explain the pre-accident conditions.

Two reasons are usually given for excluding evidence of subsequent remedial measures on the issue of negligence: (1) The evidence is thought to be of low logical relevance on this issue. (2) There is a fear that if such evidence were admitted, people would be unwilling to take post-accident precautions, to the general detriment of society.

The relevance of evidence of subsequent repairs is likely to be low for two reasons. First, it is not clear that a subsequent repair, when feasible, is substantially more likely where there has been pre-accident negligence than where there has not. Certainly a conscientious individual, newly alerted to a dangerous condition, will do everything reasonable to remedy that condition regardless of his or her earlier care.[8] If there is an intuitive sense in which this evidence appears to relate to negligence, it is probably in its strong relation to feasibility and the close relation between feasibility and negligence.

The second reason why the relevance of this evidence is likely to be low is that—feasibility aside—the evidence relates to negligence in a rather strange way. If it reflects anything, it reflects the party's *opinion* that he has been negligent.[9] But this is the kind of opinion which even experts are usually barred from giving, an opinion which summarizes a set of facts in a conclusion of law. The only reason the opinion would be allowed here, absent the subsequent repairs rule, is that it is the party's opinion; and parties are held to especially high standards of accountability for their words and actions. This is in part because courts feel that parties can always present the jury with reasons why their statements should not be taken at face value or with reasons for ignoring the apparent implications of their actions. While this may be true, it is also true that the conclusions of a non-lawyer concerning the legal consequences of certain action often will be mistaken. Where relevance depends upon treating an action as an admission of negligence (a legal conclusion), the chain of inference is particularly tenuous. The real issue may well be whether we wish routinely to force parties to explain why post-accident remedial measures are not acknowledgments of pre-accident carelessness. The subsequent repairs rule is a decision not to require such explanation.

Apart from low relevance, the reason most commonly given for the decision to exclude evidence of subsequent remedial measures is the fear that if such evidence were not excluded, individuals would be dissuaded from taking necessary safety precautions. If repetition could make for truth, this would certainly be a true explanation, for it has been repeated without questioning by many courts and most commentators. Yet, as a matter of behavioral psychology, and that is how this argument must be taken, the explanation is dubious at best. If a defendant knows enough law to realize that evidence of subsequent remedial measures will not be admissible on the issue of negligence he is also likely to realize that such evidence may be admissible for other purposes and that a failure to repair after being warned

---

8. In terms of the mathematical analysis in Chapter Three, the likelihood ratio for finding evidence of a subsequent repair is close to one.

9. Wigmore treats evidence of subsequent repairs as one kind of evidence which evinces a party's consciousness of a weak case. 2 Wigmore § 283, at 151.

by an accident may constitute gross negligence and be grounds for punitive damages.[10]

There is another possible rationale for the rule, one which courts rarely articulate, but which seems to make more sense than the instrumental explanation. This is that people who take post-accident safety measures are doing exactly what good citizens should do. In these circumstances, so long as the relevance of the activity is not great, courts do not wish to sanction procedures which appear to punish praiseworthy behavior. Perhaps courts do not articulate this reason because they are reluctant to rationalize their decisions on the basis of what truly motivates them, namely a subjective sense of the decent thing to do. They prefer instead to rest their decision on its efficacy in promoting behavior which all agree is desirable, even if they must assert by fiat an efficacy which appears unlikely.[11]

How courts rationalize their decisions is important, for their reasons, whether justified or not, exert a real influence on the law. In the subsequent repairs area, the rationale of promoting repairs applies only when the defendant is responsible for the repairs. Hence, evidence that a third party has undertaken certain repairs may come in as affirmative evidence of feasibility and, where otherwise relevant, on the issue of negligence.

Regardless of the chosen rationale, the judicial image of the defendant who has remedied a defect has been the image of a conscientious individual. Yet, today many tort defendants are large corpora-

tions. Remedial measures are often changes in safety rules or personnel, and even ordinary repairs may be the outcome of impersonal bureaucratic procedures which the plaintiff's accident may or may not have set in motion. One might wonder whether the rule respecting subsequent remedial measures should apply to corporate defendants. So long as the cause of action sounds in negligence, the rule applies to corporations in the same way it applies to individuals.

The dominant view has been the same where the case is brought on a theory of strict products liability, but the trend is to admit such evidence. An early harbinger of change was Ault v. International Harvester Company,[12] a California case in which the court held that Section 1151 of the California evidence code did not bar the introduction of testimony concerning a subsequent remedial measure in order to prove that a product was defective. The California code, like the federal rule, bars evidence of subsequent remedial measures only when offered to prove negligence or culpable conduct in connection with an event. The court held that proving a defect in a product did not necessarily show negligence or culpable conduct within the meaning of the statute. Suggested policy arguments for applying the rule in the products liability context were rejected.

Since negligence is not an issue when a case is brought on a theory of strict products liability, those who seek the protection of FRE 407 argue that the manufacture or distribution of a defective product is a

---

10. But, a committee of the Department of Justice commenting on the proposed federal rules wrote, "We understand that a number of insurance companies advise their insureds not to undertake any remedial measures until any accident litigation is concluded." (Cited in 2 Weinstein's Evidence ¶ 407[01], at n. 7). If this was true, it was given the common law rule.

11. We do not mean to suggest that absolutely no one would be deterred from making repairs if the prohibition on the admission of subsequent repair evidence were lifted. We just do not believe that the number of repairs deterred would be sufficient to justify the prohibition on admitting repair evidence.

12. 13 Cal.3d 113, 117 Cal.Rptr. 812, 528 P.2d 1148 (1975).

form of culpable conduct and that the policy considerations that justify the rule mean that its applicability should not turn on whether an action sounds in strict liability or negligence. As of this writing there is some division of opinion in the federal courts, but the majority are following *Ault*.[13]

In terms of our analysis the basic justification for abandoning the remedial measures rule in products liability cases has to do with the way in which the evidence is relevant. In a products liability case the plaintiff must usually show that there was a defect in the way in which a product was designed or manufactured. Except where the defect is obvious (as when a Coke bottle explodes), the plaintiff must usually show that some alternative way of manufacture or design was both safer and feasible. A subsequent improvement is highly probative on both these points. While even a non-negligent defendant may correct an apparent defect after an accident, a business is not likely to change a product unless the change promotes safety and is feasible.[14] Indeed the question of whether a product is defective is so likely to lead to defense arguments properly controvertible by evidence of subsequent remedial measures that it makes sense to drop the rule in these cases and admit the evidence as part of the plaintiff's affirmative case.[15]

13. The second portion of FRE 407 which mentions issues on which evidence of subsequent repairs is admissible *if the issue is controverted* mandates results that would probably be reached on a pure relevance analysis. If the evidence is relevant to some issue other than negligence or culpable conduct it is presumptively admissible under FRE 402. However, if that issue is not controverted the opposing party should be willing to admit the facts in question or stipulate to them so that the evidence of the repair is excludable under FRE 403. Thus, the "if controverted" language of FRE 407 serves to alert the judge confronted with subsequent repair evidence to the need to exercise that discretion accorded by FRE 403.

14. Such evidence is not dispositive of the matter. It is possible, for example, that the technology needed to make the product safer was available after the accident but not at the time of manufacture.

15. A warning: we as authors shall not shy away from taking positions on controversial matters. We think it increases the interest of the discussion and has scholarly merit. We shall try to be obvious when we do this and to call your attention to what we are doing. You should view these arguments critically; not every scholar or court would accept them. You should ask yourself whether our arguments are reasonable and whether the assumptions on which they are based are tenable. In the instant case, for example, one might argue that if there were ever a case in which the possible introduction of subsequent repairs evidence would discourage such repairs it is here since corporations are likely to know the law. We reject this argument because very often corporations have no choice but to repair: the repairs may be mandated by government agencies; the prospect of repeated products liability claims will make immediate repairs the less costly alternative whatever the current litigation costs; or, and perhaps most importantly, the danger that unfavorable publicity will interfere with sales of non-defective products. Who has the better of this argument, we or our imaginary opponents? Is it relevant that the dissenting justice in Ault points out that in the first trial the jury was unable to reach a verdict, but in the second trial counsel's changed tactics, including constant emphasis on the remedial measure, resulted in a verdict for $700,000? What other arguments can be made against the position taken in the text?

One of the authors has rethought his position since the publication of the first edition of the book and has concluded that in many design defect cases the evidence problem is that proof of design changes may confuse jurors as to the state of the art at the time when the product was manufactured. It is the possible confusion with respect to when defendants had what knowledge that makes product cases very much like negligence cases in many instances. See S. Saltzburg & K. Redden, Federal Rules of Evidence Manual 181–82 (3d ed. 1982). At other points in the text you will also see that we disagree in our analyses of various rules and cases. We hope that our acknowledgement of this fact will stimulate you to accept our invitation to disagree with us and to question the arguments that we make.

Problem IV–1. The plaintiff's wife and children were killed as the result of a collision with a railroad train. The collision occurred at a crossing protected by wigwag signals. The plaintiff brought an appropriate action to recover damages. At trial, the plaintiff seeks to introduce:

(a) A photograph of the intersection taken two weeks after the accident. The photograph shows the way the crossing looked at the time of the accident, except that by the time the picture was taken the railroad had replaced the wigwag signal with a flashing red light accompanied by a wooden barrier to block automobile traffic when a train was coming.

(b) Testimony that a week after the accident the railroad replaced the wigwag signal with a flashing red light and a wooden barrier.

(c) The same evidence as in (b) if the railroad alleged in its pleadings that the county highway commission and not the railroad was responsible for maintaining the safety of railroad crossings.

(d) The same evidence as in (b) if an expert testifying on behalf of the railroad told the jury that a wigwag signal was the safest kind of automatic device for the type of crossing in question.

(e) Testimony from the train's engineer describing how the railroad determines speed limits for different portions of its track and stating that the speed limit for the portion of the track on which the accident occurred had been reduced from 90 m.p.h. to 70 m.p.h. nine months after the accident.

Should any of this evidence be admitted over objections based on FRE 407?

Problem IV–2. The plaintiff, Susan Storm, rented a car from the Kiwi Rent-A-Car Company. She was driving down Route 17 when the car ahead of her stopped for a deer. Storm jammed on her brakes, but the brakes didn't hold, and she went plowing into the car ahead. She sues Kiwi for renting an unsafe car. **Can she learn through the use of some discovery device whether Kiwi had the car brakes repaired after the accident?** Assume that she learns that Kiwi took the car to the Sunshine Garage after the accident and had the front end repaired and the rear brake linings replaced. **Can she introduce evidence that the brake linings were replaced after the accident to support her claim that Kiwi had rented her an unsafe car? Can she call Sally Sunshine, the chief mechanic of the Sunshine Garage, to testify to what she saw when she took apart the brakes and looked at the linings?** Assume that Sunshine tossed the linings into the trash pursuant to standard business practice. **Would these be admissible if they had been found by an investigator working for Storm?**

Problem IV–3. Juan Garcia was injured when his car, a 1981 Aardvark, went off the road while he was trying to negotiate a sharp curve. He says that just as he entered the curve the steering wheel on his vehicle locked causing the mishap. He claims that the locking was attributable to a defective pin in the steering wheel column and sues Auto Company, the maker of the vehicle, on both negligence and strict liability theories. In support of his claim Garcia introduces the testimony of an expert who examined his car after the crash.   He would also like to introduce a recall letter distributed by Auto Company pursuant to the National Traffic and Motor Vehicle Safety Act of 1966 which says in part: "It has come to our attention that in certain of our 1981 Aardvarks one of the steering column pins was damaged in the assembly process.   While this damage is unlikely to cause problems, it may in rare instances cause steering malfunctions.   Therefore, if you own a 1981 Aardvark please take it to any Auto Company dealership for an inspection of the pin and, if it is defective, its replacement at no cost to you."   The letter was mailed three months after Garcia's accident.   **Is it admissible in support of the negligence claim?   In support of the product liability claim?   Would your answer be the same if the letter had been mailed three months before Garcia's accident?**

B.   COMPROMISES AND OFFERS TO COMPROMISE

FRE 408 provides:

Evidence of (1) furnishing or offering or promising to furnish, or (2) accepting or offering or promising to accept, a valuable consideration in compromising or attempting to compromise a claim which was disputed as to either validity or amount, is not admissible to prove liability for or invalidity of the claim or its amount.   Evidence of conduct or statements made in compromise negotiations is likewise not admissible.   This rule does not require the exclusion of any evidence otherwise discoverable merely because it is presented in the course of compromise negotiations. This rule also does not require exclusion when the evidence is offered for another purpose, such as proving bias or prejudice of a witness, negativing a contention of undue delay, or proving an effort to obstruct a criminal investigation or prosecution.

In providing that offers of compromise are not admissible to prove liability for or invalidity of a claim or its amount, FRE 408 follows the common law.   The justification commonly given for this principle is twofold.   First is the familiar claim of low relevance: a compromise offer may reflect a desire to buy peace, rather than a subjective belief that one is liable.   However, McCormick has shown the weakness in this rationale.   He points out that while an offer to pay a small fraction of a contested claim may well reflect a desire to buy peace, an offer to pay a large fraction, say $85,000 on a $100,000 claim, reflects a clear belief in the general weakness of one's position.   If we were only worried about relevance, we might leave it to the courts to separate offers apparently extended in a desire to buy peace from offers which strongly imply a consciousness of liability.[16]

The second justification for the rule is that compromise is a favored method of settling disputes which the rules of evidence should promote.   This argument is based on the assumption that individuals

---

16.   McCormick, § 274, at 663.   Even where offers are for a substantial portion of a disputed claim, the type of "opinion" problems mentioned in connection with evidence of subsequent remedial measures would apply here.   Moreover, in multiparty contexts, a defendant might settle against one party for a significant sum to negate any possibility of damage from expanding notions of collateral estoppel.   See, e.g., Bernhard v. Bank of America Nat. Trust & Sav. Ass'n, 19 Cal.2d 807, 122 P.2d 892 (1942).   But McCormick's point is still well taken: such information could be given to the jurors so they could better assess the weight to be given the settlement offer.

would be reluctant to negotiate compromises if they knew evidence of their offers could be used against them in court. This assumption, unlike the similar assumption with respect to remedial measures, appears reasonable. Since parties often negotiate compromises through lawyers, they may be expected to know the law and be influenced by it. Also, there are no pressures, apart from the pending litigation, which encourage parties to take the socially desirable course of action. McCormick thought this rationale so strong that he felt the rule regarding offers to compromise should be conceptualized as one of privilege rather than one of relevance. It would, however, be a strange privilege in which the degree of protection depended on the issues to which the evidence was relevant.[17]

In excluding evidence of conduct or statements made in compromise negotiations, FRE 408 gives more protection than does the common law. At common law, only the actual compromise offer and those statements inextricably linked with the offer are protected. Many courts have been reluctant to find inextricable linkages. If, for example, the defendant in a libel action states, "You are correct, the story is false and I will offer you $10,000 to soothe your feelings," the admission that the story is false might not be rendered inadmissible by the compromise rule since the court might conclude that it was not part of the settlement offer. If, on the other hand, the plaintiff had let it be known that no amount of money would induce him to settle without a verbal retraction, the entire statement would be excludable as an offer of settlement.

You might wonder how attorneys in common law jurisdictions can ever negotiate if they have to be so careful about what they write or say. The answer is that they do not have to be so careful. The rule admitting statements which are independent of the compromise offer may be avoided if the attorney specifies that all factual statements are hypothetical or if, following the English practice, discussion or correspondence is labeled in advance "without prejudice."

The federal rule would be preferable to the situation which exists in most states if its only advantage were to allow attorneys and their clients to negotiate without constantly qualifying any factual statements. But its value extends beyond this. In many situations individuals unaware of the technicalities of the compromise doctrine attempt to settle matters themselves. Under the common law, but not under the federal rule, they may find that the lack of legal advice has led them to make admissible statements which would have been inadmissible had they been cast in hypothetical form. It is not surprising that the Internal Revenue Service was one government agency to oppose this liberalization of the compromise rule. Of course the federal rule will not prevent all disputes in this area. There are still the questions of what constitutes a compromise attempt and what it means for a claim to be disputed as to either "validity or amount."

The federal rule is also more liberal than prevailing practice because it covers com-

---

17. **In arguing that compromise should be viewed as a question of privilege, McCormick seemed moved by a desire to find a single reason which could best explain the decided cases. But there is no good reason why the rule cannot be justified on more than one ground. Indeed, we have argued that multiple justification is an essential feature of the relevance rules. Having said this, let us suggest another possible jus-** **tification which also sounds more in privilege than relevance. This is that an individual who is taking the socially desirable action of attempting to compromise should not in an honorable and decent world find that a rejected offer will be used against him. Like the similar rationale suggested for subsequent remedial measures, this one, if it exists, is felt by judges more often than it is articulated.**

pleted compromises as well as offers. In many states evidence of a completed compromise which was not carried out will be admitted on the issues of liability or amount if the action which was the subject of the completed compromise is reinstated. The theory is that the purpose of settlement not being attained, a protection designed to promote settlement should not attach. Evidence of the completed compromise may of course come in, even under the federal rule, if suit is brought to enforce the compromise agreement as a contract.

As with all the relevance rules, evidence of an offer to compromise is not excluded for all purposes. The federal rule suggests some of the purposes for which evidence of an offer to compromise may be admitted. Courts are sometimes confused in one common situation: the threeway accident in which A pays B a compromise settlement and B then testifies for A against C. If C seeks to introduce evidence of the compromise settlement, the courts sometimes exclude it on the theory that it is being used by C to show A's negligence in the accident. In fact, it may be offered to show that A and B have had prior dealings which are likely to make B particularly well disposed toward A's side of the case. A careful attorney will make this theory clear. In these circumstances the more generous A's settlement, the more the evidence tends to show bias on B's part.[18] If the settlement appears to be well within the bounds of reason, exclusion may be justified as an exercise of judicial discretion since this is the kind of evidence which the jury might not be able to confine to its proper purpose.[19]

C. OFFERS TO PLEAD GUILTY: THE PLEA OF NOLO CONTENDERE AND WITHDRAWN PLEAS OF GUILTY

The criminal counterpart of the compromise and offer to compromise is the plea of guilt and the offer to plead guilty. The applicable federal rule is Rule 410:

Inadmissibility of Pleas, Plea Discussions, and Related Statements. Except as otherwise provided in this rule, evidence of the following is not, in any civil or criminal proceeding, admissible against the defendant who made the plea or was a participant in the plea discussions:

> (1) a plea of guilty which was later withdrawn;

> (2) a plea of nolo contendere;

> (3) any statement made in the course of any proceedings under Rule 11 of the Federal Rules of Criminal Procedure or comparable state pro-

---

18. A special problem arises if B's acceptance of A's offer is clearly inconsistent with the story that B tells from the stand, as would be the case if B suggests that he and not A was responsible for the accident. Here, even though the compromise suggests A's liability, its value for impeachment is so great that it should be admissible. Analytically, admission could be justified by arguing that it is not presented to show liability but merely to show that B's story on the stand is inconsistent with a position he took on compromise negotiations. The problem with such an analysis under FRE 408, is that B's settlement would be offered for its bearing on B's culpability, which the federal rule appears not to permit.

19. There are two other rationales, not usually recognized, that may help explain both the basic common law rule excluding compromise evidence and the expanded federal rule excluding factual admissions. Often such evidence will require one attorney to testify against another, something the law discourages. The difficulties are exacerbated if the opposing attorneys must switch from being advocates to being witnesses in the course of the trial. It is also possible that allowing the admission of settlement offers may encourage parties to "make a record", wasting resources in the process.

cedure regarding either of the foregoing pleas; or

(4) any statement made in the course of plea discussions with an attorney for the prosecuting authority which do not result in a plea of guilty or which result in a plea of guilty later withdrawn.

However, such a statement is admissible (i) in any proceeding wherein another statement made in the course of the same plea or plea discussions has been introduced and the statement ought in fairness be considered contemporaneously with it, or (ii) in a criminal proceeding for perjury or false statement if the statement was made by the defendant under oath, on the record and in the presence of counsel.

This rule follows prevailing practice in excluding evidence of offers to plead guilty or nolo contendere. Its rationale is similar to the twofold rationale given for the exclusion of offers to compromise. However, the relevancy argument is stronger in this context, while the policy argument may be more questionable. We have already detailed some of the reasons which might lead an innocent defendant to agree to plead guilty. Unlike the civil compromise, the relationship of the plea to the original charge is not necessarily a good indicator of the extent to which the plea in fact reflects consciousness of guilt. In some plea bargaining systems, charges are

seldom reduced, but extensive negotiation occurs over the sentence to be imposed upon conviction.[20]

The strength of the policy justification for protecting offers to plead depends in part on one's general view of plea bargaining as a mode of criminal justice. The plea bargaining system has come under heavy attack in recent years.[21] Individuals committed to its abolition might well criticize an evidence rule that fosters such negotiations. However, even critics generally recognize that so long as society is unwilling to put more resources into its criminal justice system, the plea bargain is likely to remain a necessary way of moving cases through lower courts in urban areas. The defendant who "cops a plea" is serving the needs of the system while he serves his own best interest. In states with no specific rule relating to offers to plead guilty, the matter is usually treated under the principles which apply to compromise negotiations generally.

The plea of nolo contendere is recognized in the federal courts and a majority of states. Acceptance of the plea is generally discretionary with the court, and in many states it is available only in misdemeanor cases. When a plea of nolo contendere is accepted, it is usually followed by all the consequences of an accepted plea of guilty,[22] except that evidence of the plea may generally not be introduced in a civil case as an admission of those facts necessary to a determination of guilt.[23]

---

20. See D. Newman, Conviction: The Determination of Guilt or Innocence Without Trial (1966).

21. See, e.g., Alschuler, The Defense Attorney's Role in Plea Bargaining, 84 Yale L.J. 1179 (1975); Doan, Illegitimacy of Plea Bargaining, 38 Fed.Prob. 18 (Sept.1974); Note, The Unconstitutionality of Plea Bargaining, 83 Harv.L.Rev. 1387 (1970).

22. There are variations among the states; in some the plea has been held not to trigger statutes denying licenses to those convicted of crimes and in a few it may not be used to impeach the credibility of a witness where a

plea of guilty could be so used. See generally, Note, The Plea of Nolo Contendere, 25 Md.L.R. 227 (1965).

23. A valid guilty plea may be introduced in a civil suit as an admission of those facts necessary to a determination of guilt. Usually a party may controvert the implied admissions of the guilty plea, but some courts have held that where the civil action turns on the same issues as the criminal action, the guilty plea is res judicata on all averments in the indictment. The plea of nolo has typically avoided these results, but a minority of courts are now holding that

In antitrust litigation the plea of nolo contendere is particularly important because the Clayton Act provides that:

A final judgment or decree * * * rendered in any civil or criminal proceeding brought by * * * the United States under the antitrust laws to the effect that a defendant has violated said laws shall be prima facie evidence against such defendant in any action or proceeding brought by any other party against such defendant under said laws. * * *

But,

[T]his section shall not apply to consent judgments or decrees entered before any testimony has been taken. * * * [24]

The federal courts have held that a plea of nolo contendere, but not a plea of guilty, is a consent judgment within the meaning of the Act and hence inadmissible in any subsequent treble damage action. This gives a defendant a strong incentive to plead nolo contendere even if the probability of conviction appears low, since the criminal penalty is likely to be substantially less than the civil liabilities which might arise from a series of private treble damage actions. Given this incentive to plead nolo contendere, the relevance of the plea as an admission of guilt is likely to be particularly low in the antitrust area. Since the plea circumvents the general Congressional intention to aid civil litigants in antitrust actions,[25] trial judges face difficult policy problems in deciding whether to accept the plea when it is offered. If you

were the judge, what factors would influence your decision? Of what relevance should FRE 410 be to your decision?

The withdrawn plea of guilty poses special problems. Most states follow the federal rule and consider the withdrawn guilty plea inadmissible in both criminal and civil litigation. Where guilty pleas may be withdrawn only with the permission of the court, there is a relevance argument supporting this position; namely that the court in deciding to allow withdrawal is likely to have found that the plea was not completely voluntary, that it was based on incomplete information, or that it was for some other reason defective. Where guilty pleas made at an early stage can be withdrawn as a matter of right, the inference of unreliability does not exist and some courts admit the plea in subsequent litigation while others bar it.[26] Courts which exclude the plea argue that to decide otherwise would effectively vitiate the permission or right to withdraw, since the defendant would almost certainly be convicted if the jury knew that at one point he was willing to admit his guilt. This position has also been supported with the suggestion that fifth amendment values are compromised where withdrawn guilty pleas are allowed into evidence, since the defendant will almost certainly have to take the stand to explain away the evidence of his prior guilty plea.

Very few cases have arisen where the defendant has made an improvident, unqualified[27] admission while negotiating a

---

a plea of nolo may be allowed in as an admission where the criminal and civil cases encompass the same matters. If this position prevails, the plea will eventually only serve as a way of saving face for those who find it psychologically difficult to admit guilt. Perhaps it will follow the path it followed in England, the land of its birth; no case reports a plea of nolo after 1702.

24. 15 U.S.C. § 16(a)(1955).

25. Congress could remove the plea of nolo contendere as an option in antitrust litigation, but it has never chosen to do so.

26. The defendant is not in any state barred from explaining how he happened to mistakenly plead or from otherwise controverting the admissions implied by the plea. Some would question, however, whether an explanation could ever be constructed which would convince a jury.

27. That is, not in hypothetical form. Also prosecutors as a matter of comity are probably unwilling to hold attorneys to the facts they admit in plea bargaining negotiations. It is clear that some defense counsel do admit their client's guilt while negotiating pleas. See Alschuler, supra note 29.

plea of guilty or nolo contendere with a prosecutor, but in these circumstances it is likely that a jurisdiction would follow its general rule respecting independent statements in compromise negotiations. FRE 410 makes it clear that such statements are inadmissible unless the conditions of subsection (i) or (ii) are met.

Since the rule only bars the use of statements *"against the defendant"* it is possible that statements made in plea discussions will be admissible against third parties or against the government.[28] Where this occurs it triggers subsection (i) and opens the door to statements that elucidate, place in context or otherwise affect the meaning of the statement originally introduced. The obvious purpose is to prevent a defendant from taking advantage of FRE 410 by introducing a statement that is exculpatory only when taken out of context.

Subsection (ii) will apply almost exclusively to statements made in the course of Rule 11 proceedings or comparable state procedures since it is only in these circumstances that statements made in connection with plea bargains are likely to be under oath, on the record and in the presence of counsel. Rule 11 of the Federal Rules of Criminal Procedure specifies those procedures that must accompany the entry

of a guilty plea in federal court. For present purposes the most important of these is that before accepting a plea the court must determine that the plea is voluntary and has some basis in fact.[29]

Determining voluntariness and basis in fact usually require the court to question the defendant. Some courts do not place defendants under oath for such colloquies. But if the defendant is placed under oath, subsection (ii) of FRE 410 allows his statements to be used against him in a later prosecution for perjury, provided that counsel is present and the statements are on the record, as the statements are required to be. Where these conditions are met, one who has admitted his guilt in the course of a "cop out" ceremony is at least in theory vulnerable to a charge of perjury should he later claim he was innocent of the crime charged. In rare cases there is the potential for unfairness here since innocent defendants can be induced to plead guilty by attractive bargains, and they may feel they must assert their guilt for the bargain to be accepted.[30]

The current version of Rule 410 is the third that has been part of the Federal Rules. The most important difference between this version and the one it replaced

---

28. Courts apparently have discretion to exclude prosecutors' statements when offered by defendants for the kinds of policy reasons that support FRE 410. See, e.g. United States v. Verdoorn, 528 F.2d 103 (8th Cir. 1976). The drafters of the current version of FRE 410 make it clear in their commentary that the "against defendant" language is not to be taken as an expression of disapproval of such decisions.

29. Problems can arise where defendants have jointly participated in a plea discussion. It may happen that one defendant wishes to bolster his case by introducing a statement made in the joint discussion. If the statement or other statements that ought in fairness to be considered along with it inculpates the codefendant, the codefendant is clearly entitled to an instruction that the statements may not be used against him and should probably be granted a separate trial upon request.

30. Occasionally a case will come to light where the accused, unsure of his role, wishes to both deny involvement yet plead guilty. Consider the following dialogue taken from a transcript reproduced in A. Blumberg, Criminal Justice, 131–136 (1967):

Mr. McManus: If your Honor pleases, the defendant John Dukes desires to plead guilty, as charged, in each and every count in the indictment.

The Court: John Dukes, do you wish to plead guilty to the crimes of robbery in the first degree, the first count, grand larceny in the first degree, the second count, assault in the second degree, the third count in the indictment?

Defendant Dukes: Yes, I do.

The Court: And are you guilty of the crimes charged therein?

Defendant Dukes: Yes.

is that under the prior rule statements made in connection with an offer to plead guilty were protected regardless of to whom the statements were addressed. This led suspects who had made improvident admissions to the police, postal inspectors, IRS agents and the like to claim that their statements were made in connection with offers to plead guilty. Courts treated such claims as raising factual issues that had to be resolved in order to determine whether FRE 410 applied. To simplify the task of the trial judge and to prevent defendants from dishonestly claiming the protection of FRE 410 for statements they later came to regret, the rule now protects only statements made in the course of plea discussions with attorneys for the prosecuting authority.

This change should certainly cure the problem that gave rise to it. It also means that people who offer the police inculpatory information in the honest belief that they are negotiating a plea will find their statements used against them. It remains to be seen whether police authorities will try to extract information by pretending that they have authority to negotiate plea bargains. FRE 410 does not exclude the statements of any who are so duped, but it is likely that the courts either by interpreting the *Miranda* rule or in their exercise of their supervisory power would refuse to admit such evidence.[31]

The Court: Do you admit, by your plea of guilt, that in _____ County, on May 23, 1964, in the vicinity of Texarkana Avenue at 2nd Street, about 4:10 a. m., you unlawfully took certain property owned by Nelson Stanley, having a value of about one hundred seventy dollars, from the person or in the presence of Nelson Stanley but against his will, by means of force or violence or fear of immediate injury to his person, and were you at the time aided, that is, assisted in the commission of this robbery by your co-defendants?

Defendant Dukes: No, sir.

The Court: Did you perpetrate this robbery alone?

Defendant Dukes: Well, I was alone. It was a crowd of fifteen people there, and I went to the crowd of fifteen, and I picked the wallet up off the ground. I went to the defense of the complainant but by me being in the crowd he picked me out.

The Court: I don't quite understand.

Defendant Dukes: It was only supposed to be ninety dollars involved.

The Court: I am not concerned about the amount of money involved. I am concerned only about the circumstance under which you got possession of this money. Did you take it by force from the person or the possession of this victim, Nelson Stanley?

Defendant Dukes: No, sir.

The Court: Did you threaten him?

Defendant Dukes: No, sir.

The Court: Then I cannot accept a plea to the indictment, Mr. McManus. Do you want to confer with your client?

* * *

Mr. McManus: *I have conferred, your Honor. You know, sometimes, when it comes to this point, they somehow or other gag, so to speak, to use a vulgar expression* [Blumberg's italics]*, but what confused him I think was the amount of money.* He claims it was ninety dollars.

* * *

The Court: Do you want me to take this plea? Do you still wish to plead guilty to the three counts in the indictment?

Defendant Dukes: Yes, sir.

* * *

The Court: By your plea of guilty, do you admit that on May 23, 1964, at about 4:10 in the morning, in the vicinity of Texarkana Avenue and 2nd Street, you, together with one or more other persons who aided you in the commission of this crime, unlawfully took certain moneys owned by Nelson Stanley from his presence or from his person but against his will, by means of force or violence, or by fear of immediate injury to his person?

Defendant Dukes: Yes, sir. Me alone.

* * *

The Court: Now, you are pleading to an indictment which charges that you, together with others, acting in concert with you, committed a robbery. Is that the fact?

Defendant Dukes: I didn't understand that, your Honor. Yes.

31. The most recent version of FRE 410 also differs from the preceding version in that subsection (i) had no counterpart in the ear-

D. PAYMENT OF MEDICAL EXPENSES

FRE 409 restates the common law with respect to the payment of medical and similar expenses after accidents:

> Evidence of furnishing or offering or promising to pay medical, hospital, or similar expenses occasioned by an injury is not admissible to prove liability for the injury.

The rule is justified by a belief that people are likely to act from humanitarian motives in providing post-accident medical care to others and from a feeling that where this is the case evidence of such payment is of low relevance. A legacy of this rationale is that in some states such evidence will be excluded only if it has been motivated by humanitarian considerations and, in almost all states, admissions made in connection with furnishing care will be allowed in on the issue of liability, if relevant.[32]

The rule is also justified by the social desirability of promoting post-accident offers of medical care and by a feeling that it would be improper to turn such a worthy deed against the one responsible. (Do these justifications suggest that statements made in connection with the rendering of such aid should also be excluded?) There is a final justification for this rule which has arisen since it was first formulated. This is the fact that many insurance policies today provide that payment for the medical expenses of injured third parties is authorized within certain limits regardless of the negligence of the policy holder. Where payments are made under such clauses, relevance to the issue of liability is obviously low.

Though FRE 409 does not specifically so state, the existence of post-accident medical payments is admissible on issues other than the liability of the one who paid.

E. LIABILITY INSURANCE

FRE 411 codifies the common law on liability insurance:

> Evidence that a person was or was not insured against liability is not admissible upon the issue whether he acted negligently or otherwise wrongfully. This rule does not require the exclusion of evidence of insurance against liability when offered for another purpose, such as proof of agency, ownership, or control, or bias or prejudice of a witness.

Such evidence is inadmissible whether offered by plaintiff to show that a defendant who had no fear of paying accident costs was likely to have been careless at a particular time or offered by a defendant who wishes to argue that the absence of insurance or the existence of low policy limits provides a circumstantial guarantee that he was likely to have been acting carefully at a particular time.

We discussed the reasons for this rule, low relevance and a high possibility of prejudice, when we used it as an example in our discussion of the mathematical model of relevance in Chapter Three. Because the existence of insurance is likely to lower a jury's regret at finding liability in the defendant, plaintiffs' counsel often try to remind juries that insurance is involved in the case. This is often done on voir dire where prospective jurors may be asked whether they have any connections

---

lier version; the earlier version only protected statements "relevant to" pleas or offers while the current version contains no such limitation, and the earlier version made evidence of pleas and related statements inadmissible against the "person making the plea or offer" while the current version makes them inadmissible against the "defendant who made the plea or was a participant in the plea discussion."

32. In the "humanitarian consideration" jurisdictions, the statement admitting liability is usually the justification for admitting the evidence of the payment as well.

with the insurance business. (Such questions are proper even where the defendant is not insured. Do you see why?) Opportunities for pointing to an "insurance connection" are also possible during the trial, most commonly where the defendant feels forced to put an insurance company investigator on the stand.

Problem IV–4. Driver, driving Owner's car without his permission, collides with Plaintiff at an intersection. Plaintiff sues Owner, claiming the cause of the accident was the defective condition of the brakes on Owner's car. Driver is called to testify for Plaintiff and Owner wants to introduce evidence of the fact that Driver agreed to settle out of court with Plaintiff by paying Plaintiff $500. **Is she permitted to do so?**

Problem IV–5. In the same case set forth in the preceding problem, Plaintiff and Owner engage in pre-trial settlement negotiations during which Plaintiff says, "Look, you and I both know that the accident was Driver's fault, but he and I have settled, and I know you're going to lose if a jury gets this case, especially since Driver will testify for me—so let's settle. I'll take $1,000." **Can this offer and accompanying statement be introduced into evidence?** Suppose Owner begins negotiations by saying "Look, I can't waste my time. You'll take $100 to get off my back or you'll find there are a lot worse accidents than the one you were in." **Admissible?**

Problem IV–6. On the same facts as the preceding problem, but as soon as Owner is notified of the accident, she calls Plaintiff and says, "I'm truly sorry about that accident. Tomorrow my lousy brakes were supposed to be fixed. How about if I give you a couple of hundred bucks and we call it even?" **Admissible? On what issues?**

Problem IV–7. Juvenile contracts to purchase an automobile, the seller being under the impression that the youth is well over the age at which he is bound by his contracts. Having agreed to purchase the car for $2,000, and having paid $200 down, Juvenile drives the car for one month, gets in an accident and returns the car, dents and all, to Seller. Seller indicates that the car is worth only $1500 after it is repaired and that the repairs will cost $100. Adding $500 depreciation to the $100 repair costs, Seller sends Juvenile a bill for $400. Two months pass and Juvenile reaches the age of legal majority. He writes Seller, "I know I owe you money for the car and I usually honor my debts. I'd like to do so here, but after all, you did sell the car to a minor. I'll give you half the $400 and we'll call it a day. A check for $200 is enclosed. **Seller sues for the remainder and wants to introduce the letter. Can he?**

Problem IV–8. The Acme Encyclopedia Company sells most of its books on a door-to-door basis. It will hire anyone who has access to a car as a sales representative. Acme pays all of its sales representatives on a straight commission basis. The sales representatives are expected to pay all their expenses, except that any salesperson who has been with the company more than three months receives 15 cents a mile for automobile expenses while on company business and is covered by a $200,000 liability insurance policy for any accidents which occur while on company business. [The company occasionally dismisses an individual with a very poor sales record after the three month period is up, but this is rare.] Larry Cary has been a salesman for Acme for seven months. One evening, while going to visit a prospective purchaser, he hits Peggy Pedestrian causing severe injuries. Pedestrian sues Acme for $500,000. Acme's attorneys are thinking of defending on the ground that they are not responsible for Cary's actions because Cary was an independent contractor who set his own hours, chose his own route and contacted his own prospects. **What factors should the attorneys consider before deciding whether to raise this defense?**

Problem IV-9. Rollo Rich, enjoying a chaufferless spin in his Rolls Royce, hit Sluggo Snyder while Sluggo was crossing the street. Rollo, very contrite, got out of his Rolls, helped Sluggo up and said, "I'm very sorry. I feel terrible. I've never driven this car before. I don't know how it happened, but it must have been all my fault. I want you to get the best medical care. Go to the Ritz Hospital and tell them that I will pay all your bills." Sluggo went to the Ritz, a luxurious private hospital, rather than to the public hospital to which he ordinarily would have gone, and ran up $2600 in health care expenses during a twelve day stay. When he was released, Rollo refused to pay, informing him that, "Since you recklessly ran in front of my car, I have no obligation to pay your bills." **If Sluggo sues Rollo in tort, can any or all of Rollo's post-accident statements come in on the issue of negligence? Will they come in on any other issue? Suppose that Sluggo borrows the money to pay the Ritz and then sues Rollo for breach of contract. Will any portion of these statements be admissible in that action?**

Problem IV-10. In the same situation as problem 9 above, Rollo has no insurance. **May he introduce evidence that he lacks insurance to support his argument that he was driving extra-carefully on the day in question? May Rollo introduce evidence that his Rolls Royce is a custom built model and that he has lavished the greatest love and care on it as evidence that he was likely to have been driving particularly carefully at the time of the accident?**

Problem IV-11. SilverScreen (SS), a movie production company, buys its film from Photo Company, a film manufacturer. In each cannister of film is the usual notice stating that in the event that the film provided by Photo Company should prove defective, Photo Company's liability is limited to the replacement cost of the film. Of course, no SS executive ever has the occasion to open a new cannister of film and the cinematographers who do open the cannisters discard the notices without examining them. SS, upon developing fifty cannisters of film shot for their new epic was dismayed to find that more than half the film they developed had scratches that rendered it worthless. SS sued Photo for the cost of reshooting the scratched film and for lost profits resulting from the delay. Photo responded that the scratches were due not to defective film but to the negligence of SS as it developed the cannisters and, in the alternative, that should it be found liable its liability was limited to the replacement cost of the film. SS denied

the allegation of contributory negligence and said that it was not bound by
the disclaimers in the cannisters because not one of its executives had seen
them.   Photo responded that it was an industry custom to limit liability as
they had done and that the SS executives would, as experienced film producers, know of the custom whether or not they had personally read the disclaimers.   Photo company would like to introduce evidence that SS had an
insurance policy that indemnified them against, among other things, defective film.   SS argues that evidence of the policy should not be admitted because it is only suing for that portion of its losses that was not covered by
insurance.   **Is evidence of the policy admissible on either the issue of SS's
contributory negligence or the issue of Photo's claim of limited liability?**

Problem IV–12.   The defendant is charged with the felony of breaking
and entering.   The prosecutor offers to reduce this charge to a misdemeanor, loitering around a building at night.   The defendant refuses and the
prosecution presses the original felony charge.   **Can the defendant introduce evidence of the prosecutor's offer to accept a misdemeanor plea?**
Assume that the defendant had asked the prosecutor, "Why the big reduction?" and the prosecutor had responded, "Frankly, I don't believe the principal eyewitness."   **Could the defendant introduce this statement?**   Suppose the prosecutor had replied, "Well, your prints don't match the prints
on the burglary tools," and there was no effort by the prosecution at trial to
introduce the burglary tools or evidence of fingerprints.   **Is the statement
admissible?**

Problem IV–13.   Assume that in the plea negotiations referred to in
the preceding problem the defendant had told the prosecutor, "Ain't no way
I'm gonna plead, I have two buddies who will swear I was at the pool hall
that night."   **Can the prosecutor introduce this statement if the defense
rests without presenting any evidence?   If the defendant testifies that he
wasn't at the scene of the crime, but at no time indicates where he was?
If the defendant testifies that he was home in bed at the time of the burglary?   If the defendant presents his two roommates, each of whom testifies that the defendant was home in bed at the time of the burglary?**

Problem IV–14. Tim Brutus, a "professional" burglar is picked up for
questioning after a series of burglaries which bear his mark.   After fifteen
minutes of police questioning he asks if he can see the prosecutor.   The
prosecutor enters the interrogation room and says, "I suppose you're going
to insist that we let you go because we have nothing on you except the *modus*.   Well, I have news for you, we've been trying to pin one of your jobs
on you for years and I've told the cops that this time they have free rein to
do whatever is needed to get you to crack."   Brutus replied, "Actually, I
called you because I wanted to wipe the slate clean and save you trouble.
I know your case is weak because I'm careful, but if you will accept a plea
to a misdemeanor I'll take six months in connection with whatever one of the
jobs you want, and so long as you won't bring charges I'll help the cops clear
another twenty jobs in which they don't even have a suspect.   What do you
say?"   The prosecutor replied, "I thought the message was clear.   This time
we're going to send you away no matter what.   We're not going to deal." **At**

Brutus' trial may the state introduce his statements? May Brutus introduce the prosecutor's first remarks? If Brutus is allowed to introduce the prosecutor's first remarks, will this open the door to the introduction of Brutus' statements?

Problem IV–15. Sandra Cooper is charged with forgery with intent to defraud. She is responsible for distributing funds under a federally sponsored university financial aid program. Under the rules of the program whenever funds are disbursed to a needy student the student must sign his name acknowledging receipt of the funds. Cooper admits signing the names of students and not giving them the money, but says she did it because she had delayed in submitting a funding request and so needed cash to meet the expenses of another program for which she was responsible. She said that it was her intention to give the students whose names she had forged the money due them as soon as the funds for her other program were received. The forged signatures had been discovered in the course of a university audit which revealed that Cooper's accounts were short $1100. Immediately after the audit, Cooper's supervisor approached her and told her that she was guilty of gross mismanagement and that unless she repaid the $1100 immediately she would be fired. Cooper did this and remained on the job, performing satisfactorily until she left for another position. At her trial for forgery with intent to defraud, the government seeks to show that when she was confronted with the deficit of $1100 she immediately repaid the money. **Should the testimony of Cooper's supervisor to this effect be allowed?**

Problem IV–16. The city of Troy wishes to condemn part of the farmland owned by Helen Homer in order to build a horsepath. Assume that the following statements were made by the city's representatives when negotiating with Homer and her attorneys over the price of the land: (1) We'll give you $4500 for your land. (2) The market value of your land is $5000; we'll give you $4500. (3) We'll give you 10% less than the market value of your land which, according to our calculations, comes to $4500. **If the city argues in court that the market value of the land is only $4000, which, if any, of the above statements would be admitted as tending to prove that the market value of the land is more than $4000?**

Problem IV–17. The Internal Revenue Service notifies Dr. Dorothy Blair, a physician, that they believe she has substantially understated her income in recent years and they wish to audit her books. After her books have been audited she is "invited" to see the IRS agent in charge of her case. He begins his conversation by giving her *Miranda* warnings. When she asks why he did that, he replies that she is in big trouble because the audit shows that she has understated her income for the years 1981 and 1982 by more than $100,000. The penalty he tells her is up to ten years in prison. She asks whether there is anything she can do to keep out of trouble. He replies that if she immediately pays the entire amount owing plus interest and the applicable penalties and if she will agree to plead guilty to a misdemeanor tax offense should the IRS decide to prosecute her criminally, he is confident based on his experience that felony charges will not be brought. Blair responds that she is sure that her understatements were for no more than $60,000, but since she should have known better and she wants to keep her license she will pay the IRS what they want and will plead guilty to a misdemeanor should criminal charges be brought. **If Blair changes her mind and decides not to pay the $100,000 and the IRS after a reaudit sues her civilly for $55,000 will Blair's statements to the IRS agent be admissible against her? If the IRS charges Blair with criminal tax fraud, a felony, will the government be able to introduce her statements to the agent to show that she knew she had understated her income by about $60,000 and that she was willing to plead guilty to a misdemeanor offense? If she had paid the sum demanded, could evidence of that payment be introduced against her in a criminal case?**

Problem IV–18. Harry Converse was involved in an automobile accident with Paula Potts in which Potts suffered severe injuries. Potts sued Converse for $200,000. Converse was present at a settlement hearing at which his offer of $60,000 was rejected. At the trial Converse denies negligence. **May Potts introduce evidence that during the negotiations Converse appeared very tense, that he was wringing his hands throughout, and that he finally started crying and got up and left when Potts started talking about the extent of her injuries? Would your answer be different if Converse's attorney had opened the negotiations with the statement, "Now, of course, all this is without prejudice"?**

F. SIMILAR HAPPENINGS

There are a variety of reasons why a party might wish to introduce evidence of an event similar to the event which is the subject matter of the litigation. The plaintiff in a negligence action might wish to introduce evidence that other people tripped and fell on a certain stair tread in order to prove that the tread was dangerous or that the landlord had notice of the defect. A party to a condemnation proceeding might wish to introduce evidence of the price at which similar parcels of land sold in order to demonstrate that the opponent's suggested price is unreasonable. In most jurisdictions, there are no hard and fast rules excluding evidence of similar events when such evidence is relevant to matters at issue,[33] but courts approach evidence of similar happenings skeptically. Minimal logical relevance will often not justify admission. Courts pay special attention to the degree of similarity between the collateral event which is offered as evidence and the event which is at issue in the case. Evidence of the collateral event will usually be admitted only where there is substantial similarity between the two events.[34]

There are good reasons for this judicial attitude. Introducing evidence of similar events may raise collateral issues concerning the accuracy with which the event is reported, it might unfairly surprise a party

---

33. There is no federal rule which deals specifically with evidence of similar happenings.

34. We are commenting here on what appears to be a judicial mood as evidenced in numerous decisions. Unfortunately we cannot be more specific in stating exactly how great the similarity between two events must be before evidence of the collateral event is allowed in. This will vary from court to court, from case to case, and from issue to issue.

who was prepared only to deal with those matters alleged in the pleadings, and it may, particularly if there is controversy about an event, lead a jury to mistakenly believe that the resolution of the controversy before it should turn largely on its views concerning the similar event. Such evidence might also prejudice the jury if the collateral event suggested that one party was in the past guilty of some form of culpable conduct.

We can see these problems in the stair tread example. It might not be clear that the earlier accidents were due to a defective tread; the defendant might argue that he could have shown the accidents were not due to the tread had he only known that evidence was going to be offered for this purpose.[35] The jury might get so caught up in the issue of what caused the other accidents that they would give their findings on this matter undue weight when deciding the case presented. Finally, the jury might decide that because the defendant is apparently responsible for other accidents which were never the subject of suit, it is only fair that the defendant pay for the plaintiff's accident if plaintiff's case is at all reasonable.

There are many different situations in which attempts are made to introduce similar fact evidence. The stair tread illustration is an example of one common use: in a negligence case to show that a situation was dangerous and/or that a party had or should have had notice of a dangerous situation. Similar accidents have also been introduced in negligence and products liability actions to prove the existence of a particular physical condition or defect and to show that the plaintiff's injury was caused

by the allegedly defective or dangerous situation. If, for example, the plaintiff fell down the defendant's stairs but did not know why, evidence that three other people had tripped over a loose tread on that stair would suggest that the plaintiff too had tripped over the loose tread.

It should be obvious that the circumstances must be relatively similar for an accident to be relevant to issues relating to negligence. If the other accidents occurred on a different stair than the plaintiff's accident, they would have little bearing on the cause of the plaintiff's misstep or on the question of whether the defendant should have been put on notice that the stair on which plaintiff tripped was dangerous.[36] Time may also be important in deciding whether two accidents share the requisite degree of similarity. An accident in the winter when surfaces are icy may not be relevant to an action for an injury which occurred in the summer when surfaces are dry. If the similar stair tread accidents had occurred two years before the accident sued upon, they would probably be excluded from evidence. Too many alterations in the condition of the stairs may have occurred between the dates of the two accidents.

Usually it is the plaintiff who wants to introduce evidence of similar accidents. The counterpart in the defendant's case is proof of the absence of other accidents as tending to show a safe condition or the defendant's reasonableness in not anticipating a dangerous condition. Evidence that thousands of people a day climb a staircase without tripping is strong evidence that a fall was caused by a stumbling

---

35. Discovery or notice procedures might alleviate this problem.

36. **Where a condition is relatively uniform throughout, a defect in one part might suggest defects in another or put a reasonable person on notice that there are likely to be defects in another part. In the stair-tread example, if the tread were of the same age and material throughout, courts might** differ on the question of whether an accident on one stair might be introduced on any issue when an action was brought for an accident which occurred on another stair. It would be most likely to be admitted in support of the proposition that the defendant upon learning of one accident had a duty, as a reasonable person, to inspect the condition of all the treads.

plaintiff and not a defective tread. Though a majority of courts admit safety history to prove lack of danger, there are difficulties in proving a negative which leads some courts that admit evidence of similar accidents to exclude evidence of this type. A major difficulty is that a lack of complaints does not mean that accidents of a similar sort have not been occurring. Those who stumble without falling may be too busy to register a complaint, and complaints to one employee may not be passed on to the person who testifies that he has not heard of any trouble. Also, the condition of areas continually changes. The plaintiff may in fact be among the first to encounter a newly dangerous situation. Of course, the absence of complaints would still be relevant on the issue of notice.[37]

Courts often refuse to admit evidence of contracts between a party and a third party when a contract between the plaintiff and defendant is in dispute. The maxim *res inter alios acta* (a thing done between others) is often invoked as a substitute for close analysis. There is sense at the core of this maxim, for parties are unequal in their bargaining power and skill. The fact that Honest Joe, the used car dealer, offered Tough Tessa a '71 Chevy for $500.00 does not mean that he did not sell the same car to Simple Simon for $750.00. But clearly the earlier offer is relevant on the issue of what Joe did ask, particularly if Simon claims he only asked $500.00. Some courts, more attentive to the relevance of the evidence than others, would admit this evidence for what it is worth.

When neither contracting party is involved in the instant litigation the courts almost always exclude evidence of their dealings. Even if Joe is no better in dealing with Tessa than Shirley is in dealing with Simon, the courts will, with one exception, simply not hold Joe to the results of Shirley's dealing. The exception is when fair market value is in issue. Then, if the commodity is a standard one, the courts will receive not only the testimony of witnesses who know of similar sales but also price lists and market reports. If the commodity is not a standard one, such as a unique jewel or a thoroughbred horse, other sales will not be directly admitted on the issue of value, though they may enter into the reasoning of an expert asked to make a considered appraisal. Land poses particular problems in this respect since the law has traditionally regarded each parcel of land as unique. Nevertheless, where courts must establish the market value of land, as in condemnation proceedings, most will admit evidence as to the price at which other parcels of land sold if the condition of the other parcels is sufficiently similar to the condition of the land in question. Again, courts will relax the similarity requirements where the other sales are offered as part of the basis of an expert's opinion and not as independent evidence of value.[38]

There are a few other areas in which courts have developed general policies with respect to similar fact evidence. Where a civil suit is based on action which is criminal in nature, as in an action for fraud, the

---

37. Many cases of this type involve businesses which have a duty to inspect their premises to protect their invitees, so notice is often not a material issue in these cases. Notice would still be relevant if, for example, the plaintiff sought punitive damages or if the danger were of such a type or of such a short duration that reasonable inspection would not have revealed it.

38. Some courts are reluctant to allow even an expert appraiser to report very dissimilar sales as part of the basis for an

opinion. They fear the jury might treat the sales as independent evidence of value, and they are skeptical of the usefulness of dissimilar sales in forming expert opinions. However, even if an attorney is barred from asking an expert about dissimilar sales on direct examination, the opposing counsel may open the door to this evidence if he probes deeply into the basis of the expert's opinion on cross-examination.

court will admit evidence of the defendant's similar past actions for the same purposes that such evidence might be admitted in criminal cases: to show guilty knowledge, tortious intent, or plan or design, if one or more of these is a material element in the plaintiff's case.

Most courts will also admit evidence that a party has previously raised fraudulent claims similar to the present claim. This kind of claim is different from other kinds of similar fact evidence because it is designed to undercut a party's case by impeaching the credibility of the party's allegations, not by suggesting facts which are inconsistent with them. Difficult problems arise where a defendant with no good evidence of plaintiff's previous fraud seeks to introduce evidence that the plaintiff has brought numerous similar claims in the past, the theory being that the improbability that one person would be so often and similarly victimized means that the plaintiff's claim is likely to be, intentionally or unconsciously, unfounded. Absent independent evidence of fraud, courts are reluctant to accept this kind of evidence. Where such evidence is admitted, it is more likely to be admitted for the purpose of testing credibility on cross-examination than as part of the defendant's case-in-chief.

A related use of similar fact evidence for impeachment occurs where a witness has told the same story in virtually the same language at a preliminary hearing, in a deposition, or at an earlier trial. Here evidence of the earlier testimony will be let in to show that a witness' story has been well prepared and lacks the spontaneity which the performance from the witness box might otherwise suggest. It also carries the damning, but by no means necessarily correct, inference that the witness only remembers a constructed version of events and not the incidents which actually occurred.[39]

In recent years some commentators have suggested that a party should be allowed to show accident proneness as evidence of negligence or contributory negligence. This is not really similar circumstance evidence since the only necessary similarity between those incidents which give rise to the inference of accident proneness is that the same party be involved in all of them.[40] To date courts have been reluctant to allow such evidence in on the issue of negligent causation in an accident,[41] but some courts have admitted evidence of a reputation for accident proneness or involvement in a series of accidents on the issue of whether an employer was negligent in hiring or continuing to employ a particular individual.

39. Occasionally a lawyer may achieve the same effect where there is no previously recorded testimony by distracting the witness' attention on cross-examination with some innocuous questions and then running the witness once, twice, or three times through a verbatim account of the testimony given on direct examination. Keep this in mind when you read Wellman's suggestion in the next chapter that a cross-examiner should always avoid repeating the direct examination.

40. Commentators have suggested that psychological testing and expert testimony should be required if an effort is made to establish accident proneness. James and Dickinson, Accident Proneness and Accident Law, 63 Harv.L.Rev. 769 (1950); Maloney and Rish, The Accident-Prone Driver, 14 U.Fla.L.Rev. 364 (1962).

41. There are at least two good reasons for this. First, accident proneness does not mean that one's negligence was responsible for a particular accident or series of accidents. Ordinary clumsiness or inattentiveness or a predilection for risk may mean that one is likely to be in more than his share of accidents without engaging in behavior which ever rises to the level of negligence or contributory negligence. Second, involvement in a series of accidents may simply involve an unusual run of bad luck. Assume, for example, that in the course of a year 100 accidents were going to happen in a village of 100 people and that these accidents were going to be assigned to people at random by drawing the names of the people who were to have accidents out of a hat and replacing them once the accident had been assigned. (This kind of random assignment gives rise to a Poisson dis-

Problem IV–19. Diane Dell is charged with embezzlement. She denies having committed the offense, but admits that in her capacity as store clerk she removed certain funds from the cash register each week and kept them for her own use. Dell's story is that her employer suggested to her that she should take $30.00 from the cash drawer each week as additional compensation. This was to be in lieu of a salary increase. According to Dell, the employer's motive was to avoid paying increased social security taxes. Dell wishes to introduce evidence that the employer filed embezzlement charges against three other employees. In two of the cases the accused employees were tried and acquitted. In the third the prosecution dropped the charges after investigating the facts. **Is the evidence offered by Dell admissible? Is some portion of this evidence more objectionable than other portions? Does it matter whether the two acquittals came in one trial or at separate trials? If you were the judge, would you desire any further information before making your ruling?**

Problem IV–20. The plaintiff sells paint to the defendant. The defendant wishes to return one can, stating that some paint that he has previously bought from the plaintiff was defective. The plaintiff refuses to accept the return and sues the defendant. The defendant then seeks to introduce evidence that paint of the same brand as that he tried to return, bought from the same salesman five months earlier, was applied to a roof, ruined the shingles and caused leakage. **Is the evidence admissible? Would you answer this question differently if the case arose in 1910 which was before chemical techniques for the analysis of paint quality had been developed?**

Problem IV–21. The same facts as the previous problem, but the defendant is suing the plaintiff for damages to his roof. **Can he introduce evidence that application of the paint five months earlier had damaged a similar roof?**

Problem IV–22. The plaintiff in a negligence action sues a streetcar company, claiming that a driver was careless in starting too suddenly while the plaintiff was alighting. The defendant wishes to show that 17 prior claims have been brought by the plaintiff's relatives against the streetcar company for injuries allegedly sustained while alighting from cars. **Should evidence of this be admitted?**

Problem IV–23. The same type of situation as in problem 22 where the plaintiff is suing for injuries alleged to have resulted when alighting from a streetcar. The defendant wishes to show that during the previous year the plaintiff has brought negligence actions against two other persons. The defendant wants the jury told that it may take into consideration the fact

tribution.) Most people in the village would have their fair share of the total accidents: one. But others would be lucky and have no accidents, while some unlucky souls would have two, three or even four accidents. The poor person with four accidents might appear to be accident prone because it could be shown that the odds were very low that he would have as many as four accidents if accidents were assigned by chance. But, by the same token the odds might be very high that someone in the village would have as many as four accidents in these circumstances. Of course, the "someone" with four accidents would always be the person labeled accident prone.

that it is unusual for a person not engaged in hazardous activities to suffer over a short period of time repeated injuries due to the negligence of different persons. **Is the evidence admissible and the requested instruction proper?**

Problem IV–24. City X wishes to condemn land owned by the defendant. In order to prove the market value of the land, the city wishes to introduce testimony as to the purchase price paid on two recent sales of comparable property in the neighborhood. **Should the testimony be admitted? Would it matter if the two earlier sales had been made to the city after the city threatened to condemn the land? Assuming that this evidence is unavailable, could the city introduce evidence that offers to purchase at certain prices had been made?**

Problem IV–25. The plaintiff sued for damages allegedly received when she slipped on the sales floor of the defendant's office building and broke her hip. The alleged cause of the injury was the wet and slippery condition of a linoleum floor. It appears that the accident happened sometime about or after 11:30 a. m. It was a cold day. There had been a slight snowfall earlier that day. A few minutes after the plaintiff had been taken away to the hospital, and shortly before noon, a young doctor entered the same room where the plaintiff had met with her accident. The doctor was called as a witness by the plaintiff and after preliminary questions asking the time and place he entered the defendant's building, this occurred: "Q. Tell us what, if anything, happened as you went in after leaving the door?" Defendant: "This is objected to as incompetent and immaterial, as to what happened when this doctor went in the front door. There is no showing that it has any relation to the case." The objection was sustained. The plaintiff offered "to prove by this witness that about 15 minutes before 12 on February 13, 1973, and at the time when the plaintiff was at the hospital after she had been injured, he walked into the sales room of the defendant's place of business, and within four or five feet after leaving the door his feet slipped out from under him, he caught himself without falling, but that the floor was wet and he slipped and nearly fell." **What is the basis for the defendant's objection? What is the plaintiff's argument? What is the proper ruling? Would the case be different if the doctor's fall had occurred on the equally dismal day of February 11? On February 15?**

Problem IV–26. The plaintiff descended a stairway in a theater, caught her foot in a space between the end of a row of seats and the edge of a step, and broke her ankle. She sues, claiming negligence. **Can the defendant introduce testimony by the theater manager that in fifteen years no one had suffered a similar accident?**

Problem IV–27. Publishing Company, Inc. is indicted under an obscenity statute for publishing and selling in New York City *Lord Chastity's Mistress*, an illustrated novel about an adulterer. The Supreme Court test for obscenity is whether to the average person, applying contemporary community standards, the dominant theme of the materials taken as a whole appeals to prurient interest and is without redeeming social importance. Publishing Company, over the prosecution's objections, seeks to introduce in evidence, through a qualified expert, an illustrated edition of Lady Chatterley's Lover by D. H. Lawrence.   It seeks to prove by the testimony of the expert that Lady Chatterley's Lover and Lord Chastity's Mistress are comparable in theme, treatment and illustration and that the former has been a best seller throughout New York City and State for the past three years. **Should the Court admit the evidence?   Would testimony that the book in controversy is a best seller in Boston, Mass. be admissible?**

Problem IV–28.   An employee of a railroad company is killed as she attempts to mount the stepboard of a moving locomotive.   Her widower sues the company to recover for the alleged wrongful death of his wife.   In the complaint, the widower alleges that the defendant was negligent in failing to promulgate and enforce a rule specifically providing that no member of the crew should be permitted to board a locomotive or mount its stepboard while the locomotive was in motion.   The plaintiff wishes to introduce evidence that at the time of the accident the rules of eight other railroad companies in the area specifically forbade mounting stepboards on moving locomotives or riding locomotives while standing on the stepboard.   **Can this evidence come in?**

Problem IV–29.   An expert at accident reconstruction testifies that after a careful investigation she has concluded that the defendant's car was not speeding at the time of the accident that is the basis for the instant lawsuit. **Can she be asked if she works for Nostate, the defendant's insurance company?   Can she then be asked whether she has not testified 20 times before for that insurance company and never once concluded that a Nostate driver was speeding at the time of an accident?**

Problem IV–30.   The Foxy-Loxy Supermarket has a strange way of marketing their epoxy.   The managers have glued 600 tubes of epoxy glue together so that they form a large "V" with a single tube at the bottom. This tube is glued to the shelf with a large banner strung between the two sides of the "V" reading, "The Strength of Epoxy."   The manager of the Foxy-Loxy claims that this promotion has increased epoxy sales to three times their previous level.

One day Sam Slade was shopping in the Foxy-Loxy when the bottom tube came loose and the entire "V" fell on Sam with such force that it broke Sam's arm.   Sam has learned that there were at least two previous occasions when the "V" broke loose from its moorings, once breaking the collarbone of a woman shopper and the other time fracturing the skull of a child. In a suit brought against the supermarket, Sam seeks to introduce evidence of these other accidents.   The attorney for the supermarket objects, pointing out that Fred Cox, the manager of the supermarket, will testify that both previous accidents were apparently caused by someone reaching in from the aisle behind the epoxy display and accidentally pushing the "V".   After the second accident a barrier was put up so that someone reaching from the adjacent shelf could not accidentally hit the "V".   **Given Cox's testimony, is there any theory on which Slade might succeed in having this evidence admitted?**

Suppose that Slade learns that the bottom tube of epoxy on which the entire "V" rested was not glued down with epoxy, but was instead attached with a weaker glue, somewhat less likely to permanently damage the shelf. Slade would like to get this evidence before the jury because he thinks that if the jury learns that the advertising slogan was deceptive they will be particularly hard on the Foxy-Loxy. **Is there any theory on which Slade is likely to get evidence on the type of glue used before the jury? If Foxy-Loxy realizes Slade's ulterior motive, what instructions will they be entitled to with respect to this evidence? What instructions will they request?**

Problem IV–31. Carl Clumsy enters Thomas Green's Rare Book Emporium & Tobacco Shoppe one rainy day, slips, hits a ladder which jars a shelf, dislodging a musty history book which falls, hitting Clumsy on the head.* Clumsy claims that he slipped on some water which Green had let accumulate. Green claims that there was no water on the floor and that Clumsy tripped over his own two feet. **Could Green at trial introduce the testimony of Clumsy's former dance teacher who will state she eventually gave up on him because he was forever "tripping over his own feet"? Could Green introduce the testimony of several witnesses who will testify that they have seen Clumsy bump into things, break things, and fall for no apparent reason? Could Green follow these witnesses with a psychiatrist who will testify that, on the basis of what she has heard in court, Clumsy is accident prone? Could Green introduce evidence that Clumsy has a mild form of epilepsy, one symptom of which is falling down without a fit for no apparent reason?** [* Aren't you glad this isn't a torts course!]

Problem IV–32. The defendant rents the plaintiff 200 acres of pasture land for $600 to be used to feed the plaintiff's cattle during the growing season. One day the plaintiff visits the land and finds the defendant's cattle grazing on the land as well as his own. The plaintiff sues and the defendant defends on the ground that when he rented the land he reserved the right to pasture up to fifty of his own cattle there. The plaintiff says there was no such reservation. **Can the plaintiff introduce the testimony of a third party who will state that eight days before the plaintiff rented the land from the defendant, the defendant had offered the grazing rights to him for $575 and had not mentioned any reservation of rights with respect to his own cattle? Would your answer be the same if the earlier asking price was $625? $750?**

G. EVIDENCE OF OTHER CRIMES

Evidence that a defendant on trial for one crime has been involved in some other crime or bad act is, with certain narrow exceptions, inadmissible in all U. S. jurisdictions if it is *only* relevant in its tendency to prove that the defendant had a propensity to commit crimes of the sort for which he is on trial.[42] In other words, a

---

42. Questions involving the admission of other crimes evidence rarely arise except in criminal cases. However, the general rule would apply in civil cases as well. In a civil action for fraud, for example, one could not show that the defendant had engaged in other fraudulent acts if the only relevance of the evidence was to demonstrate that the defendant had the character of a con man.

party (almost always the prosecutor) cannot, with rare exceptions, introduce evidence of a person's previous crimes or other immoral acts in order to show that the person's character is consistent with the commission of the crime in question. We shall call this principle the *propensity rule* to emphasize the forbidden inference.

There are two versions of this rule. FRE 404(b) exemplifies what Stone has called the original rule: [43]

> *Other crimes, wrongs, or acts.* Evidence of other crimes, wrongs, or acts is not admissible to prove the character of a person in order to show that he acted in conformity therewith. It may, however, be admissible for other purposes, such as proof of motive, opportunity, intent, preparation, plan, knowledge, identity, or absence of mistake or accident.

This rule only specifies the condition of inadmissibility: such evidence may not be used for proving the character of a person in order to show he acted in conformity therewith. When evidence of other crimes [44] is relevant *in any other way* it is admissible, subject only to the court's residual authority to exclude for reasons such as prejudice, waste of time, surprise, and confusion. This is known as the "inclusionary" version of the rule since permitted purposes *include* everything except propensity. In some jurisdictions the rule is that other crimes evidence is *excluded* except when offered for certain specific purposes. These purposes usually include those purposes presented illustratively in Rule 404(b). Some courts have added other categories to this list. This is known as the "exclusionary" version of the rule.

Even though the inclusionary approach of FRE 404(b) is cited by some courts as justifying a receptive attitude toward evidence of other crimes, appellate decisions suggest that it matters little whether a jurisdiction adopts the inclusionary or exclusionary version of the propensity rule. Those courts which exclude evidence of other crimes except when offered for specific purposes exhibit great ingenuity in fitting other crimes evidence into one of the permitted categories. So long as some permitted purpose is specified, many courts do not press prosecutors to show how the evidence is in fact relevant to that purpose or take a very broad view of what is relevant. Of course, appellate decisions reflect only imperfectly what occurs at the trial level. It may be that prosecutors in exclusionary states are restricted more in their efforts to introduce other crimes evidence at trial than those in inclusionary jurisdictions. We cannot know this from the case law because prosecutors generally cannot appeal verdicts of not guilty.

Some might argue that a basic theme of this chapter—that the relevance rules arise in situations of low probative value where appellate courts feel free to pay particular attention to policy considerations—breaks down when the propensity rule is examined. "Criminal disposition", as evidenced by prior bad acts and other crimes, might seem to be a good predictor of future criminal involvement. Certainly recidivism rates suggest that information that an individual has committed one crime is likely to be highly relevant in deciding whether he has committed another crime, particularly if the two crimes are similar in nature. But this argument misses a subtle point.

43. Stone, The Rule of Exclusion of Similar Fact Evidence: American, 51 Harv. L.Rev. 988 (1938).

44. When we refer to "other crimes" in this section we mean to include other immoral acts which may not amount to actual criminality.

By "immoral" we do not mean to assert our personal views; we refer to acts that the party offering the evidence believes are "bad" enough to establish a propensity.

The issue is not whether the fact that X has committed one crime is *in all cases* relevant to the issue of whether X has committed another crime. Rather, it is whether the evidence is relevant in those cases where X chooses to go to trial. Here there is considerable reason to believe that the evidence is less relevant than one might intuit. For a variety of reasons, which will become clear in this chapter and the one following, an individual with a past record is severely disadvantaged if he chooses to go to trial. Thus we can expect that guilty individuals with past records are disproportionately likely to take advantage of any leniency associated with pre-trial guilty pleas.[45] However, the innocent with past records are probably more likely to stand trial, since there are issues of principle and basic justice involved and since the fact of innocence suggests the prosecutor's case will be weak. Furthermore, police work is organized so that persons mistakenly charged are likely to have criminal records. This is most obvious where the decision to charge results from mistaken eyewitness identification, perhaps the most common source of unfounded convictions.[46] The identification process very often begins with the presentation to witnesses of pictures from the police files. One does not get his picture in those files unless he has been in trouble with the law. It is also true when police concentrate their attention on a group of "usual suspects."[47] One is not a "usual suspect" without a history of past crimes. Finally, the advantage which past crimes evidence gives the prosecutor at trial means that a weak case is less likely to be dropped with a repeat offender than with one accused for the first time. Thus, it is not surprising that many of those brought to trial have past offenses. Yet it is by no means clear that this history means that they are any more likely to have committed the crime with which they are charged than the group of first offenders who go to trial on the merits. First offenders need not weigh the burden of a past record when deciding to choose a trial and they have probably been selected in ways less likely to ensnare the innocent. Thus, among the group of individuals who refuse to plead, the existence of a record may have no association or, indeed, a negative association with the probability of guilt. This is true even if a propensity to future crime in fact exists among the entire group of those who have committed past offenses.[48] This is an impor-

---

45. This would be because the person with a record would estimate a lower chance of being found not guilty than a person without a record and would thus perceive the likely risk of going to trial, with the generally more severe sentences that follow conviction, as greater. Where the defendant was innocent, however, a sense of the injustice inherent in a conviction by plea or trial might lead to a smaller difference in the extent to which the previous record influenced the decision to plead. This general argument breaks down where the bargains available to first offenders offer substantially more inducement to plead guilty than the bargains available to those with records. Where extreme penalties follow necessarily upon a plea, as with third time felons in some states, the argument will not hold since the defendant has nothing to lose by going to trial.

46. See E. Borchard, Convicting the Innocent (1932), and Chapter Five, infra, at pp. 274–75 (remarks of Rep. Dennis).

47. For the extreme case which maximizes the possibility of catching the innocent, see the last scene of the movie Casablanca, with Humphrey Bogart, Claude Rains and Ingrid Bergman. In more typical situations, usual suspects are those who are known to operate in a manner similar to that used by the one who committed the crime.

48. In terms of the mathematical analysis of Chapter Three, what we are saying is that among those defendants whose cases are tried on the merits, the conditional probability that the defendant will be found to have committed a past offense is not significantly greater if the defendant is in fact guilty of the crime charged than the conditional probability that the defendant would have such a record if he were in fact innocent of the crime charged.

tant point. The failure of appellate courts to appreciate it may account in part for their general willingness to fit other crimes evidence into some appropriate category and thus avoid overturning the decision below.[49]

Even those who believe that evidence excluded by the propensity rule is not of low relevance generally accept the rule as a sound principle of evidence law. There are a number of strong arguments which support the rule. The first is the fact that evidence of other crimes is likely to be very prejudicial. If the jurors learn that the defendant has committed crimes which did not result in convictions, there is a danger that they will vote to convict, not because they find the defendant guilty of the charged crime beyond a reasonable doubt, but because they believe the defendant deserves to be punished for a series of immoral actions. In other words, the jurors will not feel great regret if they make the mistake of convicting a defendant innocent of the crime charged, because they will be sure that the defendant is guilty of some

crime. Where defendant's other crimes have resulted in convictions, the prejudicial effect reflects a similar diminution in the jury's regret at convicting an innocent defendant, but this is traceable to different causes. One reason why the conviction of innocent defendants is abhorrent is the stigma and accompanying disabilities which attach to the felony conviction. The jury's knowledge that defendant will, if convicted, be labeled a felon, that the label will shame his family, that he will have difficulty being bonded, that he will be barred from many licensed professions, and that a variety of other similar disabilities will attach regardless of sentence constitutes an important reason why juries may give defendants the benefit of the doubt.[50]

The person who has been once convicted of a felony is already suffering from many of these disabilities. The cost to him of a second conviction is not as great as the cost of a first. So the jury is likely to anticipate less personal damage if they mistakenly convict someone with a record than if they mistakenly convict someone

---

49. So far as we know this argument is original here. Do you accept it? Are the premises on which it is based valid? Do you see any weaknesses with it? If valid, what effects should it have on the propensity rule and the decision to admit other crimes evidence for non-propensity purposes?

One of the authors believes that the argument is difficult to sustain and both agree it is unnecessary to justify the rule. One author would argue that many past offenders are learning that sentences imposed after trial in many jurisdictions are not appreciably higher than those imposed on defendants who plead. The "bargain" in these jurisdictions is no bargain at all. In this author's view, the basic reason for rules like FRE 404(b) is that juries tend to misestimate the likelihood that a person who has committed some prior acts committed another one. A way of testing this hypothesis is to ask yourself how likely it is that a person once convicted of rape will commit a second rape. Your answer may suggest a fairly high probability, at least based on past samples of evidence classes. Obviously, there is no "scientifically correct" answer, since we hardly want to make the so-

cial arena an experiment in crime. But there is sufficient evidence to suggest that the odds are quite low that a person once convicted of rape will be convicted a second time. This may be because incarceration is somewhat lengthy and removes people convicted of rape from the streets or for other reasons. It is impossible to be sure. What seems apparent, however, is that people unfamiliar with the data tend to make probability estimations that are very high and thus that misestimation problems are real in this area. This, plus the jury's lessened regret at possibly convicting a person who is known to be "bad," are for both authors strong justifications for the rule. See the discussion in the text following this note and Note 51 infra.

50. This statement may be somewhat more assertive than it should be. It should be taken as an hypothesis which the authors believe is true, but which you might not want to accept. We do not have the empirical research on the jury which one must have in order to provide firm support for this statement.

who has never before been in trouble with the law.[51]

Another reason often given in support of the propensity rule is that jurors faced with evidence of other crimes are likely to have estimation problems; that is, the jurors are likely to overestimate the probative value of the evidence. If the jurors are sure that one crime leads to another, they may not give other evidence in the case, particularly that evidence which tends to exonerate the defendant, the weight which it deserves.

Two other justifications for the propensity rule have to do with the difficulties that the presentation of collateral evidence causes at trial. The defendant may be surprised when the evidence is introduced and be unable to muster contradictory evidence without a continuance, or, if the defendant does contest the accusation of other crimes, the jurors may be confused by the conflict on the collateral issue and, in attempting to resolve this conflict, they may fail to focus on more important issues in the case. We have already discussed these kinds of difficulties in connection with other relevance rules. We shall not repeat this discussion.

The last reason which we shall mention in support of the propensity rule is frequently neglected in the literature discussing the rule, but it may be the most basic reason of all. It has to do with the optimistic belief, fundamental in our social system that people are not necessarily limited by their past acts, that the criminal can reform, and that once a criminal has "paid his debt to society" he should be taken for all purposes as an upstanding member of society regardless of what we know about the probability of recidivism.[52] The presumption of innocence attaches in the same way regardless of past record. We may in fact not act upon these propositions in our day-to-day relationship with people or in institutionalized modes of dealing with former convicts; but they present a noble ideal for which to strive. And evidence law, like the law in other areas, occasionally embodies ideals which may conflict with more reason-based judgments.[53]

51. Trial counsel apparently feel this way. Where defendants have truly unblemished records, this will be emphasized in every possible way at the trial and in oral argument. The argument is likely to go far beyond the single assertion that someone with an unblemished record is unlikely to have committed a particular crime. It is likely to emphasize the many costs associated with a first conviction. Occasionally props are used. The defendant's wife and small children may be conspicuously present. Even a court far removed from the trial may be encouraged to decide appeals favorably to the defendant because of "favorable" information about the defendant that comes to its attention. Consider, for example, the extraordinary granting of bail pending appeal to the Supreme Court in Chambers v. Mississippi, 405 U.S. 1205 (1972), discussed in Chapter Seven. One cannot help but wonder whether the information contained in the bail petition affected the determination of the merits.

52. Obviously our day-to-day actions and our treatment of convicts fall short of this ideal.

53. It appears that the tendency of evidence law to embody ideals has been diminishing as the underpinnings of modern society become increasingly scientific. Certainly the dominant trend among evidence scholars is to justify evidence rules with respect to only one ideal, the ideal of finding truth. Unfortunately we know no sure way to do this, so the justification for evidence rules has most often been phrased in terms of relatively ungrounded psychological intuitions (we at times have been forced to rely on such intuitions in this book) and on uncritical acceptance of the analytic assumption that the trial system works exactly as abstract analysis suggests it should work (we have tried to avoid this as much as possible). Wigmore, who devoted his life to the rationalization of evidence law, is more responsible than any other individual for this trend, but the trend itself probably reflects the basic values of a society which at least until recently felt science could solve everything. This problem can best be seen in arguments in the area of privilege. See Chapter Eight, infra.

Unless one is willing to make the almost certainly mistaken assumption that the jury can follow instructions and consider other crimes evidence only for the limited purpose on which it is admitted,[54] the dangers which the propensity rule is designed to guard against exist when other crimes evidence is admitted for any purpose. Despite this, most commentators feel that the increased relevance of and need for other crimes evidence on issues other than propensity justify the decision to admit. This decision is wise in many cases, but courts too often admit other crimes evidence in situations where the evidence is likely to have severe prejudicial effects yet aid little in the resolution of the matter on which it was presumably admitted. We will point out instances of this when we discuss those reasons commonly advanced to justify the admission of such evidence.

However, before we do, there is one final point which we wish to emphasize. When other crimes evidence is allowed in, the problems of surprising the defendant and trying collateral issues may be exacerbated because the immoral activity credited to the defendant need not have resulted in a criminal conviction. The activity might never have led to an indictment, it might not contravene the criminal law,[55] or it might have resulted in a trial at which the defendant was acquitted. The last situation is particularly troublesome. Although a verdict of not guilty does not necessarily mean that the probabilities favored a finding of innocence, there are many reasons why we may wish to treat a not guilty verdict as completely exonerative.[56] There are, however, situations where it makes sense to allow behavior which has been the subject of an acquittal to be introduced at a later criminal trial. Suppose, for example, that the defendant's wife has drowned in the bathtub the day after willing the defendant her entire fortune. The defendant claims to have found her dead upon returning from a local bar. A suspicious prosecutor might try the de-

---

54. For a psychologist's view and a simple experiment which suggests jurors do not completely adhere to instructions see Doob and Kirshenbaum, Some Empirical Evidence on the Effect of § 12 of the Canada Evidence Act Upon an Accused, 15 Crim.L.Q. 88 (Dec.1972). Dale Broeder, after conducting jury interviews as part of the Chicago Jury project, concluded that jurors have an almost universal inability and/or unwillingness either to understand or follow the court's instruction on the use of a defendant's prior criminal record for impeachment purposes. The jurors almost universally used defendant's record to conclude that he was a bad man and hence was more likely than not guilty of the crime for which he was then standing trial. Note, Other Crimes Evidence at Trial: Of Balancing and Other Matters, 70 Yale L.J. 763 (1961).

55. Remember we are using the term "other crimes" to include immoral behavior generally.

56. For certain legal purposes this may be constitutionally required. In Ashe v. Swenson, 397 U.S. 436 (1970), the Supreme Court held that collateral estoppel is part of the fifth amendment's guarantee against double jeopardy. The Court held that where the defendant's acquittal of one robbery had to be based on a jury conclusion that he was not proven to be one of the robbers, the defendant could not be tried for another robbery occurring at the same time and place. The Federal Circuit Courts of Appeal are divided on the question of whether and to what extent Ashe prevents the prosecution from introducing evidence of the defendant's alleged involvement in crimes of which he has been acquitted. Compare Wingate v. Wainwright, 464 F.2d 209 (5th Cir. 1972) with United States v. Rocha, 553 F.2d 615 (9th Cir. 1977). Several states also bar the introduction of evidence of other crimes for which the defendant has been tried and acquitted.

Whatever the legal implications of a not guilty verdict, it appears that society in its day-to-day actions does not treat an acquittal as completely exonerative. See: Schwartz and Skolnick, Two Studies of Legal Stigma, 10 Social Problems 133 (1962), for a study which demonstrates that prospects of employment decrease when one who has been tried for and acquitted of a crime informs a prospective employer of this fact.

fendant for murder, and a jury might acquit believing that the prosecutor's evidence did not sufficiently rebut the possibility of an accident to overcome the presumption of innocence. But if the same thing happened a second and a third time, the argument of accident would become very weak. Yet, unless evidence of the earlier crimes were admitted, the defendant might be able to go on murdering wealthy wives with impunity, so long as the prosecutor brought charges after each one. Situations like this, however, are rare. When a defendant has been charged with a crime and acquitted, courts should not admit evidence of the earlier crime unless later developments suggest the jury verdict was mistaken.[57] This position is the authors'. It is not the general position of the appellate courts.

When the state seeks to introduce evidence of other crimes or wrongful acts that have not eventuated in criminal convictions, complications arise if the defendant argues that his participation in the act was not wrongful or denies all involvement in it. It is clear that a prosecutor may not offer evidence of another crime or act which is relevant only if it is wrongful unless he has a good faith belief that the act was wrong and that the defendant was involved in it. It is less clear what the standard of proof should be if the prosecutor has a good faith belief which the defendant contests. Some federal circuits have adopted or seem to be leaning toward a test of "clear and convincing evidence." Unless there is clear and convincing evidence that the wrongful act or crime is attributable to the defendant evidence suggestive of it may not be admitted. However, the Fifth Circuit, sitting *en banc* in the case of United States v. Beechum,[58] adopted a different, less stringent test. The judge, we are told, "need not require the Government to come forward with clear and convincing proof" but must instead apply FRE 104(b) and "determine whether there is sufficient evidence for the jury to find that the defendant in fact committed the extrinsic offense."[59]

---

57. **We mean here not mistaken as a matter of law—since the verdict might have been clearly correct given the evidence before the jury—but mistaken as a matter of fact. In other words, additional evidence is now available, which if available at the time of the first trial might have caused the jury to assess the probability of guilt high enough to support a conviction.**

58. 582 F.2d 898 (5th Cir. 1978).

59. Id. at 913. Note that there is some ambiguity here, since the Fifth Circuit never specifies the standard by which the jury must be able to conclude that the defendant committed the extrinsic offense. If the judge had to determine that there was enough evidence so that it was reasonable for a jury to find that the defendant had committed the extrinsic offense beyond a reasonable doubt more evidence would be required than if there only had to be enough evidence to justify a jury finding by a preponderance of the evidence. The reference to FRE 104(b) and the general tenor of *Beechum* suggest that it was the preponderance standard that the majority had in mind. The weakness behind the reference to FRE 104(b) is that the Advisory Committee notes to FRE 104(b) suggest that the rule exists because confiding preliminary questions of the kind covered by that subsection to the judge would greatly restrict and in some cases virtually destroy the function of the jury as a trier of fact. For one author, this is not a danger when the admissibility of other crimes evidence under FRE 404(b) is in question. He would argue that other crimes evidence is like other evidence (e.g., illegally seized evidence) which may, if it is admissible in a particular case, have substantial probative value, but is virtually never coextensive with an issue the jury must resolve and the decision to exclude such evidence will rarely if ever render evidence that the prosecution later wishes to offer irrelevant. For the other author, the danger is present whenever other crimes evidence is essential to the prosecution's case and the trial judge is inclined to exclude it, even though it is more probable than not that the evidence is probative in just the way the prosecution suggests. After you have read our discussion of the role of judge and jury in Chapter Twelve, you will be in a better position to decide between the authors.

As a matter of pure legal analysis, it is unclear whether the majority in *Beechum* or the five judges who joined in a stinging dissent have the better of the argument. As a matter of policy one of the authors of this book believes that the characteristics of other crimes evidence argue in favor of a "clear and convincing" test. Evidence of other crimes carries with it the danger that it will be used for the forbidden propensity inference and has substantial prejudicial potential even when admitted for a permitted purpose.[60] The decision to allow the evidence for purposes other than propensity reflects a judgment by the drafters of the rule that when the evidence is relevant in certain ways its probative value is likely to outweigh whatever prejudice accompanies it. If, however, a wrongful act is improperly attributed to the defendant, the inferences that justify the admission of other crimes evidence will subvert rather than enhance the cause of justice.

Consider, for example, a hypothetical set of situations in which the evidence suggests that there is a 51% chance that the defendant was involved in the crime charged. In almost half these cases (49%) any weight which the jury gave to the evidence for its permitted purposes would be mistaken because the defendant would not, in fact, have been involved in other wrongful behavior. Add to this the dangers of prejudice and the likelihood of the impermissible propensity inference and the evidence is likely to distort rather than enhance the fact-finding process in the long run.

Furthermore, to the extent that there is a genuine dispute about the defendant's involvement in the other crime or about its wrongful nature, the defendant will want to contest the matter before the jury. Because such disputes draw the jury's attention away from the central issue in the case, either the parties will be severely limited in the amount of evidence they can offer or there will be a substantial danger that the jury will be misled or confused. If the parties are severely limited in their ability to present evidence to the jury, the jury's judgment about the defendant's other criminal activity may be erroneous because the jurors will not be given all the evidence bearing on the matter. A preliminary hearing before the judge does not pose the problems of misleading or confusing the jury, and, because of procedural advantages when the jury is absent, it will not require as much time. In addition, a defendant may testify on preliminary matters without giving up his fifth amendment right to refuse to testify at trial. This means that one may expect the issue of the defendant's involvement in some other crime to be more thoroughly explored before the judge than before a jury. Since the case for admitting other crimes evidence is usually close to begin with, it makes sense to give the preliminary factual determination to the judge and to require the judge to make this determination by more than the mere preponderance of the evidence.

The other author takes a different approach to FRE 404(b). In his view most courts do not sufficiently appreciate the fact that all other crime (or other act) problems have two elements. The first is the likelihood that the defendant did the other act; the second is the probative value of the act once the defendant's culpability is established. The combination of these elements yields the probative value of the evidence. This value must be weighed against the possible prejudicial effect, including confusion of issues, that would arise if the evidence were admitted.

This author believes that if courts approach other crimes evidence in this way, no single standard like clear and convinc-

---

60. Although a court would no doubt lump the two together in applying the balancing test of FRE 403, we are distinguishng the prejudicial potential of the evidence (i.e. its ten- dency to change the jury's regret matrix) from the fact that it is likely to be used impermissibly (i.e. by giving probative weight to propensity).

ing evidence is appropriate. In some instances judges may insist upon such a showing because in the circumstances of the case a fairly high level of certainty is necessary for the probative value of the evidence to outweigh its prejudicial impact. In other instances, where prejudicial impact is likely to be low and the probative value of the act, if it is believed to be the act of the defendant, is great, the "more probable than not" standard should be used to determine admissibility.

This view is consistent with our earlier argument that acts for which a person has been acquitted might be used as evidence if it subsequently appears that the acquittals were factually wrong. In the case where a man is charged with drowning his wife, evidence of previous deaths of wives in the tub should be admitted even if the proof that any one of the previous wives

was murdered falls short of clear and convincing evidence. A trial judge ought to be satisfied that the proof establishes that the deaths occurred. This is sufficient for the evidence to be more probative than prejudicial.

One trouble with a uniform standard like clear and convincing evidence is that it focuses on the prior act in isolation rather than on how it fits into the fabric of evidence in the case being tried.[61] If a jury believes that some other act probably occurred, that may help explain how the crime charged occurred. Thus a more flexible balancing approach is useful.

If such an approach is adopted, as it apparently was by the majority in *Beechum*, then it becomes clear why the *Beechum* majority had no occasion for a lengthy discussion of what responsibilities the trial

61. The author who advanced the first argument presented in the text believes that the trial judge may consider evidence adduced in the case at hand when deciding whether there is clear and convincing evidence that the defendant was involved in another crime or bad act. Thus, the judge in deciding whether to admit under FRE 404(b) evidence that the defendant's first wife drowned in her bathtub may consider the fact that the defendant's second wife drowned in her tub as did the wife for whose murder the defendant is currently charged. In the mind of one author this coincidence is so unlikely to be a series of accidents or the work of a third party that it may be properly seen as clear and convincing evidence that the death of the defendant's first wife was a crime in which he was involved. Thus, even applying the clear and convincing test the jury should learn of it.

The author who rejects the clear and convincing evidence test, observes that such a test may require the judge to have an entire trial outside the hearing of the jury in order to decide whether evidence is sufficiently probative to be admitted. He regards this as unworkable and too costly. Where authors differ as strongly as we do here, the last word turns not on reason, but rather on who last has access to the manuscript. In this case it is the first author. He points out that (1) it is not clear why the standard of proving the preliminary question should determine the scope of the

necessary inquiry, (2) that the spectre of an entire trial to determine a preliminary question of fact is frequently raised but rarely substantiated, (3) that the preliminary question may be decided on a motion in limine if the concern is to avoid delays once the jury is seated, (4) that a number of circuits have been applying the clear and convincing test with no suggestion that it is unworkable, and (5) that even if a full trial were necessary under the first author's rule, it would be worth it if the result was that people would not be convicted because of inferences of guilt from crimes which a searching inquiry would show they had not committed.

This discussion of detail should not draw your attention from what is the fundamental difference between the authors. One prefers a firm rule; the other prefers greater judicial discretion. As we proceed through the book you will see that the preference for rules or discretion is fundamental in many of the policy debates that divide evidence scholars.

You should also note that under the first of our two suggested analyses FRE 403 balancing continues to play a role. Where the prejudicial effect of other crimes evidence substantially outweighs its probative value, the evidence should be excluded under FRE 403 even though it is relevant on some issue other than propensity.

judge has in screeening other crimes evidence. The judge's responsibilities are exactly the same here as when any other evidence is offered for a permissible purpose and an objection is made under FRE 403. The judge focuses on the probative value the evidence might have if admitted and balances this against the prejudicial effect attributed to the evidence.

Which of these approaches do you favor? Whatever your answer, you should remember that FRE 404(b) applies in both civil and criminal cases. It has become a useful rule in cases charging discrimination in employment or housing. In the civil context, it may well be that the prejudicial effect of evidence of prior crimes and bad acts is typically less than in criminal cases. If so, courts and commentators who prefer a clear and convincing standard for criminal cases may require less in a civil context.

1.   SITUATIONS OF ADMISSIBILITY—INTRODUCTION[62]

Obviously the first question a judge must decide when the prosecution offers to prove a crime other than the one charged is whether the issue for which the evidence is offered is one in dispute. Most courts see this as a simple mechanical process: an issue is in dispute when it is an element of the offense charged and the defendant has not expressly stipulated to that element. The failure to perceive that an issue is not really in dispute is particularly common when prior crimes are introduced to show a defendant's state of mind in situations where the only real issue is identity. Suppose the defendant is charged with bribing college basketball players in violation of a statute making it an offense to pay players money with "the intent of influencing their play" and defends solely on the grounds that he had nothing to do with the payment of bribes.[63] Evidence that defendant had bribed players in other states would have a bearing on intent. Such evidence tends to indicate that any money given the players involved in the instant case was not a token of affection, an under the table scholarship or the result of a mistake. But where payment is denied, intent, though technically part of the prosecution's case, is not really in issue. By arguing mistaken identity the defendant is implicitly conceding that whoever paid the bribe did so with the requisite criminal intent. The jury is likely to draw from the evidence not an inference of intent, but rather the inference that one who has allegedly bribed other basketball players is likely to have bribed the players in question.[64] Some courts have recognized this problem and have held that no evidence is admissible to prove intent when the nature of the crime charged clearly implies it, but they are in a minority.[65] And even the courts which make an

---

62. This section of this chapter, in which we discuss the issues on which other crimes evidence may be offered, draws heavily on, and at times copies, arguments made by Professor David Chambers of the University of Michigan Law School in an unpublished manuscript entitled "Evidence of Other Crimes in the Prosecutor's Case-In-Chief."

63. Cf. State v. Goldberg, 261 N.C. 181, 134 S.E.2d 334, certiorari denied, 377 U.S. 978 (1964).

64. The evidence, of course, may be probative on this issue, but if the court wants to admit the evidence on this issue it should face up to what it is doing.

65. E.g., when murder by poison is charged. See, e.g., People v. Molineux, 168 N.Y. 264, 61 N.E. 286 (1901). The theory of the majority, which admits such evidence, is that the burden is on the prosecutor to prove all elements of the offense beyond a reasonable doubt and the prosecutor should not be forced to take the risk that the jury will acquit because of a doubt as to intent, even if the defense offers no evidence on the issue. Query whether this risk is appreciable where the nature of the crime or the prosecutor's uncontroverted evidence clearly indicates criminal intent.

exception for intent often fail to realize that other crimes evidence may be offered on other issues which are equally undisputed.

The defendant may sometimes counter the prosecution's introduction of other crimes evidence to prove intent by stipulating that if it can be shown that he committed the crime for which he is being tried he will agree that the crime was committed with the requisite criminal intent. One danger with such a stipulation is that the hypothetical phrasing or the judge's instructions, unless carefully worded, may confuse the jurors, leading them to believe that the defendant is somehow conceding guilt.

In jurisdictions which attempt to limit other crimes evidence only to those issues actually in dispute, the defendant's attorney must be careful not to open the door to other crimes evidence by questioning matters which appear undisputed. If, for example, the defendant on direct or cross-examination admits that he might have given the deceased the substance which poisoned him, but, if so, it was by accidentally mistaking it for the deceased's medicine, the prosecutor would be allowed to reject the suggestion of accident by showing that the defendant had been involved in previous poisonings or attempted poisonings.

Having found (rightly or wrongly) that a given issue is in dispute, the court must determine whether the evidence offered is relevant to that issue through some chain of reasoning not involving the defendant's criminal propensities. We have already suggested that courts often do little more than determine whether the evidence may be colorably categorized under a permitted purpose. Now we shall look at some of the most common purposes for which other crimes evidence is admissible and briefly discuss problems peculiar to these areas.

2. RES GESTAE

Courts generally hold that crimes committed or detected simultaneously with the crime charged are admissible in order that the jury may get a fuller understanding of the events surrounding the crime charged. This exception is sensible, for often the story of one crime cannot be told without some discussion of other crimes. If the defendant were on trial for a murder committed during the course of a robbery, the murder could not be fully described without mentioning the robbery. But courts often fail to limit evidence of other crimes to that which is needed for a full understanding of the crime charged. In Texas, for example, a prosecutor was allowed to introduce, in a trial for drunken driving, evidence of a gun found concealed in the defendant's car at the time of his arrest.[66]

3. INTENT

We have given examples of other crimes being used to prove intent in our discussion of whether issues are in dispute. Where other crimes evidence is used for this purpose it is assumed that defendant's commission of the act for which he is on trial is conceded or may be proved by other evidence. Evidence of prior similar crimes comes in to show that the act was not done innocently but was done with the requisite criminal intent. Recall the example of the man who claims he poisoned another by mistake and consider how the jury will evaluate this story when it learns that the victim was the third person to be poisoned due to the defendant's "mistake". Obviously such evidence may be highly probative on the issue of intent. It also may be necessary because there may be little other evidence available to counter the

66. Dowdy v. State, 385 S.W.2d 678 (Tex.Cr.App.1964).

defendant's claim of honest error. The major problem with this evidence is that if the defendant has not been clearly established as the perpetrator of the current crime, the jury, despite instructions, is almost sure to consider the evidence on this issue as well. The major safeguard which can be expected of courts in this area is that they be sure that an issue of intent has been fairly raised in the case before admitting such evidence.[67] An instruction on the limited use which may be made of such evidence is, of course, appropriate, though it may be of limited value.

4. MOTIVE

There are two different situations in which evidence is admitted under the motive exception. The first is where the existence of another crime provides the motive which explains the criminal behavior with which the defendant is charged. A clear example is where it can be shown that a homicide victim was an eyewitness to the defendant's prior criminal activities.

Introducing other crimes evidence is particularly important in circumstances such as these because the jury might regard the absence of evidence suggesting a motive as some reason to believe that the defendant did not commit the crime charged.[68] The case for other crimes evidence is less compelling where the jury is not likely to see the absence of such evidence as an indication of innocence. For example, the desire for wealth is so common that there is no need to show a special desire in order to secure a conviction for theft or robbery. Nevertheless, some courts will admit evidence tending to show that a defendant is a drug addict with an expensive "habit" in order to establish a motive for a theft crime. Such evidence is not logically irrelevant, but it is so fraught with the danger of prejudice that its probative value is almost certain to be outweighed by its prejudicial effect.[69]

Other crimes evidence has also been used to suggest the existence of a motive without shedding light on why the defendant should be so motivated. Where the defendant has assaulted a murder victim several times in the past, evidence of other crimes might be allowed in to show that defendant "hated" the victim. Although this connection between other crimes and motive has been suggested by no less an authority than Wigmore,[70] in reality it is but propensity evidence under a different name. All that has been shown is the propensity of the defendant to attack the victim. From this, hate is inferred. From hate, one infers that the defendant attacked the victim on the occasion of the homicide. But the same inference, from previous assaults to the assault charged, could be made without positing the intervening emotion of hate (or jealousy or a sadomasochistic relationship or * * *). Perhaps similar crimes perpetrated on the same victim are so probative of other crimes directed against the victim that they should be admitted on the straightforward ground that their relevance in determining who victimized that

---

67. In what circumstances should the prosecutor be able to argue that he must be allowed to introduce such evidence in his case-in-chief to avoid a directed verdict? [Note again the importance of substantive law to decisions on evidentiary matters.] What factors should a court consider in deciding whether to allow the prosecutor to present such evidence as part of his case-in-chief?

68. See R. Lempert, Modeling Relevance, 75 Mich.L.Rev. 1021 (1977), and S. Saltzburg, A Special Aspect of Relevance: Coun-

tering Negative Inferences Associated With the Absence of Evidence, 66 Calif. L.Rev. 1011 (1978).

69. Note we are talking here about the introduction of such evidence as part of the prosecution's case-in-chief. The balance between probative value and prejudicial effect might be dramatically different after the defendant's case has been presented.

70. 2 Wigmore § 306, at 206.

individual outweighs the associated dangers. We tend to doubt this, but we feel even more strongly that the courts should face the policy issues directly rather than avoid them by applying the mistaken label of motive.[71]

5. COMMON PLAN OR SCHEME

Perhaps the most elastic and bewildering of the common exceptions to the propensity rule is that which courts typically label "common plan or scheme." As with "motive", this label is applied in two distinct circumstances. The first and less common situation is where one crime is in fact predicated on the commission of another. Consider, for example, a plot to bomb a police station and then rob a bank while the police are distracted. Where this situation exists the case for admission is strong. One cannot fully understand the crime charged without knowing of the associated crime.[72]

The common plan or scheme exception is more frequently used where two or more crimes appear to have been plotted by the same individual because they exhibit a similar unusual pattern. The theory is that the similarity between the other crimes and the crime charged means it is likely that the same individual was responsible for all of them. Thus, anything which serves to link the defendant with similar crimes also serves to link the defendant with the crime charged. Since courts usually require other crimes admitted under this theory to bear some peculiar similarity to the crime charged,[73] some courts classify the exception in these circumstances not as "common plan or scheme" but rather as "novel means", "distinctive modus operandi" or, on occasion, "identity." These latter characterizations are more accurate than "common plan or scheme." "Distinctive modus operandi" summarizes the rationale on which the evidence is admitted and "identity" points out the purpose for which this kind of evidence is invariably used.

Where this exception to the propensity rule is used to establish identity, the other crimes evidence is only as strong as the evidence which links defendant to the other crimes. If the crime charged is the last in a series of bizarrely similar crimes, one may be satisfied that the same person committed them all. Yet if there is no evidence linking the defendant to the earlier crimes, evidence of these crimes can only be prejudicial. Though it may be less intuitively obvious, the situation is the same if the defendant is linked to the earlier crimes by evidence virtually identical to that which links him to the crime charged. Consider, for example, a series of armed robberies in which ballistics tests indicate that all shots fired were from the same gun.[74]

71. To some extent this has happened in the area of sex crimes, which we will discuss below. While some courts still admit evidence of prior criminal sex acts with the same person as bearing on motive, others are more frank and state that evidence of a propensity to engage in certain sex acts with the same person is so probative on the issue of whether a given sex act has been engaged in with a given person that it should be admissible despite important reasons for keeping it out.

72. The associated crimes need not be close in time. In the Ponzi type confidence game evidence of other crimes is properly admitted though the crimes may be days, weeks, or even months apart. In a Ponzi game, the operator uses the money from later investors to pay large rates of returns to early investors. Profits are earned when news of these returns attracts even larger sums of money from even later investors. Clearly the jury must be informed of the entire scheme, even though the defendant is only charged with swindling a small percentage of those whom he in fact defrauded; otherwise the fraudulent game cannot be fully appreciated.

73. McCormick describes this nicely: "The device used must be so unusual and distinctive as to be like a signature." § 190, at 449. However, some courts see writing where others would see blank walls.

74. Cf. Williams v. State, 143 So.2d 484 (Fla. 1962).

Suppose the defendant is picked up for speeding and the gun which fired those shots is found in his car. He is charged with the one robbery on which there is some eyewitness identification. He answers the charge by attempting to discredit the eyewitness and claiming that he bought the gun from a stranger in a bar two days prior to his arrest. Obviously the jury will not be substantially aided in evaluating defendant's story by knowing that the same gun was used in three, five, or fifty robberies rather than one, but they may be prejudiced by their knowledge of other crimes. The reason for this is that the more robberies it appears the defendant might have committed, the more they will regret the mistake of acquitting a guilty defendant,[75] so the less substantial the evidence needed to convict. If, however, there is other evidence that the defendant committed one or more of the other robberies, the fact that the defendant possesses the gun used in all of them will strengthen the state's case to the extent that the defendant is clearly identified as the one who brandished the gun in the other robberies.

6. IDENTITY

Almost all courts admit other crimes evidence for the purpose of proving identity, but they are not very consistent in defining situations where other crimes evidence may be used to prove this. If all evidence were allowed which tended to prove identity, the exception would swallow the propensity rule, for propensity evidence is just one form of evidence which may be used to identify the defendant as the perpetrator of the crime in question. Many courts, following Wigmore,[76] apply this exception where novel means or a similar modus operandi are used in the crimes charged and the other crimes. We have discussed this application in the previous section.

The major independent content given to the identity exception is in demonstrating that some item acquired in a previous crime was used while committing the charged crime, as when a gun stolen from a sporting goods store is later used in the robbery of a liquor store. Here the link between the two crimes is relatively strong; there is no need to puzzle over degrees of similarity. But again, the evidence is only valuable to the extent that the defendant is linked to the prior crime.

7. KNOWLEDGE AND GUILTY KNOWLEDGE

Occasionally the state will have to prove, as part of the prosecutor's case-in-chief or to meet a defense, that the defendant knew certain facts. In some situations evidence of other crimes tends to demonstrate such knowledge. Suppose, for example, that the

75. **The behavioral hypothesis implicit here is that if the jurors think the defendant may be guilty of only one crime, they will not feel that the mistake of acquitting necessarily frees a basically evil person, one committed to a life of crime or one who has already done sufficient social harm to justify severe retribution. Where they know that defendant, if guilty, has committed a number of crimes, the jury will probably evaluate the above factors quite differently and their regret at acquitting a guilty defendant will rise substantially. One might argue that if we are really sure the same person has committed all the crimes in question the jurors should know, for it is appropriate that their regret at convicting the innocent or acquitting the guilty be adjusted accordingly. But, this would suggest that the more harm done the less the evidence which should be required to convict, a proposition which clearly contravenes the notion of a general presumption of innocence. To some extent a tendency to reduce the evidence needed to convict as the harm of the crime increases would be countered by the fact that the more shameful the crime charged and the more severe the possible penalties, the greater the jurors' regret at convicting the innocent. But this countervailing pressure is not present when we discuss other crimes evidence. The defendant is charged with the same crime and faces the same penalty however great the harm suggested by crimes not charged.**

76. 2 Wigmore § 306, at 207.

defendant is charged with passing a counterfeit twenty dollar bill. The defendant denies knowing the bill was counterfeit. If the state can show that the defendant had in the past engaged in counterfeiting, this would tend to show that he had the expertise to recognize a counterfeit twenty when he saw one. The same inference might be drawn from the defendant's possession of equipment used to counterfeit money. Courts which do not acknowl-

edge this exception usually admit this type of evidence under the rubric of intent.

Guilty knowledge is something else; this refers to crimes which defendant is unlikely to have committed were he not guilty of the crime charged. Jail breaks and the bribing of witnesses are examples of crimes admitted to show guilty knowledge or, as it is sometimes called, consciousness of guilt.

8. PROPENSITY TO CRIME

When we stated the propensity rule we qualified our statement in a way which probably alerted you to the fact that there are some situations where the rule breaks down entirely and the jury is presented other crimes evidence explicitly to show a propensity to crime. In rare instances this appears justified because the defendant's propensity to crime has become an issue in the case. This is most common where the defense of entrapment is raised and the state in rebuttal needs to show that the defendant is the sort of person who would commit the crime charged without the importuning of government agents.[77] Even here prejudicial effect may outweigh probative value. This is particularly true if the other crimes are old ones, since propensity to commit crime, like other character traits, changes continually over time. The cure, however, is probably to change the substantive law of entrapment rather than the evidentiary analysis which permits propensity evidence.[78]

A second situation where many courts admit other crimes evidence to show propensity is where defendant is charged with

a sex crime. This use directly contravenes the propensity rule, since the evidence of other crimes is admitted to support the specific inference that the defendant who committed one sex crime probably committed another. In the majority of jurisdictions, however, this exception is tempered by the requirement that the other sex crimes be shown to have occurred with the partner or victim of the crime charged. The theory is that what is being shown is not general propensity to crime but propensity to criminal activity with the same person.[79]

The exception arose at a time when consensual sex crimes, such as adultery and fornication, more often reached trial. In this context, the exception makes sense, for the probative value of earlier acts in an ongoing relationship appears especially high. However, as with common plan evidence, evidence of other sex crimes will be more prejudicial than probative when the evidence linking the defendant to the other crime is either weak or basically the same as that linking the defendant to the crime charged.[80] The evidence is also

---

77. Other crimes evidence may only be admitted for this purpose after the defense has been raised. If the government submits such evidence prematurely, the error will be cured when the defense is subsequently raised.

78. See Sorrells v. United States, 287 U.S. 435 (1932); Sherman v. United States, 356 U.S. 369 (1958); United States v. Russell, 411 U.S. 423 (1973).

79. The exception is supported in some states on the grounds that it shows a motive,

i.e., a passion for sex with a particular person, but as we have shown in our discussion of "motive" the label is really an excuse for admitting what is analytically propensity evidence.

80. A special case may arise where a woman claims the defendant engaged in numerous acts of sexual intercourse with her and the defendant claims that he never engaged in any. Unlike other common scheme cases, the other crimes evidence might have some

substantially less probative when only one or two similar crimes are alleged to have been committed, because one cannot then assume that a relationship exists which makes repetition of the crime particularly likely.

So long as the same victim requirement applies in the area of sex crimes, evidence of other sex crimes is likely to be inadmissible on propensity when the more serious sex crimes are charged. Violent rapists and people who sexually assault children may never attack the same person twice. However, some courts faced with these violent offenses have broadened the existing sex crime exception to allow evidence of similar crimes with different victims. The theory is that a violent or "abnormal" sexual assault indicates a perverted personality, hence a particularly high probability that one sex crime will be followed by another. Research, however, does not suggest that rapists and child molesters have particularly high rates of recidivism.[81]

The jurisdictions which declare evidence of other sex crimes with different victims admissible to show propensity are a distinct minority, but appellate courts dealing with other sex crimes evidence are so adept at finding other exceptions under which the other crimes evidence may be admitted that one must conclude that the propensity rule has broken down in this area. To give just one example, consider the Iowa case of State v. Schlak.[82] There the defendant was accused of sexually molesting a fifteen year old girl, and the court upheld the admission of evidence of other attacks on different victims on the grounds that they showed a motive, the motive being the defendant's "desire to gratify his lustful desire by grabbing or fondling young girls * * *." Clearly the evidence is only relevant in that it suggests a propensity to assault young girls. One wonders whether the Iowa court would have condoned the admission of evidence of other thefts in a trial for theft on the grounds that it showed the defendant's "desire to satisfy his greedy nature by grabbing other people's belongings." Perhaps they would if theft left them as upset and uncomprehending as a sexual assault on a fifteen year old.

9. PROPENSITY TO LIE

A final common use of other crimes evidence is to suggest a propensity to lie. This use is very different from the other uses we have discussed thus far. It is a way of undermining the credibility of all witnesses including the defendant, not, in theory, a way of directly suggesting guilt. We discuss this matter at length in Chapter Five on impeachment.

10. OTHER CRIMES: SUMMARY

We have devoted a good deal of space to questions involving evidence of other crimes. It is a complicated and fascinating topic. It poses the problem of relevance versus prejudice in its starkest form. It vividly demonstrates that rules of evi-

independent probative value because one might think that a person is more likely to fabricate one sex act than many and is unlikely to make mistakes about who her partner is over a series of sex acts. Also the probative value of the evidence may increase if the victim withstands cross-examination, since it should be easier to shake testimony which reports many non-existent crimes than testimony which fabricates only one.

81. Gregg, Other Acts of Sexual Misbehavior and Perversion as Evidence in Prosecutions for Sexual Offenses, 6 Ariz.L.Rev.

212, 231–234 (1965). Of course recidivism is not always the issue; one may be more interested in the probability of repeating before the first arrest. But if recidivism rates are not particularly high in this area, it suggests that such crime is often not the result of an overriding character trait. Gregg cites research which suggests that some sexual perversions are highly repetitive and others much less so or not at all. Id. at 232.

82. 253 Iowa 113, 116, 111 N.W.2d 289, 291 (1961).

dence are not always neutral rules of procedure without systematic implications for the fate of litigating parties. On the contrary, any change which increases the probability that other crimes evidence will be admitted should increase the rate at which defendants are convicted.[83] Some of these "new" convictions will involve individuals who are guilty while others will involve those who are innocent. As is often the case when we wish to evaluate evidence rules, we do not have the information needed to make even a good guess as to the percentage of "new" convictions in each category.

This discussion should also suggest the way in which courts can manipulate labels to reach decisions which are not justified by rigorous analysis. You should be aware that one reason why courts do this is that lawyers fail in their task. Too often, lawyers only argue that precedent is more consistent with their preferred categorization than with that of their opponents. Such argument is often fruitless, for appellate judges are adept at distinguishing or ignoring precedent they wish to avoid. The good advocate is able to explain why "favorite" cases make sense, forcing the court to face the full disquieting implications of an adverse decision. Inability to do this is one legacy of learning rules without learning the reasons behind them.

Problem IV–33. Harold Wolfman, owner of the Fly-By-Nite Construction Company, has been convicted on two counts of fraud. The first count involved a contract to waterproof the roof of a home owned by an elderly couple living in Garden City, New York. It was shown that this work, which was completed in the spring of 1981, consisted of painting the roof of the house with an ordinary black paint that had no special waterproofing qualities. The second count involved an agreement to install a new furnace in the home of a retired widower living in Rock Hill, North Carolina. It was shown that the furnace, which was installed in October of 1981, was about fifteen years old and in rather poor shape. Wolfman's defense to the first count was that he was cheated by his workers who didn't do the job on their work order. His defense to the second count was that a mix up in the central office led to the shipment of a used furnace rather than a new one. The jury didn't credit either defense, perhaps because Wolfman in both instances answered complaints by personally assuring his customers that quality work had been done and by promising that as soon as things had "aged sufficiently" the repairs would work as intended. He also threatened each customer with "foreclosing a mechanics lien on your entire house if you don't pay your three installments when they are due." Wolfman contends on appeal that he is entitled to a retrial because the trial judge did not grant his motion to sever the two counts of the indictment and to try him separately on each. **Should the conviction be reversed on these grounds?**

Problem IV–34. Sandy Sypher is charged with the armed robbery of a bank. She and her two accomplices escaped with about $25,000. The prosecutor wishes to place a government informer on the stand who will testify that the day after the robbery Sypher gave him $1000.00 in new bills and told him to buy her "the best heroin money can buy." **Should this tes-**

---

83. It should also increase guilty pleas as well, which means that the average rate of conviction at trial might not change very much.

timony be allowed? **Should it be allowed if the informer had immediately turned the money over to the police who discovered in Sypher's
$1000.00 some of the "bait bills" taken in the bank robbery?**

Problem IV–35. Quaalude is a Schedule II controlled substance. It
is considered a drug with a high potential for abuse, but it has a currently
accepted medical use so its distribution is not entirely banned. Dr. August,
a physician, was charged with two counts of prescribing Quaalude without a
legitimate medical purpose. Larry Walls testified that he went to August,
asked for Quaalude, and after a brief discussion with the doctor obtained a
prescription for thirty pills. The doctor charged him $10.00 for this service
and recommended that he take the prescription to Glass Drugs if he had any
trouble filling it. Dr. August testified that Walls said he worked on an assembly line and was tired and could not sleep. Quaalude, Dr. August testified, is a depressant and can induce sleep. The jury acquitted August on
this count. Walls testified that a month later he returned to Dr. August
and received a prescription for another thirty pills even though he never requested a prescription and August didn't ask him any questions relating to
his physical condition. The jury convicted August on this count. To but-
tress its case the government introduced 478 prescriptions issued by Dr. August for Quaalude and other Schedule II drugs over a twenty month period
between August 9, 1975 and April 26, 1977. All had been filled at Glass
Drugs and, over one three month period, they accounted for 47% of the
Schedule II drug prescriptions filled by that pharmacy. A police officer testified that thirteen of those named on the prescriptions filed at Glass Drugs
had "track marks" which are indicative of drug addiction, and a pharmacist
at Glass Drugs testified that he had filled about twelve prescriptions for
Quaalude issued by Dr. August and all were for young people about twenty
years of age. **Did the trial court commit reversible error in allowing the
evidence pertaining to the other prescriptions to be introduced?**

Problem IV–36. Doaks is accused of burglary. The burglar was surprised in the house by the owner but escaped with some sterling silver. The
principal evidence against Doaks is the testimony of a pawnshop owner who
says she is "almost certain" that Doaks is the man who tried to pawn silver
stolen from the house and the testimony of a handwriting expert who says
that the writing on the pawn ticket is "consistent with Doaks writing and
there is about an 80 to 90 percent chance that he is the person who filled out
the pawn ticket." The government would also like to introduce a witness
who will testify that Doaks is the person he surprised in the course of a burglary three days before the burglary for which Doaks is on trial. This burglary occurred a few doors away from the burglary with which Doaks is
charged. In each case the burglar jimmied open the back door of the house
in the early morning hours. Nothing was taken in this other burglary, but
the burglar was surprised in the dining room suggesting that he was looking
for silver. **Should the eyewitness to the first burglary be allowed to testify? Should he be allowed to testify if Doaks had been tried for the first
burglary and acquitted after presenting an alibi defense? Should he be
allowed to testify if Doaks had been convicted at the first trial on the
strength of the eyewitness' testimony?**

Problem IV–37. Farmer is charged with the murder of Woody, his hired hand who disappeared in 1909. After Woody's disappearance Farmer had taken possession of Woody's horse and his personal property. Ten years later Woody's skeleton was found in Farmer's livery barn. During the trial the prosecution wishes to introduce evidence that Farmer had two other hired hands who had disappeared, one in 1906 and one in 1913. In each case Farmer had taken possession of his workers' personal property after their disappearance. A search for their remains was made after Woody's skeleton turned up and the skeletons of each were found, one in a cave on Farmer's farm and the other near one of Farmer's outbuildings. **Should the evidence be admitted when Farmer is tried for Woody's death? Does it do anything more than show that someone has a propensity to murder Farmer's help? Would the case for admission be stronger if the other two deaths involved not other hands but a neighboring farmer in one instance and an itinerant peddler in the other? Had the bodies of the others not been found should evidence of their disappearance and of Farmer's subsequent possession of their personal property be allowed?**

Problem IV–38. In November of 1981 Officer Rich of the Iowa City Police Department issued three speeding tickets to Nancy Jean. Shortly thereafter he, his wife, and the police department began to receive numerous telephone calls in which the caller remained silent or hung up. These calls continued for almost a year. During that period Rich and his wife received two threatening letters, both in March of 1982, which referred to Rich as a "pig" and threatened a gruesome death for him and his family. Jean was later arrested and charged on two counts of mailing threatening letters. At the trial the government introduced evidence that Rich had given Jean three speeding tickets, evidence that one of the anonymous telephone calls had been traced to her telephone, testimony of a friend of Jean's that Jean had admitted making the calls, and testimony from the arresting officer that when he went to arrest Jean he found in her home three handguns, two rifles, a jar of cyanide poisoning, and a homemade gasoline bomb. At trial Jean objected to the admission of the evidence pertaining to other crimes. **Was this evidence properly introduced? On what theories?**

Problem IV–39. Dan Dooley is charged with the illegal sale of narcotics. At trial, the prosecution seeks to introduce evidence that Dooley attempted to hire someone to kill the main prosecution witness. Dooley objects. **Does the testimony come in?**

Problem IV–40. Sam Block is accused of bribing Jerry Lamp, an I.R.S. agent involved in a tax audit of Block's company. It is clear from the evidence that Block paid Lamp $2,500 to avoid a finding that would have cost him $5,000. Block's defense is that he was entrapped. He claims that Lamp first suggested the bribe and encouraged him to pay it. Block has learned that Lamp was involved in seven other bribery attempts during the previous three years. Four of these cases resulted in guilty pleas and three cases were still pending at the time of Block's trial. Block would like to introduce this evidence as part of his defense, arguing that it suggests that Lamp was prone to solicit bribes. **May the evidence be introduced?**

Problem IV–41. The defendant is prosecuted for throwing acid in the complainant's face. The complainant states that he did not see the defendant do the act, but heard his voice. The defendant and his daughter counter with evidence that the daughter threw the acid to repel an improper sexual advance. **Can the defendant introduce evidence that the complainant had previously made such advances to his daughter and to her classmates at school?**

Problem IV–42. The defendant is charged with taking indecent liberties with his 11-year old stepdaughter, Sandra. Sandra testified that on Sunday afternoon, May 6, 1982, the defendant took her to the basement of an unfinished house adjacent to her home and committed on her what amounted to an unaccomplished act of sexual intercourse. Over the defendant's objection, Sandra disclosed that during the previous year, at intervals of 2, 3 or 4 weeks, the defendant had compelled her to indulge in acts of fellatio with him in the bathroom of their home. In addition, the Court permitted another stepdaughter, Pamela, then 10 years old, to testify that every week or two for an unspecified period of time, the defendant had forced her to commit similar acts of perversion. A stepson, Gerald, also 10, testified to one such offense committed by his stepfather in April, 1982. Counsel for the defendant requested an instruction that the jury disregard all evidence concerning these prior illegal acts. The instruction was denied. The defendant appeals. **What ruling should the appellate court make and why? Would the situation be different if the only other alleged violation was one with Sandra? One act with Pamela? 10 acts with Pamela? 10 acts with Gerald? Add 10 years to the children's ages; what does this do to the problem?**

Problem IV–43. In Commonwealth v. Kline, 361 Pa. 434, 65 A.2d 348 (1949), the defendant was charged with statutory rape. On cross-examination the defendant responded to the question whether he had ever committed indecent exposure by denying that he ever exposed himself. The prosecution thereupon presented two witnesses who testified that the defendant had exposed himself to a third party within two weeks of the crime charged. The Supreme Court of Pennsylvania held that the evidence was properly admitted to show a design to commit the offense charged. **Do you agree? Is there any other theory on which this evidence might have come in?**

Problem IV–44. In McKenzie v. State, 250 Ala. 178, 33 So.2d 488 (1947), the accused was charged with assault with intent to rape A in June, 1946. A testified that the defendant drove her outside of town, made improper advances, threatened her with bodily harm if she did not accede to his sexual demands, and finally took her home. The defendant admitted almost all of the details, but denied the intent to rape. The prosecution offered evidence that two months later the defendant drove B to the identical spot, where almost the same thing happened. This evidence was introduced at trial to prove intent. **Was it properly admitted? Would your answer be any different if the other incident had occurred two months before the crime charged? What if B had been raped?**

Problem IV–45. Ralph Rakestraw was held up at gunpoint one night while returning home from work. He reported the crime to the police, who showed him pictures from their "mug files." He identified a picture of Dick Deadeye as a picture of the one who robbed him, and later picked Deadeye out of a lineup. At Deadeye's trial the prosecutor asked Rakestraw the following questions:

Q. What happened next? **A.** The police showed me pictures from their files.

Q. And did you recognize any of the pictures? **A.** Yes, I picked out one which belonged to the person I thought had robbed me.

Q. [The prosecutor hands Rakestraw a card on which there are two pictures, one full face and one in profile, both of a man wearing a striped shirt with the number 057962 superimposed at shoulder level.] Do you recognize this picture? **A.** Yes, that's him. These are the pictures I picked out.

Q. Will you show those pictures to the jury? **A.** [Rakestraw hands the pictures back to the prosecutor who hands them to the jury foreperson. They are passed from hand to hand.]

If you were Deadeye's attorney, would you have objected at any point in this questioning? On what theory? Do you think that your objection would have been sustained? Why or why not?

Problem IV–46. In July 1975 thirty blank vehicle registration certificates were stolen from a state office building in Lansing, Michigan. Defendant Hank Corcoran was arrested for selling a stolen automobile in Norman, Oklahoma, which had been registered in the name of Lloyd Ives on one of the purloined certificates. The state's evidence against Corcoran consists largely of the eyewitness testimony of the man who bought the stolen automobile. Corcoran defends on the ground that he was home with a cold the day the alleged sale took place. **Can the state introduce the testimony of another eyewitness who will identify Corcoran as the person she bought a stolen car from in Carson City, Nevada?** (Assume the car was registered in the name of the Lloyd Ives on one of the stolen certificates.) **What is the state's theory?**

Problem IV–47. **On the same facts as the previous case, will Corcoran be able to introduce an FBI agent who will testify that Corcoran was positively identified by two individuals in California as the person who sold them stolen cars registered under the name Lloyd Ives on the stolen certificates, but that charges were dropped when it turned out that the sale leading to the second identification had occurred at the very time the defendant was in court being arraigned on charges in connection with the first sale?**

Problem IV–48. Maude Margarette is charged with robbing a grocery store after pulling a snub-nosed revolver on the proprietor. The prosecution has two other grocery store owners who will identify Maude as the person who robbed their stores at the point of a snub-nosed revolver. **Should the testimony from these witnesses be allowed? Would the prosecution's chance of getting this testimony admitted be greater, less or the same if**

the person allegedly involved in the three robberies were a man rather than a woman?

Problem IV–49. Assume that in the preceding case the evidence of other crimes is held to have been properly admitted on the ground of identity. Suppose the prosecutor in his closing argument makes the following statement: "You see the defendant sitting there all dressed up; she's trying to pretend she's a lady. And you see those kids in the first row that she turns and talks to every time she gets a chance; she's trying to pretend she's just a mother. Well she's not a lady. She's not a mother. You've heard the witnesses. Three good hardworking people testified that Maude Margarette robbed them at gunpoint. Why, she's just a common criminal. That's why she robbed Sam's grocery. She's just a common criminal, a common armed robber, who does nothing well but rob." **If you were an appellate judge, would you consider this argument grounds for reversal? Is it evidence in the case? Would your decision be different if you knew that the children in the first row were unrelated to Maude? As a trial judge would you seek to ensure that evidence of maternity or the lack of any relationship was in the record? If so, how would you go about making this kind of record?**

H. CHARACTER EVIDENCE GENERALLY

The propensity rule is a special bar raised against one type of character evidence. The general principle is stated in FRE 404(a):

CHARACTER EVIDENCE GENERALLY. Evidence of a person's character or a trait of his character is not admissible for the purpose of proving that he acted in conformity therewith on a particular occasion, except:

(1) *Character of accused.* Evidence of a pertinent trait of his character offered by an accused, or by the prosecution to rebut the same;

(2) *Character of victim.* Evidence of a pertinent trait of character of the victim of the crime offered by an accused, or by the prosecution to rebut the same, or evidence of a character trait of peacefulness of the victim offered by the prosecution in a homicide case to rebut evidence that the victim was the first aggressor;

(3) *Character of witness.* Evidence of the character of a witness, as provided in Rules 607, 608, and 609.

The first thing to note about this rule is that it only bars the circumstantial use of character evidence to show action in conformity with character. In certain cases the character of a person will itself be in issue. Here evidence of character is essential and the rule does not apply. If, for example, A calls B a thief and B responds with a suit for slander, B's character will be in issue if A raises the defense of truth. Where an employer is sued on the theory that he negligently hired an incompetent servant, the character of the servant will be an issue in the case. Where character is an issue in the case, as it is in these examples, it may be proved by specific acts which reflect on the individual's character. In the slander case A could show that B had been convicted three times for shoplifting. In the negligence case the plaintiff could show that the employee was often drunk on the job or that he had been involved in a series of avoidable accidents. In the negligence case many courts would allow the employee's character for competence to be proved by opinion evidence as well; but opinion evidence is not usually allowed when *moral* traits such as honesty or peacefulness must be proved.

When the determination of an individual's character is not essential to the resolution of a case, the evidence is barred for many of the same reasons which support the other relevance rules: the hazards of prejudice, confusion of the jury, waste of time, and surprise. Some would argue that character evidence is quite probative whenever an individual's actions must be proved.[84] This is more doubtful than is generally assumed. First, there is the problem we alluded to in our discussion of other crimes; however relevant character evidence is in the abstract, its incremental relevance in the context of a specific case is likely to be low.[85] Second, evidence bearing on character is likely to be conflicting. Most individuals have engaged in actions sufficiently inconsistent to suggest diametrically opposed character traits, and most people can point to individuals who hold very different evaluations of their character. Finally, there is a good deal of psychological evidence that attributes which we think of as character traits are dynamic rather than static aspects of personality. They differ over time and as contexts change.[86] Thus, evidence that a building inspector regularly takes bribes might have little bearing on the issue of whether he acted honestly as church treasurer.[87]

Subparagraphs (1), (2), and (3) under FRE 404(a) state exceptions to the charac-

ter rule. Subparagraph (1) follows the common law: an accused may open the door to character evidence by attempting to prove that he possesses character traits which make it unlikely that he committed the crime for which he is on trial. The rationale for this rule is that with the danger of prejudicing the defendant gone, the probative value of the evidence outweighs the disadvantages of allowing admission. In fact, knowledge of the accused's good character may prejudice the jury in his favor, since their regret at mistakenly convicting an innocent defendant of good character is likely to be quite high, while their regret at mistakenly acquitting a guilty defendant is likely to be less than it would otherwise be. Perhaps it is wise to give an accused who has led a previously exemplary life this kind of advantage, but the ability to get strong character witnesses does not necessarily guarantee that one's previous life has been exemplary.

If the accused does offer character evidence, the prosecution is allowed to present similar evidence in rebuttal. For this reason a defendant who attempts to exonerate himself through character evidence is said to have "put his character in issue." This nomenclature is unfortunate, for it invites confusion with the situation where the quality of an individual's character is in fact *an issue* in the case. Where character evidence is used circumstantially, as in FRE 404(a)(1), it is not "in issue" except in the sense that the validity of any item of admissible evidence is open to dispute.

At common law and under the federal rules the 404(a)(1) type exception applies only to *pertinent* traits of character. Thus, one accused of embezzling might offer

---

84. E.g., McCormick, § 188, at 444.

85. See footnote 45 supra and the accompanying text.

86. See, e.g., W. Mischel, Personality and Assessment (1968).

87. Even if this is relevant, a jury, believing that character is unchanging, may substantially overestimate its weight.

evidence that he is trustworthy or honest, but not evidence that he is peaceable or nonviolent. One charged with assault would be in the opposite situation. Of course, general traits, such as the trait of law-abidance, appear relevant to rebut almost any accusation. Courts differ in the degree to which they will admit such general character evidence and in the leeway they give defendants when more specific traits are presented.

This exception is usually limited to criminal cases. But, a growing number of jurisdictions extend the rule to those civil cases where the plaintiff's complaint charges behavior which would be actionable under the criminal law as well. A small number admit character evidence in all civil cases when there are no eyewitnesses to the event to which the evidence is circumstantially relevant. Jurisdictions which generally do not admit character evidence in civil cases usually make an exception when an action for civil assault is countered by a claim of self-defense. If there is some dispute about who committed the first act of aggression, each party will be allowed to show his own reputation for peaceableness and his opponent's reputation for turbulence and violence. The drafters of the federal rules considered the question of whether the circumstantial use of character evidence should be allowed in civil cases and rejected that option.

Subparagraph (2) of FRE 404(a) restates the common law with respect to evidence pertaining to the character of victims generally. Such evidence is most commonly

offered to support a claim of self-defense in an assault or homicide case or a claim of consent in a rape case.[88] However, FRE 412 and similar state "rape shield" statutes now bar character evidence when it is offered for the latter purpose. Though the federal rule does not so provide, most courts require defendants to introduce other evidence of self-defense or consent before character evidence is introduced. Do you think this requirement is sensible?

Where the defendant pleads self-defense to homicide, the federal rule adopts what was at common law the minority position. Before states began revising their evidence codes on the model of the federal rules, defendants in most jurisdictions could plead self-defense and adduce noncharacter evidence that the deceased was the first aggressor without opening the door to evidence that the deceased had a peaceable character. Do you think the federal rule is preferable to the once prevailing view?

Subparagraph (3) of FRE 404(a) deals with the use of character evidence to impeach witnesses, a topic discussed more fully in Chapter Five. To anticipate briefly, one can generally present witnesses to testify that some other witness' reputation for truth and veracity is bad. This may be countered by testimony that that witness' reputation for truth and veracity is good.

Where character may be proved as circumstantial evidence of conduct under one of the exceptions described above, special rules of proof apply. In most states, such proof is limited to testimony concerning the subject's reputation in some relevant com-

---

88. **When self-defense is claimed, the accused sometimes introduces evidence of the victim's reputation for violence not to show that the victim was the first aggressor but to show that the defendant acted reasonably in using force on the victim. Evidence offered for this purpose does not contravene the basic rule excluding character evidence, since it is not offered to show that the victim acted in accord with his character. It is offered to shed light on the defendant's good faith belief that he** needed to act. **But it is important to note that the evidence is independently admissible on the issue of who was the first aggressor. Hence it is admissible for two purposes, both of which are deemed proper by the rule, and there is no need to balance utility for one purpose against the danger of misuse for another. The likely misuse is that the jury may decide that conviction is too severe a punishment for one who attacked a most deserving victim.**

munity for the character trait in question. Specific acts consistent with the subject's alleged reputation may not be shown, thus reversing the preferred mode of proof when character is truly an issue in the case. Dean Ladd has suggested the following rationale for this limitation.

> The object of the law in making reputation the test of character is to get the aggregate judgment of a community rather than the personal opinion of the witness which might be considered to be warped by his own feeling or prejudice. Even reputation must, to be admitted, be general in a community rather than based upon a limited class. While it is not necessary that a character witness know what the majority of a neighborhood think of a person, he must know of the general regard with which the party is commonly held.

> It is the general concurrence of a great number of people reflecting the sentiment toward the party whose character is subject to inquiry that is necessary to establish a reputation and to warrant its use as evidence. In this, the theory of the law is that trustworthiness is gained from the expressions of many people in their estimation of a person which would not be obtained by the individual opinion of a single witness however well acquainted he might be with the party's character. The requirement that the reputation be broadly general rather than that of a particular group * * * again emphasizes the effort to get away from the secularized and consequently biased estimate of character * * * The reputed character of a person is created from the slow spreading influence of community opinion growing out of his behavior in the society in which he moves and is known and upon

this basis is accepted as proof of what his character actually is.[89]

———

Ladd's justification may have made some sense when most communities were small and everyone talked about everyone. Then reputation had an attractive concreteness in that numerous individuals might be expected to know someone's reputation and agree on it. But in modern urban society individuals are more anonymous. Indeed, the courts have decided that comment is not necessary for reputation. Testimony that nothing bad has been heard about a person is sufficient to support the inference of good reputation. The courts have also altered the historical limitation which defined "relevant community" as the neighborhood in which one lived. Now the workplace is commonly accepted as a relevant community, and some courts accept reputation in other places where individuals have spent considerable amounts of time.

Perhaps a better explanation than Ladd's of the reputation limitation is that it reflects the law's basic ambivalence to the circumstantial use of character evidence. Testimony as to reputation is typically bloodless, ritualistic and a bit dull. Dean Ladd has suggested that the following pattern of questions is ideal in a case in which Y, defendant in a homicide action, has asked W to testify as to his character.[90]

(1) General questions identifying W, the character witness, and suggesting that the jury can rely on his evaluation of statements about Y.

(2) General questions to show that W personally knew Y, so that the jury may be sure that W is associating what he has heard with the right individual.

89. Ladd, Techniques and Theory of Character Testimony, 24 Iowa L.Rev. 498, 513 (1939).

90. Id. at 519–527.

(3) Q. Mr. W, have you heard remarks or comments concerning Y made by people generally in and about the community of Z town? A. Yes, I have.

(4) Q. Have these remarks and comments been many or few in number? A. I have heard a large number of people talk about Y on many occasions.

(5) Q. Were these persons members of some particular group of people? A. No. The remarks I have heard came from various individuals in different occupations in the community.

(6) Q. Over how long a period of time have you heard comment and talk about Y by people generally in and about Z town? A. For the last several years and quite recently.

(7) Q. Have these comments and remarks related to Y's character as a quiet, peaceable, law-abiding citizen? A. Yes, there have been many remarks about Y concerning his disposition as a peaceful, quiet and law-abiding citizen in the community.

(8) Q. Does Y have a *general* reputation for being a quiet, peaceable, law-abiding citizen in and about the community of Z town? [Italics in original to emphasize that Y's reputation is not confined to a specific group.] A. Yes, he does.

(9) Q. Do you know the *general* reputation of Y for being a quiet, peaceable, law-abiding citizen in and about the community of Z town prior to and on (the date of the commission of the offense)? A. Yes, I do.

(10) Q. Will you please state to the jury whether that reputation was good or bad? A. It was good.

————

Clearly such a presentation is not designed to maximize the emotional or prejudicial appeal of the evidence in question. And while it might put some jurors to sleep, it is unlikely to draw their attention from the central issues in the case. Also, the use of reputation evidence is unlikely to give rise to disputes concerning the existence of collateral facts, something that might occur if character could be proved by specific acts. Although the reputation ritual seems silly when first contemplated, perhaps it is a wise compromise.

In order to maximize the impact of favorable character evidence, lawyers try to get witnesses whose personal distinction lends weight to their testimony. Lawyers also attempt to impress the jury by the sheer number of people who will report the defendant's reputation as good. As in all cases where evidence is redundant, judges have discretion to limit the number of character witnesses who will be heard.

The goal in introducing character evidence is often not only to promote the inference that the defendant's reputation is so good he must be innocent, but also to suggest that because upstanding witnesses think so highly of the defendant he must be innocent. Furthermore the impression one often gets from reading or listening to testimony about reputation is that the witness is really presenting a personal opinion about the defendant's character in the guise of reporting reputation. If this is the case, would it not be wiser to discard the reputation limitation and allow witnesses to state openly their opinion of the defendant's character?

Wigmore certainly thought so. He wrote:

Put any one of us on trial for a false charge, and ask him whether he would not rather invoke in his vindication, as Lord Kenyon said, "The warm affectionate testimony" of those few whose long intimacy and trust has made them ready to demonstrate their faith to the jury, than any amount of colorful assertions about reputation. Take the place of a juryman, and speculate whether he is helped more by the witnesses whose personal intimacy gives to their belief a first and highest value, or by those who merely repeat a form of words in which the term "reputation" occurs.[91]

This view prevailed with the drafters of the Federal Rules. FRE 405 on methods of proving character provides in subsection (a):

> *Reputation or opinion.* In all cases in which evidence of character or a trait of character of a person is admissible, proof may be made by testimony as to reputation or by testimony in the form of an opinion. On cross-examination, inquiry is allowable into relevant specific instances of conduct.

If this rule only allowed opinions from witnesses whose close relationship to the defendant suggests a special ability to evaluate his character, there might be little reason to quarrel with this change.[92] However, the rule on its face contains no such limitations. Nothing in the rule would prevent a police officer who knows the defendant only as an arrestee from responding to the defendant's character evidence with an opinion that the defendant is violent and untrustworthy, or a psychiatrist from testifying that he has formed an opinion that certain witnesses for the side not paying his fee are not telling the truth. Whether such testimony will actually be admitted depends on the type of foundation which the courts will require before allowing opinions as to character.[93]

Character testimony is unusual in the law in that it is one of the few instances where a party can freely choose witnesses.[94] One might suppose that this would give defendants such a significant advantage that character evidence would be introduced in almost every case. However, the prosecution has two offsetting advantages which mean that defendants often offer character evidence at their peril. The first, and less important, we have already touched upon. When defense witnesses testify that the defendant's reputation is good, prosecution witnesses may testify that it is bad. The second, codified in the last sentence of FRE 405(a), means that although instances of good conduct may not be mentioned by character witnesses on direct examination, such witnesses on cross-examination can be asked about specific instances of bad conduct. Unless a defendant has led a previously blameless life, inquiry along these lines may be devastating.

At common law, proper form is to ask the defendant's character witness whether *he has heard* about defendant's bad acts, *not whether he knows of them.* The reason for this is that the question is allowed on the theory that people evaluate others on the basis of their bad actions as well as their good. If the character witness has not heard of the defendant's bad acts, it suggests that he may not be very familiar with the defendant's reputation. If the witness admits to having heard of bad acts and nonetheless has concluded that defendant's reputation is good, the evidence says something about his standard of judgment.[95]

---

91. 7 Wigmore § 1986, at 166.

92. But consider our earlier suggestion that the reputation limitation may strike a reasonable balance between a desire to admit certain evidence and a desire to minimize prejudice and other problems.

93. The Federal Rules on opinion evidence (Article VII) are generally more receptive to such evidence than the common law. However, they do not clearly require that testimony of the type described in the text be

admitted or excluded. See Chapter One for a more detailed discussion of the opinion rule.

94. Expert testimony is another. Usually non-party witnesses are those who were fortuitously present when some crucial event occurred.

95. Where opinion evidence is given, as under FRE 405(a), the prosecution should be able to ask the opinion witness if he "knows" of defendant's bad acts. However, it may be argued that this question is unnecessarily

Under this theory, it is not analytically necessary for the defendant to have committed the act in question. An unfounded accusation of immorality may be just as damaging to one's reputation as a well-founded one. But here the theory breaks down. It is clear that the imputation of bad acts to the defendant may be very prejudicial, even if ostensibly done to question the credibility of a character witness. Thus, most courts require that the prosecutor have a good faith belief that the defendant has committed the act alleged before propounding such questions.

Since reputation may be affected adversely by arrests or criminal acts which have not resulted in conviction for a crime, character witnesses may be asked if they have heard of such events. When this occurs a character witness may be asked on redirect examination to explain why the event did not affect the defendant's reputation. He may explain that most people believe the event did not occur, that charges were dropped or that the defendant was found innocent after trial. Where the witness has no independent explanation, the defense counsel may ask questions of the type: "Have you also heard that charges were dropped for lack of evidence?"

Special problems are posed by the scope of cross-examination in character cases.

Bad acts referred to on cross-examination should be acts which relate to the character trait about which the witness has testified. Thus, it is technically improper to ask a witness who has testified that defendant has a good reputation for peacefulness whether he has heard that defendant was once convicted for embezzlement. However, courts vary greatly in the degree to which they enforce the "same trait" limitation.

There is often a question of when an act is sufficiently ancient that one would not expect a knowledgeable reputation witness to have heard of it. At least, this is technically the issue in deciding how far back a cross-examiner may go for instances of bad acts. But a court, aware that the jury will treat the suggestion of defendant's bad acts as reflecting directly on character, should be at least as concerned with the point at which past acts are no longer probative of current character as they are with the technical issue.[96] The leading case on this issue and on the general question of testing reputation witnesses for knowledge of specific acts is Michelson v. United States.[97]

In this case the defendant, Michelson, was tried in 1947 for bribing a revenue agent. Michelson pleaded entrapment, and the issue came down to the question of whom

suggestive. See S. Saltzburg & K. Redden, Federal Rules of Evidence, Manual 1, 59 (3d ed. 1982).

96. This area is an example of a basic problem which permeates the law of evidence and makes the study of evidence so interesting. Treating evidence law as a self-contained system of rules and assumptions, certain procedures or rationales make complete analytic sense although they make little or no sense in the context of a jury trial. The tension between evidence law as an abstract scheme of analysis and as a procedural scheme applied before juries is constantly visible in court decisions. At times, a ruling will be justified on the basis of obviously artificial abstract analysis. At other times, an analytically perfect answer will be rejected because one knows the system cannot make the fine discrimination possible in abstract analysis. Thus, analytically the prosecution should be allowed to ask a character witness if he has heard of an actual but unfounded charge leveled against the defendant. Such charges affect reputation and knowledge of the charge has some bearing on the degree to which the witness is acquainted with defendant's reputation. Yet most states will not allow such questions because of the danger that they will unfairly prejudice the jury. One might conclude that well-founded charges "fairly" prejudice the jury since questions about such charges are allowed. This conclusion is worth thinking about.

97. 335 U.S. 469 (1948).

to believe, the defendant or the revenue agent. Michelson called five character witnesses, three of whom testified that he had a very good reputation for honesty, truthfulness, and being a law-abiding citizen, and two of whom stated they had never heard anything against Michelson. Two of the witnesses stated they had known the defendant for about thirty years, and the others stated they had known him for at least fifteen years. On cross-examination four of these witnesses were asked, "Did you ever hear that on October 11, 1920, the defendant, Solomon Michelson, was arrested for receiving stolen goods?" The question was apparently asked in good faith; a paper record of the arrest, which the defense did not challenge, was exhibited.[98] Despite this, the defense argued that the question constituted reversible error. The defendant's claim was rejected in an opinion by Justice Jackson which still stands as perhaps the most intelligent of judicial essays on the proof of character by reputation evidence. Reading the opinion, one feels that it might have been circulated to the other justices with a note that it was being written for the casebooks rather than the U.S. Reports.

Jackson saw three issues which had to be disposed of in order to affirm the decision below. First was the issue of whether an inquiry about an arrest was proper. He answered this in the standard manner, pointing out that even a false arrest may cloud one's reputation and stating that an inquiry into arrests tests the witness' qualifications to report community opinion.

Second was the issue of whether, in a trial for bribery, an inquiry into the crime of receiving stolen goods was proper. This question was forced on the Court by the Circuit Court of Appeals which, in affirming Michelson's conviction, suggested that the Supreme Court should reverse the circuit's decision by adopting the Illinois rule, which only allows inquiries about arrests on similar or identical charges. Jackson, after noting that the Illinois rule was inconsistent with the great weight of authority, argued that the *Michelson* case itself showed the proposal to be inexpedient. Michelson, he pointed out, had offered evidence of good character broader than the crime charged, including the traits of honesty, truthfulness and being a law-abiding citizen, characteristics which seem as incompatible with receiving stolen goods as they do with offering a bribe to a revenue agent.

The third issue was the lapse of time between the 1920 arrest and the events which gave rise to the trial. Here Jackson equivocated. After suggesting that the judge would have had discretion to exclude the inquiry, he pointed out that two of the witnesses traced their acquaintance with Michelson to a time before the earlier arrest, that Michelson himself had pointed out a 1927 conviction for violating a New York City trademark law with regard to watches and that there had been no objection at trial on the specific ground of lapse of time.

What makes the Jackson opinion memorable is not the specific decisions which were reached on the issues in the case. Jackson disposed of the first two in a nar-

---

98. **The judge's charge to the jury in this case included the following:**

I instruct the jury that what is happening now is this: the defendant has called character witnesses, and the basis for the evidence given by those character witnesses is the reputation of the defendant in the community, and since the defendant tenders the issue of his reputation the prosecution may ask the witness if she has heard of various incidents in his career. I say to you that regardless of her answer you are not to assume that the incidents asked about actually took place. All that is happening is that this witness' standard of opinion of the reputation of the defendant is being tested. Is that clear?

Id. at 472, n. 3.

rowly analytic manner and never really faced up to the third. Rather, it is that Justice Jackson throughout the opinion explicitly recognizes the various anomalies of the reputation rule and acknowledges the likelihood that the jury will not comprehend limiting instructions. In the end, however, he attempts to convert inconsistency and illogic into virtues:

> We concur in the general opinion of courts, text-writers and the profession that much of this law is archaic, paradoxical and full of compromises and compensations by which an irrational advantage to one side is offset by a poorly reasoned counterprivilege to the other. But somehow it has proved a workable even if clumsy system when moderated by discretionary controls in the hands of a wise and strong trial court. To pull one misshapen stone out of the grotesque structure is more likely simply to upset its present balance between adverse interests than to establish a rational edifice.[99]

This is an important statement. Too often in analyzing rules of evidence, what is seen as illogical analytically is thought to be nonsensical practically.[1] Even commentators who are quick to criticize other aspects of evidence law as being illogical have cited this statement with approval. However, too often this statement has been accepted as establishing a justification for the current rules respecting the cross-examination of reputation witnesses. It is not a justification for the status quo so much as it is a call for thoughtless surrender. Even if Justice Jackson is correct and the character rule is an irrational set of compromises, the conclusion that changing any aspects of the scheme can only be detrimental does not follow. All the argument fairly suggests is that one should be careful and alert to the unexpected in deciding what to change. To give just one example, Justice Jackson's argument suggests no good reason why a rule should not be formulated prohibiting cross-examination as to twenty year old arrests and convictions.[2] Indeed the drafters of the federal rules may have made such a change. Rule 609 on impeachment by prior convictions appears to establish a strong presumption that so long as ten years have passed since a witness' release from confinement, convictions more than ten years old should not be used to impeach credibility. Though FRE 405(a) mentions no time limit, the courts may well read 405(a) to be consistent with 609. Even if the courts reject this approach, there is general discretion under FRE 403 and at common law to exclude evidence of bad acts which is so dated that its prejudicial impact is likely to exceed its probative worth.

Problem IV–50. Harriet Simpson is on trial for passing bad checks. Her defense is that because of an arithmetical error she made while balancing her checkbook she did not realize that she had no money in her account when she wrote the checks in question. She has two people who are willing to testify as character witnesses on her behalf. The first is the minister of her church, Reverend Samual Brown who has known her since she began attending the First Congregational Church some seven years before. He is

------

99. Id., at 486.

1. Recall our suggestion that the apparent illogic of the basic reputation limitation may represent a wise compromise between competing interests.

2. We are obviously making some very strong statements of our own here. Do you find as much in Justice Jackson's analysis as we do? Do you agree with our criticism of the Justice's conclusion? Do you think our specific suggestion is wise?

of the opinion that she is truthful, honest and peaceful and he is willing to testify that she has a good reputation for truthfulness, honesty and peacefulness among the parishioners of the First Congregational Church. The second is Rebecca Rubinfeld, Harriet's best friend and neighbor. Their acquaintance goes back some twenty years to the time they were sorority sisters in college. Rebecca is the godmother of Harriet's children and has lived in the same neighborhood as Harriet for six years. Before that the friends lived about nine miles apart and saw each other at least once a week except during the years 1981 and 1982 when Rebecca's job took her to Paris. Rebecca too believes that Harriet is truthful, honest and peaceful, and she is willing to testify that Harriet has a good reputation for these traits in their neighborhood. The trial occurs in 1983. **Plan your direct examination of these two witnesses. Have a friend play the role of the witnesses and ask the questions you would ask if you were introducing the testimony of these witnesses at a trial.**

Problem IV–51. In the same situation as that specified above you are the prosecutor and Simpson has introduced whatever testimony is appropriate from her character witnesses. Your investigators have uncovered the following information: In 1960, at the age of 17, Harriet was arrested on a charge of passing bad checks. She was convicted in juvenile court of the offense but the conviction was expunged after a two year probationary period. In 1963, while at college, she pled guilty to a charge of shoplifting. In 1964, while at college she was brought before her college's Honor Committee on charges of plagiarism. It appears that she had to rewrite the paper in question but was not otherwise sanctioned. In 1971, 1974 and 1977 she was charged with passing bad checks. Each time she attributed the checks to her carelessness in balancing her accounts and each time charges were dropped when she repaid the funds owing. In 1977 she was divorced by her husband who charged adultery. In 1978 she was charged with assault and battery. She pled self defense but was convicted by a jury. In 1978, 1979 and 1980 she pled guilty to charges of drunk driving, and in 1980 she pled guilty to the crime of driving on a revoked license. In 1979 she was charged with shoplifting and resisting arrest. She was acquitted on the count of shoplifting but convicted on the charge of resisting arrest. In 1979 she was dimissed from her position as deputy director of the United Way fund drive. It was rumored that she had appropriated some funds to her own use, but the United Way organization never complained to the police and charges were never brought. In 1980 she was charged with assault, but charges were dropped when the victim expressed a desire not to prosecute. It appears that Harriet's troubles from 1978 on were due largely to a drinking problem, for in 1980 she joined Alcoholics Anonymous and except for her recent problem with a bad check she has not been in trouble with the law since. **Plan your cross-examination of Simpson's character witnesses. Have a friend play the role of these witnesses and ask the questions you would ask at a trial.**

Problem IV–52. Donald Doak, the proprietor of a neighborhood grocery store, swore to a criminal complaint charging Meg Peters with shoplifting. A jury acquitted Peters of the charge, and Peters has sued Doak for malicious prosecution. Peters wishes to introduce testimony by a local banker that her reputation for honesty in the community in which she lives and works is excellent. **Is this evidence admissible?**

Problem IV–53. The plaintiff sues the defendant for the wrongful death of her son. She alleges that the defendant was negligent in retaining one Peter Elrod as a blasting crew foreman and that Elrod's negligence in failing to warn of an imminent detonation was the proximate cause of her son's death. The plaintiff seeks to introduce general reputation evidence concerning the foreman's character for carelessness, testimony from two people who had worked with Elrod that in their opinion he was the most careless foreman they had worked under, and testimony describing three instances when the foreman had failed to give sufficient warning that a blast was imminent. **Is any of this evidence admissible? On what issues?**

Problem IV–54. Palmer sues Dillon for assault and battery. Dillon pleads self-defense and denies being the aggressor. **May Dillon introduce testimony regarding Palmer's reputation for violence? May Dillon introduce evidence of specific violent acts by Palmer? May Palmer introduce such evidence about Dillon? Does your decision with respect to one depend on what the other does? Would your answers change if Dillon were being prosecuted criminally for the assault? For homicide growing out of the assault? If it were a criminal trial could the state introduce evidence that Palmer had a good reputation for peacefulness and nonviolence?**

Problem IV–55. Ivan Skivar had just arrived in Dodge City after a twelve day trip by stagecoach from New York. He planned to stay there for two days and see some sights, for he had never been in the West before, and then continue on to San Francisco. However, his plans have been disrupted; he now finds himself in jail charged with murder. Skivar's story is that he had just arrived in town when Abdul Lamear stuck out a foot and tripped him. Lamear seemed to think that the sight of Skivar on the ground with his baggage scattered in all directions was very funny, for he laughed uproariously. Ivan responded with a few choice expletives (here deleted). At this point, Lamear pulled out his dagger and charged Skivar, stabbing him in the arm. Skivar tried to get away but Lamear grabbed him by one arm and placed a knife at his throat. Skivar, having been warned about the "Wild West," had a derringer up his sleeve. Fearing for his life, he shot Lamear.

May Skivar introduce witnesses who will testify that Lamear had a bad reputation for violence and hostility? May Skivar introduce witnesses who will testify as to other occasions when Lamear played crude practical jokes on strangers? As to other occasions when Lamear flew into a murderous rage when cursed by another? The stage coach driver had told the the prosecutor that on the trip from New York he witnessed several occasions when Skivar tried to pick fights and he felt that the other passengers were afraid of Skivar. **Is the prosecutor likely to get this evidence in?**

Problem IV–56. Sol Levine is an author who has had only limited success. He lives alone in a high rise apartment on the income from a small inheritance which his grandparents left him. His one passion is bridge. He plays duplicate bridge three or four times a week at the Star Bridge Club. **If he is accused of assault may he introduce testimony from others who play regularly at the Star that he has a good reputation for peacefulness and non-violence? If he is accused of thievery, may he introduce testimony from these individuals that he has a good reputation for honesty and truthfulness?**

Problem IV-57.   Assume that in the preceding fact setting, precedent in the jurisdiction makes it clear that the desired character evidence is admissible. **Must the court hear from each of the fifteen Star regulars whom Levine would like to have testify?   Would the situation be any different if Levine had brought suit for libel and the defense had introduced witnesses who had testified that before the libel (which accused Levine of being dishonest and violent) Levine's reputation for peacefulness and honesty was terrible?**

Problem IV-58.   James "The Blade" Slade, a well-known mobster, had taken a special interest in "Sad Sam" Cunningham, a young personable bookie, and had tried to persuade Sam to come work for the mob. Apparently Slade wanted Sam to be his successor and had told him the detailed history of the Midwest mob and his own role in it. One day, Sam is found in an alley with a knife through his heart. Slade is charged with murder.

Assume that the prosecution has evidence that "Sad Sam" had the reputation in the underworld as an individual who was "no squealer," but who was so open and friendly that he couldn't resist interrogation. The prosecution also has evidence of specific instances when Sam, while located in a different city, cracked under interrogation and gave the police information which was instrumental in breaking up an organized gambling ring. Finally, assume that the prosecutor has been told by an experienced detective, who had arrested Sam twice, that if they had begun to interrogate Sam about "The Blade's" activity Sam would have resisted at first but eventually would have told the police everything that he knew. **Would the prosecution be able to introduce any of this evidence in Slade's trial?   As prosecutor, is there any other information which you would like to have before attempting to introduce this evidence?**

Problem IV-59.   Sam Bullard, claiming to be a skilled and experienced bank guard, signs a contract to work for a period of four months as a guard at the Lakeview Last National Bank. The contract provides that he may be fired for dishonesty or incompetence. After two weeks, Bullard is fired. He sues Last National for breach of contract. The bank offers the testimony of an expert who viewed Bullard at a previous job. The expert testifies that, in his opinion, Bullard is incompetent. **Should the testimony be admitted?   Are there additional facts you wish to know?   Should it be admitted if punitive damages are demanded on the ground that the contract was breached only after the bank discovered that Bullard was married to a person of a different race?**

Problem IV-60.   The defendant is charged with sexual abuse of a nine-year old child. He offers a psychiatrist who, on the basis of an examination, will testify that the defendant is not a sexual deviate and could not commit the crime charged. **Is this testimony admissible?** [See Curran, Expert Psychiatric Evidence of Personality Traits, 103 U.Pa.L.Rev. 999 (1955); Falknor & Steffen, Evidence of Character: From the "Crucible of the Community" to the "Couch of the Psychiatrist," 102 U.Pa.L.Rev. 980 (1954).]

Problem IV–61. The defendant is charged with fraud in the sale of land. Wishing to introduce character testimony, he hires a private investigator to canvas the community and ascertain his reputation for honesty. The investigator interviews a substantial portion of the community, asking citizens if they know the defendant's reputation for honesty and also if they have an opinion as to his character for honesty. **Can the investigator testify as a character witness? If she can, what sort of cross-examination might be expected?**

I. HABIT: ROUTINE PRACTICE

Here is a puzzle for you. FRE 406 on evidence of habits and routine practices is unique among the relevance rules. Read it, and see if you can figure out how it is unique before you read on.

Evidence of the habit of a person or of the routine practice of an organization, whether corroborated or not and regardless of the presence of eyewitnesses, is relevant to prove that the conduct of the person or organization on a particular occasion was in conformity with the habit or routine practice.

Rule 406 is unique because it should be unnecessary. It is the only relevance rule which does not state a principle of exclusion. Under this rule the introduction of habit evidence is subject only to the principles of rules 402 and 403; without this rule the introduction of habit evidence would be subject to the same principles and no others.

The rule, however, is here for a purpose. It is to make clear that there is a distinction between character and habit evidence, and to make sure that the federal courts do not follow the lead of those

states that have adopted the so-called "eyewitness" rule, or of the few that purport to exclude evidence of habit entirely.

Under the eyewitness rule, evidence of habit is admissible only if there are no eyewitnesses who can testify about the events which were allegedly the occasion for the habitual activity. The rule appears responsive to relevance concerns. If eyewitnesses are available to describe what happened, one may reconstruct the event without resorting to habit evidence. But this justification for the eyewitness rule is misguided. Perception and memory are subject to many kinds of distortion.[3] Evidence of an established habit may be more reliable as an indicator of behavior than the testimony of an eyewitness. This is particularly likely where the eyewitness is identified with the party opposing the habit testimony. For example, a locomotive engineer who states that the plaintiff's decedent did not look both ways at a railroad crossing would not be particularly credible. The availability of even such interested eyewitness testimony will preclude the admission of habit evidence in most eyewitness rule jurisdictions.

There are reasons why courts have been so grudging in their acceptance of habit

---

3. See the selection from Stewart, Perception, Memory, and Hearsay: A Criticism of Present Law and the Proposed rules of Evidence, reprinted in Chapter Six.

evidence. The most important is probably a confusion between habit and character. Speaking loosely, one may talk of a habit for care, a habit for robbing, or a habit of dropping things. Used this way habit suggests little more than a tendency toward certain kinds of action. Such "habits" are akin to, if not identical with, the kind of character evidence excluded by the propensity rule.[4] But, "habit" need not be defined so loosely. McCormick distinguishes character from habit as follows:

> Character is a generalized description of one's disposition, or of one's disposition in respect to a general trait, such as honesty, temperance, or peacefulness. "Habit" * * * is more specific. It describes one's regular responses to a repeated specific situation. If we speak of character for care, we think of the person's tendency to act prudently in all the varying situations of life. * * * A habit, on the other hand, is the person's regular practice of meeting a particular kind of situation with a specific type of conduct, such as the habit of going down a particular stairway two stairs at a time * * * The doing of the habitual acts may become semi-automatic.[5]

McCormick's definition seems consistent with the way the term "habit" is ordinarily used. When the term is defined in this way, evidence of habit seems not to be subject to the usual objections which justify the relevance rules. Courts contemplating habit evidence do not face a situation where general low relevance justifies a peculiar attentiveness to other considerations. When there is convincing evidence that behavior is semi-automatic, it is not unreasonable to give that evidence more weight than the conflicting testimony of an eyewitness. But even if habit evidence were likely to be less probative,

a *rule* of exclusion is probably not justified, because habit evidence seems peculiarly unlikely to prejudice a jury. Although there may be exceptions, most of the detailed patterns of living which constitute habits are unlikely to move a jury to sympathy, hatred, or any of the other emotions which can distort the evaluative process. Problems of estimation and surprise do exist, but they seem no greater with respect to habit evidence than they are with respect to most of the evidence routinely admitted at trials.

There are, however, three problems linked with habit evidence which may motivate those courts that adopt the more restrictive attitudes. The first is that individuals can consciously take advantage of the fact that they are known to have certain habits. A murderer, in the habit of taking the six o'clock bus home from work, may kill someone at six-fifteen, counting on evidence of habit to establish an alibi. A court might wish to exclude evidence of habit in those exceptional cases where the charge or claim suggests a motive for non-habitual behavior. But, the alternative of leaving the matter to the jury seems at least as reasonable. The jury should be able to appreciate the degree to which motive will lead one to deviate from habit.

The second problem is that even well-established habits do not always govern behavior. A person in the habit of climbing two stairs at a time may while lost in thought be content with one stair per step. Accident cases seem particularly likely to occur on the rare occasions when habits are inadvertently ignored. It seems quite unlikely that the plaintiff's decedent, killed in a railroad accident, stopped and looked both ways at the tracks, whatever his usual habits. This difficulty raises problems of relevance in context, but these, again, are problems which the jury appears quite ca-

---

4. Yet some states will admit evidence of a "habit for carefulness" if there are no eyewitnesses to an accident or other injury.

5. McCormick § 195, at 462–3.

pable of handling. Jurors can determine when claims of habit are inconsistent with events and when there is no necessary inconsistency. They should also appreciate the fact that the existence of a habit does not guarantee conforming behavior.[6]

The third difficulty with habit evidence is that it seems particularly easy to fabricate and particularly difficult to refute. Habit evidence is often offered in cases where the individual whose behavior is in issue is dead and the estate is bringing suit. Here, the person or persons who know the most about the deceased's behavior are likely to have an interest in the suit. It would not, for example, be very difficult for a surviving spouse to consciously or unconsciously translate the behavior of stopping at most stop signs into the habit of *always* stopping at stop signs. The usual way of proving habit, the opinion of a knowledgeable witness, lends itself to such distortion.[7] In these circumstances it might be very difficult for the opposing party to come up with anyone who can dispute the habit testimony.

The fear that certain types of testimony are particularly amenable to perjury or distortion is a factor which should be considered in weighing evidence policy. But, with the possible exception of the much criticized Dead Man's statutes, nowhere in the law of evidence does a rule of exclusion rest primarily on these grounds.

There is one final factor which may justify a restrictive attitude toward habit evidence. Restrictive rules in this area provide an extra guarantee that character evidence will remain inadmissible. If the liberal federal rule on habit evidence were adopted in all states, some states might confuse character with habit and admit evidence which is justifiably excluded. This argument is not insubstantial, but on balance the authors feel that evidence as probative as habit evidence should not be routinely excluded or limited simply because the courts cannot always be trusted to do their job properly.

Courts are much less troubled in accepting evidence of the habits or customs of business. The need for regularity in business and organizational sanctions which may exist when custom is violated provide extra guarantees that the questioned activity followed the usual custom.[8] In this area the liberal standard of the federal rules generally prevails. However, in many states the individual whose customary behavior is at issue must testify that, though he does not remember the activity, he is sure that on the occasion specified he followed the usual custom.

Problem IV–62. Pedro Gomez was an experienced pilot who worked for Alta Airlines. He was responsible for taking delivery of new airplanes

6. They may well find for the claimant who is supported by habit testimony an overwhelming percentage of the time. But this is not necessarily irrational. If the habit in fact exists, there is a strong likelihood that behavior was in accordance with it. On balance, more incorrect decisions would be expected if the habit evidence were kept from the jury.

7. Usually habit may also be proved, at the discretion of the court, by testimony reporting repeated instances of the habitual conduct.

8. For example, consider the issue of whether a letter placed in an "out" box was mailed. A mail clerk's testimony that it was his routine to mail letters placed in out boxes and that he followed this routine on the day the letter was placed in the outbox would everywhere be accepted as evidence that the letter was mailed, even if the clerk did not remember posting the letter in question. In many jurisdictions even the clerk's testimony would not be necessary. One who knew of the business routine could testify to it.

manufactured by the Kadet Aeronautics Company. When a new plane was ready for delivery Gomez would fly to Santa Fe where Kadet was located, get in the plane along with one of Kadet's experienced test pilots and fly with the test pilot back to Alta's headquarters. Gomez was killed when a plane that was being delivered to Alta crashed into a mountain in dense fog. Gomez' widow sued Kadet charging negligence. Kadet claimed that Gomez was piloting the plane and was contributorily negligent. When the plane took off Gomez was in the left seat and Kadet's test pilot, who also died in the crash, in the right. The plane had dual controls and could be flown from either seat. At the trial Kadet wishes to introduce evidence that it is the custom in the industry for the pilot in the left seat of a dual control plane to do the actual flying. They also seek to introduce evidence that on each of the four previous occasions when Gomez picked up a plane for Alta he sat in the left seat and did the actual flying. **Should evidence of the industry custom or of the fact that Gomez sat in the left seat and flew the plane on four previous occasions be admitted?**

Problem IV–63. Bill Miller is charged with murder in connection with the death of his former partner. It is well known that there was considerable bitterness between the partners at the time their joint venture broke up, and the partner's death occurred soon enough after the termination of their association that Miller stood to collect a substantial sum on an insurance policy that each partner had taken out with the other as beneficiary. Miller wishes to introduce evidence that he is an active and devoted member of the Corinthians, a small religious sect whose principal tenets include a commitment to peacefulness and non-violence. He also wishes to testify that except when he is ill he spends his Wednesday evenings from 7:00 p. m. until 10:00 p. m. at the Corinthian Church attending their Holy Wednesday religious services. Miller's partner was killed at 8:30 p. m. on a Wednesday. **Should the evidence that Miller wishes to offer be allowed?**

Problem IV–64. Mack Kennedy suffered unexpected complications in the course of an operation that left him paralyzed from the waist down. It is clear that the paralysis did not result from negligence but is a rare, unavoidable complication associated with the operation in question. Kennedy sues, alleging that the hospital breached a duty to him by not warning him that paralysis was a complication that might result from the operation. The hospital wishes to introduce an internal practice manual that instructs its physicians to warn patients that the danger of paralysis is a possible complication of the operation in question. The physician, Sue Black, who told Kennedy about the operation, has since died. The hospital wants to introduce the testimony of the chief resident who will say that while she was not present when the operation in question was described to Kennedy she has been present on at least fifty occasions when Dr. Black, an intern whose work she supervised, explained operations to patients. In each case she observed Dr. Black give whatever warnings were required by the hospital manual. **Should the hospital be allowed to introduce its manual or the testimony of its chief resident?**

Problem IV–65. John Casey is a secretary for the Superior Corporation. He and four other secretaries form a "mini-pool." The secretaries in the pool take a coffee break at 9:30 every day. One of their number is responsible for picking up donuts for the break in the morning before coming to work at 8:15. They always buy from the High Quality Bakery. This task rotates: on Tuesdays it is John's turn. One Tuesday John does not show up at work. It later turns out that he is in the hospital. John claims that as he was mounting the stairs to the High Quality Bakery at 8:05 a. m. he slipped on a loose brick and fell, striking his head. He got up, forgetting his errand, and wandered off, eventually collapsing near his office two blocks from the bakery. He was found at about 8:10 a. m. and taken to the hospital for treatment of a severe concussion. John sues High Quality. The bakery manager is ready to testify that she was in the bakery shop from 7:45 a. m., that she could see the steps of the bakery through the front glass window, and that she saw no one fall on the steps on the day in question. **Can John introduce evidence of the secretaries' customs with respect to their coffee break in an effort to show that he in fact fell on the steps of the High Quality? Would the case for admissibility be stronger or weaker if John's testimony about the location of the accident was apparently shaken by a vigorous cross-examination? Can he introduce evidence that the bakery repaired a loose brick on their steps some 80 days after his accident?**

Problem IV–66. The autos of Leslie Fosdick and Richard Tracy collide head-on at 60 m. p. h., killing both. It is unclear who was responsible. Tracy's widow wishes to bring a wrongful death action against Fosdick's estate, alleging that it was her gross negligence which was responsible for the collision. She claims that Fosdick was drunk at the time. An investigator working for her attorney has discovered the following information: (1) Fosdick has a reputation in the town in which she lived as a drunkard and as a reckless driver. (2) Fosdick was ticketed 10 times over the preceding two years for driving while under the influence of alcohol. Twice she was convicted of this offense and eight times she pleaded guilty to the lesser offense of reckless driving. (3) A local police officer is willing to testify that even when sober Fosdick was the worst driver she ever saw. (4) A woman who owns a gas station next to a local bar could testify that on at least fifteen occasions during the six months preceding the accident she saw Fosdick stagger to her car obviously drunk, get in and drive off. **If the case goes to trial, do you think Ms. Tracy will be able to get in any or all of the information which the investigator has found? The investigator reports that he has not yet been able to determine whether there were any eyewitnesses to the accident. Does it matter whether or not there were any?**

Problem IV–67. The same facts as the preceding problem. The attorney representing the surviving members of Fosdick's family and Fosdick's estate has asked you whether as a matter of strategy it might be a good idea to counterclaim, also on the theory of wrongful death, on the ground that Tracy's negligence caused the accident. You question her, and she tells you that she has found one eyewitness who will testify that he thinks Tracy's car may have swerved into Fosdick's shortly before the crash, but that, most unfortunately, there are two additional eyewitnesses who think Fosdick's car swerved into Tracy's. She doesn't really expect to prevail on the counterclaim, but thinks that if the jury feels that there was a possibility of Tracy's negligence they might diminish Tracy's award accordingly. **As an evidence specialist what advice do you give her?** Assume the trial is in an "eyewitness jurisdiction."

Problem IV–68. Cars driven by Jones and Smith collide head-on. Smith is killed instantly but Jones survives. The skid marks are such that it is impossible to state which car was over the center line. You are the attorney representing Smith's estate. You have five witnesses available all of whom will testify that Smith was in the habit of always driving on the extreme right hand side of the road. Indeed his reluctance to move to the left, even to pass, was something of a joke among his friends. You would love to get this evidence in, but you know that your jurisdiction follows the eyewitness rule even when, as in this case, a party is the sole eyewitness. **What else would you wish to know about the law in your jurisdiction before you give up and plan your case on the assumption that this evidence will prove inadmissible?**

SECTION III. CONCLUSION

We have now discussed all the rules in Article IV of the Federal Rules of Evidence except one, FRE 412, the federal "rape shield" law. FRE 412 seeks to exclude certain evidence of the past sexual behavior of alleged rape victims insofar as the Constitution allows. Thus, the parameters of the rule cannot be fully understood unless one knows something about the applicable constitutional law. For this reason we postpone our discussion of FRE 412 until Chapter Seven where we discuss the confrontation and compulsory process clauses of the sixth amendment.

In presenting the relevance rules in this chapter we have tried to suggest that there is a unity of theme to these disparate rules. With one exception, they are all instances where evidence of the type precluded seems likely to be generally of low relevance. This frees the court to give special attention to those factors which suggest that an exclusionary rule is appropriate. The factors that most commonly lead to this conclusion are: prejudice, surprise, the possibilities of confusion and waste of time inherent in disputations over collateral facts,

and extrinsic policy reasons peculiar to the specific rules. We have argued that in the one area where this analysis does not apply, the area of habit evidence, an exclusionary rule is not appropriate. The federal rules have taken this position.

Our suggestion that the kinds of evidence we have been discussing are generally of low probative value does not mean the excluded evidence is worthless. These forbidden kinds of evidence almost always have some probative value and on occasion may be quite persuasive. If there were not substantial reasons favoring the exclusion of such evidence, the general decision would be to admit.

In many ways this discussion of the relevance rules, with its emphasis on reasons for exclusion, presages the rest of the course. Much of evidence law deals with justifications for excluding evidence assumed to be of some probative value. In the hearsay area, statements are excluded because we fear that they are so unreliable that the jury will be unable to give them their proper weight. In the privilege area, we reject information in order to protect certain valued relationships. We reject some opinions because there are certain issues on which we want the jury's decision to be entirely its own. In these areas and others there is often a tension between the factors justifying exclusion and the fact that, if properly used, relevant evidence is always of some value to a decision maker. As in the relevance area, we will see that this tension often leads to more exceptions than there are rules. We will also see that, as Justice Jackson stated in *Michelson,* what appears to be an illogical series of compromises may, on balance, make a good deal of sense.

Throughout this chapter we have posed questions and problems. We would like to leave you with the most fundamental question in this area. *Are the relevance rules necessary? Would it not make more sense to abolish the specific rules and exceptions and instead allow courts to decide these matters guided by general principles of the type specified in FRE 402 and 403?* There are not necessarily any correct answers to these questions, but your ability to formulate the kinds of considerations which bear on an answer will say a good deal about what you have learned thus far.

BIBLIOGRAPHY

McCormick, Chs. 17–19 (1972).

2 Weinstein's Evidence ¶¶ 404[01]–411[11] (1981).

Bell, Admissions Arising Out of Compromise—Are They Relevant?, 31 Tex.L.Rev. 239 (1953).

Falkner, Extrinsic Policies Affecting Admissibility, 10 Rutgers L.Rev. 574 (1956).

Falkner & Steffen, Evidence of Character: From the "Crucible of the Community" to the "Couch of the Psychiatrist," 102 U.Pa.L.Rev. 980 (1954).

Fannin, Disclosure of Insurance in Negligence Trials—The Arizona Rule, 5 Ariz.L.Rev. 83 (1963).

Green, Relevancy and Its Limits, Law & Social Order 553 (1969).

Hale, Some Comments on Character Evidence and Related Topics, 72 So. Cal.L.Rev. 341 (1949).

Kuhns, The Propensity to Misunderstand the Character of Specific Acts Evidence, 66 Iowa L.Rev. 777 (1981).

Ladd, Determination of Relevancy, 31 Tulane L.Rev. 81 (1956).

Levin, Rationale of Habit Evidence, 16 Syracuse L.Rev. 39 (1964).

Likert, Precautionary Measure and Compromises, 1945 Wis.L.Rev. 309.

Schmertz, Relevance and Its Policy Counterweights: A Brief Excursion Through Article IV of the Proposed Rules of Evidence, 33 Fed.B.J. 1 (1974).

Schwartz, The Exclusionary Rule on Subsequent Repairs—A Rule in Need of Repair, The Forum 1 (1971).

Slough, Relevancy Unraveled, 5 Kan.L.Rev. 424, 675 and 6 Kan.L.Rev. 38 (1957).

Slough & Knightly, Other Views, Other Crimes, 41 Iowa L.Rev. 325 (1956).

Stone, The Rule of Exclusion of Similar Fact Evidence: America, 51 Harv.L.Rev. 988 (1938).

Tracy, Admissibility of Statements of Fact Made During Negotiations for Compromise, 34 Mich.L.Rev. 514 (1936).

Williams, The Problem of Similar Fact Evidence, 5 Dalhousie L.J. 281 (1979).

Chapter Five

EXAMINATION AND IMPEACHMENT: THE DEVELOPMENT OF TESTIMONY

SECTION I.   THE EXAMINATION OF WITNESSES

A.   DIRECT EXAMINATION

The basic rules of direct examination were introduced in Chapter One. We discuss them in more detail here.[1] The direct examiner is the person at whose instance a witness is placed on the stand. Direct examination is usually used to introduce those facts that are essential to a claim or defense.   It may also be used to lay the foundation for exhibits or subsequent testimony and to raise questions about the quality of an opponent's case. However it is used, the direct examiner, unlike the cross-examiner, typically hopes that the fact finder will accept his witnesses' testimony as true.   In the Whale case, for example, Officer Norton testified on direct examination that he purchased marihuana from Whale.   The prosecutor had to elicit this information in order to survive a motion for a judgment of acquittal at the close of his case-in-chief.   He had to convince the jury that Norton was truthful in order to prevail in the end.   When Whale took the stand to give his version of the events, Whale hoped, in vain as it turned out, that he rather than Norton would be believed.   Both Norton and Whale told their stories on direct examination.   Each was presented to the jury as a truth-teller.   One was believed; one was not, and the verdict turned on the difference.   The jury's choice turned in part on the quality of the direct examinations, in part on the way the witnesses withstood cross-examination, and in part on the way these crucial stories fit in with the other evidence in the case.

At common law direct examination is restricted in ways that cross-examination is not.   The two most important restrictions are that the direct examiner must ordinarily ask only nonleading questions and the direct examiner cannot impeach those witnesses he calls to testify.

The Federal Rules maintain the restriction on the use of leading questions.   FRE 611(c) provides, "Leading questions should not be used on the direct examination of a witness except as may be necessary to develop his testimony.   Ordinarily leading questions should be permitted on cross-examination.   * * *"   Leading questions are questions that suggest the answer desired.   They are prohibited on direct examination because of the expectation that a party will call "friendly" witnesses, and the fear that a friendly witness will be prone to adopt whatever words the lawyer puts in his mouth.   Since the persuasive power of a witness' story depends on his knowledge and credibility it is important that the jury hear the witness' story in his own words.[2]   Where the assumption of a

---

1. Expert testimony may sound very different from the testimony of ordinary witnesses and experts may draw on sources that ordinary witnesses cannot.   However, except insofar as experts may be examined by hypothetical questions, there is no difference in the way experts and non-experts may be questioned.   Examination by hypothetical questions is discussed in Chapter Ten.

2. For a careful attempt to analyze why objections to leading questions are made and how judges should respond to them see Denbeaux & Risinger, Questioning Questions: Objections to Form in the Interrogation of

friendly witness is clearly mistaken, as where a witness is identified with an opposing party, the restriction on the use of leading questions is relaxed.[3]

The stories that witnesses tell on direct examination are, no doubt, more spontaneous and more prone to surprise than they would be if leading questions were routinely employed. However, this does not mean their stories are likely to surprise. Lawyers must, if they are to be effective advocates, prepare the witnesses on whom they are going to rely. At a minimum this means talking to witnesses and learning the details of their stories. When witnesses are both crucial and cooperative a rehearsal of the direct examination will be in order. It is the truly exceptional situation in which a lawyer calls a witness whose testimony he cannot predict.

A good direct examination anticipates questions that might be raised on cross-examination. A cross-examiner can focus on ambiguity or on an unintended nuance and make the witness seem less competent or less credible than he is. Careful preparation, including a mock examination, can help avoid these problems. But not all defects in testimony are semantic. Witnesses may have memory problems and

information gaps. A direct examination that candidly acknowledges a witness' imperfections may leave a jury more willing to trust the witness than an examination that glosses over flaws in the witness or his testimony only to have them revealed on cross-examination. The law in many states recognizes this by allowing the direct examiner to reveal not only failures of memory or knowledge, which the ethical attorney would be required to reveal in any event, but also personal shortcomings, such as the prior conviction of a felony, which might be used for impeachment on cross-examination. When the direct examiner reveals such flaws of character, it is called "drawing the sting." The imagery captures an important reason for bringing out such information on direct. One can be sure that the direct examiner will present the information in a less damning way than the adversary.

A direct examiner may want a witness to testify on only one aspect of a case. Where direct testimony is so confined, cross-examination is, in most American jurisdictions, similarly restricted. FRE 611(b) follows the majority of states in limiting cross-examination to the scope of direct. It also follows the common law in treating mat-

Witnesses, 33 Ark. L. Rev. 439 (1980). The authors suggest seven ways that judges might respond to improper leading questions and argue that in some instances a mistrial should be declared following an intentional course of improper questioning. Conley, Barr & Lind's article, The Power of Language: Presentational Style in the Courtroom, 1978 Duke L.J. 1375, suggests another function of leading questions. They may help overcome style problems of witnesses who seem less "powerful" than other witnesses.

3. **FRE 611 permits leading questions to be used on the direct examination of witnesses who are hostile to the direct examiner, adverse parties, and persons identified with adverse parties. The idea here is that in some situations, it is doubtful that the person who calls a witness has an opportunity to prepare the witness. It is doubtful, for example, that an adverse party will cooperate with his opponent's lawyer.**

Also, someone who has shown hostility— i.e., some bias towards a party or a clear reluctance to help one party and a preference for the other—is not going to happily take the witness stand on behalf of the side he disfavors. Thus, there is good reason to permit the attorney to ask pointed questions of these witnesses.

If a direct examiner is permitted to ask leading questions, it might be argued that the cross-examiner, who is assumed to be favored by the witness and who may have had an opportunity to prepare the witness before trial, should not be permitted to lead the witness. It can be argued in response, however, that the cross-examiner may not have prepared the same things as the direct examiner and that leading questions should therefore be permitted. Generally speaking, the judge has discretion to control the kind of questions that are put to such witnesses.

ters that bear on credibility as always within the scope of the direct.

The "scope of direct rule" means that where a direct examiner has already established or can establish a point, let us call it A, by reliable testimony, he may call a witness whose testimony on A would be unhelpful for the sole purpose of addressing another point, B. The direct examiner may also avoid raising an issue, let us again call it A, as part of his case-in-chief by making sure none of his witnesses discuss it. In neither of these circumstances is the witness barred from ever testifying about A, but if the cross-examiner wants to elicit such testimony, he must wait until his case-in-chief and then call the witness as his own. Even in the so-called "wide open rule" jurisdictions where cross-examination can exceed the scope of direct, the cross-examiner may, in the discretion of court, be required to use non-leading questions to probe matters that were not covered in the direct examination. Where this is the case, the attempt to develop new information by non-leading questions may undercut the effects of a rigorous cross-examination and so may not be attempted.

Only in special circumstances, typically where the opposing witness is hostile, does the direct examiner have occasion to object to the testimony he is eliciting. The direct examiner must live with unwelcome answers so long as they are fairly responsive to the questions he has asked. On occasion direct testimony will reveal harmful information that would have been objectionable in the adversary's case-in-chief. In such circumstances, the direct examiner may attempt to withdraw the question and strike the answer, but the court may well hold that the examiner has opened the door and must live with the answer he has received.

It is the prospective cross-examiner who must be concerned with objecting. He must worry about whether testimony is more prejudicial than probative, and he must be alert to testimony that runs afoul of some specific prohibition. Testimony may be objectionable, but if the cross-examiner is silent, the direct examination will proceed.

This does not mean that the direct examiner is unconcerned with the rules of evidence. First, he must be certain that all his evidence can be presented in accordance with the rules. Second, he should try to present it in this way. Even though otherwise inadmissible evidence will be received if the opponent does not object, it is unethical to present evidence knowing that there is no good faith argument for admissibility. It is also likely to be bad strategy. Offering testimony that is riddled with objectionable material offers the opponent an opportunity to disrupt one's cases, generates a string of adverse rulings from the bench, and may sorely try the judge's patience. In the extreme case where it appears that a lawyer has intentionally tried to insert objectionable material, a mistrial may result if the jury has been exposed to the evidence. Thus, the direct examiner in preparing witnesses to testify should instruct them on what is and is not permitted.[4]

At one time a direct examiner could not impeach a witness unless the witness were obviously hostile.[5] Now, under FRE 607,

---

4. For a good discussion of various techniques of handling witnesses on direct examination, see A. Morrill, Trial Diplomacy 32–52 (2d ed. 1972).

5. Unfriendly witnesses were often not considered hostile at common law. Hostility was either defined in terms of status (opposing parties and those closely identified with them) or by the quality of the testimony given. Testimony that positively hurt the direct examiner's case was, in many states, considered a sufficient indicator of hostility to justify cross-examination by leading questions and a right of impeachment. However, testimony that failed to enhance the direct examiner's case as the direct examiner expected was not treated as a sufficient indicator of hostility to justify proceeding as if on cross-examination.

any party can impeach any witness. This change in the common law is unimportant when a witness is friendly, but it may matter when a witness is neutral, or unfriendly but not obviously hostile. The right to impeach one's own witness is particularly important when a witness changes a story he has previously told the direct examiner or is reluctant to testify to what he does know. Techniques of impeachment are discussed in Section II, below.

———

Problem V–1. Imagine the following colloquy between a defense lawyer and a witness one week before the witness is scheduled to testify for the defendant in an automobile accident case.

LAWYER (L): Let's go over part of your testimony to make certain you are ready to testify.

WITNESS (W): Fine, how should we proceed?

L. I'll ask you questions, the same questions that I shall ask at trial. Then I'll cross-examine you. My first question is whether you were in the vicinity of Broad and Main Streets on January 22, 1974? **W.** Yes, I was there at noon.

L. What did you see? **W.** I saw an automobile accident.

L. Did you notice exactly what caused the accident? **W.** Yes.

L. What? **W.** The driver of the '69 Chevy ran a red light.

L. Do you see the driver in court today? **W.** Yes.

L. Where? **W.** There.

L. Did you see the '73 Volkswagen as it approached the light? **W.** Yes, it had a green light and proceeded accordingly.

L. Now let me cross-examine you. How far from the light were you when you saw the accident? **W.** About twenty yards.

L. How far is twenty yards—give me an approximation here in the courtroom. **W.** I never thought about that.

L. Did you actually see the green light for the defendant? **W.** Yes.

L. How could you see both lights at the same time? **W.** I couldn't have. But I know that defendant was in the right.

L. Perhaps you saw one light or the other and drew a reasonable inference about the other light. You'd better think about that. While you're at it, you might want to work on estimating how far twenty yards is. **W.** Wow, this is harder than I thought.

L. A witness can be eaten alive on cross-examination if even small mistakes or inconsistencies appear. Let me try a few more questions. First, you said you were at the corner at noon, are you sure? **W.** Well, it was approximately noon. Perhaps I should say that.

L. Perhaps, try this one. Are you certain that the defendant had the right of way? **W.** Yes, very certain.

L. Because you saw the traffic light, right? **W.** Yes.

L. How many minutes or seconds did you spend looking at the light? **W.** Oh, I see the problem.

L. Why were you staring at a light on the corner where you were not going to cross? **W.** I don't know. I'd better think about my reason and maybe be a little less certain about things.

L. Let me try to suggest to you ways of expressing your recollection which don't leave you open for vigorous cross-examination. I think we can anticipate the problems and deal with them.

Is the attorney acting ethically? If there are problems with this conduct, what are they? What does this dialogue suggest about effective tactics on cross-examination? Get together with a friend. Discuss the details of an accident. Conduct a direct examination. Now tell your friend to make up the details of an accident but not discuss them with you. Conduct the direct examination on the assumption that your friend is a friendly but unprepared witness.

Problem V–2. Sylvester Stallion, a rock and roll singer with a local band, brings a medical malpractice suit against Dr. Rolan Ginger, who treated Stallion for a bad back. Ginger performed a spinal fusion which Stallion now claims was unnecessary as well as unsuccessful. Stallion, unable to get an expert witness to support his claim, calls Ginger himself to testify as part of the plaintiff's case. Stallion's attorney asks for permission to put leading questions to Ginger and the court grants the request. A portion of the direct examination is set forth below:

Q. Doctor, you cannot say that the spinal fusion you performed actually was necessary, can you?

A. Yes, I think it was necessary.

Q. But doctor, you might be wrong, isn't that correct?

A. Yes, I suppose so, but I don't think I am wrong.

Q. Other doctors might disagree with you, isn't that possible?

A. Anything is possible.

Q. A spinal fusion that is performed when it is not necessary would be a rather bad thing, wouldn't you agree?

A. Yes, any unnecessary surgery, especially something like a fusion, which itself can cause permanent inconvenience, is serious.

Q. How sure should you be that a fusion is necessary before recommending it?

A. I like to be as sure as I can be.

Q. In this case, did you recommend that the patient Stallion get a second opinion?

A. No I did not.

Q. Wouldn't a second opinion have made you a little more comfortable?

A. Perhaps, but I did not think it was necessary.

Q. Then you cannot say you were as sure as you could have been, is that correct?

A. I was sure enough.

Q. But not as sure as you might have been had there been a second opinion similar to yours.

A. Of course not.   I suppose I could have been even more sure.

Q. Is it possible that other doctors would have been less likely to recommend surgery than you?

A. It is possible.

Q. Is it possible that many doctors would have not recommended surgery at the time you did?

A. I don't know what many would have said.   I know what I thought was correct.

Q. Then you cannot deny that many doctors would not have recommended surgery?

A. I cannot say.

Q. If many would have, they might think you exercised bad judgment, isn't that so?

A. I don't know what they would think.

Q. You can't deny it though, can you?

A. I can't deny that any more than I can answer other questions about what people whom I don't know think about something.

Is this sufficient to make out a prima facie claim of negligence?   What facts has the examiner actually established?   How would the direct examination have looked if Stallion had found a friendly expert?

B. CROSS-EXAMINATION

We have touched briefly upon cross-examination in previous chapters.   In this chapter we examine it more fully.   The word "cross-examination" brings to mind a devastating assault on the credibility of opposing witnesses, but "cross-examination" is not necessarily synonymous with "attack."   Often the cross-examiner does not even aspire to the destruction of a witness' credibility;   raising even slight doubts about credibility may be a significant ac-complishment.   At times one may even have a stake in the credibility of an adversary's witness, for witnesses can be led to restate facts on cross-examination so that damaging testimony may be transformed into neutral or even helpful evidence.   The way in which the cross-examiner treats a witness depends on many things: the importance of the witness' testimony, the strength of the witness' story, the lawyer's assessment of the likelihood that the witness will be believed, the probability that the witness will succumb under vigorous questioning, the lawyer's judgment as to whether the witness might prove helpful, the need for helpful evidence, and some feeling as to how the jury will react to particular approaches to different witnesses. Often the wisest course is not to cross-examine at all.

A lawyer who concludes that the potential advantages of attack or the disadvantages of failing to attack outweigh the dangers involved may strive to do more than merely demonstrate that there are gaps or weaknesses in testimony. Sometimes, the lawyer would like to show that the testifying witness is not worthy of belief. In Section II of this chapter we will discuss some of the devices available to the lawyer who has this goal in mind.

It is difficult to generalize about effective techniques of cross-examination. Sometimes there seem to be as many views on the subject as there are trial lawyers. Similarly, identifying and categorizing common errors, particularly errors of strategy, is not easy. Perhaps the most we can hope to accomplish is to present those ideas about cross-examination that appear to receive general approbation. Wellman's book, *The Art of Cross-Examination,* first published in 1903, is considered by many to be the single best treatment of this topic. It is a fascinating book, well worth reading in its entirety.

WELLMAN, THE ART OF CROSS-EXAMINATION

7–11, 19–23, 142–45, 193–96, 204–06
(4th ed. 1936)

THE MANNER OF CROSS-EXAMINATION

It needs but the simple statement of the nature of cross-examination to demonstrate its indispensable character in all trials

of questions of fact. No cause reaches the stage of litigation unless there are two sides to it. If the witnesses on one side deny or qualify the statements made by those on the other, which side is telling the truth? Not necessarily which side is offering perjured testimony,—there is far less intentional perjury in the courts than the inexperienced would believe.[6] But which side is honestly mistaken,—for, on the other hand, evidence itself is far less trustworthy than the public usually realizes. The opinions of which side are warped by prejudice or blinded by ignorance? Which side has had the power or opportunity of correct observation? How shall we tell, how [to] make it apparent to a jury of disinterested men who are to decide between the litigants? Obviously, by the means of cross-examination.

If all witnesses had the honesty and intelligence to come forward and scrupulously follow the letter as well as the spirit of the oath, "to tell the truth, the whole truth, and nothing but the truth," and if all advocates on either side had the necessary experience, combined with honesty and intelligence, and were similarly sworn to *develop* the whole truth and nothing but the truth, of course there would be no occasion for cross-examination, and the occupation of the cross-examiner would be gone. But as yet no substitute has ever been found for cross-examination as a means of separating truth from falsehood, and of reducing exaggerated statements to their true dimensions.

* * *

Cross-examination is generally considered to be the most difficult branch of the multifarious duties of the advocate. Success in the art, as someone has said, comes more often to the happy possessor of a genius for it. Great lawyers have often failed lamentably in it, while marvellous succes

6. **If this is actually the case, and most people believe that it is, ask yourself whether you approve of the various im-** peachment devices discussed in Section II of this chapter?

has crowned the efforts of those who might otherwise have been regarded as of a mediocre grade in the profession. Yet personal experience and the emulation of others, trained in the art, are the surest means of obtaining proficiency in this all important prerequisite of a competent trial lawyer.

It requires the greatest ingenuity; a habit of logical thought; clearness of perception in general; infinite patience and self-control; power to read men's minds intuitively, to judge of their characters by their faces, to appreciate their motives; ability to act with force and precision; a masterful knowledge of the subject-matter itself; an extreme caution; and, above all, the *instinct to discover the weak point* in the witness under examination. One has to deal with a prodigious variety of witnesses testifying under an infinite number of differing circumstances. It involves all shades and complexions of human morals, human passions, and human intelligence. It is a mental duel beween counsel and witness.

In discussing the methods to employ when cross-examining a witness, let us imagine ourselves at work in the trial of a cause, and at the close of the direct examination of a witness called by our adversary. The first inquiries would naturally be: Has the witness testified to anything that is material against us? Has his testimony injured our side of the case? Has he made an impression with the jury against us? Is it necessary for us to cross-examine him at all?

Before dismissing a witness, however, the possibility of being able to elicit some new facts in our own favor should be taken into consideration. If the witness is apparently truthful and candid, this can be readily done by asking plain, straightforward questions. If, however, there is any reason to doubt the willingness of the witness to help develop the truth, it may be necessary to proceed with more caution, and possibly to put the witness in a position

where it will appear to the jury that he could tell a good deal if he wanted to, and then leave him. The jury will thus draw the inference that, had he spoken, it would have been in our favor.

But suppose the witness has testified to material facts against us, and it becomes necessary to break the force of his testimony, or else abandon all hope of a jury verdict. How shall we begin? How shall we tell whether the witness has made an honest mistake, or has committed perjury? The methods to be used in his cross-examination in the two alternatives would naturally be quite different. There is a marked distinction between discrediting the *testimony* and discrediting the *witness*. It is largely a matter of instinct on the part of the trained examiner. Some people call it the language of the eye, or the tone of the voice, or the countenance of the witness, or his "manner of testifying", or all combined, that betrays the wilful perjurer. It is difficult to say exactly what it is, excepting that constant practice seems to enable a trial lawyer to form a fairly accurate judgment on this point. A skilful cross-examiner seldom takes his eye from an important witness while he is being examined by his adversary. Every expression of his face, especially his mouth, even every movement of his hands, his manner of expressing himself, his whole bearing— all help the examiner to arrive at an accurate estimate of his integrity.

Let us assume, then, that we have been correct in our judgment of this particular witness, and that he is trying to describe honestly the occurrences to which he has testified, but has fallen into a serious mistake, through ignorance, blunder, or what not, which must be exposed to the minds of the jury. How shall we go about it? This brings us at once to the first important factor in our discussion, the *manner* of the cross-examiner.

It is absurd to suppose that any witness who has sworn positively to a certain set of facts, even if he has inadvertently stretched the truth, is going to be readily induced by a lawyer to alter them and acknowledge his mistake. People as a rule do not reflect upon their meagre opportunities for observing facts, and rarely suspect the frailty of their own powers of observation. They come to court, when summoned as witnesses, prepared to tell what they think they know; and in the beginning they resent an attack upon their story as they would one upon their integrity.

If the cross-examiner allows the witness to suspect, from his manner toward him at the start, that he distrusts his integrity, he will straighten himself in the witness chair and mentally defy him at once. If, on the other hand, the counsel's manner is courteous and conciliatory, the witness will soon lose the fear all witnesses have of the cross-examiner, and can almost imperceptibly be induced to enter into a discussion of his testimony in a fair minded spirit, which, if the cross-examiner is clever, will soon disclose the weak points in the testimony. The sympathies of the jury are invariably on the side of the witness, and they are quick to resent any discourtesy toward him.[7] They are willing to admit his *mistakes,* if you can make them apparent, but are slow to believe him *guilty of perjury.* Alas, how often this is lost sight of in our daily court experiences! One is constantly brought face to face with lawyers who act as if they thought that every one who testifies against their side of the case is committing wilful perjury. No wonder they accomplish so little with their *cross*-examination! By their shouting, browbeating style they often confuse the wits of the witness, it is true; but they fail to discredit him with the jury. On the contrary, they elicit sympathy for the witness they are attacking, and little realize that their "vigorous cross-examination," at the end of which they sit down with evident self-satisfaction,

has only served to close effectually the mind of at least one fair-minded juryman against their side of the case, and as likely as not it has brought to light some important fact favorable to the other side which had been overlooked in the examination-in-chief.

* * *

THE MATTER OF CROSS-EXAMINATION

If by experience we have learned the first lesson of our art,—to control our *manner* toward the witness even under the most trying circumstances,—it then becomes important that we should turn our attention to the *matter* of our cross-examination. By our manner toward a witness we may have in a measure disarmed him, or at least thrown him off his guard, while his memory and conscience are being ransacked by subtle and searching questions, the scope of which will be hardly apparent to himself; but it is only with the matter of our cross-examination that we can hope to destroy him.

What shall be our first mode of attack? Shall we adopt the fatal method of those we see around us daily in the courts, and proceed to take the witness over the same story that he has already given our adversary, in the absurd hope that he is going to change it in the repetition, and not retell it with double effect upon the jury? Or shall we rather avoid carefully his original story, except in so far as is necessary to refer to it in order to point out its weak spots? Whatever we do, let us do it with quiet dignity, with absolute fairness to the witness; and let us frame our questions in such simple language that there can be no misunderstanding or confusion. Let us imagine ourselves in the jury box, so that we may see the evidence from their standpoint. We are not trying to make a reputation for ourselves with the audience as

7. **Is it possible that juries tend to be sympathetic to some witnesses and not to others? For example, would cross-examination of a police officer be viewed by a jury** in the same way as cross-examination of one of the defendant's accomplices? If not, might browbeating sometimes be useful?

"smart" cross-examiners. We are thinking rather of our client and our employment by him to win the jury to his side of the case. Let us also avoid asking questions recklessly, without any definite purpose. Unskilful questions are worse than none at all, and only tend to uphold rather than to destroy the witness.

All through the direct testimony of our imaginary witness, it will be remembered, we were watching his every movement and expression. Did we find an opening for our cross-examination? Did we detect the weak spot in his narrative? If so, let us waste no time, but go direct to the point. It may be that the witness's situation in respect to the parties or the subject-matter of the suit should be disclosed to the jury, as one reason why his testimony has been shaded somewhat in favor of the side on which he testifies. It may be that he has a direct interest in the result of the litigation, or is to receive some indirect benefit therefrom. Or he may have some other tangible motive which he can gently be made to disclose. Perhaps the witness is only suffering from that partisanship, so fatal to fair evidence, of which oftentimes the witness himself. is not conscious. It may even be that, if the jury only knew the scanty means the witness has had for obtaining a correct and certain knowledge of the very facts to which he has sworn so glibly, aided by the adroit questioning of the opposing counsel, this in itself would go far toward weakening the effect of his testimony. It may appear, on the other hand, that the witness had the best possible opportunity to observe the facts he speaks of, but had not the intelligence to observe these facts correctly. Two people may witness the same occurrence and yet take away with them an entirely different impression of it; but each, when called to the witness stand, may be willing to swear to that impression as a fact. Obviously, both accounts of the same transaction cannot be true; whose impressions were wrong? Which had the better opportunity to see? Which had the keener power of perception? All this we may very properly term the matter of our cross-examination.[8]

It is one thing to have the opportunity of observation, or even the intelligence to observe correctly, but it is still another to be able to retain accurately, for any length of time, what we have once seen or heard, and what is perhaps more difficult still— to be able to describe it intelligibly. Many witnesses have seen one part of a transaction and heard about another part, and later on become confused in their own minds, or perhaps only in their own modes of expression, as to what they have seen themselves and what they have heard from others. All witnesses are prone to exaggerate, to enlarge or minimize the facts to which they take oath.

A very common type of witness, met with almost daily, is the man who, having witnessed some event years ago, suddenly finds that he is to be called as a court witness. He immediately attempts to recall his original impressions; and gradually, as he talks with the attorney who is to examine him, he amplifies his story with new details which he leads himself, or is led, to believe are recollections and which he finally swears to as facts. Many people seem to fear that an "I don't know" answer will be attributed to ignorance on their part. Although perfectly honest in intention, they are apt, in consequence, to

8. It should be obvious that the opening for cross-examination may only be apparent because of information learned from investigation and discovery. Partisanship, inadequate opportunity to observe, and similar factors that tend to discredit testimony may not identify themselves on direct examination. Without information obtained before trial, cross-examination will often be ineffective. Or worse, questions may inadvertently be asked on cross-examination which heighten the impact of the witness' story.

complete their story by recourse to their imagination. And few witnesses fail, at least in some part of their story, to entangle facts with their own beliefs and inferences. * * *

All these considerations should readily suggest a line of questions, varying with each witness examined, that will, if closely followed, be likely to separate appearance from reality and to reduce exaggerations to their proper proportions. It must further be borne in mind that the jury should not merely see the mistake; they should be made to appreciate at the time why and whence it arose. It is fresher then and scores a more lasting effect than if left until the summing up, and then drawn to the attention of the jury.

The experienced examiner can usually tell, after a few simple questions, what line to pursue. Picture the scene in your own mind; closely inquire into the sources of the witness's information, and draw your own conclusions as to how his mistake arose, and why he formed his erroneous impressions. Exhibit plainly your belief in his integrity and your desire to be fair with him, and try to beguile him into being candid with you. Then when the particular foible which has affected his testimony has once been discovered, he can easily be led to expose it to the jury. His mistakes should be drawn out often by inference rather than by direct question, because all witnesses have a dread of self-contradiction. If he sees the connection between your inquiries and his own story, he will draw upon his imagination for explanations, before you get the chance to point out to him the inconsistency between his later statement and his original one. It is often wise to break the effect of a witness' story by putting questions to him that will acquaint the jury at once with the fact that there is another more probable story to be told later on, to disclose to them something of the defense, as it were. Avoid the mistake, so common among the

inexperienced, of making much of trifling discrepancies. It has been aptly said that "juries have no respect for small triumphs over a witness' self-possession or memory." Allow the loquacious witness to talk on; he will be sure to involve himself in difficulties from which he can never extricate himself. Some witnesses prove altogether too much; encourage them and lead them by degrees into exaggerations that will conflict with the common sense of the jury. Under no circumstances put a false construction on the words of a witness; there are few faults in an advocate more fatal with a jury.

If, perchance, you obtain a really favorable answer, leave it and pass quietly to some other inquiry. The inexperienced examiner in all probability will repeat the question with the idea of impressing the admission upon his hearers, instead of reserving it for the summing up, and will attribute it to bad luck that the witness corrects his answer or modifies it in some way, so that the point is lost. He is indeed a poor judge of human nature who supposes that if he exults over his success during the cross-examination, he will not quickly put the witness on his guard to avoid all future favorable disclosures.

* * *

CROSS-EXAMINATION TO THE "FALLACIES OF TESTIMONY"

* * *

No one can frequent our courts of justice for any length of time without finding himself aghast at the daily spectacle presented by seemingly honest and intelligent men and women who array themselves upon opposite sides of a case and testify under oath to what appear to be absolutely contradictory statements of fact.

It will be my endeavor in what follows to deal with this subject from its psychological point of view and to trace some of the *causes* of these unconscious mistakes of witnesses, so far as it is possible. The inquiry is most germane to what has preceded, for unless the advocate comprehends something of the *sources* of the fallacies of testimony, it surely would become a hopeless task for him to try to illuminate them by his cross-examinations.[9]

It has been aptly said that "Knowledge is only the impression of one's mind and *not the fact itself,* which may present itself to many minds in many different aspects." The *unconscious sense impressions*—sight, sound, or touch—would be the same to every human mind; but once you awaken the mind to consciousness, then the original impression takes on all the color of motive, past experience, and character of the individual mind that receives it. The *sensation* by itself will be always the same. The variance arises when the sensation is *interpreted* by the *individual* and becomes a *perception* of his own mind.

When a man on a hot day looks at a running stream and *sees* the delicious coolness, he is really adding something of himself, which he acquired by his past experience, to the *sense impression* which his eye gives him. A different individual might receive the impression of tepid insipidity instead of "delicious coolness," in accordance with his own past experiences. The material of sensation is acted on by the mind which clothes the sensation with the experiences of the individual. Helmholtz distinctly calls the perception of *distance,* for example, an unconscious *inference,*— a mechanically performed act of judgment.

The *interpretation* of a sensation is, therefore, the act of the individual, and different individuals will naturally vary in their interpretations of the same sensation

according to their previous experiences and various mental characteristics. This process is most instantaneous, automatic, and unconscious. "The artist immediately sees details where to other eyes there is a vague or confused mass; the naturalist sees an animal where the ordinary eye only sees a form." An adult sees an infinite variety of things that are meaningless to the child.

Likewise the same impression may be differently interpreted by the same individual at different times, due in part to variations in his *state of attention* at the moment, and in the degree of the mind's readiness to look at the impression in the required way. A timid man will more readily fall into the illusion of ghost-seeing than a cool-headed man, because he is less attentive to the actual impression of the moment.

Every mind is attentive to what it sees or hears, more or less, according to circumstances. It is in the region of hazy impressions that the imagination is wont to get in its most dangerous work. It often happens that, when the mind is either inactive, or is completely engrossed by some other subject of thought, the sensation may neither be perceived, nor interpreted, nor remembered, notwithstanding there may be evidence, derived from the respondent movements of the body, that it has been felt; as, for example, a person in a state of imperfect sleep may start at a loud sound, or turn away from a bright light, being conscious of the sensation and acting automatically upon it, but forming no kind of appreciation of its source and no memory of its occurrence. Such is the effect of sensation upon *complete* inattention. It thus appears that it is partly owing to this

9. The suggestion is that it is wise for counsel to attempt to isolate the causes of fallacious testimony and to endeavor to educate the trier of fact as to the causes. Why is this a good practice? Is the trier of fact concerned about the reasons for witness errors or only about whether errors have in fact been made? Is there another

reason for inquiring into the causes of error? Might an inquiry indicate whether cross-examination is likely to work? Are you convinced that cross-examination is as useful for testing a witness' interpretation of facts as for testing whether a witness paid attention to detail?

variation in *intensity* of attention that different individuals get such contradictory ideas of the same occurrence or conversation. When we add to this variance in the degree of attention, the variance, just explained, in the individual *interpretation* or coloring of the physical sensation, we have still further explanation of why men so often differ in what they think they have seen and heard.

Desire often gives rise to still further fallacy. Desire prompts the will to fix the attention on a certain point, and this causes the emphasis of this particular point or proposition to the exclusion of others. The will has the power of keeping some considerations out of view, and thereby *diminishes* their force, while it fixes the attention upon others, and thereby *increases* their force.

*   *   *

Still another most important factor and itself the source of an enormous number of "fallacies of testimony" is memory. * * * Sometimes the trace has been partially obliterated; and what remains may serve to give a very erroneous (because imperfect) view of the occurrence. *When it is one in which our own feelings are interested, we are extremely apt to lose sight of what goes on against them, so that the representation given by memory is altogether one-sided.*

*   *   *

TWO "LURKING, IF NOT GREAT DANGERS" THAT CONFRONT A CROSS-EXAMINER
BY MAX D. STEUER

Cross-examination is usually regarded as the means by which adverse witnesses are discredited, and it is for that purpose that it is usually employed by the Bar. The importance of it in that regard is self-evident. If through the instrumentality of the cross-examination the integrity of the witness is destroyed, even though it be not with respect to the particular testimony given at the trial, if his general reputation for truth and veracity is shown to be bad by his own utterances, clearly the examiner has very greatly helped his case. In this effort, however, there are two lurking, if not great, dangers. One is to cross-examine when it is quite unnecessary and the other to overdo the cross-examination. A recent experience will perhaps tend to illustrate the point.

A defendant in a criminal case was charged with having bribed a government inspector. Witnesses were called to establish the good reputation for truth and veracity of the defendant. There was a time when such testimony was of real and substantial value. At the present time, particularly in the federal court, under the rules there in vogue, that character of testimony has become of very slight importance. In this particular case, a number of witnesses took the stand to testify that the defendant bore an excellent reputation for truth and veracity. In each instance, the prosecutor undertook to cross-examine the reputation witness. What I am endeavoring to demonstrate is the ill effect of cross-examining when it really is not necessary or of over-doing it. The judge had several times stated that the direct examination was limited to the inquiry as to whether or not the witness knew the reputation for truth and veracity of the defendant by the speech of the people in his vicinity, and if he indicated that he did, to state whether that reputation was good or bad. He made it quite obvious that he did not consider testimony of that kind very significant in a case where a man was charged with bribing a government official, and particularly where it was conceded that money had passed from the defendant to the official after the latter had made known to the United States Attorney that it had been proffered and arrangement had been made so that the defendant should be caught in the act. Nevertheless, as has been stated, several witnesses were called to testify and in each instance they were asked, and this particular witness had put to him, the question:

Q. "When you came to know him and knew people who knew him, from the way that they have spoken of him, do you know what his reputation is in the community?"

The Prosecutor. "I object to the question as immaterial."

The Court. "Isn't it in the same form you expressed with the previous witness, by knowing the speech of those who know him?"

Defendant's Counsel. "Yes. I think very frequently you gather what a man's reputation is by the way people talk."

The Court. "There is a stereotyped form that you know well. Just ask him about it. You have asked that question many, many times."

Q. "By the speech of the people, have you come to know the reputation of the defendant for truth and veracity?" **A.** "I have."

CROSS-EXAMINATION:

Q. "Mr. Witness, you are not giving us hearsay statements of others, you are giving us your own opinion?" **A.** "I do."

The Prosecutor. "I move to strike it out as incompetent."

The Court. "Strike it out."

The Witness. "The opinion of others that I have heard—"

The Court. "Let us boil it down. You were asked by defendant's counsel if you know by the speech of those who knew him what his reputation was. You say you do?"

The Witness. "Yes."

The Court. "Tell us in a few words what that reputation is, not what you thought, but what you have heard."

The Witness. "I have heard that he is a very fine family man, he is a good father to his children, he is a good husband to his wife, that he lives in a very noble way in his neighborhood."

The Prosecutor. "I object and move to strike out the answer."

The Court. "It only has a bearing on his reputation for veracity and honesty. What is his reputation for veracity and honesty?"

The Witness. "Very good, first class."

The Court. "That is all that is necessary."

If there had not been a word of cross-examination, the usual humdrum of the witness being permitted to be asked one question or direct examination—to which the answer would be "very good, excellent, or even the best," practically no attention would be given to the testimony and nothing of importance would be elicited.[10] Here, by reason of an attempted cross-examination, the witness was permitted to say that the defendant "is a very fine family man, he is a good father to his children, he is a good husband to his wife, that he lives in a very noble way in his neighborhood." How much that testimony had to do with the disagreement of the jury in that particular case, nobody will ever know. But there may have been several men who reached the conclusion that if a man is "a very fine family man," is "a good father to his children," is "a good husband to his wife," and does "live in a very noble way in his neighborhood," it is difficult to believe that a person of that type would stoop to bribing a public official. At any rate, the testimony was made much more important and impressive after the cross-examination than [it] could possibly have been at the conclusion of the direct. Instances of that kind of course, can be multiplied. They occur with the utmost frequency, and it is important for a lawyer who prepares himself for the trial of causes to bear that in mind.

* * *

SOME COMMENTS ON THE "USES AND ABUSES" OF CROSS-EXAMINATION BY EMORY R. BUCKNER

More cross-examinations are suicidal than homicidal. There are two reasons for this: a mistaken conception as to the function of cross-examination, and faulty technique.

The purpose of cross-examination should be to catch truth, ever an elusive fugitive. If the testimony of a witness is wholly false, cross-examination is the first step toward its destruction. If the testimony of a witness is partly true and partly false, cross-examination is the first step in an effort to destroy that which is false. One should willingly accept that which he believes to be true whether or not it damages his case. If the testimony of a witness is false only in the sense that it exaggerates, distorts, garbles, or creates a wrong sense of proportion, then the function of cross-examination is to whittle down the story to its proper size and its proper relation to other facts. A composite photograph of a man's face with its ears ten times enlarged is not a true photograph of the man. If the cross-examiner believes the story told to be true and not exaggerated, and if the story changes counsel's appraisal of his client's case, then what is indicated is not a "vigorous" cross-examination but a negotiation for adjustment during the luncheon hour. If this fails, counsel should accept the story and get his settlement by the judgment of the court or verdict of the jury. No client is entitled to have his lawyer score a triumph by superior wits over a witness who the lawyer believes is telling the truth. Lawyers can do more for the improvement of the administration of justice in their daily practice than by serving on committees or making speeches at bar associations, however helpful that may be.[11]

As to technique. The worst cross-examiners belong to the major school. They

10. **The problem with the author's conclusion is that he himself concedes that at one time character evidence was important. Remember that there are two aspects to character evidence: what is said and who says it. Individuals who are held in high regard by the community still may have an impact on a jury in some cases. This may be particularly important in criminal cases where the jury may nullify application of the law to a particular individual.** Did the prosecutor err in cross-examining if he feared nullification in the particular case described? Note that the judge, not the prosecutor, opens the door to the damaging statements. Can a lawyer anticipate the judge's interference? Had the court not intervened, would the prosecutor have been entitled to have the witness' testimony stricken?

11. **Is an attorney entitled to make judgments about the credibility of wit-**

take careful notes of the witness's testimony, thus dividing their attention and sacrificing careful listening and study of the character and personality of the witness. When they rise they begin at the beginning and stoutly march through to the end. The court or jury always listens more attentively to cross-examination than direct examination. The direct examiner frequently puts too much of himself and too little of the witness in the direct testimony. Cross-examination is a combat and therefore always interesting. The lawyer who begins at the beginning and shouts his way to the end generally achieves the result of underscoring the important parts of the testimony, thus emphasizing by repetition the damage he may have suffered. He is a Micawber, always hoping that something will "turn up." Sometimes, though rarely, it does. A deliberately and wisely enforced repetition of the whole story from beginning to end sometimes is indicated to bring out the phonograph record quality of a coached witness.

A cross-examiner should limit himself to the vital points of the story he is seeking to discredit or to reduce to its proper proportions. A witness makes an unimportant error,—the train he took, the floor on which he got off, the route he drove in his car. The truth, if developed, will neither help nor hurt either side. Time is consumed, the evidence marshaled, the admission of error finally triumphantly wrung from the witness, all to no purpose. In the meantime, the cross-examiner has lost momentum, the high spots of his case are forgotten. In cross-examination as well as in direct examination, opening, and summation, the best advocate is he who never

leaves the turnpike of his case, who is never lured into attractive country roads, who never stops to buy frankfurters or cider on the way. The *motif* of the case, whether plaintiff's or defendant's, must ever recur. Cross-examination can frequently be skillfully and legitimately used as a sounding-board for the plaintiff's case or the defendant's defense.

Except where the circumstances make it wholly natural, there should be no place in cross-examination for indignation, shouting, belligerent hostility. A kindly voice and courtesy dig a better trap than high blood pressure. A jury regards the combat as unequal because of the skill and experience of the lawyer. Their sympathies are naturally with the underdog. They do not like to see him shouted at and browbeaten. Generally speaking, the adroit cross-examiner will endeavor to have the witness destroy himself and waive his personal triumph, keeping his co-operation in the destruction well in the background.

In many cases there is a fruitful field for preparation of cross-examination. Every letter or other document the anticipated witness may have signed, which has a bearing on the case, should be secured if possible and carefully studied. The life history of every expected witness should be ascertained, if possible. Diligent search should be made for conversations about the case in which the witness may have indulged. Many cases are won solely by cross-examination prepared in advance. Notwithstanding this fact, immediate improvisation is what is most frequently needed.

nesses called by the other side, or are such judgments solely for the trier of fact? Is it unethical to examine the weaknesses in a truthful witness' story? Is it improper to use cross-examination to probe testimony in the hope that the witness may succumb to the pressure of vigorous examination? Is there a difference between knowingly presenting false testimony as

part of a case-in-chief and making truthful testimony appear to lack credibility? Should a lawyer be reluctant to extensively cross-examine a witness whose testimony is consistent with what the lawyer knows of the case? Think about these questions as you proceed. These issues will be the focus of the final portion of this chapter.

When the cross-examiner rises and does not know exactly what to ask or where to begin, he should say "No cross-examination!"

————

The cross-examiner may ask leading questions and may impeach witnesses in all jurisdictions. Thus, cross-examiners are less limited than direct examiners in the nature of the questions they may put. But the cross-examiner, as noted earlier, may have to restrict questioning to the scope of direct. When permitted to exceed this scope, the rule barring leading questions may be in force.

During cross-examination, it is the direct examiner who is likely to be raising objections. The evidence rules that we examined in Chapters Three and Four and others that remain to be discussed are binding on cross-examination as well as on direct examination. In addition, there are certain matters of style that may be the subject of objection. Cross-examiners should not make statements in the guise of questions, they should not badger witnesses, and at some point they must recognize that a question has been answered, however disappointing the response. When cross-examiners raise objections during their own examinations, it is usually because a witness blurts out inadmissible evidence or does not respond to the substance of the examiner's questions.

Evidence rules control the scope and subject matter of cross-examination, but the quality of a cross-examination turns, as the Wellman excerpt indicates, on tactical decisions. Cross-examiners must decide on the basis of their experience and intuition how hard to press witnesses called by opponents.

A cross-examiner may have a variety of goals in examining witnesses. These include:

1. To have the witness repeat for purposes of emphasis something said on direct examination.

2. To have the witness repeat aspects of the direct examination in a different order so as to paint a different picture of the way facts fit together.

3. To clarify something that was said on direct examination.

4. To establish additional facts through the witness.

5. To discredit a portion of what the witness has said, leaving other parts of the testimony undisturbed.

6. To discredit the witness altogether.

The goals the examiner has in mind will dictate the strategy of cross-examination.

It is often assumed that cross-examiners do not know in advance how witnesses will respond to their questions. In modern discovery systems the assumption is often invalid. In civil cases witnesses may be deposed or interviewed by all parties to litigation. In criminal cases the defendant may avoid pretrial examination, but crucial prosecution witnesses may have testified in and been cross-examined at the preliminary hearing. The more discovery a lawyer has engaged in the better able he is to conduct a safe cross-examination that extends beyond the information elicited on direct examination.[12]

The following example may assist you in understanding what makes cross-examination effective. This example is taken from Goldstein and Lane, Trial Technique § 19.33 (1966). **What are the goals of the examiner? Is this a**

12. Bergman, Commentary, A Practical Approach to Cross-Examination: Safety First, 25 U.C.L.A. L.Rev. 547 (1978), outlines a safety model of cross-examination that may be especially useful when the attorney has not had much chance before trial to talk with a witness called by an opponent.

weak or strong cross-examination? Why? Would you have asked all the questions asked by this cross-examiner? Why or why not? What should the defendant's attorney do when given the chance for redirect exam?

[This is] a case involving a claim that an explosion and fire took place in a well on the farm of the defendant. The plaintiff, a real estate broker and builder, had come upon the premises to examine it for possible purchase for subdividing purposes. As he approached a well on the farm, in the presence of the farmer, he put a cigarette in his mouth and struck a match to light the cigarette. All of a sudden there was an explosion and before he knew it he was on fire.

The plaintiff had proved by a university chemistry professor who had done research work in the field for the Armed Forces and who had considerable experience during the war in gases and explosives that he had inspected the well after the fire and found various types of materials, decayed and foul smelling, forming gases capable of exploding into fire.

The farmer in his defense, on direct examination, claimed that there was no explosion and no fire of any consequence. His testimony tended to make light of the affair and to minimize the occurrence.

* * *

CROSS-EXAMINATION

Owned farm 15 years.

Q. You've owned that farm for some years, is that right? A. Yes.

Q. How long? A. 15 years.

Q. You bought it from another farmer? A. Yes.

Q. Do you know how long he had owned it? A. Yes, about ten years.

Q. The well involved here was on the farm before you bought the farm? A. Yes.

Well abandoned for 10 years.

Q. That was an abandoned well? A. Yes, it was.

Q. How long had it been abandoned? A. Oh, about ten years.

Q. You've had some stormy weather during that time, is that right? A. Well, we have the same weather that everyone has in this territory.

Q. What I mean is that you have had the usual average weather each year of rain and wind? A. Well, I suppose so.

Q. There was some water at the bottom of the well? A. Some.

Well not covered—not cleaned.

Q. Now, after the well was abandoned, you didn't cover it up? A. Nope.

Q. You had another well that you used closer to the house, is that right? **A.** Yes.

Q. In fact, you removed the equipment from the well involved here to the new well? **A.** That's right.

Q. You didn't clean out the well after that? **A.** When?

Q. Well, when you removed the equipment? **A.** No.

Q. The next year? **A.** No.

Q. The year after that? **A.** No.

Q. Well, during the next two years? **A.** Nope.

Q. That is also true during the next five years? **A.** Yes.

Wind had blown things in well.

Q. The wind had blown a lot of things into the well? **A.** I suppose some.

Q. It was somewhat smelly down there? **A.** Well, I didn't go down to smell it.

Q. But you knew it smelled like an unused well? **A.** I guess so.

Q. Now, on June 16th you went around the farm with Mr. Jones? **A.** Yes, I did.

Q. When you arrived near the well you were a little behind Mr. Jones, is that correct? **A.** Yes.

Q. The weather was warm? **A.** Yes.

Q. It was about 85° that afternoon? **A.** Yes.

Q. Mr. Jones stopped at the well? **A.** Yes.

Cigarettes lighted—wind blowing.

Q. He took out a package of cigarettes? **A.** Yes.

Q. Then he offered you one? **A.** Yes.

Q. You took one and then he took one; is that correct? **A.** Yes.

Q. The wind was blowing a little? **A.** Yes.

Q. In fact, more than a little? **A.** Yes.

Narrow questions only permitting narrow answers.

Q. He struck a match for you and managed to light your cigarette? **A.** Yes.

Q. Then he tried to light his but the wind started to blow and he was unable to light his cigarette with the first match? **A.** Yes.

Q. Then he got closer down to the well and he struck another match? **A.** Yes.

Explosion—flames—screams.

Q. Then you heard a noise and saw some flames?   A. Yes.

Q. You saw the flames?   A. Yes.

Q. You heard Mr. Jones scream?   A. Yes.

Q. That was a scream of pain?   A. Yes.

Q. You saw that his shirt was in flames?   A. Yes.

Q. You saw him trying to put it out?   A. Yes.

Defendant helps plaintiff.

Q. You tried to help him?   A. Yes.

Q. You got your hands burned?   A. Yes.

Q. Rather severely?   A. Yes.

Q. It was quite painful for you?   A. Yes.

Q. In fact, you were burned so that you looked around for something to help put out the fire?   A. Yes.

Q. You didn't succeed in putting out the fire up to that point?   A. No, sir.

Q. The flames got worse?   A. Yes.

Q. Mr. Jones was desperately trying to put out the flames?   A. Yes.

Q. In fact, you could hardly see him?   A. Yes.

Q. The flames had spread to his head, face, neck, and back?   A. Yes.

Q. And he was in pain?   A. Yes.

Empty cement bags to smother flames saved Jones' life?

Q. You finally put out the flames and probably saved his life?   A. Yes.

Q. How?   A. There were some empty cement bags left over from some work we were doing and I used those to smother the flames.

Q. You saw that Mr. Jones' arms, neck, chest and face were blackened?   A. Yes.

Q. He was screaming in pain?   A. Yes.

Q. He was pleading with you to get him to a doctor or to a hospital?   A. Yes.

Q. You used your truck and took him to the hospital in the city?   A. Yes.

Counsel: That is all.

Problem V–3. In a suit brought by Penny Phillips against Sam Donald arising out of an automobile accident at a main intersection in Phoenix, Arizona, Phillips has called Warren Oaky to testify that Donald's car entered the intersection after the traffic light turned red. On cross-examination the following colloquy ensues:

Defense Counsel: Weren't you drinking heavily on the evening of the accident, so heavily in fact that you were intoxicated at the time you say you saw Donald enter the intersection?

Plaintiff's Counsel: Wait a minute. May we approach the bench?

Court: Yes, please do.

Plaintiff's Counsel: Your honor, we wish to know what basis there is to support a suggestion that this witness had been drinking.

Court: What is the basis?

Defense Counsel: Your honor. We have no evidence that the witness was drinking. But we are entitled to ask the question anyway. After all, the witness might answer "yes," and then we would have established something important. If the witness answers "no," then the matter is over.

How would you rule as the trial judge? Should a court require a factual basis for questions like this one? Should a different standard apply if the witness is a party?

C. EXAMINATION OF WITNESSES BY THE COURT

FRE 614 codifies the common law by allowing the court to call its own witnesses and examine them and in providing that the judge may examine witnesses called by the parties. When the judge calls a witness all parties are entitled to question that witness as if on cross-examination. This is in part because parties who did not plan to call a witness may not be prepared to interrogate by nonleading questions. It is also the case that judges sometimes call witnesses to free the party seeking the witness' testimony from the strictures of the rule prohibiting leading questions. This is most often done at the state's behest in criminal cases, where a witness is likely to be uncooperative, but cannot be fairly characterized as hostile.

In jury trials, judges should not impose their views on the jury. Where judicial interrogation of just one side's witnesses has been extensive appellate courts screen the questioning closely to be sure that the judge has not placed his imprimatur on one litigant to the detriment of the other. How willing appellate courts are to permit judicial interrogation may depend on the role that the trial judge is expected to play in handling a jury. At common law the trial judge had the power to summarize the evidence and to comment upon it. Although this power is retained by the federal judiciary, most states have taken from the judge the power to comment on the evidence.[13] Where judicial control over the jury is expected to be slight, it is likely

13. The movement to eliminate the judge's common law power to comment on the evidence began in the late eighteenth century in North Carolina. Johnson, Province of the Judge in Jury Trials, 12 Am.Jud. Soc'y 76, 78 (1928). There is no hard and fast line between summary and comment. Some juris-

dictions allow both; some bar both; and some allow summary but not comment. Even where the power to summarize and to comment exists, often judges forego it. See H. Kalven & H. Zeisel, The American Jury 421 (1966). This topic is considered at greater length in Chapter Twelve.

that appellate courts will be more concerned about judicial influence through interrogation than in jurisdictions in which the judge is allowed to comment directly on the evidence and so guide the jury.

It is generally believed that trial judges are freer to ask questions in nonjury trials than they are when cases are tried to a jury. Distinguishing bench from jury trials makes sense, since parties cannot complain that the judge is unduly influencing himself by his questions. However, even in a bench trial there are reasons why the judge should leave the questioning largely to the attorneys. The judge who becomes active early in a case

may commit himself to a certain view before he fully understands all the evidence. Also, too active participation may result in less careful listening. Furthermore, judges often ask leading questions and, while attorneys may object, a judge's leading questions may influence a witness in a way that a lawyer's questions would not.[14]

This does not mean that the judge should be reluctant to ask a witness to clarify an obscure point or to explain a puzzling answer. It does mean that the judge ought to hesitate before exploring new material with a witness and that the judge should avoid excessive use of leading questions. Consider the following problem:

Problem V–4. Walsh and Jeffers are charged with killing a prison guard in a courthouse in Powhatan, Virginia. At the time of their separate trials, Virginia has a mandatory death penalty for the crime charged. There is some evidence that the men were attempting to escape when the guard was killed. After the two cases are severed for trial, Jeffers' lawyer moves for a change of venue. In support of his motion he offers testimony by a witness who supposedly is qualified to serve as a barometer of community sentiment. **How effective is the cross-examination? What is the impact of the questioning by the Court?**

THOMAS R. LEW, introduced on behalf of the Defendant, after being first duly sworn, testified as follows:

DIRECT EXAMINATION

BY MR. HAVLICECK:

Q. Please state your name and address. A. Thomas R. Lew, Powhatan, Virginia.

Q. What is your occupation? A. Attorney.

Q. How long have you been practicing? A. Since January 1972.

---

14. For a suggestion that judges who wish to have additional witnesses called or additional topics explored should do so by asking the lawyers to call the witnesses and to ask the questions, see Saltzburg, The Unnecessarily Expanding Role of the American Trial Judge, 64 Va.L.Rev. 1 (1978).

Judge Wyzanski has suggested that judges should be more restrained when commenting in some kinds of trials (e.g., criminal trials and suits for defamation) than in others (e.g., complex civil litigation). A Trial Judge's Freedom and Responsibility, 65 Harv.L.Rev. 1281 (1952).

The role of the judge is explored in greater depth in Chapter Twelve.

Q. How long have you been a resident of Powhatan County? **A.** Since September of 1971.

Q. And is your brother also an attorney and resident of Powhatan County? **A.** Yes, he has been for ten years.

Q. How long would you say your association with Powhatan County has lasted? **A.** Off and on over a ten year period since my brother moved here.

Q. And you feel that you have legal knowledge of the county pulse so to speak? The general feeling contained in the county? **A.** Being at the Court House Square, I feel that I do.

Q. Would you say the Court House Square forms the heart of the county? [The courthouse in which the killing took place is the same place the trial is to be held.] **A.** Yes.

Q. Would you describe to the Court in your own words the general county feeling that has been manifested concerning the death of Captain Moon? [the deceased prison guard] **A.** Well, most everyone is quite upset about it. Shocked by the fact that a man was shot and killed right in the courthouse itself. It was the topic of conversation for several weeks thereafter.

Q. And did you have occasion to go into grocery stores and other stores in the county and overhear others discussing this topic? **A.** I couldn't give you any specific examples, but it would come up from time to time at social gatherings or whenever people got together.

Q. And how large is Powhatan County as far as the population? **A.** About 8000.

Q. Do you know if many of the guards live throughout Powhatan County? **A.** I know some of the guards that I do know do live in Powhatan County.

Q. Now, did you know that Captain Moon had any children in school? **A.** Yes.

Q. In the Powhatan Public School system? **A.** Yes.

Q. Now, did you know that he was a participant in community affairs and activities? **A.** I understand that he was active in the public school system.

Q. Based on your knowledge and your involvement in local affairs and in your opinion, do you think the defendant could obtain a fair trial by a jury in Powhatan County? **A.** I do not.

Q. Why do you say this? **A.** Because everyone and everybody in the county who's going to be on the jury, I say I don't know who's going to be on the jury, but I'm sure they've heard, and this of course is my own opinion, and that's what you asked for.

Q. Yes? **A.** Has heard about it and probably has preconceived notions as to the guilt or innocence of the defendants.

Q. Now, would you say that the State Farm is something of an industry to the county? **A.** Industry—

THE COURT: I'll take judicial notice of the fact that the State Farm in Powhatan is somewhat of an industry to the County of Powhatan. [This signifies that the court will accept the fact as true without requiring proof.]

Q. Would you also say that it is an issue or source of contention among county residents? **A.** To some extent, yes.

Q. And do you recall any of this becoming manifested during this recent case where I believe an escapee from, I think it was Beaumont, was involved in the rape of a county woman? **A.** Yes. Yes. That was when I first moved to Powhatan and the trial was held.

Q. Do you recall the sentiment of those people at that time? **A.** People were—particular people who live out on Route 711 were upset because of the fact the Farm has this proximity and that this man had escaped—Beaumont, excuse me.

Q. Do you feel the greater proportion of the population of Powhatan County would either be—would have some contact with the guards, either on a direct basis, being related or being neighbors or would have some sort of feeling towards the institution just because it's there? **A.** I really couldn't answer that. I wouldn't know exactly, not having been here that long.

THE COURT: You must admit, that would be a right difficult question to answer.

MR. HAVLICECK: It might be an impossible question to answer.

MR. HAVLICECK: I have no further questions.

CROSS-EXAMINATION

BY MR. DAVIS:

Q. Mr. Lew, the Court House Square is the pulse of the county, is that correct? **A.** As far as I'm concerned it is.

Q. Do you know how many people are in the Court House Square? **A.** No, I wouldn't want to guess.

Q. You don't have any idea? **A.** No. The reason I say that is because—

Q. No more than about 50, is it? **A.** No, I wouldn't say so.

Q. The population is 8000? This is where most of your conversation has occurred, around the Court House Square? **A.** Well, I'm talking about the clerk's office.

Q. You say everyone's quite upset, that's 15 people? **A.** This is—

Q. Fifteen people? **A.** I would say everyone is upset.

Q. Everyone is upset? You've talked to 15 people? **A.** You asked for my opinion.

Q. How many people have you talked to? **A.** I just picked 15 out of the air.

Q. Fifteen out of the air? **A.** It could have been 10, it could have been 60.

Q. It could have been 60? It could have been 60— **A.** It could have been.

Q. You've been here since September, you've been practicing law since January? **A.** Right.

Q. You've never handled any jury felony cases? Have you ever handled any felony cases, period? **A.** No.

Q. But that's your opinion you came up with? **A.** Yes.

Q. All right. You say Captain Moon's children are in school? **A.** Yes.

Q. Are you familiar with the age limit of the jurors serving on jury duty? **A.** I don't understand the question.

THE COURT: They have to be 21.

A. Oh, I know that, but—

Q. School children can't serve as jurors? **A.** That wasn't my—okay.

Q. You say I'm sure they've heard about this but you don't know definitely whether they have? **A.** Who's this?

Q. The people—the majority of residents in the county? **A.** Oh, naw,—

Q. How about a third of the residents in the county? **A.** In my opinion?

Q. You're only issuing your opinion, and your opinion is based on surmise and speculation? **A.** Yes.

Q. All right, sir. Now, you say that it has been a source of contention to the county residents, the rape case that you described? **A.** Yes, sir.

Q. I see. How many people do you know on Route 711? **A.** Ah, quite a few.

Q. How many? **A.** Five families.

Q. Five families? That would be roughly 10 people? **A.** I don't—

Q. Have you talked to all 10 people about this? **A.** No.

Q. You have not? **A.** No.

Q. How many people have you talked to on 711? **A.** Somewhere between one and 10.

Q. One and 10? And you say they're upset, the ones you've talked to? **A.** (Inaudible)

Lempert & Saltzburg Mod.Approach To Evid.—8

MR. DAVIS: I have no further questions.

THE COURT: Mr. Lew, let me ask you this.

EXAMINATION OF THE WITNESS

BY THE COURT:

Q. You say on the question of this trial you talked to people, have people expressed any opinion as to the case? **A.** Yes, sir.

Q. Now, do you think those same people, based on the law and evidence that comes with the case, would be so prejudiced that they could not give a fair and impartial trial to the accused? **A.** In my opinion, I don't think they could get a fair trial in Powhatan.

Q. The opinion is one thing but what it's based on is something else. Do you think of the three people that you mentioned earlier, if they heard the case and the evidence completely exonerated one of the accused or both of the accused, do you think they would convict them anyway? **A.** I'll have to say no.

Q. So, they might have—what they surmise or what they heard, they might have formed an opinion, but you don't think that they would disregard the instructions of the Court to give a fair and impartial trial, do you? **A.** No, sir.

Q. Or if there happened to be a plea of insanity, which we heard earlier or some indication of that, and it was proved by clear and convincing evidence or the preponderance of the evidence required by law, do you think the people would be so biased or prejudiced that they would not give a fair and impartial trial to the accused? **A.** If such was the case, I feel that they could but I think—my feeling is that the populace of Powhatan County have a preconceived notion about this.

Q. Then let me ask you this. Then your opinion is based purely on your ideas and not the facts that you have gathered? **A.** Right.

Q. And this is just a personal opinion on your part? **A.** Right, backed up by conversations with the people.

Q. Now, at the time the alleged offense took place, was there any gathering of the citizens of Powhatan at the courthouse or anything of that nature? **A.** There were quite a few people around.

Q. —but I mean to do anything to the accused? **A.** Oh, no.

Q. It was nothing like a lynch mob or anything of that order? **A.** No, sir.

Q. In fact, hasn't it been rather calm and cool in Powhatan? Haven't the citizens acted calm and cool, although they may have discussed it? **A.** Uh huh.

Q. Have you heard any inflammatory remarks against the accused in any way? **A.** No, sir.

Q. All right. I don't live up here but I haven't heard of anything like that. Of that nature. But don't you really feel that, should they get a jury that did not know Captain Moon, and that might be really a problem being he was so well known up here,— **A.** Well, Your Honor,—

Q. I'm trying to get to what your opinion is based on. See, I have to kinda skim your testimony because of the fact that you represent one of the defendants. **A.** Well,—

Q. So, now I'm trying to get your— **A.** If I said yes, then I would be casting aspersions on the people of Powhatan County, that they're so bigoted or biased that they couldn't. My personal opinion is that it would be very difficult. Let me put it that way.

Q. Is what you're saying, it would be difficult to pick a jury, but there is a great possibility that a jury could be picked that would be fair and impartial and give the accused a fair and impartial trial? **A.** I wouldn't say a great possibility. I would say there would be a much greater possibility somewhere outside of Powhatan County.

Q. Oh, yes, we could move it to New York State, but we would have no jurisdiction up there. But this is a matter of proof by the accused only. But have you heard any real inflammatory things in the county? "We ought to kill those people," and things like that? **A.** Well, a few comments like that were made.

Q. Well, were they inflammatory or were they just— **A.** They weren't said to incite a mob action or—

Q. All right, sir.

THE COURT: We'll let Mr. Lew off the hook now.

Looking back over the cross-examination, are you surprised that the witness was counsel for one of the defendants? Are you surprised this was only brought out by the judge at the end of the witness' testimony? Are you troubled by the role that the trial judge assumed? Should a judge be hostile to a change of venue motion? Was this one? Should the judicial role in ruling on such motions be different from the judicial role at the trial on the merits?

SECTION II.   IMPEACHMENT

Cross-examination is an important method of discrediting adverse testimony. By pointing out gaps in a witness' testimony, or by exposing failures of memory and perception, the adroit examiner may transform what might have been a devastating indictment into a harmless narrative.

However, occasions arise when an attorney meets a witness whose story sounds true, whose memory seems unimpaired, and whose trial demeanor is superb. The lawyer who conducts a rigorous cross-examination is in danger of finding himself in the position of a boxer who, after throwing a flurry of harmless punches, has succeeded only in convincing the judge that the defense is impenetrable. What is needed is the heavy blow which destroys the adversary's balance and opens him up to further attack. This "equalizer" may be impeachment.

Impeachment, like some cross-examination, is designed to discredit a witness' testimony. In ordinary cross-examination, discrediting is usually accomplished by showing flaws in the testimony; in impeachment this is most often done by showing flaws in the witness. In the one, the witness' integrity, honesty and ability is usually left intact; in the other they are likely to be questioned if not destroyed. While the honest witness may cooperate with the cross-examiner in spelling out the limitations of his testimony, cooperation is unlikely when the witness believes the attack has become personal and threatens to diminish his stature in the eyes of the decisionmaker.

At common law, impeachment is forbidden on direct examination except in special circumstances. The traditional justification for this rule is that a party "vouches for the credibility of his witnesses." The reasoning is that impeachment is only necessary where a witness is untrustworthy. Since parties should not present testimony they believe is untrustworthy, they have no need to impeach their own witnesses. McCormick points out the flaw in this reasoning. In most cases "the party has little or no choice of witnesses. He calls only those who happen to have observed the particular facts in controversy."[15] Weinstein and Berger claim "an endorsement of the guaranteeing theory undermines the law's truth-seeking function." They argue that it discourages parties from presenting all possible sources of information and may prevent the trier-of-fact from properly weighing evidence.[16]

Another justification for limiting impeachment on direct examination is that the right to impeach one's own witness would give an attorney the means of coercing favorable testimony. This assumes weak-willed witnesses, unethical attorneys and the availability of the most embarrassing of the impeachment devices. If this combination did exist, impeachment would not be necessary to coerce favorable testimony; an out-of-court threat to reveal the information would serve just as well. Moreover, if impeachment were as coercive as this justification assumes, permitting cross-examiners to impeach might give them the means to discourage timid witnesses from testifying or enable them to bully witnesses into forsaking on cross-examination what they said during direct examination.

A third justification for forbidding impeachment on direct examination is more tenable than the others. Juries may treat evidence relevant solely for impeachment (usually prior inconsistent statements) as substantive evidence in the case. Allowingimpeachment on direct examination opens up the possibility that a lawyer will call a witness for the sole purpose of presenting the witness' inconsistent out-of-court statements to the jury. Where inconsistent statements are hearsay, this limitation on impeachment makes sense, though a narrower limitation, preventing attorneys from calling witnesses solely to impeach expected adverse testimony, might do as well. The most straightforward argument against this third justification is the increasingly popular claim that the prior out-of-court statements of a witness present and available for cross-examination should be admissible as substantive evidence. If this were the rule, impeachment by prior inconsistent statements would not present the jury with otherwise inadmissible evidence.[17]

15. McCormick § 38, at 75.
16. 3 Weinstein's Evidence ¶ 607[01].

17. For a discussion of this position see Chapter Six, infra.

Of course, the danger that impeachment will be misused for substantive purposes is present on cross-examination as well as direct. But the cross-examiner does not call witnesses in order to impeach; he deals with those his opponent has put on the stand. And, although a party does not choose all his witnesses, he has enough opportunity to present favorable witnesses so that the need for impeachment is almost always greater on cross-examination than on direct.

The weakness of these justifications for forbidding impeachment on direct examination and the fact that there are circumstances where the need to impeach one's "own witness" is clear have led to several inroads into the common law rule. Many courts allow impeachment of witnesses whose damaging testimony comes as a surprise to the party offering it. Witnesses considered by the court to be hostile may be impeached, as may witnesses, such as opposing parties, who are declared hostile as a matter of law. Witnesses may also be impeached where the party conducting the direct examination has no choice in receiving the witness' testimony. This is the case where a witness must be called as a matter of law; e.g., an attesting witness to a will. In addition, the judge may call someone as the court's witness, thus opening him up to impeachment by both sides. Finally, the rule against impeachment does not prevent counsel from seeking to refresh a witness' recollection by asking the witness whether he has previously told a different story. The witness who answers affirmatively may revert to his former story. If he does not, at least evidence of the earlier story is before the jury, and even a negative answer may encourage jurors to question the witness' testimony.

The arguments against limiting impeachment on direct examination prevailed with the drafters of the Federal Rules. FRE 607 provides that any party may attack the credibility of any witness. Weinstein and Berger suggest that in state criminal cases the defendant may have a constitutional right to the kind of umlimited impeachment allowed by the federal rule.[18] Thus far, this suggestion has not prevailed, but in particular cases courts have held that the defendant's need to present evidence impeaching an important witness outweighs the state's interest in applying the restrictive rule.[19]

Attempts at impeachment, like cross-examination generally, may, if not carefully handled, do more harm than good. A witness may explain away an inconsistent statement to the detriment of the party asking the question, and a lawyer who browbeats a witness or unfairly embarrasses him may create sympathy both for the witness and for the party for whom he is testifying.

At common law witnesses who could be impeached on direct examination could invaribly be interrogated by leading questions. Under FRE 607 any witness may be impeached by any party, but the Federal Rules also provide that leading questions should not usually be used on direct examination except where witnesses are hostile or adverse (FRE 611(c)). Clearly FRE 607 appears to apply more broadly than FRE 611. The following comment suggests that if the rules are read together the distinction in practice may not be great.

Is any witness who gives unfavorable testimony to a party a hostile or adverse witness within the meaning of Rule 611? This is a difficult question to answer. At common law more of a showing of hostility was needed than simply a demonstration that the witness had adverse testimony to give. The requirement of a greater showing before leading ques-

---

18. 3 Weinstein's Evidence ¶ 607[01].

19. See Chambers v. Mississippi, 410 U.S. 284 (1973), discussed in Chapter Seven infra.

See also United States v. Torres, 477 F.2d 922 (9th Cir. 1973); United States v. Prince, 491 F.2d 655 (5th Cir. 1974).

tions were allowed went hand in hand with the rule that a party could not impeach his own witness. This tandem tended to place the direct examiner in an uncomfortable position in dealing with witnesses whose testimony he wished to probe, and even to pick apart, in order to prove his case. Since Rule 607 provides that a party can impeach his own witness, and since one form of impeachment is asking the witness leading questions designed to test his credibility, one might think that whenever a witness gives damaging testimony against the party calling him, that party should be able to ask leading questions for purposes of impeachment. Such a reading of the new Rules would result in prohibition of leading questions on direct examination where the witness is favorable to the party calling him, but would recognize that leading questions may be a form of impeachment when a witness gives unfavorable testimony. To us this reading makes good sense. But the proper relationship between impeachment and scope of examination will probably have to be developed in the future on a case-by-case basis.[20]

Now that we have outlined general aspects of impeachment, we turn to specific techniques that are to some extent regulated by evidence rules. In examining these techniques you will find that just as there were two ways of approaching cross-examination (attacking the testimony and attacking the witness), there are two ways of impeaching a witness. One approach is to challenge the witness generally. For example, when impeachment is by prior convictions or prior bad acts, the impeaching party is suggesting that the witness' character is such that he should not be believed regardless of what he is testifying to or on whose behalf. The other approach questions the witness' credibility in the context of a specific case. For example, a witness, like the father of the plaintiff, may be shown to be biased in a particular case without necessarily implying that he is generally unworthy of belief. Nothing, of course, precludes the examiner from discrediting a witness in both respects.

A. IMPEACHMENT BY PRIOR CONVICTIONS

One of the most debatable and frequently debated ways of impeaching a witness is by showing that the witness has a criminal record. Where the witness is the defendant, the tension between preventing prejudice and testing credibility is clear. In Chapter Four we discussed the dangers which exist when evidence of other crimes is introduced even for permitted purposes. The situation is similar when a prior conviction is used to impeach. Although the purpose of offering the evidence is, at least in theory, neither to establish that the defendant's character is bad nor to suggest that he has a propensity to commit crimes, a jury may have difficulty in accepting the idea that evidence admissible to suggest perjury may not be used to prove the defendant has otherwise broken the law.

Most common law jurisdictions allow impeachment by a showing of any felony conviction or of any conviction involving dishonesty or false statement regardless of punishment.[21] This mode of impeachment can only be explained by history, for neither experience nor logic suggests that the ordinary felon is more likely to perjure himself at trial than a similarly situ-

---

20. S. Saltzburg & K. Redden, Federal Rules of Evidence Manual 402 (3d ed. 1982).

21. **A few jurisdictions use the term "infamous crimes." Several others restrict** **impeachment to felonies. Other states have slightly different statutes. We shall refer to the generalized approach of common law states as the traditional rule.**

ated first-time offender. Historically all felonies were capital, so in theory, the problem of receiving testimony from convicted felons never arose. By the 16th century some felonies were no longer capital, and by the 17th century some which were capital were routinely commuted, although serious legal disabilities continued to be imposed on convicted felons. The particular disability we are concerned with is that convicted felons were barred from testifying in courts of law. Eventually this proved untenable, in part because it often takes the testimony of one thief to catch another. So felons were allowed to testify, and the disqualification of conviction was transformed into grounds for impeachment. The notion that a felony conviction reflects adversely on credit was apparently a subsequent justification that became the exclusive rationale.[22] The debate surrounding impeachment by prior conviction has been intense, in part because the modern rationale appears so clearly contrived with respect to crimes which in no sense suggest dishonesty.[23]

We suspect that if proponents of the rule were to state honestly their reasons for supporting impeachment by crimes with no apparent relationship to veracity, the basic reason would be that this mode of impeachment is a device which redresses the balance of advantage between prosecutors and defendants. The feeling that many criminal defendants, whether previously convicted or not, tell lies on the stand is supported by numerous examples of defendants who have protested their innocence in the face of overwhelming evidence of guilt. Impeachment by prior conviction minimizes the advantages which might otherwise flow from a false story, but not necessarily because it suggests the defendant is particularly likely to lie. Usually it is because evidence of prior crimes suggests to the jury that the defendant is particularly likely to have committed the crime charged and that the mistake of convicting an innocent person is not as regretable as it otherwise might be. Of course, these inferences are technically impermissible, and they equally penalize ex-convicts who are telling the truth while having no impact on first-time offenders who fabricate denials. These are perhaps the reasons why this justification is not given.[24]

When a third-party witness is impeached by a prior conviction, there is a chance that the jury will overreact to the conviction. Honest testimony may be discounted, and the party identified with a "convict-witness" may suffer guilt by association. Where the victim of a crime is impeached by a prior record, a guilty defendant may be set free, in part because it is felt that

22. See 2 Wigmore § 519; Ladd, Credibility Tests—Current Trends, 89 U.Pa.L.Rev. 166, 175–76 (1940).

23. Note that the situation is different if there is some reason to suggest the witness has an interest in lying about a matter. There one might argue that the fact that the witness violated the law once to promote self-interest suggests he might be more likely than most to do it again, through perjury. Ironically, this argument appears less applicable the greater the witness' interest in lying, because the more one has to gain by lying the more likely that interest alone will lead to perjury. This is why we do not think prior convictions are likely to distinguish greatly between the veracity of stories told by recidivists and similarly situated non-recidivist defen-

dants. This argument is entirely theoretical, for we know of no empirical research into these matters.

24. Another possible reason is that it is wrong. This is a novel, if not radical explanation, of the prior convictions rule. It is based on speculation rather than good empirical evidence about the way judges and prosecutors feel. Are you skeptical of this explanation? If our assumption—and we must emphasize that it is an untested assumption—that many defendants will commit perjury is true, does this justify a rule which permits impeachment by prior conviction if our further assumption about the way in which such evidence affects defendants is correct? Are juries likely to be oblivious to the obvious interests of testifying defendants?

the victim deserved his fate. The rule may also do a disservice in that some victims and witnesses may seek to escape the responsibility of testifying in order to avoid the unpleasant experience of having their character assailed in the courtroom.

When the accused in a criminal case has a prior record, he is impaled on the horns of an unhappy dilemma. The privilege against self-incrimination gives the accused a right to remain silent, but exercise of that right may be costly. The jury, although instructed to disregard the accused's silence in judging guilt and innocence, may focus on unanswered questions in deciding the merits of a case. If the defendant might have answered the questions, silence is likely to hurt despite an instruction to the contrary.[25] Silence hurts most where the defendant's testimony might, *if believed*, be highly probative of innocence. The catch is that a prior criminal record makes it unlikely that the defendant will be believed, not because the jury necessarily finds the conviction probative of credibility, but rather because the jury treats the conviction as further evidence that the accused committed the crime charged. Professors Kalven and Zeisel have gathered data which measures this disadvantage. They report that when juries learn of defendants' prior records, acquittal is about 40% less likely than it is for defendants without prior records.[26]

Weinstein and Berger suggest that a system which poses this dilemma for defendants contradicts certain basic values:

A defendant with a criminal past is therefore forced by the orthodox rule of impeachment into a choice between Scylla and Charybdis, a choice which some suggest does not square with our supposed allegiance to the doctrine that all are innocent until proven guilty.[27]

A case for the traditional rule of impeachment was made by Rep. Hogan of Maryland during the debates on the Federal Rules of Evidence:

[T]he rules of evidence should not permit a witness to testify on behalf of a criminal defendant with the appearance of an unblemished citizen, whereas in fact that witness has been convicted of felonies. This is not to say that people with criminal records necessarily lie, but it is to say that juries should weigh the criminal record in determining credibility.

[N]o one can object to permitting a witness to be held up to a jury as unworthy of belief because he or she had been convicted of stealing, but that surely does not exhaust the subject matter. How credible is a witness who has been convicted, let us say, for kidnapping, or for espionage, or for inciting civil disorders, or for aircraft piracy, or for assassination, or for any of a number of * * * other crimes * * *[28]

Other members of Congress had different views.

Rep. Dennis:

The general rule, as most of us who practice law know, in most places, is that we allow unrestricted cross-examination of any and all previous convictions which any witness may have had. The theory

---

25. See Note, To Take the Stand or Not to Take The Stand, The Dilemma of the Defendant With a Criminal Record, 4 Colum.J.L. & Soc.Prob. 215, 221–22 (1968). This study indicates that judges and attorneys believe an instruction to disregard prior conviction evidence on the issue of guilt is not likely to be followed. Id. at 218–19.

26. The American Jury 160 (1966).

27. 3 Weinstein's Evidence ¶ 609[02].

28. 120 Cong.Rec. Pt. II, at 2376 (Feb. 6, 1974).

Although many jurisdictions have moved toward protecting criminal defendants, and in some cases even defense witnesses, from impeachment by prior convictions, California voters recently approved (56% of the voters approving) a "victims rights" initiative which, among other things, changes evidentiary rules in criminal cases. The initiative amends the state constitution to permit the introduction

of that is that we permit it on the ground that it goes to his credibility as a witness.

Now, it is a great anomaly that we do that, because unless the man takes the witness stand, if he is a criminal defendant, it is absolutely impossible, ordinarily, to put in any evidence concerning his previous convictions, which have nothing to do with the case on trial at all, but if he has the temerity to take the witness stand, we open all that up, on the theory that it goes to his credibility as a witness.

Now * * * that is one of the most unfair rules of law that we have. And when I say so, I am not speaking from theory; I am speaking from experience * * *

I spent 4 years as a prosecuting attorney in the State of Indiana, prosecuting on behalf of the State. I spent another year in the Army as a judge advocate officer, prosecuting for the Government, and I have defended a lot of defendants in criminal cases since. My experience is that, from either side of the table, this is utterly unfair. We put the fellow, who ever had any record, in this box. Either he can refuse to take the stand, as he is entitled to under the Fifth Amendment, and let the case go, or else he takes the stand and they crucify him with these previous irrelevant crimes which have nothing to do with what he is now on trial for.

Studies have shown that the one single reason, the one greatest reason, for mis-

carriages of justice is faulty eyewitness testimony.

However, about the next highest is this very rule, because people are either frightened off the stand, and do not tell their story, or else they take the stand and are crucified by being asked about entirely irrelevant offenses.[29]

* * *

Rep. Wiggins:

* * *

There is serious doubt in my mind, and I speak from considerable professional experience, that it is possible for a man to receive a fair trial if the jury knows he has committed, for example, the crime of child molesting. I think it is almost impossible for that man to receive a fair trial under those circumstances. It is so bad in my estimation * * * that the admission of evidence of unrelated crimes when the defendant himself is on the stand, borders upon a denial of due process, and I would expect sometime down the road for the Supreme Court to recognize that it is a denial of due process and preclude such evidence as a matter of constitutional law.[30]

A century and a half before these debates, Jeremy Bentham questioned the fundamental equation between the felony record and veracity:

Two men quarrel; one of them calls the other a liar. So highly does he prize the reputation of veracity, that, rather than suffer a stain to remain upon it, he

of evidence that is illegally seized under the California Constitution and also permits prior felony convictions of all sorts to be used to impeach criminal defendants and their witnesses. In one of the first California cases to be affected by the new law, a defendant charged with attempted murder was impeached with an earlier child molesting conviction, and his corroborating witness was impeached with a marihuana sale conviction that occurred in 1964. (Mathews, Controversial California Law Eases Path from Court to Cell, Wash. Post, July 7, 1982, at A6, col.

1.). Although the initiative is certain to be challenged in years to come on various constitutional grounds, its success suggests that large segments of the public, like Representative Hogan, believe that certain rules are overly protective of criminal defendants. As you read further think about this issue and ask yourself whether you would change federal rule 609 and permit all prior felonies to be used to impeach criminal defendants.

29. Id. at 2377.

30. Id. at 2379.

determines to risk his life, challenges his adversary to fight, and kills him. Jurisprudence, in its sapience, knowing no difference between homicide by consent, by which no other human being is put in fear—and homicide in pursuit of a scheme of highway robbery, of nocturnal housebreaking, by which every man who has a life is put in fear of it,—has made the one and the other murder, and consequently felony. The man prefers death to the imputation of a lie,—and the inference of the law is, that he cannot open his mouth but lies will issue from it. Such are the inconsistencies which are unavoidable in the application of any rule which takes improbity for a ground of exclusion.[31]

The federal courts have been sensitive to the criticisms. Fearing the misuse of prior convictions, every federal circuit had followed the lead of the District of Columbia, which in its landmark decision in Luck v. United States,[32] required the trial judge to balance the contributions of impeachment to the search for truth against the dangers of jury misuse.

Chief Justice Burger (then Circuit Judge) explained Luck in a later case:

The rationale of our Luck opinion is important; it recognized that a showing of prior convictions can have genuine probative value on the issue of credibility, but that because of the potential for prejudice, the receiving of such convictions as impeachment was discretionary. The defendant who has a criminal record may ask the court to weigh the probative value of the convictions as to the credibility [sic] against the degree of prejudice which the revelation of his past crimes would cause; and he may ask the court to consider whether it is more important for the jury to hear his story than

to know about prior convictions in relation to his credibility. We contemplated the possibility of allowing some convictions to be shown and some excluded; examples are to be found in those which are remote and those which have no direct bearing on veracity, and those which because of the peculiar circumstances at hand might better be excluded. The Luck opinion contemplated an on-the-record consideration by the trial judge whose action would be reviewable only for abuse of discretion, and that once the exercise of discretion appeared, the trial court's action be "accorded a respect appropriately reflective of the inescapable remoteness of appellate review." This is a recognition that the cold record on appeal cannot present all facets and elements which the trial judge must weigh in striking the balance.

Luck also contemplated that it was for the defendant to present to the trial court sufficient reasons for withholding past convictions from the jury in the face of a statute which makes such convictions admissible. * * * The underlying assumption was that prior convictions would ordinarily be admissible unless this burden is met. "The trial court is not required to allow impeachment by prior conviction every time a defendant takes the stand in his own defense."

* * * The impact of criminal convictions will often be damaging to an accused and it is admittedly difficult to restrict its impact, by cautionary instructions, to the issue of credibility. The test of Luck, however, is that to bar them as impeachment the court must find that the prejudice must "far outweigh" the probative relevance to credibility, or that even if relevant the "cause of truth would

---

31. Bentham, Rationale of Judicial Evidence 406 (Bowring's ed. vol. VII 1827), quoted in 2 Wigmore § 519, at 611.

32. 121 U.S.App.D.C. 151, 348 F.2d 763 (1965). The Ninth Circuit did not go as far as the other circuits in following the lead of Luck.

be helped more by letting the jury hear the defendant's story than by the defendant's foregoing that opportunity because of the fear of prejudice founded upon a prior conviction."

The burden of persuasion in this regard is on the accused; and, once the issue is raised, the District Court should make an inquiry, allowing the accused an opportunity to show why judicial discretion should be exercised in favor of exclusion of the criminal record. This, admittedly, places a very difficult burden on trial judges and some added guidelines are needed even at risk of adding to the burdens of the trial courts.

In considering how the District Court is to exercise the discretionary power we granted, we must look to the legitimate purpose of impeachment which is, of course, not to show that the accused who takes the stand is a "bad" person but rather to show background facts which bear directly on whether jurors ought to believe him rather than other and conflicting witnesses. In common human experience acts of deceit, fraud, cheating, or stealing, for example, are universally regarded as conduct which reflects adversely on a man's honesty and integrity. Acts of violence on the other hand, which may result from a shorter temper, a combative nature, extreme provocation, or other causes, generally have little or no direct bearing on honesty and veracity. A "rule of thumb" thus should be that convictions which rest on dishonest conduct relate to credibility whereas those of violent or assaultive crimes generally do not; traffic viola-

tions, however serious, are in the same category. The nearness or remoteness of the prior conviction is also a factor of no small importance. Even one involving fraud or stealing, for example, if it occurred long before and has been followed by a legally blameless life, should generally be excluded on the ground of remoteness.

A special and even more difficult problem arises when the prior conviction is for the same or substantially the same conduct for which the accused is on trial. Where multiple convictions of various kinds can be shown, strong reasons arise for excluding those which are for the same crime because of the inevitable pressure on lay jurors to believe that "if he did it before he probably did so this time." As a general guide, those convictions which are for the same crime should be admitted sparingly; one solution might well be that discretion be exercised to limit the impeachment by way of a similar crime to a single conviction and then only when the circumstances indicate strong reasons for disclosure, and where the conviction directly relates to veracity.[33] * * *

The *Luck* rule, however, was a target for those who accused the courts of "being soft on crime" and Congress rejected it in the District of Columbia Court Reform and Criminal Procedure Act of 1970, 14 D.C.Code § 305. The House Report on the bill explained:

A demonstrated instance of willingness to engage in conduct in disregard of accepted patterns is translatable into willingness to give false testimony.[34]

33. Gordon v. United States, 127 U.S.App.D.C. 343, 383 F.2d 936, 939 (1967), certiorari denied, 390 U.S. 1029 (1968).

34. **H.R.Rep. 907, 91 Cong., 2d Sess. at 62 quoting from the March 1969 proposal by the Advisory Committee on the Rules of Evidence to the Committee on Rules of Practice and Procedure of the Judicial Conference of the United States. The District of Columbia bill passed the House of**

Representatives by a vote of 332 to 64. 116 Cong.Rec. H 6743–44, 91st Cong. This assumption is as unsupported by empirical research as some of the contrary assumptions which we have hypothesized. It also does not respond to the issue raised by *Luck*, which is whether prejudicial value outweighs probative value, not whether probative value exists at all.

The debate on the federal rules of evidence gave Congress an opportunity to reconsider the necessity and fairness of impeachment by prior convictions. Despite the Justice Department's importuning for the traditional rule, Congress codified much of the *Luck* rule in FRE 609(a). A conviction punishable by death or more than one year in prison is admissible if "the court determines that the probative value of admitting this evidence outweighs its prejudicial effect to the defendant" (a balancing test more favorable to the defendant than the *Luck* test). But if a prior conviction involved "dishonesty or false statement, regardless of the punishment," it is automatically admissible, unless introduction of the evidence would deny a fair trial in violation of the fifth or fourteenth amendments.[35]

35. To make it easy for you to follow the textual discussion, we include the text of FRE 609 here:

IMPEACHMENT BY EVIDENCE OF CONVICTION OF CRIME

(a) General Rule. For the purpose of attacking the credibility of a witness, evidence that he has been convicted of a crime shall be admitted if elicited from him or established by public record during cross-examination but only if the crime (1) was punishable by death or imprisonment in excess of one year under the law under which he was convicted, and the court determines that the probative value of admitting this evidence outweighs its prejudicial effect to the defendant, or (2) involved dishonesty or false statement, regardless of the punishment.

(b) Time Limit. Evidence of a conviction under this rule is not admissible if a period of more than ten years has elapsed since the date of the conviction or of the release of the witness from the confinement imposed for that conviction, whichever is the later date, unless the court determines, in the interests of justice, that the probative value of the conviction supported by specific facts and circumstances substantially outweighs its prejudicial effect. However, evidence of a conviction more than 10 years old as calculated herein, is not admissible unless the proponent gives to the adverse party sufficient advance written notice of intent to use such evidence to provide the adverse party with a fair opportunity to contest the use of such evidence.

(c) Effect of Pardon, Annulment, or Certificate of Rehabilitation. Evidence of a conviction is not admissible under this rule if (1) the conviction has been the subject of a pardon, annulment, certificate of rehabilitation, or other equivalent procedure based on a finding of the rehabilitation of the person convicted, and that person has not been convicted of a subsequent crime which was punishable by death or imprisonment in excess of one year, or (2) the conviction has been the subject of a pardon, annulment, or other equivalent procedure based on a finding of innocence.

(d) Juvenile Adjudications. Evidence of juvenile adjudications is generally not admissible under this rule. The court may, however, in a criminal case allow evidence of a juvenile adjudication of a witness other than the accused if conviction of the offense would be admissible to attack the credibility of an adult and the court is satisfied that admission in evidence is necessary for a fair determination of the issue of guilt or innocence.

(e) Pendency of Appeal. The pendency of an appeal therefrom does not render evidence of a conviction inadmissible. Evidence of the pendency of an appeal is admissible.

"Dishonesty" is an ambiguous word. There is evidence that it is intended to signify "any crime which may injuriously affect the administration of justice, by the introduction of falsehood and fraud." Hearings on Federal Rules of Evidence Before Senate Committee on the Judiciary, 93rd Cong., 2d Sess., at 17 (1974). See also H.Rep. No. 93–1597, 93rd Cong., 2d Sess. at 9.

Under FRE 609(a) a conviction may be proved by asking the witness to admit the conviction or by offering a public record. However, the offer must be made while the witness is on the stand. This allows the witness to question the validity of the rec-

The time elapsed since the conviction in question has been one aspect of the *Luck* balancing test. Rule 609(b) explicitly provides that if ten years has elapsed from the release of the witness from confinement, or from the date of conviction if no confinement penalty was imposed, the conviction is not admissible unless the probative value of the conviction supported by specific facts and circumstances *substantially* outweighs its prejudicial effect. This allows somewhat more leeway for impeachment than an earlier draft which barred the use of stale convictions and took 10 years as the definition of stale.

The balancing test of FRE 609(a) on its face is concerned only with prejudice to the defendant. Several courts have read this rule literally, holding that witnesses in civil litigation or for the government in criminal cases are impeachable whenever they have been convicted of a felony. Other courts have suggested that while the special balancing test of 609(a) protects only criminal defendants, other litigants may utilize Rules 102, 403 and 611(a) to bar unduly prejudicial impeachment. The legislative history of FRE 609 indicates that Congress hurried to agree on a compromise and paid little attention to the exact meaning of the balancing test.

A few state courts have decided to limit those prior convictions that may be used to impeach criminal defendants to perjury and similar offenses. They are, in effect, saying that except where past crimes relate directly to truth and veracity the prejudice to a defendant will invariably outweigh whatever light past offenses shed on the defendant's credibility.

Recall that in the Whale case the conviction was reversed because the jury learned of the sentence that Whale had received following a prior conviction. Federal courts are divided on what a jury should be permitted to learn beyond the mere fact of conviction. Disclosing the sentence makes sense only if there is good reason to believe that a conviction is more probative of credibility when the accompanying sentence is high than when it is low. Whether or not the sentence is revealed, most jurisdictions permit the person impeached to make a short statement explaining the circumstances of the prior conviction. There is danger in doing so, however, since the door may be opened to a brief rejoinder by the other side.

When the balancing test of FRE 609(a) must be applied, criminal defendants often seek to learn before trial whether impeachment by prior convictions will be allowed should they choose to testify. Generally, trial judges are not required to grant the request for a pretrial ruling, but they often will do so, thus, allowing the defendant to make a more informed decision about whether to take the stand. On other occasions trial judges wait until the end of the prosecution's case to make a ruling, believing that it is impossible to know how probative impeachment of the defendant may be without having some idea of the importance of credibility issues in the case. In still other cases no advance ruling will be made because the judge believes that a fully informed decision cannot be made until after the defendant has testified.

If the judge makes a binding pretrial ruling allowing prior convictions to be used for impeachment, the defendant is entitled to claim error on appeal even though he does not take the stand.[36] Since this al-

---

ord, point to the pendency of an appeal, and say either at that time or on re-direct examination, a few words by way of explanation. Some states do not allow witnesses to be questioned about prior convictions; they require proof by public record. Do you see any reasons for this approach?

36. Cf. New Jersey v. Portash, 440 U.S. 450 (1979) (defendant who obtained a ruling that if he testified his grand jury testimony could be used to impeach him could appeal the ruling even though he did not take the stand).

lows a defendant who never intended to testify a riskless way to receive a ruling that might amount to reversible error, some courts have refused to make pretrial rulings or have conditioned them upon the defendant's stipulation that if the convictions at issue are excluded, he will testify.[37]

Courts differ on whether pardons render convictions inadmissible. Federal Rule 609(c) provides that a pardon or similar procedure, based on a finding of the rehabilitation of the person convicted, renders a conviction inadmissible, but only if the person has not thereafter been convicted of another crime punishable by death or imprisonment for more than one year. If a pardon or other procedure is based on a finding of innocence, the underlying conviction can never be admitted into evidence. Frequently it is difficult to know why a pardon was granted. The rule does not indicate whose burden it is to show the grounds for a pardon, but most courts seem to assume that the pardons are not on grounds of innocence and make the impeached witness prove otherwise. It is not clear that a pardon based on the executive's doubts about guilt qualifies as one based on a finding of innocence, but un-

der the 609(a) balancing test such convictions might be excluded as not probative enough to warrant admission. If a pardon is followed by a subsequent conviction, thus rendering the pardoned offense admissible, the question arises as to whether the pardon may be shown to mitigate the effects of the impeaching evidence. FRE 609(c) appears to make pardons not based on innocence irrelevant if there are subsequent convictions.

Although the prevailing view has been that evidence of juvenile adjudications is not admissible, FRE 609(d) admits, in criminal cases, evidence of juvenile convictions of witnesses other than the accused, if evidence of similar convictions would be admissible to attack the credibility of an adult and such evidence is necessary to a fair determination of guilt or innocence. Constitutional problems might arise if criminal defendants could not impeach the prosecution witnesses in these circumstances.

Subdivision (e) of the rule tracks the common law in providing that the fact that a conviction is on appeal does not render it inadmissible. But the pendency of the appeal may be disclosed to the jury.

Problem V–5. Sharon Dixon is charged with possession of marihuana with intent to distribute. She claims that the twenty pounds of marihuana found in a suitcase in her apartment belonged to a friend and that she did not know about the presence of the substance on her property. After she takes the stand and makes her claim of being an innocent victim of circumstance, the following colloquy ensues:

CROSS-EXAMINATION

Prosecutor: Have you ever been convicted of a felony?

Defense counsel: Your honor, may we be heard outside the presence of the jury?

Court: Yes, ladies and gentlemen of the jury you will please return to the jury room while the court meets with counsel.

---

37. See, e.g., United States v. Cook, 608 F.2d 1175 (9th Cir. 1979) (en banc), certiorari denied, 444 U.S. 1034 (1980) (to obtain an in limine ruling the defendant must state he will testify if the ruling is granted and the prior convictions are excluded, and he must indicate the nature of the testimony he will give).

D.C.: Your honor, the only previous conviction suffered by the defendant is a prior conviction for possession of marihuana with intent to distribute. She was convicted ten years ago and was put on parole after serving two years. For eight years she has been clean. Her prior conviction should be excluded as being more prejudicial than probative.

P: Nonsense, the conviction is essential to show that this testimony about being an innocent victim is false.

Court: I believe that only if the jury knows about the prior conviction can it properly evaluate her defense. So I shall let it in.

The Jury Returns

P.: Ms. Dixon, have you ever been convicted of a felony?

D.: Yes. Once.

P.: When?

Defendant: Ten years ago.

P.: What was the charge?

Defendant: Possession of marihuana with intent to distribute.

P.: What sentence did you get?

D.C.: I object your honor. We don't care about the sentence. Just the crime.

Court: No I will let her answer.

Defendant: Five years.

P.: How much time did you serve?

D.C.: Again we object.

Court: Again, you are overruled.

Defendant: Two years. I was on parole for three.

P.: How much marihuana did you have when you were arrested before?

D.C.: That's irrelevant.

Court: No, I think it sheds light on the conviction. I'll allow it.

Defendant: Eighty pounds.

P.: Where did you keep it?

D.C.: That's irrelevant and even more prejudicial.

Court: That's enough from you, counsel. I have indicated that I am going to permit this line of questioning.

Defendant: In my house.

REDIRECT EXAMINATION

D.C.: Why did you get involved with marihuana ten years ago?

P.: That doesn't matter.

Court: Come here to sidebar and tell me what you are trying to prove.

Sidebar Conference

D.C.: We are trying to show that when she committed the offense ten years ago her mother was dying of cancer and she needed money to pay medical bills.

P.: I think that is inflammatory and has nothing to do with the value of the evidence of the conviction offered for impeachment purposes.

D.C.: Sure it does. It explains why she was willing to break the law once but that she is not a perjurer.

Court: That is too prejudicial. You may ask her whether she had a need for money at the time and that's all.

D.C.: That's not good enough.

Court: That's all.

Which of the judge's rulings would you affirm? Which would you overturn?

Problem V–6. Harold Levat stands charged with the brutal rape of Suzanne Shannon. He claims to be the victim of mistaken identification and takes the stand to testify that at the time Ms. Shannon was raped, he was drinking in a bar with Stanley Surret, one of his best friends. Ten years ago Levat was convicted of a felony, statutory rape. The prosecutor indicates that he will ask about the felony on cross-examination. The defendant objects and urges that it would be more prejudicial than probative. **How should the judge rule?** Assume that the conviction was for rape, not statutory rape. **Does the argument for admission become stronger, weaker, or remain the same? What if the judge indicates that he will permit the defendant to be asked whether he has previously been convicted of a felony, but will not allow the specific felony to be mentioned? Does this remove any problem of undue prejudice? What does it do to the probative value of the evidence?**

Once Levat leaves the stand, he calls Surret to corroborate his story. Surret has previously been convicted of armed robbery (twice) and of assault with intent to rape. The armed robbery convictions are only a year and two years old, but the assault conviction is seven years old. The prosecutor wants to ask about all three convictions, and the defense objects to them all. **Which, if any, would you allow the prosecutor to use for impeachment?**

Problem V–7. Shirley Bassin is one of several defendants charged with conspiracy to violate the Food Stamp Act by pretending to have "families" larger than really existed. Her defense is that the dependents she claimed actually were living with her and were dependent upon her. The prosecution wants to impeach her with a two year old conviction for petit larceny, a misdemeanor. The defendant objects. The following exchange takes place:

P.: Your honor, We have a witness who will testify that the petit larceny involved the defendant's walking into a store to pick up a package that belonged to someone else who had already paid for it. This was a misrepresentation of identity and qualifies for admission under FRE 609(a)(2).

D.C.: Your honor, there is nothing on the face of the conviction to indicate that the defendant did anything but get involved in petty theft.

Court: Well, I am inclined to permit the witness to inform the jury about the circumstances of the prior conviction and to allow the jury to consider the conviction in assessing the credibility of the defendant.

D.C.: Your honor. The rule does not permit any more than a mention of the conviction. Getting into a dispute about who did what and so on is going to be a waste of time and highly prejudicial. We think everything, all mention of the conviction and the details, should be excluded; but certainly if anything is to be allowed, it should only be the fact of the conviction. And we'll stipulate to that if you overrule our basic objection.

What should the judge do?

Problem V–8. Three Philadelphia banks have been robbed in the last two weeks and only one surveillance film has aided the police in identifying the robber. In each robbery a man wearing a golden bandanna approached a teller, revealed a small automatic pistol and asked for money. The one film, while not very clear, has led the grand jury to charge Ralph Riley with all three robberies. Riley, who is unemployed, denies guilt and plans to defend on the ground that he was looking for work during the entire two week period that the robberies encompassed. Riley is thinking about taking the stand in his own defense, but is concerned about a prior bank robbery conviction that is eight years old. He asks the trial judge to rule that the conviction cannot be used to impeach him. The judge indicates that he will permit the impeachment if Riley testifies. Riley does and on direct examination the following testimony is elicited by defense counsel:

Q. Have you ever been convicted of a felony?

A. Yes, I have.

Q. What felony did you commit?

A. Bank robbery.

Q. When?

A. Eight years ago.

The prosecutor objects that this is not really proper impeachment, but merely an attempt to steal the government's thunder by anticipating cross-examination. **Should the objection be sustained or overruled?**

The direct examination continues:

Q. On your prior felony, did you plead guilty or did a judge or jury find you guilty?

A. I pleaded guilty.

Q. Why?

A. Because I was guilty.

Q. And why are you pleading not-guilty now?

A. Because I am not guilty.

If the prosecutor objected to this line of questions, should the objection be sustained?

Problem V–9. Flora Hytel is charged with conspiring with her good friend Joe Lobanks to embezzle money from the bank at which she worked. According to the government, Hytel would pay Lobanks more than the face value of the checks he cashed and the two would later split the difference. Lobanks has pleaded guilty to the crime. When he takes the stand to testify for the government, the government asks whether he has been convicted of a felony. Lobanks is about to answer that he has pleaded guilty to conspiring with Hytel when defense counsel objects and asks that all reference to the conviction be barred. **If the defense is willing to forego impeachment of the witness, should the prosecutor be permitted to bring up the conviction? If the defendant's questions imply that the witness is testifying favorably to the government in exchange for a promise of leniency, should the government be permitted to bring out the fact of the guilty plea?**

Problem V–10. Steven Stone and Prentice Pike were involved in a traffic accident which resulted in the demolition of Pike's motorcycle by Stone's truck. Stone claims that Pike attempted to pass him on the right and that as a consequence he did not see the bike. Pike claims that Stone tried to run him off the road. Claim and counterclaim are consolidated for trial. Stone has previously been convicted of child molesting while Pike has been convicted of assaulting a police officer. Each party wants to use the other's conviction for impeachment and each wants to suppress the use of his own conviction. **What rulings would you make as the trial judge?**

Problem V–11. Izzie Lawson is charged with hiring Tiger McGrath to assassinate his former business partner, Linda Day. According to the government's theory of the case, Lawson became upset with Day for switching partners and decided to seek revenge. Lawson denies hiring McGrath and claims that someone, perhaps even Day, set him up. Lawson has previously been convicted of tax evasion. So has Day. The tax charges stem from an overly generous tax return that the two filed on behalf of the partnership. Day testifies at trial that Lawson threatened her when she told him about her plan to switch business partners. Lawson wants to take the stand to deny the threats and to deny hiring McGrath, but he does not want his prior conviction used against him. He asks the judge to permit him to impeach Day but to prevent the state from impeaching him with the tax evasion conviction. **What should the judge do? Would your decision be the same if the convictions were for aggravated assault arising out of an incident when they jointly attacked a third party?**

Problem V–12. Margaret Mudge, state senator, sues Rebecca Pott, newspaper editor, for libel. The case centers around an article published by Pott accusing Mudge of taking bribes. Mudge claims the story was false and published with knowledge that it was false. Both parties agree the story was false, and the issue at trial is whether the story was published with knowledge that it was false or with reckless disregard of truth or falsity. Pott testifies that several sources of information, persons whose names she refuses to reveal because of a reporter's privilege, gave her the information she used in the story and that she in good faith believed it was true. Mudge calls Ronald Farber to testify that Pott told him she wanted to nail Mudge "one way or another no matter what it takes."

Farber is impeached by two previous convictions, one for bribing a government officer and another for perjury before a grand jury. Both convictions are on appeal at the time of the Mudge-Pott trial. A jury returns a general verdict for Pott. Shortly thereafter, Farber's convictions are reversed on the ground that a diary seized in violation of the fourth amendment was used in his trial. Mudge moves for a new trial on the basis of Farber's technically clean record. **Should Mudge get a new trial? Would the situation be different if the convictions were reversed on the ground that the jury verdicts were against the weight of the evidence? Would the situation be different if Farber were an important witness for a defendant in a criminal trial? If Farber were the defendant? Should impeachment by a conviction still on appeal be permitted?**

Problem V–13. Paul Parker sues his next door neighbor, Nix Nosey, for stealing a billfold from the glove compartment of his car. Paul testifies that soon after he saw Nix close the door of his car he found his billfold missing. Nix admits opening the door of the car, but says he did so only to turn off Paul's lights. He testifies he did not take any billfold or even open the glove compartment. Seven years earlier Nix was convicted on three charges of receiving stolen goods. Paul offers these convictions for impeachment purposes. Nix objects that their prejudicial effect outweighs any impeachment value. **How should the court rule?**

B. IMPEACHMENT BY OTHER BAD ACTS

Most trial witnesses do not have criminal records. But most witnesses, like most people, have done things at some time that might be termed "bad acts." One could easily draft an extensive list of common acts suggesting dishonesty: lying to parents, plagiarism, "borrowing" goods without permission, not returning borrowed goods, breaking promises, evading taxes; the list could go on and on. The issue courts face is whether any or all of these actions should be grounds for impeaching witnesses who testify in civil or criminal trials. The controversy surrounding the use of prior convictions to impeach might lead one to expect that evidence of bad acts would be inadmissible for this purpose, particularly since bad acts, unlike prior crimes, have not been independently proved. But, courts are aware that dishonesty is not limited to criminals. Indeed, dishonesty is often more evident in acts that are merely bad than in acts which result in criminal convictions. Moreover, many, though not all, prior bad acts will have less potential for prejudice than most criminal convictions.

Even if evidence of particular bad acts is useful in assessing credibility, the use of bad acts raises the question of the extent to which courts are willing to focus on isolated aspects of a witness' life in order to test that witness' credibility. The value of a searching inquiry into a witness' moral history is likely at some point to be outweighed by the time taken, the dangers of distracting the jury, and the possibility of discouraging witnesses from volunteering evidence.

FRE 608(b) reflects the common law's compromise between the value of prior bad acts on the issue of credibility and the danger that they will become too much the focus of attention.

Specific instances of the conduct of a witness, for the purpose of attacking or supporting his credibility, other than conviction of crime as provided in rule 609, may not be proved by extrinsic evidence. They may, however, in the discretion of the court, if probative of truthfulness or untruthfulness, be inquired into on cross-examination of the witness (1) concerning his character for truthfulness or untruthfulness. * * * [38]

Under the federal rule and in most common law jurisdictions any witness, including the accused in a criminal case,[39] may be asked about specific instances of conduct if relevant to credibility. But the witness' answer is conclusive; if the prior acts are denied, no additional evidence can be introduced to contradict the witness' story. The examiner may, however, continue to inquire about bad acts until it is clear that the witness is firm in his denial:

Nor is it improper for a district attorney to continue his cross-examination about a specific crime after a defendant has

---

38. The rule also provides that a witness may be asked specific questions "(2) concerning the character for truthfulness or untruthfulness of another witness as to which character the witness being cross-examined has testified." This is the *Michelson* rule, discussed in Chapter Four, applied to character evidence for truth and veracity. The knowledge of reputation, or the basis of an opinion of a character witness, may be tested.

Although most common law jurisdiction permitted questions about prior bad acts, a substantial minority of jurisdictions did not. In fact, the majority of federal courts did not permit this form of impeachment before the Federal Rules of Evidence were enacted. See Orfield, Impeachment and Support of Witnesses in Federal Criminal Cases, 11 U.Kan.L.Rev. 447, 460–64 (1963). Interestingly, the Advisory Committee did not note the existing state of federal law, but focused more on state decisions. The Congress was more concerned with rule 609 than with this rule and apparently did not realize that bad act impeachment had not been permitted by most federal courts. Some commentators have been quite critical of this mode of impeachment. See McCormick § 42; Brooks, The Treatment of Witnesses in the Proposed Federal Rules of Evidence, 25 Rec. of N.Y.C.B.A. 637 (1970). But see Hale, Specific Acts and Related Matters as Affecting Credibility, 1 Hastings L.J. 89 (1950).

39. The last paragraph of FRE 608(b) provides that the "giving of testimony, whether by an accused or by any other witness, does not operate as a waiver of his privilege against self-incrimination when examined with respect to matters which relate only to credibility." This is a protection for any witness but especially for the accused in a criminal case. It ensures that if he takes the stand to testify, he will not be forced to incriminate himself with respect to other crimes, inquired into under the guise of impeachment by prior bad acts. Weinstein and Berger suggest that the accused need not admit other criminal activity if it falls within this paragraph. 3 Weinstein's Evidence ¶ 608[05]. But is this the rule? Might the witness be provided immunity for his answers? This would seem to remove any threat of self-incrimination.

The Advisory Committee on the Federal Rules said that this provision rejects the doctrine of People v. Sorge, 301 N.Y. 198, 93 N.E.2d 637 (1950). Does it? In Sorge, a defendant on trial for committing abortions was cross-examined about four other abortions on different women. The court held this was a proper subject of "cross-examination for credit." Most jurisdictions allow cross-examination only with respect to those bad acts which relate directly to credibility. A majority of states put some restrictions on particular kinds of bad acts, such as arrests. Would cross-examination as in Sorge be improper under the Federal Rule? Would introducing extrinsic evidence?

denied committing it. As long as he acts in good faith, in the hope of inducing the witness to abandon his negative answers, the prosecutor may question further * * * In other words, a negative response will not fob off [preclude] further interrogation of the witness himself, for, if it did, the witness would have it within his power to render futile most cross-examination. The rule is clear that while a witness' testimony regarding collateral matters may not be refuted by the calling of other witnesses or by the production of extrinsic evidence * * * there is no prohibition against examining the witness himself further on the chance that he may change his testimony or his answer.[40]

Of course, such probing is likely to suggest that the witness in fact committed the bad acts in question. Unless the attorney has good reason to believe this is the case, extensive probing on the matter would be unethical.

Why should extrinsic evidence of bad acts be barred if extrinsic evidence of prior convictions is permitted? Weinstein and Berger suggest that:

[T]he difference in treatment is mandated by considerations of policy against unduly extending the trial, surprise and prejudice.[41]

Are these reasons persuasive? Isn't the trial judge's power to balance the probative value of evidence against countervailing considerations a better means of avoiding these dangers than a blanket rule? Wouldn't a notice requirement provide adequate protection against unfair surprise? As for prejudice, isn't that limited when bad act evidence is limited to credibility, and isn't it likely to arise from the questioning permissible under the current rule? In fact, the restriction on the use of extrinsic evidence to prove bad acts is probably a compromise between total exclusion and treatment analogous to con-

victions. The compromise makes a certain amount of sense since convictions may usually be proved by the introduction of indisputable official records, but proof of bad acts might require extensive testimony and always be open to question.

Perhaps the strongest argument which can be made in favor of bad act evidence lies in the examples which may be given of witnesses whose testimony was properly destroyed through the use of this kind of evidence. Consider just one classic instance:

Henry E. Lazarus, a prominent merchant in this city, was indicted a few years ago by the Federal Grand Jury, charged with the offense of bribing a United States officer and violation of the Sabotage Act, but was honorably acquitted by a jury after a thirty minute deliberation. It was during the height of the war and Mr. Lazarus was a very large manufacturer of rubber coats and had manufactured hundreds of thousands for the Government under contract. The Government for its protection employed large numbers of inspectors, and in the heat and excitement of war times these inspectors occasionally tried to "make good." One of these efforts resulted in the indictment of Lazarus.

The chief witness against Lazarus was Charles L. Fuller, Supervising Inspector attached to the Depot Quartermaster's Office in New York City. Fuller testified that Lazarus gave money to him to influence him in regard to his general duties as an inspector, and to overlook the fact that Lazarus was manufacturing defective coats and thereby violating the Sabotage Act.

Martin W. Littleton acted as chief counsel for the defense and was fully appreciative of Mr. Lazarus' high character and of his conscientious discharge of his duties in the manufacture of material for the Government. He was also well informed as to the general character and history of

---

40. People v. Sorge, 301 N.Y. 198, 200, 93 N.E.2d, 637, 639 (1950).

41. 3 Weinstein's Evidence ¶ 608[05].

Fuller. After Fuller testified in chief, he was first questioned closely as to the time when be became an employee of the Government, counsel knowing that he was *required to make and sign and swear to an application as to his prior experience.*

A messenger had been sent to the Government files to get the original of this application, signed by the witness, and came into court with the document in his hand just as counsel was putting the following question:

Q. "Did you sign such an application?" **A.** "I did, sir."

Q. "Did you swear to it?" **A.** "No, I did not swear to it."

Q. "I show you your name signed on the bottom of this blank, and ask you if you signed that?" **A.** "Yes, sir."

Q. "Do you see it is sworn to?" **A.** "I had forgotten it."

Q. "You see there is a seal on it?" **A.** "I had forgotten that also."

Q. "This application appears to be subscribed on the 24th of May, 1918, by Charles Lawrence Fuller." **A.** "It must be right if I have sworn to it on that date."

Q. "Do you remember in May, 1918, that you signed and swore to this application?" **A.** "That is so, I must have sworn to it, sir."

Q. "Do you remember it?" **A.** "Let me look at it and I can probably refresh my memory."

(Paper handed to witness)

Q. "Look at the signature. Does that help you?" **A.** "That is my signature."

Q. "You said that. Do you remember in May, 1918, you signed and swore to this?" **A.** "Well, the date is there."

Q. "Do you know that?" **A.** "Yes, sir, I must have sworn to it. I don't remember the date."

Q. "Don't you remember you signed your name, Charles Lawrence Fuller, there?" **A.** "I did, sir."

Q. "And you swore to this paper and signed it?" **A.** "That date is correct there, yes, sir."

Q. "Don't you remember you swore to it the date you signed it?" **A.** "I swore to it."

Q. "Was your name Fuller?" **A.** "Yes, sir."

Q. "Has your name always been Fuller?" **A.** "No, sir."

Q. "What was your name?"

The witness protested against any further inquiry along that line, but counsel was permitted to show that his name at one time was Finkler and that he changed his name, back and forth, from Finkler to Fuller.

Counsel then proceeded to bring the witness down to the actual oath he had taken in his application.

Q. "Now, Mr. Fuller, in your application you made to the Government, on which I showed you your signature and affidavit, you attached your picture, did you not?" **A.** "Yes, sir."

Q. "And you stated in your application you were born in Atlanta, Georgia, did you not?" **A.** "Yes, sir."

Q. "You were asked, when you sought this position, these questions: 'When employed, the years and the months,' and you wrote in, 'February, 1897 to August, 1917, number of years 20; Where employed—Brooklyn; Name of Employer—Vulcan Proofing Company; Amount of salary,—$37.50 a week; also superintendent in the rubber and compound room.'"

Q. "You wrote that, didn't you?" **A.** "Yes, sir."

Q. "And swore to that, didn't you?" **A.** "Yes, sir."

Q. "Now, were you employed from February, 1897, to August, 1917, twenty years, with the Vulcan Proofing Company?" **A.** "No, sir."

Q. "That was not true, was it?" **A.** "No, sir."

Q. "And had you been assistant superintendent of the rubber and compound room?" **A.** "No, sir."

Q. "That was false, wasn't it?" **A.** "Yes, sir."

Q. " 'And through my experience as chief inspector of the rubber and slicker division,' that was false, wasn't it?" **A.** "Yes, sir."

Q. "You knew it was false, didn't you?" **A.** "Yes, sir."

Q. "And you knew you were swearing to a falsehood when you swore to it?" **A.** "Yes, sir."

Q. "And you swore to it intentionally?" **A.** "Yes, sir."

Q. "And you knew you were committing perjury when you swore to it?" **A.** "I did not look at it in that light."

Q. "Didn't you know you were committing perjury by swearing and pretending you had been twenty years in this business?" **A.** "Yes, sir."

Q. "And you are swearing now, aren't you?" **A.** "Yes, sir."

Q. "In a matter in which a man's liberty is involved?" **A.** "Yes, sir."

Q. "And you know that the jury is to be called upon to consider whether you are worthy of belief or not, don't you?" **A.** "Yes, sir."

Q. "When you swore to this falsehood deliberately, and wrote it in your handwriting, and knew it was false, you swore to it intentionally, and you knew that you were committing perjury, didn't you?" **A.** "I did not look at it in that light."

Q. "Well, now, when you know you are possibly swearing away the liberty of a citizen of this community, do you look at it in the same light?" **A.** "Yes, sir, I do."

Mr. Littleton then uncovered the fact that the witness, instead of having been twenty years superintendent of a rubber room with the Vulcan Proofing Company, as he had sworn in his own handwriting, was a stag entertainer in questionable houses, was a barker at a Coney Island show, was an advance agent of a cheap road show and had been published in the paper as having drawn checks that were worthless, the witness fully admitting all of the details of his twenty years of questionable transactions. The result was his utter collapse so far as his credibility was concerned, and the Government's case collapsed with him.

The point of the cross-examination and the design of the cross-examiner was to get the witness at the outset of his cross-examination in a position from which he could not possibly extricate himself, by confronting him with this document, written in his own handwriting in which he would be obliged to admit that he had sworn falsely. The witness having been thoroughly subjugated by this process would then, as he actually did, confess to twenty years of gadding about in questionable employment, under different names, and thus completely destroy himself as a reliable witness in the eyes of the jury.[42]

This is a dramatic example of prior bad act impeachment. It is unclear, however, whether the utility of such impeachment in cases like Lazarus' outweighs the arguable unfairness of asking witnesses about unproved acts in the general run of cases.[43]

Because the federal rule bars extrinsic evidence from being used to contradict a witness who denies a prior act, it sometimes is said that the rule invites any witness to deny all acts whether or not they have occurred. A witness who lies about a prior act is subject to a prosecution for perjury following the lie, however. The rule simply bars litigation about the prior act within a trial that is concerned with other acts.[44]

Problem V–14. Susan Stoll has been indicted along with two other women, Harriet Hampton and Molly MacLaine, for criminal conspiracy to defraud by misrepresenting the financial condition of a business concern. She is being tried separately. The defense calls Harriet Hampton to testify on behalf of Stoll. She testifies at some length concerning the preparation and results of an important audit she had conducted as an accountant for Stoll and MacLaine. The prosecution on cross-examination wants to ask the following question: "You testified concerning these transactions in the case of the State against Hampton, and the State against MacLaine, giving then the same explanations that you have given us here, did you not?" Stoll objects. **What is the proper ruling? If the prosecution wants to establish that this witness testified to the same thing in her own trial and was convicted, would you permit this line of inquiry? How far would you allow**

---

42. Wellman, The Art of Cross-Examination 37–41 (4th ed. 1936). For an enlightening modern case, see Johnson v. Brewer, 521 F.2d 556 (8th Cir. 1975).

43. **It can be argued that in some ways individuals are held more responsible for their prior bad acts than for their criminal convictions. A convicted criminal can be pardoned; prior bad acts are never forgiven under the rules of evidence. A conviction ordinarily will require mens rea, whereas a prior bad act may focus solely on action.**

44. It is precisely because the witness must answer questions about bad acts honestly or risk perjury charges that a direct examiner might choose to bring out the prior bad acts of a witness he has called if he believes that an opponent will do so on cross-examination.

it to go?   Would you allow the prosecutor to ask Hampton whether she had perjured herself in the earlier trials?

Problem V–15.   In the criminal conspiracy case described in the preceding problem, the defendant was acquitted.   Two years later she is again indicted, this time for tax fraud.   After Susan testifies in her own behalf, the prosecutor asks whether she was ever involved in a criminal conspiracy to defraud.   An objection is raised by the defendant together with a request to the court to bar the prosecutor from pursuing this line of questioning. **Should the objection be sustained and the request granted?   Assuming the objection is not sustained and the question allowed, formulate those questions which you would ask as prosecutor if Susan's answer is that she never was involved in a criminal conspiracy.**

Problem V–16.   Maria Cox stands charged with illegally importing marihuana and with possessing marihuana with the intent to distribute.   Her version of the facts is that she had gone from Texas to Mexico to have her hair done and had parked her auto in a free customer lot, leaving the keys with an attendant.   Unbeknownst to her, ten kilos of marihuana were in her car when she brought it back to the United States.   During the cross-examination of Cox, the government offers two documents: First, a sworn statement made fourteen years earlier in which Cox states that she had used another name, had entered the United States with a false birth certificate, and had worked as a prostitute in the United States and Mexico;   second, an FBI rap sheet which listed a 1958 violation of the immigration laws, a 1960 civil deportation proceeding, a 1960 fine for vagrancy, and the arrest for the marihuana offenses giving rise to the instant case.   Cox objects to the use of the documents and to any questions concerning the matters they mention. **Should her objection be sustained in whole or in part?**

Problem V–17.   Fidel Ostrow is a prisoner in a federal penitentiary located at Lewisburg, Pa.   He has sued two prison guards, claiming that they assaulted him and thereby deprived him of his civil rights.   During cross-examination of Ostrow, the guards' lawyer asks whether Ostrow had written a letter to another inmate telling him how to "set up" a suit against a guard.   Ostrow admits that he had written a letter telling another inmate how to file suit.   The guards' attorney then successfully offers into evidence a letter from Ostrow to another inmate which could be read as an explanation of how to "set up" a brutality claim.   Ostrow objects to the introduction of the letter.   **Should it be excluded under Rule 608(b)?**

Problem V–18.   Bernard Sugar, the district attorney for Wabash County, is indicted for accepting bribes from local "numbers" operators in return for leaving them alone.   At trial Sugar takes the stand and denies ever accepting money as payment for overlooking criminal activity.   On cross-examination, the special prosecutor appointed to represent the state initiates the following exchange:

Q.   Did you ever mishandle a client's money while you were in the private practice of law?

A.   No, never.

Q. Isn't it a fact that you commingled Sara Jane Dodley's trust funds with your own bank account just five years ago?

A. That's a lie.

Q. Didn't Sara Jane Dodley file a complaint against you with the local bar association?

A. I don't recall. She may have, but if she did she lied.

Q. Didn't the state bar association reprimand you for the way you handled the trust funds of Sara Jane Dodley?

A. No, they never really reprimanded me.

Q. Let me show you this letter you received from the bar association to refresh your recollection. Now I repeat, were you reprimanded?

A. No.

During the course of the colloquy defense counsel persistently objected, but to no avail. **Would you have permitted this examination? Would you allow the prosecutor to introduce the letter that was handed to Sugar?**

C. IMPEACHMENT BY CHARACTER EVIDENCE

Impeachment by prior convictions and impeachment by prior bad acts are forms of character evidence. They are based on the supposition that a person who has acted wrongfully in the past has a special propensity to lie under oath. Such evidence is considered relevant no matter what the case or the witness' testimony in the case. A propensity to lie makes any testimony suspect. If these modes of impeachment are questionable, it is because one wonders whether the character they imply is indicative of a tendency to lie.

A related mode of impeachment, which is also applicable regardless of case or testimony, obviates the need to infer character from action. When an opposing witness is known to have a dishonest character, this may be shown directly. Lawyers speak of this mode of impeachment as proving a bad character for truth and veracity.[45]

Character evidence relating to credibility is accepted by the same courts that clas- sify character evidence as irrelevant when it is offered to prove the merits of a case. A justification for the different treatment is that a witness' credibility must be examined once testimony is taken, while character need not be inquired into on the merits since the question is not whether a party is more likely than most people to have done something, but whether he actually did it in the case before the court. This is a specious distinction. If evidence of a bad reputation for truth and veracity is admitted to impeach a witness, it comes in on the theory that someone who generally lies is likely to lie on the witness stand. This use of character evidence does not differ in any appreciable way from use of evidence that X has a reputation as a dangerous driver to show that X probably drove dangerously on a particular occasion. Many of the dangers of prejudicing a party by showing that he is a bad person exist when a party is shown to be a liar. Indeed, attacks on credibility raise additional problems of prejudice since every

---

45. 3A Wigmore §§ 920–930.

witness is subject to such impeachment, whereas it is usually only the character of the parties which is relevant to the merits of a case. Of course, when the character of witnesses other than the parties is impugned, the evidence is likely to be less devastating than when the character of the parties is attacked.

When character evidence is offered for impeachment purposes, it must be proved in the same way as character evidence which relates circumstantially to the merits of the case. In jurisdictions that do not follow the Federal Rules, this usually means that proof is limited to reputation evidence.[46] However, there is one common escape from this rule found in many jurisdictions. After testifying that a witness' reputation for truth and veracity is bad, the reputation witness may be asked, in most jurisdictions, whether he would believe the witness under oath. He is allowed to leave the jury with his negative opinion.[47]

Under FRE 608(a) character evidence in the form of opinion may be used. This is, of course, consistent with Rule 405, discussed in Chapter Four.[48]

A very few courts have permitted evidence of a witness' general moral character to be introduced to impeach credibility. It has been argued that character witnesses who testify about reputation for truth and veracity are in fact relying more on general moral reputation than on a specific reputation for honesty. But even if this is the case, admitting general reputation for immorality increases the probability that the witness and the party associated with him will be prejudiced by the character evidence. When evidence of general bad character is admitted as bearing on the credibility of a party witness, the likelihood of prejudice is great.

Character witnesses offered for impeachment can in theory be cross-examined by "have you heard" or "do you know" questions in order to probe the standards they are applying and to test their familiarity with the relevant behavior of those they have been called to impeach. However, while one act of cheating or lying might taint a person's reputation forever, few honest acts establish a lasting reputation. (Perhaps if a witness found and returned a lost money bag, evidence of this would be useful on cross-examination.) Otherwise, the right to cross-examine a witness to bad character about what he has heard or knows is likely to be less helpful than the right to examine a witness to good character about isolated bad acts.

Problem V–19. In a negligence action arising out of an automobile accident, would you admit for impeachment, after the plaintiff indicates that the accident was the defendant's fault, evidence that the plaintiff is reported to be a careless driver? Would you permit an eyewitness to a robbery to be impeached by a reputation for daydreaming and inattentiveness? In a

46. In a few jurisdictions, opinion evidence has been admitted to prove general good character, but only reputation evidence has been admitted on the question of truth and veracity. There appears to be no good reason for the difference.

47. When a witness has been impeached in this way, other witnesses may be called to state that the witness has in fact a good reputation for truth and veracity. They will be allowed to give their opinions that they would believe him under oath.

48. When reputation evidence is used, the reputation should be the witness' reputation as of the time of the trial, rather than the reputation at the time of the events giving rise to the trial. Like reputation evidence which relates to the merits, reputation for truth and veracity originally had to refer to reputation in some neighborhood or community. Now, in most jurisdictions, character witnesses may refer to reputation in some other relevant "community," such as a place of work.

custody fight would you permit one spouse to impeach the other's testimony about qualifications to care for children by a reputation for unchastity or for drunkenness? Would you allow evidence of specific instances of conduct in any of the above cases? **If you answer yes to all these questions, is it because you are prepared to discard the entire propensity rule? If you answer yes to some, what justifies the line you are drawing? If you consistently answer no, are you opposed to this evidence because it is not relevant, because it is relevant but dangerous, or because you think the law should be consistent and either accept or reject character evidence without regard to whether it is tied to a substantive or impeachment purpose?**

Problem V–20. Charles Fairfax is on trial for perjury. He takes the stand and denies the substance of the charges under oath. **Should the prosecution be able to introduce witnesses who will testify that Fairfax has a bad reputation for truth and veracity? Would your answer be the same if Fairfax were being tried for assault with a deadly weapon?**

D. IMPEACHMENT BY PRIOR INCONSISTENT STATEMENTS [49]

When a person first says one thing and then another, the inconsistency casts doubt on the truth of both statements. Reasonable minds want to reconcile the statements somehow, to have the inconsistency explained, to discover which statement or which parts of which statements are correct. Thus, when a witness testifies at trial, evidence of her prior inconsistent statements may be introduced to impeach her testimony.

In comon law jurisdictions a rigid foundation is required when prior statements of a witness are used for this purpose. Before introducing extrinsic evidence of a prior inconsistent statement, the witness must be reminded of the statement and given an opportunity to deny making it or to explain away the inconsistency.[50] The examiner typically asks the witness whether or not she recalls making a prior statement to an identified party at or about a certain time. The rationale for this requirement is that if the witness says that she does remember making such a statement, recalls the statement, and explains it, there is no need for extrinsic evidence. If the witness denies making the statement, the prior inconsistent statement usually may be proved by other evidence. However, certain inconsistent statements, termed "collateral," are not provable by extrinsic evidence, even if dishonestly denied. These are discussed below. As was true of stipulations, the witness who admits a prior statement must make more than a qualified or tentative admission to

49. FRE 613, discussed infra, assumes that this is a permissible form of impeachment, but does not say so explicitly. Since the fact that a witness has told varying stories would seem to be relevant to assessing credibility and Rule 402 admits relevant evidence absent some exclusionary rule, it appears that forms of impeachment not explicitly approved by the Federal Rules of Evidence are permissible.

50. The reminder that a witness must be given is relatively simple. It might be as follows: "Let me call your attention to a conversation you had with Ed Jones on June 4, 1980. Do you recall telling him that you had been drinking on the night of the accident?"

Extrinsic evidence is evidence other than the testimony of the witness being examined. Usually it will involve testimony from other witnesses, but it may involve an admissible document.

forestall other proof. The details of the previous declaration are fair game for the examiner and they must be conceded before extrinsic proof will be barred.

FRE 613(b) modifies the common law requirement that a foundation be laid *before* the impeachment by providing:

> Extrinsic evidence of a prior inconsistent statement by a witness is not admissible unless the witness is afforded an opportunity to explain or deny the same and the opposite party is afforded an opportunity to interrogate him thereon, or the interests of justice otherwise require. This provision does not apply to admissions of a party-opponent as defined in rule 801(d)(2).[51]

The modification occurs because the inconsistent statement may be used as long as *at some point,* but not necessarily before extrinsic evidence is offered, there is an opportunity for the impeached witness to confront the alleged inconsistent statement. Edward Cleary, the Reporter for the Advisory Committee, explained the modification as follows:

> The objectives of the [common law] procedure are: (1) to save time, since the witness may admit having made the statement and thus make the extrinsic proof necessary; (2) to avoid unfair surprise to the opposite party by affording him an opportunity to draw a denial or explanation from the witness; and (3) to give the witness himself, in fairness, a chance to deny or to explain the apparent discrepancy. These are desirable objectives. The second and third can, however, be achieved by affording an opportunity to explain at any time during the trial, and no particular time sequence is required. Only the first of the objectives named above, saving time, points in the direction of the traditional foundation requirement on

cross-examination, and even here countervailing factors are present: the time saved is not great; the laying of the foundation may inadvertently have been overlooked; the impeaching statement may not have been discovered until later; and premature disclosure may on occasion frustrate the effective impeachment of collusive witnesses. The argument may be made that the recalling of a witness for further cross-examination will afford an adequate solution for these difficulties and hence the traditional procedure should be retained. The argument is not a sound one. In the first place, recall for cross-examination has traditionally been very much within the discretion of the judge and seems likely to continue so. And secondly, the admissibility of prior inconsistent statements ought not to be enmeshed in the technicalities of cross-examination when all that is being sought is the presentation of an opportunity to deny or explain.

> In view of these considerations, the Advisory Committee concluded that the objectives could better be achieved by allowing the opportunity to deny or explain to occur at any time during the trial, rather than limiting it to cross-examination.

> Moreover, occasionally situations may arise where the interests of justice will warrant dispensing entirely with the opportunity to explain or deny. Thus if a witness becomes unavailable through absence or death, the judge ought to have discretion to allow the impeaching statement.

> In my view, the existing practice would continue in general to be followed under the rule. It is convenient and effective to raise the matter on cross-examination, and doing so would avoid

---

51. The last sentence excepts from any foundation requirement statements that qualify as admissions of a party. The reason for

this will be obvious when party admissions are discussed in the next chapter.

problems that might ultimately arise if witnesses become unavailable before the end of the trial. The rule ought, however, to remain as drawn, leaving the practical approach to the good sense of the practitioner.[52]

———

We wonder about the wisdom of this modification. The Reporter acknowledges that it can waste time. It may also give prior statements which a witness would readily acknowledge more impact than they might warrant, because the statements will not be followed immediately by an explanation. Finally, the change inconveniences witnesses who wish to minimize the time they must take from work or other activities. Under the federal rule a witness who apparently has nothing more to add must stay in court until the other party's case-in-chief or case-in-rebuttal has concluded, or there is a risk that a prior statement may be introduced when the alleged declarant is unavailable to acknowledge or explain it.[53] In these circumstances, the costly alternative of a continuance may be necessary to insure fairness. The change is directed at legitimate problems: the problems which Cleary alludes to of an inadvertent failure to lay a foundation, late discovery of the inconsistent statement, and the danger of

prematurely alerting collusive witnesses to the evidence available for impeachment.[54] However, these problems might be better dealt with by adding to the standard common law foundation requirement a sentence such as the following:

The trial judge shall permit witnesses to be recalled for purposes of laying a foundation for impeachment if satisfied that failure to lay a foundation earlier was not intentional, or if intentional, was for good cause; even if no foundation is laid, an inconsistent statement may be admitted in the interests of justice.[55]

Do you prefer the rule as written or our alternative?

Though the federal rule is not clear on this, it would appear that there are still situations in which the cross-examiner must confront the witness with her inconsistent statement or lose all chance of bringing it up. This is when the inconsistent statement involves "collateral" matters; that is, the statements do not have as their subject: (1) facts relevant to the issues in the case, or (2) facts which are themselves provable by extrinsic evidence to discredit the witness. Facts showing bias or interest, and presumably facts showing the witness had no opportunity to know the material matters testified to would fall in the second class.[56]

52. Letter from Edward W. Cleary to Hon. William L. Hungate, May 8, 1973, in Supplement to Hearings Before the Subcomm. on Criminal Justice of the House Comm. on the Judiciary, 93rd Cong., 1st Sess., at 74–75 (1973).

53. **The federal rule does not explicitly place the burden of recall on either side, although it might seem to rest on the party seeking an explanation of the prior statement since that party is the one that would be hurt by impeachment. There is a good argument, however, that the burden should rest with the party doing the impeachment, since that party knows that it has impeachment evidence that it intends to use and can make arrangements to ensure that the impeached witness has an adequate opportunity to explain or deny the inconsistent statement.**

54. The sequestration of witnesses, often a wise tactic when witnesses are suspected of collusion, may diminish this difficulty considerably.

55. While this would also require witnesses to be recalled in certain circumstances and might necessitate continuances, these situations are likely to arise less frequently than those situations where the federal rule would allow the proof of inconsistent statements by extrinsic testimony subject to later explanation.

56. McCormick § 361, at 71. McCormick notes that some courts have adopted a somewhat narrower test of collateralness: whether the party would have been entitled to prove the matter as part of his case.

At common law extrinsic evidence of inconsistent statements could not be introduced if the evidence were collateral in this sense. Presumably the practical effect of this prohibition does not totally disappear under the Federal Rules. Suppose a witness states she had just come from a business deal when she saw the defendant attack the plaintiff. A jury which knew that the witness had stated earlier that she had just come from a poker game might be led to question the witness' veracity on facts directly in issue. But unless the examiner confronts the witness with her earlier inconsistent statement, the jury might never learn of it. If the witness denies a prior inconsistent but collateral statement, the examiner, as with prior bad acts, might be precluded from introducing extrinsic evidence. This is not because there is any federal rule barring "collateral" statements. Rather, it is because the trial judge will want to avoid extensive disputes about minor facts and has the flexibility to do so under FRE 403. Where the inconsistency seems probative of credibility despite its minimal substantive implications the court may let it in.

In common law jurisdictions, before a witness could be questioned about a prior written statement, the statement had to be shown to the witness and the rest of the foundation laid. This is known as the rule of the Queen's case (Queen Caroline).[57] The United States Supreme Court approved the rule in 1855,[58] but commentators have been highly critical of it because it gives the witness faced with a statement she cannot deny a chance to fabricate an explanation of the statement. If a witness could be questioned about a statement without seeing it, cross-examination might be more effective.[59] Even prior to the adoption of the Federal Rules of Evidence most federal courts had abandoned the doctrine. Judge Learned Hand noted that the doctrine "is everywhere more honored in the breach than in the observance."[60] Critics of the doctrine do not assert that there should be no foundation; they simply urge that calling the witness' attention to when and where an allegedly contradictory statement was made is sufficient.[61]

FRE 613(a) modifies the common law along the lines suggested above:

> In examining a witness concerning a prior statement made by him, whether written or not, the statement need not be shown nor its contents disclosed to him at that time, but on request the same shall be shown or disclosed to opposing counsel.

Many opinions discuss the degree of inconsistency that is required before extrinsic evidence of a previous statement will be permitted. Generally the terminology used is that the statement must contain a *material* inconsistency, a vague formulation that gives great discretion to the trial judge. Many courts and commentators make the mistake of using the terms "immaterial" and "collateral" interchangeably. "Immaterial" in this context refers to the degree of inconsistency and "collateral" to the relationship of the inconsistent statements to a matter in issue. Rather than invoking one term or the other without much thought, careful courts recognize that the trial judge makes a relevancy ruling in determining whether to admit inconsistent statements.[62] Previous statements may or

57. 2 Brod. & Bing. 284, 129 Eng.Rep. 976 (1820).

58. The Charles Morgan, 115 U.S. 69, 77–78 (1855).

59. There is the corresponding danger that a basically honest witness might be led by a skillful cross-examiner into a situation where a contradiction appears much more damning than it in fact is. To some degree this danger always exists on cross-examination, whatever the modes of impeachment allowed.

60. United States v. Dilliard, 101 F.2d 829, 837 (2d Cir. 1938), certiorari denied, 306 U.S. 635 (1939).

61. Id.

62. Some courts make the mistake of not admitting statements unless they can only be interpreted as inconsistent. If another

may not be helpful in assessing the credibility of the witness. Assuming they are helpful, they may demand more court time than is justified by their value. Moreover, some statements may be made under circumstances that might be unduly prejudicial—e.g., where a defendant, while testifying, has made a statement only slightly inconsistent with a statement made while in custody for another crime.

You may wonder if the relevance of prior statements should be assessed only on the basis of their implications for credibility, since they may also shed light on the merits of the case. It is true that prior inconsistent statements are relevant to the substantive issues in a case, but, as Chapter Six will explain in greater detail, inconsistent out-of-court statements are usually inadmissible hearsay when offered for the truth of what they assert.[63] Where such statements are introduced, the jury is instructed that it can only use the statements to test credibility, not for substantive purposes.[64]

Of course, the jury may not fully adhere to the instruction and may consider a statement offered—in theory—to show that a vacillating witness cannot be trusted as reason to believe the truth of what it asserts. The problem is particularly acute where the direct examiner chooses to impeach a witness by a prior inconsistent statement, for the question arises as to whether the direct examiner called the witness as a way of bringing the inconsistent statement to the jury's attention. On its face FRE 607 appears to allow this, for it allows any party to impeach a witness including the party calling him. However, courts do not have to interpret the rule so as to allow this. If a witness' in-court testimony does not aid the calling party, its relevance will be limited, at least on the point for which it is offered. Thus, the testimony may be barred under FRE 403, and impeachment will not be necessary.

A few commentators have argued for readoption of the common law rule, which in most instances limited the direct examiner's use of prior inconsistent statements to situations in which a witness' testimony surprised the direct examiner and tended to undercut his case.[65] One of the authors accepts this argument for he considers a relatively liberal attitude toward the impeachment of one's own witnesses by prior inconsistent statements to be an invitation to abuse that is best avoided by a "bright line" rule. Given the federal rule's limitation of cross-examination to the scope of direct, if a party knows that a witness' testimony will be unhelpful with respect to a particular matter, he should not interrogate the witness on the matter in question. He should certainly not be allowed to interrogate the witness in order to introduce an out-of-court statement that would be

interpretation might reconcile the statements, the prior statement is excluded. This prevents the jury from learning whether the witness would have explained away the inconsistency by supplying a consistent interpretation. Se Hale, Impeachment of Witnesses By Prior Inconsistent Statements, 10 So.Cal.L.Rev. 135, 161 (1937). The error is similar to the use of the "plus" concept employed by some courts in relevance determinations, a use which is criticised in Chapter Three.

63. You will also find that almost everything a party says is admissible for substantive purposes under the "admissions" exception to the hearsay rule. Thus, much of our discussion, such as the discussion of the Rule in the Queen's Case, will not apply where the witness is a party because the statement can be admitted for a purpose other than impeachment.

64. FRE 801(d)(1)(A) allows prior statements made under oath subject to the penalty of perjury to be used on substantive issues. Cal.Evid.Code, Ann. § 1235 (West 1966) allows all prior inconsistent statements to be used for substantive as well as impeachment purposes. Most commentators applaud this approach. But see our discussion of this issue in Chapter Six infra.

65. See, e.g., Graham, The Relationship Among Federal Rules of Evidence 607, 801 (d)(1)(A), and 403: A Reply to Weinstein's Evidence, 55 Tex.L.Rev. 573 (1977).

otherwise inadmissible. The other author, who believes a "bright line" rule is an overreaction, would leave more to judicial discretion. He offers the following example:

The victim of an assault takes the stand and testifies that the assailant was 5'10" tall, approximately 150 lbs., white, male, wearing a red shirt, and a blue hat. He had previously told the prosecutor that the shirt was blue and the hat red. Other witnesses who did not observe the assailant as clearly as the victim did have described an assailant of similar height and weight, but wearing a blue shirt and a red hat. The prosecutor has discovered in his final interview with the witness that he now firmly believes that his previous statement was either a mistake on his part or a mistake in recordation. The prosecutor believes that he must ask the victim to describe the assailant, but he is worried that the jury might find a reasonable doubt on the basis of conflicts among witnesses unless he impeaches the testimony about the red shirt and blue hat with the prior statement.

This example suggests to one of us that the prosecutor should be permitted to call the victim as a witness, that he should be permitted to ask for a description of the assailant, and that he should be permitted to use the prior statement to show that the victim was less certain as to the shirt and hat colors than as to other matters. Permitting partial impeachment of a witness' story may serve to encourage prosecutors and other attorneys to develop testimony so as to actually reveal defects in their cases that ought to be known to the trier of fact. Conversations of this author with federal judges who now utilize a balancing approach under FRE 403 when presented with problems like the one posed in the example convince him that the dangers of too liberal receipt of impeachment evidence are exaggerated and pale in significance to the balancing that judges are now asked to do in connection with FRE 404(b) and 609(a)(1). This author emphasizes that impeachment does not necessarily mean attacking a witness generally; it may mean a more specific form of attack that endeavors to preserve the integrity of much of the witness' testimony while challenging only a portion. Under this approach, careful lawyers would ask trial judges for permission to impeach their own witnesses before calling them, at least whenever they expect a problem to arise.[66]

Problem V–21. Pedestrian is struck at an intersection by an automobile driven by Driver. In Pedestrian's suit for damages, he presents testimony of a highway patrolman who states he saw Driver's car shortly before the accident traveling at a speed in excess of the posted limit. **Can Driver ask the patrolman whether he preferred charges for speeding against Driver? Can Driver introduce an accident report which does not mention Driver's speeding? How would he go about doing this?**

---

66. One limitation on the use of prior inconsistent statements is found in Doyle v. Ohio, 426 U.S. 610 (1976), which prevents a defendant's silence after receiving *Miranda* warnings from being used to impeach his trial testimony. We leave this case, Harris v. New York, 401 U.S. 222 (1971) (permitting statements made in violation of *Miranda* to be used for impeachment), Jenkins v. Anderson, 447 U.S. 231 (1980) (permitting a witness to be impeached with evidence of pre-arrest silence), United States v. Havens, 446 U.S. 620 (1980) (permitting cross-examination of a defendant that refers to illegally seized evidence that the government could not use in its case-in-chief), and Fletcher v. Weir, 102 S.Ct. 1309 (1982) (permitting a witness to be impeached by post arrest silence where he had not been given *Miranda* Warnings) for courses in criminal procedure.

Problem V–22. Green is charged with selling drugs. The prosecution's key witness is Porter, an addict who had told detectives months before Green's arrest that Green was his supplier. When Porter takes the stand, he cannot remember anything about the drug sales. **Should the prosecutor be permitted to introduce Porter's prior statements to impeach his testimony?** Assume that Porter remembers the events and shortly before the trial tells the prosecutor that it was Nolan, not Green, who sold the drugs. **May a prosecutor who calls Porter expecting him to testify that Nolan was his supplier impeach Porter with his prior statements when he does so testify?** **If Porter were to stick with his identification of Green but to claim at trial that he had received the drugs at Nolan's house, should the prosecutor be permitted to impeach him with pretrial statements that he had received the drugs at Green's house? Would you expect the defense to bring out the prior statements in any of these scenarios?**

Problem V–23. Arthur Grinder has given very damaging testimony against Stan Seagull. Seagull knows a witness, Joel Comisar, who will testify that Grinder bragged to him, in the Hutchins Bar, sometime in August of 1975, that in an unrelated trial two years before he received $500 to change earlier identification testimony and deny ever recognizing the defendant. **Can Seagull ask Grinder if he has ever accepted a bribe to give false testimony at a trial? If Grinder denies this can Seagull ask him if he ever stated that he was so bribed? If so, formulate the questions which Seagull should use. If Grinder denies making the statement, can Seagull put Comisar on the stand to testify to what Grinder told him?**

Problem V–24. In the same setting as the preceding problem, assume that Grinder, while at the bar, had told Comisar that Seagull was a "damned son of a bitch." If Grinder is asked if he had ever said anything very derogatory about Seagull and he answers, "I don't like him and I haven't hidden that fact but I've never said anything terribly derogatory," **what questions would you as Seagull's attorney ask next? What objections might Grinder's attorney have if it became obvious you were laying a foundation for Comisar's testimony? Do you think a court should ultimately let Comisar testify to the statement in the bar?**

E. IMPEACHMENT FOR BIAS

Cross-examination to show bias or prejudice or some other interest in the outcome of a case is permitted wherever a witness has offered testimony potentially important to the outcome of the case. The United States Supreme Court has emphasized the importance of a liberal rule regarding cross-examination for bias:

It is the essence of a fair trial that reasonable latitude be given the cross-examiner, even though he is unable to state to the court what facts a reasonable cross-examination might develop. Prejudice ensues from a denial of the opportunity to place the witness in his proper setting and put the weight of his testimony and his credibility to a test, without which the jury cannot appraise them. * * * To say that prejudice can be established only by showing that the cross-examination, if pursued, would necessarily have brought out facts tending to discredit the testimony in chief, is to deny a substantial right and withdraw one of the safeguards essential to a fair trial.[67]

In most jurisdictions the courts impose the same foundation requirement with respect to bias that they do with respect to inconsistent statements.[68] They require that the witness be asked about his biases or interests as a precondition for introducing extrinsic evidence tending to show bias. If the witness fully admits the facts claimed to show bias, the cross-examiner is prevented from introducing further evidence. If the witness denies bias, or does not fully admit those facts which suggest bias, the cross-examiner has a right to present other evidence on the issue. Unlike prior inconsistent statements, testimony as to bias or interest is never collateral. In a substantial minority of jurisdictions there is no foundation requirement for such testimony. There is an apparent feeling that, while a prior inconsistent statement may reflect a mere mental error, bias either exists or does not exist, and the witness himself may be the last person to recognize it.

The majority view is preferable. Except in the most unusual circumstances, bias will be proved by offering evidence of the witness' statements or actions, or by proof of a relationship between the witness and someone else. It is not difficult to ask the witness whether a statement, action, or relationship is properly attributed to him. No good reason appears for not asking the question as part of cross-examination; it saves time and avoids problems similar to those discussed in connection with prior inconsistent statements. Of course, the court should have discretion to waive the foundation requirement in those rare instances where justice requires it.[69]

Courts are very concerned that defendants in criminal cases have every opportunity to demonstrate the bias of prosecution witnesses. In Davis v. Alaska, the Supreme Court held that the denial of cross-examination to show bias violated the confrontation clause of the sixth amendment as applied to the states through the fourteenth amendment. The confrontation clause will be discussed in Chapter Seven. For the moment, you should read the opinion for the example of bias evidence it provides and the importance that the Court attributes to this form of impeachment. This means that you can omit the portion of the opinion headed "(3)." In Chapter Seven you will be asked to return to this point and read the entire opinion.

---

67. Alford v. United States, 282 U.S. 687, 692 (1931).

68. Article VI of the Federal Rules of Evidence does not explicitly mention bias although it is a permissible form of impeachment permitted under FRE 607. In all probability, most courts will continue to afford the impeached witness a chance to explain alleged bias, but in light of the abandonment of the common law foundation requirement with respect to inconsistent statements, it is doubtful that a foundation will have to be laid before the witness is impeached.

There are some common law jurisdictions that require a foundation for proving bias through the statements of a witness but do not require a foundation where bias is to be proved through the acts of the witness. The distinction is hard to justify. The purpose of requiring a foundation for impeachment evidence is to save time where the witness admits the impeaching facts, to avoid subjecting the witness to a third party's attack on his credibility, and to give the witness an opportunity to show that apparent bias did not in fact exist. The prior foundation requirement serves these purposes equally well whether bias is evidenced by an act or a statement. One might argue that foundations should never be required for impeaching evidence, but if they are to be required, acts and statements should be treated in the same way.

69. E.g., where evidence of bias does not become known to the opposing party until after the witness has been dismissed.

DAVIS v. ALASKA

Supreme Court of the United States, 1974.
415 U.S. 308, 94 S.Ct. 1105, 39 L.Ed.2d 347.

Mr. Chief Justice BURGER delivered the opinion of the Court.

We granted certiorari in this case to consider whether the Confrontation Clause requires that a defendant in a criminal case be allowed to impeach the credibility of a prosecution witness by cross-examination directed at possible bias deriving from the witness' probationary status as a juvenile delinquent when such an impeachment would conflict with a State's asserted interest in preserving the confidentiality of juvenile adjudications of delinquency.

When the Polar Bar in Anchorage closed in the early morning hours of February 16, 1970, well over a thousand dollars in cash and checks was in the bar's Mosler safe. About midday, February 16, it was discovered that the bar had been broken into and the safe, about two feet square and weighing several hundred pounds, had been removed from the premises.

Later that afternoon the Alaska State Troopers received word that a safe had been discovered about 26 miles outside Anchorage near the home of Jess Straight and his family. The safe, which was subsequently determined to be the one stolen from the Polar Bar, had been pried open and the contents removed. Richard Green, Jess Straight's stepson, told investigating troopers on the scene that at about noon on February 16 he had seen and spoken with two Negro men standing alongside a late-model metallic blue Chevrolet sedan near where the safe was later discovered. The next day Anchorage police investigators brought him to the police station where Green was given six photographs of adult Negro males. After examining the photographs for 30 seconds to a minute, Green identified the photograph of petitioner as that of one of the men he had encountered the day before and described to the police. * * *

At trial, evidence was introduced to the effect that paint chips found in the trunk of petitioner's rented blue Chevrolet could have originated from the surface of the stolen safe. Further, the trunk of the car contained particles which were identified as safe insulation characteristic of that found in Mosler safes. The insulation found in the trunk matched that of the stolen safe.

Richard Green was a crucial witness for the prosecution. He testified at trial that while on an errand for his mother he confronted two men standing beside a late-model metallic blue Chevrolet, parked on a road near his family's house. The man standing at the rear of the car spoke to Green asking if Green lived nearby and if his father was home. Green offered the men help, but his offer was rejected. On his return from the errand Green again passed the two men and he saw the man with whom he had had the conversation standing at the rear of the car with "something like a crowbar" in his hands. Green identified petitioner at the trial as the man with the "crowbar." The safe was discovered later that afternoon at the point, according to Green, where the Chevrolet had been parked.

Before testimony was taken at the trial of petitioner, the prosecutor moved for a protective order to prevent any reference to Green's juvenile record by the defense in the course of cross-examination.   At the time of the trial and at the time of the events Green testified to, Green was on probation by order of a juvenile court after having been adjudicated a delinquent for burglarizing two cabins.   * * *

In opposing the protective order, petitioner's counsel made it clear that he would not introduce Green's juvenile adjudication as a general impeachment of Green's character as a truthful person but, rather, to show specifically that at the same time Green was assisting the police in identifying petitioner he was on probation for burglary.   From this petitioner would seek to show—or at least argue—that Green acted out of fear or concern of possible jeopardy to his probation.   Not only might Green have made a hasty and faulty identification of petitioner to shift suspicion away from himself as one who robbed the Polar Bar, but Green might have been subject to undue pressure from the police and made his identifications under fear of possible probation revocation.   Green's record would be revealed only as necessary to probe Green for bias and prejudice and not generally to call Green's good character into question.

The trial court granted the motion for a protective order, relying on Alaska Rule of Children's Procedure 23,[a] and Alaska Stat. § 47.10.080(g) 1971).[b]

Although prevented from revealing that Green had been on probation for the juvenile delinquency adjudication for burglary at the same time that he originally identified petitioner, counsel for petitioner did his best to expose Green's state of mind at the time Green discovered that a stolen safe had been discovered near his home.   Green denied that he was upset or uncomfortable about the discovery of the safe.   He claimed not to have been worried about any suspicions the police might have been expected to harbor against him, though Green did admit that it crossed his mind that the police might have thought he had something to do with the crime.

Defense counsel cross-examined Green in part as follows:

"**Q.**   Were you upset at all by the fact that this safe was found on your property?   **A.**   No, sir.

"**Q.**   Did you feel that they might in some way suspect you of this?   **A.**   No.

"**Q.**   Did you feel uncomfortable about this though?   **A.**   No, not really.

"**Q.**   The fact that a safe was found on your property?   **A.**   No.

"**Q.**   Did you suspect for a moment that the police might somehow think that you were involved in this?   **A.**   I thought they might ask a few questions is all.

a.   Rule 23 provides:

"No adjudication, order, or disposition of a juvenile case shall be admissible in a court not acting in the exercise of juvenile jurisdiction except for use in a presentencing procedure in a criminal case where the superior court, in its discretion, determines that such use is appropriate."

b.   Section 47.10.080(g) provides in pertinent part:

"The commitment and placement of a child and evidence given in the court are not admissible as evidence against the minor in a subsequent case or proceedings in any other court   * * *."

"**Q.** Did that thought ever enter your mind that you—that the police might think that you were somehow connected with this? **A.** No, it didn't really bother me, no.

"**Q.** Well, but . . . . **A.** I mean, you know, it didn't—it didn't come into my mind as worrying me, you know.

"**Q.** That really wasn't—wasn't my question, Mr. Green. Did you think that—not whether it worried you so much or not, but did you feel that there was a possibility that the police might somehow think that you had something to do with this, that they might have that in their mind, not that you . . . **A.** That came across my mind, yes, sir.

"**Q.** That did cross your mind? **A.** Yes.

"**Q.** So as I understand it you went down to the—you drove in with the police in—in their car from mile 25, Glenn Highway down to the city police station? **A.** Yes, sir.

"**Q.** And then went into the investigators' room with Investigator Gray and Investigator Weaver? **A.** Yeah.

"**Q.** And they started asking you questions about—about the incident, is that correct? **A.** Yeah.

"**Q.** Had you ever been questioned like that before by any law enforcement officers? **A.** No.

"MR. RIPLEY: I'm going to object to this, Your Honor, it's a carry-on with rehash of the same thing. He's attempting to raise in the jury's mind * * *.

"THE COURT: I'll sustain the objection."

Since defense counsel was prohibited from making inquiry as to the witness' being on probation under a juvenile court adjudication, Green's protestations of unconcern over possible police suspicion that he might have had a part in the Polar Bar burglary and his categorical denial of ever having been the subject of any similar law-enforcement interrogation went unchallenged. The tension between the right of confrontation and the State's policy of protecting the witness with a juvenile record is particularly evident in the final answer given by the witness. Since it is probable that Green underwent some questioning by police when he was arrested for the burglaries on which his juvenile adjudication of delinquency rested, the answer can be regarded as highly suspect at the very least. The witness was in effect asserting, under protection of the trial court's ruling, a right to give a questionably truthful answer to a cross-examiner pursuing a relevant line of inquiry; it is doubtful whether the bold "No" answer would have been given by Green absent a belief that he was shielded from traditional cross-examination. It would be difficult to conceive of a situation more clearly illustrating the need for cross-examination. * * *

The Alaska Supreme Court affirmed petitioner's conviction, concluding that it did not have to resolve the potential conflict in this case between a defendant's right to a meaningful confrontation with adverse witnesses and the State's interest in protecting the anonymity of a juvenile offender since "our reading of the trial transcript convinces us that counsel for the defendant was able adequately to question the youth in considerable detail concerning the possibility of bias or motive." Although the court admitted that Green's denials of any sense of anxiety or apprehension upon the safe's being found close to his home were possibly self-serving, "the suggestion was nonetheless brought to the attention of the jury, and that body was afforded the opportunity to observe the demeanor of the youth and pass on his credibility."

The court concluded that, in light of the indirect references permitted, there was no error.

Since we granted certiorari limited to the question of whether petitioner was denied his right under the Confrontation Clause to adequately cross-examine Green, the essential question turns on the correctness of the Alaska court's evaluation of the "adequacy" of the scope of cross-examination permitted. We disagree with that court's interpretation of the Confrontation Clause and we reverse.

(2)

The Sixth Amendment to the Constitution guarantees the right of an accused in a criminal prosecution "to be confronted with the witnesses against him." * * * Confrontation means more than being allowed to confront the witness physically. "Our cases construing the [confrontation] clause hold that a primary interest secured by it is the right of cross-examination." Douglas v. State of Alabama, 380 U.S. 415, 418 (1965). * * *

Cross-examination is the principal means by which the believability of a witness and the truth of his testimony are tested. Subject always to the broad discretion of a trial judge to preclude repetitive and unduly harassing interrogation, the cross-examiner is not only permitted to delve into the witness' story to test the witness' perceptions and memory, but the cross-examiner has traditionally been allowed to impeach, i.e., discredit, the witness. One way of discrediting the witness is to introduce evidence of a prior criminal conviction of that witness. By so doing the cross-examiner intends to afford the jury a basis to infer that the witness' character is such that he would be less likely than the average trustworthy citizen to be truthful in his testimony. The introduction of evidence of a prior crime is thus a general attack on the credibility of the witness. A more particular attack on the witness' credibility is effected by means of cross-examination directed toward revealing possible biases, prejudices or ulterior motives of the witness as they may relate directly to issues or personalities in the case at hand. The partiality of a witness is subject to exploration at trial, and is "always relevant as discrediting the witness and affecting the weight of his testimony." We have recognized that the exposure of a witness' motivation in testifying is a proper and important function of the constitutionally protected right of cross-examination.

In the instant case, defense counsel sought to show the existence of possible bias and prejudice of Green, causing him to make a faulty initial identification of petitioner, which in turn could have affected his later in-court identification of petitioner.

* * *

The accuracy and truthfulness of Green's testimony were key elements in the State's case against petitioner. The claim of bias which the defense sought to develop was admissible to afford a basis for an inference of undue pressure because of Green's vulnerable status as a probationer, as well as of Green's possible concern that he might be a suspect in the investigation.

We cannot accept the Alaska Supreme Court's conclusion that the cross-examination that was permitted defense counsel was adequate to develop the issue of bias properly to the jury. While counsel was permitted to ask Green *whether* he was biased, counsel was unable to make a record from which to argue *why* Green might have been biased or otherwise lacked that degree of impartiality expected of a witness at trial. On the basis of the limited cross-examination that was permitted, the jury might well have thought that defense counsel was engaged in a speculative and baseless line of attack on the credibility of an apparently blameless witness or, as the prosecutor's objection put it, a "rehash" of prior cross-examination. On these facts it seems clear to us that to make any such inquiry effective, defense counsel should have been permitted to expose to the jury the facts from which jurors, as the sole triers of fact and credibility, could appropriately draw inferences relating to the reliability of the witness. Petitioner was thus denied the right of effective cross-examination which "would be constitutional error of the first magnitude and no amount of showing of want of prejudice would cure it."

(3)

The claim is made that the State has an important interest in protecting the anonymity of juvenile offenders and that this interest outweighs any competing interest this petitioner might have in cross-examining Green about his being on probation. The State argues that exposure of a juvenile's record of delinquency would likely cause impairment of rehabilitative goals of the juvenile correctional procedures. This exposure, it is argued, might encourage the juvenile offender to commit further acts of delinquency, or cause the juvenile offender to lose employment opportunities or otherwise suffer unnecessarily for his youthful transgression.

We do not and need not challenge the State's interest as a matter of its own policy in the administration of criminal justice to seek to preserve the anonymity of a juvenile offender. Here, however, petitioner sought to introduce evidence of Green's probation for the purpose of suggesting that Green was biased and, therefore, that his testimony was either not to be believed in his identification of petitioner or at least very carefully considered in that light. Serious damage to the strength of the State's case would have been a real possibility had petitioner been allowed to pursue this line of inquiry. In this setting we conclude that the right of confrontation is paramount to the State's policy of protecting a juvenile offender. Whatever temporary embarrassment might result to Green or his family by disclosure of his juvenile record—if the prosecution insisted on using him to make its case—is outweighed by petitioner's right to probe into the influence of possible bias in the testimony of a crucial identification witness.

* * *

The State's policy interest in protecting the confidentiality of a juvenile offender's record cannot require yielding of so vital a constitutional right as the effective cross-examination for bias of an adverse witness. The State could have protected Green from exposure of his juvenile adjudication in these circumstances by refraining from using him to make out its case; the State cannot, consistent with the right of confrontation, require the petitioner to bear the full burden of vindicating the State's interest in the secrecy of juvenile criminal records. The judgment affirming petitioner's convictions of burglary and grand larceny is reversed and the case is remanded for further proceedings not inconsistent with this opinion.

It is so ordered.

[The concurring opinion of Mr. Justice Stewart and the dissenting opinion of Mr. Justice White, with whom Mr. Justice Rehnquist joins, are omitted.]

———

Notice that bias is usually a case-specific form of impeachment. A witness appropriately impeached for bias in one case may be quite trustworthy in another. In *Davis*, for example, the Court did not suggest that Green was generally prone to lie. What concerned the Justices is that Green's status as a juvenile offender made him particularly vulnerable to police pressure and gave him a special incentive to cast aspersions since the situation is such that he too might fall under suspicion. Generally speaking, impeachment for case specific reasons like bias will be more probative than impeachment by techniques that suggest a general propensity to lie. They may also be less threatening to a witness because they do not call his entire character into question. Nevertheless, witnesses may be disgraced in the context of a case, and, as the following problem reveals, impeachment for bias may be fraught with prejudicial potential.

Problem V–25. In Grudt v. City of Los Angeles, 2 Cal.3d 575, 86 Cal.Rptr. 465, 468 P.2d 825 (1970), a case in which the wife of a man shot by the police filed a wrongful death action against the City of Los Angeles and named police officers. Following a jury trial, judgment was entered for the defendants. The California Supreme Court reversed the judgment below. That part of the court's opinion that discusses bias evidence is here reproduced:

[The first two paragraphs, summarize the police testimony.]

[A]t 12:15 a. m., John Grudt, a 55-year-old carpenter who was slightly hard of hearing, was observed by two plainclothes police officers as they drove an unmarked blue 1960 Plymouth four-door sedan without siren or red light. Grudt was driving northbound on Western Avenue at about 35 to 40 miles per hour and narrowly missed running down two women in the crosswalk. The officers determined to stop Grudt for questioning because he was driving in a high crime area, but they did not intend to arrest him for traffic violations. They pulled along the side of Grudt's moving car, and the officer on the passenger side raised his badge, shined his flashlight on it, and shouted "Police Officer. Pull Over." Grudt continued driving and turned right at the next corner with the officers in pursuit. The officers again pulled alongside, the passenger showed his badge, and the driver flashed his bright lights and sounded his horn, but Grudt did not yield. Grudt made two more right turns and returned westbound on Western Avenue. The officers became alarmed when Grudt was seen to reach under the front seat of his car, although he did not exhibit any weapon.

Two other plainclothes policemen, Officers Kilgo and Rinehart, driving an unmarked 1961 pink-beige Dodge four-door sedan, heard a police broadcast that plainclothes officers were pursuing a 1959 green and white Ford northbound on Western Avenue. According to Officer Kilgo's testimony, he and Rinehart positioned their vehicle partially across Western Avenue at the intersection of 22d Street, and Officer Rinehart waved a red light to alert oncoming traffic. Grudt's vehicle and another unidentified vehicle just ahead stopped at the intersection, where there were no traffic signals. Officer Kilgo alighted from his vehicle and loaded his double-barreled shotgun as he approached Grudt's car. The other car drove away and Kilgo tapped loudly on the closed left front window of Grudt's car with the muzzle of his shotgun. Grudt looked at Kilgo and "was surprised and appeared to be frozen to the wheel." Kilgo, realizing Grudt might have been frightened at seeing him without his uniform and carrying a shotgun, lifted his shotgun in the air, leaned forward and pointed to his badge displayed on his left front pocket. Thereupon, Grudt turned his wheels toward the left and accelerated his car. The car brushed Kilgo back and he feared that it was heading towards Officer Rinehart, who was standing in front and to the left of the Grudt car. Kilgo fired a shotgun blast through the left rear window of the vehicle. Rinehart testified that Grudt's vehicle struck his leg and that he jumped to his right and fired four rounds from his revolver into the left front window. About three seconds elapsed from the time that Kilgo saw Grudt "frozen to the wheel" to the moment of the shots.

Grudt died within seconds of the shooting.   *   *   *

Edward A. Plankers, a meatcutter, testified for plaintiff and contradicted the officers' version of the shooting. He was on his way home from work and was driving north on Western Avenue in the left-hand lane. He stopped for a red traffic light at the intersection of the on-ramp to the Santa Monica freeway, about 40 feet north of 22d Street. Grudt's car stopped abreast of his car and to his right. Plankers was emphatic that neither he nor Grudt stopped at the intersection of 22d Street. Just before the light changed, Plankers saw a man with a shotgun coming toward them and he "didn't know what to think." He started off when the light changed and had not gone far when he heard a shot. He had looked back in his rearview mirror as he drove off, and he testified that Grudt's car did not move before the shot was fired.   Plankers' testimony was partially corroborated by the testimony of James Graves, who was on foot on the freeway overpass at the time of the shooting.   He saw Kilgo approaching with the shotgun; he saw another car that had been beside Grudt's car speed away; and he saw police cars approaching.   He dropped to the ground when he heard the shots.

William Harper, a consulting physicist, also testified for plaintiff. Based upon his examination of the 1959 Ford driven by Grudt the night he was killed and the officers' testimony as to where Grudt stopped and where Officer Rinehart was standing, Harper concluded that the steering wheel of the Grudt vehicle would have required more than two and a half complete turns to its maximum left position in order to strike Rinehart.   After such a turn, it was Harper's opinion that the vehicle could not return to a parallel position of the kind that it admittedly occupied after the shooting without some human intervention.

*   *   *

Plaintiff's [claim] raises questions regarding the proper scope of impeachment of witnesses in a context which is of first impression.   Edward Plankers and, to a lesser extent James Graves, testified for plaintiff to a version of the shooting incident which conflicted with the testimony of the police officers who were on the scene.   Over objection, defense counsel impeached both men with evidence of prior criminal arrests, on the theory that such arrests were relevant to show bias against the police officers on trial.

The impeachment of Mr. Graves occurred during the course of his cross-examination on two different days of the trial.   On the first day, the following colloquy occurred:

"**By Mr. Daly: Q.**   Mr. Graves, have you ever been convicted of a felony? **A.**   Convicted? No."

"**Q.**   Did you ever plead guilty to a felony? **A.**   No."   Counsel for plaintiff, Mr. Belli, objected.

"**The Court:**   It's a proper question.   Have you ever been convicted of a felony?   You may answer that yes or no."

"**The Witness:**   I've violated a probation, if that is a conviction; but behind the probation I was found not guilty, but I was put on probation, and a fine, which I did violate."

Further inquiry along these lines was postponed until the following morning, when the trial judge made this ruling:

"**The Court:**   All of the testimony of this witness in reference to being convicted of a felony or being on probation is stricken from the record, and the jurors are to disregard it and treat it as though they had never heard of it. *   *   * "

"**Mr. Belli:**   Excuse me.   Just a minute.   Will your Honor, respectfully, instruct the jury that the witness has not been convicted of a felony?"

"**The Court:** The defendant [*sic*, witness] has not been convicted of a felony."

"**Mr. Belli:** Thank you."

"**The Court:** He has been arrested. All other testimony in reference to this witness regarding arrest or felony is stricken from the record, other than the fact that he suffered an arrest."

After plaintiff's counsel objected to the judge's references to arrest and his motion for mistrial was denied, defense counsel proceeded to further cross-examine Graves. On recross-examination, the following colloquy ensued:

"**Mr. Daly:** Let the record indicate that this is for the purpose not of impeachment but for the purpose of bias, motive and prejudice." Mr. Belli's objection was overruled.

"**Q. By Mr. Daly:** Mr. Graves, on April 4, 1959, were you arrested for statutory rape by the City of Los Angeles police officers?" Mr. Belli's objection was overruled.

"**Q. By Mr. Daly:** Were you arrested on April 4, 1959, for statutory rape by the City of Los Angeles Police Department? **A.** Yes, I was.

"**Q.** And were you arrested on 11–13–59 for traffic warrants by the Los Angeles Police Department?" Mr. Belli's objection was overruled.

"**Q. By Mr. Daly:** Were you arrested in 1961 for narcotics? **A.** Not that I recall." Mr. Belli's objection was overruled and his motion for mistrial was denied.

"**Q. By Mr. Daly:** Were you arrested on June 27, 1961, by the Los Angeles Police Department for more traffic warrants? **A.** Perhaps." Mr. Belli's objection was overruled.

"**Q. By Mr. Daly:** October 14, 1963, were you arrested for more traffic warrants?" Mr. Belli's objection was overruled and his motion for mistrial was denied.

"**The Witness:** It's possible." Mr. Belli's motion for mistrial was denied.

"**Q. By Mr. Daly:** July 24, 1964, were you arrested for failing to appear on traffic warrants?" Mr. Belli's objection was overruled.

"**Q. By Mr. Daly:** June 13, 1965, were you arrested for violation of 459 of the Penal Code, burglary? **A.** No." Mr. Belli's objection was overruled.

"**Q. By Mr. Daly:** On March 10, 1966, were you arrested for 459 P.C., charged with 484 Penal Code, petty theft?" Mr. Belli's objection was overruled.

"**The Witness:** Yes."

The impeachment of Mr. Plankers was accomplished by extrinsic evidence. First, Leroy Craig testified without objection that he had been a coworker of Plankers at a grocery store, that late in 1963 Plankers told him that he and his family were being harassed by the police and that his son had been arrested in an auto theft ring and his wife had been arrested for drunk driving, and that Plankers said, "I'll get even with those goddam cops." Later, over objection, Officer Owen McGough was allowed to testify that Plankers' son, a juvenile, had been arrested in July 1963 for receiving stolen property. Also, Officer Pollack was permitted to testify over objection that Mrs. Plankers was arrested for driving under the influence of alcohol on September 16, 1963.
* * *

" '[T]he proper scope for the exercise of discretion by the trial court is in limiting cross-examination to a disclosure of such facts only as may show the existence of hostility, and rejecting any matters which might be pertinent only to a justification of hostility on the part of the witness, for it is the existence of the feeling which is material, and not the right or wrong in the transaction which occasions it." * * *

" '[T]he inquiry for impeachment is usually confined to the *prominent* motives for untruthful testimony; *interest* in the suit which *necessarily* tends to bias, and *other circumstances* showing bias which are not too remote."

The only evidence admitted to impeach Plankers and Graves which meets either of the above tests is the testimony of Leroy Craig relating to the attitude of Plankers. Testimony that Plankers had complained of harassment and had vowed to "get even" with the police, if believed, had some tendency to indicate that Plankers was biased against the police generally and therefore may have been biased against Officers Kilgo and Rinehart in particular. But the evidence that Plankers' wife was arrested for drunk driving and his son for receiving stolen property and that Graves was arrested on several misdemeanor and felony charges did not bear a remote relation to any alleged bias of Plankers or Graves against the two individual officers on trial. The thread of inferences from past arrests by the police, to hostility against police in general, to a willingness to distort testimony in a civil action involving individual police officers unknown to the witness is so tenuous as to render invalid the professed purpose of the defense counsel in offering the evidence.

* * *

Do you agree with the Court's decision here? Is it consistent with Davis v. Alaska? Should bias be defined more broadly in criminal cases for witnesses testifying against the defendant than in civil cases? If the cross-examination of Graves as to bias was anticipated, could the witness have been better prepared to deal with it? How might Belli have dealt with the inference that Graves was biased on redirect examination or in his argument to the jury?

Problem V–26. Herm Stromand has voted for the Radical Socialist Victory Party and once contributed $10.00 to a Radical Socialist candidate.

A major tenet of the party is that capitalism is evil and that private industry should be taken over by the government. The party also claims that productivity could be increased if the capitalist class were put to work on farms or on assembly lines. As might be expected, the party is not very popular in the United States. It is often a target for criticism in the press, and its candidates have frequently been harassed while campaigning for office.

Assume that Stromand has witnessed an accident in which a car driven by John Gault, a noted capitalist theoretician and wealthy steel magnate, struck an impoverished worker on his way to the factory. **If Stromand testifies that Gault was recklessly speeding at the time of the accident, should Gault be able to question Stromand about his voting preferences or introduce extrinsic evidence bearing on this? Would the situation be different if Stromand was a leading member of the RSVP and had been its candidate for high office in the past? If such evidence were introduced, could the plaintiff's attorney introduce a police officer who would testify that immediately after the accident Stromand told him, "The driver of the Cadillac was speeding."**

Problem V–27. Assume the same facts as in the preceding problem, except Gault is charged with manslaughter in the death of the pedestrian. **Should the court rule the same way on the impeachment questions?**

Problem V–28. Assume the same facts about Stromand and Gault as in the preceding two problems, but assume that Stromand is charged with having picked Gault's pocket at a race track. **If Stromand takes the stand to deny the charge, may he be impeached by reference to his RSVP activities?**

Problem V–29. Cynthia Simon files suit against a police officer claiming that he violently beat her during a drug raid. She testifies to this effect. The defense calls two police officers who testify that the defendant officer did not beat, assault or mistreat Simon. Simon wants to show that these officers had been disciplined for the excessive use of physical force in connection with unrelated drug raids. The defense objects. **How should the court rule? If the court allows the impeachment may Simon introduce departmental records that show the officers had been suspended for unnecessary violence without first questioning the officers about these suspensions?**

F. IMPEACHMENT BY MENTAL OR SENSORY DEFECTS

All authorities agree that evidence of sensory incapacity can be used for impeachment purposes. If someone testifies that he overheard a conversation taking place 8 feet away, evidence that the person was hard-of-hearing is information that a jury should have. Similarly, color blindness or other visual problems may reduce the impact of eyewitness testimony. Incapacities that prevent a person from coherently reporting what he has perceived may also be used for impeachment. Mental incapacity may also be shown by way of impeachment. Where mental incapacity is extreme, a witness may be deemed incompetent to testify, but this is very rare.[70]

McCormick states that "[A]bnormality] we have seen is a horse of a different color" from "defects of mind within the range of normality."[71] He argues that some qualities are regarded as normal but unusual while other qualities are regarded as abnormal. Evidence of abnormality is admissible, but evidence of only *de minimus* departures from normality is not. To McCormick, a witness who is drunk is abnormal as is one who is under the influence of narcotics, but a showing of alcoholism or addiction does not establish abnormality. Thus an alcoholic may be viewed as normal and so not impeachable by evidence of alcoholism, but anyone who is intoxicated is no longer normal and so is impeachable by evidence of drunkenness. If this were intended as an hypothesis to reconcile the myriad of conflicting authorities in American jurisdictions, it might be useful. However, when offered as a tool for deciding future cases, the analysis is dangerous. It seeks to divide the world of mental and sensory problems into rigid categories, recognizing some for impeachment purposes, but not others. We fail to see a "bright line" between the person with hearing difficulties who swears he overheard a particular conversation and the alcoholic who swears he was 100 per cent sober on a particular occasion. It is better policy to evaluate the probative value of impeachment evidence, like substantive evidence, in the context of particular cases and to admit probative evidence unless some other interest demands exclusion. In our view, Wigmore was clearly wrong, both as a matter of policy and a matter of law, when he suggested that extrinsic evidence of a witness' incapacity to observe or remember specific events is never admissible.[72]. A decision to automatically admit or exclude extrinsic evidence of drug addiction or alcoholism is similarly misguided.

An important question, addressed by courts with some frequency in recent years, is to what extent a judge should seek expert assistance for the jury on matters of credibility. An interesting case on this point is United States v. Benn.[73] Two defendants were convicted of assault with intent to commit rape while armed and assault with a dangerous weapon. The victim was a mentally retarded girl of 18. A competency hearing was held and she testified about what happened to her. The trial court found that the victim had the "rudimentary qualifications to tell what she recalls," and declared her to be competent. The appellate court affirmed:

The competency of the witness to testify before the jury is a threshold question of law committed to the trial court's decision. It remains for the jury, of course, to assess the credibility of the witness and the weight to be given her testimony. Competency depends upon the witness' capacity to observe, remember, and narrate as well as an understanding of the duty to tell the truth. It also requires an assessment of the potential prejudicial effects of allowing the jury to hear the testimony. Mental re-

70. Given FRE 601 and similar state rules, disqualification will be an extremely rare event. The test is no longer one of competency, but one of relevance under FRE 401, 402 and 403. Issues regarding the ability to take and understand some variety of oath may arise under FRE 603.

71. McCormick § 45, at 94.

72. 3A Wigmore § 993. The states are divided; some do adopt Wigmore's position.

Do you agree with the authors' position? What arguments can you think of on behalf of Wigmore? Should a witness open himself to proof that he is a moron or alcoholic simply because he is doing his civic duty and testifying at a trial?

73. 155 U.S.App.D.C. 180, 476 F.2d 1127 (1973).

tardation may be so severe, capabilities so impaired, and the testimony so potentially prejudicial that it should be barred completely by the judge. Or there may be sufficient indications of a witness' capacity and of the reliability of her testimony that it should be heard and assessed by the jury, albeit with a cautionary instruction.

A mentally defective rape prosecutrix presents a particularly difficult problem for both judge and jury. It is generally agreed that sexual assault charges by mentally abnormal girls should be subjected to great scrutiny. There is real danger of contrivance or imagination— the events may seem real to the girl even though they exist only in her own mind. Yet that testimony may arouse enough sympathy to make an innocent man the real victim.

To assist the court in making its competency decision, to aid the jury in assessing credibility, or to serve both purposes, the trial judge may order a psychiatric examination to obtain expert testimony concerning the degree and effect of a witness' disability. Wigmore has suggested that the danger of false accusations and the potential for prejudicial impact is so severe in sexual assault cases that every sex offense complainant should be examined. We think, however, that any such rigid rule is precluded by countervailing considerations. For example, a psychiatric examination may seriously impinge on a witness' right to privacy; the trauma that attends the role of complainant to sex offense charges is sharply increased by the indignity of a psychiatric examination; the examination itself could serve as a tool of harassment; and the impact of all these considerations may well deter the victim of such a crime from lodging any complaint at all. Since there is no exact measure for weighing these kinds of dangers against the need for an exami-

nation, the decision must be entrusted to the sound discretion of the trial judge in light of the particular facts.

In the present case the trial court found that the prosecutrix demonstrated an understanding of her duty to tell the truth and a capability to observe and remember. A comprehensible narrative does emerge from the sum of her testimony. Also, as the cautious trial judge noted before allowing the witness to testify, there was substantial corroboration to her testimony giving extrinsic assurance of its reliability. Finally, the judge had the benefit of the girl's father's testimony as to her retardation to assist him. Accordingly, the trial judge's determination of the prosecutrix's competency, without a psychiatric examination, will not be disturbed.

The dangers which must be considered in determining whether a mentally retarded rape prosecutrix is a competent witness must also be considered by the jury in assessing her credibility, particularly since "the jury's estimate of the truthfulness and reliability of a given witness may well be determinative of guilt or innocence * * *." The jury may be aided in its task by the results of a psychiatric examination, even when such an examination is not necessary to the judge's determination of competency. When an examination should be ordered to aid the jury is also a judgment, involving a balancing of need against dangers, which is committed to the discretion of the trial judge. Here, the strong indications of reliability of the prosecutrix's testimony weigh heavily against the need for an examination. Also, the jury was not left to make its credibility decision without information as to the witness's defect; it had the frank and comprehensive testimony of the girl's father to assist it. In these circumstances, we cannot say that the trial judge erred in failing to order a psychiatric examination of the witness to aid the jury.[74]

———————

Generally speaking, young children are treated in a manner similar to the way we treat the mentally deficient. The judge takes the witness on what is called "voir dire" and asks questions to determine whether the child is able to understand the obligation to tell the truth and to report correctly facts within his knowledge. There is no magic age at which a child is disabled from testifying. Extreme youth, unlike mental deficiency, will always be obvious without the need for extrinsic evidence. A common concession to the lawyer examining a child or mentally deficient individual is that great leeway will be allowed in the use of leading questions. Opposing counsel must take care to ensure that the witness is actually testifying.[75]

Most courts have been reluctant to concede any role for experts in helping a jury assess the credibility of normal witnesses. A juror's assessment of the witness' nervousness, error, and self-contradiction, was, and, is preferred to the use of lie detectors, hypnosis, and truth drugs as aids in evaluating credibility. Though the polygraph is now commonly used by government agencies and private businesses to test prospective and current employees, polygraph evidence is still generally kept from juries. Ironically, many police departments and prosecutors now conduct polygraph examinations of consenting suspects, agreeing to drop charges if the examination indicates that the suspect's protestations of innocence are truthful. The *quid pro quo* is that the suspect usu-

ally agrees to plead guilty to some charge if the examination indicates he is lying.

One reason why judges hesitate to accept scientific or medical judgments on truth is that highly qualified examiners are essential to the fair administration and interpretation of the scientific tests. A second reason is that the tests, even if expertly administered, are not infallible. Courts are afraid that the popular conception of "truth serum" or the "lie detector" would lead jurors to pay too much attention to such evidence and too little to other evidence in the case. Judges also may fail to appreciate the differences among the various scientific devices and techniques that aid in uncovering the truth. Hypnosis, for example, apparently acts to heighten consciousness so that a psychiatrist can more effectively probe the suppressed thoughts of his client, while truth drugs generally dull consciousness inhibiting attempts to conceal important facts. The courts, fearful that both procedures allow too much room for suggestion, lump them together in the class of inadmissible evidence. Both techniques are problematic, but they require separate analysis. Finally, whatever their value to truth-seeking, there is an apparent inhumanity to trial by medicine or machine. This is probably an important reason for the unusual skepticism which courts have directed to this variety of scientific evidence.

Nevertheless, the trend in recent years has been one of slightly greater receptivity to these truth-seeking devices. Hypnosis and drug-aided analysis have been recognized as valid aids in diagnosing conditions which are relevant at the trial, but they are still not accepted as bearing directly on

———————

74. Id. at 1130. Courts are understandably sympathetic to witnesses who do not wish to have their psychiatric histories paraded before juries, especially when their relationship to a case is remote. See, e.g., United States v. Glover, 588 F.2d 876 (2d Cir. 1978); United States v. Lopez, 611 F.2d 44 (4th Cir. 1979).

75. At times this will raise an interesting question of tactics. A lawyer may prefer to argue that a witness in fact stated nothing on his own rather than have rephrased questions—or worse yet, questions asked on cross-examination—make it clear that the witness is speaking from personal knowledge.

truth.[76] The polygraph, however, has proved its worth to many former opponents.[77] Where parties stipulate before testing that the results of a polygraph examination will be admissible, courts are generally willing to hold the parties to their stipulation and allow test evidence to reach the jury on the issue of truth and veracity.[78] However, such evidence is still almost universally excluded absent stipulation.

The breakthrough in the unilateral admission of polygraph testimony may come in criminal cases where the defendant's word is pitted against the testimony of one or two prosecution witnesses. Here the issue of whom to believe is crucial, and the lie detector is sufficiently accurate that it may provide a better guide than the other evidence likely to be available. A defendant whose story has been verified in a lie detector examination could conceivably cite Chambers v. Mississippi [79] in support of his claim that the sixth amendment obligates the court to take the testimony of the lie detector expert. Justice is so likely to be advanced by such testimony that basic fairness may demand it. An important countervailing argument is that lie detection is subjective enough that, absent very close regulation, an open door to such testimony might in the long run give rise to groups of prosecution and defense-oriented experts and a new, fruitless battle of experts. Also, if juries knew that polygraph evidence were always admissible, they might draw a negative inference when such testimony was not offered, thus putting an additional price on the accused's invocation of the fifth amendment right to remain silent. This might be acceptable if lie detector evidence were always accurate, since the decision to remain silent might be a good indication that a lie detector test was taken and failed. But even its strongest proponents admit that lie detectors are wrong about one time in 20, and it appears that inconclusive results can be expected from about one person of every ten tested. Among people actually facing trial these proportions might be much higher.[80]

76. See, e.g., Lemmon v. Denver & Rio Grande R. R. Co., 9 Utah 2d 195, 341 P.2d 215 (1959); Sallee v. Ashlock, 438 S.W.2d 538 (Ky.1969).

77. See, e.g., A. Moenssens, R. Moses & F. Inbau, Scientific Evidence in Criminal Cases (1973). For a sophisticated case against the use of lie detectors see Skolnick, Scientific Theory and Scientific Evidence: An Analysis of Lie-Detection, 70 Yale L.J. 694 (1961).

78. See, e.g., United States v. Ridling, 350 F.Supp. 90 (E.D.Mich.1972); United States v. Dioguardi, 350 F.Supp. 1177 (E.D.N.Y.1972); Williams v. State, 378 A.2d 117 (Del.1977). But see United States v. Zeiger, 350 F.Supp. 685 (D.D.C.1972), reversed 155 U.S.App.D.C. 11, 475 F.2d 1280 (D.C.Cir. 1972); United States v. DeBetham, 470 F.2d 1367 (9th Cir. 1973); United States v. Wilson, 361 F.Supp. 510 (D.Md.1973); United States v. Urquidez, 356 F.Supp. 1363 (C.D.Cal.1973). See also United States v. Lanza, 356 F.Supp. 27 (M.D.Fla.1973) (lie detector evidence admissible in discretion of trial judge, but rejected in instant case). In Walther v. O'Connell, 72 Misc.2d 316, 317, 339 N.Y.S.2d 386, 387 (1972), the Civil Court of the City of New York used lie detector evidence to resolve a dispute between plaintiff and defendant as to whether the former loaned money to the latter. "Even the wisdom of a King Solomon would be tried in deciding a case such as this," said the Court. Thus, the Court ordered both parties to take lie detector tests and admitted the evidence. Some cases admitting polygraph evidence pursuant to stipulation are State v. Harrison, 90 N.M. 439, 564 P.2d 1321 (1977); State v. Olmstead, 261 N.W.2d 880 (N.D.1978); Cullin v. State, 565 P.2d 445 (Wyo.1977). For a summary of recent federal cases ruling on the admissibility of polygraph tests, see Annot., 43 A.L.R.Fed. 68 (1979). Also of interest is Annot. 88 A.L.R.3d 227 (1978) (propriety of telling jury that accused took polygraph test where results are inadmissible).

79. 410 U.S. 284 (1973). This case is reproduced in Chapter Seven. For a discussion of polygraph evidence and other scientific evidence see Chapter Ten. The discussion here is only a brief introduction to the polygraph and similar mechanical methods of assessing credibility.

80. See Skolnick supra note 77, at 714–721.

Problem V–30. Gene Bandy is charged with conspiring to distribute heroin. Two key government informers, Sydney Sharp and June Greedy, testify that they saw Bandy sitting in a car with several other defendants shortly before the other defendants delivered half a kilo of heroin to a warehouse where the police were waiting. Bandy wants to cross-examine Sharp and Greedy concerning their use of heroin. He wants to ask them whether they are or ever have been heroin addicts, whether they had used heroin during the forty-eight hours prior to the time they allegedly saw him with the other defendants in the case, whether they had used heroin at any time in the three days since the trial began, and whether any drug agents have ever supplied them with heroin or the money to purchase it. **May these questions be posed? If Sharp denies ever using heroin, may Bandy call one of Sharp's friends who will testify that Sharp is addicted to heroin, that Sharp had been taking heroin bought with money furnished by the police on the morning that he claims to have seen Bandy in the car and that Sharp shot up with heroin about twelve hours before he testified? If Greedy testifies that she was addicted to heroin but does not remember whether she had taken heroin about the time she saw Bandy in the car, may Bandy introduce one of Greedy's friends who will testify that Greedy had shot heroin on the morning of the day that she claims to have seen Bandy?**

Problem V–31. In the trial referred to in the preceding problem, Bandy's fiancée Jean is called by the defense to testify that she heard Bandy's codefendants talking about heroin, but that the topic never came up in front of Bandy, and Bandy himself never spoke of drugs. **Can the codefendants impeach Jean by showing that twelve years ago she was committed to a mental institution following her then-fiancé's death? Can they show that two years ago she had spent three weeks in a mental institution suffering from delusions and that she has been under a psychiatrist's care ever since?**

G. CONTRADICTORY TESTIMONY: THE COLLATERAL ISSUE RULE

Perhaps the simplest way to discredit a witness and his testimony is to introduce contradictory testimony. This is allowed only where the contradictory testimony is independently relevant to a material issue in the case or relevant, apart from the contradiction, to the credibility of a witness otherwise subject to impeachment. We met one variant of this rule in our discussion of prior inconsistent statements, when we noted that extrinsic evidence of inconsistent statements could not be introduced where the subject matter of those statements was "collateral." The rule applies to contradiction generally. Suppose, for example, that a witness to a robbery, after identifying the robber, has stated on cross-examination that the robber's coat was blue. The defendant might seek to present three witnesses who will testify that the robber's coat was yellow, for this might lead the jury to question the memory or perceptual abilities of the identity witness. However, unless the court determines that the color of the coat is an important fact to be proved in the case, the matter will be deemed collateral, hence not a subject for independent proof. This does not mean that other witnesses may not be offered whose testimony does not agree with that of the first witness put on the stand, nor does it mean that other witnesses cannot describe the event, including the color of the witness' coat. It does mean that if *all* that a defense witness can state is that the culprit's coat was not the color testified to by a prosecution witness, this testimony will not be received. Obviously the collateral issue rule saves time and avoids distracting conflicts over side issues.[81] However, this does not mean the rule should be rigidly applied to preclude impeachment whenever a contradiction is collateral. There is no reason why the trial judge cannot balance the probative value of impeachment evidence bearing on collateral matters against its costs, as is done in other areas.[82] In many reported cases such a balance has been struck. One rarely finds a case reversed because impeachment was allowed on collateral matters, although this will happen if the impeaching evidence is highly prejudicial.

Some common law courts create an explicit exception from the "no impeachment on a collateral matter" rule for situations in which it is reasonable for a jury to believe that a witness who is mistaken in some particulars is likely to be mistaken about more important matters. Under the Federal Rules of Evidence the trial judge is expected to look to rules like FRE 403 and balance the probative value of evidence against the time needed to deal with it and the confusion it is likely to engender.

Problem V–32. The defendant is charged with committing a robbery in Seattle on July 14, 1961. A witness for the defense testifies that the defendant, a regular patron in his Portland, Oregon, restaurant, was in the restaurant at the time of the robbery in Seattle, Washington. On cross-examination, the witness states that he thinks the defendant has been in the restaurant every day for the past two months. To contradict this, the prosecution offers the testimony of a police officer to the effect that he saw the defendant in Seattle on June 12, 1961, and that the defendant stated that he had been there for a couple of days. The police officer also states that the defendant said that he had come from Portland. **Should this testimony be admitted? Is the place where the defendant was seen at all important? Assuming that it was error to admit this testimony, is it sufficiently harmful that an appellate court should reverse?**

81. To continue our example: If the defense could introduce two witnesses only to state the coat was yellow, the prosecutor in rebuttal might introduce three more witnesses who state it was blue. At this point it is not clear how the evidence bears on the identity witness' memory or perceptual ability, and a good deal of time has been lost over a side issue. Note, if the defense counsel has the robber's coat or a color picture of the robbery, these could be presented to the jury as exhibits and the identity witness could be confronted with them on cross-examination. What is the difference between the use of real evidence and the testimony of a witness who will state the coat was yellow?

82. However, defense attorneys might be upset by this suggestion. If most trial judges are prosecution oriented, as many defense counsel think, this discretion might be used consciously or unconsciously to give the prosecutor more leeway in impeachment than the defense. It may also be that defense witnesses are generally more impeachable by evidence of such detail. But the problems of discretion cannot be avoided at trial, and given the reluctance of appellate courts to reverse where impeachment is mistakenly allowed on collateral issues, it is clear that discretion is not avoided in this area even with the current rule.

Problem V–33. Should it make any difference whether the fact that would be contradicted by extrinsic testimony is elicited on direct, rather than cross-examination? Some courts say it does. **Can you reconcile this position with the policy underlying the general prohibition against impeachment on collateral matters? Do the different functions of direct and cross-examination bear on this? Is the position a wise one?**

Problem V–34. Beverley Pully stands indicted for the murder of his wife, Vicki. At trial, Beverley defends by calling his friend, Edward, who testifies that on the night of the murder, at about the time the wife was shot, Beverley was on a fishing trip with him in a town 600 miles away. The prosecution's theory of the case is that Edward was indeed in the distant town, but that Beverley was not with him. As part of his attack on Edward, the prosecutor asks the following questions and receives the answers indicated:

Q. Where were you on the evening of May 1, 1973, the night of the murder? **A.** At Hadfield on the Cape, 600 miles from this burgh.

Q. Why were you so far from home? **A.** We went fishing and we just wanted to relax.

Q. You never went fishing, did you? **A.** Sure we did.

Q. What did you do in the evening that day? **A.** We went to the movies.

Q. What did you see? **A.** I don't remember. It might have been "My Fair Lady."

Q. Isn't it true that you never went to the movies that night? **A.** We did go to the movies.

Q. Isn't it also true that you were alone and that you visited a brothel? **A.** That's a lie.

Upon completion of the examination, the prosecutor wishes to introduce extrinsic evidence to show: (1) that the temperature on May 1, 1973, was 40° at the Cape and seas were too high for boats to set sail; (2) that "My Fair Lady" was not at any of the theaters in Hadfield or in any of the surrounding towns on May 1, 1973; (3) that the witness did visit a brothel at 7:00 p. m. on May 1, 1973. **Can any or all of this evidence be introduced?**

Problem V–35. The defendant is arrested for selling narcotic drugs in Ann Arbor, Michigan. The sole witness against him is Smith, an undercover narcotics agent. At the trial Smith testifies to the circumstances of the sale. Cross-examination includes the following testimony:

Q. Were you a narcotics agent in Charlottesville, Virginia? **A.** Yes.

Q. You were the key witness there in several cases, weren't you? **A.** Yes.

Q. Did you ever perjure yourself in a narcotics trial? **A.** No.

Q. Did you ever lie to the prosecutor about the circumstances of a so-called "buy"? **A.** No.

Q. Isn't it true that on October 14, 1974, after you testified in a case, the prosecutor made the following statement in a Charlottesville Court?:

Your Honor, it is my duty to inform the court that this witness Smith lied when he said the defendant sold him the drugs. We have learned that Smith gave the money we supplied him with to a male friend to be transmitted to his girl friend, and that the male friend supplied the drug. We move to dismiss the prosecution and guarantee we will never use this witness again.

A. No.

You are defense counsel. **Prepare an argument which might lead a judge who takes a strict view of the collateral issue rule to admit extrinsic evidence of this incident. How would you argue to a judge who views the rule less strictly?**

H. RELIGIOUS BELIEFS

FRE 610 provides:

Evidence of the beliefs or opinions of a witness on matters of religion is not admissible for the purpose of showing that by reason of their nature his credibility is impaired or enhanced.

This is the rule in what seems to be a growing majority of jurisdictions. Those jurisdictions that permit impeachment by religious belief limit questioning to queries that shed light on a witness' belief in a God who will punish false testimony. McCormick suggests that courts and legislatures should forbid such questions:

[The] reason of course is that there is no basis for believing that the lack of faith in God's avenging wrath is today an indication of greater than average untruthfulness. Without that basis, the evidence of atheism is simply irrelevant upon the question of credibility.[83]

McCormick may or may not be right, but we prefer to rest the argument on other grounds. Even if one concedes the power of religious feeling and with it the relevance of religious belief, one may conclude that impeachment on the ground of irreligion is properly forbidden. Two factors support this conclusion. First is the prejudicial effect which evidence of certain faiths or lack of faith might have on the jury. Second is the basic value incorporated in Article 6 of the Constitution[84] and reflected in the no establishment and free exercise clauses of the first amendment, that people in this country are not to be officially judged by their religious ties regardless of its relevance. Penalties for perjury, cross-examination and the modes of impeachment discussed in this chapter provide substantial guarantees that the truth will be discovered. Whatever incremental guarantee is provided by impeachment on the basis of religious belief is outweighed by prejudice and policy.[85]

---

83. McCormick § 48, at 102.

84. "[B]ut no religious test shall ever be required as a Qualification to any office or public trust under the United States."

85. Do you agree, or should courts be given the kind of flexibility we have been arguing for in other areas?

I. REHABILITATING IMPEACHED WITNESSES

Many cases turn on the relative credibility of opposing witnesses. Just as the lawyer endeavors to question the credibility of opposing witnesses, so he will wish to strengthen the credibility of his own. As with impeachment, there are important limitations on counsel's ability to introduce evidence for this purpose.[86]

The most basic limitation is that no support for the credibility of a witness is permitted until credibility is attacked.[87] Support offered after a witness' credibility has been attacked is known as "rehabilitation." Usually rehabilitative evidence must respond as directly as possible to the theory of the impeaching evidence. For example, a witness impeached by evidence of bad reputation, conviction of a crime or prior bad acts usually may be rehabilitated by evidence of a good reputation for truth and veracity. If, however, the impeachment evidence has been introduced to show bias, only evidence which rebutted the inference of bias generally would be proper.

Analytically, of course, evidence of a reputation for truth and veracity is relevant to rebut any kind of impeachment which raises questions concerning the witness' honesty. The honest witness is less likely to be influenced by bias than the dishonest one. The inference of untruthfulness which flows from evidence of prior inconsistent statements, a harsh, skeptical cross-examination, or the contradictory evidence of other witnesses is less powerful if it is known that the witness has a good reputation for honesty. Courts differ on their willingness to allow evidence of a good reputation for truth and veracity to serve as a general technique of rehabilitation. Many hold that evidence of prior inconsistent statements opens the door to such evidence. Fewer would allow this type of rehabilitation where there has been a suggestion of bias, harsh cross-examination, or the mere presentation of conflicting evidence.

It may be that no hard and fast rule is well-suited to the host of rehabilitation problems that confront the courts. Impeachment is an integral part of the adversary system. Often it enables the jury to learn important facts about the witness and the witness' relation to the parties. But, as helpful to the trier of fact as this may be, impeachment is as one-sided as untested direct examination. Information used to discredit is often not as well-established as the examiner's confident questioning suggests. Explanation and rebuttal are often necessary to place impeachment evidence in its proper context. For this to happen, the rehabilitation rules must provide the parties with a fair opportunity to meet the thrust of the opposi-

---

86. We are talking here about specific evidence which is only relevant for its bearing on credibility. In many ways counsel is able to introduce evidence which does bear on credibility; the most important is counsel's right to explain to the jury the qualifications of his witnesses. This is most obvious with expert testimony. The impressive credentials which counsel elicit are not so much to persuade the court that the expert should be permitted to render opinions (lesser credentials will justify this) as they are to persuade the jury that the expert's testimony is to be believed. Ordinary witnesses may be questioned to show that they were in a good position to observe the matter, that glasses, hearing aids or other devices necessary to perception were used, and that they have some peculiar reason to remember the matter well. Attorneys will also use other more subtle ways to reinforce the credibility of their witnesses. For example, dress and hairstyles may be arranged for the occasion, or the witnesses may be instructed to look directly at the jury during important parts of their testimony.

87. See, e.g., FRE 608(a)(2): "[E]vidence of truthful character is admissible only after the character of the witness for truthfulness has been attacked by opinion or reputation evidence or otherwise."

tion's impeachment evidence. With this in mind, it is easy to agree with Wigmore that rehabilitation of a witness should be permitted where the denial of prior bad acts does not dissipate the suspicion that the accusing questions had a ring of truth to them.[88] One can also think of circumstances where it is sensible to permit character evidence to rebut the inference a jury might otherwise draw from prior inconsistent statements.[89] In fact, it is easy to see the sense in many of the more flexible decisions and the difficulties in purporting to adhere to standards that do not yield to the needs of individual cases.

There is one aspect of rehabilitation that generally is covered by rules: the use of prior consistent statements.

After a prior inconsistent statement is introduced to impeach a witness, the party offering the witness may want to rehabilitate the witness by introducing prior consistent statements to show that the witness' story is consistent with earlier statements. The hope is that the jury will believe that the report of an inconsistent statement is false or the result of a simple failure of communication. In most states prior consistent statements can only be used to rebut an express or implied charge of recent fabrication or of improper influence or motive, but there are a few states that admit a witness' prior consistent state-

ments in almost all situations where prior inconsistent statements have been used. Trial judges often have considerable discretion to determine whether or not the impeaching statement was such as to suggest a plan or contrivance to falsify evidence.[90]

Rehabilitation by prior consistent statements is not, however, limited to situations where impeachment has been by inconsistent statements. Where there is a suggestion through some means other than impeachment by prior inconsistent statements of recent fabrication or other improper influence, evidence of prior consistent statements made before the improper influence came to bear may be introduced to rebut the allegation.

Regardless of how one's witness has been impeached, the task facing the proponent of a prior consistent statement is to show that the statement was made before those motives arose which have allegedly led the witness to testify falsely at trial. When this can be shown, the consistent statement negates the opponent's claim that the trial testimony is the product of some recent event that has given the witness an incentive to deceive. When consistent statements do not predate the alleged incentives to deceive they are usually not admitted. Courts do not perceive them as particularly probative.

Problem V–36. On September 1, 1982, at 11:15 p. m. Ruth Roman phoned the police to report a forcible rape. She stated that an intruder forced his way through a window and raped her at knifepoint. Then the assailant fled. Ruth estimated that 5 or 6 minutes passed before she had composure enough to phone the police. David Den is arrested and charged with rape. His defense is consent. **Should the prosecutor be able to in-**

---

88. 4 Wigmore § 1104.

89. What would these circumstances be? Where might the admission of such evidence be less reasonable? Isn't the fact that character traits are apparently not independent of context important in resolving these questions?

90. Like prior inconsistent statements, prior consistent statements are not admitted on substantive issues in common law jurisdictions; rather they are used to enhance credibility. FRE 801(d)(1)(B) opens the door for use of consistent statements as substantive evidence.

troduce Ruth's phone call to bolster her testimony denying consent? If Ruth waited a day before calling the police, should the call still be admitted? A week?

Problem V–37. Max Kurfee is on trial for manslaughter stemming from an illegal abortion. The most damaging testimony against him is given by Shirley Curtain, his alleged accomplice, who describes in detail Max's participation in the abortion and the resulting consequences. On cross-examination, Max's attorney establishes that at a grand jury hearing a year before trial Shirley gave testimony which in no way inculpated Max. The defense also brings out the fact that a month later Shirley again appeared before the grand jury and told a story substantially the same as the one she told at trial. The prosecutor seeks to introduce testimony that on the day following the abortion, thirteen months before trial, Shirley told the father of the victim a story which was substantially the same as the story she told at trial. The defense argues that there was no claim of recent fabrication since the defense itself had pointed to Shirley's consistent testimony 11 months before trial and that the prosecutor suggested no reason why Shirley should have falsified her original grand jury testimony. **How should the judge decide?**

Problem V–38. Phyllis Deppety is charged with robbing a bank. One of the most important government witnesses is a teller who has had problems recalling the features of the woman who robbed him. The government arranges a pretrial hypnotic session with a qualified psychiatrist. Under hypnosis, the teller remembers facts about the robber that are detrimental to Deppety. The psychiatrist tells the witness to recall the facts when he awakes from the trance. He does and testifies against Deppety. Deppety cross-examines the witness and elicits the fact that he had been hypnotized. The government then calls the psychiatrist to testify that 1) hypnosis as he practiced it is a reliable technique for assisting recall and 2) the witness was testifying truthfully and accurately. Deppety objects. **What would you as the trial judge want to know about hypnosis in ruling on the objection? Would the witness ever be permitted to testify that Deppety was telling the truth?** [91]

Problem V–39. The government's case against Sergio Stein, accused of masterminding drug trafficking in Cleveland, depends on the testimony of a pusher who has turned state's evidence. Anticipating defense impeachment, the government brings out on direct examination of the pusher that he previously has been convicted of murder and extortion. After the pusher leaves the stand, the government calls three witnesses to testify that despite the pusher's past violence, his reputation for truth and veracity is excellent. The defense objects. **How would you rule as trial judge?**

Problem V–40. In the government's prosecution of Stein described in problem 39, the defense impeached the pusher by showing he had pled guilty to, but had not been sentenced for selling heroin. Defense counsel also asked the pusher whether he expected that he would be given special considera-

---

91. Chapter Eleven on expert testimony contains some transcript material on hypnosis and its possible uses.

tion as a result of his testifying against Stein.   The answer was "no."   The government later called an FBI agent to testify that the witness did not need to depend on what he said about Stein to win favorable treatment, since he had already provided the FBI with information that led to the discovery of an illicit methaqualone drug factory.   Stein objects to this evidence.   **Should it be admitted?   If the pusher admitted that he had been told that if he testified against Stein he would be given probation rather than the ten year sentence he could ordinarily expect, should his direct testimony be stricken upon the motion of Stein's attorney?**

SECTION III.   REVIEW PROBLEMS

The following problems test your understanding of the textual material in this Chapter.

Problem V–41.   This question involves a suit arising out of a contract for the construction of a home.   The contractor, Conley, has sued the owner, Oliver, for a balance of $6,000 due on a $60,000 written contract, plus $5,000 for certain work and materials alleged by the contractor to have been supplied at the owner's oral request.   Oliver's defense is (1) that certain of the work and materials supplied under the contract were defective and not in accordance with the specifications, resulting in damages to him in excess of $6,000, and (2) that there was no enforceable subsequent agreement varying the terms of the written contract.

The incidents described in each of the following questions have reference to the foregoing facts.   They occurred at the trial of the case.   Assume that the written contract and the plans and specifications incorporated by reference therein have been identified and received in evidence without objection.

One of the issues was whether the poured concrete basement floorslab was four inches thick, as required by the specifications.   In his case-in-chief, Oliver called Franklin as his witness.   Franklin gave his residence address as 1300 Brook Street, testified that he had been Conley's foreman on the job at the time of construction, that he no longer worked for Conley, and that both he and Conley were present when the concrete was poured.   Franklin testified further, over Conley's objection, that immediately after the concrete pouring had been completed he said to Conley, "You know perfectly well that's not four inches thick," and that Conley made no reply.

On cross-examination the following questions were put:

Question: "Were you fired by Conley?"

Oliver's Attorney: "Objection."

The Court: "Sustained."

Question: "Aren't you a chronic alcoholic?"

Oliver's Attorney: "Objection."

The Court: "Sustained."

Do you agree with these rulings?   Why or why not?

On cross-examination, Conley's attorney also asked Franklin, "You testified that you live at 1300 Brook Street.   As a matter of fact, don't you live at 1200 River Street?"   Franklin answered: "No, I do not.   I live at 1300 Brook Street."

In rebuttal Conley's attorney called a woman (not Franklin's wife) and sought to prove by her that Franklin lived with her at 1200 River Street. **Should the Court admit this testimony over objection?**

Problem V–42.   Don R. King, a noted philosopher and amateur volleyball star, sued the defendant company for injuries he allegedly suffered when his leg became infected as a result of using the defendant's product "Sun Tan Superior" while playing volleyball on the California beaches.   At trial, testimony was introduced by the defendant that plaintiff had gone to one Dr. Axelson and had told Dr. Axelson that he had fallen on a rusty rake while chasing a volleyball at the Liberty Street Club and that as a result of this fall his leg had become infected.   After the defendant rested, King sought to take the stand for a second time to testify that he frequently had shown his infected leg to friends and told them that it had become infected as a result of using "Sun Tan Superior."   **Should this testimony be admitted on this foundation if the defendant objects?   Would some different foundation make it more likely that the evidence would be admitted?   Should King be allowed to put friends on the stand to testify to what he told them?**

Problem V–43.   Pop Yokum was arrested and charged with unlawfully (1) manufacturing intoxicating liquor, and (2) possessing intoxicating liquor with intent to sell, barter, exchange or otherwise dispose of the same.   At Yokum's trial, evidence was offered by the State which showed that certain police officers, armed with a search warrant, entered a house and found Yokum sitting at a table with another man and a woman and with a bottle of intoxicating liquor upon the table.   They also found a still in an old barn nearby.

In presenting its case, the state offered:

(a) A witness who was asked the question, "Are you acquainted with the reputation of Yokum for truth and veracity in the community in which he resides, and if so, is that reputation good or bad?"

(b) Evidence that five months previously, Yokum had been convicted of selling intoxicating liquor in violation of law.

(c) Evidence that two years previously, Yokum had pleaded guilty to a charge of drunken driving.

Upon Yokum's objection, the trial court refused to allow any of this evidence in.   **Were these rulings correct?**   The same evidence was offered by the prosecution in rebuttal at the close of the defendant's case.   [Yokum had testified.   When asked on cross-examination if he'd ever been convicted of a crime, Yokum had replied, "Nothing serious."]   **Should the court allow any of the above evidence in over objection at this stage?**

Problem V–44.   David Dukes is being tried for the forcible rape of Sue Morley.   Sid, a witness from a neighboring town, testifies for David.   The prosecution waives cross-examination, whereupon the defendant's attorney offers a witness to tesify that Sid has a fine reputation for truth and veracity in his town.   The prosecution objects.   **What ruling should the trial judge make?**   Horace, David's brother and another defense witness, testifies that he overheard Sue invite the defendant to become intimate with her.   Sue had never been asked on cross-examination if she made such a statement.   **Is Horace's testimony admissible?   On cross-examination, may Horace be asked whether he was ever arrested?**   Joan, a prosecution witness, testifies that immediately after the purported rape Sue told her of the incident.   On cross-examination, Joan is asked whether she is awaiting trial for a misdemeanor.   The prosecution objects.   **What result?**

Problem V–45.   The plaintiff is involved in an automobile collision with a car owned by the defendant and driven by Michael Driver.   At the trial of the negligence action, the plaintiff calls Driver and asks the following questions: "Is it true that your salary is paid by the defendant?   Is it true that if the defendant loses this suit, she is threatened with loss of her insurance, which means loss of your job?"   **If there are objections to the questions. how should the trial judge rule?   Would the judge rule differently if Driver were named as a party?   If Driver answers "no" to the second question, should extrinsic evidence be permitted on this issue?**

Problem V–46.   In 1967 Orville Wrong filed suit against the executor of the estate of defendant on a rejected creditor's claim, seeking an accounting and alleging that before his death defendant had wrongfully appropriated the design of a fuel-saving auto engine invented by plaintiff.   The executor's answer denied that Wrong had invented the engine and alleged as an affirmative defense that Wrong had sold any interest he had in the invention to defendant.   A witness was called to testify on Wrong's behalf.   The witness indicated that Wrong had engaged in a certain kind of research and had reached a certain stage of experimentation in 1963.   On cross-examination, counsel asked: "Isn't it a fact that Wrong owes you a large sum of money and that he has been unable to pay?"   Wrong objects to the question.   **What ruling?**   After that, counsel for defendant asks the witness: "Isn't it a fact that in 1964 you heard Wrong say to defendant, 'I'll sell you my interest in the engine for $10,000'?"   Again Wrong objects.   **What ruling?**

Problem V–47.   Elizabeth Souris is sued for damages arising from an automobile accident.   She testifies in her own defense.   The plaintiff, Peter Lapin, introduces two prior inconsistent statements allegedly made by Elizabeth to witnesses shortly after the accident.   Thereafter, Elizabeth seeks to introduce witnesses to testify to her good character for truth and veracity.   Peter objects.   **What is the proper ruling?**   Assume that these witnesses are permitted to testify that Elizabeth has a good reputation for truth and veracity.   **May Peter thereafter impeach the character witnesses for the defendant by showing that they have bad reputations for truth and veracity?   May the witnesses be asked on cross-examination if they have heard that Elizabeth was convicted of drunk driving, arrested for shoplifting, suspended from college (some 9 years earlier) for plagiarism, divorced on the grounds she "cheated on her husband," and claimed to be the head of a coven of witches?**

SECTION IV. THE ETHICS OF IMPEACHMENT

John "Mad Dog" Stork is charged with aggravated assault and battery and possession of an unlicensed gun. The undisputed facts of this gruesome case are as follows: At 7:30 p. m., June 13, 1976, Abe Aged, a 78-year-old retired school teacher, was taking his after dinner walk along Fisherman's Wharf in San Francisco. A man emerged from a bar with a young woman. Spying Aged, the man said, "Honey, here comes some money!" Before she could respond, the man pulled a gun from his pocket and beat Aged near death. Two witnesses saw part of the incident: Mary, a sixteen year old girl who was sitting on a bench near the scene of the crime, and Harvey, a youthful unemployed musician, who often walked along the waterfront at night. Both Mary and Harvey identifed Stork from a group of ten photos compiled by the police. The woman with Stork was never identified.

At trial, Stork, who has a long record of prior convictions, never testifies. The only prosecution witnesses are Mary, Harvey and the victim. Stork is acquitted, largely because of the skill of his lawyer, Thayer McCormick. After the verdict is returned, McCormick returns triumphant to his law office where two associates, Louise Hand and Taft Howard, await an expected celebration. The following conversation takes place:

McCormick: Well, it's over. One of the toughest cases I ever tried.

Hand: Congratulations, boss. How did you beat three eyewitnesses?

McCormick: I really didn't beat three. Aged was still suffering from that assault. He could barely describe what happened, and he never tried to identify Mad Dog. The girl was so nervous she was easy pickings. The musician's drug record made him useless.

Hand: I sat in for most of the girl's testimony. How did you manage to rattle her so badly?

McCormick: I interviewed her before trial, and it must have been her first experience with the courts, because she cooperated like I was the prosecutor. I pinned her down with dozens of leading questions. Sibley, our office boy, wrote up a statement and she signed it. It haunted her at trial. So many inconsistencies. I built a mountain from those molehills.

Howard: You sure did. When I was in the courtroom, she seemed to think she was on trial. When she said, "I don't know. I don't know. Maybe I didn't see anything", I knew you had her. But how did you know about the musician's drug use?

McCormick: Sibley again. Of all the strange things, Sibley used to smoke dope with this guy. I never guessed that a pothead in this office would help win a case, but I'll be—it did. I asked the witness right before recess whether he was high that night. He denied it. Then I asked him whether he didn't often smoke marijuana by the Wharf. He denied it. I asked for a recess. Then I brought Sibley to the counsel's table. When that witness returned, he looked like he saw a ghost. Before long he admitted smoking grass. I took a long shot and asked him about pills. That's when he refused to answer. He wasn't much good to anybody after that.

Hand: Just between us, was Mad Dog guilty in fact?

McCormick: I don't know or care. He told me at the time he was in Oakland at the Dixie Grill. But I talked to 15 people there that night. Nobody saw him. Yet, no one said it was 100% impossible that he was there. Maybe $99^{44}/_{100}\%$, you know. (Winking)

Howard: Did you really think the girl was lying?

McCormick: It's not my job to make that judgment. For what it's worth though, I can honestly say I think she was truthful. If she hadn't made those prior statements,

Mad Dog would easily have been convicted.

Hand: Did you have qualms about breaking down an honest witness?

McCormick: Like I said, my job is to represent my client. I don't judge honesty. Anyway, I enjoyed Professor Freedman's article, Professional Responsibility of the Criminal Defense Lawyer: The Three Hardest Questions on Professional Ethics.[92] It was written in 1966, but it is still timely. Here, read these portions; I keep them on my bookshelf:

At the outset, we should dispose of some common question-begging responses. The attorney is indeed an officer of the court, and he does participate in a search for truth. These two propositions, however, merely serve to state the problem in different words: As an officer of the court, participating in a search for truth, what is the attorney's special responsibility, and how does that responsibility affect his resolution of the questions posed above?

The attorney functions in an adversary system based upon the presupposition that the most effective means of determining truth is to present to a judge and jury a clash between proponents of conflicting views. * * *

* * *

The adversary system has further ramifications in a criminal case. The defendant is presumed to be innocent. The burden is on the prosecution to prove beyond a reasonable doubt that the defendant is guilty. The plea of not guilty does not necessarily mean "not guilty in fact," for the defendant may mean "not legally guilty." Even the accused who knows that he committed the crime is entitled to put the government to its proof. Indeed, the accused who knows that he is guilty has an absolute

constitutional right to remain silent. The moralist might quite reasonably understand this to mean that, under these circumstances, the defendant and his lawyer are privileged to "lie" to the court in pleading not guilty. In my judgment, the moralist is right. However, our adversary system and related notions of the proper administration of criminal justice sanction the lie.

Some derive solace from the sophistry of calling the lie a "legal fiction," but this is hardly an adequate answer to the moralist. Moreover, this answer has no particular appeal for the practicing attorney, who knows that the plea of not guilty commits him to the most effective advocacy of which he is capable. Criminal defense lawyers do not win their cases by arguing reasonable doubt. Effective trial advocacy requires that the attorney's every word, action, and attitude be consistent with the conclusion that his client is innocent. As every trial lawyer knows, the jury is certain that the defense attorney knows whether his client is guilty. The jury is therefore alert to, and will be enormously affected by, any indication by the attorney that he believes the defendant to be guilty. Thus, the plea of not guilty commits the advocate to a trial, including a closing argument, in which he must argue that "not guilty" means "not guilty in fact."

There is, of course, a simple way to evade the dilemma raised by the not guilty plea. Some attorneys rationalize the problem by insisting that a lawyer never knows for sure whether his client is guilty. The client who insists upon his guilt may in fact be protecting his wife, or may know that he pulled the trigger and that the victim was killed, but not that his gun was loaded with blanks and that the fatal shot was fired from across the street. For anyone who finds this reasoning sat-

92. 64 Mich.L.Rev. 1469, 1470–75 (1966).

isfactory, there is, of course, no need to think further about the issue.

It is also argued that a defense attorney can remain selectively ignorant. He can insist in his first interview with his client that, if his client is guilty, he simply does not want to know. It is inconceivable, however, that an attorney could give adequate counsel under such circumstances. How is the client to know, for example, precisely which relevant circumstances his lawyer does not want to be told? The lawyer might ask whether his client has a prior record. The client, assuming that this is the kind of knowledge that might present ethical problems for his lawyer, might respond that he has no record. The lawyer would then put the defendant on the stand and, on cross-examination, be appalled to learn that his client has two prior convictions for offenses identical to that for which he is being tried.

* * *

The first of the difficult problems posed above will now be considered: Is it proper to cross-examine for the purpose of discrediting the reliability or the credibility of a witness whom you know to be telling the truth?

* * *

Viewed strictly, the attorney's failure to cross-examine would not be violative of the client's confidence because it would not constitute a disclosure. However, the same policy that supports the obligation of confidentiality precludes the attorney from prejudicing his client's interest in any other way because of knowledge gained in his professional capacity. When a lawyer fails to cross-examine only because his client, placing confidence in the lawyer, has been candid with him, the basis for such confidence and candor collapses. Our legal system cannot tolerate such a result.

* * *

Therefore, one must conclude that the attorney is obligated to attack, if he can, the reliability or credibility of an opposing witness whom he knows to be truthful. The contrary result would inevitably impair the "perfect freedom of consultation by client with attorney," which is "essential to the administration of justice."

Hand: It makes sense all right. But it is a strange system in which the prosecutor is bound to act morally, but not defense counsel. The ABA has established as part of its Standards for Criminal Justice, the Prosecution and the Defense Function, Standard 5.7, The Prosecution Function (App.Draft 1971).

Examination of witnesses.

(a) The interrogation of all witnesses should be conducted fairly, objectively and with due regard for the dignity and legitimate privacy of the witness, and without seeking to intimidate or humiliate the witness unnecessarily. Proper cross-examination can be conducted without violating rules of decorum.

(b) The prosecutor's belief that the witness is telling the truth does not necessarily preclude appropriate cross-examination in all circumstances, but may affect the method and scope of cross-examination. He should not misuse the power of cross-examination or impeachment to discredit or undermine a witness if he knows the witness is testifying truthfully.

* * *

The commentary to the rule is interesting:

a. Avoiding unnecessary embarrassment or humiliation

The scope of examination has always been subject to control in the court's discretion in order to prevent abuse of witnesses. At one time a privilege to refuse to answer degrading questions was recognized. Some states retain this privilege in statutes protecting witnesses from "irrelevant, improper or insulting questions, and from harsh or insulting demeanor." Clearly "a lawyer should never be unfair or abusive or inconsiderate to adverse witnesses or opposing litigants, or ask any question intended only to insult or degrade the witness." The more difficult issue is the lawyer's duty when the question will yield some benefit to his case but at inordinate cost to the reputation of the witness. Highly experienced trial lawyers consulted by the Advisory Committee agreed that in this situation trial counsel must carefully balance the importance of the evidence in question against the humiliation and disgrace to the witness. Especially in the case of impeaching evidence, where the humiliation it will cause the witness is out of proportion in comparison with its impeachment value, the prosecutor should forego the question. For example, if the rules of evidence in force in the jurisdiction permit impeachment by showing convictions for crimes which do not have a direct bearing on the truth-telling propensities of the witness, the prosecutor should not bring to light a long-forgotten criminal conviction of the witness simply to discredit him.

b.   Undermining a truthful witness.

A question of long standing and not completely resolved is whether in cross-examination of a witness an advocate should be restrained by his belief that the witness has testified truthfully. Numerous experienced defense counsel of the American, Canadian and British bars, consulted by the Advisory Committee, expressed the view that counsel generally is not permitted to substitute his personal opinion for the available fact-finding processes of the trial and may properly invoke the usual cross-examination technique to test the witness's capacity and opportunity for observation and the ability to recall. However, many lawyers expressed the view that the manner and tenor of cross-examination ought to be restricted where examining counsel has knowledge of the truthfulness of the testimony given by the witness.

There was a consensus among the experts consulted, and one shared by the Advisory Committee, that the difficult and delicate decisions presented by the wide range and variety of situations cannot be made the subject of rigid standards. There was general agreement that cross-examination is perhaps the best known human device for ascertaining truth and revealing falsehood. Essentially an "invention" of the common law system, the power to cross-examine adverse witnesses is a monopoly of lawyers and ought not be misused for destroying known truth. The power to cross-examine is a power vested in a lawyer by virtue of his being an officer of the court. It is a power shared by the court itself but not often used. Strong arguments were advanced by highly skilled and experienced trial advocates that if the cross-examiner knows that the testimony of a particular witness is true, he may not properly use this "monopoly power" he possesses as an officer of the court for a purpose alien to its avowed objective by using it to destroy or undermine truth. This is the view shared widely by most British barristers and judges. Some, however, take the view that within limits a cross-examiner may employ conventional cross-examination techniques notwithstanding he knows that the testimony is true. Some also pointed out that the problem rarely arises and that when it does a lawyer is ill-advised to try to undermine a known truth-teller.

* * *

McCormick: I saw that, but it only covers the prosecutor. The defendant has a right to vigorous counsel under the sixth amendment. If a witness is less than perfect, it's our job to point that out.

Howard: Of course, you really set up the girl.

McCormick: I tested her, that's all.

Hand: What about the musician. Was he really stoned?

McCormick: I don't know. He panicked and he undercut the value of his own testimony. The cops said he was so sure that Mad Dog's picture was the right one, he would bet his life on it.

Howard: It sounds like Mad Dog was really guilty. Don't you worry about a guilty man going free?

McCormick: Son, let's get one thing straight. Guilty is a legal conclusion. A man is presumed innocent until proven guilty. If not proven guilty, he's always innocent. A guilty man never goes free.

Hand: That's right. That's the American way.

A voice from an adjoining room is heard. It is the law student clerk, Mary Bentham.

Bentham: How sure you are that adversariness is the American way and that victory is justice. How you wrap yourself in the sixth amendment and lawyer's duty. Is it not the case that the lawyer can be said to serve us all, not only the client and the court? Is there nothing to the argument that the client should get all that fairly may be said to be coming and no more? Who represents those witnesses who, without asking for the privilege, observe violent crime and do not shrink from the duty of reporting it? Who will be there the next time to come into court to be destroyed by the guns of counsel? What sort of profession is it that speaks of ethics generally, but never feels any ethical responsibility to the government and people who allow lawyers special privileges? What kind of profession is so myopic that only its clients matter? What is there to be proud of in the criminal bar? I ask you what loss would be suffered if lawyers left

witnesses alone who speak the truth, except to examine them for the errors that we all make? Most of all, I wonder what justice means to you. Obviously not a fair trial. Obviously not fair treatment of witnesses. Obviously not a true result. Then what?

McCormick: Mary, my friend, you have not yet passed the bar, have you?

Bentham: I shall take it soon. But, no, I have not passed it.

McCormick: Well! You see!

Hand: I see.

Howard: I see.

[The phone rings; Hand answers it. She hangs up.]

McCormick: What is it, Louise? You look pale.

Hand: An old woman's been found dead. She was pushed to the ground and her purse stolen. She died when her head hit a step. Two witnesses have identified a picture of Mad Dog. The police want us to call if he comes here. What shall we tell them?

———

What is your reaction to the ethical questions raised by the above scenario?

The preceding conversation may appear fanciful, but the problems are real and will probably be with us as long as the adversary system. In one of the most thoughtful commentaries on these matters, Federal District Judge Marvin Frankel has expressed a fear that finding truth is not high enough on the priority list of our adversary system.[93] He offers a tentative draft of a new disciplinary rule designed to ensure that lawyers are searching for truth as well as representing clients. Judge Frankel's proposed rule 7–102 of the Code of Professional Responsibility provides as follows:

93. Frankel, The Search for Truth: An Umpireal View, 123 U.Pa.L.Rev. 1031 (1975).

(1) In his representation of a client, unless prevented from doing so by a privilege reasonably believed to apply, a lawyer shall:

   (a) Report to the court and opposing counsel the existence of relevant evidence or witnesses where the lawyer does not intend to offer such evidence or witnesses.

   (b) Prevent, or when prevention has proven unsuccessful, report to the court and opposing counsel the making of any untrue statement by client or witness or any omission to state a material fact necessary in order to make statements made, in the light of the circumstances under which they were made, not misleading.

   (c) Question witnesses with a purpose and design to elicit the whole truth, including particularly supplementary and qualifying matters that render evidence already given more accurate intelligible, or fair than it otherwise would be.

(2) In the construction and application of the rules of subdivision (1), a lawyer will be held to possess knowledge he actually has or, in the exercise of reasonable diligence, should have.

The rule would replace the following parts of the currently prevailing rule:

(A) In his representation of a client, a lawyer shall not:

   * * *

   (3) Conceal or knowingly fail to disclose that which he is required by law to reveal.

   (4) Knowingly use perjured testimony or false evidence.

   (5) Knowingly make a false statement of law or fact.

   (6) Participate in the creation or preservation of evidence when he knows or it is obvious that the evidence is false.

   (7) Counsel or assist his client in conduct that the lawyer knows to be illegal or fraudulent.

   * * *

(B) A lawyer who receives information clearly establishing that:

   (1) His client has, in the course of the representation, perpetrated a fraud upon a person or tribunal shall promptly call upon his client to rectify the same, and if his client refuses or is unable to do so, he shall reveal the fraud to the affected person or tribunal.

   (2) A person other than his client has perpetrated a fraud upon a tribunal shall promptly reveal the fraud to the tribunal.

Believing that the adversary system works better than Judge Frankel suggests, Professor Uviller proposes what he views as a less drastic alternative. First he notes the current coverage of Disciplinary Rule 7–102, set forth above, and of Rules 1–102 and 7–101, set forth below:

DR 1–102 Misconduct:

(A) A lawyer shall not:
   * * *

   (4) Engage in conduct involving dishonesty, fraud, deceit, or misrepresentation.

   (5) Engage in conduct that is prejudicial to the administration of justice.

DR 7–101 Representing a Client Zealously:

(A) A lawyer shall not intentionally:

   (1) Fail to seek the lawful objectives of his client through reasonably available means permitted by law and the Disciplinary Rules, except as provided by DR 7–101(B). A lawyer does not vi-

olate this Disciplinary Rule, however, by acceding to reasonable requests of opposing counsel which do not prejudice the rights of his client by being punctual in fulfilling all professional commitments, by avoiding offensive tactics, or by treating with courtesy and consideration all persons involved in the legal process.

(2) Fail to carry out a contract of employment entered into with a client for professional services, but he may withdraw as permitted under DR 2–110, DR 5–102, and DR 5–105.

(3) Prejudice or damage his client during the course of the professional relationship, except as required under DR 7–102(b).

(B) In his representation of a client, a lawyer may:

(1) Where permissible, exercise his professional judgment to waive or fail to assert a right or position of his client.

(2) Refuse to aid or participate in conduct that he believes to be unlawful, even though there is some support for an argument that the conduct is legal.

Professor Uviller suggests two new rules:

It is unprofessional conduct for a lawyer during the trial of a matter in which he represents a party to express, convey, or indicate to the factfinder by word, gesture, or in any manner whatever his personal opinion or belief concerning any of the facts in issue or the veracity of any testimony or other evidence.

It is unprofessional conduct for a lawyer to counsel or countenance testimony by a witness in his favor which, although true in part stated, omits matters which if stated might reasonably alter the meaning or significance of the testimony.[94]

Professor Freedman, whose views were cited in the colloquy above, rejects such proposals:

A trial is, in part, a search for truth; accordingly, * * * basic rights are most often characterized as procedural safeguards against error in the search for truth. We are concerned, however, with far more than a search for truth, and the constitutional rights that are provided by our system of justice serve independent values that may well outweigh the truth-seeking value, a fact made manifest when we realize that those rights, far from furthering the search for truth, may well impede it. * * *

[T]he point that I now emphasize is that in a society that respects the dignity of the individual, truth-seeking cannot be an absolute value, but may be subordinated to other ends, although that subordination may sometimes result in the distortion of the truth * * *[95]

From another perspective, Professor Damaska implies that some of the failings (or successes depending upon your perspective) of the adversary system are best explained by looking at the Anglo-American emphasis on individualized justice. Truth in the abstract may not be as important as truth through the eyes of a particular defendant.[96]

How do you feel about these various arguments? What do you think the canons should provide?

94. Uviller, The Advocate, The Truth and Judicial Hackles: A Reaction to Judge Frankel's Idea, 123 U.Pa.L.Rev. 1067, 1080–81 (1975).

95. Freedman, Judge Frankel's Search for Truth, 123 U.Pa.L.Rev. 1060, 1063, 1065 (1975).

96. Damaska, Presentation of Evidence and Factfinding Precision, 123 U.Pa.L.Rev. 1083, 1103–1106 (1975). See also Damaska, Evidentiary Barriers to Conviction and Two Models of Criminal Procedure, 121 U.Pa. L.Rev. 578 (1973); Damaska, Structures of Authority and Comparative Criminal Procedure, 84 Yale L.J. 483 (1975).

BIBLIOGRAPHY

ABA Standards, The Prosecution and the Defense Function (App. Draft 1971; 2d Draft 1979).

McCormick, Chs. 4–5.

Morgan, Basic Problems of Evidence 62 (1962).

Steven & Steven, Trial Lawyer (1950).

Wellman, The Art of Cross-Examination (4th ed. 1944).

3 Weinstein's Evidence ¶ 607[01] et seq. & ¶ 611[02]–[04].

3A Wigmore, Chs. 31–36.

Bergman, Commentary, A Practical Approach to Cross-Examination: Safety First, 25 U.C.L.A.L.Rev. 547 (1978).

Conley, Barr & Lind, The Power of Language: Presentational Style in the Courtroom, 1978 Duke L.J. 1375.

Denbeaux & Risinger, Questioning Questions: Objections to Form in the Interrogation of Witnesses, 33 Ark.L.Rev. 439 (1980).

Frankel, The Search for Truth: An Umpireal View, 123 U.Pa.L.Rev. 1031 (1975).

Freedman, Professional Responsibility of the Criminal Defense Lawyer: The Three Hardest Questions in Professional Ethics, 64 Mich.L.Rev. 1469 (1966).

Hale, Specific Acts and Related Matters As Affecting Credibility, 1 Hastings L.J. 89 (1950).

Ladd, Credibility Tests—Current Trends, 89 U.Pa.L.Rev. 166 (1965).

Ladd, Some Observations on Credibility, Impeachment of Witnesses, 52 Cornell L.Q. 238 (1967).

Ladd, Techniques and Theory of Character Testimony, 24 Iowa L.Rev. 498 (1935).

Maguire & Quick, Testimony: Memory and Memoranda, 3 How.L.J. 1 (1957).

McCormick, The Scope and Art of Cross-Examination, 47 Nw.U.L.Rev. 177 (1956).

McGowan, Impeachment of Criminal Defendants by Prior Conviction, 1970 Law & Social Order 1.

Nizer, The Art of Jury Trial, 32 Cornell L.Q. 59 (1946).

Lloyd, Impeachment of Witness, Common Law Principles and Modern Trends, 34 Ind.L.J. 1 (1918).

Saltzburg, The Unnecessarily Expanding Role of the American Trial Judge, 64 Va.L.Rev. 1 (1978).

Slovenko, Witnesses, Psychiatry and the Credibility of Testimony, 19 U.Fla.L.Rev. 1 (1966).

Spector, Impeaching the Defendant by His Prior Convictions and the Proposed Federal Rules of Evidence: A Half Step Forward and Three Steps Backward, 1 Loyola U.L.J. 247 (1970).

Swancara, Impeachment of Non-Religious Witness, 13 Rocky Mt.L.Rev. 336 (1941).

Thomas, Rehabilitating the Impeached Witness with Consistent Prior Statements, 32 Mo.L.Rev. 472 (1968).

Uviller, The Advocate, The Truth and Judicial Hackles: A Reaction to Judge Frankel's Idea, 123 U.Pa.L.Rev. 1067 (1975).

Weihofen, The Effect of a Pardon, 88 U.Pa.L.Rev. 177 (1939).

Chapter Six

HEARSAY

SECTION I. HEARSAY POLICY

A. INTRODUCTION

Wigmore has called the hearsay rule "that most characteristic rule of the Anglo-American law of evidence—a rule which may be esteemed, next to jury trial, the greatest contribution of that eminently practical legal system to the world's methods of procedure."[1] Some have argued that the hearsay rule, on balance, hinders rather than contributes to the practical resolution of legal disputes, but all would acknowledge the centrality of the hearsay rule to the American system of evidence law.[2] In this chapter we shall discuss the hearsay rule, the reasons which support it, and the numerous situations in which courts will allow evidence to be admitted despite its hearsay character. Later in this chapter we shall present you with several common definitions of hearsay and a detailed discussion of what hearsay actually is. But before doing this, there are certain other points we wish to make, points which require us to have some idea of what we are talking about. So, for the moment, accept this tentative, simplified version of the basic hearsay principle: *the trier of fact may only be asked to believe those statements made by witnesses testifying at the trial*. The fact finder may not be presented with state-

ments of non-witnesses and asked to believe they are true. Thus, testimony by one witness that another person said something may not be considered by the fact finder as evidence that what that other person said is true.

The common law attitude toward hearsay developed as the jury was transformed from a group of neighbors chosen to resolve matters on the basis of what the jurors knew or could learn to a group of uninformed laymen charged with deciding a case solely on the basis of information presented to them. McCormick presents the following brief summary of these developments:[3]

> The development of the jury was, no doubt, an important factor [in the development of the hearsay rule]. It will be remembered that the jury in its earlier forms was in the nature of a committee or special commission of qualified persons in the neighborhood to report on facts or issues in dispute. So far as necessary its members conducted its investigations informally among those who had special knowledge of the facts. Attesting witnesses to writings were sum-

---

1. 5 Wigmore § 1364, at 27.

2. **The importance of the hearsay rule in England has substantially diminished with the demise of jury trials in most civil cases. In this country the hearsay rule is inapplicable or relaxed in the numerous cases litigated before federal and state administrative agencies. In theory, the rule applies in its full rigor to bench trials, but except where lower court decisions specifically rely on inadmissible hearsay, appellate courts will generally assume that the trial judge**

properly discounted inadmissible hearsay. Even where the trial judge excludes inadmissible hearsay, he has heard the hearsay before reaching a decision. In these circumstances, there is good reason to believe that if the hearsay is convincing most judges cannot help but be influenced by it. If you know that an opponent's case would be substantially strengthened by convincing but inadmissible hearsay, you have good reason to insist on a jury trial.

3. McCormick § 244, at 576–81.

moned with the jurors and apparently participated in their deliberations, but the practice of calling witnesses to appear in court and testify publicly about the facts to the jury, is a late development in jury trial. Though something like the jury existed at least as early as the 1100's, this practice of hearing witnesses in court does not become frequent until the later 1400's. The changeover to the present conception that the normal source of proof is not the private knowledge or investigation of the jurors, but the testimony of witnesses in open court is a matter of gradual evolution thereafter. Finally, in the early 1500's it has become, though not yet the exclusive source of proof, the normal and principal one.

It is not until this period of the gradual emergence of the witness testifying publicly in court that the consciousness of need for exclusionary rules of evidence begins to appear. It had indeed been required even of the early witnesses to writings that they could speak only of "what they saw and heard" and this requirement would naturally be applied to the new class of testifying witnesses. But when the witness has heard at firsthand the statement of X out of court that he has seen and heard a blow with a sword, or witnessed a trespass on land, as evidence of the blow or the trespass, a new question is presented. Certainly it would seem that the earlier requirement of knowledge must have predisposed the judges to skepticism about the value of hearsay.

Accordingly, it is the value of hearsay, its sufficiency as proof, that is the subject of discussion in this gestation period. In Continental Europe there had already developed a system of evaluating witnesses and their proofs quantitatively, based on a requirement of two witnesses, or their fractional equivalents, as "full proof." In this system,

Wigmore says, at this period there were rules "declaring (for example) one witness upon personal knowledge to be equal to two or three going upon hearsay." And so through the reigns of the Tudors and the Stuarts there is a gradually increasing drumfire of criticism and objections by parties and counsel against evidence of oral hearsay declarations. While the evidence was constantly admitted, the confidence in its reliability was increasingly undermined. It was derided as "a tale of a tale" or "a story out of another man's mouth." Parallel with this increasingly discredited use of casual oral hearsay was a similar development in respect to transcribed statements made under oath before a judge or judicial officer, not subject to cross-examination by the party against whom it is offered. In criminal cases in the 1500's and down to the middle 1600's the main reliance of the prosecution was the use of such "depositions" to make out its case. As oral hearsay was becoming discredited, uneasiness about the use of "depositions" began to take shape, first in the form of a limitation that they could only be used when the witness could not be produced at the trial. It will be noted that the want of oath and the unreliability of the report of the oral statement cannot be urged against such evidence but only the want of cross-examination and observation of demeanor.

It was in the first decade after the Restoration that the century or so of criticism of hearsay had its final effect in decisions rejecting its use, first as to oral hearsay and then as to depositions. Wigmore finds that the period between 1675 and 1690 is the time of crystallization of the rule against hearsay. For a time the rule was qualified by the notion that hearsay, while not independently admissible, could come in as confirmatory of other evidence, and this qualification survived down to the end of the 1700's in the limited form of admitting a witness's prior consistent statements out of court to corroborate his testimony.

Whether the rule against hearsay was, with the rest of the English law of evidence, in fact "the child of the jury" or the product of the adversary system may be of no great contemporary significance. The important thing is that the rule against hearsay taking form at the end of the seventeenth century was neither a matter of "immemorial usage" nor an inheritance from Magna Charta but, in the long view of English legal history, was a late development of the common law.

———

The impetus for the final development and rather rigid interpretation of the hearsay rule came in part from a number of celebrated trials in which obvious injustice was wrought by a reliance on hearsay. One of the most famous was the trial of Sir Walter Raleigh. Raleigh was convicted of conspiracy to commit treason on the basis of the sworn out-of-court statement of his alleged co-conspirator Lord Cobham.[4] Raleigh protested:

> But it is strange to see how you press me still with my Lord Cobham, and yet will not produce him; it is not for gaining of time or prolonging my life that I urge this; he is in the house hard by, and may soon be brought hither; let him be produced, and if he will yet accuse me or avow this confession of his, it shall convict me and ease you of further proof.[5]

Cobham was never produced.

The prosecution also introduced hearsay through the testimony of a live witness:

Attorney-General.—"I shall now produce a witness viva voce:"

He then produced one *Dyer*, a pilot, who, being sworn, said, "Being at Lisbon, there came to me a Portuguese gentleman, who asked me how the King of England did, and whether he was crowned? I answered him, that I hoped our noble king was well, and crowned by this; but the time was not come when I came from the coast of Spain. 'Nay,' said he 'your king shall never be crowned, for Don Cobham and Don Raleigh will cut his throat before he come to be crowned.' And this, in time, was found to be spoken in mid July."

Raleigh.—"This is the saying of some wild Jesuit or beggarly priest; but what proof is it against me?"

Attorney-General.—"It must perforce arise out of some preceding intelligence, and shews that your treason had wings." * * *

The attorney-general's response to Raleigh only serves to emphasize the weakness of Dyer's testimony.[6]

The injustices of Raleigh's case and other political trials had a substantial impact on the subsequent development of English criminal procedure; they justified a strict hearsay rule and influenced the framers of the United States Constitution to incorporate in the sixth amendment a right to confront adverse witnesses.[7]

---

4. J. G. Phillimore, History and Principles of the Law of Evidence 157 (1850).

5. The accusation was later allegedly withdrawn, but the withdrawal was also allegedly recanted.

6. Phillimore, supra note 4.

7. The "confrontation clause" and the most important of the cases interpreting it will be discussed in detail in Chapter Seven. For the present it is important only to note that this constitutional guarantee applies only in criminal cases and that while it is designed to promote many of the same values as the hearsay rule, it does not necessarily follow the contours of this rule and its exceptions.

B. INFERENCES FROM TESTIMONY

History provides one kind of explanation for the hearsay rule. It explains how the rule and its exceptions arose out of earlier procedures or circumstances and it depicts the ways in which past generations rationalized the rule. However, the historical explanation does not bind us. To evaluate the continuing vitality of the rationales which have been offered for the hearsay rule and the possible existence of other justifications, one must understand what hearsay is and the dangers which the rule is intended to avoid. This can best be done by first considering the ways in which jurors make inferences from testimony. In doing so we shall borrow an idea from Professor Laurence Tribe, the device of the testimonial triangle.[8] We shall return to this device throughout our discussion of hearsay.[9]

Consider a trial in which the owner of a red auto is charged with leaving the scene of an accident. To establish that it was defendant's car which hit the victim, the prosecution calls an eyewitness, W, and after the usual preliminaries asks her if she noticed the color of the car which struck the victim. She replies, "The car was red." Figure One illustrates the double inference which the jury must draw from this statement if they are to conclude from it that the car was in fact red.

First the jurors must infer that W really believes what she has said; i.e., they must affirmatively answer what we have called the left leg question—"Does the actor really have the belief?" After inferring that W believes what she has said, the jurors must infer that W's belief is not mistaken; i.e., they must affirmatively answer what we have called the right leg question—"Does that belief really reflect reality?" Only if the jurors are prepared to answer both questions affirmatively—to make the double inference from statement to belief and belief to reality—may they conclude on the basis of W's testimony that the car which struck the victim was indeed red.

The triangle suggests that the jurors face two main problems in making each inference. If they are to conclude that W really believed what she appeared to say, they must first be sure that she and they inter-

8. Tribe, Triangulating Hearsay, 87 Harv.L.Rev. 957 (1974).

9. In doing so we shall modify Tribe's triangle in certain particulars. You should read the article cited in the preceding footnote for Tribe's original presentation.

The triangle is designed to aid you in understanding what is and is not hearsay. If the triangle does not aid you, but you nevertheless understand hearsay there is no need to master the triangular approach. If you have trouble understanding hearsay and you do not find the triangular approach helpful, you might be able to develop an approach that is personally more congenial. Professor Saltzburg, for example, has suggested that hearsay may be "straightened out" and offers the following diagram:

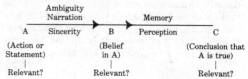

He writes: The linear diagram has several advantages. It makes it clear that one cannot go from A to C without passing through B and that one must reach C to find that a statement is hearsay. Thus, when the words of an oral contract are important, testimony about an out-of-court declaration is admissible because there is no need to leave A, the actual utterance of the words, to decide that the evidence is relevant. And if the words are circumstantial evidence of something other than their truth, it is not necessary to go beyond A or B. Finally, the linear diagram shows that if one travels from A through B to a conclusion not asserted by the declarant, some of the traditional hearsay problems still exist even though modern codes would not treat such a statement as hearsay.

Saltzburg, A Special Aspect of Relevance: Countering Negative Inferences Associated with the Absence of Evidence, 66 Calif.L.Rev. 1011 (1978).

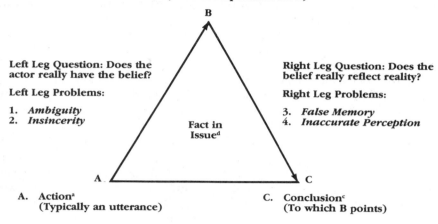

FIGURE ONE
THE TESTIMONIAL TRIANGLE

B. **Belief**[b] **(Of actor responsible for A)**

B

Left Leg Question: Does the   Right Leg Question: Does the
actor really have the belief?   belief really reflect reality?

Left Leg Problems: Right Leg Problems:

1. *Ambiguity*   3. *False Memory*
2. *Insincerity*   4. *Inaccurate Perception*

Fact in
Issue[d]

A   C

A. **Action**[a]   C. **Conclusion**[c]
    (Typically an utterance)   **(To which B points)**

[a] *W*'s statement "The car was red."
[b] *W*'s belief that the car was red.
[c] The fact that the car was red.
[d] The color of the car.

pret words in the same way. There should be no ambiguity in what was said. If the jurors discover that *W* has only recently learned to speak English and that she has frequently confused red with yellow, they will be wary of giving too much weight to her testimony. The jurors must also conclude that *W* was not trying to deceive when she stated the car was red. If they learn that *W* has been defendant's sworn enemy for years, they are again likely to discredit her testimony.

In answering the right leg question the jurors must decide whether a sincere belief is mistaken. Here the major problems are mistakes of memory and perception. The jurors, to continue with our example, would be more likely to accept *W*'s belief if her description were given one day rather than one year after the accident. If *W* were shown to be color blind, her belief, however sincere, would be discounted entirely.[10]

These problems of inference exist whenever jurors are asked to believe a witness' testimony. Obviously, we do not exclude ordinary testimony because there is a danger that the jurors may be deceived. While we are aware of this possibility, there are certain features of testimony given in the courtroom which are thought to minimize the danger: the testimony is given under oath, the jurors are able to observe the witness' demeanor,

10. You should note that it is only in an extreme situation such as color blindness when color is in issue that a trier of fact is likely to reject a statement entirely. Even successful efforts to discredit testimony will often leave the trier with the conclusion that the disputed fact is somewhat more likely than it would have been without the testimony, though not nearly as likely as if the testimony had not been discredited. This is one reason why witnesses are no longer disqualified for interest and why only prima facie showings of competency and firsthand knowledge are required before witnesses are allowed to testify. The court assumes that the trier will treat the evidence "for what it's worth." (Incidentally, because *W* is a woman she is very unlikely to be colorblind.)

testimony typically relates crucial information in the context of a larger story while hearsay often consists only of crucial statements, and the opposing party may test a witness' story by cross-examination.

Of these safeguards the opportunity to cross-examine is the most important. Ideally, cross-examination may clear up ambiguity, expose insincerity, and point out those factors which should lead jurors to suspect a witness' memory or to question his ability to observe clearly the events described. In practice, cross-examination rarely destroys a witness' testimony, but it often leads to the qualification of unqualified assertions, indicates motives to deceive, and suggests to the jurors the kind of critical stance they should take toward the testimony. The oath is thought to have been effective in promoting honesty at a time when people were more religious and belief in an avenging God more general, but now it is thought to be helpful only insofar as it emphasizes the solemnity of the occasion and raises in potential liars the fear of perjury.[11] Appellate courts often rely on the trier's opportunity to view the witness' demeanor as justification for not reversing decisions below, but there is no good evidence that the opportunity to observe the demeanor of testifying witnesses aids in evaluating credibility. The shifty-eyed may be simply nervous or astigmatic, while the cool and collected may be experienced liars. Most commentators on the hearsay rule do not mention the contextual setting as an aid to the evaluation of courtroom testimony,[12] but the authors feel that hearing the testimony in the context of a larger story is often important in evaluating credibility. Even where there is no cross-examination, the jurors may perceive inconsistencies in the various portions of a witness' testimony, and the jurors' realization that not all pertinent facts were perceived or remembered may lead them to question the accuracy of those facts which were reported. Context, like cross-examination, aids jurors in evaluating all testimonial dangers; oath and demeanor only aid in the evaluation of sincerity.

C. THE HEARSAY DANGERS

Consider our earlier example of the hit-and-run driver, but this time assume that W arrived after the driver had fled but in time to hear an observer, O, state, "A red car hit the victim." Figure Two depicts the series of inferences which the trier of fact

---

11. There is no good empirical evidence on the value of the oath in promoting reliable testimony. We tend to disagree with most modern commentators, feeling that they attribute too much weight to the value of the oath in times past and too little weight to the prevalence and sincerity of religious beliefs today. Also, the solemnity of the oath may cause even non-religious witnesses to testify more carefully. Therefore, we doubt that the moral impact of the oath on the veracity of witnesses has changed over the centuries as drastically as some commentators suggest. The fear of perjury, on the other hand, though not made much of, is, if anything, overemphasized. Perjury is very difficult to prove and the offense is rarely prosecuted, especially where the alleged lie has been told in ordinary civil litigation. In the absence of good evidence, the value of the oath should not be unduly discounted, but what constitutes undue discounting is open to considerable speculation.

12. This may be because a witness who is properly identified and shown to have firsthand knowledge will be allowed to testify to a single fact set in no context other than the context the adversary attempts to establish through cross-examination, while a witness usually will not be allowed to testify in court without taking an oath, without appearing before the fact finder, and without subjecting himself to cross-examination. However, the fact that a situation does not necessarily exist with respect to courtroom testimony does not mean that it should not be recognized as a strength of courtroom testimony and a weakness of hearsay if it in fact exists in most cases.

will have to make to conclude from *W*'s report of *O*'s statement that a red car in fact hit the victim. The factfinder will have to infer from *W*'s testimony that *W* believes she heard *O*, the declarant, make the statement; from *W*'s belief, that *O* in fact made the statement; from the fact that *O* made the statement, *O*'s belief that the car which hit the victim was red; and from *O*'s belief, the fact that the car was red. These inferences respecting the meaning, veracity and accuracy of *O*'s statement have none of the safeguards which commonly exist when jurors are asked to evaluate courtroom testimony. Because *O* is an out-of-court declarant the jurors cannot view his demeanor, have none of the assurance an oath brings, and will not see the declarant tested by cross-examination. These deficiencies constitute the most commonly mentioned hearsay dangers. To them we add the likelihood that the declarant's statement will be reported as a discrete item of information and so not be subject to the consistency checks possible when a statement is part of a larger story.

To these dangers, all of which are associated with the declarant's testimony and not that of the witness, some commentators have added the danger of mistakes in transmittal. We are all aware how secondhand stories are sometimes mistaken. Wigmore has rejected this argument as an independent justification for the hearsay rule on the ground that the testimony reporting an out-of-court statement is subject to the same safeguards which exist to maximize the reliability of all testimonial evidence. Wigmore's premises are correct, but his conclusion reflects a failure to appreciate important differences between ordinary testimony and reports of hearsay. First, it is likely that the dangers of honest mistakes about crucial matters are greater when statements are reported than when more complex events are described. The failure to hear the single word "not" may transform a statement from one of exculpation into an admission of guilt or liability. The failure to appreciate one detail of a complex scene is unlikely to be so crucial, particularly since other testimony may fill in the detail without forcing jurors to choose between inconsistent stories. If a mistake in reporting is an honest one, the witness will not be deterred by the oath nor should its falsity be reflected in the witness' demeanor.

Second, and more importantly, cross-examination appears likely to be less effective

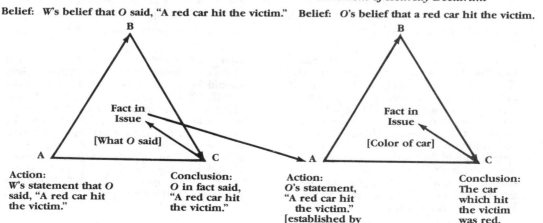

FIGURE TWO

Testimony Given in Court   *Statement of Hearsay Declarant*

Belief: *W*'s belief that *O* said, "A red car hit the victim."   **Belief:** *O*'s belief that a red car hit the victim.

B

Fact in Issue

[What *O* said]

A   C

Action: *W*'s statement that *O* said, "A red car hit the victim."

Conclusion: *O* in fact said, "A red car hit the victim."

B

Fact in Issue

[Color of car]

A   C

Action: *O*'s statement, "A red car hit the victim." [established by *W*'s testimony.]

Conclusion: The car which hit the victim was red.

in testing mistaken reports of out-of-court statements than it is in testing most other mistaken testimonial claims. This seems particularly true where deceit is intentional. The lying witness does not have to carefully fit a story into the context of facts too well-established to deny, so the story cannot be broken down by showing it does not fit. All the witness must do is testify to his good hearing and what was heard. If asked how what he heard may be reconciled with other facts in the case, the witness may reply that he knows nothing beyond what some—perhaps unidentified—other has said. How does one deal on cross-examination with the victim's friend who claims to have heard, upon arriving at the scene of the accident, a stranger in the crowd say, "The driver of the car was speeding"? If the friend testified that he saw the car speeding, one could quiz him on his ability to judge speed, his vantage point, his failure to warn, and his failure to report the driver to the police. Inconsistency in answering such questions might convince the jury that the witness was not to be trusted. Such inconsistency is more difficult to show when only hearsay is reported.[13]

D. THE HEARSAY DILEMMA

We have now canvassed the reasons usually given for the exclusion of hearsay. Presumably we have convinced you that evidence of hearsay is likely to be less reliable than similar testimony presented, subject to cross-examination, before the trier of fact. It does not follow from this that hearsay evidence is valueless or that any or all hearsay should be excluded. While there may be a danger that jurors will be misled if hearsay evidence is admitted, there may be a greater danger that they will make mistakes if such evidence is excluded. Consider the case of the hit-and-run driver described above. Suppose there is some evidence connecting the defendant to the scene of the crime: a fender is freshly dented in a way consistent with the accident, and the accident occurred at 5:10 p. m. on the defendant's regular route from work. Are the jurors likely to reach a better decision if they learn from W, a witness whose credibility is tested, that she heard O, an apparently disinterested observer, state that the car in the accident was red, or are they likely to reach a better result if this evidence is kept from them?

Perhaps hearsay should be routinely admitted. After all, even though people prefer to act on the basis of firsthand information, important decisions are often based entirely on secondhand and thirdhand reports. Can we not trust jurors to view hearsay with appropriate skepticism and give it its proper weight? If we are not willing to go this far, should we perhaps trust judges to exclude the most dan-

---

13. In addition to these arguments the fact that hearsay involves inferences about the veracity and accuracy of two declarants may also complicate the jury's decision as to the proper weight to be accorded the hearsay declaration. If a juror decides there is a fifty percent chance that a witness' statement is accurate, how much weight should that statement be given in the jury's deliberations? If the jury believes that a witness' report of an out-of-court declaration has a fifty percent chance of being accurate, and if accurate, the out-of-court statement has an eighty percent chance of being true, how much weight should be given to the out-of-court statement? Mathematically, the hearsay situation is as tractable as the other, but jurors, who will reach both conclusions on intuitive rather than mathematical bases, may be more likely to make mistakes in deciding the appropriate weight to be accorded hearsay statements than in evaluating the proper weight of disputable courtroom testimony.

gerous hearsay and to call the jury's attention to the limitations of what is admitted? These are good questions, often posed by critics of the hearsay rule. They raise the somewhat different issues of whether hearsay should be grounds for exclusion and, if so, whether exclusion should be by rule or by discretion. As with many difficult questions, there are no clearly correct answers. We will discuss these issues in more detail in Section IV of this Chapter.

In the American legal system hearsay is not routinely admitted, nor is the decision to admit hearsay left to the discretion of the judge. Yet hearsay evidence is routinely offered and often admitted. The common law has moderated the tension of a rule excluding potentially unreliable but perhaps helpful information by formulating a series of exceptions, really rules in themselves, which specify a series of situations in which hearsay may come in. The guiding principle behind most common law exceptions embodies two criteria, *necessity* and *reliability*. Where evidence of a particular type is not likely to be available unless hearsay statements are accepted, or where particular types of hearsay appear to carry special guarantees of reliability, exceptions to the hearsay rule are likely. We shall discuss these exceptions to the hearsay rule and the rationales commonly given for them in Section III of this Chapter.

For the present, it is sufficient to note that while scholars are agreed that the exclusion of all hearsay would be untenable, many see the proliferation of hearsay exceptions as part of the problem rather than the solution. The federal rules list twenty-seven specific exceptions and two general exceptions to the hearsay rule. Some commentators have spotted even more in the various states. One may wonder whether a rule which requires twenty-nine exceptions should exist. Indeed, one may ask whether it makes sense to call something a rule when it has twenty-nine exceptions. When you have mastered the exceptions, we will return to these questions. As you read about the rule and its exceptions, consider alternative ways in which our legal system might deal with hearsay. How satisfactory are the compromises that the common law courts have evolved?

SECTION II. DEFINING HEARSAY

A. GENERAL DEFINITIONS

In the preceding discussion of hearsay policy we did not attempt to define precisely the concept of hearsay because we only needed to know the general characteristics of hearsay evidence. A general appreciation of the hearsay concept will not be sufficient when you are faced with close questions of admissibility at trial. Fine distinctions between different types of out-of-court statements and the uses to which they are put will determine what the jury will be allowed to hear. In this section we shall try to explain in detail what is and what is not hearsay, and we shall alert you to kinds of evidence whose hearsay status is not clear.

If you were to comb the case law and legal literature you would probably discover literally hundreds of different definitions of hearsay, but most of these could be categorized in terms of one of two polar types: (1) those which focus on the type of statement and the purpose for which it is offered, and (2) those which focus on purported defects in testimony classified as hearsay. Dean Ladd's definition is an example of the first type:

[Hearsay] consists of a statement or assertive conduct which was made or occurred out of court and is offered in court to prove the truth of the facts asserted.[14]

Jones on Evidence provides an example of the second:

[B]y "hearsay" is meant that kind of evidence which does not derive its value solely from the credit to be attached to the witness himself, but rests also in part on the veracity and competency of some other person from whom the witness has received his information.[15]

The two approaches to definition should lead to similar classifications except in one circumstance: where a witness is citing or is confronted with his own out-of-court statement. Under Ladd's definition the statement would be classified as hearsay; under Jones' definition it would not. Since most courts treat such statements as hearsay, and since Ladd's approach to definition lends itself to more precise explication, we shall base our discussion of hearsay on a definition of this kind. But before we offer our definition there is one other definition you should consider, the definition presented in FRE 801:

(a) *Statement.* A "statement" is (1) an oral or written assertion or (2) nonverbal conduct of a person, if it is intended by him as an assertion.

(b) *Declarant.* A "declarant" is a person who makes a statement.

(c) *Hearsay.* "Hearsay" is a statement, other than one made by the declarant while testifying at the trial or hearing, offered in evidence to prove the truth of the matter asserted.

(d) *Statements which are not hearsay.* A statement is not hearsay if—

(1) *Prior statement by witness.* The declarant testifies at the trial or hearing and is subject to cross-examination concerning the statement, and the statement is (A) inconsistent with his testimony, and was given under oath subject to the penalty of perjury at a trial, hearing, or other proceeding, or in a deposition, or (B) consistent with his testimony and is offered to rebut an express or implied charge against him of recent fabrication or improper influence or motive, or (C) one of identification of a person made after perceiving him; or

(2) *Admission by party-opponent.* The statement is offered against a party and is (A) his own statement, in either his individual or a representative capacity, or (B) a statement of which he has manifested his adoption or belief in its truth, or (C) a statement by a person authorized by him to make a statement concerning the subject, or (D) a statement by his agent or servant concerning a matter within the scope of his agency or employment, made during the existence of the relationships, or (E) a statement by a coconspirator of a party during the course and in furtherance of the conspiracy.

You should note that the basic definition of hearsay presented in 801(c) is very much like Ladd's definition, but the specific exclusions of 801(d)(1) reflect to some extent an acceptance of Jones' perspective.[16] The specific exceptions of 801(d)(2) also reflect something of this perspective in a way which will be made clear when we discuss the admissions exception to the hearsay rule.[17]

14. M. Ladd, Cases on Evidence 384 (2d ed. 1955).

15. 2B Jones, Evidence § 81 (S. Gard. ed. 1972).

16. How does the approach of the federal rules lead to classifications different from those which would be made if the Jones type definition were fully accepted? We will treat 801(d)(1) in more detail in our discussion in Section IV of this chapter.

17. See Section III infra.

The definition around which we shall organize our discussion is short and simple:

Hearsay is an out-of-court "statement" offered for the truth of the matter asserted.

Three aspects of this definition require elucidation. First, what is meant by the word "statement"? (The quotation marks, which we shall hereafter discard, no doubt alerted you to the likelihood that it means

something more than "an oral or written declaration or remark.") Second, what does it mean for a statement to be "offered for the truth of the matter asserted"? And third, what does it mean for a statement to be "out-of-court"? These questions can best be answered in reverse order. Until we specify the meaning of the word "statement", you may take the term in its ordinary meaning of "a declaration or remark".[18]

B. "OUT-OF-COURT"

"Out-of-court" statements are any statements except statements made by witnesses during the trial while testifying before the trier of fact. Thus, assuming the other elements of the definition are met, any oral or written statement attributable

to someone other than the witness will be hearsay as will the witness' own statements if not made while testifying at the trial. Hearsay includes witnesses' statements embodied in depositions, made in earlier trials, or spoken in the judge's chambers.[19]

C. "THE TRUTH OF THE MATTER ASSERTED"

A statement is "offered for the truth of the matter asserted" when its relevance to some fact in issue lies not in the fact that the statement was spoken or written, nor in some inference which can be drawn from the fact that such a statement was spoken or written, but rather in a conclusion which is justified only if the statement is true. More simply, a statement is not hearsay unless it is offered to establish facts therein asserted.[20]

To see why the definition of hearsay should be so limited, consider the testimonial triangles A, B, and C in Fig-

ure Three.[21] Triangle A portrays the situation where the relevant issue is whether a statement was spoken. Here one goes directly from the report of the statement to the fact in issue. This might be the case, for example, if the issue were whether someone was conscious after an accident. The fact that a person spoke is good evidence of consciousness, but whether what was said was true does not matter. In these circumstances we have to ask neither the right nor the left leg question, so the four primary hearsay dangers do not exist.[22]

18. This is by far the most common meaning of the word for purposes of the hearsay rule. But you shall later see that in this context it has been extended to include certain nonverbal behavior.

19. Compare FRE 801(d)(1).

20. McCormick tells us that hearsay is limited "to situations where the out-of-court assertion is offered as equivalent to testimony to the facts so asserted by a witness on the stand". McCormick § 246, at 585. Can you see why this will be the case only when statements are offered to prove the truth of what they assert?

21. You should note that we have dropped the triangular depiction of the witness' testimony; these triangles depict only the statement of the out-of-court declarant.

22. There still exist potential dangers in the report of aural rather than visual stimuli, but standing by itself this should not be enough to keep a testimonial report of the statement out, particularly since, as you shall see, the question of whether the statement was made may be of great legal importance. In these circumstances there is no choice but to admit testimonial evidence which bears on this issue. There may also be a context problem, but to the extent the

Triangle B portrays the situation which usually exists when a statement is relevant because, regardless of its truth, it supports some inference which bears on a fact in issue. Usually the inference will be from the belief of the declarant to the fact. In an extortion case, for example, it is necessary to show that the victim was in fear. Sam's statement, "Joe is going to break my knuckles if I don't pay up," suggests that Sam was afraid of Joe, even if Joe, in fact, would have done nothing of the kind. Since the concern is whether the belief exists and not whether it is true, we never have to ask the right leg question, "Does the belief reflect reality?" Thus the right leg dangers of faulty memory and misperception do not exist. You might wonder whether the non-existence of only two of the hearsay dangers justifies a decision to classify the reported statement as not hearsay. Since the right leg problems are probably the most significant hearsay dangers, and since many hearsay exceptions are justified by only some support to one of the legs, it makes sense to classify statements used so as to eliminate right leg dangers entirely as not hearsay.

Triangle C depicts the situation where the relevance of the statement depends upon the truth of the conclusion which the statement appears to reach. Here all hearsay dangers are present, so a statement used this way is properly classified as hearsay. When, for example, we use

FIGURE THREE

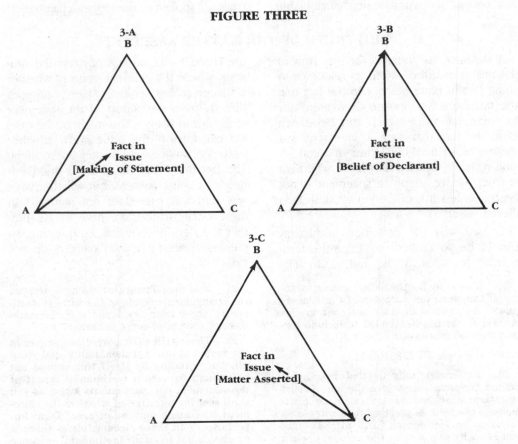

context consists of other statements, their relevance will usually lie solely in the fact that they were made, and often the relevant context may be set by a situation or event rather than by associated statements.

declarant's out-of-court statement that the light was red to establish that the light was red, it is important that the declarant really believed the light was red and that his belief reflected reality.

To define hearsay in terms of the triangle, *an out-of-court statement is hearsay if and only if the inference which the proponent seeks to establish depends upon affirmative answers to both right and left leg questions.* This is only true of the last of our examples. In pictorial terms a

statement is not hearsay unless the proponent is asking the trier to travel up the left leg and down the right leg of declarant's triangle as a prelude to applying the statement to a fact in issue. We exclude such statements as hearsay because without the aid of the oath, demeanor, context, and above all the *opportunity* for cross-examination[23] we do not feel that the trier has sufficient basis for responding affirmatively to either of the crucial questions.

1. VERBAL ACTS

Concrete examples of situations in which out-of-court statements are not considered hearsay should increase your understanding of this discussion. Perhaps the most important of these situations occurs when the very speaking of words has legal significance; indeed the issue of whether or not certain words were spoken may be the central issue in a case. Consider an action disputing the existence or contents of an oral contract. The out-of-court statements constituting the contract will no more be hearsay than the printed statements of a written contract. The issue in the contract action is not whether the statements are in some sense true but rather whether they were spoken. If words sufficient to constitute a contract were spoken, legal rights and duties turn on this very fact. Take another example: suppose A calls B "a liar and a thief" and B responds with an action for slander. Testimony by B that A spoke[24] these words would not be reporting hearsay. B is not testifying in order to convince the jury that what A said is true. Indeed, in many jurisdictions B would collect nothing if the

jury were so convinced. B is repeating the accusation because an action for slander requires proof that offensive words were spoken. Furthermore, the words must be attributed to A if he is to be held responsible for damages. Finally, consider a case in which the issue is whether X is the surviving spouse of Y. Testimony that X and Y responded "I do" to the traditional questions of the marriage ceremony and that a minister then pronounced them husband and wife would not be reporting hearsay because the statements in question are part of the very act of getting married. It matters not that neither partner ever intended to love, honor or cherish the other; having participated in the prescribed ceremony they are married just the same. Even if the ceremony were so irregular as to establish no legal tie, testimony reporting the exchange of vows would not be hearsay. It would merely be some evidence that there was a legally sufficient ceremony, evidence which in the hypothesized circumstances would be countered by other stronger evidence. Statements like these are not hearsay be-

---

23. It is important to note that it is the opportunity for cross-examination which is crucial, not cross-examination itself. If the adversary chooses not to cross-examine, it is assumed that cross-examination would not have revealed substantial weaknesses in the offered assertions.

24. Everything we say in this section applies in the same way where the out-of-court statements are written rather than oral. You

should note that "hearsay" technically refers to the out-of-court statements reported in courtroom testimony. However, testimony reporting such statements is often objected to as "hearsay." In this Chapter we shall use the term "hearsay" to refer to both out-of-court statements offered for the truth of what they assert and to testimony reporting such statements.

cause the fact they were spoken carries legal consequences. Such statements are generally called *"verbal acts"*.[25] In terms of the testimonial triangle, verbal acts fit the situation depicted in Figure 3A. The jurors are asked to reason from the fact that certain words were spoken to a fact in issue. Verbal acts are another aspect of evidence law that cannot be understood without a thorough understanding of relevant substantive law.

2. VERBAL PARTS OF ACTS

In some situations conduct is ambiguous, but accompanying words clarify the conduct, indicating its proper legal significance. Such explanatory words are known as the "verbal part of the act" and as such are not considered hearsay. For example, one friend hands another $20 and says, "Take this as a loan," or a depositor hands a teller $10,000 with a note that the money is to be placed in his child's trust account. Without the accompanying words the legal status of the conduct would be unclear. With the words we know that the friend was not giving twenty dollars away and that the depositor was surrendering control over $10,000.

There are many circumstances in which verbal parts of acts are relevant in the way depicted in Figure 3–A, but in other situations they appear relevant in the sense depicted in Figure 3–B. A bank depositor may be bound by the objective indications he gave of creating a trust, regardless of what he may have believed he was doing. But in the case of the friendly loan, the evidence appears relevant because it negates donative intent. This inference about donative intent seems to require the jury to reason from the making of the statement to the donor's belief about the transaction. It is the donor's belief or intent that determines how the transaction should be characterized. Since reasoning from a statement to intent does not require a full trip around the triangle, explanatory statements that are relevant in this way are not hearsay. Most courts, however, do not engage in such fine analysis. They treat all clarifying statements as part of the acts they accompany and assume the jury can reason directly from them to facts in issue. Figure 3–A depicts the dominant analysis.

This assimilation of statement to act is reflected in declarations by some courts that such statements are not hearsay because they are part of the *res gestae*, that is part of the thing done. If this were the only way the phrase *res gestae* were used, it might be a convenient way to classify the verbal parts of acts to explain why they are not hearsay. But, as we shall see, this phrase is also used to encompass several different hearsay exceptions, all of which carry guarantees of reliability apart from their close relationship to a legally relevant act. The multiple meanings of the phrase *res gestae* invite confusion, so we shall try to avoid using this phrase in our discussion.

3. STATEMENTS MANIFESTING AWARENESS

Often a claim or defense rests to some extent upon the allegation that an individual was or should have been aware of a particular fact. Where this is so, the fact that an individual made or heard a particular statement may be strong evidence that the requisite awareness was present. Consider a homicide case in which the defendant, Green, argues that although he fired first, the shooting was a reasonable act of self-defense. Given this defense it would not be hearsay to show that the de-

25. Some courts and commentators call such statements "operative facts" or "operative legal facts."

fendant had heard or been told of the decedent's statement: "The next time I see Green I am going to kill him." A person with reason to think another is out to kill him is more justified in interpreting an ambiguous action as a deadly threat than one with no reason to be wary. The use of statements to show awareness is also common in negligence actions. Consider an auto accident traceable to a defect in the defendant's brakes. If a garage attendant had told the defendant that his brakes were bad, the attendant's statement would not be hearsay if used only to show that the defendant was or should have been aware of his brake problems. It is generally negligent to drive with defective brakes when one has reason to know of the defect, but negligence may not exist when there is no reason to know of the problem. The analysis would be similar if the defendant had said to another, "My brakes are bad." Testimony reporting this statement would not be hearsay if used only to show the defendant's knowledge that his brakes were bad. It would be admissible because the defendant's knowledge is taken into account in determining negligence. It would be hearsay if offered to show the actual condition of the defendant's brakes.

Where statements are offered to show *an effect on the listener* the situation is that depicted by the triangle in Figure 3–A. Whether the declarant believed what he said or whether what he said was in fact true is irrelevant; the statement is offered only to show that the listener was or should have been alerted to certain facts. Thus, when a threat to kill is shown as part of a claim of self-defense, the proper issue is whether the defendant was reasonably justified in taking the threat seriously, not whether the threat was made in earnest or in jest. Where a garage attendant advises a driver that his brakes are bad, the rea-

sonable response is to have the brakes checked, regardless of whether the attendant was serious, intended a joke, or intentionally lied in order to increase his business.

But, you might object, if the attendant intended a joke or a lie, would not this suggest that the defendant's decision not to have his brakes checked was reasonable? The answer is that this would only suggest reasonableness to the extent that the defendant had cause to suspect a joke or a lie. This kind of question—the reasonableness of discounting information or ignoring a warning—will almost always affect only the weight to be accorded evidence; it will not determine admissibility. When focusing on an evidentiary problem it is too easy to think that the resolution of an admissibility issue automatically determines the outcome of the case. This is not so, no matter how crucial the issue on which the evidence bears. In the accident example, if the defendant could show that he knew the attendant had never inspected the brakes, he would probably be found not negligent in ignoring the warning. It is not inconsistent for a judge to admit disputed evidence on a central aspect of a party's case and then direct a verdict for the opposite party on the ground that that aspect was not sufficiently proven. This might occur because the evidence, though admissible, was insufficient standing alone or was so refuted by the opposing party that a jury could not reasonably find in favor of the proponent on the crucial point. A trial is unlike an abstract textual discussion in that it will often be unclear exactly how a disputed warning was meant,[26] but the listener will usually be in court to explain how it was interpreted.[27]

Where a statement is offered to show the *declarant's knowledge,* the situation is

---

26. Since we are talking about out-of-court statements, the declarant is not likely to be available to explain his intentions.

27. It should be noted that in negligence cases there is an additional protection in that the only warnings likely to be admitted on the notice issue will be those

usually that depicted in Figure 3–B. The speaker's belief, or point B on the triangle, is the fact in issue, so left leg problems will exist but right leg ones will not. If the defendant believes his brakes need repair, as evidenced by his statement to this effect, and he does nothing, he is not acting as a reasonable person regardless of the actual condition of his brakes. Very often where the declarant's belief is in issue the speaker will be available to testify to his beliefs at the time of the statement.[28]

The two examples involving the negligent driver are also examples of situations where a statement which is not hearsay for certain purposes is hearsay for others. Neither the warning by the garage attendant nor the statement of the driver is hearsay when offered to show that the defendant was or should have been aware of the defective condition of his brakes, but each would be hearsay if offered to show that the brakes were in fact defective. For this latter purpose a full trip around declarant's triangle would be necessary to reach the desired conclusion. The jurors would want to be sure that the declarant believed what he said and that this belief reflected reality. Where a statement supports both a prohibited hearsay inference and a permissible non-hearsay inference, the statement is admissible to prove the permissible inference. However, the opponent will be entitled to an instruction that the statement should not be considered for any hearsay purpose. Also, the tendency of the statement to prove the hearsay inferences may not be considered on a motion for a directed verdict.

Occasionally, a statement will be offered to show knowledge or awareness, where awareness is not an issue in the case but is rather a fact tending to prove some other matter in dispute. In one well known case, Bridges v. State, a man was accused of enticing a young girl to come into his room for the purpose of engaging in certain illicit activity. The girl's out-of-court description of the room was held to have been properly admitted over a hearsay objection because it was offered not to show how the man's room in fact looked, but rather to show that the girl had knowledge of the room which she could not have acquired had she not seen it. The girl's description would not have tended to prove that she had been in the defendant's room had there not been other admissible evidence which showed that the room in fact looked as described.[29]

4. STATES OF MIND

The substantive law takes intent into account for so many different purposes that parties are often required to furnish evidence about mental outlook. When such evidence is needed we say that "state of mind" is a fact in issue.[30] State of mind often may be proved circumstantially from statements of the person whose mental

---

which turn out to have been justified, however they were meant. Often later events are themselves evidence that the warning was meant seriously. If, for example, the defendant claims a garage attendant was jesting when he told the defendant his brakes needed repair, the fact that the brakes did indeed need repair in some evidence that the attendant was not jesting.

28. Where a statement is offered to show the speaker's knowledge or belief, it will often be the statement of a party. Here detailed analysis is not necessary, for we shall see that the statements of parties are routinely admitted under the admissions exception to the hearsay rule.

29. Bridges v. State, 247 Wis. 350, 19 N.W.2d 529 (1945).

For one of the authors, *Bridges* is the most difficult "awareness" case to treat as nonhearsay. The difficulty arises from the fact that the girl also asserted that she could give the description because she was in the room, not because anyone gave her the description. This aspect of her testimony is almost surely hearsay.

30. "Awareness," discussed above, is really one kind of state of mind. It is discussed separately for three reasons: because this type of state of mind evidence is so common that it merits special attention, because statements which provide a lis-

outlook is in issue. Statements used in this way are not hearsay because the jurors are not concerned with whether the statements reflect reality; they are only concerned with what the fact that the statements were spoken implies about the declarant's beliefs.[31]

This is most obvious where sanity is disputed. No terrestrial lawyer would introduce declarant's statement "Little green Martians are following me" as proof that the declarant is in fact being shadowed by extraterrestrial beings. If the statement were introduced, it would be because the very making of the statement is a symptom of mental disorder. Indeed the jury may not have to find that the declarant believed the statement in order to find mental illness. Except where a finding of insanity is in one's self interest, one would have to be somewhat disturbed to make claims known to be absurd. Whether or not the declarant was thought to believe the statement, it would not be offered for the truth of the assertion about green Martians. It would not pose the right leg question and thus would not be considered hearsay.

A similar analysis applies to statements offered to prove other mental states such as fear, intent to steal, alienated affections or donative intent. For example, if A sues B for alienating the affections of his wife, he does not introduce his wife's statement, "A, you're a vermin" to show his lowly estate but rather because the wife's statement is some evidence that at the time it was made she no longer loved him. Or consider a dispute over a will where ambiguous language could be interpreted as

giving everything to son C or to daughter D. The testator's statements "My son C hates me" and "D is my most devoted child" are not introduced to prove C's hatred or D's devotion. Indeed the testator may have been completely mistaken about their true feelings toward him. It does not matter; true or not, the statements suggest that if the testator intended to give all his wealth to just one child, that child was D. They indicate the testator's belief that C was unworthy and D deserving.

Perhaps the most perplexing analytical problem in the hearsay area arises with statements which assert a state of mind which is, in fact, in issue. Suppose in a suit for the alienation of affections the husband seeks to introduce the wife's statement, "I don't love you any more." The statement asserts one of the basic facts which the husband must prove, and the jury is asked to treat the assertion as true. At the same time, the very fact that the statement is made is circumstantial evidence that the assertion is true, since people do not usually make such statements if they still love their spouses. Analytically there are at least two reasons why it makes sense to classify a statement asserting the state of mind it is offered to prove as non-hearsay. The first is that when a statement may be used for both a hearsay and a non-hearsay purpose, the statement will generally be admitted for the non-hearsay purpose regardless of the probability that the jurors, despite instructions, will treat the statement as support for the forbidden hearsay inference.[32] Second, it should be clear that the jurors are only being asked to con-

---

tener with a reason to be aware of something will often be relevant as non-hearsay evidence without any need to determine the state of mind in fact induced, and because this kind of state of mind evidence seldom asserts the fact in issue and so does not pose the difficult analytic problems to be discussed below.

31. By this point you should be able to apply the triangular analysis and figure out which of the Figure Three triangles applies.

From now on we will leave this to you as an exercise.

32. Of course, under the basic principles of relevance a court would have discretion to exclude a statement if on balance the need for the statement in support of the non-hearsay inference is likely to be outweighed by the danger that the jurors will regard the statement as support for the hearsay inference. Courts are very reluctant to exclude statements on these grounds.

clude that the declarant has the belief reflected in the statement. There is no need for the jurors to decide whether the belief is well-founded. Thus we face the same 3–B type situation encountered with many other statements classified as not hearsay. On the other hand, the fact that the statement may be used to prove, albeit circumstantially, the truth of the matter therein asserted suggests the definitional problem will be less confusing if such statements are considered hearsay.

Fortunately the question of how to classify such statements has little practical importance. As you will learn in the next section, there is an exception to the hearsay rule for statements evincing states of

mind, so the kinds of statements we are talking about would be admitted into evidence regardless of how they are classified. For the purpose of dealing with the problems in this book or examination questions we make the suggestion that you arbitrarily classify as hearsay statements offered to prove precisely the state of mind asserted. We do this because it accords with the view of most commentators and because most courts if faced with a hearsay objection to such a statement will more easily follow the claim that the statement comes within the state of mind exception than they will a sophisticated argument as to why the statement is not hearsay.[33]

5. IMPEACHMENT

Perhaps the most common non-hearsay use of out-of-court statements is impeachment. Prior inconsistent statements used to impeach the testimony of a witness are admitted not to prove the truth of the matter asserted, but rather to suggest that the observations of an individual who says one thing at one time and something inconsistent at another cannot be completely trusted. From this perspective it is the fact that the inconsistent statement was made

which is important, and not its truth value. A similar analysis applies to the use of prior consistent statements to disprove a charge of recent fabrication. In both instances a party is entitled to have the jury instructed that it is not to consider the statement as bearing on anything other than credibility.[34] We have discussed impeachment by prior inconsistent statements in Chapter Five and the matter will be touched on again in Section IV of this Chapter.

6. OPINION SURVEYS

Opinion surveys are becoming an increasingly common source of out-of-court statements admitted as not hearsay. Statements generated by such surveys typically escape the hearsay objection because they are used to show a belief or state of mind and not the truth of what is believed.[35] For example, consider a trademark case in which respondents are shown the defendant's product and asked to state the name of the manufacturer. The fact

that some proportion of the respondents name plaintiff corporation is not offered to show that plaintiff manufactured defendant's product but rather to show that defendant's product looks so much like plaintiff's trademarked design as to invite confusion. Or consider a survey offered in support of a change of venue motion. A report that 75% of those interviewed state that the defendant is guilty is obviously not offered to show that the defendant is in fact

33. Instructors who feel differently should feel free to override the authors and instruct their students to treat such statements as non-hearsay.

34. But see FRE 801(d)(1).

35. There may be other objections which lead courts to refuse to admit survey results, and a hearsay problem may exist if a researcher reports statements recorded by absent interviewers, since the recording is an out-of-court assertion about what was said, offered to show what was said.

guilty; rather it is offered to show that opinion in the community is such that the defendant cannot get a fair trial.

It is possible that errors in drafting a questionnaire could result in answers asserting the matter which the proponent of the survey will wish to prove. These an-swers might be open to hearsay objections. Obviously the development of admissible survey data requires the joint work of social scientists with expertise in survey methodology and lawyers who fully understand the rules of evidence.

D. "STATEMENT"

Now we have only to define the word "statement" and our definition of hearsay will be complete. Up to a point this task is a simple one; we can follow the definition of FRE 801(a): A "statement" is (1) an oral or written assertion or (2) nonverbal conduct of a person if it is intended by him as an assertion. There are many kinds of nonverbal conduct which are clearly intended as assertions: pointing to an individual in a line up, a nodding response to a question, or the sign language of the deaf. Clearly the same kinds of hearsay dangers are present whether one points to an individual as an assailant or specifies "third from the left," whether one answers "yes" to a question or nods affirmatively, and whether one talks with one's voice or with one's hands.

1. SILENCE

It is difficult to determine whether some kinds of non-verbal conduct manifest an intent to assert. Suppose, for example, one person accuses another of picking his pocket and the other says nothing. By not responding, is the accused intending to acquiesce in the accusation? Consider the following argument which has been offered in support of this analysis: If the accused were not guilty, he would rise in righteous indignation and deny the charge; since the accused said nothing he must have intended not to assert his innocence (this step of the argument is somewhat strained); so by implication silence asserts guilt. Thus silence becomes hearsay. It might appear more reasonable to classify such silence as circumstantial evidence of guilt, but it should be recognized that, however one categorizes the evidence, the basic hearsay dangers are present. Silence is relevant to guilt only if the implication of guilt reflects the accused's belief and only if the accused's belief in fact reflects reality.[36] The most severe hearsay danger is obviously the extreme ambiguity of the failure to respond to an accusation. Most courts have treated silence in the face of comments expected to elicit denials if untrue as hearsay.[37] However, classifying si-

36. **You may wonder how consciousness of guilt may not reflect actual guilt. It might be, for example, that the accused has picked the pocket of some unknown stranger and he wrongly believes the stranger is his accuser, or it might be that the accused, not knowing the legal elements of a particular crime, wrongfully believes he is guilty.**

37. **Often one sees trial judges determining whether an out-of-court statement is admissible by whether or not it was made in the presence of the defendant or, in a civil case, a party. This rule of thumb is an analytically unsound reflection of the fact that** some statements made in the presence of the defendant will, if not replied to, be admitted under the admissions exception to the hearsay rule while many statements made in the presence of a party will be circumstantially relevant and not hearsay, e.g., a statement offered to show that the defendant was aware of something. Except in these two instances, the fact that a statement was made in the presence of a party should not affect admissibility. As a trial attorney you should be prepared to point out why certain statements made in the presence of the defendant are hearsay assertions which fit into no available exception.

lence as hearsay rarely leads to exclusion since some exception to the hearsay rule, most often the admissions exception, is usually available.[38]

2. NON-ASSERTIVE CONDUCT

Throughout this section we have emphasized that statements are hearsay only when their relevance to the litigation depends upon the double inference from a statement (an action) to belief and from belief to reality. One of the most intriguing questions in the hearsay area is whether an act performed without any intent to assert (i.e., non-assertive conduct) should be treated as hearsay when its relevance depends upon the same double inference. Suppose, for example, that a well-known sea captain is first seen inspecting all parts of a vessel with great care and is later seen embarking with his family on that vessel. If the vessel sinks at sea, should testimony reporting the captain's apparent inspection be admitted to refute a claim of unseaworthiness, or is it objectionable as hearsay? If the witness had only heard the captain state that the ship was seaworthy the answer would be clear; absent a hearsay exception the witness could not testify to this declaration. Should the rule be any different when the jurors are asked to infer from non-assertive conduct that the captain would have declared the boat seaworthy had he been asked? Both the actual assertion of the declaration and the assertion implied by the captain's conduct require a full trip around the testimonial triangle before they are relevant to the litigation. First, the jurors must conclude that the captain held the belief asserted in his statement or allegedly implied by his conduct. Then they must conclude that his belief reflected reality. Why should the one situation be considered hearsay and the other not?

This specific problem of whether non-assertive conduct should be treated as hearsay received its earliest and most thorough discussion in the now famous (among evidence teachers at least) English case of Wright v. Doe d. Tatham.[39] The case involved a contest over a will by which a testator, John Marsden, left his estate to his steward, Wright. Admiral Tatham, Marsden's heir at law, attempted to void the will, claiming that when Marsden wrote it he was mentally incompetent. The case wound its way through eight years of litigation, including several trials and numerous appeals, before it was finally resolved by the House of Lords in 1838 in favor of Admiral Tatham. Virtually all the great English attorneys of the day were in some way, either as lawyers or judges, involved in the case. The central evidentiary issue concerned the admissibility of certain letters written to Marsden by persons since deceased. There was nothing special about the letters, but their tone suggested that the writers believed they were corresponding with a person of ordinary understanding and intelligence. Wright sought to introduce the letters for their tendency to show that Marsden was mentally competent. The King's Bench and eventually the House of Lords decided that the hearsay rule prevented Wright from introducing the letters as evidence of Marsden's sanity. In the words of Baron Parke: "[P]roof of a par-

---

Even if you can do this, you may not prevail in the trial court, and you may find some jurisdictions where the appellate courts have transformed this rule of thumb into a rule of law. This matter is discussed briefly in connection with the Whale case in Chapter One.

38. See Section III.B. of this Chapter for a discussion of this exception.

39. Adolph & El. 313, 112 Eng.Rep. 488 (Exch.Ch. 1837). This case is reprinted in Section V of this Chapter.

ticular fact, which is not of itself a matter in issue, but which is relevant only as implying a statement or opinion of a third person on the matter in issue, is inadmissible in all cases where such a statement or opinion not on oath would be of itself inadmissible. * * * " [40]

American courts have generally dealt with the problem of whether non-assertive conduct is hearsay by failing to recognize that such conduct might present a hearsay problem.[41] The states that have recognized the problem have generally sided with the English court and treated the conduct as hearsay. But these cases are old and the trend, even before the federal rules, was probably in the opposite direction.[42] Where the case law is unclear, modern statutes are quite clear. The Uniform Rules, the New Jersey Evidence Code, the California Evidence Code and the Federal Rules all exclude non-assertive conduct from their definitions of hearsay.

As is so often true, there are arguments supporting both the older cases and the modern codes. In *Wright,* for example, the letters to Marsden posed each of the four basic hearsay problems. First, the correspondents might not have been sincere. Even if they doubted Marsden's sanity, they might have written their letters as if he were sane in order to spare his feelings. There is also considerable ambiguity as to the extent to which the letters, even if sincere, reflect a belief in Marsden's sanity. For example, one letter suggests that Marsden have his lawyer meet with the attorney for the local parish to resolve a certain dispute. It is not the kind of letter one would ordinarily write to someone of suspect mental capacity, but it might well have been written regardless of the addressee's mental capacity if the writer knew it would be opened and read by the addressee's steward. Problems of perception and memory are also present. One letter, written by a cousin who some years earlier had migrated to America, is fraught with these difficulties.

On balance, however, the decision of recent codifiers not to treat non-assertive conduct as hearsay is probably wise. As a practical matter, the problem of analyzing non-assertive conduct for its hearsay character is likely to lead to inconsistent decisions at the trial level and error reversible on appeal. More fundamentally, the four hearsay dangers will generally pose a far greater threat to the credibility of intended assertions than they will to the

---

40. Id. at 388–89, 112 Eng.Rep. at 516–17.

41. **In preparing this book the authors directed a research assistant to explore the case law in the states and determine which states treated non-assertive conduct as hearsay and which did not. The task of assigning positions to states proved impossible because only a few common law states have recognized the problem sufficiently well to state a position. One wonders whether the issue would not have disappeared entirely by now if the problem were not so intriguing to commentators and teachers of evidence.**

42. **The 1972 revision of McCormick's hornbook states that the trend "is in the opposite direction" [§ 250 at 598]; but the cases cited indicate that the revisors did not fully understand the problem. For example, Belvidere Land Co. v. Owen Park Plaza,** Inc., 362 Mich. 107, 106 N.W.2d 380 (1960) **is cited with summary, "evidence of receipt of telephone calls and visitors asking for Owen Park Plaza to show confusion with Owen Park Apartments." State v. Izzo, 94 Ariz. 226, 383 P.2d 116 (1963) is cited with the summary, "evidence that wife did not return home night before her murder as proof of her fear of accused husband." Triangular analysis makes it clear that the classification of the evidence in these cases as not hearsay does not depend on its non-assertive character. The evidence is offered only to show belief and not to show the truth of what is believed, so in neither case does it pose right leg problems. If sophisticated evidence scholars such as the revisors of the McCormick hornbook can misanalyze evidence questions in this way, it is no wonder that courts have not appreciated the problem.**

credibility of assertions implied from conduct. This is most obvious with respect to the danger of insincerity. Although the *Wright* case is a counter-example, usually the lack of assertive intent will negate any motive to conceal true beliefs.[43]

The problems of memory and perception are also frequently attenuated when assertions are implied from action. Conduct often occurs soon after supporting facts are perceived. Moreover, the translation of a mistaken belief into action usually carries more adverse consequences than the statement of a mistaken belief, hence an individual who acts on a belief is more likely to have carefully checked his perception and memory than one who merely speaks his mind.

Ambiguity, unlike the other basic dangers, is more likely to exist when non-assertive conduct must be interpreted than when intended statements must be understood. Individuals who speak try to make themselves clear. Actions are much less likely to carry a clear massage. The sea captain described at the beginning of this section might have been looking for a lost wallet and not inspecting the ship at all. He is unlikely, however, to turn to an observer and proclaim that he is not conducting an inspection. Yet, the fact that non-assertive conduct is more likely to be ambiguous does not necessarily mean that the danger caused by ambiguity is likely to be greater with assertions implied from non-assertive conduct than with intended assertions. The ambiguity of action is so evident that jurors are likely to appreciate this source of unreliability when asked to make inferences from conduct. Jurors are less apt to be wary of ambiguity when a hearsay statement appears clear on its face.[44]

Despite our feeling that the federal rules follow the wiser course in not treating assertions implied from conduct as hearsay, you should treat non-assertive conduct offered for the truth of an implied assertion as hearsay in dealing with the problems presented in this book and in your general study of evidence law. There are three reasons for this. First, if you are practicing in a jurisdiction which treats implied assertions as hearsay, you will have to be able to analyze conduct to see whether it is used in this way. Second, if you are practicing in a jurisdiction where this matter has not been resolved, you may want to raise the issue of hearsay to keep out crucial evidence. Finally, even if you are in federal court or some other jurisdiction which does not treat conduct as hearsay, you should be better able to per-

---

43. Close questions may arise as to whether an assertion is intended, e.g., if a person winces when a doctor touches a particular area, is the response involuntary or intended as an assertion of pain? If we know the person is seeing the doctor in connection with pending litigation, we may have substantial doubts about the purported lack of intent to assert.

44. Professor Tribe apparently feels that the fact that implied assertions are more likely than explicit assertions to mistakenly represent belief (because they are interpretations of ambiguous actions) cancels any advantage implied assertions enjoy on sincerity grounds. He also appears less confident than we that the decision to act on a belief rather than merely express it often suggests a substantial diminution in the usual hearsay dangers of memory and perception. This leads him to a compromise position on the issue of whether conduct should be treated as hearsay. He would classify non-assertive conduct as hearsay, but would admit evidence of such conduct as an exception to the hearsay rule whenever the out-of-court actor could not be made available for in-court testimony. Tribe, Triangulating Hearsay, 87 Harv.L.Rev. 957, 972 (1974). But for the practical problems of analyzing non-assertive conduct, we might agree with Tribe's position. However, we would still argue that assertions implied from non-assertive conduct are less likely to pose significant hearsay dangers than much of the hearsay which is currently admitted under those exceptions to the hearsay rule which do not depend on the unavailability of the hearsay declarant. You will better appreciate our position after you read the next section of this chapter on the hearsay exceptions.

suade the jury of the weakness of your opponent's evidence if you realize that inferences drawn from conduct present some of the same dangers which render hearsay unreliable. Of course, if you are practicing in federal court or in any of the state courts with evidence codes modeled on the federal rules, you would not object to non-assertive conduct as hearsay and would cite FRE 801(a) should an opponent object on hearsay grounds to evidence of non-assertive conduct that you offer.

3. ASSERTIONS IMPLIED FROM INTENDED ASSERTIONS

The problem of assertions implied from non-assertive conduct has received considerable attention in the literature. Much less attention has been paid to the problem of assertions implied from other assertions. Suppose, for example, that Able is found shot in the chest. When asked to describe what has happened he states, "Adams killed me." If Able survives and Adams is tried for assault with a deadly weapon would Able's statement be hearsay on the issue of whether it was Adams who shot him? According to our definition it is technically not hearsay since the statement is not offered to prove that Adams *killed* Able, the matter asserted. But the statement is offered to show that a belief implied by the intended assertion—namely the belief that Adams was the assailant—is true. In these circumstances anything which casts doubt on the sincerity, meaning or reliability of the intended statement will cast similar doubt on that statement's implications. Thus, an out-of-court statement, offered not for its literal truth but for the truth of some proposition therein implied, should be considered hearsay so long as the validity of the desired implication depends on the existence and accuracy of a belief arguably implied by the intended statement. Most courts, without seeing any problem, have treated the implications of intended statements in this way.

Often it is not easy for a trial judge to decide whether a declaration should be read as intending to assert something that arguably may be implied from the statement. If the declaration cannot be read this way, the implied assertion is not hearsay under the federal rules. Of course, as it becomes clearer that the defendant was not thinking about the proposition his statement is offered to prove, the statement may become less probative of the proposition it allegedly implies. As is the case with non-assertive conduct generally, a diminution in sincerity problems may be accompanied by an increase in ambiguity.

E. OTHER HEARSAY-RELATED PROBLEMS

1. HEARSAY DISTINGUISHED FROM LACK OF FIRSTHAND KNOWLEDGE

Occasionally the hearsay rule is confused with the rule limiting testimony to what witnesses can describe on the basis of firsthand knowledge. If a witness known not to be present at the scene of an accident states, "Hannah told me the accident was caused when the Porsche ran a red light," the witness is testifying from firsthand knowledge. He knows firsthand what Hannah told him and he is testifying to nothing more than her statement. If the statement is offered to prove the Porsche ran a red light, the proper objection is hearsay. If the witness had said instead, "The accident was caused when the Porsche ran a red light," the proper objection would not be hearsay but would be lack of firsthand knowledge. Here the witness is reporting an event with which he has had no personal contact. It is, of course, likely that the witness is merely reporting the statements of others without attribution, in which case the firsthand knowledge objection is really an objection to anonymous hearsay. But the firsthand knowledge objection also protects against statements based on dreams, crystal ball gazing, and deductions unsupported by what the witness does know.[45]

The objection that a witness lacks firsthand knowledge is in some ways more fundamental than the hearsay objection.

There are no formal exceptions to the firsthand knowledge rule.[46] Furthermore, if it can be shown from the surrounding circumstances that a hearsay declarant lacked firsthand knowledge of the subject of his declaration, evidence of that declaration will ordinarily be excluded even if it would otherwise come within some exception to the hearsay rule.

2. MULTIPLE HEARSAY

Occasionally one hearsay declaration will be embedded in another. This frequently happens where a party seeks to introduce a written report (the first level of hearsay) of another's out-of-court statement (the second level of hearsay). For example, an insurance company might want to introduce, on the issue of arson, a report in which a deceased investigator wrote, "I talked to the fire chief today and he said the fire resulted from arson." The report would be offered for the truth of what it asserts—that the fire chief made the reported statement. The fire chief's statement would also be offered for the truth of what it asserts—that the fire was due to arson. In these circumstances the evidence of the chief's statement would be admissible only if it qualified under some hearsay exception and only if the report in

which it was included also qualified under some exception. Where hearsay is only two levels deep, it is called double hearsay; where it is more than two levels deep, it is called multiple hearsay. We leave it to you to conjure up an example of the latter. When you do, remember that the principle of admissibility is always the same: a hearsay statement is admissible only if it meets some exception to the hearsay rule and only if each level of hearsay in which the statement is incorporated also qualifies under some exception to the hearsay rule. FRE 805 codifies this principle:

> Hearsay included within hearsay is not excluded under the hearsay rule if each part of the combined statements conforms with an exception to the hearsay rule provided in these rules.

3. MACHINE OR ANIMAL "STATEMENTS"

The hearsay rule responds to the frailties of human declarations and the degree to which these frailties can be better assessed if the declarant testifies in person before the trier of fact subject to cross-examination. The rule does not apply to statements which emanate from non-human sources, whose "testimony" cannot be tested by cross-examination. Thus a speed measuring device might flash numbers on a screen as cars speed by. Although the

machine's reading is a kind of out-of-court "declaration," a report of that reading is not hearsay. Of course, the admissibility of the reading depends on some evidence of the machine's accuracy and on evidence that it was used properly at the time in question. But this kind of foundation testimony is not a response to a hearsay objection. A similar analysis applies to the "statements" of animals, such as the "statement" an injured watchdog makes by growling at one

---

45. In this latter instance the firsthand knowledge objection might overlap with objections based upon the opinion rule.

46. But in some situations, expert testimony will be allowed on the basis of infor-

mation which the expert cannot be said to know firsthand. Also, a party's own statements may be admitted against him although they are not based on firsthand knowledge.

of five men in a lineup. We think by now you can see why the hearsay objection would not apply to a report of a dog's out-of-court behavior. We leave to you the determination of the required foundation for receiving such evidence.

Occasionally a machine, usually a computer, will retrieve or compile human statements which have been fed into it. In such a case there is a two-fold problem. First, the accuracy of the machine in compiling or reporting statements given to it must be shown. Then, the statements which have been compiled or reported must be shown to qualify under some hearsay exception if the compilation or report is offered for the truth of what is therein asserted.

The problems that follow test your ability to identify hearsay. In trying to solve the problems, you may want to refer back to the text. We encourage you to use triangular analysis because we think it helpful, but if you find some other approach works better for you, feel free to use it.

Problem VI–1. A widow sues defendant railroad and seeks to recover damages for the death of her husband, killed when armed robbers held up the railroad station at which he was employed. She claims the railroad should have been aware of the danger to her husband from robbers. To prove this, the widow offers to show that during the preceding four years there had been ten robberies or attempted robberies at railroad stations located between 4.7 and 29.8 miles from the deceased's station. She also wants to introduce witnesses to testify that there were conversations between the ticket-agents' union and the railroad concerning the need for increased protection from the dangers of armed robbery. However, none of these conversations specifically referred to the station of her husband. **Is any of the evidence hearsay? Would you admit it all?**

Problem VI–2. Frank Farmer was driving his automobile south on First Street. Sue Smith was driving west on Second Avenue. Their vehicles collided in the intersection of First Street and Second Avenue. The intersection was not controlled by any traffic sign or signal, and is located in a jurisdiction where a statute provides that upon simultaneous approach to an intersection in the absence of excessive speed, the vehicle on the right has the right of way. Smith brought an action against Farmer for personal injuries, alleging excessive speed and failure to maintain lookout or control. Farmer, in his answer to Smith's complaint, denied any negligence and affirmatively alleged that Smith was contributorily negligent in failing to yield the right of way. Witnesses are available to testify as follows:

(a) A witness for Smith, also driving south, will testify that 3½ miles north of the scene of the accident, Farmer passed her car at an estimated speed of 70 miles per hour, that Farmer's car rapidly disappeared, and that she saw it next a few minutes later at the intersection of First Street and Second Avenue, badly damaged. **Is there any hearsay problem here?**

(b) A bystander will testify that after the accident she went to Smith's car. Smith was conscious and said, "I was already in the intersection when he came barging in." **Is this hearsay?**

(c) Suppose Smith dies and damages are sought for her pain and suffering during the brief period she remained alive after the accident. **Can you think of any non-hearsay purpose for which evidence of Smith's statement would be relevant?**

Problem VI–3. Carl Rhinehart is on trial for fraud in connection with a series of shady stock and real estate transactions. In each case the alleged swindler identified himself as Cale Hannibal of 675 Bathurst Avenue, North Arlington, New Jersey. Three of the victims of the fraudulent transactions have identified Rhinehart as the man who passed himself off as Cale Hannibal. Rhinehart claims that this is a case of mistaken identity. In order to establish that there is no Cale Hannibal of 675 Bathurst Avenue in North Arlington, New Jersey, the prosecution puts a police officer, Henry Johnson, on the stand. Johnson testifies that he visited North Arlington, a town of about 20,000 people located on one square mile of land in northern New Jersey, and that he looked in a city directory and a telephone directory and found no one listed with the last name of Hannibal. He also testifies that he went to a number of bars, two bowling alleys, both high schools and a local football game asking people if they had ever heard of Cale Hannibal. No one reported knowing or having heard of Hannibal. Finally he testifies that he cruised through the town for over two hours going down every side street which he saw and he never found a street named "Bathurst Avenue." Rhinehart objected to each item of Johnson's testimony as hearsay and each objection was overruled. **Was the judge's decision to overrule these objections correct? How is this evidence relevant? What is the best argument which can be made that this evidence is hearsay? The best argument that it is not hearsay?**

Problem VI–4. On February 3rd, Marsha Cook was attacked and severely beaten by some unknown assailant. She was in a coma for a week. When she came out of the coma, a nurse was sitting in the room reading a paper. The nurse, seeing Marsha open her eyes, went to her. Suddenly the color drained from Marsha's face, she pointed to the back of the newspaper, then withdrew her hands, covered her eyes and said, "He's the one." Harry Medford, the man whose picture was on the back of the page, was arrested and charged with assault. The prosecution, in its effort to prove that Medford was the assailant, puts the nurse on the stand to testify to Marsha's words and action. **If the defense objects that the nurse's testimony is hearsay should an objection be sustained? Would you reach a different decision if the picture showed Medford being booked for armed robbery than you would if the picture showed Medford receiving the Jaycee's Young Man of the Year Award? Would your decision be any different if you knew that Marsha had later failed to pick Medford out of a lineup?**

Problem VI–5. Heir is contesting Testatrix's will on the ground that Testatrix was mentally incompetent to make a will. Legatee, who is fighting to support the will, has available a letter written by an old college friend of Testatrix about the time the will was drafted. The letter begins, "It is some three years since we have last met, but you are still my wisest and most generous friend." The letter goes on to seek both a loan and advice about certain "delicate matters of business and family." Legatee also has available a copy of Testatrix's response denying the loan but giving four pages of detailed advice. **Are these letters admissible over a hearsay objection?**

Problem VI–6. In the early days of the television blacklist, producers would call a particular number, give a name, and a voice would state whether or not that individual was blacklisted as a communist or communist sympathizer. Warren Walters, a newspaper columnist, is being sued by Harry Harkness, an actor turned politician, for writing a column urging people not to vote for Harkness because "Harkness is either a communist or the next closest thing." Walters defends on the grounds that (1) the accusation was true or (2) he (Walters) had good reason to believe the charge was true. He offers evidence that he received the number of "Blacklist Central" from a producer friend, that he called the number, and that when he spoke the name "Harry Harkness" into the phone a voice responded, "Harry Harkness doesn't check. You can't use him on any television show." **Is this evidence objectionable as hearsay when offered in support of either or both of Walters' defenses?** Suppose "the voice" is put on the stand to testify in support of the defense of truth. He says he can state unequivocally that Harkness is a communist because he remembers reading Harkness's name on a red colored paper headed "Known Communists." **Is this testimony objectionable? Why or why not?**

Problem VI–7. Vince Kearny is accused of arson. Near the burned house, rags were found, some of which were believed to have been soaked in oil and used to start the fire. The state called in "Old Boston," a bloodhound of distinguished pedigree. She sniffed the remaining rags and took off cross-country, eventually coming to Kearny's house. When Kearny's brother opened the door, she moved past him to Kearny standing in a corner. **Is testimony reporting Old Boston's behavior admissible over the objection that it is hearsay?**

Problem VI–8. One rainy day the plaintiff slips and falls on the floor of the Foxy-Loxy Supermarket, breaking a hip. The plaintiff claims that the floor was dangerously slippery because of the rain and that the manager was negligent in not putting down some substance to soak up the water and improve the traction. The supermarket manager testifies that the floor always gets wet when it rains and that in twelve years at the same location no one has ever complained about the floor being slippery. **Should a hearsay objection to this testimony be sustained? What arguments, if any, could be made that the evidence is not hearsay? If the manager testifies that in the twelve years she has worked there neither she nor any of the employees of the store has ever slipped when the floor was wet, would this testimony be objectionable as hearsay? Would any other objection be available?**

Problem VI–9. Phil Morris sues Tobacco Company alleging that their cigarettes caused the lung cancer from which his wife died. To prove that his wife was suffering from cancer Morris offers X-rays showing cancerous lesions in his wife's lungs and a nurse's testimony that Ms. Morris' attending physician ordered chemotherapy, a common treatment for cancer. Defendant objects.   **Are the X-rays hearsay?   Is the nurse's testimony hearsay?   Would the nurse's testimony about the chemotherapy be hearsay if Morris were seeking damages for his wife's pain and suffering as well as for her death?**

Problem VI–10.   Morgan Banker sues the Tabloid Press for publishing in an editorial in one of its daily newspapers the following alleged libel: "It is well known that Banker embezzled $10,000 from the Charlotte-Ann National Bank of which he was at the time cashier."

Banker, alleging malice on the part of Tabloid in publishing the libel, seeks punitive damages.   Tabloid's defense to the charge of malice is that at the time the statement was published, Tabloid reasonably believed it to be true.   At trial, Banker produces a secretary who worked in Tabloid's editorial office at the time of the publication.   She testifies, over Tabloid's objection, that the day before the editorial was published she overheard a conversation between the author of the editorial and the president of the bank in which the president said, "I tell you, Banker did not steal the $10,000; it was loaned to him by the bank on my authority."   **On what issues, if any, is the evidence hearsay?   On what issues, if any, is it not?**

Problem VI–11.   Plaintiff Fred Boyd was injured in an automobile accident.   In order to demonstrate Boyd's disabilities Boyd's attorney commissioned a twenty-five minute motion picture of Boyd performing various acts around the home and taking various medical tests.   The acts were chosen to demonstrate particular aspects of Boyd's impairment.   For example, one sequence shows Boyd attempting to touch his knees with his hands but being unable to do so.   Another shows him grimacing with pain while reaching above his head to take a can of soup from a kitchen shelf.   A third shows that he is unable to cut a piece of meat without assistance.   The defendant objects to the admission of the movie, claiming that it is hearsay.   **Is the defendant's characterization of the film correct?**

Problem VI–12.   David Cole is charged with possession of heroin.   An informant, one Mazor, told his contact in the Drug Enforcement Administration (DEA) that he would lead him to the home of his source.   Mazor went up to Cole's house, but Cole wasn't there, so he left.   Later that day, the DEA agent secured a warrant to search Cole's home.   A half ounce of heroin was found underneath the mattress of the bed in Cole's guest room.   Cole claims that he regularly lets friends use his guest room and that a friend must have left the drug there.   At the trial the DEA agent describes Mazor's behavior in explaining why he decided to search the house.   Cole objects to the description as hearsay.   **Is the objection well-founded?   If Cole sued the DEA for a violation of his civil rights, alleging that their agent searched his home without probable cause, would the agent's description of Mazor's behavior be objectionable as hearsay?**

Problem VI–13.   In the following vignettes W is always a witness testifying in court, D is a defendant in a civil or criminal action, P is the plaintiff in a civil action or the prosecutor in a criminal case and X may or may not be a hearsay declarant. Read each problem and determine whether W's testimony is objectionable as hearsay.

1. On the issue of whether D struck P, W's testimony that she saw D strike P.

2. On the issue of whether D struck P, W's testimony that X told her that he saw D strike P.

3. On the issue of whether D struck P, W reads the entry that she made in her diary on the day of the alleged fight, "Today I saw D strike P."

4. On the issue of whether D struck P in self defense, W testifies that she heard X say to D shortly before the fight, "You better watch out, P is out to get you."

5. The same testimony as in #4 on the issue of whether P was the first aggressor in his fight with D. D offers W's testimony.

6. On the issue of whether X was a citizen, W's testimony that she saw X swear allegiance to the United States as part of the citizenship ceremony.

7. On the issue of whether Z was X's sole heir, X's will in which it is written, "I leave all my wordly possessions to Z who is the most loving and honest of my seven children."

8. The same will as in #7 on the issue of whether Z was more honest than his six siblings.

9. The same will as in #7 on the issue of whether X loved Z more than he loved his other children.

10. On the issue of whether X had drunk a fifth of whiskey before leaving the Happy Hour Bar, W's testimony that just before he left she heard X say in a very slurred voice, "I got to go now—ha, ha, ha— I did pretty good, killed me a fifth of Mountain Jack in—ha, ha— forty-five minutes—ha, ha, ha."

11. The same testimony as in #10 on the issue of whether X was drunk when he left the Happy Hour Bar.

12. On the same issue as in #10, W's testimony that she saw X enter a booth alone with a fifth of Mountain Jack Whiskey, and that when she next passed the booth about forty minutes later she noticed that there was only about an ounce or two left in the bottle.

13. On the same issue as in #10, W's testimony that as X stood at the cash register she saw the bartender ring up charges of $13.97. $13.97 is the price (tax included) of a fifth of Mountain Jack Whiskey at the Happy Hour Bar.

14. On the issue of whether X, a child, was saddened when the cat knocked over his goldfish bowl, W's testimony that X cried as he picked up the dead goldfish.

15. On the issue of whether P had suffered a disabling back injury in an auto accident, a movie taken by one of D's investigators two

months after the accident.   The movie showed P shoveling snow and changing the tire on a car.

16. On the issue of whether a burglar had entered a house before day-break, testimony by W, a farmer, that she heard the cock crow about fifteen minutes after she had been awakened by the sounds of an intruder.

17. On the issue of whether X and Y had been involved in some sort of wager, W's testimony that she saw X and Y shake hands and heard X say, "It's a bet."

18. On the issue of D's loyalty to the United States, testimony that the FBI, after a security check, had cleared D for access to top secret information.

19. On the issue of whether X, who had moved to Hawaii some twelve months before, had the requisite domiciliary intent to qualify as a resident for voting purposes, W's testimony that X had once said to her, "The tropical breezes, the sun, the sand, the perfume of plumerias, I know of no place that is nicer."

20. On the same issue as in #19, W's testimony that X had told her, "Because I love Hawaii so much, I intend to live here forever."

Problem VI–14.   Test your understanding of hearsay and review the chapter on relevance by considering the following transcript.   **How would you rule on the points raised by counsel?   What additional points would you make?**

THE DANGEROUS TOY CASE

For Christmas a mother purchased a Matteline toy gun for her five-year-old child at Gambels Department Store.   The gun is an advance on former cap guns, giving off smoke and a spark when fired.   Plastic projectiles emerge from the gun.   The fifth time the child fired the gun it exploded, shooting a plastic projectile into his right eye, thereby causing permanent damage. The mother sues both the Gambels store and Matteline, the manufacturer. Her lawyer is not certain whether to urge negligence and breach of express warranties in addition to strict liability.   **What impact, if any, will this choice have on the course of the trial?**   The following is a transcript of testimony given at the trial.

THE MOTHER'S TESTIMONY

DIRECT EXAMINATION

Q.   State your name please.   **A.**   Mrs. Cecilia Jones.

Q.   Your address.   **A.**   104 Broad Street, Philadelphia, Pennsylvania.

Q.   Mrs. Jones, are you married or single?   **A.**   Married.

Q. How many children do you have? **A.** Three.

Q. What does your husband do? Objection by defense counsel— "Your Honor, why don't we get on with this case? All of this is immaterial and irrelevant. The jury ought to be able to hear the facts of the case and not the personal history of Mrs. Jones. **[How should the court rule? Why is this kind of testimony offered?]**

Q. Mrs. Jones, would you please focus on the date of December 15, 1979? **A.** Okay.

Q. Have you some recollection of that date? **A.** Yes, very clear recollection.

Q. Would you tell the jury and the court what, if anything, happened out of the ordinary that day? **[Why is this question phrased so awkwardly?]** **A.** Okay. Shortly after eating lunch on December 15, 1979, I decided to do some early Christmas shopping at the downtown Gambels store, in Center City, Philadelphia; I went down to the store and began looking for Christmas toys for my three children. One of the toys I saw was the gun made by Matteline and it interested me.

Q. What, if anything, did you do after seeing the gun? **A.** I went over to one of the clerks in the store and I said I would like to get some information about this gun.

Q. What, if anything, did he say?

[If the defense objects that this question will elicit hearsay what should the plaintiff's counsel argue? How should the court decide?]

A. He said, "Sure, ask anything you want." I said that I had been concerned about whether the gun was safe.

Q. Did he respond? **A.** Yes. He said, "Let me tell you the truth about these toys that we carry. Many of these guns are dangerous. The manufacturers are rushing to manufacture as many guns as possible before the Federal Trade Commission clamps down on manufacturers and requires them to make safe products. So for the most part these guns are not terribly safe, but the Matteline is the safest gun we have." **[Should Mrs. Jones be allowed to testify over objection to these statements by the employee?]**

Q. What did you do after receiving this information? **A.** I was beginning to be satisfied that the Matteline gun was a good buy, but I really was interested in why the guns were dangerous. I asked the clerk just what it was about the Matteline gun that made it safe as compared to the other guns that he thought were so dangerous.

Q. What did he say? **A.** He said that the other guns would often splinter, crack or break apart. Some, which utilized explosive smoke devices, would explode or burst apart, projecting particles at high speed which endangered children. He said the Matteline gun was well manufactured, well made, and was the kind of gun that would not break apart, that could be battered about, dropped on the floor, kicked around, and fought over without much danger, if any, to children. **[Is this testimony objectionable as hearsay? On relevance grounds?]**

Q. What, if anything, did you do then? **A.** I bought the gun in reliance on the statements made by the clerk.

Q. What did you do next with respect to the gun? **A.** Well, I took it home, wrapped it up, and put it with the Christmas gifts. It stayed with the presents till Christmas morning.

Q. What happened next? **A.** On Christmas morning, my children opened their presents and my youngest son took his gun and started playing with it. He fired a number of times, and then it exploded, shooting a projectile into his eye. I took him to the doctor and the doctor told me that there was permanent eye damage. **[Is there anything objectionable here?]**

Q. Mrs. Jones, would you have bought the gun if it were not for the statements by the clerk? **A.** No.

Q. Mrs. Jones, did you rely on the statements by the clerk? **A.** Yes.

Q. Mrs. Jones, did you trust the clerk? **A.** Yes.

CROSS-EXAMINATION

Q. Mrs. Jones, do you remember that you are sworn to tell the truth? **A.** Yes.

Q. And you are doing so? **A.** Yes.

Q. Mrs. Jones, would you please tell the court precisely what it was that your older child said to the younger child when he unwrapped the gift?

Plaintiff's counsel: Objection. Such statement would be hearsay and in any event it is immaterial.

[Following a conference with the attorneys the court overrules the objection. **Is this ruling correct? Why? What went on during the bench conference?**]

A. My oldest son told my youngest son that it looked as though the gun was broken. There seemed to be a crack along the top of the gun and he said that maybe it ought to go back to the store.

Q. Did the youngest son take the gun to you and show it to you? **A.** Yes, he did, and I told him that that crack had been there when I bought the gun and that I did not think it was a crack, I thought it was just a part of the look of the gun.

Q. Mrs. Jones, how many years have you shopped at Gambels? **A.** Oh, about fifteen years on and off.

Q. What do you know about the temporary clerks who work there prior to Christmas?

[Before the answer is rendered, counsel for the plaintiff objects and says, "Your Honor, I fail to see the relevance of this kind of question. Mrs. Jones is not an employee of Gambels, has no relationship with Gambels and cannot be expected to have knowledge concerning the employees of Gambels." The court overrules the objection. **Is the court's ruling correct? Why did defense counsel ask this question?**]

A. Well, I know that many of them are college students and many of them are young people.

Q. Did you know this prior to the time that you purchased the gun? **A.** Yes.

Q. Where did you get this knowledge? **A.** Well, I remember many friends of the family had children who had grown up and worked at Gambels, and I knew many of them and they told me that they had worked there only temporarily and that Gambels was very good about hiring people prior to Christmas. Many young people I know have talked to me about working at Gambels. **[Should this answer be stricken from the record if it is objected to as hearsay?]**

Q. Mrs. Jones, you receive the *Call-Bulletin*, don't you? **A.** Yes. We receive the newspaper every evening.

[Where did the lawyer get the information on which this question is based?]

Q. Do you regularly read it? **A.** Yes.

Q. Mrs. Jones, isn't it true that one week before you purchased the Matteline gun, the *Call-Bulletin* carried a story concerning an FTC investigation into all Matteline products, stating that the products were unsafe, they were likely to cause damage and recommending that consumers be very wary of such products? **[Is counsel's reference to this story objectionable as hearsay? Is the decision to ask this question strategically wise?]**

A. Well, I cannot say whether or not the newspaper carried such a story, all I know is I did not read it.

[Who has been cross-examining Mrs. Jones, counsel for Gambels or counsel for Matteline?]

RE-DIRECT EXAMINATION

Q. Mrs. Jones, have you ever heard or had occasion to hear any of your friends or neighbors or relatives talk about children's toy guns? **A.** No.

Q. Mrs. Jones, had you ever heard anything about the Matteline guns or other Matteline products prior to purchasing the toy for your child on December 15? **A.** No.

Q. Mrs. Jones, between December 15 and Christmas 1979, had you occasion to hear or read or see anything that might have caused you to doubt the wisdom of your purchase. **A.** No.

[At this point defense counsel moves to strike the above testimony as hearsay. How should the court rule?]

Q. Mrs. Jones, what, if anything, did you do with respect to the Gambels store after your son's accident?

[Why did the lawyer wait until this point to ask this question? Should it be permitted over objection?]

A. Well, I phoned up the store after I got back from the doctor's office. I was furious. I don't know precisely who it was that I talked to, but I do know she was very apologetic, she said, "I'm sorry, Mrs. Jones, that you have had such difficulty, sometimes our people go overboard in trying to sell their products and we will certainly see that everything is taken care of."

Q. What did you take that to mean?

[Would you object to this inquiry?]

A. I thought that she meant she was sorry that the product was bad, that she knew I had relied on their advice, and that she would see that the doctor bills were paid. I thought she was very nice at the time.

Q. Were you surprised when the defendant resisted paying the bills? **[Should this question be allowed over objection?]** **A.** Yes, very surprised.

RE-CROSS EXAMINATION

Q. Mrs. Jones, are you really trying to tell us that you called up Gambels and that Gambels admitted that it was wrong, although they had no idea who told you about the gun, they had no idea when you bought the gun, and they had no idea what gun it was? **A.** Yes, I am telling you just that.

Q. Mrs. Jones, are you telling us that you phoned up and have no idea whom you talked to, but an unnamed person guaranteed that everything would be taken care of? **A.** Well, that's the way I took it.

Q. That is all, Mrs. Jones.

[Why does the cross-examiner stop here? Is there any objection that might have been made to these questions?]

THE CHILD'S TESTIMONY

Q. State your name please. **A.** Michael Jones.

Q. Michael, where do you live? **A.** With my mother.

Q. How old are you? **A.** Five.

[**Should such a young child be permitted to testify? How should the court proceed before reaching a decision?**]

Q. Do you remember the accident to your eye? **A.** Yes, I remember.

Q. Would you please tell us the circumstances? **A.** Well, I opened my Christmas gift that my mom gave me. It was a gun. My brother, he said, "It looks like something is wrong with the gun." I asked my mom. My mom told me the man at the store said the gun was okay and I went and used it. Then it blew up and hit me in the face. [**Are there any hearsay problems here?**]

Q. That's all. Thank you.

The defendants offered into evidence a written rule of Gambels Department Store that employees are not to give any written or oral warranties with respect to any products, nor are they to say that any product is especially good or especially bad. The plaintiff objects to the introduction of this into evidence. [**Is it hearsay? Is it relevant? How would you rule?**]

Next the defendants seek to introduce a survey taken of all the persons who had worked in the toy department between September 1, 1969, and January 1, 1970. The survey shows that no person remembered Mrs. Jones or remembered ever giving any special advice regarding Matteline guns and that no person remembered telling any customer that these guns were safe or safer than any other guns sold in the toy department. The plaintiff objects to the introduction of this survey. [**What is the likely basis for this objection? How would you rule?**]
The defendants rest.

Finally, on rebuttal, the plaintiff seeks to introduce evidence of the fact that when she sent the bill for the doctor's services to the defendant, the defendant did not respond for five months. [**How, if at all, is this evidence relevant?**]

The trial ends. You are the judge. Would you change any of your rulings after the trial is over and you have an overview of the entire proceeding?

SECTION III. EXCEPTIONS TO THE HEARSAY RULE

A. INTRODUCTION

Judge Weinstein has written, "In the sea of admitted hearsay, the rule excluding hearsay is a small and lonely island."[47] In this section we shall discuss the principal exceptions to the hearsay rule—rivers of admissibility flowing together to create Weinstein's "sea of admitted hearsay." In the final section of this chapter we shall

47. Weinstein, Probative Force of Hearsay, 46 Iowa L.Rev. 331, 346 (1961).

examine the ways in which judges and scholars have tried to modify or avoid the rigidities of the hearsay system.

The hearsay exceptions we shall examine in this section are really rules in themselves, rules which specify the situations in which hearsay statements are admissible for all relevant purposes. Morgan and Maguire have suggested that a picture of the hearsay rule and its exceptions "would resemble an old-fashioned crazy quilt made of patches cut from a group of paintings by cubists, futurists and surrealists."[48] This crazy quilt quality comes in part from the fact that no single rationale justifies the many hearsay exceptions. The admissions exception has been justified by the "nature of the adversary system," the ability of a party to explain his own out-of-court statements, and the notion that it ill becomes a party to claim that his own statements cannot be believed. Several exceptions, most notably the exceptions for prior testimony and past recollection recorded, are justified by the existence of some opportunity for cross-examination, either at the time the statements were made (but not in front of the current trier of fact) or in front of the current trier of fact (but at a time when the circumstances leading to the statement have been largely forgotten). The remaining exceptions, by far the largest group, are justified by the claim that the circumstances surrounding certain statements negate at least some of the hearsay dangers.

The "quilt" is further complicated in two ways. First, some exceptions admit hearsay evidence only after its proponent has shown the declarant to be unavailable at trial, while other exceptions allow hearsay to be used regardless of declarant's availability. Second, the confrontation clause of the sixth amendment guarantees that "in all criminal prosecutions, the accused shall enjoy the right * * * to be confronted with the witnesses against him." This provision is clearly designed to promote some of the same values as the hearsay rule, but the extent to which it limits the traditional exceptions to the hearsay rule or prevents the adoption of new exceptions is less clear. The confrontation clause applies only in criminal cases, thus the potential scope of hearsay exceptions may be different in criminal and civil cases.[49] We will examine confrontation clause problems in detail in Chapter Seven.

Among courts and scholars the dominant attitude is that the probative value of hearsay evidence usually outweighs the danger that it will mislead the jury. This attitude toward hearsay leads to the liberal interpretation of hearsay exceptions, a push to create more exceptions, findings of harmless error when hearsay is mistakenly admitted, and the prevailing view that a fact finder may rely on otherwise inadmissible hearsay where it is received without objection.[50] As we look at the exceptions, you should ask yourself whether the dominant attitude is justified. Be aware in reaching

---

48. Morgan and Maguire, Looking Backward and Forward at Evidence. 50 Harv.L.Rev. 909, 921 (1937).

49. In some cases it might be so unreasonable for a civil jury to base a judgment on certain hearsay that the use of that evidence would violate the due process clause of the fifth or fourteenth amendment. Thus, there might be constitutional limitations on the admissibility of hearsay evidence even in civil cases.

50. This prevailing attitude is supported by the fact that the hearsay rule either does not apply or is greatly relaxed in many of the trial-type hearings conducted by arbitration panels, administrative agencies and other quasi-judicial bodies. There is no evidence that fact-finding before these bodies is inferior to the fact-finding which occurs in courts, nor is there evidence that it is better. One can, however, find some clearly expressed judicial feelings that agency findings are not as reliable as judicial findings. These feelings may explain the grudging reception that some courts have given FRE 803(8)(C), an exception to the hearsay rule that we discuss below.

your judgment that if hearsay is admitted, the jurors are free to disregard or discount it. If hearsay evidence is excluded, not even the most cautious inferences from the evidence are possible.

B. ADMISSIONS

The admissions exception occupies an important place in the scheme of hearsay exceptions. It is frequently invoked, and often serves to justify the admission of evidence which is crucial or devastating. This is because it allows a party to introduce into evidence almost any nonprivileged statement made by the opposing party.

We have already suggested that the admissions exception is something of an anomaly among the hearsay exceptions. It is the only exception which admits statements that do not in theory carry some special guarantee of reliability or provide some extra test of declarant's credibility. Some commentators have seen an extra guarantee of reliability in the fact that the opposing party may deny or explain his statement. But the admissions exception applies to statements made by predecessors, associates and agents of a party, none of whom need be present at trial for the statement to qualify as an admission. An extra guarantee of reliability has also been seen in the fact that admissions will usually be against the declarant's interest when made. But this is not a requirement of the admissions exception. A statement which is self-serving or neutral when made is just as readily admitted under the exception as a statement against interest.[51] Those who abandon the search for special indicia of reliability often assert that the admissions exception is justified by "the nature of the adversary system." Morgan, for example, writes: "The admissibility of an admission made by the party himself rests not upon any notion that the circumstances in which it was made furnish the trier means of evaluating it fairly, but upon the adversary theory of litigation. A party can hardly object that he had no opportunity to cross-examine himself or that he is unworthy of credence save when speaking under sanction of oath."[52] Despite the frequency with which this statement is quoted or similar sentiments expressed, it is difficult to see why an admissions exception is inherent in the adversary theory of litigation. This theory does not necessarily suggest that anything a party has ever said should be admissible against him in litigation; one might just as plausibly

---

51. **There is, as you shall learn, a general hearsay exception for statements which when made are against the declarant's interests. The kinds of adversely affected interests which will render a statement admissible are limited and the exception usually requires that a declarant be unavailable. These differences make it clear that this exception and the admissions exception are distinguishable. Nevertheless many trial courts and some appellate courts confuse the two, referring to an exception for "admissions against interest," usually in situations where the admissions exception is the appropriate one. To the purist there is no "admissions against interest" exception despite the many statements whose admissibility has been justified by** this phrase. **You will be wise to take the purist position. To do otherwise invites confusion between the rationales and the applicability of the two exceptions. Such confusion could lead you to overlook the availability of a valid hearsay exception or it might lead you to cite the wrong exception and thus fail to preserve an important point for appeal. If you understand the distinction, you can always adapt to the "admissions against interest" vernacular of some trial courts. If you confuse the admissions and statement against interest exceptions, you will have difficulties when you practice in courts which require them to be treated separately.**

52. E. Morgan, Basic Problems of Evidence 266 (1962).

argue that the adversary system, resting as it does on a right to counsel, implies that a party should never be confronted with uncounseled out-of-court statements.[53] However one may view the adversary system and its implications, the adversary theory does not explain the admissibility of statements made by a party's unavailable agents, partners, co-conspirators and predecessors in interest, all of which may be admissible as admissions. If we discard Morgan's assertion about the adversary theory of litigation and focus instead on his second sentence—"A party can hardly object * * * that he is unworthy of credence save when speaking under sanction of oath"—we are close to the probable rationale. The exception really seems rooted in ideas about the *responsibility* which individuals have for their actions.[54] People are expected to tell the truth as a matter of course, not because the law requires veracity in everyday speech, but because accepted notions of morality require it. The law recognizes in the hearsay rule the fact that people do not always speak the truth; but this recognition does not mean that parties before the court will be assumed to have failed in their moral duty to tell the truth or be relieved of the responsibility for their actions if they have failed.

Notions of responsibility also explain why one will be held to the statements of agents, partners and coconspirators.[55] Add to this idea of responsibility the fact that admissions often carry some extra guarantee of veracity by being against interest when made and the fact that parties or their associates are often available to explain statements offered as admissions, and there is a plausible basis for a hearsay exception. Include the special probative value which a party's own knowledge often gives to his statements and the case for the exception may be compelling.[56]

The admissions exception is also peculiar in other respects. Other hearsay exceptions only overcome the objection that the declarant's out-of-court statement is hearsay. If the declarant's statement is cast in the form of an inadmissible opinion[57] or is obviously not based on firsthand knowledge, the statement will be excluded on these grounds. A party's opinion, however, will be received against him and it will be assumed that he has checked his sources when he is not relying on firsthand knowledge. A party can always explain to the jury why his opinion was mistaken or his conclusions unreliable. Hence, in most jurisdictions the opinion rule and

---

53. Note how far the law has come toward this position in the criminal area. Usually the only hearsay exception which renders an out-of-court confession admissible is the admissions exception. The Supreme Court in its *Escobedo* [378 U.S. 478 (1964)] and *Miranda* [384 U.S. 436 (1966)] decisions has attempted to reduce the incidence of uncounseled admissible confessions.

54. See, e.g., Lev, The Law of Vicarious Admissions—An Estoppel, 26 U.Cinn.L.Rev. 17 (1957). "[A] man's acts, conduct, and declarations, wherever made * * * are admissible against him, as it is fair to presume they correspond with the truth; and it is his fault if they do not." Truby v. Seybert, 12 Pa.St. 101, 104 (1849).

55. Some might argue that this search for a probable rationale for the admissions exception is misguided, that the exception is explainable only by the historical fact that the

admissibility of admissions antedated the hearsay rule. Of course, the admissibility of all kinds of hearsay antedated the rule and indeed made it necessary. See Hetland, Admissions in The Uniform Rules: Are They Necessary? 46 Iowa L.Rev. 307, 309 (1961).

56. By this analysis the case for an exception grows weaker as the connection between the party and the person whose statement is offered grows more tenuous.

57. Some courts relax the stringency with which they apply the opinion rule when an opinion of marginal admissibility is embodied in hearsay. The reason is that the answer of an absent declarant cannot be reformulated in more concrete terms; so, unless the court receives the opinion embodied in the hearsay, it must do without all the information the declarant's opinion would have provided the fact finder. See footnote 20 in Chapter One.

firsthand knowledge objection are unavailable when hearsay is offered as an admission. The advisory committee's notes make it clear that the federal rule is intended to follow general practice in this respect. However, the justification for eliminating opinion rule and personal knowledge requirements applies with full force only when the out-of-court statement is the party's own or one that he has adopted. When a statement is by an agent or coconspirator of a party, courts may reimpose the firsthand knowledge requirement and be more reluctant to admit opinion.

The admissions exception is like other hearsay exceptions in that a party is in no sense bound by his out-of-court statements and so may offer evidence which contradicts them.[58] In this, the hearsay or "ev-

idential" admission differs from what might be called a "judicial" admission, that is, an admission made in the pleadings of a case or in response to a request for admission under the rules of civil procedure. A judicial admission is binding on a party and may not be controverted.[59] The hearsay admission may also differ in this respect from statements made by parties testifying in court. While the better rule allows a party to introduce evidence which contradicts his own courtroom testimony, some states will not allow a party to dispute in any way the factual assertions of his own testimony, and others forbid contradiction when a party testifies unequivocally to matters within his peculiar knowledge.[60]

The drafters of the Federal Rules, focusing on the unique way in which the admissions exception is rationalized,[61] chose

---

58. A party may, of course, always argue that a statement was not made or is quoted incorrectly or out of context.

59. A party who wishes to dispute a judicial admission must amend it or withdraw it. Usually this will require the court's permission. See, e.g., Fed.R.Civ. P. 36.

60. This means that in certain jurisdictions a party's version of important events, if adverse to his legal interest, will be considered conclusive as to the facts testified to even if other witnesses for the party testify to a different, more favorable version of the event in question. Thus, if the plaintiff testifies that he went through a stop sign, this testimony could justify a directed verdict against him even if other credible witnesses testify that the plaintiff did not go through the stop sign or that there was no stop sign at the intersection. Whether the testimony would be conclusive would depend on whether the jurisdiction in question held that this was an event about which the party easily could have been mistaken, one of the situations where the "no contradiction" jurisdictions make an exception and do not bind parties to their testimony. Other exceptions include situations where a party's testimony appears to result from inadvertence or a mistake of language, is avowedly uncertain, or is merely negative in effect. A party is also free to contradict himself during the course of his own testimony; it is the unequivocal meaning of his own testimony taken as a

whole which determines which facts have been so established by the party's own testimony that they may not be controverted. See McCormick § 266.

61. The Advisory Committee states in the notes accompanying FRE 801: "Admissions by a party-opponent are excluded from the category of hearsay on the theory that their admissibility in evidence is the result of the adversary system rather than satisfaction of the conditions of the hearsay rule."

This classification is probably a mistake. Lawyers will still have to explain why out-of-court statements of parties are not hearsay. To state simply "It is not defined as hearsay" explains nothing, so the lawyers will no doubt explain that the statement is an admission. Hence, the exception will probably live on in the courtroom even if made unnecessary by the rules. We should note that if the drafters of the Federal Rules did make a mistake, they have considerable company among evidence scholars. For more than half a century distinguished scholars have debated whether parties' statements are admissible under a hearsay exception or whether they are admissible on some nonhearsay ground. Perhaps the most cogent argument that admissions are not hearsay is made by Strahorn, who argues that they are relevant conduct of the speaker. Strahorn, A Reconsideration of the Hearsay Rule and Admissions, 85 U.Pa.L.Rev. 564 (1937). This argument to exclude statements which would fall within this exception from their definition of hearsay. In practice, the drafters' decision should make no difference in the utilization of admission evidence. Under both the federal rule and the common law, statements for which parties are held responsible will be admitted to prove the truth of the matter asserted.

Federal Rule 801(d)(2) specifies five kinds of statements which are admissible as admissions:

Admission by party-opponent.
The statement is offered against a party and is (A) his own statement, in either his individual or a representative capac-ity or (B) a statement of which he has manifested his adoption or belief in its truth, or (C) a statement by a person authorized by him to make a statement concerning the subject, or (D) a statement by his agent or servant concerning a matter within the scope of his agency or employment, made during the existence of the relationship, or (E) a statement by a coconspirator of a party during the course and in furtherance of the conspiracy.

FRE 801 (d)(2) follows the general contours of the common law admissions exception, but it is slightly more liberal in certain respects and may be more limited in others.

1. PERSONAL ADMISSIONS

Subsection (A) specifies the clearest kind of admission—a statement made by a party and offered against him in his individual or representative capacity. The federal rule is intended to admit a party's statement against him in a representative capacity even though the statement was not made in such capacity. For example, a trustee, while gossiping to a friend, may make statements pertaining to property in the trust he manages. If the trustee is sued as the party responsible for that property, these statements will be admitted as admissions. In admitting such statements, the federal rule is more liberal than the law in some states. The liberality of the federal rule makes sense, because as long as the trustee is sued in his representative capacity, he will almost always be available to explain what he meant by the statement, whatever the capacity it was made in.[62]

Since any statement made by a party may constitute an admission, you should have little difficulty in dealing with parties' statements as long as you are alert to the many different ways in which statements may be made and to the fact that a statement which constitutes an admission may be held inadmissible for policy reasons

---

reflects the position taken by Wigmore in the first edition of his treatise, where he argues that admissions are admissible for their impeachment effect because they are inconsistent with the claims implicit or explicit in the party's case. 4 Wigmore § 1048 (1st ed. 1904).

62. The problem of different capacities can be severe for some. Consider the lament of the Lord Chancellor in Gilbert and Sullivan's "Iolanthe," who is in love with his ward: The feelings of a Lord Chancellor who is in love with a Ward of Court are not to be envied. What is his position? Can he give his own consent to his own marriage with his own Ward? Can he marry his own Ward without his own con-sent? And if he marries his own Ward without his own consent, can he commit himself for contempt of his own Court?

* * *
* * * I am here in two capacities, and they clash, my Lord, they clash. I deeply grieve to say that in declining to entertain my last application to myself, [to marry my Ward] I presumed to address myself in terms which render it impossible for me ever to apply to myself again. It was a most painful scene, my Lord, most painful!

Lord Tolloller was sympathetic: This is what it is to have two capacities! Let us be thankful that we are persons of no capacity whatever.

which have nothing to do with the hearsay rule. Statements made in the course of compromise negotiations are admissions, but they are excluded for reasons specified in Chapter Four. Confessions are a type of admission, but their admissibility depends on the circumstances in which they were received. Withdrawn guilty pleas are admissions, but other policies, like those expressed in FRE 410, may prevent the admission of withdrawn pleas of guilty or of statements made in connection with them. Guilty pleas not withdrawn are also admissions as are civil pleadings later amended or a party's pleadings in one case when offered against the party in another.[63] However, when civil pleadings or guilty pleas to minor offenses are offered as admissions there is often a substantial relevance hurdle to overcome. Thus, inconsistent or hypothetical pleadings allowed under rules of civil procedure are usually not admissible, and guilty pleas to traffic offenses are commonly excluded in related civil actions since the cost of contesting a traffic ticket is often greater than the fine.

In those jurisdictions which define conduct as hearsay, the admissions exception is extended to include the conduct of a party when that conduct would otherwise be objectionable as hearsay.[64] Thus, jurors may treat evidence of the defendant's flight after a crime or his attempt to bribe witnesses as an admission of guilt or consciousness of a weak case. A party's failure to testify (in a civil case only) or to produce a witness close to him or to produce some item of real evidence in his possession or his refusal to submit to a requested physical exam will each justify the inference that had the party produced the evidence, it would have favored his opponent. Of course, the jury is not compelled to draw inferences from such conduct, and, except where the implications of conduct are almost indisputable, courts are generally unwilling to allow the party to prove an essential element of a case solely on the basis of inferences which may be drawn from the other party's conduct.

Admissions in criminal cases pose a special value conflict. Allowing admissions that tend to incriminate puts substantial pressure on the accused to take the stand to explain away his statements. The pressure is particularly strong where the admission is fabricated, quoted out of context, or otherwise inaccurate, since in these circumstances the accused will have something important to explain. Yet if the accused takes the stand to explain an admission, even a fabricated one, he will be forced to forfeit some of the protection provided by the fifth amendment and will open himself up to cross-examination and impeachment. On the other hand excluding an accused's statements may prevent the state from introducing important relevant evidence. Courts do not attempt to strike a balance. Admissions may be used against criminal defendants so long as the statements are, as a matter of constitutional law, otherwise admissible.

---

63. Of course, a party's pleadings in one case may be admissions in that case. Usually, of course, they will be judicial admissions—except by amendment a party cannot controvert facts pleaded. Where a party in arguing to the jury wants to use another's pleadings as a basis for some adverse inference not conceded on the face of the pleading, this may be done in a majority of jurisdictions by simply quoting the pleading as part of the record. In a substantial minority of jurisdictions, the party must first introduce the relevant portion of the pleading as part of his own evidence, giving the pleader an opportunity to explain why he has so pleaded.

64. If a jurisdiction does not treat conduct as hearsay there is, of course, no hearsay problem, so the evidence should be admissible without any special justification as long as it is relevant and does not contravene any other recognized policy. Nevertheless, courts in jurisdictions which do not recognize conduct as hearsay may still, in deciding to admit certain evidence, speak of "admissions by conduct."

2. ADOPTIVE ADMISSIONS

Subsection (B) of FRE 801(d)(2) refers to what at common law are called adoptive admissions. This variant of the admission exception recognizes that parties often assent to statements which others make. It holds parties responsible for statements they have assented to in the same way that they are responsible for their own assertions.

Where assent is clear, the justification for admitting adoptive admissions is almost as strong as the justification for admitting the party's own assertions. If A says, "X is true" and B, a party to the case, expressly agrees, it is difficult to see why the treatment of A's statement should be any different than when B himself is the declarant. Problems arise when it is not clear that the party's acquiescence in another's statement is knowing and voluntary. Suppose, for example, that the beneficiary under a life insurance policy complies with policy requirements for proving death by submitting a death certificate, which attributes the insured's demise to some excluded cause. Should the death certificate be admitted on the cause of death issue or should the insurance company be required to present the maker of the certificate if it wishes to get his opinion into evidence? The claim that the beneficiary adopted the maker's judgment may be entirely unrealistic. The death certificate was mailed to prove that the insured died, not how he died. The beneficiary may not have chosen the doctor who filled out the death certificate, he almost certainly lacked the expertise to evaluate the doctor's judgment, and he might well have been unaware that the technical attribution of cause would, if true, bar recovery under the policy. Yet, in most jurisdictions statements in the certificate, unless disclaimed when it was submitted, would be treated as adoptive admissions. Exclusion is more likely—though by no means guaranteed— if the policy required a specific mode of proving death or if the beneficiary were aided in his effort to present an acceptable proof of death by an insurance agent.

Even more difficult problems are presented when it is not clear whether a party has in fact acquiesced in the statement of another. The admission by silence—the classic example of the adoptive admission—poses this problem. If one person confronts another with the statement "You're the one who robbed me," is the other's silence evidence of acquiescence in this accusation? The other may not have heard the accusation, he may not have understood it, or he may by his silence have intended to treat a false accusation with the disdain it deserved. Courts generally hold that unanswered statements are not admissible under an adoption rationale if the judge determines that the listener for some reason did not appreciate the accusation or if the context is such that the denial of even an untrue accusation would not be expected. In other situations courts feel that the probability of contradiction if the statement were untrue is great enough that the jury should be able to learn of the interchange and decide for itself the extent to which a party's silence can be taken as acquiescence in the statement of another.

Perhaps the most disquieting feature of the admission by silence is that it allows one who knows of the exception to generate evidence in his favor. For example, if you are ever in an automobile accident, will you not now immediately accuse the other driver of being responsible in the hope that he will not respond and that his silence may be used against him? In the situation most prone to abuse—that of the arrestee—the right to silence and the requirement that the accused be warned of his right establish a setting where even the innocent may be unlikely to deny false accusations. Consequently, silence in the face of accusations made while in police custody is not admissible to support an inference of guilt or to impeach a witness if *Miranda* warnings have been given.[65]　Silence during the period after arrest but before *Miranda* warnings have been given is admissible for impeachment,[66] but the Supreme Court has not confronted the issue of whether such silence may be offered by the state in its case-in-chief as an adoptive admission.　Since the accusation that defined the substance of the admission could, if a response were called for, be considered questioning in violation of *Miranda*, it is likely that, unless *Miranda* is reversed, the use of post arrest but pre-warning silence will be confined to impeachment purposes.

3. AUTHORIZED ADMISSIONS

Subsections C, D and E of FRE 801(d)(2) refer to kinds of statements which the common law would treat under the heading of *representative* or *vicarious* admissions.　Subsections C and D distinguish two kinds of vicarious admissions and, following the modern trend, liberalize the conditions of admissibility with respect to each.　Subsection E, dealing with statements of coconspirators, codifies the law with respect to a particularly important type of vicarious admission.

Statements falling under Subsection C may be thought of as authorized admissions.　Where a party specifically authorizes someone to speak for him, statements made by the speaker in his capacity as spokesperson will be admitted as if they were the party's own statements.[67]　The case for admitting this kind of vicarious admission is not as strong as the case for personal or adoptive admissions since the party may have no firsthand knowledge of the facts admitted and may have done nothing to manifest agreement with the spokesperson's statements.　On the other hand, the party presumably has chosen a trustworthy spokesperson, so it does not seem fundamentally unfair to allow the agent's statements into evidence.　Furthermore, the spokesperson, unless dead or otherwise unavailable, is likely to be friendly to the party and willing to testify on his behalf.

This extension of the admissions exception is essential in the case of corporate parties who can only speak through designated individuals.　Eliminating this extension would limit the admissibility of statements made on behalf of corporations and would put people generally in a situation where they were better off speaking through third parties than speaking for themselves.　Only individuals who could not or did not know enough to secure representatives to speak for them would make out-of-court statements that were routinely admissible.　This distinction, which in practice would be a distinction between most individuals and most businesses, strikes the authors as unfair.　It is one good reason to treat authorized statements as admissions.

At common law a distinction is made between two kinds of authorized statements, those which a spokesperson is authorized to make to some third party and those which are to be reported only to the authorizing party.　Statements of the first kind are admissible against the party while statements of the latter type are considered hearsay.　Thus the results of internal reviews, inspections and other investigations are protected from disclosure at trial.[68]

65.　Doyle v. Ohio, 426 U.S. 610 (1976).

66.　Fletcher v. Weir, 102 S.Ct. 1309 (1982).

67.　Sometimes the decision to admit such statements is defended with an adoptive admissions rationale.　The party is assumed to have designated as spokesperson someone he believes is trustworthy and so adopted in advance that person's statements as his own.

68.　Of course, the opposing party can always call the investigator and, absent some privilege, learn what he has discovered.　But since the investigator is almost sure to be an unfriendly witness, this procedure may prove perilous.

So long as one justifies admissions on the basis of responsibility or other characteristics of the adversary system, a distinction based on the authorized recipients of statements makes sense. When a party has taken precautions so that third parties will not learn what his agents have said, why should he be responsible for statements which leak out against his orders? An answer sometimes given to this argument is that the individual presumably chose someone he trusted to make the report and can hardly complain when the report of a trusted agent is admitted against him. This is a rational response, but one which is hard to deal with. Either you believe responsibility should extend this far, or you believe that one should be able to limit his responsibility by specifying that a report is for his eyes only.

A much stronger case can be made for admitting internal reports if we discard the responsibility justification for admissions and look at the kinds of factors which justify most hearsay exceptions. Internal reports are likely to have such significant indicia of reliability that their admission makes sense on these grounds alone. First, one making an internal report has little or no motive to present information which falsely portrays a situation as less favorable to those who sought the report than it in fact is.[69] Second, those who prepare internal reports usually have an insider's access to individuals and information, so their reports are likely to be based on the full and frank disclosure of their various informants. Finally, internal reports are usually prepared for business purposes and so may share the guarantees of reliability which inhere in routinized business activity. Without specifying their reasons in detail, the drafters of the federal rules make it clear that Subsection C applies to all authorized statements whether made to principals or third parties. A number of states, probably a majority, agree with the position of the drafters.

4. VICARIOUS ADMISSIONS OF AGENTS

Subsection D treats the vicarious admissions of agents[70] generally. At common law the distinction between a vicarious admission of an agent and an authorized admission is unclear, since the statements of any agent are admitted only if the agent has authority to speak for the principal about the matter in question. Thus, the post-accident statements of truck drivers have been excluded when offered against truck owners on the ground that the drivers had authority to drive for the owners but not to speak for them. Subsection D of FRE 801(d)(2) avoids this result. It follows the now dominant modern trend and admits statements by agents so long as they relate to matters within the scope of the agency relationship. Specific authority to speak is not the test. The theory of the admissions exception provides no good rationale for extending admissibility this far.[71] Nevertheless the extension is probably a wise one. McCormick notes that there are reasons to believe that agent's statements made during and about their agency have some special likelihood of reliability: "The

---

69. Since bearers of sad tidings sometimes suffer for their news, there might be an incentive to report a situation as being more favorable than it in fact is, but a party confronted by a report to himself can hardly complain that the facts reported may be distorted in his favor.

70. We use the term "agent" in this section when referring to employees and other agents. We use the term "agency" to encompass the employment relationship.

71. McCormick writes, "[I]f the admissibility of admissions is viewed as arising from the adversary system, responsibility for statements of one's employees is a consistent aspect." McCormick's § 267, at 641. Responsibility for the statements of agents may be consistent with vicarious liability, but we see no particular relationship between such responsibility and the adversary system. Do you? Is McCormick's statement more convincing if confined strictly to agency relationships still in existence at the time of the trial?

agent is well informed about acts in the course of the business, his statements offered against the employer are normally against the employer's interest, and while the employment continues, the employee is not likely to make the statements unless they are true."[72]

Even in common law states the failure to classify the unauthorized statements of agents as admissions often provides little protection for principals in suits arising out of accidents in which agents have been involved. Clever counsel will usually find some way to get an agent's statement admitted. The statement may be admissible under some other hearsay exception, a sympathetic court may be persuaded that one who had authority to engage in an action (e.g., driving) had implicit authority to comment on his action (e.g., fill out an accident report), or, as a last resort, the agent might be sued jointly with the principal and the statement introduced against the agent as a personal admission.[73] In these circumstances it is probably better to discard the common law limitation entirely than to have it operate so inconsistently that its protection appears arbitrary.

Before an agent's statement may be introduced as an admission of the principal, the fact of agency must be shown. Agency cannot be shown by statements which would be inadmissible unless an agency relationship exists. Suppose, for example, Smith upon crashing into the plaintiff should state, "I'm Smith. I'm White's trusted agent. I ran a red light." Smith's relationship to White could not be proved by Smith's declaration that he is White's trusted agent. Thus, Smith's admission that he ran a red light would be admissible against White only if the plaintiff had competent evidence, apart from Smith's statement, proving that Smith was White's agent at the time of the accident.[74]

In those jurisdictions which hold principals responsible only when their agents have authority to speak, neither speaking authority nor agency may be proved by the statements of the putative agent. Where agency is shown by independent evidence, the courts are divided on whether the agent's statements may be used to establish the scope of the agency.

5. PARTNERS AND COCONSPIRATORS

When business partners make statements relating to partnership activities, the statements of one will usually be admissible against the partnership in suits arising

out of partnership activity. Although a partnership, like any business, might authorize only certain of its members to speak for it, courts have generally assumed that

72. Id.

73. In the last instance the principal would be entitled to an instruction that the statement could not be used against him. Where the statement is essential to the establishment of the agent's liability, some courts have held that the jury may find the agent liable but may not find against the principal despite the doctrine of respondeat superior. Other courts will find against the principal if respondeat superior would otherwise apply. Compare Madron v. Thompson, 245 Or. 513, 419 P.2d 611 (1966) with Branch v. Dempsey, 265 N.C. 733, 145 S.E.2d 395 (1965). If the employee's statements are admitted along with other evidence sufficient to support a finding of negligence, the principal will be held liable

in all jurisdictions despite the fact that the jury may have been influenced by the employee's admission.

Is it ethical to sue an impecunious employee for the sole purpose of offering his statements against him with the hope that the jury will disregard the court's instructions and use the statements against the employer? Should courts refuse to allow joinder in these circumstances? See Goodhart v. United States Lines Co., 26 F.R.D. 163 (S.D.N.Y. 1960).

74. There might, of course, be an exception to the hearsay rule other than the admissions exception that renders everything Smith said after the accident substantively admissible.

partners who purport to speak for the partnership have, as part owners, the authority to do so.[75] Subsection E of FRE 801(d)(2), which characterizes statements "by a coconspirator of a party [made] during the course and in furtherance of the conspiracy" as admissions, adopts a common law position usually justified on the grounds that coconspirators are "partners in crime" and that the statements of one, like the statements of any partner, should be admissible against the others. However, despite the analogy between business partners and partners in crime, statements of coconspirators are not, in fact, treated like those of business partners. Even if one accepts the agency rationale for admitting statements of partners, one must conclude that the rationale breaks down when used to justify the admission of most statements by coconspirators.

Statements of business partners are most often introduced when the partnership as a firm is involved in litigation, usually civil litigation arising out of some tort, contract or property problem. A partner's statements are admitted against the partner-

ship, the entity which explicitly or by assumption has authorized its partners to speak for it. It is true that courts speak of the statements as being admitted against the fellow partners, but this reflects the substantive law of partnership, which obligates partners personally when the partnership's assets do not cover judgments against it and enables partners to share the proceeds when the firm prevails as plaintiff.[76] Except insofar as a partner may be obligated by his relationship to the partnership, the out-of-court statements of his partners are inadmissible against him.[77] This is best seen when one partner's statements implicate another in a crime. Unless the offense is one for which the firm might be held liable (e.g., a violation of some regulatory legislation), criminal activity is assumed to be beyond the scope of the partnership, rendering the statements of one partner inadmissible against the other because they do not relate to partnership business.

The situation of conspirators differs from that of business partners in that conspirators' liability does not derive from the un-

---

75. Questions arise as to whether a partner is speaking for the partnership. A number of cases have held that the casual statements of partners, admitting liability in an accident, for example, do not bind the partnership.

76. Consider the following example on the issue of whether it is authority given by the firm or authority given by affected partners which is crucial.

Assume that an ongoing partnership decides to make partner A its spokesperson with respect to litigation growing out of accidents. Partner B objects strenuously, saying that A will never speak for him, but B is outvoted and chooses not to leave the partnership. If there is an accident and A makes an improvident statement without which there would not be proof sufficient to find the firm liable, the statement will be introduced as an admission even if B is the only partner with assets sufficient to satisfy a judgment against the firm. B will have to pay the judgment, not because he in any sense authorized A's statement, but because he belongs to a firm which author-

ized that statement and his relationship to that firm makes him ultimately responsible for the firm's debts.

77. Of course, a partner's relationship to a firm may be such that a court could hold that he had in fact authorized another partner to speak for him. If, for example, one partner, as firm bookkeeper, noted that another earned $100,000, a court might admit this statement as an admission of the partner's earnings when the partner is prosecuted for only reporting a gross income of $50,000. However, admissibility would not turn on the fact that the report on earnings was made by a partner, but rather that the partner, as part owner of the firm, had authorized the bookkeeping partner to state his earnings for him. The situation would be the same if the bookkeeper were an employee and the partner a sole proprietor who hired him. There might, of course, be other obstacles to admitting this evidence, such as the attitude which common law courts have taken toward the admissibility of internal reports.

satisfied obligations of an enterprise which they have joined for their common betterment. It derives instead from the fact that the activity of the enterprise they have joined is itself illegal.[78] Statements of conspirators which "are in furtherance of the conspiracy" are verbal actions taken for illegal ends. As such the statements of conspirators are not hearsay if offered against one who is being tried on a conspiracy count, for they are offered not for their truth but simply to show what the conspirators did. Just as conspirators are mutually responsible for physical action taken on behalf of the conspiracy so are they responsible for verbal action.[79] In other situations, however, the statements of conspirators pose the usual hearsay problems.

Consider the following example. Rogers and Brady are charged with conspiring to rob a bank. As part of its proof, the government offers the testimony of a sporting goods salesman that he sold two ski masks to Rogers who said he was buying one for himself and the other for his friend Brady. The purchase of the masks might be offered as an overt act of the conspirators, and if so, it would be admissible including the conversation, if it were deemed to be a relevant portion of that act. However, if the statement to the clerk is offered to prove that the second mask was for Brady, it is hearsay and poses the usual dangers of out-of-court statements offered for their truth.[80]

The federal rule provides an exception for statements of conspirators that are properly classified as hearsay under the definition we have been using. It is, of course, unnecessary to rely on an exception when a statement is not offered for its truth, but some courts confuse the hearsay and nonhearsay uses of conspirators' statements. You should not. If you are alert to the proper nonhearsay uses, you may avoid many of the problems that arise under this complicated hearsay exception.

The federal rules follow the common law in providing that one conspirator's statements may be treated as the admissions of another only if the statements were made in furtherance of their conspiracy and during its existence. Taking the "in furtherance" requirement seriously might lead a

---

78. **The activity of a criminal conspiracy is usually illegal whether done in concert or by individuals acting on their own, but this is not always the case. There are some activities which are illegal only when done in concert with others. This does not change the analysis here.**

79. **We take it that the theory of conspiratorial responsibility is that when individuals cooperate to achieve illegal ends they should all be held liable for the illegality achieved since they would not be considered coconspirators if each did not in some way advance or attempt to advance the illegal goals of the group. One may also be liable for the act of joining an illegal conspiracy. In this instance one is only responsible for one's own actions in joining. Statements which constitute joining together in an illegal conspiracy, since they are acts which are themselves illegal, are not hearsay if used to show membership.**

80. **The argument thus far is that if the admissions exception for statements of coconspirators were strictly limited to situa-**

tions where the statements were made to further the ends of the conspiracy (rather than to boast about the success of a conspiracy, to complain about its failures, or to point the finger at one particular conspirator) most statements that would apparently qualify for the exception could be introduced for the nonhearsay purpose of showing the actions of the conspiracy. But one might reasonably claim that a hearsay exception is required if such statements are to be introduced for the truth of what they assert rather than as acts of the conspiracy. If a hearsay exception is required in order to use coconspirators' statements for the truth of what is asserted, then, in theory, a defendant would be entitled to an instruction that coconspirators' statements would be admissible as acts for which he is responsible but not for the truth of what they assert. It is difficult to see how the jury could make this separation. These verbal acts might have been effective in furthering the ends of the conspiracy because as assertions they were credible.

court to hold that the reference to Brady in our preceding example is inadmissible against him because the reference was not needed to induce the clerk to sell the masks and so did not further the ends of the conspiracy. However, some courts slight the "in furtherance" requirement. Statements admitted under the coconspirators exception are often statements in which one conspirator points the finger at another or recounts in narrative fashion the past illegalities of the conspiracy. While it is conceivable that such statements may be made in situations where they advance the ends of the conspiracy, this is rarely the case.

The exception for coconspirator's admissions is not limited to the situation where conspiracy is charged. When a person is charged individually with a crime, the statements of fellow conspirators are admissible against him provided the judge makes a preliminary finding that the declarant and the defendant conspired together and that the other conditions for coconspirators' admissions are met.[81] Since conspiracy is not charged the statements of fellow conspirators are immaterial if offered as acts of the conspiracy, but they may be quite incriminating if received for the truth of what they assert.

The justification for an exception that admits the hearsay of one conspirator against another is unclear. Consider a situation in which there is evidence that Able, Baker, and Charley have conspired to kidnap X, but Able alone is charged with kidnapping and attempting to murder X. If Baker said to Charley, after X had been wounded trying to escape, "We should take away Able's gun; he shot X last night and if his aim wasn't bad we'd all be up for murder," this statement would be admis-

sible against Able as a vicarious admission that he shot X.

Able need not have been present when Baker made the statement; there need be no evidence that Able authorized Baker to make the statement on his behalf; the statement is irrelevant as an act of the conspiracy because the prosecution has not chosen to charge Able with conspiracy, and Baker may have had every motive to place the blame for the shooting on Able. Yet, the jury will receive Charley's testimony reporting Baker's statement. All the hearsay dangers are present in this situation. An analogous example in the partnership context would be a situation in which Able, while on partnership business, is involved in an accident allegedly due to his drunk driving. *P,* the victim of the accident, chooses to sue Able in his individual capacity and not the firm. *P* has available the statement which Able's partner Baker made to another partner Charley, the day after the accident: "Charley, we shouldn't let Able drive on partnership business; he was drunk last night and is likely to be drunk again." Few courts would hold that the fact that Baker made the statement while discussing partnership business renders it admissible against Able when Able is sued in an individual rather than business capacity.

If the coconspirators exception cannot be justified on the traditional theory of authorized admissions and if it cannot be justified by the analogy to the exception for statements of partners because conspirators' statements are admitted where partners' statements are excluded, how then can this variant of the admissions exception be justified? One of the authors sees no good analytic justification for admitting the

---

81. **In many jurisdictions the exception in these circumstances is referred to as an exception for "joint venturers" rather than "coconspirators." To admit the statements of one against the other, the prosecutor must only show by a preponderance** of the evidence that a joint venture existed. A joint venture for criminal purposes is, of course, a conspiracy whether or not the crime of conspiracy has been charged or can be proven beyond a reasonable doubt.

statements of coconspirators in cases where conspiracy is not charged or in cases where, because the "in furtherance" requirement is not strictly construed, the statement is not a material act of the conspiracy. This author sees a possible behavioral explanation for the exception, and perhaps a justification, in the fact that the exception makes it easier to secure criminal convictions. Thus, prosecutors have pressed for interpretations of the law that would admit such statements. When faced with criminal defendants presenting unsympathetic cases, courts have accepted the easy analogy to partnerships and have decided the evidence should be admitted without closely analyzing the situation. In reaching this position, courts have probably been misled by the fact that when conspiracy is charged and the conditions of the exception taken seriously, statements of coconspirators are not analytically hearsay.

The other author believes that reliability and necessity justify the exception. Active conspirators are likely to know who the members of the conspiracy are and what they have done. When speaking to advance the conspiracy, they are unlikely to describe non-members as conspirators, and they usually will have no incentive to misdescribe the actions of their fellow members. This analysis changes substantially if a conspiracy has broken up in disagreement or through arrest; it will also not apply if the conspirators have a particular motive to misrepresent, as where a powerful figure is claimed to be involved in the conspiracy in order to persuade others to join or cooperate. The element of necessity arises because the members of a crim-

inal conspiracy will have a fifth amendment privilege to refuse to testify to anything pertaining to the conspiracy.[82] Thus, hearsay may be the only way to introduce the observations of one conspirator against another. Since much of the conspiratorial activity is likely to have been kept secret, the observations of the conspirators may be the only proof of certain crucial matters.

More importantly, the conspirators exception requires that the government show the existence of and membership in a conspiracy relying exclusively, or largely, on independent evidence, a requirement we discuss below. This independent evidence rule and the fact that the exception is limited to statements made during and in furtherance of the conspiracy restrict the class of admissible statements to those that are likely to be reliable. And unlike partners who may be deposed and whose statements concerning other partners may in fact be declarations against interest in many contexts, conspirators rarely can be forced to lay the evidentiary foundation for other hearsay exceptions. The same fifth amendment that stands in the way of deposing those accused of criminal activity will prevent calling them against their will to inquire into the possibility that other more standard hearsay exceptions might cover statements by one conspirator offered against another.

The author who finds it difficult to justify the exception analytically believes these policy arguments are substantial and should be taken seriously. He is not convinced because he is troubled by how far the ar-

---

82. The prosecutor might circumvent the fifth amendment problems by granting use immunity. The value of immunity to conspirators may be very low, since conspirator A who has immunity for his statements may be convicted on the testimony of conspirator B who has immunity for his statements, and vice versa. This possibility may mean that conspirators will choose the penalties of contempt rather than testify under a grant of use immunity, in which case the necessity for a hearsay exception will still exist. An exception may be necessary where conspirators are tried together. It is unlikely that one defendant could be forced to take the stand at his own trial to testify against a codefendant under a grant of use immunity.

guments take us from the general justification for the admissions exception. The exception is justified in part because of the availability of the declarant to deny or explain the statements attributed to him. The above rationale for admitting the hearsay of fellow conspirators turns in part on the unavailability of the declarant. It is also not clear to one author that the special reliability attributed to the statements of conspirators concerning their conspiracy differs in any way from the special reliability of any statement made by an individual in a position to know what he is talking about with no apparent motive to deceive. Yet in the general case this special reliability is not enough to overcome the hearsay objection. You will have to decide whose analysis you prefer. We have, no doubt, made it clear that we are unable to persuade each other.

This discussion of how the coconspirators exception has been and should be analyzed is complicated because the issues it deals with are complicated. The state of the law regarding conspirators admissions is not so complicated. We will try to state it simply.

The first task faced by the proponent of coconspirator's hearsay is to show that the declarant and the party defendant were in fact part of the same conspiracy.[83] Over the years the courts, including the different federal circuit courts of appeal, have used a variety of standards and procedures to make this determination. Some gave the preliminary question to the judge, some gave it to the jury and some required both judge and jury to find a conspiracy before a coconspirator's statement could be used against a party. In some courts the finding of conspiracy had to be "beyond a reasonable doubt," in some it had to be by "a fair preponderance of the evidence," and in some it was sufficient if a *prima facie* case of conspiracy was made out. The circuit courts of appeal have responded to the federal rules so as to eliminate much of this confusing diversity, and it is likely that the state courts will follow the federal lead.

It is now generally agreed that the decision on the existence of the conspiracy is a preliminary question of fact that is assigned to the judge by FRE 104(a), and the prevailing view is that the judge must determine the matter by a preponderance of the evidence.[84] Three ways of proving the conspiracy are common. First, the judge may conduct a "minitrial" out of the presence of the jury to determine whether it is more likely than not that the declarant and the defendant were conspirators. Second, it may be the case that by the time the coconspirator's statement is offered, the government has already introduced enough

---

83. This is one of many areas in which the admissibility of evidence turns on some finding of fact. The topic is discussed generally in Chapter Twelve. We discuss the specific case of the coconspirator's exception at this point because the issue of what showing is necessary before the statement of a coconspirator can be admitted has been the source of considerable confusion and dispute over the years.

84. The Fifth Circuit, sitting *en banc* in the case of United States v. James, 590 F.2d 575 (5th Cir. 1979), prescribed a twofold test. "[A]s a preliminary matter, there must be substantial, *independent evidence* of a conspiracy, at least enough to take the question to the jury" (emphasis in original). At the end of the trial the court upon an appropriate motion "must determine as a factual matter whether the prosecution has shown by a preponderance of the evidence * * * (1) that a conspiracy existed, (2) that the coconspirator and the defendant against whom the coconspirator's statement is offered were members of the conspiracy, and (3) that the statement was made during the course and in furtherance of the conspiracy."

In the 9th Circuit the test has been stated to be "whether there is sufficient, substantial evidence apart from the statements which establishes a prima facie case of the conspiracy and the defendant's slight connection to the conspiracy. United States v. Batimana, 623 F.2d 1366, 1368 (9th Cir. 1980). As we write, the Ninth is the only circuit that adheres to the "prima facie evidence" approach.

evidence to allow the judge to determine that a conspiracy probably existed. Finally, the coconspirator's statement may be introduced subject to "connecting up", i.e., to the later introduction of evidence sufficient to allow the judge to determine that a conspiracy probably existed.[85] Should the government fail to offer evidence sufficient to support such a finding the defendant may be entitled to a mistrial because a belated instruction to disregard is unlikely to remove the effects of a coconspirator's incriminatory statements from the minds of the jury. For this reason, the first two methods of establishing the preliminary fact of conspiracy are preferable to the third, but the third may be the only practicable way to proceed in case with many defendants and numerous statements.

In one respect the federal rules have led to a division of opinion that did not exist before. The standard learning is that in deciding whether to admit the hearsay statement of a coconspirator (or of any agent) the court cannot consider the statements whose admissibility is in issue. As the Supreme Court said in Glasser v. United States, admissibility must depend on independent evidence in order to prevent a statement from "lift[ing] itself by its own boot straps to the level of competent evidence."[86] However, FRE 104(a) provides that in determining preliminary questions of admissibility the judge is not bound by the rules of evidence except the rules of privilege. Most courts that have examined the matter treat the rule in *Glasser* as an exception to FRE 104(a),[87] but a few circuits believe the federal rule overrules *Glasser* and allows the hearsay of a conspirator to be considered in deciding whether that hearsay should be admitted. However, even these courts say that such statements should be given little weight on the preliminary issue.

Once two people are shown to have been participants in the same conspiracy, the statements of one are treated as admissions of the other if two conditions are met. The first condition is that the statements must have been made in furtherance of the conspiracy. However, in many jurisdictions this condition exists more in theory than in fact.

As we noted earlier, courts often pay little attention to whether a conspirator's statement actually furthered the conspiracy. Statements which do no more than confess to illegal actions or inculpate fellow conspirators have often been introduced under this exception.

85. **Note that the defendant might be able to transform both the second and third ways of preceding into a minitrial by requesting a FRE 104(c) hearing after the government has presented its case to the jury. If the defendant is not allowed to present evidence to the judge, the preponderance of the evidence standard is reduced to the requirement of a prima facie case since there will be no evidence suggesting the non-existence of a conspiracy except that which the defendant might adduce on cross-examination of the state's witnesses.**

If a defendant requests an FRE 104(c) hearing, the judge might insist that the defendant present his case, promising a reconsideration of his judgment, at the close of all the evidence. If this procedure is adopted, the court is, in effect, adopting the Fifth Circuit's test in U. S. v. James, supra note 84.

86. 315 U.S. 60, 75 (1942).

87. **While this may seem to contravene the specific language of FRE 104(a) it is not inappropriate. Neither the drafters of the federal rules nor the Congress thought of all the situations where the rules might change existing practice. There are both gaps in the rules and areas where it makes sense to interpret the language of the rules in light of the prevailing common law practice. See generally, S. Saltzburg & K. Redden, Federal Rules of Evidence Manual, 735–44 (2d ed. 1977). Note that all courts agree that the statements in issue must be examined to determine whether they were "in furtherance of" the conspiracy. The *Glasser* rule restricts the use of conspirators' statements for their truth until adequate other evidence of a conspiracy is presented. It is only this restriction that is now challenged by some courts.**

The second condition is one we have not yet discussed: to be admissible, the co-conspirator's statement must have been made during the life of the conspiracy. Once a conspiracy has ended, the statements of its former members are admissible only against themselves. In most jurisdictions this condition has been taken more seriously than the "in furtherance" requirement. Conspiracies are considered to have ended when the conspiracy has achieved its goal or has in some way been broken up or disbanded. Thus, the arrest or indictment of the conspirators or a voluntary decision by the conspirators to disband will be treated as terminating the conspiracy. There is some dispute as to when a conspiracy has achieved its goal. Usually it will be with the completion of the criminal act, but the exact point of completion may not be clear. Some courts have held that a conspiracy to rob a bank does not end with the successful getaway but rather with the splitting up of the proceeds, whenever that occurs. A conspiracy to engage in a series of crimes will not be treated as over simply because arrest intervenes before the next crime may be carried out.

Prosecutors have tried to argue that any successful conspiracy gives rise to another conspiracy, a conspiracy to conceal criminal involvement and so escape punishment. If this argument were accepted, a conspiracy would not end for purposes of the admissions exception even with arrest, because conspirators who plead not guilty are still working together to conceal their involvement. Most courts do not perceive conspiracies in the "concealment phase." [88] Individuals may also leave conspiracies before the conspiracy has ended. When a conspirator's involvement has clearly been terminated, statements made by coconspirators after the date of termination will not be admissible against him. The converse is not true, however. When a conspirator enters an ongoing conspiracy, he is held implicitly to have adopted the earlier statements of fellow conspirators, so these statements may be introduced as admissions against him. This view of adoption, like so many of the arguments used to justify the coconspirators' exception, is a fictive assumption with little to commend it. [89]

6. PRIVITY

The last major heading under which many courts will admit statements as admissions is privity. If an individual acquires an interest directly from another, statements made by the other while possessing that interest may be introduced as admissions against the later possessor. The claim has been made that the statements of predecessors in interest are but one type of vicarious admission, the argu-

88. The Supreme Court has specifically rejected the idea of an implied conspiracy to conceal for the purpose of determining admissible hearsay, Krulewitch v. United States, 336 U.S. 440 (1949), but it has also held that where this view does prevail, as in Georgia, the admission against the defendant of statements made in the "concealment phase" does not necessarily violate the confrontation clause of the sixth amendment. Dutton v. Evans, 400 U.S. 74 (1970). This case is reproduced in Chapter Seven.

89. Is the fact that it makes conviction more probable reason to commend it? Is conviction of the innocent or just that of the

guilty made more probable? Should a conspirator be held responsible for the illegal actions committed by fellow conspirators before he joined? Note that if conspiracy is charged and must be proved, statements made in furtherance of the conspiracy before a person joined may not be hearsay if offered to prove that an illegal conspiracy existed which the person, contrary to law, did in fact join. Note also that a court that carefully examines the "in furtherance" requirement may find that it is not easily satisfied by statements about a third party who has not yet joined a conspiracy.

ment being that an individual adopts his predecessors' statements concerning an interest when he comes into possession of that interest. This justification is untenable if intended as a description of what actually occurs when one acquires another's interests, since courts will admit statements under the privity doctrine even though the successor in interest was unaware of the predecessor's comments. If an individual "adopts" a predecessor's statements when succeeding to an interest, it is only because the law determines that the statements will be adopted for purposes of the admissions exception, whatever the successor's intent. In most cases there is no behavioral justification for admitting the earlier statement under the theory of vicarious admissions.

There are two justifications for admitting statements by predecessors in interest which make some sense. The first is that if it were the predecessor rather than the successor who was litigating the matter, the predecessor's statements could be offered against him as personal admissions. If the statements had substantial probative value, the predecessor's chances of prevailing in the litigation would diminish accordingly. Why, courts have asked, should the transfer of a claim increase the probability that it will be effectively asserted?[90] The second reason is that most admissions offered under the privity theory are particularly likely to be reliable, since most will have been against the declarant's interest when made. If they are reliable, justice will be enhanced by making them available to the fact finder.

The second reason is a powerful one, but it does not prove the need for an exception based on privity. Instead, it argues that there should be an exception for hearsay statements which were against interest when made. There is in fact such an exception. Reliance on this exception instead of the admissions exception has the virtue of excluding statements by predecessors which are of questionable reliability because they were not against interest when made. The drafters of the federal rules, following the decision of the drafters of the Model Code of Evidence and the Uniform Rules of Evidence, make no provision for admitting statements by predecessors in interest as admissions. It is assumed that where such statements have particular probative value, they will be admissible under the declaration against interest exception.

Statements by joint obligors or other individuals jointly sharing an identical interest have been treated in the same way as other statements of parties in privity; statements of one come in as admissions of the other at common law and are inadmissible as admissions under the federal rules. Despite the federal rule, in some joint interest situations it is impossible in any practical sense not to use the statements of one joint holder against another, since the relief ordered by the court if either holder is liable will run against the jointly held property. Where identity of interest is alleged to exist either through a conjoint relationship or through succession, the technical analysis of what constitutes an identity of interest is very important. Thus, the statements of joint tenants or joint owners will be received against each other but the statements of tenants in common or co-legatees will not. The statements of an insured will be received against a beneficiary where the insured retained the power to change the designation of the beneficiary but not otherwise. To successfully deal with these evidence problems in practice, you must first master the substantive law which relates persons to property and other interests.

---

90. In some circumstances, such as those covered by the holder in due course doctrine, the legislature has decided that the transfer of a claim to another should have exactly this effect. Where this kind of decision has been made, admissions by privity are irrelevant and hence inadmissible.

Problem VI–15. Hatfield and McCoy have long disputed the ownership of a pond that borders on both their farms. Hatfield claims the pond is his and has said so on many occasions. McCoy has done likewise. All this changed, however, the day that Sammy Smith dove into the pond, hit his head on a rock and drowned. When the Smiths brought suit against Hatfield, his defense was that the pond belonged to McCoy so he was not responsible for the injuries of those using it. Hatfield wishes to introduce the statements of McCoy as evidence that McCoy owns the pond. **May he do so?** The Smiths wish to introduce Hatfield's assertions of title to prove that he owns the land. **May they do so?** The Smiths would also like to introduce a witness who will testify that Hatfield's father, from whom Hatfield inherited the land, often claimed ownership of the pond. **May they do so?** Hatfield would like to introduce a witness who will testify that she heard his grandfather, from whom his father inherited the land, say, "I sure wish I owned the pond that borders the McCoy's property. I tried to fool the kids once by telling them that their pappy had sold it to mine, but when I couldn't produce a deed they weren't buying." **May Hatfield introduce this witness?**

Problem VI–16. Lady Macbeth is charged with the murder of Duncan, King of Scotland. A physician is willing to testify that he saw her walk in her sleep one night, and that while she was still asleep she said, "Out, damned spot! Out, I say! * * *. Yet who would have thought the old man to have had so much blood in him," and "Here's the smell of the blood still. All the perfumes of Arabia will not sweeten this little hand." **Will the prosecutor be allowed to introduce the doctor's testimony over a hearsay objection?**

Problem VI–17. Harriet Hanson and her child Dolly go to Sarah Lee's beauty parlor. Lee suggests that Dolly play with her own children in her back yard. A few minutes later the adults hear cries. Lee goes outside and brings in a crying Dolly. According to Hanson, Lee said, "I'm so sorry, my dog has bitten your child." According to Lee she said, "I'm so sorry my daughter says our dog has bitten your child." **Does it matter which version of Lee's statement is correct? Why?**

Problem VI–18. Carrie Smith sues the driver of an automobile in which she was riding for damages arising out of an accident. Her husband Peter, who was in the car but not injured, sues for loss of consortium. The jurisdiction has a rule that guests like the Smiths assume the risk that defects in the host's vehicle may lead to accidents unless the host driver knows or should know of the defective condition and fails to inform a guest of it. The defendant testifies that he thought that the tire that blew out and caused the accident was in good condition and that the tire was in fact in good condition, the blowout being caused by broken glass in the road. Peter testifies that he helped change the tire shortly before the accident and it appeared to be in good condition, but that when they took it to the garage to inflate it a man, whose tire gauge they had borrowed, said that the tire was in poor condition and that with the 38 pounds of air they had put in it, it might blow to pieces in a few miles. The defendant had replied that he would take a chance on the tire and, as Peter recounts it, he said that he would do the same. **Are any of the statements at the garage admissible?   Against which parties?   On which issues?**

Problem VI–19.   The testator Harold Hawk has just died and four beneficiaries are meeting with Erica Darling, executrix for Hawk's estate. Darling opens Hawk's safe and pulls out seven bundles of money, saying there's $500.00 in each bundle.   At this point Susan Sparrow, one of the beneficiaries, says, "No, there's $5,000.00."   Darling doesn't respond to this statement but moves on to other matters.   Darling is later charged with the crime of not reporting as part of Hawk's estate the $35,000 taken from the safe.   **Can another beneficiary testify to the statements of Darling and Sparrow concerning the amount of money in the bundles in order to show that the bundles did contain $5,000.00 each?**

Problem VI–20.   Driver ran into and injured Walker, a pedestrian. Passenger was with Driver in his car.   Walker sues Driver, alleging that Driver was drunk and ran into Walker when Walker was in a marked crosswalk.   Walker's counsel wants to have a police officer testify to Passenger's statement made to the officer in Driver's absence, "We were returning from a party at which we had all been drinking."   Driver objects.   **What result? Would the result be any different if the statement had been made in Driver's presence?**   Suppose the officer had said to Driver, "The accident was all your fault."   When Driver failed to respond, the officer continued, "I'm putting you under arrest because you are drunk."   Driver responded with an expletive.   **Is any of this interchange admissible?**

Problem VI–21.   Alfred Hitchcock claims to have bought a movie camera from the DeMille Camera Shop on June 12, 1975.   The camera carries a guarantee from the manufacturer extending one year from the date of purchase.   On May 15, 1976, the camera inexplicably stops working and Hitchcock sends it back to the manufacturer for repairs under the warranty.   Two weeks later Hitchcock receives a note from the manufacturer stating that they will not repair the camera under the warranty without proof of purchase.   Hitchcock, having lost his receipt, goes back to DeMille and asks for a duplicate.   The clerk makes out a new receipt, which Hitchcock receives and mails to the manufacturer.   Two weeks later he gets another letter from the manufacturer stating that the camera will not be repaired for free because the warranty had expired before the camera had been sent in.   Hitchcock sues the manufacturer for the cost of repairs.   At the trial, the manufacturer wishes to introduce a copy of the receipt which Hitchcock had sent in.   On the receipt in the space marked "Date of Purchase", the clerk had written 5/12/75.   **Is this receipt admissible?   Would it be admissible if Hitchcock had not mailed the receipt himself but had instead requested the clerk to mail the receipt directly to the manufacturer?**

Problem VI–22.   Fred Johnson sues Walt Wreckless after the cars in which they were driving collided.   Johnson puts his passenger, Sam Schwartz, on the stand to testify to Wreckless' negligence.   On cross-examination Schwartz is asked if Johnson had been drinking before the accident.   He responds, "Fred and I each had two beers before we set out in the car.   Fred had been driving for about an hour when this other guy hit us." Johnson recovers $20,000 from Wreckless. A month later James Wreckless, the local prosecutor, brings charges against Johnson for "driving after drinking." **At the trial can the prosecutor introduce Schwartz's statement that Johnson had had two beers? Would the situation be any different if Schwartz's testimony had been in a deposition which Johnson introduced in the civil suit when Schwartz proved unavailable?**

Problem VI–23. Laura Morgan is charged with possessing phenmetrazine, a controlled substance, with intent to distribute. She was arrested in rather strange circumstances. The police had secured a warrant to search a single family house after furnishing the judge with an affidavit from Detective Mathis which said that a reliable informant had told him that a man between 22 and 24 years of age known as Timmy had within the past 48 hours been selling drugs from inside the house. When the police arrived to execute the warrant Timmy was not there, but Morgan was with a group of four others in the hallway. She was holding a snarling German shepherd on a leash. According to the police, they saw Morgan reach into a pocket just as they opened the door, throw twelve pink pills on the floor, and try to crush them with her feet. A search of the basement led to the seizure of 77 additional pink pills and $4280 secreted in a hole in the ceiling. Chemical analysis revealed that the pink pills contained phenmetrazine.

At the trial the government introduces the testimony of the owner of the house who says that Morgan came to the house every day to feed and exercise her dogs who were kept chained in the basement. The owner also testifies that no one has lived in the basement since she moved the dogs down there more than a year ago. On cross-examination she admits that her son, Timmy, lives with her in the house. As part of her defense, Morgan would like to introduce the affidavit of Detective Mathis that was used to secure the search warrant. She would also like to ask a police officer whether Detective Mathis said to him after Morgan's arrest, "I expect she just bought these. She's not the distributor." **Is evidence of Detective Mathis' affidavit or of the statement he made after Morgan's arrest admissible against the government?**

Problem VI–24. Stanley Owner owned Greenacre, a 200 acre tract of land with a 23 room mansion located at one end. When Stanley died he bequeathed a 50% interest in Greenacre to each of his two children, Fay and Ray. Mark Trueblood, Owner's trusted servant for 22 years, brings suit to void the bequest as it applies to Greenmansion and the surrounding five acres of land, alleging that some seven years earlier he had turned down an offer of more lucrative employment when Owner promised him that Greenmansion would be his if he stayed on for an additional five years. **In a suit against Fay and Ray can Mark testify that Owner told him when he threatened to leave some seven years before, "I can't match the Vanderwink's salary offer, but if you stay with me another five years Greenmansion will be yours."? Can Mark testify that five years to the day after this conversation Owner had told him, "Well, it's five years since we made our deal, Mark. Greenmansion is yours. I'll continue to live in it, but we know**

that you've now earned the title. I'll be sure that legal title passes to you on my death."? **Can Mark introduce against either Fay or Ray or both of them Ray's statement two days after Owner's death, "Well Mark, I understand that Greenmansion has been yours for two years now. I wish dad had told me sooner. I'll really miss the place."?** Disregard any Statute of Frauds or Dead Man's Statute problems in formulating your answers.

Problem VI–25. Able sells land to Baker who thinks that Able has good title to the land free from all encumbrances. One day, when Baker is walking on the far corner of his land, he notices a man herding sheep. When Baker asks the man to leave his land, the man replies that he has an easement from Able that gives him the right to graze sheep on this portion of the land. Baker subsequently sues to eject the sheep from the land, but Able is no longer within the jurisdiction of the Court. The sheepherder wishes to introduce the testimony of Able's brother, who will testify that, just before leaving the jurisdiction, Able said, "I really put one over on old Baker. He won't discover the sheep and the easement until I'm long gone." **Is the statement admissible?**

Problem VI–26. Ellen Masters, a police officer, shot and killed Fred Jacobs. Masters alleges that the killing occurred when Jacobs, despite being handcuffed, broke away and attempted to flee. She claims she fired one warning shot, and when Jacobs didn't stop she fired the shot which apparently killed him. Jacobs' family claims that he was intentionally shot through the back at close range. They bring a civil suit seeking damages for Masters' actions. In answering the third paragraph of plaintiff's complaint, which asserts that Masters fired a shot at close range killing plaintiff, Masters responds with an answer which "admits the third paragraph of plaintiff's complaint insofar as it claims that defendant fired a shot killing plaintiff, but neither affirms nor denies plaintiff's claim that the shot came from close range." The answer is filed by Masters' lawyer and is signed by her as attorney for the defendant, but it is not signed by Masters herself.

On the morning of the trial Masters' attorney says to her secretary before leaving for the courthouse, "I think they're caving. I think they will settle for under $15,000. They'll be fools if they do. If they had decent experts it would be clear to them that the shot was fired from less than four feet away." It turned out that Masters' attorney knew what she was talking about, for the case was settled for $10,000 during the recess following the selection of the jury. The Police Officer's Benevolent Association paid 95% of the settlement on Masters' behalf.

Later, following considerable political pressure, Masters is charged with murder based on the same incident. **At the trial may the prosecution introduce Masters' pleading in the civil case to show that Masters shot Jacobs? May the prosecution introduce the secretary's testimony as to what Masters' attorney had said on the morning of trial, in order to prove that the shot was fired from four feet or less? May evidence of the final settlement be introduced for any purpose?**

Problem VI–27.   Belcher Power and Light Company owns a dam on the Huron River.   About 3 a. m., following a heavy rainstorm, the dam gave way, sending water cascading through the town of Hutchins about 12 miles downstream.   The residents of Hutchins sue Belcher for 50 million dollars in damages, alleging that it was negligent in building and maintaining the dam.   **Can any of the following information be introduced against Belcher at trial?**   (a) The statement of an engineer, who had been sent to repair a sluicegate, to an onlooker, who turned out to be the mayor of Hutchins, "This repair won't do much good if there's a heavy storm.   The whole system is bad."   (b) The same statement made by the engineer to her husband when she went home that night.   (c) The statement of the president of the company, upon being called by reporters at 3:20 a. m. and informed of the disaster, "Oh my God;   the sluice system must have failed.   We were negligent in maintaining it."   (d) A report in the company files prepared by an outside consulting firm some twelve years earlier when the decision to build the dam was made, stating, "The soil at the suggested dam site is too porous.   In case of heavy rain there would be a danger of collapse."   **Would your decision as to the report be different if it were offered not to show negligent construction, but as a justification for punitive damages?**

Problem VI–28.   Charles Street, who works part time delivering groceries for the Foxy-Loxy Super Market, crashed into Marvin Gardens about five o'clock one evening.   After the collision James Place, a passerby, came up to Street and asked what happened.   Street replied, "I was speeding, trying to deliver my last bag of groceries for the F & L, when I missed the stop sign and collided with the car in the intersection."   Later Street repeats the same story to the police officer sent to investigate the accident.   **If Gardens sues Foxy-Loxy, can either of Street's statements come in on the issue of his negligence?   Can either statement come in on the issue of whether Foxy-Loxy is liable for Street's negligence on the theory of respondeat superior?   Is there any other information which you would wish to have before answering these questions?   What might you do as Gardens' attorney if you thought the court would rule that these statements were inadmissible against the supermarket?**

Problem VI–29.   On the same facts as the above, Street pleads guilty to tickets issued for speeding and for failing to stop at a stop sign.   **Would Street's pleas be admitted against Foxy-Loxy?   Against Street if Gardens had sued him?   Would the situation be any different if Gardens' heirs, suing Foxy-Loxy for wrongful death, wished to introduce the fact that Street had pleaded guilty to a charge of negligent homicide following the accident?   If Street had pleaded innocent, could a jury verdict of "guilty" be introduced against either Street or Foxy-Loxy in a civil suit arising out of the same incident?**

Problem VI–30.   Virgil Flame drives a truck for the Keepon Trucking Company, a sole proprietorship owned by Henry Keepon.   One evening Virgil misjudges his distance while pulling into a rest area and scrapes a parked car.   He offers Carol Sonda, the irate owner, $150.00, saying, "Your damages can't be more than $50.00.   If you don't call the cops, I'll give you $150.00".   Sonda asks why and Virgil replies, "This rig's ten tons over the weight limit. I have Keepon's map to avoid the scales, but I never thought I might get caught up this way." **If Keepon is later charged with knowingly sending out trucks over the highway weight limit, may Sonda testify to any of the remarks which Virgil made to her?** Assume there is no other evidence that the map referred to exists or that Keepon knew the truck was over the weight limit, but it is admitted that Virgil was working for Keepon at the time he made these remarks.

Problem VI–31. Harry Tracy and Senator Coolidge are charged with offering and taking a bribe respectively. At their joint trial, the prosecution seeks to introduce the testimony of an aide to the Senator who will testify that he overheard his boss saying on the telephone, "I just accepted some money from Tracy to vote for the farm bill." **Is this admissible or should it be excluded on the ground that it is hearsay? If it is admissible, should it come in against both parties, and if not, what can counsel for the party entitled to protection do to ensure that the statement will not be used against her client?**

Problem VI–32. Castor and Pollux are partners who operate the C-P Appliance Store in the Bronx. In early May of 1975, Castor, who has been thinking of moving to Florida, offers to sell his fifty per cent share of the business to Ajax for "its market value of $50,000." Ajax declines, so Castor sticks with the business. Two months later the Discount Appliance Center opens an outlet across from C-P. C-P cannot meet the competition and in a month is driven out of business. Later it turns out that Discount had engaged in predatory pricing for the purpose of driving C-P out of business. Pollux brings a treble damage action against Discount in which he claims actual damages of $150,000, giving rise to treble damages of $450,000. **On the issue of the value of Pollux's interest in the partnership, can Discount introduce Ajax to testify that Castor offered him a 50% interest in the store for $50,000? If Castor had offered to sell Ajax the entire store for $100,000, would Ajax be allowed to testify to this?**

Problem VI–33. There is good evidence that Tinker, Evers, and Chance conspired together to rob the Glendale Bank. Tinker, allegedly the brains behind the operation, recruited Evers and Evers recruited Chance. Tinker and Chance have never met. Evers and Chance were arrested two weeks after the robbery when they tried to pass some marked bills. Tinker was arrested a week later. Tinker was tried alone. He was charged with bank robbery, extortion by threat and receipt of stolen property knowing it was stolen. Chance has offered to turn state's evidence. He is willing to testify to the following remarks which Evers made to him during the planning stage of the robbery. **"Tinker has this all set up. This is the map of the bank which he's drawn and here's a key to the alley door which he gave me. Tinker will be at the end of the alley with the getaway car."** Two days before the robbery it appeared that Evers was getting cold feet. He said to Chance, **"Maybe we shouldn't go through with this. Tinker is clever, but I'm not sure how well he will do his part. I don't think a VW has enough acceleration to be the getaway car, and with his noisy muffler and pink decals the cops could spot us a mile away. Shall I tell Tinker it's off?"** Chance had persuaded Evers to continue in the scheme. The night of the robbery, while getting soaked by the rain in a trench outside of town, Evers had said, **"That bastard Tinker is responsible for our problems. He never showed up in the car. We were lucky to escape on foot."** [It turned out that Tinker had been stopped a block from the bank about the time of the robbery and given a ticket for driving with a defective muffler.] After Evers and Chance were arrested but before Tinker was arrested, Evers had told Chance, **"I've gotten word to Tinker where we hid the money. He'll get us the best lawyer in the business."** In addition, during the robbery, Chance had said to the bank president who was in his office when the break-in occurred, **"If you don't fill this sack with money, I will blow off your head."** This was contrary to Tinker's plans, since Tinker had planned the robbery for a time when no one was expected to be in the bank.

To which of Evers' statements will Chance be allowed to testify? Will he be allowed to repeat his own statement to the bank president? Does the admissibility of any of these statements depend on whether Tinker is charged with conspiracy to engage in the offenses charged?

Problem VI–34. White and Black are the president and vice-president of COLORS, a company they organized to "exploit the vast mineral wealth of the West." Green is by title the company's chief engineer. There are no other employees. COLORS holds the mineral rights to several thousand acres of land in Colorado and Wyoming, but the land has been thoroughly explored and at current market prices there are no minerals on the land worth extracting. Nevertheless, Green roams the country securing investors with promises of large returns from soon to be developed gold mining and oil shale operations. White and Black maintain a New York office. It is their task to maintain the semblance of an active energy exploration company and to entertain potential large investors whom Green lures to the city. One day when Green is in New York, he stops by the office while White and Black are together opening the mail. Black hands him a check from a letter he has just opened. It is made out to COLORS in the amount of $75,000. "Here's a nice return from your travels," says Black. "It's that sucker you met at the Kansas convention. What was he, a potato farmer?"

When the conspiracy is eventually broken up by the police, Black flees the jurisdiction, Green turns state's evidence and White is tried alone for fraud. **At White's trial may Green relate his conversation with Black to show that White was involved in a fraudulent activity? May it be introduced to show that White was involved in a conspiracy if White is charged with conspiracy to defraud?**

Problem VI–35. A, B, C, D, and E are on trial for a conspiracy to defraud the United States Government and the Veterans Administration by submitting false information to the V.A. with respect to certain requests for V.A. guaranteed home mortgages. The first such request was on August 1, 1962 and the last such request on September 20, 1967. A was a V.A. loan reviewer from April 1960 until she resigned from the V.A. on September 30, 1967. B, C, D, and E were, respectively, officers for two banks, one insurance company and a real estate agency. At the joint trial the prosecution seeks to introduce evidence of instances where B, C, D, and E conspired with X, an official with the FHA, to submit fraudulent data to secure

FHA guaranteed mortgages. These instances occurred in October, November and December of 1967. *A* seeks to have the jury instructed that this evidence has no bearing on her activity in the conspiracy and should not be considered by the jury on the issue of whether *A* is guilty of participating with *B, C, D,* and *E* in an illegal conspiracy to defraud the V.A. The trial judge refuses to give the requested instruction. **Has the trial judge made a mistake?**

C. OTHER EXCEPTIONS

In theory the remaining exceptions to the hearsay rule may all be justified on one of two grounds; either the statements they admit are thought to have been of particular reliability when made, or the statements in some way have been or may be tested by cross-examination. Most of the exceptions are of the first type; they reflect psychological assumptions about situations in which statements are likely to be trustworthy. Exceptions of the second type include situations in which cross-examination has occurred immediately following the statement but not in front of the current trier of fact and situations in which cross-examination occurs in front of the current trier of fact but not at the time of the out-of-court statement. The general argument supporting both types is that the required conditions tend to negate one or more of the hearsay dangers.

The hearsay exceptions may also be divided into two groups on the basis of whether the declarant's unavailability at trial is a prerequisite to the application of an exception. Exceptions have not been conditioned upon the declarant's unavailability where courts have felt that a witness' account of an out-of-court statement was likely to be as probative of the issue in question as the declarant's courtroom testimony or where the difficulty of proving unavailability or subpoenaing available witnesses was likely to outweigh the incremental benefits of courtroom testimony. Thus, judgments about when unavailability should be required, like judgments about

creating exceptions in the first place, have turned on judicial intuitions about the situations in which out-of-court statements are likely to be trustworthy.

These intuitions and the exceptions based upon them quite naturally reflect the common sense psychology popular at the time the exceptions were formed. As psychology advances and we learn more about the process of narrative description, we are better able to appreciate the wisdom behind certain exceptions and the tenuous nature of others. The following extract from an article by Professor Stewart is an aid to critical evaluation of the hearsay exceptions. In the portion of the article reproduced here, Professor Stewart presents a modern psychological perspective on the processes of perception and description which should help explain the threats posed by those dangers that have thus far been summarized by the words ambiguity, insincerity, false memory, and inaccurate perception.

STEWART, PERCEPTION, MEMORY, AND HEARSAY: A CRITICISM OF PRESENT LAW AND THE PROPOSED FEDERAL RULES OF EVIDENCE

1970 Utah L.Rev. 1, 8–23.[91]

* * *

The crucial questions in hearsay law concern the determinants of perception, memory, narration, and prevarication. Historically, exceptions to the law of hear-

---

91. The full article discusses the hearsay exceptions found in the Federal Rules of Evi-

dence in the light of the observations reported in this excerpt.

say have been founded upon assumptions of testimonial reliability based largely on the subjective and unsystematic study of human testimony, with more than a small touch of a highly rationalistic view of man. These assumptions have been carried forward in the Proposed [Federal] Rules of Evidence. * * *

* * *

Inconsistent perceptions and memories of the same events by different people arise out of complicated neurological, psychological, and physiological processes. Although functions of different neurological processes, perception and memory are both interdependent aspects of cognition. Memory does not exist without perception, and there is no psychologically meaningful perception without memory.

* * *

In organizing raw sensory input, the central nervous system is not a passive or photographic recorder. Basic interpretative principles make an automobile headlight observed from an angle appear circular even though optically the image is eliptical, and the size of an object at a distance appears much the same size as when it is nearer, even though the size of the retinal image may change many times. Injury, pathology, drugs, youth, and senility can seriously impair the accuracy of these processes.

It is, however, the behavioral and motivational factors that are particularly powerful in producing distortion in testimony. The law has long been aware of the effect of bias on testimonial accuracy. But powerful intrapsychic processes also produce substantial distortion in testimony without influence from the type of bias generally recognized, and without any intent to falsify. Bartlett, in a landmark study of memory states:

The first notion to get rid of is that memory is primarily or literally reduplicative or reproductive. * * *

* * * In fact, if we consider evidence, rather than presupposition, remembering appears to be far more decisively an affair of construction rather than one of reproduction.

A number of studies illustrate the point and demonstrate the substantial degree of perceptual and memory error in recounting the types of events that frequently are the subject of litigation. * * *

C. S. Morgan concluded that a typical report of a casual, but somewhat out of the ordinary event would give a substantially accurate report of the event but would contain roughly 20% to 25% error. Morgan also found a significant incidence of reporting nonfacts. For example, a question asking whether the 150 subjects had observed a nonexistent fact produced an affirmative response from 18%.

William Marston tested a group of 18 lawyers immediately after a staged event in which a boy entered a classroom, handed the instructor a large envelope, scraped his baseball glove with a knife while awaiting an answer, and then exited. Marston found that free recall reports rendered immediately after the event were 94.05% accurate, but mentioned only 23.2% of the details in the incident. Not one person, for example, mentioned the knife. In contrast, nonleading direct questions produced answers more complete but less accurate, i.e., 31.2% complete and 83.2% accurate (with an individual high of 94.5% and individual low of 64.2%). Leading questions in the nature of cross-examination resulted in an average completeness of 28.5% of the details and an average accuracy of 75.5%.

Essentially, the same scene was portrayed a second time for another small group who had reason to expect a reenactment of the event. This group proved to be less accurate than the first. The reason may be found in the reduced incidence of caution (measured by "I don't know" answers) compared with the first group. Marston concluded that there may be an inverse correlation between the number of inaccuracies and the degree of caution exercised. Perhaps a valid explanation is that a person who is expected to provide an accurate description is more prone to guess.

Brown demonstrated the particular unreliability of eye witness identification of persons and also provided further evidence that people honestly testify to the occurrence of events they have not witnessed. A workingman appropriately dressed walked across a classroom passing in front of the instructor's desk to tinker with the radiator. He made some inquiry about the heat, retraced his steps, and left as unceremoniously as he had entered. The instructor treated the incident in a casual manner. Sixteen days later the workingman returned with five other men of similar appearance and dress, and the subjects were asked to identify the workingman from among those in the group. Thirty students who had had some experience with surprise tests were 76.6% accurate in their identification. Sixty-four students who had had no such prior experience were 65.5% accurate. Sixteen students who likewise had had no prior experience with surprise tests were presented with a lineup of workingmen which did not include the man who had entered the class-

room. Ten, or 62.5%, identified the wrong man, and only four were correct in saying that he was not there. A group of seventeen students who also had had no prior experience with such tests and had actually not seen the event were treated by the experimenter as if they had. In effect they were asked to identify a man involved in an incident which they had never seen. Twelve or 70.5% said they didn't remember the incident, but five or 29.5% stated they recalled the incident and "identified" the man.

Perception of height, weight, age, and personal identification are especially vulnerable to inaccuracy. A drama of a startling and exciting nature was conducted before 150 sophomore college girls. Two high school boys chasing a third charged into a class that was in session. All three rushed about shouting and overturning furniture in full view of the girls. The duration of the incident was one minute and 30 seconds. The subjects rendered a free recall narration of their perceptions immediately after the event. One week later and seven weeks later (a much shorter period than it usually takes to get to trial) objective tests composed of true-false, completion, and multiple choice items were given. The range of judgments of height, weight, and age were after one week and seven weeks as follows:

HEIGHT

	First Week	Seventh Week
First Boy	4'8" to 7'	4' to 6'
Second Boy	4' to 6'4"	4'8" to 5'10"
Third Boy	4' to 5'10"	4'8" to 5'10"

WEIGHT

	First Week	Seventh Week
First Boy	90 lbs. to 170 lbs.	105 lbs. to 165 lbs.
Second Boy	100 lbs. to 160 lbs.	95 lbs. to 150 lbs.
Third Boy	85 lbs. to 150 lbs.	80 lbs. to 145 lbs.

AGE

	First Week	Seventh Week
First Boy	11 years to 20 years	10 years to 19 years
Second Boy	12 years to 19 years	11 years to 19 years
Third Boy	10 years to 18 years	10 years to 19 years

As Bartlett stated, the reason memory is not primarily "reduplicative" and is more "an affair of construction rather than reconstruction" is because "every human cognitive reaction—perceiving, imagining, remembering, thinking, and reasoning"— is "an effort after meaning." As the individual strives to organize and adjust to his environment, the meaning of his experiences is perceived and remembered in terms of cultural and emotional values, attitudes, habits, and anxieties. These factors act as powerful filters determining what and how an individual perceives and remembers.

At a basic level, the individual must be selective in both informational input from the environment and the retention of that input. Innumerable stimuli bombard each individual at any given moment. Purposeful behavior is possible only by selecting from among relevant stimuli and organizing them in a psychologically meaningful manner. Experimental studies demonstrate that individuals have limited spans of conscious apperception and cannot focus on more than a few stimuli at the same time. Memory also works on a principle of selectivity. Thus, what a person perceives and remembers "is apt to be a generalization. If this were not so, he might be hopelessly lost in detail."

Accordingly, a principle of economy influences people to perceive and remember by formulating a general overall impression, with only a few details standing out. The overall impression may produce an associated affective attitude. The impression and the affective attitude produced by it provide the framework for supplying details not observed or remembered, but which then appear in the guise of original perceptions. Memory of a poorly defined perceptual pattern is especially susceptible to substantial alteration by attitudes which shape the image of the event and conform it to preconceptions constructed from the associated affect.

Such memories are very unfaithful to their originals. Recall of faces is particularly subject to the distortive influence of affective attitudes since people often initially respond to others in an emotional way. Long after the visual image decays, the affect endures. A description of a face may be constructed in part from a stereotype associated with the observer's emotional response to the face or from a conventional personality type associated with the face in question.

Stereotypes generally exert an important influence on cognitive functioning. A person may conform a percept to a stereotype because his mental set expects the usual or common event or because memory of the event is more easily retained if it fits a known pattern. Moreover, stereotypes are often the basis for supplying facts to fill in memory gaps and reconstruct details that were not perceived or are forgotten. Thus, a beard, for example, may appear on the face of a man who never wore one, or a gun in the hand of a person who never possessed one. A sour faced clergyman may become pleasant in his mien, and a woman the victim of aggression, not the aggressor.

The manner in which individuals encode visual and verbal perceptions in the brain also contributes to the plastic nature of memory and in particular to transference of details and fusion of memories. Perceived material may be stored by visual imagery or by verbal labels applied to the perceived object. Since visual imagery is the mode of dreaming, day-dreaming, and imagining as well as a mode of memory, confusion as to the source of images and the blending of different images is easily accomplished. Moreover, the more strongly one wishes that reality had been different, or the stronger the power of suggestion or of group pressure to conform, the easier it is for the daydream, suggestion, or imagined event to become "reality" in the mind of the witness. Verbalized memory may produce distortion in yet another way. Application of a verbal label to an ambiguous stimulus may result in modification of the perception to conform with the verbal label.

The difference between verbal and visual encoding may also have other significant legal consequences. Despite the great reliance placed on demeanor evidence by the courts, demeanor may in fact lead the trier of fact astray. Bartlett found that persons who remember by visual imagery are subjectively more confident that their reproductions are accurate than are verbalizers. Verbalizers, although generally no less accurate than visualizers, are more hesitant and uncertain in their reproductions and hence do not appear as confident.

Memory is also molded by the influence of rationalization which is sometimes an unconscious and sometimes a conscious process. Rationalization provides an explanation for an event so that the material can be satisfyingly dealt with. "The general function of rationalization is in all the instances the same. It is to render material acceptable, understandable, comfortable, straightforward; to rob it of all puzzling elements. As such it is a powerful factor in all perceptual and in all reproductive processes. The forms it takes are often directly social in significance." Over a period of time the mind easily traverses the course, "could it possibly have been X," to "it must have been X," to "it was X." In the initial stages, the process may be conscious; at a later stage the conclusion emerges as a remembered "fact."

Numerous other factors influence perception and memory. The mental "set" or expectation of an individual will tend to focus attention on particular objects to the exclusion of others. Favorable material is more readily remembered than unfavorable. Excitement, a factor evidence law relies upon as a warrant for trustworthiness, produces a significant degree of error,

sometimes of the most bizarre type. Repression of memories of acts or thoughts strongly inconsistent with a person's self-concept may transpose reality diametrically, as is well known in rape cases.

Perception and memory are especially unreliable when, as is always the case when hearsay evidence is adduced, the initial stimulus is words. People generally retain verbal descriptions of events less accurately than they do visual perceptions. When a hearsay narrative of an event is rendered by one person to another, significant distortion is particularly likely, because the initial stimulus is filtered through two different cognitive processes. The point is illustrated by Allport and Postman in their classic study, *The Psychology of Rumor:*

[An] important source of invention and falsification comes about through verbal misunderstandings. When a person does not see the initial incident, and when he has no prior knowledge as to its nature, he becomes exclusively dependent upon his own auditory impressions for his understanding. The auditory apparatus is faulty in many people, but even those with normally acute hearing often mishear, or misinterpret, words for which they have no supporting mental context. Consider the following reproductions [which are related by one subject immediately to another].
* * *

Fourth Reproduction: Picture is of a subway or streetcar. There is a Negro in it and a laborer with a razor. They are going along a street. There are signs outside: *vote for somebody and for some camp.* On the right side there is a woman asleep, a man with a beard, and a priest.

Fifth Reproduction: Picture is of a streetcar or subway. There is—somebody or other—a Negro and a laborer with a razor. On the right side of the car there is a lady asleep, a man with a beard, *campaign* signs to vote for somebody, a priest.

Sixth Reproduction: Scene is a streetcar or subway.   There is a Negro man and laborer with a razor in his hand.   Sitting down are a lady sleeping, an old man with a beard, a priest.   There are signs: A camp sign and a sign to vote for somebody.

Bartlett also studied the essential elements of hearsay.   A short prose selection was presented to subjects who read the selection through twice.   After an interval of 15 to 30 minutes, a subject reproduced the material to another (who had not read it) who in turn did the same.   As the material passed through several phases of reproduction the distortions were increasingly magnified.   It is infrequent that more than one step of hearsay is admissible in court, although not impossible, but Bartlett's findings also apply to one-step reproductions, although in a less extreme form. He found that proper names and titles are especially unstable;   that there is a strong tendency to develop a concrete version of the account with the result that general opinions, reasoning, and arguments are transformed and omitted;   that the language is transformed into more conventional and popular phrases;   that in all cases there was much abbreviation;   that rationalization resulted in changes in various types;   and that the changes that are introduced may be radical.

Epithets are changed into their opposites;   incidents and events are transposed;   names and numbers rarely survive intact for more than a few reproductions;   opinions and conclusions are reversed—nearly every possible variation seems as if it can take place, even in a relatively short series.   At the same time, the subjects may be very well satisfied with their efforts, believing themselves to have passed on all impor-

tant features with little or no change, and merely, perhaps, to have omitted unessential matters.

Allport and Postman built upon the earlier work of Bartlett.   They found that the oral transmission of verbal material from one person to another is distorted by three basic processes.   First, "leveling" eliminates details so that the account becomes shorter and easier to manage.   Accounts having 20 or more details were reduced to five, with the process of elimination beginning with the first transmission.   There is, however, a limit to leveling.   Short concise statements are far less subject to distortion and are likely to be faithfully reproduced.

Second, "sharpening" produces selective perception, retention, and reporting of a limited number of details.   This process relates to leveling in that focusing on selected stimuli results in the ignoring of other stimuli.[a]   A special aspect of sharpening is "closure," or the tendency to make a report coherent and meaningful by supplying material even though the material was not perceived.   Errors of this type usually occurred in the report of the first subject.

Finally, "assimilation" describes the process by which memory drops, transposes, imports, and falsifies details as a result of the "intellectual and emotional context existing in the listener's mind."   Things are perceived and remembered as they usually are despite the nature of the stimulus.   In one experiment, a Red Cross ambulance is recalled as carrying medical supplies rather than explosives.   In another, a policeman is seen as arresting a Negro rather than protecting him.   "In short, when an actual perceptual fact is in conflict with expectation, expectation may prove a stronger determinant of perception and memory than the situation itself."

a. Names of places and persons are especially subject to being dropped.

In sum, cognitive processes of the human organism are not the equivalent of a photographic process which renders and preserves an essentially accurate counterpart of some event. Although the legal system uses the organism as a source of "facts," perception and memory operate in a way that enables a person to cope with his environment within the limitations that inhere in the neurological and psychological functioning of the organism. The degree of correspondence between the testimony of an event and the reality it purports to represent may, therefore, vary widely according to the effect of numerous factors. The imperatives of successful adaptation do not require that the individual's cognitive process operate in all instances to provide information having the degree of objective accuracy necessary for accurate, after-the-fact reconstruction which is attempted by judicial fact determination.

There is no reason to suppose that witnesses called to testify typically perceive and remember more accurately the type of events involved in the studies than the subjects in the experiments did. The studies discussed are based upon fact situations that in all instances provide a multitude of stimuli which transcend the normal span of apperception. Although not highly unusual, they were not routine occurrences of the kind that a person expects to happen periodically. Moreover, the studies did not involve the subjects personally as participants in the action, nor did the subject matter of the studies necessarily have a high degree of interest to the subjects because of related prior experiences. They did, however, evoke the attention of the subjects, they were not complicated, there was for the most part no distraction, and memory periods were short. In short, the studies were based on situations that are often similar to events which become the subject matter of testimony admitted under various exceptions to the hearsay rule.

* * *

The right to cross-examine is of the greatest importance to the integrity of the factfinding process and is the keystone of both the hearsay rule and the right of confrontation. Blunt though it may be for the discovery of subconscious distortion, cross-examination is the principal legal instrument for testing the accuracy of a witness's perception, memory, and communication. By means of cross-examination the witness may be required to explain ambiguous, unclear, or inconsistent testimony; personality traits that influence cognitive functioning may be disclosed; the effect of the witness's mental set at the time of perception, possible suggestive influences, and numerous other factors which affect a witness's mental processes may be investigated. Obviously, a witness who testifies to hearsay can usually provide the trier of fact with none of the same information.

A person who relates a hearsay is not obliged to enter into any particulars, to answer any questions, to solve any difficulties, to reconcile any contradictions, to explain any obscurities, to remove any ambiguities; he entrenches himself in the simple assertion that he was told so, and leaves the burden entirely on his dead or absent author.

* * *

Evidentiary reliability is also thought to be promoted by the oath and demeanor evidence. Despite skepticism regarding the value of the oath, some evidence exists that sworn testimony is more accurate than unsworn testimony. That result may follow, not from fear of divine sanction, but from the greater caution that witnesses probably exercise when under oath. Although highly regarded by the judges and attorneys, the value of demeanor evidence as a means of determining testimonial reliability has yet to be demonstrated factually. Effort is being expended on research in the accuracy of interpersonal perception, but the results are far from conclusive. Some evidence that demeanor may be deceptive is Bartlett's finding that a witness's feeling of certainty as to the accuracy of his testimony does not correlate with greater accuracy in fact.

Of course, the appearance of a witness having firsthand knowledge is an essential condition of cross-examination, the oath, and demeanor evidence, but for pragmatic reasons the law has never excluded all hearsay. Since adjudication operates in a forced decision context and cannot indulge the luxury of the scientific world in putting off a decision to await better evidence (which rarely would be forthcoming anyway), doubt must be treated as a factor in decision making, not as a barrier to it. As Professor Kalven has observed, "[A] trial is an exercise in the management of doubt." Rules governing burden of proof are a chief means of determining the effect doubt is to have in adjudication, but the hearsay rule also bears on the issue. The more relevant evidence excluded by the hearsay rule, the more likely it is that a factual dispute will be decided by a somewhat arbitrary rule governing the burden of proof than on the basis of some evidence.

* * *

An additional body of research, important to the evaluation of hearsay, was not published until after Stewart wrote his article. This is the work on leading questions and eyewitness reports by Elizabeth Loftus and her associates.[92] In a series of experiments Loftus found that the way in which questions are worded profoundly affects the answers received. In one experiment Loftus found that subjects asked

if they got headaches *frequently,* and if so how often, reported an average of 2.2 headaches per week. Subjects asked if they got headaches *occasionally,* and if so how often, reported an average of .7 headaches per week. In another study, 100 students viewed a short film showing a multiple car accident. Following the film the students were queried about what they had seen. One group was asked "the" questions such as, "Did you see *the* broken headlight?" The other group was asked "a" questions such as, "Did you see *a* broken headlight?" The group asked "the" questions was considerably more likely to report having seen the item inquired about regardless of whether it had actually appeared in the film. In a related experiment, subjects who viewed a series of accident films were asked to estimate how fast two cars were going when they *smashed (collided, bumped, hit* or *contacted*) each other. Estimates of speed varied depending upon the word used. The range was from 40.8 m.p.h. for those hearing the word "smashed" to 31.8 m.p.h. for those hearing the word "contacted." Question effects were also found to persist over time. A week after viewing an accident film, without again seeing it, subjects who had been asked the "smashed" and "hit" forms of the question were asked a new series of questions about the accident. Subjects previously queried with "smashed" were more than twice as likely to report having seen broken glass in the film than subjects queried with "hit". There was in fact no broken glass in the film. Those previously queried with "smashed" apparently remembered the accident as more severe and added details that accorded with a high speed collision. This general finding is replicated in other

92. See e.g., Loftus, Reconstructing Memory: The Incredible Eyewitness, 8 Psych. Today 116 (1974); Loftus & Palmer, Reconstruction of Automobile Destruction: An Example of the Interaction Between Learning and Memory, 13 J. Verbal Learning & Verbal Behavior 585 (1974); Loftus & Zanni, Eyewitness Testimony: The Influence of the Wording of a Question, 5 Bull. of Psychonomic Society 86 (1975). In the text we only discuss the implications of this research for the hearsay rule but it also suggests the wisdom of the rule forbidding leading questions on direct examination.

research by Loftus. The way in which individuals are questioned about an event, shortly after that event, affects their descriptions of the event at later points in time.

For our purposes, the most important implication of this research is that out-of-court statements elicited by questions are particularly prone to be distorted in ways suggested by the questioner. Yet unless the questions that elicited the statements are reported exactly as asked, there may be no way for the fact finder or counsel to evaluate this possible source of distortion. Loftus suggests that the language of her questions implicitly conveyed information to her respondents which was incorporated into their memory images of the events they were asked to describe. She suggests that information conveyed about events by means other than questions may cause similar distortion. Based on Loftus' research, it appears that we may add to the classic hearsay dangers the danger that perceptions reported in out-of-court statements may be distorted by the circumstances in which the statements were elicited. This danger is not completely cured by the substitution of the declarant's live testimony for his hearsay declaration, since the declarant's testimony may also be affected by the circumstances in which the out-of-court statements were first elicited. However, when live testimony is presented, cross-examination is available to probe for distortion.

As you study the hearsay exceptions that follow, ask yourself in what ways you would expect the evidence they admit to be distorted. Are any or all of the exceptions justified by the likelihood that if the conditions of the exception are met distortions will either not occur or be revealed? Also think about the wisdom of creating certain hearsay exceptions which are not conditioned on the declarant's unavailability. Would the declarant's testimony leave the jury with a more accurate impression of what occurred than the hearsay admitted by exceptions not conditioned upon unavailability? Finally, consider the possibility of a middle ground between availability and unavailability. Are there situations in which it makes sense to admit the hearsay of available declarants provided the proponent of the hearsay places the declarant on the stand for cross-examination?

1. AVAILABILITY IMMATERIAL

a. Present Sense Impressions

We shall first examine those hearsay exceptions which apply without regard to a declarant's availability. FRE 803 provides a convenient codification of these exceptions which we shall follow in our explication. FRE 803(1) provides:

> *Present sense impression.* A statement describing or explaining an event or condition made while the declarant was perceiving the event or condition, or immediately thereafter.

At common law there is a general hearsay exception admitting spontaneous declarations. However, most jurisdictions require some guarantee of spontaneity in addition to the coincidence of statement and event. Usually the guarantee has been found in the fact that the event described so excited the declarant as to still his reflective capacity, thus reducing the likelihood of fabrication. For more than half a century commentators have argued that requiring excitement as a guarantee against fabrication does more harm than good. Hutchins and Slesinger, reviewing the psychological literature in 1928, argued that excitement, however effective it may be in stilling reflection, so distorts perceptual processes that the conclusions of an excited onlooker are almost certain to be unreliable.[93] According to these authors,

---

93. Hutchins and Slesinger, Some Observations on the Law of Evidence, 28 Colum.L.Rev. 432 (1928).

it is the contemporaneous unexcited statement which should be admitted: "With emotion absent, speed present, and the person who heard the declaration on hand to be cross-examined, we appear to have an ideal exception to the hearsay rule." The absence of emotion enhances the reliability of perception, speed avoids memory problems while limiting the time for reflection and falsification, and the presence of the person hearing the statement often means that an observer of the event described is present for cross-examination.

Many states explicitly recognize this exception.[94] Some courts, however, have not analyzed the exception closely, but have instead admitted contemporaneous but unexcited utterances under the rubric of *res gestae*. In some states which adopt the *res gestae* approach the exception is read narrowly so as to admit only statements which directly relate to the act generating the litigation;[95] some states allow only witnesses who have observed the event in question to testify to the unexcited statements of others concerning it; some states allow an exception for unexcited utterances only if the declarant is unavailable; and some give the trial judge discretion to admit or exclude such statements.

In an important recent article, Professor Waltz presents ten propositions that he terms the "undisputable characteristics of the 803(1) exception.[96] They are: (1) The described event or condition need not have caused excitement; (2) the declaration need not directly relate to the principal litigated event; (3) the declarant need not have been a participant in the perceived event; (4) the declarant must have been a percipient witness; (5) the declarant need not be identified; (6) the declarant need not be shown to have been oath-worthy; (7) subject matter is restricted to a description of the observed event; (8) minimal time-lapse is permissible; (9) present sense impressions are not cumulative (i.e., a declarant's present sense impression is not inadmissible simply because the declarant is a witness who testifies to the described event from the stand); and (10) impressions in opinion form are admissible. Tracing the history of the present sense impression and the cases and commentary that influenced the drafters of the federal rule, Professor Waltz goes on to argue that there should be a corroboration requirement, but that corroboration may be supplied not only by witnesses who heard the declarant's statement but also by the circumstances surrounding the described event and by witnesses who observed the event without hearing what the declarant said.

---

94. In Houston Oxygen Co. v. Davis, 139 Tex. 1, 161 S.W.2d 474 (1942), often cited as the leading case on this aspect of spontaneous exclamations, a passenger in one car was willing to testify that the driver had commented about another car speeding by, "they must have been drunk, that we would find them somewhere on the road wrecked if they kept that rate of speed up." The remark proved accurate; the car did crash four miles further on. The occupants of the car sued the Houston Oxygen Company, which sought to introduce the statement in question. The court reviewed the arguments given on behalf of admitting unexcited spontaneous declarations, added to the above arguments the fact that a witness who heard a misstatement might have checked it at the time, and concluded, "[C]omments strictly limited to reports of present sense impressions, have such exceptional reliability as to warrant their inclusion within the hearsay exception for Spontaneous Declarations."

95. In *Houston Oxygen*, described in the previous footnote, this approach would mean that unexcited statements describing the accident would have been admitted but not unexcited statements, like the ones admitted in that case, made four miles from the scene of the accident.

96. Waltz, The Present Sense Impression Exception to the Rule Against Hearsay: Origins and Attributes, 66 Iowa L.Rev. 869 (1981).

Problem VI–35a. The argument for admitting unexcited statements describing present sense impressions has usually been based on a comparison between statements of this kind and excited utterances, which all would agree are admissible.   The claim is that since excited utterances are admissible and since contemporaneous but unexcited utterances are likely to be more reliable than excited utterances, it follows *a fortiori* that there should be an exception for spontaneous but unexcited utterances.   But this does not follow.   One could just as easily conclude that neither excited utterances nor unexcited spontaneous statements should be admitted as exceptions to the hearsay rule.   **Which do you think is the better position?   Should there be an exception for spontaneous unexcited utterances or should we perhaps rethink our exception for excited utterances?   Assuming we are to have a hearsay exception for unexcited utterances, should the exception apply regardless of the availability of the declarant?   How does the extract from Stewart's article bear on this question?   Might it make sense to require the proponent to show a declarant's unavailability before admitting such statements in the declarant's absence, but to allow the statements to be admitted if the proponent presents the declarant and puts him on the stand?**

---

b.   Excited Utterances

FRE 803(2) codifies the common law rule on excited utterances:

> *Excited utterance.*   A statement relating to a startling event or condition made while the declarant was under the stress of excitement caused by the event or condition.

We have already mentioned the excited utterance in our discussion of present sense impressions.   It appears that some variant of this exception is found in every state.   Some courts refer to it as the excited utterance exception, some as the spontaneous exclamation exception and some do not distinguish excited statements from other statements which are admitted under the heading *res gestae*.   The basic justification for the exception is the belief that excitement stills reflective capacity, so statements made by individuals feeling the stress of startling events are unlikely to be colored by self-interest or other motives to deceive.   This may be true, but excitement tends to distort perception and may cloud memory.   There is reason to believe that excited utterances are, on balance, less reliable than much of the hearsay we refuse to admit.   Whatever the indications of the unreliability of excited utterances, elimination of the exception is not likely.   The trend in evidence law is to the contrary.   Commentators argue that hearsay should be admitted more freely and the jury trusted to give the evidence its proper weight.   Perhaps allowing the presumed honesty of an out-of-court declarant to outweigh even an added probability of misperception is not completely misguided.   There is something particularly offensive about the thought of jury judgments being based on intentional deception, but mistakes due to errors of perception and memory may be accepted as an inevitable cost of the way we have chosen to resolve legal disputes.[97]

97. Alternatively, one might argue that the decision to exclude hearsay is of such questionable wisdom that anything which suggests added reliability to an out-of-court

The two basic conditions of the excited utterance exception are that the event giving rise to the statement be sufficiently startling to still reflection and that the statement be made while the declarant is still under the influence of the startling event. Few questions are raised about the first issue. Accidents, injuries, crimes and other extraordinary events are all thought to be sufficiently startling to affect the sensibilities of witnesses in the desired fashion. Problems do arise in the rare instance where the only evidence that a startling event occurred is the statement of an obviously excited declarant. Here courts split: most allow the declarant's excited statement to be used to establish the event; some do not. Since this situation will seldom exist except where the effect of the described event on the declarant is in issue, the better procedure is to admit the evidence. If the statement and surrounding circumstances provide sufficient evidence for a reasonable jury to conclude that the event in question has occurred, the matter should reach the jury; if not, a directed verdict is in order. Thus, if a dying man claims that he stumbled down an open manhole and his heirs sue the city, the man's statement, coupled with the presence of an open manhole near where he was found, should be enough to get the case to the jury. If, however, the man claimed he was hit when an airplane crashed while taking off from the airport and his heirs sue the airport, the absence of any other evidence that a plane crashed should lead the judge to direct a verdict for the airport even after admitting the excited statement.

More difficulties have been caused by the requirement that the declarant be under the influence of the exciting event. Although in determining admissibility courts have listened to testimony about the declarant's apparent state of excitement (and note that this determination is for the court), generally they have paid a good deal more attention to the time dimension. Statements made during the exciting event or within a half an hour afterward are usually admitted, statements made an hour or more after the event are usually excluded, while statements made within thirty minutes to an hour of the event are dealt with in the way that all excited utterances should in theory be dealt with, by a close look at the surrounding circumstances.[98] Occasionally an exciting event will create a condition such as the pain of an injury which interferes with reflection and endures over time. Where this is the case, courts are receptive to the claim that excitement has persisted over time. Indeed, there are cases where time is, in effect, suspended. Courts have admitted statements made by individuals immediately upon waking from comas, hours or even days after the event described, apparently on the theory that while the patient was unconscious the excitement did not abate.

In determining whether an individual is speaking under the exciting influence of an event, courts also look closely at the apparent spontaneity of the declarant's statement. Statements which are obviously self-serving arouse judicial suspicion and remarks made in response to questions are usually excluded, although the response to

---

statement justifies admissibility, regardless of features which suggest the likelihood of unreliability.

98. In litigating you should not rely on the fact that appellate opinions suggest that a rule of thumb is applied where utterances are less than thirty minutes or more than an hour after the event. A rule of thumb is not a rule of law. Good lawyers per-

suade courts to examine surrounding circumstances and there are many exceptions to these "rules." Some statements have been excluded which were made within five minutes of a startling event and others have been included although made several hours after the event. Trial judges' decisions on matters of this sort are usually respected on appeal.

a simple, "What happened?" may be allowed. Courts are also reluctant to admit statements under this exception if the declarant's actions between the event and the statement suggest an ability to reflect about other matters.

There is an interesting difference between FRE 803(1) and FRE 803(2). The exception for present sense impressions admits statements "*describing* or *explaining* an event or condition," while the exception for excited utterances admits statements "*relating to* a startling event or condition." This difference means that statements admitted under 803(2) need not directly recount the event perceived, so long as they relate to it in some way. Some states do not follow the federal rule in this respect. In these states, admissible excited utterances are only those which directly elucidate the exciting event. The

battleground, as you might guess, is over the admisssion of excited utterances to prove agency. In jurisdictions following the federal approach, the excited post-accident statement of a truck driver that he worked for a particular company would be admissible against that company to prove agency. Other states would exclude this evidence because it does not in some way explain the accident. Where an agency relationship is asserted, the federal rule is preferable because agency usually reflects a continuing relationship likely to remain in a person's mind so long as he is working for a particular employer. Where details of past activity are important, even details relating to agency, the federal rule raises the possibility of memory problems, problems which are less likely to exist when the exception is limited to utterances explaining the startling event.

Problem VI–35b. **Which of the hearsay dangers are substantially reduced when evidence is introduced under the exception for present sense impressions? Which of the dangers are substantially reduced when evidence is introduced under the exception for excited utterances? What is the justification for allowing excited utterances to be introduced regardless of the declarant's availability? Do you find this justification sufficient?**

c. Statements of Physical Condition

The admissibility of a declarant's statements concerning his own physical condition depends in part on the person to whom the statement is made. Where the statement is made to a layperson, FRE 803(3) expresses the general rule:

Then existing mental, emotional, or physical condition. A statement of the declarant's then existing state of mind, emotion, sensation, or physical condition (such as intent, plan, motive, design, mental feeling, pain, and bodily health), but not including a statement of memory or belief to prove the fact remembered or believed unless it relates

to the execution, revocation, identification, or terms of declarant's will.

Where the statement is made to a physician, FRE 803(4) applies. Federal policy in this area is considerably more liberal than the old common law:

Statements for purposes of medical diagnosis or treatment. Statements made for purposes of medical diagnosis or treatment and describing medical history, or past or present symptoms, pain, or sensations, or the inception or general character of the cause or external source thereof insofar as reasonably pertinent to diagnosis or treatment.

Statements of physical condition made to lay persons are admissible under the general exception for spontaneous statements which reflect states of mind.[99] Two basic requirements must be met before statements will be admitted under this exception. First, the statement must reflect a condition which exists when the statement is spoken. The statement "I have a terrible headache" would be admissible under this exception; the statement "I had a terrible headache yesterday" would not be. Second, the statement must be spontaneous. Under the federal rule and in most courts the mere concurrence of the statement and the condition described provides sufficient evidence of spontaneity unless the particular circumstances surrounding the statement suggest that the declarant was trying to manufacture evidence in his favor.[1] Some courts, however, have decided that certain classes of statements cannot be considered spontaneous. There are judicial opinions that purport to exclude any self-serving statements, opinions which exclude self-serving statements made after the commencement of litigation and even opinions which hold that involuntary expressions of physical condition such as grunts and groans are admissible, but not verbalizations such as "I hurt." The decisions in courts which have taken these views are often inconsistent and, except where courts have firm views about the admissibility of self-serv-

ing statements made pending litigation, it is likely that most if not all appellate courts today would grant the trial judge discretion to admit self-serving statements as well as verbal descriptions of physical conditions.

Statements admitted under the exception for bodily condition are usually statements about pain. If an individual told a lay person that his kidney was infected or his appendix inflamed, the statement, unless offered for the inference of pain, would probably be excluded on firsthand knowledge or opinion rule grounds. Where the statements are about a condition which the declarant can perceive and evaluate, such as the declaration, "I have red spots on my chest," the statements should be admitted although the case for the exception is somewhat weaker here than when the exception is used to admit statements of pain. This is because the necessity element is not as great; spots, unlike pain, are readily observable by third parties. Also a possibility of misperception exists. When present pain is described there is no memory problem, few problems of perception, and, in theory, a diminished likelihood of falsehood since the statement must be spontaneous. However, the difficulty of developing any judicial test for spontaneity other than the apparent coincidence of statement and feeling means that the spontaneity requirement offers little

---

99. In dealing with problems involving the exception for statements of bodily condition, you may refer either to the general exception for "states of mind" or the more specific variant, "statements of bodily conditions." Courts and professors differ in their preferences. Under the federal rules the phrase "then existing physical condition" characterizes the appropriate exception.

1. Under the federal rules it is not clear that the judge would have discretion to exclude statements describing existing bodily conditions even in these circumstances. Under the rule it appears that the evidence should come in for what it is worth. But

if a judge did exercise discretion to exclude, it is unlikely that this would be held to be an abuse of discretion, since FRE 403 provides general authorization for balancing probative value against such dangers as unfair prejudice and misleading the jury. Even if it were so held, the error would probably be held harmless, since statements made with the intent of manufacturing evidence have little probative value. Given FRE 803(3), the better procedure is probably for the federal judge to admit the statement. He can use his power to comment on the evidence to call the jury's attention to its deficiencies.

protection against the witness who wishes to fabricate evidence of pain.

People who visit doctors usually know that the quality of their treatment depends in part on their willingness to be candid in describing their physical condition. This added guarantee of reliability has induced courts to be particularly receptive to statements made to physicians for treatment purposes. Any statement regarding physical condition which would be admissible if made to a layperson will, of course, be admissible if made to a treating physician. Even self-serving statements are not barred. The modern trend goes still further, admitting the patient's statements describing past symptoms if made for the purposes of treatment, as well as statements about causes of ailments, if, at the time of the statement, disclosure of cause appeared important to diagnosis and treatment. Even states which do not admit statements of past symptoms as substantive evidence may allow a treating physican to recount such statements as the basis for an opinion rendered in court. Statements introduced only as the basis for an opinion are not hearsay.

Physicians employed both to testify and treat are usually regarded as treating physicians, but most courts refuse to apply the hearsay exception to statements made to physicians employed only to testify. The reason for the distinction between treating and testifying physicians is obvious: When a physician is only hired to testify, the declarant's motives to falsify the extent of his ailments are not counterbalanced by the realization that treatment and health may depend upon the honesty of what is reported. Thus, even statements of then existing physical conditions are usually barred if made to physicians employed solely for their expert testimony. But non-treating physicians usually will be allowed to recount statements of existing conditions and descriptions of past symptoms for

the purpose of explaining how they arrived at their expert opinions. Some states do not allow this, even though the statements are introduced solely for the non-hearsay purpose of showing the basis for an expert opinion. These states regard statements to non-treating physicians as especially suspect and do not believe jurors can confine the statements to permissible non-hearsay purposes.

FRE 803(4) takes a different view. In providing an exception for statements made for the purposes of medical diagnosis *or* treatment it makes no distinction between the diagnoses of treating physicians and the diagnoses of doctors employed solely to testify. Admissible statements include those which describe past symptoms as well as those which describe the cause or source of the ailment to the extent that this is pertinent to diagnosis as well as treatment. Furthermore, because FRE 803(4) refers to statements made "*for purposes* of medical diagnosis or treatment" it is not limited to statements made to a physician. Thus statements made to a nurse, a medical student, an ambulance driver, someone masquerading as a physician or a member of one's family would probably qualify under this exception if the patient thought the statements were for purposes of treatment or diagnosis. Under the theory of the exception, at least as it relates to treatment, this makes sense, for it is the patient's belief in making the statement which provides a guarantee of truthfulness. Since most reported cases involve statements made directly to physicians, it is not clear how the more restrictive common law courts would react when asked to admit statements made to third parties. It is likely that where the third party obviously was taking the information for transmittal to a physican, such as a nurse taking a patient's history, the statement would qualify as fully as if it were made to the physician. Where the third party was not one who was obviously going to transmit the statement to a treating physician, the courts would probably be skeptical of the patient's claim that the statement was made to secure medical treatment.

———

Problem VI–35c. Do you think that the liberal view that FRE 803(4) takes toward the admission of statements made to physicians is wise? The drafters justify their decision to admit statements made to a physician solely for the purpose of securing his testimony in court on the ground that, "While these statements were not admissible as substantive evidence, the expert was allowed to state the basis of his opinion including statements of this kind. The distinction thus called for was one most unlikely to be made by juries." Yet, as we have just noted, not all jurisdictions allow physicians engaged only to testify to repeat those patients' statements that formed a basis for their diagnoses. **If the drafters were really worried that jurors might not follow instructions to treat patients' statements solely as the basis of a diagnosis, might it not have been wiser for them to preclude doctors from testifying to such statements even for this purpose? Are you as sure as the drafters that the distinction between statements admissible as substantive evidence and statements admissible for substantive purposes is a distinction juries are most unlikely to make?** Remember that the jury is in some ways as strong as its strongest link; although only a few jurors understand certain instructions and take them seriously, the few may convince the other jurors, hang the jury, or arrange a compromise which reflects their appreciation of how the evidence was intended to be used. **Even if the drafters are correct about jury behavior, might not a party still benefit from the fact that his opponent's statements to a physician are presented as the basis for an expert opinion rather than as substantive evidence of the condition to which they refer? How?**

———

d. Other Existing States of Mind

We have already noted that state of mind is often an issue in litigation. Where this is the case, statements which circumstantially suggest the state of mind of a declarant are not hearsay.[2] However, where a statement asserts the very state of mind in question, most courts would view the assertion as hearsay because the jury is usually asked to take the statement at face value rather than to reason circumstantially from it. The hearsay analysis is, however, relatively unimportant because hearsay statements asserting relevant states of mind are admissible under FRE 803(3) and similar common law exceptions.[3] Thus, in a dispute over a will the testator's statement "I

2. Some courts, preferring a quick decision to close analysis, explain the admissibility of such statements by the "state of mind" exception and not by the fact they are not hearsay. Usually nothing turns on this, but see the footnote which follows.

3. The distinction between a statement which is considered not hearsay and a statement which is considered hearsay but admitted under some exception to the hearsay rule is not always a meaningless one. In some jurisdictions one might be entitled to an instruction that hearsay evidence merits less weight than non-hearsay evidence, and occasionally one will be in a jurisdiction where the substantive law in certain areas requires corroboration of admissible hearsay but does not require corroboration of a non-hearsay statement.

want my son Eldridge to have all my money" would be admitted under the state of mind exception on the issue of testamentary intent. An immigrant's statement "I intend to stay here forever" offered to show domiciliary intent or a husband's statement "I no longer love my wife" offered to prove absence of love in a suit for the alienation of affections are also admissible as states of mind.

Note that the federal rule admits statements describing the declarant's *then existing* state of mind. This requirement means that assertions of states of mind qualify for the exception only if they purport to describe what is being felt at the time they are made. Thus the statement "I am happy now" qualifies, while "I was happy yesterday" does not. Suppose that a person's state of mind on Tuesday is an issue in a case. His statement on Monday expressing his then existing state of mind will not be excluded as hearsay. If the statement is excluded, it will be because the court does not believe that there is a substantial relationship between the person's state of mind on Monday and how he felt on Tuesday. This might be the case, for example, if tragedy struck between the time of the person's statement and the time when his state of mind is in issue.

The general principle is that whether a state of mind at one time tends to prove a state of mind at another time is a *relevance* and not a *hearsay* question. Thus if a testator says "I don't want Clarence to inherit a cent," and the following day goes to his safe deposit box, takes out his will leaving everything to Clarence, and rips it up, it is his state of mind at the time he destroyed the will, and not his state of mind on the preceding day, which determines whether the tearing was done with intent to revoke. Nevertheless, the testator's earlier statement will be admissible to establish his feelings towards Clarence *at that time* and the jury will be allowed to reason from his feelings at the time of the statement to his probable state of mind at the time he ripped up the will. The obvious inference is that feelings toward Clarence existing one day persist until the next. If the destruction of the will followed the declaration about disinheriting Clarence by a year instead of a day, evidence of the statement might well be excluded, not because it is hearsay on the issue of the testator's intent at the time of the ripping, but rather because the testator's state of mind on one occasion is not very relevant to his state of mind a year later.[4] Similarly, the declarant's statement "I intend to live in Hutchins forever" made a week before his move to that town is admissible because it is relevant to his state of mind at the end of the move.

A similar analysis applies when the state of mind in issue is the declarant's state of mind at some point prior to the making of the statement. Thus, if a testator rips his will up on Monday and on Tuesday states, "I don't want Clarence to inherit a cent," the statement would be admissible under the state of mind exception and would not be excluded under a relevance analysis, because the testator's attitudes on Tuesday are likely to have a close relationship to what he felt on Monday. Note that had the testator said, "When I ripped up the will, I didn't want Clarence to inherit a cent," the statement would not be admissible under the general state of mind prin-

---

To the extent that state of mind problems are not easily classified, they suggest that such instructions might better be abandoned or changed to minimize the difference between admissible hearsay and statements not subject to the hearsay rule.

4. Of course this would depend on the exact circumstances of the case. If there were a series of statements extending through the year, all might be relevant to show the firmness of the testator's intent. Or the court might regard the matter differently if the testator did not have access to either his will or a lawyer until a year after he had made the statement.

ciple because it does not refer to a then existing attitude. However, the last clause of FRE 803(3), consistent with the practice in most states, creates a special exception for statements describing past states of mind or other past facts when those facts relate to the execution, revocation, identification or terms of the declarant's will.

The state of mind exception is generally justified on the ground that what we have called right leg dangers pose no threat when statements are used to show then existing states of mind. The "then existing" requirement eliminates memory problems and the declarant is presumed to have no difficulty in perceiving his own feelings.[5] These guarantees are thought to be so strong that the unavailability of the declarant need not be shown, for if he were to testify, "his own memory of his state of mind at a former time is no more likely to be clear and true than a bystander's recollection of what he then said."[6] Wigmore claims that the exception is also supported by a guarantee of sincerity, since statements describing then existing states of mind are likely to be spontaneous.[7] However, the declarant's assertion is usually the only evidence that the declaration is coincident with an existing state of mind. Nothing prevents a designing declarant from asserting whatever state of mind it would be convenient to possess. Nevertheless, with the exception of statements relating physical conditions, courts do not usually exclude statements relating states of mind because they were made in response to questions or because the declarant had an obvious motive to falsify. In this respect the exception differs from other hearsay exceptions requiring spontaneity.

Suppose that the testator we have been discussing had said, "I don't want Clarence

to inherit a cent because he is an alcoholic who spends all his money on whiskey." Neither the rationale for the state of mind exception nor the literal language of FRE 803(3) apply to the description of Clarence's drinking behavior. Yet courts often admit statements which assert both a feeling and the circumstances giving rise to that feeling.

One justification is that descriptive statements which accompany assertions of feelings shed light on how deeply the asserted feelings are held. Consider, for example, a trial for extortion by threat in which the prosecution must prove that the victim was put in some fear. If the prosecution could present a witness to testify only to the victim's statement, "I am afraid of D," D's counsel might successfully soften the impact of the statement by arguing that it was a single assertion based on mistake, that the victim's fear was unreasonable, or that the victim's other behavior suggested he wasn't serious when he indicated fear of D. If, however, the prosecution's witness reported the victims entire statement, "I'm afraid of D; he had his henchmen beat me within an inch of my life and now he threatens to kill me if I don't pay him the money," it would be very difficult to convince a jury that the victim's fear was not real. The problem, of course, is that the reported statement would also lead the jury to believe that D's henchmen had beaten the victim to within an inch of his life and that D had threatened to kill the victim if the money were not paid. On these issues, the victim's reported statements are inadmissible hearsay. The prejudicial impact of admitting the statements for the light they shed on the victim's state of mind is obvious. In situations like this the trial judge has great discretion. He may sever the statements, admitting only those which directly assert feelings, or he may admit the

5. Whatever the views of some schools of psychiatry, the law in this area does not entertain the question of whether the declarant really thought what he thought he thought.

6. Mutual Life Ins. Co. of New York v. Hillmon, 145 U.S. 285, 295 (1892).

7. 6 Wigmore § 1714.

entire declaration in order to show the strength with which the feeling in question was held. In the latter instance an appellate court is likely to affirm so long as the trial judge has clearly instructed the jury that the statements may not be used as evidence of the truth of what they assert. Reversal is most likely where there is so much other evidence establishing the relevant state of mind that it appears the declaration was introduced to suggest the truth of what was asserted rather than for proper probative purposes.

Where there is no direct assertion of feelings, statements may be offered as indirect evidence of a state of mind and not for the truth of what they assert. For example, the testator's statement, "Clarence cannot be trusted with money because of his drinking problem," tends to show that the testator did not intend to leave his money to Clarence when he made his will. Statements used in this way to imply a state of mind are not technically hearsay and there is no way to eliminate the prejudicial aspects of such statements while still using them to establish the relevant mental condition. In both situations, if the prejudicial effect of the statements appears great, but not great enough to be excluded under FRE 403, counsel should consider whether it would be wise to stipulate to the state of mind in issue.

Thus far we have been discussing situations where state of mind is in some way in issue. More difficult problems are posed when statements asserting or implying a state of mind are introduced to establish *behavior* consistent with that state of mind. One can distinguish two situations in which state of mind evidence has been offered to prove behavior. The first is where the evidence is offered as proof that the declarant has acted in a way consistent with his state of mind. This is the situation when statements of intent are

offered to show action in accord with intent, a matter discussed below. The second is when an existing state of mind is offered to show the behavior which caused it, as where the statement "I fear D because he threatened to kill me" is offered to show that D threatened to kill the declarant or more generally that D did something to put the declarant in fear. Another example would be the statement, "Dr. Shepard has poisoned me," offered to show that the declarant believes Dr. Shepard has poisoned her and, hence, that Dr. Shepard probably did poison her.

One can reason circumstantially from a belief to the actions of others because most beliefs about others are based on their actions. However, if a hearsay exception were allowed in the second situation described above, the exception would swallow the hearsay rule, for one would be reasoning from the declarant's belief to the action asserted or implied by the statement in almost the same way one reasons in the pure hearsay situation. The only difference would be the chimerical difference between the one stage process of accepting a statement because the declarant's words are considered reliable and the two stage process of inferring a belief from the declarant's statement and then attributing that belief to the causes which the statement specifies. In both instances one concludes that the declarant's statement is true and in both instances the truth of the statement depends on the accuracy of declarant's perceptions and the quality of his memory.

Realizing the extent to which the hearsay rule would be undermined if beliefs could be shown to prove the facts they are purportedly based upon, courts have generally not admitted out-of-court statements for this purpose. The case usually cited for this proposition is Shepard v. United States.[8] In that case the prosecution had

---

8. 290 U.S. 96 (1933). This case is reprinted in Section V of this Chapter.

introduced the deceased's statement, "Dr. Shepard has poisoned me," to prove Shepard's action under the dying declaration exception to the hearsay rule. On appeal the court held that the conditions of a dying declaration were not met. The prosecution then tried to justify the statement on the ground that it tended to negate the suggestion in the defendant's case that the declarant, defendant's wife, had committed suicide. This justification was rejected on two grounds. First, since the statement was offered at trial for the truth of the matter asserted it could not be defended on appeal on the ground that it might have been properly admitted had the jury been instructed to use it in a more narrow fashion. Second, even if offered to negate an implication of suicide, the statement was so likely to be used as proof of Shepard's action that its admission was not justified. Justice Cardozo put the matter as follows: "It will not do to say that the jury might accept the declarations for any light that they cast upon the existence of a vital urge, and reject them to the extent that they charged the death to someone else. Discrimination so subtle is a feat beyond the compass of ordinary minds. The reverberating clang of those accusatory words would drown all weaker sounds. It is for ordinary minds, and not for psychoanalysts, that our rules of evidence are framed. * * * When the risk of confusion is so great as to upset the balance of advantage, the evidence goes out."[9] Cardozo continued (and it is in this dictum that he makes the point for which the case is so often cited), "There are times when a state of mind, if relevant, may be proved by contemporaneous declarations of feelings or intent. * * * So * * * declarations by an insured that he intends to go upon a journey with another, may be evidence of a state of mind lending probabil-

ity to the conclusion that the purpose was fulfilled. Mutual Life Ins. Co. v. Hillmon, * * *. The ruling in that case marks the high water line beyond which courts have been unwilling to go. * * * Declarations of intention, casting light upon the future, have been sharply distinguished from declarations of memory, pointing backwards to the past. There would be an end, or nearly that, to the rule against hearsay if the distinction were ignored."[10]

Yet, where a declarant's descriptions of the defendant's activities are offered to show the declarant's fear, some courts have not followed *Shepard* but have invited the jury to treat the declarant's fear as evidence that the defendant did something which engendered fear. The California Supreme Court in People v. Merkouris[11] wrote in successive sentences:

The declarations that defendant had threatened the victims were admissible, *not to prove the truth of that fact directly,* but to prove the victims' fear. Where, as here, the identification of defendant as the killer is in issue, the fact that the victims feared defendant is relevant because it is some evidence that they had reason to fear him, that is, that *there is a probability that the fear had been aroused by the victims' knowledge of the defendant indicating his intent to harm them* rather than, e.g., that the victims' fear was paranoid.[12]

In other words, the victims' statements about the defendant's threats were admitted not to show that threats were made but as evidence that the victims feared the defendant, which suggested that the defendant had indicated his intent to harm (i.e. threatened) them. If this rationale confuses you, don't worry, the fault is in the rationale and not you. This case is perhaps best understood as an example of the

9. Id. at 104.

10. Id. at 104–06.

11. 52 Cal.2d 672, 344 P.2d 1 (1959), certiorari denied, 361 U.S. 943 (1960).

12. Id. at 682, 344 P.2d at 6 (emphasis added).

way in which appellate courts strain to approve evidentiary rulings below when they wish to affirm the results reached.

The rule of the *Merkouris* case has been eliminated in California by that state's modern evidence code, but one will occasionally find other states rendering decisions of this sort when statements relate the cause of fear. In most other instances, however, states follow federal practice and do not admit statements of memory or belief to prove the fact remembered or believed.[13] The one common exception is codified in FRE 803(3), where the memory or belief relates to the execution, revocation, identification or terms of declarant's will. The general feeling is that testators have peculiar knowledge about facts relating to their own wills. Since the testator is dead when his will reaches probate, his earlier statements about his will may be the most reliable evidence available to the trier of fact. The problem with the exception is that individuals may be moved to lie about their wills to keep peace in the family or to manipulate certain individuals, and persons reporting conversations with a testator may have substantial interests in falsifying their reports of what the testator said. This has led some jurisdictions to admit such statements by testators only where they are corroborated by other evidence in the case.

The leading case on the issue of whether statements of intent can be introduced to show action in accord with expressed intent is Mutual Life Ins. Co. of New York v. Hillmon,[14] one of the most famous cases in the law of evidence. This case arose when Sallie Hillmon brought suit against three companies which had insured the life of her husband, John Hillmon, claiming that a body found at Crooked Creek, Kansas, was his. The insurance companies defended on the ground that the body was that of one Walters who had accompanied Hillmon to Crooked Creek. The evidence identifying the corpse was conflicting.[15]

---

13. In **United States v. Brown**, 160 U.S.App.D.C. 190, 490 F.2d 758 (1973), as amended, (1974), the court described three purposes for which statements admitting fear are commonly allowed in evidence. In each case the statements are, at least in theory, intended to describe a state of mind inconsistent with the activity which the defendant attributes to the declarant. They are not intended to be used as proof that the defendant's behavior was responsible for the declarant's state of mind:

[T]he courts have developed three rather well-defined categories in which the need for such statements overcomes almost any possible prejudice. The most common of these involves defendant's claim of self-defense as justification for the killing. When such a defense is asserted, a defendant's assertion that the deceased first attacked him may be rebutted by the extrajudicial declarations of the victim that he feared the defendant, thus rendering it unlikely that the deceased was in fact the aggressor in the first instance. Second, where defendant seeks to defend on the ground that the deceased committed suicide, evidence that the victim had made statements inconsistent with a suicidal bent are highly relevant. A third situation involves a claim of accidental death, where, for example, defendant's version of the facts is that the victim picked up defendant's gun and was accidentally killed while toying with it. In such cases the deceased's statements of fear as to guns or of defendant himself (showing he would never go near defendant under any circumstances) are relevant in that they tend to rebut this defense. Of course, even in these cases, where the evidence is of a highly prejudicial nature, it has been held that it must be excluded in spite of a significant degree of relevance. [at 767]

14. 145 U.S. 285 (1892). This case is reprinted in Section V of this Chapter.

15. This case involved as defendants a number of insurance companies that had issued policies on the life of John Hillmon. The litigation began in 1880 and continued into 1903. There were six trials in all. In the first two the jury hung 7–5 and 6–6. The Supreme Court's well-known decision was on review from a plaintiff's judgment rendered in the third trial. Remand resulted in two more trials to hung juries followed by a second verdict for plaintiff which the Supreme Court also reversed. During the interim, however, most of the insurance company defendants settled, in part because in 1896 the

In order to support their theory that the body at Crooked Creek did belong to Walters, the insurance companies sought to introduce several letters which Walters had written to his fiancee in which he mentioned his relationship with Hillmon and stated his intention to accompany him on his trip. The Supreme Court held that the letters should have been admitted under the state of mind exception to the hearsay rule. Mr. Justice Gray wrote:

But whenever the intention is of itself a distinct and material fact in a chain of circumstances, it may be proved by contemporaneous oral or written declarations of the party.

The existence of a particular intention in a certain person at a certain time being a material fact to be proved, evidence that he expressed that intention at that time is as direct evidence of the fact, as his own testimony that he then had that intention would be. After his death there can hardly be any other way of proving it; and while he is still alive, his own memory of his state of mind at a former time is no more likely to be clear and true than a bystander's recollection of what he then said, and is less trustworthy than letters written by him at the very time and under circumstances precluding a suspicion of misrepresentation.

The letters in question were competent, not as narratives of facts communicated to the writer by others, nor yet as proof that he actually went away from Wichita, but as evidence that, shortly before the time when other evidence tended to show that he went away, he had the intention of going, and of going with Hillmon, which made it more probable both that he did go and that he went with Hillmon, than if there had been no proof of such intention.[16]

In terms of the approach which we have taken to hearsay problems, the court's ruling makes sense. In reasoning from the declarant's intentions to his actions, no right leg problems exist. We are not worried that the declarant misperceived his own intentions or that he did not remember them. However, the inference from the fact that the intention existed to the fact that the action occurred is not necessarily a strong one. The declarant may have changed his mind after expressing his intentions or intervening circumstances may have prevented him from acting as he intended. But these difficulties raise issues of relevance and not issues of hearsay. For example, had Walters been cross-examined at the time he wrote his letters, the examination would have revealed little about the probability that future circumstances would lead Walters to change his mind or prevent him from carrying out his actions.[17] The situation is very different in the *Shepard* case. While Mrs. Shepard could not have misperceived or forgotten her recollection, she might well have misperceived or forgotten the event itself. Consequently, when reasoning from her memory to the facts remembered we encounter two of the basic dangers the hearsay rule is designed to avoid, dangers which may be assessed by cross-examination at the time a statement is made.

Despite the absence of right leg problems when statements of intent are offered

---

State Insurance Commissioner of Kansas barred three companies from doing business in that state because of the public's disapproval of the companies' resistance to the Hillmon claims. For a fascinating account of the facts of this case see Wigmore, Principles of Judicial Proof, 856–896 (1913). For a classic analysis of the legal issues it raises see Maguire, The Hillmon Case—Thirty-Three Years After, 38 Harv.L.Rev. 709, (1925).

16. Id. at 295–96.

17. Cross-examination would not be entirely useless in this respect because it could reveal something about the strength of his intentions—a left leg issue. However, we have already seen that circumstances which eliminate the problems of either leg are enough to justify a hearsay exception even though cross-examination might help assess problems associated with the other leg.

to show subsequent action, a strong case can be made that this exception should be conditioned on unavailability. Professor Tribe argues as follows:

> It is true that cross-examination contemporaneous with the utterance will not give any substantial assurance with respect to the infirmities [change of mind and intervening circumstances] peculiarly associated with statements of intention, but that should indicate only that one must reconsider the notion that cross-examination be contemporaneous with the utterance. When an utterance relates to past events, the strongest cross-examination is one that occurs as soon as possible after the utterance, so the declarant's testimony will have little time to harden. But when an utterance relates to future events, the best time for cross-examination is after the future events have (or have not) taken place. To insist in such a case that the hearsay rule is designed only to exclude evidence which can be made more trustworthy by *contemporaneous* cross-examination is to admit statements which are as unreliable as any hearsay utterance, in situations which are no less amenable than others to the beneficial pressure to bring declarants to court for cross-examination.[18]

Tribe's argument may be persuasive, but the problem an unavailability requirement would correct exists more in theory than in practice. It is so clear that an individual's in-court testimony is more probative as to whether a particular action occurred than are his earlier expressions of intent to engage in that action that this aspect of the state of mind exception is typically used only where the declarant is unavailable.

In *Hillmon*, the Supreme Court stated that Walters' declarations of his intent to go to Colorado with Hillmon were admissible not only to show that he did go, but also to show that he went with Hillmon. Most courts follow the Supreme Court in this respect and allow a statement of an intention to engage in some action with another to support the inference that that action was done with the other and, since the two are not separable, to support the inference that the other did the action with the declarant. The House Committee in approving FRE 803(3) explicitly disavowed this aspect of *Hillmon*, but it is not clear how much weight this legislative history will, or should be, accorded.

Close analysis reveals that when statements of intent are used to show the actions of another they pose all the hearsay dangers. The statement "I intend to do something with X" tends to prove that the declarant and X did something together only if the inference inherent in the statement "X intends to do the same thing with me" is correct. This, of course, depends upon the declarant having correctly perceived and remembered X's intentions. The right leg dangers are back. Therefore the better policy would be to exclude statements of this sort when they are the only evidence that the declarant did the act and did it with X.

Where the declarant clearly did the intended act and the only issue is whether it was done with X, there is a strong argument for admitting the statement if the declarant's intention were such that it is unlikely that the act would have been done without X. For example, in People v. Alcalde,[19] a woman told her roommate that she intended to have dinner with Frank on a particular evening. She left her house that evening and the next morning was found murdered. In these circumstances it is arguable that the statement was prop-

---

18. Tribe, supra note 8, at 971. One of us believes that Tribe's argument is less persuasive if one concludes that forward looking statements ought to be admitted in part because triers of fact expect to see evidence of intent in many instances, and without it they may infer that a person did not do an act. This analysis is explored in Saltzburg, supra note 9, at 1637–43.

19. 24 Cal.2d 177, 148 P.2d 627 (1944).

erly admitted for the light it shed on the identity of the woman's escort on the night before she was found dead. There is no dispute that the woman dressed for dinner and went out. It is very unlikely, given her intentions, that she would at this point have accepted an invitation with anyone other than Frank. While it is possible that she might have gone out on her own had Frank never come by, it seems at least as likely that she would have returned to her apartment in these circumstances. Thus, the fact that she went out and did not return has some probative value on the issue of whether she went out with Frank.[20] This probative value does not turn entirely on the accuracy with which she perceived Frank's intention when she stated she was going out with him. Even if she were wrong about Frank's intention, she might have called Frank to reconfirm the date or gone to his apartment or bumped into him, with the same result. It is less likely that she would have sought the opportunity to go out with someone else. And, despite the theoretical existence of hearsay dangers, it is unlikely that Frank's intention was misperceived. People are usually careful about arranging dates.

One author does not accept this analysis. He points out that it is possible that the deceased would have said she was going out with Frank even if a date with Frank had not been arranged. People without dates may boast to their roommates that they are going out in order to be thought of as popular. They may unintentionally misidentify dates through simple slips of the tongue, or they may intentionally misidentify their dates because they do not want the name of their real escort to be known. People also engage in wishful thinking and express a belief that they are going out with someone in the hope that this belief will come to pass.

If the original analysis is accepted, how does one distinguish the declaration at issue in *Alcalde* from any other out-of-court declaration which arguably would not have been made had the declarant not believed it true? If, despite the deceased's statement, there was a significant possibility in *Alcalde* that a date had not been arranged with Frank, can one still justify the admission of the deceased's statement on the issue of whether Frank went out with her? Do the arguments of the first author provide sufficient justification for treating the arguments of the second author as going to weight rather than admissibility?[21] Needless to say, we disagree.

Problem VI–36. James Glenn is charged with stabbing and killing Juanita Johnson. If allowed to testify over Glenn's hearsay objection, a police officer, Pearlman, will relate the following story:

20. Recall the discussion of the likelihood ratio in Chapter Three. What is the likelihood the woman would have gone out had Frank not come by, given her intent? (Let us say .5.) What is the likelihood that she would have gone out with Frank had he come by? (Let us say almost 1.0.) Thus, knowing that she had the intention to go out with Frank and in fact went out would almost double our prior estimate of the odds that she went out with Frank. Do the estimates we have used to reach this conclusion strike you as realistic? In thinking about this, is it important whether there is any other evidence concerning a planned date with Frank?

21. Justice Traynor dissenting in the Alcalde case writes: "Since the evidence is overwhelming as to who the deceased was and where she was when she met her death, no legitimate purpose could be served by admitting her declarations of what she intended to do on the evening of November 22nd. The only purpose that could be served by admitting such declarations would be to induce the belief that the defendant went out with the deceased, took her to the scene of the crime and there murdered her." 24 Cal.2d 177, 190, 148 P.2d 627, 633 (1944).

I was working at the counter when Ms. Johnson entered the station. As she approached, she appeared as though she might fall, but instead she lunged the several steps necessary to reach me. She leaned up against the counter and grasped my wrist saying, "Please help me. Please help me. He did it." I responded, "Who is he and what did he do?" She replied, "James did it." I thought at first she said, "James Lynn," but I was only certain about the "James." I was unable to clearly make out the last name so I said, "Who?" She replied, "James Glenn." I then asked, "Where does he live?" and she replied, "3407 Sherman." Then I asked, "What did he do to you?" She replied, "I don't know because he got me in the back."

A deputy medical examiner for the government testified that there was such a large amount of whiskey in Ms. Johnson's blood that a normal person would have had to consume ten ounces of whiskey in one hour to reach that percentage. But there is also evidence that Ms. Johnson was a chronic alcoholic with greater than average tolerance for alcohol. **Should Officer Pearlman's testimony be admitted?**

Problem VI–37. Harriet Jones was injured when the car she was driving collided with a truck. She was trapped in the car and in severe pain prior to her removal. Subsequently she brought an action against the owner of the truck for damages. At trial, a witness called by Jones testifies that he arrived at the scene minutes after the accident occurred. While comforting Ms. Jones he heard her exclaim, "Why didn't he watch where he was going?" Defendant objects to the admission of this testimony. **What result?** Jones offers the witness' testimony that immediately after the accident the truck driver said, "It's all my fault. My employer, Daniels Trucking, will pay." **Is this admissible?**

Problem VI–38. In early December Phyllis Shingle was attacked and almost killed by a man who attempted to rob her. Fortunately her screams attracted a passerby and the man fled. She was unable to identify her assailant from pictures in police files and the man was never found. Six months later she opened her door to a pizza delivery man and let out a sudden scream. Her roommate came running. "That's the one who attacked me," she said, pointing to the door. But the delivery man had dropped the pizza and fled. **If the delivery man is tried for the robbery attempt, may Phyllis' roommate testify to Phyllis' statement of identification?**

Problem VI–39. Patrolwoman Carla Westerly arrived at the scene of an automobile accident between a Cadillac and a Volkswagen about five minutes after it occurred. She is willing to testify that just after she extricated the plaintiff from the Volkswagen, a man who had just walked out of a drugstore saw the body and becoming very agitated said, "How horrible, I think I'm going to faint. I'm sure the Cadillac was going too fast." **May Westerly's testimony be introduced at trial on behalf of the plaintiff as some evidence that the driver of the Cadillac was speeding?**

Problem IV–40. Cassidy claims that as she was being helped from her burning car after colliding with a red Ford, she heard an hysterical voice which she thinks was a man's, but which she cannot further identify, say,

"The red car went through the light. The driver must have been asleep." **Can Cassidy testify to hearing these statements as part of her effort to prove that the defendant drove his car through a red light because he was asleep?** After Cassidy was pulled out, the person aiding her asked what happened. Cassidy replied, "I'll tell you as soon as we get away from this car. If the gas tank ignites it might explode." Once they were safely away Cassidy said, "That car went through a light and plowed into me." The helper asked, "Do you know why he missed the light?" Cassidy replied, "No", and the helper asked, "Are you sure? The police will want to know." Cassidy responded, "His head was slumped over. I think he was asleep." Assume Cassidy dies and her widower brings a wrongful death action. **Can he introduce the helper to testify to what Cassidy told him?**

Problem VI–41. Carl Crawford sues Nora Johnson for personal injuries allegedly sustained in an automobile accident. It is undisputed that cars driven by Crawford and Johnson collided at an intersection controlled by a traffic light. Each claims to have had the green light. Crawford wishes to call to the stand Dr. Holmes, his personal physician. It was Dr. Holmes who treated Crawford for injuries after the accident. Dr. Holmes would testify, "I examined Mr. Crawford shortly after the accident. Crawford related to me the circumstances of the accident, including the fact that the other driver ran a red light and caused the accident. My examination revealed that pieces of windshield glass were lodged in plaintiff's forearm. I removed them, gave other treatment to plaintiff, and took down the history of the accident." Johnson objects to this testimony. **What result?**

Problem VI–42. Sheila Hauser is suing Dr. Lewis Coles, an anesthesiologist, for injuries suffered during the course of a routine appendectomy. Dr. Mary Schwartz, an anesthesiologist agrees to examine Hauser in order to give Hauser's attorney her opinion as to whether there has been negligence and to help him develop his theory of the case. She has stated, however, that she will under no circumstances testify in court in a malpractice action against another physician. Hauser tells Dr. Schwartz during the course of the examination that her left leg is entirely numb, that she never had any problems with the leg before the operation, and that she has had severe pains in her neck and head which have not left her since the operation. She also tells the doctor that when she awoke after the operation she heard Dr. Coles exclaim, "Thank goodness! I was afraid I hadn't given her enough oxygen!" After the examination, Dr. Schwartz writes a report for Hauser's attorney in which she notes what Hauser has told her and states that it is her opinion that the numbness Hauser reports is permanent and may eventually lead to the loss of the leg, that there is a fifty percent chance that the reported pains will disappear in time and that she believes the disabilities were due to the fact that Dr. Coles negligently failed to administer a sufficient amount of oxygen during the operation. Lincoln Franks, Dr. Schwartz's nurse, was present during the entire examination and is willing to testify for Hauser. **Will a court allow him to testify to any of the statements which Hauser made to the doctor? May Hauser's attorney offer any or all of Dr. Schwartz's report into evidence? Would your answer to these questions be the same if Schwartz had agreed to testify for Hauser before conduct-**

ing her examination? **If Schwartz's report were helpful to Coles, could he secure its admission?**

Problem VI–43. Sammy Peoples and Alice Mooney, two nine-year old children, were trick-or-treating one Halloween night when they came to the house owned by "old Mr. Crabtree." Alice said to Sammy, "I'm afraid to get anything from him. I've heard he put a razor blade in Carol's apple last year." Sammy said he wasn't afraid and went to Crabtree's house. He came back shortly with a candy apple, looked it over closely and said, "No razor blade in here." Then he took a bite and said, "This tastes strange, sweet but bitter." He took two more bites and threw the apple down. About two minutes later he complained to Alice, "My stomach hurts. I'd better go home." He came home and his mother asked him, "What is wrong?" He replied, "My stomach started hurting right after I ate old Crabtree's apple." Then he vomited. Ms. Peoples tried calling a doctor and when she could not get one she took Sammy to the emergency room of the local hospital. She told the orderly who admitted them that "My son told me that his stomach began to hurt right after he ate an apple which Tyrone Crabtree had given him. He started throwing up and then went into convulsions so I brought him here."

Assume that Crabtree is charged with poisoning Sammy Peoples and with attempted murder. **Will any of the following testimony be admitted either to prove the facts asserted or for some other purpose: Sammy's testimony about what Alice said about her reasons for not going to Crabtree's house? Alice's testimony about what Sammy said about the taste of the apple and about his stomach hurting? Ms. Peoples' testimony about what Sammy told her when she asked what was wrong? The orderly's testimony about what Ms. Peoples told him when Sammy was admitted to the hospital?**

Problem VI–44. Kenneth Kasper is suffering from severe headaches and muscle spasms which lead him to consult a neurologist. He tells the neurologist the following story: "I work cleaning out old wells and mines and other places like that. Well, last Wednesday I was down in a well picking up debris when this guy who worked for the Ace Exterminating Company started to release this gas into the well. They were supposed to kill the rats and bugs that lived at the bottom. Well, they'd been told I would be by either that day or the next to clean out the debris, but they never even looked to see if I was there before they started pumping the gas. They should have seen my other ladder lying on the grass and my van was parked outside. Well, I knew what was happening and I hightailed it up the ladder and chewed them out. Well, I didn't feel so bad immediately, but by that night my hand was shaking and I began to get real severe headaches, so I went to see my doctor but he couldn't see nothing. The headaches have continued; my head feels like it's splitting in two now, and occasionally my muscles will twitch so bad I can't hang on to anything. I had a two minute attack driving over here and I had to stop the car. Can you help me?"

The neurologist was unable to help Kasper, so on the advice of a friend he went to see a physical therapist. The physical therapist, who was not an M.D., was also unable to help Kasper, so on the advice of another friend he went to see a physician who had studied in China and was now a full time acupuncture therapist. Kasper did not believe at all in acupuncture (he thought the photos from China were phonies), but he thought the treatment could not hurt and he was desperate for help. Acupuncture did not help, but Kasper left convinced it was not the fraud he thought it was. This experience led him to become interested in faith healing and non-Western medicine. Eventually he heard of a Dr. Quick, a man with no medical training, who healed by holding his hands above the affected parts and saying prayers in five languages to each of the four winds. Kasper was convinced Quick could help him. He went to Quick, was treated by him and was cured. Before treating Kasper, the physical therapist, the acupuncture specialist and the faith healer all asked him what had caused the problem. Kasper told each of them exactly what he had told the neurologist.

Assume that Kasper sues the Ace Exterminating Company. **May the neurologist, the physical therapist, the acupuncture specialist, or the faith healer testify on Kasper's behalf to any of the information Kasper gave them before they began their respective treatments?**

Problem VI–45. James Drifter has begun seeing a psychiatrist because, "It's time I went to a shrink and straightened myself out." On his tenth visit to his psychiatrist they are discussing one of Drifter's dreams when the psychiatrist says, "I think that you are trying to hide something which you are feeling very guilty about." Drifter replies, "I can't keep anything from you. I robbed the First National Bank two months ago so I would be able to afford these visits. Now I see where some innocent kid is going to take the rap." The next day Drifter takes his own life after first sending the doctor a note saying, "Tell the court what I've told you. The kid is innocent." **May the psychiatrist testify as to what Drifter told him when "the kid" is tried for bank robbery? May Drifter's note to the psychiatrist be introduced?**

Problem VI–46. At the age of sixteen, Ross Cornwell was tragically injured on a railroad turntable, losing both his legs. This occurred on July 3, 1976. On July 31st his parents filed suit on his behalf against the railroad company. On August 5th his older sister, who had just returned from Europe, saw him for the first time since the accident. She asked him how he was and he replied, "Terrible." He proceeded to list all the things he was never going to do again: play baseball, dance, ride, swim, etc. He then said that he also felt constant pain in his toes and in his calf although he knew his legs had been amputated. Finally he confided in his sister, "I am going to kill myself." Ross did not kill himself, and at the trial six months later was getting around quite nicely on a pair of artificial legs. The Cornwells' lawyer seeks to have Ross' sister testify to what Ross told her on her first visit with him, claiming that it is relevant on the damage issue. **May the sister testify to everything Ross said, some of what he said, or none of what he said? Would the situation be any different if the visit had occurred on July 25 rather than August 5th?**

Problem VI–47. Karen Ikeda, born and raised in the Midwest, chose to attend a state school in Florida. During her first year there she sent a series of glowing letters to her parents in which she described the school, the town it is located in and above all the weather.   Among other things, she wrote: "I am never so happy as when I feel the warm wind in my face; I intend never to face another Midwestern winter; I feel at home, and, I don't believe I will ever leave Florida."   Immediately upon graduating from college, Karen left Florida to do graduate work at the University of Michigan.   The state of Florida, which had classified Karen as a resident at the end of her first year, sues to recover the difference between resident and non-resident tuition on the ground that Karen had falsely stated that she had intended to remain a Florida resident when in fact she was only there for the temporary purpose of attending college.   Karen argues that at the time she applied for residency status she did intend to remain in Florida indefinitely.   She seeks to introduce the letters she wrote to her parents during the first year.   **Are any of the statements in these letters hearsay on the purpose for which they are offered?   If they are hearsay, is there any exception available to justify their admission?**

Problem VI–48.   The party was just getting under way when Fred was called to the telephone.   Putting down the phone, Fred went quickly to get his coat.   Sara, his date, looking rather annoyed, said, "Where are you going? The party's just begun."   Fred took Sara into the hall with him and said in a low voice, "Don't tell anyone, but last week I was with Sam when he hooked a van full of cigarettes.   He just called to say he's found a buyer.   I'm going to meet him at the last truck stop on the Carolina Turnpike and we're going to start for New York tonight.   Do you remember Cary?   He moved to New York a while back.   We're going to deliver the cigarettes to him because he has some good connections up there.   I'm sorry to spoil your fun, but I'll bring you back something really nice."   With that Fred left.

Fred and Sam were arrested in a stolen truck three days later in North Carolina, just over the Virginia border.   Fred's story is that the call he received at the party was from an "old flame" asking him to pick her up at a truck stop because her car had broken down.   He says that when he got there he learned that a trucker had helped her fix the car and she had gone off with him.   The trucker who told him this was the partner of the trucker who had gone off with the girl, and he was furious because now he had no relief driver and was already behind schedule.   This trucker offered Fred $500.00 if he would share the driving to New York and drive the empty van back.   Fred said that he agreed to do this, but got out in New York before the cigarettes were delivered, meeting the trucker again at an agreed upon rendezvous point.   Sam claims that he had hitch-hiked to New York several days before to see a rock concert.   He says he was sitting in a bar in New York when he was astonished to see his friend Fred enter.   Quickly he arranged a ride back.   Fred tells the same story of their meeting.   When they were arrested Fred had $600.00 in his wallet and a box containing a $250.00 cashmere woman's sweater from Saks Fifth Avenue.   Sam had $300.00 in his wallet and the stub for a rock concert that had been held on Long Island some three days before Fred received the call at the party.   About $20,000 was found stuffed into a hole in the driver's seat.   Both Fred and Sam disclaim all knowledge of it.   About a week after Fred and Sam were arrested the police raided a drugstore in Manhatten that Cary manages.   They found no sign of the cigarettes or of any other stolen goods. It is indisputable that the truck in which Sam and Fred were found had been hijacked with a load of cigarettes on board.

Fred, Sam and Cary are charged with grand theft, the interstate transportation of a stolen vehicle, selling untaxed cigarettes and conspiring to engage in these activities. **Is Sara's testimony reporting what Fred told her at the party admissible against Fred, Sam or Cary on any of the following issues: (1) whether Fred, Sam, and Cary were members of the same conspiracy; (2) whether Fred had gone to the last truckstop on the Carolina Turnpike; (3) whether Fred had met Sam at this truck stop; (4) whether Sam and Fred drove to New York together; (5) whether the stolen van had been driven across state lines; (6) whether Sam had stolen the van and (7) whether the cigarettes were delivered to Cary?**

Problem VI–49. Osa Johnson was walking through her living room one day when she happened to glance out the picture window and see her neighbor changing a tire on his car. "Well, I guess Smitty's back is better", she remarked to her husband, "He's changing the tire on their car." Martin Johnson merely grunted. He did not look up from the football game he was watching on television. Assume that two weeks after this, Henry (Smitty) Smith's case against the Flagship Trucking Company is brought to trial. Negligence is conceded and the only issue is damages. **In order to refute Henry's claim that he is unable to do even light physical work because of his back condition, may Flagship introduce Martin who will testify to his wife's statement? If Osa testifies to having seen Smitty change a tire, may she be asked by the defendant what she said at the time?**

Problem VI–50. Abe Henderson, the surviving son of billionaire Paul G. Jetty's closest friend, is summoned to see the old man as he lies sick in the hospital. Jetty asks to see Abe alone. They are together for twenty minutes until the visit is broken up by a doctor. Leaving the room, Abe runs into Henrietta Jetty, Paul Jetty's only child and heir at law. "Your father's a remarkable man," Abe tells Henrietta. "Here he's pushing 90 and may be on his deathbed, but he's a complete gentleman and as alert as ever." Henrietta, without answering, brushes past Abe into her father's room. The next day Jetty dies. It turns out that three days before his death Jetty had made a will in which he left his entire fortune to Abe Henderson, the son of his old friend. In his will Jetty states that he feels he provided sufficiently for his daughter while she was alive, that she was not grateful for what he had done, and that he was not going to provide for her upon his death. Henrietta sues to break the will, claiming that her father was not mentally competent to make a will at any time during the last three months of his life. **Can a doctor who overheard what Abe said to Henrietta upon leaving Jetty's room testify to Abe's statement? Would the case for admitting the statement be any different if Jetty had left all his money to the Cancer Society rather than to Abe Henderson?**

---

e. Past Recollection Recorded

Sometimes an individual makes certain observations, records those observations in writing, and then forgets what has been observed and recorded. This often happens to individuals such as inventory takers or accident investigators who routinely record detailed information or numerous observations of a similar sort. It may also occur, given a long lapse of time, even where events are unique and important. When a trial witness has forgotten relevant information, he may be allowed to read his recorded observations to the jury, and the jury may be allowed to treat this recorded recollection as if it were courtroom testimony.[22] The exception invoked to admit the evidence is the exception for past recollection recorded. FRE 803(5), the federal rule admitting recorded recollection, follows the general contours of the common law exception:

Recorded recollection. A memorandum or record concerning a matter about which a witness once had knowledge but now has insufficient recollection to enable him to testify fully and accurately, shown to have been made or adopted by the witness when the matter was fresh in his memory and to reflect that knowledge correctly. If admitted, the memorandum or record may be read into evidence but may not itself be received as an exhibit unless offered by an adverse party.

First the record must relate to something the witness once knew firsthand. Second, the witness' memory of the event described must have faded to the point where he can no longer testify fully and accurately about the event in question. Here the federal rule strikes something of a compromise. The dominant form of the common law rule is that the forgetting must be more complete; it is said that the witness must lack a present recollection of the event. However, some jurisdictions, giving great weight to the minimal memory problems when recollection has been recorded, admit such memoranda without

regard to the maker's memory on the theory that the recording is likely to be more accurate than the maker's memory at the time of trial. Third, the record must be shown to have been made or adopted by the witness when the matter was fresh in his memory. Here the position of the federal rule is somewhat more liberal than that of the common law. The latter required that the memorandum be made at or near the time of the event described. Thus, the admission of a memorandum made several days after the event described, but at a time when the witness is willing to testify that his recollection was still fresh, is more likely to be admitted under the federal rule than at common law. Finally, there is the requirement that the record accurately reflect the witness' knowledge at the time it was written. This requirement is also stated in somewhat stronger terms in the common law cases; the witness, it is said, must vouch for the accuracy of the memorandum. What this means in practice is that the witness must testify either that he remembers making an accurate recording of the event in question although he no longer remembers the facts recorded, or, if the witness has entirely forgotten the situation in which the recording was made, that he is confident he would not have written or adopted some description of the facts unless that description truly described his observations at the time.

These are the basic requirements for the exception. Memoranda or other records may be introduced under this exception even where the witness did not make the record. It is sufficient that the witness adopted the record as a reflection of his knowledge. Thus, if a witness dictated an account of his observations to a third party and checked it for accuracy or read an account prepared by a third party which reported the same facts that the witness ob-

---

22. Some courts treat recorded recollection as incorporated into a witness' courtroom testimony and so presenting no hearsay problems. This is incorrect because a witness cannot be cross-examined about the details of a statement when he no longer remembers the event described in that statement.

served, the account will be admitted as the witness' recorded recollection so long as the other conditions for the exception are met. If the witness dictated an account while the matter was fresh in his mind but without checking the transcription for accuracy, courts will admit the account if the witness testifies that his oral statements accurately reported what he observed and the transcriber testifies that the transcription accurately recounts what he heard the witness say. This is really a hearsay on hearsay problem. The witness' out-of-court statements are hearsay which, if the witness can be believed, accurately portray what he observed. The transcription is hearsay which, if the transcriber can be believed, accurately reports what he heard. The simultaneous transcription is crucial to this extension of the past recollection recorded exception, since an important justification for this exception is the fact that there is little danger that the witness' words will be reported incorrectly. Most courts do not allow one witness to testify orally to a report of another, even if the other swears his report was accurate when made and the testifying witness states that he has a clear memory of what the other said.

Several rules peculiar to writings apply when the exception for recorded recollection is invoked. The "best evidence rule" [23] requires that the memorandum introduced be the original memorandum unless the proponent can show that the original is unavailable through no fault of his own. In most jurisdictions, the memorandum is treated as an ordinary item of documentary evidence and may be taken to the jury room when deliberations begin. The drafters of the federal rule thought there was no reason to give recorded recollection potentially greater impact than ordinary testimony, so FRE 803(5) provides that the memorandum may not be offered as an exhibit unless the adverse party requests it.

There is no single strong justification for the exception for recorded recollection, but the case for the exception is strong when one considers the variety of safeguards involved. The requirement of a recording ensures that the declarant's language will be accurately transmitted to the trier of fact. The requirement that the record be made when memory is fresh avoids problems of forgetting. The declarant's presence as a witness allows the attorneys to clear up ambiguities in the language of the hearsay statement and gives the fact finder some sense of the declarant's integrity and an opportunity to evaluate his capacity to observe.

This exception is also unusual in that the declarant must be both present and, in a sense, unavailable at the same time. The declarant must be in court to testify to the circumstances which qualify the declaration for admissibility as past recollection recorded. On the other hand, he must lack a clear memory of the event described, so in effect he is not available to be examined about it.

The exception for past recollection recorded should not be confused with the use of recorded information to refresh memory. A witness whose memory of an event is hazy may be given a copy of a statement, a picture, a map or some other item to aid recall. If the witness' memory is jogged by the information, he is allowed to relate his refreshed recollection of the event. In theory there is no hearsay problem. Since the witness is testifying to a current, albeit revived, memory, he may be cross-examined on the story he has told. In practice, the witness' recollection often appears remarkably similar to the information contained in the item used to freshen his memory, and one sometimes wonders whether the witness' memory is not in fact limited to what he has just read. This impression is enhanced in courts where the

---

23. See our discussion of this rule in Chapter Eleven.

witness is allowed to jog his memory throughout his testimony by consulting the memorandum used for refreshment.

A few courts do not allow memory to be refreshed except from memoranda which meet the test for past recollection recorded. Prevailing practice is to the contrary. Since witnesses with refreshed memory purport to be speaking from present recollection, the information used to revive their recollection never enters into evidence, is not seen by the jury, and is not hearsay. Thus, courts generally place few restrictions on the kinds of items which may be used to revive recollection. There need be no guarantee that the information is reliable, it need not have been prepared at or near the time of the events described, the witness is not required to have been involved in its preparation and he is not required to have seen it before trial. Whatever is used to revive recollection must, however, be shown to opposing counsel and may be used by him as a basis for cross-examination. In the extreme case where it appears that the item could not or has not refreshed recollection, the testimony of the witness may be barred by the court or, if already given, stricken from the record.[24]

f. Business Records

i. *The Shopbook Rule*

Historically, business records, despite their hearsay nature, have been admissible under two distinct exceptions. The first, the "shopbook rule," is rooted in the early English custom which allowed a merchant doing business on account to enter his books into evidence to prove the defendant owed him money. This exception, as it developed in this country, was justified on the ground of necessity. In the 18th and early 19th centuries the common law barred interested parties from testifying on their own behalf. Had there not been a hearsay exception for shopbooks, merchants might have had no way to establish legitimate debts. The weight given to necessity as a justification is evident in those jurisdictions which would not apply the shopbook exception if the merchant kept a clerk. Here the need for shopbook evidence was diminished because the clerk, a technically uninterested party, could testify to the debt. The fact that necessity was the main justification for the exception does not mean that the courts were not concerned with reliability. Indeed, the self-serving nature of shopbook entries caused considerable concern. To ensure reliability, different jurisdictions required one or more of the following guarantees: (1) a "suppletory oath" taken by the merchant as to the justness of his accounts, (2) inspection by the court to determine if the books were fairly kept in the regular course of business, (3) testimony that the merchant kept honest books, and (4) proof apart from the books that at least some portion of the goods charged to an account were actually delivered.[25]

24. **Counsel may refresh a witness' recollection in private before he takes the stand. In these circumstances opposing counsel is unlikely to know that the witness' recollection has been revived by reading certain information. If counsel does learn that recollection has been revived, courts probably have discretion to order that those memory aids used by the adversary be turned over to counsel for inspection and for use in cross-examination. However, such orders are rarely entered. FRE 612 provides that one party can see material used by a witness to prepare for testifying in** court **"if the court in its discretion determines it is necessary in the interests of justice." The Advisory Committee that first drafted the rule wanted to go beyond this limited position and provide the same right to examine documents used to refresh recollection before trial as exists with respect to documents used at trial. The Congress rejected this approach.**

25. **In some jurisdictions the exception was further limited in that the transactions could not exceed a certain value and the books could not be used to prove loans or goods and services furnished under special**

ii. Regularly Kept Records

The second exception admits the regularly kept records of business establishments. Guarantees of reliability are found in three basic requirements: "(a) the entries must be original entries made in the routine of business, (b) the entries must have been made upon the personal knowledge of the recorder or of someone reporting to him, [and] (c) the entries must have been made at or near the time of the transaction recorded." [26] It has been argued that where an entry is made in the course of a business routine, the routine itself lends a guarantee of reliability since one is not likely to develop a routine of erroneous recording. Business records are also likely to be reliable because customers can be expected to complain about errors, and the firm can be expected to discipline those who make erroneous entries in disregard of the business routine. [27] At common law this exception was also rooted in necessity, for it could only be invoked where the recorder and any informants were first shown to be unavailable.

iii. Statutory Reform

The common law exception for regularly kept records might have been gradually liberalized by the courts to meet the exigencies of modern business practice and to take account of various non-business situations where routine records are as likely to be as reliable as records kept in business. Some courts moved in this direction, but others did not. The aspects of the common law exception which caused the most difficulty were those which were particularly unsuited to large-scale businesses. Chief among these were the requirement that each entry be qualified in court by the person who made it and the related requirement that all employees transmitting information to the entrant be called as witnesses if the entrant did not have firsthand knowledge of the matter recorded. These requirements could only be avoided by evidence that the relevant persons were unavailable. [28]

The impracticability of these requirements is obvious. In a large business there might be literally dozens of bookkeepers responsible for making entries in a single account. Dozens of other individuals might be involved in transmitting the information recorded in a single entry. Indeed, in a business where numerous individuals report or record similar information there might be no way to determine who among a group of employees was responsible for the entry of interest. The New York case of Rathborne v. Hatch [29] provides an example of the impracticability of the common law requirements. In Rathborne a broker's books were offered to prove the price at which certain shares of stock were purchased. The book entry

contract or other debts not charged to an open account. The first limitation probably reflects judicial suspicion of the self-serving nature of entries in tradesmen's books while the second reflects the necessity principle, since other transactions were likely to be provable by contracts or receipts apart from the tradesmen's books. As used in the text accompanying this note, the word "necessity" signifies that courts thought they had a need for the rule because the evidence it admits might not be available absent an exception. In truth, however, they could have eliminated one form of necessity by changing the competency rules, as they subsequently did. Another form of necessity would have remained, i.e., the impossibility of remembering the details of business transactions without reference to records. This is the necessity that most concerns us today.

26. McCormick § 306, at 720.

27. 5 Wigmore § 1522.

28. The fact that individuals who participated in making the record were available to appear did not mean that the unavailability requirement of the common law exception was not met. Usually the witnesses would have forgotten the transaction in question and so were unavailable to testify to it. They were brought to court to testify to their usual business practices. Note the substantial overlap with the exception for past recollection recorded.

29. 80 App.Div. 115, 80 N.Y.S. 347 (1903).

was based on a report from the broker's floor member to one of a group of tele-phone boys responsible for relaying the information to the bookkeeper. The floor member testified that he had accurately re-layed the information to the telephone boys, but because the telephone boys were neither called to testify that they transmit-ted the information correctly nor shown to be unavailable, the book entry was not ad-mitted.

Difficulties of this sort coupled with the restrictive interpretations some courts gave to the term "business" generated consid-erable pressure for reform. Interest in reform led to two model statutes, the Commonwealth Fund Act, first proposed in 1927, and the Uniform Business Records as Evidence Act, drafted in 1933. Most states have adopted one or the other of these acts. While the two statutes differ some-what in language, they have been inter-preted to mean about the same thing. In addition, many states which purport to fol-low the common law have interpreted the common law so that it is generally con-sistent with these acts.[30]

These statutes read as follows:

Commonwealth Fund Act

Any writing or record, whether in the form of an entry in a book or otherwise, made as a memorandum or record of any act, transaction, occurrence or event shall be admissible in evidence in proof of said act, transaction, occurrence or event, if the trial judge shall find that it was made in the regular course of any business, and that it was the regular course of such business to make such memorandum or record at the time of such act, transac-tion, occurrence or event or within a reasonable time thereafter. All other circumstances of the making of such writing or record, including lack of per-sonal knowledge by the entrant or maker, may be shown to affect its weight, but they shall not affect its admissibility. The term business shall include business, profession, occupation and calling of every kind.

Uniform Business Records as
Evidence Act

"§ 1. Definition: The term 'business' shall include every kind of business profession, occupation, calling or oper-ation of institutions, whether carried on for profit or not.

"§ 2. Business Record. A record of an act, condition or event, shall, in so far as relevant, be competent evidence if the custodian or other qualified witness tes-tifies to its identity and the mode of its preparation, and if it was made in the regular course of business, at or near the time of the act, condition or event, and if, in the opinion of the court, the sources of information, method and time of preparation were such as to justify its admission." 9A U.L.A. 506 (1965).

The first thing to note is that both stat-utes eliminate the common law require-ment that all individuals who prepared or furnished recorded information be in some way accounted for. The Uniform Act does this by providing that only the custodian or other qualified witness need be called to establish the foundation for the record. The Commonwealth Fund Act accom-plishes the same result by placing no re-strictions on who may qualify a record and by specifically indicating that records shall not be rendered inadmissible because they were made by individuals who lacked per-sonal knowledge of the events recorded. Both acts eliminate the unavailability re-quirement, since neither conditions ad-missibility on the absence of witnesses who can testify to the events recorded. Also, both acts define business very broadly to include businesses, professions, occupa-tions, and callings. Institutions are spe-cifically included in the definition of busi-

---

30. Laughlin, Business Entries and the Like, 46 Iowa L.Rev. 276 (1961).

ness under the Uniform Act, a result which Commonwealth Fund jurisdictions reach by interpretation of the terms "business" or "calling."

iv. Business Duty and Informants

Two important cases interpreting the Commonwealth Fund Act set limits on the expansive language of that act. These cases have generally been followed by courts admitting business records. The first, Johnson v. Lutz,[31] involved an accident report prepared by a police officer based on the statements of those present at the scene of the accident. Despite the Act's language that the lack of personal knowledge by the entrant or maker should affect weight and not admissibility, the New York Court of Appeals held that the record was inadmissible when offered for the truth of the statements therein recorded. They interpreted the "lack of personal knowledge" language as applying only where those providing information incorporated in the record had a business duty to transmit information to the entrant or maker. Although some commentators have criticized this decision as imposing limitations not found in the language of the Act, others, including the authors, believe the decision was both wise and in accord with the intended meaning of the Act. The language, which Johnson is claimed by some to contravene, was designed to eliminate the inconvenience of accounting for all employees who had played a part in transmitting the information recorded. This is justified because the same guarantees of reliability which apply to the person making the record apply to all employees in the chain of information. All are presumed to be acting in accord with some routine and all are subject to the sanctions of superiors for mistakes in transmission. These safeguards do not apply to statements made by declarants in a non-business capacity. The statement of one who observed an accident would not

be admissible if testified to by someone at the scene. There is no good reason why it should be more readily admitted if recorded in a police report. If the statement qualifies under some other exception to the hearsay rule, prevailing practice allows the report to be introduced to prove that the statement was made and allows the statement to be received under the applicable exception. For example, if the statements reported by the officer in Johnson were made by the party against whom the report was offered, the report would be admitted as a business record and the reported statements as admissions.

v. Regular Course of Business

The second major case, Palmer v. Hoffman,[32] arose out of a grade crossing accident in which the plaintiff was injured and his wife killed. The defendant railroad sought to introduce statements made by the train's engineer (who had died before trial) to his superior in the presence of an official from the Massachusetts Public Utilities Commission. The question facing the court was whether the engineer's statements were made "in the regular course" of business within the meaning of the federal statute (essentially the Commonwealth Fund Act). The railroad argued that it was part of their regular business to investigate accidents and take the statements of employees involved, but the Supreme Court refused to admit the statements. "Their primary utility," wrote Justice Douglas, "is in litigating, not in railroading."[33]

From one perspective the railroad's argument is clearly correct. A railroad could no more stay in business without investigating its accidents than it could without maintaining its locomotives. Nevertheless, there is considerable sense in the Court's position. Accident reports are not "typical of entries made systematically or as a matter of routine to record events or

31. 253 N.Y. 124, 170 N.E. 517 (1930).
32. 318 U.S. 109 (1943).

33. Id. at 114.

occurrences, to reflect transactions with others, or to provide internal controls."[34] Hence, they do not share the trustworthiness associated with established routine. In addition, it is not clear that inaccuracy in reporting accidents will be punished by the business since whatever exonerates the employee limits the grounds on which the company may be held liable.

The Court of Appeals had reached the same result as the Supreme Court, but the majority had justified exclusion largely on the basis of the self-serving nature of the engineer's statements.[35] This rationale has been criticized on the ground that many of the statements in a party's books are self-serving in character.[36] But the critics miss the point: debts recorded in a party's books do serve that party's interests, but unless suit to collect that debt is contemplated the party has no interest in overstating the amount owed. The situation is different when litigation appears likely. At this point the need to present one's case in the most favorable light is obvious, and even basically honest individuals may be tempted to distort evidence.[37] Moreover, in any large scale business, the benefits of misreporting accounts accrue to the company and not to the record keeper. However, when an employee fills out an accident report he has at least two reasons to attempt to exonerate himself. First, victims of the accident may choose to sue him personally. Absent some privilege, his report, if discovered, may be introduced against him as an admission. Second, an employee's job may be in jeopardy if the company attributes the accident to his carelessness.

From what we have said, you can see that we favor the *Palmer* approach generally.

But we deem it inadvisable to set up hard and fast rules. Knowing the dangers presented by self-serving records, courts should be able to ascertain when the records are reliable enough, given the need for them, to warrant admission.

Most jurisdictions follow Palmer v. Hoffman when a business attempts to introduce accident reports or other self-serving records made at a time when litigation appeared likely. Courts differ, however, in the seriousness with which they take the Supreme Court's rationale. Absent some motive to misrepresent, records made for proper business purposes usually will not be excluded from evidence simply because the business rarely has the occasion to make such records. Most courts feel that an activity may be in the regular course of business without being so frequent as to be routine.

vi. *Opinions in Business Records*

Where an opinion is incorporated in a business record the court will examine the nature of the opinion to determine admissibility. The more speculative the opinion, the greater the probability of exclusion. Problems with opinions frequently arise when parties seek to introduce diagnoses contained in hospital records. So long as a diagnosis reflects a standard expert judgment based on a set of reasonably objective criteria, courts have little trouble in admitting it. A diagnosis of a fractured elbow or appendicitis would be admitted in most, if not all, jurisdictions. A court is less likely to admit a diagnosis when the diagnostic criteria are less certain, and it is unlikely to admit opinions which go beyond diagnosis into the etiology or prognosis of a condition. Faced

---

34. Id. at 113.

35. Hoffman v. Palmer, 129 F.2d 976 (2d Cir. 1942).

36. Laughlin, supra note 30, at 276 and 289. See also Judge Clark's dissent in Hoffman v. Palmer: "I submit that there is hardly a grocer's account book which could not be excluded on that basis." [The basis re-

ferred to is "a powerful motive to misrepresent."] 129 F.2d 976, 1002 (2d Cir. 1942).

37. As the extract from Stewart, reproduced supra in the text accompanying note 91, indicates, a person may not even be aware of the way in which his interests have affected his memory and perceptions.

with an entry on a patient's chart which reads, "Diagnosis: substantial lung damage resulting from black lung disease due to working in a poorly ventilated coal mine," most courts would admit the entry to show lung damage, some would admit it to show black lung disease, but few, if any, would admit it to show that the disease was caused by poor working conditions.

Professor Laughlin has suggested that, "If the person making the entry could have testified to his opinion, a record of that opinion should be admissible." [38]   This suggestion makes considerable sense when lay opinions are recorded, since admissible lay opinion pertains to evaluations on which most people would not differ or to events which cannot readily be described in more concrete terms.   However, it is less satisfactory where expert opinion is involved because the examination of experts is designed to do more than relate facts or illuminate hearsay dangers.   Expert testimony should elucidate the bases of the expert's reasoning and indicate the way in which different facts affect the expert's ultimate conclusion.   Cross-examination is a test of expertise and of the thoroughness and care with which the expert approached the problem set for him. Without some understanding of how the expert reached his opinion, the jury is often unable to appreciate the full implications of the facts it finds.   It is also unable to evaluate the reasonableness of the expert's opinion vis-a-vis the opinions of experts giving conflicting testimony.   In these circumstances it seems that the prevailing view is a sensible one.

vii.   Computer Records

Records stored on computers also pose special problems. They require a more technical foundation than the typical business record and may necessitate providing the opposing counsel with programming information and/or the opportunity to run tests on the proponent's machine. In addition, there are technical objections which can be made to the introduction of computer print-outs as business records. The print-outs themselves are often prepared specifically for the litigation in question, and the information reported in the print-outs may not have been entered into the computer at or near the time of the transactions to which the information pertains. These objections are generally dismissed by courts, and properly so. So long as the information on which a print-out is based was entered before the prospect of litigation arose, the fact that the print-out is prepared for use in court should not be disturbing. The print-out simply reproduces stored information in a form which humans can appreciate. Absent intentional fraud, which would require the cooperation of an expert programmer, there is little reason to be suspicious of the reproduction.[39] The time at which data is entered on the computer is unimportant if the data accurately reproduces records made at or near the time of the transaction.

Perhaps the most disquieting aspect of routinely admitting computer print-outs as

---

38.   Laughlin, supra note 30, at 304.

39.   **One might be suspicious of any programming changes occurring after the prospects of litigation arose. A computer can be ordered to select or present information in many different ways, some of which may be more favorable to a party than others. Selective changes motivated by the prospect of litigation could most easily be checked by running earlier versions of the program on the proponent's data base. Also an expert may be able to appreciate what a relatively uncomplicated**

program can or cannot do. It is possible that a party might erase from a computer's memory information which it believes would hurt its case. In one sense this is no different from removing data from business files. However, it would probably be much easier to remove records from a computer without a trace, since a computer print-out or even a file of stored data will not show the kinds of gaps which might be apparent if one tried to destroy a business entry. We offer you a sample trial involving computer records in Chapter Eleven.

business records is the problem of human error. Mistakes made in entering data into a computer are not corrected by the machine. Suppose, for example, a customer's bill for $10.10 is accidentally entered into the computer as $101.00. If the store's copy of the bill is then destroyed, the customer, unless he has been careful to keep a copy of the bill, may find that it is his word against the computer. The decision to admit computer records in these circumstances places the burden of keeping original records on individuals rather than organizations. This seems unfair when the errors to be avoided are the organization's. Yet an important reason why organizations store data in computers is the high cost of storing papers. Perhaps businesses should be required to keep the original records of any transactions until their dealings indicate that there is no dispute about the accuracy of their computer entries. Only then would the computer entry be admissible in lieu of the original. Do you find this a sensible compromise?

viii. Absence of an Entry

Where as a matter of business routine a particular entry could be expected in a business record if an event occurred, most courts will allow the absence of an entry to be shown as evidence that the event did not occur. Thus, in a dispute over payment of a debt, the fact that no payment has been entered in the creditor's books will be admitted as evidence that the debtor did not pay. Where hospital records do not note that a patient suffered a heart stoppage, the absence of such notation would be admitted as evidence that the patient's heart never stopped while he was in the hospital.

ix. Other Statutes—the Federal Rule

In addition to the basic business records exception there are other statutes affecting the admissibility of business records in certain jurisdictions. Special statutes are particularly likely with respect to bank records, hospital records, or corporate records generally. These should be consulted when the records of a covered organization are involved. Also some states retain versions of the shopbook exception on their statute books. It is difficult to imagine a situation where a shopbook entry would not be admissible under either the exception for business records or that for past recollection recorded, but where such statutes still exist they may serve as alternative grounds of admissibility.

Until the Federal Rules of Evidence were enacted, the Federal Business Record Act was modeled on the Commonwealth Fund Act. FRE 803(6) replaces the rule modeled on this act. FRE 803(7) applies where the lack of an entry is offered to prove the nonoccurrence of some matter. The drafters saw fit to include the latter exception, although it seems that the lack of an entry would not be hearsay as that term is defined in the Federal Rules.

FRE 803(6):

  Records of regularly conducted activity. A memorandum, report, record, or data compilation, in any form, of acts, events, conditions, opinions, or diagnoses, made at or near the time by, or from information transmitted by, a person with knowledge, if kept in the course of a regularly conducted business activity, and if it was the regular practice of that business activity to make the memorandum, report, record, or data compilation, all as shown by the testimony of the custodian or other qualified witness, unless the source of information or the method or circumstances of preparation indicate lack of trustworthiness. The term "business" as used in this paragraph includes business, institution, association, profession, occupation, and calling of every kind, whether or not conducted for profit.

FRE 803(7):

  Absence of entry in records kept in accordance with the provisions of para-

graph (6). Evidence that a matter is not included in the memoranda reports, records, or data compilations, in any form, kept in accordance with the provisions of paragraph (6), to prove the nonoccurrence or nonexistence of the matter, if the matter was of a kind of which a memorandum, report, record, or data compilation was regularly made and preserved, unless the sources of information or other circumstances indicate lack of trustworthiness.[40]

It appears that the drafters of the federal rules wished to codify what are presently the most liberal practices with respect to business entries. Data compilations are specifically made admissible, leaving no question concerning the status of computer records; business is defined to include institutions and associations as well as businesses, occupations, professions, and callings of every kind;[41] and opinions and diagnoses are specifically declared admissible. This last change may lead the federal courts to adopt a more liberal attitude in admitting diagnoses and opinions than that which has generally prevailed. Where records are based on the statements of informants, the rule of Johnson v. Lutz applies and the record is admissible only if the statement was transmitted as part of a regular business activity. The Supreme Court's argument in Palmer v. Hoffman is not, however, fully accepted. Absence of routine should render records inadmissible under this exception only where the lack of routine indicates lack of trustworthiness. Positive motives to misrepresent are more likely to result in exclusion since they strongly suggest a lack of trustworthiness.

g. Public Records and Reports

There is at common law an exception for official records and reports much like the exception for business records. The written report of a public official is admissible if the official had personal knowledge of the matter that is the subject of the report and an official duty to report on it. Some courts have used this exception to admit evaluative reports, that is reports of factual conclusions reached following an investigation, but this has not been the usual practice. However, various statutes make the results of specific evaluations admissible. At the federal level, for example, the findings of the Secretary of Agriculture are admissible as prima facie evidence of the true grade of grain, and bills of health that are prepared for ships embarking from foreign ports to the United States are, if properly executed by a consular official or other United States officer, admissible to show the sanitary history and condition of the vessel. As these examples indicate,

---

40. As the advisory committee recognizes, this exception is probably not necessary, for the failure to record something in the ordinary course of business will almost never be done with an assertive intent and so under the definition of FRE 801 the absence of a notation in a business record would not be hearsay. Where one specifically fails to record information intending to assert its nonexistence the absence of a record is hearsay, but the calculated nature of the omission could suggest that the decision to admit the information is not trustworthy. If so, 803(7) will be unavailing. In other instances, the absence of an entry may be an ordinary trustworthy declaration that nothing happened. If so, it is hearsay but admissible under FRE 803(7).

41. Under the version of this exception which was prepared by the drafters and submitted to the Congress by the Supreme Court, admissible records were not limited to those of businesses or institutions but included all records made in the course of a regularly conducted activity so long as the other conditions of the exception were met. The House of Representatives changed this so that the definition of business was generally in accord with the Commonwealth Fund Act. The Senate favored the original version and the conference compromised with language that made it clear that the records of institutions and associations were included under this exception. What do you suppose the House was worried about? Does the compromise alleviate any reasonable concerns of the House?

statutes of this sort are usually narrowly focused.

FRE 803(8), the federal rule's hearsay exception for public records and reports, makes two important changes in prior law. First, evaluative reports are now generally admissible except when offered against the defendant in a criminal case. Those statutes which specifically authorize the admission of evaluative reports are no longer necessary except insofar as they allow evaluative reports to be used by the government in criminal cases.[42] Second, the previous federal rule, codified at 28 U.S.C. 1733, applied only to the reports of federal agencies. FRE 803(8) applies to the records of all public offices and agencies, state or federal, and has been interpreted by some courts to include the public records and reports of the agencies of foreign governments. The justifications for the rule, the assumptions that public records will be reliable because public officials will perform their duties properly and that the records will be necessary because officials will be unlikely to remember what they record, are presumed to apply abroad as well as at home.

These changes have made FRE 803(8) one of the most useful and widely used exceptions to the hearsay rule. The government is in the business of producing documents. Government agents investigate and report on a wide variety of incidents, many of which are likely triggers to litigation. When there is stock fraud, the S.E.C. will investigate. After an airplane crash, the F.A.A. will have someone on the scene immediately. Numerous agencies will respond to complaints of job discrimination, and the ordinary traffic accident will inevitably generate at least one police report. In some instances statutes that impose reporting requirements or authorize investigations provide that information col-

lected or facts discovered will not be admissible in evidence. Even where statutes do not prohibit disclosure the results of governmental investigations were at one time often held confidential by the investigating agencies. Now, however, many agencies have changed their policies and the Freedom of Information Act may give one access to material that an agency does not wish to reveal. Access to governmental reports is of great value to the litigator because the government's investigative resources far outstrip those of most clients, and public investigations often begin long before lawyers are mobilized. In addition the apparent neutrality of governmental investigators means that their factual findings are likely to carry great weight in litigation between private parties.

Now that we have discussed the rule generally, we should look at its specific provisions. FRE 803(8) provides:

(8) Public records and reports. Records, reports, statements, or data compilations, in any form, of public offices or agencies, setting forth (A) the activities of the office or agency, or (B) matters observed pursuant to duty imposed by law as to which matters there was a duty to report, excluding, however, in criminal cases matters observed by police officers and other law enforcement personnel, or (C) in civil actions and proceedings and against the Government in criminal cases, factual findings resulting from an investigation made pursuant to authority granted by law, unless the sources of information or other circumstances indicate lack of trustworthiness.

Subsection A is orthodox and noncontroversial. An agency's report of its own activities may be used to show that the activities occurred. For example, the re-

---

42. As we shall see in Chapter Seven the use of evaluative reports against criminal defendants may create problems under the confrontation clause. In addition courts may reinterpret specific statutes that render evaluative reports admissible in the light of FRE 803(8).

port of a building inspector that he inspected a house located at 901 Kaplan Boulevard could be introduced to show that the inspection occurred.

Subsection B captures the essence of the common law exception. The observations of public officials are admissible so long as they were made in the line of duty and there was a duty to report them. If the building inspector observed a crack in the foundation of the house at 901 Kaplan and reported this, the report would be admissible as proof of a structural defect. If, however, the inspector had observed a marihuana plant growing in the kitchen of the house, his report would not be admissible to show that the occupant of the house was growing marihuana because the inspector had no duty to report observations unrelated to the building's condition.

Suppose the building inspector had made his report orally to a supervisor and the supervisor had not written it down. Under the literal language of FRE 803(8) it might appear that the supervisor could testify to what the inspector told her because the exception extends to statements. However, nowhere in the legislative history of the rule is there any suggestion that it will not require a writing, and one can argue that an official's statement is not the statement of an office or agency until it is written down and made part of the agency's record. Under this analysis the supervisor could not testify to the inspector's oral statement, but if the supervisor had written down the inspector's statement as part of her official duties, the supervisor's report would be admissible. As with

business records, the writing avoids reporting errors and memory problems.[43]

Section B does not apply in criminal cases to matters observed by police officers and law enforcement personnel. This exception was added on the floor of the House of Representatives largely to ensure that criminal defendants would not be tried on the basis of police reports. Contrast this language with that of section C which protects criminal defendants by providing that factual findings resulting from investigations are admissible in criminal cases only against the government. There is no obvious reason for the difference except that the language of section C was drafted by the advisory committee subject to criticism and revision while the language of section B was first offered in a House debate. The House was concerned only with the use of reports against defendants. It could have achieved this goal with an exception that did not turn on whether the case was criminal. Some courts have refused to read the exclusion of section B literally.[44] Relying on legislative history, they have interpreted B's exclusion of reported observations in criminal cases so as to conform with section C and to allow defendants to introduce police reports on their own behalf.

There is one additional problem with the Section B exclusion. Namely, a court must determine who are "other law enforcement personnel." In one case building inspectors were held not to be law enforcement personnel, in part because the maximum penalty for violating the building code was a fine.[45] In another case a

43. One district court, sitting without a jury, has focused on the word "statement" to admit the *testimony* of a postal inspector who had conducted an investigation into an alleged lottery scheme. The exception was not needed to the extent that the investigator had personal knowledge of admissible evidence, but in this case several questions asked of the inspector called for hearsay answers. Since the specific questions are not reported, one cannot tell whether the exception was cor-

rectly applied assuming that it applies to testimony in the first instance. The exception appears also to have been used to circumvent opinion rule problems, although the court does not recognize this. United States Postal Service v. Thielbar, 5 Fed.Evid.Rep. 1106 (N.D. Iowa, 1980).

44. See, e.g., United States v. Smith, 521 F.2d 957 (D.C.Cir. 1975).

45. United States v. Hansen, 583 F.2d 325 (7th Cir. 1978).

Customs Service chemist who had identified a white powder as heroin was held to fall within the scope of the ban because Customs Service chemists "are without question, important participants in the prosecutorial effort."[46]

Section C is the most controversial portion of FRE 803(8) because it opens the door to so much evidence. In construing this section one must first determine what is meant by "factual findings." Had our building inspector filed a report saying, "Because of its cracked foundation, leaking roof and rusting furnace the house at 901 Kaplan is in violation of the building code," would the assertion that the house is in violation count as a factual finding or would it be better characterized as an "opinion"? "Opinion" is a word which because of its inclusion in FRE 803(6) is in FRE 803(8) conspicuous by its absence. In Chapter One we discuss the difficulty of separating fact from opinion. Here it is impossible. A factual finding, unless it is a simple report of something observed, is an opinion as to what more basic facts imply. The building inspector is of the opinion that a house with a cracked foundation, leaking roof, and rusting furnace cannot be in compliance with the building code. He has found as a matter of fact that the house at 901 Kaplan is in violation of the code.

Sometimes when it is difficult to know the precise scope that should be accorded an evidence rule, legislative history provides a good guide as to the spirit in which it should be interpreted. Here, however, the legislative history is confused. In the House of Representatives the Committee on

the Judiciary noted its intention that "the phrase 'factual findings' be strictly construed and that evaluations or opinions contained in public reports shall not be admissible under this Rule." The Senate Committee on the Judiciary, noting the House's comment, took "strong exception to this limited understanding of the application of the rule." The Conference did not address the matter.

In our view the Senate has the better of this dispute. Not only is it impossible to separate factual findings from opinions, but, as the Senate points out, the final clause of FRE 803(8) bars factual findings that appear untrustworthy. Courts have interpreted the words "factual findings" with different degrees of liberality, but it appears that the Senate's position is prevailing. Thus, FRE 803(8)(C) has been used in a school desegregation suit to admit the finding by an HEW Hearing Examiner that a particular school had been established and maintained as a black school for segregative purposes.[47] It has been used to admit a report prepared by the Naval Rework Facility which, based upon an engineering analysis of airplane wreckage, reached conclusions about the cause of a crash.[48] And it has been used in a civil rights action to admit a finding by a state human rights agency that the plaintiff's allegation of racially motivated job termination was not supported by the facts.[49] These precedents, however, might not serve to admit the building inspector's report. For in stating that the house at 901 Kaplan is in violation of the building code the inspector is determining the legal implications of what he observed.[50] The courts are reluctant to characterize legal conclu-

---

46. United States v. Oates, 560 F.2d 45, 68 (2d Cir. 1977).

47. United States v. School District of Ferndale, 577 F.2d 1339 (6th Cir. 1978).

48. Fraley v. Rockwell International Corp., 470 F.Supp. 1264 (S.D.Ohio 1979).

49. Theobold v. Botein, Hays, Sklar & Herzberg, 465 F.Supp. 609 (S.D.N.Y. 1979).

50. However, in this situation the characterization of defects as code violations might be so ministerial or routine that a court would allow the entire report in. Note that the report is simply evidence of a code violation or, for that matter, of a rusted furnace; it is not dispositive of the matter recorded. Also it could not under FRE 803(8)(B) or (C) be admitted against a defendant in a criminal case,

sions as "factual findings," so in admitting reports under FRE 803(C) they often excise judgments of law. Thus, if an official investigation into the cause of an airplane crash concludes that the crash resulted from pilot error, the report would probably be admissible under the public records exception. But if the report went on to say that the pilot was negligent when approaching the runway, that portion would probably be excluded.

The courts are also reading the word "investigation" broadly. Administrative hearings resulting in factual findings have been treated by many courts as investigations under this rule. And there need not be a duty to investigate for a report to be admissible. It is sufficient that the investigation be authorized by law; the actual decision to investigate may have been a matter of administrative discretion.

It is quite clear that Section C admits findings that are based in part on hearsay. There are two levels at which hearsay may occur. First, a government agent may report to some other agent who prepares an official report. The analogy to business records makes it clear that this should pose no problems even if the final report quotes the first agent's statements. Second, the agency's conclusions may be based in whole or in part on the statements of those who had no duty to talk to government agents. Thus, the finding that a plane crash was due to pilot error may be based in part on the statements of those who saw the plane hit the ground. The findings of a hearing examiner may be based entirely on testimony presented to him, testimony which would be hearsay if offered by transcript in a subsequent action. The fact that a report is based on the statements of those with no official duty to speak does not mean that the factual findings it contains will be inadmissible. But hearsay statements included in such reports will typi-

cally be excluded even though they are arguably relevant for the non-hearsay purpose of showing the basis for the agency's findings. Thus, a woman's statement that she saw a plane hit the ground at a thirty degree angle cannot be introduced to show the angle at which the plane hit the ground and is likely to be excised from the report given the jury no matter what its influence on the agent who investigated the crash. The hearing transcript which accompanies the findings of a hearing examiner will be similarly excluded.

Although a hearsay basis does not render the factual findings in an official report inadmissible *per se*, it may make them vulnerable to exclusion under the trustworthiness requirement imposed by the last clause of FRE 803(8). In interpreting this clause the courts are likely to look at all the information which supports the factual findings. If, for example, an airplane accident investigator concludes on the basis of the distribution of wreckage, communications with the control tower and the observations of bystanders that a crash was due to pilot error, the report will not be excluded just because part of the evidence on which the investigator relied is, in the context of the current litigation, hearsay. However, if a bystander had said, "The plane came in so low it was clear that the pilot had made a mistake," and the finding of pilot error were based entirely on this statement, the report would almost certainly be rejected because an official imprimatur does not increase the reliability of out-of-court statements. A similar decision might be reached where a factual finding was supported by non-hearsay as well as hearsay evidence, but the hearsay was important to the final conclusion and came from an untrustworthy source. Where a factual finding is based on an evaluation of the conflicting out-of-court statements [51] of two parties and their wit-

so confrontation clause problems would not arise.

51. Note that the statements are "out-of-court" and hence hearsay only in the con-

nesses, as is often the case in an administrative hearing, the fact that the examiner heard the statements in a court-like setting and could evaluate conflicting stories should make the examiner's findings sufficiently trustworthy to be admitted.

The placement of the final clause of FRE 803(8) creates an ambiguity in the rule. It is not clear whether the trustworthiness requirement modifies all three sections of FRE 803(8) or just section C. From a grammatical standpoint one may argue that if the clause were intended to modify just section C the comma after the word "law" would not be necessary. The stronger argument, however, is on policy grounds. If there is reason to believe that an official record or report is untrustworthy, an important justification for the exception (the presumed reliability of official actions) is removed and the record should not be admitted. This is consistent with the treatment that would be given to similar information found in business records.

Ordinarily the hearsay exceptions operate without reference to each other. If a statement is admissible under one exception it is not excluded simply because it does not quite meet the conditions of another exception. It should be obvious that many of the records which would qualify under FRE 803(8) would also be admissible under FRE 803(6). Some courts have held, however, that by enacting a separate

exception for public records and reports Congress meant to preclude recourse to the exception for business records when public records were offered. This is important in criminal cases. FRE 803(8)(B) bars the observations of law enforcement personnel in criminal cases and FRE 803(8)(C) protects defendants from the introduction of factual findings resulting from investigations. FRE 803(6) contains no such limitations. The better procedure is to interpret the rules together, but not to read one as barring resort to the other. Thus, if a police report describes the suspicious behavior of a criminal defendant, a prosecutor should not be able to avoid Congress' specific judgment on the one occasion when they considered the admissibility of such evidence by offering it as a business record. On the other hand, if the police record reports a routine matter which when recorded had no obvious relevance to any criminal action (e.g., a ledger containing the serial numbers of guns legally registered in a city) the record should be admitted to prove the truth of what it asserts. Since it is barred by the literal language of FRE 803(8)(B), a prosecutor should be able to resort to FRE 803(6) or, perhaps, FRE 803(24). Congress was not thinking of this kind of record when it enacted FRE 803(8) and the value judgments that are embodied in that rule are not undercut if such records are admitted.

Problem VI–51. At 11:30 p. m. on December 3, 1982, a car driven by Neil Nyland collided with one driven by Belinda Bryce, causing considerable damage to both vehicles and severely injuring Ms. Bryce. Rachel Duty, a passenger in Nyland's car, suffered minor injuries. The day after the accident Sam Kalven, an accident investigator for Nyland's insurance company, interviewed Nyland and Duty. Both told stories which tended to exonerate

text of the litigation in which the factual findings of the hearing examiner are offered. In the hearing before the examiner the statements of the parties and their witnesses would have been given in court subject to cross-examination. It is in part

because of the testimonial quality of the evidence presented in administrative hearings that courts have found the factual findings of hearing examiners admissible under FRE 803(8)(C).

Nyland.   Three days after the accident Kalven interviewed Bryce and took her statement.   Bryce's story was somewhat mixed.   She placed the responsibility for the accident on Nyland, but she stated that she had had several drinks shortly before the accident, that she had left a party early because she felt sleepy, and that she had left her eyeglasses at the party. Shortly after the interview, Bryce brought suit against Nyland alleging that his negligence was responsible for the accident.   The case did not reach trial until two and a half years later.   At the trial Nyland's lawyer (DC) put both Duty and Kalven on the stand.   The following material is extracted from their testimony:

TESTIMONY OF RACHEL DUTY

DC: [*after asking a series of preliminary questions*]   Now Ms. Duty, can you tell the jury the way this intersection looked at the time of the accident?

Duty: Well, my memory is rather vague.   I'm not sure I can describe it.

DC: Let me show you this picture, perhaps that will refresh your memory.   [*He first hands a copy to plaintiff's counsel who immediately rises to her feet.*]

PC: Your Honor, a picture can't be used to refresh memory.   Besides, according to the date on the back, this picture was taken two weeks ago.   It's now summertime.   The accident occurred two and a half years ago during the winter.   This can't be used to refresh memory.

Court: It's only to refresh memory.   I'll let that in.

[Is the court's ruling on this point correct?]

DC: Your Honor, I'd like to show this picture to the jury as well.

[How should the court respond to this request?   How should it rule if plaintiff's counsel made the request?]

* * *

DC: Thank you, Ms. Duty.   That was a very complete description. Now I would like to call your attention to the accident itself. Can you tell the jury in your own words what happened as you approached the intersection?

Duty: I'm afraid I cannot.   My mind is a complete blank.   I only remember that I went into the dashboard cutting my nose.

DC: Do you remember describing the accident to this man (pointing to Kalven) the day after it occurred?

Duty: Yes, I do.

DC: Will you read this please?   [*He hands her two typed sheets of paper.*]   Does that refresh your memory?

Duty: Well, it sounds familiar, but I can't say that I have a live memory of what it describes.

DC: Tell me, Ms. Duty, is that your signature at the bottom of this page? [*He hands her a handwritten page.*] Your Honor, the plaintiff has stipulated that the typed pages I previously handed Ms. Duty are a true copy of this original.

Duty: Yes, that's my signature.

DC: Did you sign this statement after it was taken down?

Duty: I must have, I haven't signed it since then.

DC: Your Honor, I would like to offer this paper in evidence either as a business record or as past recollection recorded.

PC: Your Honor, I would like to ask Ms. Duty just one question before you make your ruling.

Court: Proceed.

PC: Ms. Duty, did you read this paper before you signed it?

Duty: I don't remember.

PC: You couldn't swear that you read it could you?

Duty: Why, no.

PC: In fact, you probably didn't read it, isn't that so?

Duty: I don't know. I guess there's a fifty-fifty chance I didn't read it.

PC: Ms. Duty, can you read the handwriting on this report for the jury right now?

Duty: [*hestitating and stumbling*] I * * * was a passenger * * * in the * * * cab, no car * * *.

PC: Thank you Ms. Duty, that will be all. Your Honor, this cannot be admissible as the witness' past recollection recorded and it's not a business record. We object to its admission.

[How should the court rule? Why? Is there any way DC might have strengthened the case for admitting this as a business record? As past recollection recorded?]

Court: I'll admit that as recorded recollection.

DC: Thank you, Your Honor. May the clerk enter this in evidence as Defense Exhibit Three?

PC: Your Honor, she can read that to the jury, but the clerk can't enter it in evidence.

[How should the court rule? Does it matter whether or not you are in federal court?]

*   *   *

TESTIMONY OF SAM KALVEN

[*After some preliminary questions the following occurs*:]

DC: Now Mr. Kalven, will you tell the jury when you first saw the plaintiff Belinda Bryce?

Kal: I first saw her three days after the accident.

DC: How did you happen to see her?

Kal: I was sent to interview her.

DC: Were you sent on business?

Kal: Yes, I was.

DC: And did you interview her as part of your business responsibility?

Kal: Yes, I did.

DC: Now, do you often interview people in connection with your business?

Kal: Yes, I do.

DC: These interviews are routine for you?

Kal: Yes, they are.

DC: Did Ms. Bryce talk to you?

Kal: Yes, she did.

DC: Did you make a record of that interview?

Kal: Yes, I regularly make records when I interview people on business.

DC: Do you have the record with you?

Kal: Yes, I do. [*He produces five typed pages.*]

DC: Your Honor, we would like to introduce the second and third pages of this report, which has been marked Defense Exhibit Four, into evidence as a business record.

Court: Any objection counsel?

PC: Yes, let me state first that I don't think this report qualifies, but, if he wants to admit it, he should admit the whole report not just selected pages.

DC: But only pages 2 and 3 are relevant to our case, Your Honor.

[How should a court respond to the claim that the whole report should be admitted if any of it is to be entered?]

Court: [*after ruling on the above claim*] Well, shall I admit the report now, counselor, or do you want to pursue your argument that none of the report should be admitted?

PC: I would like to ask Mr. Kalven a few questions, Your Honor. Mr. Kalven, this report was made three days after the accident, isn't that so?

Kal: Yes, it was.

PC: And it's possible that Ms. Bryce might have forgotten certain facts about the accident in the interim is it not?

Kal: Yes, it is.

PC: Tell me, Mr. Kalven, is Ms. Bryce employed by the same company which employs you?

Kal: No, she is not.

PC: And just what company is it that employs you?

Kal: The Security Investigation Company.

PC: And that is a wholly owned subsidiary of what company?

DC: [*rising to his feet*] May we approach the bench, Your Honor? [*at the bench*: Your Honor, that question was asked just to show that the Security Investigation Company works only for the Security Insurance Company. She asked that question just to alert the jury to the fact that the insurance company is the real defendant. There is no need for that question. It's already been established that the report was made in the regular course of Kalven's business as an investigator. It is irrelevant just whom the investigation was being conducted for.]

[How should the court rule on this argument?]

PC: Mr. Kalven, when Ms. Bryce made her statement to you she was under no business duty to tell you anything, was she?

Kal: That is correct.

PC: Your Honor, that report can't come in as a business record. The witness admitted that the report wasn't made at or even near the time of the accident and the declarant Ms. Bryce was under no business duty to tell Mr. Kalven anything.

[How should the court rule on this question? Are PC's arguments good ones? Could PC have come up with any stronger arguments in support of her claim that the report is inadmissible as a business record? How should DC respond to the arguments PC has made?]

DC: [*After the court rules the record does not qualify as a business record.*] Mr. Kalven, do you have a present memory of what Ms. Bryce told you when you interviewed her?

Kal: No, I do not.

DC: Now when you record someone's statement, do you make an accurate record of what they have said?

Kal: Yes, I do.

DC: You transcribe what they say?

Kal: No, I do not.

DC: [*obviously surprised and disappointed*] You don't?

Kal: No.

DC: What do you do?

Kal: Well, I take down in my own words, summarizing as I go along, the gist of what was said.

DC: [*recovering*] Are these summaries accurate?

Kal: Yes, they are.

DC: You are positive that this summary, even though you don't remember it now, was, when you took it down, faithful to what Ms. Bryce had told you?

Kal: Yes, I am.

DC: Mr. Kalven, will you please read your notes to the jury as your past recollection recorded?

PC: Objection, Your Honor. This record wasn't made when the accident was fresh and the witness has already said that it is not a transcription of what my client told him but rather a summary in his own words. This doesn't qualify for the exception.

[How should the court rule?]

Problem VI–52. Steve Kew was driving along Sloan Street when a little girl, Mary Ames, ran in front of him from between two parked cars. He tried to stop, but he could not stop before his car struck her. Seeing no one around, he picked her up, put her in his car, and sped to the emergency room of the local hospital. While at the hospital an attendant filled out an admission form. In the space labeled *cause of injury* the attendant wrote "Hit by car. Mr. Kew says that the patient jumped out from between two parked cars and that he couldn't stop because his brakes were bad." **If Mary's parents later sue Steve, may Steve introduce his copy of his form in order to show that Mary had suddenly jumped in front of his car? May the parents introduce the hospital's copy in order to show that Steve's brakes were bad?**

Problem VI–53. Following the above accident Mary Ames was given emergency treatment and admitted to the hospital. Mary's parents want to introduce the following extracts from her hospital chart under the business entry exception. **May they introduce any or all of this information to prove Mary's injuries?**

1. (By a doctor) X-rays reveal broken ribs and chipped collarbone. Patient complains of numbness in right leg. Nerve damage suspected.
2. (By a nurse) Patient in obvious pain. Administered sedative.
3. (By a doctor) Right foot still numb. Nerve damage caused when she was thrown on her back. Recommend physical therapy. Patient will never walk without a slight limp.

May the defendant Kew introduce the following extracts from the hospital records?

1. (By a nurse) Mary is remarkably cheerful. She brightens up life for everyone on the ward and is being showered with attention by both patients and staff. Yesterday when she got the Teddy Bear, she said she didn't think she ever wanted to go home.
2. (By a physical therapist) Numbness not serious. Only outpatient care is needed now. She will be walking normally within two years.
3. (By a doctor) Patients and staff must not sympathize with Mary when she limps. I think she is exaggerating walking difficulties to get attention.

Problem VI–54. Michael Minton, a successful lawyer, died at the age of 63. Minton had been interested in numismatics from the time he was a child and by his mid-thirties he was known as much for the quality of his coin collection as he was for his legal skills. Minton was continually buying, selling and trading coins. It is estimated that two-thirds of his $1,200,000 estate was represented by his coin collection or income which he had earned from sales of his coins. Shortly after Minton's death, the Midas Coin Company brought suit against the estate, alleging that Minton had neither paid for nor returned an 1803 silver dollar delivered on approval along with an 1865 gold five dollar piece and an 1861 silver three cent piece. The other two coins had been returned. The estate defends on the ground that the silver dollar was never received. In support of this defense the estate introduces Florence Minton, Michael's widow, who testifies to the regularity and care with which Michael kept track of his coins in a large leather-covered book which he called his "Coin Register". She also testifies that whenever Michael received a coin on approval, he either wrote a check for the coin immediately or left the coin locked in a drawer for his chauffeur to pick up and return to the appropriate company. The five dollar gold piece and the silver three-cent piece were delivered the evening before Michael's death. Mrs. Minton also testifies that her husband dictated notes to her every night concerning his numismatic activities. He had often expressed the hope of compiling them into a book which he had tentatively titled, *I Made a Mint on Coin Collecting: The Autobiography of a Numismatic Nut* [Minton's sense of humor left something to be desired.] Finally, Mrs. Minton testifies that she transcribed his words accurately and had never known Michael to lie.

The estate, in order to prove that the silver dollar never was delivered, offers as a business record the final page of Minton's "Coin Register" which reads as follows:

Date	Coin	Cond.	Rec'd.	Ret'd.	Bt.	Sd.	Am't.	Party
7/26	(1891cc) $1 ag.	V.F.	X	X			($15.75)	Univ.
7/26	(1882) Ind. 1¢	Unc.	X		X		($32.50)	Midas
7/30	(1796) lg. 1¢	V.F.				X	($400)	Reese
7/30	(1849) $1 au.	Unc.			X		($300)	Reese
8/3	(1865) $5 au.	Fine	X	X			($350)	Cn. X.
8/3	(1899) $10 au.	V.F.	X		X		($140)	Cn. X.
8/3	(1917) $20 au.	Unc.	X		X		($380)	Cn. X.
8/5	(1865) $5 au.	V.F.	X	X			($550)	Midas
8/5	(1861) 3¢ ag.	Fine	X	X			($20.00)	Midas

The estate claims that the absence of any notation acknowledging receipt of the silver dollar should be admitted as evidence that the coin never arrived. **How should the court rule?**

The estate also wishes to introduce as a business record a portion of the material which Minton had dictated to his wife the night that he died. This extract reads: "I don't know why I do business with Midas. Their coins are seldom in the promised condition and the company is so unreliable. They were supposed to deliver the silver dollar with the coins that arrived today. If the dollar was truly uncirculated, it would be the prize of my collection. If they have sold it to another, I shall cancel my business with them." **Is this writing admissible?**

The estate also wishes to put Minton's chauffer on the stand to testify that he went to the locked drawer where coins are left for him to return and he only found the five dollar gold piece and the three cent silver piece. **Should this testimony be allowed?**

Problem VI–55. Rules of the Camdan Chemical Company require all employees wishing to leave early to report to their supervisor and require the supervisor to report the reasons why the employee wishes to leave to the head supervisor who has authority to grant permission. One day Shelley Fraser, the supervisor of the chemical lab, called Harry Armstrong to report that Alex Earnst had requested permission to leave early because he felt sick following an accident in the chemical lab which had released a dense cloud of yellow gas. Permisson was given. Two days later Earnst died. His widow sued for survivor's benefits under the state Workers Compensation Statute. There is some evidence that Earnst's death was caused by chemical burns to his lungs. **In order to prove that the cause of death was work-related, may Mrs. Earnst introduce Armstrong to report what Fraser said to him on the theory that this was a business record?**

Problem VI–56. Joan Sanders witnessed an auto accident and heroically helped two teenagers escape from a burning car. She was burned slightly in the effort and was in some pain when the police arrived fifteen minutes later. She briefly told the police that she had seen a blue Cadillac swerve across the center line into the car driven by the teenagers. She was then taken to the hospital for treatment. Five days later, at a friend's suggestion, she wrote down a more detailed description of what she had seen.

At the trial two years later, will the police report be admissible under the business records exception against the driver of the Cadillac? Will the statement Sanders wrote five days after the accident be admissible as Sanders' past recollection recorded? What questions would you ask Sanders in an attempt to qualify this statement as past recollection recorded?

Problem VI–57. Salesperson A at the J. C. Nickel's Department Store sold a television set to the defendant for $550 and wrote a receipt charging the T.V. to the defendant's account. The store's copy of the receipt went to floor manager B, who gave it to bookkeeper C, who copied it into a day book. Day book entries were given to bookkeeper D, who copied all information relating to sales on account into a ledger book. Ledger books were sent once a week to the chain's central data processing facility where E coded the information and gave it to F, who punched it on machine-readable cards and then gave the cards to G, who entered them on the Nickel's computer. The computer had been programmed by H, I and J to send monthly bills to all those with open charge accounts and to print weekly lists of all accounts which were three months overdue. Names on this list and amounts owed were mailed to the credit managers of the stores where the transactions occurred and the credit managers wrote letters to the delinquent debtors. The weekly lists were then destroyed. Assume that the defendant's name has reached the credit manager in this way and the appropriate dunning letter has been written. Two days after the letter was mailed to the defendant, the central data processing facility was gutted by fire, destroying the ledger books stored there and the computer. **If Nickel's sues the defendant for money owing on the television and the defendant states she never owed any money, may the letter from the credit manager be introduced as a business record to establish the existence and the amount of the debt? If you were the attorney for Nickel's, what would you do to establish a foundation for admitting the letter as a business record? What is the minimum number of witnesses you would have to call?**

Problem VI–58. Paul Oakes is charged with possession of heroin. The government intends to call as its final witness Dr. Waterman, a chemist who analyzed the white powder taken from Oakes and identified it as heroin. Waterman is employed by the United States Customs Service. On the day of the trial Waterman is present, looking somewhat ill, but he is unable to testify because of unexpected delays in the presentation of the government's case. On the next day Waterman is unable to testify because he is suffering from a high fever and severe bronchial infection. Rather than seeking a continuance, the government calls Dr. Bartels, a chemist who works with Waterman in the Customs Service Laboratory. Dr. Bartels testifies to the routine procedures that are used in preparing worksheets and final reports. She identifies two government exhibits as a worksheet and a final report of a chemical analysis done by her colleague Waterman (whose handwriting she recognizes) in the Customs Service Laboratory. The documents describe the substance taken from an envelope marked "P. Oakes" as a white powder and identify it as heroin. The government seeks to introduce these documents as either business records or as public records and reports. **Are they admissible under either or both theories?**

Problem VI–59. Hungate is charged with burglary. The strongest evidence against him is a fingerprint found on a sterling silver knife that was dropped by the burglar as he fled. The defense argues that the fingerprint was planted on the knife some two months after the robbery because Hungate testified against a police officer in a civil rights action charging police brutality. In its case in rebuttal the government introduces a clerk who works in the FBI's fingerprint identification laboratory. She testifies that as soon as a print enters the office for analysis it is stamped with its date of receipt and a sequential identification number. The government then introduces the identification card which contains Hungate's print. It is dated eight days after the burglary. The government also introduces the ten identification cards that follow Hungate's card in numerical sequence. The first six have the same date as Hungate's card and the last four are dated nine days after the burglary. The government offers this card to show the date on which the print was received as either a business record or a public record or report. **Should the card be admitted?**

Assume that the fingerprint found on the knife did not belong to Hungate. He offers the FBI report containing the fingerprint found on the knife to prove the truth of what it asserts: namely that "the instant print is not that of the suspect Hungate or of anyone living in the victim's house. It is consistent with the prints of Fred Smith, who according to our records has three convictions for petty larceny and an arrest for burglary, but there are too few points to make a definite match." In offering the evidence Hungate's attorney only cites FRE 803(8). The trial court refuses to admit the evidence under that exception and, following his conviction, Hungate appeals. **Did the trial judge commit reversible error?**

Problem VI–60. Early on the evening of September 19, 1982 a truck traveling west on U.S. Route 20 collided with a car traveling south on State Route 6, killing four of the five teenagers riding in the car. Route 20 is a four lane divided highway, while Route 6 is a two lane country road. The intersection is controlled by a light which is always red in the direction of Route 6 and green in the direction of Route 20, except when a car on Route 6 trips a sensor. When this occurs, if six seconds pass without any vehicle tripping a sensor on Route 20, the light turns to amber on Route 20 for four seconds and then after one second of red on both roads it turns to green on Route 6 and red on Route 20.

At the time of the accident Sergeant Bonny Hendricksmeyer, a twenty-eight year veteran of the state highway patrol, was on duty at a local patrol office. She reached the scene of the accident about six minutes after the collision. She carefully examined the physical circumstances of the accident and noted the tire marks on the highway and the damage done to the vehicles. Several days later she interviewed the surviving passenger from the car and the truck driver. The passenger had no recollection of the event and the truck driver said he could not say what color the light was because he had been blinded by the sun. He did say that he did not see any eastbound traffic on Route 20 stop or slow down and that he saw the car emerge from behind a house on Route 4. After finishing her investigation Hendricksmeyer filled out an accident report. The report quoted what the truck driver had said verbatim. It also contained the observation that "apparently the car entered the intersection against a red light", and she had checked a box under the heading "contributing circumstances" which read "failure of vehicle #2 [the car] to yield the right of way." Nearby in the margin were the words, "teenage driver!".

At the trial the defendant company which is being sued on a *respondeat superior* theory calls the truck driver who repeats the observations he made to the officer and is vigorously cross-examined about them. The company also calls Hendricksmeyer and asks her to describe in detail the accident scene as it appeared to her and the investigation she conducted. However, the defense does not ask Hendricksmeyer whether she had reached any judgments regarding the cause of the accident. Later in the trial, after Hendricksmeyer has been excused, the company offers her accident report. **Should it be admitted over the plaintiff's objection?**

Problem VI–61. In 1978 the Secretary of HEW, pursuant to authority granted him by law, ordered the Surgeon General to establish a task force to study problems associated with DES, a drug once used for contraceptive and other purposes but now thought to cause cancer and chromosomal damage. The task force consisted of a group of doctors and other experts employed by various departments of the federal government. In addition a large group of consultants participated in the hearings of the task force and in the preparation of the final report. The consultants included both doctors and non-professionals, some of whom were active in organized efforts to expose the allegedly harmful effects of DES (e.g., the president of DES Action and the director of the Health Research Group, a Ralph Nader organization). No representative of the pharmaceutical industry was on the task force or among its consultants. The group did no original research, but reviewed the scientific literature relating to DES and met on eight occasions to talk about the health effects of DES. At these meetings a wide variety of persons, not otherwise associated with the project, presented their views and data to the task force. The final report of the task force finds that there are serious dangers associated with DES; it makes a number of "action recommendations" and discusses their scientific basis, and it recommends further research to fill in the gaps in what is known about DES.

Plaintiff brings an action against a manufacturer of DES. She alleges that she has certain deformities attributable to the fact that her mother was given DES. She would like to introduce the report of the HEW task force to establish the dangers of DES and the fact that it can cause conditions such as hers. **Should the report be admitted?**

---

h. Other Exceptions

There are numerous other exceptions to the hearsay rule which do not require prior proof of the declarant's unavailability. The number and nature of these exceptions varies from state to state. We present the specific exceptions found in FRE 803 as examples of the kinds of additional exceptions which will be found in the various states. The notes authored by the Advisory Committee (ACN) are included to give you some idea of the policies that lie behind these exceptions and of their relationship to the common law.[52]

Most of the remaining FRE 803 exceptions are relatively non-controversial and

52. The Advisory Committee prefaces its comments on the exceptions:

The exceptions are phrased in terms of nonapplication of the hearsay rule, rather than in positive terms of admissibility, in order to repel any implication that other possible grounds for exclusion are eliminated from consideration.

The present rule proceeds upon the theory that under appropriate circumstances a hearsay statement may possess circumstantial guarantees of trustworthiness sufficient to justify nonproduction of the declarant in person at the trial even though he may be available. The theory finds vast support in the many exceptions to the hearsay rule developed by the common law

track the common law. However, a few are truly innovative. FRE 803(16) transforms a rule of authentication into a hearsay exception. At common law an ancient document, that is one that was at least thirty years old, was presumed genuine unless the circumstances in which it was found suggested otherwise. However, the statements it contained were not admissible for their truth unless they qualified under some hearsay exception. Now the appellation "ancient" attaches after twenty years and the presumption of genuineness brings with it a hearsay exception.

FRE 803(18) broadens a rule of impeachment and transforms it into a hearsay exception. At common law an expert witness could be impeached by statements from the scholarly literature that were inconsistent with his testimony, provided that he relied on that literature or, in many states, acknowledged it to be authoritative. A party could not however offer a book or pamphlet as substantive evidence to support his case. Under FRE 803(18) a party may read the jury statements from any reliable authority on any science or art to prove what the statements assert. An expert must be on the stand when the work is offered and so may comment on what is read. However, the expert need not acknowledge the work as authoritative so long as the proponent can prove its stature by some other means. The rule is particularly useful when a party has difficulty acquiring a distinguished expert to testify on his behalf. In some localities this is reputed to be the case in tort actions for professional malpractice. It appears from the rule that if a party's own undistinguished expert relies on a treatise, the language of the treatise may be read as further support for the party's position.

FRE 803(22) admits with certain limitations judgments entered upon guilty pleas or guilty verdicts to prove facts essential to the judgment. Guilty pleas are, of course, admissions when offered against the person who pled, but the rule makes them more broadly admissible. Jury verdicts are hearsay when used to prove facts essential to the judgment because they are, in effect, the jurors' out-of-court assertions that particular facts have been found. The difficult problem posed by this exception is the determination of exactly what facts are essential to a judgment, for these are the only facts that one can be sure the jury has found. Until there are more cases interpreting the rule, one cannot be sure where this line will be drawn. Because FRE 803(22) is only a hearsay exception, a party can dispute the implications of a guilty plea or verdict that is offered against him. However, in some jurisdictions rules of *res judicata* or collateral estoppel may make a guilty plea or verdict incontrovertible when offered in related litigation to prove certain facts.

The most important of the remaining 803 exceptions is FRE 803(24), the residual or "catchall" exception. As its name implies, it is potentially applicable to any kind of hearsay. Because of its importance, we treat it separately in Section IV of this chapter.

(9) *Records of vital statistics*. Records or data compilations, in any form, of births, fetal deaths, deaths, or marriages, if the report thereof was made to a public office pursuant to requirements of law.

[ACN] Records of vital statistics are commonly the subject of particular statutes making them admissible in evidence. The rule is in principle nar-

---

in which unavailability of the declarant is not a relevant factor. The present rule is a synthesis of them, with revision where modern developments and conditions are believed to make that course appropriate.

In a hearsay situation, the declarant is, of course, a witness, and neither this rule

nor Rule 804 dispenses with the requirement of firsthand knowledge. It may appear from his statement or be inferable from circumstances. See Rule 602.

rower than Uniform Rule 63(16) which includes reports required of persons performing functions authorized by statute, yet in practical effect the two are substantially the same. * * *

(10) *Absence of public record or entry.* To prove the absence of a record, report, statement, or data compilation, in any form, or the nonoccurrence or nonexistence of a matter of which a record, report, statement, or data compilation, in any form, was regularly made and preserved by a public office or agency, evidence in the form of a certification in accordance with rule 902, or testimony, that diligent search failed to disclose the record, report, statement, or data compilation, or entry.

[ACN] The principle of proving non-occurrence of an event by evidence of the absence of a record which would regularly be made of its occurrence, developed in Exception (7) with respect to regularly conducted [business] activities, is here extended to public records of the kind mentioned in Exceptions (8) and (9). Some harmless duplication no doubt exists with Exception (7). * * *

The rule includes situations in which absence of a record may itself be the ultimate focal point of inquiry, e.g. People v. Love, 310 Ill. 558, 142 N.E. 204 (1923), certificate of Secretary of State admitted to show failure to file documents required by Securities Law, as well as cases where the absence of a record is offered as proof of the nonoccurrence of an event ordinarily recorded.

The refusal of the common law to allow proof by certificate of the lack of a record or entry has no apparent justification. The rule takes the opposite position, as do Uniform Rule 63(17); California Evidence Code § 1284; * * * Congress has recognized certification as evidence of the lack of a record. 8 U.S.C. § 1360(d), certificate of Attorney General or other designated officer that no record of Immigration and Naturalization Service of specified na-

ture or entry therein is found, admissible in alien cases.

(11) *Records of religious organizations.* Statements of births, marriages, divorces, deaths, legitimacy, ancestry, relationship by blood or marriage, or other similar facts of personal or family history, contained in a regularly kept record of a religious organization.

[ACN] Records of activities of religious organizations are currently recognized as admissible at least to the extent of the business records exception to the hearsay rule, and Exception (6) would be applicable. However, both the business record doctrine and Exception (6) require that the person furnishing the information be one in the business or activity. The result is such decisions as Daily v. Grand Lodge, 311 Ill. 184, 142 N.E. 478 (1924), holding a church record admissible to prove fact, date, and place of baptism, but not age of child except that he had at least been born at the time. In view of the unlikelihood that false information would be furnished on occasions of this kind, the rule contains no requirement that the informant be in the course of the activity.

(12) *Marriage, baptismal, and similar certificates.* Statements of fact contained in a certificate that the maker performed a marriage or other ceremony or administered a sacrament, made by a clergyman, public official, or other person authorized by the rules or practices of a religious organization or by law to perform the act certified, and purporting to have been issued at the time of the act or within a reasonable time thereafter.

[ACN] The principle of proof by certification is recognized as to public officials in Exceptions (8) and (10), and with respect to authentication in Rule 902. The present exception is a duplication to the extent that it deals with a certificate by a public official, as in the case of a judge who performs a marriage ceremony. The area covered by the rule is, however, substantially larger and extends the certification procedure to clergymen and the like who perform marriages and other ceremonies or administer sacraments. Thus certificates of such matters as baptism or confirmation, as well as marriage, are included. In principle they are as acceptable evidence as certificates of public officers.

When the person executing the certificate is not a public official, the self-authenticating character of documents purporting to emanate from public officials, see Rule 902, is lacking and proof is required that the person was authorized and did make the certificate. The time element, however, may safely be taken as supplied by the certificate, once authority and authenticity are established, particularly in view of the presumption that a document was executed on the date it bears.

* * *

(13) *Family records.* Statements of fact concerning personal or family history contained in family Bibles, genealogies, charts, engravings on rings, inscriptions on family portraits, engravings on urns, crypts, or tombstones, or the like.

[ACN] Records of family history kept in family Bibles have by long tradition been received in evidence. Opinions in the area also include inscriptions on tombstones, publicly displayed pedigrees, and engravings on rings.

* * *

(14) *Records of documents affecting an interest in property.* The record of a document purporting to establish or affect an interest in property, as proof of the content of the original recorded document and its execution and delivery by each person by whom it purports to have been executed, if the record is a record of a public office and an applicable statute authorizes the recording of documents of that kind in that office.

[ACN] The recording of title documents is a purely statutory development. Under any theory of the admissibility of public records, the records would be receivable as evidence of the contents of the recorded document, else the recording process would be reduced to a nullity. When, however, the record is offered for the further purpose of proving execution and delivery, a problem of lack of firsthand knowledge by the recorder, not present as to contents, is presented. This problem is solved, seemingly in all jurisdictions, by qualifying for recording only those documents shown by a specified procedure, either acknowledgment or a form of probate, to have been executed and delivered. Thus what may appear in the rule, at first glance, as endowing the record with an effect independently of local law and inviting difficulties of an *Erie* nature * * *, is not present, since the local law in fact governs under the example.

(15) *Statements in documents affecting an interest in property.* A statement contained in a document purporting to establish or affect an interest in property if the matter stated was relevant to the purpose of the document, unless dealings with the property since the document was made have been inconsistent with the truth of the statement or the purport of the document.

[ACN] Dispositive documents often contain recitals of fact. Thus a deed purporting to have been executed by an attorney in fact may recite the existence of the power of attorney, or a deed may recite that the grantors are all the heirs of the last record owner. Under the rule, these recitals are exempted from the hearsay rule. The circumstances under which dispositive documents are executed and the requirement that the recital be germane to the purpose of the document are believed to be adequate guarantees of trustworthiness, particularly in view of the nonapplicability of the rule if dealings with the property have been inconsistent with the document. The age of the document is of no significance, though in practical application the document will most often be an ancient one.

*   *   *

(16) *Statements in ancient documents.* Statements in a document in existence twenty years or more the authenticity of which is established.

[ACN] Authenticating a document as ancient, essentially in the pattern of the common law, as provided in Rule 901(b)(8), leaves open as a separate question the admissibility of assertive statements contained therein as against a hearsay objection. 7 Wigmore § 2145a. Wigmore further states that the ancient document technique of authentication is universally conceded to apply to all sorts of documents, including letters, records, contracts, maps, and certificates, in addition to title documents, citing numerous decisions. Id. § 2145. Since most of these items are significant evidentially only insofar as they are assertive, their admission in evidence must be as a hearsay exception. The former position is believed to be the correct one in reason and authority. As pointed out in McCormick § 298, danger of mistake is minimized by authentication requirements, and age affords assurance that the writing antedates the present controversy.

For a similar provision, but with the added requirement that "the statement has since generally been acted upon as true by persons having an interest in the matter," see California Evidence Code § 1331.

(17) *Market reports, commercial publications.* Market quotations, tabulations, lists, directories, or other published compilations, generally used and relied upon by the public or by persons in particular occupations.

[ACN] Ample authority at common law supported the admission in evidence of items falling in this category. While Wigmore's text is narrowly oriented to lists, etc., prepared for the use of a trade or profession, authorities are cited which include other kinds of publications, for example, newspaper market reports, telephone directories, and city directories. The basis of trustworthiness is general reliance by the public or by a particular segment of it, and the motivation of the compiler to foster reliance by being accurate.

*   *   *   Uniform Commercial Code § 2–724 provides for admissibility in evidence of "reports in official publications or trade journals or in newspapers or periodicals of general circulation published as the reports of such [established commodity] market."

(18) *Learned treatises.* To the extent called to the attention of an expert witness upon cross-examination or relied upon by him in direct examination, statements contained in published treatises, periodicals, or pamphlets on a subject of history, medicine, or other science or art, established as a reliable authority by the testimony or admission of the witness or by other expert testimony or by judicial notice. If admitted, the statements may be read into evidence but may not be received as exhibits.

[ACN] The writers have generally favored the admissibility of learned treatises, with the support of occasional decisions and rules, but the great weight of authority has been that learned treatises are not admissible as substantive evidence though usable in the cross-examination of experts. The foundation of the minority view is that the hearsay objection must be regarded as unimpressive when directed against treatises since a high standard of accuracy is engendered by various factors: the treatise is written primarily and impartially for professionals, subject to scrutiny and exposure for inaccuracy, with the reputation of the writer at stake. Sound as this position may be with respect to trustworthiness, there is, nevertheless, an additional difficulty in the likelihood that the treatise will be misunderstood and misapplied without expert assistance and supervision. This difficulty is recognized in the cases demonstrating unwillingness to sustain findings relative to disability on the basis of judicially noticed medical texts. The rule avoids the danger of misunderstanding and misapplication by limiting the use of treatises as substantive evidence to situations in which an expert is on the stand and available to explain and assist in the application of the treatise if desired. The limitation upon receiving the publication itself physically in evidence, contained in the last sentence, is designed to further this policy.

The relevance of the use of treatises on cross-examination is evident. This use of treatises has been the subject of varied views. The most restrictive position is that the witness must have stated expressly on direct his reliance upon the treatise. A slightly more liberal approach still insists upon reliance but allows it to be developed on cross-examination. Further relaxation dispenses with reliance but requires recognition as an authority by the witness, developable on cross-examination. The greatest liberality is found in decisions allowing use of the treatise on cross-examination when its status as an authority is established by any means. The exception is hinged upon this last position, which is that of the Supreme Court, Reilly v. Pinkus, 338 U.S. 269, (1949), and of recent well considered state court decisions.

In Reilly v. Pinkus, supra, the Court pointed out that testing of professional knowledge was incomplete without exploration of the witness' knowledge of and attitude toward established treatises in the field. The process works equally well in reverse and furnishes the basis of the rule.

The rule does not require that the witness rely upon or recognize the treatise as authoritative, thus avoiding the possibility that the expert may at the outset block cross-examination by refusing to concede reliance or authoritativeness. Moreover, the rule avoids the unreality of admitting evidence for the purpose of impeachment only, with an instruction to the jury not to consider it otherwise. The parallel to the treatment of prior inconsistent statements will be apparent. See Rules 613(b) and 801(d)(1).

(19) *Reputation concerning personal or family history*. Reputation among members of his family by blood, adoption, or marriage, or among his associates, or in the community, concerning a person's birth, adoption, marriage, divorce, death, legitimacy, relationship by blood, adoption, or marriage, ancestry, or other similar fact of his personal or family history.

(20) *Reputation concerning boundaries or general history*. Reputation in a community, arising before the controversy, as to boundaries of or customs affecting lands in the community, and reputation as to events of general history important to the community or State or nation in which located.

(21) *Reputation as to character*. Reputation of a person's character among his associates or in the community.

[ACN] Trustworthiness in reputation evidence is found "when the topic is such that the facts are likely to have been inquired about and that persons having personal knowledge have disclosed facts which have thus been discussed in the community; and thus the community's conclusion, if any has been formed, is likely to be a trustworthy one." 5 Wigmore § 1580, p. 444. On this common foundation, reputation as to land boundaries, customs, general history, character, and marriage have come to be regarded as admissible. The breadth of the underlying principle suggests the formulation of an equally broad exception, but tradition has in fact been much narrower and more particularized, and this is the pattern of these exceptions in the rule.

Exception (19) is concerned with matters of personal and family history. Marriage is universally conceded to be a proper subject of proof by evidence of reputation in the community. As to such items as legitimacy, relationship, adoption, birth, and death, the decisions are divided. All seem to be susceptible to being the subject of well founded repute. The "world" in which the reputation may exist may be family, associates, or community. This world has proved capable of expanding with changing times from the single uncomplicated neighborhood, in which all activities take place, to the multiple and unrelated worlds of work, religious affiliation, and social activity, in each of which a reputation may be generated. The family has often served as the point of beginning for allowing community reputation. * * *

The first portion of Exception (20) is based upon the general admissibility of evidence of reputation as to land boundaries and land customs, expanded in this country to include private as well as public boundaries. The reputation is required to antedate the controversy, though not to be ancient. The second portion is likewise supported by authority, and is designed to faciliate proof of events when judicial notice is not available. The historical character of the subject matter dispenses with any need that the reputation antedate the controversy with respect to which it is offered. * * *

Exception (21) recognizes the traditional acceptance of reputation evidence as a means of proving human character. The exception deals only with the hearsay aspect of this kind of evidence. Limitations upon admissibility based on other grounds will be found in Rules 404, relevancy of character evidence generally, and 608, character of witness. The exception is in effect a reiteration, in the context of hearsay, of Rule 405(a). * * *

(22) *Judgment of previous conviction.* Evidence of a final judgment, entered after a trial or upon a plea of guilty (but not upon a plea of nolo contendere), adjudging a person guilty of a crime punishable by death or imprisonment in excess of one year, to prove any fact essential to sustain the judgment, but not including, when offered by the Government in a criminal prosecution for purposes other than impeachment, judgments against persons other than the accused. The pendency of an appeal may be shown but does not affect admissibility.

[ACN] When the status of a former judgment is under consideration in subsequent litigation, three possibilities must be noted: (1) the former judgment is conclusive under the doctrine of res judicata, either as a bar or a collateral estoppel; or (2) it is admissible in evidence for what it is worth; or (3) it may be of no effect at all. The first situation does not involve any problem of evidence except in the way that principles of substantive law generally bear upon the relevancy and materiality of evidence. The rule does not deal with the substantive effect of the judgment as a bar or collateral estoppel. When, however, the doctrine of res judicata does not apply to make the judgment either a bar or a collateral estoppel, a choice is presented between the second and third alternatives. The rule adopts the second for judgments of criminal conviction of felony grade. This is the direction of the decisions, which manifest an increasing reluctance to reject *in toto* the validity of the law's factfinding processes outside the confines of res judicata and collateral estoppel. While this may leave a jury with the evidence of conviction but without means to evaluate it, * * * it seems safe to assume that the jury will give it substantial effect unless defendant offers a satisfactory explanation, a possibility not foreclosed by the provision. But see North River Ins. Co. of City of New York v. Militello, 104 Colo. 28, 88 P.2d 567 (1939), in which the jury found for plaintiff on a fire policy despite the introduction of his conviction for arson. * * *

Practical considerations require exclusion of convictions of minor offenses, not because the administration of justice in its lower echelons must be inferior, but because motivation to defend at this level is often minimal or nonexistent. Hence the rule includes only convictions of felony grade, measured by federal standards.

Judgments of conviction based upon pleas of *nolo contendere* are not included. This position is consistent with the treatment of *nolo* pleas in Rule 410. * * *

While these rules do not in general purport to resolve constitutional issues, they have in general been drafted with a view to avoiding collision with constitutional principles. Consequently the exception does not include evidence of the conviction of a third person, offered against the accused in a criminal prosecution to prove any fact essential to sustain the judgment of conviction. A contrary position would seem clearly to violate the right of confrontation. Kirby v. United States, 174 U.S. 47 (1899), error to convict of possessing stolen postage stamps with the only evidence of theft being the record of conviction of the thieves. The situation is to be distinguished from cases in which conviction of another person is an element of the crime, e.g., 15 U.S.C. § 902(d), interstate shipment of firearms to a known convicted felon, and, as specifically provided, from impeachment.

* * *

(23) *Judgment as to personal, family, or general history, or boundaries.* Judgments as proof of matters of personal, family or general history, or boundaries, essential to the judgment, if the same would be provable by evidence of reputation.

[ACN] A hearsay exception in this area was originally justified on the ground that verdicts were evidence of reputation. As trial by jury graduated from the category of neighborhood inquests, this theory lost its validity. It was never valid as to chancery decrees. Nevertheless the rule persisted, though the judges and writers shifted ground and began saying that the judgment or decree was as good evidence as reputation. The shift appears to be correct, since the process of inquiry, sifting, and scrutiny which is relied upon to render reputation reliable is present in perhaps greater measure in the process of litigation. While this might suggest a broader area of application, the affinity to reputation is strong, and paragraph (23) goes no further, not even including character.

The leading case in the United States, Patterson v. Gaines, 47 U.S. (6 How.) 550, 599 (1847), follows in the pattern of the English decisions, mentioning as illustrative matters thus provable: manorial rights, public rights of way, immemorial custom, disputed boundary, and pedigree. * * *

Problem VI–62. Anthony Gebippe died and left his entire estate to the Indiana University Foundation by a will dated six months before his death.

It is alleged that part of the estate included a large house and land in Bedford, currently occupied by Harry Gebippe, Anthony's son.

Harry has challenged the will in probate court, alleging that on the date of death the property in Bedford belonged to him (Harry), not his father. He further challenged the will on the grounds that Anthony was not competent at the time he executed the will in question.

(1) Harry offers into evidence a certified copy of a deed, dated June 15, 1955, which appears to pass title to the Bedford property from Anthony to Harry. The certification indicates that the original is on file with the clerk of court. The lawyer for the Foundation objects on hearsay grounds. **Is the document admissible?**

(2) Harry offers into evidence a written court judgment finding Anthony to be dangerous because of mental disease and ordering him (Anthony) committed to the State Hospital. The judgment is dated the day after the will was signed. **Is it admissible over a hearsay objection?**

(3) In order to prove the value of several copyrights that are part of the estate, Harry offers a certified copy of Anthony's 1979 tax return obtained from the I.R.S. **Would this document be admissible over a hearsay objection?**

(4) Finally, Harry wishes to produce a certified copy of Anthony's death certificate on which the cause of death is listed as brain tumor, signed by Dr. Frank Stein of the State Hospital for the Insane. **Is it admissible over a hearsay objection?**

----

2. HEARSAY EXCEPTIONS CONDITIONED ON UNAVAILABILITY

a. Requirement of Unavailability

i. The Meaning of "Unavailable"

As a precondition to admitting certain kinds of hearsay evidence the proponent must first show that the declarant is unavailable. One would suppose that hearsay which is admissible only if the declarant is first shown to be unavailable is somewhat less reliable than hearsay admitted without regard to availability. This is the prevailing view. In their commentary accompanying the federal hearsay rules the advisory committee writes:

Rule 803 * * * is based upon the assumption that a hearsay statement falling within one of its exceptions possesses qualities which justify the conclusion that whether the declarant is available or unavailable is not a relevant factor in determining admissibility. The instant rule [804] proceeds upon a different theory: hearsay which admittedly is not equal in quality to testimony of the declarant on the stand may nevertheless be admitted if the declarant is unavailable and if his statement meets a specified standard. The rule expresses preferences: testimony given on the stand in person is preferred over hearsay, and hearsay, if of the specified quality, is preferred over the complete loss of the evidence of the declarant.

The committee is probably correct in concluding that courtroom testimony is preferable to the kinds of hearsay admissible under the FRE 804 exceptions, but they may be mistaken in the implication that all exceptions conditioned upon unavailability admit less reliable hearsay than the exceptions which are not. Compare the exception for present sense impressions with the exception for former testimony or the excited utterance exception with the exception for statements against interest. Perhaps a thorough rethinking of the relative reliability of hearsay versus courtroom testimony would have led the drafters of the hearsay exceptions to condition more of the exceptions on unavailability.

At common law, the requirement of unavailability was defined separately for each of the exceptions conditioned on it. At one extreme, dying declarations were admissible only if the declarant were dead; at the other, former testimony was admissible if the declarant were either dead, physically unable to attend the trial, mentally incapacitated, rendered incompetent by statute, or claiming a privilege not to testify.[53] It has been argued that linking specific exceptions to particular causes of unavailability makes little sense. So long as the proponent of the out-of-court statement is not responsible for the declarant's absence, neither the need for the declarant's statement nor its reliability is likely to vary with the cause of unavailability. The federal rule incorporates this view. Circumstances which constitute unavailability are the same wherever this is a precondition for an exception. An increasing number of states take a similar position, though some still tie dying declarations to the declarant's demise.

FRE 804(a) specifies the circumstances in which a declarant will be considered unavailable:

Definition of unavailability. "Unavailability as a witness" includes situations in which the declarant:

(1) Is exempted by ruling of the court on the ground of privilege from testifying concerning the subject matter of his statement; or

(2) Persists in refusing to testify concerning the subject matter of his statement despite an order of the court to do so; or

(3) Testifies to a lack of memory of the subject matter of his statement; or

(4) Is unable to be present or to testify at the hearing because of death or then existing physical or mental illness or infirmity; or

(5) Is absent from the hearing and the proponent of his statement has been unable to procure his attendance (or in the case of a hearsay exception under subdivision (b)(2), (3), or (4), his attendance or testimony) by process or other reasonable means.

A declarant is not unavailable as a witness if his exemption, refusal, claim of lack of memory, inability, or absence is due to the procurement or wrongdoing of the proponent of his statement for the purpose of preventing the witness from attending or testifying.

The states generally follow the federal rule in accepting death, physical disability, mental illness, absence from the jurisdiction and privilege as grounds for unavailability.[54] The final provision, that unavailability is not established where the proponent of the hearsay is responsible for the declarant's absence, also codifies current practice. A few states are unwilling to find unavailability where a declarant present at the trial refuses to testify. The fear is that the proponent of the hearsay has secured this refusal. More states balk

---

53. In some jurisdictions, persisting in a refusal to testify and claiming a failure of memory could be added to this list.

54. In those states which separate the conditions of unavailability from the particular exceptions, these reasons would be sufficient to establish unavailability under any exception. In those states which link permissible grounds of unavailability to particular exceptions, these reasons apply at least to the exception for former testimony, since unavailability is defined most broadly in connection with this exception.

when a witness claims lack of memory. The worry here is that forgetfulness is feigned to avoid cross-examination. The federal rule makes no mention of statutory incompetency as a ground of unavailability, an oversight in view of FRE 601.[55] In state courts, statutory incompetency is usually an accepted source of unavailability. The federal courts are likely to reach the same result despite the codifiers' oversight.[56]

FRE 804(a)(5) is somewhat more restrictive than the rule in most states. Usually the unavailability requirement is held to be satisfied if a declarant can be shown to be absent from the jurisdiction and thus beyond the process of the state court. Under the federal rules showing the witness to be beyond the reach of process is not enough. One must be unable to secure the witness' attendance by means other than a subpoena and, in the case of certain of the 804(b) exceptions, attempts to depose must have been unsuccessful before the witness' absence will be accepted as tantamount to unavailability.

ii. *Constitutional Aspects*

In civil cases the states may continue to accept absence from the jurisdiction as sufficient to establish unavailability. But in criminal cases, the right to confrontation guaranteed by the sixth amendment requires the state to do more than show mere absence as a precondition to invoking hearsay exceptions which require unavailability. Just how much more must be done is not clear. Two decisions by the Supreme Court deal with this issue.

In 1968, in Barber v. Page,[57] the Court held that the declarant's absence from the jurisdiction did not by itself overcome confrontation clause objections to the use of prior testimony. In *Barber* the state of Oklahoma sought to introduce a transcript of testimony which one Wood had given at a preliminary hearing against his codefendant Barber. At the trial, as a precondition to introducing the transcript, the prosecutor had shown that Wood was in a federal prison in Texas some 225 miles from the Oklahoma courthouse. Although there were serious questions about whether the conditions of the prior testimony exception had been met at the earlier hearing, the Court was willing to assume that there were no constitutional impediments to using Wood's testimony upon a sufficient showing of unavailability.[58] The Court held that a sufficient

---

55. FRE 601 as transmitted to the Congress provided, "Every person is competent to be a witness except as otherwise provided in these rules." Had this been enacted, there would have been no reason to include incompetency as a ground for unavailability in 804(a). However, Congress amended the rule in diversity actions, so now state Dead Man's Statutes will render witnesses incompetent in federal court in some cases. One may assume that the implications of this amendment for the unavailability requirement were overlooked when FRE 804(a) was approved.

56. In situations where state law governs the trial of an issue, or part of an issue, and where state rules of incompetency govern, problems may develop in determining whether state law rejecting out-of-court statements is premised on the fact that the statements are hearsay or on the declarant's general incompetence. If the out-of-

court statements are rejected because state hearsay exceptions are conditioned on tests of unavailability different from the tests found in the Federal Rules, there seems to be no strong reason to exclude the statements of declarants whose unavailability has been established under the federal but not the state rule. If the state law establishes an incompetency, i.e., a rule that an individual in the declarant's position may not testify to certain facts even in court, FRE 601 suggests that the federal court should bow to the state rule.

57. 390 U.S. 719 (1968).

58. It is, of course, the state's function to determine in the first instance the showing which is required to invoke a particular hearsay exception. The Supreme Court on review may only reverse if the state's version of the exception violates the defendant's right to confrontation or other constitutional right.

showing had not been made. They found that Oklahoma had made no effort to secure Wood's presence once it determined that he was located in another state. Yet the policy of the federal prisons to honor *subpoenas ad testificandum* virtually guaranteed that the state could have secured Wood's presence had it tried.

It seemed that the reversal in *Barber* established a principle which was both simple and sensible: in a criminal case a declarant absent from the jurisdiction may be considered unavailable for confrontation clause purposes only if the state makes a good faith effort to secure the declarant's attendance at trial and fails. However, in Mancusi v. Stubbs,[59] decided four years after *Barber*, the Court indicated that it was not content with simplicity and sensibility.[60] *Mancusi* involved the validity of Stubbs' conviction for murder upon retrial, an earlier Tennessee conviction having been overturned on constitutional grounds. Holms, the key witness against Stubbs in the earlier trial, had in the interim moved to Sweden. Tennessee made no effort to contact Holms or to persuade him to appear at the retrial.[61] The Court held that, although Holms was a crucial witness and although no effort had been made to secure his attendance, use of his prior testimony did not violate the confrontation clause. The Court justified its holding on two grounds. The first is that had Holms been contacted and refused to attend the

retrial he, unlike Wood, could not have been compelled to appear. Thus, it is not clear that the state could have prevented Holms' absence. Second, and more fundamentally, Stubbs' earlier opportunity to examine Holms was found to be substantially more conducive to full and effective cross-examination than Barber's opportunity to examine Wood. Holms was a crucial witness against Stubbs testifying at a trial before a judge. Wood was Barber's codefendant testifying at a preliminary hearing before a magistrate. Stubbs had in fact cross-examined Holms since his defense depending largely on his ability to shake Holms' testimony. Barber's attorney had not cross-examined Wood, and it is not clear that he had reason to do so.

It appears that the lesson of *Mancusi* is that the confrontation clause allows a state to establish the unavailability required to introduce prior testimony either by failing in a good faith effort to secure the declarant's presence or by showing that the declarant could not be compelled to be present and that the declarant's prior testimony was thoroughly tested by cross-examination.[62]

One may wonder why the Court came out as it did in *Mancusi*; the good faith standard of *Barber* is not too much to ask of prosecutors and is likely to generate far less reversible error than the complicated balancing of the later case. *Mancusi* is

---

59. 408 U.S. 204 (1972).

60. From the tone of our comments you have no doubt gathered that we approve of *Barber* and not of *Mancusi*. The opinions are both short; read them for yourself and decide if you agree with us. Justice Marshall, who wrote the opinion for eight members of the Court in Barber, dissented in *Mancusi*, but only Justice Douglas joined him. In the four years between *Barber* and *Mancusi*, Chief Justice Warren and Justices Black, Fortas and Harlan left the Court and were replaced by Chief Justice Burger and Justices Blackmun, Powell and Rehnquist.

61. A subpoena had been mailed to Holms' last known United States address in Texas.

Tennessee called Holms' son to establish Holms' presence in Sweden; so it appears the state knew where Holms could be reached.

62. In Ohio v. Roberts, 448 U.S. 56 (1980), the Supreme Court reaffirms the "good faith" test. While the dissenting Justices disagree, it appears to us as it appeared to the majority that the prosecution made enough inquiries to know that at the least it would have taken an extraordinary effort to locate the missing witness, and that even with an extraordinary effort the missing witness might not have been found. *Mancusi* is cited with approval in *Roberts*. The case is presented in Chapter Seven.

particularly puzzling because it appears that the Court intentionally reached out to limit its holding in *Barber*. On the facts of *Mancusi*, the question the Court answered was of uncertain importance and perhaps moot.[63] In addition, the argument based on the quality of the earlier cross-examination is somewhat suspect, since Stubbs' first conviction had been overturned on the ground of inadequate assistance by counsel.[64] It appears to us that this case is best explained on sociopolitical grounds. It is but one of a number of recent Supreme Court efforts to free state hearsay exceptions from the constraints of the confrontation clause. This effort will be discussed in more detail in Chapter Seven.

Until the implications of the confrontation clause for the hearsay exceptions are made clear, one should not be misled by the fact that the two cases which explore the states' obligation to secure witnesses at trial both involve the admissibility of recorded testimony in situations where the declarant was absent from the jurisdiction. Confrontation clause problems may exist whenever a declarant is not put on the stand in a criminal case. It is conceivable that the introduction of hearsay under one or more of the FRE 803 exceptions will violate the confrontation clause if the de-

clarant is in fact available. However, such a ruling is very unlikely, since the Court implicitly approved the rule 803 exceptions when it transmitted them to Congress.[65] The confrontation clause may also be read as requiring an attempt to depose unavailable witnesses similar to that required by FRE 804(a)(5). This is most likely where unavailability results from the declarant's inability to be physically present at trial.

b. Former Testimony

FRE 804(b)(1), the federal rule on former testimony, is consistent with current practice among the states:

(1) *Former testimony*. Testimony given as a witness at another hearing of the same or a different proceeding, or in a deposition taken in compliance with law in the course of the same or another proceeding, if the party against whom the testimony is now offered, or, in a civil action or proceeding, a predecessor in interest, had an opportunity and similar motive to develop the testimony by direct, cross, or redirect examination.

The case for this exception appears particularly strong. Since the exception is limited to earlier testimony, it admits only statements given under oath in situations

---

63. The validity of Stubbs' second Tennessee conviction was not raised on an appeal from that conviction. Its validity became an issue when Stubbs was convicted in New York because the Tennessee conviction, if valid, would have triggered a New York second offender statute. However, Stubbs also had another earlier conviction on appeal. If this conviction were sustained, it would also have triggered the second offender statute and there would have been no need to decide the validity of the Tennessee conviction.

64. The basis for this decision was the fact that counsel had been appointed only four days before trial. Justice Rehnquist, who wrote the opinion in Mancusi, argued that Tennessee had apparently never really passed on the adequacy of Stubbs' counsel but had instead adopted a per se rule—not constitutionally required—that no one appointed four days in advance of a murder

trial **could give adequate representation. After getting this far in the evidence course, do you believe that an attorney's cross-examination could adequately test a witness when there were at most three days available for investigation?**

65. Cf. Hanna v. Plumer, 380 U.S. 460 (1965). But the Advisory Committee and the Congress, and one might assume the Supreme Court as well, took the position that constitutional issues raised by the rules should be left, for the most part, to case by case consideration, thus allowing the rules to be scrutinized as applied. The Supreme Court has, however, indicated how it might resolve one crucial issue. In Ohio v. Roberts, the majority said, "Reliability can be inferred without more where the evidence falls within a firmly rooted hearsay exception." 448 U.S. 56, 68 (1980).

of some solemnity. The testimonial limitation also suggests that the statements admitted will be provable by transcript, thus limiting the danger that they will be misrepresented. Furthermore, the party against whom the statement is offered must have had the opportunity to test the declarant's credibility by direct or cross-examination and must have had a motive to do so similar to the motive at the current trial. Finally, the time lapse between the earlier hearing and the trial at which the testimony is offered may be great enough that the earlier statements appear more reliable than the courtroom testimony which could be offered at the later date.[66] Indeed, the only apparent advantage of courtroom over prior testimony is the opportunity it affords the jury to view the witness' demeanor.

These factors have led most commentators to take a very favorable view of this exception. Wigmore went so far as to argue that the earlier opportunity for cross-examination removes prior testimony from the hearsay category.[67] Others have wondered why prior testimony should be conditioned on the declarant's unavailability when less reliable hearsay exceptions require no such showing.[68] Most believe that the exception should be broadened by expanding the category of individuals against whom prior testimony may be introduced.

Unfortunately, the case for the exception, as it is often applied, is not as compelling as the case which exists in theory. This is because courts have ignored the realities of legal practice in interpreting two conditions of the exception designed to ensure the adequacy of the earlier cross-examination. The first is the requirement of an earlier opportunity for cross-examination and the second the need for similarity of issues.

i. Opportunity for Cross-Examination

The courts have interpreted the requirement of an earlier opportunity for cross-examination to mean just that. So long as there was an opportunity to cross-examine the declarant when he gave his earlier testimony, the testimony is admissible in the later action without regard to whether cross-examination actually took place and without regard to the quality of any actual cross-examination. In many cases this focus on the opportunity rather than the actuality of cross-examination makes sense. Often a decision not to cross-examine is based on a feeling that a witness is telling the truth or that further probing will only hurt one's case. However, where an attorney has not had sufficient time to prepare a case, the failure to cross-examine (or a weak cross-examination) may only reflect the fact that the lawyer had no opportunity to collect the kind of information on which a successful cross-examination might have been based.

It would be a mistake to assume that the problem of inadequate preparation does not exist at trial, but, except where the representation of counsel has been proved inadequate, it may not be unfair to hold a party responsible for failures of this sort.[69] The situation is different where the earlier

---

66. **This last argument is not as powerful as it might appear. Studies indicate that most forgetting occurs within a few days after an event. Thus an individual who testifies at a hearing three months after an event is likely to remember very little more about the event than an individual who testifies a year later. The memory advantage of prior testimony will be most substantial when the earlier hearing occurred only a day or two after the event in question.**

67. 5 Wigmore § 1370. Wigmore's position on this has not been generally accepted.

68. **One reason is that it would be possible to build an entire case out of prior testimony whenever an earlier trial was reversed or when all important witnesses were deposed. It is very unlikely that one could similarly avoid all live testimony by means of other hearsay exceptions. Is this danger a real one?**

69. **As a practical matter, it would be very difficult, absent a showing of coun-**

testimony is given in some non-trial setting such as a preliminary hearing. Here counsel might well have entered the case so recently that there was no time to prepare for cross-examination. Indeed he may not have been aware of the identity of the prosecution's witnesses or the theory of the prosecution's case until he heard the testimony at the exam. Yet most courts do not ask whether the opportunity to cross-examine witnesses in such a setting is a realistic one. So long as the opportunity for cross-examination existed, the preliminary hearing testimony of witnesses unavailable at trial is admitted as former testimony. Courts seldom appear concerned that the basic safeguard supporting the former testimony exception is missing.

The opportunity for cross-examination may also be hampered where former testimony is offered against the party who presented the witness at the earlier hearing. Under the federal rule and in most states the opportunity to develop testimony by direct and re-direct examination is considered an adequate substitute for cross-examination. Yet, in many jurisdictions parties face restrictions in attacking the credibility of their own witnesses, even if some portion of a witness' testimony has been damaging. Furthermore, if the witness' testimony is preponderantly favorable, the party may have no motive to attack his general credibility. Although these factors decrease the likelihood of a search-

ing examination, the majority position is probably a wise one. If a witness' testimony is totally unexpected or devastating, impeachment is ordinarily allowed, and if a party believes that favorable testimony from a witness is honest, the party's failure to clarify harmful matter by redirect examination carries the suggestion that the party was not sure the matter would be clarified in his favor.[70]

ii. Identity of Issues: Motive to Cross-Examine

The second requirement which exists to ensure the adequacy of the earlier cross-examination is the requirement summarized at common law by the phrase, "identity of issues." Though some courts have applied this test literally to exclude earlier testimony when the later case involved different claims or defenses, courts today usually avoid such formalism. Opinions talk in terms of a "substantial" identity of issues, and substantial identity is usually found where "the issues in the first proceeding and hence the purpose for which the testimony was there offered, [were] such that the present opponent * * * had an adequate motive for testing on cross-examination the credibility of the testimony now offered."[71] However, courts also find substantial identity of issues where issues appear similar but where the earlier motive to cross-examine may have been very different from the motive to cross-examine at the time of trial. The defendant

---

sel's incompetence, to distinguish situations where weak or no cross-examination was attributable to lack of information which due diligence might have uncovered from situations where a failure to cross-examine reflected a belief that the witness was telling the truth or that cross-examination would only uncover further adverse information. Furthermore, the party is directly responsible for any failures of cross-examination at the trial in question. It does not seem unfair to extend this responsibility to a subsequent trial so long as the consequences of the first trial were sufficiently adverse that the party could

have been expected to make a serious effort to present a strong case.

70. In some jurisdictions earlier testimony by a party's own witness will be admitted as an adoptive admission, thus avoiding the analytic difficulties of applying the former testimony exception. Of course, the reliability of the prior testimony in this instance will not depend on the theory used to justify admissibility.

71. McCormick § 257, at 622. McCormick suggested that the requirement should be phrased in these terms. This suggestion has been adopted in the federal rule.

at a preliminary hearing may have no motive to cross-examine a witness at that time since he may not want to reveal available impeachment evidence, or, if he does choose to cross-examine, he may only be interested in probing the witness for discovery purposes. Yet courts usually find the identity of issues in these circumstances substantial enough to justify the admission of preliminary hearing testimony against a defendant. Courts also allow testimony recorded in depositions taken for discovery purposes to be introduced at a later trial if the declarant is unavailable. Here again a party may have little reason to test the declarant's credibility at the time the evidence is taken, though there may be substantial reason to do so at trial.[72] The focus of the federal rule on motive as opposed to identity or substantial identity of issues may lead the federal courts to pay closer attention to the party's actual motivation at the earlier trial. However, the Advisory Committee's reference to preliminary hearing testimony in connection with the similar motive requirement suggests that this result was not necessarily intended.[73]

iii. The Same Party Requirement

The other basic requirements of the former testimony exception are generally interpreted so as not to undercut the justifications for the exception. The requirement that the earlier testimony be under oath is adhered to, though an affirmation given at the first hearing in lieu of an oath satisfies this requirement. The final requirement at common law—that there be an identity of parties—has been relaxed by the courts to avoid needless formalism. The early decisions required mutuality. Prior testimony was inadmissible unless the offering party and his opponent had both participated at the hearing in which the testimony was first given. This requirement makes little sense. While the mutuality requirement means that the evidence is in principle available to either party, it is not mutual availability which justifies the exception. The exception is justified by the testing of the declarant's story which occurred or could have occurred at the earlier hearing. Since the proponent of the former testimony would not be offering it if he were not satisfied with the original rendition, the opponent is the only person with reason to complain that the earlier testimony is unreliable. Thus, it is the opponent's opportunity and incentive to test the witness at the earlier hearing which are crucial. The identity of the person first offering the evidence does not affect the rationale for the exception. Courts today realize this and focus on the identity of the person against whom the evidence is offered. That person must be the same person against whom the evidence was originally offered or someone in privity with that person.[74]

---

72. Generally speaking, testimony incorporated in depositions is treated as former testimony, but in many jurisdictions there are special rules relating to the taking of depositions and the situations in which evidence contained in depositions is admissible.

73. See the Advisory Committee's comments on FRE 804(b)(1). The Committee, after stating that identity of issues is significant only as bearing on motive and interest, cites California v. Green, 399 U.S. 149 (1970), for the proposition that testimony given in preliminary hearings satisfies confrontation clause requirements. The implication of the cite at that point is that such testimony satisfies the similar motive requirement as perceived by the Committee. If this is the case, the claim that a subtle shift in strategy changed the motive for cross-examination between one trial and a later one is not likely to be well-received. Should it be?

74. It appears that at one time privity was accepted as a way of meeting the same party requirement for many of the same reasons which justified admissions by privity. Both reflected the tendency of the common law to merge the identity of parties with property when property interests acquired in certain ways were in dispute. The modern justification for holding that the participation by one in privity at the earlier hearing satisfies the same party requirement is the belief that the predecessor had the same motive to cross-examine as the successor in interest.

Consider the following example. P, a pest control specialist, sues D for breach of contract alleging that D hired him to exterminate termites and carpenter ants in a building he owned and then never let him on the premises. D defends, alleging that he never hired P because he never had a termite or carpenter ant problem. At the trial P introduces an expert who testifies that he examined D's building and saw signs of a severe termite infestation but no signs of carpenter ants. Soon after this trial X, a cabinet maker, rents space in the building from D who covenants that the building is free from termites and carpenter ants. Later X sues D, alleging that the building was infested by termites when he rented it. If the expert who testified for P in the case of P against D is unavailable, X may introduce the expert's prior testimony since it is being offered against D who was a party to the earlier suit. The result would have been the same if the building had been rented by D's son who had inherited it from D since the son would be in privity with D. However, had X alleged that the building was infested by carpenter ants when he rented it, the expert's testimony that there were no carpenter ants would not have been admissible against X because X was not a party to the case of P against D nor was he in privity with a party.

Many commentators and several courts have sought to expand the exception for prior testimony by eliminating all identity requirements. They argue that so long as the party against whom the testimony was originally introduced had the opportunity to test the evidence at the earlier trial and had incentives similar to those of the party at the subsequent hearing, the earlier testimony will have been sufficiently tested to justify its presentation to the jury. The federal rule as submitted to Congress adopted this position, but the House Committee on the Judiciary changed the exception to its present form, believing it unfair to make one party responsible for the way in which another handled a witness. The question is a close one, but it seems to us that the federal rule is defensible. Cross-examination is as much art as science. Different attorneys approach the examination of witnesses in different ways. Any good attorney will assess the entire case in deciding whether to cross-examine. Fear of a devastating reply may lead some attorneys to waive cross-examination or to avoid a line of questioning despite a good chance that the results will be favorable. Others may spare the impeachable witness to avoid arousing jury sympathy. Obviously decisions like this are more likely in a case that is otherwise strong, but they will also vary with the lawyer's skills and proclivities and with the client's demands. It seems to us, as it seemed to the members of the House Committee, that it is unfair to hold an individual who played no role in determining the scope of the earlier examination—not even the vicarious role of client—to the tactics and skill which influenced the earlier exam. The problem is even more acute when the testimony was less critical in the earlier case than in the later action or when the stakes in the earlier case were insufficient to justify searching cross-examination.[75] In theory these factors suggest that either the opportunity or motives for cross-examination were not the same in the earlier trial, and the evidence should be excluded on

---

75. **This may be because funds were not available to conduct the kind of investigation needed for successful cross-examination or because there was insufficient money to pay counsel for more than a perfunctory effort. Obviously these conditions may also have existed at an earlier hearing involving the very party against whom the evidence is later offered. At least in these circum-** stances the party can call the court's attention to the earlier deficiency. Also, it somehow does not seem quite as unfair to make a party suffer the consequences of earlier poverty or an unwillingness to invest funds as it does to make one suffer the consequences of someone else's poverty or penuriousness.

these grounds. However, the tendency of courts to ignore reality when assessing opportunity and motive suggests that the "same opponent" requirement serves as a safeguard to prevent the admission of prior testimony that has not been adequately tested by cross-examination.[76]

What makes the policy question difficult is that there is a powerful countervailing argument. Former testimony, even if elicited by an unrelated party, is often likely to be more complete and accurate than much of the testimony that is admitted under the other hearsay exceptions we have examined. If the choice is—as it always is where unavailability is shown—between accepting evidence that is imperfect and foregoing it altogether, reasonable minds can easily conclude that acceptance is preferable.

iv.   Proving Prior Testimony

Statements admitted under the prior testimony exception are often recorded by a court reporter at an earlier hearing and transcribed for presentation in the later hearing. When this is done, the danger that the earlier statements will be misreported is minimal. One might think that, when transcripts are available, prior testimony must always be proved in this way, but there is no such requirement in the federal rules nor is there at common law. Certified transcripts admitted under the official records exception to the hearsay rule are just one way of proving what has been said at an earlier hearing. Earlier testimony may also be proved by the testimony of an observer who purports to remember what was said, by the testimony of an observer with recollection refreshed from stenographer's notes or other memoranda, or by the notes of an observer of the trial if the notes qualify as recorded recollection. In none of these situations is the witness required to report exactly what was said. So long as the witness claims to be reporting accurately the substance of what was said, the phrasing of the earlier testimony need not be reproduced.

v.   Objections to Prior Testimony

When prior testimony is introduced, problems arise as to whether objections may be made which were not made at the earlier hearing. McCormick summarizes the law in this area:

There are sweeping statements in some opinions that this may always be done, and in others that it is never allowable. The more widely approved view, however, is that objections which go merely to the form of the testimony, as on the ground of leading questions, unresponsiveness, or opinion, must be made at the original hearing, when they can be corrected, but objections which go to the relevancy or the competency of the evidence may be asserted for the first time when the former testimony is offered at the present trial.[77]

Problem VI–63. We have criticized the way in which the prior testimony exception is implemented on the ground that courts often ask neither

76. This approach is similar to that taken by most American courts with respect to collateral estoppel. One is not generally bound by another's loss or partial loss even though his interest in litigating a factual issue is identical to the loser's. The trend is to expand in certain circumstances the reach of collateral estoppel, and we would not oppose this if the circumstances are truly special. Similarly, one might envision special circumstances in which one not a party to previous litigation or in privity with a party might be bound by someone else's cross-examination, but this should not often be the case. For symbolic perhaps more than practical reasons, each citizen has been given his or her personal day in court.

77. McCormick § 259, at 623.

whether the earlier situation provided a realistic occasion for effective cross-examination nor whether there really was an incentive to cross-examine the witness when the testimony was given. **Is there a reasonable argument to be made that the exception for prior testimony should apply regardless of the opportunity or motives which existed for earlier cross-examination?** The earlier testimony would have been under oath, the situation would have been a solemn one and the witness would have known how much was at stake for the parties. In addition, an exception for uncross-examined prior testimony could require that the earlier testimony be proved by a trial transcript. **If you were a member of Congress, would you support a move to add such an exception to the hearsay rules? Why or why not?**

Problem VI–64. Peggy Jones sues Dr. Warren for malpractice, alleging that while he was treating her, he was suffering from chronic alcoholism and insane delusions. Ms. Jones has available two affidavits which were filed in the local probate court in an emergency commitment hearing. Each affidavit is by a local psychiatrist who knew Dr. Warren well, and each states that he is suffering from insane delusions brought on by chronic alcoholism and is likely to kill himself. They are dated January 15, 1982, the last day when Dr. Warren treated Ms. Jones. The emergency commitment hearing was held *ex parte* and Dr. Warren was committed to a local mental hospital on the strength of the affidavits. Two days after the emergency commitment the court, according to its usual practice, ordered a full hearing on whether Warren should remain committed. The psychiatrists who had signed the affidavits testified to the substance of the affidavits and they were cross-examined by the counsel whom the court had appointed to represent Warren. Warren was not present, having refused to come to court. The court again ordered Warren committed, finding that he presented a danger to himself due to insane delusions stemming from chronic alcoholism. **At the trial for malpractice, may Ms. Jones introduce (1) the affidavits in which the psychiatrists reported their opinions, (2) the testimony of the psychiatrists given in the full hearing held by the probate court, and (3) the judgment by the court, after the full hearing, finding Warren a danger to self, due to insane delusions stemming from chronic alcoholism, and ordering Warren committed?**

Problem VI–65. Jack Horner is a truck driver for the Royalle Pie Company. Returning from a delivery one evening, Horner's truck skids on some ice and swerves into two men walking by the side of the road. Dave Fisher, one of the injured men, elects to sue Horner personally. At trial Fisher calls Horner as a hostile witness. Under cross-examination Horner admits that he was returning from a delivery for the Royalle Pie Company and that he was probably driving five or ten miles over the speed limit when the truck went into the skid. Horner's lawyer, paid by Royalle, fails to examine Horner further at this point. The trial results in a verdict for Fisher. Three months later, Ted Bunter, the other injured man, brings suit against Royalle on a *respondeat superior* theory. In the interim Horner has died. **May Bunter introduce Horner's testimony in the earlier trial to establish that Horner was acting in the course of his employment at the time of the accident? To show that he was driving in excess of the speed limit**

when the truck hit the ice?   Does it matter whether Royalle is repre-sented in the later action by the lawyer they had hired for Horner in the earlier action?   Would your answers be different if Horner's lawyer had been retained privately by him rather than by the company?

Problem VI–66.   On the same facts as the preceding question, assume that Horner's lawyer has Horner testify in his own behalf.   Horner testifies that the men hit were both wearing dark clothes and facing away from traffic, that they were walking at the side of the road although there was a sidewalk by the road, and that his speed, though faster than the official limit, was about five miles an hour slower than the prevailing speed on the highway in question.   **In the later action could Royalle introduce this testimony against Bunter?   Could it be introduced against Fisher, if the earlier trial ends in a hung verdict and Fisher decides to sue Royalle after Horner dies?**

Problem VI–67.   Nora Arnold has been indicted for perjury on the ground that she lied to a congressional committee when she told the committee that she had never been a member of the Communist Party.   **May her statement "I was never a Communist," which she made at the hearing, be intro-duced against her at the perjury trial?   On what theory?   May this state-ment be proved by the testimony of a staff assistant who was present at the hearing rather than by a transcript of what was said?**

Problem VI–68.   Karen Peabody was an eyewitness to a robbery.   She testified against the defendant at a preliminary hearing, identifying him as the man she had seen fleeing the store with a drawn gun.   She was ques-tioned by the defense counsel at the preliminary hearing but did not change her story.   When the case reached trial, Ms. Peabody was in the hospital with injuries suffered in an automobile accident.   The doctor's estimate was that she would not be able to leave the hospital for two weeks.   **In these circumstances may the prosecution introduce her testimony from the pre-liminary hearing?   Would the situation be different if she were in inten-sive care following severe burns, and the doctor estimated that she would not be able to leave the hospital for from six months to a year?**

Problem VI–69.   Esther Levy, a tourist in Hawaii, was injured on state property and sued the State under the Hawaii Tort Liability Act.   At the first trial the State won a directed verdict, but the Hawaii Supreme Court reversed the trial court, entered judgment for Levy, and ordered a new trial on the issue of damages.   Ms. Levy, who had returned to her home state of New York in the interim, never testified at the second trial.   Instead a transcript of the testimony which she gave at the first trial was entered into evidence.   At the second trial, damages in excess of fifty thousand dollars were awarded.   The State appealed, claiming that the transcript of plain-tiff's testimony in the earlier trial was improperly admitted.   **How should the court rule on appeal?**

Problem VI–70.   Harry Heston was tried for running an illegal num-bers operation.   At the trial, Heston's lieutenant, White, turned state's evi-dence and testified, "Heston raked in a hundred grand a year from the numbers operation." Despite White's testimony, Heston was acquitted. Shortly afterward, White was found shot once through the head. The police had a strong suspicion that Heston was responsible, but were never able to pin the crime on him. About a year later the IRS brought an action against Heston for taxes owed on $300,000 a year which the IRS claimed Heston had earned in his numbers racket but never reported. **May Heston, in an effort to minimize the claimed delinquency, introduce evidence that White, at the earlier trial, had stated that Heston only made $100,000 per year?**

Problem VI–71. Peter Prince sued Sharon Samuel in small claims court, arguing that an electric heater which Sharon's Appliance Store had sold him was defective. He claimed that it did not regulate itself properly, sometimes failing to go on and sometimes turning itself off. Sharon claimed that she had examined the heater once when Prince had returned it and had found nothing wrong. She argued that Prince had not regulated it correctly or that Prince had abused it in some way after it had been examined in her store. Lawyers are not allowed in small claims court in the jurisdiction in question, but each party questioned the other vigorously, if not necessarily to great effect. Their testimony was given under oath. The judge ordered Sharon to pay Prince $10.00 to cover any problems with the heater which were the store's fault, and both went away feeling they had won. Three days later fire broke out in Prince's room, killing him. Prince's estate brings suit against Sharon's Appliance Store and against the Kilowatt Company which had manufactured the heater. Sharon is present at the trial. **Is the testimony which Prince gave in the small claims court admissible against either defendant? Is Sharon's testimony admissible against either defendant? Is Sharon's testimony admissible on behalf of either defendant?**

Problem VI–72. Hancher is charged with assault with a deadly weapon. The charges stem from a bar fight in Iowa City in which Hancher pulled a knife on one Dick Druid. Hancher claims Druid was coming at him with a broken beer bottle and that he just pulled the knife to scare Druid off. The crucial witness at the preliminary hearing was an eighteen year old girl named Sandy Struthers. She testifies that Druid didn't have a bottle in his hand and that Hancher first pulled his knife when Druid's back was turned. As Struthers finishes her testimony, Hancher leans over and whispers to his attorney, who had been appointed two days before the hearing, "Ask her whether she's Druid's girlfriend. I know her and she would say anything for him. And she was in the bathroom when the fight started. She didn't see him break the bottle." The attorney whispers back, "That's the kind of stuff we save for the trial. You're going to be bound over regardless."

A year later, and two weeks before trial, the prosecutor sends a subpoena to Sandy Struthers' house ordering her to show up at the trial. Struthers' parents call the prosecutor and tell him that their daughter left town six months before and they have no idea how to locate her. They say that they heard from her once, a month after she left, when she telephoned from Phoenix, and that they also had indirect contact some three months earlier when a social worker called from San Francisco to verify the fact that Sandy was no longer their dependent. The prosecutor tells them that if they should hear from their daughter during the next two weeks they should try to learn how she can be reached and they should be sure to call his office. At the trial the prosecutor calls Struthers' parents to verify her unavailability and then offers a transcript of her testimony at the preliminary hearing. **Should the transcript be admitted? If it is admitted, can the defendant show that Struthers was Druid's girlfriend and that she was in the bathroom when the fight started? If this is allowed, how can he make this showing?**

---

c. Dying Declarations

The accepted rationale for the dying declaration exception is the assumption that one who knows he is about to die is unlikely to lie. At the time this exception was defined, this assumption was probably justified. Heaven and hell were real places to many people, and bearing false witness was a serious sin. In today's more secular society the validity of the assumption is doubtful.

i. Common Law Requirements

At common law five conditions must be met before a dying declaration will be admitted. First, the evidence must show that the declarant was aware of his impending death. It is said that even the hope of recovery must be gone. The requisite awareness is commonly shown by the declarant's own statements, by statements made to the declarant, circumstantially from the nature of the declarant's wounds, or in some jurisdictions, by the opinions of those in attendance that the declarant was aware he was about to die. Second, the declarant must in fact be dead, though it is not required that death follow soon after the statement, and the rebirth of hope between the statement and the declarant's death does not render the statement inadmissible. Third, the use of the statement is usually limited to actions for homicide. However, there are a number of decisions admitting the dying declarations of women where criminal abortion has been charged, and, in recent years, a few states have, by statute or decision, admitted dying declarations in civil cases. Where dying declarations are admissible

they may be admitted on behalf of either the prosecution or defense. Fourth, the declarant must be the victim of the homicide charged. Fifth, the declaration must relate to the homicidal act or to those immediate circumstances surrounding the act. In addition to these specific requirements, the states are generally concerned that the deathbed statements be the witness' own good faith declarations. Where the declarant has indicated that he is telling only part of the story or where the declarant had special reasons to avenge himself against someone, dying declarations have been excluded. Dying declarations, like most admissible hearsay, must be based on firsthand knowledge. The opinion rule may also present problems, though it is often relaxed when hearsay is involved.

The states are split on the weight to be accorded dying declarations. In some, a party may be entitled to an instruction that dying declarations do not have the same value as sworn testimony. In others, there is no error in telling the jury that dying declarations "stand on the same plane of solemnity as statements made under oath." In most jurisdictions a dying declaration is sufficient to establish crucial facts in issue.

ii. The Federal Rule

FRE 804(b)(2) liberalizes the common law exception in two ways:

Statement under belief of impending death. In a prosecution for homicide or in a civil action or proceeding, a statement made by a declarant while believing that his death was imminent, concerning the cause or circumstances of what he believed to be his impending death.

The most important change is that the exception is no longer limited to homicide cases. In federal court, dying declarations will be admitted in civil cases so long as they concern the cause or circumstances of what the declarant believed was his impending death. An earlier draft of the rules would have admitted dying declarations in all cases to prove the circumstances of apparently impending death, but the House Committee on the Judiciary, doubting the reliability of deathbed statements, decided to limit the use of dying declarations in criminal cases to homicide prosecutions "where exceptional need for the evidence is present." The other change made by the federal rule is that the declarant need not be dead to be considered unavailable. Any of the causes of unavailability specified in FRE 804(a) will do.

Those who favor the admissibility of dying declarations in civil cases argue that if dying declarations are reliable enough to be admitted in homicide actions, where the defendant's life may be at stake, it follows *a fortiori* that they should be admissible in civil actions where so much less is involved. This argument is vulnerable at two points. It is not clear that the admissibility of dying declarations in homicide actions is justifiable today on reliability grounds alone, and there is good reason to expect that dying declarations admitted in civil actions will be less reliable than the dying declarations admitted in criminal cases.

iii. A Justification for Homicide Cases

Most would admit that the religious justification for the dying declaration excep-

tion has largely disappeared in modern society, but one still might argue that an individual aware he is about to die has little interest in deceiving listeners about the cause of his impending death. In cases of homicide this argument seems plausible. Although situations can be imagined where a dying person would lie to implicate an enemy or protect a loved one, the usual expectation is that the victim will want his killer brought to justice. This expectation alone, however, does not clearly justify the exception. While it provides some guarantee of reliability, countervailing factors exist which suggest unreliability. Chief among these is the probability that the declarant will have been under great stress before, during and after the homicidal attack. Stress, as the Stewart article makes clear, interferes with accurate perception and can lead to memory or narration problems. Yet stress may not be the threat to perception in this area that it is in others. The most significant of the facts commonly proved by dying declarations, the identity of a previously known killer, seems unlikely to be either misperceived or forgotten.[78] Where the declarant describes the circumstances of the homicide, the more detailed the account, the greater the threat posed by problems of perception. If the case for the dying declaration in homicide cases were based entirely on the probable honesty of deathbed cases discounted by the likelihood of misperception, it would be a weak one, perhaps defensible, perhaps not. But there is another factor which has nothing to do with reliability. This is the peculiar need which is felt to bring murderers to justice (to some extent this should be counterbalanced by our abhorrence of convicting the innocent) coupled with a desire to avoid rules of evi-

---

78. Problems may exist where circumstances suggest that the declarant saw his assailant when in fact he didn't. Here the declarant's accusation will be merely an assumption about who was out to get him. If other statements by the declarant indicate he was lacking firsthand knowledge the statement will be excluded, but if there is no evidence to suggest this, the statement will be admitted on the assumption that the declarant perceived that which his statement indicates.

dence which make it obvious that a criminal is better off if his victim dies than if he survives.[79] Perhaps this factor properly sways the balance toward admissibility.

However sensible this analysis,[80] it is at best a rationale for the exception and not the reason why dying declarations are admitted today. The dying declaration is, like certain other rules of evidence, rooted more in history than in reason. Courts have received dying declarations from the time that hearsay was first distinguished from courtroom testimony. They continue to apply this exception—sometimes citing the old rationales and only rarely wondering if they still apply—because its acceptability has been so often validated that the question of reliability is no longer open.[81]

iv. Extension to Civil Cases

The extension of the exception to civil cases is not, of course, historically legitimated. While it is not unreasonable to argue that evidence reliable enough for homicide cases is reliable enough for civil actions, there is reason to wonder whether the dying declaration exception in homicide cases is today justifiable on reliability grounds alone.[82] And, even if dying declarations carry substantial guarantees of reliability in homicide cases, this does not mean that similar reliability will exist in civil actions. There are reasons to believe that dying declarations admitted in civil cases will be substantially less reliable than those admitted in homicide actions. These reasons follow from the fact that dying declarations in civil cases will usually relate to an accident in which the declarant was involved rather than an assault of which the declarant was the victim. Incentives to falsify are much more likely when one is fatally injured in an accident than when one is fatally assailed. At a conscious level, a declarant who has knowledge about the laws of civil liability will wish to protect his estate and enhance the prospect that his heirs will have a valid cause of action. This may be done by denying one's own responsibility and attributing responsibility to the other party. Subconsciously, the declarant may feel guilty, both because he is leaving his family and because his accident involvement has harmed others. In his attempt to cope with guilt the declarant may, without being aware of it, seek to minimize his role in causing the accident while emphasizing the responsibility of others. The third factor likely to make dying declarations less reliable in civil cases than in homicide actions is the likely subject matter of the statements. Straightforward accusations of responsibility or simple descriptions of assaults are common in homicide cases. In civil cases, reports of the complicated details of the accident and its aftermath are likely. Here the stress of the accident situation and the resulting fatal injury may be expected to make reported perceptions particularly unreliable.

One might justify the extension of the dying declaration to civil cases on the grounds that the rule excluding hearsay is fundamentally mistaken or that the need for hearsay when individuals are unavailable overrides any justification for keeping such

---

79. **The hearsay rule and the trial system give the criminal an interest in the victim's death. The dying declaration exception only removes that interest in very specific circumstances, but these are probably the circumstances in which it would otherwise be most obvious that the criminal has gained by a fatal rather than a merely injurious assault.**

80. We make no claim that our attempt to present a secular justification for the dying

declaration exception is satisfactory. We view the case for the exception as a close one.

81. See e.g., Mattox v. United States, 146 U.S. 140 (1892).

82. This assumes that one is committed to a hearsay rule with exceptions based on reliability. Those who feel the hearsay rule should be abolished might rationally support any excuse for extending a hearsay exception.

statements out.   Also, there is no clear evidence of gross injustice in those jurisdictions which do admit dying declarations in civil cases.   But, if one is truly concerned with limiting new hearsay exceptions to situations of special reliability, a dying declaration exception in civil cases appears to one author to be a questionable candidate for innovation.

The other author finds the preceding analysis highly speculative at best and mistaken at worst.   He argues that there are also reasons why one might believe that dying declarations in civil cases are more reliable than their counterparts in criminal cases.   In a criminal case the victim is not at fault (or usually not, since self defense is a possibility).   Most dying declarations relate to actions of other people in criminal cases.   In a civil case the actions of the declarant are often important.   It may be that declarants are better able to speak about their own actions than those of others.   Stress may be somewhat less sig-

nificant when individuals are talking about their own actions.   Moreover, to the extent that the declarant may have been at fault in a civil action, feelings of guilt may promote honesty.   And, there may be some reason to think that declarants pay better attention to their own actions than to those of others.   Finally, declarations that contain excessive, self-serving details are likely, if false, to be contradicted by other evidence, and even if true, they may be viewed skeptically by jurors.

Does this analysis convince you that dying declarations in civil cases are at least as justified as those in criminal actions?   Does it convince you that we really do not know how the reliability of dying declarations in civil cases compares with their reliability in criminal actions?   This difference between the authors should reveal the extent to which armchair psychology influences judgments about rules of evidence.   Whose armchair psychology do you agree with?[83]

Problem VI–73.   Sam Peck is charged with murder.   He allegedly killed a bank guard in the course of an armed robbery.   As he was leaving he also shot a pedestrian, Carl Adams, on the sidewalk outside the bank.   When the police arrived Adams was lying in a pool of blood.   As they were placing him on a stretcher, Adams said to one of the officers, "That bastard who shot me was Sam Peck.   We went to high school together, and he knew I recognized him.   Well I've had it and I'm going to heaven, but I hope he roasts in hell."   In spite of what he said Adams recovered.   However, he died of a heart attack a year later while Peck was still at large.   Eventually, Peck was captured and brought to trial.   **At that trial may the state offer Adams' statement to identify Peck as the bank robber?   Had Adams died of the gunshot wound, could the state introduce his statement if Peck were tried for murdering him?**

Problem VI–74.   Candy Young is found shot in the back.   **Will her statement "Billy Olds shot me" be admitted if there is evidence that when she made this statement she knew she was about to die?**   Assume that after stating that she expects to die, Candy makes a more elaborate state-

---

83.   The dispute about whether dying declarations should be admitted in civil cases is not as important as it might seem since statements that qualify as dying declarations are often admissible under other hearsay exceptions.   Most commonly, they qualify as excited utterances since courts are quite willing to find that an excited state exists during a period of intense suffering following an event.

ment, "Billy Olds and I had a fight.   I told him I never wanted to see him again.   He slapped me.   I kicked him.   He pulled a gun and hit me on the shoulder with the butt.   I gave him a karate chop to the stomach and he fell down.   I turned and ran and then he shot me."   **Is a court more or less likely to admit this statement than they are the simple statement, "Billy Olds shot me"?   If Tom Novack is charged with Young's murder, will the statement be admissible on his behalf?**

Problem VI–75.   Jim Short is found dying of stab wounds.   A police officer accompanies him to the hospital in an ambulance.   On the way the officer, who knows Short, says, "Jim, the driver tells me you lost too much blood.   He says he's never seen anyone in your condition survive.   You know you don't have long to live, don't you?"   Jim nods yes.   The officer continues, "Now Jim, this is Sandy's doing isn't it?"   Jim nods yes.   "He pulled a knife on you didn't he?"   Jim nods yes.   "He slashed you because he knew you were ready to testify against him on the drug case, isn't that the reason?"   Jim nods yes.   "He wanted to do more than scare you.   He wanted to be sure you wouldn't live to tell your story.   Isn't that what happened?"   Jim nods yes and expires.   **If Sandy is charged with murdering Short, will the officer's questions and Jim's answers be admissible against Sandy at trial?**   Suppose that the police officer, after establishing that Jim was aware of his impending death, had merely asked Jim what had happened and Jim had replied, "Sandy was out to get me because he knew I intended to spill on him," and then died before saying anything more.   **If there were other evidence linking Sandy to the killing, would this statement be admissible to establish Sandy's motive?   If there were no other evidence linking Sandy to the killing, would the statement be admissible to show that Sandy was the killer?**

Problem VI–76.   Pat Kelley was dying of cancer.   She was in great agony and knew she had at most a week or two to live.   One evening a nurse looked in and noticed that Pat was in a shallow sleep looking particularly pale.   He shook her awake and asked her if she had had her medicine for the evening.   She replied that she did not remember having any of her hospital medicine but that her sister had given her two pills to swallow before she left.   The nurse gave Pat her medicine and departed.   That night Pat died.   A routine autopsy showed that the cause of her death was not cancer but poison.   Her sister is charged with manslaughter for this "mercy killing."   **May the state introduce Pat's statement that her sister gave her two pills to swallow as part of its effort to establish that the sister was responsible for the poisoning?**

---

d.   Statements Against Interest

At common law there is a hearsay exception for statements which at the time they are made appear so contrary to the declarant's <u>pecuniary</u> or <u>proprietary</u> interest that it is unlikely that they would have been made had they not been true.   State-

ments admissible under this exception assert facts suggesting that the declarant is potentially worse off than he would have appeared to be had the statement not been made.   Almost always, the *making* of such statements will be against the declarant's interest as well, since such statements can be introduced as admissions if the declarant tries to assert a contrary position in any legal action. For example, a creditor's statement acknowledging payment of a debt is considered to be a statement against interest, for it makes the creditor appear worse off financially than if the debt were thought to be still owing. Furthermore, if the creditor sues to collect the debt, his acknowledgement of payment can be introduced as an admission, thus diminishing his chance of collecting on the debt. The exception for statements against interest is based on the reasonable assumption that a person is unlikely to intentionally depict a situation as less favorable to him than it in fact is. A creditor's statement acknowledging payment of a debt is most unlikely if payment did not occur since the motives for such a lie are few. The exception provides substantially less protection against the dangers of misperception or faulty memory than it does against the danger of prevarication. Still there is some protection, since individuals are likely to check those memories and perceptions which suggest they are less well off than they might otherwise be.

The basic requirements for the statement against interest exception are few. The declarant has to be unavailable, the declaration must be against a pecuniary or proprietary interest of the declarant when made, and the usual firsthand knowledge requirement applies. To these some states add a further requirement. The declarant must have had no probable motive to falsify. This requirement assumes importance in jurisdictions which admit, as parts of statements against interest, portions not against interest. This is done on the theory that the aspect of the statement which is against interest guarantees the credibility of the entire statement. Jurisdictions vary in the extent to which this "piggybacking" is allowed.

Historically, statements against interest were admitted only where the declarant's unavailability was due to death. By the 1940's a number of states had come to recognize insanity as well, and today the trend is toward allowing the exception whenever a legitimate cause of unavailability is shown. The requirement of unavailability and the strictness with which it has been construed may seem strange given the apparent trustworthiness of declarations against interest. It has been suggested that the exception is so limited because it is often used to introduce associated statements which are neutral or even self-serving in character.[84] Such statements contain no guarantee of reliability apart from their close association with a statement which is predominantly disserving. Thus, in the early English case of Higham v. Ridgway [85] the entry of a male midwife reporting payment on Oct. 25, 1768 of money due for attendance at the birth of a son on April 22, 1768 was admitted as a declaration against interest to show the date on which the son was born. If the entry appears particularly reliable on the issue of the son's birthdate, it is because it appeared in a business record and not because it accompanied the acknowledgement of a debt paid. American courts differ in their willingness to admit neutral or self-serving statements as statements against interest. To the extent that the exception is limited to only those portions of statements that were clearly against interest when made, the case for a strict application of the unavailability requirement is weakened.

i. The Against Interest Requirement

Most of the difficulties associated with the statement against interest exception are difficulties in determining when a statement is sufficiently against interest to qualify under the exception. Statements often found to be against pecuniary or proprie-

---

84. Jefferson, Declarations Against Interest: An Exception to the Hearsay Rule, 58 Harv.L.Rev. 1 (1944).

85. 10 East 109, 103 Eng.Rep. 712 (K.B. 1808).

tary interest include: declarations acknowledging indebtedness, declarations acknowledging payment of a debt, declarations of contingent contractual liability, statements of agents acknowledging receipt of money on behalf of principals, declarations admitting less than a fee simple interest in property, declarations by an heir acknowledging that property has been left by will to another, declarations by beneficiaries of insurance policies tending to defeat claims thereunder and statements acknowledging tortious liability in specific amounts. Courts have been divided on the question of whether statements which tend to establish or extinguish tort liability qualify as statements against interest. The prevailing view is that they do qualify.

Often it is not clear on the face of a statement whether it was against interest when made. This will depend on facts existing at the time of the statement. Thus X's statement "Last year Y bought out my interest in the X Department store" would be against interest if the X store were flourishing, but not if it were insolvent. Similarly a statement by A that B owns Blackacre shares the guarantees of a statement against interest only if A believes he has some colorable claim to Blackacre.[86] It is for the court, not the jury, to find the contextual facts on which admissibility is conditioned.

While the situation at trial cannot determine whether a statement was against interest when made, it may influence the decision on admissibility in two ways. It may be a clue as to whether a statement was in fact against interest when made. For example, a statement acknowledging a life

estate in land is generally assumed to be against interest because of the presumption that the possessor of land holds the fee. However, if the plaintiff sues the possessor alleging that the possessor's leasehold has expired, the possessor's earlier statement acknowledging a life estate appears not to have been against interest when made. The subsequent suit makes it likely that declarant knew at the time of his statement that although he may have had some claim to a life estate rather than a leasehold, he had no colorable claim to possession in fee simple.

The situation at the time of the suit may also be important because an earlier statement may be against interest only with respect to certain inferences. If the statement is offered to support those inferences it will be admitted; otherwise it will be excluded. Consider, for example, an income tax return which reports an annual income of $10,000. If the statement were offered to show that the declarant earned at least that much, it should be admitted since the taxpayer had financial incentives to minimize the amount of income reported. The same incentives mean that the statement should not be admitted under this exception to show that the declarant earned no more than $10,000.

A declaration may have both self-serving and disserving aspects. Where assertions are separable a court has three options: (1) to admit the entire declaration on the strength of the part which is disserving, (2) to admit the entire statement if the disserving part predominates and to exclude it entirely if the self-serving part predominates, or (3) to admit only those parts of the statement which are disserving.

86. **Regardless of what A knows, if he should later learn that he has a claim to Blackacre this statement would be admissible against him as a personal admission. This has led some courts to admit such statements against third parties as declarations against interest. The better practice is not to admit these statements against** third parties because the statements do not have those extra indicia of reliability which justify the exception. Thus A, not knowing he has some claim to Blackacre, might well be careless about the truth if he were arguing that his friend B and not his enemy C was the rightful owner.

American courts usually choose either the second or third option. Both McCormick[87] and Jefferson[88] suggest that the third option is preferable. Where a single assertion is both self-serving and disserving the third option is not possible. Here the courts take the second approach. If the statement seems on balance self-serving, it will be excluded; if it is on balance disserving it is admitted. One situation where this kind of balancing is required is where a creditor's statement acknowledges part payment of a debt. If at the time of the statement the statute of limitations has run on the debt and if part payment would revive it, the statement is excluded because the creditor's interest in reviving the legal obligation outweighs his interest in not acknowledging payments never received. If the statute has not run, an acknowledgment of part payment is considered a statement against interest.

Neutral observations that are part of a statement against interest are more likely to be admitted than self-serving comments, and they will not cause the disserving portion to be excluded. In deciding whether to admit the neutral portions of a statement against interest, a court will look at how closely related the neutral portion is to the disserving portion and at whether there are other indicia of reliability. If circumstances, including a close relationship to the disserving portion, suggest that the neutral portion is reliable, it will usually be admitted.

ii. *Statements Against Penal Interests*

Commentators have argued that the declaration against interest exception is unduly narrow because it is limited to statements against pecuniary or proprietary interests. The claim is that admissions of criminal responsibility and statements made despite the probability of social disgrace carry guarantees of reliability akin to those that justify the admission of statements against fiscal interests. There are a few cases admitting statements against social interest and more admitting acknowledgments of criminal responsibility. The catalyst for the latter decisions is Justice Holmes' brief but eloquent dissent in the case of Donnelly v. United States.[89] Donnelly had been convicted and sentenced to die for a murder which he claimed one Joe Dick had committed. There was some evidence suggesting that Dick had committed the crime and Dick had confessed to the crime before he died. However, the jury never learned of the confession because it did not qualify as a statement against interest. The majority in *Donnelly* upheld the lower court because the statement did not relate to Dick's pecuniary or proprietary interests. Holmes disagreed:

> The confession of Joe Dick, since deceased, that he committed the murder for which the plaintiff in error was tried, coupled with circumstances pointing to its truth, would have a strong tendency to make anyone outside of a court of justice believe that Donnelly did not commit the crime. I say this, of course, on the supposition that it should be proved that the confession really was made, and that there was no ground for connecting Donnelly with Dick * * *. [T]he exception to the hearsay rule in the case of declarations against interest is well known; no other statement is so much against interest as a confession of murder, it is far more calculated to convince than dying declarations, which would be let in to hang a man; and when we surround the accused with so many safeguards, some of which seem to me excessive, I think we ought to give him the benefit of a fact that, if proved, commonly would have such weight.

---

87. McCormick § 279, at 677.

88. Jefferson, supra note 84, at 50.

89. 228 U.S. 243, 277–78 (1913).

Despite Holmes' eloquence, there are good reasons to be wary of statements admitting criminal involvement. Police report that they commonly receive false confessions to publicized crimes. Should the jury learn of these it might necessitate a detailed explanation of why each confessor could not have committed the crime charged. It is also possible that a criminal on his deathbed or safely outside the jurisdiction will seek to protect his buddies by confessing to crimes which they have committed.[90] Perjury, a third danger, is a possibility whenever a statement against interest is admitted. It may, however, be more of a danger when statements against penal interest are introduced in criminal cases. There is often more at stake in such cases and criminals may be more likely than noncriminals to perjure themselves or to know people who will perjure themselves for friendship or payment or out of fear. All three reasons become less persuasive where there is substantial independent evidence connecting the declarant to the crime.

FRE 804(b)(3) strikes a balance by admitting statements against penal interest, provided that corroborating circumstances indicate trustworthiness if the statement is offered to exculpate an accused. Except for the general changes made in the unavailability requirement, this is the major difference between the federal declaration against interest exception and the common law:

Statement against interest. A statement which was at the time of its making so far contrary to the declarant's pecuniary or proprietary interest, or so far tended to subject him to civil or criminal liability, or to render invalid a claim by him against another, that a reasonable man in his position would not have made the statement unless he believed

it to be true. A statement tending to expose the declarant to criminal liability and offered to exculpate the accused is not admissible unless corroborating circumstances clearly indicate the trustworthiness of the statement.

In jurisdictions which do not adopt this reform there are two other approaches available to a defense attorney who wants to use the inculpatory statements of an unavailable third party to exculpate a client. The first is a constitutional argument. It is possible that the compulsory process clause of the sixth amendment as interpreted in Chambers v. Mississippi[91] gives the defendant a constitutional right to introduce third party admissions of criminal responsibility so long as other evidence connects the third party with the crime. The second approach takes account of the fact that criminal behavior is often tortious. Where this is the case, one may argue that a statement admitting a crime is also against pecuniary interest. The difficulty with this approach is that courts willing to treat acknowledgments of criminal behavior as contrary to pecuniary interest often admit such statements only in civil cases. In criminal cases tried under the federal rules, statements that tend to expose the declarant to civil as well as criminal liability may still be held to trigger the corroborating circumstances requirement.

Although the exception for statements against penal interest was passed with cases like *Donnelly* in mind, it is today commonly invoked by the prosecution. Criminals often implicate others in the course of admitting their own criminal involvement. Some courts treat such implications as the neutral portion of disserving statement. They examine the circumstances closely for other indicia of reliability. If such indicia are present, the

---

90. Ironically, the police, in order to make their record look good, may also elicit confessions to crimes which the confessor did not commit. See J. Skolnick, Justice Without Trial pp. 164–181 (1966).

91. 410 U.S. 284 (1973). This case and its implications are fully discussed in Chapter Seven.

statements are usually admitted. Other courts are likely to exclude references to third persons if redaction of the hearsay statement is possible. In one situation, the courts are particularly wary. This is where a statement inculpating oneself and another has been given to a law enforcement officer after arrest. Courts know that statements to law enforcement officials may be part of a plea bargaining process or may be otherwise motivated by a desire to curry favor. This does not mean that such statements are never admitted. It does mean they are subject to close scrutiny.

iii. Distinguished from Admissions

You should note that very often statements against interest will be admissible under some other exception to the hearsay rule, usually an exception which will have the advantage that unavailability need not be shown. The most common alternative ground of admissibility is the admissions exception, since parties frequently introduce statements of facts detrimental to the financial interests of opposite parties, those in privity to them and their agents. The exceptions, however, are not the same. The admissions exception does not require unavailability or firsthand knowledge and admissions need not be against interest when made. Lawyers nonetheless speak of "admissions against interest." Be aware of the way in which this confuses two distinct exceptions.

Problem VI–77. Jill Hennesey, a notorious gambler, is being sued by the IRS for back taxes. The IRS claims that Hennesey failed to report as earnings $80,000 which she and a partner won in 1982 by gambling. To prove this the IRS seeks to introduce entries on some papers seized from Hennesey which record winning bets totaling $80,000. Hennesey claims that at most she owes taxes on $30,000 in winnings because the partnership lost $50,000 wagering on the horses during 1982, and the tax law allows gambling losses to be subtracted from winnings. She seeks to introduce other entries on the papers seized by the IRS which note gambling losses totaling $50,000. The entries reporting losses are interspersed with those reporting winnings. **May the government introduce the entries reporting Hennesey's successful wagers? If the government is allowed to do this, may Hennesey introduce the entries which show her bad bets? If you were Hennesey's lawyer, what arguments would you make in support of your motion to admit the entries showing the losing bets?** Assume the entries were written by the partner, since deceased.

Problem VI–78. One day A tells her cousin, "I've just conveyed Whiteacre to B in exchange for Blackacre." Some years later, after both A and B have died, oil is discovered on Whiteacre and a dispute arises between the heirs of A and those of B about who owns which property. **May B's heirs introduce A's cousin to testify to what A told him?**

Problem VI–79. Carol Pack, a thirty year old woman, sues the estate of Butler Yates, claiming that she is the adopted daughter of Yates and entitled to a share in his estate. **May Pack introduce a witness who will testify that her natural father, now nowhere to be found, once said, "Well, I've done it. I've entered into a contract with Butler allowing him to adopt Carol. He's her father now. I no longer have the rights nor the responsibility."** At the time of this statement Pack was five years old. **May the estate introduce copies of Yates' income tax returns for the years when**

Pack was 12, 13 and 14 years old to show that Carol's name is not listed among Yates' dependents?

Problem VI–80. Harriet Duncan sues Randy Goshen, alleging that he is the father of her child. Randy claims he is not the father. Randy wishes to introduce a witness who will testify that she once heard Sam Davids state that he was the father of Harriet's child. **If Randy cannot find Davids to subpoena him, will the witness' testimony be admissible?**

Problem VI–81. Horton sues Prince to quiet title to a tract of land known as "Cold Bottom." Horton claims to own the land by virtue of twenty years of open and hostile adverse possession. It is admitted by all that Horton has lived openly on the Cold Bottom tract for twenty years. The issue is whether his possession was hostile throughout this period. Prince argues that up until two years before the date the suit was filed, Horton was paying him rent for use of the land. The rent was allegedly paid through a local real estate dealer who collected money from Horton, deducted a commission and forwarded her own check for the remaining amount to Prince. The dealer is now deceased. To prove his claim, Prince seeks to present testimony by the dealer's husband that up until the time of his wife's death about two years ago, she would come home on the first day in every quarter complaining, "Well, I've gotten the money out of Horton again. I don't know why I put up with this. The commission isn't worth it. He's got to be the crookedest man I have met." The husband also remembers that his wife once told him, "When Horton gave me the rent today he said that he wouldn't be paying for long because he had a lawyer friend who told him how he could trump up a claim for adverse possession. I was going to tell him that he couldn't so long as he was paying me rent, but I figured that that would make it harder than ever to collect." **May the husband testify to any of his wife's statements? May the defense introduce checks from the deceased real estate dealer on which she has written in the lower left hand corner "Horton rent"? May the dealer's check stubs which say "Horton rent" on them be admitted on any theory?**

Problem VI–82. Stephen Bird, noted bridge authority, wrote a column in which he accused Henry Hogg and his partner Timothy Toucan of cheating in major bridge tournaments over a ten year period. Hogg sues Bird for libel. **At the trial, may Bird introduce evidence that Timothy Toucan, since deceased, had admitted before his death that he and Hogg had been cheating at bridge for many years? Would it matter whether the admission was made before or after Bird's column appeared?**

Problem VI–83. Henderson, vice president and treasurer of the Mogg Corporation, is accused by a corporate auditor of embezzlement. Eventually she admits to having taken $46,000 over a three year period. The company fires Henderson but does not press charges. Henderson leaves for a foreign country to be sure that the charges will not be brought despite the company's failure to press them. Later Mogg sues the company which had bonded Henderson for the $46,000. **In order to prove that this was the amount lost, may the company introduce Henderson's admission of this fact?**

Problem VI–84. Dovico and Gangi are jointly charged with selling narcotics. Dovico is tried and found guilty by a jury. Gangi pleads guilty. While in prison Gangi tells another prisoner that he was solely responsible for the sale and that Dovico was innocent. On the strength of this disclosure Dovico is granted a new trial. However, Gangi dies before the new trial can begin. **Should the prisoner who heard Gangi's confession be allowed to testify to it? Would the case for admission be stronger if Gangi had testified that he and a person named Cook were responsible for the sale, not he and Dovico? Would your answer to either of the above questions be different if you were in a progressive jurisdiction which had held that statements against social interest were sufficient to justify the statement against interest exception to the hearsay rule?**

Problem VI–85. Thompson, Ekols and Meeks are charged with bank robbery. Ekols chose to plead guilty and turn state's evidence while Thompson and Meeks pled not guilty and were tried together. Ekols testified as follows:

> The day before the robbery Meeks approached me and asked me if I would like some easy money. I said yes and we went to his apartment and planned the robbery. It's only a small branch and we thought they wouldn't have much security. The next morning Meeks told me that he'd gotten Roland Thompson to drive for it. Later that day Meeks and I went to his apartment. Roland was there in the parking lot. He drove us downtown and circled the block the bank was on once or twice. Then he let us out. Meeks told him to meet us at corner of First and Fifth, and he was there when we got out.

The cross-examination included the following:

D.C. You say you planned this robbery with Meeks. Was Thompson ever involved in the planning?

E. No.

D.C. Did you and Weeks ever discuss the robbery while you were in the car driving to the bank?

E. No.

D.C. Did you ever hear Meeks mention the robbery in Thompson's presence?

E. No.

D.C. After the robbery, what was Thompson's share of the proceeds?

E. He didn't get any of the money.

D.C. Isn't it true that on the morning of the robbery Meeks said, "I've suckered Thompson into driving for it."

E. No. He said, "I've gotten Thompson to drive for it." He meant Thompson agreed.

D.C. Did Meeks use the word "agreed."

E.   No.

D.C.   Thank you.   No more questions.

At the preliminary hearing in this case, right after pleading guilty, Meeks had said within the hearing of the U.S. Magistrate, the prosecuting and defense attorneys, a reporter and Thompson, "They ought to let Thompson go. He didn't have anything to do with it." At the trial the government did not seek to introduce this statement against Meeks in its case-in-chief. It was also not used for impeachment since Meeks never took the stand. Thompson, however, wanted to introduce the statement. **Should he have been allowed to place any of the witnesses to the statement on the stand to testify to what Meeks had said?**

Problem VI–86. Phyllis Harris works as a bank teller at First National. One day a woman walks up to a window and passes through a note saying, "I've got a gun. Put all your money in the bag." Phyllis puts $5,000.00 in the woman's bag and the woman flees. Later Phyllis is questioned by Special Agent Kirshner of the FBI. Although Kirshner does not arrest Phyllis, he gives her *Miranda* warnings. He suspects she is involved in the robbery both because she delayed in pressing the switch that triggers the silent alarm and because he knows that her brother Ed is a suspect in another bank robbery, at Bankers Trust. After several hours of questioning, Phyllis breaks down and confesses her complicity. She tells Kirshner:

> About five days ago Eddie called me. He said that he was one of those who robbed the Bankers Trust, but that his pictures weren't on the T.V. news because the surveillance cameras didn't catch him. I think he was proud of it. He asked me to meet him the next day, and I did. The next day he told me he wasn't really one of the robbers, but that he was outside the bank at the time, and he thought the police suspected him so he had better get out of town. He said he needed money and that his girlfriend Karen would stage a bank robbery if I would cooperate. I didn't want to do it, but he wore me down saying how it would kill mamma if he got arrested. I stopped by Karen's yesterday morning to explain the layout of the bank, and you know the rest.

Eddie Harris was arrested four years later and tried for robbing the Bankers Trust. The state's central witness is Simon, one of the robbers who was caught soon after the robbery and convicted. He identifies Eddie as a participant and says that because Eddie's location was near the bank's door, he was out of the field of the camera. The corroborating evidence is weak. One of Eddie's prints was found on the getaway car and he was absent from work the day of the robbery. To further corroborate the accomplice's testimony, the state would like to introduce Phyllis' statement. Eddie's admission that he was one of the participants but that the camera didn't catch him is considered particularly important. Phyllis, who was indicted for the second robbery but never tried, is called as a witness. She says she no longer remembers the details of her conversation with agent Kirshner and she specifically does not recall ever telling him that her brother said that he had helped rob the Bankers Trust but had not been photographed. She does say that she recalls answering all of Kirshner's questions truthfully. The state would like to call Agent Kirshner to testify to Phyllis' statement. **Is Kirshner's testimony admissible?**

---

e. Statements of Pedigree

The last of the specific hearsay exceptions for which unavailability is generally required[92] is the exception for statements of pedigree or family history. By this time you should not be surprised that FRE 804(b)(4), which codifies this exception, makes substantial changes in the common law:

> (4) *Statement of personal or family history.* (A) A statement concerning the declarant's own birth, adoption, marriage, divorce, legitimacy, relationship by blood, adoption, or marriage, ancestry, or other similar fact of personal or family history, even though declarant had no means of acquiring personal knowledge of the matter stated; or (B) a statement concerning the foregoing matters, and death also, of another person, if the declarant was related to the other by blood, adoption, or marriage or was so intimately associated with the other's family as to be likely to have accurate information concerning the matter declared.

The common law requirements for this exception which are not codified in the federal rule are that unavailability be due to death, that the statement be *ante litem motam,* i.e., made before the beginning of the controversy which ultimately gave rise to the litigation, and that the declarant be either the person whose family status is in issue or someone related to that person by blood or marriage.

The exception admits statements which are not based on firsthand knowledge.[93] This is necessary since family history is often based on secondhand information. It is felt that the kind of communication which characterizes family life makes it likely that the information is accurate.

This exception was justified at common law on two grounds: the belief that relatives have special knowledge of family history and the protection against intentional deception inherent in the *ante litem motam* requirement. Both these requirements were carried to extremes in some courts. For example, where statements specified a relationship between two parties, some jurisdictions refused to admit the statements unless the declarant could be connected to both parties. The requirement that a statement must be made before the matter in controversy arose not only barred statements arising long before any suit was filed, it also barred statements made after the controversy arose by persons shown to be unaware of the existing controversy.

In dispensing with the requirement that the declarant have some family relationship to the subject of the statement, the federal rule follows the lead of a number of states. The relaxation of this requirement appears sensible, for unrelated individuals intimately connected with a family are often as knowledgeable about the family's history as family members. The complete elimination of the requirement insulating the statement from the instant controversy is questionable. Where the only statements of family history available to a party are favorable statements made

---

92. Some states require unavailability for hearsay exceptions which apply regardless of availability in other jurisdictions.

93. Part A of 804(b)(4) eliminates this requirement specifically where the declarant is speaking about himself. Part B makes no specific mention of the requirement but the drafters almost certainly did not mean to require firsthand knowledge here either. One may be likely to have accurate information without having firsthand knowledge.

after a controversy arose, one wonders about the absence of earlier information. The drafters of the federal rule felt that the jury could evaluate these circumstances in determining the weight to be given to such statements. Perhaps they can. We believe that a compromise admitting statements whenever made, so long as the declarant is not shown to be involved in the controversy, is better than either extreme.

You should note the overlap between this rule and FRE 803(19). When statements concerning family history are numerous enough to constitute a reputation for the matter in the family, among associates, or in the community, unavailability of the declarants need not be shown and the fact may be established by anyone familiar with the reputation. An exception like 803(19) is not available in all states. Some states condition such exceptions on unavailability and some place more restrictive limits on the kinds of reputation evidence that may be presented.

Although this exception has not given rise to many reported cases, you should not ignore it. Whenever a family relationship is relevant in a case this rule may provide a useful, efficient way of offering evidence.

3. IMPEACHING A HEARSAY DECLARANT

When testimony has been admitted under an exception to the hearsay rule, the hearsay declarant may be impeached in much the same way as an ordinary witness. Witnesses may testify to the declarant's biases, inability to observe and bad reputation for truth and veracity. However, difficulties may arise if the attempt is to impeach by inconsistent statements. You will recall that at common law this mode of impeachment requires the cross-examiner, by way of foundation, to direct the witness' attention to the alleged inconsistent statement. Extrinsic evidence of the inconsistent statement is allowed only if the witness denies having made the statement and the statement does not pertain to a collateral matter. Obviously this foundation requirement cannot be met if the hearsay declarant is unavailable. So long as there never was an opportunity to meet this requirement, as with a dying declaration or a statement against interest, states are willing to waive the foundation requirement and allow extrinsic evidence of inconsistent statements which are not collateral. However, the situation is different if there was once an opportunity to meet the foundation requirement and it was not met, as with hearsay admitted under the exception for former testimony. At one time a majority of states held that the failure to establish a foundation on the earlier occasion barred impeachment by inconsistent statements when the hearsay was later introduced. The modern trend is in the opposite direction.

Where a hearsay declarant may be impeached by inconsistent statements, the impeaching party may usually introduce statements made before or after the hearsay that has been admitted. Statements made subsequent to the hearsay declaration are likely to be as probative of the declarant's credibility as those made before. Some jurisdictions, which require a foundation when former testimony is impeached, waive the foundation when the impeachment is by subsequent inconsistent statements. In these circumstances, the impossibility of laying a foundation is obvious.

The receptive attitude toward hearsay embodied in the federal rules is complemented by an equally receptive attitude toward evidence that tends to impeach the credibility of hearsay declarants. FRE 806 provides:

When a hearsay statement, or a statement defined in rule 801(d)(2), (C), (D), or (E), has been admitted in evidence, the credibility of the declarant may be attacked, and if attacked may be supported, by any evidence which would be admissible for those purposes if declarant had testifed as a witness. Evidence of a statement or conduct by the declarant at any time, inconsistent with his hearsay statement, is not subject to any requirement that he may have been afforded an opportunity to deny or explain. If the party against whom a hearsay statement has been admitted calls the declarant as a witness, the party is entitled to examine him on the statement as if under cross-examination.

SECTION IV.   MODERN TRENDS

A.   LOOKING BACKWARD AT PAST JUDGMENTS ON THE FUTURE OF HEARSAY

For years evidence scholars have been writing about "the future of hearsay," and a glance at the future has become the customary way of concluding the hearsay chapter in casebooks. Since before most of us were born, the consensus among scholars has been that the future of the common law hearsay doctrine is deservedly bleak. The most common criticisms have been that the exclusion of hearsay evidence hampers the search for truth too often to be tolerated in a rational system of evidence law and that the proliferation of hearsay exceptions has created a system of unnecessary and unmanageable complexity. Suggested improvements range from the abolition of the basic rule of exclusion to the creation of new hearsay exceptions admitting reliable evidence currently excluded.

During the past two decades, the case most often cited as an example of what the future will and should bring has been Dallas County v. Commercial Union Assurance Co., Ltd.[94] The incident giving rise to that case occurred on July 7, 1957, when "the clock tower of the Dallas County Courthouse at Selma, Alabama, commenced to lean, made loud cracking and popping noises, then fell and telescoped into the courtroom."[95] The damage exceeded $100,000. Dallas County sued its insurance carrier under a provision of the pol-

icy providing recovery for damage caused by lightning. The carrier defended claiming that the collapse was due to structural defects. Evidence on the cause of the collapse was conflicting. Perhaps the strongest evidence offered by the County was testimony that charred timbers had been found in the tower debris. In order to rebut the inference, supported by expert testimony, that the charred timbers were attributable to lightning, the insurance company introduced a copy of the *Morning Times* of Selma for June 9, 1901, which carried an unsigned story reporting a fire in the courthouse at a time when it was still under construction. The jury found for the defendant and the issue on appeal was whether this story had been properly admitted under the then governing rule, Fed.R.Civ.P. 43(a), which provided:

All evidence shall be admitted which is admissible under the statutes of the United States, or under the rules of evidence heretofore applied in the courts of the United States on the hearing of suits in equity, or under the rules of evidence applied in the courts of general jurisdiction of the state in which the United States court is held. In any case, the statute or rule which favors the reception of the evidence shall govern.
* * *

94.   286 F.2d 388 (5th Cir. 1961).

95.   Id. at 390.

The appellate court might have strained to fit the story under one of the existing hearsay exceptions, but it eschewed that route. Instead it looked at the two criteria which Wigmore thought sufficient for the creation of a hearsay exception—necessity and circumstantial guarantees of trustworthiness. Admitting that witnesses to the fire might be uncovered by a diligent search, the court nevertheless found the story to be a necessary vehicle for effectively proving the source of the charred timbers. The court assumed that it was improbable that any witness could be found with a clear recollection of events at the time the courthouse was built and that it would have been impossible for the testimony of any witness to be as accurate and reliable as the statement of facts in the contemporary news article. The court found circumstantial guarantees of trustworthiness in the fact that the individual reporting the fire had no motive to falsify and that a false report of a matter so easily checked by the readers of the paper would have subjected the reporter to considerable embarrassment. The court concludes with the following statement of the philosophy behind its opinion:

> We do not characterize this newspaper as a "business record", nor as an "ancient document", nor as any other readily identifiable and happily tagged species of hearsay exception. It is admissible because it is necessary and trustworthy, relevant and material, and

its admission is within the trial judge's exercise of discretion in holding the hearing within reasonable bounds.[96]

Despite the approval with which this opinion was greeted, it was not followed by any marked increase in the tendency of courts to ignore the parameters of the hearsay exceptions and look to the general character of the proffered hearsay.[97] Predictions that the hearsay rule would be substantially relaxed continued to be better indicators of the hopes of the prognosticators than of the probability that the courts would suddenly become substantially more receptive to the admission of hearsay.[98] But in the middle to late 1960's an important development occurred. In a number of states and at the federal level, a decision was made to codify the rules of evidence. Suddenly the numerous critics of the hearsay rule no longer had to convince conservative courts of the direction which hearsay doctrine should take. As reporters of or advisors to committees drafting these codes, the critics had the opportunity to write their preferences into law. Although some of the more extreme ideas for liberalizing the hearsay rule were never accepted or were eliminated in the enactment process, all the modern codes substantially liberalize traditional restrictions on hearsay evidence. With the enactment of the Federal Rules of Evidence and of the many state codes they have inspired, it is safe to say that the "future of hearsay" is, for better or worse, upon us.

---

96. Id. at 397.

97. There were, to be sure, some exceptions [see, e.g., United States v. Barbati, 284 F.Supp. 409 (E.D.N.Y.1968)], but there had been exceptional cases before *Dallas County* as well.

Almost no one disagrees with *Dallas County* on its facts, but one of us wonders whether the Court of Appeals might not have been too ready to assume that a reporter would not err in reporting a fire. What specific information should a court demand before concluding that a story in a newspaper must have been true?

98. It should be emphasized that trial courts have always taken liberties with the hearsay doctrine as they have with other rules of evidence. The motivation for such action ranges from a desire to get at the truth to simple misunderstanding of the rule to be applied. Appellate courts, however, in affirming cases where the admissibility of hearsay is not clear have almost always tried to rationalize the trial court's decision in terms of one of the traditional exceptions or have treated the error as harmless. Rarely have they taken the approach seen in *Dallas County* and disclaimed the need to look to particular exceptions.

The arrival of the "future" has been marked by a significant expansion of the situations in which hearsay evidence is admissible. This is accomplished in two ways: by the elimination of certain restrictive conditions which are part of the traditional exceptions and by the creation of new exceptions to the hearsay rule. In Section III of this chapter we noted the

many ways in which the specific exceptions of the Federal Rules of Evidence differ from their common law counterparts. In almost all cases deviation from tradition enhances the admissibility of hearsay evidence. Indeed certain federal hearsay exceptions, such as the exception for statements in learned treatises, are unknown at common law.

B. RELIABILITY AS A PRIMARY JUSTIFICATION

The new exceptions created by the Federal Rules of Evidence are rather narrow reactions to specific situations in which it is thought hearsay should be admissible. The exceptions which we shall discuss in this section are based on more general principles, principles which are likely to influence both those states which codify their evidence rules and those which opt for case by case reform. Perhaps the most basic and potentially the most expansive principle is the principle applied in the *Dallas County* case: *if a particular item of hearsay evidence has circumstantial guarantees of trustworthiness equivalent to the guarantees which attach to the recognized exceptions, that item of evidence should be admitted whether or not it meets the requirements of an established hearsay exception.* This principle is most likely to be applied when it is difficult to develop non-hearsay evidence which bears on the fact in issue.

This principle was pressed to the fullest in the original draft version of the Federal Rules of Evidence.[99] In this draft there were only two true exceptions to the hearsay rule. FRE 803(a) was the exception which did not turn on declarant's availability:

A statement is not excluded by the hearsay rule if its nature and the special cir-

cumstances under which it was made offer assurances of accuracy not likely to be enhanced by calling the declarant as a witness, even though he is available.

FRE 804(a) applied if the declarant were unavailable:

A statement is not excluded by the hearsay rule if its nature and the special circumstances under which it was made offer strong assurances of accuracy and the declarant is unavailable as a witness.

The specific exceptions now found in these subsections were mentioned, but only as illustrations of the situations in which the general rule should admit hearsay and not by way of limitation.

This dramatic subordination of the specific hearsay exceptions to the principles of reliability and necessity was eventually rejected as too drastic a change in established doctrine. In the version of the rules transmitted by the Supreme Court to Congress, specific exceptions were spelled out.[1] However, the principle which guided the original approach was firmly embedded in two new rules, FRE 803(24) and FRE 804(b)(6)[2], both of which provided exceptions for:

A statement not specifically covered by any of the foregoing exceptions but having comparable circumstantial guarantees of trustworthiness.

99. Proposed Rules of Evidence for the U.S. District Courts and Magistrates (1969).

1. The court approved the rules on November 20, 1972. They were submitted to

the Congress on February 5, 1973, by the Chief Justice.

2. One exception conditioned on unavailability was eliminated from the version which

The "foregoing exceptions" referred to are, of course, conditioned on unavailability only in the case of FRE 804(b)(6). Had this version been adopted, the potential for admitting hearsay not covered by specific exceptions would have been almost as great as it was in the original version. The House Committee on the Judiciary rejected these catch-all exceptions, feeling that they injected too much uncertainty into the law of evidence and that by diminishing the predictability of rulings on hearsay they impaired the ability of litigants to prepare adequately for trial.

The Senate Judiciary Committee had a different set of fears. They were afraid that unless some discretion to admit reliable hearsay was vested in the courts, the result in cases like *Dallas County* would be reversed. They proposed language giving courts discretion to admit apparently reliable hearsay where the need for such hearsay is great. With the addition in conference of a notice requirement the Senate revision was enacted as FRE 803(24) and as FRE 804(b)(5):

> A statement not specifically covered by any of the foregoing exceptions but having equivalent circumstantial guarantees of trustworthiness, if the court determines that (A) the statement is offered as evidence of a material fact; (B) the statement is more probative on the point for which it is offered than any other evidence which the proponent can procure through reasonable efforts; and (C) the general purposes of these rules and the interests of justice will best be served by admission of the statement into evidence. However, a statement may not

be admitted under this exception unless the proponent of it makes known to the adverse party sufficiently in advance of the trial or hearing to provide the adverse party with a fair opportunity to prepare to meet it, his intention to offer the statement and the particulars of it, including the name and address of the declarant.

It is clear that the spirit of the rule which Congress enacted is quite different from that of the rule as originally proposed or as transmitted by the Court. Under the earlier versions the decision to exclude hearsay was suspect; the goal was to avoid depriving the jury of reliable evidence. Under the enacted version hearsay evidence remains suspect; only in exceptional circumstances is hearsay which does not meet the conditions of a particular exception to be admitted.

However, there is considerable variation in the way in which the "catchall" or "residual" exceptions are being interpreted. Some judges remain faithful to Congressional intent and use their discretion only in exceptional circumstances. Other judges treat 803(24)[3] as a license to admit whatever hearsay they think essential to a just result. Consider, for example, the case of United States v. Lyon,[4] the trial of a man who allegedly built bombs in shoe boxes. A Mrs. Lorts, Lyon's landlady, told a police officer, who had found a bomb in a shoe box, that she had given a shoe box to Lyon. Shortly after this interview, Lyon jumped bail and remained free for eleven years. By the time of the trial, Mrs. Lorts had apparently forgotten both the incident and her description of it. The trial judge admitted

the Supreme Court transmitted to Congress. Thus, the general provision in the Court's version of 804(b) was numbered (6) while the general provision in the enacted version is numbered (5).

3. When we refer to 803(24) we mean to include 804(b)(5) as well. The only independent content of 804(b)(5) is that when a witness is unavailable a court may consider the circumstantial guarantees of trustworthiness that attach to the 804 exceptions in deciding whether evidence is admissible. A court cannot refer to these exceptions when a declarant is available. However, since the hearsay admitted by the 804 exceptions is in no obvious way less reliable than at least some of the hearsay admitted under the 803 exceptions, the distinction is of little practical importance.

4. 567 F.2d 777 (8th Cir. 1977).

the police officer's transcription of his interview with Mrs. Lorts under 804(b)(5). The appellate court approved, noting that "[t]rustworthiness was guaranteed by Smith's detailed testimony about how he took Mrs. Lorts' statement and transcribed it."[5] But this justification does not relate at all to the trustworthiness of Mrs. Lorts' statement. It means, at most, that whatever Mrs. Lorts said was accurately reported. This is an important consideration when eleven years have elapsed, but by this standard the recorded statements of any unavailable witnesses would be presumptively admissible. The court also noted that the shoe box, which was in evidence, bore the signatures of both Mrs. Lorts and the police officer and that it conformed to the description of the box that Mrs. Lorts had given the officer. Here the court is looking for circumstantial guarantees of trustworthiness,[6] but these guarantees are not akin to those that attach to other hearsay exceptions. It is only in retrospect that these facts suggest that Mrs. Lorts was telling the truth. The circumstances used to justify other hearsay exceptions suggest the special reliability of statements standing alone. By the standard applied to Mrs. Lorts' statements, any hearsay which is likely to be true because it is consistent with other evidence in a case would be presumptively admissible under the residual exceptions.

The Eighth Circuit in *Lyon* was arguably unfaithful to both the letter and the spirit of the residual exception.[7] But a court may remain faithful to the letter of the rule and still use it in a way that Congress never intended. Turbyfill v. International Harvester Company is such a case.[8] In *Turbyfill* the plaintiff and two companions while shopping on the defendant's used car lot were, with the help of the defendant's mechanic, Anderson, trying to start a balky truck. As the plaintiff was pouring gasoline from a small can into the truck's carburetor, one of his companions attempted to start the engine. The engine backfired, the gas can caught fire, and the plaintiff was severely burned. Three hours later, Anderson's supervisor told him to go into a room and write down everything he knew about the accident. Anderson died before the suit that arose out of this event reached trial. The defendant offered his statement to show how the accident occurred, and the trial judge admitted it under FRE 804(b)(5). The judge noted that the statement was offered to prove a material fact and that it was more probative on the points for which it was offered than any other evidence that the defendant could reasonably have obtained. Guarantees of trustworthiness were present because:

> He [Anderson] wrote the statement on the afternoon of the accident while the circumstances were still fresh in his mind. Moreover, the fact that he made his written account while alone in a room indicates that the account accurately reflects his knowledge of the events transcribed.[9]

The judge in this case has complied with the letter of the rule. After determining that the evidence is material and neces-

---

5. Id. at 784.

6. Id. Note, however, that if as is probably the case, Mrs. Lorts signed the box to indicate that it was the box she gave Lyon, Mrs. Lorts' signature is assertive conduct and is itself objectionable as hearsay. If she signed the box without intending to assert that it was the box she gave Lyon, it is hard to see how her signature is relevant.

7. The court's clearest violation of the letter of the rule was their failure to enforce the

pre-trial notice provision. We discuss judicial treatment of the notice provision in the text accompanying note 17 infra.

8. 486 F.Supp. 232 (E.D.Mich.1980). Professor John Kaplan rated this case among the year's six "most interesting" because of its implications for the general prohibition against hearsay. Kaplan, Mason Ladd and Interesting Cases, 66 Iowa L.Rev. 931 (1981).

9. 486 F.Supp. 232, 235 (E.D.Mich.1980).

sary, he has, as a matter of discretion, found that the hearsay carries guarantees of trustworthiness equivalent to those that guarantee other hearsay exceptions.[10] The problem is with the exercise of discretion. If Anderson's hearsay is admissible, so is any other uncoerced statement written or uttered while an event is fresh in the declarant's mind and not duplicable by other reasonably accessible evidence. Indeed, Anderson's statement is more suspect than many such statements, for Anderson was a potential defendant in Turbyfill's suit and he might also have feared that he would have been fired by his employer had his description made it appear that he was in some way responsible for what had happened.[11] To exercise discretion as the judge in *Turbyfill* did is to undercut a considered Congressional decision.[12] If *Turbyfill* were the standard for admissible hearsay, the hearsay rule would be all but destroyed. So long as hearsay was necessary, all but the most obviously contrived statements would be admitted.

Lyon and *Turbyfill* are extreme cases. They do not, however, stand alone. We could have used a number of other cases as examples of how some courts disregard a legislative history that includes language like the following:

It is intended that the residual hearsay exceptions will be used very rarely, and only in exceptional circumstances. The committee does not intend to establish a broad license for trial judges to admit hearsay statements that do not fall within one of the other exceptions contained in rules 803 and 804(b).[13]

Other courts have taken Congress' intent seriously and have cited the above language in construing the residual exception. At this point, it is not clear which view of the exception will ultimately prevail. Although the appellate courts have addressed issues on a case by case basis, no circuit has laid down a coherent framework to guide trial judges in their exercise of discretion.

10. The trial judge also cited FRE 803(5), the exception for past recollection recorded, as a justification for his decision. The judge pointed out that if Anderson were present at the trial and could not remember the circumstances of the accident, his written account would have been admissible. This is true, but this is because additional guarantees of trustworthiness are thought to attach to such statements. First of all, Anderson would have to swear that the statement was accurate when made or that he wouldn't have written an inaccurate account. Anderson could also be asked general questions about his perceptual abilities and about his feelings at the time of the accident. He might be asked whether his company disciplined employees who were responsible for accidents and whether it had ever occurred to him that he might be sued personally by Turbyfill. Throughout such questioning the jury could view Anderson's demeanor and reach some judgment about whether he was the kind of person who might falsely describe an incident in order to protect his own interests. The fact that FRE 803(5) is used to admit hearsay similar to Anderson's emphasizes the degree to which Anderson's hearsay lacks the guarantees associated with other objections.

11. In addition to Anderson's obvious motive to falsify there is the natural human instinct to deny one's responsibility for a tragic event. This may be the greater threat to accuracy.

12. One might argue that the guarantees in Turbyfill were no weaker than the guarantees that justify the admission of dying declarations or excited utterances. However, when those exceptions first arose their justifications appeared considerably stronger than they do now. It is only the psychology of the twentieth century that makes us wonder whether the enhanced sincerity in such situations is more than offset by difficulties of perception. Congress was clearly concerned with the trustworthiness of the hearsay that the residual exceptions might admit. Courts should not use exceptions attributable more to historical reasons and nineteenth century psychology than to current judgments of reliability as benchmarks for determining what circumstantial guarantees of trustworthiness are equivalent to the established exceptions.

13. Report of Committee on the Judiciary Senate, Federal Rules of Evidence No. 93-1277, at 20 (1974). Because the House of Representatives would have eliminated the residual exceptions entirely, the Senate's language indicates the most expansive

In interpreting the residual exceptions subsection (A), that the statement be offered as evidence of a material fact, and subsection (C), that the purposes of the rules and the interests of justice be served, are not problematic. If a statement is not material, it is not admissible under any hearsay exception, and if the statement is material, trustworthy and necessary, the purposes of the rules and the interests of justice will almost certainly be served by its admission. It is also possible to read "material" not in a technical sense, but as signifying a Congressional intent that the fact which the evidence is offered to prove be important to the outcome of the case. This reading, like a more technical reading, will not limit the applicability of the exceptions where they truly matter. Subsection (B), the requirement that the statement be "more probative on the point for which it is offered than any other evidence which the proponent can secure through reasonable efforts," is substantively important. It means that even under FRE 803(24) unavailability will typically be required [14] and where an available witness is outside the jurisdiction of a court an attempt to depose may be needed before the witness' hearsay will be admitted.

The courts have been most concerned with the requirement that there be circumstantial guarantees of trustworthiness equivalent to those that justify other hearsay exceptions. More hearsay has been refused for lack of trustworthiness than for any other reason, but, as in *Turbyfill,* the requirement is also, on occasion, empty. Courts searching for equivalent guarantees of trustworthiness have looked at the characteristics of the statement, the circumstances in which it was made, and the extent to which it is corroborated by other evidence. If, as appears to be the case, Congress intended that the required indicia of trustworthiness be similar in kind to those of the other exceptions, the existence of corroborating evidence should play no part in decisions regarding admissibility. The admissibility of hearsay under the specific exceptions does not turn on its consistency with the other evidence in the case. Nevertheless, if trustworthiness is the primary concern, the best indicator of trustworthiness may be whether the hearsay coincides with the other evidence in the case. The danger in using consistency as a guide is that this approach may blur the separate elements of a case. Assume, for example, that in order to convict the defendant of a crime the state must prove elements, A, B and C. Elements A and B are proved by admissible evidence while element C is only supported by hearsay. If the hearsay supporting C is deemed trustworthy because it is consistent with the evidence supporting A and B, the court may be deciding *sub silentio* that if elements A and B exist, element C probably exists as well and on this basis may allow the admission of evidence that tends to prove C.[15]

---

reading that can be given to the residual exceptions consistent with the legislative history.

14. One may conceive of situations where unavailability will not have to be shown because the hearsay is likely to be substantially more probative than the testimony of the hearsay declarant. In Dallas County, for example, memory problems mean that the newspaper story was likely to have been substantially more probative than the testimony of the reporter who wrote the story on the issue of whether there had been a fire in the courthouse sixty years before.

15. This is not necessarily the result of evaluating trustworthiness by the way in which a statement coincides with other evidence in a case. In United States v. Lyon, supra note 4, Mrs. Lorts not only said that she had given a shoe box to Lyon, but she also described the box. The fact that her description matched that of the box in which the bomb was found suggests that her entire statement was trustworthy. Even where a court does blur lines between elements to be proved, it does not necessarily mean that the decision to admit hearsay is unwise. Hearsay tending to prove element C may, in fact, be more credible because evidence tending to prove elements A and B exists. If, for example, we know that D intended to kill X, the hearsay of a declar-

The search for "equivalent circumstantial guarantees of trustworthiness" requires courts to compare hearsay that can only be admitted under the residual exceptions with hearsay that is admissible under the specific exceptions. Special problems arise if the hearsay in question has a good deal in common with hearsay that would be specifically admitted. On the one hand, the hearsay in question may share some of the indicia of trustworthiness that justify the specific exception. On the other hand, the fact that hearsay does not qualify under the specific exception may mean that it is of a kind that Congress or the Advisory Committee meant specifically to exclude. The better policy is for the courts to defer to legislative history where there is evidence that Congress or the Advisory Committee deliberated over the lines they were drawing and to make their own judgments when there is no evidence that a matter was considered.

If there is one portion of the residual exceptions that seems invulnerable to judicial discretion, it is the requirement that a statement "not be admitted under this exception unless the proponent of it makes known to the adverse party * * * in advance of trial * * * his intention to offer the statement." There are courts that read the requirement literally and say it is to be strictly construed. But other courts read it in light of its most obvious purpose which is "to provide the adverse party with a fair opportunity to prepare to meet" the statement. One of the first cases construing the exceptions held that where the government was unexpectedly confronted with otherwise inadmissible hearsay, a

continuance was sufficient to meet the purposes of the notice requirement.[16] Other courts have implied that even a continuance is not necessary if the adverse party had reason to expect that information like that contained in the hearsay would be admitted.[17] In ruling this way, the courts are not only ignoring what appears to be a clear Congressional command, but they are also treating pre-trial notice as if its sole function is to allow the adversary an opportunity to question the hearsay. Knowing before trial whether certain evidence will be admitted may also affect a party's litigation strategy and proclivity to settle. In addition, if notice must be given before trial, hearsay cannot be resorted to when a party finds that other attempts to prove a point have not been convincing. It may even be that the requirement of pre-trial notice was one means by which the Congress meant to ensure that the residual exceptions would be used "very rarely, and only in exceptional circumstances."

The future of hearsay is inextricably linked with the way that courts interpret the residual exceptions. To date, interpretations have been mixed. On the one hand, judges clearly want discretion to admit hearsay when they feel that admission will enhance the cause of justice. On the other, there is the pull of the legislative history which, on any fair reading, means that the residual exceptions should be used only sparingly and in special circumstances.

The Supreme Court has had opportunities to cast some light on the residual exceptions, but it has chosen not to do so.

---

ant who claims to have seen D shoot X is more credible than it would be without the evidence of intent.

Where the hearsay and the facts that corroborate it bear on the same element in a case, it may be that the relationship is too close to justify admitting the hearsay under the residual exceptions, for the corroborating evidence and not the hearsay is likely to be the most probative evidence that

bears on the issue in question. Since the probative value of evidence turns in part on the other evidence in a case, this may suggest to some that the limitation imposed by Section A of FRE 803(24) is unwise.

16. United States v. Iaconetti, 540 F.2d 574 (2d Cir. 1976).

17. United States v. Lyon, supra note 4, is one such case.

In one case where the record offered little to support the government's introduction of the grand jury testimony of an uncooperative government witness, Justice Stewart, joined by Justice Marshall, dissented from a denial of certiorari.[18] Justice Stewart's opinion suggests that it is "open to serious doubt whether Rule 804(b)(5) was intended to provide case-by-case hearsay exceptions, or rather only to permit expansion of the hearsay exceptions by categories."

We think that the language of the rule and the legislative history described above make it absolutely plain that what is required is a careful, sensitive, judicial examination of the offered evidence and the justifications proposed for admitting it. This kind of meticulous scrutiny does not lend itself to establishing new categories of exceptions. Evidence might be admitted in one case because of special circumstances that, if changed even slightly, should produce a different result.

The case that prompted the Stewart opinion is troublesome, but this is because of the ease with which the court of appeals approved the admissibility of very damaging evidence made in circumstances that ought to have cast doubt on its reliability. Also, the use of grand jury testimony by a witness whose uncooperative attitude made cross-examination difficult posed a potential conflict with the policies supporting FRE 801(d)(1)(A), a rule which allows the substantive admissibility of inconsistent statements only when the declarant has testified as a witness and is present for cross-examination. As we have indicated earlier, it is possible to read certain congressional judgments in the drafting of the rules as implicitly barring extensions through the residual exceptions. It makes sense to read other rules as posing no barriers to the use of the residual exceptions to admit evidence falling outside traditional exceptions.

What we have said may suggest that appellate courts have not always performed well in interpreting the residual rules. It should be noted, however, that how well they perform depends in part on the quality of arguments about evidence issues on appeal, and more importantly, in the trial courts.

You must understand the policies underlying the hearsay rule and its exceptions in order to argue about whether hearsay falling outside the traditional exceptions satisfies the demanding standard Congress established in its residual clauses. You should be ready to argue by analogy to the policy justifications for other rules and be prepared to point out how some hearsay falls short of the residual standard because the hearsay dangers that other exceptions guard against are not removed in the particular case.

Since some form of notice, or at the very least a continuance to prepare, is available when the residual exceptions are invoked, there is the opportunity to make full arguments on the hearsay question at the trial stage. Trial judges may not always have the legislative history in mind when a hearsay question arises, but you can provide them with it. The better you know the rationales for the standard exceptions, the more able you will be to argue for and against admission under the residual exceptions.

C. NECESSITY AS A PRIMARY JUSTIFICATION

Exceptions like those in *Dallas County* are justified primarily on the ground that the excluded hearsay is considerably more reliable than most out-of-court statements.

---

18. United States v. Garner, 574 F.2d 1141 (4th Cir. 1978), certiorari denied, 439 U.S. 936 (1978).

The necessity for the evidence, although a factor to be weighed, is of secondary importance.[19] However, some have suggested that necessity alone should suffice as a justification for a hearsay exception. Those who take this position feel that the costs of excluding hearsay are clear, while the possibility that hearsay will mislead the jury is problematic. Given this perceived imbalance, they argue that where the declarant is unavailable, his statements should be admitted unless there exist peculiar reasons to believe them unreliable.[20] But, as a factor to be weighed in creating hearsay exceptions, necessity cuts two ways. Hearsay is most necessary to a party when it is the only available evidence tending to prove an important aspect of his case. It is precisely in these circumstances that the concern for reliability should be greatest, because the decision in the case may turn on whether or not the hearsay is admitted. What is necessary to the proponent of hearsay may be devastating for the opponent. When the necessity for hearsay carrying no special indicia of reliability is great, it is not clear whether justice is more likely to be advanced by the admission of such hearsay or by its exclusion.

Those who argue that necessity is sufficient justification for a hearsay exception point to an exception available in civil actions in Massachusetts since 1898:

No declaration of a deceased person shall be excluded as evidence on the ground of its being hearsay if it appears to the

satisfaction of the judge to have been made in good faith before the beginning of the suit and upon the personal knowledge of the declarant.[21]

Despite long and apparently favorable experience with this exception in two states, the proposed principle justifying the admission of hearsay largely on the basis of necessity has been the least well received of the principles we discuss in this section. It is accepted to a limited extent, in certain states which in abolishing their "Dead Man's Statutes" provided a hearsay exception for statements of decedents in actions involving their estates. The principle was also embodied in the version of the Federal Rules transmitted by the Supreme Court to the Congress. In that version, rule 804(b)(2) provided:

Statement of recent perception. A statement, not in response to the instigation of a person engaged in investigating, litigating, or settling a claim, which narrates, describes, or explains an event or condition recently perceived by the declarant, made in good faith, not in contemplation of pending or anticipated litigation in which he was interested and while his recollection was clear.

This proposed federal exception is both broader and more restrictive than the Massachusetts rule. It is broader in two respects: it recognizes more than death as a cause of unavailability and it applies to criminal as well as civil actions. It is more restrictive in that it is limited to statements

---

19. In the version of FRE 803(24) and 804(b)(5) adopted by the Congress this is not true. The requirement that the statement be more probative on the point for which it is offered than any other evidence which the proponent can procure through reasonable effort means that the necessity element should weigh heavily in the decision whether to admit hearsay under these provisions.

20. This position is codified in Rule 503(a) of the Model Code of Evidence (1942), which provides that, "Evidence of a hearsay declaration is admissible if the judge finds that the declarant is unavailable as a

witness". **This radical restructuring of the hearsay rule has been felt by many to be a principle reason why the Model Code has not been adopted in any jurisdiction.**

21. Mass. Acts and Resolves 1898, ch. 535, p. 522. In 1920 a Committee of the Commonwealth Fund concluded after polling the Massachusetts Bar that the statute "is sound in theory and beneficent in operation." 4 Weinstein's Evidence 804–103. The Massachusetts statute has been copied in Rhode Island. It is claimed that experience with the statute in that state is also favorable.

of recent perceptions, thus minimizing memory problems, and in that it specifically excludes the kinds of statements which might be taken by insurance adjusters or other persons investigating claims. Despite the efforts of the drafters to include more indicia of reliability in the federal rule than in the Massachusetts statute, the exception was deleted in Congress on the ground that statements which would be admitted by the exception did not bear "sufficient guarantees of trustworthiness to justify admissibility."[22] This Congressional decision rejects the principle that necessity alone is sufficient justification for a hearsay exception. However, statements which would have been admissible under this proposed exception are not necessarily inadmissible under the adopted version of the federal rules. Where a case can be made that a statement is particularly reliable, admission under FRE 804(b)(5) is possible if not likely.

D. PRIOR STATEMENTS OF AVAILABLE WITNESSES: A PROBLEM IN POLICY ANALYSIS

The third basic principle which is transforming hearsay doctrine in many jurisdictions is the idea that prior out-of-court statements of individuals available to testify should be admitted as substantive evidence. We shall discuss this principle in detail because it provides an excellent example of the difficulties of policy analysis in the hearsay area. As you read the arguments concerning the substantive use of prior inconsistent statements, consider how you as a policy-maker would resolve the issues. Remember that a rule permitting the substantive use of prior inconsistent statements is asymmetric in that its benefits accrue almost entirely to the party having the burden of proof, that is, the prosecution in criminal cases and the plaintiff in most aspects of civil actions. The defending party is likely to be content with the traditional rule admitting prior inconsistent statements for impeachment only since if the jury disbelieves the testimony of crucial prosecutorial or plaintiff's witnesses, the defendant will prevail.

The major justification offered to support a hearsay exception for prior statements by available declarants is that the declarant's presence at trial provides an opportunity for cross-examination which protects against many of the same dangers that the hearsay rule is designed to avoid. The jury can observe the declarant's demeanor and develop some notion of whether he is the type of individual who usually tells the truth. Ambiguity in the declarant's earlier statement may be cleared up by the later cross-examination. Finally, the declarant will usually be able to describe the context in which the earlier statement was uttered, thus allowing some test of his opportunity to observe and his motives to falsify. The problem with this analysis is that a hearsay exception for earlier statements will rarely be necessary where the declarant adopts his earlier statement or repeats it from the stand. In these circumstances the substance of the earlier statement is also proved by the declarant's courtroom testimony. Yet only where the declarant adopts or reiterates the earlier statement is the opportunity for cross-examination likely to be fully effective as a means of testing the credibility of the earlier assertion.

The exception may be essential to a party's case where the substance of the earlier statement cannot be proved by declarant's courtroom testimony. If the declarant does not remember the incident described in the earlier statement or if the declarant's courtroom testimony is inconsistent

22. Report of Committee on the Judiciary, House of Representatives, 93rd Congress, 1st Session, Federal Rules of Evidence, No. 93–650, at 6 (1973).

with his earlier statement, evidence of that statement may be the only way of proving what is asserted therein. Yet in these circumstances the utility of courtroom cross-examination will often be quite limited. The declarant may fob off any attempt to develop the inconsistencies in or the implausibility of his earlier statements by saying, "I don't remember." He may deal similarly with efforts to secure an admission that his vantage point was obscured or his judgment biased. Whether the declarant's failure of memory is feigned or honest, the jurors are likely to be placed in a situation where they have only a bare accusation or simple description without any of the contextual information crucial to a rational determination of the weight the statement should be accorded. While cross-examination may help clarify ambiguous language and might give the jurors an idea of the declarant's general trustworthiness, the more significant hearsay dangers remain.

One might expect the opportunity for cross-examination to be more meaningful where the declarant's story from the stand is inconsistent with his earlier statement. In this situation the declarant not only remembers the event, he has probably stated from the stand that version of the event which the cross-examiner would have tried to elicit had the witness testified instead to the substance of the earlier inconsistent statement. Justice White, writing for the majority in California v. Green, put the argument this way: "The most successful cross-examination at the time the prior statement was made could hardly hope to accomplish more than has already been accomplished by the fact that the witness is now telling a different, inconsistent story, and—in this case—one that is favorable to the defendant." [23]

But this argument ignores those dramatic features which may determine the impact of the witness' recantation. Consider the following situations in each of which the witness eventually withdraws a statement accusing Green of selling him marihuana. Situation B is most like California v. Green.

Situation A: Where the witness on direct examination accuses Green of selling marihuana and the cross-examiner gets the witness to repudiate the accusation.

Prosecutor [On direct examination]: And will you tell us who sold you the marijuana which was found in your possession? **W:** It was Martin Green.

P: And how did this sale occur? Did he hand you the marihuana? **W:** No, he pointed to some bushes near his parents' house and said I would find the baggies there. I did, I found twenty-nine.

P: Thank you, your witness.

Defense Counsel [On cross-examination]: Is marihuana the only drug you have ever used? **W:** No, it is not.

D: What other drugs have you used? **W:** Well, I've dropped acid, that is, used LSD.

D: What are the effects of dropping acid? **W:** Well, it makes you super high. It changes your sense of things, of time, of space. Your world is different, everything is alive.

23. 399 U.S. 149, 159 (1970).

D: In short, it distorts your perceptions considerably; isn't that right? **W:** Yes.

D: You might be talking to someone and not remember who he is afterwards? **W:** Yes.

D: The features of the person you are talking to might be different, you might see a nose exaggerated or proportions changed? **W:** Yes.

D: Now, when was the last time you had dropped acid before you arranged this marihuana purchase? **W:** Well, actually I had taken some about twenty minutes before I got the call from Green telling me where to go to pick up the marihuana.

D: LSD distorts the perception of voices does it not? **W:** It may.

D: You really can't be certain it was Green's voice you heard on the phone, can you? **W:** No.

D: It's quite possible that someone else had called you up, your best friend, for example; yet you might have thought it was Green who called you when the effects wore off? **W:** Yes.

D: You then went to pick up the baggies. Did you not? **W:** Yes, I guess so.

D: What do you mean, I guess so? **W:** Well, I was still high, so fact and fantasy are really mixed up in my mind. If I hadn't had the baggies on me when the police came I wouldn't know what I had done.

D: You really aren't sure where you got the marihuana, are you? **W:** No.

D: You wouldn't want to swear under oath that Green was your supplier. Would you? **W:** No.

D: In short, you have no idea where the marihuana came from; isn't that so? **W:** Yes.

Situation B: Where the witness acknowledges but repudiates and explains his earlier inconsistent statement.

Prosecutor [On direct examination]: Now can you tell us who sold you the marihuana? **W:** No, I cannot.

P: Your honor, the witness' statement is inconsistent with his earlier statements on this subject. The prosecution is surprised by this testimony and would like to question him as if on cross-examination in order to clarify certain matters.

J: Go ahead.

P: Do you mean that you cannot swear that it was Green who gave you the marihuana? **W:** No, I cannot.

P: Do you remember giving a statement to a police officer shortly after you were arrested with the marihuana? **W:** Yes, I do.

P: And that was soon after you purchased the marihuana, at a time when your memory of the event was considerably fresher than it is now.   **W:** Yes.

P: Do you remember giving Officer Johnson, the officer who arrested you, the following statement, "I bought the dope off of Green.   He had the baggies under a bush on his folks' property.   I gave him the money and he told me where to look."   **W:** Yes, I said that.

P: Thank you.

Defense Counsel [On cross-examination]:   You've just testified that you cannot be sure that Green sold you the marihuana, isn't that right?   **W:** Yes, it is.

D: In fact, you have no reason to believe it was Green who sold you the marihuana, do you?   **W:** No.

D: Could you explain why you're unsure about who sold you the marihuana?   **W:** Yes.   You see, I had just dropped acid at the time I bought the marihuana.   That's LSD.   It distorts your perception. You can't be sure of anything.   I had this call on the phone telling me about the dope.   The voice might have sounded like Green's, but it could have been anybody's.   Then I went out to pick the stuff up.   But, I was so high I couldn't tell fact from fantasy.   When the police came I thought the police might go easy on me if I could name my supplier, so I just picked Green's name out because I knew him as an acquaintance.   But he wasn't a friend.

D: Thank you.

Prosecutor [On redirect examination]:   Just one more question.   When you were arrested you never told the officer that you had just been taking LSD, did you?   **W:** No.

P: That is all.

Defense Counsel [On recross-examination]:   Why didn't you tell the arresting officer you were high on LSD?   **W:** I was afraid I would get busted for that, too.

Situation C: Where the witness denies making an earlier inconsistent statement.

Prosecutor [On direct examination]:   Now, can you tell us who sold you the marihuana?   **W:** No, I cannot.

P: Your honor, the witness' statement is inconsistent with his earlier statements on this subject.   The prosecution is surprised by this testimony and would like to question him as if on cross-examination in order to clarify certain matters.

J: Go ahead.

P: Do you mean you cannot swear that it was Green who sold you the marihuana?   **W:** No, I cannot.

P: Do you remember giving a statement to a police officer shortly after you were arrested with the marihuana? **W:** No, I don't. I never gave a statement.

P: You are denying that you ever gave any statement to the arresting officer? **W:** Yes, I never said anything.

P: That is all, thank you.

*   *   *

P: [Questioning Officer Johnson. The circumstances of the arrest have just been described.]: What did you say next? **J:** I said that he was only a juvenile and if he would cooperate things might go easier for him.

P: What did he say? **J:** He said, "I bought the dope off of Green. He had hid the baggies under a bush on his folks' property. I gave him the money and he told me where to look."

P: You're sure he identified Green? **J:** Yes, I'm certain.

P: Thank you, officer.

In each of these situations the witness has told two stories. One accuses the defendant of supplying him with marihuana; the other professes an inability to identify the supplier. Yet, the situations are clearly not equivalent. In situation A, the jury sees the prosecution's witness discredited on cross-examination. Here they are likely to discount the accusation entirely. In situation B there is no discrediting of the witness, just an explanation of why his earlier statement was inaccurate. If the jury accepts the explanation it may discount the accusation; if it does not, the later courtroom repudiation will be of little help to the defendant. In situation C, where there is no cross-examination of the witness because he has denied ever accusing the defendant, and has said he cannot identify the source of the marihuana, the jury is faced with the simple question of whom to believe. If the witness is believed, the defendant was never identified as the supplier; if the police officer is believed, the identification stands with full force. These examples should make it clear that the repudiation of an earlier story on direct examination is not necessarily equivalent to the retraction of that story on cross-exam-

ination. For the advocate, the way in which a jury learns facts is often almost as important as the facts the jury learns.

But does this make the case against the exception? The right of cross-examination which is at the heart of the hearsay rule is not a right to discredit an opponent's testimony in the most dramatic way possible. (Dramatic discrediting only occasionally occurs.) It is a right to test an opponent's story so that the jury may better assess its validity. Where a witness *remembers* making an earlier inconsistent statement, the cross-examiner's main disadvantage is that he cannot attack the witness' general credibility because he wants the jury to believe the witness' testimony. But the *substance* of the witness' inconsistent statement may be tested almost as thoroughly at the trial as it could have been at the time the statement was made. The California Law Revision Commission put the argument this way:

> The declarant is in court and may be examined and cross-examined in regard to his statements and their subject matter. * * * The trier of fact has the declarant before it and can observe his de-

meanor and the nature of his testimony as he denies or tries to explain away the inconsistency. Hence, it is in as good a position to determine the truth or falsity of the prior statement as it is to determine the truth or falsity of the inconsistent testimony given in court.[24]

If testimonial repudiation of an earlier out-of-court statement is likely to be less convincing than the repudiation of direct testimony on cross-examination, it is because the jury may not believe that contemporaneous cross-examination would have shaken the earlier out-of-court statement. The crucial factor will be whether the witness can offer a satisfactory explanation for the discrepancy between his out-of-court statement and his courtroom testimony. Absent a convincing explanation, it is not irrational for the jury to believe that "the inconsistent statement is more likely to be true than the testimony of the witness at the trial because it was made nearer in time to the matter to which it relates and is less likely to be influenced by the controversy which gave rise to the litigation."[25] However, it does not necessarily follow that we want to allow convictions or judgments to rest largely on out-of-court statements that have been contradicted by sworn testimony. There is something incongruous about resting a verdict on the judgment that someone who cannot be believed under oath was credible in an earlier unsworn statement. In addition, the prior statement may have been elicited by the kind of leading questions which would have been barred on direct examination as unduly suggestive.

The case against an exception is considerably stronger where the witness denies making the inconsistent statement or asserts he has no memory of it. If the de-

nial is coupled with a failure to remember the incident described or with a claim to have never known the facts of the incident, the opposing attorney has no way of testing the truth of the inconsistent statement on cross-examination.[26] One cannot extract from a witness the details of an incident which he claims to have forgotten or to have never known about in the first place. Virtually all the hearsay dangers are present.

Prospects for a meaningful cross-examination are only slightly more favorable where the witness remembers the incident but denies the inconsistent statement. The witness has already told a story favorable to the cross-examining party, so that party has no incentive to question the witness' credibility or his opportunity to observe. There is little the examiner can do to show that the earlier statement, if made, is not to be believed, since the witness has denied making the earlier statement. However cooperative the witness, there can be no explanation for a discrepancy which is not acknowledged. The cross-examiner is at a similar disadvantage if the witness claims to have forgotten whether he has ever told an inconsistent story.

Where the making of the inconsistent statement is denied, the disputed issue is usually whether the statement was made. Unfortunately, this issue is likely to be reduced to a swearing contest between the witness who claims he never made the alleged statement and some other witness who claims to have heard it. The report of a discrete statement is very difficult to shake on cross-examination. Hearing a discrete statement is consistent with almost any context and with many different relationships between speaker and auditor. Only where the circumstances sug-

24. California Law Revision Commission. Comment on Sec. 1235 of the California Evidence Code (1965).

25. Id.

26. There is a question of whether a statement asserting lack of memory or non-

involvement in an event is inconsistent with an earlier statement describing some aspect of the event. In the related area of impeachment, some courts have held that it is.

gest difficulty in overhearing or bias on the part of the reporting witness is cross-examination likely to be effective. Rationally disproving a witness' claim that nothing was said is even more difficult, unless the statement has been reliably recorded or independent witnesses are available to substantiate it. Thus, in deciding whether the inconsistent statement was made the jury will often have little to guide it except its evaluation of the witnesses who report and deny the statement.[27] Where, as is often the case, the reporting witness is a police officer or the denying witness is someone who has been in trouble with the law, the jury is likely to believe that the earlier statement was made and to treat it as true. With the dispute focused on the making of the statement, the possibility that the statement was made but was inaccurate may well be ignored.

Even in situations where cross-examination cannot effectively test prior inconsistent statements, the policymaker must recognize that a strong case can be made for admitting inconsistent statements as substantive evidence. Recall situations B and C. Do they not suggest the possibility that the witness was in some way "reached" between the time he made the earlier statement and the trial? A witness may be threatened or bribed or the code which prohibits "squealing" may reassert itself once the pressure applied to elicit the earlier statement has disappeared. False testimony due to any of these reasons poses a peculiar threat to the integrity of the trial process and should be discouraged in every way possible.

However, the integrity of the trial may be equally threatened in a system which admits unacknowledged prior inconsistent statements as substantive evidence, for there is a danger that allegedly inconsistent statements will be misreported or fabricated for the purpose of securing a conviction or judgment. The policymaker cannot ignore a growing body of evidence that perjury is not an uncommon aspect of police work. A Chicago police officer put the matter this way:

> A vice officer spends quite a bit of time in court. You learn the judges, the things they look for. You become proficient in testifying. You change your testimony, you change the facts. You switch things around 'cause you're trying to get convictions. You figure he's only a criminal, so you lie about it. The judges are aware of it. The guy who works in plain clothes is usually ambitious and aggressive and will take the time to go to court.[28]

---

27. Some might argue that the jury's judgment in this matter will usually be accurate because the jury has the opportunity to observe the demeanor of the witnesses while they make their contradictory statements. Unfortunately, there is, to our knowledge, no good evidence that demeanor is a substantial aid in the evaluation of credibility. The relationship between demeanor and credibility is often assumed because it is a convenient justification for a number of legal rules. However, the assumption has never been rigorously tested.

28. **Terkel, Working, at 194 (1974).** It appears that police perjury occurs most frequently in cases where the police seek the admission of evidence, usually narcotics or gambling material, which was seized in violation of fourth amendment standards. **Mapp v. Ohio, 367 U.S. 643 (1961), was apparently followed by such a substantial decrease in the number of individuals arrested with narcotics reported as hidden on their person and by such a substantial increase in the number of arrested people reported as holding narcotics in plain view or dropping it to the ground as to compel the conclusion that police testimony, rather than suspect behavior, was what had changed. The phenomenon is so common that these cases have become collectively known as "dropsy" cases. See, e.g., Oteri and Perretta, "Dropsy" Evidence and the Viability of the Exclusionary Rule, 1 Cont. Drug Prob. 35 (1971). Matters reached the point where Frank S. Hogan, the District Attorney for New York County, joined with defense counsel in an appeal of a narcotics conviction to suggest that in dropsy cases**

Clearly perjured testimony by individuals sworn to uphold the law offends the integrity of the criminal justice system at least as much as false recantations by bribed or threatened witnesses.[29]

Given these competing factors, how should we resolve the difficult policy issue of whether to create a hearsay exception for prior inconsistent statements? Two intermediate positions currently exist. The first, the position of the common law, is not intended as a compromise but is one in effect. At common law prior inconsistent statements are admitted to impeach a witness but not to prove the substance of what was asserted. Although the jury may be instructed to consider these statements only on issues of credibility, few believe that the jurors entirely disregard the substantive implications of what they learn.[30] Thus, statements ostensibly admitted for impeachment purposes may significantly

advance a party's affirmative case. However, the formal limitation on admissibility provides the opposite party with two important safeguards. The first is that limitations on impeaching one's own witnesses mean that one may not introduce a witness for the sole purpose of presenting the jury with an inconsistent out-of-court statement.[31] This prevents a party from building a case largely on out-of-court statements, but it can also destroy a case where a crucial witness has been persuaded to change an earlier honest account. Whether this limitation is wise is a difficult question. The second safeguard is that the distinction between substance and impeachment, however meaningless it may be to the jury, may be dispositive when a directed verdict is requested. If evidence of facts asserted only in statements admitted for impeachment is essential to a party's case, the other party will be entitled to a directed verdict. If

the burden of proving a legal search should be on the state. People v. Berrios, 28 N.Y.2d 361, 321 N.Y.S.2d 884, 270 N.E.2d 709 (1971). However, police perjury is apparently not confined to cases where technical rules prevent the conviction of obviously guilty defendants. Paul Chevigny documents a number of instances in which police officers apparently responded to charges that they used excessive force against an individual by filing and swearing to fabricated charges of resisting arrest. Police Power (1969). Oteri and Perretta, in their article on "Dropsy," suggest that there have been cases where the police testify falsely to confessions or other implicatory statements. 1 Cont. Drug Prob. 35, 39 (1971). (See, e.g., Veney v. United States, 120 U.S.App.D.C. 157, 344 F.2d 542, certiorari denied, 382 U.S. 865 (1965). It also appears that one undercover police officer may have arrested as many as seventy individuals on the false charge of selling hard drugs. The officer was arrested and convicted of perjury when he swore to an affidavit charging another undercover policeman, imported to test his credibility, with selling him heroin. Supercop Busted, 310 Civil Liberties 7 (Jan. 1976).

29. To make a wise decision the policymaker would want to know something about

the incidence of these two types of perjury. This information is not available. If it were and we were to learn that false testimony reporting inconsistent statements was only half as common as false denials, would it follow that a hearsay exception admitting inconsistent statements is justified?

30. Although one refers to "the jury" as a single body it should be remembered that juries are not monolithic; they are collections of individuals. While some jurors may pay no attention to instructions, others may take them quite seriously. If only one juror treats an instruction as strictly controlling it may still have an impact on the deliberative process and the ultimate verdict.

31. In practice this limitation may be circumvented by courts which are uncritically receptive to claims of surprise. A party who knows the opponent's witness will tell a story more favorable to him than the witness' earlier story should try to have this made clear before the witness' testimony is presented to the jury so that the opposing party may not claim surprise. A party is, unfortunately, most likely to know this when he has played some part, proper or not, in securing the recantation of the witness' earlier story.

the statement is admitted for substantive as well as impeachment purposes, the directed verdict will not issue. This seems to be a valuable limitation on the use of inconsistent statements. If a case is so weak that it could not get to the jury unless a prior inconsistent statement were given substantive effect, the case probably should not get to the jury at all. The difficulties in effectively cross-examining a witness about an earlier inconsistent statement coupled with the danger of mistake or fabrication should lead courts to ignore the substance of prior inconsistent statements in determining whether a party has presented sufficient evidence to reach the jury. We are approaching the situation of the *Raleigh* case when a conviction is allowed to turn on out-of-court statements repudiated under oath. Consider the irony of allowing a conviction to rest on the unexamined out-of-court testimony of a witness whom the jury has found incredible under oath.[32]

Some commentators have suggested that even if there is a hearsay exception for prior inconsistent statements, notions of due process may still lead courts to direct verdicts where an essential element of a party's case rests solely on the inconsistency. This is a result to be hoped for. However, unless the Supreme Court reverses the trend of its recent confrontation clause cases, there is little reason to expect this position to be adopted as a general rule.

A second intermediate position is the one adopted in FRE 801(d)(1). The federal rule offers substantial protection against the danger that an out-of-court statement will be fabricated or misreported and also provides whatever assurances are gained when statements are given under oath. Because the committee which drafted the rule was persuaded that the opportunity to examine the declarant in court negated most hearsay dangers, some prior inconsistent statements are excluded from the definition of hearsay. The same result could have been reached by creation of a hearsay exception.[33] FRE 801(d)(1) provides that a statement is not hearsay if:

> The declarant testifies at the trial or hearing and is subject to cross-examination concerning the statement, and the statement is (A) inconsistent with his testimony, and was given under oath subject to the penalty of perjury at a trial, hearing, or other proceeding, or in a deposition, or (B) consistent with his testimony and is offered to rebut an express or implied charge against him of recent fabrication or improper influence or motive, or (C) one of identification of a person made after perceiving him.

Subsection (A) of the federal "exception" relates to inconsistent statements generally. Where statements admitted under this provision have been made in other trials, hearings or depositions, the additional safeguard of contemporary cross-examination will often be present, but neither actual cross-examination nor the opportunity to cross-examine are conditions of the "exception". The language admitting inconsistent statements made under oath at "other proceedings" was included at the insistence of the Senate so that grand

---

32. One might object that if the jurors are persuaded that the witness' new story is attributable to a bribe or threat, they should be allowed to credit the earlier version. The jury can do that under the current system; if there is evidence that a party was responsible for the bribe or threat, the statements which the party sought to change may be received against him as adoptive admissions, and the bribe or threat may be used to show consciousness of guilt.

33. In the original draft of FRE 801(d)(1) all prior inconsistent statements were admissible. The Congress substituted a substantially more restrictive version because it felt that prior inconsistent statements generally were subject to certain of the hearsay dangers. Nevertheless, the Congress did not change the approach of the drafters by converting this provision into a hearsay exception.

jury testimony would be admissible where it varied from the declarant's courtroom statements.[34] Because of its *ex parte* nature and the pressure prosecutors can put on witnesses to testify, one may argue that statements made to grand juries should be regarded with more suspicion than other inconsistent statements meeting the conditions of this "exception".

It is hard to see the necessity of subsection (B) of FRE 801(d)(1). If a statement is consistent with trial testimony, the jury already has substantive evidence of the matter testified to. The utility of the earlier statement is solely to enhance the credibility of the courtroom testimony. When used for this purpose, it is not hearsay under the traditional definition.

Before the states began copying the federal rules only a few admitted prior inconsistent statements for all substantive purposes.[35] but more than half had an exception akin to FRE 801(d)(1)(C). This exception is justified on the ground that out-of-court identifications are often more reliable than the ritualistic courtroom identification of the person who occupies the chair next to defense counsel. If a lineup has been properly conducted and the defendant identified, the out-of-court identification should carry more weight with the jury than courtroom finger pointing. The exception also makes considerable sense when a witness has identified someone, either through photographs or in person, shortly after first perceiving him. It is known that recollection fades rapidly, so an identification made shortly after an individual has been first perceived is much more likely to be accurate than an identification made at some substantially later date. The federal rule, however, is not limited to the situations where the exception makes the most sense. If read literally, prior statements of identification will be admissible under this rule no matter how suggestive or casual the conditions under which they were made and no matter how great the length of time between the perception and an identification. In some circumstances, however, there may be constitutional problems which will prevent the admission of out-of-court identifications, FRE 801(d)(1)(C) notwithstanding.[36] Courts may also interpret the rule as applying only where a statement of identification has been made *soon* after the person identified was initially perceived.

In contemplating the future of hearsay you should be aware that the future has to some extent been constitutionalized in criminal cases. The confrontation clause of the sixth amendment may require the exclusion of certain kinds of hearsay evidence while the compulsory process clause of the same amendment may mandate the admission of certain hearsay. These matters will be discussed in detail in Chapter Seven. You should also remember that modern trends in other areas of evidence may have important implications for the rules of hearsay. FRE 703, for example, relaxes the hearsay rule substantially in the case of experts who need to rely on the work of others.

Problem VI–87. Freddy Farmer farms land which borders on government property. One day Freddy is stopped for speeding. In his car the

34. It should also apply to statements made to congressional committees and in other circumstances where testimony is under oath.

35. See Blakey, Substantive Use of Prior Inconsistent Statements Under The Federal Rules of Evidence, 64 Ken.L.J. 3 (1975), for a thoughtful analysis of the prior inconsistent statement problem.

36. See United States v. Wade, 388 U.S. 218 (1967); Gilbert v. State of California, 388 U.S. 263 (1967); Stovall v. Denno, 388 U.S. 293 (1967); and Simmons v. United States, 390 U.S. 377 (1968).

police spot a basket full of gold.　Freddy claims to have found the gold on his property.　The government claims the gold was illegally taken from government property and so should revert to the government.　To support this claim the government seeks to introduce a map, found in the basket, which was drawn by Pauline Prospector shortly before her death five years earlier. The map purports to locate a cache of gold on government property near the border of Freddy's farm.　**Is the map admissible to show the location of the gold?**

Problem VI–88.　A bartender received a counterfeit ten dollar bill as payment for a drink.　Realizing it was counterfeit, she told the manager to call the police.　When the police arrived, she pointed to the man who gave her the bill and he was arrested.　At the defendant's trial a year later the bartender states that she can no longer remember what the man who passed the ten dollar bill looked like, but she does remember that at the time she pointed out the culprit to the arresting officer.　The arresting officer testifies that the defendant is the man whom the bartender pointed out.　**Is the officer's testimony that the bartender pointed to the defendant admissible over defendant's hearsay objection?　Would the situation be any different if the police officer testified to the earlier identification but the bartender either denied making the identification or stated that she had forgotten the incident and did not remember whether she had received a counterfeit bill or whether she had identified the person who passed it to her?**

Problem VI–89.　The defendant, in a jurisdiction that follows the Federal Rules of Evidence, introduces a witness who testifies that he was near Bill's Bar at the time it was robbed and that he never saw the defendant. On cross-examination the prosecutor calls the witness' attention to a statement he had made under oath to a grand jury two weeks after the robbery. In this statement the witness said that he saw the defendant walk down a side street about fifty feet from the bar five minutes before the robbery. The witness remembers the statement but says that he now knows he was mistaken and that it was someone else he had seen.　The defendant moves for a directed verdict, claiming that there is no credible evidence placing him near the scene of the crime.　The prosecutor argues that under FRE 801(d)(1)(A) the inconsistent statement of the defendant's witness may be treated by the jury as substantive evidence that the defendant was near the scene of the crime.　The defendant argues that 801(d)(1)(A) does not apply because he had called the witness first and so could only question the witness on redirect examination and not on cross-examination.　He claims that FRE 801(d)(1) requires that a witness be subject to cross-examination concerning an earlier inconsistent statement before that statement can be used substantively.　**Who should prevail?**

Problem VI–90.　Professor Ellen Carter was a distinguished medical sociologist famous for her careful ethnographies of hospital life.　In an article written shortly before her death and published in a major sociology journal, she described conditions at "Oceanview Hospital."　She wrote that because of inadequate staffing at Oceanview it was customary for nurses and even orderlies to prescribe medicine for patients.　According to Professor

Carter, physicians usually initialed these prescriptions without seeing the patient and after the drug had been administered. The claim was supported by the detailed description of a case in which drugs were mistakenly prescribed by three different nurses before a doctor finally diagnosed the patient and prescribed the correct drug. The mistaken prescriptions resulted in serious injury to the patient. The article quotes the head of the hospital as saying, "Our nurses were responsible for those mistakes. We just don't have enough doctors to examine each patient every time we prescribe drugs."

Henry Moler sues Bayside General Hospital for injuries suffered following the administration of three different drugs, none of which was correctly prescribed. He claims that although prescriptions for the drugs were initialed by a staff doctor, they were in fact prescribed by nurses. He contends that the hospital was aware of this practice and so asks for punitive as well as actual damages. The details of Moler's case are precisely the details of the case described in Carter's article. The hospital administration reluctantly stipulates that "Oceanview Hospital" is the pseudonym which Professor Carter used for Bayside General Hospital in a series of articles based on her research at that institution. Moler offers Carter's article to prove that the drugs administered to him were prescribed by nurses and to show the kind of gross negligence on the part of the hospital which would justify punitive damages. The hospital objects to the introduction of this article on the ground that it is hearsay. **How should a court rule?**

Problem VI–91. In exchange for dropping a drug charge and lifting a detainer for a parole violation, Brown agreed to cooperate with agents from the Drug Enforcement Agency (DEA). He was particularly important in an investigation involving Charles East. On three occasions, Brown was strip-searched to ascertain that he had no heroin in his possession, given money and sent to meet East. Each time he returned from the meeting with heroin which he gave to the DEA agent in charge of the case. His phone calls to East to arrange his purchases were monitored and on one occasion the DEA agents were able to photograph East and Brown together. After each purchase the DEA agent prepared a statement summarizing what had occurred which Brown read, corrected and signed. On March 16, 1976 Brown appeared before a grand jury and described his dealings with East and with others involved in the heroin traffic. The statements signed by Brown were read to the grand jury and the government's attorney periodically asked him if they were correct. On March 19 Brown was found dead in his car with four bullets through the back of his head. A month later, a week before East's case was scheduled to come to trial the government notified East that it intended to offer under FRE 804(b)(5) a transcript of Brown's grand jury testimony, including the prepared statements that Brown had said were accurate. At the time this notice was given the government stipulated that it had no evidence that tended to connect East to Brown's death. **Should the judge admit the evidence?** Suppose that Brown had not died in the manner described, but had died of a heart attack on the third day of trial shortly before he was scheduled to be called as a witness. At that point the government stated its intention to offer the transcript of Brown's grand jury testimony under 804(b)(5). **Should the transcript be admitted?**

Problem VI–92. Stan Mead is indicted for bank robbery. During the trial the government sought to place William Carmel on the stand to testify as follows:

I work at the bank that was robbed. About five minutes after the robbers fled I was locking the entrance door when a customer knocked on the door. I recognized him as someone whom I had seen in the bank about once a month during the preceding five years, but I don't know his name and I haven't seen him since. Anyway, there was a kid of about twenty sitting in a car outside the door giving this customer the make and license plate number of the getaway car. I didn't hear what the kid said, but I saw the kid's lips move, and the customer relayed the information through the door. I didn't open the door because it's our policy to keep the building secure after a robbery. He told me the car was a "tan Dodge Valiant" with license plate number 700 QRS.

In addition to this testimony, the government has a witness who will testify that he worked for a while as a taxicab driver with Mead and he used to see him driving an off-white Dodge with license plate number 700 QRS. This witness' testimony is, however, somewhat open to suspicion for a car with plate number 700 QRS is registered to him. However, he claims that he once lost his wallet and when he regained it, it contained a registration certificate for a car with the plate number in question registered to his name by, he believes, Mead. The government investigation has verified that the registration was not in the witness' handwriting and that he does not drive a Dodge. The other evidence that significantly implicates Mead is the testimony of three eyewitnesses who had viewed a photo spread. One of the eyewitnesses says that although Mead's face was masked, his eyes, mustache, ears and part of his face were visible. This witness feels that he can identify Mead positively on that basis. A second eyewitness says that she saw Mead's face from the tip of his nose to his chin before it was masked and was able to see certain features through the mask because it did not distort them. A third witness says that Mead's picture closely resembled the appearance of the robber.

The trial judge elects to admit the evidence under FRE 804(b)(5). He offers the defendant a five day continuance to prepare for this evidence, but the defense counsel declines the offer saying that since the government claims it has searched thoroughly for the unknown declarants she doesn't believe that a continuance would be of much help. The defendant appeals arguing that the decision to admit Carmel's testimony was in error. On appeal the state defends the decision under FRE 804(b)(5) and claims the testimony was admissible under FRE 803(1) as well. **How should the appellate court rule?**

E. OVERALL EVALUATIONS: A CASE AGAINST LIBERALIZATION

As the lawyers, judges, legislators, and educators of tomorrow, the future of hearsay is in your hands. By this point you should understand the current hearsay system and be aware of some of the factors that must be considered in evaluating proposals for change.   In concluding this section, we would like to present you with further arguments for and against change.

As you have, no doubt, divined by now, our position is a conservative one.   We do not advocate radical changes in traditional hearsay doctrine.   Those who oppose the liberalization of the hearsay rule are often thought fundamentally to distrust the jury system.   But this is not where our conservatism is rooted.   We take the positions we do because of certain beliefs about testimonial accounts of statements and about the system of justice in this country.

1.   THE DANGER OF HEARSAY

We believe that the probability that an out-of-court statement will be significantly distorted when recounted in court, though not great, is not negligible.   There are normal difficulties in perceiving speech, there is the natural tendency for people to translate what they hear into what they want to hear, and there is the danger of perjury. We do not wish to overemphasize this last danger, for it is probably the least common of the three.   We suggest only that there are enough cases in which witnesses tell contradictory stories that the danger cannot be regarded as *de minimis*.[37]

The usual response to these justifications for the hearsay rule is that these are dangers which exist whenever perceptions are reported and that testimony reporting statements may, like any other testimony, be tested through cross-examination.   This response is formally correct.

These dangers do exist whenever perceptions are reported, and individuals who testify to statements may be cross-examined about what they have heard. But, we feel that the dangers are greater with reports of statements than with reports of visual stimuli and that the opponent's ability to correct for these dangers is less.   Our reasons for feeling this way are: (1) Small mistakes in overhearing statements may completely change the meaning of what is reported.   Consider for example, the simple mistake of hearing "has" when the declarant has said "hasn't." Since most witnessed events are more complex than statements, small mistakes in perceiving them are less likely to distort their meaning.   (2) Cross-examination is less likely to be effective in testing reports of statements than in testing reports of more complex events.[38]   (3) Significant statements are often directed at just one

37. **Where witnesses appear to contradict each other the contradiction is often only apparent or due to honest mistakes in perception or to the unconscious reconstruction of events in ways which favor the witness' interests.   It is, in part, because these possibilities exist whenever one testifies falsely under oath that prosecutions for perjury at trial are uncommon.   However, a low rate of prosecution does not mean that perjury itself is uncommon.**

38. **By this we do not mean that the dramatic revelation of perjury is more likely when testimony reports events other than statements.   Although this may be so, our concern is with cross-examination used more prosaically to demonstrate why a witness' account, whether honest or dishonest, may be doubted.   This usually involves setting a witness' statement in a context and demonstrating through the witness' own**

testimony that certain aspects of that context hindered perception or that there are inconsistencies or implausibilities in the description of the context which render the witness' crucial evidence somewhat suspect.   This type of examination is particularly valuable from a systemic point of view, for if it fails to shake the witness, it quite appropriately increases the credibility of a witness' account.   We suggest in our discussion of prior inconsistent statements the difficulties of setting discrete statements in contexts which allow meaningful cross-examination.   (We intentionally do not mention cross-examination to show bias, also an important goal of cross-examination.   The possibility for a meaningful cross-examination with this goal should not vary with the type of perception reported.)   If a witness claims to have heard but a single statement, he may plausibly claim that that was all that was said

person, while significant events are often observed by many. Thus the possibility of questioning a misreported statement through the testimony of other witnesses will generally be less than the possibility of questioning an erroneous observation through the testimony of others. Furthermore, it will be particularly hard to prove perjury when statements are attributed to an anonymous or unavailable declarant, so the temptation to perjury may increase.

2. THE BALANCE OF ADVANTAGE

Our second reason for regarding proposals to liberalize the admission of hearsay with some skepticism is our concern with the way in which the proposed changes would affect the balance of advantage in litigated cases. Despite the important rights enjoyed by the accused in criminal cases, we feel that the balance of advantage lies with the state in criminal cases [39] and with wealthy organizations in civil actions.[40] Organizations, unlike most individuals, usually have substantial resources available for the generation of evidence and often have the further advantage that litigation and the anticipation of litigation is, for them, routine. This means that organized parties are likely to have access to more hearsay evidence than the individuals they oppose. Often the hearsay will be of a particularly suspect kind,

to him or that after the statement the speaker lowered his voice. While the examiner may question the witness about his surroundings, a failure to closely observe one's surroundings does not necessarily suggest inattention to matters overheard. The witness must, of course, convince the jury that he was in a position to overhear, but usually this will only involve establishing his distance from the conversation. The attorney who investigates the scene is unlikely to find barriers to sound which would render certain versions of how a statement was heard suspect. Unreliable aspects of visual observations are much more susceptible to exposure through cross-examination. If a witness remembers only a single aspect of an event, that in itself is suspect. The inability to place the events observed in context may suggest visual inattention. (We suspect that a failure to remember what was said during an event one observed would be regarded by the jury with much less suspicion than a failure to remember other things which were seen.) If events can be placed in context, cross-examination can be much more effective, both as a means of revealing possible error and as a way of showing that the witness probably does know what he is talking about. Finally, barriers to sight are much more common than barriers to sound. A witness' ability to explain his position with respect to such barriers will be an important test of his ability to observe. Of course, there are many occasions when testimony reporting statements is set in a context which allows for meaningful cross-examination. It is interesting to note that this is particularly likely in situations where statements are not hearsay or where we currently admit hearsay. Verbal acts are often part of a sequence of events and meaningful only as part of that sequence, or they may be so important, as in an oral contract, that a witness' attention will be called specifically to them, thus minimizing the danger of honest error. Most of the hearsay exceptions either require that statements be in writing or are conditioned on the ability of the witness to describe other aspects of the context in which they were uttered.

This argument is based on our subjective judgments about when cross-examination is likely to be effective. These judgments have not been rigorously tested. You should not consider them proven simply because you read our views here. As you develop experience in litigation, you will be able to make your own judgments about these observations.

39. See, e.g., Goldstein, The State and The Accused: Balance of Advantage in Criminal Procedure, 69 Yale L.J. 1149 (1960). This thoughtful discussion is somewhat dated today because of the many changes which have occurred in criminal procedure since it was written. However, we feel that Goldstein's conclusion, that the balance of advantage lies with the state, still holds today.

40. See Galanter, Why the "Haves" Come Out Ahead: Speculations on the Limits of Legal Change, 9 L. & Soc.Rev. 95 (1974).

though this may not be evident on the face of the statements. Where the information is recorded in files, it may have been recorded selectively by agents who elicited information by leading questions or who included only what they thought their superiors most wanted to hear, and it may include statements by individuals of doubtful credibility.[41] When witnesses to hearsay are uncovered, the organization may have special claims on the witnesses which render their accounts suspect.[42]

Even if these problems did not exist, one might still have reservations about a change in evidence law which is likely to disproportionately advantage certain litigants. True, there is considerable disparity in the capacity of parties to uncover evidence and one would not, for example, want to bar eyewitness testimony simply because organized parties are more likely to find eyewitnesses than unorganized ones. But the fact that imbalance necessarily exists does not justify its exacerbation.

Liberalization of the hearsay rule will also change the balance between those bearing the burden of proof, generally prosecutors and plaintiffs, and their opponents, generally defendants, since it makes it easier to introduce the evidence necessary to establish a prima facie case. Again we do not see any need to make the prosecutor's task easier, and because of the dangers we perceive with hearsay, we are reluctant to expand the situations in which hearsay enables a party to avoid a directed verdict.[43]

---

41. Where a statement is recorded in organizational records there is a double hearsay problem. But the fact that the statement was recorded accurately can be proved by the traditional business records or past recollection recorded exceptions. Only the substantive admissibility of the recorded statement turns on some liberalization of the hearsay rule. Many proposals for liberalizing the hearsay system do not admit multiple hearsay because of the weakness of rumor. However, if all but one element of a chain qualified under a highly regarded exception such as that for business records, it is unlikely that the substantive statement would be excluded as the last element of multiple hearsay. Thus, the problems alluded to in the text are likely to remain even in jurisdictions sensitive to the weakness of rumor.

42. Consider testimony by accused criminals who are hoping for easy treatment from a prosecutor's office or testimony by insurance adjustors reporting statements they attribute to unavailable informants. People often have a few friends who can be pressed into stretching the truth but seldom have the potential range of influence of organizations. Organizations have a particular advantage in that they may generate pressure for stories which favor them without ever requesting deceit. A criminal may feel (correctly) that if he can offer the police or prosecution testimony of value to them, he will be treated better regardless of the veracity of his testimony. The police and prosecution will want to believe the statement because they think they are trying a guilty person. Similarly, the insurance adjustor is likely to believe (again correctly) that adjustors who report hearsay which favors the company are likely to do better with the company in the long run than adjustors who report hearsay that undermines the company's interests. True, the jury may discount such statements because of those who report them, but even if the statement is discounted, the opponent is considerably worse off than if the statement had been excluded.

43. A judge, in passing on a directed verdict, will view the evidence in the light least favorable to the movant. Unless testimony reporting a statement is incredible, the judge may well find that a reasonable jury can credit hearsay which he himself does not credit. If that hearsay reports the crucial facts necessary for a prima facie case, a directed verdict will be avoided. Yet the jury may view the hearsay with the same skepticism as the judge and nonetheless find for its proponent. Sympathy for an injured plaintiff may lead to a plaintiff's verdict in a situation where there is insufficient proof of negligence if hearsay is discredited. Knowledge of a defendant's criminal record or conclusions drawn from his failure to take the stand may lead to a conviction even when the jury has discredited hearsay evidence necessary for a prima facie case of criminal responsibility.

3. JUDICIAL DISCRETION

Most proposals for reforming the hearsay rule expand judicial discretion. This is evident in proposals to admit hearsay so long as some standard of reliability and necessity is met. It is also true of proposals to abolish the hearsay rule entirely, for much of what the hearsay rule excludes is arguably irrelevant or unduly prejudicial. This brings us to the third reason for our conservative stance toward hearsay reform. Put simply, we do not trust trial judges. If we thought that the country's trial judges were almost always highly capable and completely impartial, we might reluctantly support hearsay reform despite our reservations. The hearsay rule does exclude considerable relevant evidence, a cost which must be acknowledged by its defenders.

Unfortunately, the trial bench in this country is not uniformly excellent. Although many trial judges in this country are capable and impartial, there are others who are neither. In almost any large city and in many smaller ones, lawyers can tell stories of judges noted for their incompetence or unfairness. Abraham Blumberg, a lawyer-sociologist, characterized one of nine judges of a criminal court he studied as an "Intellectual-Scholar." The other eight fell into the categories "Routineer-Hack," "Political Adventurer-Careerist," "Judicial Pensioner," "Hatchet Man," and "Tyrant-Showboat-Benevolent Despot."[44] The captions give you an idea of what Blumberg thought of their performance.

Furthermore, it appears that trial judges who are biased are more likely to favor the prosecution than the defense. There are a variety of institutional reasons for this, including the system of electing judges which prevails in many jurisdictions, the fact that many judges have had prosecutorial experience, and the need for cooperation between judges and prosecutors in the general administration of the criminal courts. These factors all suggest that increasing judicial discretion in the hearsay area will make it somewhat easier for prosecutors to secure convictions.

4. SYSTEMIC EFFECTS

Finally, we believe the current system is working reasonably well and we fear the impact in the long run of substantially liberalizing the hearsay rule. It is notable that in the literature critical of the hearsay rule, examples are rarely given of cases where the exclusion of hearsay has led to unjust results. Yet this would surely be the strongest indictment that one could bring against the rule. One reason for the lack of outrageous cases is that the hearsay rule is already applied more liberally than it is written. Competent attorneys can usually find some way to introduce reliable hearsay essential to their case. When judicial creativity is added to the long list of exceptions, the hearsay rule becomes an even greater conceptual nightmare, but a nightmare which is probably more agonizing to those who contemplate it than to those who practice with it. On aesthetic grounds alone, one can appreciate the desire of scholars to rationalize this area of evidence law. But one should be wary of changing a system which apparently delivers justice, however neat and attractive the suggested alternative.

There is also the danger that liberalization of the hearsay rule will change attitudes toward hearsay in a way detrimental to our system of justice. Today hearsay is suspect, an attitude which is probably colored by the general rule excluding hearsay evidence. If the hearsay rule were formally or effectively abolished, attitudes

---

44. Blumberg, Criminal Justice 138 (1967).

toward hearsay might change. Judges who today strive to find some rationale for admitting exceptionally reliable hearsay not clearly falling under an established exception might under a more liberalized system admit, "for what it's worth," the hearsay they now exclude. This is the familiar decision when evidence is of generally low relevance. However, hearsay evidence with low probative value differs from evidence of low logical relevance. The low probative value of hearsay usually stems from the fact that it is difficult to evaluate the trustworthiness of the reported statements. Reported hearsay, *if believed,* may be quite probative of a fact in issue. The consequences of admitting less probative hearsay should usually be slight, for the jury is likely to dismiss hearsay of low probative value as incredible. However, in some cases the consequences may be great, either because the hearsay enables a party to avoid a directed verdict or because the jury does not appreciate the weakness of the evidence. Furthermore, there is the danger that if judicial attitudes toward the hearsay rule change, the attitudes of lawyers will change as well. Where hearsay evidence is easily accessible, they may devote less attention to finding nonhearsay evidence on the same point. This means that over time an increasing proportion of trial evidence will be hearsay rather than firsthand testimonial accounts.[45] At the very least such a change would decrease the appearance of fairness; it is likely to lead to substantial injustice as well. We are not saying that changes such as these will occur. They are, however, possibilities which must be taken into account when evaluating the more radical proposals for hearsay reform.

Although we have stated that our position on hearsay reform is a conservative one, it should be obvious to you that its implications are in another sense "liberal." Most suggested hearsay reforms are likely to be of more benefit to prosecutors than defendants. A conservative view of reform is consistent with the civil libertarian position on the criminal process. Thus, it is not surprising that attitudes toward the criminal process are often related to attitudes toward the hearsay rule.

When Congress enacted the Federal Rules of Evidence, the House's "liberal" Committee on the Judiciary consistently tried to restrict the scope of suggested hearsay exceptions while the Senate's more "conservative" committee favored the expansive positions of the draft rules. Similarly, those who believe that many criminals escape conviction because of the difficulties of proving guilt beyond a reasonable doubt, are likely to end up on the side which favors hearsay reform. Those who believe that the danger of convicting innocent people already exists and who take seriously the notion that it is better to acquit several people who are guilty than to convict one who is innocent, will probably oppose most suggested reforms. To those who think that the integrity and competence of police, prosecutors and judges is high and that witnesses almost always tell the truth, the hearsay rule may appear to be an archaic impediment to the search for truth. To those who think that the integ-

---

45. We recognize that the fact that courtroom testimony is usually more convincing than hearsay provides an incentive for attorneys to find non-hearsay evidence to prove crucial elements of their cases. However, were the hearsay rule abolished the incentive would be less than it is under the current system. Now the inability to present non-hearsay evidence on a particular point may entitle an opponent to a directed verdict or mean that the jury learns nothing about a particular matter. One might also expect that the bureaucratic pressures which often exist in the offices of prosecutors and public defenders will enhance the desirability of using hearsay, because hearsay evidence is easily routinized in advance of trial. Furthermore, there will be some witnesses whose trial presence is likely to be so shaky that one would prefer their hearsay statements to their testimony. The hearsay rule exists, in part, so that the weaknesses of such witnesses may be exposed to the jury.**

rity or competence of police, prosecutors and judges is at times suspect and that error, intentional or not, is common in testimony, the hearsay rule is more likely to appear as an imperfect but important guarantor of the integrity of the trial process.

F.　OVERALL EVALUATIONS:　THE CASE FOR REFORM

In this discussion of hearsay we have not hesitated to give you our own views on specific rules and proposals for change. We have at the same time tried to point out the ways in which our opinions differ from those of other writers, and we have tried to acknowledge the strength of the positions we ultimately reject. We regard many of the questions in this area as close ones. In trying to present our views in simplified fashion we may have overstated the conviction we feel. At the same time, we may have also failed to do justice to those who take a contrary position. The acknowledgment of an opposing view is not the same as the development of its argument. In closing this section we shall let one of the most distinguished proponents of hearsay reform speak for himself. After you have read his views on reform you will be in a better position to evaluate intelligently the conflicting arguments.

WEINSTEIN, PROBATIVE FORCE OF HEARSAY

46 Iowa L.Rev. 331–355 (1961).

The present evidence rules fall short of providing a satisfactory solution to the hearsay problem. They exclude evidence that has a higher probative force than evidence they admit. They fail to provide adequate procedural devices to minimize the possibility of misjudging the probative force of hearsay admitted. While coming closer to the mark, the Uniform Rules on hearsay suffer from similar defects.

I. NATURE OF HEARSAY PROBLEM

For the purpose of this discussion, the term hearsay is used broadly to encompass any action or declaration involving a hearsay danger. A hearsay danger exists when a trier of fact is asked to conclude that a proposition about a matter of fact is true because an extra-judicial declarant stated it was the case or did an act, verbal or otherwise, from which it can be inferred that he believed it to be true. To accomplish what is requested of him, the trier must rely upon one or more elements of the declarant's credibility—his ability and opportunity to observe, remember, or communicate accurately or his intention to state what he believes to be true. A person is an extra-judicial declarant unless, when he made the declaration or did the act, he was under oath, before the trier, and subject to cross-examination—in which case he is a witness.

The probative force of a line of proof is its power to convince a dispassionate trier of fact that a material proposition, sometimes referred to as an "ultimate fact," is probably true or false. It may also be defined as the increment, resulting from admission of evidence, in the "degree of belief which it is *rational* to entertain" with respect to a proposition about a matter of fact. Convincing power or probative force of any statement is affected by the trier's assessment of the credibility of the declarant with respect to the specific statement. If circumstantial steps are involved in the line of proof, it will also be affected by the probability of whatever hypotheses are involved in the circumstantial steps.

General credibility of a declarant depends upon his general attitude towards truth as well as his normal ability to observe, remember, and communicate his thoughts accurately. His specific credibility, while dependent upon general credibility, may vary depending upon the occasion he had to make the observation attributed to him, the circumstances surrounding his statement, and his relationship to the case—i.e., a generally honest man may yield to the temptation to exaggerate to help a dear friend or to hurt an enemy. Since specific credibility of the same witness or extra-judicial declarant may vary from one statement to another, it will also be determined by taking into account the statement's consistency with other information in the case, its internal consistency, and its conformity with the trier's pre-existing general knowledge. This reasoning is reversible; where the trier finds that a particular declaration does not accord with his experience or other credible evidence, he finds the declarant's specific credibility low and may infer from this a low general credibility. The probative force of hearsay may, therefore, increase as it is fitted into a mosaic of other evidence. On the other hand, the increment of convincing power of hearsay may be reduced as the number of lines of proof tending to prove the same material proposition increases—i.e., as evidence becomes cumulative.

In sum, in order to determine how much weight should be given to any hearsay, a trier must be able to determine the credibility of the extra-judicial declarant when he made the statement attributed to him, and to do this the statement must be viewed as part of the other evidence in the case. It is obvious that the trier has exactly the same problem with respect to a witness. Hearsay is thus a special form of testimonial proof. The main justification for treating it differently from other testimonial proof must be that the trier can more readily come to a correct conclusion with respect to credibility if he observes the declarant making his statement, or doing the act, under the stress of a judicial hearing when he is under oath, being observed by an adverse party, and subject to almost immediate searching cross-examination to test the various elements of his credibility. This explains the theoretical justification— but not the practical absurdity in many instances—for treating the out of court statement of the witness himself as hearsay.

Since no one can read another man's mind or judge his capacities directly, evidence of specific credibility, including demeanor, is always circumstantial; and even the demeanor of an extra-judicial declarant may be described by the witness reporting his statement. Many kinds of evidence bearing upon credibility do not require the presence of the declarant. So, for example, reputation, inconsistent statements, prior bad acts, and motive to falsify are available in evaluating the veracity of the extra-judicial declarant. Even as to such discrediting evidence, however, there may be some advantage in introducing it when the declarant's reaction to it may be observed. This is one justification for the rule requiring a foundation by questioning the witness about certain kinds of evidence before using them in attacking him.

* * * Does it follow, then, that all hearsay should be treated as testimonial proof and permitted to come in subject to proof and disproof of credibility?

II. SOLUTIONS TO HEARSAY PROBLEMS

A. *Admitting Hearsay Freely*

There are three separable but related objections to free admission of hearsay. They do not, however, require the absolute exclusionary hearsay rule, for each of them may be considered by the court in determining when hearsay should be admitted and by the trier in deciding how much probative force to give hearsay once it is admitted.

First, lawyers assume that the ability of the trier to assess credibility is greater when he can observe demeanor and reaction to cross-examination. Even if this assumption is not subject to proof by acceptable psychological tests and theory, it is shared by jurors and it seems to accord with our common experience. In the trial of cases, if the trier feels more assurance that he can arrive at truth, and if the parties agree that this is the case, we are entitled to assume it to be true—in the absence of a demonstration to the contrary—in constructing procedural rules. Trials are designed to settle disputes in a way that gives the litigants and public a sense of fairness. Until, therefore, it is demonstrated that the reliability of a statement cannot be better assessed by observing the demeanor of the person while he is making it, we are justified in placing reliance on this first factor.

Assurance of the trier, however, dictates only a rule of preference, not of exclusion. Moreover, it suggests that the risks in using hearsay are exaggerated because the trier tends to recognize the difficulty in evaluating the probative force of hearsay and does not rely heavily upon it when he is aware that it is hearsay. * * * Courts and many commentators, however, are probably correct in suggesting that juries are generally not as apt to be as critical of hearsay as trained judges. If this is true—and the danger is easily magnified—it can be met by permitting courts to comment on the weight to be given evidence. Lawyers can and do carry the main burden of showing the dangers by their arguments.

The second factor is one of trial convenience. Where credibility is assessed primarily on the basis of demeanor, an opposing attorney can see a witness for the first time and cross-examine solely on the basis of trial observation, hints from his client or expert, and what he believes about the witness's background and the facts of the case. It is better if he is prepared in advance, of course—and all the tactics books warn against the danger of unprepared cross-examinations. But the trial can go on without any extensive before-trial examination of the witness's background or preparation for proof and disproof of his credibility by other witnesses and documents. This permits cheaper preparation and a shorter trial, and by avoiding the need for continuances to permit investigation it makes the present form of dramatic jury trial more practicable.

A third factor is the possibility during the course of cross-examination of prevailing

upon the honest witness to change his testimony or upon the craven one not to varnish the truth. While it is possible to cause the dishonest witness to contradict himself or change his demeanor, Professor Morgan has pointed out that "if a witness is willing to commit perjury and counsel is willing to co-operate, neither oath nor cross-examination will be of much avail to expose the wilful falsehood unless either witness or counsel is unusually stupid."

B. Excluding Hearsay

What, then, of the other possible alternative—excluding all hearsay? Obviously, this approach would deny to the trier much useful information which should be available if he is to have a substantial chance of coming to a correct conclusion on the facts. In view of the paucity of other information bearing on many issues of fact, much hearsay must be admitted. No one, including Gilbert, has sought to apply literally his quaint statement that "a mere *hearsay* is no evidence," written as the hearsay rule was becoming fixed as a rule of exclusion in the early part of the eighteenth century. The logic of this approach must yield to the practicalities of our trial practice.

C. Class Exceptions

Wigmore's rationale for the hearsay exceptions expresses a compromise position between allowing all hearsay or no hearsay. Where, he argues, there is great necessity for a class of hearsay and there are general circumstantial grounds for concluding that a class of hearsay is reliable, an exception for the class may be created. This analysis, made possible by treating admissions and former testimony as not requiring the test of cross-examination and by applying variable standards of need and credibility to different classes, has satisfied the conscience of the bar but not that of recent commentators. It should be emphasized that Wigmore's rationale—as well as that of most of the cases—makes admissible a class of hearsay rather than particular hearsay for which, in the circumstances of the case, there is need and assurance of reliability. Nevertheless, Wigmore's analysis might have supported an exception based upon the individual case rather than upon a class—although it would have compounded his difficulty in synthesizing the cases for his treatise.

The second factor underlying the hearsay rule referred to above—i.e., that of trial convenience—might be used to support a class theory of exceptions. Since the classes of hearsay are defined in advance, the argument would go, lawyers cannot claim surprise when they are used. This rationale is not persuasive because, in the individual litigation, a lawyer may be surprised by his opponent's reliance on particular hearsay even though it falls within a class recognized as an exception. He may not, in fact, have time to investigate and obtain data to attack the extra-judicial declarant's credibility. Having *a priori* classes does, however, cut down the amount of hearsay that may be offered and thus offers him some protection. It also permits the judge to rule mechanically on admissibility without having to think of the particular circumstances of the case—and, as with many of our procedural rules, a judge may, in refusing to think, find satisfaction in the knowledge that this self-denial is required of him.

D. Admission Based Upon Probative Force With Procedural Safeguards

1. Greater Discretion In Judge

Apart from the greater burden on the judges, it would seem desirable to abandon the class exception system and substitute individual treatment if such a practice were to be combined with advance notice to the opponent when hearsay was to be introduced. Hearsay would then be admissible when it met the usual standard for admission of any line of proof—i.e., a reasonable man might be appreciably more satisfied about the truth or falsity of a ma-

terial proposition with the evidence than without it. To prevent burdening the trial with a great deal of evidence of small probative force, it would be well to permit the court a greater freedom to exclude than it normally exercises. Where its probative force was minimal because it was cumulative, other evidence would normally be preferred to hearsay.

The concept that admission should depend upon probative force weighed against the possibility of prejudice, unnecessary use of court time, and availability of more satisfactory evidence is an application of the well recognized principle * * * giving the court discretion to exclude admissible evidence. Where the extra-judicial declarant was available to the proponent but was not produced, the argument of spoliation could be permitted in evaluating probative force, but it would seem better to exclude the evidence or at least require that the extra-judicial declarant be made available for cross-examination, for the burden on the opponent to produce the witness for examination should be minimized. The right to treat such a witness as upon cross-examination with the right to attack credibility should, of course, be protected.

The circumstantial proof of credibility which gave rise to the class exception may continue to be utilized in the particular case in assessing probative force. Nevertheless, a series of independent letters written by disinterested ministers who were eyewitnesses to an event and who are shown to have acute vision, sound memories, and clear powers of communication might well be given more weight than many dying declarations or implied admissions which may be made by a party having no knowledge of the event or may have been made many years before by a predecessor in interest who had every motive to lie. On the other hand, hearsay coming within one of the traditional exceptions may rightly be given greater weight by a trier than testimony on the witness stand. Some faith must be reposed in triers to assess the evidence as "responsible persons" engaged "in serious affairs."

2. Notice of Intention to Use Hearsay

Notice and a minimum standard of credibility as a basis for admission of hearsay is worth increased attention now in view of the widespread growth of discovery-disclosure procedures in civil cases and the availability of pre-trial hearings in many jurisdictions. * * *

It is not suggested that this warning procedure is wholly satisfactory. Often an attorney is surprised by testimony at the trial and wants to meet it with hearsay. Advance notice of such possible use is often not practical; where the case is tried with a jury an adjournment is often difficult. A notice requirement should not, of course, be strictly enforced for every mite of hearsay. Nevertheless, the law ought to have some regard for the pitiful plaint of one lawyer, when his opponent introduced damaging testimony regarding an alleged conversation with an agent: "We should have some opportunity to run it down."

3. Judge's Comment on Evidence

To minimize the possibility of overestimation of the probative force of hearsay under a rule of discretion, the trial court's power to comment freely on the weight of such evidence should be recognized. If the jurisdiction does not generally recognize this right in the judge, a specific rule to this effect should be embodied in any codification of the law of evidence.

4. Review by Appellate Court and Greater Trial Court Control Over Jury

More explicit recognition of the power of appellate courts in evaluating hearsay should also be recognized if a new hearsay approach is adopted. Appellate courts have sought to insure reasoned consideration of hearsay by applying mechanical

tests of probative force in reviewing verdicts and decisions as well as administrative orders. Reliance on such "rules of law" disguises the fact that courts are reviewing the reasonableness of findings of fact but, like other procedural subterfuges, often leads to indefensible results. There is no reason for appellate courts to be embarrassed about exercising a higher degree of control when a finding is based upon hearsay rather than upon testimony of a witness in court; since the credibility of the statement does not depend upon the trier's observation of the extra-judicial declarant's demeanor, but rather upon a calculated evaluation of the surrounding circumstances found in the record, the appellate court may well feel itself in as good a position as the trier to evaluate the probative force of a statement. If its force is slight or so questionable as to be entitled to little weight, the appellate court will feel strongly impelled to discount it.

This attitude of more stringent review is part of a general pattern in cases involving circumstantial proof. Appellate courts, while normally denying the exercise of any substantial degree of control, use mechanical tests such as the inference on an inference rule, and these tests are in truth applied selectively to insure what the court believes is a sound result. Care must therefore be taken in evaluating cases in which appellate courts have taken the position that hearsay has no probative force. The rule may have been applied selectively as a means of exercising control over a trial judge or jury which has made a finding of fact unacceptable to an appellate judge with limited powers to substitute his judgment for the trier's.

III. CURRENT TRENDS AND CRITICISMS OF HEARSAY RULE

The current tendency is clearly towards much freer admissibility of hearsay. But without frank recognition of the rapid change in our attitude towards the exclusionary rules, we abandon the possibility of providing reasonable procedural protections.

In addition to the tendency to ignore hearsay dangers by providing a narrow definition of hearsay and by expanding the exceptions [,] * * * there is in the cases and in practice a tendency to admit hearsay where there can be no serious doubt of the credibility of the extra-judicial declarant—i.e., where probative force is high. * * * So quickly has the exclusionary power of the hearsay rule waned that there are few cases today where the outcome of a well-tried case would have been different had it not been for the hearsay rule, where a good court was prevented from admitting persuasive hearsay. Not all lawyers and courts, of course, have fully exploited present tendencies.

Scholars have reached surprising agreement on the desirability of replacing our present hearsay rule with one based upon probative force in the particular case. In the last century Bentham in England and Appleton in this country recognized the ability of triers to assess probative force of hearsay and proposed that the best-evidence concept be applied to hearsay. More recently Thayer declared that "the attempt to make the group [of classes], in the form in which they finally chanced to settle, fit into a scheme having any measure of theoretical consistency is an undertaking so Procrustean as to defy even the brilliant ingenuity of Professor Wigmore"; the class system he denominated as "crude and primitive." Chamberlayne, in his important treatise, made a full scale and well reasoned attack on the "archaic" hearsay rules as "an anomaly absolutely defying the established principles of a sound judicial administration," and referred to the exceptions as having developed in "the stone age of judicial evolution." McCormick has noted that "the value of hearsay declarations or writings, and the need for them, in particular situations cannot with any degree of realism be thus minutely ticketed in advance. * * *

Too much worthless evidence will fit the categories, too much that is vitally needed will be left out." Morgan has repeatedly insisted that much of the hearsay excluded "raises the hearsay dangers to no greater extent than evidence now admitted under the hearsay exceptions." He has demonstrated by a series of devastating hypotheticals how much evidence of high probative force may be excluded and how much of low convincing power admitted under our present rules. The notes to the Model Code of Evidence state that in many exceptions "the necessity resolves itself into mere convenience and the substitute for cross-examination is imperceptible." Summarizing their view of this pastiche in a manner probably considered derogatory when it was written a quarter of a century ago, Professor Maguire joined with Morgan to write: "[A] picture of the hearsay rule with its exceptions would resemble an old-fashioned crazy quilt made of patches cut from a group of paintings by cubists, futurists and surrealists." * * *

Wigmore, whose masterly treatise has prevented our complex hearsay rule from collapsing of its own weight, judged it one "which may be esteemed, next to jury-trial, the greatest contribution of that eminently practical [Anglo-American] legal system to the world's jurisprudence of procedure." Nevertheless, he favored rules making a general exception "for *all statements of deceased persons*," giving the court discretion not to exclude hearsay where it would interrupt the narrative of the witness and allowing it to permit authenticated statements to be admitted. "What the times now demand," he declared, "is an attempt to simplify the use of the Hearsay rule."

IV. EVALUATION OF HEARSAY WHEN THE EXCLUSIONARY RULE IS NOT RECOGNIZED

In the sea of admitted hearsay, the rule excluding hearsay is a small and lonely island. No serious claim has been made that adjudications in which hearsay is received on a discretionary basis and given reasonable probative force fail to resolve satisfactorily issues of fact.

Continental systems manage well without our rules. The matter is left to the judge's *intime conviction,* his common sense. The lack of experience of lawyers from other countries with our exclusionary rules makes it impossible to use them before international tribunals.

In this country the hearsay rule is strictly applied in the order of one percent of the civil litigations commenced. Arbitrators are not bound by the rules and it is estimated that seventy percent or more of private civil litigation not involving accident cases are tried before arbitrators; lawyers appear in most of these cases and have shown no general dissatisfaction with the process. Indeed, the Judicial Conference of New York has recently recommended adoption of a new procedure in which the hearsay rule would be ignored, calculated to woo cases back to the courts from arbitrators.

Workmen's accident cases, which clogged our courts earlier in this century, as well as the many other kinds of litigation handled by administrative agencies, have been resolved without utilizing mechanical rules excluding hearsay. * * * The probative force of hearsay should remain "constant at all levels of the adjudicatory process." It seems clear that the administrative process is having an ameliorative effect on court trials; the proper standards for decisions based upon hearsay in both is that of "convincing evidence."

Where our procedure is not adversary, as in grand jury proceedings and hearings on the issuance of search and arrest warrants, some of our courts have recognized convincing hearsay as a basis for action. When sentencing reports of probation officers or social workers' reports used in custody cases must be kept confidential, there is little doubt that the hearsay may be relied upon; the important problem is one of providing procedural devices which will

permit the parties to meet the hearsay and so reduce its apparent force. Even more acute are similar problems in security cases.

When judges try cases which involve such small amounts that relaxation of the hearsay rule reduces the cost of trial to reasonable proportions, or so complex that admission of hearsay shortens the trial to acceptable lengths, the hearsay rule is ignored. Sitting without juries, judges have been told to err in favor of admission rather than exclusion of evidence. Experience with the ability of human beings to weigh hearsay should affect jury trials.

Even in the class of cases where courts might be inclined to enforce present rules of evidence strictly, the exclusionary hearsay rule has little direct impact. Only a small percent of commenced civil cases which are not terminated by defaults reach trial; most are settled and a few are disposed of by summary judgment or other motion. Hearsay may be elicited by deposition under the widely adopted Federal Rules [of Civil Procedure] and, for most cases, the sessions at which depositions are taken constitute the "trial," for the litigation is commonly terminated on the lawyer's evaluation of the depositions.

V. EVALUATION OF HEARSAY WHEN NO OBJECTION IS MADE TO ITS ADMISSION

In all but a few jurisdictions, hearsay admitted without objection may be considered by the trier of facts and given whatever weight it is entitled to under the circumstances. One court has explained this sound approach by noting:

The hearsay rule is merely an exclusionary principle limiting admissibility and in no sense a canon of relevancy. It involves no assertion that hearsay statements are without probative force or that they furnish to logical basis for conclusions of fact. On the contrary, if relevancy were not assumed, no special rule of exclusion would be required. * * * [H]earsay testimony when admitted without objection is to be considered and given its logical probative effect.

This position has also been supported on the theory that the hearsay rule is based on the right of the opposing party to cross-examine the declarant under oath and that this right is waived by the failure to object.

* * *

VI. CONCLUSION

There is no reason to believe that our judges are less able to assess the probative force of hearsay than are their civil counterparts or arbitrators or administrative hearing officers. There is little reason to believe that jurors—a much more highly educated and sophisticated group than their English seventeenth and eighteenth century predecessors—are not also capable of assessing hearsay's force without giving it undue weight. As Morgan has pointed out, the present hearsay rules rely upon "an entirely unrealistic assumption of naive credulity of jurors." The arguments of the opposing counsel in the case and caution of the judge—assuming the court is given necessary power to comment on the evidence—furnish sufficient guidance.

Much wider discretion should be vouchsafed the court to admit hearsay of high and assessable probative force. Exercise of discretion rather than mechanical rules requires more thought and consideration of such factors as surprise, possible prejudice through overestimation of force, and the availability of other evidence more easily assessed. Since it is desirable that the extra-judicial declarant be called to give evidence directly where important evidence is involved, rather forceful application of a best-evidence concept should be encouraged; it presents less dangers than does reliance on an argument of spoliation.

Discretion to admit hearsay should be exercised in advance of the trial wherever possible so that the opponent will have the opportunity to investigate and produce evidence in derogation of particular hearsay. The pre-trial hearing furnishes a useful opportunity for the court to exercise this discretion.

Since hearsay's probative force can be estimated on the record by the inferential methods used in estimating any circumstantial proof, appellate courts are in a position to exercise greater control over trial decisions based on hearsay. Instead of applying mechanical rules such as the "no probative weight" test of a small minority of states or the "not sufficient weight to make a prima facie case" test of a larger number, they ought to assume the greater power of reviewing the evidence—a review which, of course, ought to be exercised with restraint.

Problem VI–94.   You are on a legislative committee which is drafting a new code of evidence for your state.   One member of the committee has proposed that the traditional hearsay rule be replaced with a rule which defines hearsay and then provides: The admissibility of hearsay evidence shall be within the discretion of the judge.   In determining the admissibility of hearsay the judge shall consider the probable reliability of the hearsay declarations and the availability of the declarant for courtroom testimony.   **Would you support such a hearsay rule?   Why or why not?   What is your ideal hearsay rule?**

SECTION V.   THREE CLASSIC CASES

In this book we have deliberately eschewed using cases to teach settled principles of evidence law.   There are, however, some cases which are so closely associated with certain evidentiary principles that they have become part of the culture of the legal profession. When such cases exist, we mention them in the text and sometimes we describe them in detail. We recognize, however, that some students may want to read these classic cases themselves and some teachers may feel that the principles they embody will be better remembered if their seminal language is read along with our textual treatment. The three cases that follow would head almost everyone's list of classics. Their importance was obvious at the time they were handed down, and they continue to be associated with the principles they espouse.

———

Wright v. Doe dem. Tatham, grew out of a disputed bequest. John Marsden, a wealthy landowner, had left two manor houses, a rectory and a large amount of land to his steward, Wright. Admiral Sanford Tatham, Marsden's heir at law, claimed that the bequest was a result of Wright's overreaching and that the will devising the properties was invalid because Marsden's mental state was throughout his life such that he was not competent to make a will. The case turned on the admissibility of three letters, all of which were of a kind that one might write to a person of ordinary intelligence. The judges who heard the case on a first appeal to Kings Bench and a subsequent appeal to the Exchequer Chamber were all of the opinion that the letters could not be introduced to show that their authors had acted as if Marsden were competent. When used this way the letters were hearsay, for their relevance depended on the truth of beliefs that the letters implied. Thus, *Wright* has come to stand for the proposition that what we now call implied assertions or nonassertive conduct should be treated as hearsay. The trend, as you know, is in the opposite direction. As you read the case, you might want to think further about this trend and ask yourself whether *Wright* should have come out differently. The judges in *Wright* were also unanimously of the view that if Marsden had acted in response to the letters the letters could be introduced to help the jury evaluate the rationality of Marsden's response. The judges of Kings Bench did not believe that there was enough evidence that Marsden had reacted to the letters to render them admissible. The judges of Exchequer Chamber were split three-three on this issue, so a verdict for Tatham was affirmed by an equally divided court. The case generated numerous opinions, the most informative of which are those by Lord Denman speaking for Kings Bench and by Baron Parke on review in Exchequer Chamber. We present the essential portions of each and follow them with the letters on which a fortune turned.

WRIGHT v. DOE dem. TATHAM

7 AD. & E. 313 (1837).

Lord DENMAN C.J.

This case rests at present on a single question—that of the admissibility of certain letters tendered on a trial [of] whether the testator was competent to make a will; which the plaintiff denied, alleging his entire natural incapacity. Such an issue opens a wide door for the admission of evidence, as every transaction of the testator's life, every expression he ever used, and his manner of conducting himself in the most ordinary concerns, may have a bearing on the question.

The letters tendered, written at the time of their several dates, by respectable persons now deceased, who were acquainted with the testator, had been found in his house, with the seals broken, shortly after his death. No other circumstance was proved relating to them: no act of the testator's was shown to have produced them, or to have followed upon them.

But it has been strongly contended before us, as it was at the trial, and as it has been argued in a former stage of the cause, that the contents of these letters ought to be laid before the jury, as showing in what manner the testator was treated by the writers; and such treatment, abstracted from all corresponding conduct on his part, was said to be evidence to disprove his alleged imbecility.

Without dispute, any, the least, act done by the testator with reference to the letters would have made them evidence; for such act could not be properly explained without recourse to them: and, if received, no rule of law could have prevented their full effect from being produced on the minds of the jury.   *   *   *

The manner in which a man is treated by persons ignorant of his intellectual character would be obviously of no value. But, even if well acquainted with him, their treatment does not prove their opinion. The respectful phrases may be ironical, or employed for the very purpose of circumventing the party addressed, on the presumption of his inbecility. *   *   *

The learned counsel will, however, remind us that they disclaim the letters as proofs of the opinion of the writers, or of any fact mentioned in them, and that their only object is to show the treatment which the testator received from other persons. But if it be admitted,—and we think it cannot be denied,—that the letters would prove absolutely nothing if they proceeded from persons unacquainted with the deceased, or if they were insincere and hypocritical, it inevitably follows that their relevancy to the question depends on their representing the real opinion of the writers.   *   *   *

*   *   *

The hardship of excluding these letters was powerfully urged, since it was said that the jury were in fact much influenced by the manner, in which the testator was treated by children pursuing him in the street like one deprived of reason.[a] But the answer is, that   *   *   *   the insults offered to him as an idiot by boys, when he walked out, are not evidence as the acts of the boys: their treatment of him as such is nothing; but the manner in which he received that treatment falls within the scope of our rule, and may certainly furnish strong proofs in affirmance or refutation of the proposition under inquiry.

The argument for the defendant appears, indeed, to be founded on a fallacious use of the word treatment. The behaviour of A. to B. may, without

a. The plaintiff, Tatham, had introduced at trial evidence that the boys of the town where Marsden lived would pursue him calling out names such as "Silly Marsden" and "Crazy Jack."

impropriety of language, be called treatment of him, though he be absent or asleep, and wholly unconscious of what is done.   A. might thus evince his high or mean opinion of B.'s understanding and character; but such proof of his opinion is allowed to be no evidence in a Court of Justice.   If such behaviour were observed by A. towards B. in his presence, and while he was in a state of consciousness, his conduct in return, with reference to the forms of society and to the natural feelings of human nature in similar circumstances, may afford strong evidence of the state of his intellect.   In this latter case, the treatment of B. by A. must be given in evidence, not as treatment, but because B.'s conduct thereupon cannot be understood without it.   This bears an exact resemblance to letters sent and answered, or dealt with in any way: the former case is that of letters merely written and received, without proof that the party receiving them did anything in respect to them.   *   *   *

This must be considered as the judgment of my brothers Littledale and Coleridge, and myself.   Our two brothers, having been engaged in the cause while at the Bar, have taken no part in the deliberation.

PARKE B.   The question for us to decide is, whether all or any of the three rejected letters were admissible evidence, on the issue raised in this case, for the purpose of showing that Mr. Marsden was, from his majority in 1779 to and at the time of the making of the alleged will and codicil in 1822 and 1825, a person of sane mind and memory, and capable of making a will?

It is contended, on the part of the learned counsel for the plaintiff in error   *   *   *   that each of the three letters was evidence of an act done by the writers of them towards the testator, as being a competent person; and that such acts done were admissible evidence on this issue proprio vigore, without any act of recognition, or any act done thereupon by him.

*   *   *

First, then, were all or any of these letters admissible on the issue in the cause as acts done by the writers, assuming, for the sake of argument, that there was no proof of any act done by the testator upon or relating to these letters or any of them,—that is, would such letters or any of them be evidence of the testator's competence at the time of writing them, if sent to the testator's house and not opened or read by him?

Indeed this question is just the same as if the letters had been intercepted before their arrival at his house; for, in so far as the writing and sending the letters by their respective writers were acts done by them towards the testator, those acts would in the two supposed cases be actually complete.   It is argued that the letters would be admissible because they are evidence of the treatment of the testator as a competent person by individuals acquainted with his habits and personal character, not using the word treatment in a sense involving any conduct of the testator himself; that they are more than mere statements to a third person indicating an opinion of his competence by those persons; they are acts done towards the testator by them, which would not have been done if he had been incompetent, and from which, therefore a legitimate inference may, it is argued, be derived that he was so.

Each of the three letters, no doubt, indicates that in the opinion of the writer the testator was a rational person. He is spoken of in respectful terms in all. Mr. Ellershaw describes him as possessing hospitality and benevolent politeness; and Mr. Marton addresses him as competent to do business to the limited extent to which his letter calls upon him to act; and there is no question but that, if any one of those writers had been living, his evidence, founded on personal observation, that the testator possessed the qualities which justified the opinion expressed or implied in his letters, would be admissible on this issue. But the point to be determined is, whether these letters are admissible as proof that he did possess these qualities?

I am of opinion that, according to the established principles of the law of evidence, the letters are all inadmissible for such a purpose. One great principle in this law is, that all facts which are relevant to the issue may be proved; another is, that all such facts as have not been admitted by the party against whom they are offered, or some one under whom he claims, ought to be proved under the sanction of an oath.   *   *   *

That the three letters were each of them written by the persons whose names they bear, and sent, at some time before they were found, to the testator's house, no doubt are facts, and those facts are proved on oath; and the letters are without doubt admissible on an issue in which the fact of sending such letters by those persons, and within that limit of time, is relevant to the matter in dispute; as, for instance, on a feigned issue to try the question whether such letters were sent to the testator's house, or on any issue in which it is the material question whether such letters or any of them had been sent. Verbal declarations of the same parties are also facts, and in like manner admissible under the same circumstances; and so would letters or declarations to third persons upon the like supposition.

But the question is, whether the contents of these letters are evidence of the fact to be proved upon this issue,—that is, the actual existence of the qualities which the testator is, in those letters, by implication, stated to possess: and those letters may be considered in this respect to be on the same footing as if they had contained a direct and positive statement that he was competent. For this purpose they are mere hearsay evidence, statements of the writers, not on oath, of the truth of the matter in question, with this addition, that they have acted upon the statements on the faith of their being true, by their sending the letters to the testator. That the so acting cannot give a sufficient sanction for the truth of the statement is perfectly plain; for it is clear that, if the same statements had been made parol or in writing to a third person, that would have been insufficient; and this is conceded by the learned counsel for the plaintiff in error. Yet in both cases there has been an acting on the belief of the truth, by making the statement, or writing and sending a letter to a third person; and what difference can it possibly make that this is an acting of the same nature by writing and sending the letter to the testator? It is admitted, and most properly, that you have no right to use in evidence the fact of writing and sending a letter to a third person containing a statement of competence, on the ground that it affords an inference that such an act would not have been done unless the statement was true, or believed to be true, although such an inference no doubt would be raised in the conduct of the ordinary affairs of life, if the statement were made by a man of veracity. But it cannot be raised in a judicial inquiry; and, if such an argument were admissible, it would lead to the indiscriminate admission of hearsay evidence of all manner of facts.

Further, it is clear that an acting to a much greater extent and degree upon such statements to a third person would not make the statements admissible. For example, if a wager to a large amount had been made as to the matter in issue by two third persons, the payment of that wager, however large the sum, would not be admissible to prove the truth of the matter in issue. You would not have had any right to present it to the jury as raising an inference of the truth of the fact, on the ground that otherwise the bet would not have been paid. It is, after all, nothing but the mere statement of that fact, with strong evidence of the belief of it by the party making it. Could it make any difference that the wager was between the third person and one of the parties to the suit? Certainly not. * * *

Let us suppose the parties who wrote these letters to have stated the matter therein contained, that is, their knowledge of his personal qualities and capacity for business, on oath before a magistrate, or in some judicial proceeding to which the plaintiff and defendant were not parties. No one could contend that such statement would be admissible on this issue; and yet there would have been an act done on the faith of the statement being true, and a very solemn one, which would raise in the ordinary conduct of affairs a strong belief in the truth of the statement, if the writers were faithworthy. The acting in this case is of much less importance, and certainly is not equal to the sanction of an extra-judicial oath.

Many other instances of a similar nature * * * were supposed on the part of the plaintiff in error, which, at first sight, have the appearance of being mere facts, and therefore admissible, though on further consideration they are open to precisely the same objection. * * * To [this] class belong the supposed conduct of the family or relations of a testator, taking the same precautions in his absence as if he were a lunatic; his election, in his absence, to some high and responsible office; the conduct of a physician who permitted a will to be executed by a sick testator; the conduct of a deceased captain on a question of seaworthiness, who, after examining every part of the vessel, embarked in it with his family; all these, when deliberately considered, are, with reference to the matter in issue in each case, mere instances of hearsay evidence, mere statements, not on oath, but implied in or vouched by the actual conduct of persons by whose acts the litigant parties are not to be bound.

The conclusion at which I have arrived is, that proof of a particular fact, which is not of itself a matter in issue, but which is relevant only as implying a statement or opinion of a third person on the matter in issue, is inadmissible in all cases where such a statement or opinion not on oath would be of itself inadmissible; and, therefore, in this case the letters which are offered only to prove the competence of the testator, that is the truth of the implied statements therein contained, were properly rejected, as the mere statement or opinion of the writer would certainly have been inadmissible.

[Parke goes on to say that Marsden did not react to the letters in a way that would render them admissible for the light they shed on his reactions.]

The Letters

I. From CHARLES TATHAM, Mr. Marsden's cousin, who, at the time of writing, was in America.

"My Dear Cousin.—You should have been the first person in the world I would have wrote too had nt. my time Imployd by affairs that called for my more imeadeate atention in the first place I am calld upon by my Buseness it being the first consideration must by no means be neglected. As for my Brother his goodness is Such that I know he will Excuse me till I am more disengaged was I to write to him in my present Embarased situation I might perhaps only do justice to my own feelings & he might construe it deceit (so different an oppinion have I of him to Mankind in Genl. who above all things are fond of Flattery. I shall now proceed to give you a small Idea of what has passd. since my Departiure from Whitehaven as I supose Harry long ere now has told you the rest. We saild the 14th. July & had Good Weather the Chief of the Way but as you know nothing of Sea fareing matters it is not worth While to Dwell upon the Subject. We Reachd. the Cape of Verginia the 13th Septr. but did not get heare till the begining of the present Month so we were about twenty Days in coming 350 Miles. When I arivd. I was no little consirned to find the Town in a Most Shocking Condition the People Dieing from 5 to 10 per day & scarsely a Single House in Town cleare of Descease which proves to be the Putrid Fevour—I am going to Philadilphia in a few days if God Spares my Life and permits me my Health & their I intend to stay till Affairs here bare a more friendly Aspect & so the Next time you here from me will be I expect from that Place tho' Youl Please to direct to me here as Usual. God Bless You my Dear Cousin and may You still be Blessd with health which is one of the greatest Blessings we require here is the sinseare wish of Dr Cosn. Your Affect. Kinsman & verry Humble Servt.   "CHA. TATHAM.

"P.S. Pray give my kind Love to my Aunt My Brother & My Cousin Betty allso my Complements to all the rest of the Family and all others my former Aquintances, &c.

"Alexandria, 12th Octr. 1784."

Addressed "John Marsden Esquire Wennington Hall, Lancaster."

II. From the Rev. OLIVER MARTON, Vicar of Lancaster.

"Dear Sir.—I beg that you will Order your Attorney to Wait on Mr. Atkinson, or Mr. Watkinson, & propose some Terms of Agreement between You and the Parish or Township or disagreeable things must unavoidably happen. I recommend that a Case should be settled by Your and their Attorneys, and laid before Councill to whose Opinion both Sides should submit otherwise it will be attended with much Trouble and Expence to both Parties.—I am, Sr. with compliments to Mrs. Coockson, Your Humble Servant, &c.   "OLIVER MARTON.

"May ye 20th 1786.

"I beg the favour of an Answer to this.

"John Marsden, Esq. Wennington."

III. From the Rev. HENRY ELLERSHAW, on resigning the perpetual curacy of Hornby, to which Mr. Marsden had appointed him.

"Dear Sir.—I should ill discharge the obligation I feel myself under, if, in relinquishing Hornby, I did not offer you my most grateful acknowledgments for the abundant favours of your Hospitality and Beneficence. Gratitude is all that I am able to give you, and I am happily confident that it is all that you expect; I have only therefore to assure you, that no Circumstances in this World will ever obliterate from my Heart and Soul the remembrance of your benevolent Politeness. May the good Almighty long bless you with Health and Happiness, and when his Providence shall terminate your Xtian Warfare upon Earth, may the Angels of the Lord welcome you into Blessedness everlasting. It will afford me Pleasure to continue my Services during the Vacancy, if agreeable to you. With every sentiment of Respect and Affection to yourself and the worthy family at the Castle, I hope you will ever find me, Your grateful, faithful & obliged Servt.

"HENRY ELLERSHAW.

"Chapel le dale.

"3d Oct: 1799—Please to deliver the Inclosed to Mr Wright."

Sallie Hillmon's efforts to recover on three insurance policies her husband had taken out became a cause celebre in their time. The case was in litigation for more than two decades. It required six trials and two appeals to the Supreme Court. At trial Mrs. Hillmon never lost, although on four occasions the jury was hung. In the Supreme Court she never won. Nevertheless popular sentiment was such, including for one brief period the barring of the three insurance companies that were resisting Mrs. Hillmon's claims from doing business in Kansas, that she eventually received most of what she had sought. The Hillmon Case, by which we mean the opinion on the first appeal to the Supreme Court, stands for the proposition that statements of intent may be used for their tendency to show action in accord with intent. It also discusses the state of mind exception more generally and suggests that where one's intended actions are inextricably linked with the likely actions of another, statements of intent may be used to show that one acted with the other. These propositions which have made the case a classic were, in fact, not essential to the Supreme Court's decision. The Court reversed the verdict at trial because in joining the three defendants the trial judge had improperly restricted them to the number of peremptory challenges that would be available to a single party. The admissibility of Walters' letters was discussed only because the issue was "so likely to arise upon another trial." We present only that portion of the opinion which bears on this issue.

MUTUAL LIFE INSURANCE CO. v. HILLMON

Supreme Court of the United States, 1892.
145 U.S. 285.

On July 13, 1880, Sallie E. Hillmon, a citizen of Kansas, brought an action against the Mutual Life Insurance Company, a corporation of New York, on a policy of insurance, dated December 10, 1878, on the life of her husband, John W. Hillmon, in the sum of $10,000, payable to her within sixty days after notice and proof of his death.   On the same day the plaintiff brought two other actions, the one against the New York Life Insurance Company, a corporation of New York, on two similar policies of life insurance, dated respectively November 30, 1878, and December 10, 1878, for the sum of $5000 each;   and the other against the Connecticut Mutual Life Insurance Company, a corporation of Connecticut, on a similar policy, dated March 4, 1879, for the sum of $5000.

In each case, the declaration alleged that Hillmon died on March 17, 1879, during the continuance of the policy, but that the defendant, though duly notified of the fact, had refused to pay the amount of the policy, or any part thereof;   and the answer denied the death of Hillmon, and alleged that he, together with John H. Brown and divers other persons, on or before November 30, 1878, conspiring to defraud the defendant, procured the issue of all the policies, and afterwards, in March and April, 1879, falsely pretended and represented that Hillmon was dead, and that a dead body which they had procured was his, whereas in reality he was alive and in hiding.   *   *   *

On February 29, 1888, after two trials at which the jury had disagreed, the three cases came on for trial, under the order of consolidation.   *   *   *

At the trial the plaintiff introduced evidence tending to show that on or about March 5, 1879, Hillmon and Brown left Wichita in the State of Kansas, and travelled together through Southern Kansas in search of a site for a cattle ranch;   that on the night of March 18, while they were in camp at a place called Crooked Creek, Hillmon was killed by the accidental discharge of a gun;   that Brown at once notified persons living in the neighborhood;   and that the body was thereupon taken to a neighboring town, where, after an inquest, it was buried.   The defendants introduced evidence tending to show that the body found in the camp at Crooked Creek on the night of March 18 was not the body of Hillmon, but was the body of one Frederick Adolph Walters.   Upon the question whose body this was, there was much conflicting evidence, including photographs and descriptions of the corpse, and of the marks and scars upon it, and testimony to its likeness to Hillmon and to Walters.

The defendants introduced testimony that Walters left his home at Fort Madison in the State of Iowa in March, 1878, and was afterwards in Kansas in 1878, and in January and February, 1879;   that during that time his family frequently received letters from him, the last of which was written from Wichita;   and that he had not been heard from since March 1879.   The defendants also offered the following evidence:

Elizabeth Rieffenach testified that she was a sister of Frederick Adolph Walters, and lived at Fort Madison.

"Witness further testified that she had received a letter written from Wichita, Kansas, about the 4th or 5th day of March, 1879, by her brother Frederick Adolph;   that the letter was dated at Wichita, and was in the handwriting of her brother;   that she had searched for the letter, but could not find the same, it being lost;   that she remembered and could state the contents of the letter.

Thereupon the defendants' counsel asked the question: "State the contents of that letter." To which the plaintiff objected, on the ground that the same is incompetent, irrelevant, and hearsay. The objection was sustained, and the defendant duly excepted. The following is the letter as stated by witness:

"Wichita, Kansas,

"March 4th or 5th or 3d or 4th—I don't know—1879.

"Dear sister and all: I now in my usual style drop you a few lines to let you know that I expect to leave Wichita on or about March the 5th, with a certain Mr. Hillmon, a sheeptrader, for Colorado or parts unknown to me. I expect to see the country now. News are of no interest to you, as you are not acquainted here. I will close with compliments to all inquiring friends. Love to all.

"I am truly your brother,
FRED. ADOLPH WALTERS."

Alvina D. Kasten testified that she was twenty-one years of age and resided in Fort Madison; that she was engaged to be married to Frederick Adolph Walters; that she last saw him on March 24, 1878, at Fort Madison; that he left there at that time, and had not returned; that she corresponded regularly with him, and received a letter about every two weeks until March 3, 1879, which was the last time she received a letter from him; that this letter was dated at Wichita, March 1, 1879, and was addressed to her at Fort Madison, and the envelope was postmarked "Wichita, Kansas, March 2, 1879;" and that she had never heard from or seen him since that time.

The defendants put in evidence the envelope with the postmark and address; and thereupon offered to read the letter in evidence. The plaintiff objected to the reading of the letter, the court sustained the objection, and the defendants excepted.

This letter was dated "Wichita, March 1, 1879," was signed by Walters and began as follows:

"Dearest Alvina: Your kind and ever welcome letter was received yesterday afternoon about an hour before I left Emporia. I will stay here until the fore part of next week, and then will leave here to see a part of the country that I never expected to see when I left home, as I am going with a man by the name of Hillmon, who intends to start a sheep ranch, and as he promised me more wages than I could make at anything else I concluded to take it, for a while at least, until I strike something better. There is so many folks in this country that have got the Leadville fever, and if I could not of got the situation that I have now I would have went there myself; but as it is at present I get to see the best portion of Kansas, Indian Territory, Colorado, and Mexico. The route that we intend to take would cost a man to travel from $150 to $200, but it will not cost me a cent; besides, I get good wages. I will drop you a letter occasionally until I get settled down; then I want you to answer it." * * *

The court, after recapitulating some of the testimony introduced, instructed the jury as follows: "You have perceived from the very beginning of the trial that the conclusion to be reached must practically turn upon one question of fact, and all the large volume of evidence, with its graphic and varied details, has no actual significance, save as the facts established thereby may throw light upon and aid you in answering the question, Whose body was it that on the evening of March 18, 1879, lay dead by the camp-fire on Crooked Creek? The decision of that question decides the verdict you should render."

The jury, being instructed by the court to return a separate verdict in each case, returned verdicts for the plaintiff against the three defendants respectively.

Mr. Justice GRAY, after stating the case as above, delivered the opinion of the court. * * *

There is, however, one question of evidence so important, so fully argued at the bar, and so likely to arise upon another trial, that it is proper to express an opinion upon it.

This question is of the admissibility of the letters written by Walters on the first days of March, 1879, which were offered in evidence by the defendants, and excluded by the court. In order to determine the competency of these letters, it is important to consider the state of the case when they were offered to be read.

The matter chiefly contested at the trial was the death of John W. Hillmon, the insured; and that depended upon the question whether the body found at Crooked Creek on the night of March 18, 1879, was his body, or the body of one Walters.

Much conflicting evidence had been introduced as to the identity of the body. The plaintiff had also introduced evidence that Hillmon and one Brown left Wichita in Kansas on or about March 5, 1879, and travelled together through Southern Kansas in search of a site for a cattle ranch, and that on the night of March 18, while they were in camp at Crooked Creek, Hillmon was accidentally killed, and that his body was taken thence and buried. The defendants had introduced evidence, without objection, that Walters left his home and his betrothed in Iowa in March, 1878, and was afterwards in Kansas until March, 1879; that during that time he corresponded regularly with his family and his betrothed; that the last letters received from him were one received by his betrothed on March 3 and postmarked at Wichita March 2, and one received by his sister about March 4 or 5, and dated at Wichita a day or two before; and that he had not been heard from since.

The evidence that Walters was at Wichita on or before March 5, and had not been heard from since, together with the evidence to identify as his the body found at Crooked Creek on March 18, tended to show that he went from Wichita to Crooked Creek between those dates. Evidence that just before March 5 he had the intention of leaving Wichita with Hillmon would tend to corroborate the evidence already admitted, and to show that he went from Wichita to Crooked Creek with Hillmon. Letters from him to his family and his betrothed were the natural, if not the only attainable, evidence of his intention.

The position, taken at the bar, that the letters were competent evidence, within the rule stated in Nicholls v. Webb, 8 Wheat. 326, 337, as memoranda made in the ordinary course of business, cannot be maintained, for they were clearly not such.

But upon another ground suggested they should have been admitted. A man's state of mind or feeling can only be manifested to others by countenance, attitude or gesture, or by sounds or words, spoken or written. The nature of the fact to be proved is the same, and evidence of its proper tokens is equally competent to prove it, whether expressed by aspect or conduct, by voice or pen. When the intention to be proved is important only as qualifying an act, its connection with that act must be shown, in order to warrant the admission of declarations of the intention. But whenever the intention is of itself a distinct and material fact in a chain of circumstances, it may be proved by contemporaneous oral or written declarations of the party.

The existence of a particular intention in a certain person at a certain time being a material fact to be proved, evidence that he expressed that intention at that time is as direct evidence of the fact, as his own testimony that he then had that intention would be. After his death there can hardly be any other way of proving it; and while he is still alive, his own memory of his state of mind at a former time is no more likely to be clear and true than a bystander's recollection of what he then said, and is less trustworthy than letters written by him at the very time and under circumstances precluding a suspicion of misrepresentation.

The letters in question were competent, not as narratives of facts communicated to the writer by others, nor yet as proof that he actually went away from Wichita, but as evidence that, shortly before the time when other evidence tended to show that he went away, he had the intention of going, and of going with Hillmon, which made it more probable both that he did go and that he went with Hillmon, than if there had been no proof of such intention. In view of the mass of conflicting testimony introduced upon the question whether it was the body of Walters that was found in Hillmon's camp, this evidence might properly influence the jury in determining that question.

The rule applicable to this case has been thus stated by this court: "Wherever the bodily or mental feelings of an individual are material to be proved, the usual expressions of such feelings are original and competent evidence. Those expressions are the natural reflexes of what it might be impossible to show by other testimony.   *   *   * "

In accordance with this rule, a bankrupt's declarations, oral or by letter, at or before the time of leaving or staying away from home, as to his reason for going abroad, have always been held by the English courts to be competent, in an action by his assignees against a creditor, as evidence that his departure was with intent to defraud his creditors, and therefore an act of bankruptcy.   *   *   *

In actions for criminal conversation, letters by the wife to her husband or to third persons are competent to show her affection towards her husband, and her reasons for living apart from him, if written before any misconduct on her part, and if there is no ground to suspect collusion.   *   *   *

So letters from a husband to a third person, showing his state of feeling, affection and sympathy for his wife, have been held by this court to be competent evidence, bearing on the validity of the marriage, when the legitimacy of their children is in issue.

* * *

Upon an indictment of one Hunter for the murder of one Armstrong at Camden, the Court of Errors and Appeals of New Jersey unanimously held that Armstrong's oral declarations to his son at Philadelphia, on the afternoon before the night of the murder, as well as a letter written by him at the same time and place to his wife, each stating that he was going with Hunter to Camden on business, were rightly admitted in evidence. Chief Justice Beasley said: "In the ordinary course of things, it was the usual information that a man about leaving home would communicate, for the convenience of his family, the information of his friends, or the regulation of his business. At the time it was given, such declarations could in the nature of things, mean harm to no one; he who uttered them was bent on no expedition of mischief or wrong, and the attitude of affairs at the time entirely explodes the idea that such utterances were intended to serve any purpose but that for which they were obviously designed. If it be said that such notice of an intention of leaving home could have been given without introducing in it the name of Mr. Hunter, the obvious answer to the suggestion, I think, is that a reference to the companion who is to accompany the person leaving is as natural a part of the transaction as is any other incident or quality of it. If it is legitimate to show by a man's own declarations that he left his home to be gone a week, or for a certain destination, which seems incontestable, why may it not be proved in the same way that a designated person was to bear him company? At the time the words were uttered or written, they imported no wrongdoing to any one, and the reference to the companion who was to go with him was nothing more, as matters then stood, than an indication of an additional circumstance of his going. If it was in the ordinary train of events for this man to leave word or to state where he was going, it seems to me it was equally so for him to say with whom he was going." Hunter v. State, 11 Vroom (40 N.J. Law) 495, 534, 536, 538.

Upon principle and authority, therefore, we are of opinion that the two letters were competent evidence of the intention of Walters at the time of writing them, which was a material fact bearing upon the question in controversy; and that for the exclusion of these letters, as well as for the undue restriction of the defendants' challenges, the verdicts must be set aside, and a new trial had.

————————

Shepard v. United States is most important because it emphasizes the limits of *Hillmon*. Forward looking statements of intent are admissible to show actions in accordance with intent. Backward looking statements of memory or belief are not admissible to show actions consistent with a memory or belief. The case is also valuable for its discussion of the common law dying declaration, and it nicely illustrates how a statement can be hearsay on one issue and not on another. In the latter instance *Shepard* tells us that if a statement is erroneously admitted under an exception to the hearsay rule, reversal may not generally be avoided by showing a proper non-hearsay use of the statement on appeal. Finally, *Shepard* may be profitably read for the richness of Justice Cardozo's prose.

SHEPARD v. UNITED STATES

Supreme Court of the United States, 1933.
290 U.S. 96.

Mr. Justice CARDOZO delivered the opinion of the Court.

The petitioner, Charles A. Shepard, a major in the medical corps of the United States army, has been convicted of the murder of his wife, Zenana Shepard, at Fort Riley, Kansas, a United States military reservation. The jury having qualified their verdict by adding thereto the words "without capital punishment" * * *

The crime is charged to have been committed by poisoning the victim with bichloride of mercury. The defendant was in love with another woman, and wished to make her his wife. There is circumstantial evidence to sustain a finding by the jury that to win himself his freedom he turned to poison and murder. Even so, guilt was contested and conflicting inferences are possible. The defendant asks us to hold that by the acceptance of incompetent evidence the scales were weighted to his prejudice and in the end to his undoing.

The evidence complained of was offered by the Government in rebuttal when the trial was nearly over. On May 22, 1929, there was a conversation in the absence of the defendant between Mrs. Shepard, then ill in bed, and Clara Brown, her nurse. The patient asked the nurse to go to the closet in the defendant's room and bring a bottle of whisky that would be found upon a shelf. When the bottle was produced, she said that this was the liquor she had taken just before collapsing. She asked whether enough was left to make a test for the presence of poison, insisting that the smell and taste were strange. And then she added the words, "Dr. Shepard has poisoned me."

The conversation was proved twice. After the first proof of it, the Government asked to strike it out, being doubtful of its competence, and this request was granted. A little later, however, the offer was renewed, the nurse having then testified to statements by Mrs. Shepard as to the prospect of recovery. "She said she was not going to get well; she was going to die." With the aid of this new evidence, the conversation already summarized was proved a second time. There was a timely challenge of the ruling.

She said, "Dr. Shepard has poisoned me." The admission of this declaration, if erroneous, was more than unsubstantial error. As to that the parties are agreed. The voice of the dead wife was heard in accusation of her husband, and the accusation was accepted as evidence of guilt. If the evidence was incompetent, the verdict may not stand.

1. Upon the hearing in this court the Government finds its main prop in the position that what was said by Mrs. Shepard was admissible as a dying declaration. This is manifestly the theory upon which it was offered and

received.   The prop, however, is a broken reed.   To make out a dying declaration the declarant must have spoken without hope of recovery and in the shadow of impending death.   The record furnishes no proof of that indispensable condition.   *   *   *   Fear or even belief that illness will end in death will not avail of itself to make a dying declaration.   *   *   *   The patient must have spoken with the consciousness of a swift and certain doom.

What was said by this patient was not spoken in that mood.   There was no warning to her in the circumstances that her words would be repeated and accepted as those of a dying wife, charging murder to her husband, and charging it deliberately and solemnly as a fact within her knowledge.   To the focus of that responsibility her mind was never brought.   *   *   *   She did not speak as one dying, announcing to the survivors a definitive conviction, a legacy of knowledge on which the world might act when she had gone. *   *   *

2.   We pass to the question whether the statements to the nurse, though incompetent as dying declarations, were admissible on other grounds.

The Circuit Court of Appeals determined that they were.   Witnesses for the defendant had testified to declarations by Mrs. Shepard which suggested a mind bent upon suicide, or at any rate were thought by the defendant to carry that suggestion.   More than once before her illness she had stated in the hearing of these witnesses that she had no wish to live, and had nothing to live for, and on one occasion she added that she expected some day to make an end to her life.   This testimony opened the door, so it is argued, to declarations in rebuttal that she had been poisoned by her husband.   They were admissible, in that view, not as evidence of the truth of what was said, but as betokening a state of mind inconsistent with the presence of suicidal intent.

(a) The testimony was neither offered nor received for the strained and narrow purpose now suggested as legitimate.   It was offered and received as proof of a dying declaration.   What was said by Mrs. Shepard lying ill upon her deathbed was to be weighed as if a like statement had been made upon the stand.   There is no disguise of that purpose by counsel for the Government.   They concede in all candor that Mrs. Shepard's accusation of her husband, when it was finally let in, was received upon the footing of a dying declaration, and not merely as indicative of the persistence of a will to live.   Beyond question the jury considered it for the broader purpose, as the court intended that they should.   *   *   *   A trial becomes unfair if testimony thus accepted may be used in an appellate court as though admitted for a different purpose, unavowed and unsuspected.   *   *   *

(b) Aside, however, from this objection, the accusatory declaration must have been rejected as evidence of a state of mind, though the purpose thus to limit it had been brought to light upon the trial.   The defendant had tried to show by Mrs. Shepard's declarations to her friends that she had exhibited a weariness of life and a readiness to end it, the testimony giving plausibility to the hypothesis of suicide.   By the proof of these declarations evincing an unhappy state of mind the defendant opened the door to the offer by the Government of declarations evincing a different state of mind, declarations consistent with the persistence of a will to live.   The defendant would have no grievance if the testimony in rebuttal had been narrowed to that point. What the Government put in evidence, however, was something very different. It did not use the declarations by Mrs. Shepard to prove her present thoughts and feelings, or even her thoughts and feelings in times past. It used the declarations as proof of an act committed by some one else, as evidence that she was dying of poison given by her husband. This fact, if fact it was, the Government was free to prove, but not by hearsay declarations. It will not do to say that the jury might accept the declarations for any light that they cast upon the existence of a vital urge, and reject them to the extent that they charged the death to some one else. Discrimination so subtle is a feat beyond the compass of ordinary minds. The reverberating clang of those accusatory words would drown all weaker sounds. It is for ordinary minds, and not for psychoanalysts, that our rules of evidence are framed. They have their source very often in considerations of administrative convenience, of practical expediency, and not in rules of logic. When the risk of confusion is so great as to upset the balance of advantage, the evidence goes out.

These precepts of caution are a guide to judgment here. There are times when a state of mind, if relevant, may be proved by contemporaneous declarations of feeling or intent. Mutual Life Ins. Co. v. Hillmon, 145 U.S. 285. Thus, in proceedings for the probate of a will, where the issue is undue influence, the declarations of a testator are competent to prove his feelings for his relatives, but are incompetent as evidence of his conduct or of theirs. * * *

In damage suits for personal injuries, declarations by the patient to bystanders or physicians are evidence of sufferings or symptoms, but are not received to prove the acts, the external circumstances, through which the injuries came about. * * * So also in suits upon insurance policies, declarations by an insured that he intends to go upon a journey with another, may be evidence of a state of mind lending probability to the conclusion that the purpose was fulfilled. Mutual Life Ins. Co. v. Hillmon, supra. The ruling in that case marks the high water line beyond which courts have been unwilling to go. * * * Declarations of intention, casting light upon the future, have been sharply distinguished from declarations of memory, pointing backwards to the past. There would be an end, or nearly that, to the rule against hearsay if the distinction were ignored.

The testimony now questioned faced backward and not forward. This at least it did in its most obvious implications. What is even more important, it spoke to a past act, and more than that, to an act by some one not the speaker. Other tendency, if it had any, was a filament too fine to be disentangled by a jury.

The judgment should be reversed and the cause remanded to the District Court for further proceedings in accordance with this opinion.

BIBLIOGRAPHY

McCormick, Chs. 24–34.

4 Weinstein's Evidence ¶ 800[01]–806[01].

4 Wigmore Ch. 37, 5 Wigmore Chs. 45 et seq.

Bein, Prior Inconsistent Statements: The Hearsay Rule, 801(d)(1)(A) and 803(24), 26 U.C.L.A.L.Rev. 967 (1979).

Donnelly, The Hearsay Rule and Its Exceptions, 40 Minn.L.Rev. 455 (1956).

Falkner, The Hearsay Rule and Its Exceptions, 2 U.C.L.A.L.Rev. 43 (1954).

Falkner, Hearsay, 1969 Law & Social Order 591.

Falkner, Indirect Hearsay, 31 Tul.L.Rev. 3 (1956).

Falkner, Silence as Hearsay, 89 U.Pa.L.Rev. 182 (1940).

Falkner, Vicarious Admissions and the Uniform Rules, 14 Vand.L.Rev. 855 (1961).

Gamble, The Tacit Admission Rule: Unreliable and Unconstitutional—A Doctrine Ripe for Abandonment, 14 Ga.L.Rev. 27 (1979).

Graham, Prior Consistent Statements: Rule 801(d)(1)(B) of the Federal Rules of Evidence, Critique and Proposal, 30 Hast.L.J. 575 (1979).

Hutchins & Slesinger, Memory, 41 Harv.L.Rev. 860 (1928).

Hutchins & Slesinger, Some Observations on the Law of Evidence: Spontaneous Exclamations, 46 Colum.L.Rev. 432 (1946).

Imwinkelried, The Scope of the Residual Hearsay Exceptions in the Federal Rules of Evidence, 15 S.D.L.Rev. 239 (1978).

Jefferson, Declarations Against Interest: An Exception to the Hearsay Rule, 58 Harv.L.Rev. 1 (1944).

Ladd, The Hearsay We Admit, 5 Okl.L.Rev. 271 (1952).

Maguire, The Hearsay System: Around and Through the Thicket, 14 Vand.L.Rev. 741 (1961).

Maguire, The Hillmon Case—Thirty Three Years After, 38 Harv.L.Rev. 709 (1925).

Maguire & Vincent, Admissions Implied from Spoliation or Related Conduct, 45 Yale L.J. (1935).

Marcus, Co-Conspirator Declarations: The Federal Rules of Evidence and Other Recent Developments From a Criminal Law Perspective, 7 Am.J.Crim.Law 287 (1979).

McCormick, The Borderland of Hearsay, 39 Yale L.J. 489 (1930).

Morgan, Admissions, 12 Wash.L.Rev. 18 (1937).

Morgan, Declarations Against Interest, 5 Vand.L.Rev. 751 (1952).

Morgan, Foreword, Model Code of Evidence (1942).

Morgan, Hearsay Dangers and the Application of the Hearsay Concept, 62 Harv.L.Rev. 177 (1948).

Morgan, Rationale of Vicarious Admissions, 42 Harv.L.Rev. 461 (1929).

Morgan, Res Gestae, 12 Wash.L.Rev. 91 (1937).

Note, The Unavailability Requirements of Rule 804(a) of the Federal Rules of Evidence, 56 N.Dak.L.Rev. 387 (1980).

Park, McCormick on Evidence and the Concept of Hearsay: A Critical Analysis Followed by Suggestions to Law Teachers, 65 Minn.L.Rev. 423 (1981).

Quick, Some Reflections on Dying Declarations, 6 How.L.J. 109 (1960).

Rucker, The Twilight Zone of Hearsay, 9 Vand.L.Rev. 453 (1950).

Slough, Spontaneous Statements and State of Mind, 46 Iowa L.Rev. 224 (1961).

Strahorn, A Reconsideration of the Hearsay Rule and Admissions, 85 U.Pa.L.Rev. 484 (1937).

Tague, Perils of the Rulemaking Process: The Development, Application and Unconstitutionality of Rule 804(b)(3)'s Penal Interest Exception, 69 George.L.J. 851 (1981).

Tracy, The Introduction of Documentary Evidence, 24 Iowa L.Rev. 436 (1935).

Travers, Prior Consistent Statements, 57 Neb.L.Rev. 974 (1978).

Tribe, Triangulating Hearsay, 87 Harv.L.Rev. 957 (1975).

Waltz, The Present Sense Impression Exception to the Rule Against Hearsay: Origins and Attributes, 66 Iowa L.Rev. 869 (1981).

Weinstein, Probative Force of Hearsay, 46 Iowa L.Rev. 331 (1961).

Chapter Seven

CONFRONTATION AND COMPULSORY PROCESS

SECTION I.   INTRODUCTION

There are a number of situations in which the ordinary rules of evidence are supplemented or supplanted by constitutional doctrines.   The most familiar of these have to do with the admission of real evidence acquired in the course of a search, the admission of confessions made to police officers, and the related privilege against self-incrimination.   Any trial attorney who takes criminal cases[1] must be thoroughly familiar with the law in these areas, for the admissibility of crucial evidence often turns on the way these doctrines are interpreted.   Because of their importance, it was with some reluctance that we decided against extended treatment of these doctrines in this volume.[2] There were three reasons for this decision.   First, the law in these areas is generally unrelated to the other evidence rules discussed in this book.   Second, you will find that this book already contains more than enough material to fill the typical evidence course.   A serious classroom treatment of these topics would require substantial deletions in the other material

covered.   Finally, these constitutional principles are so important that in most law schools they are treated in detail in courses in criminal procedure or constitutional law.

However, two clauses of the sixth amendment relate so closely to the rules of evidence discussed in this volume that we feel they merit extended treatment.[3] The first, the confrontation clause, may mean that in a criminal case hearsay evidence is not admissible against an accused even though it meets the conditions of a traditional or an innovative exception to that rule.   The confrontation clause also poses difficulties in joint trials where evidence is admissible only against one defendant.   The second, the compulsory process clause, may mean that certain evidence if offered by the defendant in a criminal case must be admitted even though it is excludable or inadmissible under the jurisdiction's ordinary rules of evidence.

The approach taken in this chapter differs from the general approach of this book.   Here appellate opinions form the core of

1.   **Generally speaking, the only cases in which the admissibility of evidence will be controlled by these doctrines and the doctrines discussed in this chapter will be criminal cases. though they may also apply in cases whici, while nominally "civil", carry substantial adverse consequences for the subject of the action.   The protection afforded by these doctrines, particularly the privilege against self-incrimination as now interpreted, is often important in settings other than the judicial trial, and the violation of certain constitutional restrictions on the gathering of evidence may give rise to civil actions.**

2.   But see our summary of the law relating to the fifth amendment privilege against

self-incrimination in Chapter Eight, infra, and our brief introduction to the fourth amendment in the final chapter.

3.   **The sixth amendment provides:**

In all criminal prosecutions, the accused shall enjoy the right to a speedy and public trial, by an impartial jury of the State and district wherein the crime shall have been committed, which district shall have been previously ascertained by law, and to be informed of the nature and cause of the accusation; to be confronted with the witnesses against him; to have compulsory process for obtaining Witnesses in his favor, and to have the Assistance of Counsel for his defence.

our presentation. This is because your task in this chapter is different from the task you face in other parts of this book. There is no body of rules, informed by history and a century of common law decisions, to be learned as a starting point. Instead you must deal with a judicial mood; one that as of this time has been expressed in too few cases to allow us to be certain where it will lead. The direction of future cases will depend in large part on the arguments which lawyers like yourself bring to bear in litigation and in the legal literature. As you will see, the common thread that links cases in the confrontation and the compulsory process areas is that the cases force courts to explore the relationship between rules of evidence and fairness at trial.

SECTION II.   THE CONFRONTATION CLAUSE

The confrontation clause provides that in all criminal prosecutions the accused shall enjoy the right to be confronted with witnesses against him.[4] The language is rather opaque. At one extreme it may mean simply that the accused has a right to be present at his trial and learn what evidence is admitted to convict him. At the other extreme it could be read to bar the introduction of any hearsay evidence in a criminal trial. The framers of the Bill of Rights never expressed clearly their intended construction of this clause, nor are there any early Supreme Court cases interpreting the provision. Wigmore believed that the confrontation clause meant only that testimony required by the hearsay rule to be taken in court had to be taken subject to cross-examination.[5] Under this view the confrontation clause has no bearing on traditional hearsay exceptions and places no limits on the ability of states to create new exceptions.[6] Professor Graham has characterized Wigmore's view as "highly partisan and probably inaccurate."[7] Other writers, who have independently examined the origins of the clause, agree with Graham's characterization.[8]

Most scholars agree that the framers drafted the confrontation clause to curb abuses associated with such celebrated English trials as the trial of Sir Walter Raleigh. We have already described this trial in the chapter on hearsay. By way of review consider Professor Graham's description:

On November 17, 1603, Sir Walter Raleigh * * * went on trial for high treason. His conviction for having conspired to deprive the King of his government, to alter religion and bring in "the Roman superstition," and to procure foreign enemies to invade the kingdom was eventually to cost Raleigh his head; but it gained him fame as the supposed cause of the confrontation clause of the Sixth Amendment.

4.   The Supreme Court has also held that the due process clause requires that the values of confrontation and compulsory process be preserved in certain proceedings which are not formally criminal. It appears that the scope of this due process right is not as extensive as the sixth amendment rights. See, e.g., **Greene v. McElroy**, 360 U.S. 474 (1959); **Morrissey v. Brewer**, 408 U.S. 471 (1972); **Wolff v. McDonnell**, 418 U.S. 539 (1974).

5.   5 Wigmore § 1395, at 150–51.

6.   However, the due process clause might still place some limits on the creation of new exceptions.

7.   Graham, The Right of Confrontation and the Hearsay Rule: Sir Walter Raleigh Loses Another One, 8 Crim. L. Bull. 99, 104 (1972).

8.   See, e.g., Larkin, The Right of Confrontation: What Next? 1 Texas Tech. L. Rev. 67, 69 (1969); Baker, The Right to Confrontation, The Hearsay Rules, and Due Process—A Proposal for Determining When Hearsay May Be Used in Criminal Trials, 6 Conn. L. Rev. 529, 534–538 (1974).

The principal, indeed the only, evidence to support Raleigh's conviction was the confession of Lord Cobham, an alleged coconspirator. This document obtained by officers of the Crown in proceedings at which Raleigh was neither present nor represented by counsel, was used against Raleigh, though he was able to show that Cobham had later recanted. Raleigh, though not a lawyer and not permitted counsel, responded with an eloquent demand for confrontation:

"The proof of the Common Law is by witness and jury; let Cobham be here, let him speak it. Call my accuser before my face, and I have done."

Raleigh's repeated demands for confrontation were answered by Justice Warburton in terms familiar to those who have heard the modern claims for law and order:

"I marvel, Sir Walter, that you being of such experience and wit should stand on this point; for so many horse-stealers may escape, if they may not be condemned without witnesses."

The only witness produced to testify *viva voce* at Raleigh's trial was one Dyer, a pilot who had been in Portugal at the time the conspiracy was supposed to have been afoot. He testified:

"I came to a merchant's house in Lisbon to see a boy that I had there; there came a gentleman into the house, and inquiring what countryman I was, I said an Englishman. Whereupon he asked me if the King was crowned? And I answered, No, but that I hoped that he would be so shortly. Nay, saith he, he shall never be crowned; for Don Raleigh and Don Cobham shall cut his throat ere that day come."

Modern lawyers would recognize this as the rankest sort of hearsay; a con-cept that did not evolve until much later. Raleigh shrewdly responded in terms of weight rather than admissibility: "This is the saying of some wild Jesuit or beggarly priest; but what proof is it against me?" Although his contemporaries tended to agree that none of the evidence proved Raleigh guilty, he was convicted.[9]

————

The United States Supreme Court had no occasion to interpret the confrontation clause until the case of Mattox v. United States[10] about a century after the clause's enactment. That case involved one Clyde Mattox who had had an earlier murder conviction overturned by the Supreme Court. In the period between the trial resulting in the overturned conviction and Mattox's retrial two crucial witnesses died. At the retrial the state introduced a transcription of the testimony which the deceased witnesses had given at the earlier trial. Mattox claimed that this procedure violated his right to confrontation. The Court affirmed the conviction, making it clear that the confrontation clause did not, at least in certain circumstances, prevent a prosecutor from introducing out-of-court statements. Speaking through Justice Brown the Court wrote:

The primary object of the constitutional provision in question was to prevent depositions or *ex parte* affidavits, such as were sometimes admitted in civil cases, being used against the prisoner in lieu of a personal examination and cross-examination of the witness in which the accused has an opportunity, not only of testing the recollection and sifting the conscience of the witness, but of compelling him to stand face to face with the jury in order that they may look at him, and judge by his demeanor upon the stand and the manner in which he gives

9. Graham, supra note 7, at 99–101.

10. 156 U.S. 237 (1895).

his testimony whether he is worthy of belief. There is doubtless reason for saying that the accused should never lose the benefit of any of these safeguards even by the death of the witness; and that, if notes of his testimony are permitted to be read, he is deprived of the advantage of that personal presence of the witness before the jury which the law designed for his protection. But general rules of law of this kind, however beneficent in their operation and valuable to the accused, must occasionally give way to considerations of public policy and the necessities of the case. To say that a criminal, after having once been convicted by the testimony of a certain witness, should go scot free simply because death has closed the mouth of that witness, would be carrying his constitutional protection to an unwarrantable extent. The law in its wisdom declares that the rights of the public shall not be wholly sacrificed in order that an incidental benefit may be preserved to the accused.

We are bound to interpret the Constitution in the light of the law as it existed at the time it was adopted, not as reaching out for new guaranties of the rights of the citizen, but as securing to every individual such as he already possessed as a British subject—such as his ancestors had inherited and defended since the days of Magna Charta. Many of its provisions in the nature of a Bill of Rights are subject to exceptions, recognized long before the adoption of the Constitution, and not interfering at all with its spirit. Such exceptions were obviously intended to be respected. A technical adherence to the letter of a constitutional provision may occasionally be carried farther than is necessary to the just protection of the accused, and farther than the safety of the public will warrant. For instance, there could be nothing more directly contrary to the letter of the provision in question than the admission of dying declarations. They are rarely made in the presence of the accused; they are made without any opportunity for examination or cross-examination; nor is the witness brought face to face with the jury; yet from time immemorial they have been treated as competent testimony, and no one would have the hardihood at this day to question their admissibility. They are admitted not in conformity with any general rule regarding the admission of testimony, but as an exception to such rules, simply from the necessities of the case, and to prevent a manifest failure of justice. As was said by the Chief Justice when this case was here upon the first writ of error, the sense of impending death is presumed to remove all temptation to falsehood, and to enforce as strict an adherence to the truth as would the obligation of an oath. If such declarations are admitted, because made by a person then dead, under circumstances which give his statements the same weight as if made under oath, there is equal if not greater reason for admitting testimony of his statements which were made under oath.

The substance of the constitutional protection is preserved to the prisoner in the advantage he has once had of seeing the witness face to face, and of subjecting him to the ordeal of a cross-examination. This, the law says, he shall under no circumstances be deprived of, and many of the very cases which hold testimony such as this to be admissible also hold that not the substance of his testimony only, but the very words of the witness, shall be proven. We do not wish to be understood as expressing an opinion upon this point, but all the authorities hold that a copy of the stenographic report of his entire former testimony, supported by the oath of the stenographer that it is a correct transcript of his notes and of the testimony of the deceased witness, such as was produced in this case, is competent evidence of what he said.[11]

———

Four years later in the case of Kirby v. United States[12] the Court made it clear that the *Mattox* decision did not mean that the confrontation clause was to be interpreted narrowly. The *Kirby* case involved a statute making it a crime to receive stolen property with an intent to convert. The statute provided that judgments of conviction against the principal felons should be evidence that the property of the United States alleged to have been stolen was in fact stolen. In overturning this provision the first Justice Harlan wrote:

> The record showing the result of the trial of the principal felons was undoubtedly evidence, as against *them,* in respect of every fact essential to show *their* guilt. But a fact which can be primarily established only by witnesses cannot be proved against an accused—charged with a different offense for which he may be convicted without reference to the principal offender—except by witnesses who confront him at the trial, upon whom he can look while being tried, whom he is entitled to cross-examine, and whose testimony he may impeach in every mode authorized by the established rules governing the trial or conduct of criminal cases.[13]

Harlan acknowledged that dying declarations were admissible despite the confrontation clause. He noted the necessity for such evidence, the pre-constitutional origins of the exception, and the fact that the circumstances surrounding the dying declaration made it "equivalent to the evidence of a living witness upon oath."[14]

From 1899 until 1965 the Supreme Court rarely dealt with confrontation clause issues and there is no significant Supreme Court interpretation of that clause during this period.[15] Then in 1965, in the case of Pointer v. State of Texas,[16] the Supreme Court applied the confrontation clause to the states. In the ensuing four years the Court decided a series of cases which made it appear that the confrontation clause placed substantial limits on the extent to which the government could introduce hearsay and other uncross-examined evidence in criminal cases. There was considerable doubt whether certain traditional and many proposed hearsay exceptions could withstand constitutional muster. But with the case of California v. Green[17] in 1970, the Court began a change of direction. Today it is not clear to what extent, if any, the confrontation clause limits the use of hearsay evidence in criminal cases.[18] Whether Cobham's confession would be admitted against Raleigh is again an open question.

We shall briefly summarize the major cases which mark the rise of the confrontation clause as a limitation on the state's power to admit unconfronted evidence. Then we shall present for your perusal

11. Id. at 242–44.

12. 174 U.S. 47 (1899).

13. Id. at 55.

14. Id. at 61.

15. Note, however, Motes v. United States, 178 U.S. 458 (1900), in which the Supreme Court refused to admit on confrontation clause grounds the testimony of a government witness given at a preliminary hearing and subject to cross-examination by at least some defendants, where the witness had escaped due to the negligence of the government and where it appeared that the witness could not have fled so far as to have been outside the jurisdiction of the trial court at the time of the trial. See also West v. State of Louisiana, 194 U.S. 258 (1904).

16. 380 U.S. 400 (1965).

17. 399 U.S. 149 (1970).

18. **Confrontation has been found to be an element of due process, so even if the confrontation clause is held to place no limits on the ability of states to create hearsay exceptions, the due process clause may prevent the admission of certain unconfronted evidence in some cases.**

several of the important cases which indicate that its limitations may not be as far reaching as at one time seemed possible. We shall conclude with a case which suggests another way in which the confrontation clause affects the validity of state rules of evidence.

A. POINTER v. STATE OF TEXAS, 380 U.S. 400 (1965)

Pointer grew out of a robbery in which Pointer and a codefendant, Dillard, were arrested for allegedly robbing one Kenneth W. Phillips. At a preliminary hearing before a Texas judge, Phillips identified Pointer as the man who had robbed him. Pointer, who had no counsel, did not try to cross-examine Phillips, although Dillard did. By the time of the trial Phillips had moved to California. After showing that Phillips had moved from the jurisdiction, the state introduced, over Pointer's objection, a transcript of Phillips' preliminary hearing testimony. The Court held that this violated Pointer's right to confrontation. The case is most important for its holding that the confrontation clause applies to the states in the same way that it applies to federal proceedings. Justice Black, writing for the majority, notes that "a major reason underlying the constitutional confrontation rule is to give a defendant charged with crime an opportunity to cross-examine the witnesses against him"[19] but Justice Black also speaks of "the right of confrontation and cross-examination,"[20] thus implying that the right of cross-examination does not necessarily exhaust the meaning of the confrontation clause. The Justice is careful to note that nothing in the *Pointer* opinion is meant to override previous case law which sanctioned the admission of dying declarations and the prior testimony of deceased witnesses. He leaves the reader wondering whether in the setting of a preliminary hearing the right of confrontation is not in fact coextensive with the right to effective cross-examination, for he states that the *Pointer* case "would be quite a different one had Phillips' statement been taken at a full-fledged hearing at which petitioner had been represented by counsel who had been given a complete and adequate opportunity to cross-examine."[21]

B. DOUGLAS v. STATE OF ALABAMA, 380 U.S. 415 (1965)

Douglas v. Alabama, a case decided on the same day as *Pointer,* grew out of a charge of assault with intent to commit murder. Lloyd, who had been charged along with Douglas, had confessed, been tried separately and been convicted. At Douglas' trial, Lloyd was called by the prosecution as a principal witness, but he refused to testify on fifth amendment grounds despite the judge's instruction that the fifth amendment privilege did not apply once an initial conviction had been entered. The prosecutor, citing Lloyd's failure to cooperate, asked and received permission to examine Lloyd as a hostile witness. Under the guise of cross-examination to refresh memory, the prosecutor read a document which purported to be Lloyd's confession to him, pausing every few sentences to ask Lloyd, "Did you make that statement?" Lloyd continued in his refusal to answer, but the entire confession, including parts which implicated Douglas, was read to the jury in this fashion. Later three law enforcement officers identified the prosecutor's document as a

19. 380 U.S. at 406–07.
20. Id. at 405.
21. Id. at 405.

transcription of Lloyd's confession. The document itself was never offered into evidence.

The Court, speaking through Justice Brennan, found that "[i]n the circumstances of this case, petitioner's inability to cross-examine Lloyd as to the alleged confession plainly denied him the right of cross-examination secured by the Confrontation Clause."[22] The case is interesting when one remembers that the confrontation clause gives criminal defendants the right to be confronted with *witnesses against them*. Yet, Lloyd's confession was never in evidence, so technically, Lloyd was never a witness against Douglas. The Court eschewed such formal analysis. It took the reasonable position that although the confession was not technically testimony, it might have been seen as such in the eyes of the jurors and that Lloyd's continual failure to respond on fifth amendment grounds might have been seen as an implied admission that the confession was an accurate account of what had happened.

Justices Harlan and Stewart concurred in both *Pointer* and *Douglas* on due process grounds.

C.   BARBER v. PAGE, 390 U.S. 719 (1968)

We discussed *Barber* in the preceding chapter on hearsay because it relates so closely to the unavailability requirement associated with certain hearsay exceptions. You will recall that *Barber* involved the efforts of the state of Oklahoma to introduce, as former testimony, statements which one Woods had made at a preliminary hearing. The state claimed that the unavailability requirement for this exception was satisfied because Woods was, at the time of Barber's trial, in federal prison in Texas.   The Supreme Court, in an opinion by Justice Marshall, reversed, holding that, "a witness is not 'unavailable' for purposes of the [prior testimony] exception to the confrontation requirement unless the prosecutorial authorities have made a good-faith effort to obtain his presence at trial."[23] The Court also held that Barber's failure to cross-examine Woods through his counsel at the preliminary hearing did not amount to a waiver of cross-examination at trial. The Court went on to note that:

We would reach the same result on the facts of this case had petitioner's counsel actually cross-examined Woods at the preliminary hearing.   The right to confrontation is basically a trial right. It includes both the opportunity to cross-examine and the occasion for the jury to weigh the demeanor of the witness. A preliminary hearing is ordinarily a much less searching exploration into the merits of a case than a trial, simply because its function is the more limited one of determining whether probable cause exists to hold the accused for trial. While there may be some justification for holding that the opportunity for cross-examination of a witness at a preliminary hearing satisfies the demands of the confrontation clause where the witness is shown to be actually unavailable, this is not, as we have pointed out, such a case.[24]

D.   BRUTON v. UNITED STATES, 391 U.S. 123 (1968)

This case grew out of a joint trial of Bruton and Evans for armed postal robbery.

Evans had orally confessed to a postal inspector that he and Bruton had committed

---

22.   380 U.S. 415, 419 (1965).
23.   390 U.S. 719, 724–25.

24.   Id. at 725–26.

the robbery in question. At the trial Evans' confession was introduced against Evans, and the judge instructed the jury that they should not treat the confession as evidence against Bruton. Evans never took the stand, so Bruton had no chance to examine Evans about the substance of his confession. This case is similar to *Douglas* in that technically there was no evidence introduced against the appellant, for the prosecutor offered Evans' confession as Evans' personal admission and never claimed that it was admissible against Bruton. But as in *Douglas* the Court was unwilling to be bound by the formal posture of the case. Overruling an earlier decision,[25] it held that the jury could not be expected to follow the judge's limiting instructions. Thus Evans' confession was, in effect, evidence against Bruton as well as Evans. Since Bruton had never had an opportunity to examine Evans on the confession, Bruton's confrontation clause rights were violated by its introduction at his trial.[26]

The reach of *Bruton* was subsequently limited by Harrington v. California[27] which

held that a *Bruton* violation could be harmless error and suggested that no *Bruton* problem exists when a codefendant whose confession is introduced takes the stand and admits making the statement. In Parker v. Randolph,[28] a decade later, four of the eight justices who heard the case were willing to hold that where the confessions of nontestifying codefendants interlocked—i.e., defendant *A*'s confession implicated both himself and *B*, and vice versa—*Bruton* violations would always be harmless so long as the jury was given a proper limiting instruction.

These are the major cases imposing confrontation clause restrictions on the government's ability to introduce evidence against accused persons.[29] In the three cases that follow, the California Supreme Court, the United States Court of Appeals for the Fifth Circuit and the Ohio Supreme Court extended the right of confrontation in ways they thought mandated by the Court's prior decisions. All three courts were mistaken.

---

25. Delli Paoli v. United States, 352 U.S. 232 (1957).

26. The implications of Bruton are potentially great, for there are many areas in which judicial instructions are thought sufficient to cure the errors which occur at trials or to ensure that evidence is used for a permitted purpose and not an impermissible one. Where constitutional rights are not threatened by the impermissible use of evidence, the limiting instruction may often be the best way we have to minimize improper impact while getting on with the practical business of finishing trials. The Bruton Court is probably correct in its conclusion that the jury cannot be expected to follow an instruction to completely disregard certain persuasive evidence, but it is by no means clear that limiting instructions are totally without effect. Bruton appears to stand for the proposition that where a natural but impermissible use of certain evidence will violate a person's constitutional rights, the Court will not assume that an instruction limiting the evidence to permissible uses provides adequate

protection for the person's constitutional rights. But cf. Harris v. New York, 401 U.S. 222 (1971), where the Court held that statements substantively inadmissible, because they were taken in violation of the Miranda rules, could be used for impeachment purposes. It is at least as unlikely that a properly instructed jury would confine a defendant's inculpatory statements to impeachment purposes as it is that the Bruton jury would have considered Evans' confession only against him.

27. 395 U.S. 250 (1969); see also the case of Nelson v. O'Neil discussed in the text at note 35, infra.

28. 442 U.S. 62 (1979).

29. A number of less important cases were decided during the same period. These include: Brookhart v. Janis, 384 U.S. 1 (1966) (holding that under the facts of the case petitioner, by requesting a bench trial which court and counsel assumed would follow the pattern of a rather esoteric and unofficial Ohio substitute for the plea of *nolo contendere* had not thereby intelligently waived his rights

E.   CALIFORNIA v. GREEN, 399 U.S. 149 (1970)

Mr. Justice WHITE delivered the opinion of the Court.

Section 1235 of the California Evidence Code, effective as of January 1, 1967, provides that "[e]vidence of a statement made by a witness is not made inadmissible by the hearsay rule if the statement is inconsistent with his testimony at the hearing.   *   *   * "   In People v. Johnson, 68 Cal.2d 646, 441 P.2d 111 (1968), cert. denied, 393 U.S. 1051 (1969), the California Supreme Court held that prior statements of a witness that were not subject to cross-examination when originally made, could not be introduced under this section to prove the charges against a defendant without violating the defendant's right of confrontation guaranteed by the Sixth Amendment and made applicable to the States by the Fourteenth Amendment.   In the case now before us the California Supreme Court applied the same ban to a prior statement of a witness made at a preliminary hearing, under oath and subject to full cross-examination by an adequately counseled defendant.   We cannot agree with the California court for two reasons, one of which involves rejection of the holding in People v. Johnson.

I

In January 1967, one Melvin Porter, a 16-year-old minor, was arrested for selling marihuana to an undercover police officer.   Four days after his arrest, while in the custody of juvenile authorities, Porter named respondent Green as his supplier.   As recounted later by one Officer Wade, Porter claimed that Green had called him earlier that month, had asked him to sell some "stuff" or "grass," and had that same afternoon personally delivered a shopping bag containing 29 "baggies" of marihuana.   *   *   *   A week later, Porter testified at respondent's preliminary hearing.   He again named respondent as his supplier, although he now claimed that instead of personally delivering the marihuana, Green had showed him where to pick up the shopping bag, hidden in the bushes at Green's parents' house.   Porter's story at the preliminary hearing was subjected to extensive cross-examination by respondent's counsel—the same counsel who represented respondent at his subsequent trial.   At the conclusion of the hearing, respondent was charged with furnishing marihuana to a minor in violation of California law.

Respondent's trial took place some two months later before a court sitting without a jury.   The State's chief witness was again young Porter.   But this time Porter, in the words of the California Supreme Court, proved to be "markedly evasive and uncooperative on the stand."   He testified that respondent had called him in January 1967, and asked him to sell some unidentified "stuff."   He admitted obtaining shortly thereafter 29 plastic "baggies" of marihuana, some of which he sold.   But when pressed as to whether respondent had been his supplier, Porter claimed that he was uncertain how he obtained the marihuana, primarily because he was at the time on "acid" (LSD), which he had taken 20 minutes before respondent phoned.   Porter

under the confrontation clause, and that counsel could not waive these rights on his client's behalf by entering a plea apparently inconsistent with the client's desires);   Roberts v. Russell, 392 U.S. 293 (1968) (applying Bruton retroactively); and Berger v. California, 393 U.S. 314 (1969) (applying Barber retroactively).

claimed that he was unable to remember the events that followed the phone call, and that the drugs he had taken prevented his distinguishing fact from fantasy.

At various points during Porter's direct examination, the prosecutor read excerpts from Porter's preliminary hearing testimony. This evidence was admitted under § 1235 for the truth of the matter contained therein. With his memory "refreshed" by his preliminary hearing testimony, Porter "guessed" that he had indeed obtained the marihuana from the backyard of respondent's parents' home, and had given the money from its sale to respondent. On cross-examination, however, Porter indicated that it was his memory of the preliminary testimony which was "mostly" refreshed, rather than his memory of the events themselves, and he was still unsure of the actual episode. Later in the trial, Officer Wade testified, relating Porter's earlier statement that respondent had personally delivered the marihuana. This statement was also admitted as substantive evidence. Porter admitted making the statement, and insisted that he had been telling the truth as he then believed it both to Officer Wade and at the preliminary hearing; but he insisted that he was also telling the truth now in claiming inability to remember the actual events.

Respondent was convicted. The District Court of Appeals reversed, holding that the use of Porter's prior statements for the truth of the matter asserted therein, denied respondent his right of confrontation under the California Supreme Court's recent decision in People v. Johnson, supra. The California Supreme Court affirmed, finding itself "impelled" by recent decisions of this Court to hold § 1235 unconstitutional insofar as it permitted the substantive use of prior inconsistent statements of a witness, even though the statements were subject to cross-examination at a prior hearing. * * *

II

The California Supreme Court construed the Confrontation Clause of the Sixth Amendment to require the exclusion of Porter's prior testimony offered in evidence to prove the State's case against Green because, in the court's view, neither the right to cross-examine Porter at the trial concerning his current and prior testimony, nor the opportunity to cross-examine Porter at the preliminary hearing satisfied the commands of the Confrontation Clause. We think the California court was wrong on both counts.

Positing that this case posed an instance of a witness who gave trial testimony inconsistent with his prior, out-of-court statements, the California court, * * * held that belated cross-examination before the trial court, "is not an adequate substitute for the right to cross-examination contemporaneous with the original testimony before a different tribunal." We disagree.

Section 1235 of the California Evidence Code represents a considered choice by the California Legislature between two opposing positions concerning the extent to which a witness' prior statements may be introduced at trial without violating hearsay rules of evidence. The orthodox view, adopted in most jurisdictions, has been that the out-of-court statements are inadmissible for the usual reasons that have led to the exclusion of hearsay statements. * * *

In contrast, the minority view adopted in some jurisdictions and supported by most legal commentators and by recent proposals to codify the law of evidence would permit the substantive use of prior inconsistent statements on the theory that the usual dangers of hearsay are largely non-existent where the witness testifies at trial.   *   *   *

Our task in this case is not to decide which of these positions, purely as a matter of the law of evidence, is the sounder.   The issue before us is the considerably narrower one of whether a defendant's constitutional right "to be confronted with the witnesses against him" is necessarily inconsistent with a State's decision to change its hearsay rules to reflect the minority view described above.   While it may readily be conceded that hearsay rules and the Confrontation Clause are generally designed to protect similar values, it is quite a different thing to suggest that the overlap is complete and that the Confrontation Clause is nothing more or less than a codification of the rules of hearsay and their exceptions as they existed historically at common law. Our decisions have never established such a congruence;   indeed, we have more than once found a violation of confrontation values even though the statements in issue were admitted under an arguably recognized hearsay exception.   See Barber v. Page, 390 U.S. 719 (1968);   Pointer v. Texas, 380 U.S. 400 (1965).   The converse is equally true: merely because evidence is admitted in violation of a long-established hearsay rule does not lead to the automatic conclusion that confrontation rights have been denied.

Given the similarity of the values protected, however, the modification of a State's hearsay rules to create new exceptions for the admission of evidence against a defendant, will often raise questions of compatibility with the defendant's constitutional right to confrontation.   Such questions require attention to the reasons for, and the basic scope of, the protections offered by the Confrontation Clause.

The origin and development of the hearsay rules and of the Confrontation Clause have been traced by others and need not be recounted in detail here.   It is sufficient to note that the particular vice that gave impetus to the confrontation claim was the practice of trying defendants on "evidence" which consisted solely of ex parte affidavits or depositions secured by the examining magistrates, thus denying the defendant the opportunity to challenge his accuser in a face-to-face encounter in front of the trier of fact. Prosecuting attorneys "would frequently allege matters which the prisoner denied and called upon them to prove.   The proof was usually given be reading depositions, confessions of accomplices, letters, and the like;   and this occasioned frequent demands by the prisoner to have his 'accusers,' i.e. the witnesses against him, brought before him face to face   *   *   *."

But objections occasioned by this practice appear primarily to have been aimed at the failure to call the witness to confront personally the defendant at his trial.   So far as appears, in claiming confrontation rights no objection was made against receiving a witness' out-of-court depositions or statements, so long as the witness was present at trial to repeat his story and to explain or repudiate any conflicting prior stories before the trier of fact.

*   *   *   Viewed historically, then, there is good reason to conclude that the Confrontation Clause is not violated by admitting a declarant's out-of-

court statements, as long as the declarant is testifying as a witness and subject to full and effective cross-examination.

This conclusion is supported by comparing the purposes of confrontation with the alleged dangers in admitting an out-of-court statement. Confrontation: (1) insures that the witness will give his statements under oath—thus impressing him with the seriousness of the matter and guarding against the lie by the possibility of a penalty for perjury; (2) forces the witness to submit to cross-examination, the "greatest legal engine ever invented for the discovery of truth"; (3) permits the jury that is to decide the defendant's fate to observe the demeanor of the witness in making his statement, thus aiding the jury in assessing his credibility.

It is, of course, true that the out-of-court statement may have been made under circumstances subject to none of these protections. But if the declarant is present and testifying at trial, the out-of-court statement for all practical purposes regains most of the lost protections. If the witness admits the prior statement is his, or if there is other evidence to show the statement is his, the danger of faulty reproduction is negligible and the jury can be confident that it has before it two conflicting statements by the same witness. Thus, as far as the oath is concerned, the witness must now affirm, deny, or qualify the truth of the prior statement under the penalty of perjury; * * *

Second, the inability to cross-examine the witness at the time he made his prior statement cannot easily be shown to be of crucial significance as long as the defendant is assured of full and effective cross-examination at the time of trial. The most successful cross-examination at the time the prior statement was made could hardly hope to accomplish more than has already been accomplished by the fact that the witness is now telling a different, inconsistent story, and—in this case—one that is favorable to the defendant. We cannot share the California Supreme Court's view that belated cross-examination can never serve as a constitutionally adequate substitute for cross-examination contemporaneous with the original statement. The main danger in substituting subsequent for timely cross-examination seems to lie in the possibility that the witness' "[f]alse testimony is apt to harden and become unyielding to the blows of truth in proportion as the witness has opportunity for reconsideration and influence by the suggestions of others, whose interest may be, and often is, to maintain falsehood rather than truth." That danger, however, disappears when the witness has changed his testimony so that, far from "hardening," his prior statement has softened to the point where he now repudiates it.

The defendant's task in cross-examination is, of course, no longer identical to the task that he would have faced if the witness had not changed his story and hence had to be examined as a "hostile" witness giving evidence for the prosecution. This difference, however, far from lessening, may actually enhance the defendant's ability to attack the prior statement. For the witness, favorable to the defendant, should be more than willing to give the usual suggested explanations for the inaccuracy of his prior statement, such as faulty perception or undue haste in recounting the event. * * *

Similar reasons lead us to discount as a constitutional matter the fact that the jury at trial is foreclosed from viewing the declarant's demeanor when he first made his out-of-court statement. The witness who now relates a different story about the events in question must necessarily assume a position as to the truth value of his prior statement, thus giving the jury a chance to observe and evaluate his demeanor as he either disavows or qualifies his earlier statement. * * *

It may be true that a jury would be in a better position to evaluate the truth of the prior statement if it could somehow be whisked magically back in time to witness a gruelling cross-examination of the declarant as he first gives his statement. But the question as we see it must be not whether one can somehow imagine the jury in "a better position," but whether subsequent cross-examination at the defendant's trial will still afford the trier of fact a satisfactory basis for evaluating the truth of the prior statement. On that issue, neither evidence nor reason convinces us that contemporaneous cross-examination before the ultimate trier of fact is so much more effective than subsequent examination that it must be made the touchstone of the Confrontation Clause.

Finally, we note that none of our decisions interpreting the Confrontation Clause requires excluding the out-of-court statements of a witness who is available and testifying at trial. The concern of most of our cases has been focused on precisely the opposite situation—situations where statements have been admitted in the absence of the declarant and without any chance to cross-examine him at trial. These situations have arisen through application of a number of traditional "exceptions" to the hearsay rule, which permit the introduction of evidence despite the absence of the declarant usually on the theory that the evidence possesses other indicia of "reliability" and is incapable of being admitted, despite good-faith efforts of the State, in any way that will secure confrontation with the declarant. Such exceptions, dispensing altogether with the literal right to "confrontation" and cross-examination, have been subjected on several occasions to careful scrutiny by this Court. * * *

* * *

We find nothing, then, in either the history or the purposes of the Confrontation Clause, or in the prior decisions of this Court, that compels the conclusion reached by the California Supreme Court concerning the validity of California's § 1235. Contrary to the judgment of that court, the Confrontation Clause does not require excluding from evidence the prior statements of a witness who concedes making the statements, and who may be asked to defend or otherwise explain the inconsistency between his prior and his present version of the events in question, thus opening himself to full cross-examination at trial as to both stories.

III

We also think that Porter's preliminary hearing testimony was admissible as far as the Constitution is concerned wholly apart from the question of whether respondent had an effective opportunity for confrontation at the subsequent trial. For Porter's statement at the preliminary hearing had already been given under circumstances closely approximating those that surround the typical trial. Porter was under oath; respondent was represented by counsel—the same counsel in fact who later represented him at the trial; respondent had every opportunity to cross-examine Porter as to his statement; and the proceedings were conducted before a judicial tribunal, equipped to provide a judicial record of the hearings. Under these circumstances, Porter's statement would, we think, have been admissible at trial even in Porter's absence if Porter had been actually unavailable, despite good-faith efforts of the State to produce him. That being the case, we do not think a different result should follow where the witness is actually produced.

This Court long ago held that admitting the prior testimony of an unavailable witness does not violate the Confrontation Clause. Mattox v. United States, 156 U.S. 237 (1895). That case involved testimony given at the defendant's first trial by a witness who had died by the time of the second trial, but we do not find the instant preliminary hearing significantly different from an actual trial to warrant distinguishing the two cases for purposes of the Confrontation Clause. * * * In the present case respondent's counsel does not appear to have been significantly limited in any way in the scope or nature of his cross-examination of the witness Porter at the preliminary hearing. If Porter had died or was otherwise unavailable, the Confrontation Clause would not have been violated by admitting his testimony given at the preliminary hearing—the right of cross-examination then afforded provides substantial compliance with the purposes behind the confrontation requirement, as long as the declarant's inability to give live testimony is in no way the fault of the State. * * *

* * * [N]othing in Barber v. Page or other cases in this Court indicates that a different result must follow where the State produces the declarant and swears him as a witness at the trial. It may be that the rules of evidence applicable in state or federal courts would restrict resort to prior sworn testimony where the declarant is present at the trial. But as a constitutional matter, it is untenable to construe the Confrontation Clause to permit the use of prior testimony to prove the State's case where the declarant never appears, but to bar that testimony where the declarant is present at the trial, exposed to the defendant and the trier of fact, and subject to cross-examination.[a] As in the case where the witness is physically un-

---

a. The explanation advanced for the contrary conclusion seems to be that where the witness is dead or otherwise unavailable, the State may in good faith assume he would have given the same story at trial, and may introduce the former testimony as reasonably reliable and as prompted by the factor of "necessity." On the contrary, it is argued, where the witness is present to testify but does not relate the same story, "necessity," "reliability," and the assumption that the story would be the same are all destroyed. But the only "necessity" that exists in either case is the State's "need" to introduce relevant evidence that through no fault of its own cannot be introduced in any other way. And the "assumption" that the witness would have given the same story if he had been available at trial, is little more than another way of saying that the testimony was given under circumstances that make it reasonably reliable—there is nothing in a witness' death by itself, for example, which would justify assuming his story would not have changed at trial. Finally, the "reliability" of the statement is based on the circumstances under which it was given—cir-

producible, the State here has made every effort to introduce its evidence through the live testimony of the witness; it produced Porter at trial, swore him as a witness, and tendered him for cross-examination. Whether Porter then testified in a manner consistent or inconsistent with his preliminary hearing testimony, claimed a loss of memory, claimed his privilege against compulsory self-incrimination, or simply refused to answer, nothing in the Confrontation Clause prohibited the State from also relying on his prior testimony to prove its case against Green.

IV

There is a narrow question lurking in this case concerning the admissibility of Porter's statements to Officer Wade. In the typical case to which the California court addressed itself, the witness at trial gives a version of the ultimate events different from that given on a prior occasion. * * * Here, however, Porter claimed at trial that he could not remember the events that occurred after respondent telephoned him and hence failed to give any current version of the more important events described in his earlier statement.

Whether Porter's apparent lapse of memory so affected Green's right to cross-examine as to make a critical difference in the application of the Confrontation Clause in this case is an issue which is not ripe for decision at this juncture. * * * Its resolution depends much upon the unique facts in this record, and we are reluctant to proceed without the state court's views of what the record actually discloses relevant to this particular issue. * * *

We therefore vacate the judgment of the California Supreme Court and remand the case to that court for further proceedings not inconsistent with this opinion.

The concurring opinion of Chief Justice Burger is omitted.

Mr. Justice HARLAN, concurring.

The precise holding of the Court today is that the Confrontation Clause of the Sixth Amendment does not preclude the introduction of an out-of-court declaration, taken under oath and subject to cross-examination, to prove the truth of the matters asserted therein, when the declarant is available as a witness at trial. With this I agree.

The California decision that we today reverse demonstrates, however, the need to approach this case more broadly than the Court has seen fit to do, and to confront squarely the Confrontation Clause because the holding of the California Supreme Court is the result of an understandable misconception, as I see things, of numerous decisions of this Court, old and recent, that have indiscriminately equated "confrontation" with "cross-examination."

cumstances that remain unaffected regardless of whether the witness is present or absent at the later trial. Surely in terms of protecting the defendant's interests, and the jury's ability to assess the reliability of the evidence it hears, it seems most unlikely that respondent in this case would have been better off, as the dissent seems to suggest, if Porter had died, and his prior testimony were admitted, than he was in the instant case where Porter's conduct on the stand cast substantial doubt on his prior statement. As long as the State has made a good-faith effort to produce the witness, the actual presence or absence of the witness cannot be constitutionally relevant for purposes of the "unavailability" exception.

* * *

If "confrontation" is to be equated with the right to cross-examine, it would transplant the ganglia of hearsay rules and their exceptions into the body of constitutional protections. The stultifying effect of such a course upon this aspect of the law of evidence in both state and federal systems need hardly be labored, and it is good that the Court today, as I read its opinion, firmly eschews that course.

* * * History seems to give us very little insight into the intended scope of the Sixth Amendment Confrontation Clause. Commentators have been prone to slide too easily from confrontation to cross-examination.

Against this amorphous backdrop I reach two conclusions. First, the Confrontation Clause of the Sixth Amendment reaches no farther than to require the prosecution to *produce* any *available* witness whose declarations it seeks to use in a criminal trial. Second, even were this conclusion deemed untenable as a matter of Sixth Amendment law, it is surely agreeable to Fourteenth Amendment "due process," which, in my view, is the constitutional framework in which state cases of this kind should be judged. * * *

* * *

A

* * * [T]he Confrontation Clause was apparently included without debate along with the rest of the Sixth Amendment package of rights—to notice, counsel, and compulsory process—all incidents of the adversarial proceeding before a jury as evolved during the 17th and 18th centuries. If anything, the confrontation guarantee may be thought, along with the right to compulsory process, merely to constitutionalize the right to a defense as we know it, a right not always enjoyed by the accused, whose only defense prior to the late 17th century was to argue that the prosecution had not completely proved its case. * * *

* * *

From the scant information available it may tentatively be concluded that the Confrontation Clause was meant to constitutionalize a barrier against flagrant abuses, trials by anonymous accusers, and absentee witnesses. That the Clause was intended to ordain common law rules of evidence with constitutional sanction is doubtful, notwithstanding English decisions that equate confrontation and hearsay. Rather, having established a broad principle, it is far more likely that the Framers anticipated it would be supplemented, as a matter of judge-made common law, by prevailing rules of evidence.

B

Judicial Precedent.

* * *

Notwithstanding language that appears to equate the Confrontation Clause with a right to cross-examine, and, by implication, exclude hearsay, the early holdings and dicta can, I think, only be harmonized by viewing the confrontation guarantee as being confined to an availability rule, one that requires the production of a witness when he is available to testify. This view explains the recognition of the dying declaration exception, which dispenses with any requirement of cross-examination, and the refusal to make an exception for prior recorded statements, taken subject to cross-examination by the accused, when the witness is still available to testify.

* * *

II

Recent decisions have, in my view, fallen into error on two scores. As a matter of jurisprudence I think it unsound, * * * to incorporate *as such* the guarantees of the Bill of Rights into the Due Process Clause. While, in this particular instance, this would be of little practical consequence if the Court had confined the Sixth Amendment guarantee to an "availability" requirement, some decisions have, unfortunately, failed to separate, even as a federal matter, restrictions on the abuse of hearsay testimony, part of the due process right of a reliable and trustworthy conviction, and the right to confront an available witness.

By incorporating into the Fourteenth Amendment its misinterpretation of the Sixth Amendment these decisions have in one blow created the present dilemma, that of bringing about a potential for a constitutional rule of hearsay for both state and federal courts. However ill-advised would be the constitutionalization of hearsay rules in federal courts, the undesirability of imposing those brittle rules on the States is manifest. Given the ambulatory fortunes of the hearsay doctrine, evidenced by the disagreement among scholars over the value of excluding hearsay and the trend toward liberalization of the exceptions, it would be most unfortunate for this Court to limit the flexibility of the States and choke experimentation in this evolving area of the law. * * *

What I would hold binding on the States as a matter of due process is what I also deem the correct meaning of the Sixth Amendment's Confrontation Clause—that a State may not in a criminal case use hearsay when the declarant is available. There is no reason in fairness why a State should not, as long as it retains a traditional adversarial trial, produce a witness and afford the accused an opportunity to cross-examine him when he can be made available. That this principle is an essential element of fairness is attested to not only by precedent, but also by the traditional and present exceptions to the hearsay rule which recognize greater flexibility for receiving evidence when the witness is not available. Furthermore it accommodates the interest of the State in making a case, yet recognizes the obligation to accord the accused the fullest opportunity to present his best defense. For those rare cases where a conviction occurs after a trial where no credible evidence could be said to justify the result, there remains the broader due process requirement that a conviction cannot be founded on no evidence.

III

Putting aside for the moment the "due process" aspect of this case, it follows, in my view, that there is no "confrontation" reason why the prosecution should not use a witness' prior inconsistent statement for the truth of the matters therein asserted. Here the prosecution has produced its witness, Porter, and made him available for trial confrontation. That, in my judgment, perforce satisfies the Sixth Amendment. * * *

The fact that the witness, though physically available, cannot recall either the underlying events that are the subject of an extra-judicial statement or previous testimony or recollect the circumstances under which the statement was given, does not have Sixth Amendment consequence. * * *

* * *

Mr. Justice BRENNAN, dissenting.

Respondent was convicted of violating California Health and Safety Code § 11532 which prohibits furnishing narcotics to a minor. The only issue at his trial was whether he had in fact furnished Porter, a minor, with marihuana. On the direct testimony, it does not appear that he could have been constitutionally convicted, for it seems that there would have been insufficient evidence to sustain a finding of guilt. * * *

[T]he evidence on which respondent was found guilty consisted of two pretrial statements by Porter. The first was the account given Officer Wade. It was unsworn and not subject to defense cross-examination. Porter's demeanor while making the statement was not observed by the trial factfinder. The statement was made under unreliable circumstances—it was taken four days after Porter's arrest for selling marihuana to an undercover agent and while he was still in custody.[b] No written transcript of the statement was introduced at trial. Officer Wade recounted it simply as he remembered Porter's words. The second statement was given by Porter during respondent's preliminary hearing. It was sworn and subject to cross-examination. Defense counsel, however, did not engage in a searching examination. * * *

* * * In my view, neither statement can be introduced without unconstitutionally restricting the right of the accused to challenge incriminating evidence in the presence of the factfinder who will determine his guilt or innocence.

I

* * *

There is no way to test the recollection and sift the conscience of a witness regarding the facts of an alleged offense if he is unwilling or unable to be questioned about them,[c] defense counsel cannot probe the story of a silent witness and attempt to expose facts that qualify or discredit it. * * * If the witness claims that he is unable to remember the pertinent events, it is

b. Porter declared under oath on May 12, 1967, that "when I was arrested and was in custody, the police kept telling me that they knew it was JOHN GREEN I was involved with and that unless I implicated him that they would see that I was out of circulation for a long time * * *."

c. If, on the other hand, the witness is willing and able to testify at trial about the operative events, the demands of the Confrontation Clause may be met, even though the witness contradicts his pretrial assertions. I see no need on the facts presented here, however, to resolve this issue.

true that this assertion can be challenged, and that in making and defending it the witness will be affected by his oath, the penalty for perjury, and the courtroom atmosphere. It is equally true that the trial factfinder can observe and weigh the witness' demeanor as he makes and defends such a claim. But a decision by the factfinder that the witness is lying sheds no direct light on the accuracy of any pretrial statement made by him; that statement remains without the support or discredit that can come only from the probing of its factual basis while the witness stands face to face with the accused and the factfinder. * * *

This Court has already explicitly held in Douglas v. Alabama, 380 U.S. 415, 419–420 (1965), that the Confrontation Clause forbids the substantive use at trial of a prior extrajudicial statement, when the declarant is present at trial but unwilling to testify about the events with which his prior statement dealt. * * *

For purposes of the Confrontation Clause, there is no significant difference between a witness who fails to testify about an alleged offense because he is unwilling to do so and a witness whose silence is compelled by an inability to remember. * * * In both cases, if a pretrial statement is introduced for the truth of the facts asserted, the witness becomes simply a conduit for the admission of stale evidence, whose reliability can never be tested before the trial factfinder by cross-examination of the declarant about the operative events, and by observation of his demeanor as he testifies about them.

Unlike the Court, I seen no reason to leave undecided the inadmissibility of Porter's statements to Officer Wade. We have before us the transcript of Porter's trial testimony. He could not remember the operative events. Whether he feigned loss of memory is irrelevant to respondent's confrontation claim. Under *Douglas* his statement to Officer Wade must be excluded as substantive evidence.

II

The question remains whether the fact that a pretrial statement was obtained at a preliminary hearing, under oath and subject to cross-examination, distinguishes that statement for confrontation purposes from an extrajudicial statement. I thought that our decision in Barber v. Page, 390 U.S. 719 (1968), resolved this issue. In *Barber* we stated that confrontation at a preliminary hearing cannot compensate for the absence of confrontation at trial, because the nature and objectives of the two proceedings differ significantly. * * *

* * * Cross-examination at the hearing pales beside that which takes place at trial. This is so for a number of reasons. First, * * *, the objective of the hearing is to establish the presence or absence of probable cause, not guilt or innocence proved beyond a reasonable doubt; thus, if evidence suffices to establish probable cause, defense counsel has little reason at the preliminary hearing to show that it does not conclusively establish guilt—or, at least, he had little reason before today's decision. Second, neither defense nor prosecution is eager before trial to disclose its case by extensive examination at the preliminary hearing; thorough questioning of a prosecution witness by defense counsel may easily amount to a grant of gra-

tis discovery to the State. Third, the schedules of neither court nor counsel can easily accommodate lengthy preliminary hearings. Fourth, even were the judge and lawyers not concerned that the proceedings be brief, the defense and prosecution have generally had inadequate time before the hearing to prepare for extensive examination. Finally, though counsel were to engage in extensive questioning, a part of its force would never reach the trial factfinder, who would know the examination only second hand. As the California Supreme Court stated:

> "[L]ost in a cold reading of the preliminary transcript is the more subtle yet undeniable effect of counsel's rhetorical style, his pauses for emphasis and his variations in tone, as well as his personal rapport with the jurors, as he pursues his cross-examination. * * *

If cross-examination at the preliminary hearing rarely approximates that at trial, observation by the trial factfinder of the witness' demeanor as he gives his prior testimony is virtually nonexistent. Unless the committing magistrate is also the trial factfinder, the demeanor purpose of the Confrontation Clause is wholly negated by substituting confrontation at the preliminary hearing for confrontation at trial. * * *

It appears, then, that in terms of the purposes of the Confrontation Clause, an equation of face-to-face encounter at the preliminary hearing with confrontation at trial must rest largely on the fact that the witness testified at the hearing under oath, subject to the penalty for perjury, and in a courtroom atmosphere. These factors are not insignificant, but by themselves they fall far short of satisfying the demands of constitutional confrontation. * * *

* * *

The Court relies heavily on the traditional practice of admitting the prior testimony of a witness who is physically unavailable at trial. It finds no ground for distinguishing between the pretrial declarant who fails to testify at trial because he is not physically present and the pretrial declarant who, though present at trial, fails to testify because he is unwilling or unable to do so. The Court reasons that the "necessity" for the introduction of either declarant's prior statement is "the State's 'need' to introduce relevant evidence," and that the testimony's "reliability" rests "on the circumstances under which it was given—circumstances that remain unaffected regardless of whether the witness is present or absent at the later trial." I disagree.

The State, obviously, does need to introduce relevant evidence. But the "necessity" that justifies the admission of pretrial statements is not the prosecution's need to convict, but the factfinder's need to be presented with reliable evidence to aid its determination of guilt or innocence. * * * When a probability exists that incriminating pretrial testimony is unreliable, its admission, absent confrontation, will prejudicially distort the factfinding process.

The reliability of pretrial testimony, in turn, is not determined simply by the circumstances under which it was given. It is also influenced by subsequent developments. If, for example, prior testimony is later disavowed by the declarant in an extrajudicial but convincing statement, it would be unrealistic to argue at a later trial, from which the declarant was physically absent, that the reliability of his prior testimony was unaffected by the intervening event.

The subsequent developments under consideration here are (1) failure to testify at trial because of physical unavailability and (2) failure to testify because of unwillingness to do so or inability to remember. In my view, these developments have very different implications for the reliability of prior testimony. Physical unavailability is generally a neutral factor; in most instances, it does not cast doubt on the witness' earlier assertions. Inability to remember the pertinent events, on the other hand, or unwillingness to testify about them, whether because of feigned loss of memory or fear of self-incrimination, does cast such doubt. Honest inability to remember at trial raises serious question about clarity of memory at the time of the pretrial statement. The deceit inherent in feigned loss of memory lessens confidence in the probity of prior assertions. And fear of self-incrimination at trial suggests that the witness may have shaped prior testimony so as to avoid dangerous consequences for himself. Reliability cannot be assumed simply because a prior statement was made at a preliminary hearing.

In sum, I find that Porter's real or pretended lapse of memory about the pertinent events casts serious doubt upon the reliability of his preliminary hearing testimony. It is clear that so long as a witness, such as Porter, cannot or will not testify about these events at trial, the accused remains unable to challenge effectively that witness' prior assertions about them. The probable unreliability of the prior testimony, coupled with the impossibility of its examination during trial, denies the accused his right to probe and attempt to discredit incriminating evidence. * * *

In the preceding chapter we are quite critical of the rule allowing prior inconsistent statements to be used substantively.[30] Review these arguments, for we shall not repeat them here. Even if these arguments convince you that the rule approved in *Green* is unwise, does it necessarily follow that the rule should be struck down as a violation of the confrontation clause? What standard can the Court use to determine whether an evidence rule violates the confrontation clause? Does it have anything more to rely upon than its sense of what is wise and what is fair?

What factors does the majority in *Green* believe important in determining whether the admission of certain evidence violates the confrontation clause? What does this tell you about the values which the majority believes the confrontation clause was

designed to protect? Do you find Justice Harlan's approach to this case more satisfactory than the approach of the majority? Is it likely to provide better guidance to the lower courts? Note the irony here. Justice Harlan believes that the Court's role in cases like this is to determine whether a state's procedures are so fundamentally unfair as to violate the due process clause of the fourteenth amendment. Yet he is able to propound a relatively unambiguous statement of what the confrontation clause means at its core. The majority eschews the generalized due process approach, yet they seem particularly concerned with what fairness requires.

A concern for fairness may be essential to any sound interpretation of the clause for one may regard the confrontation clause as one of a set of guarantees found in the

30.   See pp. 479–89 supra.

sixth amendment which, taken together, are designed to ensure that criminal trials will be fair. It does not, however, follow from this view that confrontation clause analysis must be equated with due process analysis. For it may be, as Harlan's opinion suggests, that the confrontation clause is designed to achieve fairness by specifying procedures which must be followed regardless of their implications for particular cases. It is also likely that the courts will be more sensitive to the potential unfairness of procedures that deny confrontation than to a similar potential in procedures that do not appear to conflict with specific constitutional protections.

If you believe that the confrontation clause should be read to prohibit the substantive use of all prior inconsistent statements consider the facts of Gelhaar v. State.[31] This case involved a woman who was accused of stabbing and killing her husband. The police had been called to the house immediately after the killing, and within an hour of the killing they had conducted separate interviews of the couple's two teenage children. In these interviews the children told the same basic story. They had heard a drawer open; they had heard their father say, "let's talk it over"; they had heard their mother say, "where do you want it?"; they had heard their father reply, "anywhere, anywhere"; and they had heard their father say, "call a doctor." At their mother's trial the children, called by the defense, denied any memory of what they said to the police. Instead they testified that they heard their father call their mother a "whore" and their mother accuse the father of being a "child rapist." In addition, the daughter testified that she heard her father say, "I ought to kill you for that."

Doesn't it appear that the statements made by the children to the police are the most reliable evidence in this case as to what happened on the night of the killing? Aren't they considerably more reliable than the stories told by the children months later when their mother was on trial? Should the confrontation clause be read to prohibit the substantive use of statements which appear so reliable, or is reliability not the only important issue? Is an important distinction between Green and Gelhaar the fact that in Green Porter's statements were the only evidence linking Green to the crime, while in Gelhaar the earlier statements served at least as much to impeach the children's exonerative testimony as they did to provide affirmative evidence of guilt? Indeed, had the defense not called the children, their earlier statements might never have been offered in evidence. Is there any way of reading the confrontation clause so as to prohibit the substantive admission of statements like those in Green while allowing statements of the kind found in Gelhaar? Would Justice Brennan, who dissented in Green, have dissented in Gelhaar? Is there any way of drafting a hearsay rule which would admit for substantive purposes inconsistent statements like those found in Gelhaar, yet not admit the kinds of inconsistent statements found in Green?

In comparing Green and Gelhaar ask yourself whether the statements in Gelhaar might have been admissible under a traditional hearsay exception even if the children had not been called to testify. Cases in which statements are regarded as sufficiently reliable to be admitted even if the declarant is absent are, in this important respect, quite different from those in which there are no guarantees of reliability other than those that stem from the declarant's presence on the stand. Compare the additional guarantees that may have been present in Green with those that were present in Gelhaar.

31. 41 Wis.2d 230, 163 N.W.2d 609 (1969), certiorari denied 399 U.S. 929 (1970).

In addition to sanctioning the substantive use of prior inconsistent statements,[32] *Green* seems to stand for the proposition that confrontation clause problems do not exist when the state seeks to introduce the prior testimony, including preliminary hearing testimony,[33] of witnesses present in court.[34] Justice Brennan argues that although the fact that preliminary hearing testimony is given under oath in a courtroom setting is significant, it is not sufficient to satisfy the demands of the confrontation clause where a witness is available. He believes that cross-examination at a preliminary hearing cannot be expected to approximate that at trial. He also argues that the subsequent disavowal of preliminary hearing testimony or a failure to remember matters described in such testimony renders such testimony suspect. Thus, Justice Brennan distinguishes situations like that in *Green* from situations where prior testimony is clearly admissible, i.e., situations where a witness' unavailability is due to factors beyond his control. The majority asserts that Green's opportunity to cross-examine Porter at his preliminary hearing was not sufficiently different from the opportunity he would have had to cross-examine at an actual trial to warrant distinguishing the two for purposes of the confrontation clause. They respond at greater length to Justice Brennan's second argument in a footnote we have labeled "a." How do you come out

on these issues? Do you believe with Justice Brennan that recanted prior testimony is less reliable than prior testimony which has been neither recanted nor affirmed?

Is the opportunity to cross-examine witnesses at a preliminary hearing sufficiently different from the opportunity to cross-examine at trial that these two proceedings should be distinguished for confrontation clause purposes? Assuming the opportunity is the same, should this be the end of the analysis? Is the motive for cross-examination similar in the two settings? If it is not, should this difference be given any weight in confrontation clause analysis? Suppose, for example, the state wishes to introduce uncross-examined testimony given at an earlier trial by a currently unavailable witness. The defendant argues that its admission violates the confrontation clause, because had the evidence at the second trial been presented at the earlier one, the decision to forego cross-examination would not have been made. Do you think the defendant's argument should prevail? If not, can you distinguish this situation involving two trials from situations involving a trial and a preliminary hearing?

The Supreme Court had occasion to return to the situation in which the out-of-court statements of a testifying witness are

---

32. The Court did leave open the question of whether Porter's apparent memory lapse so affected Green's ability to cross-examine Porter at the trial as to make a critical difference in the application of the confrontation clause to the facts of the case. For the California Supreme Court's treatment of the reserved question (admitting the statement) see, 3 Cal.3rd 981, 92 Cal.Rptr. 494, or 479 P.2d 998 (1971).

33. In *Green* the majority notes that Green was represented by counsel at the preliminary hearing and that there was an opportunity to cross-examine the witness Porter at that time. How important are these features to the Court's decision regarding this

testimony in *Green?* When will these factors be important in determining whether the admission of prior testimony violates the confrontation clause?

34. There is, of course, no general hearsay exception admitting the prior testimony of witnesses present in court. Thus the protection of the hearsay rule extends beyond the mandate of the confrontation clause as interpreted in *Green.* The preliminary hearing testimony introduced by the trial court in *Green* was admitted on the theory that it was inconsistent with Porter's courtroom testimony and hence admissible as an inconsistent statement regardless of the forum in which it was given.

introduced in the case of Nelson v. O'Neil.[35] This case involved codefendants, O'Neil and Runnels, who were charged with kidnapping, robbery and vehicular theft. The codefendants entered not guilty pleas and at trial they both told the same exonerative story. However, a police officer testified that Runnels had made an informal admission of the crime which also implicated O'Neil. The jury was instructed that the statement could be used against Runnels and not against O'Neil. O'Neil objected that the instruction was not sufficient to protect his confrontation clause rights under *Bruton*. However, the case differed from *Bruton* in that Runnels, during the trial, had taken the stand and denied making the statement inculpating O'Neil. The Court found this difference sufficient to justify a different result. Citing *Green*, the majority repudiated the statement in *Douglas* that " 'effective confrontation' of a witness who allegedly made an out-of-court statement implicating the defendant 'was possible only if [the witness] affirmed the statement as his,' "[36] and held that "[t]he Constitution as construed in *Bruton* * * * is violated *only* where the out-of-court hearsay statement is that of a declarant who is unavailable at the trial for 'full and effective' cross-examination."[37] The Court found that Runnels could not be considered unavailable for full and effective cross-examination in this case because

"[h]ad Runnels in this case 'affirmed the statement as his,' the respondent would certainly have been in far worse straits than those in which he found himself when Runnels testified as he did."[38] In conclusion the Court stated that, "where a codefendant takes the stand in his own defense, denies making an alleged out-of-court statement implicating the defendant, and proceeds to testify favorably to the defendant concerning the underlying facts, the defendant has been denied no rights protected by the Sixth and Fourteenth Amendments."[39]

This language implies that the Court would sustain a hearsay exception which allows the alleged out-of-court statements of one testifying codefendant to be introduced against all others. Do you have any difficulties with such an exception or with the *O'Neil* case generally? Consider the difficulties that might be present in cross-examining a codefendant which are not posed by the cross-examination of ordinary witnesses? What, if any, are their implications for confrontation clause analysis? Since after *O'Neil* one defendant may be hurt by the out-of-court admissions of a codefendant who takes the stand, the case will, in certain circumstances, make it ethically impossible for an attorney to represent two or more codefendants.

Problem VII–1.   A.   The prosecutor at a trial puts a witness, *W*, on the stand. She then reads the transcript of the testimony which *W* gave at the defendant's preliminary hearing to the jury, and without asking *W* any questions, offers *W* to the defendant for cross-examination. The earlier testimony is admitted under a new hearsay exception which provides that prior testimony made under oath and subject to cross-examination by the defendant in the case is admissible if the declarant is unavailable or if the declarant is available and present in court. **On the basis of the cases you have**

35.   402 U.S. 622 (1971).
36.   Id. at 627.
37.   Id.

38.   Id. at 628–29.
39.   Id. at 629–30.

read thus far, should a lower court hold that this exception violates the confrontation clause?

B.   The prosecutor announces to the defendant two days before trial that she intends to introduce *W*'s preliminary hearing testimony at trial without calling *W*, but that the defendant may subpoena *W* if he wishes.   At trial the earlier testimony is admitted under a new hearsay exception which provides that prior testimony made under oath and subject to cross-examination by the defendant in the case is admissible if the declarant is unavailable or if the declarant is available and subject to subpoena by the defendant and defendant has at least two days notice of the state's intention to use the prior testimony without calling the witness.   **Should a lower court hold that this exception violates the confrontation clause?   Does it differ in any meaningful way from the exception posited in Part A of this problem?**

F.   DUTTON v. EVANS, 400 U.S. 74 (1970)

Mr. Justice STEWART announced the judgment of the Court and an opinion in which The CHIEF JUSTICE, Mr. Justice WHITE, and Mr. Justice BLACKMUN join.

Early on an April morning in 1964, three police officers were brutally murdered in Gwinnett County, Georgia.   Their bodies were found a few hours later, handcuffed together in a pine thicket, each with multiple gunshot wounds in the back of the head.   After many months of investigation, Georgia authorities charged the appellee, Evans, and two other men, Wade Truett and Venson Williams, with the officers' murders.   Evans and Williams were indicted by a grand jury;   Truett was granted immunity from prosecution in return for his testimony.

Evans pleaded not guilty and exercised his right under Georgia law to be tried separately.   After a jury trial, he was convicted of murder and sentenced to death.   * * *

In order to understand the context of the constitutional question before us, a brief review of the proceedings at Evans' trial is necessary.   The principal prosecution witness at the trial was Truett, the alleged accomplice who had been granted immunity.   Truett described at length and in detail the circumstances surrounding the murder of the police officers.   He testified that he, along with Evans and Williams, had been engaged in switching the license plates on a stolen car parked on a back road in Gwinnett County when they were accosted by the three police officers.   As the youngest of the officers leaned in front of Evans to inspect the ignition switch on the car, Evans grabbed the officer's gun from its holster.   Evans and Williams then disarmed the other officers at gunpoint, and handcuffed the three of them together.   They then took the officers into the woods and killed them by firing several bullets into their bodies at extremely close range.   In addition to Truett, 19 other witnesses testified for the prosecution.   Defense counsel was given full opportunity to cross-examine each witness, and he exercised that opportunity with respect to most of them.

One of the 20 prosecution witnesses was a man named Shaw.   He testified that he and Williams had been fellow prisoners in the federal penitentiary in Atlanta, Georgia, at the time Williams was brought to Gwinnett County to be arraigned on the charges of murdering the police officers.   Shaw said that when Williams was returned to the penitentiary from the arraignment, he had asked Williams: "How did you make out in court?" and that Williams had responded, "If it hadn't been for that dirty son-of-a-bitch Alex Evans, we wouldn't be in this now."   Defense counsel objected to the introduction of this testimony upon the ground that it was hearsay and thus violative of Evans' right of confrontation.   After the objection was overruled, counsel cross-examined Shaw at length.

The testimony of Shaw relating what he said Williams had told him was admitted by the Georgia trial court, and its admission upheld by the Georgia Supreme Court, upon the basis of a Georgia statute that provides: "After the fact of conspiracy shall be proved, the declarations by any one of the conspirators during the pendency of the criminal project shall be admissible against all."   As the appellate court put it:

> " 'The rule is that so long as the conspiracy to conceal the fact that a crime has been committed or the identity of the perpetrators of the offense continues, the parties to such conspiracy are to be considered so much a unit that the declarations of either are admissible against the other.'   The defendant, and his co-conspirator, Williams, at the time this statement was made, were still concealing their identity, keeping secret the fact that they had killed the deceased, if they had, and denying their guilt. * * * "

This holding was in accord with a consistent line of Georgia decisions construing the state statute.

It was the admission of this testimony of the witness Shaw that formed the basis for the appellee's claim in the present habeas corpus proceeding that he had been denied the constitutional right of confrontation in the Georgia trial court.   In upholding that claim, the Court of Appeals for the Fifth Circuit regarded its duty to be "not only to interpret the framers' original concept in light of historical developments, but also to translate into due-process terms the constitutional boundaries of the hearsay rule."   The court upheld the appellee's constitutional claim because it could find no "salient and cogent reasons" for the exception to the hearsay rule Georgia applied in the present case, an exception that the court pointed out was broader than that applicable to conspiracy trials in the federal courts.

The question before us, then, is whether in the circumstances of this case the Court of Appeals was correct in holding that Evans' murder conviction had to be set aside because of the admission of Shaw's testimony.   In considering this question, we start by recognizing that this Court has squarely held that "the Sixth Amendment's right of an accused to confront the witnesses against him is * * * a fundamental right * * * made obligatory on the States by the Fourteenth Amendment."   But that is no more than the beginning of our inquiry.

I

It is not argued, nor could it be, that the constitutional right to confrontation requires that no hearsay evidence can ever be introduced. * * *

The argument seems to be, rather, that in any given case the Constitution requires a reappraisal of every exception to the hearsay rule, no matter how long established, in order to determine whether, in the words of the Court of Appeals, it is supported by "salient and cogent reasons." The logic of that position would seem to require a constitutional reassessment of every established hearsay exception, federal or state, but in the present case it is argued only that the hearsay exception applied by Georgia is constitutionally invalid because it does not identically conform to the hearsay exception applicable to conspiracy trials in the federal courts.

[Mr. Justice Stewart proceeds to dismiss this argument pointing out that the Federal coconspirator exception to the hearsay rule responds to policy considerations which are not related to the sixth amendment's guarantee of confrontation.]

II

It is argued, alternatively, that in any event Evans' conviction must be set aside under the impact of our recent decisions that have reversed state court convictions because of the denial of the constitutional right of confrontation. The cases upon which the appellee Evans primarily relies are Pointer v. Texas; Douglas v. Alabama; Brookhart v. Janis; Barber v. Page; and Roberts v. Russell.

* * *

It seems apparent that the Sixth Amendment's Confrontation Clause and the evidentiary hearsay rule stem from the same roots. But this Court has never equated the two, and we decline to do so now. We confine ourselves, instead, to deciding the case before us.

This case does not involve evidence in any sense "crucial" or "devastating," as did all the cases just [cited]. It does not involve the use, or misuse, of a confession made in the coercive atmosphere of official interrogation, as did *Douglas, Brookhart, Bruton,* and *Roberts.* It does not involve any suggestion of prosecutorial misconduct or even negligence, as did *Pointer, Douglas,* and *Barber.* It does not involve the use by the prosecution of a paper transcript, as did *Pointer, Brookhart,* and *Barber.* It does not involve a joint trial, as did *Bruton* and *Roberts.* And it certainly does not involve the wholesale denial of cross-examination, as did *Brookhart.*

In the trial of this case no less than 20 witnesses appeared and testified for the prosecution. Evans' counsel was given full opportunity to cross-examine every one of them. The most important witness, by far, was the eyewitness who described all the details of the triple murder and who was cross-examined at great length. Of the 19 other witnesses, the testimony of but a single one is at issue here. That one witness testified to a brief conversation about Evans he had had with a fellow prisoner in the Atlanta Penitentiary. The witness was vigorously and effectively cross-examined by defense counsel.[d] His testimony, which was of peripheral significance at

d. This cross-examination was such as to cast serious doubt on Shaw's credibility and, more particularly, on whether the conversation which Shaw related ever took place.

most, was admitted in evidence under a co-conspirator exception to the hearsay rule long established under state statutory law. The Georgia statute can obviously have many applications consistent with the Confrontation Clause, and we conclude that its application in the circumstances of this case did not violate the Constitution.

Evans was not deprived of any right of confrontation on the issue of whether Williams actually made the statement related by Shaw. Neither a hearsay nor a confrontation question would arise had Shaw's testimony been used to prove merely that the statement had been made. The hearsay rule does not prevent a witness from testifying as to what he has heard; it is rather a restriction on the proof of fact through extra-judicial statements. From the viewpoint of the Confrontation Clause, a witness under oath, subject to cross-examination, and whose demeanor can be observed by the trier of fact, is a reliable informant not only as to what he has seen but also as to what he has heard.[e]

The confrontation issue arises because the jury was being invited to infer that Williams had implicitly identified Evans as the perpetrator of the murder when he blamed Evans for his predicament. But we conclude that there was no denial of the right of confrontation as to this question of identity. First, the statement contained no express assertion about past fact, and consequently it carried on its face a warning to the jury against giving the statement undue weight. Second, Williams' personal knowledge of the identity and role of the other participants in the triple murder is abundantly established by Truett's testimony and by Williams' prior conviction. It is inconceivable that cross-examination could have shown that Williams was not in a position to know whether or not Evans was involved in the murder. Third, the possibility that Williams' statement was founded on faulty recollection is remote in the extreme. Fourth, the circumstances under which Williams made the statement were such as to give reason to suppose that Williams did not misrepresent Evans' involvement in the crime. These circumstances go beyond a showing that Williams had no apparent reason to lie to Shaw. His statement was spontaneous, and it was against his penal interest to make it. These are indicia of reliability which have been widely viewed as determinative of whether a statement may be placed before the jury though there is no confrontation of the declarant.

The decisions of this Court make it clear that the mission of the Confrontation Clause is to advance a practical concern for the accuracy of the truth-determining process in criminal trials by assuring that "the trier of fact [has] a satisfactory basis for evaluating the truth of the prior statement." Evans exercised, and exercised effectively, his right to confrontation on the factual question whether Shaw had actually heard Williams make the statement Shaw related. And the possibility that cross-examination of Williams could conceivably have shown the jury that the statement, though made, might have been unreliable was wholly unreal.

---

e. Of course Evans had the right to subpoena witnesses, including Williams, whose testimony might show that the statement had not been made. Counsel for Evans informed us at oral argument that he could have subpoenaed Williams but had concluded that this course would not be in the best interests of his client.

Almost 40 years ago, in Snyder v. Massachusetts, 291 U.S. 97, Mr. Justice Cardozo wrote an opinion for this Court refusing to set aside a state criminal conviction because of the claimed denial of the right of confrontation. The closing words of that opinion are worth repeating here:

"There is danger that the criminal law will be brought into contempt— that discredit will even touch the great immunities assured by the Fourteenth Amendment—if gossamer possibilities of prejudice to a defendant are to nullify a sentence pronounced by a court of competent jurisdiction in obedience to local law, and set the guilty free." 291 U.S., at 122.

The judgment of the Court of Appeals is reversed, and the case is remanded to that court for consideration of the other issues presented in this habeas corpus proceeding.

It is so ordered.

Mr. Justice BLACKMUN, whom The CHIEF JUSTICE joins, concurring.

I join Mr. Justice STEWART'S opinion. For me, however, there is an additional reason for the result.

The single sentence attributed in testimony by Shaw to Williams about Evans, and which has prolonged this litigation, was, in my view and in the light of the entire record, harmless error if it was error at all. Furthermore, the claimed circumstances of its utterance are so incredible that the testimony must have hurt, rather than helped, the prosecution's case. On this ground alone, I could be persuaded to reverse and remand.

Shaw testified that Williams made the remark at issue when Shaw "went to his room in the hospital" and asked Williams how he made out at a court hearing on the preceding day. On cross-examination, Shaw stated that he was then in custody at the federal penitentiary in Atlanta; that he worked as a clerk in the prison hospital; that Williams was lying on the bed in his room and facing the wall; that he, Shaw, was in the hall and not in the room when he spoke with Williams; that the door to the room "was closed"; that he spoke through an opening about 10 inches square; that the opening "has a piece of plate glass, window glass, just ordinary window glass, and a piece of steel mesh"; that this does not impede talking through the door; and that one talks in a normal voice when he talks through that door. Shaw conceded that when he had testified at Williams' earlier trial, he made no reference to the glass in the opening in the door.

* * *

I am at a loss to understand how any normal jury, as we must assume this one to have been, could be led to believe, let alone be influenced by, this astonishing account by Shaw of his conversation with Williams in a normal voice through a closed hospital room door. I note, also, the Fifth Circuit's description of Shaw's testimony as "somewhat incredible" and as possessing "basic incredibility."

* * *

The error here, if one exists, is harmless beyond a reasonable doubt.

Mr. Justice HARLAN, concurring in the result.

Not surprisingly the difficult constitutional issue presented by this case has produced multiple opinions.   *   *   *

The difficulty of this case arises from the assumption that the core purpose of the Confrontation Clause of the Sixth Amendment is to prevent overly broad exceptions to the hearsay rule. I believe this assumption to be wrong. Contrary to things as they appeared to me last Term when I wrote in California v. Green, 399 U.S. 149, 172 (1970), I have since become convinced that Wigmore states the correct view when he says:

> "The Constitution does not prescribe what kinds of testimonial statements (dying declarations, or the like) shall be given infra-judicially,—this depends on the law of Evidence for the time being,—but only what mode of procedure shall be followed—i.e. a cross-examining procedure—in the case of such testimony as is required by the ordinary law of Evidence to be given infra-judicially." 5 J. Wigmore, Evidence § 1397, at 131 (3d ed. 1940) (footnote omitted).

*   *   *

If one were to translate the Confrontation Clause into language in more common use today, it would read: "In all criminal prosecutions, the accused shall enjoy the right to be present and to cross-examine the witnesses against him." Nothing in this language or in its 18th-century equivalent would connote a purpose to control the scope of the rules of evidence.   *   *   *

Nor am I now content with the position I took in concurrence in California v. Green, supra, that the Confrontation Clause was designed to establish a preferential rule, requiring the prosecutor to avoid the use of hearsay where it is reasonably possible for him to do so—in other words, to produce available witnesses. Further consideration in the light of facts squarely presenting the issue, as *Green* did not, has led me to conclude that this is not a happy intent to be attributed to the Framers absent compelling linguistic or historical evidence pointing in that direction.   *   *   *

A rule requiring production of available witnesses would significantly curtail development of the law of evidence to eliminate the necessity for production of declarants where production would be unduly inconvenient and of small utility to a defendant. Examples which come to mind are the Business Records Act, 28 U.S.C. §§ 1732–1733, and the exceptions to the hearsay rule for official statements, learned treatises, and trade reports. If the hearsay exception involved in a given case is such as to commend itself to reasonable men, production of the declarant is likely to be difficult, unavailing, or pointless. In unusual cases, of which the case at hand may be an example, the Sixth Amendment guarantees federal defendants the right of compulsory process to obtain the presence of witnesses.   *   *   *

Regardless of the interpretation one puts on the words of the Confrontation Clause, the clause is simply not well designed for taking into account the numerous factors that must be weighed in passing on the appropriateness of rules of evidence. The failure of Mr. Justice STEWART'S opinion to explain the standard by which it tests Shaw's statement, or how this standard can be squared with the seemingly absolute command of the clause, bears witness to the fact that the clause is being set a task for which it is not suited. The task is far more appropriately performed under the aegis of the

Fifth and Fourteenth Amendments' commands that federal and state trials, respectively, must be conducted in accordance with due process of law. It is by this standard that I would test federal and state rules of evidence.

It must be recognized that not everything which has been said in this Court's cases is consistent with this position. However, this approach is not necessarily inconsistent with the results that have been reached.   *   *   *

*   *   *

Judging the Georgia statute here challenged by the standards of due process, I conclude that it must be sustained. Accomplishment of the main object of a conspiracy will seldom terminate the community of interest of the conspirators. Declarations against that interest evince some likelihood of trustworthiness. The jury, with the guidance of defense counsel, should be alert to the obvious dangers of crediting such testimony. As a practical matter, unless the out-of-court declaration can be proved by hearsay evidence, the facts it reveals are likely to remain hidden from the jury by the declarant's invocation of the privilege against self-incrimination.   *   *   * Exclusion of such statements, as is done in the federal courts, commends itself to me, but I cannot say that it is essential to a fair trial. The Due Process Clause requires no more.

*   *   *

Mr. Justice MARSHALL, whom Mr. Justice BLACK, Mr. Justice DOUGLAS, and Mr. Justice BRENNAN join, dissenting.

  *   *   *   [T]he Court today concludes that admission of the extra-judicial statement attributed to an alleged partner in crime did not deny Evans the right "to be confronted with the witnesses against him" guaranteed by the Sixth and Fourteenth Amendments to the Constitution. In so doing, the majority reaches a result completely inconsistent with recent opinions of this Court, especially Douglas v. Alabama, and Bruton v. United States. In my view, those cases fully apply here and establish a clear violation of Evans' constitutional rights.

*   *   *

In Douglas v. Alabama, this Court applied the principles of *Pointer* to a case strikingly similar to this one. There, as here, the State charged two defendants with a crime and tried them in separate trials. There, as here, the State first prosecuted one defendant (Loyd) and then used a statement by him in the trial of the second defendant (Douglas).   *   *   * Indeed, the only significant difference between *Douglas* and this case, insofar as the denial of the opportunity to cross-examine is concerned, is that here the State did not even attempt to call Williams to testify in Evans' trial. He was plainly available to the State, and for all we know he would have willingly testified, at least with regard to his alleged conversation with Shaw.[f]

---

f. My Brother Stewart comments that Evans might have brought Williams to the courthouse by subpoena. Defense counsel did not do so, believing that Williams would stand on his right not to incriminate himself. Be that as it may, it remains that the duty to confront a criminal defendant with the witnesses against him falls upon the *State*, and here the State was allowed to introduce damaging evidence without running the risks of trial confrontation.

* * *

The teaching of this line of cases seems clear: Absent the opportunity for cross-examination, testimony about the incriminating and implicating statement allegedly made by Williams was constitutionally inadmissible in the trial of Evans.

Mr. Justice STEWART'S opinion for reversal characterizes as "wholly unreal" the possibility that cross-examination of Williams himself would change the picture presented by Shaw's account. A trial lawyer might well doubt, as an article of the skeptical faith of that profession, such a categorical prophecy about the likely results of careful cross-examination. Indeed, the facts of this case clearly demonstrate the necessity for fuller factual development which the corrective test of cross-examination makes possible. The plurality for reversal pigeonholes the out-of-court statement that was admitted in evidence as a "spontaneous" utterance, hence to be believed. As the Court of Appeals concluded, however, there is great doubt that Williams even made the statement attributed to him. Moreover, there remains the further question what, if anything, Williams might have meant by the remark that Shaw recounted. Mr. Justice STEWART'S opinion concedes that the remark is ambiguous. Plainly it stands as an accusation of some sort: "If it hadn't been for * * * Evans," said Williams, according to Shaw, "we wouldn't be in this now." At his trial Evans himself gave unsworn testimony to the effect that the murder prosecution might have arisen from enmities that Evans' own law enforcement activities had stirred up in the locality. Did Williams' accusation relate to Evans as a man with powerful and unscrupulous enemies, or Evans as a murderer? Mr. Justice STEWART'S opinion opts for the latter interpretation, for it concludes that Williams' remark was "against his penal interest" and hence to be believed. But at this great distance from events, no one can be certain. The point is that absent cross-examination of Williams himself, the jury was left with only the unelucidated, apparently damning, and patently damaging accusation as told by Shaw.

Thus we have a case with all the unanswered questions that the confrontation of witnesses through cross-examination is meant to aid in answering: What did the declarant say, and what did he mean, and was it the truth? If Williams had testified and been cross-examined, Evans' counsel could have fully explored these and other matters. The jury then could have evaluated the statement in the light of Williams' testimony and demeanor. As it was, however, the State was able to use Shaw to present the damaging evidence and thus to avoid confronting Evans with the person who allegedly gave witness against him. I had thought that this was precisely what the Confrontation Clause as applied to the States in *Pointer* and our other cases prevented.

* * *

Finally, the plurality for reversal apparently distinguishes the present case on the ground that it "does not involve evidence in any sense 'crucial' or 'devastating.'" Despite the characterization of Shaw's testimony as "of peripheral significance at most," however, the possibility of its prejudice to Evans was very real. The outcome of Evans' trial rested, in essence, on whether the jury would believe the testimony of Truett with regard to Evans' role in the murder.   Truett spoke as an admitted accomplice who had been immunized from prosecution.   Relying on Georgia law, not federal constitutional law, the trial judge instructed the jury that "you cannot lawfully convict upon the testimony of an accomplice alone.   * * *   [T]he testimony of an accomplice must be corroborated   * * *.   [T]he corroboration   * * *   must be such as to connect the defendant with the criminal act." The State presented the testimony of a number of other witnesses, in addition to that of the alleged accomplice that tended to corroborate Evans' guilt. But Shaw's account of what Williams supposedly said to him was undoubtedly a part of that corroborating evidence.

* * *   Beyond and apart from the question of harmless error, Mr. Justice STEWART undertakes an inquiry, the purpose of which I do not understand, into whether the evidence admitted is "crucial" or "devastating." The view is, apparently, that to require the exclusion of evidence falling short of that high standard of prejudice would bring a moment of clamor against the Bill of Rights.   I would eschew such worries and confine the inquiry to the traditional questions: Was the defendant afforded the right to confront the witnesses against him?   And, if not, was the denial of his constitutional right harmless beyond a reasonable doubt?

* * *

I am troubled by the fact that the plurality for reversal, unable when all is said to place this case beyond the principled reach of our prior decisions, shifts its ground and begins a hunt for whatever "indicia of reliability" may cling to Williams' remark, as told by Shaw.   Whether Williams made a "spontaneous" statement "against his penal interest" is the very question that should have been tested by cross-examination of Williams himself.   If "indicia of reliability" are so easy to come by, and prove so much, then it is only reasonable to ask whether the Confrontation Clause has any independent vitality at all in protecting a criminal defendant against the use of extrajudicial statements not subject to cross-examination and not exposed to a jury assessment of the declarant's demeanor at trial.[g]   I believe the Confrontation Clause has been sunk if any out-of-court statement bearing an indicium of a probative likelihood can come in, no matter how damaging the statement may be or how great the need for the truth-discovering test of cross-examination. Our decisions from *Pointer* and *Douglas* to *Bruton* and *Roberts* require more than this meager inquiry.   Nor is the lame "indicia" approach necessary to avoid a rampaging Confrontation Clause that tramples all flexibility and innovation in a state's law of evidence.   That specter is only a specter.   To decide this case I need not go beyond hitherto settled Sixth and Fourteenth Amendment law to consider generally what effect, if any, the Confrontation Clause has on the common-law hearsay rule and its exceptions, since no issue of such global dimension is presented.   The incriminatory extrajudicial

g.   Mr. Justice Harlan answers this question with directness by adopting, to decide this case, his view of due process which apparently makes no distinction between civil and criminal trials, and which would prohibit only irrational or unreasonable evidentiary rulings.   Needless to say, I cannot accept the view that Evans' constitutional rights should be measured by a standard concededly having nothing to do with the Confrontation Clause.

statement of an alleged accomplice is so inherently prejudicial that it cannot be introduced unless there is an opportunity to cross-examine the declarant, whether or not his statement falls within a genuine exception to the hearsay rule.

In my view, Evans is entitled to a trial in which he is fully accorded his constitutional guarantee of the right to confront and cross-examine all the witnesses against him.   I would affirm the judgment of the Court of Appeals and let this case go back to the Georgia courts to be tried without the use of this out-of-court statement attributed by Shaw to Williams.

———

Dutton is a strange case, and its meaning is by no means clear.   Four justices would reverse the circuit court and affirm Evans' conviction on one theory, Justice Harlan would affirm the conviction on very different grounds, and four justices believe that the confrontation clause requires that Evans be retried.   In addition, Justice Blackmun in an opinion joined by the Chief Justice, suggests that the case might just as easily have been decided on the ground of harmless error.

The most interesting feature of Justice Blackmun's concurring opinion is that he believes any error was harmless largely because he feels that the jury was very unlikely to believe that Shaw (the witness) was telling the truth when he reported his conversation with Williams (the declarant). Until this case, one might have thought that one of the purposes of the confrontation clause was to avoid the danger that out of court statements might be intentionally misreported.   However, the plurality for reversal (henceforth the "plurality") is apparently willing to assume that the danger that an out-of-court statement will be fabricated or misreported has no place in confrontation clause analysis because the person doing the misreporting is available for cross-examination, so, in theory, inac-

curacy will be exposed.   For a similar reason Wigmore argued that the danger that a statement would be fabricated or misreported was not one of the dangers which justified the hearsay rule.   In the preceding chapter we dispute Wigmore's contention and point out the special difficulties which attend the cross-examination of those who report hearsay.[40]   Because of these difficulties we believe that the fact that Shaw's testimony "was somewhat incredible" is a reason to demand that the declarant be brought forward if available and not a reason to hold the confrontation clause inapplicable.   By concurring in the plurality opinion, Justice Blackmun and the Chief Justice are in the position of saying that they believe it very likely that Williams never made the statement attributed to him, but if in fact he made it, it was almost certainly believable since it was a spontaneous statement against penal interest by a person with firsthand knowledge.   Thus, Williams need not be present for examination, because if he told what appears to be the truth and denied making the statement, the jury would learn no more than what they probably learned through the cross-examination of Shaw, and if he repeated the statement from the stand it is unlikely that cross-examination could have shaken his credibility.[41]   The danger, of

40. See the text accompanying the first note 13 in Chapter Six supra.

41. **The plurality never deals with the dissent's claim that the statement is highly ambiguous and that Williams, had he been** present, might have admitted the statement but explained it in a way which would not have tended to incriminate Evans. Should one read the confrontation clause as designed, in part, to protect against the danger that an out-of-court statement which has

course, is that the jury will appreciate the reliability of Williams' statement if made and not appreciate the improbability that the statement was made. The possibility that this will occur may well be slight, but if it does occur grave injustice will result. If bringing an available witness to court could forestall the possibility that perjured testimony might be believed, should not the confrontation clause demand this result? But would the confrontation clause necessarily have this effect? If Williams denied under oath that he ever made the statement, would not Shaw's testimony under *Green* and *O'Neil* be admissible for substantive purposes? If so, would the defendant Evans have gained anything by the fact that Williams' presence was compelled?

Justice Harlan's opinion is interesting because he repudiates the construction of the confrontation clause that he advanced in *Green* less than a year before. Harlan now adopts Wigmore's view that the rules of evidence, and not the confrontation clause, determine whether evidence must be presented infra-judicially. However, in a part of *Green* not reproduced above, Harlan had this to say about Wigmore's views:

> Wigmore's more ambulatory view—that the Confrontation Clause was intended to constitutionalize the hearsay rule and all its exceptions as evolved by the courts—rests also on assertion without citation, and attempts to settle on grounds that would appear to be equally infirm as a matter of logic. Wigmore's reading would have the practical consequence of rendering meaningless what was assuredly in some sense meant to be an enduring guarantee. It is inconceivable that if the Framers intended to constitutionalize a rule of hearsay they would have licensed the judiciary to read it out

of existence by creating new and unlimited exceptions.[42]

Does Harlan convince you in *Dutton* that his criticism of Wigmore in *Green* was mistaken? Harlan rejects his earlier view that the confrontation clause requires the production of available witnesses in large part because he believes that this view invalidates such well-established hearsay exceptions as the business records exception. Does Harlan have to reject his earlier position entirely in order to accommodate such hearsay exceptions? Can you formulate some middle ground or, if you prefer Harlan's approach in *Green* to his approach in *Dutton*, do you believe that confrontation clause problems probably do exist when business records are introduced in criminal cases?

The plurality make much of the fact that Shaw's testimony was not in any sense "crucial" or "devastating", although they are unwilling to state that the testimony was so unimportant that any error in admitting it had to be harmless. The dissenters purport not to understand why the plurality are concerned with the importance of the evidence. Do you understand this concern? Would the plurality's concern make more sense if they were purporting to interpret the due process clause rather than the confrontation clause? Do you think the plurality would have decided differently if the other evidence against Evans had been weaker and if the statement reported by Shaw had been more incriminatory?

The plurality also focus on those indicia of reliability which characterized Williams' out-of-court statement. Why should they be concerned with this? Does the plurality intend to convert the confrontation clause into a constitutional hearsay rule which allows exceptions wherever they are justified by necessity and/or reliability? Does the plurality mean that state hearsay

---

been accurately described will be misinterpreted by the jury because of the ambiguity inherent in it?

42. 399 U.S. 149, 178–79.

exceptions dispensing with the production of available declarants, do not offend the confrontation clause so long as the exceptions can be rationally justified on grounds of reliability? How can they mean this after *Pointer* and *Barber*? Or do they only mean this where the evidence admitted is not "crucial" or "devastating"?

Although the lead opinion in *Dutton* commanded only four votes, the case is often cited by the lower courts. You should appreciate the leeway it allows. Harlan's opinion suggests that wherever a hearsay exception may be interpreted to admit the evidence, confrontation clause problems do not exist. The plurality opinion allows judges to distinguish cases on two dimensions, the importance of the hearsay evidence and the reliability of the reported statements. These are such subjective factors that different judges have reached diametrically opposed judgments on the same facts.[43]

G. OHIO v. ROBERTS, 448 U.S. 56 (1980)

Mr. Justice BLACKMUN delivered the opinion of the Court.

This case presents issues concerning the constitutional propriety of the introduction in evidence of the preliminary hearing testimony of a witness not produced at the defendant's subsequent state criminal trial.

I

Local police arrested respondent, Herschel Roberts, on January 7, 1975, in Lake County, Ohio. Roberts was charged with forgery of a check in the name of Bernard Isaacs, and with possession of stolen credit cards belonging to Isaacs and his wife Amy.

A preliminary hearing was held in Municipal Court on January 10. The prosecution called several witnesses, including Mr. Isaacs. Respondent's appointed counsel had seen the Isaacs' daughter, Anita, in the courthouse hallway, and called her as the defense's only witness. Anita Isaacs testified that she knew respondent, and that she had permitted him to use her apartment for several days while she was away. Defense counsel questioned Anita at some length and attempted to elicit from her an admission that she had given respondent checks and the credit cards without informing him that she did not have permission to use them. Anita, however, denied this. Respondent's attorney did not ask to have the witness declared hostile and did not request permission to place her on cross-examination. The prosecutor did not question Anita.

A county grand jury subsequently indicted respondent for forgery, for receiving stolen property (including the credit cards), and for possession of heroin.

* * *

Between November 1975 and March 1976, five subpoenas for four different trial dates [h] were issued to Anita at her parents' Ohio residence. The last three carried a written instruction that Anita should "call before appearing."

---

43. See, e.g., Park v. Huff, 493 F.2d 923 (5th Cir. 1974); reversed rehearing en banc, 506 F.2d 849 (1975); certiorari denied, 423 U.S. 824 (1975).

h. A number of continuances were granted for reasons unrelated to Anita's absence.

She was not at the residence when these were executed. She did not telephone and she did not appear at trial.

In March 1976, the case went to trial before a jury in the Court of Common Pleas. Respondent took the stand and testified that Anita Isaacs had given him her parents' checkbook and credit cards with the understanding that he could use them. Relying on [Ohio law], which permits the use of preliminary examination testimony of a witness who "cannot for any reason be produced at the trial," the State, on rebuttal, offered the transcript of Anita's testimony.

Asserting a violation of the Confrontation Clause * * * the defense objected to the use of the transcript. The trial court conducted a *voir dire* hearing as to its admissibility.

Amy Isaacs, the sole witness at *voir dire*, was questioned by both the prosecutor and defense counsel concerning her daughter's whereabouts. Anita, according to her mother, left home for Tucson, Ariz., soon after the preliminary hearing. About a year before the trial, a San Francisco social worker was in communication with the Isaacs about a welfare application Anita had filed there. Through the social worker, the Isaacs reached their daughter once by telephone. Since then, however, Anita had called her parents only one other time and had not been in touch with her two sisters. When Anita called, some seven or eight months before trial, she told her parents that she "was traveling" outside Ohio, but did not reveal the place from which she called. Mrs. Isaacs stated that she knew of no way to reach Anita in case of an emergency. * * * The trial court admitted the transcript into evidence. Respondent was convicted on all counts.

* * *

The Supreme Court of Ohio * * * held that the transcript was inadmissible. Reasoning that normally there is little incentive to cross-examine a witness at a preliminary hearing, where the "ultimate issue" is only probable cause, and citing the dissenting opinion in California v. Green, the court held that the mere opportunity to cross-examine at a preliminary hearing did not afford constitutional confrontation for purposes of trial. The court distinguished *Green*, where this Court had ruled admissible the preliminary hearing testimony of a declarant who was present at trial, but claimed forgetfulness. The Ohio court perceived a "dictum" in *Green* that suggested that the mere opportunity to cross-examine renders preliminary hearing testimony admissible. But the court concluded that *Green* "goes no further than to suggest that cross-examination actually conducted at preliminary hearing *may* afford adequate confrontation for purposes of a later trial." (emphasis in original). Since Anita had not been cross-examined at the preliminary hearing and was absent at trial, the introduction of the transcript of her testimony was held to have violated respondent's confrontation right. The three dissenting justices would have ruled that " 'the test is the opportunity for full and complete cross-examination rather than the use which is made of that opportunity'."

We granted certiorari to consider these important issues under the Confrontation Clause.

II

A

The Court here is called upon to consider once again the relationship between the Confrontation Clause and the hearsay rule with its many exceptions. The basic rule against hearsay, of course, is riddled with exceptions developed over three centuries.

* * *

The Sixth Amendment's Confrontation Clause, made applicable to the States through the Fourteenth Amendment, Pointer v. Texas, 380 U.S. 400, 403–405 (1965); provides: "In all criminal prosecutions, the accused shall enjoy the right * * * to be confronted with the witnesses against him." If one were to read this language literally, it would require, on objection, the exclusion of any statement made by a declarant not present at trial. * * * But, if thus applied, the Clause would abrogate virtually every hearsay exception, a result long rejected as unintended and too extreme.

The historical evidence leaves little doubt, however, that the Clause was intended to exclude some hearsay. Moreover, underlying policies support the same conclusion. The Court has emphasized that the Confrontation Clause reflects a preference for face-to-face confrontation at trial, and that "a primary interest secured by [the provision] is the right of cross-examination." In short, the Clause envisions

> "a personal examination and cross-examination of the witness in which the accused has an opportunity, not only of testing the recollection and sifting the conscience of the witness, but of compelling him to stand face to face with the jury in order that they may look at him, and judge by his demeanor upon the stand and the manner in which he gives his testimony whether he is worthy of belief." Mattox v. United States, 156 U.S., at 242–243.

* * *

The Court, however, has recognized that competing interests, if "closely examined," may warrant dispensing with confrontation at trial. * * * [E]very jurisdiction has a strong interest in effective law enforcement, and in the development and precise formulation of the rules of evidence applicable in criminal proceedings.

This Court, in a series of cases, has sought to accommodate these competing interests. True to the common-law tradition, the process has been gradual, building on past decisions, drawing on new experience, and responding to changing conditions. The Court has not sought to "map out a theory of the Confrontation Clause that would determine the validity of all * * * hearsay 'exceptions.'" But a general approach to the problem is discernible.

B

The Confrontation Clause operates in two separate ways to restrict the range of admissible hearsay. First, in conformance with the Framers' preference for face-to-face accusation, the Sixth Amendment establishes a rule of necessity.   In the usual case (including cases where prior cross-examination has occurred), the prosecution must either produce, or demonstrate the unavailability of, the declarant whose statement it wishes to use against the defendant.[i]

The second aspect operates once a witness is shown to be unavailable. Reflecting its underlying purpose to augment accuracy in the factfinding process by ensuring the defendant an effective means to test adverse evidence, the Clause countenances only hearsay marked with such trustworthiness that "there is no material departure from the reason of the general rule."

The principle recently was formulated in Mancusi v. Stubbs:

"The focus of the Court's concern has been to insure that there 'are indicia of reliability which have been widely viewed as determinative of whether a statement may be placed before the jury though there is no confrontation of the declarant,' and to 'afford the trier of fact a satisfactory basis for evaluating the truth of the prior statement.' It is clear from these statements, and from numerous prior decisions of this Court, that even though the witness be unavailable his prior testimony must bear some of these 'indicia of reliability.' "

The Court has applied this "indicia of reliability" requirement principally by concluding that certain hearsay exceptions rest upon such solid foundations that admission of virtually any evidence within them comports with the "substance of the constitutional protection."   This reflects the truism that "hearsay rules and the Confrontation Clause are generally designed to protect similar values,"   *   *   *   It also responds to the need for certainty in the workaday world of conducting criminal trials.

In sum, when a hearsay declarant is not present for cross-examination at trial, the Confrontation Clause normally requires a showing that he is unavailable.   Even then, his statement is admissible only if it bears adequate "indicia of reliability."   Reliability can be inferred without more in a case where the evidence falls within a firmly rooted hearsay exception.   In other cases, the evidence must be excluded, at least absent a showing of particularized guarantees of trustworthiness.

III

We turn first to that aspect of confrontation analysis deemed dispositive by the Supreme Court of Ohio, and answered by it in the negative—whether Anita Isaacs' prior testimony at the preliminary hearing bore sufficient "indicia of reliability."   Resolution of this issue requires a careful comparison of this case to California v. Green, supra.

A

In *Green*, at the preliminary hearing, a youth named Porter identified Green as a drug supplier.   When called to the stand at Green's trial, however, Porter professed a lapse of memory.   Frustrated in its attempt to ad-

i.   A demonstration of unavailability, however, is not always required.   In Dutton v. Evans, 400 U.S. 74 (1970), for example, the Court found the utility of trial confrontation so remote that it did not require the prosecution to produce a seemingly available witness.

duce live testimony, the prosecution offered Porter's prior statements.   The trial judge ruled the evidence admissible, and substantial portions of the preliminary hearing transcript were read to the jury.   This Court found no error.   Citing the established rule that prior trial testimony is admissible upon retrial if the declarant becomes unavailable,   *   *   *   the Court rejected Green's Confrontation Clause attack.   It reasoned:

> "Porter's statement at the preliminary hearing had already been given under circumstances closely approximating those that surround the typical trial.   Porter was under oath;   respondent was represented by counsel—the same counsel in fact who later represented him at the trial; respondent had every opportunity to cross-examine Porter as to his statement;   and the proceedings were conducted before a judicial tribunal, equipped to provide a judicial record of the hearings."

These factors, the Court concluded, provided all that the Sixth Amendment demands: "substantial compliance with the purposes behind the confrontation requirement."

*   *   *

This passage and others in the *Green* opinion suggest that the *opportunity* to cross-examine at the preliminary hearing—even absent actual cross-examination—satisfies the Confrontation Clause.   Yet the record showed, and the Court recognized, that defense counsel in fact had cross-examined Porter at the earlier proceeding.

*   *   *

We need not decide whether the Supreme Court of Ohio correctly dismissed statements in *Green* suggesting that the mere opportunity to cross-examine rendered the prior testimony admissible.   *   *   *   Nor need we decide whether *de minimis* questioning is sufficient, for defense counsel in this case tested Anita's testimony with the equivalent of significant cross-examination.

B

Counsel's questioning clearly partook of cross-examination as a matter of *form*.   His presentation was replete with leading questions, the principal tool and hallmark of cross-examination.   In addition, counsel's questioning comported with the principal *purpose* of cross-examination: to challenge "whether the declarant was sincerely telling what he believed to be the truth, whether the declarant accurately perceived and remembered the matter he related, and whether the declarant's intended meaning is adequately conveyed by the language he employed."   Anita's unwillingness to shift the blame away from respondent became discernible early in her testimony.   Yet counsel continued to explore the underlying events in detail.   He attempted, for example, to establish that Anita and the defendant were sharing an apartment, an assertion that was critical to respondent's defense at trial and that might have suggested ulterior personal reasons for unfairly casting blame on the defendant.   At another point, he directly challenged Anita's veracity by seeking to have her admit that she had given the credit cards to respondent to obtain a television. When Anita denied this, defense counsel elicited the fact that the only television she owned was a "Twenty Dollar * * * old model."

Respondent argues that, because defense counsel never asked the court to declare Anita hostile, his questioning necessarily occurred on direct examination. But however state law might formally characterize the questioning of Anita, it afforded "substantial compliance with the purposes behind the confrontation requirement," no less so than classic cross-examination. Although Ohio law may have authorized objection by the prosecutor or intervention by the court, this did not happen. As in *Green*, respondent's counsel was not "significantly limited in any way in the scope or nature of his cross-examination."

* * *

Finally, we reject respondent's attempt to fall back on general principles of confrontation, and his argument that this case falls among those in which the Court must undertake a particularized search for "indicia of reliability." Under this theory, the factors previously cited—absence of face-to-face contact at trial, presence of a new attorney, and the lack of classic cross-examination—combine with considerations uniquely tied to Anita to mandate exclusion of her statements. Anita, respondent says, had every reason to lie to avoid prosecution or parental reprobation. Her unknown whereabouts is explicable as an effort to avoid punishment, perjury, or self-incrimination. Given these facts, her prior testimony falls on the unreliable side, and should have been excluded.

In making this argument, respondent in effect asks us to disassociate preliminary hearing testimony previously subjected to cross-examination from previously cross-examined prior-trial testimony, which the Court has deemed generally immune from subsequent confrontation attack. Precedent requires us to decline this invitation. In *Green* the Court found guarantees of trustworthiness in the accouterments of the preliminary hearing itself; there was no mention of the inherent reliability or unreliability of Porter and his story.

In sum, we perceive no reason to resolve the reliability issue differently here than the Court did in *Green*. "Since there was an adequate opportunity to cross-examine [the witness], and counsel * * * availed himself of that opportunity, the transcript * * * bore sufficient 'indicia of reliability' and afforded ' "the trier of fact a satisfactory basis for evaluating the truth of the prior statement." ' "[j]

j. We need not consider whether defense counsel's questioning at the preliminary hearing surmounts some inevitably nebulous threshold of "effectiveness." In *Mancusi*, to be sure, the Court explored to some extent the adequacy of counsel's cross-examination at the earlier proceeding. That discussion, however, must be read in light of the fact that the defendant's representation at the earlier proceeding, provided by counsel who had been appointed only four days prior thereto, already had been held to be ineffective. Under those unusual circumstances, it was necessary to explore the character of the actual cross-examination to ensure that an adequate opportunity for full cross-examination had been afforded to the defendant. We hold that in all but such extraordinary cases, no inquiry into "effectiveness" is required. A holding that every case involving prior testimony requires such an inquiry would frustrate the principal objective of generally val-

IV

Our holding that the Supreme Court of Ohio erred in its "indicia of reliability" analysis does not fully dispose of the case, for respondent would defend the judgment on an alternative ground. The State, he contends, failed to lay a proper predicate for admission of the preliminary hearing transcript by its failure to demonstrate that Anita Isaacs was not available to testify in person at the trial.

* * *

A

The basic litmus of Sixth Amendment unavailability is established: "[A] witness is not 'unavailable' for purposes of * * * the exception to the confrontation requirement unless the prosecutorial authorities have made a *good-faith effort* to obtain his presence at trial."

* * *

Although it might be said that the Court's prior cases provide no further refinement of this statement of the rule, certain general propositions safely emerge. The law does not require the doing of a futile act. Thus, if no possibility of procuring the witness exists (as, for example, the witness' intervening death), "good faith" demands nothing of the prosecution. But if there is a possibility, albeit remote, that affirmative measures might produce the declarant, the obligation of good faith *may* demand their effectuation. "The lengths to which the prosecution must go to produce a witness * * * is a question of reasonableness." The ultimate question is whether the witness is unavailable despite good-faith efforts undertaken prior to trial to locate and present that witness. As with other evidentiary proponents, the prosecution bears the burden of establishing this predicate.

B

On the facts presented we hold that the trial court and the Supreme Court of Ohio correctly concluded that Anita's unavailability, in the constitutional sense, was established.

At the *voir dire* hearing, called for by the defense, it was shown that some four months prior to the trial the prosecutor was in touch with Amy Isaacs and discussed with her Anita's whereabouts. It may appropriately be inferred that Mrs. Isaacs told the prosecutor essentially the same facts to which she testified at *voir dire*: that the Isaacs had last heard from Anita during the preceding summer; that she was not then in San Francisco, but was traveling outside Ohio; and that the Isaacs and their other children knew of no way to reach Anita even in an emergency.

* * *

The evidence of record demonstrates that the prosecutor issued a subpoena to Anita at her parents' home, not only once, but on five separate occasions over a period of several months.

idating the prior testimony exception in the first place—increasing certainty and consistency in the application of the Confrontation Clause.

* * *

Given these facts, the prosecution did not breach its duty of good-faith effort. To be sure, the prosecutor might have tried to locate by telephone the San Francisco social worker with whom Mrs. Isaacs had spoken many months before and might have undertaken other steps in an effort to find Anita. One, in hindsight, may always think of other things. Nevertheless, the great improbability that such efforts would have resulted in locating the witness, and would have led to her production at trial, neutralizes any intimation that a concept of reasonableness required their execution. We accept as a general rule, of course, the proposition that "the possibility of a refusal is not the equivalent of asking and receiving a rebuff." But the service and ineffectiveness of the five subpoenas and the conversation with Anita's mother were far more than mere reluctance to face the possibility of a refusal. It was investigation at the last-known real address, and it was conversation with a parent who was concerned about her daughter's whereabouts.

* * *

We conclude that the prosecution carried its burden of demonstrating that Anita was constitutionally unavailable for purposes of respondent's trial.

The judgment of the Supreme Court of Ohio is reversed, and the case is remanded for further proceedings not inconsistent with this opinion.

It is so ordered.

Mr. Justice BRENNAN, with whom Mr. Justice MARSHALL and Mr. Justice STEVENS join, dissenting.

* * *

As the Court recognizes the Constitution imposes the threshold requirement that the prosecution must demonstrate the unavailability of the witness whose prerecorded testimony it wishes to use against the defendant. Because I cannot agree that the State has met its burden of establishing this predicate, I dissent.

* * *

From all that appears in the record—and there has been no suggestion that the record is incomplete in this respect—the State's *total* effort to secure Anita's attendance at respondent's trial consisted of the delivery of five subpoenas in her name to her parents' residence, and three of those were issued after the authorities had learned that she was no longer living there. At least four months before the trial began, the prosecution was aware that Anita had moved away; yet during that entire interval it did nothing whatsoever to try to make contact with her. It is difficult to believe that the State would have been so derelict in attempting to secure the witness' presence at trial had it not had her favorable preliminary hearing testimony upon which to rely in the event of her "unavailability." The perfunctory steps which the State took in this case can hardly qualify as a "good-faith effort." In point of fact, it was no effort at all.

The Court, however, is apparently willing to excuse the prosecution's inaction on the ground that any endeavor to locate Anita Isaacs was unlikely to bear fruit. I not only take issue with the premise underlying that reasoning—that the improbability of success can condone a refusal to conduct even a cursory investigation into the witness' whereabouts—but I also seriously question the Court's conclusion that a bona fide search in the present case would inevitably have come to naught.

Surely the prosecution's mere speculation about the difficulty of locating Anita Isaacs cannot relieve it of the obligation to attempt to find her. Although the rigor of the undertaking might serve to palliate a failure to prevail, it cannot justify a failure even to try. Just as *Barber* cautioned that "the possibility of a refusal is not the equivalent of asking and receiving a rebuff," so, too, the possibility of a defeat is not the equivalent of pursuing all obvious leads and returning emptyhanded. The duty of "good-faith effort" would be meaningless indeed "if that effort were required only in circumstances where success was guaranteed."

*   *   *

Roberts is a particularly helpful opinion because in it the Court seeks to specify the most important lessons that may be drawn from the prior case law. Nevertheless, *Roberts* leaves many questions unanswered, and the next case may lead the Justices to think further about the implications of what they have written.

Justice Blackmun, writing for the majority, tells us that the confrontation clause operates in two ways to restrict the range of admissible hearsay. First, it establishes a rule of necessity which in the usual case means that "the prosecution must either produce or demonstrate the unavailability of the declarant whose statement it wishes to use against the defendant."[44] This statement, if taken literally, would work a dramatic change in the way criminal cases are tried. It would mean that all hearsay exceptions in criminal cases require unavailability. Excited utterances, present sense impressions, statements to physicians and the rest of the FRE 803 exceptions would not be admissible unless one of the conditions listed in FRE 804(a) was

met. It is hard to believe that the Court meant to go this far.

While the Court leaves itself an "out" in the footnote we have renumbered as "i", the "out" applies only where the utility of trial confrontation seems remote. As an empirical matter, the fact that hearsay is admissible under an exception that applies regardless of availability does not necessarily mean that the utility of trial confrontation is remote. As we have seen in Chapter Six, the hearsay exceptions offer protection against some *but not all* the dangers that might be inquired into on cross-examination. Moreover, even where an exception carries with it guarantees of trustworthiness, those guarantees might be enhanced by the ability to cross-examine the declarant. Thus, a statement admitted as an excited utterance is likely to be sincere. However, cross-examining the declarant about his perceptions would be clearly useful, and there might even be value in exploring the declarant's possible motives to deceive.

---

44. 448 U.S. 56, 65 (1980).

The second way in which the confrontation clause, as explicated in *Roberts*, restricts the range of admissible hearsay is that it "countenances only hearsay marked with such trustworthiness that 'there is no material departure from the reason of the general rule.'"[45]   This has led the courts to search for indicia of reliability before admitting the hearsay of unavailable declarants against defendants in criminal cases. Justice Blackmun reaffirms the centrality of trustworthiness to confrontation clause analysis, but tells us that "[r]eliability can be inferred without more in a case where the evidence falls within a firmly rooted hearsay exception."[46]   It is only when there is no established exception that hearsay must be excluded absent a particularized guarantee of trustworthiness.

One of the authors believes that Justice Blackmun's willingness to infer reliability from the fact that hearsay meets the conditions of a traditional exception is a serious flaw in an otherwise promising analysis.   As an empirical matter, reliability cannot be inferred without more simply because an out-of-court statement falls within a firmly rooted hearsay exception. Dying declarations are admissible because of judicial fiat and centuries of precedent, not because they are invariably reliable. Neutral statements that are tied closely to statements against interest are not necessarily reliable even though they are in some jurisdictions routinely admitted under the established exception.   Justice Blackmun's mistake is to confuse "indicia of reliability" which arguably do attach whenever a statement falls within an established hearsay exception with "reliability" or "trustworthiness" which requires an evaluation of hearsay in the context within which it is uttered.   He has told us initially that trustworthiness is a central con-

cern of the confrontation clause, but he ends up with an analysis that makes only the presence of some indicia of trustworthiness important.

Roberts illustrates how this analysis works in practice.   Justice Blackmun refuses to evaluate both Roberts' contention that Anita had every reason to lie to avoid prosecution or parental reprobation and his suggestion that Anita's continued absence might be explained by her desire to avoid punishment, perjury or self-incrimination. This may be sensible, for when hearsay takes the form of prior testimony a searching inquiry into trustworthiness may not be needed.   Because prior testimony involves cross-examination or a considered decision to waive it, the fact finder is in a good position to evaluate the possibility that the declarant's statements are untrue.   Had the declarant testified in court, the fact finder would have made similar use of the cross-examination.

To focus on this aspect suggests a way to protect the values that the Court in *Roberts* sees as a central concern of the confrontation clause while still admitting most hearsay that falls under an established exception.   The trial judge, in the opinion of one author, should engage in a two-step analysis when the state offers the hearsay of an unavailable declarant.   First, the judge should ask whether, given all the available evidence,[47] the statement may be reasonably believed.   If not, it should be excluded regardless of whether it meets the conditions for a particular hearsay exception.   This result is probably required by FRE 403 regardless of the confrontation clause.   Next, the judge should ask whether the jury, consistent with the rules of evidence, may be provided with enough evidence to reach an intelligent judgment about the reliability of the statement in

---

45. Id.

46. Id. at 66.

47. Some of this evidence might not be admissible at trial.   See FRE 104(a); but c.f., FRE 806.

question. Where there is no reason to suspect the accuracy of the statement, the fact that it meets the conditions of a particular exception is enough to justify the jury's reliance on it. Where there are reasons to question the accuracy of a statement, admissibility should turn on the jury's ability to judge the credibility of the declarant. Often this will pose no problems because those facts that make the statement suspect may be presented to the jury. However, in some cases where the suspicion of inaccuracy is strong, it may be clear that only cross-examination would allow the jury to reach a *reasoned* judgment. If the declarant is unavailable for cross-examination, the evidence should be excluded.

Suppose, for example, that the declarant whose dying declaration accuses the defendant is one of the defendant's bitter enemies. While the jury could no doubt better appreciate the depth of the declarant's bias if he were cross-examined in front of them, the impeaching evidence is of a kind that would come out at trial, and even without cross-examination the jury can evaluate the declaration in light of it. If, on the other hand, there is substantial reason to believe that the declarant was hallucinating at the time he made his statement, but the evidence is unclear, the statement should be excluded because the only way to clarify the matter is by cross-examination, which, given the declarant's unavailability, is impossible. The vice of allowing the jury to convict on the basis of such a statement is not that the jury's judgment may be wrong—this can happen with live testimony. Rather it is that the jury's resolution of the crucial credibility issue will have little basis in reason. If it is clear that the declarant was hallucinating, the evidence should also be excluded, but exclusion would be by the judge under the first prong of the suggested test. Finally, if the evidence that the declarant was hallucinating is not substantial, the statement

should be admitted because the jury could *reasonably* disregard this possibility. In the latter instance, cross-examination might have changed the jury's assessment, but, by hypothesis, it is likely that the examination would have served only to confirm the jury's decision. Exclusion of hearsay that is admissible under an established exception is a drastic step given both established practice and Supreme Court precedent. It is not appropriate unless the confrontation and cross-examination of the declarant would have been the only way to reach a reasoned decision about the reliability of his out-of-court statement.

We have been focusing on the situation where the declarant is unavailable. If the language in *Roberts* quoted in the text at note 44 *supra* is taken literally, this analysis cannot justify the admissibility under FRE 803 of the hearsay of available declarants. Regardless of the guarantees that attach to a hearsay statement, cross-examination in some cases will allow a sounder assessment of the declarant's credibility. However, the rights granted parties by FRE 806 and the compulsory process rights of a criminal defendant suggest that when declarants are available a different analysis is appropriate.

The most sensible procedure, in the eyes of the author who has written the above critique, is to defer to the practice of the past century and allow hearsay to be admitted whenever it qualifies under an exception which does not require unavailability. If, however, the defendant wishes to call the declarant and question him as if on cross-examination, this should be allowed immediately after the testimony of the witness who has reported the declarant's statements. The only change this works in current practice is one of timing. However, this change is important. Cross-examination of a declarant may be much less effective after his hearsay has been assimilated into the body of the state's case, and it might disrupt the presentation of the defendant's case-in-chief if hearsay declarants could not be called for cross-examination until that time.[48] If this suggested change were made, it might be necessary to require pre-trial notice of the state's intention to offer the hearsay of available declarants. While this would be somewhat disruptive of current practice, it would be substantially less disruptive than the standard Justice Blackmun has suggested.[49] The suggested change would, without enervating the hearsay exceptions that do not require unavailability, give prosecutors additional reasons to prefer live testimony to the hearsay of available declarants, for they could not secure the benefits of presenting testimony that was not soon challenged and by using live witnesses they could maintain greater control over the order in which they presented their evidence.

Make no mistake about it. The preceding test is not the Court's test in *Roberts*. It is one author's attempt to resolve a conflict that is implicit in that case but was not perceived by the Court, perhaps because it is unlikely to arise when hearsay is admitted under the prior testimony exception. If the next case involves the uncross-examined testimony of a witness at a preliminary hearing or hearsay admissible under some other exception, the Court might find that the facts of the case lead them to retreat from Blackmun's equation of reliability with the existing exceptions. Should they do so, the proposed test is one way of protecting the values of confrontation while holding the disruption of standard practice to a minimum.

For the other author, *Roberts* contains seeds of wisdom, but invites some modifications that would improve doctrinal clarity and provide reasonable answers to most confrontation problems. These modifications are developed below in seven steps.

First, it is necessary to explain what the word "confrontation" means in the sixth amendment context. The words "confrontation" and "cross-examination" are often used interchangeably, even though confrontation is probably a more inclusive term than cross-examination. The background of the confrontation clause, its relatively brief history in the Supreme Court, and its relationship to hearsay doctrine suggest that the right of confrontation is provided in order to protect a defendant's right to challenge the accuracy and reliability of evidence presented against him.

---

48. For one of the few articles that appreciates the way in which issues of timing bear on sixth amendment rights see, Westen, Order of Proof: An Accused's Right to Control the Timing and the Sequence of Evidence in His Defense, 66 Calif.Law Rev. 935 (1978).

49. It is possible that some defendants would wish to call available hearsay declarants to increase the costs of trial to the state or otherwise harass the prosecution and state officials. It might be appropriate to require the defendant to specify the reason why he thought it important to be able to confront the declarant. If it was quite clear that the defendant was at best engaged in a "fishing expedition"—as, for example, might often be the case where the hearsay was part of a routine business record—the court might deny the request to subpoena the witness but allow the defendant to depose the witness if he wished and thus establish some need for the witness' presence. Since depositions involve additional costs for defense counsel as well as the prosecution, it is unlikely that such requests would be lightly made. If the deposition suggested that there was possible utility to trial confrontation, the state should be required to produce the declarant. If the deposition promised to be as useful as the declarant's testimony in revealing reasons not to trust the reported hearsay, it might be sufficient to read the deposition into the record after the hearsay had been offered.

Special problems might arise where the prosecution intends to call a declarant whose hearsay is reported by some earlier prosecution witness. So long as the prosecutor acts in good faith, the better policy is probably to allow the prosecutor to present this witness at the time he chooses.

There are several different ways to challenge a witness. One way is to probe any testimony that the witness gives or any statement he has made with questions designed to point out defects in the witness' story. Another is to demonstrate to the jury that the bearing and delivery of the witness—often referred to as demeanor—suggest that the witness should be viewed with caution, or perhaps dismissed as unworthy of belief. Still another is to contradict the witness with other evidence. A final way is to impeach the witness—i.e., to show that the witness is generally unworthy of belief or that in the particular case there is some reason to question or to distrust him. These modes of challenge should be kept in mind as the analysis continues.

Second, the government should have an obligation to produce at trial persons on whose statements it intends to rely as truthful, at least where it is reasonably possible for the government to do so. The rationale for this rule, which is consistent with the Court's statement in *Roberts,* is that the sixth amendment right is afforded to the defendant. It is his right to confront witnesses, and it is his choice as to which forms of confrontation he wishes to pursue. The government may not dictate the choice by action or inaction designed to make a witness unavailable.

When the government relies on hearsay evidence, by definition it is asking the trier of fact to accept the evidence as if it were provided on the witness stand. Since the government is using out-of-court declarations for their truth, the defendant has the same interest in challenging—i.e., confronting—a hearsay declarant, who is a witness against him, as he would any witness who came to court to tell the same story the declarant tells. Obviously, however, if the declarant is not present there typically will be no demeanor evidence. (Even a videotape may not provide identical demeanor evidence to that provided at trial.) If the declarant is not present there cannot be cross-examination. And some forms of impeachment may only be possible if the declarant admits the truth of certain facts; there may be no other source of proof at trial. Thus, if the declarant is not produced, one or more modes of confrontation may be denied a defendant. Only when the hearsay declarant's presence is assured can the defendant fully exercise his right to confront the witnesses against him. The government may not deny him this right. When a declarant is unavailable, not due to any fault of the government, the defendant also is denied confrontation opportunities. But the courts have long recognized that while the sixth amendment prevents the government from denying confrontation opportunities, it does not require the government to produce unavailable witnesses. That would be to require the impossible.

Under this analysis, it is not required that the government actually call a witness on whose out-of-court statements it wishes to rely. It is sufficient that, where possible, the state assures the defendant of an opportunity to put the witness on the stand. In some instances the government may satisfy its duty to the defendant by providing notice before trial of an intention to use hearsay evidence together with the name of the declarant, but if the government has permitted the declarant to depart the jurisdiction notice may be inadequate. Thus, as *Motes* (supra note 15) requires, the government must endeavor in good faith to see that its hearsay declarants are available should the defendant wish to put them on the stand in order to exercise confrontation rights.

Third, the requirement that the declarant must be produced provides no threat to such traditional "efficiency" exceptions to the hearsay rule as the business and public records exceptions, at least not in the typical case. When a business record or a public record is utilized, the government often is relying only on the credibility of the custodian or other qualified representative of the business who lays the foundation required under typical statutes and rules such as FRE 803(6). The declarant is an entity and the key witness is the person who explains why the entity's records should be believed. Confrontation of this person satisfies the goals of the sixth amendment.

Of course, there are cases in which it is clear that one particular person has formulated a record and where the records may involve opinions and other matters observed only by that person—medical records are a good example. In such a case, the confrontation clause should require that the person who made the record be produced, where possible, so that he can be examined by the defense. One cannot assume that defendants are usually less concerned with examining those who make business records than they are with examining other hearsay declarants. Defendants have the right to examine whomever the government relies upon to argue that its hearsay should be accepted as true.

This analysis might initially appear to call into question rules like FRE 803 that are fairly inclusive and that do not require a showing of unavailability as a prerequisite to admitting hearsay. But it does not. The government can still use hearsay qualifying under an exception even if a witness is available. It simply must make an effort to assure that a defendant can examine the declarant if he chooses to do so. In many instances, even without the proposal advanced here, the government probably will choose to produce, and even to call to the stand, the declarant, since in-court testimony often is preferred over hearsay. The analysis offered here would deny, however, any opportunity to the government to offer hearsay in circumstances in which a defendant might unnecessarily be denied his choice of confrontation challenges to the hearsay declarant.

Fourth, the defendant has the right to test hearsay declarants by cross-examining them about their statements and to impeach them in the same way he could impeach other government witnesses. Thus, rules like FRE 806 have strong constitutional roots, and no common law rule barring impeachment of one's own witness could constitutionally be enforced against a defendant who called the government's hearsay declarant for cross-examination about his statement or for impeachment. The testing of hearsay declarants need not occur at the moment their statements are offered. As long as the jury understands that the witness who reports a hearsay statement cannot vouch for its truthfulness, a subsequent examination of the hearsay declarant should suffice to satisfy confrontation needs.

Fifth, whenever the state chooses to rely on hearsay as truth—and this may occur whether or not the hearsay declarant is called to testify—the government must lay a foundation from which a reasonable trier of fact could draw the inference that the out-of-court statement should be believed. The background of the confrontation clause leads to a conclusion that a jury cannot be permitted to jump from the fact that someone made a statement out of court to the conclusion that the statement is true. What is needed is some evidence—i.e., actually presented in court and itself subject to examination—that sufficiently informs the jury of the circumstances surrounding the statement to warrant the jury's believing it and to enable the jury to assess its weight.

Sixth, this surrounding circumstance evidence must itself be admissible, since the jury can only evaluate a hearsay statement in light of the other evidence that reaches it. Confrontation requires not only that the other evidence be sufficient to warrant an inference that the statement is true, but also that the defendant be given an opportunity to show the jury why it should not draw the inference or why it should give the statement little, if any, weight. Note that the government need not actually convince the judge that its hearsay is true, and it need not remove all doubts about the truth and reliability of the statement. But it must establish a sufficient foundation for the jury to believe and assess the significance of the hearsay upon which it relies. Since the traditional hearsay exceptions satisfy this requirement, they should pose no serious confrontation problems.

Seventh, the trial judge must zealously guard against any prosecutorial argument that goes beyond the foundation evidence and that assumes facts not presented to the jury. Where, for example, the prosecutor has obtained admission of evidence as an excited utterance, he cannot argue that the hearsay declarant was in a good position to observe events, unless there is some nonhearsay evidence to support this argument.

This completes this author's analysis. You can see that it attempts to impose order on the Supreme Court's cases and to meet some of the concerns raised by Justice Harlan as he shifted positions from *Green* to *Dutton*. It goes well beyond Justice Blackmun's opinion in *Roberts,* but is not necessarily inconsistent with it. It would afford a post-hoc opportunity to limit *Dutton* as a case in which the hearsay declarant was actually available to be called at trial had Evans wished to examine him. It would have afforded Raleigh a right to have Cobham produced and required rejection of the testimony of the statements Raleigh described as those of a "wild Jesuit or beggarly priest."

Returning to the *Roberts* opinion, you should note that the case is important in another respect. The Court explicitly affirms *Barber's* holding that unless the state has made a *good faith* effort to secure the appearance of absent declarants, their

hearsay will be barred by the confrontation clause. In reaffirming *Barber* the Court is implicitly retreating from *Mancusi*,[50] for in *Roberts* as in *Barber* the measure of good faith is clearly separated from the reliability of the hearsay that is sought to be admitted. Even if there is a remote possibility "that affirmative measures might produce the declarant, the obligation of good faith *may* demand their effectuation." (Emphasis in original.)[51] The question is whether the effort is reasonable, for "good faith" does not demand a futile act.

Under the Court's test, the question of whether the state made a good faith effort to produce a witness presents a factual question. In *Roberts*, the Justices split on this issue. The positions of both the majority and the dissent are reasonable. The prosecutor could have made more substantial efforts to find Anita, but given what the prosecutor knew it is likely that a rather expensive investigation would have been required to find Anita, and even an expensive investigation might not have succeeded. The problem with the good faith standard is that the words "good faith" and the admonition that the Constitution does not command a futile act are not very helpful in determining the kinds of efforts that are required when a witness is not so obviously available that a failure to call him is an act of bad faith.

We believe good faith should be interpreted as requiring a prosecutor who knows how to reach a witness to make some effort to procure the witness' attendance, even if the effort is likely to prove futile. Thus, in *Mancusi* the prosecutor should have contacted the absent witness and offered to pay the transportation expenses and witness fees that would have been tendered any other witness. The state should not have been allowed to assume that because the witness could not

---

50. To refresh your memory of Mancusi v. Stubbs see our discussion in the text of Chapter Six at the second note 59.

51. Roberts v. Ohio, supra note 44 at 74.

be subpoenaed he would not, if requested, come. Similarly, the possibility that a witness may claim a right to remain silent under the fifth amendment should not obviate the obligation to bring that witness to court. At a minimum, the good faith test should be read as requiring a recent affidavit in which the declarant asserts his intention to remain silent. Even this should not be sufficient if there is a possibility that the state has encouraged the defendant to remain silent or if there is a question about the witness' right to claim the privilege. In addition, some states have allowed prosecutors to place witnesses on the stand despite their asserted intention to "take the fifth" in situations where the witness' implied admission of criminal behavior is likely to suggest the defendant's guilt. The rationale offered is that until the witness finds himself in the solemn setting of the witness box, one cannot be sure that he will persist in his claim of privilege. In jurisdictions where this is the standard applied when the prosecution wants a witness to be present, it should be applied when the defendant makes that demand.

One of us would go further and read "good faith" to impose an additional requirement when a witness cannot be located or when a witness who can be located cannot be compelled to testify. In these circumstances the state should be required to engage in the kind of search or other effort to secure testimony that might have been expected had the hearsay not been available. In *Mancusi*, for example, the witness was the principal witness in a murder case. Had his hearsay not been available, the state, while it could not have compelled his return, surely would have made special efforts to encourage him to testify. The prosecutor might, for example, have offered him full compensation for the time he spent away from home. At a minimum, he would have attempted to secure his deposition. Stubbs should have been able to demand that similar efforts prove futile before the state was allowed to introduce hearsay. In *Roberts*, Anita's testimony was apparently not central to the state's case. She had been called by the defendant at the preliminary hearing, not by the state, and there is every reason to believe that had her hearsay not been available the state would have engaged in only a minimal search before presenting a case based entirely on her parents' testimony. In these circumstances, if the hearsay is reliable the defendant should be able to demand no more under his right to confrontation.[52] By this standard, the more crucial the hearsay, the more diligent the required search.

Although the other author would not impose this burden on prosecutors, both authors agree that from the inception of a case prosecutors must make every effort to ensure that any witness whose statements

52. Note that defendants in criminal cases also have the right under the sixth amendment to compulsory process to secure witnesses in their favor. This right may allow defendants to insist that the state make special efforts to secure witnesses whom they wish to call. Note also that under the test suggested in the text the effort the state must make to satisfy the confrontation clause is measured by the effort the state would have engaged in had they thought that a witness' testimony would have been as valuable as his unconfronted hearsay. Thus, the textual analysis of *Roberts* might, as a factual matter, be mistaken. The state's failure to call Anita at the preliminary hearing may have been because until they heard her testimony they did not believe that she had anything useful to say, or it may have been because they wanted to withhold what they perceived to be their strongest evidence until the trial. Knowing what Anita would have testified to, the state might have made substantial efforts to locate Anita for the trial had her hearsay statements been inadmissible. A trial judge can assess the importance of evidence in the context of the case. At this remove we cannot; so the textual speculation about the importance of Anita's hearsay may be flawed.

might be offered as evidence by the government is available at trial, and that the opportunity for a deposition is provided the defendant where there is any reasonable probability of nonappearance by a declarant. It should not be sufficient for prosecutors to undertake searches for missing witnesses prior to trial. They must endeavor to prevent declarants from becoming unavailable and to alert defendants to potential problems of unavailability. Lest this be unduly burdensome, prosecutors should only be required to exercise reasonable care in dealing with witnesses.

In thinking about problems of confrontation, you should keep in mind the fact that the Constitution only sets a standard beyond which a state may not go. It is not the measure of a defendant's right to exclude evidence. Typically, a state's domestic rules of evidence will give defendants the right to exclude hearsay that might be admitted consistent with the constitutional command. Domestic hearsay rules become an increasingly important guarantor of fair trials as the Supreme Court's interpretation of the confrontation clause grows increasingly relaxed. As a matter of law, a state may do whatever the Constitution allows. As a matter of policy, asserting authority to the limit of what is not constitutionally forbidden is almost always unwise.

————

Problem VII–2. Assume the same facts as in *Dutton* except (1) Truett's testimony did not mention Evans but instead implicated Williams and a friend of Williams whom he (Truett) did not know; and (2) Shaw testified that Williams had said, "Me, Truett, and Evans killed the cops. Evans was the trigger man." **Do you think the Court would have decided this case in the same way it decided** *Dutton*? Assume that this case arose today, and that you were asked to write an opinion affirming the conviction that was consistent with both *Dutton* and *Roberts*. **What would you write?**

Problem VII–3. Judi Villars and Sam Turk are jointly tried for conspiring to blow up the Washington Monument. At their joint trial, recordings of statements that Sam made to FBI undercover agents are introduced. The statements describe the scheme in detail as well as the leading roles that he and Judi are to play in it. Sam cross-examines one agent who was wired for sound. The agent admits that he knows of no steps that were made to carry out the plot, but he responds "No" when he is asked, "Isn't it true that Sam's opening remark, which is drowned out by that truck noise in the background, was, 'Last week you asked me how I would call attention to the danger of nuclear war. I wouldn't do this, but let me tell you my wildest dream about how to get the nation's attention'?" Judi's confession to the police is also introduced. The confession describes the plan in detail and inculpates Sam as well as herself. Generally it is consistent with Sam's remarks, but it differs dramatically on some important details. Neither Sam nor Judi testify on their own behalf. At the end of the trial the judge instructs the jury that Sam's remarks may only be considered against him and Judi's confession may only be considered against her. Sam and Judi both appeal their convictions, citing Bruton v. United States and arguing that their rights under the confrontation clause have been violated. **Should their convictions be reversed? Would you reach a different decision if their out-of-court statements were completely consistent? Would you reach a**

different decision if their out-of-court statements had been "redacted"; that is wherever Sam had referred to Judi by name that portion of the tape had been "bleeped" out and wherever Judi mentioned Sam the reference was reported to the jury as "Mr. X"?

Problem VII–4. Assume that in the case described in the preceding problem Judi's conviction was reversed after an appellate court found that her confession was coerced and involuntary. At her retrial Sam is called by the state. He correctly points out that he faces additional charges growing out of his alleged plans to blow up the Washington Monument, and he refuses to testify, claiming his privilege against self-incrimination. The prosecution then offers, as a statement against interest, those portions of Sam's remarks that do not inculpate Judi in order to establish that there was a scheme to blow up the landmark. Judi protests and demands that the state grant Sam use immunity rather than use his hearsay. There is a statute that provides that a court cannot grant use immunity except upon the application of the Attorney General of the United States. The prosecutor tells the judge that the Attorney General has considered the matter and has decided that it is not in the national interest to grant use immunity to Sam. Judi then insists that because Sam will not testify before the jury, his hearsay statements must be excluded. **How should the judge rule?**

Problem VII–5. On August 7, 1982 Frank Head, the district attorney of Piedmont County, was killed when dynamite wired to the ignition system of his car exploded. A lengthy investigation culminated in the arrest of four people: Black, Shay, Pine and Stark. Shay and Black pled guilty to murder while Pine was convicted after trial. At Stark's trial evidence was introduced that he, Pine and Black were involved in a conspiracy to illegally distribute liquor in Piedmont County, and that Head, at the time of his death, had been acting vigorously to break up the conspiracy. Head had seized large quantities of illegal alcohol, padlocked a building owned by Stark and filed criminal charges that had resulted in fines of more than $6,000. There is also evidence that Stark is the leader of the conspiracy and that Pine is his lieutenant and "enforcer." It appears that, on occasion, Stark was referred to by the conspirators as the "old man" and that he was known in some portions of the community by this sobriquet.

The only evidence that linked Stark to the conspiracy to murder Head, other than the evidence establishing motive, was the testimony of Shay. Shay said that he was approached by Pine and offered $5,000 if he would murder Head. He declined, saying he wanted at least $7,500. Pine responded saying he did not think "the man" would pay more than $5000 but that he would inquire. According to Shay, Pine returned an hour later, saying, "The old man won't go up anymore, but I'll add $500 to make it $5500." Shay accepted the offer. Shay also testified that at one time he thought of pulling out, but Black told him that if he backed out, the "old man" would have "something done" to him and his family. Shay admitted on cross-examination that other than what Pine told him, he knew nothing as to Stark's "having any connection" with the money given to him by Pine and that he had never had any contact with Stark regarding the killing. Shay's testimony reporting what Pine and Black had told him was admitted against Stark as a coconspirator's admission. The state never called Pine or Black. Had Stark called them, he would, by offering testimony in his defense, have forfeited his right under state law to make the final closing argument to the jury. Stark appealed his conviction for murder, claiming that his right to confrontation had been denied. **Should an appellate court reverse Stark's conviction?**

Problem VII–6. Harry Gebippe is charged with sale of cocaine to an undercover police officer posing as a law student on the afternoon of September 2. Harry denies that the sale took place, and claims he was bird watching in Yellowood State Forest at the time.

The state calls Adam Bentley. Bentley takes the stand and testifies that he and Cliff Davis were in Nick's on September 2nd in the late afternoon when six cops came running up with guns drawn, pointed at the table next to them, yelling for everyone to freeze. Bentley testifies that he and Davis were right in line with some of the guns. One cop grabbed a guy sitting at the next table, threw him against the wall, handcuffed him, and dragged him away. Davis, while they were cuffing the guy, said, "My God, they've grabbed Gebippe. He's in my evidence class."

The defense objects on confrontation clause grounds, citing Ohio v. Roberts, and says that no hearsay is admissible unless the state establishes unavailability. The state responds that excited utterances do not require unavailability, citing the same case for the preposition that established hearsay exceptions are deemed reliable enough to meet confrontation requirements. **Should the testimony be allowed?** Assume that the state has subpoenaed Davis, and announces that he is available in the witness room should the defense wish to call him. **Now should the hearsay be admitted?** Assume that the judge requires the state to call Davis. Davis testifies he remembers saying that Gebippe was being arrested, but is no longer entirely sure it really *was* Gebippe. **Now will the hearsay statement be admissible? If the testimony is admitted could Gebippe be convicted if that is the only evidence the state has? Does it matter whether Davis testifies if this is the only evidence?**

Problem VII–7. Henry Clark, desk clerk at the Sweetwater Motel, is found at 4 a. m. one morning sprawled dead behind his desk. He was shot in the course of an apparent robbery. The evidence shows that the death occurred between 2:45 and 3:15 a. m. David Dick, a former acting manager of the Sweetwater, is accused of the murder. At the trial the prosecutor wishes to introduce under FRE 803(6) an entry in the motel logbook which reads, "2:35 a. m., David, former acting manager, has been here." As a foundation for this evidence, the prosecutor offers the testimony of the hotel manager who states that desk clerks are instructed to note the presence of any suspicious individuals in the logbook and the time at which they were seen. The manager further states that to his knowledge Clark had been introduced to Dick on one occasion. The log entry is clearly in Clark's handwriting. Dick objects to the introduction of the log entry stating that its use at trial would violate his right to confrontation under the Sixth Amendment. **How should the court rule?**

Problem VII–8. Payne, who pled guilty to a conspiracy to pass counterfeit money, is called by the government as a witness in the trial of his brother for the same conspiracy. At the trial Payne claims to remember neither the event nor his guilty plea, and he states that he can neither confirm nor deny the making of a statement he is alleged to have given to a federal agent several months before the trial. Payne explains his failure of memory by saying that he has had a fall that has caused memory problems, that he has recently been a patient at a state mental hospital and that he is still on medication prescribed by psychiatrists at the hospital. The state then calls a federal agent who testifies that Payne admitted his involvement in the conspiracy in a statement given to the agent and that in that statement Payne also implicated his brother. The agent also testifies that at the time of the statement Payne seemed to be in good health and his memory seemed to be much better than it is at the trial. The statement itself is in the agent's handwriting and unsigned. The agent explains that this is because the interview with Payne had to be terminated prematurely when Payne complained of dizzy spells and lapses of memory. The prosecutor then asks the agent to read the statement to the jury. At this point, the defendant, Payne's brother, objects, claiming that the statement is inadmissible hearsay under both the Federal Rules and the common law and that if the statement were admissible under some hearsay exception, its introduction would nonetheless violate the confrontation clause. **How should a court rule on the two issues which the defendant poses?**

Problem VII–9. Kienlen is charged with bank robbery. He defends on the ground of insanity. His chief defense witness is Dr. Gonzales, the psychiatrist who had admitted Kienlen to State Mental Hospital three months before the robbery. Dr. Gonzales testifies that in his opinion Kienlen at the time of the robbery was suffering from a psychosis which left him, at best, in tenuous contact with reality. The psychiatrist also testifies that after reaching his conclusion he examined the discharge records concerning Kienlen's various stays at State Hospital. On cross-examination the prosecutor reads to Dr. Gonzales from records, including discharge records, which were made during Kienlen's previous stays in the hospital. The general import of the records is that Kienlen was never diagnosed psychotic while in the hospital, that his problem was poor social adjustment, and that he used hospitalization as a way to escape responsibility. After reading from each record, the prosecutor asks Dr. Gonzales whether the information in that record causes him to change his opinion, and the doctor responds in each instance that it does not. Counsel for the defendant objects to the reading of these letters on confrontation clause grounds. The trial judge overrules the objection stating that he will instruct the jury to use the information only for impeachment purposes. Kienlen is convicted and appeals on confrontation clause grounds. **How should an appellate court rule? Are there alternative procedures available that will permit adequate cross-examination of the witness?**

H. THE RIGHT TO CONFRONT TESTIFYING WITNESSES

The preceding cases all involve efforts by defendants in criminal cases to use the confrontation clause to prevent the admission of inculpatory evidence. The cases make it clear that there are some circumstances in which the confrontation clause will bar the admission of out-of-court statements, but it is also clear that there are many circumstances in which the clause does not bar unconfronted evidence. While *Roberts* attempts to synthesize past case law, its shortcomings are such that we can still say that the Supreme Court has yet to offer a satisfactory theory distinguishing situations in which confrontation is required as a condition for the admissibility of evidence from situations in which confrontation is excused.[53] Wigmore's treatment, denying the clause any role in determining what evidence may be admitted, is still cited, despite its inconsistency with many judicial decisions. Indeed, we saw in *Dutton* that no less a personage than Justice Harlan was converted to this view. The failure of the Court to develop a consistent theory reflects, in part, general dissatisfaction with the hearsay rule, a feeling that recent liberalization of the hearsay doctrine is wise, and a desire not to hamper future experimentation in the hearsay area with constitutional restrictions.

Whatever its role in determining the admissibility of evidence there is little doubt that the confrontation clause guarantees certain modes of trial procedure. Most would agree that Wigmore's analysis presents at least the minimum content of the clause: testimony received in court in a criminal case is received subject to the defendant's rights to be present when the testimony is taken and to test the testimony by cross-examination.[54] These rights are reflected in the general rule, applicable in both civil and criminal proceedings, that when an individual who has testified for one party refuses to answer questions on cross-examination, that individual's direct testimony shall, at the request of the other party, be stricken from the record.[55]

Like other rights, these rights may be waived. At trial, cross-examination is often foregone, and the admission of uncross-examined testimony of unavailable witnesses will not violate the confrontation clause so long as there was an opportunity for effective cross-examination at the hearing at which the testimony was given. The right to be present at one's trial is, if anything, even more fundamental than the right to cross-examination, but it may be forfeited even where it is not intentionally waived. In Illinois v. Allen[56] the Supreme Court held that an obstreperous defendant could lose his right to be present if, after being warned by the judge that he would be removed if he persisted in his

---

53. For valuable scholarly attempts at synthesis see Graham, The Right of Confrontation and the Hearsay Rule: Sir Walter Raleigh Loses Another One, 8 Crim.Law Bull. 99 (1972) and Westen, Confrontation and Compulsory Process: A Unified Theory of Evidence for Criminal Cases, 91 Harv.L.Rev. 567 (1978). For an interesting treatment of one area in which confrontation clause problems commonly arise see Davenport, The Confrontation Clause and the Co-Conspirator Exception in Criminal Cases: A Functional Analysis, 85 Harv.L.Rev. 1378 (1972).

54. The defendant's rights with respect to non-testimonial evidence are somewhat less clear. Presumably documents can only be received subject to the defendant's right to examine them and challenge their authenticity. However, in Snyder v. Commonwealth of Massachusetts, 291 U.S. 97 (1934), the Supreme Court held, by a vote of 5 to 4, that a prisoner had no right under the fourteenth amendment to be present at a jury view of the scene of his alleged crime.

55. Where the state's witnesses in a criminal case refuse to submit to cross-examination, the confrontation clause requires that the testimony be stricken from the record. In a civil case, the due process clause of the fourteenth amendment may require a similar result. Problems arise where the refusal of the witness to submit to cross-examination is not willful, as where disability or death intervenes between direct and cross-examination, or where the refusal to submit to cross-examination is only partial, as where a witness submits to detailed cross-examination on the subject matter of his direct testimony, but pleads the fifth amendment when asked about matters which might impeach his credibility. For a discussion of these issues see McCormick § 19.

56. 397 U.S. 337 (1970).

disruptive behavior, he continued to behave in such a way that an orderly trial could not be carried on in the courtroom.[57]

The right to confront opposing witnesses does not mean that defendants in criminal cases have an unlimited or uncontrolled right to engage in cross-examination. Cross-examination must pertain to relevant matters, and state rules limiting the scope of cross-examination to matters either covered in direct examination or relevant to impeachment continue to apply.[58] In addition, judges have discretion to control examinations which are unduly repetitive or argumentative or which involve the badgering or intimidation of witnesses. If, however, a judge takes a very restrictive view of what is proper on cross-examination and limits the defendant's cross-examination on any of the above grounds, confrontation clause problems may exist.[59]

The most interesting questions in this area arise when the state for policy reasons forbids an admittedly relevant line of cross-examination. The Supreme Court, to date, has been reluctant to allow such limitation. In Alford v. United States[60] a unanimous court held that it was error to bar the cross-examiner from asking a witness for the prosecution where he lived. The Court stated:

> It is the essence of a fair trial that reasonable latitude be given the cross-examiner, even though he is unable to state to the court what facts a reasonable cross-examination might develop. * * *

* * * The question "Where do you live?" was not only an appropriate preliminary to the cross-examination of the witness, but on its face, without any such declaration of purpose as was made by counsel here, was an essential step in identifying the witness with his environment, to which cross-examination may always be directed.[61]

The Court also pointed out that on the facts of Alford there was an additional reason why the question in dispute should have been allowed. The defense had reason to believe that the witness, although not convicted of a crime, was in the custody of federal authorities. The Court recognized that this fact might have suggested that the witness' testimony was "affected by fear or favor growing out of his detention,"[62] something the witness was "entitled to show by cross-examination."[63] The Court apparently decided Alford on the basis of its supervisory power over the lower federal courts, for there is no mention of the confrontation clause in the Court's opinion.

In Smith v. State of Illinois,[64] the Court overturned a conviction for the sale of narcotics because the trial judge had sustained objections to questions asking the state's principal witness what his true name was and where he lived. The witness had

---

57. Obstreperous behavior may also justify such measures as gagging or shackling a defendant. It has been suggested that the best way of dealing with such defendants might be to remove them to a room from which they could view the proceedings by closed circuit television and communicate with their attorneys by telephone.

58. However, the defendant may have a right under the compulsory process clause to call the state's witness as his own if he wishes to explore matters beyond the scope of the direct examination. And there may be the further right, an amalgam of the confrontation and compulsory process rights, to question the witness as if on cross-examination, if he is in fact hostile. See Chambers v. Mississippi, infra.

59. This does not mean that undue restriction of cross-examination will always lead to the reversal of a conviction. In the light of other evidence and the cross-examination which did take place, the error may be judged harmless beyond a reasonable doubt.

60. 282 U.S. 687 (1931).

61. Id. at 692–93.

62. Id. at 693.

63. Id.

64. 390 U.S. 129 (1968).

admitted he was testifying under an alias. The reversal rests squarely on the sixth and fourteenth amendments. *Alford* is cited as setting the standard which is appropriate when the confrontation clause is applied to such cases. Justice White, in a concurring opinion in which Justice Marshall joins, notes that the Court in *Alford* recognized that questions which tend merely to harass, annoy or humiliate a witness may go beyond the bounds of proper cross-examination. Justice White suggests that inquiries which tend to endanger the personal safety of the witness should be placed in the same category. Lower courts since *Smith* have sustained objections to questions seeking a witness' current address where there was reason to fear that the information might endanger the witness.[65]

Both *Alford* and *Smith* are cases in which the trial judge decided that there were policy reasons why a witness should not be required to answer certain questions. Davis v. Alaska presents a more interesting and difficult case. In *Davis* the policy decision is the state's, not a judge's. Furthermore, the Court does not challenge the state's assertion that it has good reasons for deciding that certain lines of inquiry should be impermissible.

DAVIS v. ALASKA

Supreme Court of the United States, 1974.
415 U.S. 308, 94 S.Ct. 1105, 39 L.Ed.2d 347.

[Davis v. Alaska is printed in Chapter Five supra, at pages 314–19. You should re-read *Davis* at this time.]

Do you think that the Court in *Davis* would have come out the same way had Green's juvenile conviction only tended to impeach by showing general bad character? What if the conviction were for fraud or perjury, thus suggesting that Green was disposed to deceit? Do you think the Court would have decided differently if Green's testimony had not been crucial and devastating? Do you think the Court would have come out the same way if the defense through its questions had sought to invade a well-established privilege? Consider the following problems which pose this last issue and others. For some of the problems, none of the preceding cases will seem directly on point. But what are their implications?

Problem VII–10. Walter Witness testifies against his alleged coconspirator, David Defendant. At the trial the defense establishes that Walter had gone to see his attorney shortly after he was arrested for the crime in question. The defense counsel says that she has good reason to believe that the story Witness told his attorney is inconsistent with the story he has just told at trial. She then asks Witness whether he had mentioned Defendant's name to his attorney when he described the machinations of the conspiracy. Witness refuses to answer on the basis of the attorney-client privilege. **May Witness be compelled to answer? If Witness persists in his refusal, does Defendant have any right to have Witness' testimony on direct examination stricken from the record? May he demand any lesser protection? Would the situation be any different if Witness were claiming the fifth amendment privilege against self-incrimination rather than the attorney-**

---

65. See, e.g., United States v. Battaglia, 432 F.2d 1115 (7th Cir. 1970), certiorari denied, 401 U.S. 924 (1971).

client privilege? Suppose Witness' attorney were willing to testify to what Witness told him. **Could Witness assert the privilege to prevent his attorney from testifying?** [Assume in dealing with this problem that Witness' conversation with his attorney qualifies for the protection of the attorney-client privilege. Thus, were it not for the confrontation clause, Witness clearly could refuse to testify to this conversation and could prevent his attorney from testifying.]

Problem VII–11. In a criminal case a witness testifies for the prosecution. After the direct examination of the witness, the judge orders a fifteen minute recess during which time the witness suffers a heart attack and dies. The defense requests that the witness' testimony on direct examination be stricken from the record because the defense had no opportunity to cross-examine the witness. **How should the court rule? Does it matter whether the testimony of the dead witness was crucial to the prosecution's case or merely dealt with a peripheral issue? How does this factor cut? Will there be situations in which the remedy of striking the testimony from the record will not be sufficient and a mistrial will have to be declared?**

Problem VII–12. Delia Dawn, accused of murder, argues that at the time of the killing she was insane within the meaning of the law. A key witness for the state is Helen Trueblood, a distinguished psychiatrist, who examined Dawn shortly after the murder and reached the opinion that Dawn was sane at the time of the killing. To accommodate Dr. Trueblood, who is extremely busy, the state records her testimony on videotape in her office the day before the trial begins. The defense counsel is present to cross-examine the doctor, and Dawn is released from jail for the event. At the trial the prosecution requests permission to play the videotape for the jury, citing a recently enacted state statute which provides, "Whenever a witness finds it difficult or impossible to attend a trial by reason of illness, disability, location or grave inconvenience, the witness' testimony may be taken by videotape and offered to the jury on the same basis as any other courtroom testimony." Provisions are also included relating to notice, the setting of a mutually convenient time and location, the apportionment of expenses ["in a criminal case if the state wishes to offer videotape evidence the state shall pay the reasonable expenses of the defense"], and procedures for judicially supervised editing to cull objectionable testimony. Dawn objects to the presentation of this tape claiming that replacing the courtroom testimony of a living witness with videotaped testimony violates her rights under the confrontation clause. **How should the court rule on Dawn's objection? Are the confrontation clause claims stronger or weaker if Dawn's defense is that she did not commit the crime in question and the doctor is testifying as an eyewitness to the murder rather than as an expert witness?**

Problem VII–13. Carrie Cody was kidnapped in Oklahoma by Hal Minnow, an escaped prisoner, and forced to drive to St. Louis. There Minnow called his old friend Louie Bonfield, and they arranged to meet at a motel. At Minnow's instruction, Bonfield rented a room in his name and Cody was taken there. During the next two days Bonfield watched over Cody while Minnow slept and during the brief intervals that Minnow left the room. He also did some grocery shopping for the three of them, rented a car at Minnow's request, and gave Minnow $500.00.   At 3:00 a. m. on the third day, both Minnow and Bonfield fell asleep at the same time and Cody escaped. Bonfield was charged as an accessory after the fact to the kidnapping.   His story is that the only reason he cooperated with Minnow was to protect Cody. He says that he had persuaded Minnow not to harm her, that he had subtly tried to reassure Cody, and that had Minnow ever been gone long enough he would have helped Cody escape.   Some three months after her traumatic experience, Cody went into a psychological decline.   She was unable to work and eventually reached the point where she could not stand being in crowds or near people whose faces she considered "hostile."   Her psychiatrist characterizes these problems as a delayed reaction to the kidnapping.   Bonfield's trial was postponed on three occasions because Cody was not in fit condition to testify.   Finally, in early May, the prosecutor arranged to take a video-taped deposition in Cody's hospital room.   Bonfield's attorney was in the room, but upon the advice of Cody's psychiatrist Bonfield was not.   Instead, unbeknownst to Cody, he watched the entire proceedings by closed circuit television from another hospital room.   He had a buzzer so that he could alert his attorney that he wished to communicate with him.   He did this several times, suggesting questions that he might ask.   At the trial, which occurs in early July, the prosecution offers Cody's videotaped deposition. When asked whether Cody is unavailable the prosecutor replies, "I told Cody's psychiatrist to call me if there were any change in her condition, and I have not heard from him."   Citing the confrontation clause, Bonfield objects to the admission of Cody's deposition.   **Should the objection be sustained? Would you as a judge rule differently if the prosecutor had said that he had called Cody's psychiatrist the morning before trial and had been told that she was still in the hospital and that her condition had deteriorated from what it was at the time of the deposition?**

SECTION III.   THE COMPULSORY PROCESS CLAUSE

The compulsory process clause of the sixth amendment provides that "[i]n all criminal prosecutions, the accused shall enjoy the right * * * to have compulsory process for obtaining witnesses in his favor." Together with the confrontation clause, which applies to witnesses against the accused, the compulsory process clause gives defendants the constitutional right to present available exculpatory evidence to the trier of fact.   The clause is the culmination of centuries of development in English criminal procedure.   From the time the jury trial first

developed until the fifteenth century, jurors were chosen because they were witnesses to the event, and neither side could call independent witnesses.   This was followed by a period extending until about 1600 when only the prosecution could call witnesses.   During the seventeenth century the accused gained the right to call witnesses, but could neither compel their attendance nor have them testify under oath.   Finally, by an act of Parliament in 1702, criminal defendants were given the right to have their witnesses sworn.[66]   Although the Parliamentary act contains no

66.   The provision that witnesses could be sworn did not, however, apply to the accused, who was not allowed to testify under

oath in his own favor.   This disability was not removed until the nineteenth century.

mention of the subpoena power, it was interpreted to give a right of compulsory process as well.

The inability to call defense witnesses, like the inability to confront the prosecution's witnesses, resulted in clear injustice in a number of celebrated trials. Indeed, William Penn, while in England, was the celebrated victim of tactics preventing the presentation of a full defense.[67] Trials like Penn's were well-known in the colonies and the procedures used were abhorred. Penn himself drafted provisions for the charters of the colonies of New Jersey and Pennsylvania designed to prevent tactics like those of which he was the victim.

Thus, by the time of the American Revolution, the right to subpoena defense witnesses was considered fundamental to the Anglo-American system of criminal justice. Nine of the newly independent colonies provided specifically in their constitutions or attached bills of rights for the defendant's right to produce witnesses in his favor. It is not surprising then that the compulsory process clause, like the confrontation clause, was included in the sixth amendment without significant commentary or debate.

However, unlike the confrontation clause, the compulsory process clause was the focus of an early case which helps clarify the framers' intent. In 1807 Chief Justice Marshall had occasion to interpret the clause while sitting as a circuit judge in the trial of Aaron Burr. The Chief Justice gave the clause a broad reading, consistent with the notion that the clause was intended to constitutionalize the accused's right to present the evidence needed for an effective defense.

Burr had attempted to subpoena a letter in the hands of President Jefferson. The government argued that this removed the case from the sixth amendment, which explicitly extends the right of process only to witnesses and not to their papers. Marshall rejected this "literal distinction" as "too much attenuated to be countenanced in the tribunals of a just and humane nation."[68] In addition, Marshall held that only a minimum showing of materiality was needed to justify production of the letter, since the accused could not be expected to know exactly what the letter contained or how the testimony to be developed at trial would make it relevant. Finally, Marshall held that when, in the ordinary course of proceeding, the indictment would be tried at the term to which the subpoena was made returnable, the subpoena would issue even though the indictment had not been handed down at the time the subpoena was sought. The Chief Justice felt that inherent in the compulsory process clause was the right of process at an early enough stage so that the accused had an effective opportunity to prepare a defense.[69]

---

67. Penn was charged with delivering a sermon on London's streets to an unlawful assembly of Quakers. His effort to defend himself without counsel was interrupted by the court and he was forcibly removed to a walled-off corner of the courtroom while the trial proceeded in his absence. Penn was acquitted when the jury ignored the judge's instructions to convict. The jury was then ordered fined and imprisoned, giving rise to the celebrated *Bushell's Case*, in which the Kings Bench determined that a jury could not be punished for reaching a verdict with which the court disagreed.

68. United States v. Burr, 25 Fed.Cas. 30, 35, No. 14,692d (C.C.D.Va. 1807).

69. Marshall also held that the President could be the object of a *subpoena duces tecum*, and that even, if the President had the right personally to decide that certain portions of the subpoenaed material were too sensitive to be revealed (which Marshall found unnecessary to decide), where the government attorney made this decision on the President's behalf, a continuance would be ordered unless the entire letter was produced. These holdings do not tell us as much about the central meaning of the compulsory process clause as the holdings mentioned in the text, but they emphasize the importance which Marshall attached to the clause and Marshall's feeling that the clause should be read broadly.

After this auspicious beginning, the jurisprudence of the compulsory process clause lapsed into a 160 year decline. From 1807 until 1967 the Supreme Court only addressed the clause five times, twice in dictum and three times while declining to construe it.[70]   Then came the case which follows.

WASHINGTON v. STATE OF TEXAS

Supreme Court of the United States, 1967.
388 U.S. 14, 87 S.Ct. 1920, 18 L.Ed.2d 1019.

Mr. Chief Justice WARREN delivered the opinion of the Court.

We granted certiorari in this case to determine whether the right of a defendant in a criminal case under the Sixth Amendment to have compulsory process for obtaining witnesses in his favor is applicable to the States through the Fourteenth Amendment, and whether that right was violated by a state procedural statute providing that persons charged as principals, accomplices, or accessories in the same crime cannot be introduced as witnesses for each other.

Petitioner, Jackie Washington, was convicted in Dallas County, Texas, of murder with malice and was sentenced by a jury to 50 years in prison. The prosecution's evidence showed that petitioner, an 18-year-old youth, had dated a girl named Jean Carter until her mother had forbidden her to see him.   The girl thereafter began dating another boy, the deceased.   Evidently motivated by jealousy, petitioner with several other boys began driving around the City of Dallas on the night of August 29, 1964, looking for a gun.   The search eventually led to one Charles Fuller, who joined the group with his shotgun.   After obtaining some shells from another source, the group of boys proceeded to Jean Carter's home, where Jean, her family and the deceased were having supper.   Some of the boys threw bricks at the house and then ran back to the car, leaving petitioner and Fuller alone in front of the house with the shotgun.   At the sound of the bricks the deceased and Jean Carter's mother rushed out on the porch to investigate.   The shotgun was fired by either petitioner or Fuller, and the deceased was fatally wounded. Shortly afterward petitioner and Fuller came running back to the car where the other boys waited, with Fuller carrying the shotgun.

Petitioner testified in his own behalf.   He claimed that Fuller, who was intoxicated, had taken the gun from him, and that he had unsuccessfully tried to persuade Fuller to leave before the shooting.   Fuller had insisted that he was going to shoot someone, and petitioner had run back to the automobile. He saw the girl's mother come out of the door as he began running, and he subsequently heard the shot.   At the time, he had thought that Fuller had shot the woman.   In support of his version of the facts, petitioner offered the testimony of Fuller.   The record indicates that Fuller would have tes-

----

70. The brief history presented above is drawn from Westen, The Compulsory Process Clause, 73 Mich.L.Rev. 71, 75–108 (1975) [hereinafter Compulsory Process I].   For a fuller history of the clause, refer to the cited portion of Westen's article and sources cited therein.   See also Westen, Compulsory Process II, 74 Mich.L.Rev. 191 (1975).

tified that petitioner pulled at him and tried to persuade him to leave, and that petitioner ran before Fuller fired the fatal shot.

It is undisputed that Fuller's testimony would have been relevant and material, and that it was vital to the defense. Fuller was the only person other than petitioner who knew exactly who had fired the shotgun and whether petitioner had at the last minute attempted to prevent the shooting. Fuller, however, had been previously convicted of the same murder and sentenced to 50 years in prison, and he was confined in the Dallas County jail. Two Texas statutes provided at the time of the trial in this case that persons charged or convicted as coparticipants in the same crime could not testify for one another, although there was no bar to their testifying for the State. On the basis of these statutes the trial judge sustained the State's objection and refused to allow Fuller to testify.

* * *

I.

We have not previously been called upon to decide whether the right of an accused to have compulsory process for obtaining witnesses in his favor, guaranteed in federal trials by the Sixth Amendment, is so fundamental and essential to a fair trial that it is incorporated in the Due Process Clause of the Fourteenth Amendment. * * *

* * * This Court had occasion in In re Oliver, 333 U.S. 257 (1948), to describe what it regarded as the most basic ingredients of due process of law. It observed that:

> "A person's right to reasonable notice of a charge against him, and an opportunity to be heard in his defense—a right to his day in court—are basic in our system of jurisprudence; and these rights include, as a minimum, a right to examine the witnesses against him, to offer testimony, and to be represented by counsel." 333 U.S., at 273 (footnote omitted).

The right to offer the testimony of witnesses, and to compel their attendance, if necessary, is in plain terms the right to present a defense, the right to present the defendant's version of the facts as well as the prosecution's to the jury so it may decide where the truth lies. Just as an accused has the right to confront the prosecution's witnesses for the purpose of challenging their testimony, he has the right to present his own witnesses to establish a defense. This right is a fundamental element of due process of law.

II.

Since the right to compulsory process is applicable in this state proceeding, the question remains whether it was violated in the circumstances of this case. The testimony of Charles Fuller was denied to the defense not because the State refused to compel his attendance, but because a state statute made his testimony inadmissible whether he was present in the courtroom or not. We are thus called upon to decide whether the Sixth Amendment guarantees a defendant the right under any circumstances to put his witnesses on the stand, as well as the right to compel their attendance in court. The resolution of this question requires some discussion of the common-law context in which the Sixth Amendment was adopted.

Joseph Story, in his famous Commentaries on the Constitution of the United States, observed that the right to compulsory process was included in the Bill of Rights in reaction to the notorious common-law rule that in cases of treason or felony the accused was not allowed to introduce witnesses in his defense at all. Although the absolute prohibition of witnesses for the defense had been abolished in England by statute before 1787, the Framers of the Constitution felt it necessary specifically to provide that defendants in criminal cases should be provided the means of obtaining witnesses so that their own evidence, as well as the prosecution's, might be evaluated by the jury.

Despite the abolition of the rule generally disqualifying defense witnesses, the common law retained a number of restrictions on witnesses who were physically and mentally capable of testifying. To the extent that they were applicable, they had the same effect of suppressing the truth that the general proscription had had. Defendants and codefendants were among the large class of witnesses disqualified from testifying on the ground of interest. A party to a civil or criminal case was not allowed to testify on his own behalf for fear that he might be tempted to lie. Although originally the disqualification of a codefendant appears to have been based only on his status as a party to the action, and in some jurisdictions co-indictees were allowed to testify for or against each other if granted separate trials, other jurisdictions came to the view that accomplices or co-indictees were incompetent to testify at least in favor of each other even at separate trials, and in spite of statutes making a defendant competent to testify in his own behalf. It was thought that if two persons charged with the same crime were allowed to testify on behalf of each other, "each would try to swear the other out of the charge." This rule, as well as the other disqualifications for interest, rested on the unstated premises that the right to present witnesses was subordinate to the court's interest in preventing perjury, and that erroneous decisions were best avoided by preventing the jury from hearing any testimony that might be perjured, even if it were the only testimony available on a crucial issue.

The federal courts followed the common-law restrictions for a time, despite the Sixth Amendment. In United States v. Reid, 12 How. 361 (1852), the question was whether one of two defendants jointly indicted for murder on the high seas could call the other as a witness. Although this Court expressly recognized that the Sixth Amendment was designed to abolish some of the harsh rules of the common law, particularly including the refusal to allow the defendant in a serious criminal case to present witnesses in his defense, it held that the rules of evidence in the federal courts were those in force in the various States at the time of the passage of the Judiciary Act of 1789, including the disqualification of defendants indicted together. The holding in United States v. Reid was not satisfactory to later generations, however, and in 1918 this Court expressly overruled it, refusing to be bound by "the dead hand of the common-law rule of 1789," and taking note of "the conviction of our time that the truth is more likely to be arrived at by hearing the testimony of all persons of competent understanding who may seem to have knowledge of the facts involved in a case, leaving the credit and weight of such testimony to be determined by the jury or by the court * * *." Rosen v. United States, 245 U.S. 467, 471.

Although *Rosen v. United States* rested on nonconstitutional grounds, we believe that its reasoning was required by the Sixth Amendment. In light of the common-law history, and in view of the recognition in the *Reid* case that the Sixth Amendment was designed in part to make the testimony of a defendant's witnesses admissible on his behalf in court, it could hardly be argued that a State would not violate the clause if it made all defense testimony inadmissible as a matter of procedural law. It is difficult to see how the Constitution is any less violated by arbitrary rules that prevent whole categories of defense witnesses from testifying on the basis of *a priori* categories that presume them unworthy of belief.

The rule disqualifying an alleged accomplice from testifying on behalf of the defendant cannot even be defended on the ground that it rationally sets apart a group of persons who are particularly likely to commit perjury. The absurdity of the rule is amply demonstrated by the exceptions that have been made to it. For example, the accused accomplice may be called by the prosecution to testify against the defendant. Common sense would suggest that he often has a greater interest in lying in favor of the prosecution rather than against it, especially if he is still awaiting his own trial or sentencing. To think that criminals will lie to save their fellows but not to obtain favors from the prosecution for themselves is indeed to clothe the criminal class with more nobility than one might expect to find in the public at large. Moreover, under the Texas statutes the accused accomplice is no longer disqualified if he is acquitted at his own trial. Presumably, he would then be free to testify on behalf of his comrade, secure in the knowledge that he could incriminate himself as freely as he liked in his testimony, since he could not again be prosecuted for the same offense. The Texas law leaves him free to testify when he has a great incentive to perjury, and bars his testimony in situations where he has a lesser motive to lie.

We hold that the petitioner in this case was denied his right to have compulsory process for obtaining witnesses in his favor because the State arbitrarily denied him the right to put on the stand a witness who was physically and mentally capable of testifying to events that he had personally observed, and whose testimony would have been relevant and material to the defense. The Framers of the Constitution did not intend to commit the futile act of giving to a defendant the right to secure the attendance of witnesses whose testimony he had no right to use. The judgment of conviction must be reversed.

It is so ordered.

The concurring opinion of Justice Harlan is omitted.

Professor Westen comments on Washington v. Texas as follows:[71]

    * * * Chief Justice Warren's opinion compares in scope with Marshall's sweeping opinions in United States v. Burr. Marshall extended compulsory process to the period before trial and made it a means for discovery; Warren read it to reach beyond the mere production of witnesses and made it a means by which to have defense witnesses heard.

                  * * *

71. Westen, Compulsory Process I, at 111–17.

* * * The Court framed the compulsory process question broadly. The defendant was denied the benefit of Fuller's exculpatory testimony not because the state refused to compel Fuller's attendance at trial, but because under the statute his testimony was inadmissible: "We are thus called upon to decide whether the Sixth Amendment guarantees a defendant the right under any circumstances to put his witnesses on the stand, as well as the right to compel their attendance in court." The Court answered the question in the defendant's favor. It declared the accomplice statute unconstitutional under the compulsory process clause because it denied the defendant "the right to put on the stand a witness who was physically and mentally capable of testifying to events that he had personally observed, and whose testimony would have been relevant and material to the defense."

* * *

Washington's importance is greater than its immediate holding. First, the Court's use of history was significant, not only in concluding that compulsory process governs the testimonial competence of defense witnesses as well as their personal attendance, but also in defining the constitutional standard for determining the validity of specific rules of competence. Justice Harlan, while agreeing that Texas denied the defendant a fair trial by rendering his accomplice incompetent to testify in his behalf, denied that the error had anything to do with "compulsory process." The Court, he said, had "to strain this constitutional provision * * *" to reach its result. As another commentator put it: "The compulsory process clause * * * cannot be construed to give the defendant a substantive right to have the testimony of his witness entered into evidence. It gives the defendant only the right to have

compulsory process to obtain witnesses in his behalf—to have subpoenas issued for their appearance in court."

The Court rejected Harlan's literal construction in favor of a historical construction. Without detailing the long history of the defendant's right to present witnesses in his favor, the Court concluded that the clause was originally intended to permit witnesses to testify for the defense: "The Framers of the Constitution did not intend to commit the futile act of giving to a defendant the right to secure the attendance of witnesses whose testimony he had no right to use." * * * Rather, the explicit right to subpoena witnesses carries with it an implicit right to put them on the stand to be heard.

* * *

Second, * * * *Washington* is important for the standard of analysis it ultimately adopted. The Court construed the compulsory process clause to embody the principle that the government cannot "arbitrarily" disqualify witnesses from testifying for the defense. The controlling factor is the standard it used in deciding whether the accomplice rule was "arbitrary." The Texas rule—formerly well-accepted at common law and routinely applied in the federal courts—was not irrational. It assumed that accomplices were unreliable witnesses because "each would try to swear the other out of the charge."

The Court nevertheless found the rule "arbitrary," not because it failed to prevent perjury, but because it employed means that were too drastic under the circumstances. Without so stating, the Court implied that the state had no "compelling interest" in using disqualification as a means for avoiding perjury. The Court concluded that Texas could adequately satisfy its interest in avoiding perjury without excluding the accomplice's testimony, by leaving its weight and credibility to the jury. It implied, in other words, that, given the

benefits of cross-examination and cautionary instructions, a jury determination of
credibility constituted an adequate and
constitutionally permissible alternative for
minimizing the dangers of perjury; therefore, despite its legitimate interest in
avoiding perjured testimony, the state was
not justified in imposing the onerous and
unnecessary burden of disqualification on
the defendant's constitutional right to
present witnesses.

* * *

Finally, the case is important because it
was decided on the specific words of the
compulsory process clause, rather than on
the general notions of "fairness" underlying the due process clause. Justice Harlan, who concurred in the result, argued
that the conviction should be reversed on
its "peculiar" facts because it denied the
defendant a fair trial. Rejecting the ad hoc
approach of due process adjudication, the
Court provided guidance for future cases
by giving definite meaning to the more
specific terms of the sixth amendment.

———

Since *Washington* the Court has concerned itself with compulsory process on
several occasions. In United States v. Augenblick[72] the Court held that the failure
at a court-martial to produce lost Jencks Act
material was not a violation of constitutional dimensions, nor was the failure to
call a witness who might have known where
the material could be found but whose

preliminary hearing testimony apparently
suggested that he did not. In dictum the
Court acknowledges the possibility that in
some situations the failure to produce a
Jencks Act type statement might be a denial of compulsory process. In Webb v.
Texas[73] the Court found the compulsory
process clause violated when a trial judge
so harshly admonished a defense witness
about the penalties for false testimony as
to suggest a judicial expectation of perjury
and, in effect, drove the witness from the
stand. In Cool v. United States,[74] a judicial instruction that the jury should disregard testimony by the defendant's alleged
accomplice unless "convinced it is true
beyond a reasonable doubt" was found to
obstruct impermissibly the defendant's
right, guaranteed in *Washington*, to present an accomplice's testimony. Finally
dictum in United States v. Nixon[75] treated
the compulsory process clause as a constitutional indication that the nature of the
presidency does not imply an absolute
privilege to withhold evidence on the
grounds of the general presidential interest in confidentiality. Chief Justice Marshall's earlier opinion on this point is
mentioned with approval.

For our purposes, however, by far the
most interesting post *Washington* case on
compulsory process is one in which the
Supreme Court tries to avoid making constitutional law and in which the compulsory process clause is nowhere specifically
mentioned.

———

CHAMBERS v. MISSISSIPPI

Supreme Court of the United States, 1973.
410 U.S. 284, 93 S.Ct. 1038, 35 L.Ed.2d 297.

Mr. Justice POWELL delivered the opinion of the Court.

Petitioner, Leon Chambers, was tried by a jury in a Mississippi trial
court and convicted of murdering a policeman. * * * [T]he petition for

72. 393 U.S. 348 (1969).
73. 409 U.S. 95 (1972).
74. 409 U.S. 100 (1972).
75. 418 U.S. 683 (1974).

certiorari was granted, 405 U.S. 987 (1972), to consider whether petitioner's trial was conducted in accord with principles of due process under the Fourteenth Amendment.   We conclude that it was not.

I

The events that led to petitioner's prosecution for murder occurred in the small town of Woodville in southern Mississippi.   On Saturday evening, June 14, 1969, two Woodville policemen, James Forman and Aaron "Sonny" Liberty, entered a local bar and pool hall to execute a warrant for the arrest of a youth named C. C. Jackson.   Jackson resisted and a hostile crowd of some 50 or 60 persons gathered.   The officers' first attempt to handcuff Jackson was frustrated when 20 or 25 men in the crowd intervened and wrestled him free.   Forman then radioed for assistance and Liberty removed his riot gun, a 12-gauge sawed-off shotgun, from the car.   Three deputy sheriffs arrived shortly thereafter and the officers again attempted to make their arrest.   Once more, the officers were attacked by the onlookers and during the commotion five or six pistol shots were fired.   Forman was looking in a different direction when the shooting began, but immediately saw that Liberty had been shot several times in the back.   Before Liberty died, he turned around and fired both barrels of his riot gun into an alley in the area from which the shots appeared to have come.   The first shot was wild and high and scattered the crowd standing at the face of the alley.   Liberty appeared, however, to take more deliberate aim before the second shot and hit one of the men in the crowd in the back of the head and neck as he ran down the alley.   That man was Leon Chambers.

Officer Forman could not see from his vantage point who shot Liberty or whether Liberty's shots hit anyone.   One of the deputy sheriffs testified at trial that he was standing several feet from Liberty and that he saw Chambers shoot him.   Another deputy sheriff stated that, although he could not see whether Chambers had a gun in his hand, he did see Chambers "break his arm down" shortly before the shots were fired.   The officers who saw Chambers fall testified that they thought he was dead but they made no effort at that time either to examine him or to search for the murder weapon.   Instead, they attended to Liberty, who was placed in the police car and taken to a hospital where he was declared dead on arrival.   A subsequent autopsy showed that he had been hit with four bullets from a .22-caliber revolver.

Shortly after the shooting, three of Chambers' friends discovered that he was not yet dead.   James Williams, Berkley Turner, and Gable McDonald loaded him into a car and transported him to the same hospital.   Later that night, when the county sheriff discovered that Chambers was still alive, a guard was placed outside his room.   Chambers was subsequently charged with Liberty's murder.   He pleaded not guilty and has asserted his innocence throughout.

The story of Leon Chambers is intertwined with the story of another man, Gable McDonald.   McDonald, a lifelong resident of Woodville, was in the crowd on the evening of Liberty's death.   Sometime shortly after that day, he left his wife in Woodville and moved to Louisiana and found a job at a sugar mill.   In November of that same year, he returned to Woodville when his wife informed him that an acquaintance of his, known as Reverend Stokes, wanted to see him.   Stokes owned a gas station in Natchez, Mississippi, several miles north of Woodville, and upon his return McDonald went to see him.   After talking to Stokes, McDonald agreed to make a statement to Chambers' attorneys, who maintained offices in Natchez.   Two days later, he appeared at the attorneys' offices and gave a sworn confession that he shot Officer Liberty.   He also stated that he had already told a friend of his, James Williams, that he shot Liberty.   He said that he used his own pistol, a nine-shot .22-caliber revolver, which he had discarded shortly after the shooting.   In response to questions from Chambers' attorneys, McDonald affirmed that his confession was voluntary and that no one had compelled him to come to them.   Once the confession had been transcribed, signed, and witnessed, McDonald was turned over to the local police authorities and was placed in jail.

One month later, at a preliminary hearing, McDonald repudiated his prior sworn confession.   He testified that Stokes had persuaded him to confess that he shot Liberty.   He claimed that Stokes had promised that he would not go to jail and that he would share in the proceeds of a lawsuit that Chambers would bring against the town of Woodville.   On examination by his own attorney and on cross-examination by the State, McDonald swore that he had not been at the scene when Liberty was shot but had been down the street drinking beer in a cafe with a friend, Berkley Turner.   When he and Turner heard the shooting, he testified, they walked up the street and found Chambers lying in the alley.   He, Turner, and Williams took Chambers to the hospital.   McDonald further testified at the preliminary hearing that he did not know what had happened, that there was no discussion about the shooting either going to or coming back from the hospital, and that it was not until the next day that he learned that Chambers had been felled by a blast from Liberty's riot gun.   In addition, McDonald stated that while he once owned a .22-caliber pistol he had lost it many months before the shooting and did not own or possess a weapon at that time.   The local justice of the peace accepted McDonald's repudiation and released him from custody. The local authorities undertook no further investigation of his possible involvement.

Chambers' case came on for trial in October of the next year.   At trial, he endeavored to develop two grounds of defense.   He first attempted to show that he did not shoot Liberty.   * * *

Petitioner's second defense was that Gable McDonald had shot Officer Liberty.   He was only partially successful, however, in his efforts to bring before the jury the testimony supporting this defense.   Sam Hardin, a lifelong friend of McDonald's, testified that he saw McDonald shoot Liberty.   A second witness, one of Liberty's cousins, testified that he saw McDonald immediately after the shooting with a pistol in his hand.   In addition to the testimony of these two witnesses, Chambers endeavored to show the jury that McDonald had repeatedly confessed to the crime.   Chambers attempted to prove that McDonald had admitted responsibility for the murder on four separate occasions, once when he gave the sworn statement to Chambers' counsel and three other times prior to that occasion in private conversations with friends.

In large measure, he was thwarted in his attempt to present this portion of his defense by the strict application of certain Mississippi rules of evidence. Chambers asserts in this Court, * * * that the application of these evidentiary rules rendered his trial fundamentally unfair and deprived him of due process of law. It is necessary, therefore, to examine carefully the rulings made during the trial.

II

Chambers filed a pretrial motion requesting the court to order McDonald to appear. Chambers also sought a ruling at that time that, if the State itself chose not to call McDonald, he be allowed to call him as an adverse witness. Attached to the motion were copies of McDonald's sworn confession and of the transcript of his preliminary hearing at which he repudiated that confession. The trial court granted the motion requiring McDonald to appear but reserved ruling on the adverse-witness motion. At trial, after the State failed to put McDonald on the stand, Chambers called McDonald, laid a predicate for the introduction of his sworn out-of-court confession, had it admitted into evidence, and read it to the jury. The State, upon cross-examination, elicited from McDonald the fact that he had repudiated his prior confession. McDonald further testified, as he had at the preliminary hearing, that he did not shoot Liberty, and that he confessed to the crime only on the promise of Reverend Stokes that he would not go to jail and would share in a sizeable tort recovery from the town. He also retold his own story of his actions on the evening of the shooting, including his visit to the cafe down the street, his absence from the scene during the critical period, and his subsequent trip to the hospital with Chambers.

At the conclusion of the State's cross-examination, Chambers renewed his motion to examine McDonald as an adverse witness. The trial court denied the motion, stating: "He may be hostile, but he is not adverse in the sense of the word, so your request will be overruled." On appeal, the State Supreme Court upheld the trial court's ruling, finding that "McDonald's testimony was not adverse to appellant" because "[n]owhere did he point the finger at Chambers."

Defeated in his attempt to challenge directly McDonald's renunciation of his prior confession, Chambers sought to introduce the testimony of the three witnesses to whom McDonald had admitted that he shot the officer. The first of these, Sam Hardin, would have testified that, on the night of the shooting, he spent the late evening hours with McDonald at a friend's house after their return from the hospital and that, while driving McDonald home later that night, McDonald stated that he shot Liberty. The State objected to the admission of this testimony on the ground that it was hearsay. The trial court sustained the objection.

Berkley Turner, the friend with whom McDonald said he was drinking beer when the shooting occurred, was then called to testify. In the jury's presence, and without objection, he testified that he had not been in the cafe that Saturday and had not had any beers with McDonald. The jury was then excused. In the absence of the jury, Turner recounted his conversations with McDonald while they were riding with James Williams to take Chambers to the hospital. When asked whether McDonald said anything regarding the shooting of Liberty, Turner testified that McDonald told him that he "shot him." Turner further stated that one week later, when he met McDonald at a friend's house, McDonald reminded him of their prior conversation and urged Turner not to "mess him up." Petitioner argued to the court that, especially where there was other proof in the case that was corroborative of these out-of-court statements, Turner's testimony as to McDonald's self-incriminating remarks should have been admitted as an exception to the hearsay rule. Again, the trial court sustained the State's objection.

The third witness, Albert Carter, was McDonald's neighbor. They had been friends for about 25 years. Although Carter had not been in Woodville on the evening of the shooting, he stated that he learned about it the next morning from McDonald. That same day, he and McDonald walked out to a well near McDonald's house and there McDonald told him that he was the one who shot Officer Liberty. Carter testified that McDonald also told him that he had disposed of the .22-caliber revolver later that night. He further testified that several weeks after the shooting, he accompanied McDonald to Natchez where McDonald purchased another .22 pistol to replace the one he had discarded. The jury was not allowed to hear Carter's testimony.   *   *   *

In sum, then, this was Chambers' predicament. As a consequence of the combination of Mississippi's "party witness" or "voucher" rule and its hearsay rule, he was unable either to cross-examine McDonald or to present witnesses in his own behalf who would have discredited McDonald's repudiation and demonstrated his complicity.   *   *   *   Chambers' defense was far less persuasive than it might have been had he been given an opportunity to subject McDonald's statements to cross-examination or had the other confessions been admitted.

III

The right of an accused in a criminal trial to due process is, in essence, the right to a fair opportunity to defend against the State's accusations. The rights to confront and cross-examine witnesses and to call witnesses in one's own behalf have long been recognized as essential to due process.   *   *   * Both of these elements of a fair trial are implicated in the present case.

A

Chambers was denied an opportunity to subject McDonald's damning repudiation and alibi to cross-examination. He was not allowed to test the witness' recollection, to probe into the details of his alibi, or to "sift" his conscience so that the jury might judge for itself whether McDonald's testimony was worthy of belief. The right of cross-examination is more than a desirable rule of trial procedure. It is implicit in the constitutional right of confrontation, and helps assure the "accuracy of the truth-determining process."   *   *   * Of course, the right to confront and to cross-examine is not absolute and may, in appropriate cases, bow to accommodate other legitimate interests in the criminal trial process. But its denial or significant diminution calls into question the ultimate " 'integrity of the fact-finding process' " and requires that the competing interest be closely examined.

In this case, petitioner's request to cross-examine McDonald was denied on the basis of a Mississippi common-law rule that a party may not impeach his own witness. The rule rests on the presumption—without regard to the circumstances of the particular case—that a party who calls a witness "vouches for his credibility."

*   *   *

Whatever validity the "voucher" rule may have once enjoyed, and apart from whatever usefulness it retains today in the civil trial process, it bears little present relationship to the realities of the criminal process. It might have been logical for the early common law to require a party to vouch for the credibility of witnesses he brought before the jury to affirm his veracity. Having selected them especially for that purpose, the party might reasonably be expected to stand firmly behind their testimony. But in modern criminal trials, defendants are rarely able to select their witnesses: they must take them where they find them. Moreover, as applied in this case, the "voucher" rule's impact was doubly harmful to Chambers' efforts to develop his defense. Not only was he precluded from cross-examining McDonald, but, as the State conceded at oral argument, he was also restricted in the scope of his direct examination by the rule's corollary requirement that the party calling the witness is bound by anything he might say. He was, therefore, effectively prevented from exploring the circumstances of McDonald's three prior oral confessions and from challenging the renunciation of the written confession.

In this Court, Mississippi has not sought to defend the rule or explain its underlying rationale. Nor has it contended that its rule should override the accused's right of confrontation. Instead, it argues that there is no incompatibility between the rule and Chambers' rights because no right of confrontation exists unless the testifying witness is "adverse" to the accused. The State's brief asserts that the "right of confrontation applies to witnesses 'against' an accused." Relying on the trial court's determination that McDonald was not "adverse," and on the State Supreme Court's holding that McDonald did not "point the finger at Chambers," the State contends that Chambers' constitutional right was not involved.

The argument that McDonald's testimony was not "adverse" to, or "against," Chambers is not convincing. The State's proof at trial excluded the theory that more than one person participated in the shooting of Liberty. To the extent that McDonald's sworn confession tended to incriminate him, it tended also to exculpate Chambers. And, in the circumstances of this case, McDonald's retraction inculpated Chambers to the same extent that it exculpated McDonald. It can hardly be disputed that McDonald's testimony was in fact seriously adverse to Chambers. The availability of the right to confront and cross-examine those who give damaging testimony against the accused has never been held to depend on whether the witness was initially put on the stand by the accused or by the State. We reject the notion that a right of such substance in the criminal process may be governed by that technicality or by any narrow and unrealistic definition of the word "against." The "voucher" rule, as applied in this case, plainly interfered with Chambers' right to defend against the State's charges.

B

We need not decide, however, whether this error alone would occasion reversal since Chambers' claimed denial of due process rests on the ultimate impact of that error when viewed in conjunction with the trial court's refusal to permit him to call other witnesses. The trial court refused to allow him to introduce the testimony of Hardin, Turner, and Carter. Each would have testified to the statements purportedly made by McDonald, on three separate occasions shortly after the crime, naming himself as the murderer. The State Supreme Court approved the exclusion of this evidence on the ground that it was hearsay.

The hearsay rule, which has long been recognized and respected by virtually every State, is based on experience and grounded in the notion that untrustworthy evidence should not be presented to the triers of fact. Out-of-court statements are traditionally excluded because they lack the conventional indicia of reliability: they are usually not made under oath or other circumstances that impress the speaker with the solemnity of his statements; the declarant's word is not subject to cross-examination; and he is not available in order that his demeanor and credibility may be assessed by the jury. A number of exceptions have developed over the years to allow admission of hearsay statements made under circumstances that tend to assure reliability and thereby compensate for the absence of the oath and opportunity for cross-examination. Among the most prevalent of these exceptions is the one applicable to declarations against interest—an exception founded on the assumption that a person is unlikely to fabricate a statement against his own interest at the time it is made. Mississippi recognizes this exception but applies it only to declarations against pecuniary interest. It recognizes no such exception for declarations, like McDonald's in this case, that are against the penal interest of the declarant.

This materialistic limitation on the declaration-against-interest hearsay exception appears to be accepted by most States in their criminal trial processes, although a number of States have discarded it. Declarations against penal interest have also been excluded in federal courts under the authority of Donnelly v. United States, although exclusion would not be required under the newly proposed Federal Rules of Evidence. Exclusion, where the limitation prevails, is usually premised on the view that admission would lead to the frequent presentation of perjured testimony to the jury. It is believed that confessions of criminal activity are often motivated by extraneous considerations and, therefore, are not as inherently reliable as statements against pecuniary or proprietary interest. While that rationale has been the subject of considerable scholarly criticism, we need not decide in this case whether, under other circumstances, it might serve some valid state purpose by excluding untrustworthy testimony.

The hearsay statements involved in this case were orginally made and subsequently offered at trial under circumstances that provided considerable assurance of their reliability. First, each of McDonald's confessions was made spontaneously to a close acquaintance shortly after the murder had occurred. Second, each one was corroborated by some other evidence in the case— McDonald's sworn confession, the testimony of an eye witness to the shooting, the testimony that McDonald was seen with a gun immediately after the shooting, and proof of his prior ownership of a .22-caliber revolver and subsequent purchase of a new weapon. The sheer number of independent confessions provided additional corroboration for each. Third, whatever may be the parameters of the penal-interest rationale, each confession here was in a very real sense self-incriminatory and unquestionably against interest. McDonald stood to benefit nothing by disclosing his role in the shooting to any of his three friends and he must have been aware of the possibility that disclosure would lead to criminal prosecution. Indeed, after telling Turner of his involvement, he subsequently urged Turner not to "mess him up." Finally, if there was any question about the truthfulness of the extrajudicial statements, McDonald was present in the courtroom and was under oath. He could have been cross-examined by the State, and his demeanor and responses weighed by the jury. The availability of McDonald significantly distinguishes this case from the prior Mississippi precedent, Brown v. State, supra, and from the *Donnelly*-type situation, since in both cases the declarant was unavailable at the time of trial.

Few rights are more fundamental than that of an accused to present witnesses in his own defense. E.g., Webb v. Texas, 409 U.S. 95 (1972); Washington v. Texas, 388 U.S. 14, 19 (1967); In re Oliver, 333 U.S. 257 (1948). In the exercise of this right, the accused, as is required of the State, must comply with established rules of procedure and evidence designed to assure both fairness and reliability in the ascertainment of guilt and innocence. Although perhaps no rule of evidence has been more respected or more frequently applied in jury trials than that applicable to the exclusion of hearsay, exceptions tailored to allow the introduction of evidence which in fact is likely to be trustworthy have long existed. The testimony rejected by the trial court here bore persuasive assurances of trustworthiness and thus was well within the basic rationale of the exception for declarations against interest. That testimony also was critical to Chambers' defense. In these circumstances, where constitutional rights directly affecting the ascertainment of guilt are implicated, the hearsay rule may not be applied mechanistically to defeat the ends of justice.

We conclude that the exclusion of this critical evidence, coupled with the State's refusal to permit Chambers to cross-examine McDonald, denied him a trial in accord with traditional and fundamental standards of due process. In reaching this judgment, we establish no new principles of constitutional law. Nor does our holding signal any diminution in the respect traditionally accorded to the States in the establishment and implementation of their own criminal trial rules and procedures. Rather, we hold quite simply that under the facts and circumstances of this case the rulings of the trial court deprived Chambers of a fair trial.

The judgment is reversed and the case is remanded to the Supreme Court of Mississippi for further proceedings not inconsistent with this opinion.

It is so ordered.

[The concurring opinion of Justice White, and the dissenting opinion of Justice Rehnquist are omitted.]

The cases decided before *Chambers* in which the Court overturned criminal convictions on compulsory process grounds all involved evidentiary rules or judicial actions that were both somewhat aberrant and biased against the interest of defendants.[76] *Chambers* is significant because it found constitutional infirmities in trial court rulings which were consistent with well-established principles of evidence law. While one might argue that the voucher rule is a discredited anachronism,[77] there was nothing idiosyncratic about the trial court's refusal to declare McDonald a hostile witness. More importantly, the application of the Mississippi hearsay rule was entirely orthodox and on its face favored neither the defense nor the prosecution in the long run.[78] The Court notes the modern trend expanding the declaration against interest exception to include statements against penal interest and suggests that such statements are particularly reliable if corroborated, but the Court makes no mention of the fact that even under a modern code, such as the Federal Rules of Evidence, these statements would not have been admissible as statements against interest. Do you see why? It is because in the federal rules and in most states this exception is conditioned upon the declarant's unavailability. When the declarant is available, live testimony is preferred and statements against interest are excluded. Apparently the Court is willing to find that a traditional application of a traditional hearsay exception violates a defendant's rights under the due process clause. It is true that the Court ultimately rests its determination that Chambers was denied a fair trial on the conjunction of two different rulings below. Nevertheless the opinion reads as if the hearsay ruling alone would have been sufficient to justify reversal. It was the exclusion of the apparently reliable confessions that made the trial most unfair.

Although the Court purports to reverse Chambers' conviction in the name of due process, the values protected by the compulsory process clause are clearly implicated. Justice Powell cites *Webb* and *Washington* as illustrating the proposition that "[f]ew rights are more fundamental than that of an accused to present witnesses in his own defense."[79] It is this element of due process that is violated by

---

76. Cf. Wardius v. Oregon, 412 U.S. 470 (1973). This case overturned Oregon's "notice of alibi" statute. In *Wardius* the petitioner, who had not given the required notice of alibi, was prevented from putting an alibi witness on the stand and from giving alibi testimony himself. The petitioner cited the compulsory process clause as grounds for reversal, but the Court chose not to explore that issue. Instead the conviction was reversed with a finding that the Oregon procedure violated due process because it forced the defendant to give notice of alibi witnesses without imposing any reciprocal discovery obligation on the state.

77. If the second aspect of the voucher rule—that a party calling a witness is bound

by what the witness says—means, as the Court seems to imply, that Chambers could not have disputed McDonald's testimony in his argument to the jury or through other witnesses, the Mississippi rule differs in this respect from prevailing evidence law.

78. Indeed, one wonders why the prosecution didn't object on hearsay grounds to the introduction of McDonald's sworn statement. Had McDonald been declared hostile, might not the introduction of the sworn confession and the renunciation it elicited have opened the way to the admission of the other confessions, not for hearsay purposes but as prior inconsistent statements?

79. 410 U.S. at 302.

the Mississippi court's application of its hearsay rule.

Indeed, one may argue that the Court's rejection of the Mississippi voucher rule in Part II-A of this case, although couched in terms of the value of confrontation, is better analyzed in terms of compulsory process. McDonald was not called by the state as a witness against Chambers. He was present because Chambers had subpoenaed him, exercising a right guaranteed under the compulsory process clause. Once it became clear from the stand that McDonald would not testify voluntarily in Chambers' favor, the only way in which Chambers could extract favorable evidence from McDonald was by examining him as a hostile witness and, if necessary, impeaching his testimony. So long as the techniques of confrontation are used by defendants attempting to gain favorable evidence from witnesses not offered by the prosecution, the compulsory process clause and not the confrontation clause seems the appropriate basis for any constitutional right to proceed as if on cross-examination.[80] Chief Justice Marshall made it clear in the trial of Aaron Burr that the compulsory process clause was not intended to be a "dead letter;" it was intended to guarantee to the accused an *effective* opportunity to present a defense. At times, the right to present testimony in one's favor may be ineffective without the opportunity to treat one's "own witnesses" as hostile. In these circumstances the compulsory process clause may require that this opportunity be given.

One may ask why this case was decided on generalized due process grounds rather than on the more specific grounds of the confrontation and/or compulsory process clauses. Professor Westen suggests two reasons: First, Justice Powell, the author of the *Chambers* opinion, opposes incorporating the specifics of the Bill of Rights into the due process clause of the fourteenth amendment. Second, the defendant had not mentioned the compulsory process clause as the basis of his rights in the court below.[81] To these reasons we would add two others. The only compulsory process clause precedent for holding invalid the Mississippi law was *Washington*, but that case struck down a restriction on witnesses without regard to the facts of the particular case. Certainly it would have been difficult for the Court to say that the Mississippi rule regarding out-of-court statements was arbitrary in the way the Texas law was. Thus, the Court may not have cited the compulsory process clause because it did not believe the clause was applicable. It is possible to read *Chambers* not as an extension of *Washington*, but as a considered refusal to give *Washington* a broad reading. Finally, the Court was aware that in this case it was invalidating the application of well-established state rules of evidence. It felt the facts of *Chambers* made its decision appropriate,[82] but it did not want to suggest the creation of a rule which would generalize the results of this case. The due process approach allows the Court to tailor its decision rather strictly to the facts presented.

The Court's concern with restricting the implications of *Chambers* is evident in the rather peculiar lines which close Justice Powell's opinion:

80. So long as the Court is willing to read the meaning of the phrase "Witnesses against him" in the confrontation clause as broadly as it did in *Chambers*, the issue of whether a confrontation or compulsory process right is involved may have no practical importance. Close analysis will be similarly unimportant if the Court persists in taking a generalized due process approach to questions of the kind posed in *Chambers*.

81. Westen, Compulsory Process I, supra note 70, at 151, n. 384.

82. *Chambers* is rare among cases to reach the Supreme Court in that it appears likely that the defendant was innocent. Thus the majority may have been motivated in this case more by a desire to do substantive justice than by a notion of procedural justice. The case was posed, however, in procedural justice

In reaching this judgment we establish no new principles of constitutional law. Nor does our holding signal any diminution in the respect traditionally accorded to the States in the establishment and implementation of their own criminal trial rules and procedures. Rather, we hold quite simply that under the facts and circumstances of this case the rulings of the trial court deprived Chambers of a fair trial.[83]

But, when the Court decides a case on constitutional grounds, it is difficult for it to avoid making constitutional law, however hard it tries. Justice Kaus of California found in *Chambers* "the potential of becoming the most important constitutional law case in the field of criminal evidence that has come down in the last few years." But he also cautioned, "It depends, of course, on how it will be interpreted."[84] To date, interpretations have varied.

Looking only at the numbers, one finds that the courts have usually declined the invitation to declare established exclusionary rules unconstitutional, either generally or in the context of a particular case. However, in cases where the possibility of injustice is patent, courts have been willing to overturn traditional evidentiary limitations. Most often this is done in the name of "due process" rather than "compulsory process." Thus, *Chambers* has been cited in a case that says the state of Wisconsin cannot, in a first degree murder trial, preclude psychiatric testimony on the issue of intent;[85] in a case holding that a state cannot bar evidence that one of its undercover drug agents was involved in a "frame-up" in another state;[86] in a case which suggests that the statement against penal interest exception should be read broadly when the corroborated statements of an unavailable witness are offered to exonerate the accused;[87] in a case holding that so long as a third party's confession bears "a semblance of reliability," a criminal defendant has a constitutional right to call that person as a witness and, if he denies responsibility for the crime of which the defendant is accused, to introduce that person's confession;[88] and in a case which holds that in certain circumstances where credibility is crucial a defendant has a due process right to introduce exonerative polygraph evidence.[89]

The Supreme Court has also had occasion to follow *Chambers*. Green v. Georgia[90] involved two men, Moore and Green, who had been convicted of the rape and murder of a woman. At Moore's trial Thomas Pasby, one of the state's witnesses, testified that Moore had told him that he had killed the woman, shooting her twice after ordering Green to run an errand. At the death penalty phase of Green's trial, Pasby's testimony, which would have duplicated the testimony he had given in Moore's trial on behalf of the state, was held to be inadmissible hearsay. Unfairness was compounded when the prosecutor, while addressing the jury, had the temerity to argue:

83.   410 U.S. at 302–03.

84.   Proceedings of the 1973 Sentencing Institute for Superior Judges, 112 Cal.Rptr. (app.) 97 (1973) (remarks of Justice Otto M. Kaus).

85.   Hughes v. Mathews, 576 F.2d 1250 (7th Cir. 1978).

86.   Johnson v. Brewer, 521 F.2d 556 (8th Cir. 1975).

87.   United States v. Benveniste, 564 F.2d 335 (9th Cir. 1977).

88.   Welcome v. Vincent, 549 F.2d 853 (2d Cir. 1977).

89.   State v. Dorsey, 87 N.M. 323, 532 P.2d 912 (App.1975); Cf. McMorris v. Israel, 643 F.2d 458 (7th Cir. 1981); For a case that invokes the compulsory process clause rather than the due process clause as the source of a right to submit polygraph evidence see State v. Sims, 52 Ohio Misc. 31, 369 N.E.2d 24, 6 O.O.3d 124 (C.P. Cuyahoga County 1977). The court in *Sims* does not cite *Chambers*.

90.   442 U.S. 95 (1979).

"We couldn't possibly bring any evidence other than the circumstantial evidence * * * that we had pointing to who did it * * * I don't know whether Carzell Moore fired the first shot and handed the gun to Roosevelt Green and he fired the second shot or whether it was vice versa or whether Roosevelt Green had the gun and fired the shot or Carzell Moore had the gun and fired the first shot or the second, but I think it can be reasonably stated that you Ladies and Gentlemen can believe that each one of them fired the shots so that they would be as equally involved and one did not exceed the other's part in the commission of this crime."[91]

The Court, pointing to the disserving character of Moore's statement and the fact that the state had thought it sufficiently reliable to use in prosecuting Moore, held that Green's right to a fair trial on the issue of punishment had been denied and vacated his death sentence.

The Court would, no doubt, have reached the same result had the prosecutor not made the argument he did. However, the prosecutor's remarks highlight a feature that *Chambers* and most of its progeny share. When courts follow *Chambers* to reverse criminal convictions, it is almost always the case that a prosecutor's adversarial instincts have overcome his official commitment to promote justice. Prosecutors are not required to object to all evidence excludable under domestic rules of evidence, and they should not do so when evidence is sufficiently crucial and reliable that its consideration seems essential to a fair verdict. When the state relies on exclusionary rules to secure the conviction of one whose guilt appears, in the light of all the evidence, to be at best questionable, *Chambers* is a valuable precedent for securing justice on appeal. But whatever

the potential of *Chambers, Washington* and the compulsory process clause for mandating more drastic changes in state rules of evidence,[92] it remains as of this writing inchoate.

It is possible to contemplate compulsory process challenges to almost any ruling excluding defense evidence, and some commentators have argued that most exclusionary rules should give way to a defendant's need to introduce evidence on his own behalf. But the history of the compulsory process clause does not suggest that it was intended to supplant local evidence rules. The framers of the sixth amendment knew about rules of disqualification, rules of privilege (they wrote one particularly important one into the fifth amendment), and rules excluding hearsay. Nothing about the language of the compulsory process clause or early practice in the federal courts suggests that the clause was designed to overturn ordinary domestic rules of evidence.

There is, however, in our view, a core value that emerges from the background of the compulsory process clause, and helps makes sense of it. This value is equality in the right to produce evidence in court.

The framers of the sixth amendment were familiar with English procedures that at one time or in some courts denied the right to counsel, precluded confrontation, and prevented defendants from offering their own witnesses. The framers, no doubt, understood that the state can and might be expected to draft rules of evidence and procedure that preserve its interests. No constitutional provision is needed to protect the government's interest in fair treatment. But the state—anxious to suppress crime, punish wrongdoers and assuage community fears—might be tempted to seek an edge in its legal battles against those who stand accused.

91. Id at note 2.

92. For one view of how drastic these changes may and should be, see the two articles by Westen cited in note 70 supra.

The sixth amendment provides protections—originally vis-a-vis the federal government and now vis-a-vis state governments as well—designed to guarantee defendants the same fair chance to be heard that political power and control over rule-making give the government.

At the heart of the right to equal standing in the courts is the compulsory process clause. Just as the government can assert its power to compel witnesses to attend and to testify, so can the accused. He has the right to command this governmental power on his own behalf. Whenever a rule enables the government to produce witnesses that the accused cannot, that rule is, under the sixth amendment, suspect. It is but a small step from this realization to the position that rules that do not interfere with the defendant's subpoena power but prevent the witnesses a defendant calls from testifying are likely to offend the core principle of compulsory process unless the rule would have similarly barred the state from introducing the evidence in question.[93]

This step may help explain the Aaron Burr case. President Jefferson had in his possession evidence that might have assisted the defense. He could have offered this or any other evidence in his possession to the prosecution if the state wished to introduce the evidence against Burr, the accused. Chief Justice Marshall's subpoena for evidence that could help Burr might be seen as reflecting the view that the defense can call for evidence favorable to it just as the government can. The chief executive officer of the land cannot choose to supply only that which helps the government.

In *Washington v. Texas* it was a rule rather than executive discretion that denied the defendant evidence that would have been available to the state. The discriminatory state policy was, despite the offered rationale, immediately suspect. The Chief Justice did not say that the Texas law would have been sustained if it were evenhanded, but it is difficult to imagine a state today adopting a rule of incompetency that might deny it the only witnesses who might be available in criminal cases.

The principle of evenhandedness may also help explain some of the Court's lesser known decisions. The finding of no constitutional violation in *Augenblick*, the case involving lost Jencks Act material, may in part have reflected the fact that the evidence was lost to both sides. In *Webb*, a judge admonished a defense witness as he admonished no other witness in the case. In *Cool*, the jury was instructed to evaluate the crucial exculpatory testimony of the defendant's accomplice by a stricter standard than that applied to the testimony of other witnesses in the case. And in *Green*, the Court found that the defendant's rights were violated when he was precluded from introducing in a sentencing hearing an out-of-court statement that the state had been allowed to use to show the guilt of the co-defendant, who uttered it.

These cases strongly support the notion that equal access to witnesses is a fundamental right, strongly associated with the term compulsory process. Treating this right as the core of compulsory process suggests an additional reason why the *Chambers* Court did not rely on this clause in overturning Leon Chambers' conviction. The justices may not have perceived a po-

---

93. What we are asserting here is a general principle. There might, on occasion, be good policy reasons that allow the state to introduce evidence the accused could not. Thus, the state can introduce an accused's out-of-court statements as admissions, but the accused cannot, as a general rule, introduce his own hearsay. This is because the accused is always free to take the stand to testify to his out-of-court declarations, but the state cannot place the accused on the stand against his will. Whether a rule treats the state and defendants sufficiently the same will depend at some level on the characteristics of the evidence involved. Note how in *Washington* the Court rejected the state's attempt to suggest a distinction between accomplices who testify for the state and those who testify for the accused. But c.f., FRE 804(b)(3).

tential for unequal application in the Mississippi rules.

United States v. Valenzuela-Bernal [94] which is, as we write, the Supreme Court's most recent compulsory process clause case appears, at first blush, to be inconsistent with the above analysis. The case arose following an incident in which Ricardo Valenzuela-Bernal was stopped while driving a car with five passengers, all of whom had illegally entered the country. The passengers fled, but three of them, along with Valenzuela-Bernal were arrested. One passenger was detained as a material witness, and Valenzuela-Bernal was charged with the single count of transporting this passenger in violation of the law. The other two passengers were questioned and, after an Assistant United States Attorney had concluded "that the passengers possessed no evidence material to the prosecution or defense of respondent for transporting illegal aliens," they were deported.

Some may argue that the governmental action violates the mutuality principle that we see as the heart of the compulsory process clause. Had the government required the testimony of the other two passengers, these aliens would have been detained whether or not they wished to remain in the country.[95]   However, the Supreme Court's decision is not, in fact, inconsistent with the principle we espouse. Five members of the Court, speaking through Justice Rhenquist, held that at least in the special case where the government has a substantial policy interest in deporting aliens, government action that negates an accused's ability to subpoena witnesses will not mandate the dismissal of an indictment unless the defendant can make "some showing that the evidence lost would be both material and favorable to the defense." The Court, in effect, reads a test of harmlessness into the compulsory process clause of the sixth amendment [96] for at least those situations in which the state action that deprives the defendant of a potential witness is taken to further a substantial Congressional policy.   The test requires some reason to believe that the government's action has hurt the defendant's case before reversal will be justified.[97]   As two justices point out in separate concurring opinions, Valenzuela-Bernal had no plausible theory to suggest that the testimony of the deported witnesses would have helped his case.

If equality in the opportunity to present witnesses is, as we believe even after *Valenzuela-Bernal,* what the Court sees at the heart of the compulsory process guaran-

---

94.   102 S.Ct. 3440 (1982).

95.   Some may argue that there is mutuality here since once the government chose to deport the passengers, they were equally unavailable as witnesses to both the prosecution and the defense.   A concern for mutuality is also evident in the thoughtful concurring opinion of Justice O'Connor.   She would have had the Court require, in the exercise of its supervisory power, that defense counsel be given access to potential witnesses and the opportunity to show the need for their testimony before they were deported.

96.   The Court also applied the harmlessness test to the due process claim that the defendant raised under the fifth amendment. In addition, the majority noted that the usual test of harmless error should apply.   Reversal of a conviction is not required simply because a defendant can show that a witness has been wrongfully deported under the *Valenzuela-Bernal* test.   In addition there has to be a reasonable likelihood that the missing testimony could have affected the judgment of the trier of fact.

97.   The Court recognizes the special difficulties that a witness might encounter in a showing how the testimony of a deported witness might have helped him when he had not had access to that witness prior to the government's action.   The majority places some importance on the fact that the defendant was present throughout the commission of the crime and so knew better than anyone else what the deported witnesses said to him that might bear on the crime charged.   In a footnote, the Court distinguishes the *Burr* case which found it unreasonable to require Aaron Burr to explain the relevancy of General Wilkinson's letter to President Jefferson upon which the President's allegation of treason was based on the ground that Burr had never read the letter and so was unaware of its contents.

tee, evenhanded hearsay rules that endeavor to keep unreliable evidence from fact finders are likely to be sustained, as are other rules that apply equally, in theory and in practice, to prosecution and defense. Nevertheless, there will be times when a rule that as a general matter works well may produce what seems to be a clear injustice. In these instances the due process clause should provide sufficient authority for ignoring the rule. Such cases should be relatively rare. In common law jurisdictions, judges can mold rules to suit particular cases and avoid constitutional problems. Modern codes, like the Federal Rules of Evidence, invariably include grants of discretion, such as the catch all hearsay exceptions, that allow judges to do justice in those rare cases that cry out for exceptions from a wise general rule.

The following problems suggest some situations in which you as an attorney may wish to advance compulsory process arguments. They also pose the question of where the limits of compulsory process should be set. The problems refer specifically to the compulsory process clause, but in answering them you should assume the defendant invokes the due process clause as well.

Problem VII–14. The defendant is accused of robbing a supermarket. A witness who saw the getaway car has testified that a small person or a child was in the car with defendant when he drove away. The defendant claims he was hiking in the woods with his seven year old son at the time of the robbery. In support of this alibi the defendant would like to put his son on the stand. The prosecution objects and the following dialogue occurs between the judge and the child:

Judge: Do you know what an oath is?

Child: No.

Judge: Do you know what a lie is?

Child: Yes, it's not telling when you did something wrong.

Judge: Do you know what God does to people who lie?

Child: I don't know about God.

Judge: Do you ever lie?

Child: [squirms but says nothing.]

Judge: Do you know what happens when you lie?

Child: Sometimes you get spanked and sometimes no one knows.

At this point the judge rules that the child does not understand the nature of the oath and so will not be allowed to testify. The defendant claims this decision violates his rights under the compulsory process clause. **How should the court rule?** Assume the prosecutor sought to introduce the child as a witness against the defendant in this case and the court ruled the child competent. **How should the court rule on the defendant's argument that putting this child on the stand violates his rights under the confrontation clause?**

Problem VII–15.   Bowie and Keen are charged with bank robbery.   A joint trial has been scheduled.   Bowie asks that the court try her separately and after Keen.   In support of her motion for a later separate trial she introduces an affidavit from Keen which states: "If I am tried before Bowie and am either convicted or acquitted, I shall testify that I had never met Bowie until the time we were both arrested, and I shall offer further testimony in her favor.   However, if we are tried jointly or if Bowie is tried first, I shall have to claim my fifth amendment right and refuse to testify."   **Is the judge required by the compulsory process clause to grant Bowie's motion?**

Problem VII–16.   In the same circumstances as the preceding problem assume that the trial was severed, but that Keen's earlier trial had ended with the jury hung 8–4 for acquittal, and the prosecutor had tentatively decided not to seek a retrial.   When Bowie called Keen, the prosecutor objected even to placing Keen on the stand because Keen had stated that as long as she was subject to retrial she would be forced to claim her right to remain silent.   The judge determined that this was true and refused to place Keen on the stand.   Bowie asked the judge to grant use immunity so that Keen could be forced to testify.   After determining that the prosecutor had no desire to seek use immunity for Keen's testimony, the judge rejected Bowie's request, explaining (correctly) that use immunity was only authorized by statute at the behest of the attorney general.   Bowie argued that the judge's refusal to grant immunity and the prosecutor's refusal to request it violated her rights under the compulsory process clause.   **How should the court rule?**   Bowie also argued that if the judge would not grant immunity, Keen should at least be placed on the stand so that the jury might see that she chose to claim her fifth amendment privilege.   Bowie argued that since her case was built on the theory that she had been mistaken for someone else, her failure to put anyone on the stand who could apparently testify to this fact would result in an unjustified inference that no such person existed.   Hence she had a right under the compulsory process clause to put Keen on the witness stand even if Keen intended to invoke her fifth amendment privilege.   **How should the court rule on this argument?**

Problem VII–17.   In the same circumstances as the preceding two problems, assume that Keen, instead of invoking the fifth amendment, stated that since she was not involved in the bank robbery, she had no idea whether or not Bowie was involved, having never met her until the time they were both arrested.   Bowie requests permission to question Keen as a hostile witness.   **Does either the confrontation clause or the compulsory process clause require the court to grant this request?**

Problem VII–18.   In the same circumstances as the preceding three problems assume that Keen was put on the stand and refused to testify on fifth amendment grounds.   Bowie then sought to introduce Keen's statement in the affidavit she had submitted to the trial court in Problem VII–15.   The prosecutor objected that the statement was hearsay.   **How should the court rule on Bowie's claim that she has a right under the due process clause and under the compulsory process clause to have this hearsay**

statement admitted on her behalf?   Should the court's ruling be any different if Bowie has two witnesses who will testify that they saw Keen and an unidentified female partner (not Bowie) rob the bank?   If she has two witnesses who will testify that while in jail Keen told them that the police had made a mistake when they arrested Bowie?

Problem VII–19.   Dabny is accused of manslaughter and of leaving the scene of an accident in which two pedestrians were hit by a car.   In the accident, one pedestrian was killed, and the other was knocked unconscious and was still in a coma at the time of Dabny's trial.   Dabny moved for a continuance until such time as the victim in the coma recovered and could testify on his behalf.   The judge, after hearing medical testimony that the victim in the coma might recover the next day, the next year, or not at all, refused to grant a continuance.   **Did this decision violate Dabny's rights under the compulsory process clause?   Would the situation be any different with respect to Dabny's rights under the compulsory process clause if the doctors had testified that within six months the victim would either be dead or fully recovered?**   Assume that three months after Dabny was tried and convicted the victim recovered.   Dabny seeks a new trial at which the victim's testimony could be taken.   He claims to have this right under the compulsory process clause.   **How should a court rule?   Would Dabny's rights be any different if he had obtained an affidavit from the victim stating that he was hit by a yellow car and Dabny's car was blue?**

Problem VII–20.   Marcia Fields is accused of attempted extortion.   The principal evidence against her is voiceprint evidence, a new scientific technique admissible in the jurisdiction in question but subject to challenge before the jury.   Fields seeks to subpoena a leading authority on voiceprints who has expressed considerable skepticism about the accuracy with which they can be used to identify individual speakers.   The expert ordinarily commands a fee of $10,000—ten times more than the fees demanded by less eminent and presumably less persuasive experts in this field.   Fields can afford to pay at most $200.   Citing the compulsory process clause, Fields claims that the court must either order the state to pay the expert's $10,000 fee or order the expert, under threat of contempt, to testify as an ordinary witness with no special fee.   There is a statute in the jurisdiction which provides that in the case of indigent defendants the state will pay up to $500 in expert witness fees, and there is clear precedent that experts will not be required to testify to matters within their expertise unless they agree to do so.   **How should the court rule on Fields' claim?**

Problem VII–21.   In the same case as the preceding problem, assume that Fields had taken a polygraph (lie detector) examination and that the expert who examined her was prepared to testify that she was telling the truth when she stated that she had not made the threatening phone calls which gave rise to this prosecution.   The jurisdiction has a clear precedent of not admitting polygraph evidence in any circumstances.   Fields argues that the compulsory process clause gives her the right to have this evidence placed before the jury.   **How should the court rule?   Does it matter**

whether the consensus of polygraph experts is that the machine is 30% accurate, 60% accurate, or 90% accurate?   Would the situation be different if Fields were charged with selling narcotics and the only evidence against her was the testimony of an informer who alleged that he had made a buy?   In these circumstances would Fields have the right under the confrontation clause to insist that the informer take a polygraph examination?

Problem VII–22.   Lorenzo Bolt is tried for the murder of Willie Mitchell.   At trial, the State calls to the witness stand two persons who saw the shooting of Mitchell.   They testify that Mitchell parked his taxicab on Liberty Street, next to a public telephone booth, and was checking a tire when a dark-colored car pulled up alongside of him.   Within a few seconds, a shot was heard.   Mitchell was seen running across the street, clutching his chest, as the car drove off.   Defense counsel, during cross-examination of one of these witnesses, attempts to impeach her testimony by referring to a written statement she had given police.   The trial judge refuses to allow counsel to introduce the statement or cross-examine the witness in any manner concerning it, on the ground that she had not signed a receipt, acknowledging delivery of a copy.   The trial judge relies upon legislative provisions governing the use of certain prior statements.   The three sections essentially provide that where a public employee has taken a written statement from a person in any investigation that person may not be examined or cross-examined by any "examiner, solicitor, lawyer or prosecuting officer" concerning the statement, nor may it be introduced or used in any manner unless the person giving it has received a copy, signed a receipt for the same and has had a reasonable time to read it over.   Defendant claims these sections violate the sixth amendment.   **Will he prevail?**

Problem VII–23.   Professor Westen writes:

> *Privileges that cannot be accommodated.*   There remains a group of privileges that cannot be narrowed or modified in light of the right of compulsory process without defeating their purpose, such as the absolute privilege in some states for newsmen to conceal their sources, the statutory privilege of witnesses in some states to remain silent in the face of incriminating questions unless granted transactional immunity, and certain federal privileges applicable in state criminal proceedings. They cannot be waived or controlled by the party initiating the prosecution and cannot survive even limited disclosure to the defense.   Any disclosure of a federal "state secret" or a newsman's source, except perhaps *in camera*, would defeat the state's strong interest in the privilege.
>
> Conflict between compulsory process and such absolute privileges may be resolved in two ways: Either the accused must go forward with his defense without the benefit of the privileged information or the prosecution must strike the portion of its case to which the information relates.   The decision may depend on the materiality of the privileged information and the possibility of curing prejudice by permitting the jury to draw a favorable inference from the witness' silence. *Ultimately, how-*

ever, where the defendant can show that the information is indispensable to rebuttal or to an affirmative defense the court must dismiss the charges.[98]   (emphasis added)
Do you agree with Professor Westen's conclusion?

Problem VII–24.   In concluding his first article, Professor Westen compares the confrontation clause with the compulsory process clause:

> Compulsory process is more important to the accused than confrontation because in most cases it can substitute for confrontation, while confrontation cannot replace the functions served by compulsory process.   The essential difference between the two is their allocation of the burden of producing witnesses.   Confrontation allocates to the prosecution the burden of producing witnesses against the accused, while compulsory process allocates to the accused the burden (and the means) of producing witnesses in his favor.   Thus, unless a prosecution witness has become unavailable, the right of confrontation only relieves the defendant of the burden of issuing subpoenas for the witnesses whose out-of-court statements are introduced against him.   Abolition of the right of confrontation would not automatically result in trials by affidavit and hearsay; it would simply shift to the defendant the administrative burden of producing the adverse declarants for cross-examination, along with producing the separate witnesses in his favor.   Abolition of compulsory process, on the other hand, would be more drastic: It would leave the defendant face to face with the witnesses against him, but with no means to produce the witnesses in his favor.[99]

This analysis implies that the protection of the confrontation clause is ultimately unnecessary.   **Do you agree that this is the case?**

SECTION IV.   "RAPE SHIELD" LAWS

Rape is a particularly serious crime.   In many jurisdictions only intentional homicide may be punished more severely.   Rape can be especially brutal or degrading, and it is no wonder that the victim of a violent rape may be haunted by the experience for years.   But a rape need not be violent to cause serious psychological damage.   The crime is inescapably sexual and sexual identity is, for most people, a core component of self-concept.   Thus rape, whether or not it is accompanied by violence, may be perceived by the victim as a uniquely *personal* attack.   Outside of prisons, jails and other institutions, it is, almost exclusively, an attack by men against women.

At the same time, rape is an unusual crime.   The acts of sexual intercourse, that in both a legal and a psychological sense uniquely define the offense, are enjoyed each day by many adults.   The line between the legal and the illegal is one of free and intelligent consent.[1]   A man engaging in sexual intercourse with a woman

----

98. Westen, Compulsory Process I, supra, note 70 at 173–74.

99. Id. at 183.

1. In some circumstances consent or a lack of consent may be assumed.   Thus, in most jurisdictions, a woman is presumed to consent to sex with her husband, so a man can-

may on one day be acting legally and on the next be guilty of rape. Moreover, since consent to sexual intercourse is not implied from consent to only slightly less intimate acts, a man may be guilty of rape even though the victim has consented to or taken the initiative in those erotic activities that are common preludes to sexual intercourse.[2] Rape is also a crime of specific intent. This means that a man's culpability turns on his belief about whether a woman consented at the time of the act as well as on what the woman actually felt. Since communications about sexual matters are often non-verbal, determining what a man might reasonably have believed can be difficult.[3]

Rape trials pose special problems. Because the crime is so serious, it is important that the issues of consent and intent be thoroughly explored in any case where they are legitimately in issue. To be mistakenly convicted of rape is at least as likely to ruin a man's life as the experience of being raped is to ruin a woman's. A woman's past sexual experience and an accused's knowledge of aspects of that experience will often be probative of matters in issue. For example, when a genuine issue of consent is raised, evidence that the victim was a virgin is typically received for its tendency to negate consent. If evidence of virginity negates consent, evidence of nonvirginity must, as a matter of

logic, support that defense, although the support need not be strong.

Allowing those charged with rape to introduce evidence of a woman's past sexual activity to show consent is problematic in several respects. First, the state may be prejudiced by the evidence. Jurors may think that forcible sex with one who has been promiscuous or "lived in sin" is not so serious as to be deserving of substantial punishment and so may acquit one they think guilty or may require the state to meet an inordinately high burden of proof. Second, the evidence may lead to estimation problems, for the jury may substantially overestimate the probative value that attaches to a history of sexual experience. Most women who have had intercourse with several men over a period of a year may be quite reluctant to consent to sex with strangers, but jurors may believe that they are likely to do so.

The tendency to misuse evidence of sexual history in these ways has almost certainly diminished in recent years. The incidence of pre-marital and extra-marital sex is today sufficiently high and well known that most jurors are unlikely to define a woman's character by her sexual life or to believe that because a woman consented to sex with one or two men she will consent with all. The feeling that the unmarried rape victim had, if she was not at the time of the assault a virgin, "nothing to

not rape his wife. In all jurisdictions certain categories of people, such as girls below a certain age, are presumed incapable of giving consent. Typically such presumptions are irrebuttable; so they are really rules of law excluding otherwise culpable behavior from the definition of a crime or creating new crimes in which consent is not an issue. As attitudes change some of these presumptions, like the presumption that a man cannot rape his wife, are increasingly coming under attack. Our textual discussion involves only those situations where acts of sexual intercourse would not have been criminal had the woman consented.

2. In some jurisdictions the crime of rape has, as a legal matter, turned entirely on

whether there was sexual intercourse without consent. Thus, the lover who insists on intercourse when his beloved would "rather not" is, in theory, vulnerable to the same punishment as the stranger who brutally assaults a woman. Today rape laws are being revised, and modern laws graduate the offense according to the degree of force involved.

3. Some people involved in the movement to reform rape laws and enact rape shield statutes would dispute this proposition. They believe that the difficulty of determining whether certain acts of sexual intercourse are forcible or voluntary is often exaggerated in commentaries on the legal aspects of rape.

lose" is, one hopes, far behind us. We do not mean to say that we have reached that happy state where a rape victim's history of past sexual activity will in no way prejudice the state, but it is important that in balancing prejudicial value against probative effect that prejudice not be overweighted by reference to the standards of a bygone era.[4]

The third problem with admitting evidence of a woman's sexual history when rape is charged is its effect on the victim. Rape, as we have noted, can be both brutal and degrading. A trial for rape should not add to the victim's trauma. Yet, to some extent it inevitably will. At a minimum the woman will have to recount her experience and confront her alleged assailant. What is not inevitable is the exposure of the victim's sex life and the attempt to portray her, by virtue of her past behavior, as one who would consent to the activity by which she feels victimized. The victim who is forced to disclose her sexual history may not only suffer psychic pain, she may also find that ongoing relationships with friends and family are disrupted. Some women may not report rapes or may later withdraw their complaints in order to avoid testifying, and those who follow through may suffer for it. Thus, the state has a substantial policy interest in protecting the rape victim's interest in the privacy of her sex life. However, this policy interest has nothing to do with the quality of fact-finding at trial. Protecting privacy interests may enhance or impede justice depending on the circumstances of the case.

In recent years, almost every jurisdiction in this country has enacted some sort of "rape shield" law. Rape shield laws may prevent defendants in rape cases from exploring certain aspects of the sexual histories of their alleged victims, from offering certain kinds of evidence that bear on sexual history or from offering evidence of sexual history for certain purposes. They also commonly impose special procedures, usually requiring notice and a hearing, before evidence of sexual history can be introduced for permitted purposes. These laws have been passed largely to protect the privacy interests of rape victims, but they have also been justified by their tendency to prevent the prejudice and estimation problems we mention above.[5]

Despite their commonality of purpose, rape shield statutes come in many different forms. Tanford and Bocchino, after examining forty-six such laws, report that "almost every conceivable use of sexual history evidence is * * * admissible under at least one rape victim shield law."[6] Some shield statutes do little more than caution a court to be sure that sexual history evidence is more probative than prejudicial while others seek to limit substantially the admissibility of relevant evidence.

---

4. One of us is less sanguine about this assertion than the other. Both of us agree that its validity may depend on the part of the country, or even the part of the state, in which one resides. Everywhere there may be substantial vestiges of a dual morality, the public views and the private life. We know little about how much of their private lives jurors share with one another. Jurors who are sexually active may never admit this fact in the jury room. Many jurors may still live in a "we" and "they" world when it comes to sexual matters. Jurors may find their own behavior unacceptable as a standard for others.

5. An important stimulus to these laws has been cases suggesting that an unchaste woman cannot be expected to tell the truth or cases admitting evidence of unchastity on the issue of consent where any suggestion that the woman consented to the assault in question is absurd. It is not clear that cases of this sort have ever been frequent, but they have occurred and their existence has helped make the case for rape shield laws. For examples of such cases see, Berger, Man's Trial, Woman's Tribulation: Rape Cases in the Courtroom, 77 Colum.L.Rev. 1, 12–20 (1977).

6. Tanford & Bocchino, Rape Victim Shield Laws and the Sixth Amendment, 128 U.Pa.L.Rev. 544 (1980).

The latter necessarily raise constitutional problems. A legislature cannot by fiat change the logical relevance of evidence in a case, nor can it by statute infringe on a defendant's constitutional rights. To the extent shield laws bar relevant evidence on cross-examination they may interfere with a defendant's rights under the confrontation clause, and to the extent that they preclude the introduction of exonerative evidence, they may interfere with rights to compulsory process or to due process of law. Shield statutes also raise policy problems, for the heinous nature of the crime of rape makes it particularly important that we do not change our procedures so as to enhance the probability of convicting the innocent.

FRE 412, the federal rape shield statute, is the product of a coalition between Congressional liberals, strongly influenced by the concerns of the "women's movement" and Congressional conservatives with "law and order" concerns. It was enacted without any input from the Federal Rules Advisory Committee or from the Court. It is, from the victim's standpoint, one of the more protective of the rape shield laws that have been enacted. From the defendant's standpoint it excludes a wide range of potentially relevant evidence. When you read the statute, you will see why we postponed discussion of it until this point in the course. Certain aspects require reference to the Constitution, and other portions are fraught with constitutional problems.

Rule 412.

RAPE CASES; RELEVANCE OF VICTIM'S PAST BEHAVIOR

(a) Notwithstanding any other provision of law, in a criminal case in which a person is accused of rape or of assault with intent to commit rape, reputation or opinion evidence of the past sexual behavior of an alleged victim of such rape or assault is not admissible.

(b) Notwithstanding any other provision of law, in a criminal case in which a person is accused of rape or of assault with intent to commit rape, evidence of a victim's past sexual behavior other than reputation or opinion evidence is also not admissible, unless such evidence other than reputation or opinion evidence is—

(1) admitted in accordance with subdivisions (c)(1) and (c)(2) and is constitutionally required to be admitted; or

(2) admitted in accordance with subdivision (c) and is evidence of—

(A) past sexual behavior with persons other than the accused, offered by the accused upon the issue of whether the accused was or was not, with respect to the alleged victim, the source of semen or injury; or

(B) past sexual behavior with the accused and is offered by the accused upon the issue of whether the alleged victim consented to the sexual behavior with respect to which rape or assault is alleged.

(c)(1) If the person accused of committing rape or assault with intent to commit rape intends to offer under subdivision (b) evidence of specific instances of the alleged victim's past sexual behavior, the accused shall make a written motion to offer such evidence not later than fifteen days before the date on which the trial in which such evidence is to be offered is scheduled to begin, except that the court may allow the motion to be made at a later date, including during trial, if the court determines either that the evidence is newly discovered and could not have been obtained earlier through the exercise of due diligence or that the issue to which such evidence relates has newly arisen in the case. Any motion made under this paragraph shall be served on all other parties and on the alleged victim.

(2) The motion described in paragraph (1) shall be accompanied by a written offer

of proof. If the court determines that the offer of proof contains evidence described in subdivision (b), the court shall order a hearing in chambers to determine if such evidence is admissible. At such hearing the parties may call witnesses, including the alleged victim, and offer relevant evidence. Notwithstanding subdivision (b) of rule 104, if the relevancy of the evidence which the accused seeks to offer in the trial depends upon the fulfillment of a condition of fact, the court, at the hearing in chambers or at a subsequent hearing in chambers scheduled for such purpose, shall accept evidence on the issue of whether such condition of fact is fulfilled and shall determine such issue.

(3) If the court determines on the basis of the hearing described in paragraph (2) that the evidence which the accused seeks to offer is relevant and that the probative value of such evidence outweighs the danger of unfair prejudice, such evidence shall be admissible in the trial to the extent an order made by the court specifies evidence which may be offered and areas with respect to which the alleged victim may be examined or cross-examined.

(d) For purposes of this rule, the term "past sexual behavior" means sexual behavior other than the sexual behavior with respect to which rape or assault with intent to commit rape is alleged. (As added by P.L. 95–540, § 2(2), Oct. 28, 1978).

Section (a) of FRE 412 bars reputation or opinion evidence of an alleged rape victim's past sexual behavior regardless of purpose. So long as specific acts evidence is admissible and is at least as probative as reputation or opinion evidence on the points for which it is offered the ban should pose no constitutional problems. However, in certain situations the constitutionality of this ban is deservedly suspect. One such situation is where the defendant's intent is in issue and the victim's reputation, as known to the defendant, has some bearing on his likely intent. Suppose, for example, two college students are engaged in erotic petting when the woman, at the point of intercourse, arguably refuses. Her version is that she pushed him away and said, "That's it. I want to get dressed—quickly." His version is that she may have said that, but that he thought her pushing was teasing and what he thought she meant was, "Do it quickly, I want to get dressed." If the woman had, within the defendant's fraternity, a reputation for promiscuity and was also known to have little patience for afterplay, the evidence would be clearly relevant on the issue of whether the defendant intended to have intercourse without consent. It appears to the authors that the exclusion of reputation evidence in such circumstances would be unconstitutional. A second situation in which the ban of section (a) is suspect is where reputation or opinion evidence appears reliable and is the best available evidence of the victim's relevant sexual behavior. Suppose, for example, that the defendant claims the victim is a prostitute who threatened to accuse him of rape when he refused to give her an extra hundred dollars. The defendant offers as witnesses two of the victim's associates and one of her "clients," but all three refuse to testify, citing the fifth amendment. The defendant then calls an experienced vice squad officer who will testify that while he has never seen the woman engage in an act of sex for pay, he has observed her behavior on the streets as well as a steady stream of men entering her apartment and he is of the opinion that she is a prostitute. Can such testimony be banned consistent with the constitution? We think not.[7]

7. It might be argued that since section (a) does not bar testimony concerning the acts that underlie the officer's opinion, the bar is, as it relates to the statement of opinion, constitutional. In our view, the validity of this position turns on whether the jury could fully

Subsection (b)(1) cannot pose constitutional problems except insofar as section (c) is constitutionally suspect, for under (b)(1) all evidence which is constitutionally required to be admitted is admissible so long as the procedures of subdivision (c)(1) and (c)(2) are followed. The problem is to determine when evidence of an alleged rape victim's past sexual behavior is constitutionally required to be admitted. The basic test should be one of relevance, although it is possible that more than minimal logical relevance will be required. This provision should eliminate abuses frequently cited by those who advocate rape shield laws. First, the defendant should not be allowed to introduce evidence of the complaining witness' promiscuity for "whatever bearing it has on her credibility." The inference from sexual activity to character to credibility is so attenuated, if it exists at all, that the Constitution should not be interpreted so as to require the admission of sexual history evidence for this purpose. This does not mean that evidence of past sex acts will never be admissible for its bearing on credibility. Where, for example, a rape victim flaunts her virtue on direct examination, the defendant should, under the confrontation clause, have a right to probe that victim's virtue on cross-examination and to introduce extrinsic evidence contradicting the woman's self-portrait in appropriate circumstances. Second, where the circumstances of a rape suggest that there was a very low probability of consent, the Constitution should not be read so as to require the admission of sexual history evidence for whatever bearing it might have on that issue. Thus, if a woman is raped and beaten by a stranger in a parking lot and afterwards complains immediately to the police, evidence that the woman was promiscuous or, indeed, was a prostitute should not be admissible simply because the defendant has the gall to claim that the woman consented.

Changes of the sort we mention are entirely salutary, but a law that commands the exclusion of all evidence whose admission is not constitutionally mandated should not have been required to achieve them. Judges should have been excluding such evidence all along under their basic authority to bar evidence which, in the context of a case, is either irrelevant or unduly prejudicial or confusing. Many courts were doing this before the term "rape shield" was invented. We shall not try to anticipate other changes that subsection (b)(1) will bring. Ultimately, the meaning of this clause will have to be determined by the developing case law.

Subsection (b)(2) contains provisions which are found in many rape shield laws. It lists categories of past sexual behavior which are so likely to be relevant that they are presumptively admissible. Subsection (b)(2)(A) is standard, but the federal rule, unlike many state statutes, does not include pregnancy or disease under this head. If a woman claims that she became pregnant or contracted a disease as a result of a rape, the defendant will have to resort to section (b)(1) to show that there is another man who may have been the source of the condition. Subsection (b)(2)(B) is another common exception. It is felt that a woman's past history of sex with the one she accuses is ordinarily probative of consent on a given occasion.

Section (c) establishes procedures that defendants wishing to offer evidence of the victim's sexual history must follow. Subsection (1) is likely to be held constitutional, although there is precedent in the

---

appreciate the implications of the underlying facts without guidance from the expert. It is, of course, true that rape prosecutions are unlikely to occur in the situations described in this paragraph. However, there are cases in which, if the man's story is to be believed, the situation was much like that we describe, and, regardless of how realistic the examples are, they are appropriately posed to test the constitutional limits of section (a).

"notice of alibi" area which holds that when a state demands discovery of an accused's evidence, it must in some way reciprocate.[8] Subsection (2) poses more serious problems for the procedures described may interfere with an accused's right to jury trial. Under subsection (2) if the relevance of evidence that an accused seeks to offer depends on the fulfillment of a condition of fact, the judge is to determine the issue. The rule does not speak to the standard that the judge should apply. If the judge must only decide whether there is enough evidence for a reasonable jury to find the fact in question, there are no problems with this procedure. But if, as is more likely to be the case, the judge is to determine by the preponderance of the evidence whether a preliminary fact exists, the judge may reach a decision that a reasonable jury would not reach, and on the basis of that decision withhold evidence the admission of which would be constitutionally required if the judge shared the jury's view of the preliminary fact.

Suppose, for example, that a defendant claims that he never had sexual intercourse with the alleged rape victim. As evidence that he did, the state shows that ten days after the alleged rape the woman was found to have a venereal disease from which the defendant was known to have suffered. The defendant wishes to offer evidence that at about the time of the alleged rape the woman had intercourse with two other men. He argues that under FRE 412(b)(1) he is entitled to show these acts of intercourse in order to rebut the inference that he was the source of the disease. When the other acts are offered for this purpose, their probative value turns on whether either of the men was suffering from the disease that the woman later contracted. Suppose the evidence on this is conflicting, but the judge believes that it is

more likely than not that neither of the two men suffered from the disease in question. Under subsection (c)(2), it appears that the judge should exclude the evidence. If the judge does this the jury learns of no alternative explanation for the woman's diseased condition. Yet had the jurors heard the evidence presented to the judge in chambers they might have concluded that one or both of the other men were carriers of the disease the victim contracted. Furthermore, the evaluation problem may be inextricably linked with factual issues which, because they are committed to the jury, the judge is likely to ignore in the context of a preliminary hearing. Assume the medical evidence relating to the two men we have been discussing suggests that it is more likely than not that neither was diseased at the time in question. Also assume that the jury finds the alleged victim's testimony about being raped somewhat incredible and tends to believe the defendant's alibi testimony. Nevertheless, the fact that defendant had the disease that the victim indisputably contracted leads the jury to ultimately credit the victim and discredit the defendant. However, just as evidence of a victim's disease can properly lead a fact finder to reevaluate other evidence that a person was involved in a rape, so can evidence of the victim's disease lead to a reevaluation of the probability that one of the victim's known paramours was free from disease. If the defendant's alibi evidence is strong, it becomes unlikely that the defendant was the source of the disease and it becomes more likely that a paramour was diseased despite the weight of the medical evidence to the contrary. Because, as our examples illustrate, the procedures prescribed by subsection (c)(2) take from the jury factual issues that have been historically within its province and because the resolution of the preliminary question may be inextric-

8. Compare Williams v. Florida, 399 U.S. 78 (1970) with Wardius v. Oregon, 412 U.S. 470 (1973).

ably linked with facts that are for the jury to determine, giving the preliminary factual question to the judge may contravene the defendant's sixth amendment right to jury trial as well as his right to due process of law.

Subsection (c)(3), like subsection (c)(1) should pass constitutional muster. Note that the court's responsibility to compare "probative value" with "unfair prejudice" does not authorize it to consider the embarrassment or pain which the disclosure of past sexual activity will cause the victim. "Prejudice" is a term of art, and as such it refers to certain ways in which a party's case may be improperly weakened. In a rape case, the state and not the victim is the party. Only the state may be prejudiced. Also, the last clause of (c)(3) should not be read to take away what the first clause gives. Once the judge determines that the probative value of certain evidence outweighs the danger of unfair prejudice the specification of what areas may be inquired into must be coextensive with the relevance determination. To hold otherwise would raise serious constitutional problems.

Rape shield statutes are relatively new. Courts are only now beginning to confront the constitutional issues that they raise. We have given you our analysis of where serious problems lie and how they should be resolved. We cannot be certain that courts will share these views. We now offer you a set of problems so that you may apply not our analysis but your own reading of the cases and commentary that make up the bulk of this chapter.

Problem VII–25. Suppose that the state of Hutchins "in order to protect the reputation of our beloved dead and to prevent the pain and suffering of their near kin" passes a statute that provides: "In a trial for homicide reputation or opinion evidence of the past violent behavior of the deceased victim is not allowed. Evidence of past violent acts which the deceased perpetrated on persons other than the accused is inadmissible, but evidence of past violent acts by the deceased on the accused may be admitted on the issue of self defense." **Is this statute unconstitutional on its face? Can you think of circumstances where it would be unconstitutional as applied? If the statute provided that evidence of violent acts by the deceased was inadmissible except where the evidence was constitutionally required to be admitted, would this be a wise legislative policy? What are the salient differences between this statute and the federal rape shield statute? What are the salient differences between rape victims and homicide victims?**

Problem VII–26. Three youths are accused of dragging a seventeen year old girl 500 feet down an alley, forcing her into a vacant house, and raping her. The youths argue that once in the building the girl consented to the sex act. They seek to present evidence that six months before the alleged rape the girl had had sexual intercourse with her boyfriend, who now lives in another state. They also wish to offer evidence that sometime after the alleged rape, the girl had moved into a motel with a forty year old man. When questioned about this incident by the juvenile authorities, she had first denied having had sexual intercourse with the man, but later admitted it. **Is this evidence admissible in a jurisdiction without a rape shield law? Is**

it admissible in federal court?   Is it important that she never claimed that the forty year old man raped her?

Problem VII–27.   Mack Lane is charged with raping a sixteen year old friend of his.   She testifies that she was walking home with him one evening when he lured her into a house where he and three friends had sexual intercourse with her.   She claims that she struggled but that she could do nothing as she was held down by three youths during the acts.   She says that when the last of the youths left the room where they had placed her, she telephoned her sister and asked her to come get her, but did not say that she had been raped.   However, before her sister arrived a friend of hers opened the door, found her and escorted her outside.   She immediately ran to a nearby police car screaming that she had been raped.   The doctor who examined her found no signs of external bruises or injuries but he did find internal scratches consistent with either normal or multiple intercourse.   At the trial, Lane wants to introduce evidence that the victim had engaged in other acts of intercourse in the past and that she had a bad reputation for chastity.   He claims that this is probative both of her veracity and on the issue of her consent.   Lane would also like to introduce evidence that on two other occasions his friend had run screaming to police cars claiming she had been raped by several men and on each occasion she had later admitted that she had engaged in consensual intercourse with just one person.   **Is any of the evidence that Lane wishes to offer admissible in a jurisdiction with no rape shield law?   Is any of it admissible in federal court?   Does it matter whether the witnesses to the other accusations are police officers or friends of Lane?   Would you permit Lane to show that the girl's father has on a number of occasions beaten her because of his suspicion that she had been engaging in sexual activity?**

Problem VII–28.   Fred is accused of raping Paula.   There was no evidence of violence and Paula did not complain of the rape until two days after it allegedly occurred.   Fred claims that Paula is a prostitute who filed the rape charge when a check he had given her bounced.   Thus Fred's defense is consent.   **May Fred introduce the testimony of two men who will say that they had paid Paula to have sex with them?   Does it matter how long before the rape complaint these acts occurred?   If Fred's two witnesses plead the fifth amendment, would Fred be able to introduce the testimony of a vice squad officer to the effect that Paula has a reputation as a prostitute and that in his opinion Paula was a prostitute?   Would your ruling on this question change if the officer testified in a preliminary hearing that in ten years in the business Paula had not once complained of rape?   If Paula takes the stand to testify that Fred raped her and says that fear made her refrain from reporting the rape, may Fred ask her on cross-examination whether she has worked in the past as a prostitute?   May Fred ask whether she didn't consent to sex with him on the condition that he pay $50.00?**   Assume that the judge refuses to admit any testimony regarding Paula's other sexual activities or alleged activities as a prostitute.   **Have any of Fred's constitutional rights been violated?   Would they be violated if in trying to introduce the evidence Fred had not complied with the applicable parts of FRE 412(c)?   Do your answers** to any of the above questions change if it was shown by the testimony of third parties that Paula had complained within hours of the alleged rape and that when Paula came to the police station she was badly bruised and cut in several places? If there were subsection (c) hearings on any of these issues, what would happen at such hearings?

Problem VII–29. Dave is being tried in federal court for assaulting Phyllis with intent to rape. Sam testifies for the prosecution that he heard screams and ran in the direction in which they were coming. He heard Phyllis sobbing, "You can't do it, don't kill me." He identifies Dave as the man he saw running away from the scene. Dave claims that Phyllis had consented to intercourse and in fact was saying, "You can do it, thrill me." **May Dave ask Sam on cross-examination whether he wasn't in fact living with Phyllis and regularly having intercourse with her though they weren't married? If Sam denies this may Dave call Phyllis as his witness and ask her whether she was living with Sam to show their relationship by extrinsic evidence?** Suppose Dave claims that he had propositioned Phyllis because his fraternity brothers had said that she was "easy" and "would do it anywhere." **Could he testify to this? Could Dave introduce five of his fraternity brothers who would testify that they had propositioned Phyllis during the past three months and she had always consented to sex? May he introduce this testimony if his witnesses will all testify that when asked to have sex Phyllis responded "You can do it, thrill me."?**

Problem VII–30. Harry is accused of raping Meg. Meg complained shortly after the alleged act. A physical examination revealed that she had recently had sexual intercourse and that she was bruised over much of her body. Harry offers evidence that he and Meg had been married for six years but had been divorced a year and a half ago. He also offers to testify and presents a mutual friend who will testify that when married he and Meg were into "kinky" sex and it was common for one of them to beat the other as part of the foreplay leading to the sex act. Harry claims the act was consented to, and argues that Meg reported the rape because when she asked him when he would come again he said that his visit was in the form of a farewell because he was getting remarried. The judge following a section (c) hearing rules that Harry cannot present the evidence because it is more prejudicial than probative. **Are any of Harry's constitutional rights violated because he cannot inquire into these matters in his cross-examination of Meg?**

Problem VII–31. In the same circumstances as in the preceding problem, suppose Harry and Meg were never married, but Harry wishes to offer testimony that they had engaged in sex in the fashion described several times before. The judge refuses to even conduct a section (c) hearing, holding that since the behavior Harry describes is illegal under the laws of the jurisdiction in question Meg could not consent to such treatment and so the evidence is irrelevant on the issue of consent. **How should a higher court decide the inevitable appeal?** Suppose the judge holds a section (c) hearing and Meg testifies that while she had known Harry for about a month before the incident, she had never had sex with him. The judge, admitting he has nothing to go on except differences in demeanor, finds Meg's story more credible and prevents Harry from describing his version of their past sexual encounters to the jury. **Has the judge committed reversible error?** Suppose Harry demands that the judge consider in the section (c) hearing a polygraph examination he had submitted to and asks that Meg be required to submit to one as well? **How should the judge rule?** Suppose Harry wants the jury to consider the results of a polygraph examination which indicate that he is telling the truth when he says that Meg consented on the occasion in question and he wants Meg to be ordered to submit to a similar exam, the results of which would be given the jury. **How should the judge rule?**

BIBLIOGRAPHY

McCormick § 255.

4 Weinstein's Evidence ¶ 800[04].

5 Wigmore Ch. 47.

Berger, Man's Trial, Woman's Tribulation: Rape Cases in the Courtroom, 77 Colum.L.Rev. 1 (1977).

Davenport, The Confrontation Clause and the Co-Conspirator Exception in Criminal Prosecution: A Functional Analysis, 85 Harv.L.Rev. 1398 (1972).

Flanagan, Compelled Immunity for Defense Witnesses: Hidden Costs and Questions, 56 Notre Dame Lawyer 447 (1981).

Graham, K., The Right of Confrontation and the Hearsay Rule: Sir Walter Raleigh Loses Another One, 8 Crim.L.Bull. 99 (1972).

Graham, M., The Confrontation Clause, the Hearsay Rule, and the Forgetful Witness, 56 Tex.L.Rev. 151 (1978).

Griswold, The Due Process Revolution and Confrontation, 119 U.Pa.L.Rev. 711 (1971).

Levie, Hearsay and Conspiracy, 52 Mich.L.Rev. 1159 (1954).

Marcus, The Confrontation Clause and Co-Defendant Confessions: The Drift From Bruton to Parker v. Randolph, 1979 U.Ill.L. Forum 559 (1979).

Read, The New Confrontation-Hearsay Dilemma, 45 So.Cal.L.Rev. 1 (1972).

Snow, Co-Conspirators Exception to the Hearsay Rule: Procedural Implementation and Confrontation Clause Requirements, 63 J.Crim.L. 1 (1972).

Tanford & Bocchino, Rape Victim Shield Laws and the Sixth Amendment, 128 U.Pa.L.Rev. 544 (1980).

Westen, The Future of Confrontation, 77 Mich.L.Rev. 1185 (1979).

Westen, Confrontation and Compulsory Process: A Unified Theory of Evidence for Criminal Cases, 91 Harv.L.Rev. 567 (1978).

Westen, Order of Proof: An Accused's Right to Control the Timing and Sequence of Evidence in His Defense, 66 Calif.L.Rev. 935 (1978).

Westen, Compulsory Process II, 74 Mich.L.Rev. 191 (1975).

Westen, The Compulsory Process Clause, 73 Mich.L.Rev. 71 (1974).

Chapter Eight

PRIVILEGES

SECTION I. INTRODUCTION

The evidence rules discussed in previous chapters are designed, for the most part, to aid "the search for truth." However evanescent truth may be, the law of evidence generally assumes that truth can be approached in litigation if suitable rules govern the adversary process. The basic rule, you will remember, is that relevant evidence is generally admitted unless there is a clear danger that it will lead to inaccurate fact-finding. Exclusionary rules are inescapably suspect in a system that seeks to learn all facts in order to reconstruct past events as accurately as possible. Beneath the stone left unturned may lie the key that will unlock the mystery of the past. Yet, despite continual attack and perpetual suspicion, exclusionary rules somehow survive. The remarkable tenacity of the hearsay rule is the best example. At times, however, the fear of "lost evidence" and doubts about how well rules of exclusion serve their intended purposes lead courts and legislatures to relax exclusionary principles. The relaxation of an exclusionary rule may improve the law of evidence. We have suggested, for example, that the decision to admit evidence of subsequent remedial measures in products liability cases may in some circumstances be a salutary one. At other times the pressure generated by the belief that truth can be reasonably approximated leads to the relaxation of exclusionary rules that might better be left alone. In discussing the way hearsay is treated in the Federal Rules of Evidence, we pointed to a number of instances where we thought this was the case.

Whatever the merits of the exclusionary rules which have been treated in previous chapters, it is important to note that most of them are traditionally justified on the ground that they enhance truth-seeking by excluding weak evidence, prejudicial evidence, or other evidence that is somehow disruptive of an orderly inquiry into past events. The exclusionary rules of privilege presented in this chapter are usually justified on entirely different grounds. When a privilege exists, an individual may not be compelled to disclose information about a particular event. Privileges to withhold information may hamper the search for truth. This is recognized. Privileges persist because some values are regarded as important enough to justify restrictions on the search for truth.

The privileges that involve a "professional" counselor and a "nonprofessional" seeking advice—most commonly the attorney-client privilege and the doctor-patient privilege—are designed to promote free communication on topics relevant to the professional's services. Other privileges are designed to establish zones of private activity or private communication. Spouses may have a privilege so broad as to preclude any testimony from one spouse concerning the other. In addition, they often have one that protects their private communications. The fifth amendment gives criminal defendants the well-known privilege not to testify against themselves. The government has special privileges. It may be permitted to conceal the identity of certain informants and it may refuse to reveal state secrets. News reporters may claim a privilege to protect their sources similar to the government's privilege to protect informants, and businesses may claim a privilege to protect trade secrets similar to that which exists to protect state secrets. Other privileges exist in some jurisdictions.

Most privileges are not constitutionally based. They exist in some places and not in others. They take different forms in different jurisdictions. Interest groups often seek privileges for information they believe should be held in confidence, and critics of the privilege system seek to limit or repeal existing privileges. In virtually every state you are assured of finding some form of attorney-client privilege, priest-penitent privilege, spousal privilege, and governmental privileges. The privilege against self-incrimination also applies throughout the United States.[1] The incidence of other privileges varies markedly.

There is constant tension between the desire to protect those values which privileges promote and the need for evidence in litigation. The general view is that the need for evidence is so great that the proponent of any privilege bears a heavy burden of persuasion.[2]

In rejecting President Nixon's claim of executive privilege in the investigation of the events that ultimately led to Mr. Nixon's resignation, Chief Justice Burger writing for the Supreme Court discussed the need for evidence as follows:

We have elected to employ an adversary system of criminal justice in which the parties contest all issues before a court of law. The need to develop all relevant facts in the adversary system is both fundamental and comprehensive. The ends of criminal justice would be defeated if judgments were to be founded on a partial or speculative presentation of the facts. The very integrity of the judicial system and public confidence in the system depend on full disclosure of all the facts, within the framework of the rules of evidence. To ensure that justice is done, it is imperative to the function of courts that compulsory process be available for the production of evidence needed either by the prosecution or by the defense.

Only recently the Court restated the ancient proposition of law, albeit in the context of a grand jury inquiry rather than a trial:[3]

"that 'the public * * * has a right to every man's evidence,' except for those persons protected by a constitutional, common-law, or statutory privilege * * * "[4]

It seems almost inconceivable today that there was a time when cases were tried without witnesses, as in fifteenth century England,[5] or on the basis of depositions, as in the same country two centuries later.[6] It is even stranger to realize that once the modern witness appeared, he was not compelled to testify; in fact he *was not welcomed.*[7] The doctrine of maintenance was most inhospitable to witnesses, providing that anyone who urged a jury to decide for one or another party to a dispute was a meddler who could be sued for his interference.[8] Except for persons

---

1. Although we prefer not to conceptualize them in this way, one may think of the rules regarding improper confessions and illegally seized evidence as rules of privilege. As constitutional rules of evidence they apply throughout the United States.

2. One should note that privileged information may be available from non-privileged sources. This fact does not mean the privilege is not serving some valuable purpose. The course of litigation may be affected even where the privileged information is otherwise available, for the burden of developing privileged information from non-privileged sources may be considerable.

3. Quoting from Branzburg v. Hayes, 408 U.S. 665, 688 (1972).

4. United States v. Nixon, 418 U.S. 683, 709 (1974).

5. See J. Thayer, A Preliminary Treatise on Evidence at The Common Law 122–34 (1898).

6. See 8 Wigmore § 2190, at 62.

7. Id. at 63 (emphasis in original).

8. See Thayer, supra note 5, at 126–29.

sought out by the jury or persons such as servants, counsel, or tenants "bound to be" with a party, those wanting to testify were regarded as nuisances.[9] The demise of this attitude is marked by the Statute of Elizabeth in 1562–63, which required testimony from all persons served with process and a tender of expenses. Until the seventeenth century, England prevented accused criminals from introducing any witnesses,[10] and rules forbidding testimony by parties and those having a pecuniary or proprietary interest in the lawsuit endured long after that.[11] It is no wonder that litigation (even criminal litigation) turned more on argument than on fact.[12]

Today expectations are quite different. Almost all the rules which disqualified witnesses have disappeared, replaced by the idea that anyone with relevant information has a responsibility to testify. Claimed exemptions from this responsibility are regarded with suspicion.

More than a third of a century ago the eminent Professor Edmund M. Morgan wrote:

If a party is entitled to present as a witness any person having communicable relevant information, should any such person have a privilege not to testify at all, or not to testify concerning specified matters? Or should a party have a privilege to prevent him from testifying to such matters? If these questions are to be answered in the affirmative, it will be not because there is any danger that the testimony will be untrustworthy or be incapable of valuation by the trier, but rather because of a legislative or judicial conviction that the benefit to a social interest accruing from the suppression of such evidence outweighs the harm done thereby in the investigation of particular disputes.

Too often such a legislative or judicial conviction seems to be based on inadequate data or on sentiment rather than on fact. For example, judicial opinion long asserted that to permit a husband or wife to testify for or against one another would be to destroy marital harmony. Experience under statutes, some of which make spouses competent but not compellable witnesses against each other, and others of which make them both competent and compellable, has exploded this idea, but it still remains the foundation of the rule privileging confidential communications between husband and wife. Likewise the theory that public health is promoted by statutes making communications between physician and patient privileged rests solely on *a priori* grounds. No statistics as to health in states where no such

---

9. Wigmore, supra note 6, at 64.

10. Id. at 67.

11. See Chapter One, supra, at note 4.

12. See Faretta v. California, 422 U.S. 806, 824 n. 21 (1975), quoting from 1 Stephen, History of the Criminal Law of England 325–26 (1883) (describing trials in the 16th and 17th centuries):

The trial would begin with accusations by counsel for the crown. The prisoner usually asked, and was granted, the privilege of answering separately each matter alleged against him:

" * * * [T]he trial became a series of excited altercations between the prisoner and the different counsel opposed to him. Every statement of counsel operated as a question to the prisoner, * * * the prisoner either admitting or denying or explaining what was alleged against him. The result was that * * * the examination of the prisoner * * * was the very essence of the trial and his answers regulated the production of the evidence * * *. As the argument proceeded the counsel [for the Crown] would frequently allege matters which the prisoner denied and called upon them to prove. The proof was usually given by reading depositions, confessions of accomplices, letters and the like * * *. When the matter had been fully inquired into * * * the presiding judge 'repeated' or summed up to the jury matters alleged against the prisoner, and the answer, given by him; and the jury gave their verdict."

privilege exists, as compared with those in states where it is recognized, can be tortured into a support for it; but the law reports and the experience of judges and lawyers furnish ample evidence that such a privilege operates to suppress the truth and to further injustice. Consequently, a thoroughgoing reformation of the law of evidence would begin with the abolition of all privileges, and then re-create only such of them as reason and experience justify.[13]

More recently, McCormick wrote:

The development of judge-made privileges virtually halted a century ago. In more recent times the attitude of commentators, whether from the bench, the bar, or the schools, has tended to view privileges from the standpoint of the hindrance to litigation resulting from their recognition. In this regard, the granting of a claim of privilege can serve only to "shut out the light" so far as the party seeking to bring the privileged matter into the lawsuit is concerned. The commentators generally advocated a narrowing of the field of privilege. * * *[14]

How have privileges managed to survive in the face of numerous attacks by scholars and judges and an historical trend that would suggest their ultimate demise? McCormick explains:

The privileges have survived largely unaffected by these winnowings of the law by eminent scholars and jurists who saw them as suppressing the truth, for it is evident that for many people, judges, lawyers and laymen, the protection of confidential communications from enforced disclosure has been thought to represent rights of privacy and security too important to relinquish to the convenience of litigants. Growing concern in recent times with the increase in official prying and snooping into the lives

of private individuals has reinforced support for the traditional privileges and no doubt aided in the creation of new ones.[15]

Professor Louisell put the case for privileges this way:

I believe that the historic privileges of confidential communication protect significant human values in the interest of the holders of the privileges, and that the fact that the existence of these guarantees sometimes results in the exclusion from a trial of probative evidence is merely a secondary and incidental feature of the privileges' vitality. These convictions contrast with much recent thinking which regards the privileges chiefly from the viewpoint of their exclusionary function in litigation, and deprecates their social and moral significance and worth. It is my opinion that the current analysis of the privileges is unsatisfactory and is contributing to confusion in judicial opinions, notably in federal cases.

Experience in the practice of law and the limited comparative law study I have been able to accomplish to date seem to confirm my convictions. The privileges apparently are widely accepted in European law and generally in western society; possibly also in eastern legal traditions. In European legal thought emphasis is placed upon the moral importance of refraining from coercion of witnesses in matters of conscience; such coercion, in the face of conflicting concepts of loyalty and duty, is considered to put witnesses in an intolerable position, resulting as to some in the likelihood of perjury. * * *

* * *

* * * Anglo-American analysis commonly proceeds from the premise that recognition of the privileges consti-

13. Some Observations Concerning A Model Code of Evidence, 89 U.Pa.L.Rev. 145, 150–51 (1940).

14. McCormick § 77, at 156.

15. Id. at 157.

tutes a perpetual threat to the ascertainment of truth in litigation. Assuming for present purposes the validity of this premise (which should be further tested by comparative law inquiry), it is nevertheless submitted that there are things even more important to human liberty than accurate adjudication. One of them is the right to be left by the state unmolested in certain human relations. At least, there is no violence to history, logic or common sense in a legislative judgment to that effect. It is the historic judgment of the common law, as it apparently is of European law and is generally in western society, that whatever handicapping of the adjudicatory process is caused by recognition of the privileges, it is not too great a price to pay for secrecy in certain communicative relations—husband-wife, client-attorney, and penitent-clergyman.

Therefore, to conceive of the privileges merely as exclusionary rules, is to start out on the wrong road and, except by happy accident, to reach the wrong destination. They are, or rather by the chance of litigation may become, exclusionary rules; but this is incidental and secondary. Primarily they are a right to be let alone, a right to unfettered freedom, in certain narrowly prescribed relationships, from the state's coercive or supervisory powers and from the nuisance of its eavesdropping. Even when thrown into the lap of litigation, they are not the property of the adversaries as such; even in litigation, they may be exclusively the property of perfectly neutral persons who wish to preserve despite litigation, just as they preserved prior to litigation, their right to be left alone in their confidences. " * * * The privilege is that the confidential matter be not revealed, not that it be not used against the holder of the privilege or any other. * * *"

It may be that Wigmore, despite his monumental contribution to the law of privileges, has conduced to the current confusion by his emphasis on strictly utilitarian bases for the privileges—bases which are sometimes highly conjectural and defy scientific validation. It will be remembered that he predicates four fundamental conditions necessary to establish a privilege as an exception to the general liability of all persons to testify fully on all facts in a judicial proceeding:

(1) The communications must originate in a *confidence* that they will not be disclosed;

(2) This element of *confidentiality must be essential* to the full and satisfactory maintenance of the relation between the parties;

(3) The *relation* must be one which in the opinion of the community ought to be sedulously *fostered*; and

(4) The *injury* that would inure to the relation by the disclosure of the communications must be *greater than the benefit* thereby gained for the correct disposal of litigation.

* * *

If it will help clarify thinking about the nature of the privileges, let us by all means use terminology appropriate to describe protection for significant human freedoms. The privileges are guarantees for the benefit of their holders; they exist from the moment of their inception in the confidential communication; they normally survive all the vicissitudes of life save only waiver by the owner; they survive even his death. The law will protect them at all stages of their existence. If they are in the form of written documents, the law will protect them against theft, trespass, subpoena, or other infringement; if oral, from all types of seizure to which such are susceptible: coercion, physical or psychological, trickery or fraud. If the holder becomes involved in litigation, a new type of attack on his privilege may or may not be made, in the discretion of his adversary. But if the attack is made, if the infringing question is propounded, the law through the judge will continue its protection by now affirmatively enveloping the holder in a cloak of silence. Realization that all this protection is for the holder of the privilege as such, regardless of whether or not in litigation he becomes an adversary or neutral witness, perhaps most keenly focuses up that the exclusionary feature of the privileges, far from defining them, is only an incident of their vitality. It is also noteworthy that, whether or not evidence rules primarily exclusionary in nature, such as the hearsay rule, are attributable to the jury trial, the composition of the tribunal has nothing to do with the privileges. It is equally important to prevent disclosure in a judge or jury trial, an administrative hearing, deposition or other discovery proceeding, or any other procedure whatsoever. Of course the privileges can be waived by the holder; but so can an automobile be sold, given away, abandoned or destroyed; so can realty be deliberately conveyed or let go for taxes.[16]

In a similar vein, Professor Krattenmaker has made these comments:

Privacy * * * is not merely secrecy but also involves the voluntary and secure control one possesses over communication of information about oneself; a person locked in a closet against his will may have secrecy but is unlikely to be enjoying privacy. Simple secrecy is in no sense a valuable right. What makes privacy both a distinct concept and a valuable right is the fact that it is voluntary and that it includes a secured ability to control by oneself how much information about oneself is disseminated and the scope and circumstances of its communication.

The rejection of a claim of privilege destroys the claimant's control over the breadth of the audience receiving personal information as well as his control over the timing and conditions of its release. Clearly then, limitations on testimonial privileges are invasions of privacy.

* * *

Professor Alan Westin has catalogued those social goals that are furthered by securing to all citizens a right to control the communication of knowledge about themselves. First, recognition of a right to privacy serves to promote and protect personal autonomy. * * *

Secondly, privacy provides a context for necessary emotional release. As society grows ever more complex and open, the individual has a greater need for respite from his public activities. * * *

Third, "[e]very individual needs to integrate his experiences into a meaningful pattern and to exert his individuality on events. To carry on such self-evaluation, privacy is essential." * * *

Fourth, the right of privacy permits citizens to engage in limited and protected communication. Confidences and intimacies can be shared with those who are trusted, and, equally important, distances can be erected as shields from premature or too widespread dissemination of information. * * *

[P]rivacy is further an end in itself—an essential condition of political liberty and our very humanity.[17]

Despite these eloquent statements on the relationship between testimonial privileges and a general value of privacy, you will see when we discuss the specific priv-

16. Confidentiality, Conformity and Confusion: Privileges in Federal Court Today, 31 Tulane L.Rev. 100, 110–11, 113–14 (1956).

17. Testimonial Privileges in Federal Courts: An Alternative to The Proposed Federal Rules of Evidence, 62 Geo.L.J. 61, 86–88 (1973).

ileges that Wigmore's more "pragmatic" analysis generally predominates.[18] In the dominant analysis privacy is valued not as an end in itself, but rather as a crucial factor in promoting relationships that society seeks to foster. The difference between privacy as an end and privacy as a means has important implications for decisions to create or limit privileges. And, for the most part privilege claims have not fared well in the past few years, especially in judicial decisions as the following commentary notes:[19]

> Recently, confidentiality has suffered a number of defeats in clashes with other values. As a result, it now seems that new privileges are not likely to be created, and established privileges are likely to be contracted.

* * *

The difficulty in identifying with precision the harm caused by incorrectly deciding a privilege claim also contributes to the judicial erosion of evidentiary privileges. To sustain the privilege claim is to deny a particular litigant specific evidence that she claims might produce a different judgment. To reject the privilege claim is to pose a more speculative threat of future harm.[19]

The preceding chapters focus almost exclusively on the trial process. The touchstone for evaluating rules of evidence has been their implications for the fact-finding process. Now you must focus your attention more broadly. You must recognize that courts, litigants, and legal disputes represent but one aspect of life, and that the costs to society of improving the adjudicatory process may outweigh any benefits. The questions for you to ponder with respect to each existing or proposed privilege are, "What are the costs?" and "What are the benefits?"

---

18. When we use the term "pragmatic" to refer to a justification for privileges, we are using it to mean "instrumental" or "goal directed." As we shall see, privileges are commonly justified and criticized in terms of the likelihood that they will have certain specific effects on particular social relationships. It is this approach to privileges that we refer to as the "pragmatic" or "instrumental" analysis.

19. Saltzburg, Privileges and Professionals: Lawyers and Psychiatrists, 66 Va.L.Rev. 597, 599 & n. 9 (1980). This point is expanded as follows:

> When assessing privilege claims, courts have had difficulty distinguishing two questions: (1) what information would exist if no privilege were recognized, and (2) once information is created in a particular case, would disclosure harm the creator of the information more than nondisclosure would harm litigants seeking evidence and impair the factfinder's ability to function? See In re Farber, 78 N.J. 259, 394 A.2d 330 (1978). In *Farber*, a news reporter had written stories concerning a doctor whom the reporter suspected of poisoning some of his patients. On the basis of the information in the stories, a prosecutor indicted the doctor. The defendant doctor wanted to subpoena the material gathered by the news reporter. The news reporter refused to honor the subpoena, because he had promised his sources that their identities would be kept confidential. If a court focuses on the second question posed above, it easily could find that the harm to the doctor of not seeing the information is greater than the harm to any particular person whose identity might be revealed as a source of information. The proper question, however, might be the first one: What will happen the next time a news reporter goes out to make an investigation?

> In dealing with privilege claims courts should focus on the ex ante issue: To what extent will the privilege promote the creation of information that might otherwise not exist? If the court focuses only on the ex post question—i.e., after information already has been created, what are the respective harms in a particular case of disclosure and nondisclosure—the court ignores the crucial aspect of privileges, which is the promoting of information-sharing and experimentation in the future, when others will think about whether to assist in the creation of information.

Id. at 600 n. 9.

Problem VIII-1. New privileges are often proposed. **Would you favor any of the privileges described below? What factors would you want to weigh in deciding whether to create a new privilege? Is there any additional information which you would like to have? Is this information currently available? If a privilege is desirable, on what basis does one choose between an absolute privilege forbidding all testimony relating to privileged information regardless of the circumstances and a qualified privilege which might not apply to certain information or in all situations?**

A. News reporters claim that they must often give sources a promise of confidentiality in order to elicit important information. Indeed, even if explicit promises are not given, an unspoken understanding may be thought to exist. Reporters feel that if they are compelled to reveal the identity of individuals giving them information in confidence, their sources will dry up. **Should there be a privilege to protect the identity of sources promised confidentiality or the identity of sources generally?** Reporters also receive a good deal of information "off the record." This information often helps them to understand the background of a story or to develop leads to on the record sources. **Should reporters be privileged to refuse to reveal the contents of off the record information? Does it matter if the identify of the off the record informant is known?**

B. In a number of cities throughout the United States, centers have been established to shelter drug addicts, runaways, pregnant teenagers and other troubled individuals. Most such centers engage in informal counseling and often intensive individual or group therapy sessions are available for the "guests". **Should information gained in informal counseling or in therapy sessions be privileged? Should the identity of the guests at such establishments be privileged?**

C. At times a party will seek to put the best friend of an opposing party on the stand. Honest testimony in these circumstances may strain even a close friendship. The best friend may be called upon to reveal information given in the strictest confidence. The temptation to perjury is obvious. **Should there be a privilege which enables an individual to keep his best friend from testifying against him? Should there be a privilege which enables an individual to prevent his best friend from testifying to anything the friend has learned from the individual in confidence engendered by the friendship?**

SECTION II. ATTORNEY-CLIENT PRIVILEGE

A. BASIC JUSTIFICATIONS

The attorney-client privilege, its roots extending to Roman law, is the oldest of the existing privileges for confidential communications. Until the end of the 18th century, the privilege was justified by its relationship to the honor of attorneys:

"He [the attorney] is not bound to make answer for things which may disclose the secrets of his clients (sic) cause." [20]

"After the retainer, they [attorneys] are considered as the same person with their clients and are trusted with their secrets, which without a breach of confidence cannot be revealed, and without such sort of confidence there could be no trust or dependence on any man * * *." [21]

In the early 19th century, a new justification emerged:

This was the theory that claims and disputes which may lead to litigation can most justly and expeditiously be handled by practised experts, namely lawyers, and that such experts can act effectively only if they are fully advised of the facts by the parties whom they represent. Such full disclosure will be promoted if the client knows that what he tells his lawyer cannot, over his objection, be extorted in court from the lawyer's lips. [22]

Both the emerging justification and the one it replaced were attacked by the English lawyer-philosopher Jeremy Bentham:

When, in consulting with a law adviser, attorney or advocate, a man has confessed his delinquency, or disclosed some fact which, if stated in court, might tend to operate in proof of it, such law adviser is not to be suffered to be examined as to any such point. The law adviser is neither to be compelled, nor so much as suffered, to betray the trust thus reposed in him. Not suffered? Why not? Oh, because to betray a trust is treachery; and an act of treachery is an immoral act.

An immoral sort of act, is that sort of act, the tendency of which is, in some way or other, to lessen the quantity of happiness in society. In what way does the supposed cause in question tend to the production of any such effect? The conviction and punishment of the defendant, he being guilty, is by the supposition an act the tendency of which, upon the whole, is beneficial to society. Such is the proposition which for this purpose must be assumed. Some offences (it will be admitted by every body) are of that sort and quality, that the acts by which they are punished do possess this beneficial tendency. Let the offence in question be of the number: it is of such only as are of that number that I speak. The good, then, that results from the conviction and punishment, in the case in question, is out of dispute: where, then, is the additional evil of it when produced by the cause in question? Nowhere. The evil consists in the punishment: but the punishment a man undergoes is not greater when the evidence on which the conviction and punishment are grounded happens to come out of the mouth of a law adviser of his, than if it had happened to come out of his own mouth, or that of a third person.

But if such confidence, when reposed, is permitted to be violated, and if this be known, (which, if such be the law, it will be), the consequence will be, that no such confidence will be reposed. Not reposed?—Well: and if it be not, wherein will consist the mischief? The man by the supposition is guilty; if not, by the supposition there is nothing to betray: let the law adviser

---

20. Waldron v. Ward, 82 Eng.Rep. 853 (K. B. 1654).

21. Gilbert, Evidence 138 (London ed. 1756), quoted in 8 Wigmore § 2290, at 543 n. 3. See generally, Radin, The Privilege of Confidential Communication Between Lawyer and Client, 16 Calif.L.Rev. 487 (1928).

Hazard, An Historical Perspective on the Attorney-Client Privilege, 66 Calif.L.Rev. 1061 (1978), for a discussion of the development of the privilege to cover legal advice when litigation was not pending or necessarily contemplated.

22. McCormick § 87, at 175.

say every thing he has heard, every thing he can have heard from his client, the client cannot have any thing to fear from it. That it will often happen that in the case supposed no such confidence will be reposed, is natural enough: the first thing the advocate or attorney will say to his client, will be,—Remember that, whatever you say to me, I shall be obliged to tell, if asked about it. What, then, will be the consequence? That a guilty person will not in general be able to derive quite so much assistance from his law adviser, in the way of concerting a false defence, as he may do at present.

Except the prevention of such pernicious confidence, of what other possible effect can the rule for the requisition of such evidence be productive? Either of none at all, or of the conviction of delinquents, in some instances in which, but for the lights thus obtained, they would not have been convicted. But in this effect, what imaginable circumstance is there that can render it in any degree pernicious and undesirable? None whatever. The conviction of delinquents is the very end of penal justice.[23]

———————

Many have tried to answer Bentham. One commentator marshals the arguments of Dean Wigmore and Professor Radin in aid of his own:[24]

* * * It has been said that this argument "cannot really be met as long as we keep on the level from which Bentham views the subject." But this is the level of pure abstraction, and the matter is not so simple as Bentham makes it appear. Furthermore, the context of the privilege in actual practice must be considered. For example, there may be a greater problem in counsel's obtaining the whole story once a person has summoned the courage to consult with counsel. Then, there is the problem of the client's feelings, the relation between the client and his lawyer as a counsellor and advocate, and finally, the position of the lawyer in the eyes of the public. * * *

* * * Dean Wigmore accepted this position and also answered Bentham by raising four objections to the latter's abstract oversimplification of the problem, to wit:

1. In civil cases there is often no hard-and-fast line between guilt and innocence.

2. In most civil cases it does not happen that all of the facts on one side are wholly right and all of those on the other side are wholly wrong. There is a mixture on both sides in varying proportions. Both plaintiff and defendant may have fear of disclosing some part of his case. The party having the better case would be deterred from seeking legal advice, and this is not good for the administration of justice.

3. To deter a wrongdoer from seeking legal advice is not an unmixed good. It depends upon the ethics of the bar. Counsel can always decline a case, persuade his client to abandon it, or settle the case when some moral claim is present. Moreover, if the privilege were abolished, there are ways in which a guilty party could derive quite as much assistance from his legal adviser as at present.

4. Contrary to Bentham the consideration of "treachery" is important. The position of counsel would be most disagreeable if he were forced to testify against his client. It would be disturbing to his peace of mind and would create an unhealthy moral state.

23. J. Bentham, 5 Rationale of Judicial Evidence 302–04 (J.S.Mill ed. 1827).

24. Gardner, A Re-Evaluation of the Attorney-Client Privilege, Pt. 1, 8 Vill.L.Rev. 279, 304–06 (1963).

Wigmore added two other points: (1) that in criminal cases, if the privilege were abolished, the prosecution might tend to rely on defense counsel's testimony to the neglect of other and better sources of truth, while the defendant would not be deterred from seeking counsel but rather from disclosing incriminating facts; and (2) that the loss to truth is comparatively small in modern times, since the parties themselves can now be examined.[25]

The late Professor Radin deemed that the main argument made by Professor Wigmore in support of the privilege is that a policy favoring frank disclosure discourages litigation.[26] Professor Radin then proceeded to show, by the use of a hypothetical example, that this result does not necessarily follow from a policy promotive of frank disclosure. But he found a justification for the privilege in a broader if more nebulous principle, which can perhaps best be described as the right of the client to command the attorney's loyalty. * * *

Professor Saltzburg has made the following argument for the privilege:

The lawyer plays a special role in the legal system. The law has been the special province of lawyers and judges for a long time. Although ancient, cumbersome procedures frequently have been replaced with more efficient processes, laws also have become more complicated as they have become more numerous. Expertise still is needed to achieve the expected efficiencies of modern process, to protect the legal rights of parties, and to discover when and how to avoid litigation.

Although a lay person can read law and gather legal knowledge to represent herself, most observers recognize that a nonprofessional, especially if involved in formal litigation, will have better success with a lawyer's assistance. The United States Supreme Court has acknowledged the necessity of legal representation by recognizing a constitutionally based right to counsel in felony and serious misdemeanor criminal cases. Although no similar right has been recognized in civil cases, legal service agencies for the poor and burgeoning prepaid legal service plans for middle class persons evidence the importance of counsel. No reasonable person voluntarily would place substantial property at risk in a legal dispute without seeking the assistance of counsel, nor invest substantial personal resources without seeking legal advice on the legitimacy of the enterprise or the risk of future liability. The need for an attorney both in and out of court is recognized widely by parties and nonparties alike.

With the importance of the lawyer to the client in mind, the justifications for the attorney-client privilege become clearer. To imagine what the relationship between an attorney and her client would be like if no privilege existed, suppose an attorney began a relationship with a client by giving her the equivalent of *Miranda* warnings. An attorney would tell the client that any-

25. 8 Wigmore § 2291. At common law parties were at one time not allowed to testify on their own behalf and had the privilege of refusing to testify at the instance of a party opponent. Wigmore suggests that it is impossible to find an adequate explanation for the availability of the privilege. It was not recognized in chancery practice, so it apparently did not reflect the notion that people could never be compelled to testify against their own interests. This privilege coupled with the attorney's privilege effectively rendered conversations between attorney and client confidential. See 8 Wigmore § 2217.

26. But see Morgan, Suggested Remedy for Obstructions to Expert Testimony by Rules of Evidence, 10 U.Chi.L.Rev. 285, 288–90 (1943). See also Louisell, supra note 16, at 112.

thing the client says could be used against her and that the lawyer might have to testify about the statement. This obviously seems to be a counter-productive beginning to a relationship in which one person renders personal help to another. More important, however, without advice on the advantages or disadvantages of making particular statements, a client who knows nothing about the law cannot decide confidently whether to talk with the lawyer. Even the *Miranda* warnings given to an accused in a criminal case include a warning about the right to counsel *before* making a statement. The lawyer cannot advise the client unless she knows the reason for the client's visit; thus, the client must talk before the lawyer can advise.

A *Miranda*-type warning could affect the attorney-client relationship dramatically. Although one cannot predict how many clients would refuse to talk to an attorney following a *Miranda* warning, some would be more sensitive about their privacy than others and thus would refuse to talk. Many who would refuse to talk might have valid claims and defenses. Advocates of privileges recognize that one naturally fears baring her soul to a stranger, especially if the stranger does not clearly share her interests. Good persons (or persons with good claims) may shrink from the attorney who gives *Miranda* warnings as quickly as bad persons (or persons with bad claims).

Even if the *Miranda*-type warning would not deter the client completely from talking to her attorney, it still might inhibit communication. A client does not arrive at the lawyer's office with relevant facts sorted, properly ordered, or distinguished from irrelevant facts. A client is not always sure what she knows and how certain she is of her beliefs. To determine accurately the client's problem, a lawyer must gain the client's

trust. Intimate, personal details otherwise may not be revealed, and the client's uncertainties about her problem may be concealed. A client is more likely to share information openly if she knows that a slip of the tongue will not be used against her in court. With this confidence, the client may overcome her concern about the particular words she uses, and communicate everything, including inconsistencies, that she knows or feels about her problem. The attorney probably will be better able to ask a penetrating question of a nervous, off-balance client if the attorney is not concerned that she may have to testify later about a premature, ill-considered statement she elicited from a vulnerable client who trusted the lawyer to protect her.

Requiring an attorney to testify in a case in which her client was a party would present interesting procedural problems. Should the client retain a second lawyer to represent her while the first lawyer testifies? Would the second lawyer then be called to testify about the client's statements concerning her relationship with the first lawyer? Could the first lawyer continue to represent the client after testifying? If not, would this nonprivilege system thus favor lawyers with "poor memories" about their client's statements? Would these lawyers be more or less scrupulous than the lawyers in whom we take the most pride today? Would this system also disadvantage clients whose lawyers seek the truth most vigorously and in its fullest particulars? These problems are litigation-oriented, and demonstrate that a client probably would find it difficult to communicate with a second lawyer after she had a bad experience with a first one.

* * *

The attorney-client privilege has remained popular for another reason that may not be apparent from many court decisions. In assessing a claim of privilege, some commentators analyze the attorney-client privilege as though it resulted in a clear loss of information that otherwise would be available to a court. This analysis, however, misconstrues a key point about the privilege—the privilege is intended to generate information. The privilege creates a zone of privacy in which an attorney and client can create information that did not exist before and might not exist otherwise. Because the same information might not exist were it not for the privilege, any loss of information when the privilege is upheld may be more imagined than real. Without the privilege, there might be less information, because the communications between attorney and client would be changed.[27]

B. THE PRIVILEGE IN DETAIL

These arguments, pro and con, address the question whether conversations between attorneys and clients should, in principle, be privileged. It is difficult, however, to evaluate the strengths and weaknesses of these arguments in the abstract, for the attorney-client privilege, like other privileges, is quite specific. Some conversations between attorneys and clients are protected by the privilege while others are not. You will see when we look at the privilege in detail that the pragmatic view of the privilege has prevailed. Generally speaking, the privilege applies where it is thought to promote attorney-client communication about legal matters and not otherwise. Later, you will find that a similar instrumental orientation is evident in most other privileges.

We shall draw on proposed Article V in the version of the Federal Rules approved by the Supreme Court and transmitted to Congress for our example of this and most other privileges. None of these privileges has been enacted into law at the federal level. Some aspects of proposed Article V proved to be quite controversial, as did the notion that Congress should legislate about matters so clearly related to substantive state policies. In the end Congress abdicated. The enacted version of Article V contains only one rule, FRE 501:

> Except as otherwise required by the Constitution of the United States or provided by Act of Congress or in rules prescribed by the Supreme Court pursuant to statutory authority, the privilege of a witness, person, government, State, or political subdivision thereof shall be governed by the principles of the common law as they may be interpreted by the courts of the United States in the light of reason and experience. However, in civil actions and proceedings, with respect to an element of a claim or defense as to which State law supplies the rule of decision, the privilege of a witness, person, government, State, or political subdivision thereof shall be determined in accordance with State law.[28]

---

27. Saltzburg, supra note 19, at 605–610.

28. **Congress also added a new section to Title 28 of the United States Code:**

"§ 2076. Rules of evidence

"The Supreme Court of the United States shall have the power to prescribe amendments to the Federal Rules of Evidence. Such amendments shall not take effect until they have been reported to Congress by the Chief Justice at or after the beginning of a regular session of Congress but not later than the first day of May, and until the expiration of one hundred and eighty days after they have been so reported; but if either House of Congress within that time shall by resolution disapprove any amendment so reported it shall not take effect. The effective date of any amendment so reported may be deferred by either House of Congress to a later date or until approved by Act of Congress. Any rule

Despite Congressional rejection of the specific rules, they are useful aids to analysis. The proposed privileges are the product of years of thought by judges, lawyers, and law teachers, who set out to review and revise the law in this area. Moreover, the Supreme Court accepted the proposed rules of privilege, suggesting that it found them satisfactory. In this chapter we look to these proposed rules for examples whenever it makes sense to do so. We begin with the recommended rule of attorney-client privilege.

Proposed Rule (PFRE) 503: LAWYER-CLIENT PRIVILEGE

(a) *Definitions*. As used in this rule:

(1) A "client" is a person, public officer, or corporation, association, or other organization or entity, either public or private, who is rendered professional legal services by a lawyer, or who consults a lawyer with a view to obtaining professional legal services from him.

(2) A "lawyer" is a person authorized, or reasonably believed by the client to be authorized, to practice law in any state or nation.

(3) A "representative of the lawyer" is one employed to assist the lawyer in the rendition of professional legal services.

(4) A communication is "confidential" if not intended to be disclosed to third persons other than those to whom disclosure is in furtherance of the rendition of professional legal services to the client or those reasonably necessary for the transmission of the communication.

(b) *General rule of privilege*. A client has a privilege to refuse to disclose and to prevent any other person from disclosing confidential communications made for the purpose of facilitating the rendition of professional legal services to the client, (1) between himself or his representative and his lawyer or his lawyer's representative, or (2) between his lawyer and the lawyer's representative, or (3) by him or his lawyer to a lawyer representing another in a matter of common interest, or (4) between representatives of the client or beween the client and a representative of the client, or (5) between lawyers representing the client.

(c) *Who may claim the privilege*. The privilege may be claimed by the client, his guardian or conservator, the personal representative of a deceased client, or the successor, trustee, or similar representative of a corporation, association, or other organization, whether or not in existence. The person who was the lawyer at the time of the communication may claim the privilege but only on behalf of the client. His authority to do so is presumed in the absence of evidence to the contrary.

(d) *Exceptions*. There is no privilege under this rule:

(1) Furtherance of crime or fraud. If the services of the lawyer were sought or obtained to enable or aid anyone to commit or plan to commit what the client

Note the special provision for privilege rules. Congress' action leaves the role of the courts slightly confused because the Rule permits the development of a law or privileges on a common law basis while the statute restricts the Court's power to change privileges. In Trammel v. United States, 445 U.S. 40 (1980), the Court concluded that the statute restricted only its rulemaking, not its adjudicatory power.

knew or reasonably should have known to be a crime or fraud; or

(2) Claimants through same deceased client. As to a communication relevant to an issue between parties who claim through the same deceased client, regardless of whether the claims are by testate or intestate succession or by *inter vivos* transaction; or

(3) Breach of duty by lawyer or client. As to a communication relevant to an issue of breach of duty by the lawyer to his client or by the client to his lawyer; or

(4) Document attested by lawyer. As to a communication relevant to an issue concerning an attested document to which the lawyer is an attesting witness; or

(5) Joint clients. As to a communication relevant to a matter of common interest between two or more clients if the communication was made by any of them to a lawyer retained or consulted in common, when offered in an action between any of the clients.

———

The privilege belongs to the client. He may refuse to disclose confidential communications made for the purpose of securing legal advice or services (as specified in subdivision (b)) and he may prevent others from disclosing such communications. Or he may waive the privilege, in which case those who were parties to the conversation have no right to refuse to testify to what they heard or said. In these particulars the proposed rule tracks the common law.

Over the years, the common law courts have grappled with a number of specific questions in determining the scope of the attorney-client privilege. Generally speaking, the proposed federal privilege codifies dominant common law positions. Do communications made to a lawyer

through her secretary remain privileged? Yes, a secretary qualifies as a "representative of a lawyer" under PFRE 503(a)(3). The same paragraph applies when one lawyer relates a client's story to another lawyer in order to secure more expert advice. Does the privilege apply if the proposed attorney turns out to be a charlatan unqualified for the practice of law? Yes, under paragraph (a)(2) the privilege will apply so long as the client reasonably believes he was talking to a lawyer. Does the privilege apply if the lawyer, after hearing the client's story, wants no part of the case? Paragraph (a)(1) makes it clear that it does. In the client's absence may the attorney claim the privilege? Paragraph (c) makes it clear that she can. Indeed, unless the lawyer knows the client intends to waive the privilege, it is the lawyer's ethical duty to assert the privilege on the client's behalf. The judge may call the lawyer's attention to this duty. Are the lawyer's lips sealed after the client dies? Generally they are, for under paragraph (c) the representative of a deceased client may claim the privilege, but the paragraph (d)(2) exception for those claiming through the same deceased client abrogates the privilege in the situation where it might otherwise be most commonly invoked. There is an assumption in this circumstance that the client probably would have wanted his confidences revealed in order to increase the likelihood that his testamentary intent will be understood and respected.

The privilege applies only to communications made for the purpose of securing *legal* services because the right to secure legal services is considered fundamental and because a client has special reason to fear that statements made to secure legal services might become legally damaging admissions. Thus, these are communications that might not be made without a privilege. When lawyers are consulted as family friends, business advisors, or political consultants, the privilege is inapplicable. It is also inapplicable to information given to lawyers that relates to matters clearly outside the scope of the legal services for which they have been consulted. Since such statements are not likely to have legal significance they are likely to be made whether or not a privilege protects them, and if they are not made a person's ability to secure legal representation has not been hampered.[29] The law is wary about creating a class of people whose status renders everything said to them in confidence beyond the reach of process. The communication must be of a type that is made for a highly valued end, and the case for a privilege becomes stronger the less likely it is that that type of communication would be made absent a privilege.

On these and other points the proposed federal rule appears clear. But the rule leaves many difficult questions unanswered. Often one must look to the common law in order to interpret the proposed rule. What, for example, qualifies as a confidential communication? Obviously oral or written assertions will qualify. But suppose a client, instead of talking about a scar on his stomach, opens his shirt, or, instead of telling his attorney what he has done with his gun, points to the gun in its hiding place; are these protected communications? Some courts have held that they are, for such gestures are meant to convey information to the lawyer's eyes only. These courts rule differently when the lawyer observes what others are free to see. A lawyer may be forced to testify to her observation that her client has a scar on his forehead or walks with a limp, even if these facts are relevant to the services for which she has been hired. Such facts are considered public facts; they cannot be conveyed in confidence. Some scholars have questioned whether observations of

counsel ever should be privileged.[30] As you examine the attorney-client privilege problems in this chapter, you should think about whether the rationales that have been offered for the privilege support treating observations as privileged. Some courts have required attorneys to answer questions about the apparent mental state of their clients on the theory that this also is a public fact. The extension is questionable, for the client's mental condition is not open to casual observation. Only the intimacy of the lawyer-client relationship allows the attorney to make reliable judgments about mental state, and it is difficult to imagine how the attorney might be cross-examined about the basis for her conclusions without revealing the substance of privileged communications.

Courts have struggled to articulate the scope of the confidential communication concept. A recurring problem has centered on whether the facts of the lawyer-client relationship should be privileged— e.g., the name of the lawyer's client, the address the client has given, the fee arrangement, details concerning the transfer of funds, and information about when the lawyer and client have met.

Consider, for instance, the identity of the client. There is a general doctrine that the identity of the client is not protected. Yet, in some cases it is. A good example is *In re* Kaplan.[31]

In *Kaplan,* an attorney representing a group of fruit buyers in a New York neighborhood was informed by one member of the association that while its members could not find parking in the neighborhood and could not arrange parking with the city, large trailer trucks parked illegally for long periods of time without any difficulty. The informing member, after

---

29. This point is explored in Saltzburg, Communications Falling Within the Attorney-Client Privilege, 66 Iowa L.Rev. 811, 817 (1981). We shall not discuss every point which the proposed rule makes clear. If a

matter is not mentioned you may assume that the proposed rule tracks the common law.

30. See, e.g., Saltzburg, supra note 29.

31. 8 N.Y.2d 214, 203 N.Y.S.2d 836, 168 N.E.2d 660 (1960).

investigating the matter, told the lawyer that the trucks had obtained their neighborhood parking privileges by paying off two powerful politicians. The lawyer who had conveyed this information to the heads of certain city departments was jailed for contempt when he refused to reveal his client's name to the New York City Commissioner of Investigation. New York's highest court reversed the contempt citation. It wrote:

> [H]ere the client's communication had already been divulged to the Commissioner and it was the client's name that deserved and needed protection for fear of reprisals, etc. Since there was no reason to doubt that the informant was a client of appellant, it was unnecessary to investigate that relationship. Since the client's communication to appellant was made in the aid of a public purpose to expose wrongdoing and not * * * to conceal wrongdoing, the seal of secrecy should cover the client's name, so long as his information was made available to the public authorities. The contary holding serves no right end, contravenes the ancient policy [of the attorney-client privilege] and embarrasses and penalizes a lawyer for taking a course consistent with his professional and civil responsibilities.

A similar issue arose in Sepler v. State.[32] In this case a woman named Judith Hyams had disappeared on September 14, 1965. The next day, an individual who was a client of two attorneys called them to seek advice on behalf of another man. The individual stated that the other man may have been involved in an abortion thought to have been performed on Ms. Hyams and wanted legal advice. The other man was then placed on the phone and gave the lawyers certain information indicating that he was to some extent implicated in the abortion and that he knew the doctor who performed it. The lawyers stated they

were not versed in criminal law and could not give any advice. Three days later, after reflecting on the matter, the lawyers telephoned Sepler, an older and more experienced lawyer, and asked him what they should do. Sepler advised them to inform the appropriate law enforcement officials and they asked Sepler to do so, but without revealing their identity. Sepler relayed the information given him to an assistant state attorney and later revealed the information that the attorneys had given him: that the individual who had called them was Dr. Herschel Gordon, that the attorneys had been told that the doctor who had arranged or performed the abortion had a name sounding "like Hilow or Hihow", and that the other man who spoke to the attorneys had a high-pitched voice, had attended the University of Pennsylvania and was thought by the attorneys to be a doctor.

Sepler was subpoenaed in a criminal investigation. He revealed everything he knew except the names of the attorney informants. For this refusal he was cited for contempt and sentenced to ten days in jail. He appealed, and the Florida Court of Appeal ruled as follows:

> The privilege relied on, though firmly established in the law of this state is not absolute and may be outweighed by public interest in the administration of justice in certain circumstances. The question presented by this case is a close one, and requires a balancing of the interests, on the one hand as to the attorney and client in their right to the protection of the privilege, and on the other hand in the public and the state for the proper administration of law and justice.
>
> * * *
>
> In the Baird case [Baird v. Koerner, 279 F.2d 623 (9th Cir. 1960)] the facts were that after the accountants and general counsel employed by certain clients

---

32. 191 So.2d 588 (Fla.App.1966).

concluded and advised them they had failed to properly report and pay amounts due on income taxes for a prior year or years, the appellant, an attorney experienced in income tax law, was employed and on his advice the client or clients made an anonymous payment of $12,706.85 to the government, through him. This was accomplished by the appellant tax lawyer forwarding a bank cashier's check for that amount with a covering letter by him explaining the same, and stating that the identity of the client-taxpayers had not been disclosed to him. No tax investigation of the clients was then in progress. In a subsequent investigation by the department appellant was called upon to disclose the identity of the accountants, the general counsel and the client. He declined to do so, basing his refusal on the attorney-client privilege. In appropriate proceedings against him which followed, a trial court approved his refusal to reveal the identity of the accountants and general counsel, but held him in contempt for refusing to identify the client or clients. The attorney appealed the portion of the order adjudging him in contempt, and the department cross-appealed from the ruling which upheld the claim of privilege against disclosing identity of the accountants and general counsel. In an extensive and well reasoned opinion the court of appeals noted the existence and purposes of the attorney-client privilege, and held it was not absolute but must yield to public interest in the administration of justice in proper circumstances, upon a balancing of the interests on consideration of the facts of each case. The appellate court held, on the facts of the Baird case, that the attorney-client privilege was to be respected, and that nondisclosure by the attorney of the identity of the client was justified and held likewise as to his refusal to reveal [the] identity of the accountants and the general counsel in that

case. The reason underlying that decision was that revealing the identity of those involved would subject the clients to income tax investigation and possible prosecution, for their admitted and disclosed nonpayment of prior taxes, although it was not shown whether their indicated guilt was such as would form a basis for criminal prosecution.

The claim of privilege is not asserted here by the attorney Sepler on the basis that revealing the identity of the lawyers would lead to an investigation or prosecution of their established client. This is so because that client's identity as Dr. Herschel Gordon was known, and it was revealed in the information given to Sepler that such client was not implicated in the Hyams matter. It does appear, however, that the unidentified other man, on whose behalf the client first called the attorneys, also stood in an attorney-client relationship with those attorneys. That client status of the other man resulted when he talked with the attorneys, revealed his situation with relation to the matter, and sought their professional aid. Therefore, that other person stands in this case in a position similar to that of the unidentified client in the Baird case. Here, as in *Baird*, denial of the attorney-client privilege would be calculated to lead to possible identification and prosecution of that unknown client based on his disclosures to the attorneys he had consulted.

An added element favoring the appellant attorney in this case is that the information he refused to disclose and for which he was held in contempt, that is, the identity of the two attorneys, did not amount to withholding information as to the crime which was under investigation by the state attorney at the time appellant was questioned. Appellant had furnished the state attorney with all information he had received bearing on the nature and reason for the girl's disappearance (other than the identity of the lawyers), including the name of their regular client, who obviously knew the other "client," and including the fact that the girl's parents could supply [the] identity of the man whom she had been seeing. Also, it appears the state attorney subsequently questioned or attempted to question the said Dr. Herschel Gordon.

* * *

We hold, therefore, that on the facts of this case the trial court should have sustained the privilege invoked by the appellant, upon a balancing of the interests in accordance with the rule announced in the Baird and Tillotson cases. Accordingly, the order appealed from is reversed.

PEARSON, Judge (dissenting).

I agree with the principle stated in the opinion that the privilege relied upon is not absolute and may be outweighed by public interest in the administration of justice in certain circumstances. I also agree that the question presented by this case required a balancing of the client's right to the privilege and the public's interest in the proper administration of law and justice.

My position is that in this case, where the investigation is into the disappearance or death of the young woman, the proper balance of interest required that the facts possessed by the appellant be made available to the investigating authorities.[33]

———

Do you agree with the balance struck by the court? Did Sepler have any obligation to disclose anything to the police? If questioned, could he have remained silent in reliance upon the privilege?

McCormick comments on cases of this sort:

One who reviews the cases in this area will be struck with the prevailing flavor of chicanery and sharp practice pervading most of the attempts to suppress the proof of professional employment, and the broader solution of a general rule of disclosure seems the one most consonant with the preservation of the high repute of the lawyer's calling. Cases may arise, however, where protection of the client's identity is conceivably in the public interest. [citing In re Kaplan][34]

Do *Baird* and *Sepler* strike you as smacking of chicanery? In cases like these, it seems that the courts, under the guise of interpreting the attorney-client privilege, are really creating a privilege akin in some cases to the informant's privilege that the government claims to protect its sources and in other cases to the immunity granted to circumvent the fifth amendment privilege against self-incrimination. By allowing lawyers to conceal their clients' identities, we allow individuals to publicize important or incriminating information without the worry that they will be adversely affected by disclosure. It may be that the legislature, rather than the court, is the proper body to decide whether such a privilege should exist. But, if the courts are to enter this area, they should focus on the desirability of this kind of protection against incrimination.

This point applies generally in the analysis of privileges. The difficult questions require policy judgments. We allow privileges because we believe that certain values should be promoted even though their advancement means a loss of evidence for the judicial process. Identifying which values deserve to be protected by privileges and when such protection is essential requires sensitivity to the host of different factual settings in which claims of privilege arise.

33. Id. at 590–92.
Lempert & Saltzburg Mod.Approach To Evid.—16

34. McCormick § 90, at 187.

Usually the attorney-client privilege is invoked to keep confidential information the client has disclosed to the lawyer. *Kaplan* was atypical because the client wanted to give information to public officials, but he wanted to do so anonymously. One decision facing the court was how to value disclosures which, like that of Kaplan's client, are apparently in the public interest. The basic choice was between encouraging such disclosures and hampering investigations conducted by official authorities.

Compare *Kaplan* with *Baird,* the income tax payment case. Did upholding the privilege serve any values other than allowing the IRS to receive money that might not otherwise have been paid? If this was the only value served, should the court have deferred to the IRS which was seeking to discover the identity of the taxpayer? Is the decision perhaps justified because if the taxpayer had not thought his identity privileged, there would have been no payment to investigate?

Sepler is different from both *Kaplan* and *Baird* because it is not clear that the client consented to any disclosures. Yet the lawyers apparently told Sepler everything their client told them, and they asked Sepler to give their information to the appropriate authorities but without revealing their identities. While the attorneys' request for ethical advice was arguably a communication to secure legal services, it is hard to characterize their request that Sepler disclose information that they had received in confidence in this fashion. What values are involved here?

It is important to remember that a client's expectation of confidentiality is protected by more than the attorney-client privilege. Two other doctrines are important.

First, the Code of Professional Responsibility imposes a duty on lawyers not to reveal client secrets or confidences. This protection is broader but more precarious than that of the privilege. It is broader because client secrets include information that the client would not want disclosed whether or not the information originated with the client or was revealed in a setting in which the privilege attaches. The protection is narrower because when secrets and confidences are not privileged, disclosure may be compelled through judicial process. There are also situations in which a lawyer is, under the Code, permitted or required to volunteer information to appropriate officials. One such situation is where disclosure is needed to thwart criminal activity likely to endanger the life of a person or to prevent serious physical harm. Many argue that where this is the case even privileged information must be disclosed.

Second, the work product concept, discussed in Chapter Two, prevents the routine discovery of information that an attorney acquires while working on a case. The degree of protection depends on the extent to which an attorney's own thoughts are embodied in the material that the adversary wants disclosed. Where an attorney's work product contains relevant information that an opponent might not otherwise have access to; e.g., statements by nonclient witnesses, disclosure may be ordered. The rationale for the work product doctrine is that in an adversary system the parties are responsible for preparing their own cases and they deserve the benefits of their thought and diligence. But this doctrine recognizes that a litigant sometimes cannot duplicate the work of the other side and that where this is the case justice may be better served if information is shared rather than kept secret by the side that discovered it. When the attorney-client privilege is properly invoked, an adversary's showing of need cannot override it. Work product protects non-privileged information—most importantly information from third parties—but its protection must give way where justice requires this.

The problem that comes next raises the "scope of privilege" issue central to *Kaplan, Baird* and *Sepler* in a somewhat different setting. Following it are six additional problems that permit you to apply the basic definition of attorney-client privilege and that reveal how important the rationale for the privilege is in the resolution of new cases.

———

Problem VIII–2. The Grundy Commission, examining vice in New York City, notes that one lawyer, Archie Andrews, handles more than a quarter of the cases in which streetwalkers are arrested for soliciting. They subpoena Andrews and ask him the following questions: Have you been personally employed by each of the alleged prostitutes you have represented in New York City courts during the past year? Who pays your fees when you represent streetwalkers charged with soliciting? Are you paid a retainer by a woman known generally as "Madame Veronica"? During the past year how much money have you received from Madame Veronica? Andrews (respectfully) declines to answer each of the above questions claiming that to do so would violate the attorney-client privilege. The Commission, according to the powers delegated to it, finds Andrews in contempt and orders him imprisoned until he responds to their questions or for sixty days, whichever comes first. Andrews appeals the order, again citing the attorney-client privilege. **How should the appellate court rule? Why?**

Assume that the appellate court rules against Andrews and lifts the stay of the sentence. Andrews answers the first question, but does not know whether he should respond to the other three. He is, in fact, paid a retainer by Madame Veronica, and this retainer amounted to $180,000 during the previous year. However, he accepted the retainer only after he assured Madame Veronica that he would keep both the fact and the amount of the retainer in the strictest confidence, and after he told her, in good faith, that if he were ever asked about his relationship with her, the attorney-client privilege would enable him to protect her identity. It is clear that Madame Veronica would not have retained Andrews but for these assurances. **How should Andrews respond to the questions pertaining to Madame Veronica? Should he choose jail?**

Problem VIII–3. Jones is charged with shooting her husband. At trial, the prosecution wishes to introduce evidence of the fact that Jones went to a noted criminal lawyer, Beeley, one hour after her husband was killed, and that prior to that visit, Beeley had never represented Jones in any matter nor had he ever been retained by Jones for any purpose. To prove these facts, the prosecution calls Beeley and asks: "Did the defendant come to your office at 1:30 p. m. on January 3, 1973 to seek legal counsel?" Jones objects to the question on the ground that her relationship with Beeley is privileged. The prosecution also asks: "Wasn't that the first time you ever met Jones?" The same objection is made. **What are the proper rulings?**

Problem VIII–4. In the above case, Wilson, an eyewitness, testifies that he saw Jones commit the murder. Beeley asks Wilson whether he talked to the prosecutor and Wilson answers, "Yes." The next questions are: "Is it not true that when you first approached the prosecutor you told him that you were not positive that you could make any identification of the perpetrator of the crime, even though you knew that the defendant had been charged with the offense and you knew her quite well? Isn't it also the case that the prosecutor advised you that someone murdered Mr. Jones, and that if it was not the defendant, then perhaps it was you, Mr. Wilson?" The prosecution objects to both questions on the ground that any advice given to the witness was given in confidence and is protected by the attorney-client privilege. **How should the court rule?** Assume that there is a motion to suppress the murder weapon, a gun, which was seized from the defendant upon her arrest. The defendant contends that there was no probable cause for the arrest and that the search and seizure made incident thereto were invalid. A police officer testifies to the circumstances surrounding the arrest. Beeley asks:

> Officer, prior to your testifying here today, did you seek legal advice from the prosecution as to the meaning of probable cause and the application of the legal definition to the facts of this case?

Once again, an objection is made on the basis of the attorney-client privilege. **What is the proper ruling?**

Problem VIII–5. Jean Prchlik is a CPA and an attorney. She is hired by Hilda Grant, a wealthy jockey, to prepare her tax return so as to minimize her tax liability. **If the State Racing Commission should call Prchlik to testify to the sources of Grant's earnings, will Grant be able to claim a privilege to prevent Prchlik from testifying to what she had learned while preparing Grant's taxes? If Prchlik gave tax advice but Grant filed her own return, does this make any difference? Assume Prchlik was a CPA but not a lawyer; would Grant be able to prevent Prchlik's testimony if Prchlik had given the same advice that a competent tax lawyer would have given?**

Problem VIII–6. Assume that Grant had been in an auto accident shortly after seeing her attorney, Prchlik, about her taxes. **If the other party to the accident sues Grant on the theory that she was drunk at the time, could they call Prchlik to the stand and ask her whether she had smelled whiskey on her client's breath? Could they ask Prchlik whether Grant's discussion of her tax matters had revealed the kind of inattention and confusion which might be associated with intoxication? Could they ask Prchlik if she had served Grant any alcoholic beverages? Do your answers to any of the above questions depend on whether Prchlik is representing Grant in the tort action?**

Problem VIII—7. Sam Tucker, a prominent attorney, will not take a case unless his potential clients' stories have been confirmed by a lie detector examination. Assume that in accordance with this policy Tucker sends Jimmy Jacobs, an accused forger, for a polygraph examination. **If the government seeks to question the polygraph examiner at trial, may Jacobs claim the attorney-client privilege to prevent the examiner from describing the ex-**

amination?   Could the privilege be claimed if the examiner was asked only two questions: "Did you administer a polygraph examination to Mr. Jacobs," and "Did you conclude Mr. Jacobs was lying"?   Do your answers to these questions depend on whether Tucker had accepted Jacobs as a client?   If Jacobs had not been indicted at the time of the examination but had approached Tucker fearing indictment, could he claim the attorney-client privilege to prevent the examiner from describing the examination to a grand jury?   If Jacobs knew of Tucker's policy and sought out the examiner before consulting Tucker, would this make a difference?

Problem VIII–8.   Assume that in the previous question Tucker had told the examiner when he sent Jacobs for the examination, "I want you to be particularly careful with this examination.   I am convinced Jacobs is telling the truth, and I intend to create new law in this case by establishing a precedent that defendants have the right to introduce polygraph evidence which exonerates them."   **Should this affect the court's ruling on whether the polygraph examiner may be called by the government and questioned about the test he administered to Jacobs?**

———

C.   PHYSICAL EVIDENCE

Does the receipt of physical evidence qualify as the receipt of a communication? The general rule is that any physical evidence which could be subpoenaed if it were in the hands of the client may be subpoenaed from the attorney.   If this were not the rule, parties could use their attorneys to hide evidence under their control.   Related to this is the obligation of attorneys not to participate in schemes to destroy or to conceal evidence.

These principles seem simple enough, but they can cause enormous difficulties for lawyers.   The next two cases are examples.

STATE EX REL. SOWERS v. OLWELL

Supreme Court of Washington, 1964.
64 Wash.2d 828, 394 P.2d 681.

DONWORTH, JUSTICE.   May an attorney refuse to produce, at a coroner's inquest, material evidence of a crime by asserting the attorney-client privilege or by claiming the privilege against self-incrimination on behalf of his client?   These are the issues raised in this appeal.

September 18, 1962, a coroner's inquest was held for the purpose of investigating the circumstances surrounding the death of John W. Warren. Several days prior to the date of the inquest, appellate was served with a subpoena duces tecum, which said, in part:

" *   *   *   bring with you all knives in your possession and under your control relating to Henry LeRoy Gray, Gloria Pugh or John W. Warren."

Thereafter, at the coroner's inquest the following exchange took place between a deputy prosecutor and appellant:

" *   *   * "

"Q.   Now, Mr. Olwell, did you comply with that?   [Subpoena]

"A.   I do not have any knives in my possession that belong to Gloria Pugh, or to John W. Warren, and I did not comply with it as to the question of whether or not I have a knife belonging to Henry LeRoy Gray.

"Q.   Now, I would ask you, do you have a knife in your possession or under your control relating to or belonging to Henry LeRoy Gray?

"A.   I decline to answer that because of the confidential relationship of attorney and client; and to answer the question would be a violation of my oath as an attorney.

" *   *   * "

"Q.   And for the record, Mr. Olwell, in the event you do have in your possession a knife or knives that would be called for under the subpoena duces tecum, I take it your answer would be that you received these at the time you were acting as the attorney for Mr. Gray, is that correct?

"A.   That is correct."

Further, on examination by the coroner, the following occurred:

"Mr. Sowers: *   *   *   As the Coroner of King County I order you to do so [answer] under the provisions of the law set forth in the legislature under R.C.W. 36.24.050.

"Mr. Olwell: I decline to surrender any of my client's possessions, if any, because of the confidential relationship of attorney and client because under the law I cannot give evidence which under the law cannot be compelled from my client himself."

The events preceding the issuance of the subpoena and the coroner's inquest   *   *   *   are substantially as follows: Henry LeRoy Gray and John W. Warren engaged in a fight on September 7, 1962, which resulted in Warren's being mortally injured by knife wounds. On or about September 8, 1962, Gray was taken into custody by the Seattle Police Department and placed in jail. During his incarceration, Gray admitted the stabbing of Warren and was willing to co-operate and to aid in the investigation of the homicide. According to a detective of the police department, Gray was not sure what became of the knife he had used in the fight with Warren.

September 10, 1962, David H. Olwell, appellant, was retained as attorney for Gray, who was still confined in jail. Mr. Olwell conferred with his client and then, between the time of that conference and the issuance of the subpoena duces tecum, he came into possession of certain evidence (a knife). It is not clear whether appellant came into possession of this knife through his own investigation while acting as attorney for Gray or whether possession of it was obtained as the result of some communication made by Gray to Olwell during the existence of their attorney and client relationship. This factor is important in determining whether the evidence could be considered as a privileged communication * * *.

Therefore, at the time of the inquest, appellant was in possession of a knife that, at that time, was considered as a possible murder weapon. * * *

* * * [A]ppellant was cited to appear in the Superior Court of King County, where he was found to be in contempt because of his actions at the coroner's inquest on September 18, 1962. Appellant was given 10 days within which to purge himself of contempt, and, upon his failure to do so, an order was entered adjudging him to be in contempt and directing that he serve two days in the county jail. From that order finding him in contempt, Mr. Olwell appeals.

The attorney-client privilege is codified in RCW 5.60.060, which provides, in part:

"The following persons shall not be examined as witnesses:

" * * *

"(2) An attorney or counselor shall not, without the consent of his client, be examined as to any communication made by the client to him, or his advice given thereon in the course of professional employment."

To be protected as a privileged communication, information or objects acquired by an attorney must have been communicated or delivered to him by the client, and not merely obtained by the attorney while acting in that capacity for the client.

This means that the securing of the knife in this case must have been the direct result of information given to Mr. Olwell by his client at the time they conferred in order to come within the attorney-client privilege. Although there is no evidence relating thereto, we think it reasonable to infer from the record that appellant did, in fact, obtain the evidence as the result of information received from his client during their conference. Therefore, for the purposes of this opinion and the questions to be answered, we assume that the evidence in appellant's possession was obtained through a confidential communication from his client. If the knife were obtained from a third person with whom there was no attorney-client relationship, the communication would not be privileged, and the third person could be questioned concerning the transaction.

* * *

In the present case we do not have a situation that readily lends itself to the application of one of the general rules applicable to the attorney-client privilege. Here, we enter a balancing process which requires us to weigh that privilege (which is based on statute and common law), and, as discussed later herein, the privilege against self-incrimination (which is constitutional), against the public's interest in the criminal investigation process. Generally speaking, the public interest at times must yield to protect the individual. Also we must not lose sight of the policy behind the attorney-client privilege, which is to afford the client freedom from fear of compulsory disclosure after consulting his legal adviser.

We must remember, also, that the attorney-client privilege is not absolute, for it can be waived by the client.

On the basis of the attorney-client privilege, the subpoena duces tecum issued by the coroner is defective on its face because it requires the attorney to give testimony concerning information received by him from his client in the course of their conferences. The subpoena names the client and requires his attorney to produce, in an open hearing, physical evidence allegedly received from the client. This is tantamount to requiring the attorney to testify against the client without the latter's consent. RCW 36.24.080 makes testifying in a coroner's inquest similar to testifying in a superior court, and, therefore, the attorney-client privilege should be equally applicable to witnesses at a coroner's inquest. We therefore, hold that appellant's refusal to testify at the inquest for the first reason stated by him was not contemptuous.

We do not, however, by so holding, mean to imply that evidence can be permanently withheld by the attorney under the claim of the attorney-client privilege. Here, we must consider the balancing process between the attorney-client privilege and the public interest in criminal investigation. We are in agreement that the attorney-client privilege is applicable to the knife held by appellant, but do not agree that the privilege warrants the attorney, as an officer of the court, from withholding it after being properly requested to produce the same. The attorney should not be a depository for criminal evidence (such as a knife, other weapons, stolen property, etc.), which in itself has little, if any, material value for the purposes of aiding counsel in the preparation of the defense of his client's case. Such evidence given the attorney during legal consultation for information purposes and used by the attorney in preparing the defense of his client's case, whether or not the case ever goes to trial, could clearly be withheld for a reasonable period of time. It follows that the attorney, after a reasonable period, should, as an officer of the court, on his own motion turn the same over to the prosecution.

We think the attorney-client privilege should and can be preserved even though the attorney surrenders the evidence he has in his possession. The prosecution, upon receipt of such evidence from an attorney, where charge against the attorney's client is contemplated (presently or in the future), should be well aware of the existence of the attorney-client privilege. Therefore, the state, when attempting to introduce such evidence at the trial, should take extreme precautions to make certain that the source of the evidence is not disclosed in the presence of the jury and prejudicial error is not committed. By thus allowing the prosecution to recover such evidence, the public interest is served, and by refusing the prosecution an opportunity to disclose the source of the evidence, the client's privilege is preserved and a balance is reached between these conflicting interests. The burden of introducing such evidence at a trial would continue to be upon the prosecution.

IN RE RYDER

United States District Court, Eastern District of Virginia, 1967.
263 F.Supp. 360.

Before HOFFMAN, Chief Judge, and LEWIS and BUTZNER, Judges.

MEMORANDUM

PER CURIAM.

This proceeding was instituted to determine whether Richard R. Ryder should be removed from the roll of attorneys qualified to practice before this court.   *   *   *

In proceedings of this kind the charges must be sustained by clear and convincing proof, the misconduct must be fraudulent, intentional, and the result of improper motives.   *   *   *   We conclude that these strict requirements have been satisfied.   Ryder took possession of stolen money and a sawed-off shotgun, knowing that the money had been stolen and that the gun had been used in an armed robbery.   He intended to retain this property pending his client's trial unless the government discovered it.   He intended by his possession to destroy the chain of evidence that linked the contraband to his client and to prevent its use to establish his client's guilt.

On August 24, 1966 a man armed with a sawed-off shotgun robbed the Varina Branch of the Bank of Virginia of $7,583.   Included in the currency taken were $10 bills known as "bait money," the serial numbers of which had been recorded.

On August 26, 1966 Charles Richard Cook rented safety deposit box 14 at a branch of the Richmond National Bank.   Later in the day Cook was interviewed at his home by agents of the Federal Bureau of Investigation, who obtained $348 from him.   Cook telephoned Ryder, who had represented him in civil litigation.   Ryder came to the house and advised the agents that he represented Cook.   He said that if Cook were not to be placed under arrest, he intended to take him to his office for an interview.   The agents left.   Cook insisted to Ryder that he had not robbed the bank.   He told Ryder that he had won the money, which the agents had taken from him, in a crap game.   At this time Ryder believed Cook.

Later that afternoon Ryder telephoned one of the agents and asked whether any of the bills obtained from Cook had been identified as a part of the money taken in the bank robbery.   The agent told him that some bills had been identified.   *   *   *

The next morning, Saturday, August 27, 1966, Ryder conferred with Cook again.   He urged Cook to tell the truth, and Cook answered that a man, whose name he would not divulge, offered him $500 on the day of the robbery to put a package in a bank lockbox.   Ryder did not believe this story.   Ryder told Cook that if the government could trace the money in the box to him, it would be almost conclusive evidence of his guilt.   He knew that Cook was under surveillance and he suspected that Cook might try to dispose of the money.

That afternoon Ryder telephoned a former officer of the Richmond Bar Association to discuss his course of action.   He had known this attorney for many years and respected his judgment.   The lawyer was at home and had no library available when Ryder telephoned.   In their casual conversation Ryder told what he knew about the case, omitting names.   He explained that he thought he would take the money from Cook's safety deposit box and place it in a box in his own name.   This, he believed, would prevent Cook from attempting to dispose of the money.   The lawyers thought that eventually F.B.I. agents would locate the money and that since it was in Ryder's possession, he could claim a privilege and thus effectively exclude it from evidence.   This would prevent the government from linking Ryder's client with the bait money and would also destroy any presumption of guilt that might exist arising out of the client's exclusive possession of the evidence.

* * *

The lawyers discussed and rejected alternatives, including having a third party get the money.   At the conclusion of the conversation Ryder was advised, "Don't do it surreptitiously and to be sure that you let your client know that it is going back to the rightful owners."

On Monday morning Ryder asked Cook to come by his office.   He prepared a power of attorney, which Cook signed, [giving him access to Cook's safe deposit box.]

* * *

Ryder did not follow the advice he had received on Saturday.   He did not let his client know the money was going back to the rightful owners.   He testified about his omission:

    " * * *   In the power of attorney, I did not specifically say that Mr. Cook authorized me to deliver that money to the appropriate authorities at any time because for a number of reasons.   One, in representing a man under these circumstances, you've got to keep the man's confidence, but I also put in that power of attorney that Mr. Cook authorized me to dispose of that money as I saw fit, and the reason for that being that I was going to turn the money over to the proper authorities at whatever time I deemed that it wouldn't hurt Mr. Cook."

Ryder took the power of attorney which Cook had signed to the Richmond National Bank.   He rented box 13 in his name with his office address, presented the power of attorney, entered Cook's box, took both boxes into a booth, where he found a bag of money and a sawed-off shotgun in Cook's box.   * * *   He transferred the contents of Cook's box to his own and returned the boxes to the vault.   He left the bank, and neither he nor Cook returned.

Ryder testified that he had some slight hesitation about the propriety of what he was doing.   Within a half-hour after he left the bank, he talked to a retired judge and distinguished professor of law.   He told this person that he wanted to discuss something in confidence.   Ryder then stated that he represented a man suspected of bank robbery.   The judge recalled the main part of the conversation:

" * * *   And that he had received from his client, under a power of attorney, a sum [of] money which he, Mr. Ryder, suspected was proceeds of the robbery, although he didn't know it, but he had a suspicion that it was; that he had placed this money in a safety deposit vault at a bank; that he had received it with the intention of returning it to the rightful owner after the case against his client had been finally disposed of one way or the other; that he considered that he had received it under the privilege of attorney and client and that he wanted responsible people in the community to know of that fact and that he was telling me in confidence of that as one of these people that he wanted to know of it.

* * *

The same day Ryder also talked with other prominent persons in Richmond—a judge of a court of record and an attorney for the Commonwealth. Again, he stated that what he intended to say was confidential.   He related the circumstances and was advised that a lawyer could not receive the property and if he had received it he could not retain possession of it.

On September 7, 1966 Cook was indicted for robbing the Varina Branch of the Bank of Virginia.   * * *

On September 12, 1966 F.B.I. agents procured search warrants for Cook's and Ryder's safety deposit boxes in the Richmond National Bank.   They found Cook's box empty.   In Ryder's box they discovered $5,920 of the $7,583 taken in the bank robbery and the sawed-off shotgun used in the robbery.

* * *

At the outset, we reject the suggestion that Ryder did not know the money which he transferred from Cook's box to his was stolen.   We find that on August 29 when Ryder opened Cook's box and saw a bag of money and a sawed-off shotgun, he then knew Cook was involved in the bank robbery and that the money was stolen.   The evidence clearly establishes this. Ryder knew that the man who had robbed the bank used a sawed-off shotgun.   He disbelieved Cook's story about the source of the money in the lockbox.   He knew that some of the bills in Cook's possession were bait money.

* * *

We also find that Ryder was not motivated solely by certain expectation the government would discover the contents of his lockbox.   He believed discovery was probable.   In this event he intended to argue to the court that the contents of his box could not be revealed, and even if the contents were identified, his possession made the stolen money and the shotgun inadmissible against his client.   He also recognized that discovery was not inevitable.   His intention in this event, we find, was to assist Cook by keeping the stolen money and the shotgun concealed in his lockbox until after the trial.   His conversations, and the secrecy he enjoined, immediately after he put the money and the gun in his box, show that he realized the government might not find the property.

We accept his statement that he intended eventually to return the money to its rightful owner, but we pause to say that no attorney should ever place himself in such a position. Matters involving the possible termination of an attorney-client relationship, or possible subsequent proceedings in the event of an acquittal, are too delicate to permit such a practice.

We reject the argument that Ryder's conduct was no more than the exercise of the attorney-client privilege. The fact that Cook had not been arrested or indicted at the time Ryder took possession of the gun and money is immaterial. Cook was Ryder's client and was entitled to the protection of the lawyer-client privilege. * * *

Regardless of Cook's status, however, Ryder's conduct was not encompassed by the attorney-client privilege. * * *

* * *

It was Ryder, not his client, who took the initiative in transferring the incriminating possession of the stolen money and the shotgun from Cook. Ryder's conduct went far beyond the receipt and retention of a confidential communication from his client. * * *

* * *

Not all papers in a lawyer's file are immune. The rule is summarized in McCormick, Evidence § 93 at p. 188 (1954):

"[I]f a document would be subject to an order for production if it were in the hands of a client, it would be equally subject if it is in the hands of an attorney."

Ryder, an experienced criminal attorney, recognized and acted upon the fact that the gun and money were subject to seizure while in the possession of Cook.

* * *

* * * In argument, it was generally conceded that Ryder could have been required to testify in the prosecution of Cook as to the transfer of the contents of the lockbox.

We conclude that Ryder violated Canons 15 and 32. His conduct is not sanctioned by Canons 5 or 37. * * *

* * * Pertinent in this case are Canons 5, 15, 32 and 37:

"5. *The Defense or Prosecution of Those Accused of Crime.* It is the right of the lawyer to undertake the defense of a person accused of crime, regardless of his personal opinion as to the guilt of the accused; otherwise innocent persons, victims only of suspicious circumstances, might be denied proper defense. Having undertaken such defense, the lawyer is bound by all fair and honorable means, to present every defense that the law of the land permits, to the end that no person may be deprived of life or liberty, but by due process of law.

"The primary duty of a lawyer engaged in public prosecution is not to convict, but to see that justice is done. The suppression of facts or the secreting of witnesses capable of establishing the innocence of the accused is highly reprehensible.

* * *

"15. *How Far a Lawyer May Go in Supporting a Client's Cause.* Nothing operates more certainly to create or to foster popular prejudice against lawyers as a class and to deprive the profession of that full measure of public esteem and confidence which belongs to the proper discharge of its duties than does the false claim, often set up by the unscrupulous in defense of questionable transactions, that it is the duty of the lawyer to do whatever may enable him to succeed in winning his client's cause.

"It is improper for a lawyer to assert in argument his personal belief in his client's innocence or in the justice of his cause.

"The lawyer owes 'entire devotion to the interest of the client, warm zeal in the maintenance and defense of his rights and the exertion of his utmost learning and ability,' to the end that nothing be taken or be withheld from him, save by the rules of law, legally applied. No fear of judicial disfavor or public unpopularity should restrain him from the full discharge of his duty. In the judicial forum the client is entitled to the benefit of any and every remedy and defense that is authorized by the law of the land, and he may expect his lawyer to assert every such remedy or defense. But it is steadfastly to be borne in mind that the great trust of the lawyer is to be performed within and not without the bounds of the law. The office of attorney does not permit, much less does it demand of him for any client, violation of law or any manner of fraud or chicane. He must obey his own conscience and not that of his client.

* * *

"32. *The Lawyer's Duty In Its Last Analysis.* No client, corporate or individual, however powerful, nor any cause, civil or political, however important, is entitled to receive, nor should any lawyer render any service or advice involving disloyalty to the law whose ministers we are, or disrespect of the judicial office, which we are bound to uphold, or corruption of any person or persons exercising a public office or private trust, or deception or betrayal of the public. When rendering any such improper service or advice, the lawyer invites and merits stern and just condemnation. Correspondingly, he advances the honor of his profession and the best interests of his client when he renders service or gives advice tending to impress upon the client and his undertaking exact compliance with the strictest principles of moral law. He must also observe and advise his client to observe the statute law, though until a statute shall have been construed and interpreted by competent adjudication, he is free and is entitled to advise as to its validity and as to what he conscientiously believes to be its just meaning and extent. But above all a lawyer will find his highest honor in a deserved reputation for fidelity to private trust and to public duty, as an honest man and as a patriotic and loyal citizen.

* * *

"37. *Confidence of a Client.* It is the duty of a lawyer to preserve his client's confidences. This duty outlasts the lawyer's employment, and extends as well to his employees; and neither of them should accept employment which involves or may involve the disclosure or use of these confidences, either for the private advantage of the lawyer or his employees or to the disadvantage of the client, without his knowledge and consent, and even though there are other available sources of such information. A lawyer should not continue employment when he discovers that this obligation prevents the performance of his full duty to his former or to his new client.

If a lawyer is accused by his client, he is not precluded from disclosing the truth in respect to the accusation. The announced intention of a client to commit a crime is not included within the confidences which he is bound to respect. He may properly make such disclosures as may be necessary to prevent the act or protect those against whom it is threatened."

The money in Cook's box belonged to the Bank of Virginia. The law did not authorize Cook to conceal this money or withhold it from the bank. His larceny was a continuing offense. Cook had no title or property interest in the money that he lawfully could pass to Ryder. * * * No canon of ethics or law permitted Ryder to conceal from the Bank of Virginia its money to gain his client's acquittal.

Cook's possession of the sawed-off shotgun was illegal. 26 U.S.C. § 5851. Ryder could not lawfully receive the gun from Cook to assist Cook to avoid conviction of robbery. Cook had never mentioned the shotgun to Ryder. When Ryder discovered it in Cook's box, he took possession of it to hinder the government in the prosecution of its case, and he intended not to reveal it pending trial unless the government discovered it and a court compelled its production. No statute or canon of ethics authorized Ryder to take possession of the gun for this purpose.

* * *

In helping Cook to conceal the shotgun and stolen money, Ryder acted without the bounds of law. He allowed the office of attorney to be used in violation of law. The scheme which he devised was a deceptive, legalistic subterfuge—rightfully denounced by the canon as chicane.

Ryder also violated Canon 32. He rendered Cook a service involving deception and disloyalty to the law. He intended that his actions should remove from Cook exclusive possession of stolen money, and thus destroy an evidentiary presumption. His service in taking possession of the shotgun and money, with the intention of retaining them until after the trial, unless discovered by the government, merits the "stern and just condemnation" the canon prescribes.

Ryder's testimony that he intended to have the court rule on the admissibility of the evidence and the extent of the lawyer-client privilege does not afford justification for his action. He intended to do this only if the government discovered the shotgun and stolen money in his lockbox. If the government did not discover it, he had no intention of submitting any legal question about it to the court.   If there were no discovery, he would continue to conceal the shotgun and money for Cook's benefit pending trial.

Ryder's action is not justified because he thought he was acting in the best interests of his client.   To allow the individual lawyer's belief to determine the standards of professional conduct will in time reduce the ethics of the profession to the practices of the most unscrupulous.   Moreover, Ryder knew that the law against concealing stolen property and the law forbidding receipt and possession of a sawed-off shotgun contain no exemptions for a lawyer who takes possession with the intent of protecting a criminal from the consequences of his crime.

We find it difficult to accept the argument that Ryder's action is excusable because if the government found Cook's box, Ryder's would easily be found, and if the government failed to find both Cook's and Ryder's boxes, no more harm would be done than if the agents failed to find only Cook's. Cook's concealment of the items in his box cannot be cited to excuse Ryder. Cook's conduct is not the measure of Ryder's ethics.   The conduct of a lawyer should be above reproach.   Concealment of the stolen money and the sawed-off shotgun to secure Cook's acquittal was wrong whether the property was in Cook's or Ryder's possession.

There is much to be said, however, for mitigation of the discipline to be imposed.   Ryder intended to return the bank's money after his client was tried.   He consulted reputable persons before and after he placed the property in his lockbox, although he did not precisely follow their advice.   Were it not for these facts, we would deem proper his permanent exclusion from practice before this court.   In view of the mitigating circumstances, he will be suspended from practice in this court for eighteen months effective October 14, 1966.

Olwell and *Ryder* taken together stand for certain fundamental principles that appear to be generally accepted, although one cannot always be confident of this, for they are rarely addressed in judicial opinions. One clear principle is that a lawyer may not destroy or conceal evidence to benefit a client and may not aid a client bent on such activity.   Another is that a lawyer may examine material in a client's possession without violating ethical or criminal proscriptions.   But if the lawyer takes possession of certain objects from the client, she may have obligations to third parties once the period needed for a reasonable inspection has passed.   If what she takes is stolen property, the lawyer is under an obligation to return it promptly to its rightful owner.   If it is contraband or an instrument used in a crime, she is probably obliged to forward what she has taken to state officials;   to keep such material is to help conceal the fruits or instrumentality of a crime, and to return it to the client once possession has passed may be to aid in its destruction.   Where the lawyer fulfills her obligation by giving the government evidence she has received in confidence, many courts would conclude that the attorney-client privilege precludes the government from tying the material to the client through his attorney.[35]

35.   For a suggestion that the source should have to be revealed and an idea how the client's communications might be protected without permitting the connection between the evidence and the client to be broken, see Saltzburg, supra note 29.

Put yourself in the position of a criminal defense lawyer whose client enters the office with a mask worn in a bank robbery. He says that before the robbery he loaned the mask to a friend. Now he wants to know what to do. You look at the mask and note that several red hairs, very much like your client's, are embedded in the fibers. What do you say? If he gives you the mask, you will have to give it to the government if it is subpoenaed. You may have an obligation to take the initiative in handing it over. If you tell your client to keep it, what more can you say? You cannot tell your client to destroy the mask. Can you warn him that if the mask is found in his possession he will be a prime suspect in the robbery regardless of his guilt or innocence? Should you warn him about criminal statutes that prohibit the destruction of evidence?

The conflict between the duty that the lawyer owes the client and the duty that she owes the legal system is obvious. The attorney-client privilege does not help resolve it, for the privilege does not by itself protect existing evidence or evidence that would have been generated absent a privilege. The privilege does, however, protect the client who discloses otherwise privileged information to his attorney.

This last point is illustrated by the Supreme Court's decision in Fisher v. United States.[36] Fisher grew out of an IRS effort to subpoena documents that certain taxpayers had given their attorneys in connection with the legal services they were receiving. On behalf of their taxpayer clients, the attorneys claimed the privilege against self-incrimination.

The Supreme Court held that the fifth amendment privilege was designed to prevent personal compulsion and so could not be invoked when compulsion in the form of the subpoenas was directed against someone (i.e., the attorneys) other than the arguable holder of the privilege (i.e., the taxpayer-clients). However, the Court went on to say that if the clients would have had a fifth amendment right to refuse to hand over the papers if the papers were in their hands, the papers would remain immune from discovery if they were given to the client's lawyers for the purpose of securing legal advice. On the facts of the case, the Court concluded, for reasons that need not concern you at this point, that the taxpayers would have had no right to refuse to produce the documents, so the lawyers were required to deliver them to the IRS.[37]

Fisher highlights some of the questions that Olwell and Ryder do not answer. For example, how certain must an attorney be that what her client has given her is evidence in a pending case before she is obliged to turn it over to the government? Does such an obligation ever arise when the material a client has turned over is neither contraband nor the fruits or instrumentality of a crime? Olwell was easy on both counts, and so was Ryder. But there are many situations in which an attorney may suspect she has something the government would subpoena if they knew about it, but no one has asked for the material and it is not obvious on its face that it relates to an ongoing proceeding or one certain to commence. If the uncertain attorney can take possession of evidence, she may become, perhaps unknowingly, a depository for evidence that the government seeks.

There is also the question of how long an attorney may keep possession of an ob-

---

36. 425 U.S. 391 (1976).

37. Note that in Fisher, Olwell and Ryder the evidence sought by the state relates to activities that might (in the latter two cases "will") give rise to criminal prosecutions. If the possibility of a criminal prosecution did not exist no fifth amendment argument could be advanced to refuse to turn over the evidence or to turn it over anonymously. Thus, in civil cases physical evidence in an opponent's possession is routinely subpoenaed and routinely turned over for inspection, copying and testing.

ject, like the knife in *Olwell,* before she is obliged to turn it over to the government? If she picks it up to look at it, has the client relinquished possession for the purposes of the laws relating to concealing evidence and the attorney's ethical obligations? A sensible rule would be that the legal obligation attaches once the attorney sufficiently removes the evidence from the possession of the client so that one who searched the client and his immediate surroundings would not find the evidence. It would also make sense to hold that the obligation attaches when the client has left the evidence with the attorney for any period of time but does not attach when the client shares evidence with an attorney but takes it away at the conclusion of their meeting. Not many cases have yet addressed this question.

Another question arises when an attorney who does not know that the government seeks certain evidence returns it to the client, and the evidence is later lost or destroyed. Can the attorney be questioned about the characteristics of the evidence? In *Olwell,* for example, if the attorney had returned the knife to Gray not knowing about the stabbing, could he be asked to describe it to a grand jury if by the time the grand jury was convened the knife could no longer be found? [38]

The problems that follow explore these and related questions.

Problem VIII–9. In State v. Olwell the Washington court suggests that it may be important whether the attorney discovered the knife sought by the government on his own or as a result of talking with his client, Gray. Is there a sensible line to be drawn here? Consider four possible settings in which facts similar to those of *Olwell* might arise. **What is the attorney's responsibility in each setting? What steps if any, should the attorney take to share the evidence with the prosecutor?**

   a.   Gray brings a knife to his attorney and asks him to hold the knife until after the trial.

   b.   During an interview with his lawyer, Gray mentions that a knife is hidden in his neighbor's yard. The attorney goes to the yard, examines the knife, and leaves it there.

   c.   Gray, claiming to be innocent, gives his attorney permission to search his house. Although Gray has said he does not own a switchblade knife, the attorney finds one.

   d.   Gray tells his attorney that the knife is in the possession of his best friend, Jeremiah Johnson.

Under which of these circumstances could the attorney be compelled to testify about the knife—e.g., its appearance or where it was located?

Problem VIII–10. Is there a difference between a knife and a writing? Or between a knife and some writings? Assume that Harris is charged with willfully evading the payment of federal income taxes. **Does his lawyer have a duty to share information with the prosecutor under any of the following circumstances? Under which circumstances might the attorney be called to testify about the writing had it been lost or destroyed?**

----

38. A suggested approach for handling these questions is found in Saltzburg, supra note 29.

a. Harris produces a bankbook showing a secret account which might prove he has received undeclared income.   He gives it to his lawyer.

b. Harris tells his lawyer that, under a false name, he has money in a bank in a distant city and that he doubts that the government has this information.

c. In response to his lawyer's request for a summary of his income, Harris prepares a detailed analysis of all receipts in the past several years.

d. In connection with the detailed report described in *c*, Harris delivers to the lawyer all the records he has kept in connection with his previous tax returns.

e. Harris drops the key to a safe deposit box on his attorney's desk. The attorney goes to the bank, opens the box, and finds $100,000 in large bills.

In the last situation should the attorney act differently if the client has consulted her as a suspect in a bank robbery in which $100,000 in large bills were taken rather than as one suspected of concealing income?

Problem VIII–11. Charles Oakes approaches Joan Bennet, an attorney, for legal advice.   He tells Bennet that the police have been questioning him about a murder and he wants Bennet to represent him.   Bennet agrees. At first Oakes denies any involvement in the murder, but upon further questioning by Bennet and with the assurance that the attorney-client privilege will protect the confidence of any communication, Oakes admits to the murder of a seventeen year old girl.   He tells Bennet that he hid the body in a cave near a lake in a state forest.   **Does Bennet have any responsibility to disclose this information to anyone?   Would she be acting ethically if she did disclose this information?**   The next weekend Bennet takes a camping trip to the state forest to check her client's story.   She finds the body in the place described.   **Was Bennet acting wisely when she went in search of the body?   Does Bennet's personal observation change her responsibilities respecting disclosure?   If the body had fallen from a ledge on which the client said he had placed it and was consequently visible from the entrance of the cave, would Bennet be acting properly if she placed the body back on the ledge?   Would she be acting properly if she left the body where it was but later told Oakes about its current position? How should Bennet respond if she simply told Oakes she had visited the cave and Oakes asked her if the body had fallen?**   Two months after agreeing to represent Oakes, Bennet receives a letter from the deceased's parents in which they describe their grief at not knowing whether their daughter is dead or alive and at the prospect that their daughter may be dead and unburied.   They ask Bennet if she can shed any light on these matters.   She responds that she knows nothing about these matters.   **Is Bennet's response proper?   If a grand jury calls Bennet to testify and asks if she knows where the body is, must Bennet answer?**

Problem VIII–12.   You are an attorney in a large city.   A man, whom you recognize as Clyde Bonnie, comes into your office and says that he expects to be picked up soon for armed robbery of a supermarket. He wants you to defend him. You tell him you will accept his case if he can pay your fee. At that he lays down a shoe box in front of you and says that it contains a Colt revolver registered in his name which he doesn't want anyone to find. He then turns to leave, but you stop him because you still haven't discussed your fee. After he hears how much you expect to be paid, he asks you to "loan" him back his "box" because he has to "visit" another supermarket. You persuade him to leave the box in your custody and he leaves, stating that he will raise the money somehow because he wants you as his "mouthpiece." Two days later, shortly after Bonnie has paid you your retainer, you read in the paper that the Foxy Loxy Supermarket has been robbed by a man armed with a knife. The general description of the robber resembles that of your client. The story also states that the same supermarket had been robbed a week before by a man armed with a Colt revolver. Two weeks pass and your client still has not been picked up for armed robbery.

Are you under any ethical duty to disclose all or part of the interchange which occurred between you and Bonnie on his first visit to your office? What should you do with the gun which is in the box? If your client is arrested and the prosecution calls you to the stand, is your client privileged to prevent you from revealing all or part of the information he communicated to you on his first visit to your office? Can you be forced, over your client's objection, to disclose that you have the gun? To turn the gun over to the state?

D. CORPORATE CLIENTS

When an individual consults an attorney, the identity of the client is clear. But, the term "client" has been interpreted to include corporations and other organizations. Few courts have been concerned with the wisdom of this interpretation.[39] There has, however, been considerable dispute over the proper scope of the privilege in the corporate context. It is generally agreed that the privilege does not apply to all communications made by corporate employees to the corporation's attorneys. The privilege will not apply if the communication was made for some corporate purpose other than securing legal advice or if the communication is treated by the corporation in such a way as to negate an intention of confidentiality. These conclusions follow from the scope of the

privilege held by individual clients. But, the privilege does not automatically apply whenever a corporation, desiring confidentiality, secures a communication from an employee solely for the purpose of securing legal advice. The clearest case of non-applicability is where an off-duty worker fortuitously witnesses an event affecting the legal liabilities of the company. There is no good reason why the employment nexus should give the worker's statements greater protection than that of any other witness. When an employee's ability to give evidence is job related, a dispute arises over the issue of whether the employee must have some particular status before his communications will be privileged. The once dominant test limited the privilege to statements made by

---

39. One district court held that the privilege was not available to corporations, but it was reversed on appeal. Radiant Burners, Inc. v. American Gas Ass'n, 320 F.2d 314 (7th Cir. 1963), reversing, 207 F.Supp. 771 (N.D.Ill.1962). Review was denied by the Supreme Court, 375 U.S. 921 (1963).

members of the corporate "control group," a group that has been loosely defined as those individuals having authority to seek out and act on legal advice. This group includes, and may be limited to, the directors and executive officers of the corporation. A broader test applies the privilege to communications of lower level corporate employees reporting information acquired and transmitted in the course of corporate duties. During the 1960's the control group test was in the ascendancy in the federal courts, but in 1970 the Seventh Circuit applied the broader test in Harper & Row Publishers Inc. v. Decker, a decision affirmed by an equally divided Supreme Court.[40] Because of the uncertainty of which test the Court would prefer, the drafters of the proposed federal rule did not specify a standard.

The Supreme Court did not indicate its preference until 1981 in Upjohn Co. v. United States. The *Upjohn* opinion is valuable not only for its discussion of the attorney-client privilege, but also for its analysis of the work product doctrine.

UPJOHN CO. v. UNITED STATES

Supreme Court of the United States, 1981.
449 U.S. 383, 101 S.Ct. 677, 66 L.Ed.2d 584.

Justice REHNQUIST delivered the opinion of the Court.

We granted certiorari in this case to address important questions concerning the scope of the attorney-client privilege in the corporate context and the applicability of the work-product doctrine in proceedings to enforce tax summonses. With respect to the privilege question the parties and various *amici* have described our task as one of choosing between two "tests" which have gained adherents in the courts of appeals. We are acutely aware, however, that we sit to decide concrete cases and not abstract propositions of law. We decline to lay down a broad rule or series of rules to govern all conceivable future questions in this area, even were we able to do so. We can and do, however, conclude that the attorney-client privilege protects the communications involved in this case from compelled disclosure and that the work-product doctrine does apply in tax summons enforcement proceedings.

I

Petitioner Upjohn manufactures and sells pharmaceuticals here and abroad. In January 1976 independent accountants conducting an audit of one of petitioner's foreign subsidiaries discovered that the subsidiary made payments to or for the benefit of foreign government officials in order to secure government business. The accountants, so informed Mr. Gerard Thomas, petitioner's Vice-President, Secretary, and General Counsel. Thomas is a member of the Michigan and New York bars, and has been petitioner's General Counsel for 20 years. He consulted with outside counsel and R. T. Parfet, Jr., petitioner's Chairman of the Board. It was decided that the company would conduct an internal investigation of what were termed "questionable payments." As part of this investigation the attorneys prepared a letter containing a questionnaire which was sent to "all foreign general and

40. 423 F.2d 487 (7th Cir. 1970), affirmed,
400 U.S. 348 (1971).

area managers" over the Chairman's signature. The letter began by noting recent disclosures that several American companies made "possibly illegal" payments to foreign government officials and emphasized that the management needed full information concerning any such payments made by Upjohn. The letter indicated that the Chairman had asked Thomas, identified as "the company's General Counsel," "to conduct an investigation for the purpose of determining the nature and magnitude of any payments made by the Upjohn Company or any of its subsidiaries to any employee or official of a foreign government." The questionnaire sought detailed information concerning such payments. Managers were instructed to treat the investigation as "highly confidential" and not to discuss it with anyone other than Upjohn employees who might be helpful in providing the requested information. Responses were to be sent directly to Thomas. Thomas and outside counsel also interviewed the recipients of the questionnaire and some 33 other Upjohn officers or employees as part of the investigation.

On March 26, 1976, the company voluntarily submitted a preliminary report to the Securities and Exchange Commission on Form 8–K disclosing certain questionable payments. A copy of the report was simultaneously submitted to the Internal Revenue Service, which immediately began an investigation to determine the tax consequences of the payments. Special agents conducting the investigation were given lists by Upjohn of all those interviewed and all who had responded to the questionnaire. On November 23, 1976, the Service issued a summons pursuant to 26 U.S.C. § 7602 demanding production of:

"All files relative to the investigation conducted under the supervision of Gerard Thomas to identify payments to employees of foreign governments and any political contributions made by the Upjohn Company or any of its affiliates since January 1, 1971 and to determine whether any funds of the Upjohn Company had been improperly accounted for on the corporate books during the same period.

"The records should include but not be limited to written questionnaires sent to managers of the Upjohn Company's foreign affiliates, and memoranda or notes of the interviews conducted in the United States and abroad with officers and employees of the Upjohn Company and its subsidiaries."

The company declined to produce the documents specified in the second paragraph on the grounds that they were protected from disclosure by the attorney-client privilege and constituted the work product of attorneys prepared in anticipation of litigation. On August 31, 1977, the United States filed a petition seeking enforcement of the summons under 26 U.S.C. §§ 7402(b) and 7604(a) in the United States District Court for the Western District of Michigan. That court adopted the recommendation of a magistrate who concluded that the summons should be enforced. Petitioner appealed to the Court of Appeals for the Sixth Circuit which rejected the magistrate's finding of a waiver of the attorney-client privilege, but agreed that the privilege did not apply "to the extent the communications were made by officers and agents not responsible for directing Upjohn's actions in response to legal advice . . . for the simple reason that the communications were not the 'client's.' "

The court reasoned that accepting petitioner's claim for a broader application of the privilege would encourage upper-echelon management to ignore unpleasant facts and create too broad a "zone of silence." Noting that petitioner's counsel had interviewed officials such as the Chairman and President, the Court of Appeals remanded to the District Court so that a determination of who was within the "control group" could be made. In a concluding footnote the court stated that the work-product doctrine "is not applicable to administrative summonses issued under 26 U.S.C. § 7602."

II

Federal Rule of Evidence 501 provides that "the privilege of a witness . . . shall be governed by the principles of the common law as they may be interpreted by the courts of the United States in light of reason and experience." The attorney-client privilege is the oldest of the privileges for confidential communications known to the common law. Its purpose is to encourage full and frank communication between attorneys and their clients and thereby promote broader public interests in the observance of law and administration of justice. * * * Admittedly complications in the application of the privilege arise when the client is a corporation, which in theory is an artificial creature of the law, and not an individual; but this Court has assumed that the privilege applies when the client is a corporation. United States v. Louisville & Nashville R. Co., 236 U.S. 318, 336, 35 S.Ct. 363, 369, 59 L.Ed. 598 (1915), and the Government does not contest the general proposition.

The Court of Appeals, however, considered the application of the privilege in the corporate context to present a "different problem," since the client was an inanimate entity and "only the senior management, guiding and integrating the several operations, * * * can be said to possess an identity analogous to the corporation as a whole." 600 F.2d at 1226. The first case to articulate the so-called "control group test" adopted by the court below, City of Philadelphia v. Westinghouse Electric Corp., 210 F.Supp. 483, 485 (ED Pa.), petition for mandamus and prohibition denied, General Electric Company v. Kirkpatrick, 312 F.2d 742 (CA3 1962), cert. denied, 372 U.S. 943, 83 S.Ct. 937, 9 L.Ed.2d 969 (1963), reflected a similar conceptual approach:

> "Keeping in mind that the question is, Is it the corporation which is seeking the lawyer's advice when the asserted privileged communication is made?, the most satisfactory solution, I think, is that if the employee making the communication, of whatever rank he may be, is in a position to control or even to take a substantial part in a decision about any action which the corporation may take upon the advice of the attorney, * * * then, in effect, *he is (or personifies) the corporation* when he makes his disclosure to the lawyer and the privilege would apply." (Emphasis supplied.)

Such a view, we think, overlooks the fact that the privilege exists to protect not only the giving of professional advice to those who can act on it but also the giving of information to the lawyer to enable him to give sound and informed advice. * * *

In the case of the individual client the provider of information and the person who acts on the lawyer's advice are one and the same.   In the corporate context, however, it will frequently be employees beyond the control group as defined by the court below—"officers and agents * * * responsible for directing [the company's] actions in response to legal advice"— who will possess the information needed by the corporation's lawyers.   Middle-level—and indeed lower-level—employees can, by actions within the scope of their employment, embroil the corporation in serious legal difficulties, and it is only natural that these employees would have the relevant information needed by corporate counsel if he is adequately to advise the client with respect to such actual or potential difficulties.   This fact was noted in Diversified Industries, Inc. v. Meredith, 572 F.2d 596 (CA8 1978) (en banc):

> "In a corporation, it may be necessary to glean information relevant to a legal problem from middle management or non-management personnel as well as from top executives.   The attorney dealing with a complex legal problem 'is thus faced with a "Hobson's choice."   If he interviews employees not having "the very highest authority" their communications to him will not be privileged.   If, on the other hand, he interviews *only* those employees with the "very highest authority," he may find it extremely difficult, if not impossible, to determine what happened.' "   Id., at 608–609 (quoting Weinschel, Corporate Employee Interviews and the Attorney-Client Privilege, 12 B.C.Ind. & Comm.L.Rev. 873, 876 (1970)).

The control group test adopted by the court below thus frustrates the very purpose of the privilege by discouraging the communication of relevant information by employees of the client to attorneys seeking to render legal advice to the client corporation.   The attorney's advice will also frequently be more significant to noncontrol group members than to those who officially sanction the advice, and the control group test makes it more difficult to convey full and frank legal advice to the employees who will put into effect the client corporation's policy.

The narrow scope given the attorney-client privilege by the court below not only makes it difficult for corporate attorneys to formulate sound advice when their client is faced with a specific legal problem but also threatens to limit the valuable efforts of corporate counsel to ensure their client's compliance with the law.   In light of the vast and complicated array of regulatory legislation confronting the modern corporation, corporations, unlike most individuals, "constantly go to lawyers to find out how to obey the law," Burnham, The Attorney-Client Privilege in the Corporate Arena, 24 Bus.Law. 901, 913 (1969), particularly since compliance with the law in this area is hardly an instinctive matter.[a]   The test adopted by the court below is difficult to apply in practice, though no abstractly formulated and unvarying "test"

---

a. The Government argues that the risk of civil or criminal liability suffices to ensure that corporations will seek legal advice in the absence of the protection of the privilege. This response ignores the fact that the depth and quality of any investigations, to ensure compliance with the law would suffer, even were they undertaken.   The response also proves too much, since it applies to all communications covered by the privilege: an individual trying to comply with the law or faced with a legal problem also has strong incentive to disclose information to his lawyer, yet the common law has recognized the value of the privilege in further facilitating communications.

will necessarily enable courts to decide questions such as this with mathematical precision. But if the purpose of the attorney-client privilege is to be served, the attorney and client must be able to predict with some degree of certainty whether particular discussions will be protected. An uncertain privilege, or one which purports to be certain but results in widely varying applications by the courts, is little better than no privilege at all. The very terms of the test adopted by the court below suggest the unpredictability of its application. The test restricts the availability of the privilege to those officers who play a "substantial role" in deciding and directing a corporation's legal response. Disparate decisions in cases applying this test illustrate its unpredictability. Compare, e.g., Hogan v. Zletz, 43 F.R.D. 308, 315–316 (ND Okl.1967), aff'd in part sub nom. Natta v. Hogan, 392 F.2d 686 (CA10 1968) (control group includes managers and assistant managers of patent division and research and development department) with Congoleum Industries, Inc. v. GAF Corp., 49 F.R.D. 82, 83–85 (ED Pa.1969), aff'd, 478 F.2d 1398 (CA3 1973) (control group includes only division and corporate vice-presidents, and not two directors of research and vice-president for production and research).

The communications at issue were made by Upjohn employees [b] to counsel for Upjohn acting as such, at the direction of corporate superiors in order to secure legal advice from counsel. As the magistrate found, "Mr. Thomas consulted with the Chairman of the Board and outside counsel and thereafter conducted a factual investigation to determine the nature and extent of the questionable payments *and to be in a position to give legal advice to the company with respect to the payments.*" Information, not available from upper-echelon management, was needed to supply a basis for legal advice concerning compliance with securities and tax laws, foreign laws, currency regulations, duties to shareholders, and potential litigation in each of these areas. The communications concerned matters within the scope of the employees' corporate duties, and the employees themselves were sufficiently aware that they were being questioned in order that the corporation could obtain legal advice. The questionnaire identified Thomas as "the company's General Counsel" and referred in its opening sentence to the possible illegality of payments such as the ones on which information was sought. A statement of policy accompanying the questionnaire clearly indicated the legal implications of the investigation. The policy statement was issued "in order that there be no uncertainty in the future as to the policy with respect to the practices which are the subject of this investigation." It began "Upjohn will comply with all laws and regulations," and stated that commissions or payments "will not be used as a subterfuge for bribes or illegal payments" and that all payments must be "proper and legal." Any future agreements with foreign distributors or agents were to be approved "by a company attorney" and any questions concerning the policy were to be referred "to the

b. Seven of the 86 employees interviewed by counsel had terminated their employment with Upjohn at the time of the interview. Petitioner argues that the privilege should nonetheless apply to communications by these former employees concerning activities during their period of employment. Neither the District Court nor the Court of Appeals had occasion to address this issue, and we decline to decide it without the benefit of treatment below.

company's General Counsel." This statement was issued to Upjohn employees worldwide, so that even those interviewees not receiving a questionnaire were aware of the legal implications of the interviews. Pursuant to explicit instructions from the Chairman of the Board, the communications were considered "highly confidential" when made, and have been kept confidential by the company. Consistent with the underlying purposes of the attorney-client privilege, these communications must be protected against compelled disclosure.

The Court of Appeals declined to extend the attorney-client privilege beyond the limits of the control group test for fear that doing so would entail severe burdens on discovery and create a broad "zone of silence" over corporate affairs. Application of the attorney-client privilege to communications such as those involved here, however, puts the adversary in no worse position than if the communications had never taken place. The privilege only protects disclosure of communications; it does not protect disclosure of the underlying facts by those who communicated with the attorney * * *. Here the Government was free to question the employees who communicated with Thomas and outside counsel. Upjohn has provided the IRS with a list of such employees, and the IRS has already interviewed some 25 of them. While it would probably be more convenient for the Government to secure the results of petitioner's internal investigation by simply subpoenaing the questionnaires and notes taken by petitioner's attorneys, such considerations of convenience do not overcome the policies served by the attorney-client privilege. * * *

Needless to say, we decide only the case before us, and do not undertake to draft a set of rules which should govern challenges to investigatory subpoenas. Any such approach would violate the spirit of F.R.E. 501. * * * While such a "case-by-case" basis may to some slight extent undermine desirable certainty in the boundaries of the attorney-client privilege, it obeys the spirit of the Rules. At the same time we conclude that the narrow "control group test" sanctioned by the Court of Appeals, in this case cannot, consistent with "the principles of the common law as * * * interpreted * * * in light of reason and experience," F.R.E. 501, govern the development of the law in this area.

III [41]

Our decision that the communications by Upjohn employees to counsel are covered by the attorney-client privilege disposes of the case so far as the responses to the questionnaires and any notes reflecting responses to interview questions are concerned. The summons reaches further, however, and Thomas has testified that his notes and memoranda of interviews go beyond recording responses to his questions. To the extent that the material subject to the summons is not protected by the attorney-client privilege as disclosing communications between an employee and counsel, we must reach the

---

41. Full understanding of the situations in which attorneys can keep matters confidential requires an understanding of the work product doctrine because when the attorney-client privilege is not available, the work product doctrine still may be. *Upjohn* is an important statement of the potential breadth of this protection.

ruling by the Court of Appeals that the work-product doctrine does not apply to summonses issued under 26 U.S.C. § 7602.[c]

The Government concedes, wisely, that the Court of Appeals erred and that the work-product doctrine does apply to IRS summonses. This doctrine was announced by the Court over 30 years ago in Hickman v. Taylor, 329 U.S. 495, 67 S.Ct. 385, 91 L.Ed. 451 (1947). In that case the Court rejected "an attempt, without purported necessity or justification, to secure written statements, private memoranda, and personal recollections prepared or formed by an adverse party's counsel in the course of his legal duties." The Court noted that "it is essential that a lawyer work with a certain degree of privacy" and reasoned that if discovery of the material sought were permitted

> "much of what is now put down in writing would remain unwritten. An attorney's thoughts, heretofore inviolate, would not be his own. Inefficiency, unfairness and sharp practices would inevitably develop in the giving of legal advice and in the preparation of cases for trial. The effect on the legal profession would be demoralizing. And the interests of the clients and the cause of justice would be poorly served." Id., at 511, 67 S.Ct., at 393–394.

The "strong public policy" underlying the work-product doctrine was reaffirmed recently in United States v. Nobles, 422 U.S. 225, 236–240, 95 S.Ct. 2160, 2169–2171, 45 L.Ed.2d 141 (1975), and has been substantially incorporated in Federal Rule of Civil Procedure 26(b)(3).[d]

* * * Nothing in the language of the IRS summons provisions or their legislative history suggests an intent on the part of Congress to preclude application of the work-product doctrine. Rule 26(b)(3) codifies the work-product doctrine, and the Federal Rules of Civil Procedure are made applicable to summons enforcement proceedings by Rule 81(a)(3). While conceding the applicability of the work-product doctrine, the Government asserts that it has made a sufficient showing of necessity to overcome its protections. The magistrate apparently so found. The Government relies on the following language in *Hickman*:

> "We do not mean to say that all written materials obtained or prepared by an adversary's counsel with an eye toward litigation are necessarily free from discovery in all cases. Where relevant and nonprivileged facts

c. The following discussion will also be relevant to counsels' notes and memoranda of interviews with the seven former employees should it be determined that the attorney-client privilege does not apply to them. See n. b, supra.

d. This provides, in pertinent part:

"A party may obtain discovery of documents and tangible things otherwise discoverable under subdivision (b)(1) of this rule and prepared in anticipation of litigation or for trial by or for another party or by or for that other party's representative (including his attorney, consultant, surety, indemnitor, in-surer, or agent) only upon a showing that the party seeking discovery has substantial need of the materials in the preparation of his case and that he is unable without undue hardship to obtain the substantial equivalent of the materials by other means. In ordering discovery of such materials when the required showing has been made, the court shall protect against disclosure of the mental impressions, conclusions, opinions, or legal theories of an attorney or other representative of a party concerning the litigation."

remain hidden in an attorney's file and where production of those facts is essential to the preparation of one's case, discovery may properly be had. * * * And production might be justified where the witnesses are no longer available or may be reached only with difficulty." 329 U.S., at 511, 67 S.Ct., at 394.

The Government stresses that interviewees are scattered across the globe and that Upjohn has forbidden its employees to answer questions it considers irrelevant. The above-quoted language from *Hickman*, however, did not apply to "oral statements made by witnesses * * * whether presently in the form of [the attorney's] mental impressions or memoranda." Id., at 512, 67 S.Ct., at 394. As to such material the Court did "not believe that any showing of necessity can be made under the circumstances of this case so as to justify production. * * * If there should be a rare situation justifying production of these matters petitioner's case is not of that type." Id., at 512–513, 67 S.Ct., at 394–395. Forcing an attorney to disclose notes and memoranda of witnesses' oral statements is particularly disfavored because it tends to reveal the attorney's mental processes.[e]

Rule 26 accords special protection to work product revealing the attorney's mental processes. The Rule permits disclosure of documents and tangible things constituting attorney work product upon a showing of substantial need and inability to obtain the equivalent without undue hardship. This was the standard applied by the magistrate. Rule 26 goes on, however, to state that "[i]n ordering discovery of such materials when the required showing has been made, the court shall protect against disclosure of the mental impressions, conclusions, opinions or legal theories of an attorney or other representative of a party concerning the litigation." Although this language does not specifically refer to memoranda based on oral statements of witnesses, the *Hickman* court stressed the danger that compelled disclosure of such memoranda would reveal the attorney's mental processes. It is clear that this is the sort of material the draftsmen of the Rule had in mind as deserving special protection. See Notes of Advisory Committee on 1970 Amendment to Rules, reprinted in 48 F.R.D. 487, 502 ("The subdivision * * * goes on to protect against disclosure the mental impressions, conclusions, opinions, or legal theories * * * of an attorney or other representative of a party. The *Hickman* opinion drew special attention to the need for protecting an attorney against discovery of memoranda prepared from recollection of oral interviews. The courts have steadfastly safeguarded against disclosure of lawyers' mental impressions and legal theories * * * ").

Based on the foregoing, some courts have concluded that *no* showing of necessity can overcome protection of work product which is based on oral statements from witnesses. Those courts declining to adopt an absolute rule have nonetheless recognized that such material is entitled to special protection.

---

e. Thomas described his notes of the interviews as containing "what I consider to be the important questions, the substance of the responses to them, my beliefs as to the importance of these, my beliefs as to how they related to the inquiry, my thoughts as to how they related to other questions. In some instances they might even suggest other questions that I would have to ask or things that I needed to find elsewhere."

We do not decide the issue at this time. It is clear that the magistrate applied the wrong standard when he concluded that the Government had made a sufficient showing of necessity to overcome the protections of the work-product doctrine. The magistrate applied the "substantial need" and "without undue hardship" standard articulated in the first part of Rule 26(b)(3). The notes and memoranda sought by the Government here, however, are work product based on oral statements. If they reveal communications, they are, in this case, protected by the attorney-client privilege. To the extent they do not reveal communications, they reveal the attorneys' mental processes in evaluating the communications. As Rule 26 and *Hickman* make clear, such work product cannot be disclosed simply on a showing of substantial need and inability to obtain the equivalent without undue hardship.

While we are not prepared at this juncture to say that such material is always protected by the work-product rule, we think a far stronger showing of necessity and unavailability by other means than was made by the Government or applied by the magistrate in this case would be necessary to compel disclosure. Since the Court of Appeals thought that the work-product protection was never applicable in an enforcement proceeding such as this, and since the magistrate whose recommendations the District Court adopted applied too lenient a standard of protection, we think the best procedure with respect to this aspect of the case would be to reverse the judgment of the Court of Appeals for the Sixth Circuit and remand the case to it for such further proceedings in connection with the work-product claim as are consistent with this opinion.

Accordingly, the judgment of the Court of Appeals is reversed, and the case remanded for further proceedings.

Chief Justice BURGER, concurring in part and concurring in the judgment.

I join in Parts I and III of the opinion of the Court and in the judgment. As to Part II, I agree fully with the Court's rejection of the so-called "control group" test, its reasons for doing so, and its ultimate holding that the communications at issue are privileged. As the Court states, however, "if the purpose of the attorney-client privilege is to be served, the attorney and the client must be able to predict with some degree of certainty whether particular discussions will be protected." For this very reason, I believe that we should articulate a standard that will govern similar cases and afford guidance to corporations, counsel advising them, and federal courts.

The Court properly relies on a variety of factors in concluding that the communications now before us are privileged. Because of the great importance of the issue, in my view the Court should make clear now that, as a general rule, a communication is privileged at least when, as here, an employee or former employee speaks at the direction of the management with an attorney regarding conduct or proposed conduct within the scope of employment. The attorney must be one authorized by the management to inquire into the subject and must be seeking information to assist counsel in performing any of the following functions: (a) evaluating whether the employee's conduct has bound or would bind the corporation; (b) assessing the legal consequences, if any, of that conduct; or (c) formulating appropriate legal responses to actions that have been or may be taken by others with regard to that conduct. Other communications between employees and corporate counsel may indeed be privileged—as the petitioners and several *amici* have suggested in their proposed formulations—but the need for certainty does not compel us now to prescribe all the details of the privilege in this case.

* * *

Weinstein and Berger, in their commentary on the federal rules, present a thoughtful discussion of the appropriate limits on the privilege of the corporate context. Although Weinstein and Berger were commenting on *Harper & Row,* not *Upjohn,* their discussion is consistent with that of the Court in *Upjohn,* especially with the Chief Justice's concurring opinion. It is not clear how the Supreme Court would have decided *Upjohn* had Weinstein and Berger's suggested requisites for the privilege not been met. However, it is perhaps significant that the Court emphasized that the employees were ordered to disclose information by the corporation's Chairman, that the employees knew that the information was being sent to the corporation's legal counsel for the purpose of securing legal advice for the corporation, that the employees were told that their communications were considered highly confidential, and that the communications were in fact kept confidential by the company.

Weinstein and Berger write:

The following approach to administration of the standard in doubtful cases is suggested.

(1) The corporation has the burden of showing that the communication was made for the purpose of securing *legal* advice, i.e. that it was made in contemplation of future professional action by the attorney. This criterion is in accord with the rationale of the privilege that the fullest disclosure to an attorney results in more competent legal advice with consequent benefits to justice. If the attorney is merely receiving routine reports that would be made in any event, these communications should not be privileged. The burden should also be on the corporation to show that counsel was not sitting in on a business conference primarily as business rather than legal advisor; whether or not the attorney was rendering legal services is the decisive question. It is irrelevant whether he was acting as house counsel or outside counsel.

(2) Consequently, the first criterion of *Harper & Row*—that the employee was required by his superior to disclose the required information—must be expanded by requiring a showing that the superior made this request so as to enable the corporation to receive legal advice. The person with the information need not be the person who recognized that there is a possible legal problem. Nor need he be the one to whom the attorney will report after he has gathered the requisite information.

(3) The question of who is a superior for the purpose of having the privilege apply when such a person advises an employee to seek legal advice is a difficult one. A desirable approach, and one avoiding the definitional problems of the control group theory, would be to resolve this question in functional terms. A superior should be taken as one who is in a position to initiate a request for legal advice and whose actions indicate that his purpose in directing

disclosure to the attorney was in contemplation of the rendition of legal services. At times, depending upon the structure of the corporation and the nature of the communication, a communication which a rather low level employee made on his own initiative may be privileged if the court can find that the employee consciously divulged his information to the attorney for the purpose of obtaining legal advice which would benefit the corporation. In any case, the corporation must show that the communication, from its inception, was intended to be made in order to obtain legal services, as opposed to being a routine report which eventually comes to the attorney's attention.

(4) The second criterion of *Harper & Row*—that the subject matter of the communication is the performance by the employee of the duties of his employment—should be applied, since it removes from the scope of the privilege communications which are within the employee's knowledge solely because he happened to witness or observe an event.

(5) The basic confidentiality requirement of the privilege should be enforced, but in a way compatible with corporate circumstances. A student note suggests:

[C]ommunications within the corporation that are necessary for completeness and accuracy of information given the attorney should be considered confidential even though they have been communicated to third persons. However, holding them confidential without any restrictions, would facilitate the creation of zones of silence. This danger would be substantially eliminated if the class of persons to whom the communication can be disclosed without losing the protection of the privilege was limited to those persons who, because of the structure of the corporation, must know of the communication in order to insure that the attorney is obtaining both full and accurate information.

Information which "is being circulated unnecessarily in the organization" should not be protected. Enforcement of this criterion would ensure that routine business records are not being immunized from discovery by the simple device of forwarding a copy to counsel. The burden is on the corporation to provide information about its own internal security practices which would support a finding of confidentiality. If a corporation wants the benefit of the privilege it should enforce a fairly firm "need to know" of the communication rule.

As a general matter, the more abstract the information and the higher in the corporate hierarchy it is generated, the more likely it is that it will be deemed privileged. Raw observations of a worker in the shop will tend to be repeated by him to persons other than the attorney, while more generalized reports above the foreman level will usually be intended for a restricted group so that it makes more sense to treat them as confidential.

All these criteria added together amount to a standard which allows for predictability since the corporation is on notice that it must be able to prove a connection between the communication and the rendition of legal advice. The corporation cannot make the requisite showing by channelling requests through a member of the control group, or by routine orders by supervisors to have their employees forward all memoranda to counsel. Rather it must be able to show that from the moment the particular communication was initiated it took measures, such as those discussed above, compatible with the communication's having been in confidence to an attorney for the purpose of seeking legal services for the corporation.

The application of this approach can be illustrated by a series of examples all stemming from a collision between a bus and an automobile in which plaintiff was riding.

(1) A lawyer for the bus company obtains a statement from an employee who happened to be on his way to work when he saw the accident. Observing accidents has nothing to do with the duties of the employee. He is simply a witness and his statement while possibly subject to the work-product doctrine of the *Hickman* case is not protected by the attorney-client privilege.

(2) The lawyer for the company obtains a statement from the driver of the bus. Here the inquiry must focus on how the communication reached the attorney. If the bus driver was required to file an accident report with the state and a copy of this is what reached the attorney, the communication would clearly not be privileged since it would not be confidential. If the driver was required to make a report which was circulated in the company for purposes other than obtaining legal advice—e.g., to provide records for disciplinary purposes, medical payments or safety checks—the requisite confidentiality would also be lacking. If the bus driver is asked to report on his accident before a group of corporate employees debating new safety measures, his communication would not be privileged merely

because house counsel sat in on the meeting.

(3) If a person from the corporation's claims department, following routine procedure, consults the corporation's attorney about a possible settlement of plaintiff's claim, this communication would be privileged if the requisite confidentiality exists. It can be assumed that he has been authorized to seek legal advice about a matter concerning the performance of his duties.

To summarize, the corporation must show that the communication was 1) not disseminated beyond those with the need to know and 2) was intended primarily for the ears of the attorney and 3) was made for the purpose of obtaining legal services for the corporation. This can be done by showing the instructions the employee was given about making his report, the status of the person giving him the instructions, the manner in which the report was filed, the purposes for which it was used, and the reason the communication was furnished to the attorney.[42]

———

The proposed federal rule and most of the rules that have been enacted by states which used it as a guideline assume that a client can be a government agency as well as a corporation. The Supreme Court has not yet decided whether the same scope should be given to the privilege for all entities.

As you go through the next set of problems, contrast the implications of the con-

---

42. 2 Weinstein's Evidence ¶ 503(b)[04]. Reprinted by permission of Matthew Bender & Company. It must be kept in mind that this is only one approach. Other thoughtful commentators have suggested different analyses. See generally Gardner, A Personal Privilege for Communications of Corporate Clients—Paradox or Public Policy, 40 U.Det.L.J. 299 (1963); Simon, The Attorney-Client Privilege as Applied to Corporations, 65 Yale L.J. 953 (1956); Note, Attorney-Client Privilege for Corporate Clients: The Control Group Test, 84 Harv.L.Rev. 424 (1970). A good, recent discussion is Weissenberger, Toward Precision in the Application of the Attorney-Client Privilege for Corporations, 65 Iowa L.Rev. 899 (1980).

trol group test with those of *Upjohn*. Remember that even if the privilege is narrowly construed, work product protection
still may be available.

———

Problem VIII–13. A. The Winkel Motor Company is thinking of marketing a new steering device but is concerned with potential liability should
the device in any way contribute to accidents. To insulate the company as
much as possible from successful lawsuits, the president of the company places
Winkel's General Counsel, Frank Edsel, in charge of the program to develop,
evaluate and market the device. The president orders that all employees
submit to Edsel, in confidence, a memorandum prepared specially for the
purpose of obtaining legal advice that describes all test data and other information about the steering device and that the employees destroy all other
copies of the data and information they have described to counsel. She then
instructs Edsel to give a legal opinion on the potential liability of the company should it market the device and to carefully scrutinize any advertising
about the device to minimize claims based on advertising. Final authority
to proceed with, abandon or to do anything else with the device rests at all
times with the board of directors and company management. **Can Edsel
ethically accept this assignment?**

B. Assume that Fielding, who purchased a car containing the steering
device, is injured, and that the alleged cause of the injury is a defect in the
device. **If Fielding sues the company, can he obtain copies of the test
data and other reports of the company regarding the device? Does it
matter whether the control group test or the test of Harper & Row is
used? Would it make any difference if the attorney for the corporation
were an outside attorney?**

C. The company has employee-investigators who are assigned to investigate the Fielding accident. These investigators photograph both the car
and the accident scene, and they interview the witnesses. They also prepare
a report containing their conclusions regarding the accident. **Are the photographs, the witnesses' statements or the report protected by the attorney-client privilege if they are transmitted to Edsel? Are they protected
by the work product doctrine?**

Problem VIII–14. Fred Stone is a janitor at the Winkel Corporation.
One day, while sweeping up, he notices a worker toss a banana peel on the
floor. He intends to sweep it up as soon as he finishes the portion of the
floor he is working on. Before he can finish, a tour group comes by and, to
his horror, Fred sees a woman (Flora Joslyn) slip on the peel, fall and break
her arm. The supervisor tells Fred to tell the company lawyer everything
he knows about the incident. This follows company policy of interviewing
all employees at the scene of an accident. Fred tells his story to the lawyer.
**If Winkel is sued by Flora, will she be able to discover what Fred told
the attorney? Does this depend on the test used? If Fred were on his
lunch hour and saw the accident from across the street from the corporation's building, would there be a privilege under any test? Will the**

situation be any different if Flora joins Fred as a defendant and the company lawyer represents Fred as well as Winkel?

Problem VIII–15. One day the president of the Winkel Music Company asks Edsel, the general counsel, to come to her office. She outlines for Edsel a major new campaign which the company is considering. The only difficulty with the campaign is that some of the material the company hopes to sell may infringe certain copyrights held by other companies and individuals. She describes the copyright situation in some detail and presents Edsel with a memorandum of law prepared for the company by an outside copyright attorney who has concluded that there is a substantial risk that some infringement suits against the company will be successful. She wants Edsel's advice as to whether the profits from the campaign are likely to offset any costs associated with possible suits for copyright infringement and the bad publicity which may stem from being sued. **If Winkel is later sued for copyright infringement, will the president's statements to Edsel concerning the copyright situation be protected by the attorney-client privilege? Will the memorandum prepared by the outside copyright attorney be protected?** Assume that Edsel also is concerned about the company's potential liability for copyright infringement, but is uncertain about the correctness of the advice given by outside counsel. Edsel supplies company employees who are veterans of the music business with copies of both the material the company plans to sell and previously copyrighted works. He asks them for their opinions as to whether the company's music is the same as or different from the copyrighted works. Each employee is told that his answers will be confidential and that the information is sought to enable the company to obtain legal advice. **If Winkel is sued for copyright infringement, will the employees' responses be privileged? Does it matter whether the company President knew of Edsel's actions and approved them? Does it matter whether she ever ordered the employees to respond to Edsel? If Edsel provided similar material to independent music experts and asked them to provide their opinions about the similarity of Winkel's music and previously copyrighted material, would their responses be privileged?**

Problem VIII–16. The town of Cookville is sued for injuries sustained by a plaintiff who tripped on an icy city sidewalk. The plaintiff asks for actual and punitive damages. The mayor of Cookville tells the attorney who has been hired to defend the case that the town had not removed the snow from city sidewalks because a particularly hard winter had left them with insufficient funds to pay for needed snow removal. The mayor admitted that $20,000 in a contingency fund, which might have paid for snow removal, was spent instead on a trip to Florida for the mayor and council members so that they could attend a conference on the cash flow problems in small towns. **If the attorney is asked what reason, if any, the mayor gave for the absence of money in the contingency fund, may she claim the attorney-client privilege on the town's behalf and refuse to answer? Does it matter if the attorney is hired not by the town but by the insurance company which writes the town's liability policy and has the contractual burden of defending any tort actions brought against the town?**

E. WAIVER

The attorney-client privilege, like all privileges, may be waived by the holder. It is waived when the client so states and will be considered waived as to a set of communications concerning an event when a client testifies to some of the communications or permits the attorney to so testify. The law will also imply a waiver whenever the holder of the privilege voluntarily discloses or allows to be disclosed any significant part of the privileged matter.

Waiver can be a tricky concept. Assume that a woman goes to a lawyer to discuss a divorce and later tells a friend of her visit to the lawyer and her reason for going there. If the woman's husband files a countersuit and demands to know what his wife told her lawyer, the privilege would apply to prevent disclosure. If, however, the woman gave her friend a complete description of her conversation with her lawyer, the privilege could no longer be asserted. A person may discuss an event or other matter that was the subject of a previous confidential talk with a lawyer without waiving the privilege, but waiver is implied once the client reveals what was communicated to the lawyer.

Waiver is not assumed if a privileged statement is disclosed in another privileged relationship. For example, if a woman tells her lawyer of privileged statements she made to a physician, disclosure

to the lawyer does not remove them from the protection of the physician-patient privilege so long as the disclosure is otherwise privileged.

The courts are divided on the fate of the privileges when the holder is erroneously compelled to disclose privileged matter or when privileged matter is disclosed under circumstances in which the holder cannot claim the privilege. Some cases suggest that the holder of a privilege who feels disclosure is improperly compelled must remain silent and risk a contempt citation. Disclosure, even in these circumstances, is considered a valid waiver.[43] It is generally understood, however, that erroneously compelled disclosures that violate an accused's fifth amendment rights are not admissible in subsequent criminal prosecutions of the accused. Some authorities advocate a similar rule for all compelled disclosure cases. Even though confidentiality is destroyed by the compulsory disclosure, the damage is minimized if the use of the evidence is restricted. PFRE 512 took this position.

Today, one of the most familiar waiver questions is whether in a case involving a multitude of documents the inadvertent inclusion in discovery materials of privileged matter is a waiver. Some courts have said yes; others have been more protective of the privilege.[44] Here again there are competing policies. Once the privi-

---

43. See, e.g., Fraser v. United States, 145 F.2d 139 (6th Cir. 1944), certiorari denied 324 U.S. 849 (1945). At common law an eavesdropper who overhears a confidential communication is not barred from testifying to the contents of that communication. Two justifications are given for the exception. The first is that privileges, since they suppress relevant evidence, should be strictly construed. The second is that an individual truly concerned with the confidentiality of his communications can take precautions to ensure that no eavesdroppers are present. The development of sophisticated techniques for electronic eaves-

dropping has made the second justification obsolete. This development convinced the drafters of the proposed federal rules to eliminate the common law's exception in the case of eavesdroppers. The proximity of an eavesdropper is still a factor which a court will consider in determining whether a conversation was intended to be confidential.

44. Compare, e.g., Hercules, Inc. v. Exxon Corp., 434 F.Supp. 136 (D.Del.1977) (narrow view of waiver) with RCM Supply Co. v. Hunter Douglas, Inc., 510 F.Supp. 994 (D.Md.1981) (waiver even though disclosures may be inadvertent).

leged information is revealed, confidentiality cannot be restored and probative evidence is available to a fact finder. But, if inadvertence is tantamount to waiver, parties may be unduly restrictive in responding to discovery requests. Furthermore, recognition of a privilege following inadvertent disclosure minimizes the harm to the party that has accidentally disclosed since what has been disclosed will not be used at trial.

F. COMMUNICATIONS WHICH ARE NOT PRIVILEGED

Communications in certain settings or about certain matters are specifically exempted from the protection of the attorney-client privilege. The five exceptions of proposed rule 503(d) codify the common law. When an attorney serves as an attesting witness, she is not acting as a lawyer and the client's obvious intent is to have her available to testify to the matter attested. When two clients consult a lawyer jointly about a matter of common interest, there is no privilege if a dispute should arise between them because there was no intent that their communications be kept secret from each other. However, each would retain a privilege as to his own communications in any litigation against third parties. If a lawyer takes her client to court or vice versa, as in a suit to recover a fee or in a malpractice case, the privilege will give way to the extent necessary to ensure that it is not used to deny either party a rightful recovery. When two persons are claiming through the same deceased client, as in a dispute over which of two wills is valid, the issue of who may properly claim the privilege as the deceased's successor is often tied up with the ultimate issue in the case. Some courts allow either side to claim the privilege. Better practice is to hold the privilege inapplicable in such disputes. This exception is supported by the sensible fiction that the deceased client would have been willing to reveal confidential communications to ensure that his affairs were settled as he intended.

The exception that has given rise to the most controversy is PFRE 503(d)(1) which abrogates the privilege when "the services of the lawyer were sought or obtained to enable or aid anyone to commit or plan to commit what the client knew or reasonably should have known to be a crime or fraud."

The McCormick treatise explains that:

> Since the policy of the privilege is that of promoting the administration of justice, it would be a perversion of the privilege to extend it to the client who seeks advice to aid him in carrying out an illegal or fraudulent scheme. Advice given for those purposes would not be a professional service but participation in a conspiracy.[45]

Wigmore suggests that tortious schemes should also be unprotected by the privilege. He argues that it is difficult to see how any "moral line" can be drawn between crime and fraud on the one hand and tortious acts on the other.[46]

One of the great difficulties in applying this exception is determining what showing of wrongful intent is necessary before the privilege will be abrogated. McCormick writes:

> Must the judge, before denying the claim of privilege on this ground find as a fact, after a preliminary hearing if contested, that the consultation was in furtherance of crime or fraud? This would be the normal procedure in passing on

---

45. McCormick § 95, at 199.

46. 8 Wigmore § 2298, at 577. See also 2 A.L.R.3d 861.

a preliminary fact, on which the admissibility of evidence depends, but here this procedure would facilitate too far the use of the privilege as a cloak for crime. As a solution, some courts have cast the balance in favor of disclosure by requiring only that the one who seeks to avoid the privilege bring forward evidence from which the existence of an unlawful purpose could reasonably be found. Even this limitation seems needless when, as is commonly the case, the examining counsel has sufficient information to focus the inquiry by specific questions, thus avoiding any broad exploration of what transpired between attorney and client.[47]

Apparently the Advisory Committee on the Federal Rules agreed with McCormick, because it noted in connection with PFRE 503:

> While any general exploration of what transpired between attorney and client

would, of course, be inappropriate, it is wholly feasible, either at the discovery stage or during trial, so to focus the inquiry by specific questions as to avoid any broad inquiry into attorney-client communications. Numerous cases reflect this approach.

We are not as confident as McCormick and the Advisory Committee that abuse of the privilege can be ascertained without undermining its legitimate exercise. There are easy cases, but we doubt that they are as common as the previous quotations might lead one to believe. In determining whether the privilege has been abrogated, "the client's guilty intention is controlling."[48] Intent is particularly hard to discover through a small number of specific questions. Perhaps the more traditional view, requiring a preliminary finding that there is prima facie evidence of wrongdoing, is preferable.

Problem VIII–17. Assume that in problem VIII–14 Fred Stone was sued along with the Winkel Corporation and that in the jurisdiction in question both Stone and the Winkel Corporation could claim the attorney-client privilege with respect to Stone's statements to the corporate attorney. **If Stone tells his wife what he told the corporate attorney, would this affect the availability of the privilege to him? The availability of the privilege to Winkel? If Stone tells his bowling buddies what he told the corporate attorney, would this affect the availability of the privilege to him? The availability of the privilege to the corporation?**

Problem VIII–18. Davis, knowing she is under investigation for fraud, consults Polk, an attorney, to secure legal advice. She tells Polk of the scheme she has been using to sell small parcels of land at large profits. The scheme is ingenious but of questionable legality, and Polk, citing his sense of ethics, refuses to take Davis as a client. Two weeks later at a cocktail party where people are talking about different get-rich-quick schemes, Polk describes the scheme which Davis has revealed to him. **Do Polk's revelations in some way violate the attorney-client privilege? Will they affect Davis' ability to claim the privilege with respect to Polk's testimony if Polk is subpoenaed after the case goes to trial? Would your answer to either of these questions be different if Polk had agreed to take Davis on as a client?** Suppose it was Davis rather than Polk who had described the scheme at the

47. McCormick § 95, at 200.   48. Id.

party. **Would Davis' revelations affect her right to claim the attorney-client privilege if asked before a Grand Jury to reveal what she told Polk?**

Problem VIII–19. Dan Nostrum, newspaper columnist and author of the best selling book, *Washington's Seamy Side*, is sued for libel by Sam Senator, a powerful politician, whose private life was explored in some detail in Nostrum's book. At the behest of Joanne Betlem, his attorney, Nostrum describes in detail how he researched the portion of the book pertaining to Senator. Although Nostrum is proud of his research methods, it is clear to Betlem that these methods were so slipshod that Nostrum might be fairly regarded as having acted in reckless disregard of the truth. Before Nostrum leaves, Betlem cautions Nostrum not to discuss their conversations with anyone. Nostrum replies, "But, I'm proud of my methods. Sam abused me in public. I have to defend my reputation by calling a press conference to defend myself." * Betlem, after almost losing her client by bluntly describing the deficiencies in his research, convinces Nostrum not to hold the press conference and to keep the discussion between them confidential. **If Nostrum is later asked what he told Betlem about his research methods, may he refuse to respond on the basis of the attorney-client privilege? Do you think your answer would hold in practice as well as in theory? Why or why not? If Nostrum is asked in a deposition to describe his research methods, may he refuse to do so on the ground of attorney-client privilege? May Betlem refuse to respond if she is asked whether she advised Nostrum not to call a press conference? May Betlem refuse to respond if she is asked what she thought of Nostrum's research methods? Does the attorney-client privilege protect all communications from attorneys to clients?**

Problem VIII–20. The FBI has a mail cover on Kent Kingston, a notorious gangster. The cover is authorized by a warrant. One item which is opened and copied is a letter by Kingston to his attorney, listing the income he has received from certain illegal ventures. Kingston wants to pay the taxes due but does not want the source of the income to be revealed. He asks if this is legally possible and, if so, how this may be done. **May the letters be introduced by the prosecution if Kingston is tried for the illegal activities giving rise to this income? Would the situation be any different if the letters were to Kingston's accountant rather than to his attorney?**

Problem VIII–21. One evening at a cocktail party, Fred Fenster cornered Henry Fish, an attorney, and proceeded to describe certain tax problems. After five minutes Fred concluded, "I know you're a specialist in tax law. What should I do?" Henry replied, "Come see me first thing tomorrow. I don't believe in doing business when my client is half drunk." **Are Fred's disclosures to Henry protected by the attorney-client privilege? Does it matter whether Fred was half drunk? Does it matter whether Fred followed up this conversation with a visit to Henry's office?** Assume Fred had never employed Henry before.

Problem VIII–22. Carla Castenada, a Cuban who speaks no English, consults an attorney about a dispute she is having with a neighbor. She brings along one Mary Sanchez to act as a translator.   During the conference with the attorney Carla discloses certain facts which undercut her claim to title in the disputed land.   Later, in one of those coincidences which happen in problems as well as real life, Mary marries Castenada's neighbor.   The neighbor dies of course, and Mary, the sole beneficiary of his will, brings suit against Castenada to quiet title in the disputed land.   **May Mary testify at the trial concerning the conversation she translated between Castenada and her attorney?**

Problem VIII–23.   Arnold and Baker are both concerned because their children have become devoted followers of the Reverend Luna's Galactic Church.   They consult a lawyer together to learn about their legal options. Arnold describes an elaborate kidnapping and reprogramming plan to the attorney and asks if it would be legal.   The attorney tells Arnold that it would not be and advises him not to implement it.   They leave.   Later Baker's son is accidently killed during a kidnap attempt which closely follows the plan Arnold described.   **If Baker sues Arnold for the wrongful death of his son, will the attorney-client privilege prevent him from testifying to the plan Arnold disclosed in the lawyer's office?   If the state prosecutes Arnold for kidnapping, will the attorney-client privilege prevent Baker from testifying as a witness for the state?**

Problem VIII–24.   Thomas Dooley asked David Guard, an attorney, to represent him in a divorce action.   During a series of interviews Dooley related to Guard the intimate details of his married life, including the fact that he had engaged in several adulterous affairs during the preceding five years. Dooley also acquainted Guard with the details of his financial condition, including the facts that: (a) he is the recipient of a trust fund paying $15,000 a year, (b) he owns a variety of stocks with a book value of $190,000 and a current market value of $310,000, (c) his earned income has increased during the preceding five years from $42,000 to $60,000 and he expects it to continue increasing at the rate of about $4000 a year during the foreseeable future, and (d) he has earned an additional sum ranging from $10,000 to $25,000 during each of the preceding three years from the illegal sale of amphetamines.   He is considering giving up this "business" because of the risk involved.   After the divorce was completed, Dooley paid Guard $5000 for general services but refused to pay an extra $5000 which Guard claimed was due him for special tax advice.   Dooley claimed that the tax advice he received from Guard was not worth more than $500.   Guard sues for his fee.   **If Guard takes the stand on his own behalf, may Dooley claim the attorney-client privilege to prevent Guard from testifying to the conversations relating to (a) his adulterous affairs, (b) his involvement in the illegal sale of amphetamines, and (c) the other details of his financial situation?**

When the divorce action mentioned above was tried Dooley, after testifying on direct examination to his financial status, was asked by his wife's attorney, "Isn't it true that your trust account paid $30,000 a year until the past month when, at your encouragement, the trustees shifted the corpus into more speculative stock?"   **If Dooley answered, "No, why three months ago I told Mr. Guard the expected earnings were only $15,000 a year," would he be able to claim a privilege if his wife's attorney then asked him what else he had told Mr. Guard about his finances?**

Problem VIII–25. Alan Kaufman, a professional basketball star, has hired Daniel Novack, an attorney, as his agent. Novack doesn't understand the tax implications of certain endorsement proposals so he refers Kaufman to a leading tax practitioner. Kaufman gives Novack a detailed account of his conversations with the tax specialist. After considering the tax consequences, the quality of the products Kaufman would be associated with, Kaufman's image, and the likelihood of future endorsement contracts, Novack advises Kaufman to sign with the Winkel Corporation. Later the IRS charges Kaufman with income tax evasion. They seek to put either the tax specialist or Novack on the stand in order to learn what Kaufman told the specialist about his tax situation. **May Kaufman claim the attorney-client privilege with respect to the testimony of either or both of them?**

Problem VIII–26. Paul Peters sues the Foxy-Loxy Supermarket for injuries allegedly suffered when Peters passed through an electronically operated entrance door to the Foxy-Loxy. The complaint alleges that as Peters approached the entrance, the door automatically opened, but that before Peters passed completely through, the door closed suddenly and with great force, striking Peters in the face, breaking his eyeglasses, and causing blindness in the right eye. Foxy-Loxy calls Sarah Andrews, an attorney, who will testify that the day after the alleged accident, Peters consulted her and asked her to sue the defendant, but that she refused the case because Peters insisted on claiming that his right eye had been blinded by the accident although he admitted that he had in fact lost the sight in that eye a year earlier in an industrial accident. Plaintiff objects to the testimony on the ground of privilege. **What is the proper ruling?**

Problem VIII–27. Martin, an actor, has just completed a very successful year in show business. In fact, his income is so great that he goes to Lewis, a tax lawyer, for legal advice. Martin has prepared a tentative return including some questionable deductions for business expenses. Lewis tells him:

> Mr. Martin, you're a better actor than tax man. These deductions you want to take are completely unwarranted. The government will challenge you on them without any doubt. In fact, some of the things you have done are plainly fraudulent, and if you were to submit your return in its current form, you might well be subject to prosecution for tax fraud.

Upset at the pessimistic reaction of Lewis, Martin takes his tax business to Shyster who tells him that the return is perfectly satisfactory. Shyster is not a tax lawyer, however. Admiralty is his specialty. But, happy to rely on this legal advice, Martin submits his return without deleting any of the claimed deductions. In a prosecution for tax fraud, the prosecution wants to call Lewis to testify to what he told Martin. Martin objects. **What result? Can the prosecutor ask specific questions of the tax lawyer to determine whether the privilege should apply without violating the privilege? What questions would you ask?**

Problem VIII–28. In the preceding problem, assume that Martin was told by Lewis that there was a 50–50 chance that his return would be viewed as fraudulent. Assume also that Martin went to another tax lawyer who said there was no possibility of fraud. **Could Lewis testify as to the state**

of mind or intent of Martin, if Martin objected on the ground of privilege?   What specific questions would you ask to determine whether the privilege applies?

Problem VIII–29.   Assume that Shyster, the admiralty lawyer consulted in Problem VIII–27, is the subject of disciplinary action by the local bar.   He is charged with incompetence, not with aiding in the commission of a fraud.   The bar wishes to demonstrate that the advice given to Martin typifies the quality of Shyster's legal work.   A trial-type hearing is held in which the rules of evidence apply.   Any decision at the hearing may be appealed to the state supreme court.   The hearing examiner compels Martin, who is called as a witness, to testify (over his and Shyster's objections) to his communications with Shyster.   **Is this decision correct?   If Shyster had been asked what he told Martin and Martin was not present because he had been imprisoned for the tax fraud described in Problem VIII–27, could Shyster claim the privilege on Martin's behalf?**

G. ETHICAL ISSUES

Questions relating to the attorney-client privilege often merge with other questions about the duty which an attorney owes her client and the court.   There are ways in which a client who has revealed information to an attorney may be disadvantaged even if the privilege is honored.   One recurring issue is whether an attorney whose client has confessed to a crime may continue to defend the client as if no confession had been made.   The tentative position of the American Bar Association is that knowledge of a client's guilt limits the ways in which a lawyer may defend her client.

ABA STANDARDS FOR CRIMINAL JUSTICE, THE PROSECUTION FUNCTION AND THE DEFENSE FUNCTION, STANDARD 7.7, THE DEFENSE FUNCTION (APP. DRAFT 1971).

Testimony by the defendant.

(a) If the defendant has admitted to his lawyer facts which establish guilt and the lawyer's independent investigation established that the admissions are true but the defendant insists on his right to trial, the lawyer must advise his client against taking the witness stand to testify falsely.

(b) If, before trial, the defendant insists that he will take the stand to testify falsely, the lawyer must withdraw from the case, if that is feasible, seeking leave of court if necessary.

(c) If withdrawal from the case is not feasible or is not permitted by the court, or if the situation arises during the trial and the defendant insists upon testifying falsely in his own behalf, the lawyer may not lend his aid to the perjury.   Before the defendant takes the stand in these circumstances, the lawyer should make a record of the fact that the defendant is taking the stand against the advice of counsel in some appropriate manner without revealing the fact to the court.   The lawyer must confine his examination to identifying the witness as the defendant and permitting him to make his statement to the trier or the triers of the facts;   the lawyer may not engage in direct examination of the defendant as a witness in the conventional manner and may not later argue the defendant's known false version of facts to the jury as worthy of belief and he may not recite or rely upon the false testimony in his closing argument.

Dean Monroe Freedman, whose views were briefly examined in Chapter Five, disagrees with the ABA's position:

THE ADVERSARY SYSTEM AND THE NECESSITY FOR CONFIDENTIALITY

The adversary system has further ramifications in a criminal case. The defendant is presumed to be innocent. The burden is on the prosecution to prove beyond a reasonable doubt that the defendant is guilty. The plea of not guilty does not necessarily mean "not guilty in fact," for the defendant may mean "not legally guilty." Even the accused who knows that he committed the crime is entitled to put the government to its proof. Indeed, the accused who knows that he is guilty has an absolute constitutional right to remain silent. The moralist might quite reasonably understand this to mean that, under these circumstances, the defendant and his lawyer are privileged to "lie" to the court in pleading not guilty. In my judgment, the moralist is right. However, our adversary system and related notions of the proper administration of criminal justice sanction the lie.

Some derive solace from the sophistry of calling the lie a "legal fiction," but this is hardly an adequate answer to the moralist. Moreover, this answer has no particular appeal for the practicing attorney, who knows that the plea of not guilty commits him to the most effective advocacy of which he is capable. Criminal defense lawyers do not win their cases by arguing reasonable doubt. Effective trial advocacy requires that the attorney's every word, action, and attitude be consistent with the conclusion that his client is innocent. As every trial lawyer knows, the jury is certain that the defense attorney knows whether his client is guilty. The jury is therefore alert to, and will be enormously affected by, any indication by the attorney that he believes the defendant to be guilty. Thus, the plea of not guilty commits the advocate to a trial, including a closing argument, in which he must argue that "not guilty" means "not guilty in fact."

[The question is posed whether it is proper to put a witness on the stand when you know he will commit perjury.]

Perhaps the most common method for avoiding the ethical problem just posed is for the lawyer to withdraw from the case, at least if there is sufficient time before trial for the client to retain another attorney. The client will then go to the nearest law office, realizing that the obligation of confidentiality is not what it has been represented to be, and withhold incriminating information or the fact of his guilt from his new attorney. On ethical grounds, the practice of withdrawing from a case under such circumstances is indefensible, since the identical perjured testimony will ultimately be presented. More important, perhaps, is the practical consideration that the new attorney will be ignorant of the perjury and therefore will be in no position to attempt to discourage the client from presenting it. Only the original attorney, who knows the truth, has that opportunity, but he loses it in the very act of evading the ethical problem.

The problem is all the more difficult when the client is indigent. He cannot retain other counsel, and in many jurisdictions, including the District of Columbia, it is impossible for appointed counsel to withdraw from a case except for extraordinary reasons. Thus, appointed counsel, unless he lies to the judge, can successfully withdraw only by revealing to the judge that the attorney has received knowledge of his client's guilt. Such a revelation in itself would seem to be a sufficiently serious violation of the obligation of confidentiality to merit severe condemnation. In fact, however, the situation is far worse, since it is entirely possible that the same judge who permits the attorney to withdraw will subsequently hear the case and sentence the defendant. When he does so, of course, he will have had personal knowledge of the defendant's guilt before the trial began. Moreover, this will be knowledge of which the newly appointed counsel for the defendant will probably be ignorant.

The difficulty is further aggravated when the client informs the lawyer for the first time during trial that he intends to take the stand and commit perjury. The perjury in question may not necessarily be a protestation of innocence by a guilty man. Referring to the * * * hypothetical of the defendant wrongly accused of a robbery at 16th and P, the only perjury may be his denial of the truthful, but highly damaging, testimony of the corroborating witness who placed him one block away from the intersection five minutes prior to the crime. Of course, if he tells the truth and thus verifies the corroborating witness, the jury will be far more inclined to accept the inaccurate testimony of the principal witness, who specifically identified him as the criminal.

If a lawyer has discovered his client's intent to perjure himself, one possible solution to this problem is for the lawyer to approach the bench, explain his ethical difficulty to the judge, and ask to be relieved, thereby causing a mistrial. This request is certain to be denied, if only because it would empower the defendant to cause a series of mistrials in the same fashion. At this point, some feel that the lawyer has avoided the ethical problem and can put the defendant on the stand. However, one objection to this solution, apart from the violation of confidentiality, is that the lawyer's ethical problem has not been solved, but has only been transferred to the judge. Moreover, the client in such a case might

well have grounds for appeal on the basis of deprivation of due process and denial of the right to counsel, since he will have been tried before, and sentenced by, a judge who has been informed of the client's guilt by his own attorney.

A solution even less satisfactory than informing the judge of the defendant's guilt would be to let the client take the stand without the attorney's participation and to omit reference to the client's testimony in closing argument. The latter solution, of course, would be as damaging as to fail entirely to argue the case to the jury, and failing to argue the case is "as improper as though the attorney had told the jury that his client had uttered a falsehood in making the statement."

Therefore, the obligation of confidentiality, in the context of our adversary system, apparently allows the attorney no alternative to putting a perjurious witness on the stand without explicit or implicit disclosure of the attorney's knowledge to either the judge or the jury. * * *

Of course, before the client testifies perjuriously, the lawyer has a duty to attempt to dissuade him on grounds of both law and morality. In addition, the client should be impressed with the fact that his untruthful alibi is tactically dangerous. There is always a strong possibility that the prosecutor will expose the perjury on cross-examination. However, for the reasons already given, the final decision must necessarily be the client's. The lawyer's best course thereafter would be to avoid any further professional relationship with a client whom he knew to have perjured himself.[49]

49. Professional Responsibility of the Criminal Defense Lawyer: The Three Hardest Questions, 64 Mich.L.Rev. 1469, 1470–72, 1475–78 (1966). Others take strong exception to this analysis. See e.g., Noonan, The Purposes of Advocacy and the Limits of Confidentiality, 64 Mich.L.Rev. 1485 (1966). In connection with this material you might find it helpful to review Section IV of Chapter Five.

Problem VIII–30. Kate Rist is charged with murdering a police officer. There were no eyewitnesses to the crime, but Rist's gun was found near the scene and it can be proved that Rist harbored a grudge against the officer. During the first of several meetings with appointed counsel, Rist admits the crime, but indicates that she wishes to put the prosecution to its proof. Independent investigation has turned up nothing for defense counsel. Shortly before trial, Rist tells counsel that she really did not do it, but that she lent her gun to a recently deceased friend. Rist says that the friend was the killer and that she had been lying to protect her friend. The lawyer finds the story incredible and asks the court for leave to withdraw, which is refused. At the trial the lawyer puts Rist on the stand, and simply asks Rist to relate her story of the night in question. Rist, after she is convicted, challenges her conviction on the ground that she was denied the effective assistance of counsel and that statements made in confidence to her attorney resulted in her being denied the right to testify like all other witnesses. **Should she prevail?**

———

H. CLOSING REMARKS

In our discussion of the attorney-client privilege we have not mentioned every situation in which the applicability of the privilege is problematic. There are a number of areas where the general principles do not provide clear guidance and the courts are understandably split. Should a corporation be able to claim the privilege against a shareholder bringing a derivative action?[50] Are discussions between an insured party and a lawyer working for an insurance company protected in a "direct action" state?[51] Do lawyers have peculiar duties to disclose information they learn in connection with mergers or the sale of stock?[52] When you are working in an area where the implications of the general principles are unclear, you will want to learn how courts have dealt with the privilege in similar situations.

As we see it, there are four particularly strong arguments which support the attorney-client privilege. Each of these, however, carries more force with respect to natural persons than with respect to organized entities.

First, a proper understanding of the privilege reveals that it suppresses very little information. This privilege does not prevent disclosure of what a person knows; it only protects the actual communications with counsel. In most civil cases, discovery devices may be used to probe the knowledge of all witnesses, including the opposing party. It is true that in criminal

50. See Garner v. Wolfinbarger, 430 F.2d 1093 (5th Cir. 1970), certiorari denied, 401 U.S. 974 (1971) (suggesting at 1103–04 that the privilege bows to a good cause showing). See generally Brodsky, The Attorney and Client Privilege in Stockholder Derivative Cases, 168 N.Y.L.J. 3 (1972); Van Dusen, The Responsibility of Lawyers: Advising Management Under the ABA Code of Professional Responsibility, 46 N.Y.S.Bar J. 565 (1974); Comment, The Attorney-Client Privilege in Shareholders' Suits, 69 Colum.L.Rev. 309 (1969).

51. See, Gottlieb v. Bresler, 24 F.R.D. 371 (D.D.C.1959) (rejecting majority common law position and concluding that statement of insured to insurer is not privileged).

52. See SEC v. National Student Marketing Corp., 360 F.Supp. 284 (D.D.C.1973) (raising question of whether a lawyer has an obligation to disclose corporate violation of securities' laws to the SEC).

cases the government may be barred from questioning the accused, but this is because of the privilege against self-incrimination, not the attorney-client privilege. If the fifth amendment results in inequities in the criminal process, this should be corrected at the constitutional level and not by interfering with the attorney-client relationship. Even in criminal cases, the privilege may not suppress as much evidence as it seems. If clients knew that whatever they told their attorneys could be revealed in court, attorneys might learn much less about their clients' activities than they currently do. This is why the sixth amendment's "right to counsel" may mandate the privilege in criminal cases.

Second, the privilege is necessary for effective representation because it facilitates the kind of interview which ensures that nothing is overlooked. The effective interviewer endeavors to extract everything the client thinks he knows. The lawyer must insist that the client reveal incriminating or embarrassing details and must also invite errors which might be harmful but for the privilege. As we suggested in Chapter Two, clients are naturally reluctant to reveal information which casts them in a bad light. The privilege helps the attorney convince the client to "come clean". Clients might be reluctant to state facts of which they were not sure if they thought their statements could be used against them. The privilege encourages clients to give their attorneys leads which might be crucial to a successful case, or, indeed, to the conclusion that there is no case worth litigating.

Third, the situation at trial might be intolerable without the privilege. Imagine a civil suit in which Passenger sues Driver for damages resulting from injuries suffered when Driver's car hit Passenger at an intersection. Passenger claims that Driver ran a red light. Driver asserts that she was not at fault because Passenger jumped in front of her car. After Passenger testifies and rests his case, Driver calls Passenger's lawyer as a hostile witness. The following dialogue portrays what might occur absent a privilege.

[BY DEFENSE COUNSEL]

Q. You represent Passenger? A. Yes.

Q. Have you represented him from the beginning of this suit? A. Yes.

Q. When was the first time you saw him? A. The 21st of September, 1973.

Q. That is 2 weeks after the accident? A. That is correct.

Q. Did he describe the accident at that time? A. Yes.

Q. Do you recall his description? A. Yes.

Q. And it goes without saying, does it not, that you heard his testimony in court today? A. Yes, that is also correct.

Q. Was today's story the same one you heard on September 21, 1973? A. Yes.

Q. Exactly? A. Yes.

Q. You mean to say you asked him the exact questions in 1973 that you asked today and he used exactly the same words to answer? A. No, not the same words, but the essence of his story did not change.

Q. You mean there were no changes in his story from then until now? **A.** Correct.

Q. Not one change? **A.** Not one major change.

Q. Were there minor changes? **A.** Yes.

Q. What were they? **A.** I cannot recall.

Q. You cannot recall any? **A.** No.

Q. How can you be certain then that they were minor? **A.** Well, if they were major, I'd remember.

Q. How many minor changes? **A.** I don't know. Several maybe.

Q. Three, ten, how many? **A.** I don't know.

Q. Might there have been ten? **A.** No.

Q. How can you be sure? Can you recall the changes better now? **A.** No, there could have been ten. O.K.

Q. And of the ten, you can't remember one? **A.** I can't tell you if there were ten.

Without the privilege, might not cases turn on the skills of lawyers as witnesses? Who would represent Passenger while his lawyer testified? What would that lawyer have to know about the case? Could she then be called as a witness? Does the fact that counsel speaks for the client throughout a trial mean that counsel's statements from the stand would "bind" the client? If they did not in law, might they in the eyes of the jury? Or, is the situation we have sketched so improbable we should not be worried about it? Can the work product rule and comity among lawyers be relied upon to prevent all such abuse?

Finally, we come to more nebulous values. The lawyer-client relationship should be one of loyalty and can be one of intimate trust. Is it right to compel attorneys to reveal confidences which were gained only because of the rapport they were able to establish in the counseling relationship? In a system in which attorneys are defined as zealous advocates on their clients' behalf, should we specify one area in which attorneys are routinely expected to betray their clients? If we did, would we get betrayal? Might we not get larger numbers

of attorneys who either render ineffective assistance because they have chosen to remain ignorant about important aspects of their clients' affairs or perjure themselves, or go to jail for their silence? If attorneys did prefer jail to testifying against their clients, would we admire them or condemn them for their choice? If we would admire them, it suggests that the privilege is rooted in deeply held values. Furthermore, in a society in which government is too often intrusive and in which numbers on computers follow one throughout life, it is good to have zones of privacy. Should the relationship with an attorney be such a zone? These values alone might not justify a privilege. (Indeed, it seems that they are all threatened more by the compelled testimony of best friends than they are by that of lawyers.) But, when these values are coupled with the other factors which support the privilege, they weigh heavily in the balance.

If the client is a corporate entity, the third point appears to have the same force as it does with respect to natural persons. The identification of lawyer with client remains real and the potential for abuse exists if communications to counsel are unprivileged. It is not clear, however, that one should expect this potential to be realized, for much of what was learned by counsel from low level corporate employees in the past has not been privileged. It has been protected only by the work product rule and a sense that opposing counsel should be called to testify only as a last resort. These protections have apparently been sufficient to prevent abuse.

The argument that the privilege encourages clients to be honest in communicating with counsel is weaker when corporations are clients. Often corporate employees are not deeply involved in the matters they discuss with the corporation's attorneys. Individuals are much more likely to be personally affected by the outcome of their involvement with the legal process. Of course, in close or small corporations, and in situations where the employee's job or reputation is at stake, the privilege may help promote honest communications to the same extent that it helps when individuals are clients. The situation is similar with respect to more nebulous values. The corporate setting typically depersonalizes the attorney-client relationship. Communications to counsel are often part of one's job or, indeed, explicitly ordered. Furthermore, loyalty to a business organization is not regarded in the same way as loyalty to a human being, though again, there will be situations in which corporate-individual differences disappear.

Finally, invocation of the privilege in the corporate setting has a greater potential for concealing information than it does when individuals are clients. Determining who in a corporation has relevant information or deposing large numbers of individuals may be costly. The office of corporate counsel may be an efficient clearinghouse for corporate information. Moreover, employees performing routine functions may forget the details of events which they have described to the corporate attorney. The attorney's records may be the only source of this information. While opening up the attorney's files might deter the collection of certain information, business needs requiring the attorney to have the information are likely to outweigh the possible costs of potential disclosure. The work product rule would still ensure a considerable degree of privacy.

We believe that, except in one circumstance, only a qualified privilege is desirable in the corporate setting. The privilege should give way upon a substantial showing of need in much the same way as "work product" protection. The exceptional circumstance, where we would apply the privilege in full, is where the corporation can demonstrate that the confidential communications were elicited under circumstances, including potential liability, virtually identical to those facing natural persons. The Supreme Court has taken a different view in *Upjohn*.

SECTION III.   PHYSICIAN-PATIENT PRIVILEGE

A.   THE PRIVILEGE GENERALLY

At common law the patient had no privilege to prevent a physician from testifying to information learned in confidence. In 1828, New York legislated a physician-patient privilege. Today the privilege exists in most of the states. In the first half of the nineteenth century, when the attorney-client privilege was justified largely on the basis of professional honor, the case for a physician-patient privilege was strong: a patient's physical condition is a private matter which the honorable doctor is bound to keep confidential. But as justifications for privileges became more pragmatic, the case for the physician-patient privilege grew weaker. The argument was made that without the privilege people would be reluctant to seek treatment for loathsome or shameful diseases like leprosy and syphilis, but the difficulties with this argument are clear. Individuals are seldom thrust involuntarily into litigation requiring embarrassing disclosures about their medical histories. People seeing doctors, unlike those who see lawyers, do not usually fear that confidential disclosures might prove harmful in forthcoming litigation because they do not usually anticipate litigation. Above all, the desire for good health is a powerful incentive to seek treatment and be honest with one's physician whatever the potential for disclosure. As Wigmore points out, there is no evidence that jurisdictions which have not adopted the privilege have lower standards of medical care than those which have adopted it.[53]

The privilege is often invoked in circumstances where the patient may have expected that his revelations to a doctor would be relevant in future litigation. Wigmore asserts that ninety-nine percent of the cases in which the privilege is claimed fall into one of three categories: actions on life insurance policies where representations of the health of the deceased are challenged by the company, tort actions for injuries where plaintiff's physical condition is at issue, and testamentary actions where the testator's mental capacity is questioned. These are all situations in which invocation of the privilege may prevent probative evidence, not otherwise accessible, from reaching the trier of fact. They are also situations in which the patient holding the privilege has knowingly become involved in a legal matter that makes his health a central issue. Wigmore comments:

> In all of these the medical testimony is absolutely needed for the purpose of learning the truth. In none of them is there any reason for the party to conceal the facts, except as a tactical maneuver in litigation.[54]

These arguments, by Wigmore and others, have generally not dislodged the privilege where it exists, but they have led to numerous exceptions which meet many of the commentators' objections. Consider, for example, the privilege as it applies in California:[55]

ARTICLE 6. PHYSICIAN-PATIENT PRIVILEGE

§ 990. "Physician". As used in this article, "physician" means a person authorized, or reasonably believed by the patient to be authorized, to practice medicine in any state or nation.

§ 991. "Patient". As used in this article, "patient" means a person who consults a physician or submits to an examination by a physician for the purpose of securing a diagnosis or preven-

53. 8 Wigmore § 2380a, at 830. The view that no privilege is needed, which prevails in approximately a third of the states, has deep common law roots. In a bigamy trial involving the Duchess of Kingston (Elizabeth) in 1776, a surgeon attempted to invoke a privilege not to answer questions concerning a previous marriage of the defendant, whom the surgeon had treated. The court ruled:

If a surgeon was voluntarily to reveal these secrets, to be sure he would be guilty of a breach of honour, and of great indis-

cretion; but, to give that information in a court of justice, which by the law of the land he is bound to do, will never be imputed to him as any indiscretion whatever.

20 How.St. Trials 355, 573 (1776). Of course, the details of the marriage were far removed from the kinds of facts generally protected by a physician-patient privilege.

54. 8 Wigmore § 2380a, at 831.

55. West's Ann.Calif. Evid.Code §§ 990–1007 (1966, as amended).

tive, palliative, or curative treatment of his physical or mental or emotional condition.

§ 992. *"Confidential communication between patient and physician"*. As used in this article, "confidential communication between patient and physician" means information, including information obtained by an examination of the patient, transmitted between a patient and his physician in the course of that relationship and in confidence by a means which, so far as the patient is aware, discloses the information to no third persons other than those who are present to further the interest of the patient in the consultation or those to whom disclosure is reasonably necessary for the transmission of the information or the accomplishment of the purpose for which the physician is consulted, and includes a diagnosis made and the advice given by the physician in the course of that relationship.

§ 993. *"Holder of the privilege"*. As used in this article, "holder of the privilege" means:

(a) The patient when he has no guardian or conservator.

(b) A guardian or conservator of the patient when the patient has a guardian or conservator.

(c) The personal representative of the patient if the patient is dead.

§ 994. *Physician-patient privilege*. Subject to Section 912 and except as otherwise provided in this article, the patient, whether or not a party, has a privilege to refuse to disclose, and to prevent another from disclosing, a confidential communication between patient and physician if the privilege is claimed by:

(a) The holder of the privilege;

(b) A person who is authorized to claim the privilege by the holder of the privilege; or

(c) The person who was the physician at the time of the confidential communication, but such person may not claim the privilege if there is no holder of the privilege in existence or if he is otherwise instructed by a person authorized to permit disclosure.

The relationship of a physician and patient shall exist between a medical corporation as defined in Article 17 (commencing with Section 2500) of Chapter 5 of Division 2 of the Business and Professions Code and the patient to whom it renders professional services, as well as between such patients and licensed physicians and surgeons employed by such corporation to render services to such patients. The word "persons" as used in this subdivision includes partnerships, corporations, associations, and other groups and entities.

§ 995. *When physician required to claim privilege*. The physician who received or made a communication subject to the privilege under this article shall claim the privilege whenever he is present when the communication is sought to be disclosed and is authorized to claim the privilege under subdivision (c) of Section 994.

§ 996. *Exception: Patient-litigant exception*. There is no privilege under this article as to a communication relevant to an issue concerning the condition of the patient if such issue has been tendered by:

(a) The patient;

(b) Any party claiming through or under the patient;

(c) Any party claiming as a beneficiary of the patient through a contract to which the patient is or was a party; or

(d) The plaintiff in an action brought under Section 376 or 377 of the Code of Civil Procedure for damages for the injury or death of the patient.

§ 997. *Exception: Crime or tort.* There is no privilege under this article if the services of the physician were sought or obtained to enable or aid anyone to commit or plan to commit a crime or a tort or to escape detection or apprehension after the commission of a crime or a tort.

§ 998. *Exception: Criminal proceeding.* There is no privilege under this article in a criminal proceeding.

§ 999. *Exception: Proceeding to recover damages on account of conduct of patient.* There is no privilege under this article as to a communication relevant to an issue concerning the condition of the patient in a proceeding to recover damages on account of conduct of the patient if good cause for disclosure of the communication is shown.

§ 1000. *Exception: Parties claiming through deceased patient.* There is no privilege under this article as to a communication relevant to an issue between parties all of whom claim through a deceased patient, regardless of whether the claims are by testate or intestate succession or by inter vivos transaction.

§ 1001. *Exception: Breach of duty arising out of physician-patient relationship.* There is no privilege under this article as to a communication relevant to an issue of breach, by the physician or by the patient, of a duty arising out of the physician-patient relationship.

§ 1002. *Exception: Intention of deceased patient concerning writing affecting property interest.* There is no privilege under this article as to a communication relevant to an issue concerning the intention of a patient, now deceased, with respect to a deed of conveyance, will, or other writing, executed by the patient, purporting to affect an interest in property.

§ 1003. *Exception: Validity of writing affecting property interest.* There is no privilege under this article as to a communication relevant to an issue concerning the validity of a deed of conveyance, will, or other writing, executed by a patient, now deceased, purporting to affect an interest in property.

§ 1004. *Exception: Commitment or similar proceeding.* There is no privilege under this article in a proceeding to commit the patient or otherwise place him or his property, or both, under the control of another because of his alleged mental or physical condition.

§ 1005. *Exception: Proceeding to establish competence.* There is no privilege under this article in a proceeding brought by or on behalf of the patient to establish his competence.

§ 1006. *Exception: Required report.* There is no privilege under this article as to information that the physician or the patient is required to report to a public employee, or as to information required to be recorded in a public office, if such report or record is open to public inspection.

§ 1007. *Exception: Proceeding to terminate right, license or privilege.* There is no privilege under this article in a proceeding brought by a public entity to determine whether a right, authority, license, or privilege (including the right or privilege to be employed by the public entity or to hold a public office) should be revoked, suspended, terminated, limited, or conditioned.

In most jurisdictions the physician-patient privilege is not as riddled with exceptions as it is in California, but most of the specific exceptions found in California are found in other jurisdictions. Most, if not all, states would prevent either by judicial decision or statute, the invocation of the privilege where a physician was consulted to facilitate the commission of a crime, in actions involving a breach of duty arising out of the physician-patient relationship, or where physicians are required to report certain conditions to public authorities. A number of states do not allow the privilege to be invoked in criminal cases and more than half do not allow it in disputes concerning worker's compensation.

California's exception for situations in which the patient has placed his condition in issue generally prevents plaintiffs from claiming the privilege in personal injury litigation. Many states do not follow California in this regard. However, some hold that the privilege is waived where the plaintiff testifies about his physical condition, and all hold it waived as to the plaintiff's testifying physicians and doctors consulted jointly with testifying physicians. Some states maintain that placing one physician on the stand to testify waives the privilege with respect to all doctors consulted about the particular physical condition. Waiver is also effected under Fed.R.Civ.P. 35 and its state counterparts if a patient examined under that rule seeks a report of the examination or deposes the examining physician.

The physician-patient privilege in California has other features generally characteristic of the privilege. The patient holds the privilege and may waive it. The privilege survives the death of the patient. The privilege extends to information which the physician learns from examining the patient even if the patient does nothing, apart from allowing the examination, to actively communicate information to the doctor. The presence of third persons or the transmittal of information to others in order to facilitate treatment or diagnosis does not abrogate the privilege. By implication, the presence of third persons not necessary to the consultation, or the patient's knowing transmittal of information to such persons, will vitiate the privilege. Finally the privilege is limited to information which the physician receives for purposes of diagnosis or treatment. Here the California statute, by using the disjunctive "or," creates a privilege that is somewhat broader than the privilege found in most jurisdictions. Usually, a diagnostic consultation is not privileged unless the diagnosis is sought at least in part, for the purpose of securing treatment. Thus, if a physician is consulted only to secure an expert diagnosis at trial, confidential communications to that physician are not privileged. Of course, the abrogation of the privilege in these circumstances is meaningless unless the party, after receiving the diagnosis, chooses not to have the physician testify.

B. AN EMERGING PRIVILEGE

The committee which drafted the federal rules was persuaded that a privilege which required the exceptions of the California privilege was hardly a privilege at all, so they chose not to include a physician-patient privilege in the proposed rules. They did, however, feel that a convincing case could be made for a psychotherapist-patient privilege:

Among physicians, the psychiatrist has a special need to maintain confidentiality. His capacity to help his patients is completely dependent upon their willingness and ability to talk freely. This makes it difficult if not impossible for him to function without being able to assure his patients of confidentiality and, indeed, privileged communication. Where there may be exceptions to this general rule * * *, there is wide agreement that confidentiality is a *sine qua non* for successful psychiatric treatment. The relationship may well be likened to that of the priest-penitent or the lawyer-client. Psychiatrists not only

explore the very depths of their patients' conscious, but their unconscious
feelings and attitudes as well. Therapeutic effectiveness necessitates going
beyond a patient's awareness and, in order to do this, it must be possible to
communicate freely. A threat to secrecy blocks successful treatment.[56]

The following rule was proposed:

PSYCHOTHERAPIST-PATIENT PRIVILEGE

(a) *Definitions.*

(1) A "patient" is a person who consults or is examined or interviewed by a
psychotherapist.

(2) A "psychotherapist" is (A) a person authorized to practice medicine in
any state or nation, or reasonably believed by the patient so to be, while engaged in the diagnosis or treatment of a
mental or emotional condition, including drug addiction, or (B) a person licensed or certified as a psychologist under the laws of any state or nation, while
similarly engaged.

(3) A communication is "confidential" if not intended to be disclosed to
third persons other than those present
to further the interest of the patient in
the consultation, examination, or interview, or persons reasonably necessary for
the transmission of the communication,
or persons who are participating in the
diagnosis and treatment under the direction of the psychotherapist, including
members of the patient's family.

(b) *General rule of privilege.* A patient has a privilege to refuse to disclose
and to prevent any other person from
disclosing confidential communications,
made for the purposes of diagnosis or

treatment of his mental or emotional
condition, including drug addiction,
among himself, his psychotherapist, or
persons who are participating in the diagnosis or treatment under the direction
of the psychotherapist, including members of the patient's family.

(c) *Who may claim the privilege.* The
privilege may be claimed by the patient,
by his guardian or conservator, or by the
personal representative of a deceased
patient. The person who was the psychotherapist may claim the privilege but
only on behalf of the patient. His authority so to do is presumed in the absence of evidence to the contrary.

(d) *Exceptions.*

(1) Proceedings for hospitalization.
There is no privilege under this rule for
communications relevant to an issue in
proceedings to hospitalize the patient for
mental illness, if the psychotherapist in
the course of diagnosis or treatment has
determined that the patient is in need of
hospitalization.

(2) Examination by order of judge.
If the judge orders an examination of the
mental or emotional condition of the
patient, communications made in the
course thereof are not privileged under
this rule with respect to the particular
purpose for which the examination is
ordered unless the judge orders otherwise.

*(3) Condition an element of claim or
defense.* There is no privilege under
this rule as to communications relevant
to an issue of the mental or emotional
condition of the patient in any proceeding in which he relies upon the condition as an element of his claim or defense, or, after the patient's death, in any
proceeding in which any party relies

---

56. Report No. 45, Group for the Advancement of Psychiatry 92 (1960) [quoted in
the Advisory Committee's note on PFRE 504,
the Psychotherapist-Patient Privilege.] Recently, this argument has been questioned.

See Shuman & Weiner, The Privilege Study:
An Empirical Examination of the Psychotherapist-Patient Privilege, 60 N.Car.L.Rev.
893 (1982.)

upon the condition as an element of his claim or defense.

———

Although the trend is toward a psychotherapist-patient privilege and away from a doctor-patient privilege, not everyone believes that a sharp line can or should be drawn between the two. Consider the following argument:

Unlike the attorney-client privilege, the doctor-patient privilege has been the subject of a devastating attack. Commentators have argued that few patients would jeopardize their treatment and lie to their doctors out of fear that any information they give a doctor could be used as evidence against them in court. Few patients are even conscious of the privilege when they visit a doctor. Because an opposing party can require a patient or doctor to testify about symptoms, past history, and the patient's visit to a doctor, commentators also have argued that the privilege's narrow scope emasculates its effectiveness.

Despite the apparent persuasiveness of this attack on the doctor-patient privilege, it ignores a strong justification for the privilege—the need for privacy. Patients depend on doctors for special counseling and personal attention, and they need a zone of privacy to seek this help. Because medicine involves intimate facts about one's body, health, and mind, the privacy of this treatment and counseling should be protected. The unhappy prospect of disease, sickness, and injury should not be aggravated by a rule that freely allows public disclosure in court papers and open trials of medical procedures and the facts surrounding medical treatment.

This justification also forms the basis for the narrower psychotherapist-patient privilege, which has enjoyed greater support than the doctor-patient privilege. * * * Psychiatric communications are uniquely sensitive, and successful treatment requires a degree of self-revelation by the patient which can only be accomplished in an atmosphere of inviolate privacy. Confidentiality is especially important in overcoming the reluctance of patients who are involved in psychotherapy not of their own volition but at the behest of a relative or under court order as a condition of parole. Even when a patient recognizes a problem, she might be unable to perceive or acknowledge its dimensions. Some patients unfortunately also may view a history of mental problems as a character flaw. Such patients may fear candor; they may be reluctant to disclose important but embarrassing details that reasonably may be perceived by them as unimportant, or as not important enough to risk embarrassment. Trust is necessary, and trust requires that the patient have confidence in the psychotherapist.[57]

This need for trust is not restricted to the relationship between a psychotherapist and her patient. Treatment of emotional problems often enters into any doctor's relationship with her patient. Doctors today do not focus solely on one aspect of a person's problems; instead, they emphasize treatment of the whole person. The line between treating the mind and treating the body generally

57. See generally R. Slovenko, Psychotherapy Confidentiality, and Privileged Communications (1966); Fisher, The Psychotherapeutic Professions and the Law of Privileged Communications, 10 Wayne L.Rev. 609 (1964); Fleming & Maximov, The Patient or His Victim: The Therapist's Dilemma, 62 Cal.L.Rev. 1025 (1974); Goldstein & Katz, Psychiatrist-Patient Privilege: The GAP Proposal and the Connecticut Statute, 36 Connecticut Bar Journal 175, 182 (1962); Slovenko, Psychiatry and a Second Look at the Medical Privilege, 6 Wayne L.Rev. 175 (1960); Note, Confidential Communications to a Psychotherapist: A New Testimonial Privilege, 47 Nw.U.L.Rev. 384 (1952).

need not be drawn. For example, a migraine headache may be caused by either emotional or physical factors; a patient may need surgery but may lack the emotional capacity to withstand some possible post-surgical problems. Doctors should consider carefully all aspects of medical problems if they are to provide adequate diagnosis and treatment. A traditional doctor-patient privilege encourages doctors to treat people as human beings, not as physical objects. A law that sharply distinguishes psychotherapists from other doctors may discourage much that is good in current medical practice.[58]

Is it possible to achieve the desirable consequences of the physician-patient privilege by enacting rules of privilege which apply in particular circumstances? This is what the drafters of the Federal Rules attempted to do in the case of psychotherapy and what Congress does in the Federal Comprehensive Drug Abuse Prevention and Control Act of 1970, where a privilege is established which protects the privacy of research subjects in drug programs.[59] Should this approach be preferred? Are statutes likely to be enacted to cover all the situations where the physician-patient privilege should exist? Your answer to these questions will probably depend on how often you think the privilege furthers the interests of society. If you think this occurs often, you will probably favor a general privilege with exceptions rather than specific legislation. Since the pragmatic justification for the physician-patient privilege is weak, your ultimate position on the privilege is likely to reflect the balance you strike between the value of privacy in confidential relationships and the needs which litigants have for relevant information. How do you strike this balance?

The following problems illustrate some of the difficulties presented by the physician-patient privilege.

Problem VIII–33. Shortly after being involved in an automobile accident, Smith goes to Drs. Jones, Schwartz and Hood. Smith complains of pains in the lower back. Drs. Schwartz and Hood diagnose "whiplash" and, for a fat fee, agree to testify on Smith's behalf. Dr. Jones, after an exhaustive examination, finds absolutely nothing wrong with Smith, and begins to suspect that perhaps Smith is faking his injuries. After further tests are conducted, Dr. Jones tells Smith:

> Smith, there is absolutely nothing wrong with you. I am convinced that you are feigning your injuries in order to bring a lawsuit. Therefore, I will refuse to treat you. In addition, I will volunteer my testimony at trial should you continue to complain about these imaginary injuries and to attribute them to the automobile accident in which you were involved.

Smith continues with his lawsuit, and Dr. Jones does just what she said, namely, she volunteers her services to the defense. When Dr. Jones seeks to testify, Smith objects. **What is the proper ruling? Does it depend on whether or not Smith has called Drs. Schwartz and Hood to testify?**

Problem VIII–34. The defendant is charged with first degree murder. The trial judge believes the defendant is not competent to stand trial and

---

58. Saltzburg, supra note 19, at 617–21.

59. 21 U.S.C. §§ 801 et seq. See People v. Newman, 32 N.Y.2d 379, 345 N.Y.S.2d 502, 298 N.E.2d 651 (1973).

orders a psychiatric examination to determine whether this belief is correct. The defendant is found competent and the trial commences. The defense claims that the defendant is not guilty by reason of insanity and introduces psychiatric evidence to show the mental condition of the defendant. In response, the prosecution seeks to introduce testimony by the doctors who examined the defendant to determine his competency. The defendant objects, and urges that any statements or any information that he may have conveyed to the doctors during the competency examination is privileged. **How should the court rule?**

Problem VIII–35. Mr. and Mrs. Taylor are married on September 1, 1972. On March 2, 1973, Mrs. Taylor gives birth to a child. Shortly thereafter, Mr. Taylor files suit for divorce on the grounds that Mrs. Taylor was pregnant at the time of their marriage, that she did not disclose that fact to him, and that he is not the father of the child. To prove that the child was a full term baby, Mr. Taylor calls the doctor who delivered the child. Mrs. Taylor's lawyer objects on behalf of the child claiming that any information that the doctor may have obtained as a result of the delivery or post-natal care is privileged. **Should the objection be sustained? Would the decision be any different if the objection were entered on the mother's behalf?**

Problem VIII–36. While crossing the street, Susan Howe is hit by a car, breaking bones in both legs. From the hospital she contacts her lawyer, Ted White, who insists that Dr. Kildare, a famous orthopedic surgeon, attend to her case. In the course of an initial diagnostic interview, Howe tells Dr. Kildare that she does not remember the details of the accident because she was drunk at the time, that she has always walked with a limp because one leg is shorter than the other, and that she hopes that the doctor will be able to correct that condition. After she is released from the hospital (without a limp) White sends her to Dr. Welby, another noted specialist. He asks Dr. Welby to evaluate her current condition with particular attention on the prognosis. He seeks Welby's opinion as an aid in estimating the value of the suit. White also intends to use Dr. Welby, as he has in the past, as a source of information on the technical medical details of the case. He has found that Welby's briefings aid him in presenting the plaintiff's case and in cross-examining the defendant's expert witnesses. Howe gives Welby the same information she gave Kildare. At trial, plaintiff Howe calls no expert medical witnesses, but the defendant seeks to call Kildare and Welby to testify to Howe's statements concerning her limp and her condition at the time of the accident, and to her physical condition at the time each of the doctors examined her. **What testimony, if any, is likely to be admitted in a jurisdiction with the general common law privilege? What testimony, if any, is likely to be admitted in a jurisdiction like California?**

Problem VIII–37. Ted Ohlin takes his ten year old son to a pediatrician for a physical examination. Present at the examination are Ted and his child, the pediatrician, a young man in a white coat who was introduced to Ted after the examination as an anthropologist doing research on the medical profession, and a nurse. From time to time another nurse enters and leaves the examination room. The office is so small that whenever the nurse opens the door people in the waiting room can hear what the doctor is saying to Ted and his son. Thus, at least six people hear the doctor diagnose the son's illness as mumps and advise the youngster to stay out of school to avoid infecting others. Following an epidemic of mumps in the son's school, the parents of those children who caught the mumps sue Ted and his son for causing the epidemic by not heeding the doctor's advice to stay away from school. **May Ted or his son claim the physician-patient privilege to prevent the pediatrician from testifying to her diagnosis or advice? Will the claim of privilege prevent the anthropologist from testifying? The nurses? The people in the waiting room? Ted, if he is called as an adverse witness?**

Problem VIII–38. Following an automobile accident, Carl Kahn was brought unconscious to the emergency room of the Lake City General Hospital. The admitting doctor, noticing that Kahn smelled of alcohol, thought he was drunk and ordered a blood test to be certain. The lab reported that Kahn had a blood alcohol level of .21, confirming the doctor's initial suspicions. On Kahn's patient chart the doctor noted the blood alcohol level as well as the following diagnosis: inebriated, slight concussion, lacerations on the face and arms, broken wrist, shock. Treatment was ordered to deal with each of these conditions, and the chart was placed at the foot of Kahn's bed where it was accessible to anyone who came by. **In a suit against Kahn by the other driver in the accident, will Kahn's claim of physician-patient privilege prevent the other driver from introducing Kahn's hospital record to show that Kahn was drunk? If the court rules that the record is protected by the privilege, may Kahn introduce the record to prove his injuries—in support of a counterclaim—without relinquishing the claim of privilege as to the diagnosis of inebriation?**

One of the difficult issues that courts have struggled with in recent years involves the relationship of counsel and a doctor, often a psychiatrist, who is retained by counsel to examine the client. If the doctor's examination is favorable to the client's theory of the case—e. g., the doctor supports an insanity defense—the doctor will be called to testify. If the doctor is unfavorable, she will be paid and discharged and another expert will be sought. Assuming that the views of another expert are more favorable, the other expert will be called to testify. But can the opponent call the first expert?[60] Problem 36 raises this in the context of a civil case. The next problem raises the problem in the context of a criminal case.

Problem VIII–39. Sabrina Dunkett is charged with murdering her husband, George Clark, following a family squabble. Dunkett has retained F. Roy Bellow, a noted criminal lawyer, to defend her. Dunkett is sufficiently wealthy that money is of no concern in mounting a defense. Bellow calls Dr. Fredericka Phipps, the most respected psychiatrist in the city, and asks

---

60. Cases examining this issue are discussed in Saltzburg, supra note 19.

Phipps to examine Dunkett with an eye towards an insanity defense. Phipps is reluctant to get involved in a criminal case. But she agrees to participate when Bellow gives her a $15,000 retainer to "examine" Dunkett, to form an opinion as to her mental condition on the night in question, and to gather information needed to advise on a course of psychiatric treatment for Dunkett if that proves advisable. She conducts the examination and submits a lengthy report to Bellow summarizing everything Dunkett told her and noting her conclusion, which is "that your client was perfectly capable of understanding and controlling her actions when she shot her husband six times." The report also states that since the shooting Dunkett has developed some emotional disturbance and asks whether she should prepare a report recommending treatment. Bellow says that advice is not needed. Knowing he cannot use Phipps as a witness, Bellow tries again. This time he retains Dr. Marvin Mageco, also a well known psychiatrist. Mageco is retained for only $10,000 and does the examination. He concludes that Dunkett was suffering a dissociative reaction on the night of the shooting and was unable to control her behavior, because of the borderline paranoid, schizophrenic condition from which she suffered. Happy to have this report, Bellow calls Mageco to testify as a witness. The government, which has learned that Dr. Phipps also examined the defendant, calls her as a witness. The prosecutor asks Dr. Phipps what Dunkett said about the night in question and whether she has formed an opinion as to Dunkett's sanity. Dunkett objects and argues that anything said to Phipps was said to her as Bellow's agent and as such is protected by the attorney-client privilege. The government says that this privilege, like the doctor-patient privilege, should be disallowed since it relates to the results of a medical examination and the defendant has chosen to place her mental condition in issue. **How should a court rule?** Dunkett also claims that since she was told at the time of the examination that Dr. Phipps might be called upon to give advice concerning the treatment of any mental problem she might have, whatever she said to Phipps is protected by the psychotherapist-patient privilege. **How should a court rule?**

SECTION IV. MARITAL PRIVILEGES

A. SPOUSAL IMMUNITY

In most states the marital relationship gives rise to two distinct privileges. One, the spousal immunity,[61] protects one spouse from adverse testimony by the other spouse. The other, the privilege for marital communications, protects confidential

---

61. Actually, this privilege has three different names in different parts of the country. Some call it spousal incapacity, some spousal immunity and some the privilege for anti-marital facts. We have chosen the spousal immunity label to make it clear that this is not a disqualification of a witness as incompetent. One of us believes that, but

for the terminology already developed, courts would find it easier to call this privilege the "marital privilege" or "married spouse privilege" when both spouses hold it, the "testifying spouse privilege" when that spouse alone holds it, and the "defendant spouse privilege" when that spouse alone holds it. The other marital privilege, which may be effective even

communications made to one's spouse during the course of a marriage. The spousal immunity is a relic of the time when both husband and wife were barred from testifying in a common law proceeding to which the other was a party. Today spouses are usually competent to testify on each other's behalf, but in most states a privilege exists in criminal cases which, when properly invoked, prevents the state from requiring that one spouse testify against the other.

Like all privileges, this one may be waived by the holder. In some jurisdictions the privilege is either held by both spouses or by the one against whom the testimony is to be given, but in other states the privilege is vested in the testifying spouse alone. It is generally agreed that "[t]he basic reason the law has refused to pit wife against husband or husband against wife in a trial where life or liberty is at stake was a belief that such a policy was necessary to foster family peace, not only for the benefit of the husband, wife and children, but for the benefit of the public as well."[62]

This has led some to argue that the privilege should rest solely with the testifying spouse since "the fact a husband or wife testifies against the other voluntarily is strong indication that the marriage is already gone."[63] When the Supreme Court first faced this issue in Hawkins v. United States, it reaffirmed the common law rule that the non-testifying spouse may claim the privilege. Justice Stewart, in a concurring opinion, emphasized the difficulty of determining when testimony is truly voluntary and pointed out the government's temerity in arguing for the "marriage gone" theory in a case where the defendant's wife had been held in jail as a material witness until she agreed to testify against her husband.[64]

In 1980, the Supreme Court reversed its position and adopted the hitherto minority view that it is the testifying spouse who has the sole right to claim the privilege. Chief Justice Burger wrote for the Court in Trammel v. United States:[65]

It is essential to remember that the *Hawkins* privilege is not needed to pro-

---

when the spouses are no longer married, would be known, as it is now, as the marital communications privilege. For purposes of an evidence course, the functional descriptions recommended here may be useful.

62. Hawkins v. United States, 358 U.S. 74, 77 (1958).

63. Id.

64. Id. at 83.

65. 445 U.S. 40 (1980). The Court related the following facts:

On March 10, 1976, petitioner Otis Trammel was indicted with two others * * * for importing heroin into the United States from Thailand and the Philippine Islands and for conspiracy to import heroin * * *. The indictment also named six unindicted coconspirators, including petitioner's wife Elizabeth Ann Trammel.

According to the indictment, petitioner and his wife flew from the Philippines to California in August 1975, carrying with them a quantity of heroin. Freeman and Roberts assisted them in its distribution. Elizabeth Trammel then travelled to Thailand where she purchased another supply

of the drug. On November 3, 1975, with four ounces of heroin on her person, she boarded a plane for the United States. During a routine customs search in Hawaii, she was searched, the heroin was discovered, and she was arrested. After discussions with Drug Enforcement Administration agents, she agreed to cooperate with the Government.

Prior to trial on this indictment, petitioner moved to sever his case from [the others]. He advised the court that the Government intended to call his wife as an adverse witness and asserted his claim to a privilege to prevent her from testifying against him. At a hearing on the motion, Mrs. Trammel was called as a Government witness under a grant of use immunity. She testified that she and petitioner were married in May 1975 and that they remained married. She explained that her cooperation with the Government was based on assurances that she would be given lenient treatment. She then described, in considerable detail, her role and that of her husband in the heroin distribution conspiracy.

tect information privately disclosed between husband and wife in the confidence of the marital relationship—once described by this Court as "the best solace of human existence." Stein v. Bowman, 13 Pet. at 223. Those confidences are privileged under the independent rule protecting confidential marital communications. The *Hawkins* privilege is invoked, not to exclude private marital communications, but rather to exclude evidence of criminal acts and of communications made in the presence of third persons.

No other testimonial privilege sweeps so broadly. The privileges between priest and penitent, attorney and client, and physician and patient limit protection to private communications. These privileges are rooted in the imperative need for confidence and trust. The priest-penitent privilege recognizes the human need to disclose to a spiritual counselor, in total and absolute confidence, what are believed to be flawed acts or thoughts and to receive priestly consolation and guidance in return. The lawyer-client privilege rests on the need for the advocate and counselor to know all that relates to the client's reasons for seeking representation if the professional mission is to be carried out. Similarly, the physician must know all that a patient can articulate in order to identify and to treat disease; barriers to full disclosure would impair diagnosis and treatment.

The *Hawkins* rule stands in marked contrast to these three privileges. Its protection is not limited to confidential communications; rather it permits an accused to exclude all adverse spousal testimony. As Jeremy Bentham observed more than a century and a half ago, such a privilege goes far beyond making "every man's house his castle," and permits a person to convert his house into "a den of thieves." 5 Rationale of Judicial Evidence 340 (1827).

It "secures, to every man, one safe and unquestionable and ever ready accomplice for every imaginable crime." Id., at 338.

The ancient foundations for so sweeping a privilege have long since disappeared. Nowhere in the common-law world—indeed in any modern society—is a woman regarded as chattel or demeaned by denial of a separate legal identity and the dignity associated with recognition as a whole human being.
* * *

The contemporary justification for affording an accused such a privilege is also unpersuasive. When one spouse is willing to testify against the other in a criminal proceeding—whatever the motivation—their relationship is almost certainly in disrepair; there is probably little in the way of marital harmony for the privilege to preserve. In these circumstances, a rule of evidence that permits an accused to prevent adverse spousal testimony seems far more likely to frustrate justice than to foster family peace. Indeed, there is reason to believe that vesting the privilege in the accused could actually undermine the marital relationship. For example, in a case such as this the Government is unlikely to offer a wife immunity and lenient treatment if it knows that her husband can prevent her from giving adverse testimony. If the Government is dissuaded from making such an offer, the privilege can have the untoward effect of permitting one spouse to escape justice at the expense of the other. It hardly seems conducive to the preservation of the marital relation to place a wife in jeopardy solely by virtue of her husband's control over her testimony.

Criticisms of the *Trammel* decision have been few. But we are critics. We believe that the Chief Justice's opinion ignores the role that the government may play in setting one spouse against the other. "Surely a court that acknowledges the privilege's importance to marital harmony by continuing to vest it in the witness spouse should not tolerate a rule that gives the government strong incentives to break up those marriages it can."[66]

PFRE 505 had continued the spousal immunity:

HUSBAND-WIFE PRIVILEGE

(a) *General rule of privilege.* An accused in a criminal proceeding has a privilege to prevent his spouse from testifying against him.

(b) *Who may claim the privilege.* The privilege may be claimed by the accused or by the spouse on his behalf. The authority of the spouse to do so is presumed in the absence of evidence to the contrary.

(c) *Exceptions.* There is no privilege under this rule (1) in proceedings in which one spouse is charged with a crime against the person or property of the other or of a child of either, or with a crime against the person or property of a third person committed in the course of committing a crime against the other, or (2) as to matters occurring prior to the marriage, or (3) in proceedings in which a spouse is charged with importing an alien for prostitution or other immoral purpose in violation of 8 U.S.C. § 1328, with transporting a female in interstate commerce for immoral purposes or other offense in violation of 18

U.S.C. §§ 2421–2424, or with violation of other similar statutes.

The proposed federal rule follows prevailing practice in some respects and is more restrictive in others. As in most states it is limited to criminal cases, and the right to claim the privilege is contingent upon the existence of a valid marriage. The privilege endures only so long as the marriage endures, ending with an annulment or divorce. Obviously, it serves no purpose after death. The exception for crimes committed by one spouse against the other or against the children of either is also standard. The extension to crimes committed jointly against a third party and the spouse codifies an accepted judicial gloss. Some states specifically deny the privilege when crimes against the marriage, such as bigamy or adultery, are charged. Had PFRE 505 been enacted, the federal courts would, no doubt, have treated such crimes as crimes against the spouse.[67] Most states do not have an exception like PFRE 505(c)(2). Individuals are allowed to and, indeed, have married to prevent testimony against them.[68] Federal courts also have permitted this.[69] PFRE 505(c)(3) reflects both Congress' decision to withdraw the privilege in any action involving the importation of aliens for immoral purposes and the Advisory Committee's extension of this policy to arguably analogous statutes. Section (b) no longer gives guidance to federal courts since it has been overruled by *Trammel.* The privilege now belongs to the witness rather than to the defendant spouse.

B. THE PRIVILEGE FOR MARITAL COMMUNICATIONS

The second of the marital privileges protects confidential communications between spouses. The traditional jus-

tification for this privilege is the assumption that it fosters confidences between spouses, thereby promoting marital har-

66. Lempert, A Right to Every Woman's Evidence, 66 Iowa L.Rev. 725, 734 (1981). This article describes the history of the spousal immunity and argues that *Hawkins* should not have been overruled.

67. See, e.g., Wyatt v. United States, 362 U.S. 525 (1960) (no privilege in Mann Act case

where husband was charged with prostituting his wife).

68. See, e.g., State v. Chrismore, 223 Iowa 957, 274 N.W. 3 (1937).

69. See, e.g., Wyatt v. United States, 362 U.S. 525 (1960).

mony.   However unrealistic this assumption, its general acceptance has had important implications for the limits of this privilege.   The privilege only protects confidential communications made to one's spouse during marriage.   Yet, because the possibility that such confidences would be later disclosed might, in theory, discourage them, privileged communications remain protected after the marriage has terminated.   This is one way in which the privilege for marital communications differs from the spousal immunity.   A second difference is that the privilege for marital communications is available in civil as well as criminal litigation.   A third is that this privilege may be claimed where neither spouse is an actual or potential party to litigation.

Different jurisdictions specify different situations in which confidential marital communications remain unprivileged.   The following exceptions are common:

1. Prosecutions for crimes committed by one spouse against the other or against the children of either.

2. Actions by one of the spouses against an outsider for an intentional injury to the marital relation.

3. Actions by one spouse against the other.

4. A criminal prosecution in which the declaration of the accused spouse would tend to justify or reduce the grade of the offense.

5. A juvenile court proceeding.

6. A proceeding between a surviving spouse and a person who claims through the deceased spouse.

7. A proceeding to establish the competence of the spouse holding the privilege.

8. Commitment proceedings.

9. If the communication was made, in whole or in part, to enable or aid anyone to commit or plan to commit a crime or a fraud.

The privilege for marital communications shares certain features with the other privileges for confidential communications.   The most obvious is the concern for confidentiality.   Unless the communication was intended to be confidential the privilege will not attach.   Since intermediaries are almost never needed to facilitate communications between husband and wife, the presence of third parties, including children old enough to understand what is said, will vitiate the privilege.   Eavesdroppers unknown to either spouse will not destroy the privilege between spouses, but they will be allowed to testify to what they have heard unless the jurisdiction has decided to protect communications not knowingly exposed to the public.   Eavesdroppers secreted by a spouse are barred from testifying on the theory that a spouse may not by out-of-court actions destroy a privilege which could not be unilaterally avoided in court.

States vary in the communications they are willing to protect.   All make privileged statements by one spouse to another and actions intended to substitute for statements.   Many states extend the privilege to private acts done by one spouse in the presence of the other.   Although there is arguably no communicative intent in these situations, there is a willingness to disclose information which would presumably not exist but for the marital relationship.   A minority of states go further and protect by privilege any information which would not be available to a spouse but for the marital relationship.   At this extreme, the classic justification for the privilege no longer applies.

As with other privileges protecting confidential communications, the prevailing view is that the privilege for marital communications resides in the communicator.   However, some jurisdictions allow either spouse to invoke the privilege.   This has been justified on the ground that "granting or withholding the privilege according to whether a spouse talks or listens perhaps results from a fictive assimilation of the position of the spouse-communicatee to that of the professional person in the professional privilege situation. Realistically, both husband and wife in a talk between them are essentially in the same position in respect of need of the privilege whether at a given moment husband or wife is speaker or listener."[70]

In the federal rules no privilege was proposed for confidential marital communications. The drafters argued:

> The traditional justifications for privileges not to testify against the spouse and not to be testified against by one's spouse have been the prevention of marital dissension and the repugnancy of requiring a person to condemn or be condemned by his spouse. These considerations bear no relevancy to marital communications. Nor can it be assumed that marital conduct will be affected by a privilege for confidential communications of whose existence the parties in all likelihood are unaware. The other communication privileges, by way of contrast, have as one party a professional person who can be expected to inform the other of the existence of the privilege. Moreover, the relationships from which those privileges arise are essentially and almost exclusively verbal in nature, quite unlike marriage.

The decision of the drafters represents an important value judgment, for the marital privileges highlight the difficult question of what values should be sufficient to sustain a privilege. The drafters are almost certainly correct: there is little reason to believe that marital conduct is directly affected by the privilege for confidential communications. Couples who never have reason to assert the privilege probably live their lives in ignorance of it. Yet, after *Trammel,* the marital communications privilege is strong again, for the Court mentions it with apparent approval.

C. EVALUATING THE MARITAL PRIVILEGES

All privileges have costs for they allow the suppression of evidence that if produced at trial might prevent errors. Thus, we can ask of every privilege whether its costs exceed the social gains attributable to it. Jeremy Bentham expressed his doubts about the value of the spousal immunity:

> Hard—hardship—policy—peace of families—absolute necessity:—some such words as these are the vehicles by which the faint spark of reason that exhibits itself is conveyed. These are the leading terms, and these are all you are furnished with; and out of these you are to make an applicable, a distinct and intelligible proposition, as you can.

*   *   *

> [As to the "policy of the situation it is precisely the opposite, for if] a man could not carry on schemes of injustice, without being in danger, every moment, of being disturbed in them,—and (if that were not enough) betrayed and exposed to punishment,—by his wife; injustice in all its shapes, and with it the suits and the fees of which it is prolific, would, in comparison of what it is at present, be rare. Let us, therefore, grant to every man a license to commit all sorts of wickedness, in the presence and with the assistance of his wife: let us secure to every man in the bosom of his family, and in his own bosom, a safe accomplice: let us make every man's house his castle; and, as far as depends upon us, let us convert that castle into a den of thieves.

---

70. Louisell & Crippin, Evidentiary Privileges, 40 Minn.L.Rev. 413, 417 (1956).

Two men, both married, are guilty of errors of exactly the same sort, punishable with exactly the same punishment. In one of the two instances (so it happens), evidence sufficient for conviction is obtainable, without having recourse to the testimony of the wife; in the other instance, not without having recourse to the testimony of the wife. While the one suffers,—capitally, if such be the punishment,—to what use, with what consistency, is the other to be permitted to triumph in impunity?

* * *

Oh! but think what must be the suffering of my wife, if compelled by her testimony to bring destruction on my head, by disclosing my crimes!—Think? answers the legislator; yes, indeed, I think of it; and, in thinking of it, what I think of besides, is what *you* ought to think of it. Think of it as part of the punishment which awaits you, in case of your plunging into the paths of guilt. The more forcible the impression it makes upon you, the more effectually it answers its intended purpose. Would you wish to save yourself from it? it depends altogether upon yourself: preserve your innocence.

* * *

The reason now given, was not, I suspect, the original one. Drawn from the principle of utility, though from the principle of utility imperfectly applied, it savours of a late and polished age. The reason that presents itself as more likley to have been the original one, is the grimgribber, nonsensical reason,— that of the identity of the two persons thus connected. Baron and Feme are one person in law. On questions relative to the two matrimonial conditions,

this quibble is the fountain of all reasoning.[71]

Bentham would, no doubt, have extended his argument to include the privilege for marital communications had that privilege been fully developed at the time he wrote.

McCormick, writing about the privilege for marital communications, suggests a second and more likely justification for the marital privileges:

Probably the policy of encouraging confidences is not the prime influence in creating and maintaining the privilege. It is really a much a more natural and less devious matter. It is a matter of emotion and sentiment. All of us have a feeling of indelicacy and want of decorum in prying into the secrets of husband and wife. It is important to recognize that this is the real source of the privilege.[72]

If these are the values which the privilege promotes, do the benefits justify the costs involved? For McCormick the answer is easy:

When we [recognize the real source of the privilege], we realize at once this motive of delicacy, while worthy and desirable, will not stand in the balance with the need for disclosure in court of the facts upon which a man's life, liberty, or estate may depend.

This feeling of disproportion between the interest of delicacy and the interest of justice has doubtless swayed the courts in limiting the privilege in groups of cases where injustice in its application was most apparent, in the illogical permission to the third party intercepting or overhearing the message to make disclosure, and in the oft-repeated admonition that the scope of the privilege should, in case of doubt, be strictly confined.[73]

71. J. Bentham, 5 Rationale of Judicial Evidence 332, 339–41, 344–45 (J. S. Mill ed. 1827).

72. McCormick § 86, at 173.

73. Id.

But does McCormick's choice of words, "indelicacy and want of decorum," bias the conclusion against these privileges? Gardner uses stronger language to describe the values involved:

> The writer submits that these two [marital] privileges rest on a stronger basis in our society, however. This basis is the concept of human dignity in connection with an especially confidential relationship, one incidentally packed with "emotional dynamite" and one which the state has a strong interest in protecting and fostering. In a personal and intimate sense the husband and wife relationship is the closest one known to man. Ideally, it involves a union of minds as well as bodies. A spouse reveals himself to his marital partner in almost every way more thoroughly than to others—even when he does so unconsciously. This intimate relationship is of great worth in the promotion of the ultimate interests of society. Immediately, the problem is one of the security of domestic institutions, but behind this is the ultimate interest of the state in the individual life.
>
> Therefore, private matters occurring in the area of the marital relationship are not to be brought out lightly in formal public hearings, such as judicial, legislative, and administrative proceedings. After the marital relationship has come to an end, the confidential matters are not so deserving of protection from public scrutiny. Nevertheless, something in the spirit is shocked and hurt at the betrayal of former confidences, at the revelation of the secrets of the bedchamber, and perhaps at the vindictiveness of alienated ex-spouses, in some cases to the point of perjury, and at the conduct of fortune hunters, who make a mockery of the institution of marriage.[74]

Gardner's reasons call to mind the revulsion felt in this country at allegations that in Stalinist Russia children were expected to and did turn in their parents for crimes against the Soviet state. Surely our revulsion stemmed as much from the use of child informants as it did from the acts made criminal. Do the marital privileges respond to similar values? In a society which intrudes in a multitude of ways into one's personal life (how many official forms have you filled out during the past year?), a zone of guaranteed privacy is a valuable end in itself.

Other reasons may be added to those furnished by Gardner. Consider the impeachment process when spouse testifies against spouse. Impeachment for bias may lead to the examination of sexual roles, conflicts, spousal jealousy and the most sensitive kinds of marital secrets. The psychological cost to both spouses may be great, and the jury may get so involved with the details of the marriage as to lose sight of the probative value of the witness' testimony. In existing marriages, the strain might lead to disruption. In terminated marriages, attacks might be more bitter and the psychological costs greater.

Abolition of both privileges might well lead prosecutors to put more pressure on spouses to testify than they do now, since spouses will often have information about their mates which others do not have access to. Remember, in *Hawkins* the prosecutor placed a woman in jail as a material witness until she agreed to testify against her husband. Do you think that an increase in this kind of behavior is acceptable? What would happen to children or other family members in this situation? Are other less coercive forms of pressure more acceptable? Should grand juries be able to force spouses to choose among contempt, perjury and betraying their loved ones? If not, what about lovers? Best friends? Is this slope so slippery that we do not want to get on it? Is the institution of marriage peculiar enough that it is

---

74. Gardner, note 24 supra, at 489–90.

a convenient and justifiable stopping point? Or do you have no difficulty in extending the privilege to spouses because you believe an ideal system would extend a privilege to less formal relationships as well?

Finally, one must consider the quantity and quality of the evidence suppressed by the privilege. Exceptions now exist to cover those situations where there is a significant likelihood that the event could not be proved but for the spouse's testimony. In most other situations there is likely to be such a substantial amount of non-privileged evidence available that the testimony of the spouse is not necessary to the decision. However, there are certainly occasions where a spouse can furnish reliable evidence crucial to a party's case, and there are, no doubt, a number of cases where the availability of corroborating evidence from a spouse would induce a party to settle or make the jury's task considerably easier.

Of course, abrogating the marital privileges does not necessarily mean that fact finders will learn what spouses know. If the marriage is a happy one, some spouses will refuse to testify despite the threat of being held in contempt. Others will perjure themselves or distort their testimony in ways which are likely to mislead the jury. The opposite danger exists where a marriage is unhappy or has been terminated with rancor. Here one spouse may be out to get the other, and testimony may be colored to achieve this end.

These arguments apply in different ways to the two privileges. The case for a priv-

ilege is probably stronger where there is an ongoing marriage than where the marriage has been terminated. Does the fact that one marital privilege appears to be more strongly supported than the other justify the abolition of the other? Obviously not; that decision depends on the strength of the support for the other. Gardner concludes:

> [T]he relationship itself is no longer in existence, and there are other policies competing for recognition, policies which pull in the opposite direction. One of these is the policy favoring accuracy in fact-finding, which in general is and should be the strongest one known to the courts, standing everready to tip the scales when the weight in the opposing balance is lightened. The writer therefore advocates that the confidential communications privilege should be qualified by statute to provide that the court should have the power to allow disclosure after the marriage has ceased to exist, if it should first be shown that the benefit to be derived from the disclosure would tend to outweigh the harm which might tend to result from such disclosure. This would leave a kind of qualified immunity, to be dissolved upon the showing of good cause.[75]

Do you think that Gardner has struck a happy balance? Do you prefer the position of the common law? Do you prefer the position of the proposed federal rules? Do you prefer the position of the Supreme Court after *Trammel*?

Problem VIII–40. A man tells his wife he has just robbed a grocery store. He doesn't see his son sitting in a chair. At the husband's trial the prosecution calls both the wife and child to testify to the man's statement. The husband seeks to exclude the testimony of both witnesses as privileged. Neither witness wants to testify. **Will he succeed in excluding the testimony of one or both of them? If so, on what ground?** Would the situ-

75. Id. at 490.

ation be any different if the man's wife had divorced him before the trial? If the wife had divorced him and the child were four years old? If the child were four months old?

Problem VIII-41. Bill and Betty Smith, husband and wife, are on trial for smuggling cocaine in a jurisdiction that gives the spousal immunity privilege to the defendant spouse. They each want to testify on their own behalf and each intends to claim that the other was solely responsible for the operation. Each claims spousal immunity to keep the other off the stand. **Should the judge apply the privilege in this case? Are there ways of handling this case without abrogating the privilege?** Assume they are on trial in a jurisdiction that follows *Trammel*, and each wants to testify as described above, but only in order to make out a defense. Neither wants to be a witness against the other. **Should the judge apply the privilege here? What would this entail?**

Problem VIII-42. Julie Adams is charged with armed robbery. She has fled and the prosecutor would like to force her husband to disclose her hiding place. The prosecutor subpoenas Mr. Adams to appear before the grand jury. He asks Mr. Adams if he knows where his wife is hiding and Mr. Adams replies that he believes he does. In response to the question of how he knows, Mr. Adams replies that his wife, fearing their phone was tapped, telephoned a friend and the friend passed the information to him. Claiming a marital privilege, Mr. Adams refuses to disclose the identity of the friend who relayed the message from his wife or the location of his wife. **In an action against Mr. Adams for contempt, should the claim of privilege be upheld? Could Mr. Adams have claimed the privilege at any earlier point? Could he have claimed any privilege if he had been divorced between the time he heard from the friend and the time he was subpoenaed before the grand jury? Would your answer to the previous question be different if it were Ms. Adams who had told Mr. Adams where she was?**

Problem VIII-43. Sued for divorce, a husband defends on grounds of cruelty. He testifies that his wife told him in secret that she had committed adultery with another man and was going to leave him. The wife objects to the introduction of this testimony on the ground that anything she may have told the husband in the confidence of the marriage was privileged. **Should the wife prevail? If the wife were prosecuted for adultery, could her husband be called to testify against her?**

Problem VIII-44. Van Duzek is charged with two counts of transporting aliens with knowledge of the alien's illegal presence in the United States. The aliens allegedly transported include one who became Van Duzek's wife one month after his indictment. She and two of her three children entered the United States at Brownsville, Texas in October 1971, with a local border-crossing card. Van Duzek met her there, and they then traveled in his car to Laredo, Texas and then to Chicago Heights, Illinois. One of the woman's children had preceded her there. She and her three children lived with Van Duzek's friends in Chicago Heights. They did not return to Mexico as planned because her fourth pregnancy made her ill. The prosecutor wants to call the wife as a witness against Van Duzek.   She does not want to testify.   **Does she have a right to refuse?**

Problem VIII–45.   One morning Eileen Simpson awoke at 6 a. m. in order to get some milk for her baby.   Entering the kitchen, she saw her husband sitting around the kitchen table with three other men.   Her husband Todd is later charged with participating in a conspiracy with these other men.   In order to prove Todd's association with the conspiracy, the prosecutor calls Eileen Simpson to testify to what she saw that morning.   The Simpsons are divorced at the time of the trial, but Todd still seeks to claim a marital privilege to prevent his wife from testifying to her observations. **How should a court rule?   Should the court rule any differently if Todd had roused his wife, brought her downstairs and introduced her to the three men?**

Problem VIII–46.   Peter Polk comes home one evening at 6 p. m.   He empties a bag containing three rings, five watches and sixteen wallets on to the living room table.   Sally Polk comes in, points to the pile and asks him where it came from.   Peter responds, "These are the profits Wilkins and I made working the East end."   **If Peter is tried for theft, may he or his wife claim a privilege to prevent his wife from testifying to what she saw or heard?   If he is sued in tort for conversion by the owner of one of the watches, may he or his wife claim a privilege to prevent his wife from testifying to what she saw or heard?   If Wilkins is tried alone for theft, may Peter or his wife claim a privilege to prevent his wife from testifying against Wilkins?   If Peter refuses to claim a privilege, may Wilkins do so?   Might he do so if Peter is in prison in a distant state?**

Problem VIII–47.   Mrs. Conrad tells her husband that she wants him to be her agent in the sale of wheat from a farm she owns.   The husband sells the wheat, but before the delivery date has arrived the price of wheat rises $.40 a bushel.   Mrs. Conrad then sells the same wheat to another buyer at a higher price.   The original buyer sues Mrs. Conrad in contract for his lost profits.   At the trial, he wishes to put Mr. Conrad on the stand and ask him whether Mrs. Conrad had told him that he was her agent for the sale of the wheat.   Mrs. Conrad claims a marital privilege.   **How should the court rule?**

Problem VIII–48.   Sara Kemper operates a small jewelry store.   One evening her husband comes home, tosses a diamond ring in her lap and says, "See what you can get for this; I won it in a crap game."   It turns out that the ring was stolen, and Sara is charged with the knowing sale of stolen property.   She seeks to have her husband testify to what he told her, but the husband refuses, saying that whatever he told her was said in the confidence of the marriage relationship.   **How should the judge rule on the husband's claim of privilege?**

Problem VIII—49.   Joy Smathers and her husband Gary were subpoenaed to testify before a United States grand jury investigating extortionate extensions of credit.   Joy appeared, refused to testify and took the fifth amendment.   She was not recalled.   Gary also invoked the fifth amendment, but received full immunity, removing the self-incrimination danger.

Gary then refused to answer certain questions because of an asserted husband-wife privilege. **Should there be a husband-wife privilege before a grand jury? Assuming arguendo that there should be, does the privilege disappear if the United States Attorney in charge of the investigation states for the record the following:**

On behalf of the United States Government, I hereby represent and agree that no testimony of Gary Smathers before the Grand Jury, or its fruits, will be used in any way in any proceeding against his wife.

Problem VIII–50. Argyle and Zanuk are both charged with bank robbery. According to the prosecution's theory of the case, they entered a bank wearing ski masks and robbed a teller at gunpoint. The prosecutor believes that Argyle's wife saw Argyle dispose of the ski masks and he wants to call the wife as a witness. Fearful of running into a spousal privilege, he calls Mrs. Argyle to testify only against Zanuk. **Is this permissible? Does it matter whether Argyle and Zanuk are indicted together? Tried together? Whether Argyle has already been tried and convicted?**

SECTION V. PRIEST-PENITENT PRIVILEGE

It is unclear whether a priest-penitent privilege existed in common law courts before the Restoration, but since then English common law courts have rejected this privilege. In the United States almost every jurisdiction has adopted the privilege, most by legislation, but some by judicial decision. Perhaps no more need be said in favor of it than that even Bentham, the sharp critic of most privileges, supported this one.[76] Even when the privilege was not recognized in common law courts, there were:

few instances, if any, in which a priest was actually compelled to disclose a statement made to him in the confessional.[77]

PFRE 506 sets forth one version of this privilege:

COMMUNICATIONS TO CLERGYMEN

(a) Definitions. As used in this rule:

(1) A "clergyman" is a minister, priest, rabbi, or other similar functionary of a religious organization, or an individual reasonably believed so to be by the person consulting him.

(2) A communication is "confidential" if made privately and not intended for further disclosure except to other persons present in furtherance of the purpose of the communication.

(b) General rule of privilege. A person has a privilege to refuse to disclose and to prevent another from disclosing a confidential communication by the person to a clergyman in his professional character as spiritual adviser.

(c) Who may claim the privilege. The privilege may be claimed by the person, by his guardian or conservator, or by his personal representative if he is deceased. The clergyman may claim the

---

76. See J. Bentham, 4 Rationale of Judicial Evidence 588–91 (J. S. Mill ed. 1827).

77. Comment, Rule 219, Model Code of Evidence (1942).

privilege on behalf of the person. His authority to do so is presumed in the absence of evidence to the contrary.

The other common version of the priest-penitent privilege is considerably more restrictive and has been thought by some to protect the confessional sacrament of the Roman Catholic church and little else. Uniform Rule 29 took this narrow approach, covering only:

a confession of culpable conduct made secretly and in confidence by a penitent to a priest in the course of discipline or practice of the church or religious denomination or organization of which the penitent is a member.

In practice the difference between the narrow and the broad rule is probably slight. Lawyers rarely seek to force clergy to disclose communications made in confidence. Perhaps there is an implicit recognition that spiritual ties, if no other, are stronger than legal obligations. Efforts to force the clergy to reveal information given in confidence might result in a substantial number of contumacious witnesses but little valuable information. Does the fact that in some religions the clergy are not allowed to reveal confidences, even with the permission of the penitent, mean that the privilege should be vested in priests as well as penitent? A few jurisdictions take this approach.

Problem VIII–51. Sue and Harold Hillmon visit their minister to discuss marital problems and to seek his counseling in the hope they can keep their faltering marriage alive. During the session Harold admits to having an affair, something Sue knew nothing about. Sue storms out of the session and sues Harold for divorce, claiming adultery. Harold claims that neither Sue nor the minister may reveal what he said during the counseling session with the minister. **Will his privilege claim be sustained?**

Problem VIII–52. One afternoon the Reverend Lewis Sims is playing golf with his friend Lloyd Butler. At the second hole Sims asks Butler, "How's business?" and Butler responds that business is terrible and he doesn't know whether he will be able to meet his next payroll. At the 11th hole Butler says to Rev. Sims, "I have a problem that's been bothering me," and proceeds to describe an extra-marital affair which he wishes to break off. Assume that Butler's company offers stock to the public a week after this golf game and the accompanying prospectus states business is booming. Butler is sued for fraud. **May he claim the priest-penitent privilege to prevent Sims from testifying to the conversation at the second hole?** Assume that Butler's wife sues for divorce charging adultery. **May Butler claim the priest-penitent privilege to prevent Sims from testifying to what Butler told him at the eleventh hole? Does your answer to either of these questions depend on whether Butler is a member of Sims' congregation?**

Problem VIII–53. The Swami Baba Mamaresh is guru to a group of devoted followers. He teaches meditation and yoga. One day he notices that one of his followers cannot settle into meditation. He asks what is wrong and the follower tells him that he held up a gas station the night before and is worried about the consequences. The Swami tells him to return the money and that the Spirit of All will forgive his sins. **If the follower is later tried for the hold up, may he claim the priest-penitent privilege to prevent the Swami from testifying to their conversation?**

Problem VIII–54. During the Viet Nam war the Reverend Weems did extensive draft counseling. One day Dick Dodger came to see him about the possibility of applying for conscientious objector status. They determined that Dodger probably could not qualify as a C.O., but Rev. Weems suggested he consider a medical deferment. Later Dodger is tried for submitting false information in connection with his application for a medical deferment. **Can he claim the priest-penitent privilege to prevent Rev. Weems from testifying to what Weems told him in the counseling session? Would the situation be any different if Dodger had spoken not to Weems, but to a lay counselor who assisted Weems when the demand for draft counseling became too great for one person?**

SECTION VI. GOVERNMENT PRIVILEGES AND THEIR "PRICE"

A. GOVERNMENT SECRETS AND THEIR PRICE

With a government of the people, by the people and for the people, it is not surprising that citizens presume that they have a right to know what their elected and appointed representatives have done and are doing. Nor is it surprising to find government officials claiming that some information cannot be made public because of the dangers of misuse. When citizen and government meet in a judicial arena, the presumption and the perceived danger collide. A privilege emerges, but the government pays for it. In the following case, the Supreme Court was called upon to strike the delicate balance between a litigant's right to information and the government's right to preserve secrets.

UNITED STATES v. REYNOLDS

Supreme Court of the United States, 1953.
345 U.S. 1, 73 S.Ct. 528, 97 L.Ed. 727.

Mr. Chief Justice VINSON delivered the opinion of the Court.

These suits under the Tort Claims Act arise from the death of three civilians in the crash of a B-29 aircraft at Waycross, Georgia, on October 6, 1948. Because an important question of the Government's privilege to resist discovery is involved, we granted certiorari.

The aircraft had taken flight for the purpose of testing secret electronic equipment, with four civilian observers aboard. While aloft, fire broke out in one of the bomber's engines. Six of the nine crew members and three of the four civilian observers were killed in the crash.

The widows of the three deceased civilian observers brought consolidated suits against the United States. In the pretrial stages the plaintiffs moved, under Rule 34 of the Federal Rules of Civil Procedure, for production of the Air Force's official accident investigation report and the statements of the three surviving crew members * * *. [The government claimed privilege and the Secretary of the Air Force filed a formal claim that disclosure would not be in the public interest. The government did offer, however, to produce the survivors for plaintiff's examination and said witnesses would be allowed to refresh their memories from any statement made by them to the Air Force, and authorized to testify as to all matters except those of a "classified nature."]

The District Court ordered the Government to produce the documents in order that the court might determine whether they contained privileged matter. The Government declined, so the court entered an order, under Rule 37(b)(2)(i), that the facts on the issue of negligence would be taken as established in plaintiffs' favor. After a hearing to determine damages, final judgment was entered for the plaintiffs. The Court of Appeals affirmed, both as to the showing of good cause for production of the documents, and as to the ultimate disposition of the case as a consequence of the Government's refusal to produce the documents.

We have had broad propositions pressed upon us for decision. On behalf of the Government it has been urged that the executive department heads have power to withhold any documents in their custody from judicial view if they deem it to be in the public interest. Respondents have asserted that the executive's power to withhold documents was waived by the Tort Claims Act. Both positions have constitutional overtones which we find it unnecessary to pass upon, there being a narrower ground for decision.

The Tort Claims Act expressly makes the Federal Rules of Civil Procedure applicable to suits against the United States. The judgment in this case imposed liability upon the Government by operation of Rule 37, for refusal to produce documents under Rule 34. Since Rule 34 compels production only of matters "not privileged," the essential question is whether there was a valid claim of privilege under the Rule. We hold that there was, and that, therefore, the judgment below subjected the United States to liability on terms to which Congress did not consent by the Tort Claims Act.

We think it should be clear that the term "not privileged," as used in Rule 34, refers to "privileges" as that term is understood in the law of evidence. When the Secretary of the Air Force lodged his formal "Claim of Privilege," he attempted therein to invoke the privilege against revealing military secrets, a privilege which is well established in the law of evidence.
* * *

Judicial experience with the privilege which protects military and state secrets has been limited in this country. * * * Nevertheless, the principles which control the application of the privilege emerge quite clearly from the available precedents. The privilege belongs to the Government and must be asserted by it; it can neither be claimed nor waived by a private party. It is not to be lightly invoked. There must be a formal claim of privilege, lodged by the head of the department which has control over the matter, after actual personal consideration by that officer. The court itself must determine whether the circumstances are appropriate for the claim of privilege, and yet do so without forcing a disclosure of the very thing the privilege is designed to protect. The latter requirement is the only one which presents real difficulty. As to it, we find it helpful to draw upon judicial experience in dealing with an analogous privilege, the privilege against self-incrimination.

The privilege against self-incrimination presented the courts with a similar sort of problem. Too much judicial inquiry into the claim of privilege would force disclosure of the thing the privilege was meant to protect, while a complete abandonment of judicial control would lead to intolerable abuses. Indeed, in the earlier stages of judicial experience with the problem, both extremes were advocated, some saying that the bare assertion by the witness must be taken as conclusive, and others saying that the witness should be required to reveal the matter behind his claim of privilege to the judge for verification. Neither extreme prevailed, and a sound formula of compromise was developed. * * * There are differences in phraseology, but in substance it is agreed that the court must be satisfied from all the evidence and circumstances, and "from the implications of the question, in the setting in which it is asked, that a responsive answer to the question or an explanation of why it cannot be answered might be dangerous because injurious disclosure could result." If the court is so satisfied, the claim of the privilege will be accepted without requiring further disclosure.

Regardless of how it is articulated, some like formula of compromise must be applied here. Judicial control over the evidence in a case cannot be abdicated to the caprice of executive officers. Yet we will not go so far as to say that the court may automatically require a complete disclosure to the judge before the claim of privilege will be accepted in any case. It may be possible to satisfy the court, from all the circumstances of the case, that there is a reasonable danger that compulsion of the evidence will expose military matters which, in the interest of national security, should not be divulged. When this is the case, the occasion for the privilege is appropriate, and the court should not jeopardize the security which the privilege is meant to protect by insisting upon an examination of the evidence, even by the judge alone, in chambers.

In the instant case we cannot escape judicial notice that this is a time of vigorous preparation for national defense. Experience in the past war has made it common knowledge that air power is one of the most potent weapons in our scheme of defense, and that newly developing electronic devices have greatly enhanced the effective use of air power. It is equally apparent that these electronic devices must be kept secret if their full military advantage is to be exploited in the national interests. On the record before the trial court it appeared that this accident occurred to a military plane which had gone aloft to test secret electronic equipment. Certainly there was a reasonable danger that the accident investigation report would contain references to the secret electronic equipment which was the primary concern of the mission.

Of course, even with this information before him, the trial judge was in no position to decide that the report was privileged until there had been a formal claim of privilege. Thus it was entirely proper to rule initially that petitioner had shown probable cause for discovery of the documents. Thereafter, when the formal claim of privilege was filed by the Secretary of the Air Force, under circumstances indicating a reasonable possibility that military secrets were involved, there was certainly a sufficient showing of privilege to cut off further demand for the documents on the showing of necessity for its compulsion that had then been made.

In each case, the showing of necessity which is made will determine how far the court should probe in satisfying itself that the occasion for invoking the privilege is appropriate. Where there is a strong showing of necessity, the claim of privilege should not be lightly accepted, but even the most compelling necessity cannot overcome the claim of privilege if the court is ultimately satisfied that military secrets are at stake. *A fortiori*, where necessity is dubious, a formal claim of privilege, made under the circumstances of this case, will have to prevail. Here, necessity was greatly minimized by an available alternative, which might have given respondents the evidence to make out their case without forcing a showdown on the claim of privilege. By their failure to pursue that alternative, respondents have posed the privilege question for decision with the formal claim of privilege set against a dubious showing of necessity.

There is nothing to suggest that the electronic equipment, in this case, had any causal connection with the accident. Therefore, it should be possible for respondents to adduce the essential facts as to causation without resort to material touching upon military secrets. Respondents were given a reasonable opportunity to do just that, when petitioner formally offered to make the surviving crew members available for examination. We think that offer should have been accepted.

Respondents have cited us to those cases in the criminal field, where it has been held that the Government can invoke its evidentiary privileges only at the price of letting the defendant go free. The rationale of the criminal cases is that, since the Government which prosecutes an accused also has the duty to see that justice is done, it is unconscionable to allow it to undertake prosecution and then invoke its governmental privileges to deprive the accused of anything which might be material to his defense. Such rationale has no application in a civil forum where the Government is not the moving party, but is a defendant only on terms to which it has consented.

The decision of the Court of Appeals is reversed and the case will be remanded to the District Court for further proceedings consistent with the views expressed in this opinion.

Reversed and remanded.

Mr. Justice BLACK, Mr. Justice FRANKFURTER, and Mr. Justice JACKSON dissent, substantially for the reasons set forth in the opinion of Judge Maris below. 192 F.2d 987.

Probably none of the rules proposed by the Supreme Court received more criticism in the Congressional hearings than PFRE 509. Some of the critics of the rule charged that it amounted to an official secrets act and that it considerably lightened the burden which the government bears when seeking to conceal information. Rep. Holtzman of New York suggested that the proposed rule would greatly alter the balance between the government's right to conceal information and the citizen's right to know. Are either or both of these points meritorious?

SECRETS OF STATE AND OTHER OFFICIAL INFORMATION

PFRE 509:

(a) Definitions.

(1) Secret of state. A "secret of state" is a governmental secret relating to the

national defense or the international relations of the United States.

(2) Official information. "Official information" is information within the custody or control of a department or agency of the government the disclosure of which is shown to be contrary to the public interest and which consists of: (A) intragovernmental opinions or recommendations submitted for consideration in the performance of decisional or policymaking functions, or (B) subject to the provisions of 18 U.S.C. § 3500; [the Jencks Act] investigatory files compiled for law enforcement purposes and not otherwise available, or (C) information within the custody or control of a governmental department or agency whether initiated within the department or agency or acquired by it in its exercise of its official responsibilities and not otherwise available to the public pursuant to 5 U.S.C. § 522. [The Freedom of Information Act]

(b) General rule of privilege. The government has a privilege to refuse to give evidence and to prevent any person from giving evidence upon a showing of reasonable likelihood of danger that the evidence will disclose a secret of state or official information, as defined in this rule.

(c) Procedures. The privilege for secrets of state may be claimed only by the chief officer of the government agency or department administering the subject matter which the secret information sought concerns, but the privilege for official information may be asserted by any attorney representing the government. The required showing may be made in whole or in part in the form of a written statement. The judge may hear the matter in chambers, but all counsel are entitled to inspect the claim and showing and to be heard thereon, except that, in the case of secrets of state, the judge upon motion of the govern-

ment, may permit the government to make the required showing in the above form *in camera*. If the judge sustains the privilege upon a showing *in camera*, the entire text of the government's statements shall be sealed and preserved in the court's records in the event of appeal. In the case of privilege claimed for official information the court may require examination *in camera* of the information itself. The judge may take any protective measure which the interests of the government and the furtherance of justice may require.

(d) Notice to government. If the circumstances of the case indicate a substantial possibility that a claim of privilege would be appropriate but has not been made because of oversight or lack of knowledge, the judge shall give or cause notice to be given to the officer entitled to claim the privilege and shall stay further proceedings a reasonable time to afford opportunity to assert a claim of privilege.

(e) Effect of sustaining claim. If a claim of privilege is sustained in a proceeding to which the government is a party and it appears that another party is thereby deprived of material evidence, the judge shall make any further orders which the interests of justice require, including striking the testimony of a witness, declaring a mistrial, finding against the government upon an issue as to which the evidence is relevant, or dismissing the action.

Is PFRE 509's treatment of state secrets consistent with *Reynolds* or does it in some way change the scope of the privilege? Do trial judges in passing upon claims of privilege have the discretion which the *Reynolds* court contemplated, or is judicial discretion in some way restricted? Does *Reynolds* sanction a general privilege for official information? Do you feel there should be such a privilege when it is not specifically provided for by statute?

The following dialogue involving Representatives Hungate, Dennis, and Holtzman, and Messrs. Santarelli and Keuch from the Department of Justice illustrates some of the reasons why codification does not resolve difficulties of interpretation and shows how small differences in wording may change the meaning of a statute:

MR. DENNIS.   Let me get onto one other thing that probably you gentlemen should be given a chance to talk about.

Rule 509, Secret of State and Other Information.   I am far from an expert in the field, but I have the impression that A(1), Secrets of State, is pretty much the present law, but A(2) Official Information, probably broadens the present law and I would be glad to hear you gentlemen on that subject.

MR. SANTARELLI.   Our view is it does not significantly broaden the present law.

*   *   *

MR. KEUCH.   I would like to echo Mr. Santarelli's comments that the rule as drafted was an attempt to track what we think is current law.   The overall test for official information was referred to earlier.   This has been the rule used to test a claim of privilege in those areas other than State secrets rule.   (sic)

I might also point out that there is also a second balancing opportunity and that is that the final section of the rule provides that if a privilege, whether it be for a secret of State of for official information, is accepted by the court, the court may make whatever further order the interests of justice require.   That may be to dismiss the testimony of a particular witness.   You may tell the Government it cannot rely on a particular area of testimony.

The Government may lose the suit in a criminal case.   An indictment may be dismissed.   This happens all the time when Government claims the privilege in the court and these privileges are recognized.   We do feel the rule correctly states the current law.

MS. HOLTZMAN.   I would like to know where the balance test comes in under rule 509(a)(2)?

MR. KEUCH.   First, the definition of official information states in the rule that it is information the disclosure of which is shown to be contrary to the public interest.   That is a burden the Government would have to meet in any claim of a privilege for official information.

MS. HOLTZMAN.   That is the balancing?   The present law as I understand it, where the executive privilege is recognized, is that further elements come into the balancing decision.   The statement that the Government has a public interest is only element number one in the balancing test and element number two is the availability of the information in other forms to the litigant and the necessity of that information to the litigant *   *   *.

And there is no provision, as I read rule 509(a)(2), with respect to the official information that permits those second aspects of the balancing test to come into consideration, so in effect   *   *   *   the only claim that is to be evaluated before this privilege can be absolutely invoked is a claim of the Government with respect to it being detrimental to the public interest.

*   *   *

MR. KEUCH.   We don't think so.   We think those claims, including the other factors you mentioned, are summarized by the rule in the ultimate test "contrary to the public interest."

That determination would take in many things.   Contrary to the Government's interest would be part of that.   But also part of the "contrary to the public interest" test would be all the factors that you commented on. Is it available elsewhere? What would be the harm to the individual involved, and matters of that type.

*   *   *

MS. HOLTZMAN.   *   *   *

I am also concerned with the statement with respect to rule 509(a)(1) that that tracks existing law. It is my understanding that, although I have not read all the cases, there is no privilege of secret of state where an allegation or claim is not made that the disclosure of this secret would affect national security, and in terms of the definition there is no requirement that a secret of state has to affect national interest or the national security in its disclosure, so to my mind it is a radical departure from existing law.

MR. KEUCH. There is an attempt not to make a radical departure. That draftsmanship comes from the last Supreme Court expression on some of these matters. Under the *Reynolds* case, the "secret of state" must be a governmental secret relating to national defense, or international relations, of the United States, and under rule 509(b) there must be a reasonable likelihood of danger that the evidence will disclose a secret of state or official information as defined in the rule.

MS. HOLTZMAN. But there is nothing in here, rule 509(a)(1) or 509(b) that says that the disclosure of this secret would affect national security, so that to my mind the breadth of this definition is so great that a claim could be made with respect to secrets affecting tariffs on Persian rugs or the government's decision whether or not to disclose information that meats that are imported are contaminated, even though the disclosure of such might not affect the national security.

MR. KEUCH. Of course, the definition does say the "secret of state" is a governmental secret relating to national defense. That tracks the present Executive order concerning the classification of information. Also, of course, the court is a participant in this process. The court may require a showing by the Government as to why this information is a secret relating to the national defense, in the example you stated.

MS. HOLTZMAN. Where in this rule do you see any ability of the court to make such a demand on the part of the Government?

MR. KEUCH. I believe under the procedures in rule (c). That may be made by affidavit or in written form or *in camera* if the judge so orders. But there is a provision for the court to require a showing.

*   *   *

MS. HOLTZMAN. But we are getting into a circular problem here. Under rule 509(a)(1) and (c) all that the Government—as I read this rule—need show in order to invoke the privilege of secret of state is that the Government, is claiming there is a secret of state relating to national defense or international relations.

The Government need not show the disclosure of this so-called secret would in any way affect national security. The Government simply claims this is a secret. I don't know what could be a secret. That term is not even defined here.

In fact, let me point out to you, that the October 1971 draft in its definition of military and State secrets said that the Government had a privilege to refuse to give evidence and prevent a person to give evidence upon a showing of likelihood of danger—"that disclosure of evidence will be injurious to national defense."

That language is eliminated and I think the elimination in the history of this provision would clearly indicate the Government would be able to invoke the privilege simply on a claim or a showing that this was a secret—not that disclosure of the secret would be detrimental to national security. So, I think it is a departure in that regard.

MR. KEUCH. We do not believe so. The first section (a)(1), tracks fairly well the present Executive order on the definition of classified information. That is secret information relating to both national defense, military matters, and also international relations.

* * *

MR. HUNGATE. If I understand—I never could keep a secret—but if I understand this colloquy, Ms. Holtzman is suggesting there is some significance in the elimination of the phrase from the first draft of these rules, while you are suggesting that it made no substantive change in the law as it exists, as stated in the cases.

MR. KEUCH. I would agree there is a difference in the burden which the Government would be required to show from the draft. We felt that it was important to bring it in accord with existing law.

MR. HUNGATE. You think it brings it into conformity with existing law and someone else might disagree.[78]

———

Subsection (a)(2) of PFRE 509, extending a privilege to official information, appears on its face to be a substantial expansion of existing law. However, while the federal government has never had a privilege for official information, there has always been protection for the kinds of information which subsection (a)(2) would

make officially privileged. Statutes make certain governmental information specifically privileged. The relevance, hearsay, and work product rules protect other information, and the courts use their discretion to protect sensitive information when the need for it does not outweigh the need for confidentiality. Most of the criticism of subsection (a)(2) centered around part (C) which would make information not available under the Freedom of Information Act (FOIA) presumptively privileged. The FOIA requires federal agencies to honor public requests for information in their possession. No particularized showing of need is required. Although the FOIA is at times used as a discovery device in connection with litigation, it is clear that the exemptions do not weigh the specific need of litigants for information against the agency's need for secrecy. Extending a privilege to everything exempt from disclosure under the FOIA would unduly broaden the protection currently accorded government information. However, 509(a)(2) doesn't necessarily do this. It only protects FOIA information, the disclosure of which is "shown to be contrary to the public interest." If this formula allows full consideration of the litigant's needs, subsection (a)(2) may only restate existing law. The danger is that giving a presumptive privilege to information not available under the FOIA will cause courts to give undue weight to the government's case for confidentiality and too little weight to the litigant's particularized needs.

The Justice Department lawyers, in defending PFRE 509, relied to a considerable extent on the authority given courts under subsection (e) to ameliorate any unfairness which might result from governmental claims of privilege. Is subsection (e) consistent with *Reynolds*? Does it give too much discretion to the judge? Does it allow too much relief to the party opposing

78. Hearings on Proposed Rules of Evidence Before the Special Subcommittee on Reform of the Federal Criminal Laws of the

House Committee on the Judiciary, 93rd Cong., 1st Sess., § 2, at 277–282 (1973).

the privilege? If the costs of revealing government information exceed the benefits, what reason is there to exact a price for secrecy?

Consider the situation with respect to other privileges. Ordinarily, if a party suppresses relevant information within his control, the other party is entitled to have the jury instructed that it may draw the inference that had the evidence been introduced it would have been unfavorable to the party suppressing it. However, when a party is privileged to suppress information, the great weight of authority holds that no adverse inference may be drawn from exercise of that privilege. Not only is the adverse party barred from commenting on the exercise of the privilege, but if the party has reason to believe a valid privilege will be claimed, he should not force his op-

ponent to invoke it in front of the jury. In the majority of jurisdictions, which follow the no adverse inference rule, it is felt that to do otherwise would undercut the value of the privilege.

Cases are no doubt lost because one party's invocation of a privilege prevents the other from establishing a successful claim or defense. Why should the exercise of governmental privileges carry the possibility of penalties which do not attach when private privileges are invoked? Perhaps because society as a whole benefits from governmental privileges, it is appropriate that society rather than an individual litigant pays the price. It certainly seems unfair to allow the government as the moving party in criminal litigation to claim a privilege for information that may be essential to an effective defense.

Problem VIII–55. The government prosecutes Laurie Rhine for attempting to give information pertaining to the national defense to a foreign power. Rhine denies the charge and demands to know what the information was which she allegedly attempted to pass. The government asserts the secret of state privilege, claiming that the disclosure of the information to the judge and jury would harm the national defense and that Rhine is aware of the information she attempted to pass. **In these circumstances should the prosecution be allowed to proceed? If so, should the judge instruct the jury that an essential element of the crime—that the information pertained to the national defense—has been proved? If the government is charging Rhine with transmitting microfilm showing the computer system of an atomic submarine, must the actual microfilm be shown to the judge and jurors and made available to the defense?**

Problem VIII–56. Young sues a military hospital claiming that hospital officials knew that the surgeon assigned to her case was not competent to do the operation required. She seeks access to certain memoranda concerning the surgeon which had been prepared for the head of the hospital. The head of the hospital claims that the memoranda in question are privileged as official information, that they were prepared for his use in making administrative decisions, and that to reveal them at a trial would discourage the candid peer review necessary for the intelligent assignment of personnel. Moreover, he notes that it is a military hospital, and the records, therefore, are military records. The judge accepts these arguments and decides that disclosure of the memoranda would be contrary to the public interest. **Is this a decision which the judge should make without regard to Young's need for the information? Should the government be able to claim a di-**

rected verdict if the memoranda are the only proof of an essential element of Young's case? Is it relevant that Young could not have brought suit against the government had the government not given its general consent to being sued in tort?

———

In United States v. Nixon, 418 U.S. 683 (1974), the Supreme Court recognized the concept of executive privilege and found that it was constitutionally based. However, the Court held it was for the judiciary to determine the limits of the privilege and that a court could demand from the President information necessary to the prosecution of a criminal case despite a claim of privilege, if the claim of privilege was not grounded in any perceived danger to the national security.

Most people are willing to concede that a claim of privilege is sometimes needed to protect against the disclosure of important government secrets, but the government's tendency to claim privileges can get out of hand. In the following opinion one federal district judge comments on the abuse of governmental privileges.

EEOC v. LOS ALAMOS CONSTRUCTORS, INC.

United States District Court, D.New Mexico, 1974.
382 F.Supp. 1373.

MEMORANDUM OPINION

WINNER, District Judge, sitting by Designation.

These consolidated cases are before the Court on discovery problems. The zeal with which plaintiff resists routine discovery necessitates a much longer opinion than discovery squabbles deserve. Moreover, the problem is a recurring one, and I want to add to the many cases on the subject my word of protest against the view of the executive branch of the government that it can govern in secret. That thinking pervades the entire executive branch, and there is little wonder that we face a crisis in public confidence in government officials and employees.

Here, plaintiff filed a skeleton complaint which pleaded few facts and which alleged by way of legal conclusion that defendant, Zia, was guilty of discriminatory practices in its employment practices. A motion to dismiss and a motion for a more definite statement were denied on the theory that the complaint is just barely sufficient under notice pleading concepts. However, at pretrial conference, plaintiff was ordered to set forth in a pretrial order a fair summary of the facts on which it relies. To date, plaintiff has ignored the Court's order, and defendant is still defending against nothing but a phantom legal conclusion sketched out in the complaint. As a last resort, defendant is now trying to find out through interrogatories what it is accused of, but plaintiff's answers to many of the interrogatories have frustrated defendant's efforts to make reasonable preparations for trial. Twenty-one interrogatories were served, and the answers to less than half of them were acceptable to defendant. * * *

* * *

My predilections as to claims of governmental privilege fully appear in 28 F.R.D. 97, 107, a paper presented by me, speaking as a lawyer, to the Tenth Circuit Judicial Conference in 1960. The intervening fourteen years have added judicial and Congressional support to the views I then expressed, and it is now generally recognized that bureaucrats cannot hide behind a privilege claim unless national security or an overwhelming public interest demands that the agency be permitted to operate behind locked doors. Those unfortunate enough to be forced into litigation with the government still face agency insistence on trial by ambush, although, as we will see presently, Congress and the courts agree that a recognition of governmental privilege is the rare exception, while full disclosure is the almost universal rule. When the government or one of its agencies comes into court [with very few exceptions], it is to be treated in exactly the same way as any other litigant. Appointment to office does not confer upon a bureaucrat the right to decide the rules of the game applicable to his crusades or his lawsuits.

Claims of governmental privilege have been made throughout almost the entire history of our nation. They started with the trial of Aaron Burr and they have continued through the Watergate cases. President Thomas Jefferson asserted an executive privilege claim as to a letter written by General Wilkinson [really just an informer] and Richard Nixon said that tapes of his conversations were privileged. Chief Justice Marshall rejected the claim of Thomas Jefferson; Chief Justice Burger rejected the claim of Richard Nixon. Treating these cases as the alpha and the omega of privilege claims, the similarity of the Chief Justices' opinions is deserving of note.

One final comment will bring this opinion to a close. There is no justification for taking as much of a court's scarce time as has been required for the hearing held on this matter and for the inordinately long opinion which has been written in faint hope that government counsel can be persuaded to live within the spirit of the rules. Entitlement to receipt of a government paycheck is not a license to interfere with or to attempt to interfere with the fair administration of justice. Government files are not sacrosanct, and government employees are going to have to learn to live with the concept that even in their official capacity, they ordinarily have no fewer and no more rights in a lawsuit than does their adversary, although, reluctantly, I must now mention a special status which has been given government litigants.

Rule 37 of the Federal Rules of Civil Procedure was amended in 1970 in an important particular. Although, prior to 1970, an award of expenses and attorneys' fees was not ordinarily made, Rule 37(a)(4) now provides:

"If the motion is granted, the court *shall*, after opportunity for hearing, require the party or deponent whose conduct necessitated the motion or the party *or attorney advising such conduct* or both of them to pay to the moving party the reasonable expenses incurred in obtaining the order, including attorney's fees, unless the court finds that the opposition to the motion was substantially justified or that other circumstances make an award of expenses unjust."

If the shoe were on the other foot, unhesitatingly I would award expenses, including attorney's fees, against defendant, and I very much would like to award them against the EEOC. Unfortunately, I can't. Rule 37(f) confers a special "privilege" on the government to be contumacious:—"Except to the extent permitted by statute, expenses and fees may not be awarded against the United States under this rule." Perhaps this doesn't immunize government counsel from an award against them personally, but in light of all of the circumstances, I think that a personal award against counsel would be unjust—at least it would be unjust this time around.

In many ways, as this opinion suggests, the problem of the privilege for official information is not with the law but with the lawyers. Government attorneys, like all attorneys, like to win their cases. If they can win on procedural grounds or enhance their chances for victory by a claim of privilege, they will usually attempt to do so, regardless of whether justice is served. If government lawyers could be trusted to claim a privilege only when official interests are real and compelling, the precise language of the privilege might not be important. Because government lawyers cannot be so trusted, any governmental privilege should contain language that gives the judge substantial discretion and discourages undue judicial deference to governmental claims.

Problem VIII–57. CAAD (Citizens Against Atomic Destruction) sues the Consolidated Electric Company to prevent them from constructing a nuclear power generating station. They allege that the proposed station will be a nuisance because its emergency core cooling system is unsafe. They seek to discover the exact plans for the cooling system. The Atomic Energy Commission presents the judge with a request signed by the chairperson of the Commission asking the court to deny discovery on the ground that the exact plans are a "national defense secret." **How should the court rule on this claim of privilege?**

Problem VIII–58. Assume that in the previous problem the government's claim of privilege is granted and the case goes to trial with discovery of the plans denied. At trial CAAD wishes to present the testimony of Leah Lempert, a nuclear engineer who had worked on the cooling system before leaving Consolidated Electric to campaign against the spread of unsafe nuclear power stations. The AEC through its chairperson claims a privilege on the ground of national defense to prevent Lempert from testifying to what she knows about the cooling system in the Consolidated Electric plant. **How should the court rule?** Assume that the judge believes the privilege must be granted because the court cannot in this area override the decision of the AEC concerning what is relevant to the national defense, but the judge also believes the privilege would not have been claimed if the core cooling system were unequivocally safe. **Is there any relief which the judge can grant CAAD consistent with PFRE 509?**

Problem VIII–59. Nancy Johnson, an attorney with the IRS, sues the agency because she feels she has been discriminated against and denied promotions because of her sex. She seeks copies of those evaluation memoranda which have been prepared respecting her work and the work of all those attorneys who joined the IRS within three years (before and after) of the date she arrived. She also wants a copy of her personnel file and a copy of the files of all attorneys in the six year period. The government claims a privilege for official information. **How should a judge rule?**

Problem VIII–60. Rachel Lindsey owns farmland which has been taken for a highway. She claims that the highest and best use of the land is for apartment dwellings and that for this purpose the land is worth $3,000 per acre. The government has offered her $280 per acre, which they claim is the land's value as farmland. Rachel has heard that the government in choosing its highway routes attempts to evaluate the different potential uses of the land it would need to take for different possible routes. She believes that the government files contain the highway department's evaluation of potential uses for her land. **If she attempts to subpoena all highway department documents relating to her land, may the government resist the subpoena by claiming a privilege for official information?** Assume Lindsey is attempting to enjoin the taking of the land entirely, claiming it is an abuse of discretion to go through her land. **May she subpoena all the information in the highway department's files relating to possible routes which the highway might take? Is this really an evidence question, or is it more a question of administrative law?**

Problem VIII–61. The Army wishes to seize 20,000 acres of land owned by Hiram Brown. Brown resists the seizure on the ground that he has heard the land will be turned over to a private corporation and hence the seizure is not for a "public purpose." He demands to know the specific use to which the land will be put. The Army introduces a letter from the Secretary of Defense stating, "I must claim the privilege for state secrets and not specify the army's intended use of this land since it relates closely to the national defense. It will be used to the benefit of the public." **What should the judge do? If this is the only evidence as to the Army's intended use, should the judge allow the condemnation?**

B. THE PRICE OF PROTECTING GOVERNMENT INFORMANTS

McCRAY v. STATE OF ILLINOIS

Supreme Court of the United States, 1967.
386 U.S. 300, 87 S.Ct. 1056, 18 L.Ed.2d 62.

Mr. Justice STEWART delivered the opinion of the Court.

The petitioner was arrested in Chicago, Illinois, on the morning of January 16, 1964, for possession of narcotics. The Chicago police officers who made the arrest found a package containing heroin on his person and he was indicted for its unlawful possession. Prior to trial he filed a motion to suppress the heroin as evidence against him, claiming that the police had acquired it in an unlawful search and seizure in violation of the Fourth and

Fourteenth Amendments. After a hearing, the court denied the motion, and the petitioner was subsequently convicted upon the evidence of the heroin the arresting officers had found in his possession. The judgment of conviction was affirmed by the Supreme Court of Illinois and we granted certiorari to consider the petitioner's claim that the hearing on his motion to suppress was constitutionally defective.

The petitioner's arrest occurred near the intersection of 49th Street and Calumet Avenue at about seven in the morning. At the hearing on the motion to suppress, he testified that up until a half hour before he was arrested he had been at "a friend's house" about a block away, that after leaving the friend's house he had "walked with a lady from 48th to 48th and South Park," and that, as he approached 49th Street and Calumet Avenue, "[t]he Officers stopped me going through the alley." "The officers," he said, "did not show me a search warrant for my person or an arrest warrant for my arrest." He said the officers then searched him and found the narcotics in question. The petitioner did not identify the "friend" or the "lady," and neither of them appeared as a witness.

The arresting officers then testified. Officer Jackson stated that he and two fellow officers had had a conversation with an informant on the morning of January 16 in their unmarked police car. The officer said that the informant had told them that the petitioner, with whom Jackson was acquainted, "was selling narcotics and had narcotics on his person and that he could be found in the vicinity of 47th and Calumet at this particular time." Jackson said that he and his fellow officers drove to that vicinity in the police car and that when they spotted the petitioner, the informant pointed him out and then departed on foot. Jackson stated that the officers observed the petitioner walking with a woman, then separating from her and meeting briefly with a man, then proceeding alone, and finally, after seeing the police car, "hurriedly walk[ing] between two buildings." "At this point," Jackson testified, "my partner and myself got out of the car and informed him we had information he had narcotics on his person, placed him in the police vehicle at this point." Jackson stated that the officers then searched the petitioner and found the heroin in a cigarette package.

Jackson testified that he had been acquainted with the informant for approximately a year, that during this period the informant had supplied him with information about narcotics activities "fifteen, sixteen times at least," that the information had proved to be accurate and had resulted in numerous arrests and convictions. On cross-examination, Jackson was even more specific as to the informant's previous reliability, giving the names of people who had been convicted of narcotics violations as the result of information the informant had supplied. When Jackson was asked for the informant's name and address, counsel for the State objected, and the objection was sustained by the court.

Officer Arnold gave substantially the same account of the circumstances of the petitioner's arrest and search, stating that the informant had told the officers that the petitioner "was selling narcotics and had narcotics on his person now in the vicinity of 47th and Calumet." The informant, Arnold testified, "said he had observed [the petitioner] selling narcotics to various people, meaning various addicts, in the area of 47th and Calumet." Arnold testified that he had known the informant "roughly two years," that the informant had given him information concerning narcotics "20 or 25 times," and that the information had resulted in convictions. Arnold too was asked on cross-examination for the informant's name and address, and objections to these questions were sustained by the court.

* * *

In permitting the officers to withhold the informant's identity, the court was following well-settled Illinois law. When the issue is not guilt or innocence, but, as here, the question of probable cause for an arrest or search, the Illinois Supreme Court has held that police officers need not invariably be required to disclose an informant's identity if the trial judge is convinced, by evidence submitted in open court and subject to cross-examination, that the officers did rely in good faith upon credible information supplied by a reliable informant. This Illinois evidentiary rule is consistent with the law of many other States. * * *

The reasoning of the Supreme Court of New Jersey in judicially adopting the same basic evidentiary rule was instructively expressed by Chief Justice Weintraub in State v. Burnett, 42 N.J. 377, 201 A.2d 39:

"If a defendant may insist upon disclosure of the informant in order to test the truth of the officer's statement that there is an informant or as to what the informant related or as to the informant's reliability, we can be sure that every defendant will demand disclosure. He has nothing to lose and the prize may be the suppression of damaging evidence if the State cannot afford to reveal its source, as is so often the case. And since there is no way to test the good faith of a defendant who presses the demand, we must assume the routine demand would have to be routinely granted. The result would be that the State could use the informant's information only as a lead and could search only if it could gather adequate evidence of probable cause apart from the informant's data. Perhaps that approach would sharpen investigatorial techniques, but we doubt that there would be enough talent and time to cope with crime upon that basis. Rather we accept the premise that the informer is a vital part of society's defensive arsenal. The basic rule protecting his identity rests upon that belief.

* * *

"We must remember also that we are not dealing with the trial of the criminal charge itself. There the need for a truthful verdict outweighs society's need for the informer privilege. Here, however, the accused seeks to avoid the truth. The very purpose of a motion to suppress is to escape the inculpatory thrust of evidence in hand, not because its probative force is diluted in the least by the mode of seizure, but rather as a sanction to compel enforcement officers to respect the constitutional security of all of us under the Fourth Amendment. If the motion to suppress is denied, defendant will still be judged upon the untarnished truth.

* * *

"The Fourth Amendment is served if a judicial mind passes upon the existence of probable cause.   Where the issue is submitted upon an application for a warrant, the magistrate is trusted to evaluate the credibility of the affiant in an ex parte proceeding.   As we have said, the magistrate is concerned, not with whether the informant lied, but with whether the affiant is truthful in his recitation of what he was told.   If the magistrate doubts the credibility of the affiant, he may require that the informant be identified or even produced.   It seems to us that the same approach is equally sufficient where the search was without a warrant, that is to say, that it should rest entirely with the judge who hears the motion to suppress to decide whether he needs such disclosure as to the informant in order to decide whether the officer is a believable witness."

What Illinois and her sister States have done is no more than recognize a well-established testimonial privilege, long familiar to the law of evidence. Professor Wigmore, not known as an enthusiastic advocate of testimonial privileges generally, has described that privilege in these words:

"A genuine privilege, on   *   *   *   fundamental principle   *   *   *, must be recognized for the *identity of persons supplying the government with information concerning the commission of crimes.*   Communications of this kind ought to receive encouragement.   They are discouraged if the informer's identity is disclosed.   Whether an informer is motivated by good citizenship, promise of leniency or prospect of pecuniary reward, he will usually condition his cooperation on an assurance of anonymity—to protect himself and his family from harm, to preclude adverse social reactions and to avoid the risk of defamation or malicious prosecution actions against him.   The government also has an interest in nondisclosure of the identity of its informers.   Law enforcement officers often depend upon professional informers to furnish them with a flow of information about criminal activities.   Revelation of the dual role played by such persons ends their usefulness to the government and discourages others from entering into a like relationship.

"That the government has this privilege is well established, and its soundness cannot be questioned."

In the federal courts the rules of evidence in criminal trials are governed "by the principles of the common law as they may be interpreted by the courts of the United States in the light of reason and experience."   This Court, therefore, has the ultimate task of defining the scope to be accorded to the various common law evidentiary privileges in the trial of federal criminal cases.   This is a task which is quite different, of course, from the responsibility of constitutional adjudication.   In the exercise of this supervisory jurisdiction the Court had occasion 10 years ago, in Roviaro v. United States, 353 U.S. 53, to give thorough consideration to one aspect of the informer's privilege, the privilege itself having long been recognized in the federal judicial system.

The Roviaro case involved the informer's privilege, not at a preliminary hearing to determine probable cause for an arrest or search, but at the trial itself where the issue was the fundamental one of innocence or guilt.   The petitioner there had been brought to trial upon a two-count federal indictment charging sale and transportation of narcotics.   According to the prosecution's evidence, the informer had been an active participant in the crime. He "had taken a material part in bringing about the possession of certain drugs by the accused, had been present with the accused at the occurrence of the alleged crime, and might be a material witness as to whether the accused knowingly transported the drugs as charged." The trial court nonetheless denied a defense motion to compel the prosecution to disclose the informer's identity.

This Court held that where, in an actual trial of a federal criminal case, "the disclosure of an informer's identity   *   *   *   is relevant and helpful to the defense of an accused, or is essential to a fair determination of a cause, the privilege must give way. In these situations the trial court may require disclosure and, if the Government withholds the information, dismiss the action.   *   *   *

                 *   *   *

"We believe that no fixed rule with respect to disclosure is justifiable. The problem is one that calls for balancing the public interest in protecting the flow of information against the individual's right to prepare his defense. Whether a proper balance renders nondisclosure erroneous must depend on the particular circumstances of each case, taking into consideration the crime charged, the possible defenses, the possible significance of the informer's testimony, and other relevant factors."

The Court's opinion then carefully reviewed the particular circumstances of Roviaro's trial, pointing out that the informer's "possible testimony was highly relevant   *   *   *," that he "might have disclosed an entrapment *   *   *," "might have thrown doubt upon petitioner's identity or on the identity of the package   *   *   *," "might have testified to petitioner's possible lack of knowledge of the contents of the package that he 'transported' *   *   *," and that the "informer was the sole participant, other than the accused, in the transaction charged." The Court concluded "that, under these circumstances, the trial court committed prejudicial error in permitting the Government to withhold the identity of its undercover employee in the face of repeated demands by the accused for his disclosure."

What Roviaro thus makes clear is that this Court was unwilling to impose any absolute rule requiring disclosure of an informer's identity even in formulating evidentiary rules for federal criminal trials. Much less has the Court ever approached the formulation of a federal evidentiary rule of compulsory disclosure where the issue is the preliminary one of probable cause, and guilt or innocence is not at stake. Indeed, we have repeatedly made clear that federal officers need *not* disclose an informer's identity in applying for an arrest or search warrant. As was said in United States v. Ventresca, 380 U.S. 102, 108, we have "recognized that 'an affidavit may be based on hearsay information and need not reflect the direct personal observations of the affiant,' so long as the magistrate is 'informed of some of the underlying circumstances' supporting the affiant's conclusions and his belief that any informant involved *'whose identity need not be disclosed*   *   *   * was "credible" or his information "reliable." '   *   *   * And just this Term we have taken occasion to point out that a rule virtually prohibiting the use of informers would "severely hamper the Government" in enforcement of the narcotics laws. Lewis v. United States, 385 U.S. 206, 210.

In sum, the Court in the exercise of its power to formulate evidentiary rules for federal criminal cases has consistently declined to hold that an informer's identity need always be disclosed in a federal criminal trial, let alone in a preliminary hearing to determine probable cause for an arrest or search. Yet we are now asked to hold that the Constitution somehow compels Illinois to abolish the informer's privilege from its law of evidence, and to require disclosure of the informer's identity in every such preliminary hearing where it appears that the officers made the arrest or search in reliance upon facts supplied by an informer they had reason to trust. The argument is based upon the Due Process Clause of the Fourteenth Amendment, and upon the Sixth Amendment right of confrontation, applicable to the States through the Fourteenth Amendment. Pointer v. Texas, 380 U.S. 400. [The Court rejects this argument and affirms the decision of the Illinois Supreme Court.]

Mr. Justice DOUGLAS, with whom the Chief Justice, Mr. Justice BRENNAN, and Mr. Justice FORTAS concur, dissenting.

* * *

There is no way to determine the reliability of Old Reliable, the informer, unless he is produced at the trial and cross-examined. Unless he is produced, the Fourth Amendment is entrusted to the tender mercies of the police. What we do today is to encourage arrests and searches without warrants. The whole momentum of criminal law administration should be in precisely the opposite direction, if the Fourth Amendment is to remain a vital force. Except in rare and emergency cases, it requires magistrates to make the findings of "probable cause." We should be mindful of its command that a judicial mind should be interposed between the police and the citizen. We should also be mindful that "disclosure, rather than suppression, of relevant materials ordinarily promotes the proper administration of criminal justice."

Does the opinion of Justice Douglas miss the point made by the majority? Is the reliability of Old Reliable in dispute, or is the dispute over whether the officers reasonably believed that the informant was reliable? In the circumstances of *McCray* is there any need to be sure that Old Reliable is not an illegal wiretap or bug? Is there a middle ground possible between keeping the informant's identity secret and revealing it to the world? Would *in camera* proceedings make sense? What about requiring the officers to take a lie detector test affirming their description of the informant? The Advisory Committee in PFRE 510 purports to codify the holdings of *McCray* and *Roviaro* (discussed in *McCray*):

IDENTITY OF INFORMER

(a) *Rule of privilege.* The government or a state or subdivision thereof has a privilege to refuse to disclose the identity of a person who has furnished information relating to or assisting in an investigation of a possible violation of law to a law enforcement officer or member of a legislative committee or its staff conducting an investigation.

(b) *Who may claim.* The privilege may be claimed by an appropriate representative of the government, regardless of whether the information was furnished to an officer of the government or of a state or subdivision thereof. The privilege may be claimed by an appropriate representative of a state or subdivision if the information was furnished to an officer thereof, except that in criminal cases the privilege shall not be allowed if the government objects.

(c) *Exceptions.*

(1) Voluntary disclosure; informer a witness. No privilege exists under this rule if the identity of the informer or his interest in the subject matter of his communication has been disclosed to those who would have cause to resent the communication by a holder of the privilege or by the informer's own action, or if the informer appears as a witness for the government.

(2) Testimony on merits. If it appears from the evidence in the case or from other showing by a party that an informer may be able to give testimony necessary to a fair determination of the issue of guilt or innocence in a criminal case or of a material issue on the merits in a civil case to which the government is a party, and the government invokes the privilege, the judge shall give the government an opportunity to show *in camera* facts relevant to determining whether the informer can, in fact, supply that testimony. The showing will ordinarily be in the form of affidavits, but the judge may direct that testimony be taken if he finds that the matter cannot be resolved satisfactorily upon affidavit. If the judge finds that there is a reasonable probability that the informer can give the testimony, and the government elects not to disclose his identity, the judge on motion of the defendant in a criminal case shall dismiss the charges to which the testimony would relate, and

the judge may do so on his own motion. In civil cases, he may make any order that justice requires. Evidence submitted to the judge shall be sealed and preserved to be made available to the appellate court in the event of an appeal, and the contents shall not otherwise be revealed without consent of the government. All counsel and parties shall be permitted to be present at every stage of proceedings under this subdivision except a showing *in camera*, at which no counsel or party shall be permitted to be present.

(3) Legality of obtaining evidence. If information from an informer is relied upon to establish the legality of the means by which evidence was obtained and the judge is not satisfied that the information was received from an informer reasonably believed to be reliable or credible, he may require the identity of the informer to be disclosed. The judge shall, on request of the government, direct that the disclosure be made *in camera*. All counsel and parties concerned with the issue of legality shall be permitted to be present at every stage of proceedings under this subdivision except a disclosure *in camera*, at which no counsel or party shall be permitted to be present. If disclosure of the identity of the informer is made *in camera*, the record thereof shall be sealed and preserved to be made available to the appellate court in the event of an appeal, and the contents shall not otherwise be revealed without consent of the government.

––––––––––

The leading cases do not address many questions that the rule attempts to resolve, and the rule does not solve all problems. Consider the following questions. What resolution, if any, does the rule provide? Is that resolution satisfactory?

1. Should any government attorney have the power to invoke the privilege, or should this power be limited to officials holding positions high in the hierarchy of executive responsibility?

2. Should danger to informants be presumed, or should a showing of danger be required in every case?

3. If an informant provides information to a state agency, should that agency, absent a particularized showing of danger to the informant, be permitted to invoke a privilege over the objection of the federal government?

4. If the government chooses to conceal the identity of an informant until trial, is it then allowed to use the informant as a witness?

5. Does the requirement that an informant be produced turn on whether the defense can show that the informant can, in fact, supply information on the merits of a case, or on whether it is possible that he will be helpful to the defense?

6. If the informant has relevant information, but the judge determines that it would harm rather than help the defense, can a privilege be sustained?

7. If the relevant information known to the informant has some slight probative value, can the identity of the informant be preserved? If so, does his information remain secret or must it be conceded by the government and submitted by affidavit or stipulation? Should civil and criminal cases be treated the same?

8. If the prosecutor places great reliance on the testimony of a single police officer, and if the defendant contends that discrepancies or gaps in the officer's testimony on a search and seizure question cast doubt on the officer's entire testimony, must the government produce at trial an informant if the informant's knowledge is limited to the search and seizure issue?

9. What is the role of the judge in an *in camera* proceeding? Who else is involved?

10. Should the *in camera* proceeding be the same in civil as in criminal cases?

You should note this rule protects only the identity of the informer. Information furnished by the informer is not privileged unless it would tend to reveal the informer's identity. Does this suggest another possible middle ground between the disclosure and the suppression of an informer's evidence? Might not an informer be given interrogatories which could be answered anonymously?

Problem VIII–62. With the help of a confidential informant, Agent George of the Bureau of Narcotics and Dangerous Drugs met Fred James, who took Agent George to Sam Conno on February 16, 1972. At that time Conno sold George two ounces of cocaine. The sale took place in a house which James and George entered while the informer remained outside in an automobile. A week later Conno was arrested. At trial, Conno claimed the defense of entrapment and demanded that the informant's identity be disclosed and that he be produced. Conno contended that the informant might be able to support his defense. At no time prior to the trial did Conno seek to subpoena James, but James was a fugitive from justice during this period and no subpoena could have been served. The government claims a right to protect the informant's identity. **Should the government's claim be honored? How should the trial judge proceed to make a ruling?**

Problem VIII–63. Tom Tale testifies that he bought heroin from Stan Seller. On cross-examination Seller wishes to ask Tale whether he had informed on Seller twice in the past, whether he was a paid informant for the Bureau of Narcotics, and whether Seller was the anonymous informer who had turned in Frank Ravitz and Betty Bonds. Tale refuses to answer each of these questions on the basis of the informer's privilege. **Should the court order him to answer? What should the court do if Tale refuses to answer despite a court order?**

Problem VIII–64. Churder is charged with transporting stolen property knowing it was stolen. He defends on the ground that he took the property with the intent of turning it over to the police at his earliest convenience. He seeks the identity of the informant who told the police he was in possession of this property. **Should this request be granted?**

Problem VIII–65. Late one night the police burst into the Kitcheners' apartment without a warrant. They terrified the Kitcheners and turned the house upside down looking for narcotics, but they found nothing. The Kitcheners believe that Art Graham, with whom they had recently quarreled, falsely reported them out of spite. They sue the police, alleging reckless reliance on an unreliable informer. The Kitcheners also intend to sue Graham if he was the informer. Interrogatories are issued to the chief of police. The first asks the chief to provide the name of the informer who told the police the Kitcheners were concealing narcotics. The second asks whether Art Graham was the informer. The chief refuses to answer either question, claiming the informer's privilege. **What should the court do in these circumstances?**

Problem VIII–66. Jane Field is arrested for possession of narcotics, following a search of her apartment that reveals a package containing half a kilo of heroin. Field states the package had come in the mail that very morning. She says that she opened it but had no idea of what it contained, since she had never seen heroin before. She also says she has no idea who sent it. She has a piece of brown wrapping paper with cancelled stamps on it which could have fit the package. At trial she demands that the police reveal the name of the individual who informed on her. **When the police refuse how should a court rule? Does it matter if the prosecution has three witnesses who will testify that they have bought heroin from Jane?**

Problem VIII–67. The state housing board brings an action to collect a civil fine of $1000 from Ivan Tucker, a landlord. The claim is that for 10 days during the month of February Tucker failed to heat his apartment to the required minimum of 62 degrees. Tucker demands to know who complained about the lack of heat. **If the board can prove its charges without relying on the testimony of any tenant, must it nonetheless disclose the complainant's identity?**

Problem VIII–68. Stephen Silt is charged with selling narcotics. A government informant not only helped to arrange the alleged sales transaction, but also was present when it took place. Silt denies the sale, claiming that the two undercover officers who claim to have purchased drugs framed him. The government claims that Silt must show that the informant would support the defendant's version of the facts before the court orders disclosure. **Is this correct? If the government files an affidavit of the infor-**

mant with the court stating that the informant agrees with the government witnesses' version of the facts, is there any need to call the informant?

SECTION VII. MISCELLANEOUS NON-CONSTITUTIONAL PRIVILEGES

A number of other privileges are found in different jurisdictions. Statutes protect the identity of news sources, certain reports required by government agencies, trade secrets, and the secret of the ballot box. Most of these miscellaneous privileges are qualified in important ways, and in some cases the qualifications vary considerably from state to state. It is often extremely difficult to draft a statute or rule that strikes an appropriate balance between the interest to be protected and the need for information in the legislative and judicial processes. Consider, for example, the wording of the two proposed federal privileges and the criticism following each:

Required Reports Privilege

PFRE 502:

A person, corporation, association, or other organization or entity, either public or private, making a return or report required by law to be made has a privilege to refuse to disclose and to prevent any other person from disclosing the return or report, if the law requiring it to be made so provides. A public officer or agency to whom a return or report is required by law to be made has a privilege to refuse to disclose the return or report if the law requiring it to be made so provides. No privilege exists under this rule in actions involving perjury, false statements, fraud in the return or report, or other failure to comply with the law in question.

The Advisory Committee indicated that:

[s]tatutes which require the making of returns or reports sometimes confer on the reporting party a privilege against disclosure, commonly coupled with a prohibition against disclosure by the officer to whom the report is made.

Why? The committee said:

A provision against disclosure may be included in a statute for a variety of reasons, the chief of which are probably assuring the validity of the statute against claims of self-incrimination, honoring the privilege against self-incrimination, and encouraging the furnishing of the required information by assuring privacy.

In essence the proposed rule reiterated a result mandated in certain federal statutes and established a federal privilege for required state reports elicited with a state guarantee of confidentiality. Senator McClellan had the following reservations:

I am somewhat troubled by the apparent scope of this new privilege. * * * To uphold values found in the privilege against self-incrimination, it may be necessary to accord protection against disclosure of information required to be filed by an individual, but why extend the privilege to an association or a corporation? Neither comes with the protection of the privilege against self-incrimination. * * * Information privileged by Federal statute ought to be accorded appropriate status under the rules. But why should the rules incorporate wholesale State law? If the litigation were between private parties or civil in character, I might readily agree that due deference to policies grounded in Federalism ought to control. But the administration of Federal criminal justice has never been thought to be generally subject to State privileges. Why should a required reports exception be carved out of this salutary general principle? I am not willing to suggest that in particular instances the courts ought not recognize such a privilege, but this should take place on a case by case basis; I would be reluctant to support a wholesale adoption of State law in this area without knowing quite what it was that was being adopted.[79]

Assuming that a guarantee of confidentiality will encourage more honest reporting, is this outcome so important that it outweighs the value of providing needed information to civil and criminal litigants? Could not honest reporting be as effectively encouraged by harsh penalties for dishonest reporting? Does the privilege respond to some of the same values as the fifth amendment's privilege against self-incrimination, even though it applies in many circumstances where the fifth amendment would not?

Trade Secrets

PFRE 508:

A person has a privilege, which may be claimed by him or his agent or employee, to refuse to disclose and to prevent other persons from disclosing a trade secret owned by him, if the allowance of the privilege will not tend to conceal fraud or otherwise work injustice. When disclosure is directed, the judge shall take such protective measure as the interests of the holder of the privilege and of the parties and the furtherance of justice may require.

Terry Lenzner, a lawyer representing the Project on Corporate Responsibility, found fault with this wording:

In the trade secret area, for example, we would suggest that information be made available to people seeking it from corporations, unless the corporation can sustain the burden of showing that it will create unfair economic advantage to its competitors or its potential competitors if that information is disclosed.

We believe that proposed rule would be closer to a codification of existing law than the proposed rules that are before you. Indeed, in the committee's advisory note on the trade secret privilege, you will see that at the bottom of the note the committee suggests that this is, in fact, an expansion of existing law under Rule 26 of the Federal Rules of Civil Procedure.

My interpretation is that it is, indeed, an expansion, because it shifts the burden of proof.

Under rule 26, the person who is seeking to protect confidential or trade secret information has the burden of obtaining a protective order or proving to a court that that information should not be disclosed for the purposes of the litigation.

Under the proposed evidence rule, however, a person, when a corporation classifies information as a trade secret, will have the burden of proving first, that without that information it will be either unjust or there will be a fraud perpetrated.

Also, rule 508 in our opinion is almost absolute in its coverage, despite the trend of Federal laws and despite the fact that courts can provide adequate protective measures if such information is given an individual seeking it.

We are also concerned because the Government, we feel, will be hindered in obtaining information for investigations and prosecutions of civil and criminal violations by corporations. And the Department of Justice and regulatory agencies may find that road blocks are

---

79. Supplement to Hearings on the Rules of Evidence Before the Subcomm. on Criminal Justice of the House Comm. on the Judiciary, 93d Cong., 1st Sess., at 49–50 (1973).

thrown up in their way and expensive delays created if this rule is passed.

Indeed, if you look at the Federal Trade Commission cases over the past 20 or 30 years, the trade secret privilege has been raised almost consistently by corporations seeking to keep information from the FTC in its prosecutive efforts.

We were disturbed to read in the testimony of the Department of Justice * * * before this subcommittee that the Department did not raise these problems or seem concerned with some of these privileges that would, in fact, inhibit and deter effective prosecutions by regulatory agencies, by the Criminal Division, and by the Anti-Trust Division.

Now, the rule, in addition to being over-expansive, does not even define what a trade secret is, or what ownership of a trade secret means. There is extensive case law in this area. And it seems to us that the drafters should have made an attempt to at least limit that definition.

In addition, since it does not define what a trade secret is and does not limit its application, it goes far beyond existing case law because it creates an absolute privilege. And Wigmore and every expert and every court that we have looked at have said that this is not an absolute privilege. It is limited only as a property right in situations where economic harm to the corporation is balanced against the need to have the information to complete the litigation.

In addition, there is no great social policy behind the trade secret as there is in the husband-wife privilege or the doctor-patient privilege. Those privileges, as we understand them, were created to encourage private confidential communications on a personal basis. Those characteristics, of course, are not involved in the trade secret privilege.[80]

————

Although the rule is not crystal clear, many people believe that its flexibility is needed to permit courts to balance the needs of businesses to preserve their competitive advantages against the needs of litigants for evidence. Those litigants who seek discovery of trade secrets are not all well intentioned and the ability to discover secrets sometimes can be used as a blackmail device. Courts sensibly try to allow businesses to retain their marketplace positions while providing litigants what will help their cases. They seem well aware that this is not an absolute privilege and requires consideration of competing interests.

SECTION VIII. THE PRIVILEGE AGAINST SELF-INCRIMINATION

A. INTRODUCTION

In this section we discuss the privilege against self-incrimination, the one privilege which is clearly required by the Constitution. In the past it has been attacked more severely than any of the privileges we have discussed and it might well not exist today but for the difficulties of constitutional amendment. We could easily spend as much space on this privilege as we have on the other privileges combined, but we shall be brief, for we assume that the privilege against self-incrimination is considered in depth in courses in criminal procedure or constitutional law.

80. Hearings on the Rules of Evidence Before the Subcomm. on Criminal Justice of the House Comm. on the Judiciary, 93d Cong., 1st Sess., at 394–95 (1973).

We shall not discuss the history of this privilege. A brief exposition is available in McCormick,[81] and more extensive histories can be found in the sources cited therein. The privilege is found in the fifth amendment to the United States Constitution and in the constitutions of every state except Iowa and New Jersey. Since the Supreme Court has held that the fifth amendment's privilege is binding on the states, only the federal constitutional provision will be examined.

As Justice Black might have said, the proper place to begin a discussion of a constitutional provision is with the language found in the constitution. The relevant portion of the fifth amendment states:

No person * * * shall be compelled in any criminal case to be a witness against himself.

It is possible to read this language as providing a privilege only for defendants in criminal cases and not for witnesses in other legal proceedings. Some early state constitutional provisions were read this way. In the landmark decision of Counselman v. Hitchcock,[82] the Supreme Court eschewed this narrow reading of the Fifth Amendment. The issue in that case was whether the privilege was available to a witness before a grand jury. The Court answered in the affirmative:

The object [of the privilege] was to insure that a person should not be compelled, when acting as a witness to any investigation, to give testimony which might tend to show that he himself had committed a crime. The privilege is limited to criminal matters, but it is as broad as the mischief against which it seeks to guard.

For many years the federal version of the privilege was not binding on the states. But in 1964, in Malloy v. Hogan,[83] the Court reversed its earlier position and incorporated the privilege into its reading of the due process clause of the fourteenth amendment.

B. TO WHOM DOES THE PRIVILEGE BELONG?

Like the attorney-client privilege, the physician-patient privilege and other privileges that we have previously discussed, the privilege against self-incrimination is a personal one. It belongs only to the one claiming that compelled testimony might tend to subject him to criminal sanctions. A codefendant has no right to raise the privilege of another codefendant, and an attorney cannot raise the privilege on the ground that her answers might tend to incriminate her clients. Where one has surrendered personal records to an accountant or other non-privileged custodian, a court is likely to find that the privilege may not be invoked by or on behalf of the owner of the records. The privilege is personal and compulsion directed at a third

81. McCormick §§ 114–17.

In choosing to de-emphasize the privilege against self-incrimination, we are aware that some courses in criminal procedure do not fully cover the privilege, but focus instead on coerced confessions and judicial scrutiny of police procedures. Since the Warren court married the privilege to the law of coerced confessions in the sixties, we believe that the policies of the privilege must certainly be discussed in criminal procedure, if only indirectly. In this section we have attempted to organize the basic fifth amendment law into a short, but coherent, presentation. The organization is ours, and the cases cited are standard fare. The reader will note that we cite few books and articles aside from the McCormick treatise. Because we are not attempting to fully cover the subject, we thought it would be most helpful to select one outside source for further reference. McCormick will lead you to most other relevant authorities. We do recommend that you read Leonard Levy's book, Origins of the Fifth Amendment (1968) and Lewis Mayers' book, Shall We Amend the Fifth Amendment? (1959).

82. 142 U.S. 547 (1892).

83. 378 U.S. 1 (1964).

party who has more than momentary possession of the records does not require the owner to do anything that might be incriminating.[84] However, in our discussion of attorney-client privilege we saw in the *Fisher* case that an attorney may assert attorney-client privilege on a client's behalf to avoid surrendering the client's records when the client could have invoked the privilege against self-incrimination to prevent surrender had a subpoena been issued to the client before the records were transferred to the lawyer. *Fisher* itself indicates that a client would not always be able to prevent surrender.

Corporations do not have a privilege against self-incrimination,[85] nor, in the usual case, do partnerships or labor unions. In United States v. White,[86] the Court said:

The test   *   *   *   is whether one can fairly say under all the circumstances that

a particular type of organization has a character so impersonal in the scope of its membership and activities that it cannot be said to embody or represent the purely private or personal interest of its constituents, but rather to embody their common or group interests only. If so, the privilege cannot be invoked on behalf of the organization or its representatives in their official capacity.

Because the corporation has no privilege, the agent of a corporation cannot claim the privilege on its behalf. Indeed, a corporate agent, by holding corporate records, is obligated to allow the government to inspect the records even if they tend to incriminate him personally.[87] However, a corporate agent does not waive his own right to keep silent about his activities on behalf of the corporation.[88]

C. COMPULSION TO INCRIMINATE AND IMMUNITY FROM CRIMINAL PROSECUTION

The privilege protects against any sort of legal compulsion to give testimony which in some way might subject one to criminal liability. So long as the testimony would tend to incriminate, the privilege applies in civil cases, bankruptcy proceedings, administrative hearings and before grand juries, legislative committees, and other official investigatory bodies.

The fifth amendment does not protect a witness against testimony that might subject him to ridicule, disgrace, or scorn. Nor will the privilege apply to testimony relating to criminal activity if there is no possibility of criminal prosecution, as, for example, where the witness has been pardoned, the statute of limitations has run,

the witness has already been convicted or acquitted, or the witness has been granted immunity.

Problems do arise in determining what are criminal proceedings. In Boyd v. United States,[89] the Supreme Court held that proceedings to forfeit a man's property because of criminal offenses, though civil in form, are in their nature criminal. The privilege is also available in prosecutions in juvenile court.[90]

Our federal system of separate, but related, sovereignties has given rise to the issue of whether individuals may refuse to answer questions posed by officials of one jurisdiction if their answers might tend to incriminate them in another. Early cases

---

84. See Couch v. United States, 409 U.S. 322 (1973).

85. See, e.g., Hale v. Henkel, 201 U.S. 43 (1906). See also Bellis v. United States, 417 U.S. 85 (1974) (no privilege for dissolved law partnership).

86. 322 U.S. 694, 701 (1944).

87. See Wilson v. United States, 221 U.S. 361 (1911).

88. See Curcio v. United States, 354 U.S. 118, 125 (1957).

89. 116 U.S. 616 (1886).

90. See Application of Gault, 387 U.S. 1 (1967).

held that the privilege did nothing to relieve this bind, but the Supreme Court's decision in Murphy v. Waterfront Commission of New York Harbor [91] indicates that the earlier decisions are no longer good law. *Murphy* involved a man subpoenaed to testify before a state commission investigating a work stoppage on the docks who was granted immunity against prosecution under state law. Nevertheless he refused to testify, citing his fear of federal prosecution. The Supreme Court held that the fifth amendment protected witnesses whose testimony was compelled in state proceedings from prosecution under federal as well as state law. The Court said that in the

exercise of its supervisory powers, it would direct lower federal courts to exclude the testimony and the fruits of testimony elicited from witnesses under state grants of immunity.

If the situation in *Murphy* were reversed—i.e., if a witness given immunity at the federal level were later prosecuted by a state—the result should be the same. Under the supremacy clause of the Constitution, the federal government can provide immunity which binds the states. The Court can also be expected to prevent one state from prosecuting a declarant on the basis of testimony elicited in another state under a grant of immunity.

D.   HOW FAR DOES THE PRIVILEGE EXTEND?

In Hoffman v. United States the Court said:

The privilege afforded not only extends to answers that would in themselves support a conviction * * * but likewise embraces those which would furnish a link in the chain of evidence needed to prosecute * * *. [I]f the witness, upon interposing his claim, were required to prove the hazard * * * he would be compelled to surrender the very protection which the privilege is designed to guarantee. To sustain the privilege, it need only be evident from the implications of the question, in the setting in which it is asked, that a responsive answer to the question or an explanation of why it cannot be answered might be dangerous because injurious disclosure could result.[92]

This language was cited with approval in Malloy v. Hogan. The *Malloy* Court also repeated the language in *Hoffman* that to deny the claim of privilege the judge must be:

"perfectly clear, from a careful consideration of all the circumstances in the case, that the witness is mistaken, and that the answer[s] *cannot possibly* have such tendency" to incriminate.[93] (emphasis in original)

Thus, assertion of the privilege is usually sufficient to forestall further questioning. The witness may claim the privilege without informing the judge, even *in camera,* of the substance of his testimony.

Malloy, Hoffman and the other cases extending the privilege apply only to testimony or written material which are products of an individual's thoughts. The fifth amendment's protection does not extend to the physical characteristics of individuals. Thus, in Schmerber v. California,[94] the Court held that taking a blood sample from an accused did not violate the Fifth Amendment. More recently, the Court has held that taking voice prints [95] and handwriting samples [96] from unwilling defendants does not contravene the privilege against self-incrimination. Nor will the

91. 378 U.S. 52 (1964). Immunity is discussed more generally infra.

92. 341 U.S. 479, 486–87 (1951).

93. Id. at 488, quoting from Temple v. Commonwealth, 75 Va. 892, 898 (1881).

94. 384 U.S. 757 (1966).

95. United States v. Dionisio, 410 U.S. 1 (1973).

96. United States v. Mara, 410 U.S. 19 (1973).

privilege prevent an accused from being placed in a lineup or being compelled to speak.[97]

It is not clear, however, what sanctions are available to the state when the accused will not cooperate in supplying physical evidence relating to his person. It would seem that, at the least, the prosecution should be able to comment on the accused's non-cooperation and to argue that such non-cooperation indicates consciousness of guilt. An action for contempt may also be available, especially where the refusal to cooperate occurs before trial.

The privilege against self-incrimination affords protection not only against legal compulsion to provide testimony and to make verbal and written statements that might be used against a declarant in a criminal prosecution, but also it protects against legal compulsion to take certain action that might be viewed as implicitly testimonial. A rule of thumb that works in almost all cases is that a person need not comply with a government order or request to take certain action if by complying the person might implicitly provide the government with information of a testimonial sort that could be used against him in a criminal case. The problem of incrimination by action already has been considered in the material on attorney-client privilege where the *Fisher* and *Olwell* cases are discussed.

The archetypical case in which the privilege may be used to justify a refusal to act involves a subpoena to a person suspected of some crime, which directs the suspect to bring documents, e.g., his financial records for the past three years, to a grand jury or to an IRS office. Were the suspect to comply with the subpoena, production of the documents would be tantamount to his saying "These are my financial records for the last three years." Such an implicit statement might be used by the government to authenticate the records and justify using them against the suspect in a subsequent criminal case. Only where a court believes that implicit authentication cannot be accomplished by production, as in *Fisher*, will production be required despite a self-incrimination claim. As a general rule, the government may not compel a person to implicitly provide information that might be incriminating any more than it may compel explicitly incriminating assertions.

Courts disagree over whether the privilege against self-incrimination protects against the use of "private papers" written by a person without any compulsion by the government. It is uncertain, for instance, whether a diary kept by a person and shown to no one before the police discover it in the course of a search may be used against the author. The government has not compelled the author to make this record, suggesting that there is no compelled self-incrimination if the evidence is used. Yet, the privacy notions that support the fifth amendment privilege as well as certain fourth amendment concepts have led some courts to create a special protection for private papers. Having noted the uncertainty, we leave the scope of searches and the permissible use of evidence seized in searches for courses in criminal procedure.

E. DEFENDANTS AND OTHER WITNESSES

The defendant in a criminal action receives greater protection from the fifth amendment's privilege against self-incrimination than does the ordinary witness in a judicial proceeding. This is because the defendant need not take the stand at all, while the ordinary witness must invoke the fifth amendment as a justification for refusing to answer specific questions. Although it is usually clear when a defen-

---

97. United States v. Wade, 388 U.S. 218, 222–23 (1967).

dant has a right not to take the witness stand, it is not clear when in the course of an investigation one becomes a defendant for fifth amendment purposes. Is it after indictment, or is it when the focus of the inquiry is on him? Is it when there is sufficient basis for indictment, or when the prosecution decides to indict? Miranda v. State of Arizona [98] suggests that so long as someone is under formal legal restraint or compulsion and is subject to interrogation, he has the right to shut off questioning with a general claim of privilege. But during investigations, before grand juries and other investigative bodies, individuals must assert their privilege in response to particular inquiries. They cannot successfully claim a right not to appear simply because they are the targets of the investigation.

F. WAIVER

When the defendant in a criminal case chooses to testify, his choice waives the privilege at least to the extent necessary for effective cross-examination. Although there is language in some cases which suggests that an accused who testifies is subject to cross-examination on the same basis as any other witness, it is not yet clear whether defendants who testify in "wide open rule" jurisdictions open themselves up to substantive examination beyond the scope of their direct testimony. To hold that they do is to base a determination of the degree to which a federal constitutional right is waived on local rules of procedure concerned not with fundamental constitutional values but rather with the promotion of orderly trials. The better procedure is to limit cross-examination of an accused to the scope of direct, regardless of the limits placed on the cross-examination of other witnesses. McCormick comments, "A rule of blanket waiver would not only discourage accused persons from testifying at all but would in effect make them prosecution witnesses, confronting them with the cruel trilemma of self-accusation, perjury or contempt." [99]

Waiver questions also arise when an individual who has testified at some stage of a proceeding elects later to invoke the privilege. Courts have taken the sensible view that an accused who takes the stand at any time during his trial waives the privilege for the trial. If he leaves the stand, he is subject to recall on the same basis as other witnesses. But, if, following a trial in which an accused has testified, the judgment is reversed, the right not to testify in a second trial probably remains. Of course, anything that the accused admitted in the first trial can be introduced against him as an admission.

The courts have not been sympathetic to ordinary witnesses who seek the protection of the privilege only after having testified to some incriminating information. In Rogers v. United States,[1] a witness before a grand jury testified that she had held the office of Treasurer of the Communist party and had at one time possessed the party's membership lists and books. She stated that she had turned the lists and books over to another person, but she claimed the privilege when asked to reveal the identity of that person. The Supreme Court affirmed a contempt citation, rejecting the claim of privilege on the ground that once a witness had revealed incriminating information, she could not refuse to fill in the details. The Court's theory was that, given what Rogers had already revealed, disclosure of her successor's identity would not have tended to incriminate. If it would have had this tendency, the privilege would still have been available.

In Ellis v. United States,[2] the United States Court of Appeals for the District of Colum-

---

98. 384 U.S. 436 (1966). *Miranda* is discussed infra in subsection H.

99. McCormick § 132, at 280–81.

1. 340 U.S. 367 (1951).

2. 135 U.S.App.D.C. 35, 416 F.2d 791 (1969).

bia, going against the great weight of authority, held that a nonindicted witness who has waived the privilege when asked to testify before a grand jury may not claim the privilege and refuse to testify at a trial based on an indictment returned by the grand jury that heard his testimony. The privilege does remain, under *Ellis,* for

questions which go beyond the substance of the witness' grand jury testimony. McCormick criticizes the decision in *Ellis,* suggesting that it may discourage witnesses from testifying before grand juries and arguing that the subsequent testimony does pose additional dangers of self-incrimination.[3]

G. REQUIRED RECORDS

Individuals engaged in certain regulated activities may not rely on the fifth amendment to avoid relinquishing records they are required to keep. The leading case is Shapiro v. United States.[4] This case involved a defendant charged with violating the Emergency Price Control Act of 1942. The defendant argued that information he had given the government pursuant to a subpoena *duces tecum* could not be used against him in a criminal trial because its production had been compelled. The Court rejected the defendant's claim and held that there's no violation of the fifth amendment where reasonable governmental regulations require regulated parties to supply the government with certain information. But, in three cases decided in 1968–Marchetti v. United States,[5] Grosso v. United States[6] and Haynes v. United States[7]—the Court found violations of the fifth amendment in requirements that individuals register or pay occupational taxes under the federal wagering tax statutes and register regulated firearms pursuant to another federal statute. The Court said in *Grosso*:

The premises of the doctrine, as it is described in *Shapiro,* are evidently three: first, the purposes of the United States' inquiry must be essentially regulatory; second, information is to be obtained by requiring the preservation of records of

a kind which the regulated party has customarily kept; and third, the records themselves must have assumed "public aspects" which render them at least analogous to public documents.[8]

In *Shapiro* these conditions were met. In the three 1968 cases, the statutes served to facilitate the discovery of crimes committed by the registrants; they did not regulate legal behavior.[9] The *Shapiro* doctrine seems to represent an easy way for the government to circumvent the fifth amendment. Assuming that the *Grosso* quotation accurately captures the essence of the doctrine, are you satisfied with the limits placed upon it? Is the public aspect part of the inquiry any control at all, or is it a reiteration that the required documents must relate to a regulatory purpose? What kinds of records do people normally keep? Business records? Is the second prong of the doctrine much of a control on the government? Finally, is there much limit today to the regulatory power of the government? Why should the government ever be able to compel people to give evidence that might tend to incriminate without guaranteeing use immunity, discussed infra, in return. Would any governmental interest be impaired by

3. McCormick § 140, at 298–99.
4. 335 U.S. 1 (1948).
5. 390 U.S. 39 (1968).
6. 390 U.S. 62 (1968).
7. 390 U.S. 85 (1968).

8. 390 U.S. 62, 67–68 (1968).

9. See also Albertson v. Subversive Activities Control Board, 382 U.S. 70 (1965) (officers of Communist Party not required to file registration statements); United States v. Freed, 401 U.S. 601 (1971) (upholding the National Firearms Act disclosure requirements as amended); California v. Byers, 402 U.S. 424 (1971) (upholding requirement that participants in auto accident stop at scene).

requiring the government to use evidence obtained pursuant to its regulatory func-

tion only in regulatory proceedings and not in criminal actions?

H. CONFESSIONS

By confessions we mean statements made by an accused in a governmental setting other than a courtroom, for example, in a police interrogation room. Confessions are admissible into evidence under the admissions exception to the hearsay rule. Some are only slightly incriminatory and are usually referred to as admissions, while others describe in gory detail the accused's involvement in the crime charged. Since the late 18th century the common law courts have refused to admit against an accused statements obtained from him through the application of physical force, by threat of physical force, or in response to promises of leniency. In this country the same result was reached at the federal level and in many states as a matter of constitutional law. The usual justification for the rule was that such statements were not reliable, but the rule was applied in cases where extrinsic evidence made it clear that the confession was completely credible. In 1936, in Brown v. State of Mississippi,[10] the Supreme Court first held that the introduction of involuntary confessions in state courts was a violation of due process. This is now a well-established rule of law.

Determining whether or not a confession is voluntary requires consideration of the totality of the circumstances surrounding a case. Relevant factors include the accused's age, his educational background, his physical and mental condition at the time of interrogation, his awareness of his rights and his familiarity with police procedures. As McCormick points out, it is difficult to establish a blanket rule that promises or suggestions of leniency automatically make a confession involuntary.[11]

Sometimes the police are responding honestly to the accused's desire to learn the potential benefits of cooperation with the police.

The well-known case of Miranda v. State of Arizona[12] has substantially changed the law with respect to interrogations conducted by the police. Miranda holds that an individual in custody may not be questioned by the police until he is warned of a right to remain silent, a right to an attorney, a right to an appointed attorney if he has no funds, and a right to have counsel present before any questioning begins. In terms of the prior law, Miranda establishes an irrebutable presumption that the confessions of an unwarned accused are involuntary. However, it may be a mistake to read Miranda in terms of the prior law. Miranda may signal a change in the basic justification for the confession rule. After Miranda, is danger of unreliability still the Court's primary concern? Are the warnings required by Miranda devices to ensure that confessions are reliable, or are they devices to minimize the pressure that police can place on suspects, and thus to minimize the likelihood that suspects will unwillingly or unwittingly provide evidence leading to their own convictions? The former concern responds more to due process values; the latter to fifth amendment values.

Miranda is among the most heavily criticized of the Warren Court decisions. It has already been substantially undercut by the case of Harris v. New York,[13] which held that statements taken in violation of Miranda could be used for impeachment purposes.

10. 297 U.S. 278 (1936).
11. § 150, at 323–324.
12. 384 U.S. 436 (1966).
13. 401 U.S. 222 (1971). But the Court has held that a suspect's silence after receiv-

ing Miranda warnings cannot be used as impeachment evidence. See United States v. Hale, 422 U.S. 171 (1975) (supervisory power) and Doyle v. Ohio, 426 U.S. 610 (1976) (constitutional rule).

I. PROCEDURAL PROTECTIONS

The substantive values promoted by constitutional rules concerning self-incrimination and confessions have, over the years, been thought to require special procedural protection.   In Jackson v. Denno [14] the Supreme Court struck down as contrary to due process a state procedure requiring the trial judge to submit the factual issue of whether a confession was voluntary to the jury.   The Court felt that jurors could not ignore matters confessed to, even if they thought the confession involuntary.   *Jackson* requires the judge to resolve factual disputes and to make a preliminary determination on voluntariness. If the judge finds the confession involuntary it must be excluded.   But, what should occur if the judge finds the confession voluntary?   Should it be presented to the jury as a voluntary confession, or is it desirable to submit the issue of voluntariness to the jury with an instruction that the jury should not consider the confession unless it finds it voluntary?   Some states use one procedure, and some the other.   Where the judge makes the sole finding on voluntariness, the jury may still discount or dismiss the confession if it believes that the confession, because it was involuntary, is unreliable.   A confession may not be admitted by a judge unless the prosecution can prove voluntariness by a preponderance of the evidence. [15]   In some states the burden on the prosecution is higher than this constitutional minimum.

The Supreme Court has not yet been faced with the issue of how a judge should proceed when the voluntariness of a confession is at issue in a case tried without a jury.   The better procedure, in our opinion, is to require the judge to make a finding on the issue of voluntariness in a separate hearing rather than to allow the judge to merge a finding on voluntariness with a decision on the merits.   The best procedure is a two judge procedure in which the issue of voluntariness is tried before a judge other than the judge assigned to hear the case on the merits. When one judge determines both voluntariness and guilt, the position of the judge is similar to that of the jury in *Jackson*. Therefore, absent a two judge procedure, counsel has a strong incentive to avoid a bench trial when the voluntariness of a confession is in issue.

In no jurisdiction may a person be convicted solely on the basis of a confession. Corroboration is always required.   In most jurisdictions the requirement is the minimal one of proving the *corpus delicti.* Where this is the case the corroboration requirement means that the prosecution must have some evidence, apart from the confession, that a crime has been committed.   Normally there is no requirement that the defendant's guilt be proved by evidence other than the confession.   The federal courts require corroboration showing the confession to be reliable. McCormick sees no practical distinction between the federal test and the test used in most states. [16]

The privilege against self-incrimination exists only where there is the possibility of criminal prosecution.   A grant of immunity which removes the threat of criminal prosecution abrogates the privilege.   The law recognizes two kinds of immunity: transactional immunity and use immunity. Where transactional immunity is granted, the witness cannot be prosecuted for the transaction about which he testifies.   Use immunity provides less protection.   The witness may be prosecuted for the transaction about which he testifies, but the

---

14.   378 U.S. 368 (1964).

15.   Lego v. Twomey, 404 U.S. 477 (1972). *Lego* is criticized in Saltzburg, Standards of Proof and Preliminary Questions of Fact, 27

Stan.L.Rev. 271 (1975).   A "beyond a reasonable doubt" burden of persuasion is proposed.

16.   McCormick § 158, at 349.

prosecution may neither introduce statements made by the witness under the grant of immunity nor other evidence which is the fruit of the witness' testimony. For many years it was thought that under the Supreme Court's decision in Counselman v. Hitchcock [17] only transactional immunity could vitiate a claim of privilege under the fifth amendment. But in Murphy v. Waterfront Commission [18] the Court held that when a state gave a witness immunity from prosecution at the state level, the constitution only required use immunity at the federal level. After *Murphy* some argued that use immunity was sufficient only in dual sovereignty situations, but in Kastigar v. United States [19] the Supreme Court made it clear that use immunity is always sufficient to supplant the privilege.

In most jurisdictions it has been held that neither the prosecuting attorney nor the courts have inherent authority to grant immunity; a statute is necessary. Congress has authorized use immunity for federal witnesses.[20] Yet, it is not clear that Congress can prevent prosecutors from granting transactional immunity. Where a witness prefers the sanctions associated with contempt to the possibility that his testimony will in some undiscoverable way be used against him, the prosecution may wish to give the witness the protection from prosecution which only transactional immunity can provide. If the witness relies on the prosecutor's promise of transactional immunity, it would seem that the witness would be forever protected, even though the prosecutor's action was not authorized by statute. The witness is protected as long as the prosecution keeps its bargain; should the prosecution attempt to breach its agreement, it is likely that the courts would hold the attempt impermissible, at least if the defendant did not know the law of immunity and the limits of prosecutorial power.[21]

The last of the procedural protections we shall discuss is the rule preventing comment when the fifth amendment is invoked. In Griffin v. State of California,[22] the Supreme Court held that the prosecution could not comment on the failure of an accused to take the witness stand. While there is general agreement with the Court's conclusion that prosecutorial comment increases the cost of the decision not to testify, many believe that this increase in "cost" is a fair price to charge for the right to remain silent and that comment does not contravene the fifth amendment. Judge Friendly argues that *Griffin* "gave inadequate weight to the language of the amendment that testimony must be 'compelled'; presenting an unpleasant consequence is not compulsion unless the unpleasantness is so great as in effect to deprive of choice." [23] Even if Friendly's reading of minimum fifth amendment requirements were correct, one might wonder why, as a policy matter, comment should be allowed when the fifth amendment is invoked. It seems somewhat incongruous to penalize silent defendants in this fashion when the general rule with respect to non-constitutional privileges is that opposing counsel may not call the jury's attention to their exercise. In practice, the no comment rule as it applies to a defendant's failure to take the stand is unlikely to matter much, for the jury can see that the defendant has not testified and is likely to wonder why. However, the no comment rule may be very important when the privilege has been claimed before grand

17.   142 U.S. 547 (1892).
18.   378 U.S. 52 (1964).
19.   406 U.S. 441 (1972).
20.   18 U.S.C. § 6002.
21.   Remember that courts do "immunize" statements obtained in violation of the fifth amendment.

22.   380 U.S. 609 (1965).
23.   The Fifth Amendment Tomorrow: The Case for Constitutional Change, 37 U.Cin.L.Rev. 671, 700 (1968).

juries, at preliminary hearings or to forestall police interrogation, although it is no
longer clear when comment on prior exercises of the privilege is permitted.[24]

J. SOME FIFTH AMENDMENT PROBLEMS

Problem VIII–69. Lee Goodwin is one of three men accused of a bank
robbery. He denies participating and is tried separately from his alleged
partners. While the alleged partners' appeals are pending, Goodwin's case
is called for trial. The two convicted codefendants indicate to the prosecutor prior to the trial that, if called, they will plead the fifth amendment.
They are called over Goodwin's objection and refuse to answer any questions, citing the fifth amendment. Goodwin is convicted. On appeal he argues that it was error to call the alleged partners since their invocation of
the fifth amendment may have led the jury to draw adverse inferences against
him. **Should Goodwin prevail on appeal? To answer this question must
you know whether the fifth amendment may be invoked after conviction
but pending appeal? What are the inferences that Goodwin fears will be
drawn against him? Is there really a substantial probability that Goodwin was prejudiced by the prosecutor's action? Are there any other constitutional arguments you would raise on Goodwin's behalf? Suppose
Goodwin wants to call the men and have them invoke their privilege not
to answer and the prosecutor objects. Should the result be different?**

Problem VIII–70. On the same facts as the preceding problem, except
that Goodwin urges that due process requires postponement of his trial or a
grant of use immunity to the alleged partners, so that he can examine them
in order to prove his innocence. **Should his constitutional claim prevail?**

Problem VIII–71. Frank Butts seeks to have his father committed to
a mental institution on the ground that he is a danger to the community.
Appearing before a magistrate in a commitment hearing, the father refuses
to answer questions, invoking the privilege against self-incrimination. **May
he be ordered to answer? Does this depend on the questions asked? What**

---

24. Griffin deals only with comments on
the failure of an accused to take the stand.
In Grunewald v. United States, 353 U.S. 391
(1957), the Court held that the prosecution
could not refer to the defendant's silence before a grand jury to impeach his testimony
when he took the stand. In United States
v. Hale, 422 U.S. 171 (1975), the Court, focusing on the particular circumstances of the
case, exercised its supervisory powers to hold
that the defendant's trial testimony could not
be impeached by reference to his silence under police interrogation. In Doyle v. Ohio,
426 U.S. 610 (1976), the Court held that the
Hale result was constitutionally required.
Silence after Miranda warnings was characterized as "insolubly ambiguous."

In Jenkins v. Anderson, 447 U.S. 231 (1980),
the Court held that a defendant who testified
could be impeached with questions about his
pre-arrest silence, since taking the stand
amounted to a waiver. This opens the door
to a similar analysis for refusals to testify before grand juries and in preliminary hearings. *Jenkins* is criticized in Saltzburg,
Foreword: The Flow and Ebb of Constitutional Criminal Procedure in the Warren and
Burger Courts, 69 Geo.L.Rev. 151, 203–205
(1980).

In Fletcher v. Weir, 102 S.Ct. 1309 (1982),
the Court held that a defendant who testified
could be impeached with his silence after arrest but before *Miranda* warnings had been
given.

is the appropriate penalty if he refuses to comply with a court order to testify?

Problem VIII-72.   You are the prosecutor in the affair known as "Watergate."   Many of the people whom you hope to prosecute are called before a Senate Select Committee investigating the same affair.   Pursuant to the applicable federal statute, the potential defendants are given use immunity for their testimony before the committee.   Fearing that your case may appear tainted by the evidence aired before the committee, you desire to increase your chances of successfully prosecuting those you expect to indict. **What actions might you take?**

Problem VIII-73.   Eustice Tilly, a well-known dandy, is charged with jewel theft.   The judge is concerned about his competency to stand trial and orders him to undergo a psychiatric examination.   Tilly refuses on the ground that any such examination would violate his privilege against self-incrimination. **Should his refusal be respected?   If Tilly had pleaded not guilty by reason of insanity, and the judge had ordered a hearing into his competency and into his mental status at the time of the alleged theft, would his fifth amendment claim be stronger or weaker than where no insanity plea was entered?**

Problem VIII-74.   In denaturalization proceedings brought against Vera Hugo, the government calls Hugo to ask her about her involvement in the Communist Party.   She refuses to answer the government's questions on the ground that her testimony might tend to incriminate her.   Subsequently, she takes the stand on her own behalf and testifies that she has never taught or advocated the overthrow of the government and that she has always believed in the Constitution of the United States.   On cross-examination, the government again attempts to inquire into her association with the Communist Party, and again she invokes the fifth amendment.   The government argues that Hugo has waived the privilege by her voluntary testimony.   **Has she?**

Problem VIII-75.   The daughter of a wealthy family is kidnapped by a radical political group on July 1, 1980.   A year later, she participates in a bank robbery and subsequently is arrested and charged with the crime.   Her defense is that she acted under duress imposed by the kidnappers.   The government's theory is that she acted voluntarily.   She takes the stand in her own defense and testifies that during the year before the robbery she had been threatened and indoctrinated, and she states that she feared for her safety if she did not cooperate.   On cross-examination the government asks her about her involvement in other illegal acts with the group during the year.   Her lawyer says that she would gladly answer if the government will give use immunity with respect to the answers.   The government refuses and asks the trial judge to order the defendant to answer the questions.   He so orders, but the defendant refuses to answer.   Forty-one questions are asked about other criminal acts and the privilege against self-incrimination is invoked as to each one, all in the presence of the jury.   The defendant is convicted and appeals.   **Should an appellate court find a violation of the defendant's rights?**

Problem VIII–76. Ralph Walenda brings a civil rights suit against his employer, Atlantic Edison Co., claiming that he was not promoted because a supervisor was biased against him on religious grounds. Walenda testifies on his own behalf concerning conversations that he had with the supervisor. On cross-examination, he is asked whether he is placing bets illegally with a bookie on his own behalf. He also is asked whether he is placing bets illegally with a bookie on behalf of other workers. To both questions Walenda invokes the privilege against self-incrimination. **Should a court uphold the privilege claim?**

Problem VIII–77. Stanley Surry and Richard Douglas put on one of the greatest bar brawls ever witnessed in Seattle before the police broke it up. Both men were arrested but the prosecutor is undecided about bringing charges. His plan is not to file immediately but to wait and see whether either or both get involved in any more trouble. He regards this approach as a kind of unofficial probation. Meanwhile Surry sues Douglas for battery, claiming that Douglas attacked him first and that he responded in self defense. Douglas is called to testify by Surry and invokes the privilege against self-incrimination. He asks that the jury be instructed that it cannot draw an adverse inference from his assertion of the privilege. Surry responds by arguing that the privilege furnishes no protection against civil liability. **How should the court rule?**

SECTION IX.   EXCLUSIONARY RULES

McCormick believes that the rule excluding evidence seized in violation of the fourth amendment and other judicially developed rules of exclusion "may be classified as privileges rather than as rules of incompetency, as they are designed to protect interests deemed of great social importance rather than to guard against evidence which is unreliable or calculated to prejudice or mislead the trier of fact."[25] However, the exclusionary rules are different from the privileges we have discussed. The exclusionary rules prevent the government from introducing evidence which has been acquired in some disfavored fashion. The privileges prevent the acquisition of evidence in the first place. However unimportant this difference, it is sufficient to lead us to leave the topic of search and seizure and the other rules of exclusion extrapolated from the Constitution by the Supreme Court for other courses.[26]

SECTION X.   THE NEWS REPORTER'S PRIVILEGE

Legislatures are constantly wooed by professions which seek to have privileges attached to their business relationships. Usually the professions may honestly claim that the relationships in which they are involved properly carry an expectation of confidentiality. However, many unprivileged relationships carry such an expectation. Privileges are reserved for situations in which society feels the potential

25.   McCormick § 164, at 365.

26.   See, e.g., United States v. Wade, 388 U.S. 218 (1967) (lineups, right to counsel); Massiah v. United States, 377 U.S. 201 (1964) (post-indictment interrogation; right to counsel); Burgett v. State of Texas, 389 U.S. 109 (1967) (void prior convictions for impeachment).

disclosure of information given in confidence would so threaten a valued relationship or be such a gross invasion of personal privacy as to outweigh a clear judicial need for accurate information. Thus, a privilege which is granted a profession represents, among other things, a legislative judgment about the social utility of the profession in question. Given this, it is not surprising that the evidentiary privilege is something of a status symbol among professions. Pressure for new privileges may reflect professional pride as much as it reflects a true need for privacy and confidentiality.

Perhaps the most interesting of the new privileges is the news reporter's privilege, which is found in some form in about half of the states. The privilege which news reporters seek, and to some extent have achieved, is designed to protect those sources which provide reporters with confidential information. Usually this protection requires only that the identity of the source remain secret. The information provided is printed for all to see. Sometimes, however, information must be kept confidential to protect the identity of a source, and on other occasions valuable background information will only be provided on the understanding that it will not be revealed.

Professor Vince Blasi, who surveyed about one thousand journalists by mail and conducted in depth interviews with forty-seven others, reports the following findings:

(1) [G]ood reporters use confidential source relationships mainly for the assessment and verification opportunities that such relationships afford rather than for the purpose of gaining access to highly sensitive information of a newsworthy character; (2) the adverse impact of the subpoena threat has been primarily in "poisoning the atmosphere" so as to make insightful, interpretive reporting more difficult rather than in causing sources to "dry up" completely; (3) understandings of confidentiality in reporter-source relationships are frequently unstated and imprecise; (4) press subpoenas damage source relationships primarily by compromising the reporter's independent or compatriot status in the eyes of sources rather than by forcing the revelation of sensitive information; (5) only one segment of the journalism profession, characterized by certain reporting traits (emphasis on interpretation and verification) more than type of beat, has been adversely affected by the subpoena threat; (6) reporters feel very strongly that any resolution of their conflicting ethical obligations to sources and to society should be a matter for personal rather than judicial determination, and in consonance with this belief these reporters evince a high level of asserted willingness to testify voluntarily and also a very high level of asserted willingness to go to jail if necessary to honor what they perceive to be their obligation of confidentiality; (7) newsmen prefer a flexible ad hoc qualified privilege to an inflexible per se qualified privilege; (8) newsmen regard protection for the *identity* of anonymous sources as more important than protection for the *contents* of confidential information given by known sources; (9) newsmen object most of all to the frequency with which press subpoenas have been issued in what these reporters regard as unnecessary circumstances when they have no important information to contribute * * *.[27]

The news reporter's privilege is unusual in two respects. First, because the identity of the source will usually be crucial, the right to assert the privilege must rest

27. Blasi, The Newsman's Privilege: An Empirical Study, 70 Mich.L.Rev. 229, 284 (1971).

in the reporter rather than the source, although it can be waived by a source willing to reveal himself. Second, reporters have claimed that this privilege exists as a matter of constitutional law. They have argued that the first amendment's guarantee of freedom of the press provides reporters with at least a qualified privilege to refuse to reveal the identity of their sources and other information gained under promises of confidentiality. In 1972 the Supreme Court, by a 5–4 vote, rejected these claims. The Court's opinion is particularly helpful in understanding the conflict of values because it provides a detailed description of some of the circumstances in which reporters have felt that a privilege was necessary.

A.   THE COURT'S OPINION

BRANZBURG v. HAYES

Supreme Court of the United States, 1972.
408 U.S. 665, 92 S.Ct. 2646, 33 L.Ed.2d 626.

Mr. Justice WHITE delivered the opinion of the Court.

*   *   *

On November 15, 1969, the Courier-Journal carried a story under petitioner's by-line describing in detail his observations of two young residents of Jefferson County synthesizing hashish from marihuana, an activity which, they asserted, earned them about $5,000 in three weeks. The article included a photograph of a pair of hands working above a laboratory table on which was a substance identified by the caption as hashish. The article stated that petitioner had promised not to reveal the identity of the two hashish makers. Petitioner was shortly subpoenaed by the Jefferson County grand jury; he appeared, but refused to identify the individuals he had seen possessing marihuana or the persons he had seen making hashish from marihuana. A state trial court judge ordered petitioner to answer these questions * * *.

The second case involving petitioner Branzburg arose out of his later story published on January 10, 1971, which described in detail the use of drugs in Frankfort, Kentucky. The article reported that in order to provide a comprehensive survey of the "drug scene" in Frankfort, petitioner had "spent two weeks interviewing several dozen drug users in the capital city" and had seen some of them smoking marihuana. A number of conversations with and observations of several unnamed drug users were recounted. Subpoenaed to appear before a Franklin County grand jury "to testify in the matter of violation of statutes concerning use and sale of drugs," petitioner Branzburg moved to quash the summons; the motion was denied, although an order was issued protecting Branzburg from revealing "confidential associations, sources or information" but requiring that he "answer any questions which concern or pertain to any criminal act, the commission of which was actually observed by [him]." Prior to the time he was slated to appear before the grand jury, petitioner sought mandamus and prohibition from the Kentucky Court of Appeals, arguing that if he were forced to go before the grand jury or to answer questions regarding the identity of informants or disclose information given to him in confidence, his effectiveness as a reporter would be greatly damaged. The Court of Appeals once again denied the requested writs.

* * *

In re Pappas, originated when petitioner Pappas, a television newsman-photographer working out of the Providence, Rhode Island, office of a New Bedford, Massachusetts, television station, was called to New Bedford on July 30, 1970, to report on civil disorders there which involved fires and other turmoil. He intended to cover a Black Panther news conference at that group's headquarters in a boarded-up store. Petitioner found the streets around the store barricaded, but he ultimately gained entrance to the area and recorded and photographed a prepared statement read by one of the Black Panther leaders at about 3 p. m. He then asked for and received permission to re-enter the area. Returning at about 9 o'clock, he was allowed to enter and remain inside Panther headquarters. As a condition of entry, Pappas agreed not to disclose anything he saw or heard inside the store except an anticipated police raid, which Pappas, "on his own," was free to photograph and report as he wished. Pappas stayed inside the headquarters for about three hours, but there was no police raid, and petitioner wrote no story and did not otherwise reveal what had occurred in the store while he was there. Two months later, petitioner was summoned before the Bristol County Grand Jury and appeared, answered questions as to his name, address, employment, and what he had seen and heard outside Panther headquarters, but refused to answer any questions about what had taken place inside headquarters while he was there, claiming that the First Amendment afforded him a privilege to protect confidential informants and their information. A second summons was then served upon him, again directing him to appear before the grand jury and "to give such evidence as he knows relating to any matters which may be inquired of on behalf of the Commonwealth before * * * the Grand Jury." His motion to quash on First Amendment and other grounds was denied by the trial judge who, noting the absence of a statutory newsman's privilege in Massachusetts, ruled that petitioner had no constitutional privilege to refuse to divulge to the grand jury what he had seen and heard, including the identity of persons he had observed. The case was reported for decision to the Supreme Judicial Court of Massachusetts. The record there did not include a transcript of the hearing on the motion to quash, nor did it reveal the specific questions petitioner had refused to answer, the expected nature of his testimony, the nature of the grand jury investigation, or the likelihood of the grand jury's securing the information it sought from petitioner by other means. The Supreme Judicial Court, however, took "judicial notice that in July, 1970, there were serious civil disorders in New Bedford, which involved street barricades, exclusion of the public from certain streets, fires, and similar turmoil. We were told at the arguments that there was gunfire in certain streets. We assume that the grand jury investigation was an appropriate effort to discover and indict those responsible for criminal acts." 358 Mass. 604, 607, 266 N.E.2d 297, 299 (1971). The court then reaffirmed prior Massachusetts holdings that testimonial privileges were "exceptional" and "limited," stating that "[t]he principle that the public 'has a right to every man's evidence' " had usually been preferred, in the Commonwealth, to countervailing interests.   *   *   *

United States v. Caldwell, arose from subpoenas issued by a federal grand jury in the Northern District of California to respondent Earl Caldwell, a reporter for the New York Times assigned to cover the Black Panther Party and other black militant groups.   A subpoena *duces tecum* was served on respondent on February 2, 1970, ordering him to appear before the grand jury to testify and to bring with him notes and tape recordings of interviews given him for publication by officers and spokesmen of the Black Panther Party concerning the aims, purposes, and activities of that organization. Respondent objected to the scope of this subpoena, and an agreement between his counsel and the Government attorneys resulted in a continuance. A second subpoena, served on March 16, omitted the documentary requirement and simply ordered Caldwell "to appear   *   *   *   to testify before the Grand Jury."   Respondent and his employer, the New York Times, moved to quash on the ground that the unlimited breadth of the subpoenas and the fact that Caldwell would have to appear in secret before the grand jury would destroy his working relationship with the Black Panther Party and "suppress vital First Amendment freedoms   *   *   *   by driving a wedge of distrust and silence between the news media and the militants."   Respondent argued that "so drastic an incursion upon First Amendment freedoms" should not be permitted "in the absence of a compelling governmental interest—not shown here—in requiring Mr. Caldwell's appearance before the grand jury."   The motion was supported by *amicus curiae* memoranda from other publishing concerns and by affidavits from newsmen asserting the unfavorable impact on news sources of requiring reporters to appear before grand juries.   The Government filed three memoranda in opposition to the motion to quash, each supported by affidavits.   These documents stated that the grand jury was investigating, among other things, possible violations of a number of criminal statutes, including 18 U.S.C. § 871 (threats against the President), 18 U.S.C. § 1751 (assassination, attempts to assassinate, conspiracy to assassinate the President), 18 U.S.C. § 231 (civil disorders), 18 U.S.C. § 2101 (interstate travel to incite a riot), and 18 U.S.C. § 1341 (mail frauds and swindles).   It was recited that on November 15, 1969, an officer of the Black Panther Party made a publicly televised speech in which he had declared that "[w]e will kill Richard Nixon" and that this threat had been repeated in three subsequent issues of the Party newspaper.   Also referred to were various writings by Caldwell about the Black Panther Party, including an article published in the New York Times on December 14, 1969, stating that "[i]n their role as the vanguard in a revolutionary struggle the Panthers have picked up guns," and quoting the Chief of Staff of the Party as declaring that: "We advocate the very direct overthrow of the Government by way of force and violence. By picking up guns and moving against it because we recognize it as being oppressive and in recognizing that we know that the only solution to it is armed struggle [*sic*]."   The Government also stated that the Chief of Staff of the Party had been indicted by the grand jury on December 3, 1969, for uttering threats against the life of the President in violation of 18 U.S.C. § 871 and that various efforts had been made to secure evidence of crimes under investigation through the immunization of persons allegedly associated with the Black Panther Party.

On April 6, the District Court denied the motion to quash, *Application of Caldwell*, 311 F.Supp. 358 (NDCal.1970), on the ground that *"every person within the jurisdiction of the government"* is bound to testify upon being properly summoned. Id. at 360 (emphasis in original). Nevertheless, the court accepted respondent's First Amendment arguments to the extent of issuing a protective order providing that although respondent had to divulge whatever information had been given to him for publication, he "shall not be required to reveal confidential associations, sources or information received, developed or maintained by him as a professional journalist in the course of his efforts to gather news for dissemination to the public through the press or other news media." The court held that the First Amendment afforded respondent a privilege to refuse disclosure of such confidential information until there has been "a showing by the Government of a compelling and over-riding national interest in requiring Mr. Caldwell's testimony which cannot be served by any alternative means."

Subsequently, the term of the grand jury expired, a new grand jury was convened, and a new subpoena *ad testificandum* was issued and served on May 22, 1970. A new motion to quash by respondent and memorandum in opposition by the Government were filed, and, by stipulation of the parties, the motion was submitted on the prior record. The court denied the motion to quash, repeating the protective provisions in its prior order but this time directing Caldwell to appear before the grand jury pursuant to the May 22 subpoena. Respondent refused to appear before the grand jury, and the court issued an order to show cause why he should not be held in contempt. Upon his further refusal to go before the grand jury, respondent was ordered committed for contempt until such time as he complied with the court's order or until the expiration of the term of the grand jury.

Respondent Caldwell appealed the contempt order, and the Court of Appeals reversed. *Caldwell v. United States*, 434 F.2d 1081 (CA9 1970). Viewing the issue before it as whether Caldwell was required to appear before the grand jury at all, rather than the scope of permissible interrogation, the court first determined that the First Amendment provided a qualified testimonial privilege to newsmen; in its view, requiring a reporter like Caldwell to testify would deter his informants from communicating with him in the future and would cause him to censor his writings in an effort to avoid being subpoenaed. Absent compelling reasons for requiring his testimony, he was held privileged to withhold it. The court also held, for similar First Amendment reasons, that, absent some special showing of necessity by the Government, attendance by Caldwell at a secret meeting of the grand jury was something he was privileged to refuse because of the potential impact of such an appearance on the flow of news to the public. * * *

II

Petitioners Branzburg and Pappas and respondent Caldwell press First Amendment claims that may be simply put: that to gather news it is often necessary to agree either not to identify the source of information published or to publish only part of the facts revealed, or both; that if the reporter is nevertheless forced to reveal these confidences to a grand jury, the source so identified and other confidential sources of other reporters will be measurably deterred from furnishing publishable information, all to the detriment of the free flow of information protected by the First Amendment. Although the newsmen in these cases do not claim an absolute privilege against official interrogation in all circumstances, they assert that the reporter should not be forced either to appear or to testify before a grand jury or at trial until and unless sufficient grounds are shown for believing that the reporter possesses information relevant to a crime the grand jury is investigating, that the information the reporter has is unavailable from other sources, and that the need for the information is sufficiently compelling to override the claimed invasion of First Amendment interests occasioned by the disclosure. Principally relied upon are prior cases emphasizing the importance of the First Amendment guarantees to individual development and to our system of representative government, decisions requiring that official action with adverse impact on First Amendment rights be justified by a public interest that is "compelling" or "paramount," and those precedents establishing the principle that justifiable governmental goals may not be achieved by unduly broad means having an unnecessary impact on protected rights of speech, press, or association. The heart of the claim is that the burden on news gathering resulting from compelling reporters to disclose confidential information outweighs any public interest in obtaining the information.

* * *

Despite the fact that news gathering may be hampered, the press is regularly excluded from grand jury proceedings, our own conferences, the meetings of other official bodies gathered in executive session, and the meetings of private organizations. Newsmen have no constitutional right of access to the scenes of crime or disaster when the general public is excluded, and they may be prohibited from attending or publishing information about trials if such restrictions are necessary to assure a defendant a fair trial before an impartial tribunal. * * *

It is thus not surprising that the great weight of authority is that newsmen are not exempt from the normal duty of appearing before a grand jury and answering questions relevant to a criminal investigation. At common law, courts consistently refused to recognize the existence of any privilege authorizing a newsman to refuse to reveal confidential information to a grand jury. * * *

* * *

A number of States have provided newsmen a statutory privilege of varying breadth, but the majority have not done so, and none has been provided by federal statute. Until now the only testimonial privilege for unofficial witnesses that is rooted in the Federal Constitution is the Fifth Amendment privilege against compelled self-incrimination. We are asked to create another by interpreting the First Amendment to grant newsmen a testimonial privilege that other citizens do not enjoy. This we decline to do. Fair and effective law enforcement aimed at providing security for the person and property of the individual is a fundamental function of government, and the grand jury plays an important, constitutionally mandated role in this process. On the records now before us, we perceive no basis for holding that the public interest in law enforcement and in ensuring effective grand jury proceedings is insufficient to override the consequential, but uncertain, burden on news gathering that is said to result from insisting that reporters, like other citizens, respond to relevant questions put to them in the course of a valid grand jury investigation or criminal trial.

This conclusion itself involves no restraint on what newspapers may publish or on the type or quality of information reporters may seek to acquire, nor does it threaten the vast bulk of confidential relationships between reporters and their sources. Grand juries address themselves to the issues of whether crimes have been committed and who committed them. Only where news sources themselves are implicated in crime or possess information relevant to the grand jury's task need they or the reporter be concerned about grand jury subpoenas. Nothing before us indicates that a large number or percentage of *all* confidential news sources falls into either category and would in any way be deterred by our holding that the Constitution does not, as it never has, exempt the newsman from performing the citizen's normal duty of appearing and furnishing information relevant to the grand jury's task.

The preference for anonymity of those confidential informants involved in actual criminal conduct is presumably a product of their desire to escape criminal prosecution, and this preference, while understandable, is hardly deserving of constitutional protection. It would be frivolous to assert—and no one does in these cases—that the First Amendment, in the interest of securing news or otherwise, confers a license on either the reporter or his news sources to violate valid criminal laws. Although stealing documents or private wiretapping could provide newsworthy information, neither reporter nor source is immune from conviction for such conduct, whatever the impact on the flow of news. Neither is immune, on First Amendment grounds, from testifying against the other, before the grand jury or at a criminal trial. The Amendment does not reach so far as to override the interest of the public in ensuring that neither reporter nor source is invading the rights of other citizens through reprehensible conduct forbidden to all other persons.   *   *   *

Thus, we cannot seriously entertain the notion that the First Amendment protects a newsman's agreement to conceal the criminal conduct of his source, or evidence thereof, on the theory that it is better to write about crime than to do something about it. Insofar as any reporter in these cases undertook not to reveal or testify about the crime he witnessed, his claim of privilege under the First Amendment presents no substantial question. The crimes of news sources are no less reprehensible and threatening to the public interest when witnessed by a reporter than when they are not.

There remain those situations where a source is not engaged in criminal conduct but has information suggesting illegal conduct by others. Newsmen frequently receive information from such sources pursuant to a tacit or express agreement to withhold the source's name and suppress any information that the source wishes not published. Such informants presumably desire anonymity in order to avoid being entangled as a witness in a criminal trial or grand jury investigation. They may fear that disclosure will threaten their job security or personal safety or that it will simply result in dishonor or embarrassment.

   The argument that the flow of news will be diminished by compelling reporters to aid the grand jury in a criminal investigation is not irrational, nor are the records before us silent on the matter.   But we remain unclear how often and to what extent informers are actually deterred from furnishing information when newsmen are forced to testify before a grand jury.   The available data indicate that some newsmen rely a great deal on confidential sources and that some informants are particularly sensitive to the threat of exposure and may be silenced if it is held by this Court that, ordinarily, newsmen must testify pursuant to subpoenas, but the evidence fails to demonstrate that there would be a significant constriction of the flow of news to the public if this Court reaffirms the prior common-law and constitutional rule regarding the testimonial obligations of newsmen.   Estimates of the inhibiting effect of such subpoenas on the willingness of informants to make disclosures to newsmen are widely divergent and to a great extent speculative.[f]   It would be difficult to canvass the views of the informants themselves; surveys of reporters on this topic are chiefly opinions of predicted informant behavior and must be viewed in the light of the professional self-interest of the interviewees.[g]   Reliance by the press on confidential informants does not mean that all such sources will in fact dry up because of the later possible appearance of the newsman before a grand jury.   The reporter may never be called and if he objects to testifying, the prosecution may not insist.   Also, the relationship of many informants to the press is a symbiotic one which is unlikely to be greatly inhibited by the threat of subpoena: quite often, such informants are members of a minority political or cultural group that relies heavily on the media to propagate its views, publicize its aims, and magnify its exposure to the public.   Moreover, grand juries characteristically conduct secret proceedings, and law enforcement officers are themselves experienced in dealing with informers, and have their own methods for protecting them without interference with the effective administration of justice.   There is little before us indicating that informants whose interest in avoiding exposure is that it may threaten job security, personal safety, or peace of mind, would in fact be in a worse position, or would think they would be, if they risked placing their trust in public

f. Cf., e.g., the results of a study conducted by Guest & Stanzler, which appears as an appendix to their article, [The Constitutional Argument for Newsmen Concealing their Sources, 64 Nw.U.L.Rev. 18 (1969)]. A number of editors of daily newspapers of varying circulation were asked the question, "Excluding one- or two-sentence gossip items, on the average how many stories based on information received in confidence are published in your paper each year? Very rough estimate." Answers varied significantly, e.g., "Virtually innumerable," Tucson Daily Citizen (41,969 daily circ.), "Too many to remember." Los Angeles Herald-Examiner (718,221 daily circ.), "Occasionally," Denver Post (252,084 daily circ.), "Rarely," Cleveland Plain Dealer (370,499 daily circ.), "Very rare, some politics," Oregon Journal (146,403 daily circ.).

This study did not purport to measure the extent of deterrence of informants caused by subpoenas to the press.

g. In his Press Subpoenas: An Empirical and Legal Analysis, Study Report of the Reporters' Committee on Freedom of the Press 6–12, Prof. Vince Blasi discusses these methodological problems. Prof. Blasi's survey found that slightly more than half of the 975 reporters questioned said that they relied on regular confidential sources for at least 10% of their stories. Id. at 21. Of this group of reporters, only 8% were able to say with some certainty that their professional functioning had been adversely affected by the threat of subpoena; another 11% were not certain whether or not they had been adversely affected. Id. at 53.

officials as well as reporters. We doubt if the informer who prefers anonymity but is sincerely interested in furnishing evidence of crime will always or very often be deterred by the prospect of dealing with those public authorities characteristically charged with the duty to protect the public interest as well as his.

Accepting the fact, however, that an undetermined number of informants not themselves implicated in crime will nevertheless, for whatever reason, refuse to talk to newsmen if they fear identification by a reporter in an official investigation, we cannot accept the argument that the public interest in possible future news about crime from undisclosed, unverified sources must take precedence over the public interest in pursuing and prosecuting those crimes reported to the press by informants and in thus deterring the commission of such crimes in the future.

We note first that the privilege claimed is that of the reporter, not the informant, and that if the authorities independently identify the informant, neither his own reluctance to testify nor the objection of the newsman would shield him from grand jury inquiry, whatever the impact on the flow of news or on his future usefulness as a secret source of information. * * *

Of course, the press has the right to abide by its agreement not to publish all the information it has, but the right to withhold news is not equivalent to a First Amendment exemption from the ordinary duty of all other citizens to furnish relevant information to a grand jury performing an important public function. * * *

Neither are we now convinced that a virtually impenetrable constitutional shield, beyond legislative or judicial control, should be forged to protect a private system of informers operated by the press to report on criminal conduct, a system that would be unaccountable to the public, would pose a threat to the citizen's justifiable expectations of privacy, and would equally protect well-intentioned informants and those who for pay or otherwise betray their trust to their employer or associates. The public through its elected and appointed law enforcement officers regularly utilizes informers, and in proper circumstances may assert a privilege against disclosing the identity of these informers. But

> "[t]he purpose of the privilege is the furtherance and protection of the public interest in effective law enforcement. The privilege recognizes the obligation of citizens to communicate their knowledge of the commission of crimes to law-enforcement officials and, by preserving their anonymity, encourages them to perform that obligation." Roviaro v. United States, 353 U.S. 53, 59.

Such informers enjoy no constitutional protection. Their testimony is available to the public when desired by grand juries or at criminal trials; their identity cannot be concealed from the defendant when it is critical to his case. Clearly, this system is not impervious to control by the judiciary and the decision whether to unmask an informer or to continue to profit by his anonymity is in public, not private, hands. We think that it should remain there and that public authorities should retain the options of either insisting on the informer's testimony relevant to the prosecution of crime or of seeking the benefit of further information that his exposure might prevent.

We are admonished that refusal to provide a First Amendment reporter's privilege will undermine the freedom of the press to collect and disseminate news. But this is not the lesson history teaches us. As noted previously, the common law recognized no such privilege, and the constitutional argument was not even asserted until 1958. From the beginning of our country the press has operated without constitutional protection for press informants, and the press has flourished. The existing constitutional rules have not been a serious obstacle to either the development or retention of confidential news sources by the press.

It is said that currently press subpoenas have multiplied, that mutual distrust and tension between press and officialdom have increased, that reporting styles have changed, and that there is now more need for confidential sources, particularly where the press seeks news about minority cultural and political groups or dissident organizations suspicious of the law and public officials. These developments, even if true, are treacherous grounds for a far-reaching interpretation of the First Amendment fastening a nationwide rule on courts, grand juries, and prosecuting officials everywhere. The obligation to testify in response to grand jury subpoenas will not threaten these sources not involved with criminal conduct and without information relevant to grand jury investigations, and we cannot hold that the Constitution places the sources in these two categories either above the law or beyond its reach.

The argument for such a constitutional privilege rests heavily on those cases holding that the infringement of protected First Amendment rights must be no broader than necessary to achieve a permissible governmental purpose. We do not deal, however, with a governmental institution that has abused its proper function, as a legislative committee does when it "expose[s] for the sake of exposure." Nothing in the record indicates that these grand juries were "prob[ing] at will and without relation to existing need." * * * The investigative power of the grand jury is necessarily broad if its public responsibility is to be adequately discharged.

The requirements of those cases, which hold that a State's interest must be "compelling" or "paramount" to justify even an indirect burden on First Amendment rights, are also met here. As we have indicated, the investigation of crime by the grand jury implements a fundamental governmental role of securing the safety of the person and property of the citizen, and it appears to us that calling reporters to give testimony in the manner and for the reasons that other citizens are called "bears a reasonable relationship to the achievement of the governmental purpose asserted as its justification." If the test is that the government "convincingly show a substantial relation between the information sought and a subject of overriding and compelling state interest," it is quite apparent (1) that the State has the necessary interest in extirpating the traffic in illegal drugs, in forestalling assassination attempts on the President, and in preventing the community from being disrupted by violent disorders endangering both persons and property; and (2) that, based on the stories Branzburg and Caldwell wrote and Pappas' admitted conduct, the grand jury called these reporters as they would others—because it was likely that they could supply information to help the government determine whether illegal conduct had occurred and, if it had, whether there was sufficient evidence to return an indictment.

Similar considerations dispose of the reporters' claims that preliminary to requiring their grand jury appearance, the State must show that a crime has been committed and that they possess relevant information not available from other sources, for only the grand jury itself can make this determination. The role of the grand jury as an important instrument of effective law enforcement necessarily includes an investigatory function with respect to determining whether a crime has been committed and who committed it. To this end it must call witnesses, in the manner best suited to perform its task. "When the grand jury is performing its investigatory function into a general problem area * * * society's interest is best served by a thorough and extensive investigation." A grand jury investigation "is not fully carried out until every available clue has been run down and all witnesses examined in every proper way to find if a crime has been committed." * * *

The privilege claimed here is conditional, not absolute; given the suggested preliminary showings and compelling need, the reporter would be required to testify. Presumably, such a rule would reduce the instances in which reporters could be required to appear, but predicting in advance when and in what circumstances they could be compelled to do so would be difficult. Such a rule would also have implications for the issuance of compulsory process to reporters at civil and criminal trials and at legislative hearings. If newsmen's confidential sources are as sensitive as they are claimed to be, the prospect of being unmasked whenever a judge determines the situation justifies it is hardly a satisfactory solution to the problem. For them, it would appear that only an absolute privilege would suffice.

We are unwilling to embark the judiciary on a long and difficult journey to such an uncertain destination. The administration of a constitutional newsman's privilege would present practical and conceptual difficulties of a high order. Sooner or later, it would be necessary to define those categories of newsmen who qualified for the privilege, a questionable procedure in light of the traditional doctrine that liberty of the press is the right of the lonely pamphleteer who uses carbon paper or a mimeograph just as much as of the large metropolitan publisher who utilizes the latest photocomposition methods. * * *

In each instance where a reporter is subpoenaed to testify, the courts would also be embroiled in preliminary factual and legal determinations with respect to whether the proper predicate had been laid for the reporter's appearance: Is there probable cause to believe a crime has been committed? Is it likely that the reporter has useful information gained in confidence? Could the grand jury obtain the information elsewhere? Is the official interest sufficient to outweigh the claimed privilege?

Thus, in the end, by considering whether enforcement of a particular law served a "compelling" governmental interest, the courts would be inextricably involved in distinguishing between the value of enforcing different criminal laws. By requiring testimony from a reporter in investigations involving some crimes but not in others, they would be making a value judgment that a legislature had declined to make, since in each case the criminal law involved would represent a considered legislative judgment, not constitutionally suspect, of what conduct is liable to criminal prosecution. The task of judges, like other officials outside the legislative branch, is not to make the law but to uphold it in accordance with their oaths.

At the federal level, Congress has freedom to determine whether a statutory newsman's privilege is necessary and desirable and to fashion standards and rules as narrow or broad as deemed necessary to deal with the evil discerned and, equally important, to refashion those rules as experience from time to time may dictate. There is also merit in leaving state legislatures free, within First Amendment limits, to fashion their own standards in light of the conditions and problems with respect to the relations between law enforcement officials and press in their own areas. It goes without saying, of course, that we are powerless to bar state courts from responding in their own way and construing their own constitutions so as to recognize a newsman's privilege, either qualified or absolute.

In addition, there is much force in the pragmatic view that the press has at its disposal powerful mechanisms of communication and is far from helpless to protect itself from harassment or substantial harm. Furthermore, if what the newsmen urged in these cases is true—that law enforcement cannot hope to gain and may suffer from subpoenaing newsmen before grand juries—prosecutors will be loath to risk so much for so little. Thus, at the federal level the Attorney General has already fashioned a set of rules for federal officials in connection with subpoenaing members of the press to testify before grand juries or at criminal trials.[h] These rules are a major step in the direction the reporters herein desire to move. They may prove wholly sufficient to resolve the bulk of disagreements and controversies between press and federal officials.

Finally, as we have earlier indicated, news gathering is not without its First Amendment protections, and grand jury investigations if instituted or conducted other than in good faith, would pose wholly different issues for resolution under the First Amendment. Official harassment of the press undertaken not for purposes of law enforcement but to disrupt a reporter's relationship with his news sources would have no justification. Grand juries

---

h. The Guidelines for Subpoenas to the News Media were first announced in a speech by the Attorney General on August 10, 1970, and then were expressed in Department of Justice Memo. No. 692 (Sept. 2, 1970), which was sent to all United States Attorneys by the Assistant Attorney General in charge of the Criminal Division. The Guidelines state that: "The Department of Justice recognizes that compulsory process in some circumstances may have a limiting effect on the exercise of First Amendment rights. In determining whether to request issuance of a subpoena to the press, the approach in every case must be to weigh that limiting effect against the public interest to be served in the fair administration of justice" and that: "The Department of Justice does not consider the press 'an investigative arm of the government.' Therefore, all reasonable attempts should be made to obtain information from non-press sources before there is any consideration of subpoenaing the press." The Guidelines provide for negotiations with the press and require the express authorization of the Attorney General for such subpoenas. The principles to be applied in authorizing such subpoenas are stated to be whether there is "sufficient reason to believe that the information sought [from the journalist] is essential to a successful investigation," and whether the Government has unsuccessfully attempted to obtain the information from alternative non-press sources. * * *

are subject to judicial control and subpoenas to motions to quash. We do not expect courts will forget that grand juries must operate within the limits of the First Amendment as well as the Fifth.

* * *

[Mr. Justice POWELL, whose vote was crucial in *Branzburg*, expressed his understanding of the Court's opinion, in which he joined, in the following brief concurring opinion.]

I add this brief statement to emphasize what seems to me to be the limited nature of the Court's holding. The Court does not hold that newsmen, subpoenaed to testify before a grand jury, are without constitutional rights with respect to the gathering of news or in safeguarding their sources. Certainly, we do not hold, as suggested in Mr. Justice STEWART'S dissenting opinion, that state and federal authorities are free to "annex" the news media as "an investigative arm of government." The solicitude repeatedly shown by this Court for First Amendment freedoms should be sufficient assurance against any such effort, even if one seriously believed that the media—properly free and untrammeled in the fullest sense of these terms—were not able to protect themselves.

As indicated in the concluding portion of the opinion, the Court states that no harassment of newsmen will be tolerated. If a newsman believes that the grand jury investigation is not being conducted in good faith he is not without remedy. Indeed, if the newsman is called upon to give information bearing only a remote and tenuous relationship to the subject of the investigation, or if he has some other reason to believe that his testimony implicates confidential source relationships without a legitimate need of law enforcement, he will have access to the court on a motion to quash and an appropriate protective order may be entered. The asserted claim to privilege should be judged on its facts by the striking of a proper balance between freedom of the press and the obligation of all citizens to give relevant testimony with respect to criminal conduct. The balance of these vital constitutional and societal interests on a case-by-case basis accords with the tried and traditional way of adjudicating such questions.

In short, the courts will be available to newsmen under circumstances where legitimate First Amendment interests require protection.

Mr. Justice STEWART, with whom Mr. Justice BRENNAN and Mr. Justice MARSHALL join, dissenting.

* * *

[W]hen a reporter is asked to appear before a grand jury and reveal confidences, I would hold that the government must (1) show that there is probable cause to believe that the newsman has information that is clearly relevant to a specific probable violation of law; (2) demonstrate that the information sought cannot be obtained by alternative means less destructive of First Amendment rights; and (3) demonstrate a compelling and overriding interest in the information.

This is not to say that a grand jury could not issue a subpoena until such a showing were made, and it is not to say that a newsman would be in any way privileged to ignore any subpoena that was issued. Obviously, before the government's burden to make such a showing were triggered, the reporter would have to move to quash the subpoena, asserting the basis on which he considered the particular relationship a confidential one.

The crux of the Court's rejection of any newsman's privilege is its observation that only "where news sources themselves are implicated in crime or possess information *relevant* to the grand jury's task need they or the reporter be concerned about grand jury subpoenas." But this is a most misleading construct. For it is obviously not true that the only persons about whom reporters will be forced to testify will be those "confidential informants involved in actual criminal conduct" and those having "information suggesting illegal conduct by others." As noted above, given the grand jury's extraordinarily broad investigative powers and the weak standards of relevance and materiality that apply during such inquiries, reporters, if they have no testimonial privilege, will be called to give information about informants who have neither committed crimes nor have information about crime. It is to avoid deterrence of such sources and thus to prevent needless injury to First Amendment values that I think the government must be required to show probable cause that the newsman has information that is clearly relevant to a specific probable violation of criminal law.[i]

Similarly, a reporter may have information from a confidential source that is "related" to the commission of crime, but the government may be able to obtain an indictment or otherwise achieve its purposes by subpoenaing persons other than the reporter. It is an obvious but important truism that when government aims have been fully served, there can be no legitimate reason to disrupt a confidential relationship between a reporter and his source. To do so would not aid the administration of justice and would only impair the flow of information to the public. Thus, it is to avoid deterrence of such sources that I think the government must show that there are no alternative means for the grand jury to obtain the information sought.

Both the "probable cause" and "alternative means" requirements would thus serve the vital function of mediating between the public interest in the administration of justice and the constitutional protection of the full flow of information. These requirements would avoid a direct conflict between these

---

i. If this requirement is not met, then the government will basically be allowed to undertake a "fishing expedition" at the expense of the press. Such general, exploratory investigations will be most damaging to confidential news-gathering relationships, since they will create great uncertainty in both reporters and their sources. The Court sanctions such explorations, by refusing to apply a meaningful "probable cause" requirement. As the Court states, a grand jury investigation "may be triggered by tips, rumors, evidence proffered by the prosecutor, or the personal knowledge of the grand jurors." It thereby invites government to try to annex the press as an investigative arm, since any time government wants to probe the relationships between the newsman and his source, it can, on virtually any pretext, convene a grand jury and compel the journalist to testify.

The Court fails to recognize that under the guise of "investigating crime" vindictive prosecutors can, using the broad powers of the grand jury which are, in effect, immune from judicial supervision, explore the newsman's sources at will, with no serious law enforcement purpose. The secrecy of grand jury proceedings affords little consolation to a news source; the prosecutor obviously will, in most cases, have knowledge of testimony given by grand jury witnesses.

competing concerns, and they would generally provide adequate protection for newsmen. No doubt the courts would be required to make some delicate judgments in working out this accommodation. But that, after all, is the function of courts of law. Better such judgments, however difficult, than the simplistic and stultifying absolutism adopted by the Court in denying any force to the First Amendment in these cases.

The error in the Court's absolute rejection of First Amendment interests in these cases seems to me to be most profound. For in the name of advancing the administration of justice, the Court's decision, I think, will only impair the achievement of that goal. People entrusted with law enforcement responsibility, no less than private citizens, need general information relating to controversial social problems. Obviously, press reports have great value to government, even when the newsman cannot be compelled to testify before a grand jury. The sad paradox of the Court's position is that when a grand jury may exercise an unbridled subpoena power, and sources involved in sensitive matters become fearful of disclosing information, the newsman will not only cease to be a useful grand jury witness; he will cease to investigate and publish information about issues of public import. I cannot subscribe to such an anomalous result, for, in my view, the interests protected by the First Amendment are not antagonistic to the administration of justice. Rather, they can, in the long run, only be complementary, and for that reason must be given great "breathing space."

*   *   *

[The separate dissenting opinion of Mr. Justice Douglas is omitted.]

———

Obviously society benefits when stories like those written by Branzburg, Pappas and Caldwell are printed. Is it just as obvious that absent a privilege such stories would not be printed? If a choice must be made between protecting confidences so that the amount of information available to the public will be increased and satisfying a weak governmental interest in acquiring evidence, what is the proper choice? Must this choice be made? Was the government's need for information in *Branzburg* and its companion cases weak? Suppose the government's need were very great. Would a reporter's privilege still be justified?

If you favor the protection of confidences, how do you distinguish the first amendment rights of ordinary citizens from those of news reporters? The first amendment guarantees freedom of speech as well as freedom of the press. If the disclosure of secrets invades the privacy of the reporter-source relationship and causes news to dry up, is it not also true that forcing individuals to reveal personal confidences may inhibit interpersonal communications by inhibiting free speech? Is there something about the role of the press in America which justifies a privilege for reporters and their sources when one is not given to ordinary citizens and those who confide in them?

The Court's opinion in *Branzburg* suggests that the absence of a privilege "involves no restraint on what newspapers may publish or the type or quality of information reporters may seek to acquire." Is this correct? Does the absence of a privilege create indirect restraints on the press every bit as powerful as direct restrictions on publishing, or are any indirect restraints substantially less threatening to the vitality and the freedom of the press? Should any indirect restraints on reporting be tolerated, or does the first amendment only prohibit indirect restraints as serious as direct restrictions on publishing? Is there some middle ground?

How great will the government's loss of information be if a privilege, even an absolute privilege, is extended to news reporters? In the short run one can point to information that would be kept from the government. In the long run will the kind of information the government is now seeking from reporters be available? If you were a reporter, what would *Branzburg* lead you to tell a source willing to furnish information on the condition that his identity be kept secret?

The Court in *Branzburg* states that grand juries have a right to every citizen's evidence. This is a glib phrase, but overbroad, as the Court itself concedes. Grand juries must bow to claims of the attorney-client, spousal, fifth amendment and other recognized privileges. The fact that grand juries have a right, and indeed a need, to receive evidence does not help determine whether other interests are sufficiently strong to override that right and need. The Supreme Court did not decide that other interests did not override the grand jury's need for evidence. It simply decided that the first amendment did not require a privilege which might frustrate grand jury investigations. Do you agree that the privilege sought by Messrs. Branzburg, Pappas and Caldwell was so tangentially related to freedom of the press that it was not mandated by the Constitution?

Assuming that a news reporter's privilege is desirable, do we really want to have new privileges created as a matter of constitutional law? Can you think of difficulties which might arise if a news reporter's privilege were based in the first amendment? Does the history of the fifth amendment provide any examples?

One of the most interesting developments following *Branzburg* is the reading that lower courts have given it. Although Justice White must have thought he was putting an end to constitutionally based newsreporter claims of privilege, he probably could not foresee that Justice Powell's separate opinion would be read by many lower courts as an invitation to protect the press on a case-by-case basis in much the way the dissenters in *Branzburg* might have provided protection.[28]

The most surprising development of all is the holding by some courts that there is a common law newsreporter-source privilege that is recognized under FRE 501.[29] Although the Supreme Court was not asked to address itself to a common law claim (and could not have decided the state cases on this basis anyway), the history related by Justice White makes it doubtful that he would have thought that reporters should get the benefit of a judicially created privilege. Since the purpose of a common law privilege is to protect the flow of information, it is hard to distinguish it from a constitutionally based privilege, especially a conditional one. If there is a difference it is that Congress could act to reject a common law privilege, but could not reject a constitutionally based one without amending the Constitution.

B. A PROPOSED STATUTE

The following statute is the second tentative draft, dated June 1, 1975, of a Uniform Reporter's Privilege Act considered for adoption by the National Conference of

---

28. See, e.g., Silkwood v. Kerr-McGee Corp., 563 F.2d 433 (10th Cir. 1977); Altemose Construction Co. v. Building & Construction Trades Council, 443 F.Supp. 489 (E.D.Pa.1977).

29. See, e.g., United States v. Cuthbertson, 630 F.2d 139 (3d Cir. 1980); Riley v. City of Chester, 612 F.2d 708 (3d Cir. 1979).

Commissioners on Uniform State Laws and eventually rejected. Is it too protective of the reporter's interests? Is it not protective enough? If this proposed statute were introduced in the legislature in your state, would you support it? What changes, if any, would you want to make? As you read this proposed statute ask yourself whether the distinctions made, between trials and other proceedings and between the disclosure of confidential sources and the disclosure of confidential information, are sensible.

PREFATORY NOTE

* * *

Since 1969 the number of subpoenas issued to reporters has greatly increased. Several factors appear to have contributed to the rise. The increased amount of journalistic and scholarly attention being paid to unlawful and dissident activities means that reporters today probably have more information of potential value to prosecutors than was true in the past. In addition, news organizations have been putting more of their resources into investigative reporting and this kind of in-depth probing is more likely to uncover information that is otherwise unavailable to litigants. Also, improvements in technology such as mobile, long-range cameras and cassette tape-recorders have enabled newsmen and scholars to keep much better records of their research, a development which not only facilitates long-range, in-depth reporting but also makes a reporter's files a more promising hunting ground for litigants in search of evidence. Moreover, the mutual distrust between law enforcement officials and newsmen that has been growing as a result of the political and cultural tensions of the last ten years has seriously undermined the informal processes of accommodation that used to resolve most subpoena disputes. Possibly the most important change is simply that the inhibitions (perhaps rooted in vague notions about the First Amendment) that used to deter litigants from subpoenaing reporters seem no longer to operate in the wake of a few well-publicized violations of the taboo and the Supreme Court's holding in Branzburg v. Hayes, 408 U.S. 665 (1972), that reporters do not have a general First Amendment privilege against compulsory process.

Whatever forces lie behind the increase in subpoenas, the phenomenon has created many instances of observed or articulated anxiety and non-cooperation on the part of news sources, expressions of alarm from journalists and scholars, and a number of shield-law proposals in Congress and the state legislatures. In the last seven years alone, twelve different state legislatures have passed new shield laws and several other states have amended their pre-existing laws.

* * *

The Uniform Reporter's Privilege Act is fashioned around two key distinctions. The first is the distinction between trials on the one hand, and investigative, accusatory, and preliminary proceedings on the other hand. Of the subpoenas that have been served on reporters in recent years, those that have been issued during the course of investigative, accusatory, and preliminary proceedings have tended to be the most numerous, most wide-ranging in scope, most dubious in motivation, most damaging to source relationships, and least justifiable in terms of evidentiary needs. From the reporter's point of view, these subpoenas comprise the crux of the problem. In providing for an absolute privilege against this type of subpoena, the Act grants reporters the essential protection they need in order to engage in the kind of in-depth investigative reporting which ultimately redounds to the benefit of law enforcement as well as most other societal interests.

The second important distinction comes into play with regard to trials. This is the distinction between evidence which discloses the identity of a confidential source and that which discloses only the content of confidential information which the reporter obtained from a source whose identity has already been published or remains undisclosed. In all proceedings except certain defamation and privacy actions, the Act grants reporters an absolute privilege to decline to give evidence which would disclose the identity of a confidential source; it is noteworthy that seventeen states already provide this much protection for the identity of a confidential source. With regard to the content of confidential information, however, the Act provides that the privilege is superseded in a trial if the reporter's evidence is indispensable to the subpoenaing party's case. In a libel case in which the plaintiff must prove that the defendant acted with negligence or reckless disregard for the truth, even the identity of a confidential source can be required to be disclosed if the source's identity is indispensable to the plaintiff's case and all other elements of the case have been established.

Although the basic privilege is limited to confidential sources and information, the Act also provides limited protection for non-confidential matter the disclosure of which would harm the future flow of information to the public to an extent unjustified by the likely evidentiary value of disclosure.

The Act defines "reporter" broadly to include authors of books, lecturers, pamphleteers, and other persons whose primary purpose in obtaining information is to contribute to public knowledge.

The most important procedural provisions are the requirement that every privilege claim be determined by a court of law and the requirement that a judge find reasonable grounds to believe that a reporter has relevant evidence before a subpoena can be issued to the reporter.

SECTION 1. [*Definitions.*]

As used in this Act:

(1) "Confidential information" means information which has been obtained by a reporter and withheld from publication pursuant to an express or implied understanding between the reporter and the source that the information would not be published.

Comment

This definition needs to be read in conjunction with Section 3, which provides that "confidential information" can under certain conditions be subpoenaed in a trial but cannot be subpoenaed in any other proceeding. * * *

(2) "Confidential source" means a source whose identity as a source of certain information has been withheld from publication pursuant to an express or implied understanding between the reporter and the source that his identity as the source of the information would not be published.

(3) "Give evidence" means to testify, produce tangible evidence, submit to a deposition, answer interrogatories, or otherwise make information available at any stage of a proceeding.

(4) "Information" means knowledge which is capable of being transmitted by oral, written, pictorial, electronic, demonstrative, or other means. The term includes, but is not limited to, assertions and documentations of fact, expressions of opinion, fictional representations and portrayals, interpretations, predictions, eyewitness observations, and names of persons who might be able to furnish additional knowledge.

(5) "Proceeding" means any hearing or procedure in which or for which the power of compulsory process may be exercised.

(6) "Publish" means to disseminate by any means information in a form available to the public.

Comment

This definition includes the disseminations of highly specialized publications such as trade journals and foreign language, college, and underground newspapers which typically are read only in narrow circles but which are available to any member of the public who desires to have access to them. On the other hand, a restricted dissemination such as a private "house organ" newsletter, a commissioned survey, or a class limited to registered students is excluded. The definition includes a lecture open to the public, even if there is a charge for admission. However, information disseminated only in personal conversation is not regarded as "published". Information which has once been given in a public proceeding is "published", even if it was given under compulsion.

(7) "Reporter" means a person who has obtained, received, or processed the desired information primarily for the purpose of publishing it or using it to obtain, interpret, or prepare other information to be published.

(8) "Source" means an individual who communicates or transmits information to a reporter, or who expressly or impliedly authorizes a reporter to observe an activity or situation which the reporter would not otherwise be able to observe.

(9) "Trial" means the adversary proceeding in which a judicial or quasi-judicial body may make a final disposition of a claim of right for civil or administrative relief, or of a prosecution of a person who has been impeached, indicted, or otherwise formally bound over for final adjudication, for an offense punishable by fine, imprisonment, removal from office, revocation of license, or loss of other valuable privilege. The term includes a separate hearing at which the judicial or quasi-judicial body may make a final ruling on an issue in the proceeding.

Comment

This definition needs to be read in conjunction with paragraph 1(5), which defines "proceeding", and Section 3, which provides that confidential information can be subpoenaed under certain conditions in a trial. * * *

SECTION 2. [*Privilege Regarding Confidential Source.*]

In any proceeding, a reporter is privileged to decline to give evidence which would disclose or materially facilitate the discovery of the identity of a confidential source.

Comment

In making the privilege absolute with respect to the identity of a confidential source, the Act follows seventeen of the twenty-five states which have passed shield laws. (Two of these states have special qualifications limited to libel cases, which is the result provided by the Act if Section 5 is included.) In some instances criminal defendants would seem to be entitled under the Compulsory Process Clause of the Sixth Amendment to learn the identity of a confidential source. However, the Act does not incorporate any notion of what exceptions are required by the Sixth Amendment but rather leaves that question to the process of case-by-case constitutional adjudication.

Evidence is considered to "disclose" the identity of a confidential source even if the subpoenaing party or the tribunal already has a good idea who the source is, for example if the reporter is asked whether his source for a statement was a particular individual and a truthful answer would confirm the suspicion. Information is privileged under this section if its disclosure would not facilitate the discovery of a source's identity by the court or the subpoenaing party but would materially facilitate discovery by other persons who might retaliate against the source.

SECTION 3. [*Privilege Regarding Confidential Information.*]

(a) In any proceeding other than a trial, a reporter is privileged to decline to give evidence which would disclose confidential information.

(b) In a trial, a reporter is privileged to decline to give evidence which would disclose confidential information unless the a court determines that the evidence:

(1) will not disclose or materially facilitate the discovery of the identity of a confidential source, and

(2) is indispensable to the establishment of the offense charged, the claim pleaded, a defense raised, or the relief sought in the trial.

SECTION 4. [*Privilege Regarding Non-Confidential Matter.*]

In any proceeding, a reporter is privileged to decline to give evidence concerning non-confidential sources he has developed, non-confidential information he has obtained, opinions, or impressions he has formed, conduct in which he has engaged, or tangible material he has obtained or produced in the course of procuring and preparing information for publication, unless the court determines that the probable value of the reporter's evidence is sufficient to justify any detriment to the flow of information to the public that may ensue if the reporter is compelled to give the evidence.

Comment

This section protects a reporter from having to give evidence of a non-confidential nature when the flow of information to the public is likely to be harmed to an unjustifiable extent if the reporter is compelled to give the evidence. An example might be a dragnet subpoena to newspapers and television stations to acquire their films and photographs of a demonstration in order to identify persons who may have engaged in illegal conduct during the demonstration. In most instances even this kind of subpoena would be permissible, but if the court determined that news coverage in the future would be harmed due to physical threats to photographers or retaliation by key sources against other journalists, the likely value of the documentary evidence could be found to be outweighed by the likely value of the future information that would be sacrificed if the evidence were to be compelled. This section gives a measure of protection to, among other things, the reporter's work product—tapes, notebooks, discarded drafts of stories, film "outtakes", lists of possible sources for stories, daily logs, and the like. One reason for providing a qualified privilege for these materials is to encourage reporters to preserve records which may have historical value.

In making the balancing determination required by this section the court should take into account not only the importance of the evidence to the proceeding for which it is sought but also the importance of the proceeding itself.

SECTION 5. [*Exception to the Privilege in Defamation and Privacy Actions.*]

In a civil action for defamation or invasion of privacy in which the plaintiff must prove that the defendant had knowledge of the falsity of his statement or acted with reckless disregard or negligence concerning its truth or falsity, and in which the plaintiff may be hindered by a claim of privilege under this Act from proving the degree of fault required to establish liability, the plaintiff may have the issue of fault tried separately from and subsequent to the trial of all other issues in the case. After a finding for the plaintiff on all other elements of the [cause of action] [claim for relief] necessary to recovery, the issue of fault shall be tried and the privilege does not apply if the court determines that the reporter's evidence is indispensable to the establishment of the requisite fault.

SECTION 6. [*Procedures.*]

(1) A claim of privilege under this Act asserted in a judicial proceeding is determined by the judge hearing the case. A claim asserted in any other proceeding is determined by the [court of general jurisdiction].

(2) Compulsory process to give evidence shall issue against a reporter only upon an order by the judge who is conducting or ruling on preliminary motions for the proceeding for which the reporter's evidence is desired or, for a nonjudicial proceeding, a judge of the [court of general jurisdiction]. The order shall be entered only upon a motion by the subpoenaing party supported by affidavit or sworn testimony and only upon a finding by the judge that there are reasonable grounds to believe that the reporter has evidence relevant to the proceeding.

(3) An order denying in whole or in part a claim of privilege under this Act is subject to an interlocutory appeal. If an appeal is taken, the order shall be stayed pending final disposition of the privilege claim. The appeal shall be given preference and heard at the earliest practicable date.

SECTION 7. [*Waiver.*]

A reporter waives the privilege with respect to particular items of evidence by voluntarily giving the evidence in any proceeding, but not by giving the evidence for the sole purpose of establishing his entitlement to the privilege. A source waives the privilege by submitting to the presiding officer of any proceeding a written notice of waiver specifying the particular items of evidence with respect to which the privilege is waived. If the reporter or the source waives the privilege with respect to particular items of evidence, the reporter may be examined regarding those items of evidence but not regarding other items of evidence for which the privilege has not been waived.

Comment

If either the reporter or the source waives the privilege in one proceeding with respect to particular items of evidence, the privilege is waived with regard to those items of evidence in all subsequent stages of that proceeding and in all subsequent proceedings. However, if a reporter is compelled to testify in one proceeding he is not considered to have waived the privilege for subsequent proceedings, although the evidence he gives under compulsion (but not that which he gives solely to establish his privilege claim) is considered "published" under Section 1(6) and hence no longer confidential so that only the limited protection provided by Section 4 would be available to the reporter. A reporter who is subpoenaed in one proceeding and does not contest the subpoena is considered to have given evidence "voluntarily".

If a reporter has more than one source for a particular item of evidence, one of the sources can waive the privilege without having to secure the consent of the other sources. However, a reporter cannot then be compelled to give particular items of evidence learned exclusively from a source who has not consented to the waiver.

If the privilege is waived with regard to a particular item of evidence, the judge should permit the reporter to be cross-examined only to the extent necessary for a fair assessment of the credibility and meaning of the particular item of evidence which the reporter has given.

An "item of evidence" is any unit of evidence which in the context of the proceeding has probative value standing alone.

*   *   *

Professor Blasi, who drafted the proposed Uniform Reporter's Privilege Act, believes that the questions presented below, as the concluding problems in this section, are among the most difficult for the policy maker contemplating the news reporter's privilege.[30]

30. Personal communication to the authors.

Problem VIII–78. If only a small percentage of reporters have the kind of source relationships that depend on the protection of a privilege is a privilege for all reporters relying on confidential sources justified? Is there any way to extend the protection of a statute to only those reporters whose source relationships would "dry up" absent a statute.

Problem VIII–79. Many reporters regard the maintenance of promised confidentiality as a matter of personal and journalistic ethics. They feel so strongly that they will accept contempt citations and go to jail rather than breach the confidences of sources. How should this fact be weighed in deciding whether to create a news reporter's privilege? Does it depend on the percentage of reporters who will eventually succumb to jailing or the threat of jailing and provide the information sought? Are there reasons to give this factor no weight even if all reporters would serve out a sentence for contempt rather than breach a promised confidence?

Problem VIII–80. Some reporters, particularly those dealing with alienated radical groups, believe that any obvious cooperation with authorities will lead their sources to distrust them. Assume that the following facts, which reflect the beliefs of these reporters, are true. Appearing before a grand jury, even if only to claim a privilege, will generate suspicion because sources will have no way of being sure about what in fact went on in the grand jury room. Participation in a "political trial" on behalf of the prosecution will cause source relationships to disappear and may destroy a reporter's ability to acquire any inside information on a particular radical movement. This is true even if the testimony at the trial is given only after contempt has been threatened and even if no confidential information is revealed. Do these facts justify the extension, to some or all reporters, of a privilege to refuse to testify to information not given in confidence and to refuse to submit documentary or photographic evidence not acquired pursuant to a promise that confidentiality would be maintained?

SECTION XI. POSSIBLE PRIVILEGES

You have now seen a variety of privileges, some with constitutional roots and most arising out of a history of protecting certain relationships or certain kinds of information. We have focused our attention on how federal courts treat privileges, although we have noted the variety of approaches that exist throughout the United States. Often, requests are made of courts and legislatures to create new privileges. Analogies are drawn to existing privileges and claims of entitlement to equal treatment are not unusual. Consider how you might respond as a judge or as a legislator to proposals for the following privileges.

A. An accountant-client privilege. Approximately one-third of the states recognize this privilege. The argument can be made that information involving one's private records and financial dealings ought to be as protected as similar information transmitted to counsel. This is an especially strong argument when an accountant is giving tax advice similar to that provided by lawyers. Is there a valid distinction to be drawn between the professions?[31]

B. Catholic Sisters and Irregularly Ordained Women-Penitent Privilege. As long as spiritual advisors provide religious counseling, they have a claim to be within the clergy-penitent privilege. This may be especially important when women are denied formal positions in the clergy but may be sought out by other women for special counseling.[32] Should such a privilege be extended?

C. A counselor-counselee privilege. In a number of cities throughout the United States, centers have been established to shelter drug addicts, runaways, pregnant teenagers and other troubled individuals. Most such centers engage in informal counseling and often intensive individual or group therapy sessions are available for the "guests." Should information gained in formal counseling or in therapy sessions be privileged? Should the identity of the guests at such establishments be privileged?

D. Friend-friend privilege. At times a party will seek to put the best friend of an opposing party on the stand. Honest testimony in these circumstances may strain even a close friendship. The best friend may be called upon to reveal information given in the strictest confidence. The temptation to perjury is obvious. Should there be a privilege which enables an individual to keep his best friend from testifying against him? Should there be a privilege which enables an individual to prevent his best friend from testifying to anything the friend has learned from the individual in confidence engendered by the friendship?

E. Parent-child privilege. In a world in which families seem to have difficulty staying together, should there be protection for the family relationship? If so, should it be in the form of a communications type privilege, an incapacity type privilege, or both? Is the parent-child or brother-sister relationship less worthy of a privilege than the husband-wife relationship?[33]

F. Peer review or business judgment privilege. If academics, doctors, other professionals and business persons discuss their own work in confidence and review privately work done by their peers, the public, arguably, will benefit from the candid exchange of criticism. Such exchanges might be tempered or diminished if efforts at self-scrutiny must be shared with the public. Should information exchanged in such peer review or confidential discussions and/or the identities of those involved be protected by a privilege?[34]

G. Social scientists often promise their subjects or respondents that information communicated to them in the course of their research will be held confidential and published in a way that precludes the identification of individual responses. Researchers are dependent on voluntary participation. Should they be able to offer the protection of a privilege? How would a social scientist be defined? By an advanced degree? A teaching position? The nature of the research?

H. Social worker-client privilege. Thousands of social workers, many of whom have advanced degrees, work in psychiatric facilities throughout the country. Many also work for family service and

---

31. Note, Evidence: The Accountant-Client Privilege Under Federal Rules of Evidence—New Statute and New Problems, 28 Okla.L.Rev. 637 (1975).

32. See Note, Catholic Sisters, Irregularly Ordained Women and the Clergy-Penitent Privilege, 9 U.Cal.Davis L.Rev. 523 (1976).

33. See Note, Recognition of a Parent-Child Testimonial Privilege, 23 St. Louis U.L.Rev. 676 (1979).

34. See, e.g., FTC v. TRW, Inc., 628 F.2d 207 (D.C.Cir.1980).

social welfare agencies. Some are engaged in private practice. As long as social workers are employed to assist in therapeutic processes, especially those relating to social adjustment, is there any reason to treat them differently from other psychotherapists?[35]

BIBLIOGRAPHY

Berger, Executive Privilege: A Constitutional Myth (1974).

McCormick, Chs. 8–13.

Wigmore, Chs. 76, 79–83, 85–87.

Berger, How the Privilege for Governmental Information Met Its Watergate, 25 Case W.Res.L.Rev. (1975).

Berger, The President, Congress and the Courts, 83 Yale L.J. 1111 (1974).

Blasi, The Newsman's Privilege, An Empirical Study, 70 Mich.L.Rev. 229 (1971).

Chafee, Privileged Communications: Is Justice Served or Obstructed by Closing the Doctor's Mouth on the Witness Stand?, 52 Yale L.J. 607 (1943).

Gardner, A Personal Privilege for Communications of Corporate Clients—Paradox or Public Policy, 40 U.Det.L.J. 299 (1963).

Gardner, A Re-Evaluation of the Attorney-Client Privilege, 8 Vill.L.Rev. 279 (1963).

Goldstein & Katz, Psychiatrist Patient Privilege: The GPA Proposal and the Connecticut Statute, 36 Conn.B.J. 175 (1965).

Guttmacher & Weihofen, Privileged Communication Between Psychiatrist and Patient, 28 Ind.L.J. 32 (1952).

Hutchins & Slesinger, Some Observations on the Law of Evidence: Family Relations, 13 Minn.L.Rev. 675 (1929).

Kobak, The Uneven Application of the Attorney-Client Privilege to Corporations in the Federal Courts, 6 Ga.L.Rev. 339 (1972).

Krattenmaker, Testimonial Privileges in Federal Courts: An Alternative to the Proposed Federal Rules of Evidence, 62 Geo.L.J. 61 (1973).

Ladd, Privileges, 1969 Law & Social Order 555 (1969).

Lempert, A Right to Every Woman's Evidence, 66 Iowa L.Rev. 725 (1981).

Louisell, Confidentiality, Conformity and Confusion: Privileges in Federal Courts Today, 31 Tul.L.Rev. 101 (1956).

Louisell & Crippin, Evidentiary Privileges, 40 Minn.L.Rev. 413 (1956).

Miller, The Challenge to the Attorney-Client Privilege, 49 Va.L.Rev. 262 (1963).

Reese, Confidential Communication to the Clergy, 24 Ohio St.L.J. 55 (1963).

Saltzburg, Communications Falling Within the Attorney-Client Privilege, 66 Iowa L.Rev. 811 (1981).

Saltzburg, Privileges and Professionals: Lawyers and Psychiatrists, 66 Va.L.Rev. 597 (1980).

Sawyer, The Physician-Patient Privilege: Some Reflections, 14 Drake L.Rev. 83 (1965).

---

35. See Testimony of Sherman Ragland, Hearings on the Rules of Evidence Before the Subcommittee on Criminal Justice of the House Committee on the Judiciary, 93rd Cong., 1st Sess., at 475–81 (1973).

Shuman & Weiner, The Privilege Study: An Empirical Examination of the Psychotherapist-Patient Privilege, 60 N.Car.L.Rev. 893 (1982).

Slovenko, Psychiatry and a Second Look at the Medical Privilege, 6 Wayne L.Rev. 175 (1960).

Stedman, Trade Secrets, 23 Ohio St.L.J. 4 (1965).

Stoyles, The Dilemma of the Constitutionality of the Priest-Penitent Privilege—The Application of the Religious Clauses, 29 U.Pitt.L.Rev. 27 (1967).

Symposium on United States v. Nixon, 22 U.C.L.A.L.Rev. 1 (1974).

Chapter Nine

ASPECTS OF PROOF: BURDENS, STANDARDS, SHORTCUTS, AND REVIEW

SECTION I. IDENTIFYING THE FACTS IN DISPUTE AND ALLOCATING BURDENS

A. THE IMPORTANCE OF THE PLEADINGS

Trials are not natural occurrences. Grievances are not inevitably settled by trials. The transformation of private grievances or violations of public law into adjudicated disputes occurs only when some individual or organization takes appropriate initiatives. In civil cases, the filing of a complaint marks the formal commencement of an adjudicated dispute; on the criminal side, such disputes are commenced by the return of an indictment, the filing of an information, or the filing of a complaint and an arrest. The process of making a dispute judicial is in one sense a process of simplification. However complicated the relationship of the parties and the law that might bear on that relationship, the dispute, as presented to the court, is made to turn on a relatively small number of legal and factual questions.

Just as disputes do not appear magically in court, questions crucial to dispute res-

olution do not arise magically at trial. The parties must specify these questions for the court. Historically this was done almost entirely by the process of pleading. The plaintiff alleged certain facts and their legal implications and the defendant denied either the facts or their legal implications or both. When the parties went to trial, they more or less knew from the pleadings the significant differences that remained to be litigated. Today pleadings continue to play a role in specifying the subject matter of litigation, but they no longer play the major role. With modern notice pleading, like that provided for in the Federal Rules of Civil Procedure, discovery reveals disputed factual and legal questions more fully than do the pleadings. Pre-trial conferences and court orders relating thereto also help define issues in a notice pleading system.

B. ALLOCATING BURDENS OF PROOF

If parties to a dispute learn during the course of the pre-trial proceedings that they agree completely on the facts relating to their dispute but disagree on the legal implications of these facts, the only difference between them is one of law. If this is the case, witnesses need not be presented. The dispute may be settled by the judge

on the basis of briefs and arguments. If the parties find that they cannot agree on the facts relating to their dispute and if legal rights or responsibilities hinge upon whose version of the facts is accepted, adjudication is available to resolve factual differences and to determine legal implications. For adjudication to occur, one party must raise the issues for the trier of fact and some party must begin the process of proof.[1]

Upon which party should the burden fall? Usually it is upon the party seeking to change the status quo at the time the litigation begins; i.e., the prosecution in a criminal case, the plaintiff in a civil action, and the moving party in motion practice. But there are issues, such as those that must be raised to make out an affirmative defense, on which defendants bear the burden of producing evidence.

The law requires the party who brings a controversy to court not only to state his claim clearly, but also to show that its factual basis is sufficiently strong that the fact finder might reasonably decide for that party. Conceptually, it is possible to separate the responsibility to state a claim, or the pleading burden, from the obligation to introduce evidence, or the production burden. Disregarding questions of constitutionality, one can imagine a system in which one party's statement of the reasons why he thinks the law should move against the other obliges the other party to introduce evidence showing why such a move is unjustified. But if such a system applied to all issues raised by the alleged cause of action, it would be fraught with difficulties. Substantial resources would be wasted by requiring defendants to disprove claims that were insubstantial to begin with, and if allegations of great generality were allowed it might be impossible for defendants to meet them. How, for example, would Able begin to defend Baker's claim, "Able injured me by his negligence" without knowing more specifically Baker's claim? Furthermore, if in our imaginary system the burden of proof in the sense of the risk of non-persuasion (which we shall call the persuasion burden) did

not shift along with the production burden, the defendant by introducing only slight evidence in response to the plaintiff's pleading could forestall a directed verdict and require the plaintiff to mount a case. If the plaintiff did mount a case, as long as the defendant were allowed to rebut it, the system would look much like the present one, except for the small initial step required of the defendant. Thus, the current system which requires the party who initiates a controversy to introduce evidence sufficient to establish a prima facie case makes sense.

Problems arise, however, because a party who initiates a law suit or brings a criminal action is only raising certain controversies; everything that becomes controversial in the course of the suit may not be at his instance. In fact, the initiating or moving party may have no way of anticipating everything that the opponent will make controversial. The law deals with this problem by special pleading requirements and by assuming that specific claims necessarily raise certain controversies. The claim of negligence, for example, necessarily raises a controversy about the defendant's lack of care, and the charge of murder necessarily raises a controversy about whether the defendant was responsible for the death of the deceased. The burden of producing evidence with respect to these necessary controversies is on the moving party as is, as a general matter, the persuasion burden.

On other matters, the law requires defendants to choose between placing issues in controversy and foregoing whatever benefits the favorable resolution of the issue will provide. The law's decision to make defendants responsible for creating certain controversies often but not always carries with it a shift in the persuasion

---

1. See generally, Cleary, Presuming and Pleading: An Essay on Juristic Immaturity, 12 Stan.L.Rev. 5 (1959).

burden. Where that burden is not fully shifted to the defendant, the defendant may face only a pleading burden or he may be required to introduce evidence sufficient to show that his claim is potentially meritorious.

It is a jurisdiction's substantive law which determines whether a matter is necessarily placed in issue by a claim, and so must be addressed by the moving party, or whether the matter is in issue only if raised by the defense. Substantive law also determines who bears the persuasion burden. Even when substantive matters bear similar labels, like first degree murder or breach of contract, jurisdictions vary in the way they allocate both the burden of production and the burden of persuasion.

Variations can exist because any definition of claims and defenses is somewhat arbitrary. In many instances an element of a claim might be reasonably characterized as part of an affirmative defense, or an element of a defense could be made part of the claim that the plaintiff must prove to prevail in the litigation. In a negligence action, for example, the plaintiff in one jurisdiction might be required to offer evidence sufficient to prove fault on the part of the defendant while the defendant is required to prove the plaintiff's lack of care if contributory negligence is his defense. In another jurisdiction the plaintiff might be required to offer evidence sufficient to prove both the defendant's fault and his own due care. In still another jurisdiction the defendant might be required to plead and offer some evidence of the plaintiff's negligence if contributory negligence is his defense, but if he does so the plaintiff might be required to prove that he acted with reasonable care.

In deciding how to define claims and whether to allocate elements of proof to claims or defenses, courts and legislatures consider factors such as the ease with which the respective parties can gather and present evidence, the fairness of making one side rather than the other bear the burden of producing evidence and the desired result if neither party produces evidence on a point. If the party with the burden of producing evidence produces nothing or produces evidence of insufficient probative value, his claim or defense will not be considered by the trier of fact. If he produces enough evidence that a jury might reasonably find in his favor or, in the case of a criminal defendant, enough to place the matter in issue, the fact finder will consider the claim or defense in light of all the evidence presented.

The question that is begged here is, of course, how much evidence does it take to satisfy the production burden. Again one must turn to substantive law, for the answer depends largely on the standard of proof by which the trier of fact is to decide the case and the way the law assigns responsibility for persuading a trier that a contention is valid.[2] For example, in a criminal action for assault and battery the prosecutor must prove the identity of the assailant beyond a reasonable doubt, while in a civil action growing out of the same attack the plaintiff must prove identity by only a preponderance of the evidence. In these circumstances, a plaintiff might get to the jury in a civil action with evidence that could not withstand a motion to dismiss in a criminal case. Moreover, if the defendant admits striking the victim but argues that it was an accident, the prosecutor in a criminal case may have to prove the non-accidental nature of the touching beyond a reasonable doubt. In the corresponding civil action the defendant who admits striking the plaintiff may have the responsibility of proving the accidental nature of the battery to the jury, or if the burden of proving the non-accidental na-

2. See generally, James, Burdens of Proof, 47 Va.L.Rev. 51 (1961).

ture of the touching remains on the plaintiff, it may be satisfied by a preponderance of the evidence. Where the burden of producing evidence shifts to the defendant, it is conceivable that a civil plaintiff could get a directed verdict on a set of facts that would entitle a criminal defendant to have the action dismissed. Such are the wonders of substantive legal differences.

The Supreme Court held in In re Winship that in criminal cases the state must prove the essential elements of the charged offense beyond a reasonable doubt.[3] Since the state must bear the persuasion burden on these issues it follows that it must bear the production burden as well because without any in the evidence an essential point cannot be proved beyond a reasonable doubt. Such evidence must be presented in the state's case-in-chief because if it is not, the defendant who chooses to present no evidence would be entitled to a judgment of acquittal. In practice, of course, defendants do not risk foregoing a defense, for they can test the soundness of the state's prima facie case by moving to dismiss at the close of the state's evidence.

In the case of affirmative defenses to criminal charges, such as duress, insanity and self-defense, the production burden is in some jurisdictions placed on defendants. The justification for the shift is that if an issue is neither necessarily nor typically raised by a criminal charge it makes sense to allow the government to assume that the issue is not raised by a case unless the defendant provides some reason to believe that it is. So long as the government bears the burden of persuasion on issues raised by affirmative defenses, the defendant's production burden will be the relatively light one of introducing evidence sufficient to show a genuine controversy.[4]

3. 397 U.S. 358 (1970). The Constitution does not explicitly require this standard in criminal cases, but the United States Supreme Court held in Winship that the due process clause of the fourteenth amendment requires that an accused in a criminal prosecution be acquitted unless the highest standard of proof known to the law is satisfied. Writing for the Court, Justice Brennan said:

The reasonable-doubt standard plays a vital role in the American scheme of criminal procedure. It is a prime instrument for reducing the risk of convictions resting on factual error. The standard provides concrete substance for the presumption of innocence—that bedrock "axiomatic and elementary" principle whose "enforcement lies at the foundation of the administration of our criminal law." Id. at 363, quoting Coffin v. United States, 156 U.S. 432, 453 (1895).

Justice Brennan also said in Winship, that "use of the reasonable doubt standard is indispensable to command the respect and confidence of the community in its applications of the criminal law. It is critical that the moral force of the criminal law not be diluted by a standard of proof that leaves people in doubt whether innocent men are being condemned." (at 365)

4. Even where one side has both the production and persuasion burdens, the other side may at some point have to come forward with evidence or risk a directed verdict—i.e., a decision that the proof is so overwhelming that the party offering it must prevail. The amount of evidence needed to avoid a directed verdict must, in civil cases, be sufficient for reasonable people to draw an inference of the existence of the particular facts sought to be proved. Putting this another way the defendant on an issue is in no danger of having a verdict directed against him unless no reasonable jury could fail to accept the proof offered by the opponent and no substantial rebuttal evidence is produced. A case so one-sided is a rare phenomenon. Even where defendants do not present a case, they invariably dispute the stories of the plaintiff's witnesses. Unless the challenge to the plaintiff's case is incredible or does not dispute the central issues, the judge must let the case go to the jury. However, the trial judge can tell the jury that it must find for the plaintiff if it finds the facts to be as the plaintiff contends.

In a criminal case tried to a jury, the jury is empowered to acquit in the face of overwhelming prosecution evidence, for it has, under the sixth amendment, the power, if not the right, to nullify the criminal law.

Shifting just the production burden on a particular issue is unlikely to cause constitutional problems so long as the issue is not necessarily raised by the crime charged and so long as the defendant is in a good position to suggest the existence of the issue if it is, within the context of the particular case, in fact problematic.

More serious difficulties arise when a state attempts to shift the persuasion burden on a particular issue to a criminal defendant. This cannot be done, consistent with *Winship*, if the issue is an essential element of the crime charged or if it becomes one when the defendant shows that the matter is, in the context of the case, controversial. Thus, the state's ability to shift persuasion burdens turns in part on whether the elements that the prosecution must continue to prove beyond a reasonable doubt are, in the light of the issues injected by the defendant, sufficient to define a crime that is sanctioned in the way the state has specified.

As of this writing it is not clear exactly what persuasion burdens can be shifted to defendants, but it is clear that some burdens that might be characterized as affirmative defenses can be shifted, while others, so long as a state chooses to define crimes in certain ways, cannot. Thus, the pre-*Winship* case of Leland v. State of Oregon[5] upheld a statute that required defendants claiming insanity to prove their insanity beyond a reasonable doubt. However, the Court in *Leland* noted that under Oregon law the state still had the burden of providing premeditation beyond a reasonable doubt and that the evidence the defendant offered to show his insanity could be considered by the jury on the premeditation issue as well. Mullaney v. Wilbur,[6] arising after *Winship*, suggested that the Court might be ready to take a different position. In *Mullaney,* the Court held unconstitutional a Maine statute which required a defendant claiming that a homicide was manslaughter and not murder to establish by a preponderance of the evidence that he acted "on sudden provocation in the heat of passion." The statute at issue in *Mullaney* required "malice aforethought" as an element of the crime but allowed malice to be presumed from "any deliberate, cruel act committed by one person against another suddenly * * *," and proof of "heat of passion" was seen as negating malice. Thus, requiring the defendant to bear the persuasion burden on the issue of "heat of passion" was seen as tantamount to requiring him to bear the burden of negating malice, an element which in the Maine statute was an essential part of the offense of murder and so under *Winship* had to be proved by the state beyond a reasonable doubt.

After *Mullaney,* the Court dismissed the appeal from a case challenging the application of *Leland* for want of a substantial federal question.[7] And in Patterson v. New York,[8] the Court upheld a statutory scheme that placed on the defendant the burden of proving extreme emotional disturbance by a preponderance of the evidence once the prosecution in a trial for second degree murder had proved an intentional homicide beyond a reasonable doubt. The defendant's showing of extreme emotional disturbance would have had the effect of reducing the offense committed from second degree murder to manslaughter. Ac-

Thus, there can be no directed verdict against a defendant in a criminal trial. A judgment of acquittal, the equivalent of a directed verdict of innocence, can, however, be entered against the government if the prosecution does not respond adequately to a defendant's affirmative defense.

5. 343 U.S. 790 (1952).

6. 421 U.S. 684 (1975).

7. Rivera v. Delaware, 429 U.S. 877 (1976).

8. 432 U.S. 197 (1977).

cording to the *Patterson* majority, the major difference between the New York scheme and the Maine scheme was that the New York statute did not require that the defendant bear the burden of persuasion with respect to a fact that was inconsistent with and hence would necessarily negate an element of the crime as the legislature had defined it. But the majority in *Patterson* appeared to view the Maine statute rather differently from the majority in *Mullaney.* Justice Powell, the author of the lead opinion in *Mullaney,* highlighted this in his dissent in *Patterson.* Regardless of how the Maine statute should be read, the implications for defendants who argue that they are guilty of manslaughter and not murder are under the two statutory schemes much the same.[9]

In civil cases and in criminal cases where it is constitutional to place the burden of persuasion on defendants the standard which proof must meet is a question of local law.[10] A legislature's choice with respect to standards of proof and the allocation of persuasion burdens reflects judgments about who should bear the risks of mistakes when there is uncertainty in a case and in what proportion the risks should be borne. In civil cases where the typical "preponderance of the evidence" standard applies, both sides bear, in theory, an approximately equal risk of an erroneous decision. The placement of the burden of persuasion is important only if the trier of fact is in equipoise, for then the party with the persuasion burden loses. Like all rules for breaking ties, this one is arbitrary, although it is sometimes justified by the argument that unless the party initiating a legal controversy can show that the status quo should be disturbed, it should

not be. The proposition sounds reasonable but it is not self-evident. The opposite rule could be justified by an equally empty shibboleth such as, "change is the parent of progress" or "a plaintiff who can move a defendant to equipoise should prevail." The important thing is that some rule is needed to break ties, and as long as that rule is known to both sides they can plan for litigation accordingly. In civil cases the standard rule is consistent with the typical allocation of pleading, production and persuasion burdens. On issues where the burden of persuasion falls upon the defendant, a tie results in a plaintiff's victory.

In a criminal case the defendant, in theory, bears little risk of mistake since the reasonable doubt standard tells the jurors that they should be quite certain of guilt before convicting.

In allocating production burdens or in choosing one standard of proof rather than another a court or legislature may consider a number of factors. If events usually develop in a certain way, the party who claims that his case is an exception to the usual rule will ordinarily have the production burden and may face a higher than average persuasion burden. If certain outcomes are particularly disvalued, the state may require a party who seeks such an outcome to be almost certainly correct in his claim if he is to prevail. Thus, a husband who seeks to bastardize his wife's child may be required to show that he is not the father by clear and convincing evidence or by proof beyond a reasonable doubt. Similar reasons of policy justify the high standard placed on prosecutors in criminal cases. The immense costs of a criminal conviction in terms of stigmatiza-

---

9. For opposing views on the permissibility of placing persuasion burdens on defendant, compare Allen, The Restoration of In re Winship: A Comment on Burdens of Persuasion in Criminal Cases After Patterson v. New York, 76 Mich.L.Rev. 30 (1977), with Underwood, The Thumb on the Scales of Jus-

tice: Burdens of Persuasion in Criminal Cases, 86 Yale L.J. 1299 (1977).

10. The Constitution may impose certain burdens of persuasion in civil cases. See, e.g., Addington v. Texas, 441 U.S. 418 (1979) (clear and convincing evidence required in civil commitment proceedings.)

tion and the potential loss of liberty or life justifies, for most people, a system which requires substantial certainty of guilt before such penalties can follow. Further justification for the "beyond a reasonable

doubt" standard can be found in the vast resources which the state, but not usually a criminal defendant, can bring to the investigation and trial of a criminal case.[11]

C. APPLYING STANDARDS OF PROOF

Problem IX-1. Chamberlain was killed while working for a railroad. His estate brought an action to recover damages for his death. The federal district court held that the estate did not meet its burden of producing sufficient evidence of negligence to warrant submitting the case to the jury. The Court of Appeals reversed. **Should the Supreme Court have found the production burden satisfied upon the facts that follow?** Chamberlain is referred to as the deceased, and the estate as the respondent.

That part of the yard in which the accident occurred contained a lead track and a large number of switching tracks branching therefrom. The lead track crossed a "hump," and the work of car distribution consisted of pushing a train of cars by means of a locomotive to the top of the "hump," and then allowing the cars, in separate strings, to descend by gravity, under the control of hand brakes, to their respective destina-

---

11. As one commentator has noted:

Attainment of certainty—no possibility of error—is beyond man's capacity; beyond the capacity of any trier of fact whether he be a learned judge or an honest, conscientious and intelligent juror. The trier of fact, therefore, whether judge or jury, can only reach conclusions which are rationally describable in terms of probabilities. This basic principle has been stated by Jevons, noted logician, as follows:

The subject upon which we now enter [probability] must not be regarded as an isolated and curious branch of speculation. It is the necessary basis of nearly all the judgments and decisions we make in the prosecution of science, or the conduct of ordinary affairs. As Butler truly said, "Probability is the very guide of life." Had the science of numbers been developed for no other purposes, it must have been developed for the calculation of probabilities. All our inferences concerning the future are merely probable, and a due appreciation of the degree of probability depends entirely upon a due comprehension of the principles of the subject. I conceive that it is impossible even to expound the principles and methods of induction as applied to natural phenomena, in a sound manner, without resting them upon the theory of probability. Perfect knowledge alone can give certainty, and in nature perfect knowledge would be infinite knowledge, which is clearly beyond our capacities. We have, therefore, to content ourselves with partial knowledge—knowledge mingled with ignorance, producing doubt. [citing Jevons, Principles of Science 224 (Am. ed. 1874)].

When people take their disputes to court, or the state prosecutes an alleged offender for a crime, what has happened in the past must be determined. The trier of fact can only rationally conclude that the assertions are possibly true; are as probably true as not true; are more probably true than not true; are highly probably true; are true beyond a reasonable doubt, almost certainly but not certainly true.

McBaine, Burden of Proof: Presumptions, 2 U.C.L.A. L.Rev. 13, 15 (1954).

For a recent case analyzing the appropriate standard of proof in mentally disordered sex offender proceedings, see People v. Burnick, 14 Cal.3d 306, 121 Cal.Rptr. 488, 535 P.2d 352 (1975).

tions in the various branch tracks. Deceased had charge of a string of two gondola cars, which he was piloting to track 14. Immediately ahead of him was a string of seven cars, and behind him a string of nine cars, both also destined for track 14. Soon after the cars ridden by deceased had passed to track 14, his body was found on that track some distance beyond the switch. He had evidently fallen onto the track and been run over by a car or cars.

The case for respondent rests wholly upon the claim that the fall of deceased was caused by a violent collision of the string of nine cars with the string ridden by deceased. Three employees, riding the nine-car string, testified positively that no such collision occurred. They were corroborated by every other employee in a position to see, all testifying that there was no contact between the nine-car string and that of the deceased. The testimony of these witnesses, if believed, establishes beyond doubt that there was no collision between these two strings of cars, and that the nine-car string contributed in no way to the accident. The only witness who testified for the respondent was one Bainbridge; and it is upon his testimony alone that respondent's right to recover is sought to be upheld. This testimony is concisely stated, in its most favorable light for respondent, in the prevailing opinion below by Judge Learned Hand, as follows:

"The plaintiff's only witness to the event, one Bainbridge, then employed by the road, stood close to the yardmaster's office, near the 'hump.' He professed to have paid little attention to what went on, but he did see the deceased riding at the rear of his cars, whose speed when they passed him he took to be about eight or ten miles. Shortly thereafter a second string passed which was shunted into another track and this was followed by the nine, which, according to the plaintiff's theory, collided with the deceased's. After the nine cars had passed at a somewhat greater speed than the deceased's, Bainbridge paid no more attention to either string for a while, but looked again when the deceased, who was still standing in his place, had passed the switch and onto the assorting track where he was bound. At that time his speed had been checked to about three miles, but the speed of the following nine cars had increased. They were just passing the switch, about four or five cars behind the deceased. Bainbridge looked away again and soon heard what he described as a 'loud crash', not however an unusual event in a switching yard. Apparently this did not cause him at once to turn, but he did so shortly thereafter, and saw the two strings together, still moving, and the deceased no longer in sight. Later still his attention was attracted by shouts and he went to the spot and saw the deceased between the rails. Until he left to go to the accident, he had stood fifty feet to the north of the track where the accident happened, and about nine hundred feet from where the body was found."

* * * It is correctly pointed out * * * that Bainbridge was in no position to see whether the two strings of cars were actually together; that Bainbridge repeatedly said he was paying no particular attention; and that his position was such, being 900 feet from the place

where the body was found and less than 50 feet from the side of the track in question.

Problem IX–2. Dyer files a complaint against MacDougall. The first count alleges that MacDougall said of Dyer at a directors' meeting of the Queensboro Corporation, "You are stabbing me in the back." The second count alleges that MacDougall has written a letter to Dorothy Hope, Dyer's sister-in-law, stating, "Dyer has made false statements to my clients in Philadelphia and presented bills for work not done." The third count alleges that MacDougall had told Dorothy Hope that Dyer had sent out a "blackmailing letter." The fourth count alleges that MacDougall had also told Almirall, a lawyer, that Dyer had sent out a "blackmailing letter." MacDougall unequivocally denies uttering the libel and slanders attributed to him, Hope denies receiving the letter which forms the basis for the second count of Dyer's complaint, and Hope and Almirall deny hearing the slander that MacDougall allegedly spoke to them. Dyer has no affirmative proof to support his counts, but urges that a jury could find sufficient evidence to justify a verdict for him if it disbelieves MacDougall and his corroborating witnesses. **Has Dyer produced sufficient evidence to take his case to a jury?**

Problem IX–3. Examine the following two jury instructions on burden of proof. Are they satisfactory? Equally so?

a) I shall now explain to you the burden of proof which the law places on the parties to establish their respective claims. When I say that a party has the burden of proof, or, in this connection, use the expression "if you find" or "if you decide," I mean the evidence must satisfy you that the proposition on which that party has the burden of proof has been established by evidence which outweighs the evidence against it. You must consider all the evidence regardless of which party produced it.[12]

b) Whenever I say a claim must be proved, I mean that all of the evidence by whomever produced must lead you to believe it is more likely that the claim is true than not true. [If the evidence does not lead you to believe it is more likely that the claim is true than not true, then the claim has not been proved].

[Proof of a claim does not necessarily mean the greater number of witnesses or the greater volume of testimony. Any believable evidence may be a sufficient basis to prove a claim].[13]

Problem IX–4. In a negligence case involving a counterclaim by the defendant, is the following instruction satisfactory? Could you write a better instruction? Make any changes you think would improve this one.

In this action there is not only the claim of the plaintiff against the defendant, but also a claim by the defendant against the plaintiff. This is known as a counterclaim.

Because there is a counterclaim in this case you may reach one of three results.

---

12. Mich. Standard Jury Instruction 21.01 (1970).

13. Minn. Jury Inst. Guide, JIG 70 (1963).

First, your verdict may be for the plaintiff on his claim and against the defendant on his counterclaim;

Second, your verdict may be for the declarant on his counterclaim and against the plaintiff on his claim; or

Third, your verdict may be against both the plaintiff on his claim and the defendant on his counterclaim.

As to plaintiff's claim, he has the burden of proof on each of the following propositions:

(a) that the plaintiff (was injured) (sustained damages);

(b) that the defendant was negligent in one or more of the ways claimed by the plaintiff as stated to you in these instructions;

(c) that the negligence of the defendant was a proximate cause of the (injuries) (damages) to the plaintiff.

The defendant has the burden of proof on his defense that the plaintiff was negligent in one or more of the ways claimed by the defendant as stated to you in these instructions; and that such negligence was a proximate contributing cause of the injury to the plaintiff.

Your verdict will be for the plaintiff on his claim, if he was (injured) (damaged), and defendant was negligent, and such negligence was a proximate cause of his (injuries) (damages); unless plaintiff himself was negligent and such negligence proximately contributed to his (injuries) (damages).

Your verdict will be for the defendant on plaintiff's claim, if plaintiff was not (injured) (damaged), or if defendant was not negligent, or if negligent, such negligence was not a proximate cause of the (injuries) (damages) or, if the plaintiff himself was negligent and such negligence was a proximate contributing cause of his (injuries) (damages).

As to the defendant's counterclaim, he has the burden of proof on each of the following propositions:

(a) that the defendant (was injured) (sustained damages);

(b) that the plaintiff was negligent in one or more of the ways claimed by the defendant as stated to you in these instructions;

(c) that the negligence of the plaintiff was a proximate cause of the (injuries) (damages) to the defendant.

The plaintiff has the burden of proof on his defense that the defendant was negligent in one or more of the ways claimed by the plaintiff as stated to you in these instructions; and that such negligence was a proximate contributing cause of the (injuries) (damages) to the defendant.

Your verdict will be for the defendant on his counterclaim if he was (injured) (damaged), and plaintiff was negligent, and such negligence was a proximate cause of his (injuries) (damages); unless defendant himself was negligent and such negligence proximately contributed to his (injuries) (damages).

Your verdict will be for the plaintiff on defendant's counterclaim if defendant was not (injured) (damaged), or if plaintiff was not negligent, or if negligent, such negligence was not a proximate cause of the (injuries) (damages), or, if the defendant himself was negligent and such negligence was a proximate contributing cause of his (injuries) (damages).

If both plaintiff and defendant were negligent and the negligence of each was a proximate cause of the injuries received by the other, then your verdict will be no cause for action on both the plaintiff's claim and the defendant's counterclaim.[14]

Problem IX–5. Lee is charged with bank robbery and murder. Prior to trial, Lee moves to suppress the money, ski masks, and automatic weapons seized in a search of his house pursuant to a warrant on the ground that the affidavit of the FBI agent who sought the search warrant was insufficient to demonstrate probable cause. Lee also moves to suppress statements elicited from him by the police at the station house shortly after arrest, claiming the statements were involuntary and obtained in violation of the fifth amendment. The Supreme Court has held that the burden on the prosecutor to prove the voluntariness of confessions may be met by a preponderance of the evidence.[15] **Do you think this minimal burden is appropriate? Would you distinguish the fourth amendment and fifth amendment questions? If a witness will testify that the teller who was killed in the robbery stated as he died, "Oscar Brown killed me," should this evidence be admissible if there is only a reasonable possibility that the teller had the sense of imminent death required by the dying declaration exception to the hearsay rule? Or should the evidence be excluded unless Lee can demonstrate by a preponderance of the evidence that the requisites for a dying declaration were met? If the declaration identified Lee and was offered by the prosecutor, what standard of proof should the prosecutor have to satisfy before the statement is admitted pursuant to the hearsay exception?**

Problem IX–6. Sid's automobile collides with Mary's. Mary files suit claiming that Sid was negligent. She also claims that she has suffered partial amnesia and is unable to recall the details of the accident. **Should the judge tell the jury that if it is satisfied that Mary is suffering from amnesia as a result of the accident, Mary's burden of proof is reduced?**

Problem IX–7. If the cause of action in a civil case parallels a criminal action, (e.g., an action for fraud or assault) **should the plaintiff have to prove wrongdoing beyond a reasonable doubt?** Most American jurisdictions require only a preponderance of the evidence. **If you were briefing a state supreme court in a case of first impression, what arguments would you make in support of some higher standard? What arguments would you make to justify the preponderance of the evidence standard?**[16]

14. Mich. Standard Jury Instruction 21.04 (1970).

15. Lego v. Twomey, 404 U.S. 477 (1972). The case is criticized and an alternative analysis suggested in Saltzburg, Standards of Proof and Preliminary Questions of Fact, 27 Stan.L.Rev. 271 (1975).

16. See generally, Cohen, Allegation of Crime in a Civil Action: Burden of Proof, 20 Toronto U.Fac.L.Rev. 20, 34 (1962).

SECTION II. SHORTCUTS TO PROOF

A. PRESUMPTIONS

1. INTRODUCTION

Professor Morgan, who understood presumptions as well as anyone, once wrote:

> Every writer of sufficient intelligence to appreciate the difficulties of the subject-matter has approached the topic of presumptions with a sense of hopelessness and has left it with a feeling of despair.[17]

A principal cause of scholarly despair is that courts use the term "presumption" to mean many different things.[18] Commentators can agree that most judicially ascribed meanings are inappropriate, but they are unable to agree precisely on the legal implications of true presumptions.

Generally speaking, presumptions involve a relationship between one fact or set of facts—the basic fact(s)—and another fact or set of facts—the presumed fact(s). Basic facts imply presumed facts, the strength of the implication varying with the presumption. Where a presumption exists, certain advantages usually accrue to a party proving the basic fact which would not accrue absent the presumption. The degree of advantage depends upon the sense in which the term "presumption" is used.

At one extreme, the term "presumption" refers to a situation where proof of the basic fact means that the existence of the presumed fact may not be controverted. Here the term is a misnomer. What really exists is a substantive rule of law equating the legal effects of proving the basic fact with the effects of proving the presumed fact. Such presumptions are called "conclusive presumptions."

At the other extreme, the term refers simply to a permissible inference, i.e., a standardized situation in which a jury may, but is not required to, infer a presumed fact from a basic fact. Here again the term is misused, for the existence of such a "presumption" has no necessary legal implications. However, even such weak presumptions as these may benefit the parties proving basic facts. They are precedents holding that the inference for which the basic fact was offered is reasonable,[19] and, as precedent, they may enable

---

17. Morgan, Presumptions, 12 Wash. L.Rev. 255, at 255 (1937).

18. Laughlin identifies eight different senses in which courts have used this term. Laughlin, In Support of the Thayer Theory of Presumptions, 52 Mich.L.Rev. 195, 196–209 (1953). Our textual introduction to presumptions examines four of the meanings that have been ascribed to the term "presumption." Other meanings are discussed in the subsections that follow.

19. **In some situations, the existence of a presumption in a statute will lead a court to accept as reasonable or permissible an inference that would not otherwise be allowed. One noted commentator observed:**

When the basic fact is established, the trier of fact is permitted to infer or deduce therefrom the existence of the presumed fact, although in the opinion of the court the inference or deduction is not rationally permissible. Thus, the court may have repeatedly held that possession of intoxicating liquor is insufficient to support a finding of illegal acquisition of the liquor. The legislature may thereafter have enacted a statute, phrased in terms of presumption or prima facie evidence, which the court interprets as providing that evidence of possession of intoxicating liquor is sufficient to justify a finding of its illegal acquisition. Such a statute is ordinarily held valid. This may mean that the court is willing to concede that its prior concept as to the value of the evidence was in error because based on inadequate experience, or it may mean that, for reasons of policy and convenience, the legislature was justified in permitting the trier of fact to give to the evidence more than its inherently logical value. Some commentators, accepting the second explanation, say that the term

a party to avoid a directed verdict. Also, in some jurisdictions the jury will be told of the existence of such presumptions, which may encourage the jury to make the presumptive inference.

In the intermediate cases, presumptions are rebuttable, but they operate to change the production burden or the risk of non-persuasion (burden of proof). Where only the production burden is changed, the party proving the basic fact (we will call this party, the *beneficiary* of the presumption, *B*) will be entitled to have the presumed fact taken as proved unless the *opposing* party (we will call this party *O*) introduces some information tending to disprove the presumed fact. If the basic fact is undisputed and *O* introduces no evidence controverting the presumed fact, *B* will be entitled to have the jury instructed that the presumed fact must be taken as proved. In these circumstances, if the presumed fact is dispositive of the case, *B* will be entitled to a directed verdict. If *O* introduces evidence disputing the basic fact, but not the presumed fact, *B* will be entitled to have the jury instructed that if they believe that the basic fact is as *B* contends, they must take the presumed fact to be established as well. If, however, *O* introduces evidence disputing the presumed fact, the jury will not be instructed in the matter. They will simply have to decide whether the strength of the inference from the basic to the presumed fact outweighs the strength of *O*'s evidence. If *B* had the burden of proving the presumed fact, that burden will remain with *B*, although in practice it may be somewhat eased in jurisdictions where the

jury is told of the existence of the presumption.

Presumptions that change the burden of proof are treated the same as presumptions that change only the production burden so long as the party opposing the presumption (*O*) does not introduce evidence disputing the presumed fact. However, if *O* attempts to controvert the presumed fact, the jurors will be instructed that they must find the presumed fact unless *O* convinces them by some appropriate standard that the presumed fact does not exist. Chart IX–1 should help you sort out the different types of presumptions. You may want to look at it now and refer back to it as you read the remainder of this section and the section on rebuttable presumptions.

A simple example may help clarify these different uses of the term presumption. In a suit for child support, Shirley claims that her ex-husband, Clem, is the father of a child born while she was separated from Clem but prior to their formal divorce. In suing for support, Shirley may benefit from a presumption that a child born to a married woman is the child of her husband. If the presumption is a conclusive presumption, Shirley has to show only that she was married to Clem at the time the child was born in order to prevail on the paternity issue. Clem would not be allowed to controvert paternity. For example, he could not introduce the results of a blood test proving he was not the father. Here what is called a presumption is really a law providing that a husband shall be treated as the father of any

presumption properly may be applied to this situation, since by a positive rule of law, an artificial effect is given to the establishment of the basic fact. Sometimes it may be hard to determine whether this effect and no more shall be given to the establishment of the basic fact in an action; but, where so determined, no serious difficulty in application is disclosed in the cases.

Morgan, Further Observations on Presumptions, 16 So.Cal.L.Rev. 245, 246 (1943). Note, however, as you read the material on criminal presumptions that the Supreme Court has made it less likely that any artificial effect will be recognized if it works to the disadvantage of criminal defendants.

Chart IX–1
Types of Presumptions

The beneficiary of the presumption (B) introduces evidence of the basic fact and the presumption:	The party opposing the presumption (O) introduces.	The consequences of the presumption are that the jurors will be instructed that:
1. Is conclusive.	No evidence bearing on the presumption.	If they find the basic fact, they must find the presumed fact. A directed verdict may be in order.
	Evidence tending to contradict the basic fact.**	If they find the basic fact, they must find the presumed fact.
	Evidence tending to contradict the presumed fact.	If they find the basic fact, they must find the presumed fact. A directed verdict may be in order.
2. Shifts the risk of nonpersuasion (burden of proof).	No evidence bearing on the presumption.	If they find the basic fact, they must find the presumed fact. A directed verdict may be in order.
	Evidence tending to contradict the basic fact.	If they find the basic fact, they must find the presumed fact.
	Evidence tending to contradict the presumed fact.	If they find the basic fact, they must find the presumed fact unless O convinces them by a preponderance of the evidence (or, in certain cases, by some higher standard) that the presumed fact does not exist.*
3. Shifts the production burden.	No evidence bearing on the presumption.	If they find the basic fact, they must find the presumed fact. A directed vedict may be in order.
	Evidence tending to contradict the basic fact.	If they find the basic fact, they must find the presumed fact.
	Evidence tending to contradict the presumed fact.	There will be no jury instruction relating the basic fact to the presumed fact.*
4. Is a permissible inference.	No evidence bearing on the presumption.	There will be no jury instruction relating the basic fact to the presumed fact.* If B has the burden of proving the presumed fact and offers no evidence tending to prove the presumed fact except that which tends to prove the basic fact, B will be able to avoid a directed verdict if the underlying inference is strong enough.
	Evidence tending to contradict the basic fact.	The same as if O introduces no evidence bearing on the presumption.*
	Evidence tending to contradict the presumed fact.	The same as if O introduces no evidence bearing on the presumption, except that if O's evidence contradicting the presumed fact is strong, B might not be able to avoid a directed verdict.*

* In some jurisdictions the jurors may be informed about the existence of the presumption.
** Whenever the evidence tending to contradict the basic fact is beyond dispute, the court will give a peremptory instruction and the presumption will not help B. This is true throughout the chart.

children born to his wife during their marriage regardless of actual paternity. The validity of the presumption depends upon whether holding a spouse responsible for the care of a child he has not fathered violates due process, not upon the reasonableness of implying paternity from the fact of marriage.

If the presumption is merely a standardized reference to a permissible inference, the presumption means that evidence of marriage has been held in previous cases to relate sufficiently to a husband's probable paternity to justify a jury verdict. Thus, a judge would not dismiss Shirley's case at the close of her case-in-chief on the ground that there was no evidence from which a reasonable jury could find paternity. Of course, if the inference is permissible, Shirley should avoid dismissal regardless of whether the judge calls the inference a presumption.

If the presumption shifts the production burden, Shirley would be entitled to a directed verdict on the issue of paternity if she introduces evidence proving marriage and Clem introduces no evidence controverting paternity. If Clem introduces evidence contesting Shirley's claim of marriage but not the paternity issue, the jury will be instructed that if they find Shirley and Clem were married at the time the baby was born, they must find that Clem was the father of the child.   If Clem introduces evidence contesting paternity, the jury will have to weigh Clem's evidence against the probability that children born to a married woman are fathered by the woman's husband.   The jury might or might not be told of the presumption, and the burden of proving paternity would still rest on Shirley.

If the presumption shifts the risk of non-persuasion, and if Clem introduces evidence contesting paternity, the jury will be told that if they find that the child was born to Shirley while she was still married to Clem, they must find that Clem is the father of the child unless convinced to the contrary by a preponderance of the evidence or, in some jurisdictions, by a higher standard such as clear and convincing evidence or proof beyond a reasonable doubt. Where a husband contests paternity, the presumption arising from the fact of mar-

riage is usually of this last type, and the husband must usually prove non-paternity by some higher standard than the mere preponderance of the evidence.

Except where presumptions are conclusive, the beneficiary of a presumption will not necessarily avoid a directed verdict at the close of *all* the evidence.   Thus, if Clem presents uncontested blood test evidence proving that he cannot be the father of Shirley's child, he might win a directed verdict in any jurisdiction where the presumption is not conclusive.   However, the stronger the presumption the less likely is a directed verdict against the beneficiary of the presumption.   Thus, if Clem presents uncontested evidence that he last saw Shirley eleven months before the birth of the child, he might win a directed verdict if the presumption is no more than a standardized reference to a permissible inference, but he will probably not win a directed verdict if the presumption operates to shift the burden of proof.

2.   REBUTTABLE PRESUMPTIONS

Most scholars agree that a true presumption is rebuttable and amounts to more than a permissible inference.   They disagree about whether true presumptions should only shift the production burden or whether they should shift the risk of non-persuasion as well.   The former position, that a presumption only shifts the production burden, is associated with James Thayer, the latter position with Edmund Morgan.   A middle position is possible. Presumptions are designed both to facilitate proof and to promote social policy, and the inferences they standardize may be weak or strong.   It may be that presumptions with certain characteristics should be of one type while those with different characteristics should be of the other.

Before we look further at rebuttable presumptions, you should have a better idea of the reasons behind their creation. Morgan offered seven reasons why courts

and legislatures create presumptions.   You will see that some reasons apply more to one type of presumption than they do to another and that some of the same factors that are important in the allocation of pleading and proof requirements are also important here:

* * *   (1) Some are designed to expedite the trial by relieving a party from introducing evidence upon issues which may not be litigated.   For example, why does a court which puts upon the prosecution the burden of proving a defendant's sanity beyond a reasonable doubt, at the same time give the prosecution the benefit of a presumption of sanity?   Simply to avoid the waste of time and effort required to take evidence on an issue which, aside from statute, is raised by the plea of not guilty but in most cases will not be raised by evidence.   The defendant must at least

show that the question raised by the pleadings is to be litigated in the evidence. (2) In some cases a presumption may be necessary to avoid a procedural impasse. Where a court has a fund to be distributed, and the determination of the rights of conflicting claimants depends upon the date of the death of X, it may be established that X disappeared more than seven years before action was brought; this raises a presumption of his death, but by the orthodox view raises no presumption as to the date of death. If he died soon after his disappearance, A will take. If he died between four and six years after his disappearance, B will take; if later, C will take. In the absence of evidence and of any presumption as to date of death, the court simply cannot decide the case. This has led some courts to raise a presumption of death on the last instant of the seventh year. (3) Some presumptions are based upon a preponderance of probability. Indeed, Mr. Justice Holmes once said that all true presumptions have such a foundation. To save time, it is well for the court to compel the trier of fact to assume the usual and to require the party relying upon the unusual to show that he has at least enough evidence to make its existence reasonably probable. (4) In some instances there will be the added element of difficulty in securing legally competent evidence in cases of the particular class. This is exemplified in the common law rule that a long continued exercise of what would be a right if properly originated raises a presumption of a legally created right. (5) Another group of presumptions owe their origin to the fact that one of the parties has peculiar means of access to the evidence or peculiar knowledge of the facts. For example, at common law, where freight is delivered in good order to an initial carrier and is delivered in bad order to the consignee by the terminal carrier, although it may have been transported over the lines of several connecting carriers, the presumption is that the damage was done by the terminal carrier. Here, there is no procedural convenience or preponderance of probability or general inaccessibility of evidence to call forth the presumption, but as between consignee and carrier, the last carrier has peculiar means of access to the facts. (6) Again, many presumptions express the result that the courts creating them deem socially desirable. This causes such courts to require the trier to assume the existence of that result in the absence of any showing to the contrary. The stock illustration has already been given, namely, that a right enjoyed by usage for a long period is presumed to have had a legal origin. That the judicial conviction of social desirability was the chief reason for this presumption is shown by its evolution from a mere inference through a presumption to a hard and fast rule of law which gives to adverse possession for the prescribed period the effect of creating a new title. (7) Finally, many, if not most, of the generally recognized presumptions are supported by two or more of the foregoing. The presumption that a child born in wedlock is the legitimate child of the husband, for instance, is supported by a heavy preponderance of probability, by the consideration of difficulty in producing legally competent evidence of the paternity of a child born to a married woman, and by considerations of policy predicated upon a society in which the their marriage and a birth during its extution by which the devolution of property is determined, and as to the intimate aspects of which accepted notions of decency and propriety demand a discreet secrecy.[20]

20. Presumptions, supra note 17, at 257–59. See also Morgan, Instructing the Jury upon Presumption and Burden of Proof, 47 Harv.L.Rev. 59 (1933).

Morgan explained the different approaches to rebuttable presumptions as follows:

(1) When evidence has been introduced which would support a finding of the non-existence of the presumed fact, the existence or non-existence of the presumed fact is to be determined exactly as if no presumption had ever been applicable or possible of application in the action. In other words, the sole effect of the establishment of the basic fact is to put upon the party asserting the non-existence of the presumed fact the risk of the non-introduction of evidence sufficient to support a finding that the presumed fact does not exist. If before the basic fact is established such evidence has been introduced, the establishment of the basic fact puts no compulsion upon the trier of fact; it is to be treated exactly as if the doctrine of presumptions had never been known. If such evidence does not come in until the basic fact has been established, but does then enter, the case thereafter proceeds as if no presumption had ever been heard of. It makes not the slightest difference whether the evidence tending to show non-existence of the presumed fact came from the party asserting such non-existence or from his opponent or from the judge. * * * [In the case of Shirley and Clem, once Shirley proves their marriage and a birth during its existence, Clem is forced to offer evidence disputing paternity. If he does not he loses. If he does the presumption disappears and the parties are left with the evidence as it bears on paternity.[21]]

(2) When "substantial evidence" has been introduced tending to prove the non-existence of the presumed fact, the existence or non-existence of the presumed fact is to be determined exactly as if no presumption had ever been applicable or possible of application in the action. When evidence which would support a finding of non-existence of the presumed fact, but which is not "substantial," has been introduced, the question of the existence or non-existence of the presumed fact is for the jury or other trier of fact, even though, without the operation of the presumption, the trier would be compelled to find the non-existence of the presumed fact. Just what constitutes "substantial evidence," as distinguished, on the one hand, from evidence which would support a finding and, on the other, from evidence which would compel a finding, is not discoverable from an examination of the cases. In the State of Washington, evidence from a disinterested witness has the effect given to substantial evidence in New York. In situations where the question is for the jury, it is problematical whether the jury is to be advised of the existence of the presumption or of its effect. [In the case of Shirley and Clem, the situation is the same as in No. 1 if Clem offers substantial evidence rebutting paternity. If Clem offers less than substantial evidence, Shirley's case will survive a directed verdict request even though it would not if Clem had offered more evidence.]

(3) When evidence has been introduced sufficient to support a finding of the non-existence of the presumed fact, the trier of fact is free to believe or disbelieve it, unless it is such that no reasonable trier could fail to believe it.

---

21. This theory is often referred to as the bursting bubble theory. The presumption bursts when sufficient contradictory evidence is introduced. Can a presumption of this sort achieve any of the goals that lead courts and legislatures to create presumptions? Can it achieve all of these goals?

Note that in each approach discussed by Morgan, the opponent of a presumption must, at a minimum, come forward with evidence. If not, the opponent loses. The differences among the approaches relate to what happens after rebuttal evidence is offered.

If the trier positively disbelieves this evidence, it has no effect and the presumption operates as if no such evidence had been introduced. If the trier believes this evidence, the existence or non-existence of the presumed fact is to be determined exactly as if no presumption had ever been applicable or capable of application in the action. The result of inability of the trier to decide whether to believe or to disbelieve the evidence is nowhere made clear. * * * [This approach] has comparatively little support. [In the case of Shirley and Clem, if the trier treats Clem's evidence as unbelievable, the presumption remains in effect and Clem loses. If the trier believes Clem's evidence, the presumption disappears. Under this approach the trier must learn about the presumption, since it may retain its effect.]

(4) When evidence has been introduced sufficient to support a finding of the non-existence of the presumed fact, the question of its existence or non-existence is for the trier of fact and the trier must find its existence unless convinced by the evidence that its non-existence is at least as probable as its existence. In other words, the establishment of the basic fact puts upon the party asserting the non-existence of the presumed fact not only the burden of producing the requisite evidence but also the risk of non-persuasion of the trier that the non-existence of the presumed fact is at least as probable as its existence. This is to say that the trier must begin with the assumption that the presumed fact exists and must continue to act upon that assumption until his mind is at least put in equilibrium on the question. This view is sometimes said to require the party asserting the non-existence of the presumed fact to balance but not overcome the presumption of its existence. A comparatively few cases support it. * * * [In the case of Shirley and Clem, after Clem offers evidence rebut-

ting the paternity claim, the trier must still find paternity unless Clem's evidence puts it in a position where it believes the odds are at least even that Clem is not the father. Clem does not bear the preponderance of the evidence burden of persuasion since he will win if the trier is in equilibrium.]

(5) When evidence has been introduced sufficient to support a finding of the non-existence of the presumed fact, the question of its existence or non-existence is for the trier of fact and the trier must find its existence unless convinced by the evidence that its non-existence is more probable than its existence. The establishment of the basic fact puts upon the party asserting the non-existence of the presumed fact not only the risk of non-production of the requisite evidence but also the risk of non-persuasion of the non-existence of the presumed fact. To use currently accepted phrases, the effect of the presumption is to fix both the burden of producing evidence and the burden of persuasion. Many jurisdictions have adopted this view with respect to certain specified presumptions. * * * [Once Shirley has proved the basic facts Clem must not only offer evidence disproving paternity, he must persuade the jury by a preponderance of the evidence that he is not the child's father. The jury learns of the presumption for they are told that if they find the basic fact the burden of proof on the paternity issue shifts to Clem.]

(6) The effect of the introduction of evidence sufficient to support a finding of the non-existence of the presumed fact depends upon the weight of the reasons which caused the creation or justify the persistence of the presumption. In some situations the first of the above described views will be adopted, in others, the fourth, and conceivably in still others, the third. Where, however, the reason for the presumption is that the

party relying upon the non-existence of the presumed fact has peculiar knowledge, or means of access to knowledge, of matters from which the existence or non-existence of the presumed fact may be inferred, he has both the burden of producing evidence to support his assertions as to those matters and the burden of persuasion that those assertions are more probably true than not. * * * [In the case of Shirley and Clem, the judge would have to decide why the presumption was created and would apply one of the aforementioned approaches as long as legislation or precedent did not specify the effect of a presumption.]

(7) When evidence has been introduced sufficient to support a finding of the non-existence of the presumed fact, the trier of fact need not assume the existence of the presumed fact, but the "presumption" is still to be treated "as evidence" of the existence of that fact. The presumption may not have any further effect—as most cases seem to indicate—or it may fix the burden of persuasion—as does, for example the presumption of legitimacy of a child born in wedlock—or it may conceivably require the party asserting the non-existence of the presumed fact to put the mind of the trier in equilibrium as explained in paragraph numbered (5) above.[22] [In the case of Shirley and Clem, the presumption is treated as if it were additional evidence even though Clem offers evidence rebutting the inference of paternity. The weight to be accorded the presumption will depend on the nature of the presumption.]

As a purely theoretical proposition, Morgan concluded that no one rule fits all presumptions and that the sixth option was the most defensible,[23] but as a practical matter he feared this approach would fail.

* * * Unfortunately, however, there are myriads of presumptions created by courts and legislatures. They can not be authoritatively classified by courts except as each one is involved in a litigated action. Wherever there is room for difference of opinion, no presumption can finally be assigned its proper place except by the appropriate court of last resort. To evolve a classification by judicial decision would require decades, if not centuries. To make a legislative classification of existing presumptions would involve immense labor and would still leave room for debate as to all subsequently created presumptions. Unless a trial judge were presented with a catalogue of classified presumptions, it would be fatuous to expect him to determine the reasons and objectives of a presumption suddenly thrust at him in the hurry of a trial, with a demand to classify it and accord it the appropriate effect. * * *[24]

Concluding that a single approach was needed, Morgan chose option five.

If a policy is strong enough to call a presumption into existence, it is hard to imagine it so weak as to be satisfied by the bare recital of words on the witness stand or the reception in evidence of a writing. And if the judicial desire for the result expressed in the presumption is buttressed by either the demands of procedural convenience or

---

22. Further Observations, supra note 19, at 247–49.

23. Id. at 250–51.

24. Id. at 254. The California Evidence Code, adopted in 1965, divides presumption into two classes: 1) those based upon public policy, which fix the burden of persuasion, and

2) those established "to implement no public policy other than to facilitate the determination of the particular action," which are given a bursting bubble or Thayerian effect. See Calif.Evid.Code § 600 et seq. (1965). A number of states have since taken a similar approach.

is in accord with the usual balance of probability, it is little short of ridiculous to allow so valuable a presumption to be destroyed by the introduction of evidence without actual persuasive effect. Indeed, the only purpose which the reception of such credible but discredited evidence can ever accomplish is to demonstrate that in the particular case the proposition that the presumed fact exists is legally disputable, and the only situation in which such a purpose can furnish a justification for creating a presumption is one where the presumption expresses a balance of probability not potent enough to overcome the burden which must normally be borne by the litigant seeking to overcome the inertia of the court.

The presumptions which have the function of authorizing a jury to draw an inference which ordinary judicial experience would deem unjustifiable may owe their creation to a realization that the generalizations which judicial experience would ordinarily condemn have been demonstrated to be warrantable in the pertinent repetitive situations, or to a conviction that the judgment likely to be exercised by a jury in such situations will produce a result which the court deems socially desirable. If the for-

mer, the court is merely proclaiming that from the basic fact A any trier may reasonably deduce the presumed fact B; if the latter, it is giving an artificial effect to an item of evidence in order that a desirable result may be reached. Insofar as A is logically potent to produce the inference B, its power should not be destroyed except by evidence which persuades the jury that the inference should not be drawn. Insofar as A is given artificial power to produce that effect for the purpose of attaining a socially desirable objective, its power ought to persist until evidence is produced which has an appreciable influence upon the mind of the trier.[25]

The Congress of the United States was unpersuaded. It rejected the Morgan approach, which had been approved by the Supreme Court, and enacted FRE 301:

> In all civil actions and proceedings not otherwise provided for by Act of Congress or by these rules, a presumption imposes on the party against whom it is directed the burden of going forward with evidence to rebut or meet the presumption, but does not shift to such party the burden of proof in the sense of the risk of nonpersuasion, which remains throughout the trial upon the party on whom it was originally cast.

Problem IX–8. During the course of hearings and debates on the federal rules, the House Subcommittee on Criminal Justice proposed the following rule:

> In all civil actions and proceedings not otherwise provided for by Act of Congress or by these rules a presumption imposes on the party against whom it is directed the burden of going forward with the evidence, and, even though met with contradicting evidence, a presumption is sufficient proof of the fact presumed to be considered by the trier of the facts.

---

25. Instructing the Jury, supra note 20, at 82–83. McCormick supported this approach. McCormick § 345, at 819 et seq.

The Subcommittee explained:

> With respect to the weight to be given a presumption in a civil case, the Subcommittee agreed with the conclusion reflected in the Court's version that the so-called "bursting bubble" theory of presumptions, whereby a presumption vanishes upon the appearance of any contradicting evidence by the other party, gives to presumptions too slight an effect. On the other hand, the Subcommittee believed that the rule proposed by the Court, whereby a presumption permanently alters the burden of persuasion, no matter how much contradicting evidence is introduced—a view adopted by only a few courts—lent too great a force to presumptions. The Subcommittee accordingly adopted an intermediate position under which a presumption does not vanish upon the introduction of contradicting evidence, and does not change the burden of persuasion; instead it is merely deemed sufficient evidence of the fact presumed to be considered by the jury or other finder of fact.

How does this rule differ from that actually enacted? Which rule do you prefer? Do you prefer a rule that shifts the risk of non-persuasion to either the above rule or the rule actually enacted? [26]   When thinking about this, consider the presumption that a letter that is mailed is received.   Assume that a plaintiff proves that a letter was mailed but the defendant testifies it was not received.   **Is the fact that the letter was mailed sufficient to take the plaintiff's case to the jury?   Under FRE 301?   Under the Subcommittee's rule?**

Problem IX-9.   Under the Morgan theory, what happens when a presumption operates against the party having the burden of proof?   Does the existence of a presumption convert a preponderance standard into something stiffer?   Consider the following facts:

Minnie Breeden was declared ineligible for Social Security disability benefits because the Social Security Administration credited her for only 18 quarters of covered employment in the ten years preceding her disability. Twenty quarters are required for coverage under 42 U.S.C. § 423(c)(1)(B) (1970).

Breeden filed an application for disability benefits in 1969.   Upon discovering that her Social Security wage records showed a deficit in covered quarters, she attempted to prove that she had earned wages between 1957 and 1963 in addition to those that appeared on her record.   Several of her employers had since gone out of business;   others had discarded records that would prove or disprove Breeden's claims.   Consequently, her supporting evidence was limited to affidavits and testimony of people who had known her during the period in question.   Most of her witnesses were relatives, some were friends, others were co-workers and acquaintances, and one was the wife of a former employer.   The testimony of any of them, if accepted, would have established coverage for more than the two quarters that Breeden lacked.   But the administrative law judge rejected all the testimony,

---

26. See generally Cal.Evid.Code § 600 (1966); Morgan, Instructing the Jury, supra note 20, at 73; Rothstein, Evidence: Trends, Developments, N.Y.L.J., June 16, 1974, at 4, col. 1.

including Breeden's own account of her work history.　He indicated distrust for the testimony of "friends and kinfolk," he faulted the witnesses for not producing written records, and he found most of their testimony inexact. He also insisted that Breeden prove her case "clearly and convincingly."

The Social Security Act creates a scale of evidentiary weight for the wage records held by the Social Security Administration.　It provides that entries in the records shall serve as evidence of the amounts of wages paid and that the absence of entries shall constitute evidence that no wages were paid. The records are open to revision for a period of three years, three months, and 15 days.　After that period expires, an entry acquires conclusive weight, but the absence of an entry merely stands as "presumptive evidence" that no wages were paid.　Consequently, a claimant cannot dispute the accuracy of a wage entry after the time limit has expired, but is allowed to prove that a blank wage record is incorrect.　**Should the existence of this presumption increase the burden by which Breeden must prove her claim from a preponderance of the evidence standard to a standard of clear and convincing evidence?**

Problem IX–10.　In Keyes v. School District No. 1, Denver, Colo.,[27] there was a difference between a majority of the court and Mr. Justice Powell.　The federal district court held that there was *de jure* segregation in one section of the Denver schools, but found that the segregation in that section had no impact on other sections of the city.

Justice Brennan's opinion for the court held that the lower courts had erred in the way they approached the integration issue.　Brennan wrote:

> [W]here, as here, the case involves one school board, a finding of intentional segregation on its part in one portion of a school system is highly relevant to the issue of the board's intent with respect to other segregated schools in the system.　This is merely an application of the well-settled evidentiary principle that "the prior doing of other similar acts, whether clearly a part of a scheme or not, is useful as reducing the possibility that the act in question was done with innocent intent." 2 J. Wigmore, Evidence 200 (3d ed. 1940). * * *

> Applying these principles in the special context of school desegregation cases, we hold that a finding of intentionally segregative school board actions in a meaningful portion of a school system, as in this case, creates a presumption that other segregated schooling within the system is not adventitious.　It establishes, in other words, a prima facie case of unlawful segregative design on the part of school authorities, and shifts to those authorities the burden of proving that other segregated schools within the system are not also the result of intentionally segregative actions.　This is true even if it is determined that different areas of the school district should be viewed independently of each other because, even in that situation, there is high probability that where school authorities have effectuated an intentionally segregative policy in a meaningful portion of the school system, similar impermissible considerations have motivated their actions in other areas of the system. * * *

27.　413 U.S. 189 (1973).

This burden-shifting principle is not new or novel. There are no hard-and-fast standards governing the allocation of the burden of proof in every situation. The issue, rather, "is merely a question of policy and fairness based on experience in the different situations." 9 J. Wigmore, Evidence § 2486 at 275, (3d ed. 1940). In the context of racial segregation in public education, the courts, including this Court, have recognized a variety of situations in which "fairness" and "policy" require state authorities to bear the burden of explaining actions or conditions which appear to be racially motivated.   *   *   *

Can you see why creation of the presumption goes considerably further than merely holding that evidence of similar acts may be useful in proving a common scheme or in establishing intent?

Justice Powell wrote:

*   *   * I would not   *   *   * perpetuate the de jure/de facto distinction nor would I leave to petitioners the initial tortuous effort of identifying "segregative acts" and deducing "segregatory intent." I would hold, quite simply, that where segregated public schools exist within a school district to a substantial degree, there is a prima facie case that the duly constituted public authorities   *   *   * are sufficiently responsible to warrant imposing upon them a nationally applicable burden to demonstrate they nevertheless are operating a genuinely integrated school system.

*   *   *

*   *   * An integrated school system does not mean—and indeed could not mean in view of the residential patterns of most of our major metropolitan areas—that every school must in fact be an integrated unit. A school which happens to be all or predominantly white or all or predominantly black is not a "segregated" school in an unconstitutional sense if the system itself is a genuinely integrated one.

*   *   *

Justices Brennan and Powell both would shift the burden of proof in cases like this. **How do their approaches differ? Is it true, as Justice Powell says, that under his test legislative intent is no longer relevant? If you were counsel for the NAACP Legal Defense Fund, litigating desegregation cases throughout the country, which approach would you favor?** In answering this question, consider whether potential plaintiffs give up possible remedies to obtain what may be an extremely attractive presumption.

Problem IX–11. McCormick poses the following hypothetical case:

A conflict between presumptions may arise as follows: W, asserting that she is the widow of H, claims her share of his property, and proves that on a certain day she and H were married. The adversary then proves that three or four years before her marriage to H, the alleged widow married another man. W's proof gives her the benefit of the presumption of the validity of a marriage. The adversary's proof gives rise to the general presumption of the continuance of a status or condition once proved to exist, and a specific presumption of the continuance of a marriage relationship. The presumed facts of the claimant's presumption and those of the adversary's are contradictory.[28]

How should the conflict be resolved? How would it be resolved under the Federal Rules? Under the Morgan view?

Problem IX–12. A problem closely related to the previous one is raised by FRE 302:

> In civil actions and proceedings, the effect of a presumption respecting a fact which is an element of a claim or defense as to which State law supplies the rule of decision is determined in accordance with State law.

Assume that under the doctrine of pendent jurisdiction, common law fraud counts are joined with federal securities claims in a federal court action for damages arising out of the sale of shares of stock by a corporation. Plaintiff claims that the directors of the corporation failed to disclose important information about the company's financial condition. But plaintiff can prove the financial condition of the company only during a period of several months before the sale of the stock and not at the exact time of the sale. **If under both state and federal law there is a presumption that a state of affairs shown to be continuous over a period of time continues beyond that period, and if state law adopts the Morgan view of presumptions, how should a federal judge instruct the jury with respect to this presumption?**

Problem IX–13. Your client, the owner of a small business, is being sued in a tort action. The plaintiff, who has brought the action in a Maryland state court, seeks $9,500 in damages. Liability turns in part on whether your client received notice of a defect in the product that she sold the plaintiff. The plaintiff has testified that he mailed a letter to your client's place of business describing the defect in the product. Having so testified, the plaintiff is the beneficiary of a presumption that a letter that is placed in the mailbox arrives at its intended destination. You have available three witnesses whose testimony might help you on this issue. One is plaintiff's ex-wife who, because of the bitter divorce they have been through, has only slight credibility. She will testify that plaintiff never mailed the letter in question. The second is defendant's long-time secretary who, because of her great loyalty to defendant, has only moderate credibility. She will testify that she opens all defendant's mail and that she never opened a letter from the plaintiff. The third, the country's leading expert on the U.S. Postal Service, has no prior involvement with the parties. She will testify that the postal service has deteriorated to the point where it is common for mail, particularly mail sent long distances, never to arrive at its destination. All three witnesses live in San Francisco. Because of the amount at stake the defendant can afford to fly only one witness for the trial. **Who should the defendant choose if the presumption is: (A) a permissive inference; (B) one which shifts the production burden; (C) one which shifts the risk of non-persuasion; (D) conclusive?**

---

28. McCormick § 345, at 823.

Problem IX–14. Richard Riley brings an action in state court against Manyunk Law School to have his transcript corrected to reflect an A in Evidence, not the C that the record now reads. Riley claims that Harvey Wallis, his professor, actually awarded him the higher grade and that the record is erroneous. Wallis is now deceased. The state court has long recognized a common law presumption that records of public agencies, including schools like Manyunk, are presumed to be maintained in a regular, accurate form. Manyunk relies upon this presumption when it calls its records custodian to testify that C is the grade that was recorded in the ordinary course of Manyunk's record-keeping. **Which of the following pieces of evidence would be sufficient to rebut the presumption under a rule similar to FRE 301: a properly authenticated letter from Wallis to Riley congratulating him on his high grade; a witness who heard Wallis tell another professor that Riley had surprised him on the exam; a witness who heard Wallis tell another professor that Riley had done surprisingly well on the exam; proof that Wallis wrote a letter of recommendation for Riley after filing his evidence grades; testimony that the records custodian had been involved with Riley in frequent arguments concerning the way the school's records were kept and that the custodian had been heard to say that she did not like Riley; testimony by another employee of the records office that in the past some errors had been made and corrected on transcripts?**

Problem IX–15. Phillip South was married for 21 years before his wife Mary in 1980 told him she would file for divorce. Phillip was shocked, but did not contest the divorce since Mary left him with their two children, Amy (16) and Daniel (17). Mary left the house and at some point in 1981 she informed Phillip that she had finalized a divorce decree. Phillip married Sheri in 1982, the same year in which they had their first child, Nancy. During a vacation trip to Mexico, Phillip and Sheri were killed in an automobile crash. The children were at home with relatives at the time. Neither parent had left a will. Thus, under state law, each legitimate child would take equally from Phillip. Amy and Daniel claim, however, that the second marriage was invalid and that Nancy is not Phillip's legitimate child. In the probate proceeding, Nancy's guardian offers a marriage certificate containing the names of Phillip and Sheri. The guardian also claims the benefit of a presumption that a marriage duly performed is valid. In response, Amy and Daniel offer evidence of the certificate evidencing the marriage of Phillip to his first wife and rely on the presumption that a marriage once in effect continues in effect. **If both sides rest at this point, who should prevail?** Assume that Nancy's guardian presents as a witness, Sheri's best friend who testifies that Sheri told her that Phillip had just been divorced. **Now who wins?** Now assume that in response to the marriage certificate offered by Nancy's guardian, a friend of Phillip's is called to testify that he saw a certificate granting a divorce to Phillip and his first wife. **Does this mean that Nancy will prevail?**

---

3. CONCLUSIVE PRESUMPTIONS

Conclusive presumptions are really substantive legal rules. Even in the civil area they may be struck down if they conflict with the due process or equal protection clauses. Consider Vlandis v. Kline.[29] In Connecticut, the tuition for nonresidents enrolled in state universities was higher than the tuition charged residents of Connecticut. The Connecticut legislature enacted two irrebuttable presumptions: that married students were not residents if at the time they applied for admission to a state college or university their legal address was outside the state, and that single students were not residents if they had a legal address outside the state at some time during the year preceding their admission. Once classified as nonresidents, students could not be reclassified while they remained enrolled. This presumption was challenged by two women claiming to be Connecticut residents. They argued for the right to controvert the presumption by showing that they were in fact residents. The Court held that when a "presumption is not necessarily or universally true in fact, and when the state has reasonable alternative means of making the crucial determination,"[30] an individual must be afforded an opportunity to rebut the presumption. Would the Court have struck down a law which did not mention residency but provided that married students with Connecticut addresses at the time they applied for admission and single students with legal addresses within Connecticut during the entire year preceding their application for admission would pay less tuition than students who did not meet these qualifications? Phrasing the question this way

should alert you to the fact that most legislation rests in part on certain implicit presumptions. Given this, does Vlandis mean that the ordinary rational basis test for measuring legislation challenged under the equal protection clause is not constitutionally sufficient?

Consider a problem posed by Chief Justice Burger, dissenting in Vlandis:

[A] State provides that a person may not be licensed to practice medicine or law unless he or she is a graduate of an accredited professional graduate school; a perfectly capable practitioner may as a consequence be barred "permanently and irrebuttably" from pursuing his calling, without ever having an opportunity to prove his personal skills.[31]

Is the state provision valid? Consider a jurisdiction where failing to stop at a stop sign is negligence *per se*. May a defendant who has hit a pedestrian after running a stop sign successfully argue that it is unconstitutional to instruct the jury that they must find him negligent if they find that he would not have hit the plaintiff had he not run a stop sign? It seems obvious that the court was not reformulating the entire law of equal protection and presumptions in Vlandis. What was it doing?[32]

A more recent case suggests that Vlandis may represent a high water mark beyond which the courts will not go in overturning conclusive presumptions. In Wein-

29. 412 U.S. 441 (1973).

30. Id. at 452.

31. Id. at 462.

32. See also Jimenez v. Weinberger, 417 U.S. 628 (1974) (invalidating a provision in the Social Security Act denying benefits to some, but not all, illegitimate children born after the parent's disability); United States Department of Agriculture v. Murray, 413 U.S. 508 (1973) (invalidating a statute denying food stamps to persons living in certain households with members eighteen years old or older claimed as dependents on tax return of persons living outside the household); Cleveland Bd. of Educ. v. LaFleur, 414 U.S. 632 (1974) (invalidating a school board re-

quirement of mandatory maternity leave without pay); Stanley v. Illinois, 405 U.S. 645 (1972) (voiding a statutory irrebuttable presumption that unmarried fathers are unqualified to raise their children); Bell v. Burson, 402 U.S. 535 (1971) (invalidating a state procedure that assumed fault from the mere fact of an accident and mandated license suspensions when uninsured motorists were unable to post bond); Carrington v. Rash, 380 U.S. 89 (1965) (voiding a state constitutional provision that any member of the armed forces who entered the service while a resident of a state other than Texas, and who moved to Texas while in the service, could not satisfy the residency requirement for voting in Texas elections).

berger v. Salfi[33] a widow who had been married less than six months sought social security survivors' benefits for herself and her daughter by a previous marriage. The Social Security Administration (SSA) denied the applications for benefits because the Social Security Act defines "widow" and "child" so as to deny benefits to widows and stepchildren whose formal relationship with the deceased commenced less than nine months before his death. Congress' intent in enacting these definitions was apparently to thwart individuals from contracting sham marriages with fatally diseased wage earners in order to collect survivors' benefits. A three-judge federal court found that the definitions in the Act incorporated constitutionally invalid "irrebuttable presumptions," because not all marriages contracted within nine months of the death of a wage earner were entered into for the purpose of securing social security benefits. The Supreme Court reversed and upheld the challenged provisions. Justice Rehnquist wrote for the majority:

The District Court relied on congressional history for the proposition that the duration-of-relationship requirement was intended to prevent the use of sham marriages to secure Social Security payments. As such, concluded the court, "the requirement constitutes a presumption that marriages like Mrs. Salfi's, which did not precede the wage earner's death by at least nine months, were entered into for the purpose of securing Social Security benefits." The presumption was moreover, conclusive, because applicants were not afforded an opportunity to disprove the presence of the illicit purpose. The court held that under our decisions in Cleveland Board of Education v. LaFleur, 414 U.S. 632, 94 S.Ct. 791, 39 L.Ed.2d 52 (1974), Vlandis v. Kline, 412 U.S. 441, 93 S.Ct. 2230, 37 L.Ed.2d 63 (1973), and Stanley v. Illinois,

405 U.S. 645, 92 S.Ct. 1208, 31 L.Ed.2d 551 (1972), the requirement was unconstitutional, because it presumed a fact which was not necessarily or universally true.

Our ultimate conclusion is that the District Court was wrong in holding the duration-of-relationship requirement unconstitutional. Because we are aware that our various holdings in related cases do not all sound precisely the same note, we will explain ourselves at some length.

* * *

* * * "A statutory classification in the area of social welfare is consistent with the Equal Protection Clause of the Fourteenth Amendment if it is 'rationally based and free from invidious discrimination.' Dandridge v. Williams, 397 U.S. 471, 487. While the present case, involving as it does a federal statute, does not directly implicate the Fourteenth Amendment's Equal Protection Clause, a classification that meets the test articulated in *Dandridge* is perforce consistent with the due process requirement of the Fifth Amendment." Richardson v. Belcher, 404 U.S. 78, 81.

* * *

Stanley v. Illinois held that it was a denial of the equal protection guaranteed by the Fourteenth Amendment for a State to deny a hearing on parental fitness to an unwed father when such a hearing was granted to all other parents whose custody of their children was challenged. This Court referred to the fact that the "rights to conceive and to raise one's children have been deemed 'essential.' * * * "

In Vlandis v. Kline, a statutory definition of "residents" for purposes of fixing tuition to be paid by students in

33.   422 U.S. 749 (1975).

a state university system was held invalid. The Court held that where Connecticut purported to be concerned with residency, it might not at the same time deny to one seeking to meet its test of residency the opportunity to show factors clearly bearing on that issue.

In *LaFleur* the Court held invalid, on the authority of *Stanley* and *Vlandis*, school board regulations requiring pregnant school teachers to take unpaid maternity leave commencing five months before the expected birth. The Court stated its long-standing recognition "that freedom of personal choice in matters of marriage and family life is one of the liberties protected by the Due Process Clause of the Fourteenth Amendment," and that "overly restrictive maternity leave regulations can constitute a heavy burden on the exercise of these protected freedoms."

We hold that these cases are not controlling on the issue before us now. Unlike the claims involved in *Stanley* and *LaFleur*, a noncontractual claim to receive funds from the public treasury enjoys no constitutionally protected status * * *. We think that the District Court's extension of the holdings of *Stanley*, *Vlandis* and *LaFleur* to the eligibility requirement in issue here would turn the doctrine of those cases into a virtual engine of destruction for countless legislative judgments which have heretofore been thought wholly consistent with the Fifth and Fourteenth Amendments to the Constitution. For example, the very section of Title 42 which authorizes an action such as this, § 405(g), requires that a claim be filed within 60 days after administrative remedies are exhausted. It is indisputable that this requirement places people who file their claims more than 60 days after exhaustion in a different "class" than people who file their claims within the time limit. If we were to follow the

District Court's analysis, we would first try to ascertain the congressional "purpose" behind the provision, and probably would conclude that it was to prevent stale claims from being asserted in court. We would then turn to the question of whether such a flat cutoff provision was necessary to protect the Secretary from stale claims, whether it would be possible to make individualized determinations as to any prejudice suffered by the Secretary as the result of an untimely filing, and whether or not an individualized hearing on that issue should be required in each case. This would represent a degree of judicial involvement in the legislative function which we have eschewed except in the most unusual circumstances, and which is quite unlike the judicial role mandated by *Dandridge, Belcher* and Flemming v. Nestor, as well as by a host of cases arising from legislative efforts to regulate private business enterprises.

*   *   *

While it is possible to debate the wisdom of excluding legitimate claimants in order to discourage sham relationships, and of relying on a rule which may not exclude some obviously sham arrangements, we think it clear that Congress could rationally choose to adopt such a course. Large numbers of people are eligible for these programs and are potentially subject to inquiry as to the validity of their relationships to wage earners. These people include not only the classes which appellees represent, but also claimants in other programs for which the Social Security Act imposes duration-of-relationship requirements. Not only does the prophylactic approach thus obviate the necessity for large numbers of individualized determinations, but it also protects large numbers of claimants who satisfy the rule from the uncertainties and delays of administrative inquiry into the circumstances of their marriages. Nor is it at all clear that individual determinations could effectively filter out sham arrangements, since neither marital intent, life expectancy nor knowledge of terminal illness has been shown by appellees to be reliably determinable. Finally, the very possibility of prevailing at a hearing could reasonably be expected to encourage sham relationships.

The administrative difficulties of individual eligibility determinations are without doubt matters which Congress may consider when determining whether to rely on rules which sweep more broadly than the evils with which they seek to deal. In this sense, the duration-of-relationship requirement represents not merely a substantive policy determination that benefits should be awarded only on the basis of genuine marital relationships, but also a substantive policy determination that limited resources would not be well spent in making individual determinations. It is an expression of Congress' policy choice that the Social Security system, and its millions of beneficiaries, would be best served by a prophylactic rule which bars claims arising from the bulk of sham marriages which are actually entered, which discourages such marriages from ever taking place, and which is also objective and easily administered.

* * *

Are you satisfied with the Court's attempt to distinguish *Salfi* from *Vlandis* and related cases? Assume the Court had written in *Vlandis*: "The administrative difficulties of individual residency determinations are without doubt matters which a state may consider when determining whether to rely on rules which sweep more broadly than the evils with which they deal. In this sense the legal address requirement represents not merely a substantive policy determination that benefits should be awarded only on a basis of genuine residency, but also a substantive policy determination that limited resources would not be well spent in making individual determinations." Is this argument less applicable to the college residency situation than to the situation of Mrs. Salfi?

Weinberger was followed by Elkins v. Moreno.[34] This case involved the question of whether *Vlandis* prevented the University of Maryland from rejecting the in-state tuition applications of certain students because they were G–4 aliens (i.e., their parents were officers or employees of international organizations.) The Supreme Court, treating an issue of state law as potentially controlling, avoided the constitutional question and declined the invitation to decide whether *Salfi* had overruled *Vlandis*. Nevertheless, the Court's approach to *Elkins* suggests that it will use due process and equal protection analyses to test the validity of presumptive provisions in statutes and regulations, not a special conclusive presumption approach.

Problem IX–16. In Western & Atlantic R.R. v. Henderson,[35] the Supreme Court held the following Georgia statute unconstitutional:

34. 435 U.S. 647 (1978). See also Usery v. Turner Elkhorn Mining Co., 428 U.S. 1 (1976). See generally Note, The Conclusive Presumption Doctrine: Equal Process or Due Process? 72 Mich.L.Rev. 800 (1974). The recent cases suggest that the conclusive presumption reasoning might no longer be used in cases like *Vlandis*. However, the court remains concerned about discrimination against "new" residents of a state. See Zo-

bel v. Williams, 102 S.Ct. 2309 (1982) (holding unconstitutional an Alaska dividend scheme that paid residents according to their length of residency). Elkins v. Moreno returned to the Supreme Court in 1982 and was decided in favor of the alien students, *sub nom* Toll v. Moreno, on Supremacy Clause grounds, 102 S.Ct. 2977 (1982).

35. 279 U.S. 639 (1929).

A railroad company shall be liable for any damages done to persons, stock, or other property by the running of the locomotives, or cars, or other machinery of such company, or for damage done by any person in the employment and service of such company, unless the company shall make it appear that their agents have exercised all ordinary and reasonable care and diligence, the presumption in all cases being against the company.

Western & Atlantic arose when a woman sued for damages resulting from the death of her husband. After she had proved that death resulted from the operation of railroad equipment, the trial judge instructed the jury that in order to win the case the railroad had to overcome, by showing that its employees exercised ordinary care and diligence, a presumption of negligence arising from the fact of the accident.

The Supreme Court said:

Legislation declaring that proof of one fact or group of facts shall constitute prima facie evidence of an ultimate fact in issue is valid if there is a rational connection between what is proved and what is to be inferred. A prima facie presumption casts upon the person against whom it is applied the duty of going forward with his evidence on the particular point to which the presumption relates. A statute creating a presumption that is arbitary or that operates to deny a fair opportunity to repel it violates the due process clause of the Fourteenth Amendment. Legislative fiat may not take the place of fact in the judicial determination of issues involving life, liberty or property.

The mere fact of collision between a railway train and a vehicle at a highway grade crossing furnishes no basis for any inference as to whether the accident was caused by negligence of the railway company or of the traveler on the highway or of both or without fault of anyone. Reasoning does not lead from the occurrence back to its cause. And the presumption was used to support conflicting allegations of negligence. Plaintiff claimed that the engineer failed to keep a lookout ahead, that he did not stop the train after he saw the truck on the crossing, and that his eyesight was so bad that he could not see the truck in time to stop the train.

Appellee relies principally upon Mobile, J. & K. C. R. R. v. Turnipseed, 219 U.S. 35. That was an action in a court of Mississippi to recover damages for the death of a section foreman accidentally killed in that State. While engaged about his work he stood by the track to let a train pass; a derailment occurred and a car fell upon him. A statute of the State provided: " * * * Proof of injury inflicted by the running of the locomotives or cars of such [railroad] company shall be prima facie evidence of the want of reasonable skill and care on the part of the servants of the company in reference to such injury." That provision was assailed as arbitrary and in violation of the due process clause of the Fourteenth Amendment. This court held it valid and said "The only legal effect of this inference is to cast upon the railroad company the duty of producing some evidence to the contrary. When that is done, the inference is at an end, and the question of negligence is one for the jury upon all of the evidence. * * * The statute does not * * * fail in due process of law, because it creates a presumption of liability, since its operation is only to supply an inference of liability in the absence of other evidence contradicting such inference." That case is essentially different from this one. Each of the state enactments raises a presumption from the fact of injury caused by the running of locomotives or cars. The Mississippi statute created merely a temporary inference of fact that vanished upon the introduction of opposing evidence. That of Georgia as construed in this case creates an inference that is given [the] effect of evidence to be weighed against opposing testimony and is to prevail unless such testimony is found by the jury to preponderate.

Does Western & Atlantic present the problem of a rebuttable or an irrebuttable presumption? Did the Court recognize the character of the Georgia presumption? Would the Georgia statute be upheld today?

---

4. PRESUMPTIONS IN CRIMINAL CASES

In criminal cases constitutional problems arise only when presumptions aid the government. Presumptions that work against the government threaten no rights protected by the Bill of Rights or the fourteenth amendment.

It is easy to see why the government seek the establishment of presumptions in criminal cases. The government is benefitted because the jury may assume a second fact is true once a first fact has been shown. Moreover, since the accused has the right to refuse to take the stand to testify, the government may need to rely on a presumption to establish facts that in a civil action might be proved by calling the defendant. Most importantly, the behavior of judges often adds to the utility of presumptions in criminal cases. Whether or not the defense offers evidence contradicting the presumed fact, the trial judge, even in a traditional Thayer jurisdiction

(where rebuttal evidence "bursts the bubble"), is likely to mention the presumption to the jury at the close of the case, almost certainly suggesting that in his view the presumed fact is likely to follow from the basic fact. This may be especially important in jurisdictions where the judge cannot comment on the weight of the evidence and in some small way may ameliorate the disadvantage that the prosecution suffers by never being entitled to a directed verdict.

Thus, an available presumption may lighten the prosecution's effective burden of proof no matter what the defendant does. It is for this reason that the Supreme Court has carefully scrutinized presumptions directed against criminal defendants. Many of the Court's precedents are summarized in the following case which sets forth the Court's test for the criminal presumptions.

BARNES v. UNITED STATES

Supreme Court of the United States, 1973.
412 U.S. 837, 93 S.Ct. 2357, 37 L.Ed.2d 380.

Mr. Justice POWELL delivered the opinion of the Court.

Petitioner Barnes was convicted in United States District Court on two counts of possessing United States Treasury checks stolen from the mails, knowing them to be stolen, two counts of forging the checks and two counts of uttering the checks, knowing the endorsements to be forged. The trial court instructed the jury that ordinarily it would be justified in inferring from unexplained possession of recently stolen mail that the defendant possessed the mail with knowledge that it was stolen. * * *

The evidence at petitioner's trial established that on June 2, 1971, he opened a checking account using the pseudonym "Clarence Smith." On July 1, and July 3, 1971, the United States Disbursing Office at San Francisco mailed four Government checks in the amounts of $269.02, $154.70, $184, and $268.80 to Nettie Lewis, Albert Young, Arthur Salazar, and Mary Hernandez, respectively. On July 8, 1971, petitioner deposited these four checks into the "Smith" account. Each check bore the apparent endorsement of the payee and a second endorsement by "Clarence Smith."

At petitioner's trial the four payees testified that they had never received, endorsed, or authorized endorsement of the checks. A Government handwriting expert testified that petitioner had made the "Clarence Smith" endorsement on all four checks and that he had signed the payees' names on the Lewis and Hernandez checks. Although petitioner did not take the stand, a postal inspector testified to certain statements made by petitioner at a post-arrest interview. Petitioner explained to the inspector that he received the checks in question from people who sold furniture for him door to door and that the checks had been signed in the payees' names when he received them. Petitioner further stated that he could not name or identify any of the salespeople. Nor could he substantiate the existence of any furniture orders because the salespeople allegedly wrote their orders on scratch paper that had not been retained. Petitioner admitted that he executed the Clarence Smith endorsements and deposited the checks but denied making the payees' endorsements.

The District Court instructed the jury that "[p]ossession of recently stolen property, if not satisfactorily explained, is ordinarily a circumstance from which you may reasonably draw the inference and find, in the light of the surrounding circumstances shown by the evidence in the case, that the person in possession knew the property had been stolen." [a]

a. The full instruction on the inference arising from possession of stolen property stated:

"Possession of recently stolen property, if not satisfactorily explained, is ordinarily a circumstance from which you may reasonably draw the inference and find, in the light of the surrounding circumstances shown by the evidence in the case, that the person in possession knew the property had been stolen.

"However, you are never required to make this inference. It is the exclusive province of the jury to determine whether the facts and circumstances shown by the evidence in this case warrant any inference which the law permits the jury to draw from the possession of recently stolen property.

"The term 'recently' is a relative term, and has no fixed meaning. Whether property may be considered as recently stolen depends upon the nature of the property, and all the facts and circumstances shown by the evidence in the case. The longer the period of time since the theft the more doubtful becomes the inference which may reasonably be drawn from unexplained possession.

"If you should find beyond a reasonable doubt from the evidence in the case that the mail described in the indictment was stolen, and that while recently stolen the contents of said mail here, the four United States Treasury checks, were in the possession of the defendant you would ordinarily be justified in drawing from those facts the inference that the contents were

The jury brought in guilty verdicts on all six counts, and the District Court sentenced petitioner to concurrent three-year prison terms. The Court of Appeals for the Ninth Circuit affirmed, finding no lack of "rational connection" between unexplained possession of recently stolen property and knowledge that the property was stolen. 466 F.2d 1361 (1972). Because petitioner received identical concurrent sentences on all six counts, the court declined to consider his challenges to conviction on the forgery and uttering counts. We affirm.

I

We begin our consideration of the challenged jury instruction with a review of four recent decisions which have considered the validity under the Due Process Clause of criminal law presumptions and inferences. Turner v. United States, 396 U.S. 398 (1970); Leary v. United States, 395 U.S. 6 (1969); United States v. Romano, 382 U.S. 136 (1965); United States v. Gainey, 380 U.S. 63 (1965).

In United States v. Gainey, the Court sustained the constitutionality of an instruction tracking a statute which authorized the jury to infer from defendant's unexplained presence at an illegal still that he was carrying on "the business of a distiller or rectifier without having given bond as required by law." Relying on the holding of Tot v. United States, 319 U.S. 463, 467 (1943), that there must be a "rational connection between the fact proved and the ultimate fact presumed," the Court upheld the inference on the basis of the comprehensive nature of the "carrying on" offense and the common knowledge that illegal stills are secluded, secret operations. The following Term the Court determined, however, that presence at an illegal still could not support the inference that the defendant was in possession, custody, or control of the still, a narrower offense. "Presence is relevant and admissible evidence in a trial on a possession charge; but absent some showing of the defendant's function at the still, its connection with possession is too tenuous to permit a reasonable inference of guilt—the inference of the one from proof of the other is arbitrary   *   *   *.' "

Three and one-half years after Romano, the Court in Leary v. United States, considered a challenge to a statutory inference that possession of marihuana, unless satisfactorily explained, was sufficient to prove that the

possessed by the accused with knowledge that it was stolen property, unless such possession is explained by facts and circumstances in this case which are in some way consistent with the defendant's innocence.

"In considering whether possession of recently stolen property has been satisfactorily explained, you are reminded that in the exercise of constitutional rights the accused need not take the witness stand and testify.

"Possession may be satisfactorily explained through other circumstances, other evidence, independent of any testimony of the accused."

[Notice that the trial judge spoke of inferences, not presumptions. However, the judge was explaining the connection between a fact as to which proof was offered and another fact. Because a judge cannot direct a verdict against a criminal defendant, there can be no presumption in the sense that a defendant will automatically lose if he offers no evidence on an issue. But an instruction like this one can give the government some benefit from the fact that the defendant has not offered rebuttal evidence.

In the first paragraph of part I of the opinion, infra, the Court uses the term "presumptions" and the term "inferences" without differentiating them.]

defendant knew that the marihuana had been illegally imported into the United States. The Court concluded that in view of the significant possibility that any given marihuana was domestically grown and the improbability that a marihuana user would know whether his marihuana was of domestic or imported origin, the inference did not meet the standards set by Tot, Gainey, and Romano. Referring to these three cases, the Leary Court stated that an inference is " 'irrational' or 'arbitrary,' and hence unconstitutional, unless it can at least be said with substantial assurance that the presumed fact is more likely than not to flow from the proved fact on which it is made to depend." In a footnote the Court stated that since the challenged inference failed to satisfy the more-likely-than-not standard, it did not have to "reach the question whether a criminal presumption which passes muster when so judged must also satisfy the criminal 'reasonable doubt' standard if proof of the crime charged or an essential element thereof depends upon its use."

Finally, in Turner v. United States, decided the year following Leary, the Court considered the constitutionality of instructing the jury that it may infer from possession of heroin and cocaine that the defendant knew these drugs had been illegally imported.[b] The Court noted that Leary reserved the question of whether the more-likely-than-not or the reasonable-doubt standard controlled in criminal cases, but it likewise found no need to resolve that question. It held that the inference with regard to heroin was valid judged by either standard. With regard to cocaine, the inference failed to satisfy even the more-likely-than-not standard.

The teaching of the foregoing cases is not altogether clear. To the extent that the "rational connection," "more likely than not," and "reasonable doubt" standards bear ambiguous relationships to one another, the ambiguity is traceable in large part to variations in language and focus rather than to differences of substance. What has been established by the cases, however, is at least this: that if a statutory inference submitted to the jury as sufficient to support conviction satisfies the reasonable-doubt standard (that is, the evidence necessary to invoke the inference is sufficient for a rational juror to find the inferred fact beyond a reasonable doubt) as well as the more-likely-than-not standard, then it clearly accords with due process.

In the present case we deal with a traditional common-law inference deeply rooted in our law. For centuries courts have instructed juries that an inference of guilty knowledge may be drawn from the fact of unexplained possession of stolen goods. James Thayer, writing in his Preliminary Treatise on Evidence (1898), cited this inference as the descendant of a presumption "running through a dozen centuries." Early American cases consistently upheld instructions permitting conviction upon such an inference, and the courts of appeals on numerous occasions have approved instructions essentially identical to the instruction given in this case. This longstanding and consistent judicial approval of the instruction, reflecting accumulated com-

b. The Turner Court also considered the validity of inferring that a defendant knowingly purchased, sold, dispensed, or distributed a narcotic drug not in or from the original package bearing tax stamps from the fact that the drugs had no tax stamps when found in the defendant's possession. The Court upheld the inference that a defendant possessing unstamped heroin knowingly purchased it in violation of the statute, but struck down the inference with regard to cocaine.

mon experience, provides strong indication that the instruction comports with due process.

This impressive historical basis, however, is not in itself sufficient to establish the instruction's constitutionality. Common-law inferences, like their statutory counterparts, must satisfy due process standards in light of present-day experience.[c] In the present case the challenged instruction only permitted the inference of guilt from unexplained possession of recently stolen property.[d] The evidence established that petitioner possessed recently stolen Treasury checks payable to persons he did not know, and it provided no plausible explanation for such possession consistent with innocence. On the basis of this evidence alone common sense and experience tell us that petitioner must have known or been aware of the high probability that the checks were stolen. Such evidence was clearly sufficient to enable the jury to find beyond a reasonable doubt that petitioner knew the checks were stolen. Since the inference thus satisfies the reasonable-doubt standard, the most stringent standard the Court has applied in judging permissive criminal law inferences, we conclude that it satisfies the requirements of due process.[e]

II

Petitioner also argues that the permissive inference in question infringes his privilege against self-incrimination. The Court has twice rejected this argument, Turner v. United States, 396 U.S., at 417–418; Yee Hem v. United States, 268 U.S. 178, 185 (1925), and we find no reason to re-examine the issue at length. The trial court specifically instructed the jury that peti-

c. The reasoning of the statutory-inference cases is applicable to analysis of common-law inferences. Common-law inferences, however, present fewer constitutional problems. Such inferences are invoked only in the discretion of the trial judge. While statutes creating criminal law inferences may be interpreted also to preserve the trial court's traditional discretion in determining whether there is sufficient evidence to go to the jury and in charging the jury, such discretion is inherent in the use of common-law inferences.

d. Of course, the mere fact that there is some evidence tending to explain a defendant's possession consistent with innocence does not bar instructing the jury on the inference. The jury must weigh the explanation to determine whether it is "satisfactory." The jury is not bound to accept or believe any particular explanation any more than it is bound to accept the correctness of the inference. But the burden of proving beyond a reasonable doubt that the defendant did have knowledge that the property was stolen, an essential element of the crime, remains on the Government.

e. It is true that the practical effect of instructing the jury on the inference arising from unexplained possession of recently stolen property is to shift the burden of going forward with evidence to the defendant. If the Government proves possession and nothing more, this evidence remains unexplained unless the defendant introduces evidence, since ordinarily the Government's evidence will not provide an explanation of his possession consistent with innocence. In Tot v. United States, the Court stated that the burden of going forward may not be freely shifted to the defendant. Tot held, however, that where there is a "rational connection" between the facts proved and the fact presumed or inferred, it is permissible to shift the burden of going forward to the defendant. Where an inference satisfies the reasonable-doubt standard, as in the present case, there will certainly be a rational connection between the fact presumed or inferred (in this case, knowledge) and the facts the Government must prove in order to shift the burden of going forward (possession of recently stolen property).

We do not decide today whether a judge-formulated inference of less antiquity or authority may properly be emphasized by a jury instruction.

tioner had a constitutional right not to take the witness stand and that possession could be satisfactorily explained by evidence independent of petitioner's testimony.   Introduction of any evidence, direct or circumstantial, tending to implicate the defendant in the alleged crime increases the pressure on him to testify.   The mere massing of evidence against a defendant cannot be regarded as a violation of his privilege against self-incrimination.

*   *   *

Mr. Justice BRENNAN, with whom Mr. Justice MARSHALL joins, dissenting.

Petitioner was charged in two counts of a six-count indictment with possession of United States Treasury checks stolen from the mails, knowing them to be stolen.   The essential elements of such an offense are (1) that the defendant was in possession of the checks, (2) that the checks were stolen from the mails, and (3) that the defendant knew that the checks were stolen.   The Government proved that petitioner had been in possession of the checks and that the checks had been stolen from the mails; and, in addition, the Government introduced some evidence intended to show that petitioner knew or should have known that the checks were stolen.   But rather than leaving the jury to determine the element of "knowledge" on the basis of that evidence, the trial court instructed it that it was free to infer the essential element of "knowledge" from petitioner's unexplained possession of the checks. In my view, that instruction violated the Due Process Clause of the Fifth Amendment because it permitted the jury to convict even though the actual evidence bearing on "knowledge" may have been insufficient to establish guilt beyond a reasonable doubt.   I therefore dissent.

We held in In re Winship, 397 U.S. 358, 364 (1970), that the Due Process Clause requires "proof beyond a reasonable doubt of every fact necessary to constitute the crime   *   *   *."   Thus, in Turner v. United States, we approved the inference of "knowledge" from the fact of possessing smuggled heroin because " '[c]ommon sense'   *   *   *   tells us that those who traffic in heroin will *inevitably* become aware that the product they deal in is smuggled   *   *   *."   (Emphasis added).   The basis of that "common sense" judgment was, of course, the indisputable fact that all or virtually all heroin in this country is necessarily smuggled.   Here, however, it cannot be said that all or virtually all endorsed United States Treasury checks have been stolen.   Indeed, it is neither unlawful nor unusual for people to use such checks as direct payment for goods and services.   Thus, unlike *Turner*, "common sense" simply will not permit the inference that the possessor of stolen Treasury checks "*inevitably*" knew that the checks were stolen.

In short, the practical effect of the challenged instruction was to permit the jury to convict petitioner even if it found insufficient or disbelieved all of the Government's evidence bearing directly on the issue of "knowledge." By authorizing the jury to rely exclusively on the inference in determining the element of "knowledge," the instruction relieved the Government of the burden of proving that element beyond a reasonable doubt.   The instruction thereby violated the principle of *Winship* that every essential element of the crime must be proved beyond a reasonable doubt.

[The separate dissenting opinion of Justice Douglas is omitted.]

Does the majority opinion refute to your satisfaction the point made by Justice Brennan in the final paragraph of his dissent?

The Supreme Court had occasion more recently to return to the subject of presumptions and inferences in criminal cases.

COUNTY COURT v. ALLEN

Supreme Court of the United States, 1979.
442 U.S. 140, 99 S.Ct. 2213, 60 L.Ed.2d 777.

Mr. Justice STEVENS delivered the opinion of the Court.

A New York statute provides that, with certain exceptions, the presence of a firearm in an automobile is presumptive evidence of its illegal possession by all persons then occupying the vehicle. The United States Court of Appeals for the Second Circuit held that respondents may challenge the constitutionality of this statute in a federal habeas corpus proceeding and that the statute is "unconstitutional on its face."   *   *   *

Four persons, three adult males (respondents) and a 16-year-old girl (Jane Doe, who is not a respondent here), were jointly tried on charges that they possessed two loaded handguns, a loaded machinegun, and over a pound of heroin found in a Chevrolet in which they were riding when it was stopped for speeding on the New York Thruway shortly after noon on March 28, 1973. The two large-caliber handguns, which together with their ammunition weighed approximately six pounds, were seen through the window of the car by the investigating police officer. They were positioned crosswise in an open handbag on either the front floor or the front seat of the car on the passenger side where Jane Doe was sitting. Jane Doe admitted that the handbag was hers. The machinegun and the heroin were discovered in the trunk after the police pried it open. The car had been borrowed from the driver's brother earlier that day; the key to the trunk could not be found in the car or on the person of any of its occupants, although there was testimony that two of the occupants had placed something in the trunk before embarking in the borrowed car. The jury convicted all four of possession of the handguns and acquitted them of possession of the contents of the trunk.

Counsel for all four defendants objected to the introduction into evidence of the two handguns, the machinegun, and the drugs, arguing that the State had not adequately demonstrated a connection between their clients and the contraband. The trial court overruled the objection, relying on the presumption of possession created by the New York statute. Because that presumption does not apply if a weapon is found "upon the person" of one of the occupants of the car, the three male defendants also moved to dismiss the charges relating to the handguns on the ground that the guns were found on the person of Jane Doe. Respondents made this motion both at the close of the prosecution's case and at the close of all evidence. The trial judge twice denied it, concluding that the applicability of the "on the person" exception was a question of fact for the jury.

At the close of the trial, the judge instructed the jurors that they were entitled to infer possession from the defendants' presence in the car. He did not make any reference to the "on the person" exception in his explanation of the statutory presumption, nor did any of the defendants object to this omission or request alternative or additional instructions on the subject.

* * *

Inferences and presumptions are a staple of our adversary system of factfinding. It is often necessary for the trier of fact to determine the existence of an element of the crime—that is, an "ultimate" or "elemental" fact—from the existence of one or more "evidentiary" or "basic" facts. The value of these evidentiary devices, and their validity under the Due Process Clause, vary from case to case, however, depending on the strength of the connection between the particular basic and elemental facts involved and on the degree to which the device curtails the factfinder's freedom to assess the evidence independently. Nonetheless, in criminal cases, the ultimate test of any device's constitutional validity in a given case remains constant; the device must not undermine the factfinder's responsibility at trial, based on evidence adduced by the State, to find the ultimate facts beyond a reasonable doubt.

The most common evidentiary device is the entirely permissive inference or presumption, which allows—but does not require—the trier of fact to infer the elemental fact from proof by the prosecutor of the basic one and that places no burden of any kind on the defendant. In that situation the basic fact may constitute prima facie evidence of the elemental fact. When reviewing this type of device, the Court has required the party challenging it to demonstrate its invalidity as applied to him. Because this permissive presumption leaves the trier of fact free to credit or reject the inference and does not shift the burden of proof, it affects the application of the "beyond a reasonable doubt" standard only if, under the facts of the case, there is no rational way the trier could make the connection permitted by the inference. For only in that situation is there any risk that an explanation of the permissible inference to a jury, or its use by a jury, has caused the presumptively rational factfinder to make an erroneous factual determination.

A mandatory presumption is a far more troublesome evidentiary device. For it may affect not only the strength of the "no reasonable doubt" burden but also the placement of that burden; it tells the trier that he or they must find the elemental fact upon proof of the basic fact, at least unless the defendant has come forward with some evidence to rebut the presumed connection between the two facts.[f] In this situation, the Court has generally

---

f. This class of more or less mandatory presumptions can be subdivided into two parts; presumptions that merely shift the burden of production to the defendant, following the satisfaction of which the ultimate burden of persuasion returns to the prosecution; and presumptions that entirely shift the burden of proof to the defendant. The mandatory presumptions examined by our cases have almost uniformly fit into the former subclass, in that they never totally removed the ultimate burden of proof beyond a reasonable doubt from the prosecution. E.g., Tot v. United States. See Roviaro v. United States, describing the operation of the presumption involved in Turner, Leary, and Romano.

To the extent that a presumption imposes an extremely low burden of production—e.g., being satisfied by "any" evidence—it may well be that its impact is no greater than that of a permissive inference, and it may be proper to analyze it as such.

In deciding what type of inference or presumption is involved in a case, the jury instructions will generally be controlling, although their interpretation may require

examined the presumption on its face to determine the extent to which the basic and elemental facts coincide. To the extent that the trier of fact is forced to abide by the presumption, and may not reject it based on an independent evaluation of the particular facts presented by the State, the analysis of the presumption's constitutional validity is logically divorced from those facts and based on the presumption's accuracy in the run of cases.[g] It is for

recourse to the statute involved and the cases decided under it. Turner v. United States, provides a useful illustration of the different types of presumptions. It analyzes the constitutionality of two different presumption statutes (one mandatory and one permissive) as they apply to the basic fact of possession of both heroin and cocaine, and the presumed facts of importation and distribution of narcotic drugs. The jury was charged essentially in the terms of the two statutes.

The importance of focusing attention on the precise presentation of the presumption to the jury and the scope of that presumption is illustrated by a comparison of United States v. Gainey with United States v. Romano. Both cases involved statutory presumptions based on proof that the defendant was present at the site of an illegal still. In Gainey the Court sustained a conviction "for carrying on" the business of the distillery in violation of 26 USC § 5601(a)(4), whereas in Romano, the Court set aside a conviction for being in "possession, or custody, or * * * control" of such a distillery in violation of § 5601(a)(1). The difference in outcome was attributable to two important differences between the cases. Because the statute involved in Gainey was a sweeping prohibition of almost any activity associated with the still, whereas the Romano statute involved only one narrow aspect of the total undertaking, there was a much higher probability that mere presence could support an inference of guilt in the former case than in the latter.

Of perhaps greater importance, however, was the difference between the trial judge's instructions to the jury in the two cases. In Gainey, the judge had explained that the presumption was permissive; it did not require the jury to convict the defendant even if it was convinced that he was present at the site. On the contrary, the instructions made it clear that presence was only " 'a circumstance to be considered along with all the other circumstances in the case.' " As we emphasized, the "jury was thus specifically told that the statutory inference was not conclusive." In Romano, the trial judge told the jury that the defendant's presence at the still " 'shall be deemed sufficient evidence to authorize conviction.' " Although there was other evidence of guilt, that instruction au-

thorized conviction even if the jury disbelieved all of the testimony except the proof of presence at the site. This Court's holding that the statutory presumption could not support the Romano conviction was thus dependent, in part, on the specific instructions given by the trial judge. Under those instructions it was necessary to decide whether, regardless of the specific circumstances of the particular case, the statutory presumption adequately supported the guilty verdict.

g. In addition to the discussion of Romano in n. f, supra, this point is illustrated by Leary v. United States. In that case, Dr. Timothy Leary, a professor at Harvard University, was stopped by customs inspectors in Laredo, Tex., as he was returning from the Mexican side of the international border. Marihuana seeds and a silver snuffbox filled with semirefined marihuana and three partially smoked marihuana cigarettes were discovered in his car. He was convicted of having knowingly transported marihuana which he knew had been illegally imported into this country in violation of 21 U.S.C. § 176a (1964 ed). That statute included a mandatory presumption: "possession shall be deemed sufficient evidence to authorize conviction [for importation] unless the defendant explains his possession to the satisfaction of the jury." Leary admitted possession of the marihuana and claimed that he had carried it from New York to Mexico and then back.

Mr. Justice Harlan for the Court noted that under one theory of the case, the jury could have found direct proof of all of the necessary elements of the offense without recourse to the presumption. But he deemed that insufficient reason to affirm the conviction because under another theory the jury might have found knowledge of importation on the basis of either direct evidence or the presumption, and there was accordingly no certainty that the jury had not relied on the presumption. The Court therefore found it necessary to test the presumption against the Due Process Clause. Its analysis was facial. Despite the fact that the defendant was well educated and had recently traveled to a country that is a major exporter of marihuana to this country, the Court found the presumption of knowledge of importation from possession irrational. It did so, not because Dr.

this reason that the Court has held it irrelevant in analyzing a mandatory presumption, but not in analyzing a purely permissive one, that there is ample evidence in the record other than the presumption to support a conviction.

Without determining whether the presumption in this case was mandatory, the Court of Appeals analyzed it on its face as if it were. In fact, it was not, as the New York Court of Appeals had earlier pointed out.

The trial judge's instructions make it clear that the presumption was merely a part of the prosecution's case, that it gave rise to a permissive inference available only in certain circumstances, rather than a mandatory conclusion of possession, and that it could be ignored by the jury even if there was no affirmative proof offered by defendants in rebuttal. The judge explained that possession could be actual or constructive, but that constructive possession could not exist without the intent and ability to exercise control or dominion over the weapons. He also carefully instructed the jury that there is a mandatory presumption of innocence in favor of the defendants that controls unless it, as the exclusive trier of fact, is satisfied beyond a reasonable doubt that the defendants possessed the handguns in the manner described by the judge. In short, the instructions plainly directed the jury to consider all the circumstances tending to support or contradict the inference that all four occupants of the car had possession of the two loaded handguns and to decide the matter for itself without regard to how much evidence the defendants introduced.

Our cases considering the validity of permissive statutory presumptions such as the one involved here have rested on an evaluation of the presumption as applied to the record before the Court. None suggests that a court should pass on the constitutionality of this kind of statute "on its face." It was error for the Court of Appeals to make such a determination in this case.

III

As applied to the facts of this case, the presumption of possession is entirely rational. * * * [R]espondents were not "hitch-hikers or other casual passengers," and the guns were neither "a few inches in length" nor "out of [respondents'] sight." The argument against possession by any of the respondents was predicated solely on the fact that the guns were in Jane Doe's pocketbook. But several circumstances—which, not surprisingly, her counsel repeatedly emphasized in his questions and his argument—made it highly improbable that she was the sole custodian of those weapons.

Even if it was reasonable to conclude that she had placed the guns in her purse before the car was stopped by police, the facts strongly suggest that Jane Doe was not the only person able to exercise dominion over them. The two guns were too large to be concealed in her handbag. The bag was consequently open, and part of one of the guns was in plain view, within easy

---

Leary was unlikely to know the source of the marihuana, but instead because "a majority of possessors" were unlikely to have such knowledge. Because the jury had been instructed to rely on the presumption even if it did not believe the Government's direct evidence of knowledge of importation (unless, of course, the defendant met his burden of "satisfying" the jury to the contrary), the Court reversed the conviction.

access of the driver of the car and even, perhaps, of the other two respondents who were riding in the rear seat.

Moreover, it is highly improbable that the loaded guns belonged to Jane Doe or that she was solely responsible for their being in her purse. As a 16-year-old girl in the company of three adult men she was the least likely of the four to be carrying one, let alone two, heavy handguns. It is far more probable that she relied on the pocketknife found in her brassiere for any necessary self-protection. Under these circumstances, it was not unreasonable for her counsel to argue and for the jury to infer that when the car was halted for speeding, the other passengers in the car anticipated the risk of a search and attempted to conceal their weapons in a pocketbook in the front seat. The inference is surely more likely than the notion that these weapons were the sole property of the 16-year-old girl.

Under these circumstances, the jury would have been entirely reasonable in rejecting the suggestion—which, incidentally, defense counsel did not even advance in their closing arguments to the jury—that the handguns were in the sole possession of Jane Doe. Assuming that the jury did reject it, the case is tantamount to one in which the guns were lying on the floor or the seat of the car in plain view of the three other occupants of the automobile. In such a case, it is surely rational to infer that each of the respondents was fully aware of the presence of the guns and had both the ability and the intent to exercise dominion and control over the weapons.

Mr. Justice POWELL, with whom Mr. Justice BRENNAN, Mr. Justice STEWART, and Mr. Justice MARSHALL join, dissenting.

* * *

Legitimate guidance of a jury's deliberations is an indispensable part of our criminal justice system. Nonetheless, the use of presumptions in criminal cases poses at least two distinct perils for defendants' constitutional rights. The Court accurately identifies the first of these as being the danger of interference with "the factfinder's responsibility at trial, based on evidence adduced by the State, to find the ultimate facts beyond a reasonable doubt." If the jury is instructed that it must infer some ultimate fact (that is, some element of the offense) from proof of other facts unless the defendant disproves the ultimate fact by the preponderance of the evidence, then the presumption shifts the burden of proof to the defendant concerning the element thus inferred.[h]

But I do not agree with the Court's conclusion that the only constitutional difficulty with presumptions lies in the danger of lessening the burden

h. The Court suggests that presumptions that shift the burden of persuasion to the defendant in this way can be upheld provided that "the fact proved is sufficient to support the inference of guilt beyond a reasonable doubt." As the present case involves no shifting of the burden of persuasion, the constitutional restrictions on such presumptions are not before us, and I express no views on them.

It may well be that even those presumptions that do not shift the burden of persuasion cannot be used to prove an element of the offense, if the facts proved would not permit a reasonable mind to find the presumed fact beyond a reasonable doubt. My conclusion in Part II, infra, makes it unnecessary for me to address this concern here.

of proof the prosecution must bear. As the Court notes, the presumptions thus far reviewed by the Court have not shifted the burden of persuasion; instead, they either have required only that the defendant produce some evidence to rebut the inference suggested by the prosecution's evidence, or merely have been suggestions to the jury that it would be sensible to draw certain conclusions on the basis of the evidence presented. Evolving from our decisions, therefore, is a second standard for judging the constitutionality of criminal presumptions which is based—not on the constitutional requirement that the State be put to its proof—but rather on the due process rule that when the jury is encouraged to make factual inferences, those inferences must reflect some valid general observation about the natural connection between events as they occur in our society.

* * *

In sum, our decisions uniformly have recognized that due process requires more than merely that the prosecution be put to its proof. In addition, the Constitution restricts the court in its charge to the jury by requiring that, when particular factual inferences are recommended to the jury, those factual inferences be accurate reflections of what history, common sense, and experience tell us about the relations between events in our society. Generally, this due process rule has been articulated as requiring that the truth of the inferred fact be more likely than not whenever the premise for the inference is true. Thus, to be constitutional a presumption must be at least more likely than not true.

II

In the present case, the jury was told:

"Our Penal Law also provides that the presence in an automobile of any machine gun or of any handgun or firearm which is loaded is presumptive evidence of their unlawful possession. In other words, [under] these presumptions or this latter presumption upon proof of the presence of the machine gun and the hand weapons, you may infer and draw a conclusion that such prohibited weapon was possessed by each of the defendants who occupied the automobile at the time when such instruments were found. The presumption or presumptions is effective only so long as there is no substantial evidence contradicting the conclusion flowing from the presumption, and the presumption is said to disappear when such contradictory evidence is adduced."

Undeniably, the presumption charged in this case encouraged the jury to draw a particular factual inference regardless of any other evidence presented: to infer that respondents possessed the weapons found in the automobile "upon proof of the presence of the machine gun and the hand weapon" and proof that respondents "occupied the automobile at the time such instruments were found." I believe that the presumption thus charged was unconstitutional because it did not fairly reflect what common sense and experience tell us about passengers in automobiles and the possession of handguns. People present in automobiles where there are weapons simply are not "more likely than not" the possessors of those weapons.

* * *

It seems to me that the Court mischaracterizes the function of the presumption charged in this case. As it acknowledges was the case in Romano, supra, the "instruction authorized conviction even if the jury disbelieved all of the testimony except the proof of presence" in the automobile. The Court nevertheless relies on all of the evidence introduced by the prosecution and argues that the "permissive" presumption could not have prejudiced defendants. The possibility that the jury disbelieved all of this evidence, and relied on the presumption, is simply ignored.

* * *

Although the Court divided 5–4 in *Allen*, there may be more agreement among the Justices than their division suggests, and *Allen* may provide more assistance to criminal lawyers and trial judges than is immediately apparent.

Both the majority and the dissent focus on the extent to which the judge is trying to control or to direct the jury with a presumption or suggested inference. As long as the judge is doing nothing more than calling the jury's attention to a possible inference and leaving the jury totally free to reject the inference on the basis of its evaluation of the evidence, neither the majority nor the dissenters are troubled. Indeed, federal judges have long asserted their common law right to comment on the evidence, and judicial comment designed not to direct but to assist the jury has not been seen as raising constitutional problems.

What the majority and dissent cannot agree on is the intended force of the presumption in *Allen*. If it was more than a simple suggestion, explaining a permissible inference, it seems that all the Justices would have been willing to subject it to stricter scrutiny. The majority saw the presumption as a suggestion, which, because it was rational, was acceptable. The dissenters regarded the instruction that the jury received on the presumption as an effort to control the jury's deliberations on a crucial issue. This they thought, could not be justified given what they saw as the rather tenuous factual support for the presumption.

One of the contributions of *Allen* is that it focuses on the language used by trial judges to explain presumptions and inferences in the Court's prior cases and analyzes how that language might have been interpreted by juries. The majority and the dissent seem to agree that in some cases the judicial language was much stronger than in others. The rule that emerges from *Allen* appears to be that the more directive the language of the judge's instructions—i.e., the more likely it is to control jury fact-finding—the greater the burden on the state to justify the use of the presumption or inference.

In dealing with presumptions, reviewing courts assume that the jury will try conscientiously to follow the judge's instructions. The fundamental question for a reviewing court is whether the trial judge had an adequate basis for the degree of control that his instructions would have had on a conscientious jury. If the judge instructs the jury that if it finds a basic fact, then the presumed fact, as an empirical matter, necessarily follows, the reviewing court will demand that the judge's empirical analysis be correct. Since the jury is presumed to accept the judge's analysis, if the judge was incorrect, the jury has been misled. To assess whether or not the trial judge was correct, a reviewing court will use the stringent test discussed in *Barnes*. Where the trial judge's instructions on the presumption describe only a permissible inference, the conscientious jury may prefer some other inference than can follow from the evidence, so the judge is exercising less control and his instructions can be more easily justified. A rational connection between the presumed and basic fact will do.

Some support for this reading of *Allen* may be found in the subsequent decision in Sandstrom v. Montana.[36] That case involved an instruction in a homicide case that "the law presumes that a person in-tends the ordinary consequences of his voluntary acts." A unanimous court struck this presumption down because the Justices believed that the jury might have concluded that the instruction was binding or that the burden of persuasion had been shifted to the defendant. Had the instruction simply noted that if the jury found the defendant's act voluntary it might, after considering the other evidence in the case, conclude that the act's consequences were intended, the Court, depending on the other evidence, might have sustained it.

Problem IX–17. Blago, a Massachusetts state police officer on duty at the Callahan Tunnel, heard one of the automatic toll collection machines signal that a vehicle had passed through without a deposit of twenty-five cents. He noted the license plate number of the car, and that the operator had shoulder length hair and wore glasses, but did not attempt to stop the car.

From the license plate number it was learned that the car was registered to the defendant, Joseph C. Pauley. Blago accordingly swore out a complaint in the East Boston District Court charging that Pauley had deposited a copper slug in the meter at the end of the Callahan Tunnel intending to evade payment of the toll.

---

36. 442 U.S. 510 (1979). Concurring in the Leary case, Justice Black made a similar point when he offered an additional reason for invalidating the statutory presumption:

The trial court in this case charged the jury that proof that petitioner merely had possession of marihuana was sufficient to authorize a finding that he knew it had been imported or brought into the United States contrary to law. It is clear beyond doubt that the fact of possession alone is not enough to support an inference that the possessor knew it had been imported. Congress has no more constitutional power to tell a jury it can convict upon any such forced and baseless inference than it has power to tell juries they can convict a defendant of a crime without any evidence at all from which an inference of guilt could be drawn. Under our system of separation of powers, Congress is just as incompetent to instruct the judge and jury in an American court what evidence is enough for conviction as the courts are to tell the Congress what policies it must adopt in writing criminal laws. The congressional presumption, therefore, violates the constitutional right of a defendant to be tried by jury in a court set up in accordance with the commands of the Constitution. It clearly deprives a defendant of his right not to be convicted and punished for a crime without due process of law, that is, in a federal case, a trial before an independent judge, after an indictment by grand jury, with representation by counsel, an opportunity to summon witnesses in his behalf, and an opportunity to confront the witnesses against him. This right to a fullfledged trial in a court of law is guaranteed to every defendant by Article III of the Constitution, by the Sixth Amendment, and by the Fifth and Fourteenth Amendments' promises that no person shall be deprived of his life, liberty, or property without due process of law—that is, a trial according to the law of the land, both constitutional and statutory.

Leary v. United States, 395 U.S. 6, 55–56 (1969).

At the trial in the Municipal Court, Blago was the only witness.   He testified to the incident at the tunnel as recounted above.   The defendant Pauley, who was present in court, had short hair and was not wearing glasses. Blago said he could not, "under oath," positively identify Pauley as the person who had deposited the slug.   Pauley stipulated that he was the registered owner of the car and that whoever was driving the car at the time and place testified to had attempted to evade payment of the toll in violation of the tunnel regulation.   The Commonwealth offered the tunnel rules and regulations in evidence, directing the court's attention to a provision that

> [i]f a vehicle is operated within tunnel property in violation of any provision of these rules and regulations and the identity of the operator of such vehicle cannot be determined, the person in whose name such vehicle is registered shall be deemed prima facie responsible for such violation.

The regulation was received over the defendant's objection and exception. The defendant offered no evidence.   The judge found him guilty and fined him $25.   No findings were made.   Pauley appealed.

Under Massachusetts case law it is clear that in a criminal case the trier of fact may convict if a prima facie case is made out.   No other evidence is necessary.   **Should an appellate court overturn the conviction and declare the presumption (i.e., the prima facie case) invalid?** [37]

Problem IX–18.   Zaremski is charged with a knowing failure to report for induction into the armed forces of the United States.   At trial, the government introduces Zaremski's selective service file into evidence and rests its case.   The file shows that Zaremski was classified 1–A and that a notice of classification was mailed to him.   It also shows that he did not comply with an order to report for induction that had been mailed two years before the trial and two months before he was scheduled to report.   Zaremski places his mother on the stand, and introduces through her certain letters from the Selective Service Administration, one of which is an order to report for induction addressed to her son.   Zaremski's mother testifies that she regularly forwarded mail to her son, but that she had not forwarded these letters. On the basis of this testimony, the defendant contends that he could not have knowingly refused to submit for induction because he had no notice of the order to report.   Assume that the government requests the trial judge to instruct the jury pursuant to a selective service regulation which provides:

> It shall be the duty of each registrant to keep his local board currently informed of the address where mail will reach him.   The mailing of any order, notice, or blank form by the local board to a registrant at the address last reported by him to the local board shall constitute notice to him of the contents of the communications, whether he actually received it or not.

Should the trial judge grant this instruction?   What form would the requested instruction take?   What are the implications of the instruction

---

37.   Some rules—e.g., Alaska R.Evid. 301—specifically state that the usual approach to presumptions applies to statutory language that a certain kind of proof is prima facie evidence of a proposition.

if granted?   If the statute so provided, should the court instruct the jury that there is a presumption that a draft registrant receives all mail sent to the address that he has furnished the draft board?   Could a judge tell the jury "that the law presumes that mail is received?"

In order to deal with the problem of presumptions in criminal cases, the Advisory Committee drafted the following rule, which was approved by the Supreme Court:

Rule 303.   Presumptions in Criminal Cases

(a) Scope.—Except as otherwise provided by Act of Congress, in criminal cases, presumptions against an accused, recognized at common law or created by statute, including statutory provisions that certain facts are prima facie evidence of other facts or of guilt, are governed by this rule.

(b) Submission to jury.—The judge is not authorized to direct the jury to find a presumed fact against the accused.   When the presumed fact establishes guilt or is an element of the offense or negatives a defense, the judge may submit the question of guilt or of the existence of the presumed fact to the jury, if, but only if, a reasonable juror on the evidence as a whole, including the evidence of the basic facts, could find guilt or the presumed fact beyond a reasonable doubt.   When the presumed fact has a lesser effect, its existence may be submitted to the jury if the basic facts are supported by substantial evidence, or are otherwise established, unless the evidence as a whole negatives the existence of the presumed fact.

(c) Instructing the jury.—Whenever the existence of a presumed fact against the accused is submitted to the jury, the judge shall give an instruction that the law declares that the jury may regard the basic facts as sufficient evidence of the presumed fact but does not require it to do so.   In addition, if the presumed fact establishes guilt or is an element of the offense or negatives a defense, the judge shall instruct the jury that its existence must, on all the evidence, be proved beyond a reasonable doubt.

Congress deleted this proposed rule because it differed from section 103(4)(b) of the Federal Criminal Code proposed by the National Commission on Reform of Federal Criminal Laws.   The proposed Criminal Code requires the court to instruct the jury that the "law regards the facts giving rise to the presumption as strong evidence of the fact presumed."   Which rule do you favor?   Why?   Remember, Congress expressed no view as to which rule was preferable;   it merely left the matter open for later consideration.   How would a court have applied PFRE 303?   The provision in the proposed Criminal Code is much clearer, but are there constitutional problems with this draft?   Would it withstand attack after County Court v. Allen?   Is it possible to decide this question without analyzing each presumption individually?

B. JUDICIAL NOTICE

1. INTRODUCTION

In both civil and criminal cases presumptions may be available to aid in establishing proof. Presumptions may substitute for proof, alter the burden of proof, or guide the weighing of evidence. Judicial notice may do everything presumptions do and more.

When courts take judicial notice, they accept as true some fact or set of facts without requiring that the fact be proved by admissible evidence. Where appropriate, the jury will be instructed to treat a noticed fact as true in the course of their deliberations. Consider a case in which it is important to know whether a contract dated November 3, 1976 was signed on a Wednesday or a Thursday. A party might ask the court to take judicial notice that November 3, 1976 fell on a Wednesday. If the court notices this fact, as it probably would, the party will be entitled to have the jury instructed that if it finds the contract was signed on November 3, 1976, it must find that the contract was signed on a Wednesday. The party seeking judicial notice might have to bring a calendar to court since the judge is unlikely to know on what day a specified date fell, but he would not have to present the calendar, or other evidence of the fact he wants noticed, to the jury.

Courts may also notice law, either on their own initiative or at the instance of a party. Parties usually cannot complain when their failure to bring a legal argument to the judge's attention results in a mistaken decision. They also cannot complain when the judge correctly applies law that the parties did not seek to apply

in the case. Judicial notice of facts and law occurs at both the trial and appellate levels.

Since it is a normal function of courts to decide questions of law, judicial notice of law is easily understood and readily accepted. But judicial notice of facts seems to contravene the notion that courts try cases on the basis of the evidence presented in court and not on the basis of information known privately to the judge or jury. Previously examined principles, such as hearsay, confrontation, chain of custody and the like, are premised in large part on the belief that evidence should be tested by an adversary before it is used by the trier of fact. Judicial notice seems inconsistent with this belief. But there are good reasons for allowing judicial notice. We shall see that judicial notice, wisely taken, does not undermine the basic nature of the adversary system.

Professor Davis believes that to sensibly discuss judicial notice, factual information should be divided into two categories. First, there are specific facts concerning who did what to whom, when, where, how and why. Professor Davis calls these "adjudicative facts" or "facts concerning the immediate parties."[38] Second, there are more general facts that do not concern the immediate parties. These include: facts not introduced into evidence but known to the fact finder and used to assess the validity and strength of adjudicative facts; information found in extra-record sources that sheds light on legislative intent or on the constitutional basis for legislative or executive action; general information rel-

38. K. Davis, Administrative Law Text § 15.03, at 296 (3d ed. 1972). See also Davis, An Approach to Problems of Evidence in the Administrative Process, 55 Harv.L.Rev. 364, 402–16 (1942); Davis, Official Notice, 62 Harv.L.Rev. 537, 549–60 (1949); Davis, Judicial Notice, 55 Colum.L.Rev. 945, 952–59 (1955); Davis, A System of Judicial Notice Based on Fairness and Convenience, in R. Pound, ed., Perspectives of Law 69 (1964); Davis, Judicial Notice, in Symposium: Proposed Federal Rules of Evidence, 1969 Law & Soc. Order 513.

evant to the legal policy decisions made by courts of last resort, and the contents of statutes, regulations, judicial decisions and other reports of official action.   Davis terms information of this general sort "legislative facts."   His distinction is recognized in the Federal Rules of Evidence.

2.   ADJUDICATIVE FACTS

FRE 201 codifies a view of judicial notice found in many common law cases:

(a) Scope of rule.—This rule governs only judicial notice of adjudicative facts.

(b) Kinds of facts.—A judicially noticed fact must be one not subject to reasonable dispute in that it is either (1) generally known within the territorial jurisdiction of the trial court or (2) capable of accurate and ready determination by resort to sources whose accuracy cannot reasonably be questioned.

(c) When discretionary.—A court may take judicial notice, whether requested or not.

(d) When mandatory.—A court shall take judicial notice if requested by a party and supplied with the necessary information.

* * *

The Advisory Committee Note accompanying FRE 201 reads in part:

"In conducting a process of judicial reasoning, as of other reasoning, not a step can be taken without assuming something which has not been proved; and the capacity to do this with competent judgment and efficiency, is imputed to judges and juries as part of their necessary mental outfit."   Thayer, Preliminary Treatise on Evidence 279–280 (1898).

As Professor Davis points out, every case involves the use of hundreds or thousands of non-evidence facts. When a witness in an automobile accident case says "car," everyone, judge and jury included, furnishes, from non-evidence sources within himself, the supplementing information that the "car" is an automobile, not a railroad car, that it is self-propelled, probably by an internal combustion engine, that it may be assumed to have four wheels with pneumatic rubber tires, and so on.   The judicial process cannot construct every case from scratch, like Descartes creating a world based on the postulate *Cogito, ergo sum.* These items could not possibly be introduced into evidence, and no one suggests that they be.   Nor are they appropriate subjects for any formalized treatment of judicial notice of facts.

Another aspect of what Thayer had in mind is the use of non-evidence facts to appraise or assess the adjudicative facts of the case.   Pairs of cases from two jurisdictions illustrate this use and also the difference between non-evidence facts thus used and adjudicative facts.   In People v. Strook, 347 Ill. 460, 179 N.E. 821 (1932), venue in Cook County had been held not established by testimony that the crime was committed at 7956 South Chicago Avenue, since judicial notice would not be taken that the address was in Chicago.   However, the same court subsequently ruled that venue in Cook County was established by testimony that a crime occurred at 8900 South Anthony Avenue, since notice would be taken of the common practice of omitting the name of the city when speaking of local addresses, and the witness was testifying in Chicago.   People v. Pride, 16 Ill.2d 82, 156 N.E.2d 551 (1951).   And in Hughes v. Vestal, 264 N.C. 500, 142 S.E.2d 361 (1965), the Supreme Court of North Carolina disapproved the trial judge's admission in evidence of a state-published table of automobile stopping distances on the basis of judicial notice, though the court itself had referred to the same table in an earlier case in a "rhetorical and illustrative" way in determining that the defendant could not have stopped her car in time to avoid striking a child who suddenly appeared in the highway and that a nonsuit was properly granted. It is apparent that this use of nonevidence facts in evaluating the adjudicative facts of the case is not an appropriate subject for a formalized judicial notice treatment.

* * *

This rule is consistent with Uniform Rules 9(1) and (2) which limit judicial notice of facts to those "so universally known that they cannot reasonably be the subject of dispute," those "so generally known or of such common notoriety within the territorial jurisdiction of the court that they cannot reasonably be the subject of dispute," and those "capable of immediate and accurate determination by resort to easily accessible sources of indisputable accuracy." * * *

The phrase "propositions of generalized knowledge" found in Uniform Rule 9(1) and (2) is not included in the present rule. It was, it is believed, originally included in Model Code Rules 801 and 802 primarily in order to afford some minimum recognition to the right of the judge in his "legislative" capacity (not acting as the trier of fact) to take judicial notice of very limited categories of generalized knowledge. The limitations thus imposed have been discarded herein as undesirable, unworkable, and contrary to existing practice. What is left, then, to be considered, is the status of a "proposition of generalized knowledge" as an "adjudicative" fact to be noticed judicially and communicated by the judge to the jury. Thus viewed, it is considered to be lacking practical significance.

Thus, facts known generally or capable of accurate determination may be judicially noticed. But what ends are served by dispensing with ordinary proof in these instances? Thayer wrote that judicial notice helps:

to shorten and simplify trials; it is an instrument of great capacity in the hands of a competent judge; and it is not nearly as much used, in the region of practice and evidence, as it should be.[39]

Wigmore agreed:

With these aspects of the principle [judicial notice] in mind, a large field opens for reducing the tedious proof of notorious facts. The principle is an instrument of a usefulness hitherto unimagined by judges. Let them make liberal use of it; and thus avoid much of the needless failures of justice that are caused by the artificial impotence of judicial proceedings.[40]

More recently, it has been said that:

[t]he obvious cost of establishing adjudicative facts in an adversary proceeding—in terms of time, energy and money—justifies dispensing with formal proof when a matter is not really disputable. Since there is no real issue of fact, the right to trial by jury is not infringed.[41]

Our adjudicatory system is grounded in the belief that the presentation of evidence in court, subject to the rules discussed throughout this book, is the preferable way of seeking truth in litigation and thereby doing justice. But we recognize that trial procedures may be costly, and we are willing to opt for a reduction in litigation costs when it appears that the integrity of the adjudicative process will not be compromised substantially. This explains certain presumptions.

---

39. J. Thayer, A Preliminary Treatise on Evidence at the Common Law 309 (1898).

40. 9 Wigmore § 2583, at 585.

41. 1 Weinstein's Evidence ¶ 201[03], at 201–24 (1975).

But what does it mean to compromise *substantially* the integrity of the adjudicative process? When can we afford to abandon the usual requirement of evidentiary proof for judicial notice of adjudicative facts? Professor Morgan concluded that we should do this only when a matter was indisputable.[42] Professor Davis disagrees, arguing:

> The basic principle is that extra-record facts should be assumed whenever it is convenient to assume them, except that convenience should always yield to the requirement of procedural fairness that parties should have opportunity to meet in the appropriate fashion all facts that influence the disposition of the case.[43]

Davis contends that "[t]he two major considerations in developing a system of judicial notice are fairness and convenience," and suggests that Morgan's view is too limited. It "sacrifices convenience much more than is necessary for protecting procedural fairness."[44] FRE 201 accords with the Morgan view and is accordingly criticized by Professor Davis.

To fully understand the competing positions, it is necessary to examine the procedural impact of judicial notice. FRE 201 provides:

* * *

(e) Opportunity to be heard.—A party is entitled upon timely request to an opportunity to be heard as to the propriety of taking judicial notice and the tenor of the matter noticed. In the absence of prior notification, the request may be made after judicial notice has been taken.

(f) Time of taking notice.—Judicial notice may be taken at any stage of the proceeding.

(g) Instructing jury.—In a civil action or proceeding, the court shall instruct the jury to accept as conclusive any fact judicially noticed. In a criminal case, the court shall instruct the jury that it may, but is not required to, accept as conclusive any fact judicially noticed.

Although the parties have a chance to be heard on the propriety of notice, once notice is taken it is conclusive in civil cases and advisory in criminal actions.[45] Professor Davis would allow parties opposing noticed facts to offer contradictory evidence and argument[46] in bench trials, but he recognizes the difficulties of using this approach in jury trials.[47]

Should there be judicial notice for the sake of convenience? Whose convenience? If the parties are contesting adjudicative facts in a particular case, what justifies a departure from the usual rules respecting the burdens and modes of proof? If judges will not notice facts unless it is clear from the evidence that the facts are almost certainly as one party contends, is judicial notice needed? If the facts are dispositive, a directed verdict may be in order; if not, cannot the jury be trusted to see the facts as the court does? If the facts are not completely clear, what justifies a judge's treating them as if they are? Are the normal allocation of burden rules inadequate to accomplish their task? If so, will not the creation of a presumption suffice? Does judicial convenience open the door to judicial bias?

---

42. See Morgan, Judicial Notice, 57 Harv.L.Rev. 269, 271–72 (1944). See also Morgan, Basic Problems of Evidence 9 (1963).

43. Administrative Law Text, supra note 38, § 15.09, at 314. (Original is in italics.)

44. Id.

45. Congress apparently believed that making judicial notice binding in criminal cases amounted to partially directing a verdict, thus invading the defendant's right to a jury trial. Do you share this belief?

46. Administrative Law Text, supra note 38, §§ 15.09–15.10, at 314–16.

47. See Davis, A System of Judicial Notice Based on Fairness and Convenience, in R. Pound, ed., Perspectives of Law 69, 76 (1964). See also McNaughton, Judicial Notice—Excerpts Relating to the Morgan-Wigmore Controversy, 14 Vand.L.Rev. 779 (1961).

The skeptical attitude toward the need for judicial notice, implicit in these questions, applies only when the court proposes to notice facts that are disputable. When facts are truly indisputable—the day on which a certain date fell, the name of the street on which the courthouse is located, the Great Lake on which the City of Chicago is located, the chemical formula for salt, or whether trout are fish—both time and money are saved by allowing the fact to be noticed. Indeed, it is at times difficult to prove by admissible evidence facts that are common knowledge. When this is the case, justice may turn on whether notice is allowed.

But consider this comment by Professor Schwartz:

[Judicial notice] fails as a means of identifying issues that need be tried because of the extraneous limitation to facts that are of "common notoriety" or "capable of immediate and accurate determination." The only significant question should be whether the particular factual issue is genuinely in dispute. * * *

* * *

* * * [A] party who is aware that there is strong proof of his contention and would be entitled to have judicial notice taken should be able to demonstrate his right to summary judgment or a directed verdict. In addition to covering all cases within the scope of judicial notice as presently conceived, the summary judgment and directed verdict procedures serve to foreclose spurious issues that are beyond reach of judicial notice. The overlap between summary judgment or directed verdict on the one hand and judicial notice on the other creates the risk that a party may invoke judicial notice, overlook the other devices, and thus be denied relief to which he is entitled. * * *

* * *

The use of judicial notice as a pretrial device is probably explicable in historical terms by the unavailability of summary judgment (and perhaps discovery devices such as requests for admissions that can also be used to eliminate spurious issues) as a means of limiting trials to matters genuinely in dispute. One other contemporary justification might be offered. Since the exclusionary rules of evidence generally do not govern what a judge may consider in determining whether to take judicial notice, judicial notice may be viewed as a means of relaxing the hearsay limitations on the use of documentary evidence. This approach to the problem is unfortunate. If reliable documentation is being excluded by the hearsay rule, the rule ought to be changed. It is anomalous indeed for a scholarly work to be characterized as a "source of indisputable accuracy" for the purpose of allowing judicial notice and yet to be excluded as hearsay at trial.

In any event, with the advent of liberal discovery and summary judgment, the judicial notice doctrine is not significant where counsel realizes that his position may be so strong that he can avoid litigating the matter at trial. Its more significant use, however, is when it is discovered after all the evidence is in that a party has failed to offer adequate proof with respect to a contention that the court nevertheless feels is true. In this situation the limitations of the judicial notice doctrine can create more serious problems. The court can supply the missing proof only if the stated requirements are met. If they cannot be met, however, the case must be decided on the existing record no matter how strong the indications are that vital evidence has been omitted.

This is obviously a bad result. If there is still time to produce reliable proof before the case is submitted for decision, the court should advise counsel to obtain it. Or if the inadequacy is detected after an initial determination, the party should be permitted to demonstrate the fact by affidavit or other irrefutable proof. More fundamentally, the court should never decide a case on a record it regards as inadequate. Rather, it should invoke the alternative provided by the proposed Rule, which assures an informed resolution of the issue with the least possible expense and burden.[48]

The question Professor Schwartz poses for Professor Davis is whether judicial notice is the appropriate guarantor of convenience. The question posed for Professor Morgan's followers and the drafters of the Federal Rules is whether the doctrine is necessary.

Judgment on the pleadings, summary judgment preceded by discovery, and directed verdicts are useful devices to ensure that needless litigation does not take place. Such procedures are alternatives to judicial notice and fit more easily into the traditional mode of trial in American courts. In some respects they accomplish more than judicial notice, because they can end disputes when particular litigants do not actually disagree on important facts, even though the facts are not of the type justifying judicial notice. But do these devices accomplish everything that can be accomplished by judicial notice?

The answer is no. In criminal cases judicial notice cannot take a core issue from the jury, but it allows the state to dispense with proof in a situation in which neither summary judgment nor a directed verdict can be ordered. In civil cases the argument that judicial notice is expendable fails to recognize that devices like summary judgment depend upon gathering proof admissible at trial, that discovery may be

---

48. Schwartz, A Suggestion for the Demise of Judicial Notice of "Judicial Facts", 45 Tex.L.Rev. 1212 (1967). The author proposes a statutory substitute for judicial notice of judicial facts.

(1) If the trial court in a case in which both sides have rested and the case has not been decided shall determine that the evidence with respect to a material issue of fact is significantly less than may be available and that there is a substantial risk that decision based on the evidence of record measured by the applicable burdens of proof and persuasion may not comport with actual fact it may

(a) in all cases where there is no jury and in jury cases where the additional evidence can be obtained without substantial delay stay all proceedings until the parties have an opportunity to obtain the additional evidence and then permit the evidence to be introduced and considered in the decision of the case, or

(b) in jury cases where the additional evidence cannot be obtained without substantial delay discharge the jury and direct retrial of the case when the additional evidence is obtained.

(2) If the trial court after the case has been decided or an appellate court shall determine that the evidence with respect to a material issue of fact is significantly less than may be available and that there is a substantial risk that decision based on the evidence of record measured by the applicable burdens of proof and persuasion may not comport with actual fact it may

(a) afford the parties the opportunity to demonstrate to the Court before whom the matter is pending their respective rights to summary judgment with respect to the issue, or

(b) remand the case for the taking of further evidence and reconsideration by the judge before whom the case was originally heard (who may be the judge issuing the order) or a retrial of the issue before a jury as may be appropriate.

(3) The party or parties against whom the issue would be resolved on the state of the record prior to the proceedings authorized by this Rule shall be responsible for all costs, including reasonable attorney's fees, incurred by the other parties in connection with proceedings authorized by this Rule.

Id. at 1213–14.

expensive,[49] and that directed verdicts are available only after proof is offered.[50] What happens to litigants who cannot afford to muster the necessary proof? Will parties with funds always find the sources needed to prevail on motions for summary judgment or by directed verdicts? Should court time be spent introducing evidence on indisputable matters? Should litigants be required to spend money to prove matters that cannot be reasonably contested? The questions are rhetorical. Obviously there are circumstances in which judicial notice makes considerable sense.

We do, however, agree with Professor Schwartz when he argues that judicial notice should not be used to fill gaps in an appellate record or as a backdoor for hearsay evidence. Rather, judicial notice should be viewed as one tool of an efficient judicial system.

Problem IX–19. A group of citizens brings an action challenging the apportionment of the state legislature. They claim that population disparities between districts are so great as to violate the principle of one-person, one-vote. **Can the district court hearing the challenge take judicial notice of census figures reporting the population of the various districts? What is the actual effect of taking notice?**

Problem IX–20. Jack L. Mills brings an action against Denver Tramway for personal injuries suffered when he was struck by one of the company's streetcars. Mills had been hit by a westbound streetcar while crossing the Tramway's tracks after alighting from an eastbound streetcar. There is evidence that Mills was contributorily negligent in failing to notice the westbound car, and that the driver of the westbound car did everything possible to stop before hitting Mills. However, there is no evidence that the driver sounded a gong or bell or other warning device. Mills' counsel requests that the jury be instructed that under the doctrine of last clear chance even though Mills did not exercise reasonable care in crossing the tracks, if the driver realized or should have realized that the accident could have been avoided by ringing the gong, Mills is entitled to recover. Tramway objects to the instruction, correctly pointing out that Mills has introduced no evidence that the streetcar that hit him had a bell or gong. Mills' counsel then asks the court to reopen the case and take judicial notice that all streetcars are equipped with bells or gongs. **Should judicial notice be taken? Is this a case in which, rather than taking notice, a court should follow Professor Schwartz's proposal?**

Problem IX–21. Lawrence was charged with grand larceny arising out of the theft of an automobile, a 1967 Ford, stolen in March, 1971. At the conclusion of the evidence, Lawrence moved for a directed verdict because no evidence had been introduced to establish the value of the stolen car. The

---

49. See, e.g., Fed.R.Civ.P. 56. Judgment on the pleadings cannot be granted where material facts are disputed in the pleadings. If facts are not disputed, judicial notice is not necessary.

50. The reason for the error is that in the preceding comment the author is concerned primarily with the use of judicial notice as a device to secure justice on a technically inadequate record. If this is the concern, judicial notice is both too narrow and unnecessary. But, as suggested by the quotations from Wigmore and Thayer, judicial notice serves other ends as well.

state's attorney might properly, and with little difficulty, have moved to re-open to supply the missing evidence. She did not do so, but instead argued that judicial notice could be taken of the value of the car. The court denied defendant's motion and included in its instructions to the jury the following:

"Grand Larceny so far as it might be material in this case is committed when the property taken is of a value exceeding $50.00."

"In this case you will take the value of this property as being in excess of $50.00 and therefore the defendant, if he is guilty at all, is guilty of grand larceny."

Has the court properly taken judicial notice in this case? Would the court's instruction be proper under FRE 201? Is judicial notice in these circumstances constitutional? Would you answer any of these questions differently if the theft had occurred in March 1981?

Assume that there is evidence that the car was in perfect condition when it was stolen and that it had been well cared for by its owner. Assume also that there is no evidence offered in the trial court on the value of the car and no instruction by the court about the value of the car, but that the court tells the jury that one element of the crime is that the property taken must have been worth more than $50. **If the jury convicts and the defendant appeals, could an appellate court take judicial notice of the value of the car? If not, must the appellate court reverse the conviction?**

Problem IX–22. Black residents of Little Rock, Arkansas bring a class action in federal court to enjoin a recreational facility called Lake Nixon Club from denying them admission because of their race. They allege a violation of Title II of the Civil Rights Act of 1964. After a trial, the district court dismisses the complaint, finding that although plaintiffs were refused admission because of their race, Lake Nixon Club was not a public accommodation within the meaning of the statute because it was not in interstate commerce. The Court of Appeals affirms, and the case reaches the Supreme Court. There is no specific evidence that interstate travelers have been served at the Club, but there is evidence that the Club contains a snack bar serving 100,000 patrons each season and that the Club advertises its facilities in local hotels, motels, and restaurants. **On the basis of these facts, should the Supreme Court take judicial notice of the "fact" that the Club must serve interstate travelers?**

Problem IX–23. Mary Longly files suit against an airline claiming that its weight program (regulating the weights of employees) discriminates against women. The trial judge rejects the challenge. Based on his more than 100 flights on the defendant airline and 500 aboard 24 other airlines, the judge takes judicial notice of the fact that the defendant's employees have a reputation for competence as well as good looks. **Has the judge acted properly?** Assume the regulation in question provides that no employee who regularly meets the public may exceed by 20% the appropriate weight with respect to their height and bone structure that is given by the "Physician's Table of Appropriate Weights." The table specifies appropriate weights for women which, depending on height and bone structure, are between six and twenty-two pounds less than the corresponding weights for men. **May the judge**

take judicial notice of the weights specified in the "Physician's Table" and of the fact that the proper weight for women is at all heights and bone structures less than the proper weight for men? Can the judge take judicial notice of the fact that it is no more difficult for women to remain within 20% of their appropriate weight than it is for men? How would you support a motion for judicial notice of these facts? How would you oppose such a motion? If the plaintiff supplies the judge with the airline's personnel records, can the judge on the basis of these records take notice of the fact that 73% of the employees who fill "public contact jobs" are women but only 21% of those occupying "internal contact jobs" are women? [The terms in quotation marks are the terms used in the company records from which the figures are taken.]

Problem IX–24. Harriet Barber is charged with auto theft. At an earlier trial on the same charges the case had been dismissed when Harriet, her counsel, three jurors and the judge came down with the flu. At the second trial Harriet moves to dismiss the charges, claiming that the state is precluded by the double jeopardy clause from trying her again for the same theft. The assistant prosecutor, new on the job and unaware of the earlier trial, responds that he does not believe there was an earlier trial, and that if there was an earlier trial, he does not believe it involved the same charges. **May the trial judge take judicial notice of the fact that there was an earlier trial on the same charges? May the trial judge also take judicial notice of the fact that at the first trial the prosecutor moved to dismiss only after Harriet's counsel stipulated that all claims of double jeopardy arising out of the dismissal would be waived? Assuming notice may be taken, how should this be done? What are the obligations of counsel? Do your answers to any of these questions depend upon whether the judge at the second trial was also the presiding judge at the first trial?**

Problem IX–25. Merry Levin is charged with negligent homicide resulting from an auto accident. She demands a jury trial. At the trial, a highway patrol officer testifies that just before the accident he had clocked Merry's car on radar and it was traveling in excess of 90 m.p.h. Merry objects to the officer's testimony on the grounds that no evidence has been introduced to show that radar is an accurate way of measuring speed nor is there evidence that the machine that clocked Merry was accurate. **May the state meet either ground for objection through judicial notice? If the judge notices that radar is an accurate way of measuring speed, may Merry introduce an "expert" to testify that radar is not an accurate way of measuring speed? Could Merry argue to the jury that radar is not an accurate way to measure speed? Would your answer to any of these questions be different if this were a civil action?**

Problem IX–26. Henry Miller sues Dennis Dam for assault and battery, claiming that Dam was trying to drive him out of the restaurant business. The first count of Henry's complaint alleges that Dam hired two thugs, Cox and Box, to beat up Henry, and that the thugs did beat up Henry, breaking his arm and causing $10,000 in damages. The second count alleges that Dam later acquired a piece of Henry's hair, took it to a "voodoo woman" and had that woman incorporate the hair into a doll-image of Henry. Dam then stuck pins into the doll and broke the doll's leg, causing Henry great pain and a broken leg. Henry claims damages of $50,000 under this count. Dam moves to strike count two of Henry's complaint, asking the court to take judicial notice of the fact that one cannot cause physical injury by manipulating a doll-image. **Should the court notice this fact? Is there any evidence that Henry might present to the judge in an effort to get the court to deny notice? Should the judge rule in the same way on Dam's motion if Henry were seeking only punitive damages for this "assault"?**

Problem IX–27. In the same situation as the preceding problem, Dam, defending himself on count one, testifies that he was not acquainted with Cox and Box and so could not have hired them to assault Henry. **If this were a bench trial, could a state judge take judicial notice of the fact that Dam, Cox and Box had pleaded guilty in federal court to a conspiracy to extort money by force and violence? Could the judge inform the jury of this fact in a jury trial? Could the judge, upon the request of Henry's counsel, take judicial notice of the fact that some six months earlier the lead story on the society page of the local paper reported the marriage of Cox's daughter to Dam's son and contained a picture of Cox and Dam together with their children?**

3. LEGISLATIVE FACTS

While Professor Davis recognizes that there is no bright line separating adjudicative and legislative facts, he does suggest that there is a practical difference between them, useful for analytical purposes. Legislative facts are those "which have relevance to legal reasoning and the lawmaking process, whether in the formulation of a legal principle or ruling by a judge or court or in the enactment of a legislative body."[51]

Professor Davis applied this distinction in the following comment on an earlier version of FRE 201:

The facts that judges use for lawmaking cannot be limited to facts that are "not subject to reasonable dispute." * * * Facts needed for judicial lawmaking are seldom developed through evidence submitted at a trial. Such facts are amost always the subject of judicial notice. And such facts are seldom of such a nature that they can be called, in the language of 201, "not subject to reasonable dispute."

* * *

When courts engage in lawmaking, they constantly use facts, through judicial notice, that they could not use if your version of Rule 201 were literally applied.

For instance, in the abortion cases, Roe v. Wade, 410 U.S. 113 (1973), and Doe v. Bolton, 410 U.S. 179 (1973), the Supreme Court's opinions are full of extra-record facts about the history of abortion, and about abortion practices throughout the world.

Chief Justice Burger said, 410 U.S. at 208: "I am somewhat troubled that the Court has taken notice of various scientific and medical data in reaching its conclusion; however, I do not believe that the Court has exceeded the scope of judicial notice acceptable in other contexts."

* * *

51. Advisory Committee Note to FRE 201.

In 1924, Mr. Justice Brandeis said in a formal opinion that "Much evidence referred to by me is not in the record." Jay Burns Baking Co. v. Bryan, 264 U.S. 504, 533 (1924). You should look at his opinion and see how much extra-record evidence he put into it. Yet that was judicial excellence, not misbehavior. It was in his capacity to bring facts to bear upon legal problems that Mr. Justice Brandeis was one of the greatest Justices we have ever had. Of course, the facts were legislative facts, not adjudicative facts. As to what the parties did—that is, as to adjudicative facts—Mr. Justice Brandeis would not go outside the record.

* * *

1. Facts that are most useful for thinking about problems of policy are often in the nature of actual conclusions that are mixed with judgment or opinion.

2. The bulk of social science in its present stage of development probably cannot be called "clearly indisputable," but it is decidedly useful in trying to work out law and policy.

3. Even though anyone would prefer to found law making and policy making upon clearly indisputable facts, the practical choice is often between proceeding in ignorance and following the uncertain, tentative, and far from indisputable teachings of social science such as they are, for the simple reason that clearly indisputable facts are often unavailable.

4. The whole vital and basic idea of the Brandeis brief and all that goes with it, including research by counsel and by judges into factual materials that are useful in thinking about policy ques-

tions, * * * assumes that courts will consider extra-record facts which bear upon disputed issues and that the facts may be presented without regard for the question whether they are indisputable.

5. The judicial making of law and policy is much strengthened, not weakened, by the judges' increasing resort to social science literature. The judicial tendency in this direction should be encouraged, and it may be most needed when the factual materials are least clear. Whenever a judge finds a problem of social policy especially difficult, he properly draws upon his education and experience, including a spectrum of facts from the most specific to the most general, and many of the facts or mixtures of facts with judgment are in the nature of faulty impressions.[52]

————————

There are few who dispute the need of appellate courts to rely on extra-record facts. But there is an understandable concern about the frequency and scope of such reliance and a feeling that certain procedural safeguards might be appropriate. Consider, for example, the decisions in the abortion cases referred to by Davis. Was it appropriate for the Court to conclude largely on the basis of medical evidence neither presented at trial nor argued at any stage of the proceedings that the fetus becomes viable approximately twenty-eight weeks after conception and that it thereafter might exist independently of the mother? If the Court believed that this information was important to its analysis, should it have circulated a draft opinion to the parties and given them a chance to dispute the facts on which it relied?

52. Letter from Kenneth C. Davis to Hon. William L. Hungate, August 7, 1973, in Supplement to Hearings on the Rules of Evidence Before the Subcomm. on Criminal Justice of the House Comm. on the Judiciary, 93d Cong., 1st Sess., at 312–317 (1973).

Problem IX–28. In Furman v. Georgia,[53] the Supreme Court held that the death sentences imposed upon two convicted rapists and one convicted murderer constituted cruel and unusual punishment in violation of the eighth amendment. Five concurring Justices agreed on a one paragraph concurring opinion, and each also wrote a separate opinion. The opinion by Justice White illustrates a unique form of judicial notice.

He wrote:

> I must arrive at judgment; and I can do no more than state a conclusion based on 10 years of almost daily exposure to the facts and circumstances of hundreds and hundreds of federal and state criminal cases involving crimes for which death is the authorized penalty. That conclusion * * * is that the death penalty is exacted with great infrequency even for the most atrocious crimes and that there is no meaningful basis for distinguishing the few cases in which it is imposed from the many cases in which it is not.[54]

Should this kind of judicial notice be encouraged? Can it be avoided? Should the states seeking to uphold capital punishment have been given the opportunity to demonstrate to White's satisfaction that there were grounds for distinguishing the few cases in which capital punishment is imposed from those in which it is not imposed? How might such an opportunity be provided?

Problem IX–29. In its last major round of obscenity cases, the Supreme Court held that states have the power to regulate materials that depict or describe sexual conduct if the regulated materials are specifically defined by state law and if prohibitions are limited to works which, taken as a whole, appeal to a prurient interest in sex, portray sexual conduct in a patently offensive way, and do not have serious literary, artistic, political, or scientific value. The issue of whether a work appeals to prurient interest is to be decided by focusing on the reaction of the average person applying contemporary community standards. The court has also stated that the determination of obscenity does not lend itself to expert testimony, but should be left to the good sense of jurors.[55] **How can the trial judge determine that an individual juror or a jury panel represents contemporary community standards unless such information as who sees and reads various kinds of books and movies is known before the jury is selected? What does it mean to represent contemporary community standards? Is the jury by definition a cross-section of the community? How does the court determine whether a work has serious value?**

---

53. 408 U.S. 238 (1972); for an excellent examination of the opinions, see P. Brest, Processes of Constitutional Decisionmaking 894–935 (1975).

In racial discrimination cases the Supreme Court often takes judicial notice. For example, in United Steelworkers v. Weber, 443 U.S. 193, 198 n.1 (1979), the Court said that "[j]udicial findings of exclusion from crafts on racial grounds are so numerous as to make such exclusion a proper subject for judicial notice."

54. 408 U.S. 238, 313 (1972).

55. See generally Miller v. California, 413 U.S. 15 (1973), and Paris Adult Theater I v. Slaton, 413 U.S. 49, 56 (1973).

Problem IX–30. When a trial judge is required to balance the probative value of evidence against its prejudicial effect in order to determine whether or not to admit evidence, the judge must of necessity consider matters on which no proof has been offered. **Does such consideration amount to judicial notice? Should the judge inform the parties of any sources she has consulted in making her ruling? Of rules of thumb she has relied upon? Should she inform the parties of the extra-record facts she intends to rely upon in reaching a decision on the merits of case? Of the facts she relies upon in evaluating the credibility of witnesses in a bench trial?**

---

4. JUDICIAL NOTICE OF LAW

It is a basic precept of American jurisprudence that questions of law are reserved for the judge.[56] In deciding questions of law, the judge is not confined to sources supplied by the parties. Generally a judge is required to take judicial notice of domestic law if asked by a party, and is expected to do so absent a request. However, a failure to notice law may not be reversible error if counsel has not pointed it out. State trial courts notice federal law and their own law. Federal trial courts notice all state law as well as federal law. Law for the purposes of judicial notice includes executive orders and proclamations, and administrative regulations published so as to be readily available. Private laws and municipal ordinances are not usually noticed.[57]

At common law, state courts did not notice the law of sister states. Today a majority of states have adopted the Uniform Judicial Notice of Foreign Law Act,[58] alleviating the burdens of a system that presumed the inaccessibility and incomprehensibility of foreign law. Some states that have not adopted the Uniform Act presume, absent proof to the contrary, that the law of a sister state is identical to its own. Otherwise, the law of sister states must be pleaded and proved. The law of foreign

---

56. Separating law from fact is not always easy, however. Is it not arguable, as the last problem may suggest, that courts should alert parties to sources of law used to resolve legal issues?

57. See generally McCormick § 335, at 776–77; 1 Weinstein's Evidence ¶ 200[02].

58. **UNIFORM JUDICIAL NOTICE OF FOREIGN LAW ACT**

§ 1. **Judicial Notice.** Every court of this state shall take judicial notice of the common law and statutes of every state, territory and other jurisdiction of the United States.

§ 2. **Information of the Court.** The court may inform itself of such laws in such manner as it may deem proper, and the court may call upon counsel to aid it in obtaining such information.

§ 3. **Ruling Reviewable.** The determination of such laws shall be made by the court and not by the jury, and shall be reviewable.

§ 4. **Evidence as to Laws of Other Jurisdictions.** Any party may also present to the trial court any admissible evidence of such laws, but, to enable a party to offer evidence of the law in another jurisdiction or to ask that judicial notice be taken thereof, reasonable notice shall be given to the adverse parties either in the pleadings or otherwise.

§ 5. **Foreign Country.** The law of a jurisdiction other than those referred to in Section 1 shall be an issue for the court, but shall not be subject to the foregoing provisions concerning judicial notice.

* * *

This act was withdrawn by the National Conference of Commissioners in 1966, but it had been adopted in several states prior to its withdrawal.

countries must still be pleaded and proved in most courts. But Fed.R.Civ.P. 44.1 now provides:

A party who intends to raise an issue concerning the law of a foreign country shall give notice in his pleadings or other reasonable written notice. The court, in determining foreign law, may consider any relevant material or source, in- cluding testimony, whether or not sub- mitted by a party or admissible under the Federal Rules of Evidence. The court's determination shall be treated as a rul- ing on a question of law.[59]

Some states have begun to modify the rule that the failure to plead and prove relevant foreign law requires that a case be dis- missed.[60]

Problem IX–31. Gena Rowlan and Debbie Harris, both of Shreveport, Virginia, vacationed in Alaska, having driven there from Virginia in Row- lan's car. While in Anchorage, Rowlan struck a parked car, seriously injur- ing Harris. When the two returned home, Harris sued Rowlan, claiming that she deliberately drove 35 m.p.h. inside the Anchorage city limits, de- spite the fact that the speed limit was 30 m.p.h. Rowlan denied the alle- gation that the speed limit was 30 m.p.h. where the accident took place. The following colloquy occurred at trial:

Judge: Now, Ms. Harris, you ask me to take judicial notice that the speed limit was 30 m.p.h. What authority do you have for that?

Harris: Judge, it's the law of Alaska. There was no sign that I can remember, but the law says that in unposted areas within cities the maxi- mum speed limit is 30 m.p.h.

Rowlan: I never heard of that law, judge. I think she's wrong. As I remember it the street we were on was a 40 m.p.h. zone.

Judge: Well, I don't have anything in front of me that would enable me to decide the point. Perhaps I should just apply our own state law, which makes 25 m.p.h. the maximum in this kind of case.

Rowlan: Judge, that is just ridiculous. What you should do is throw this case out.

At this point what should the judge do? How might the parties con- vince the judge that the speed limit was or was not 35 m.p.h.

---

59. See generally Miller, Federal Rule 44.1 and the "Fact" Approach to Determining Foreign Law: Death Knell for a Die-Hard Doctrine, 65 Mich.L.Rev. 613 (1967).

60. E.g., Leary v. Gledhill, 8 N.J. 260, 84 A.2d 725 (1951). Ascertaining international law presents difficult problems for American courts. Recently, some courts have relied upon expert witnesses in an effort to cope with the intricacies of international legal prob- lems. Whether courts should accept expert help on legal questions, and if so, what kind of help they should accept are questions now being debated by international lawyers.

For an excellent discussion of the problems courts have in ascertaining and applying in- ternational and foreign law, see Second An- nual Sokol Colloquium, 18 Va. J. Int'l L. 609 (1978).

SECTION III. APPELLATE REVIEW: SUFFICIENCY OF THE EVIDENCE AND THE EFFECT OF ERROR

One of the functions of appellate courts is to determine whether there was sufficient evidence below to warrant the decision of the trier of fact. In civil cases the question of sufficiency most often arises in appeals from rulings on motions for directed verdicts or judgments notwithstanding the verdict. Sometimes challenges are based on the alleged insufficiency of the evidence to support the findings of fact in a case tried to a judge. Whenever the judge determines to let a case go to the jury, and thus denies a request for a peremptory ruling, a disappointed litigant has a potential challenge based on the contention that there was insufficient evidence to warrant a jury verdict. Whenever the judge enters judgment on a jury verdict a similar challenge is available. Whenever the judge makes findings, he determines, explicitly or implicitly, that there is sufficient evidence to support the findings. Since the prosecution has no appeal from an acquittal in a criminal case, arguments about the sufficiency of the evidence in criminal trials are always initiated by the defendant.

It is important to remember that it is not the task of appellate judges reviewing facts to determine how they would have ruled on the evidence presented. Their task is only to determine whether the evidence was such that a reasonable trier of fact might have reached the decision below.

It should be obvious by now that in many respects courts treat criminal cases and civil cases differently. In this Chapter we have seen that the standard of proof is typically higher in criminal cases than in civil actions and that certain limitations on presumptions and judicial notice apply only in the criminal context. In previous chapters we have seen that rules of evidence may be applied differently in criminal and civil proceedings. Therefore, you should not be surprised to learn that courts review questions of sufficiency in criminal cases differently from similar questions in the civil context. As Roger Traynor, former Chief Justice of the California Supreme Court, has written:

> When it is the responsibility of the trier of fact to observe the requirement of clear and convincing evidence, as in fraud cases, or of evidence beyond a reasonable doubt, as in criminal cases, it becomes the responsibility of the appellate court to test the finding accordingly. In reviewing such cases, quite different from the ordinary civil case, the court should do more than determine simply whether the trier of fact could reasonably conclude that the alleged fact was more probable than not. It should determine whether the trier of fact could reasonably conclude that the alleged fact was * * * in criminal cases, almost certain.[61]

The view taken by Traynor is generally accepted as correct. In determining whether the evidence was sufficient to justify some finding of the trier of fact, an appellate court must judge sufficiency against the standard of proof utilized by the trier of fact. It might be reasonable to conclude that some fact was established by a preponderance of evidence, yet be unreasonable to conclude that it was established beyond a reasonable doubt.

When an appellate court examines the sufficiency of the evidence, it gives the winning party the benefit of all doubts and assumes that the proof properly offered was accepted for all that it was worth, since the judge or jury might reasonably have given it the maximum possible weight.

---

61. R. Traynor, The Riddle of Harmless Error 29 (1970).

It is not surprising that it is a rare occurrence when a judgment is overturned on appeal because of insufficient evidence at trial. To overturn a verdict on these grounds means that the trial jury or judge rendered a decision that no reasonable person could have reached. In jury trials it also means that the trial judge acted improperly in refusing to upset the jury verdict.

It is not unusual for appellate courts to find that although the record as a whole supports the verdict rendered, the trial judge erred in his decisions to admit or exclude evidence or in his instructions to the jury. When an appellate court finds error, it must decide whether the error justifies the outright reversal of the judgment entered below or a reversal coupled with a remand for a new trial.

In criminal cases for errors of constitutional magnitude the United States Supreme Court has said that the mistake cannot be disregarded unless it is clear beyond a reasonable doubt that the error did not effect the outcome of the case. If in the light of the entire record the error does not meet this test of harmlessness, a new trial will be ordered, unless the error involved the improper admission of evidence that was necessary to the government's prima facie case. In the latter instance a dismissal will be ordered, or if it is unclear whether the government's case would have withstood a motion to dismiss without the evidence, the matter will be remanded to the trial judge for the appropriate determination.

Courts treat evidentiary errors in civil cases and nonconstitutional errors in criminal cases in a variety of ways. The following article describes some of the standards of review that have been used by courts reviewing such errors. After reviewing these standards the author urges that review of error should be stricter in criminal cases and that the proper distinction is between criminal and civil cases rather than between constitutional and nonconstitutional issues. After reading the exerpt, ask yourself how you would decide whether or not an error was sufficiently damaging to warrant reversal in civil and criminal cases.

SALTZBURG, THE HARM OF HARMLESS ERROR

59 Va.L.Rev. 988, 992–93, 999, 1012–29 (1973).

* * *

It would make little sense to adopt the *Winship*[62] standard, which is designed to prevent criminal convictions if there is even a reasonable doubt in the minds of jurors as to the guilt of the person charged, and then on appeal to emasculate that evidentiary standard by allowing a conviction to stand when the trial court has violated evidentiary rules which might have influenced the jury by creating the requisite doubt. Justice Brennan said in *Winship* that:

use of the reasonable doubt standard is indispensable to command the respect and confidence of the community in its applications of the criminal law. It is critical that the moral force of the criminal law not be diluted by a standard of proof that leaves people in doubt whether innocent men are being condemned.

If the "moral force" of the criminal law is not to be diluted on appeal, convictions must be reversed where the appellate court cannot arrive at a conclusion about the impact of an error on the jury verdict with the same degree of certainty demanded at the trial.

Appeals from civil cases can properly receive somewhat different treatment be-

62. In re Winship, 397 U.S. 358 (1970).

cause of the less stringent standard of proof in civil trials. The plaintiff in a civil case may win his verdict even though the jury has substantial doubts as to the validity of his claim. So long as the jury finds it more likely than not that the claim is good, it must follow the court's instructions and return a verdict for the plaintiff. Because lawmakers have not compelled civil juries to decide cases on the basis of a high degree of certainty, it would make little sense to advocate the adoption of a harmless error standard which would compel appellate courts to be very certain as to the precise effect of errors on the trier of fact's decision. So long as the appellate court reverses when it is *probable* that the error affected the decision below, the appellate court is true to the preponderance of the evidence standard. Thus unlike criminal cases, decisions in civil cases are acceptable even though there exists almost as much chance that they are wrong as that they are right.

* * *

Special Treatment for Constitutional Error

Rather than focusing on the kind of case in which error was committed, American courts have tended to focus on the kind of error committed. If an error was of constitutional dimensions, reversal was once almost automatic. While this is no longer always the case, constitutional errors still receive different treatment from all other errors and are still far more likely to require a new trial than nonconstitutional errors. In large part this special treatment can be attributed to theories developed in the federal courts.

* * *

In Chapman v. State of California[63] the Court finally confronted the constitutional problem. * * * The defendants in *Chapman* had been convicted of robbing,

kidnapping, and murdering a bartender. At the trial, the prosecution had taken advantage of a provision in the California Constitution which permitted comment on the failure of an accused to testify; and in addressing the jury the prosecutor had made several references to the defendants' refusal to take the stand. Shortly after the trial in *Chapman*, the Supreme Court held in Griffin v. California that the prosecution's commenting on an accused's silence violated the fifth and fourteenth amendments. Nevertheless, upon appeal the California Supreme Court found harmless the constitutional error in the trial stage of *Chapman*. The United States Supreme Court's decision was predictable. Writing for a seven-man majority, Justice Black reversed the state court. His opinion was divided into three main parts. First, he considered the question whether a federal or state rule for judging the impact of error should govern constitutional violations and opted in favor of the federal rule. Second, he asked whether there could ever be harmless constitutional error and answered affirmatively. Third, he promulgated a rule for measuring the effect of error:

> [B]efore a federal constitutional error can be held harmless, the court must be able to declare a belief that it was harmless beyond a reasonable doubt.

Applying his test to the facts of the case, Justice Black had little difficulty in concluding that the error was not harmless. *Chapman* is an interesting and important case because it clearly represents a broad exertion of federal judicial power over state courts and, at the same time, a retreat from the rule of automatic reversal which the Court had previously relied upon in dealing with invasions of constitutional rights.

In *Chapman,* Justice Black rejected the California test for harmless error, which required a showing that it was reasonably *probable* that an error affected the verdict,

---

63. 386 U.S. 18 (1967).

rather than that it was reasonably *possible*. While the cryptic language of the case makes analysis difficult, Justice Black seemed to recognize that because of the enormous burden of proof placed on the prosecutor in criminal cases, a small showing of prejudice should suffice to convince an appellate court that an error during the course of the trial was reversible.[i]

* * *

THE PREFERABLE TEST OF HARMLESS ERROR IN CRIMINAL CASES

One possible test of harmfulness would be to presume prejudice where the pros-

ecutor could not demonstrate that the presumption had been misapplied. * * * Yet because prejudice to a verdict generally eludes precise evidentiary determination, the finding of harmlessness is generally based upon other than firm factual proof. Requiring the prosecution to overcome a presumption of prejudice is tantamount to mandating automatic reversal whenever there are errors during trial. Of course, the same criticism may be made of presumptions that work in favor of the prosecution by imposing the burden of proving harm upon the defendant. Again the presumption confuses rather than aids

---

i. There has been much ado about Justice Black's rejecting the test of harmless error that focused on whether, aside from the error, there was overwhelming evidence requiring conviction. This has been read as a rejection of any test phrased in terms of what a jury would have done but for the error. * * * However, there may be no significant difference between these tests so long as the Court is able to say that it is reasonably certain a jury would have convicted on the basis of the untainted evidence. What Justice Black apparently rejected was the notion that reversal was not required merely because a jury *could* have convicted on the basis of good evidence; his test insured that they *would* have.

One point must be kept clearly in mind in any discussion of harmless error cases. There may be a difference between a rule which says appellate courts will reverse criminal convictions because of trial errors if the errors might have contributed to the finding of guilt, and a rule which says appellate courts will reverse criminal convictions because of trial errors only if the other evidence (unrelated to the error) is insufficient to require a guilty verdict. The first rule can be read as requiring reversal where, irrespective of the fact that if retrial was permitted the jury might convict on the basis of proper evidence, the error could have contributed to the verdict actually reached by the jury. The second test could end with the first half of the inquiry— if the jury would have likely convicted on the basis of the proper evidence adduced, any trial errors are harmless.

The extent of difference between these two rules depends upon the degree of certainty that, but for the error, the jury would have convicted. When the second rule is read as

requiring reversal for trial errors unless it is *virtually certain* or established *beyond a reasonable doubt* that on the basis of the other evidence in the case there would have been a conviction, the two rules are substantially the same. For in order to say that the jury was almost certain to convict, it must be shown that the proof was so overwhelming, aside from the taint of the error, that all reasonable jurors would find guilt beyond a reasonable doubt. Once this strong showing is made, it is hard to believe that the first test would not also be met, i.e., that anyone could believe that the error contributed to the verdict, or that its contribution was significant enough to warrant reversal.

But if the second rule is read as requiring affirmance of a conviction so long as it is probable (more likely than not) that another jury would convict, or even worse, that it is possible they would convict, then the two rules differ. This reading would go a long way towards undercutting the standard of proof in criminal cases and towards encouraging trial errors. It would permit appellate courts to affirm convictions with the most minimal assurance that on the basis of valid evidence a jury would find the defendant guilty beyond a reasonable doubt, and it would indicate to prosecutors that their errors are not likely to be costly.

There remains the theoretical possibility that an error may be so serious that it would be almost impossible to conclude that the jury did not rely on it; yet, the evidence of guilt is overwhelming. It is doubtful that this sort of case will arise very often, since errors tend to be viewed as serious or minor depending on their importance in the context of a particular litigation.

analysis. Yet, in moving away from the presumption of prejudice which benefitted the convicted defendant, some courts adopted this standard, apparently without regard for its logical inadequacy.

In an effort to escape the old presumption which favored the defendant other courts, supported by commentators and legislators, have maintained that a conviction should only be reversed when it is clearly wrong. Whatever merit this "clearly-wrong" standard may have in a civil context, it is totally inappropriate in a criminal context where the standard of proof at trial is the proof beyond a reasonable doubt mandated by In re Winship. The "clearly-wrong" test is so far removed from this traditional trial court standard as to completely subvert it. Translated into its converse, it would be similar to a trial standard which convicted defendants if there was a bare possibility that they were guilty.

Other courts have asked whether the jury reached a correct result. This "correct-result" standard is also undesirable, since it runs counter to the principle that a citizen should be tried for criminal offenses only by a jury of his peers. To allow the court of appeals to ask whether the jury reached the correct result is, in essence, to permit the appellate judges to substitute their own judgments for the jury's. The American judicial system is concerned not with guilt in fact, but rather, in the words of Justice Rutledge's Kotteakos v. United States opinion, with "guilt in law, established by the judgment of laymen." As Justice Rutledge implied, the appellate court sits not to decide guilt or innocence, but to judge whether error may have influenced the decision of the trier of fact.

Still other courts have advocated that the appellate tribunal inquire whether it is more probable than not that the error affected the verdict. Although preferable to those tests previously discussed because it implicitly recognizes that the role of an appellate court is to examine error in light of the judgment of the trier of fact, it does not attempt to complement the burden of proof at trial. Under this test resolutions of appeals emasculate the proof beyond a reasonable doubt standard required at the trial court level by *Winship*. That standard requires reversal on appeal where there is a reasonable possibility that an error influenced the outcome; the former standard does not require reversal even when such influence is *reasonably probable,* but only when the probability of influence exceeds 50 percent.

Finally, Justice Traynor maintains that a court should reverse both civil and criminal cases unless it is "highly probable" that the error *did not* affect the judgment. Although this standard seems considerably more desirable than those previously discussed, the fact that it is an attempt to provide a uniform rule for all cases is fatal. Since a uniform appeal standard stands in direct contradiction to the separate and distinct standards used in civil as opposed to criminal proceedings at the trial court level, there is no doctrinal justification for commingling the standards of review in criminal and civil cases. To obtain his uniform standard, Justice Traynor has watered down the criminal standard in order to obtain an acceptable civil standard for judging the effects of error.

The Reasonable Possibility Standard

In order to be consistent with *Winship,* the courts of appeals should reverse trial court verdicts if there is a *reasonable* possibility that the error affected the judgment. Although it has been argued that this test is tantamount to a rule of automatic reversal, it must be remembered that it is a *reasonable* possibility of prejudice that is required, not just any possibility. The standard merely assures that appellate courts will seek the same high degree of certainty in criminal cases as will the trier of fact. It requires neither automatic reversal nor an abdication of judgment.

Rather, by requiring the court to make a judgment as to the reasonable impact of the error, it compels the court of appeals to determine whether the criminal trial was tainted with error and therefore whether the defendant is guilty in law. Although the same standard was advocated in *Chapman,* that case applied the reasonable-possibility standard only when the error during trial reached constitutional dimensions. But the standard should be applied uniformly in all criminal cases regardless of whether the trial court error was constitutional or nonconstitutional.

* * *

Instead Justice Black's opinion reflects an underlying belief either that constitutional errors are inherently more harmful than other errors, or that state courts are likely to subvert federal rights more quickly than state rights. The assumption may also be indicative of a desire to provide a deterrent to prevent violations of certain specific constitutional rights. However, it is erroneous to say that constitutional errors are more likely to have an injurious effect at trial than other errors. As Justice Harlan pointed out, the opposite may be more correct. There are relatively few rules derived from the federal constitution which bind state courts; there are hundreds of rules arising from nonconstitutional state rules of procedure, and it is these rules that provide a defendant with his primary protections.

Moreover, where federal and state protections overlap there is no inherent justification for favoring federal as opposed to state grounds. Consider, for instance, the introduction into evidence of a confession or admission which was illegally obtained. The evidence is dangerous because it is likely to carry great weight with the jury. But from the defendant's standpoint, it makes no difference whether an adverse jury verdict, based on the confession, is reversed upon the grounds that the illegal statement violates the federal rule of Miranda v. Arizona or a state rule regarding tacit admissions. Regardless of legal theory, the harm prevented is precisely the same. Similarly, although the protections provided by state hearsay rules and the sixth amendment's right of confrontation are not identical, violations of the state rule and the constitutional command are equally harmful to a defendant. It is the impact of the error upon the defendant's trial which should primarily concern the courts, not whether the error can be labelled constitutional or nonconstitutional.

* * *

Nevertheless much of the commentary about *Chapman* urges that there be a partial return to the rule of automatic reversal, and even Justice Traynor implies that such a rule is desirable in certain kinds of cases. But any attempts to catalogue the kinds of cases in advance would be an exercise in futility. Surely some classes of errors will be more or less likely to require reversal than others. Irrespective of the harmless error rule chosen, certain patterns will no doubt become apparent. But there will always be exceptions, and the use of the reasonable possibility test, which avoids automatic reversal, permits the patterns and their exceptions to develop naturally.

BIBLIOGRAPHY

Allen, Presumptions in Civil Actions Reconsidered, 66 Iowa L.Rev. 843 (1981).

Allen, Structuring Jury Decisionmaking in Criminal Cases: A Unified Constitutional Approach to Evidentiary Devices, 94 Harv.L.Rev. 321 (1980).

Davis, Administrative Law Text Ch. 15 (3d ed. 1972) (Judicial Notice).

McCormick, Chs. 35 (Judicial Notice) and 36 (Presumptions).

Thayer, A Preliminary Treatise on Evidence at the Common Law 300 (1898).

Traynor, The Riddle of Harmless Error (1970).

9 Wigmore §§ 2483–2550 (Presumptions); 2565–2583 (Judicial Notice).

Bigham, Presumptions, Burden of Proof and the Uniform Commercial Code, 21 Vand.L.Rev. 177 (1968).

Cleary, Presuming and Pleading: An Essay on Juristic Immaturity, 12 Stan.L.Rev. 5 (1955).

Davis, Judicial Notice, 1969 Law & Social Order 573.

Falkner, Notes on Presumptions, 15 Wash.L.Rev. 71 (1940).

Field, Assessing the Harmlessness of Federal Constitutional Error—A Process in Need of a Rationale, 125 U.Pa.L.Rev. 15 (1976).

James, Burdens of Proof, 47 Va.L.Rev. 51 (1961).

Laughlin, In Support of the Thayer Theory of Presumptions, 52 Mich.L.Rev. 195 (1953).

McBaine, Burden of Proof: Degrees of Belief, 32 Cal.L.Rev. 242 (1944).

McBaine, Burden of Proof: Presumptions, 2 U.C.L.A.L.Rev. 13 (1954).

McNaughton, Judicial Notice—Excerpts Relating to the Morgan-Wigmore Controversy, 4 Vand.L.Rev. 779 (1961).

Michael & Adler, The Trial of An Issue of Fact: I, 34 Colum.L.Rev. 1224 (1934).

Morgan, Further Observations on Presumptions, 16 So.Cal.L.Rev. 245 (1943).

Morgan, Instructing the Jury Upon Presumption and Burden of Proof, 47 Harv.L.Rev. 59 (1933).

Morgan, Judicial Notice, 57 Harv.L.Rev. 269 (1944).

Morgan, Presumptions, 12 Wash.L.Rev. 256 (1937).

Nesson, Rationality, Presumptions, and Judicial Comment: A Response to Professor Allen, 94 Harv.L.Rev. 1574 (1981).

Saltzburg, The Harm of Harmless Error, 59 Va.L.Rev. 988 (1973).

Saltzburg, Standards of Proof and Preliminary Questions of Fact, 27 Stan.L.Rev. 271 (1975).

Schwartz, A Suggestion for the Demise of Judicial Notice of "Judicial Facts," 45 Tex.L.Rev. 142 (1967).

Underwood, The Thumb on the Scales of Justice: Burdens of Persuasion in Criminal Cases, 86 Yale L.J. 1299 (1977).

Chapter Ten

EXPERT ASSISTANCE FOR JUDGES AND JURIES

SECTION I. INTRODUCTION TO EXPERTS

Litigation always entails the use of persons with specialized knowledge. Attorneys, for example, are persons trained in the law who have in some way demonstrated competence to handle legal questions, usually by passing a bar examination. Their expertise relates to the system of pleading and practice that molds factual and legal disputes for ultimate resolution by judges and juries. Witnesses too are specialists of a sort. They are usually produced because they are familiar with certain aspects of a dispute that are not commonly known. No special showing is needed to qualify the ordinary witness. So long as the witness has firsthand knowledge of relevant information, competence is presumed.[1]

Some witnesses, however, play a special role in litigation. We speak of them as "experts." They are able to aid the jury in its task of fact-finding, not because they have fortuitously observed events which are relevant to the jury's inquiry, but because they have specialized skill or training which enables them to perceive and interpret events in ways that ordinary laypeople cannot. In the words of one court, an expert is someone who "possesses extraordinary training [and is able] to aid laymen in determining facts."[2] FRE 702 states that witnesses may be qualified as experts "by knowledge, skill, experience, training or education." Under rule 702 experts may be called "[i]f scientific, technical or other specialized knowledge will assist the trier of fact to understand the evidence or to determine a fact in issue;" experts "may testify * * * in the form of an opinion or otherwise."[3] In these particulars the federal rule restates the common law.

McCormick comments:

An observer is qualified to testify because he has firsthand knowledge of the situation or transaction at issue. The expert has something different to contribute. This is a power to draw inferences from the facts which a jury would not be competent to draw. To warrant the use of expert testimony, then, two elements are required. First, the subject of the inference must be so distinctively related to some science, profession, business or occupation as to be beyond the ken of the average layman. Some courts emphasize that the judge has discretion in administering this aspect of the rule, and other courts will admit expert opinion concerning matters about which the jurors may have general knowledge if the expert opinion would still aid their understanding of the fact issue. This latter approach emphasizes the true function of expert testimony. Second, the witness must have sufficient skill, knowledge, or experience in that

---

1. See note 35 in Chapter One, supra, and FRE 601.

2. Twin City Plaza, Inc. v. Central Surety & Insurance Co., 409 F.2d 1195, 1203 (8th Cir. 1969).

3. The complete rule reads as follows:

If scientific, technical, or other specialized knowledge will assist the trier of fact to understand the evidence or to determine a fact in issue, a witness qualified as an expert by knowledge, skill, experience, training, or education, may testify thereto in the form of an opinion or otherwise.

field or calling as to make it appear that his opinion or inference will probably aid the trier in his search for truth. The knowledge may in some fields be derived from reading alone, in some from practice alone, or as is more commonly the case, from both. While the court may rule that a certain subject of inquiry requires that a member of a given profession as a doctor, an engineer or a chemist, be called, usually a specialist in a particular branch within the profession will not be required. The practice, however, in respect to experts' qualifications has not for the most part crystallized in specific rules, but is recognized as a matter for the trial judge's discretion reviewable only for abuse. Reversals for abuse are rare.[4]

Courts look at experts from a functional perspective. If the court is satisfied that an individual has the ability to draw inferences which the ordinary juror could not draw and that these inferences will aid the jury in rationally evaluating a fact in issue, the individual may qualify as an expert witness. People may acquire special knowledge in many ways. There is no general requirement that expertise be reflected by formal training, years of experience or advanced degrees. However, the court will be interested in such factors in determining whether the individual qualifies as an expert and whether the individual's field is an appropriate one for expert testimony. Sometimes expertise is situational. In a trial in downtown New York City one might be able to qualify an ordinary farmer as an expert on the general characteristics of fertilizer. The same farmer would probably not qualify before a jury in a rural community. Expertise is

also limited to certain topics or aspects of topics. Even in Manhattan the average farmer could not qualify as an expert on the technical chemistry of different fertilizers. This would require a knowledgeable chemist. The most expert psychiatrist could not testify that a man *was not guilty* of a crime because he was insane. Psychiatric expertise is limited to the evaluation of mental conditions; it does not extend to the determination of the legal implications of conditions found to exist. Of course, if the jury accepts the psychiatrist's judgment on sanity, a legal conclusion may follow directly.

In Chapter One we call your attention to the common law rule which purports to ban the opinion testimony of ordinary witnesses.[5] The reason for the rule is that jurors are thought to be as capable as the ordinary witness in drawing inferences from data. Neither the reason nor the rule applies in the case of experts. Indeed, experts are often called to testify because they are capable of forming opinions on matters which the jury is not expected to understand. In some jurisdictions problems arise when experts are asked to give opinions on so-called ultimate issues, matters which go to the heart of the case. Thus, some jurisdictions would bar psychiatric testimony that a criminal defendant was not capable of knowing right from wrong, because, under one test, this is precisely the question the jury must answer in determining whether the defendant is not guilty by reason of insanity. FRE 704 codifies the modern trend:

> Testimony in the form of an opinion or inference otherwise admissible is not objectionable because it embraces an ul-

---

4. McCormick § 13, at 29–30. Although a party may not be able to make a convincing case without expert testimony, generally there is no legal requirement that expert testimony be introduced to prove a particular point. The area of medical malpractice is a common exception. Some jurisdictions hold as a matter of law that expert testimony is required

to establish a prima facie case of medical malpractice, unless the negligence complained of is so obviously understandable to lay decisionmakers that the negligent act needs no expert explanation—e.g., leaving a scalpel inside a patient.

5. See note 20 in Chapter One.

timate issue to be decided by the trier of fact.

This does not mean that expert opinions will always be admissible. The opinion must still be helpful to the trier of fact. The drafters of the federal rule comment:

> The abolition of the ultimate issue rule does not lower the bars so as to admit all opinions. Under Rules 701 and 702, opinions must be helpful to the trier of fact, and Rule 403 provides for exclusion of evidence which wastes time. These provisions afford ample assurances against the admission of opinions which would merely tell the jury what result to reach, somewhat in the manner of the oath-helpers of an earlier day. They also stand ready to exclude opinions phrased in terms of inadequately explored legal criteria. Thus the question, "Did T have capacity to make a will?" would be excluded, while the question, "Did T have sufficient mental capacity to know the nature and extent of his property and the natural objects of his bounty and to formulate a rational scheme of distribution?" would be allowed.[6]

Experts are not confined to giving opinions. They are often needed to provide information which is every bit as concrete as the information presented by ordinary witnesses. Expert testimony may be required to establish that one dose of curare is commonly used in surgery and that a larger dose is invariably fatal. Such testimony is no more subjective or speculative than the testimony of an eyewitness who states she observed a red light. Without the aid of an expert, the jury may not be aware that an X-ray plate reveals a compound fracture of the tibia, but testimony to this effect may be no more opin-

ion than testimony that a car in a photograph is a 1975 Ford Pinto.

Expert testimony may have as many bases as there are sources of specialized knowledge. Where expert testimony rests on a scientific principle or on a process validated by a scientific principle, some courts have established a special barrier which must be overcome before the testimony will be admitted. They require that the principle "be sufficiently established to have gained general acceptance in the particular field in which it belongs."[7] This contrasts with the general rule which requires only that the expert testimony be likely to aid the jury in its deliberations.

The special rule regarding scientific evidence is generally traced to the case of Frye v. United States.[8] *Frye* upheld a lower court decision to exclude the results of a lie detector examination offered by a defendant in a criminal case. The court seemed to accept the statement in the defendant's brief that when a matter in issue does not lie within the range of common experience "the opinions of witnesses skilled in that particular science, art, or trade to which the question relates are admissible in evidence."[9] However, the court concluded that the lie detector test had not yet gained the required standing and scientific recognition among authorities in the fields of physiology and psychology to justify the admission of such evidence.

The *Frye* case is often cited by courts dealing with scientific evidence and is usually followed when the admissibility of lie detector evidence is in issue. In other areas, it has had a surprisingly erratic influence for a case that has received so much attention. Courts generally were not reluctant to admit the results of breath tests for alcohol or to allow identification by

---

6. Advisory Committee Note on FRE 704. FRE 704 applies to lay opinions as well as expert opinions. However, lay opinions on ultimate issues are less likely to be admitted than expert opinions because they are not as frequently helpful to the trier of fact.

7. Frye v. United States, 54 App.D.C. 46, 293 F. 1013, 1014 (1923).

8. Id.

9. Id. at 1014.

neutron activation analysis when these procedures were in their infancy and scientists differed about their validity. One court upheld a trial judge's decision to admit the results of a novel chemical test which purported to detect a poison that scientists had generally believed to be undiscoverable in the human body.[10] Many courts today take the position that any relevant scientific evidence supported by qualified expert witnesses should be received unless there are specific reasons for excluding it, such as the danger of prejudicing or misleading the jury. Some believe that FRE 401, 402 and 403 or their state counterparts require this approach. Courts that have moved away from *Frye* regard the criterion of general scientific acceptability as an appropriate condition for the judicial notice of scientific facts but not as a condition for the admissibility of controvertible testimony. Other jurisdictions still adhere to *Frye,* or at least purport to do so. However, the courts in these jurisdictions seem to relax the doctrine in some instances, while applying it at full strength in others. Whatever the test, in both *Frye* and non-*Frye* jurisdictions courts are properly concerned that evidence based on "new" scientific advances may present special problems of fairness. The problems presented later in this chapter illustrate some of the reasons for this concern.[11]

SECTION II. PRESENTATION OF EXPERT TESTIMONY

We discussed some aspects of expert testimony in the introductory material. This section will examine standard methods of presenting expert testimony and will discuss certain preliminary matters that must be attended to whenever expert testimony is offered.

As we note in the introduction to this chapter anyone can qualify as an expert who by reason of skill, experience, training, or knowledge can offer a jury composed of ordinary lay persons relevant information that they would otherwise not possess. Expert testimony is, of course, offered with the intent to influence the jury, and jurors may be particularly prone to believe those with esoteric knowledge and impressive credentials. It must be remembered, however, that experts do not in any legal sense specially bind a judge or jury. Although in some cases it may be impossible to make out a case without expert testimony, the fact that expert testimony is offered in aid of a claim or defense is no guarantee of victory. Fact finders are free to assess the credibility of expert witnesses just as they assess the

---

10. Coppolino v. State, 223 So.2d 68 (Fla.App.1969), appeal dismissed 239 So.2d 120 (Fla.), certiorari denied, 399 U.S. 927 (1969).

11. Frye rears its head at irregular intervals and in some very important cases. For example, California has reaffirmed its adherence to the test in an opinion rejecting the admissibility of voiceprints, an identification device discussed later in this Chapter. See People v. Kelly, 17 Cal.3d 24, 129 Cal.Rptr. 144, 549 P.2d 1240 (1976). For a contrary view, see United States v. Williams, 583 F.2d 1194 (2d Cir. 1978), certiorari denied, 439 U.S. 1117 (1979). The drafters of the Federal Rules of Evidence failed to confront the continuing validity of the Frye case and may have implicitly extended its life. See the final paragraph of the Advisory Committee's Note accompanying Rule 703. Our comments are based upon a reading of many cases decided since Frye in which general relevance principles seem to be applied in preference to Frye. It would be a mistake to ignore Frye in the future, even though it is now an old case, because it is often the precedent that is used by courts that want to reject expert evidence but have difficulty in writing an opinion in relevance language.

For an excellent examination of the impact that Frye has had over the years, see Giannelli, The Admissibility of Novel Scientific Evidence, Frye v. United States, A Half-Century Later, 80 Colum.L.Rev. 1197 (1980).

credibility of other witnesses. It is true that expert evidence can be so compelling in a given case as to require a directed verdict, but the same may be said of lay testimony. Usually juries may reject expert testimony as readily as nonexpert testimony, and they often have to reject some expert testimony because it is common for each side in a lawsuit to present its own experts.

Although expert testimony may be rejected by the jury, the law is not indifferent to the likely quality of what will be heard. Since experts may testify to matters on which lay witnesses have nothing to offer and since they may rely on sources of information that would be objectionable as a basis for lay testimony, special qualifications are required of those who wish to qualify as experts. Whether a witness is qualified to testify as an expert is determined by the trial judge as a preliminary matter. Often the jury will be present when this determination is made, so that they can learn of the expert's credentials. This saves time if the testimony is allowed, and it is felt that in the usual case no harm is done when the testimony is not permitted.

The test for the judge under FRE 702 is whether the person claiming expertise is sufficiently skilled or knowledgeable to assist the jury. This may require an examination of the purported expert's credentials—e.g., is the witness really an M.D. or just pretending to be one. It may also involve a decision as to the appropriateness of a witness' credentials given her expected testimony—e.g., if negligence in performing open heart surgery is alleged, a family physician might not qualify as an expert.

Occasionally a court must decide whether a witness whose technical expertise is acknowledged—e.g., a highly regarded scientist talking about physics or chemistry—should be permitted to rely on data from a machine or a computer or on specific techniques or scientific principles. Where an expert has used some electronic or mechanical device, the judge will allow the testimony if the device is of a kind that is ordinarily used by experts in the particular field and if it is reasonable to assume that the device was working properly at the time it was used. If there is some dispute about whether the device was in good working order at the time in question, most courts hold that the evidence which suggests that the device was not working goes to weight rather than admissibility. The party opposing the expert testimony can offer the jury evidence suggesting that the device was not functioning properly. If the jury believes there was a malfunction, they should discount the expert's testimony accordingly.

When a novel technique relied on by an expert is purportedly based on scientific principles, the judge must decide whether to use the *Frye* test, apply a simple relevance analysis, or take some other approach. If the judge does not believe that a scientific test employed by an expert is likely to have produced evidence helpful to the jury, an otherwise qualified expert will not be permitted to give testimony based on that test. The exclusion in federal court is justified by FRE 702 or on the "reasonable reliance" language of FRE 703. It may also be justified by reference to FRE 401, 402 and 403.

In deciding the FRE 703 issue of whether the data an expert relies upon is reasonably relied upon by similar experts, the judge might want to hear from experts other than the one who wishes to rely on the data. If the judge decides that the data is not reasonably relied upon, he may bar the expert's opinion altogether, bar it to the extent it relies on impermissible data, or only bar references to the impermissible data.

Since expertise relates to the value of testimony, one may wonder why the judge should pass on an expert's qualifications as a preliminary matter when the jury generally decides questions of credibility.

There are several reasons. First, the purported expert who lacks expertise is a bit like the proffered witness who lacks first-hand knowledge. The issue is not whether the witness is credible in the usual sense of the word. Rather it is whether the witness knows anything on which the jury should rely. Second, there is a traditional relevance analysis. If the witness who lacks expertise is presented as an expert, the technical aspects of her testimony are likely to waste time and confuse the jury. Third, the nature of the expert's testimony may make it difficult for lay jurors to assess expertise. Often the jurors would have to be provided with considerable information about the state of a scientific field in order to decide whether one purportedly trained in or relying on theories in that field has sufficient expertise to give helpful testimony. At a minimum this might require a lengthy hearing on the value of the expert's testimony which will distract the jury from its more general fact-finding tasks. Finally decisions on the admissibility of expert testimony may reflect policy judgments that should be consistent within a jurisdiction. For example, you will see in Section III of this Chapter that although polygraphy evidence often has probative value, there may nevertheless be good reasons for a general rule of exclusion. If so, the reasons will usually apply throughout the jurisdiction.

These good reasons for giving the preliminary question to the judge are not reasons for keeping potentially helpful evidence from a jury that hears experts on both sides and can understand that some experts have more to offer than others. Consequently, the test a proposed expert must pass in order to testify is not very stringent, except when *Frye* or similar policies are invoked to determine whether a subject matter is an appropriate one for experts of a particular type. A party need not offer the best available expert. He need only find someone who meets the test of FRE 702; that is, someone with suffi-

cient expertise to assist the trier of fact in situations where scientific, technical or other specialized knowledge will aid in understanding the evidence or determining a fact in issue.

So far we have been discussing the court's power to determine who may testify about what. The power the judge has under FRE 705 to control the order in which an expert presents testimony is also important. The judge can require the expert to begin with the facts and explain how they lead to her opinion, or, he can permit the expert to simply state an opinion without ever explicating its factual bases. In the latter instance, the underlying facts may be explored by the opponent on cross-examination. However, the jury is likely to be more influenced by an expert opinion the better they understand its underlying factual basis. Thus, the usual problem with experts is controlling how much they say, not getting them to say more.

The material that follows addresses many of the practical problems that arise in the use of expert witnesses. There are illustrations of how to lay foundations for experts (i.e., how to show how expert a witness really is), how to attack an expert on cross-examination, and how to challenge the validity of the data utilized by experts.

Appellate courts often say that rulings on expert testimony will not be reversed on appeal except for a gross abuse of discretion. Like many of the standards that appellate courts cite in their review of evidentiary rulings, this may be little more than a statement that appellate courts will strain to uphold trial court judgments. Although there are cases in which appellate courts reverse trial judges' rulings on expert witnesses, the basic rules, such as FRE 702–705, leave much to the trial judge's discretion. They provide an outline for lawyering. The effective lawyer must apply the outline to new facts and issues.

If you examine trends in litigation, you will find that experts testify in an increasing proportion of cases. In tort cases, engineers may testify concerning product deficiencies or on questions of causation, and economists are retained to project damage awards into the future. In school desegregation cases, experts on demographics, education and transportation may be needed. In criminal cases, psychiatrists, psychologists and other forensic scientists commonly provide help to courts and juries. In tax cases, lawyers and accountants are often called as witnesses, and in antitrust cases economists are essential. The more complicated the law becomes and the more complex the legal theories that lawyers use, the more likely it is that experts will be necessary.

In this Chapter we only discuss matters relating to the use of experts as witnesses.

You should be aware, however, that careful lawyers use experts to prepare for litigation as well as to testify. If medical, economic or other technical subjects are going to arise in litigation, lawyers can benefit from acquiring expert assistance early—before witnesses are deposed and interrogatories are answered. By the time the trial is on the horizon, positions may have hardened and experts must deal with materials developed by nonexperts. The use of experts to plan, prepare and design litigation strategies not only makes good sense; it is with increasing frequency essential to effective representation.

At common law there are three basic ways in which expert testimony may be presented. Each has its problems.

A. PERSONAL KNOWLEDGE

If an expert knows relevant facts through personal observation, the courts routinely admit testimony reporting those facts and conclusions based on them. Difficulties arise when an expert claims to "know" facts because she credits the observations of out-of-court sources with which she has become acquainted. Obviously, testimony reporting the observations of others would be hearsay. So, absent some exception, an opinion based on such facts would not be supported by admissible evidence. Professor Mitchell describes the problem:

Traditionally, the expert witness is expected to specify the data upon which his conclusions are founded. The purpose of such a requirement has been said to be to give the jury a full picture by presenting both the conclusions and the premises upon which the conclusions rest. If a professional has cause to utilize the reports of others in formulating his own opinion, the prevailing view insists that such use is improper and subject to the hearsay or want of personal knowledge objections. Any opinion

based partly on the reports, opinions, or findings, written or otherwise, of parties not before the court for cross-examination is subject to such objection. This is the rule in a majority of states, but there have been many practical criticisms of the rule. Illustrating this point, McCormick points out that a physician is often called to give his opinion although his findings are based not on personal knowledge but on hospital records, reports and charts, diagnoses and reports of attending physicians, and relevant medical literature conventionally relied on in the field. The expert in his own professional area of expertise would seem to be the one consummately capable of judging the relevancy and reliability of any such extraneous sources relative to his own diagnosis. In the majority of states, no reference can be made to technical or scientific out-of-court documentation although the expert, in keeping with accepted practice, has colored his opinion by some degree of reliance upon such sources. In some instances, the opinion so influenced may be rejected in its entirety. The minority rule would permit reference to be made to such extrajudicial professional information if, in the judgment of the expert whose opinion they influence, they are relevant, reliable and valuable.[12]

FRE 703 follows what was described as the minority view in providing:

The facts or data in the particular case upon which an expert bases an opinion or inference may be those perceived by or made known to him at or before the hearing. If of a type reasonably relied upon by experts in the particular field in forming opinions or inferences upon the subject, the facts or data need not be admissible in evidence.

Thus, in federal court, an expert witness can familiarize herself with the records in a case, rely on those records considered to be reliable by experts in her field, and testify on the basis of material that may not be directly admissible. This rule has the virtue of being true to the way in which experts typically operate in nonjudicial settings. Its supporters argue that conclusions reached through procedures which meet the standards of scientific validity are sufficiently reliable for courtroom presentation.

When an expert opinion is based upon facts which the expert has observed personally, some courts require the expert to state those facts before giving her opinion, some allow the factual basis for the opinion to be laid anytime during the direct examination of the expert, and some do not require that any foundation be established on direct examination. In jurisdictions which take this third approach, the cross-examiner may explore the factual basis for the opinion if he thinks it desirable. There is some confusion in the literature about the implications of these different procedures. Consider the following comment:

In certain fact situations the information on which the expert is partly relying is itself inadmissible, such as the situations where a scientist makes a judgment based on data gathered by others not present to testify to selection methods, or where a psychiatrist formulates an opinion from hearsay information provided by a patient's family and friends. These conditions pose real problems in jurisdictions where the expert is commanded to specify on direct his bases for the opinion. The prevailing view, if the opinion is founded in major part on inadmissible bases, is to disallow the opinion in its entirety for lack of foundation (the "want of knowledge" objection to admissibility).[13]

The conditions the author speaks of should pose problems in *any* jurisdiction, for the problems result directly from the requirement that experts base their opinions solely on firsthand information and not from the requirement that the information supporting an expert opinion be presented on direct examination. A jurisdiction that has decided that there are good policy reasons to prohibit experts from relying on inadmissible information would not allow a lawyer to present flawed expert testimony by the simple expedient of not revealing the flaws on direct examination. In such a jurisdiction, revelation of the fatal flaws on cross-examination would also lead to a striking of the opinion testimony. Of course, if the cross-examiner decides not to take up the task of showing the factual basis of an opposing expert's opinion, the court might never realize that, given its hearsay policy, the opinion is inadmissible.

The revelation of basic facts prior to the rendering of an expert opinion serves sev-

12. Mitchell, The Proposed Federal Rules of Evidence: How They Affect Product Liability Practice, 12 Duquesne L.Rev. 551, 567–68 (1974). McCormick § 15, at 34–35, notes

a trend in common law courts toward admitting opinions based on third party reports supplemented by personal observation.

13. Mitchell, supra note 12, at 573.

eral purposes. It eliminates the need for motions to strike *after* testimony is produced, thus saving time and reducing confusion. It may clarify the expert's opinion for the trier of fact; it helps avoid opinion testimony on inappropriate issues; and it helps the judge decide whether the expert's opinion will be of aid to the jury. While these purposes are legitimate, there are circumstances where it is unwise to prohibit a witness from beginning with an opinion and working backwards to the facts and situations where the basic facts are so technical that knowing them is not helpful to laypersons. FRE 705 leaves the trial judge with discretion to control the flow of proof:

> The expert may testify in terms of opinion or inference and give his reasons therefor without prior disclosure of the underlying facts or data, unless the court requires otherwise. The expert may in any event be required to disclose the underlying facts or data on cross-examination.

This approach is clearly sensible in civil cases in jurisdictions where rules of procedure like F.R.Civ.P. 26(b)(4) allow substantial pretrial discovery of the factors underlying an opposing expert's opinion. It is more questionable where discovery is more limited.

FRE 703 and FRE 705 should be read in conjunction with FRE 803 (18) which changes the common law rule regarding the use of learned treatises. At common law statements in treatises were considered hearsay if offered for their truth, and thus could not be offered as evidence. Even

though expert knowledge is often based largely on what the expert has read, some courts ignore this reality and allow experts to testify to what they know but not to what particular books say. As you saw in Chapter Six, FRE 803(18) provides a hearsay exception which states:

> To the extent called to the attention of an expert witness upon cross-examination or relied upon by him in direct examination, statements contained in published treatises, periodicals or pamphlets on a subject of history, medicine, or other science or art, established as a reliable authority by the testimony or admission of the witness or by other expert testimony or by judicial notice. If admitted, the statements may be read into evidence but may not be received as exhibits.

A treatise may not be introduced under this rule unless an expert is on the witness stand and the treatise is called to her attention on cross-examination or has been relied upon by her in direct examination. The drafters thought it important that treatises not be introduced unless an expert is available to explain the technical material it contains and to say why it should or should not be accepted. An interesting question that remains unresolved in the federal courts is whether a plaintiff suing an expert can call the defendant as a witness, direct her attention to a treatise, and then offer the treatise as evidence. Under FRE 611(c), there is little doubt that the plaintiff can call a defendant and ask leading questions, but it is not clear that this should qualify as cross-examination under FRE 803(18).[14]

B. HYPOTHETICAL QUESTIONS GENERALLY

If an expert lacks firsthand knowledge of some or of all the facts necessary to support an opinion, facts may be stated hy-

pothetically for the expert's consideration. A party taking this approach must be sure that at some point in the trial evidence is

---

14. See Maggipinto v. Reichman, 607 F.2d 621 (3d Cir. 1979).

For an example of an expert testifying from personal knowledge gained from scientific

tests, review the testimony of the chemist, Stanley Wall, in the Whale transcript in Chapter One.

introduced to support, either directly or inferentially, each of the hypothesized facts on which the opinion is based. The opinion will be stricken if the jury cannot possibly find that its factual underpinnings are true. There is, however, no requirement that the underlying facts be presented before an opinion is rendered.

In jurisdictions which would otherwise limit experts to facts they know firsthand, the hypothetical approach has the advantage that one need not pay an expert for the time needed to acquire personal knowledge of the facts relevant to an opinion. Indeed, many eminent experts might be unavailable if demands on their time could not be limited in this fashion. In theory, the hypothetical question has the additional advantage of specifying for the jury the factual assumptions on which the expert's opinion is based. However, in practice the hypothetical question is often more likely to be confusing than helpful. Questions running twenty or thirty transcript pages have been asked and the felicitous phrasing of assumed facts is common. The procedure has been often criticized:

> There are certain basic requirements for the use of the hypothetical question itself that attempt to preserve the accuracy of the process, such as the requirement that all facts assumed in the hypothetical must be supported by the evidence either directly or inferentially. But is this requirement conversely true, that all facts of record material to the question at issue must of necessity be included in the framing of the hypothetical? One of the great disadvantages in use of the hypothetical is the danger of

conscious or subconscious shading of the issue by carefully choosing the facts which are to be assumed. On the other hand, a hypothetical which embraces all facts pertinent to the question may become so cumbersome and complex as to destroy its utility for the jury. Yet the hypothetical question, that "wen on the fair face of justice," is still the primary vehicle for presenting expert testimony to the jury today. Wigmore characterizes its problems as follows:

> The hypothetical question, misused by the clumsy and abused by the clever, has in practice led to intolerable obstruction of the truth * * *. It has artificially clamped the mouth of the expert so that his answer to a complex question may not express his actual opinion on the case. The question may be so built up and contribed (sic) by counsel as to represent only a partisan conclusion. In the second place, it has tended to mislead the jury as to the purport of actual expert opinion. This is due to the same reason. In the third place, it has tended to confuse the jury, so that its employment becomes a mere waste of time and a futile obstruction * * *.[15]

Wigmore, who recognized that presentation of expert testimony need not involve hypothetical questions, suggested an alternative:

> By exempting the offering party from the *requirement* of using the hypothetical form; by according him the *option* of using it,—both of these to be left to the trial court's *discretion;* and by permitting the opposing party on *cross-exami-*

---

15. Id. at 564–65, quoting 2 Wigmore § 686, at 812–13. Wigmore condemned the hypothetical question in no uncertain terms:

[I]ts abuses have become so obstructive and nauseous that no remedy short of extirpation will suffice. It is a logical necessity, but a practical incubus; and logic here must be sacrificed * * *. It is a strange irony that the hypothetical ques-

tion, which is one of the few truly scientific features of the rules of Evidence, should have become that feature which does most to disgust men of science with the law of Evidence.

Id. at 812. See also Diamond & Louisell, The Psychiatrist as an Expert Witness: Some Ruminations and Speculations, 63 Mich. L. Rev. 1335, 1346–47 (1965).

nation, to call for a hypothetical specification of the data which the witness has used as the basis of the opinion. The last rule will give sufficient protection against a misunderstanding of the opinion, when any actual doubt exists.[16]

FRE 703 adopts Wigmore's suggestion and leaves the hypothetical question as an option. But the rule diminishes the significance of the hypothetical question by allowing flexibility in the presentation of expert testimony and by broadening the data base on which experts may rely.[17]

The following example illustrates how useful a hypothetical question can be and some typical kinds of objections to expert testimony. The testimony is drawn from a case in which a police officer shot a citizen after stopping his vehicle and ordering him and another person out of it as suspects in a prior shooting incident. The officer was sued by the estate of the deceased and testified that he thought the deceased was reaching for a gun, that the deceased had turned himself at a 45 degree angle from the car after being ordered to put his hands atop it, and that there was no time to fire a warning shot. The plaintiff responded with the expert testimony of Mr. Dahn, a ballistics expert. The examination went as follows:

Q. Mr. Dahn, will you assume these facts, and I am going to recite a rather long series of facts. At the conclusion of this question I am going to ask you if you understand the question and then if you can answer it, all right?

A. Okay.

Q. Mr. Dahn, would you assume this: Would you assume for purposes of this question that we had an east and a west alley. At the top of a chart that would be west and at the bottom it would be east. The alley is adjacent to an empty lot. The empty lot is large, sufficiently large as to not involve us.

Would you assume that a police officer is standing with his 357 magnum pistol, which carries in its barrel a 357 round, and that he is standing five feet north of the alley and ten feet west of the beginning of that lot.

Would you assume that he stays there and, in fact, shoots his weapon from that spot.

Would you assume further that there is a car, which we are calling car X, that is on a north-south direction to the alley, that is, it is facing the alley, and the front of the car faces the north. Would you assume that the front of that car X is ten feet off of the alley, from 10 to 15 feet off of the alley. Would you assume that this car is 10 feet west of the police officer.

Would you assume that the man shot was approximately even with the driver's door of car X and approximately two feet east of the door. Would

---

16. 2 Wigmore § 686, at 813.

17. **FRE 703 does not mention hypothetical questions. The Advisory Committee's note to this rule makes it clear that the hypothetical question is intended to be left as an option. This is wise, for not all uses of the hypothetical question should be condemned:**

[T]he hypothetical question still retains its usefulness in a case where, for example, the "super-expert" applies his specialized learning to testimony in a case where he had no personal contact whatever either with the persons or the matter involved in the litigation, or in a case where there is a dispute as to the basic facts and a question should be presented hypothetically as an alternative set of facts.

New Jersey Supreme Court Committee on Evidence 113 (1963).

you assume that the man was shot by the police officer, again approximately 12 to 15 feet from the man shot—they were 12 to 15 feet apart in other words.

Would you assume that the bullet entered that man's body at the tenth intercostal space in the posterior aspect, that is in the back, the upper left back. Would you assume that it lodged and several months later was surgically removed from the right lower part of his abdomen, specifically at the sixth intercostal space.

Would you assume that the pathway of the bullet as described by the surgeon and doctor familiar with this area . . . was a plane parallel to the ground without deflections upon entry.

Now, assuming all of those facts, Mr. Dahn, could you tell me to a reasonable degree of engineering certainty the angle that the man shot would bear to car X? Can you tell me that?

MR. FITZPATRICK: Your Honor, I would interpose this objection. I think on the facts related one is mistaken. It has the front of car X headed north. I think it is an agreement that it was headed south.

MR. HEGARTY: You are correct, counsel. It is south.

MR. FITZPATRICK: I would say on those facts that this is a question that requires no expert, that this is a question within the province and the abilities of the jury. An expert witness is only to be brought in where there is something that requires study and learning that the ordinary man would not have in his experience.

Now, the question also omits the fact that the person shot was in a rotary motion, that he was turning at the time. Now, all of these assumptions of distance and that I would say if an ordinary man had it and if he plotted it out on a piece of paper and then drew the car and the two men the ordinary man would be able to answer that question as well as any expert who has studied ballistics.

This is not a case that involves deflection or ricocheting or anything like that. So that is the basis for my objection of submitting this question to the expert.

THE COURT: You may reply to the objection.

MR. HEGARTY: Thank you, your Honor.

Unless the ordinary man has been trained in external ballistics, he would have no way of determining the angle that man would face to the car. As a matter of fact, when I asked Dr. Lowe if the bullet was deflected, counsel stood up and wondered and queried whether it was deflected.

The officers have testified that the man was 45° and he was on some angle to them. I believe the testimony shown by the plaintiff will reflect he was completely turned away from them.

I am offering this evidence to show that as a matter of geometric law he could not be standing at a 45° angle as a matter of geometric law.

* * *

MR. FITZPATRICK: Your Honor, if it is a matter of geometry, and I think that is all it is, the degree of angle, I would think that a jury is qualified to know whether it is 45° or 90° or 30°. And I don't think it is a matter that an expert can top a jury on, because it is just a matter of experience and position. And counsel says here he is—so that is my position, your Honor.

THE COURT: I do not believe that the information which you seem to be seeking, Mr. Hegarty, is information that must be given by an expert witness. You are asking for purely factual information. I, therefore, sustain the objection to the question.

MR. HEGARTY: I, at this time, would like to make an offer of proof, your Honor.

THE COURT: You may make an offer of proof.

Ladies and gentlemen of the jury, I will excuse you for a brief period.

* * *

Q. What would an ordinary person have to know and what education would he have to have to make a calculation as to the angle this person shot bore to the car?

A. He would need to know the—one is the response time of the individual who is shot, how fast he could move versus time that the trigger was pulled by the policeman, that is an integral factor that must be considered.

You must consider the degree of deflection that the bullet could have or the dispersion that a bullet could have from a pistol fired from a policeman. He would need to know how a bullet would enter into a material like a human body in order to be able to determine what angle the human would have been at relative to the line of sight of the policeman.

Q. Would this hypothetical person need to know anything about the velocity of particular weapons?

A. He would need to know the velocity of the particular weapons in order to determine the response time between the time the trigger was pulled until the bullet hit the person, how much movement could the person have in that particular time period.

* * *

Q. Mr. Dahn, can you answer my original hypothetical question?

A. Yes.

Q. Would you do so?

A. Yes. The angle in which the person was at at the time he was shot, including the response times out of the police officer and the response times of the bullet would be no greater than 20° relative to the westerly direction.

Q. Could it be less than that?

A. It could be less than that, yes, depending—I had, in my calculation, based the automobile 10 feet from the alley. If the automobile was greater than 10 feet from the alley, this angle would be smaller.

Q. And if the feet given to you were greater than 10 feet, for example, 10 to 15 feet, then the angle would be less than 20°, would it not?

A. It would be very close to zero degrees actually.

Q. Taking into account the facts I have given you, is it possible for a man to be facing 45° and be shot at the point I have indicated by a man who was shooting a gun at the point I have indicated that the policeman was standing?

A. It is not possible.

Q. Is it not possible, sir, as a geometric law or in a matter—to a matter—to a reasonable degree of engineering certainty?

A. Yes, that is right.

MR. HEGARTY: Your Honor, thank you. That completes my offer of proof.

* * *

Should the judge reverse his decision regarding the admissibility of Dahn's testimony following this offer of proof? Might plaintiff's counsel have avoided these difficulties if, instead of beginning with a hypothetical question, he had asked Dahn how one determined the angle at which a person was standing from the angle at which a bullet entered and lodged in his body? Could Dahn's testimony have been effectively elicited without using a hypothetical question? In the case from which this testimony is taken the trial judge did not change his mind following the offer of proof, but the appellate court reversed; holding that Dahn's testimony was mistakenly excluded. Note how important the clear offer of proof—actually, in this case, the laying of a foundation—was to the appellate court's decision.

C. HYPOTHETICAL QUESTIONS TO AN EXPERT OBSERVING THE TRIAL

It is generally permissible to have an expert witness who listens to the testimony of other witnesses give an opinion based upon the assumed truth of the previous testimony. This procedure works well where the testimony of the other witnesses is clear and non-contradictory. Otherwise, the expert must explain which facts she is relying upon in reaching a conclusion. Courts are not reluctant to allow experts to assume the truth of facts previously testified to, but when experts are asked to assume the truth of other witnesses' conclusions, judges often speak disparagingly of "inferences on inferences." Yet if the conclusions of another witness, expert or otherwise, are sound enough for the jury to rely on, they should be sound enough to provide a basis for expert testimony. McCormick properly notes that "[i]t is apparent * * * that the line between observed 'fact' and inferential 'opinion' is here, as always, a shadowy one and [that] the trial judge should be allowed a wide latitude in passing on * * * [an] objection".[18]

An example of an expert opinion based on the assumption that previous testimony is true is found in the transcript presented in the next section.

18. McCormick § 14 at 33.

Problem X–1.   Peggy Potter, a pedestrian, was injured when she was hit by a car driven by Tad Johnson.   Johnson claims that he was driving through an intersection on a green light when Potter walked in front of him. Potter claims that she was in the intersection when Johnson went through a red light and hit her.   There are no other witnesses to the accident.   Potter would like to introduce an expert at accident reconstruction who will testify that, given the point of impact on the car, the distance and direction in which she was thrown, and the speed of the car (as estimated from the skid marks after the car braked to a halt) Potter could not possibly have walked in front of the car so suddenly that Johnson had no time to stop.   **Should this testimony be admitted?   On what should the judge's decision turn?   Should the fact that there were no witnesses to the accident except the parties who tell conflicting stories have any bearing on the judge's decision?** Johnson wants to introduce a master of astrology who will testify that he has cast Ms. Potter's horoscope, and it is clear that on the day in question she was in grave danger from her own carelessness.   In addition, the astrologer will testify that Johnson's horoscope indicated that, at about the time of the accident, he would find himself in considerable trouble through no fault of his own.   **Should testimony by the astrologer be allowed?   How, if at all, may the astrologer be distinguished from the accidentologist?**

Problem X–2.   Sue Stewart is resisting the state's effort to commit her to a mental hospital.   She wishes to put Abigail Sanders on the stand to testify that although she, Sue, is somewhat eccentric, she is perfectly capable of functioning in society without endangering herself or others, and that she is not suffering from any mental disease or defect.   Sanders and Stewart have known each other as neighbors for more than fifteen years.   Sanders holds a bachelor's degree in history, acquired some twenty years ago. For the past twelve years she has written a newspaper advice column which has been syndicated to over 300 newspapers.   It is generally acknowledged that her column is one of the most sensible of its kind, that she "knows people" very well, and that she has an uncanny knack for understanding personal problems.   **Should her testimony on Stewart's mental health be admitted?   Is there any testimony she might give in addition to or instead of the testimony described?**

Problem X–3.   Elizabeth Steinberg brought an action against a plastic surgeon for malpractice alleging that because the surgeon negligently failed to remove a plaster of paris splint when she complained of a burning sensation, her skin was severely damaged.   She introduces as an expert a general practitioner who testifies that the plastic surgeon had enough evidence that the splint was doing damage that he should have been alerted to the need to remove it.   The plastic surgeon objects to this testimony on the ground that plastic surgeons are not guilty of malpractice unless they fail to exercise the skill normally exercised by plastic surgeons in the community.   He claims that the plaintiff's witness, as a general practitioner, is not competent to testify to the standard of care appropriate to plastic surgeons.   **How should the court rule?   Does it matter if the jurisdiction is one of those which has a rule that in malpractice cases a prima facie case may not be established without some expert testimony?**   Assume that the plaintiff asked the doctor, "In your opinion, was there or was there not malpractice?" and that the doctor answered, "There was malpractice." **Should an objection to the question have been sustained? Should an appellate court which determined that the question was improper reverse?**

Problem X–4. Big Gill Springsten sues James Perkins claiming that he is entitled to a one-half partnership interest in Perkins' explosives business and for a percentage of past profits. Springsten calls a certified public accountant to testify. This accountant reviewed a financial report on the partnership prepared by another accounting firm at Springsten's request. The report has been marked as Exhibit One. The testimony is as follows:

Q. All right, sir. Let me show you what has been marked as Plaintiff's Exhibit Number One and ask you whether or not you recognize that instrument.

A. I recognize it.

Q. All right, sir, and have you had occasion to familiarize yourself with that instrument?

A. Yes, sir, I have and I have discussed certain matters of it with Mr. Steve Pena, who worked for Anderson & Co., an accounting firm hired to prepare the report.

Q. Can you tell me from this instrument what amounts of money that James Perkins took from the explosives business during the years covered by this accounting, which I believe is '68 through April of '76.

A. Yes, sir.

Q. What is that figure?

A. The answer to your question involves two items, really. The total numbers, according to my computation, is $332,187.70.

Q. Now, that is your conclusion based upon your examination of this report marked as Plaintiff's Exhibit Number One, is that correct?

A. Yes, sir. It is.

Q. And that is the moneys that that report shows actually came into James Perkins' possession from the James Perkins Explosives Company?

A. Yes, sir.

Q. Are the figures in the report the type you usually rely on in making accounting judgments?

A. Yes they are.

Perkins moves to have the testimony stricken on the ground that it is without a proper foundation because the witness did not himself examine Perkins' records. **Should he prevail? How might Springsten overcome the objection?**

Problem X–5. Sylvia Swanson was injured when the door of a freight elevator in her employer's plant prematurely closed and struck her. She sued the manufacturer of the elevator claiming that the elevator's buttons were defectively designed because they could be activated inadvertently. She calls as her expert witness Maria MacDonald, a consulting engineer, who has a background not only in engineering, but in chemistry, machine guarding, toxicology and industrial hygiene and safety. On one occasion MacDonald designed machine guards for the buttons of a punch press. MacDonald never examined the elevator in question nor has she previously designed an elevator or any part thereof. As a consulting engineer her activities have principally related to fires, explosions, chemical poisoning, failures of materials, and failures of structural and hydraulic parts. The defendant objects that MacDonald is not an expert on elevators and should not be permitted to testify concerning alleged defects in the elevator's operating equipment. **Should MacDonald be permitted to testify as to the safety effects of leaving elevator buttons unguarded? Should she be permitted to give an opinion as to whether the absence of guards was a defect in the design?**

Problem X–6. The plaintiff, Betty Patton, was injured in an automobile accident. Following the accident, she suffered injuries to her spine of a relatively minor nature but also developed extreme nervousness and a severe depression with suicidal tendencies, which she attributes to the accident. The plaintiff calls a psychiatrist as an expert. She wishes the psychiatrist to testify that her psychiatric problems are due to the accident and that the extreme nervousness and severe depression are likely to endure for a substantial period of time. Among the facts which have been testified to by various witnesses are the following: (1) The accident occurred when the defendant's car struck the plaintiff's car from the rear. The plaintiff's car was stopped at the time. (2) The plaintiff claims she came to a gradual stop while the defendant claims the plaintiff stopped suddenly. The defendant claims her car was going about 10 m.p.h. at the time of the collision and the plaintiff claims the car was going about 25 m.p.h. (3) An orthopedic surgeon called by the plaintiff has given an opinion that she has suffered a five percent permanent disability of the neck and thoracic spine. (4) The plaintiff was three months pregnant at the time of the accident. The child, now two months old, is perfectly normal. (5) The plaintiff was in good physical health before the accident but had a tendency to nervousness. (6) The plaintiff had been brought up on a farm and was always very active and energetic. At the time of the accident she had a full time job to which she did not return. (7) After stopping at the intersection, the plaintiff had properly signaled for a left turn. (8) Traffic was extremely heavy at the time of the accident. (9) The impact of the collision threw the plaintiff forward onto the steering wheel; shortly thereafter she felt severe pain in her neck, back, shoulders and arms. (10) The plaintiff's spine could not be x-rayed after the accident because she was pregnant at the time. (11) Until the baby was born the plaintiff was very worried that her baby might have been injured when her abdomen hit the steering wheel. (12) The plaintiff went to see the psychiatrist who is her expert witness three months after the accident. At that time, the psychiatrist found that the plaintiff was often unable to concentrate and upon occasion did not wish to live. (13) The plaintiff's medical expenses following the accident amounted to $600, and she had to wear a special corrective girdle and a cervical collar for six months. (14) Additional medical expenses are likely.

Prepare the hypothetical question or questions which you would ask the psychiatrist in order to establish that the plaintiff's psychiatric problems are attributable to the accident and are likely to endure over a long period of time. Would you incorporate all the facts presented above in your hypothetical questions? Why or why not? How would you cross-examine the psychiatrist? If parts of the proof were left out of the hypothetical, could you work them in on cross-examination?

Problem X–7. Josiah Daniels was driving down Constitution Ave. in the District of Columbia with Ellen Swan as his passenger when he was struck from behind by a United States mail truck. Daniels sues the United States under the Federal Tort Claims Act for damages. The truck driver contends that Daniels suddenly put on his brakes with no warning whatever in order to get a better view of the Washington Monument. Daniels denies this. Shortly after the accident, a police officer arrived at the scene to investigate. Her report states as follows: "Based on the damage done to the rear of the car, the position of the vehicles, and the information provided to me by both cars' occupants, it is clear that the accident was caused by the sudden stopping of the passenger car before it was struck by the mail truck." This report is offered by the defendant truck driver as a business or public record. Assume that the trial judge believes it meets the qualifications of a hearsay exception. **Should an objection claiming that the report should not be admitted without some showing that the maker is an expert be sustained? How might that showing be made? If the showing were made, would you admit the report?**

D. ON TRIAL FOR MURDER; THE DEFENSE OF UNCONSCIOUSNESS

The quality of expert testimony varies from trial to trial, as does its importance and the way it is presented. The following transcripts, taken from an actual murder trial and a hypothetical suit for medical malpractice, illustrate ways in which expert testimony can be used and the problems faced by lawyers who must present expert testimony or cross-examine expert witnesses. As you read these transcripts, consider critically both the actions of counsel and the rules of evidence that help shape these actions.

The first transcript is taken from a trial for first degree murder in a state court. We have changed the names of partici-

pants and localities to protect the privacy of those involved. We have also edited some of the dialogue. However, we have refrained from making all possible improvements so that you can get some idea of the difficulties you may have in ensuring that you and your experts are understood.

The basic facts in this case are as follows:

Sam Green, the defendant, and Molly Glick, the deceased, were employees of Harry's Bar and Grill, a restaurant and beer parlor near the University of Tobias in Pleasantville. The deceased, a 21 year-old college student, was a waitress, and the defendant, 17 years of age, was a doorman at the establishment.

Sam testified that it was raining quite heavily the night of the killing, so Molly offered him a ride home. About 12:30 on the morning of November 8 they left Harry's, with Molly using Sam's green "army-type" jacket to shield herself from the rain when she went for her car. Sam waited for her under an awning in front of Harry's. After Molly picked him up, she drove to a parking lot near his apartment where they sat in the car and talked for about fifteen minutes. She criticized Sam for using drugs, which Sam resented, but they were again on friendly terms before Sam left the car. Sam had taken heroin early in the evening and psilocybin (a hallucinogenic drug) before leaving the restaurant. Sam said that as he was alighting from the car he felt a falling sensation, and the next thing he could remember was awakening and finding himself on the ground about fifteen feet from the car on the driver's side. When he got up, he saw a person running from the scene, Molly lying motionless in a pool of blood on the driver's side of the car and his pocket knife on the car floor. He picked up the knife and put it in his pocket. He then noticed that his hand was cut and bleeding. He concluded that he must have "freaked out" and killed her. He fled from the scene and hitched a ride with a truck driver.

Around 12:25 a. m., a college student who lived near the parking lot where the deceased and defendant had parked thought he heard a woman screaming. Responding to those screams, he left his apartment, observed a man wearing an olive army coat running from the parking lot, and saw the victim lying beside the open door of her car on the driver's side. He carried her to his apartment and called the rescue squad and the police. Molly died shortly thereafter at University Hospital. The cause of her death was multiple stab wounds. The student's description of the person running from the scene did not match Sam's appearance.

During the daylight hours of the next day, Sam was arrested at a hospital in Bradley where he had sought medical attention for his hand. After receiving *Miranda* warnings, Sam freely and voluntarily made a statement to a detective. According to the officer, Sam admitted in his statement that he killed the deceased and that the knife taken from him by the police was the murder weapon. However, there were inconsistencies in the detective's testimony as to whether Sam's admissions came without prompting or were made only in response to questioning. Another detective testified that while en route to Pleasantville, Sam told him, "I don't feel bad about taking her life. * * * I don't feel bad about taking a human being's life."

Sam never denied making statements to the police, but he maintained that he always had prefaced his statements with the reservation that he was guessing as to what had occurred because he really could not remember.

After arriving at the Pleasantville jail, the police gave Sam some clean clothes and took from him the clothing he was wearing. An analysis of defendant's clothing revealed bloodstains of Molly's blood type. Stains of Sam's blood type were also found on some of Molly's clothing. Sample puncture holes made by Sam's knife were of a different width than the wounds that had killed Molly.

All of the evidence against Sam was circumstantial, except for the alleged admissions. These have almost no probative value if Sam's version of his statements is believed. The prosecution not only lacked good eyewitness evidence, but also had great difficulty explaining how the defendant's knife could have made the wounds found on the body of the victim. Interestingly, some time after Sam's conviction for second degree murder was affirmed by the State Supreme Court, the Pleasantville prosecutor received a letter from the director of the FBI stating that an administrative review of the FBI agent who had supposedly examined the bloodstains on the clothing revealed that in another case the agent had "lied under oath in an affidavit," pretending to have conducted an examination he had not in fact carried out. The director stated that "there is no indication that the examinations [the agent] conducted in the [transcript] case were erroneous or incomplete. In view of the record, however, we could not be sure of this. * * *"

The defense asserted was unconsciousness. State law provides that:

Unconsciousness is a state of mind of persons of sound mind suffering from some voluntary or involuntary agency rendering them unaware of their acts. See C.J.S. Criminal Law § 55, at 194.

Where not self-induced, unconsciousness is a complete defense to a criminal homicide. But self-induced uncon-sciousness goes only to the grade of the offense and not to the existence of a complete defense.

To prove unconsciousness, the defense attempted to rely on psychiatric testimony. Aside from the defendant himself, the psychiatrist may have been the most important witness in the case. The transcript illustrates the problems of using psychiatric expert testimony in a common law jurisdiction, the ways a defendant seeks to circumvent the problems, and the woodenness of the common law rules. Had the defense been insanity rather than unconsciousness, the rulings would have been the same.

As you read the transcript be aware that it raises two separate questions: How should expert testimony be presented to a trier of fact? When should certain kinds of expert testimony be permitted? Focus primarily on the first question until you have a chance to complete the transcript and review the material that follows it.

R. K. LOCKET, a witness called by and on behalf of the Defendant, being first duly sworn, is examined and testifies as follows:

DIRECT EXAMINATION

BY MS. TRILO:

Q. Will you state your name, sir?   A. Dr. R. K. Locket.

Q. What is your profession?   A. I am a psychiatrist.

Q. Where are you licensed?   A. I am licensed for the State of New York and also for the District of Columbia.

Q. Where did you get your degree? Did you graduate from medical school?   A. I graduated from Western Reserve Medical School, and I got my M.D. degree in 1965.

Q. Was that an accredited medical school?   A. Oh, yes.

Q. Where did you intern?   A. A rotating internship in San Francisco at the Kaiser Hospital from 1965 * * * well, for one year from 1965 to 1966.

Q. What sort of studies did you make during your internship?   A. Well, rotating internship has four categories. I spent time on the medical unit, the surgical unit and the pediatric unit, and the obstetric unit.

Q. Did you go into a residency? **A.** Yes, I did.

Q. Where did you take your residency? **A.** I took a residency in adult psychiatry and in community psychiatry at Columbia Presbyterian Hospital in New York City; that is a three year residency and that lasted until July, 1966—from July 1966 until July 1969.

* * *

Q. During that three year time you specialized entirely in psychiatry? **A.** Yes, entirely in psychiatry and it also included a tour of duty as a resident through a neurological institute which is connected with Columbia Presbyterian Hospital.

Q. Have you ever taught psychiatry? **A.** I taught psychiatry when I was in the residency. As I became a senior resident I taught a psychiatric principles course to the junior residents and also I taught a great deal to nonprofessionals and professionals in the community health centers that I have worked in since that time.

Q. Have you ever studied under Dr. Speit? **A.** Yes, I have.

Q. Who is Dr. Speit? **A.** Speit, he is probably one of the few highly recognized medical hypnotists in this country and in the world.

Q. How long did you study under Dr. Speit? **A.** Primarily in my final year as a resident but I saw lectures by him in the previous year, too.

Q. Have you studied his works? **A.** Yes, I have.

Q. Have you practiced in your field of psychiatry with patients who have used drugs? **A.** Oh, yes, after I got out of my residency I then immediately went into the Army for two years. I was a staff psychiatrist at the De Witt Army hospital, in particular in the mental hygiene clinic there, and my duties were to evaluate enlisted men and dependents and officers if there was some reason to believe that there were some psychiatric problems. And I saw over that time hundreds of cases, I would say, involving drugs in which an evaluation of the drug history and their drug status was crucial to the evaluation that was expected of me to deliver to the command.

Q. Have you gained knowledge of the effects of various drugs on the human body? **A.** Yes. I have this experience, plus the experience when I was a resident at the New York Presbyterian Hospital, plus the experience that I have had in Washington, D.C. I have had a great number of cases in which I have gone into meticulous clinical histories surrounding the use of drugs and numerous kinds of drugs as a matter of fact.

Q. In your studies of hypnosis, have you ever had the occasion to work on a person who had amnesia? **A.** Yes, I have. I have had occasion to do that.

Q. How is hypnosis used in connection with a person who has amnesia? **A.** In the cases that I have had (and also there have been numerous cases reported in medical and psychiatric literature on this area), in essence hypnosis is used to concentrate one's ability to concentrate—one's ability to have a peak attention to a particular problem. Now, then, in this regard, the hypnosis would be used to allow the person to regress to the period of time that the amnesia occurred and to use his atypical consciousness under a trance to re-experience the experience and to recapture that memory during hypnosis.

Q. You are telling us that, with someone who had a loss of memory, through hypnosis there is a possibility of being able to recapture the memory during hypnosis? A. Yes. I have done that on several occasions, and I am aware of it being done by other doctors in cases of amnesia going back many years.

Q. When a person is submitted to a trance under hypnosis, can you, as the person putting him into that trance, tell if he is in a trance or not? A. Yes. In recent years in particular the procedure for identifying the degree of trance has been specified. It has been made uniform so that research on this subject—when a person is doing an experiment with hypnosis, he has a way of documenting the degree of trance so that the research could be repeated by other people in the field and the results could be scientifically validated.

Q. Has Dr. Speit made any study of the different degrees of trance? How can you tell if a person is in a trance while they are under hypnosis? A. Dr. Speit has been one of the men who has indeed worked out a procedure to both identify the degree of trance and to identify the susceptibility of a person to a hypnotic trance.

Q. Is there any established reliability of what is divulged by a trance or by a person under a trance? A. I am not sure what you mean by reliability.

Q. Can you tell me whether someone is being truthful when they are in a trance or if there is a probability they will be truthful while they are in a trance? A. Given certain prerequisites, and of course, truth meaning that a person is in essence giving a truthful response about his belief.

Q. About his belief? A. About his belief or I would say what his – – – in this case we are talking about memory – – – recovery of memory, past memory. I think the way I really would like to state this, I guess, is that a person is giving as fully as he is able at the given – – – the degree of trance that he is in, what his memory banks in essence are telling and whether that is related to the truth; in any other sense hypnosis would not be an instrument that could determine that.[19]

* * *

19. Can you follow this answer? Do you think the jury could? Is there anything the attorney might have done to ensure that the jury understood what was being said? In this transcript we have made slight revisions of some of the remarks of several of the participants to make them more easily comprehended than they, in fact, may have been.

It should be recognized, of course, that the confusion may be produced by transcription mistakes made by the court reporter or the transcriber. See, e.g., Phila. Inquirer, May 27, 1976, § B, at 1, col. 5. This case was recorded on tape, and the court reporter in fact did have problems deciphering the tapes.

Q. All right, sir, is hypnosis generally regarded as a valid medical tool in your profession? **A.** Hypnosis is regarded as one of the modalities that is at the command of psychiatry. It is a clinical tool like, for example, the clinical psychiatric interview is a clinical tool.

Q. Is it used as reliably in the diagnosis of a person as, for instance, the Rorschach test or other psychological or psychiatric tests? **A.** You mentioned specifically the diagnosis of a person. Hypnosis is much different than other psychological tests. In more recent years this is a fairly recent advancement, I believe. The literature of medical hypnosis is now quite interested in the correlation between personality type and the degree of susceptibility to hypnotic trance. Dr. Speit, for example, is one person who has done research in this area. And a number of other doctors across the country have been much interested in this question right now, but that is fairly recent; it is not fully developed. I would say hypnosis as of yet is not used as a definitive tool for diagnosis. It is used as a tool, for example, for recovery of early memories and uncovering dreams. It is used as a tool for doing therapy for all different kinds of problems including phobias and other kinds of psychiatric problems.

Q. Does it have a different purpose from, say, sodium pentothal or a lie detector test? **A.** Oh, yes, of course. A lie detector test is a polygraph representation of the physiological state of a person while he is giving some response and the idea is to determine whether that person is lying or at least feels he is lying. The sodium pentothal interview is a tool, a psychiatric tool, in which the idea is to inject an acting narcotic to bring a person right to the door of completely falling asleep, but not passing into that stage, so the person is still able to talk and to answer questions. But, the idea is that his defenses—his usual defenses—are almost totally eclipsed at that point as they would be in sleep, but he is not actually asleep; he is able to respond. So this tool is used when somebody has a great deal of physiological defense against becoming aware of something, and usually it is done with something in the past, and the sodium pentothal breaks down those defenses so that in the interview one then gets the relatively open expression of what the person was feeling or thinking or doing, free of the kinds of overlaying defenses which usually hide it from the person and from the interviewer.

Now, hypnosis is different from sodium pentothal in the sense that it is not bringing a person into a sleep type condition. As a matter of fact, in many respects hypnosis is the exact opposite of that. In sleep both peripheral awareness and focal awareness dissolve and the person becomes sort of unrelated to external awareness. In hypnosis, the person's peripheral awareness shrinks to practically nothing, but his central awareness, his attention, is heightened greatly. It is a kind of peak type of heightening his central awareness. In other words, it is similar to when somebody is studying a problem in his office; he can become so focused on that problem that he is totally unaware of people walking in and out of the office and doing other things. This is what hypnosis in essence is.

* * *

Q. How many people have you ever been involved with—that is directly involved with as a psychiatrist—who have been put under hypnosis? How many people have you actually put under hypnosis yourself? **A.** I would estimate that I have seen maybe, all together, 50 or 60 people under the conditions of medical hypnosis.

Q. How many have you put under hypnotic trance yourself? **A.** Between 20 and 30 people.

Q. How long have you been in the practice of psychiatry? **A.** Well, if you would include the three years of my training when I was actually doing psychiatric work and two years in the military, and the two and one half years since I have been out of the military, it turns out to be seven and one half years.

Q. What does your actual practice consist of at the present time? **A.** I work at a community mental health center half of the time. The center's name is Area G Community Mental Health Center and it is located in Washington, D.C. I am a psychiatric consultant.

Q. How many patients do you see approximately a week? **A.** I generally see between 20 and 25 patients a week.

Q. Do you do any private practice in psychiatry also? **A.** Yes, I do.

Q. And that is besides the consultation work that you do? **A.** Yes.

Q. Have you had an opportunity to interview Mr. Green, the defendant in this case? **A.** Yes, I have.

Q. How many hours have you spent in an interview with him? **A.** I have seen him on two occasions. The first occasion lasted about three hours and the second one was about two hours.[20]

Q. During those occasions was he put into a hypnotic trance? **A.** On both occasions, he was.

Q. Have you made other studies of materials that were made available to you by Mr. Green? **A.** Yes, I have.

Q. What kind of materials were made available to you? **A.** Actually there is a voluminous literature going back to teachers' reports when he was in kindergarten and on up, and reports by his school psychologists and psychiatrists from his grade school—reports from recent psychiatric evaluations which was done at the beginning of this year by Dr. Shane. I also have been able to talk to Mr. Green's parents and to his sister.

Q. How many hours total do you estimate that you have spent on this case studying Mr. Green's history? **A.** In addition to the five or six hours of actual interview, I would say at least a minimum of twelve additional hours.

20. In this case the prosecuting attorney did not know in advance of trial that a psychiatrist would be called, or that the defense of unconsciousness would be raised. You will soon observe that the prosecutor objects to the introduction of any evidence relating to hypnosis. In view of the objec- tions that are made later, are you surprised that this background information was introduced without objection? Assuming that the prosecutor was unsure of the direction in which the defense was heading, what protective moves might she have made?

Q. Have you been retained by the defense in this case?   **A.** Yes, I have.

Q. Does your retainer have anything to do with the outcome of the case? [21]   **A.** No, it hasn't.

Q. As a result of the observations that you have made, Doctor, of Mr. Green, have you been able to formulate an opinion with regard to his state of mind on November 8, 1972, at the time of the commission of the alleged offense?

MS. CYNDEN: I object, Your Honor.
JURY OUT

THE COURT: All right, will you state your objection please?

MS. CYNDEN: May it please the Court: Expert opinion is to be based on facts, Your Honor, before the jury. This witness has been asked if he has an opinion based on we know not what – – – there is nothing before the jury as to what facts or non-facts, the opinion might be based on.[22] The jury has no way to evaluate it. What the doctor may be accepting as true, or what he may be discarding which the jury accepts as true in rendering such an opinion as such would be inadmissible. From the prior questioning it would seem that his opinion, if he has one, is based on things this witness told him while under hypnosis which would be inadmissible to go before the jury, and therefore inadmissible as the basis for his opinion.[23]

MS. TRILO: May it please the Court: I am vouching for the record and to the court. I am going to put the defendant on as I told you before and I vouch that the defendant will indicate in his testimony that he has no memory of the actual event.

I thought perhaps this was the better order. I wanted to put the doctor on so that the jury would have some understanding of what happened, by expert testimony on that night to Mr. Green, and what his state of mind was, before they hear from him, and so they can make a better evaluation of his testimony as they hear it. I will vouch that Mr. Green will take the stand and he will testify that he was at the scene and that he remembers starting to get out of the automobile, remembers a falling sensation, and the next thing that he remembers is looking into the automobile, seeing the girl on the ground, and seeing blood, but there is no memory span whatsoever, Your Honor, of what he saw or what happened to that girl between the time that he said that he started to get out of the automobile. At that time he will testify about the girl, the fact they had just made a joke and he was getting ready to leave to go home, and that is the last thing that he remembers until again he looked into that automobile and saw all of that blood.

---

21. Is this an attempt to bolster credibility before it is attacked? If so, should it be permitted?

22. If an objection were made that the psychiatrist has insufficient data on which to base an expert opinion, how should the court rule? Compare the testimony of the psychiatrist in the medical malpractice case that follows.

23. This objection is printed as transcribed. Do you understand it? Would it be proper in federal court? In most common law jurisdictions? This is the prosecutor's first objection to evidence based on hypnosis. Is it too late? Has the prosecutor waived a right to object? If not, how will the jury react to the prosecutor's attempt to stop the flow of facts for which an extensive foundation has been laid?

THE COURT: What have you to say about what Ms. Cynden commented about his opinion being based on matters not before the jury?

MS. TRILO: Well, I can only say, Your Honor, that I am vouching to the court that I will put the defendant on and that the matters are going before the jury. I am going to put the defendant on, of course, with no restrictions whatsoever. She will have a full chance to cross-examine the defendant. I am going to examine him as fully as I can myself on direct examination. A great many of the things that the doctor will be testifying to will be things that Mr. Green does remember.

THE COURT: You have just asked him if he has an opinion. Now, in the absence of the jury, let's see what his opinion is.

MS. TRILO: Do you want me to repeat the question, or do you remember the question?

THE COURT: Ask him the question.

BY MS. TRILO:

Q. My question was: Have you formulated an opinion on the state of mind of Green as it was on November the 8th at the time of the commission of the crime with which he is charged here? A. Yes, I have formed an opinion on that matter.

MS. TRILO: Do you want him to state that?

THE COURT: Yes.

Q. Will you state your opinion? A. It is my clinical opinion that he was unconscious at that point.

Q. Do you have some basis for that opinion? A. Yes, I do.

MS. TRILO: Do you want to hear the basis?

THE COURT: Yes.

Q. Doctor, would you go ahead and start right from the beginning and give the basis? It will take some time, Your Honor, now, go ahead. A. Well, there are two levels for the basis, do you want me to give the full – – –

Q. Yes. I want you to go through everything that you did to formulate – – – that basis starting right from the initial contact with him if you wish, the first contact that you had with Mr. Green.

THE COURT: Just one second. Does the Commonwealth have any questions? It might save time if the Commonwealth has some questions that she wants to ask him rather than to have the entire matter – – –

MS. CYNDEN: I would like to ask him one question, Your Honor.

THE COURT: All right.

MS. CYNDEN: The question was the state of mind of Green at the time of the commission of the crime and the answer was that he was unconscious at that time.   Doctor, are you saying that he was unconscious when he committed the crime?

A.   What I am saying is at the time that the crime was committed, the defendant, Mr. Green, was unconscious.   I was not making an assertion as to who did the crime; I don't know.

Q.   Well, if Green was unconscious, is there any way of knowing who committed the crime or when it was committed? [24]   **A.**   So far as I know I can think of no way right offhand.   I have thought about the matter.   I don't know how the jury or the court here can determine the truth about this matter.

Q.   Do you think that you can?   **A.**   What I can establish is my clinical impression about the state of mind of Mr. Green at the time of the murder as clearly as possible.

Q.   Is that based in part on reports from his school records going all of the way back to grammar school?   **A.**   There are two aspects, one is — —

Q.   Could you answer yes or no, doctor, and then explain?   **A.**   In part, yes.

Q.   All right.   **A.**   The explanation is — — —

Q.   From his parents and his sister?   **A.**   In part.

MS. CYNDEN: Your Honor, I renew my objection if his opinion is based on what — — —

DR. LOCKET: I would like to explain my opinion.

MS. CYNDEN: To what his parents told him and what his sister told him and reports made by unknown persons 15 years ago.

THE COURT: Let me ask you another question.   Do you have an opinion as to what caused him to be unconscious?

DR. LOCKET: I cannot fully give an opinion on that basis because there just isn't enough evidence.   There is not enough data.   It would be a supposition that I would not put under the label of a clinical opinion.

THE COURT: Do you have an opinion as to what length of time he was unconscious?

DR. LOCKET: I cannot determine that.

MS. TRILO: May I ask him one question in that respect, Your Honor?

THE COURT: All right.

MS. TRILO: Would you have an opinion with respect to a period of time when he became unconscious and a time when he regained his consciousness?

---

24.   What is the problem the prosecutor is attempting to raise?   Does the doctor's expertise enable him to answer this question?

DR. LOCKET: Yes.

MS. TRILO: I think that is what the court was looking for.

THE COURT: Now when would those times be?

DR. LOCKET: Well, specifically when the defendant, Mr. Green, was leaving the car, opening the door, and starting to leave the car, and that is the beginning of his unconsciousness. When he starts to regain consciousness is when he is starting to get off of the ground on the opposite side of the car. In between something happened. I can't say much about what happened because I have no information about that. All that I can say is that what happened left a woman dead outside of her car, and this is, in essence, what Mr. Green witnesses in a sense for the first time. The period of unconsciousness then lasts on that basis—it is my impression that there was a murder committed during the time that he was unconscious. He was conscious at one point and she was alive, he was unconscious for a period of time, then he was conscious again and she is dead.

THE COURT: Is this based in large part on what he told you while he was under hypnosis?

DR. LOCKET: On what he told me prior to his going under a trance and on what he told me while he was in a trance. Yes.

THE COURT: Does the Commonwealth have any questions?

MS. CYNDEN: Yes, sir.

THE COURT: I wanted to ask you one other question. You said that hypnosis is not fully developed and not yet used as a definitive tool for diagnosis?

DR. LOCKET: For diagnosis, yes.

THE COURT: Well, is the reason for this that it is not accurate? Is that the reason?

DR. LOCKET: No. I didn't want to give you the impression—hypnosis is used for diagnosis, for treatment and also for recovering memory in amnesia. Now as a diagnostic tool it is in its infancy. As a treatment tool it goes way back, way back in history, back to the last century or before that. And in terms of recovering memory for periods of amnesia, it also has a very long history, which has been documented in medical literature and
– – –

THE COURT: Now didn't you say earlier that you couldn't say whether or not what he would tell you under the influence of hypnosis was the truth or not?

DR. LOCKET: Well, my impression is not just in terms of what he tells me, but in terms of the whole situation. What he tells me nonverbally, and what he demonstrates, in essence, unwittingly. We all do this at all times. What we say is only a very small portion of the data that I obtain in my listening and observing a person while he is talking. My clinical impression is a matter of taking all of these data and placing them into a pattern which is, in essence, patterned by psychiatric theory, established psychiatric theory, and seeing what fits and what doesn't fit and on the basis of that developing a clinical impression, on the basis of that – – – [25]

THE COURT: You are in effect weighing the evidence before you make a determination? [26]

DR. LOCKET: In essence, in terms of my clinical experience, in terms of my clinical knowledge, and in terms of the observable data that I see along with and including the subjective report by the subject. I take all of these into consideration, and the final impression is a synopsis of this into a meaningful pattern.

THE COURT: Do you have any more questions, Ms. Cynden?

MS. CYNDEN: No, sir.

THE COURT: Ms. Trilo, do you have any further questions relating to this?

MS. TRILO:

Q. Doctor, you said that you didn't have enough reliable data to arrive at a conclusion whether or not he was unconscious. You do have some data derived from Mr. Green, do you not, with regard to the period which you believe that he went into unconsciousness? A. I am sorry. I think what I said – – – this can be documented I suppose on that tape recorder – – – was I could not state whether Mr. Green was involved in the murder or whether someone else was. That was beyond the data that I have at my command.

Q. How did you arrive at that clinical impression? What data do you have to arrive at the clinical impression that he became unconscious? A. At this point, I think that I should give a more detailed presentation of the data, the data base that I am making my conclusion on, because otherwise it is difficult to understand what I am saying.

THE COURT: All right. A. When I first came onto this case, this would be on May the 30th of this year, and this is the first time that I met Mr. Green. This was in jail. I began my clinical interview at that point. My initial impression of Mr. Green when I first met him was that he seemed to not be as depressed as I imagined a person could be given the circumstances, and very quickly it seemed to me that he was very much interested in capturing my attention, and keeping me sort of enthralled with him. And at any time that my attention seemed to lag or slacken, he would at that point bring forth something particularly dramatic in order to recapture my attention.

This was my initial impression of him. I went through a personal history and a family history. I think my feelings relating to a person are very

25. What exactly is the expertise the doctor is claiming? Is it the ability to detect lies without a polygraph?

26. Compare the thrust of the question with the tenor of the answer. Do the judge and the psychiatrist mean the same thing by the term "weighing the evidence"?

important data in terms of my impression, diagnosis, and whatever. But I began to have a feeling that he was not a reliable historian when talking about his own biography, and that he would distort certain aspects of his biography in order to dramatize them and in order to catch my interest.[27] I paid a great deal of attention to what he said and I took a mental status examination in which I saw no evidence of any schizophrenia in him, which is important too. Then I moved, after all of this history, I moved onto his memory of what happened on that night of November the 8th, and he began telling me about what happened that afternoon and into the evening.

He related the facts of that evening in the following way. He said what he remembered was that Molly Glick had asked him if he would like a ride home, and that he had said, "No," but then said, "Yes," later. And that she had taken his coat to go retrieve her car and they drove back and as they were driving back, they stopped at a stoplight, and that a car had pulled up beside them. He remembered it having its interior light on in the compartment. I asked him at that time did he remember who was in the car, and did he see anyone in the car. He said, "No," he had no memory for that. All that he could recall was that the interior light was on in the car.

THE COURT: Now, was he under the influence of hypnosis? A. No, no, this was just a continuation of my psychiatric history into the present problem. He then told me that they drove to his house, and he mentioned that he wasn't sure how she even knew where he lived, and that not many people knew where he lived. He was surprised that she knew but he didn't ask her how she knew but she drove directly to his house.

She stopped in front of his house. He doesn't remember exactly what went on, but she said something like, "Would you like to talk?" and he said, "O.K." And she started into the parking lot across the street from his house, and there were two cars parked there or he said there were some cars parked there, and so she pulled further around the corner so presumably she could have privacy. And he said that he couldn't really remember much about the conversation that they had, except she was saying something about drugs, and didn't he know that drugs would kill him, or some such thing as that, and that he was getting angry, and was replying in the sense of saying, "Well it is my life, don't bug me about that." Then he recalls asking her if she would like to go up to his place and she said that she was too tired. He said he could sort of remember that there was something about a joke made at that point. He said something about, "O.K. I am going to go up to my place," and he started to open the door to her car. He remembers opening the door and feeling the cold rain on his face as he was getting out, and then, according to him, he had no memory for a period of time. He does not know, but his very next memory is that it happened almost right after his getting out of the car—is getting up from a crouched position and feeling sort of groggy and then noticing that the –   –   –   the first thing that he noticed

---

27. Given the nature of the judge's questions, it is likely that the judge will conclude that the psychiatrist is unreliable because he admits that the facts related to him are probably not reliable? Is the psychiatrist saying this? Or is he saying that by choosing to relate certain facts and by relating them in a particular way, Green transmitted information that amounted to reliable clues as to the condition of his mind?

was that the car light is on, and he walks over and he sees the body of Molly Glick, and then he sees his knife and he picks up his knife and puts it into his pocket.

He hears a voice say, "Hey," from behind him. He turns around and— but does not see anything. And then runs, according to him, away from the scene down some railroad tracks. There is additional information too, but this is the information that he told me at this time outside of a trance as well as he could remember it.

I asked him specific questions trying to gain more data, but this was about all that he can give me. As a matter of fact, the way that I tell it to you right now is in better order than the way he related it to me the first time. I then shortly thereafter asked him specifically if he would like to recapture that memory. I asked him that question specifically as a test, – – – because when I was in the Army, I saw many men who had gone A.W.O.L. and I found that, when I would approach them from the standpoint of recapturing their memory, they would be very suspicious of me and they would ask me all kinds of questions. "How would I do it?" "What is involved?" And they seemed to have no anxiety about the fact that they had a period of time for which they had no memory.

On the other hand, people whom I have dealt with who had bona fide amnesia—for example one man who was knocked over the head and his memory was lost and it had nothing to do with anything that could incriminate him, and other cases like this—had a great deal of anxiety that there was a period of time that they had no memory for. When I asked them if they would like to try to recapture that memory, they unqualifiedly said yes.

It is like a person who is in pain versus a person who isn't in pain but is saying that he is. That person in pain just wants to get rid of that pain, and he will say, "Yes, what can you do to help me?" and this is in essence the response that Green gave me. He said, "Yes," and then he qualified it by saying, "I am frightened about recapturing this memory. I am frightened about what I would find, but I would want to know what happened." So on the basis of that I told him that one way in which we could recapture his memory was to put him into a hypnotic trance, and he readily agreed. We were able to find a quiet room down in the basement at the jail. At this point I only had some peripheral evidence that he might be a good subject for hypnosis. Not everybody is able to go into a good trance. I did the procedure that I had learned previously from Dr. Speit, and he went into a rapid trance. I tested the trance by regressing him to the two and five years old periods of his life and determining the details that he was able to remember, and he gave me a wealth of details about things that people ordinarily have no memory for. I instructed him to tell what was going on and he used the present tense. I also observed him while he was in the trance. He began to perspire profusely. When people are in trances their temperature increases anywhere between a half of a degree to a full degree. I was satisfied at that point he was in a trance and a good trance and that he was one of those few people who can go into a good trance rapidly. I then regressed him to the night of November the 8th, and I asked him to go through the details of that evening, beginning with the time that work was starting to close. Immediately I could see that he was giving me a much more detailed description, and he used the present tense as to what happened on that evening. He described what he was doing, and who was in the room. He described the conversation that he had with the bartender, and also with Molly Glick. His description all of the way through had the same structure as what he told me before he was hypnotized, but it was filled in with a great deal of detail. Much of the detail is irrelevant, but it is there, which is another indication that we had a valid trance. He told me, I will give you the story as he told it to me the very first time I asked him to relate this material under a trance. He told me again that he was setting up the chairs, and he commented to the bartender that it was really pouring out and Molly Glick came over and said, "Would you like a ride?" He said, "No," initially, and she asked him again, and so he said, "Yes, but I have to take out the trash first," and Miss Glick said that she needed his coat in order to go out and get her car.

So he gave her his coat and finished his final tasks, and then went out under the awning of the pub to wait for the car. Molly Glick comes and picks him up and as he gets into the car—his coat, she had placed it on the seat between them. As they were driving to his place, he talks about coming to the stoplight and this car coming up next to them. He sees inside the car, he notices the interior light is on, and this time describes what he sees inside of the car, all men, one person is a small thin person driving the car. Then they pull up to his house. She says, "Would you like to talk?" according to him in a trance, and he says, "O.K." She pulls into the driveway and there are two cars parked there, and one car turns its lights out as they are pulling in and she pulls around these cars to the back of the lot. He then goes on to talk about the conversation between the two of them and gives details, more details. She is saying such things as, "Don't you know drugs will kill you? I have a good mind to turn right around and turn you in for your own good."

And he describes how he slumped in the chair of the car with his knees sort of relaxing on the dash and he is feeling angry and kind of tired and he responds, in essence the same way he told outside of the trance, "It is my life." And then he asked her if she wanted to go up to his apartment with him, and she says, "No." She is too tired, maybe some other time. And he says, "Those are nice pants that you have on," and she says, "These pants I only wear once a year during election night," and they both laughed. At this point he is getting on his coat and he says, "You are sure you don't want to come up," and she says "Yes." He says, "O.K., see you around." At this point he is slipping on his coat and he is also opening the car door, and he describes himself as kind of being a little bit twisted in his coat and starting to move out of the car. Then he describes that suddenly he is starting to fall.

He describes this as just falling straight forward, pitching forward almost out of the car. He falls onto what he feels to be almost a trampoline, a soft surface from which he sort of bounces and then comes down to rest. And then he feels gravel in his mouth and feels pain in his right hand. He starts to get up. He is just lying there on the lot. He starts to raise up and he is feeling groggy and he falls backward a little bit, tries to catch his balance and he notices the lights on in the car, walks over and looks down and sees Molly Glick's body. And he reports this, as a matter of fact, each time he reports this his face is distorted with a kind of horror, looks like horror on his face, and he says, "I see her body and I looked into the car and I see my knife in a jackknife position next to the gas pedal of the car, and there is blood all over. I reached down and pick up the knife and put it into my pocket, and in my mind I feel like I must have done it. I must have really freaked out and done it." At this point he hears a voice behind him say "Hey," and he turns around and he sees a man standing about a 100 feet behind him. He describes the man as being bigger than him, wearing a jacket that looks very much like his own but being baggier.

At this point, he thinks to himself, "Here is somebody who saw what happened, he can tell me whether I killed this woman or not." So, as he is thinking this, the figure starts to run, and he describes that he isn't a good runner, that he takes long loping steps as he is running across the parking lot in the direction of Green's place, and Green takes off after him according to what he talks about now in the trance. He runs after him and, as they both arrive at the street, a car comes and the lights of the car blind him, blind Green. As he is talking about this, he shows the characteristics of re-experiencing the event by closing his eyes very tightly as if he was seeing those bright lights. He jumps behind a bush so he is not seen. When he emerges from the bush, he sees a figure, he thinks it is the same figure now running down the street, and as he runs after this figure, the figure turns the corner and runs straight down towards the direction of some fraternities.

He is now at a junction where he can continue to chase the man or he can take another path which leads down to the railroad. He is confused about this in the trance. He says, "I don't understand why I didn't chase him. I should have chased him but I didn't. I ran down instead of chasing him down the street and I ran down the path onto the railroad tracks."

This is in essence the story he told me the first time that I put him into a trance. Now the period of amnesia is still there even though he is in a trance; the period of amnesia is still there. So I did certain hypnotic techniques to try to recapture that period of time. What this meant was that I went back and back again while he was in a trance to the period of time when he was opening up that door, and starting to emerge from the car and – – –

MS. CYNDEN: I am sorry—opening the car and – – – A. Starting to emerge from the car, I went over those events over and over and over again in a number of different ways. Now one way which I tried was to have him go through it – – – give him a hypnotic command that the events are going to slow up – – – that everything is going to go very very slow and to tell me while you are re-experiencing this event to tell me everything that you hear, see, feel, or smell as you slowly go through these events and another technique I used was to – – –

THE COURT: Let me interrupt you. Did you ever succeed while he was in a trance in having him recall that period there? He never regained his recollection?   **A.**   No, but I got additional data as I went over and over in a painstaking way, a very painstaking fashion, and there were other subtle little facts that came out, which so far as I know have never emerged in any other manner.   To give you an example, I will just relate the data that I did receive in this fashion.

THE COURT: This material, these were the reports and everything that you had?   **A.**   Each time I have gone over with him the details of these events while under a trance he gives me the same exact order of events. This is consistent with the research on memory of events—it is almost like a train of associations that you get the same sequence each time.

MS. CYNDEN: May I ask the doctor if this is equally consistent with a good rehearsal?

THE COURT: Equally consistent with what?

MS. CYNDEN: A good rehearsal.

DR. LOCKET: No, it is not equally consistent with a good rehearsal.

MS. CYNDEN: Do you mean that you can't remember to say things the same way over and over?

DR. LOCKET: No, my point is given the full context of his being in a trance and all of the things that he demonstrated he couldn't, he couldn't possibly be able to rehearse that and to know what I expected, what I was judging as his being in a trance or what I was judging in terms of what criteria I was using to judge his memory.   There is no way for him to know what I was looking for, so he could rehearse it for me.

* * *

THE COURT: Suppose we stop this right at this point.   Ms. Trilo, do you have any authority for this type of evidence in this case?

MS. TRILO: Yes, sir.

THE COURT: Will you present it please?

MS. TRILO: Your Honor, I am going to ask the doctor to complete his statement in any event.   At this point, I will – – –

THE COURT: Well for the record you can put in the doctor's report, that can go in at a future time if I don't admit it, or if I do admit it then there is no use in going any further.   Let's see what your authority is.   The doctor can stand down now if he wants to, whichever way you want to do.[28]

* * *

MS. CYNDEN:

* * *

---

28.   Defense counsel is seeking to make an offer of proof.   First degree murder is charged and a life sentence is possible.   The jury is still out.   Is the court justified in cutting off the witness?   See also the appellate opinion following the transcript.

As I gather, Your Honor, what Ms. Trilo is suggesting, if you boil it right down, is that we have wasted three days here. We should have dismissed Your Honor and the jury and let Dr. Locket decide the case. I certainly am not willing to have a witness for the defense cross-examined by Dr. Locket, which is what is being suggested here.

I have a duty to cross-examine these witnesses myself if I feel it is called for and I also have a duty to object to hearsay evidence coming in. Whether he was under a trance or might have been stating a well rehearsed story, it is equally outside the realm of our system of justice. I again renew my objection.

THE COURT: Do you have anything more, Ms. Trilo?

MS. TRILO: Yes, sir. We are not asking Dr. Locket to take over the province of the jury, Your Honor. Certainly in this phase of Dr. Locket's testimony, he will not take over the province of the jury with respect to guilt or innocence. He will really relate to the Court some things this defendant cannot relate to the Court without being put under a trance.

Ms. Cynden says that the doctor is going to state things to the Court that the defendant is not going to state. We submit, Your Honor, that we are going to put the defendant on, and we will allow the doctor to put this man under a trance, and we will take the chance of what answers he may give while here in a trance. The doctor has done it before, and we are not saying to the Court that we are going to unravel all of the period of amnesia. It is the only way that we can present the evidence. We are not taking over the province of the jury. We are not making a determination with respect to guilt or innocence.

The doctor is not going to say, "I think that he is innocent," or "I think that he is guilty." He is going to bring out the facts for the Court and the jury to consider.

* * *

THE COURT: The Court sustains the objection. This Court doesn't make the rules; I just apply them as they are already made. I have no authority to change them. This memorandum does not convince me that this is the law.[29] These memoranda do not show me any case where this exact thing had been done. It would be quite an innovation. I think it violates several rules of evidence as contained in *Bash*.[30] Since it is ultimately the province of the jury to find the facts as well as draw conclusions therefrom, the facts on which the expert grounds his opinion must be brought before the jury.

This opinion is based on hearsay statements of the defendant in part, and also in part on weighing all of the evidence that he had before him; what his family had told him, what the records showed, what his grades were in

29. See the defense counsel's memorandum reproduced after this transcript.

30. *Bash* is an evidence book that was written approximately forty years before the trial of this case. It was not updated. During in camera arguments about the admissibility of the expert testimony, defense counsel attempted to cite modern authorities from other jurisdictions, but the trial judge insisted on following *Bash*.

his school work, and that sort of thing. I feel in addition to that, that the doctor put his finger on the thing when he said his function was really weighing the evidence. And of course, that encroaches on the province of the jury, and of course, that also in *Bash* is ruled out.[31]

What you are in effect having him do is to come here and bolster what will presumably be the testimony of the defendant, and that is not proper. I have accordingly made my ruling to sustain the objection.

* * *

MS. TRILO: I just was going to ask the Court a question. Supposing we just put Green on and let the doctor hypnotize him and the doctor made no opinion or gave no opinion? Just under hypnotism—put him under hypnosis, and he could be asked questions by me and Ms. Cynden, but with no opinion by the doctor?

THE COURT: I know of no such procedure.[32]

AFTERNOON SESSION

JURY OUT

MS. TRILO: I would like to ask that Dr. Locket remain in the courtroom while Mr. Green is testifying with the expectation that I would put him on the stand again and ask him if he could formulate an opinion with regard to whether Green was conscious or unconscious at the time of the commission of the offense.

The reason why I am asking is that I wouldn't want the fact that he stayed in the courtroom to disqualify him because we are here under the rules of exclusion. I don't believe the rule of exclusion applies to him in this case because the rule is for the purpose of keeping the witnesses from getting together on the testimony that is given in the courtroom so that they can have consistent testimony, but there is no danger of that certainly here.

THE COURT: Ms. Cynden?

MS. CYNDEN: May it please the Court: I have no objection to the doctor staying in the courtroom. I would have objection to his testifying and rendering an opinion based upon what he had heard in the courtroom. One of the specific things that has to be guarded against in expert opinion is the factor of the expert who is giving the opinion weighing the evidence. And what Ms. Trilo is asking is specifically that he be allowed to weigh the evidence, and give an opinion based upon what he heard.

---

31. Is this an accurate description of the doctor's testimony? Is the doctor weighing evidence? Would the jury be deprived of the facts supporting the doctor's opinion if the defense were allowed to proceed as requested?

32. What objections might be raised to such a procedure? Are these objections important enough to warrant depriving the defendant of evidence which a trained psychiatrist insists is reliable? Is testimony under hypnosis a kind of evidence that a jury should be allowed to rely on in considering the defendant's guilt? You will be better able to deal with this last question when you have read the material that follows the transcript.

The ordinary way of asking for expert opinion is to state a hypothetical question: If such and such is a fact or if such and such is fact, all of these matters that the jury has heard, of course, then do you have an opinion, if so, what is it? This would be absolutely contrary to the ordinary way of rendering an opinion. I think now that the doctor is completely disqualified from rendering any opinion. He has already stated that he has an opinion based on evidence that is inadmissible, and the Judge has so ruled. How could he possibly now discard from his mind all of the bases for his prior opinion which has been ruled inadmissible? I just don't believe that a human being can do it. And furthermore, Your Honor, Ms. Trilo made the motion to exclude the witnesses and now she is asking that a particular exception be made to that motion. Your Honor, I would object on all of these bases.

[The judge permitted the expert to remain in the courtroom.]

* * *

[At this point the jury has returned and the defendant has testified. Both counsel have approached the bench.]

MS. TRILO: May it please the Court: I would again renew my motion that Dr. Locket be allowed to take the stand and on the basis of the information that he has available to give an opinion, if he has one, with regard to whether or not Green was unconscious during the period of time from when he started to get out of the car until he again came to and saw the blood in the car.

I again also renew my motion, Your Honor, for permission to put Green on the stand and have the doctor put him into a hypnotic trance and question him while he is in a hypnotic trance for the purpose of possibly getting more information from him than he has given here because of his loss of memory.

THE COURT: All right, the Court overrules your motion.

MS. TRILO: I except, Your Honor, on the grounds that I have previously given to the Court in my oral argument and in my memoranda.

THE COURT: The doctor's testimony about whether or not he was unconscious would be sheer speculation, and it would have to be based upon what the defendant has testified to, and I think it would encroach on the province of the jury.

MS. TRILO: Your Honor, again with regard to my motion, I asked when I made the motion, I would ask the doctor to assume if the jury believed everything that the defendant said to be true and then ask if he formulated an opinion on that—so it wouldn't be invading the province of the jury.

THE COURT: Ms. Cynden?

MS. CYNDEN: May it please the Court: You are still faced with the fact that the doctor has already shown that he has a fixed opinion on the subject, and it is based on what he said was a study of school records, conversations with his parents, and statements made to him which are inadmissible. I think it would be naive to assume that he could now remove all of that from his mind and form an opinion on an entirely separate set of facts.[33]

THE COURT: I think the last request of Ms. Trilo is in a different light because then it becomes a hypothetical—in the nature of a hypothetical question. Not her first request, that he be allowed to testify as to whether or not he was unconscious. But I think if she frames it as she last suggested, then it becomes a hypothetical question. I believe that he can and he will be permitted to answer it. But, of course, the fact that he had a previous opinion would perhaps go to the weight of it; it wouldn't go to the admissibility. I think he can be asked that.[34]

MS. CYNDEN: May it please the Court: The Commonwealth is perfectly willing to stipulate that if everything that he says is true, he was unconscious.

MS. TRILO: We would rather have the doctor testify, Your Honor, rather than have a stipulation.

MS. CYNDEN: I will withdraw the offer to stipulate; I don't believe I would like to.[35]

THE COURT: All right.

MS. TRILO: Could we talk to the doctor a few minutes?

THE COURT: No ma'am, the doctor will have to take the stand. This case has been going on for days and you have had the doctor here for three days—put the doctor on the stand.

MS. TRILO: This is the first time that we have been allowed, Your Honor, to put the doctor on and I would like to talk to him for a couple of minutes to formulate any questions.

THE COURT: Well, you can talk to him right there.

[Conference at the bench]

MS. TRILO: May it please the Court: Do I understand that your ruling is that the doctor can only testify on the basis of what Mr. Green has said? The doctor cannot give an opinion on that any more than anyone of

33. Is the prosecutor as concerned with getting at the truth as she is with winning her case? In the situation presented here, are the two goals antithetical?

34. **Notice what has happened. Defense counsel persuades the court that after the defendant testifies, the psychiatrist could be asked for an opinion on consciousness based upon the hypothesis that the defendant's testimony was truthful. Apparently the court is convinced that such an opinion will be helpful to the trier of fact. Must the court also be convinced that the psychiatrist can and will ignore all other data in rendering such an opinion? The judge, apparently, does not think so. Is the** prosecution likely to cross-examine the doctor about his earlier opinion? Would evidence of the earlier opinion detract from the weight of his courtroom opinion? Now that the door is opened to the defense watch what happens and what doesn't. What do you expect the defense attorney to be able to get in?

35. Would a stipulation have been harmful to the prosecution? Exactly what was being given away? Could the court have forced the defense to accept the stipulation instead of calling the doctor? What went through the prosecutor's mind during the brief period between the time she offered the stipulation and the time she withdraw it?

us can, as far as what he said on the stand. His opinion would have to be based on everything that he has learned about this man, and I understand that you are not going to permit this?

THE COURT: No.

MS. TRILO: All right, sir, we can't put him on because he can't give an opinion on just that, but he could give an opinion on everything he knows about with respect to his state of consciousness between the time he said that he fell out of the car and the time he looked in and saw the blood. So that I understand the basis of your ruling, this is on anything outside of what the doctor heard in the courtroom? That is why you won't let him get on there?

THE COURT: Well the jury has to have the facts on which he bases his opinion.

MS. TRILO: Well, Your Honor, that comes out on cross-examination. That is the purpose of cross-examination.

THE COURT: But that is going to involve, as I understand it, a lot of material that is not in evidence.

MS. TRILO: That is right, Your Honor.

MS. CYNDEN: Your Honor, according to the doctor this morning, it involved weighing the probative value of various statements that had been made to him by various people.

MS. TRILO: All right, I am sure Your Honor knows that experts generally do this. Certainly a doctor who tests a person on the question of insanity weighs the things that are given to him, the data given to him. He has to weigh it. He is not a machine that can objectively test things and come up with a completely objective answer. He has to be somewhat subjective, based on his own knowledge and his experience and learning. A doctor can't make himself into a machine to make such a determination, and – – –

THE COURT: Well, the Court will permit a hypothetical question based on the evidence before the jury but it will not permit an opinion on facts not before the jury.

* * *

MS. TRILO: May it please the Court: Your Honor, Dr. Locket informs us that he has with him all of the data, aside from the statements made by the defendant under hypnosis, all reports etc. throughout the defendant's childhood and on up – – – Now, we would offer that as part of his testimony. The Commonwealth has objected on the grounds that is hearsay. Your Honor, we would put him on the stand and ask him about that in order to introduce that as a basis for his testimony.

We understand the Court's ruling to be that we would have to call the principal, call the psychologist who examined him in elementary school and on up for every one of those persons in order to introduce those statements.

And therefore, that the Court does not accept a psychiatrist's history as compiled from his patient.

THE COURT: Well, does he have a verbatim record of his conversation with the defendant, the two or three hour sessions that he had?

MS. TRILO: He does not have. As a matter of fact he does have a tape recording of a large portion of one of them but he does not have a verbatim record.

Of course, there is an exception to the hearsay rule for statements made by a patient to his doctor about present mental impressions but aside from that, as we understand the law, psychiatrists always rely upon personal history. The only way a psychiatrist can give an opinion as to the present state of mind or past state of mind of any person is a personal history.

Now it is true, and it would be possible for the Court to hold, that we would have to introduce every single person who ever filed one of those reports or one of those report cards. We view that as error and except from the ruling, and we want to ask the Court if that is the ruling, if that evidence cannot come in? [36]

THE COURT: Well, the ruling is that a hypothetical question, if it is going to be based on evidence that is not before the jury, then it has got to be in the form of a hypothetical question, and therefore, not contain every element that he has had in his mind or gotten into his mind and particularly used in forming his opinion. [37]

MS. TRILO: Your Honor, I will answer that. I would put the doctor on and have him testify first before I asked him the basis on which he forms an opinion, and I would ask him in detail everything that he is going to base his opinion on.

THE COURT: So if it is not going to be based on the evidence which is before the jury, then you have got to ask him a hypothetical question.

MS. TRILO: But he is an expert, an expert witness, Your Honor, I don't have to ask him – – – a treating physician – – – a hypo-

36. Throughout the trial the defense contended that a patient's history was necessary to a psychiatric diagnosis and that psychiatrists must rely on information that courts would call hearsay in order to render opinions on mental conditions. The same contentions were made on appeal. Numerous authorities were cited in support of the proposition that a psychiatrist must be permitted to use some hearsay in making an evaluation. In other words "the validity of the psychiatrist's observations and inferences is dependent upon the totality of his approach." See Diamond & Louisell, supra note 14. See also the discussion of the New York Criminal Procedure Code providing that a psychiatrist must be given an opportunity to explain his diagnosis and its basis in Lee v. County Court of Erie County, 27 N.Y.2d 432, 318 N.Y.S.2d 705, 267 N.E.2d 452 (1971), certiorari denied, 404 U.S. 823 (1971). In this case could the defense counsel have validly argued that the patient's history, as used by the psychiatrists, was not hearsay? In chambers the defense did made this argument, claiming that the history was used not for its truth, but to explain the expert opinion. Believing that only facts otherwise in evidence could be used to support the opinion of an expert, the court rejected the argument. The court also refused to treat school records and report cards as business records.

37. The judge misunderstands the law on expert testimony. He has already ruled that facts not in evidence cannot be used for any purpose. The question is what facts should be allowed in as evidence.

thetical question.   In a negligence case I don't have to ask an expert who is going to testify about the disability of his patient a hypothetical question. I can ask him the whole history of what he found with that patient with reference to an injured leg.   Now if I bring in an expert simply for that purpose, then I have to go to the hypothetical question with him and give him all of the pertinent facts.   But this man was the treating physician.   He is the psychiatrist that took the data and read the data and used it in arriving at this decision.   I submit, Your Honor, we don't have to ask him a purely hypothetical question.

THE COURT: Let me meet with counsel.

REPORTER'S NOTE: Conference off of the record.[38]

* * *

R. K. LOCKET, a witness called by and on behalf of the Defendant, having previously been sworn, was examined and testified as follows:

BY MS. TRILO:

Q.   Will you state your name again for the jury, please?   I know you were on the stand this morning but it has been some time.   A.   Yes.   Dr. R. K. Locket.

Q.   Will you state again your occupation?   A.   I am a psychiatrist.

THE COURT: The jury has heard his qualifications this morning, you don't have to repeat them.

BY MS. TRILO:

Q.   Doctor, have you had occasion to examine the defendant, Mr. Green? A.   Yes, I have.

Q.   When you examined him did you make a diagnosis of his mental condition?   A.   Yes, I did.

Q.   In making this diagnosis were there several bases that you used to come to your conclusion?   A.   Oh, yes.

38.   From the viewpoint of the defense, the most important development in the case occurred in the off-the-record meeting that took place in chambers.   Although noting that the judge at one point apparently was willing to permit a hypothetical question that would include facts not in evidence, the defense chose not to pursue this course for two reasons: It would be hard to explain to the jury why the hypothetical facts were never put into evidence, and the trial judge might recognize his error in midstream and hold the hypothetical improper.   In lieu of the hypothetical based upon unproved facts, the defense sought to benefit from the judge's openness to hypotheticals by convincing the judge that the doctor should be permitted to state that he personally examined the defendant and to give his opinion that, assuming hypothetically that everything the defendant related in his courtroom testimony was true, the defendant was unconscious at the time of the murder.   (Was the doctor, as Ms. Trilo states before the judge intervenes, a treating physician?)

The judge made clear his intent to bar the defense from eliciting the specific data relied upon by the doctor to reach his conclusion.   Watch how the door opens wider, despite the intention of the judge, as the defense proceeds.   But remember that the defense was reacting to the earlier restrictive rulings of the court, and that it preferred to present directly all the information the doctor possessed that might tend to shed light on the defense of unconsciousness.

Q. Would you list those bases, please? **A.** I used initially a psychiatric interview which has two forms of basis of data. One being the subjective verbal report of the patient and the second being the non-verbal observation, direct observation on my part. I also used a great deal of past records of Mr. Green that were made available to me stretching way back in his history.

I reviewed all of those and I also reviewed the psychiatric evaluation that was made by Dr. Shawn earlier this year. I also talked briefly with the parents with regard to particular areas that I was interested in.

Q. Can you relate anything specific in your conversations, in your interviews—in your psychiatric interviews with the defendant—on which you base your diagnosis?

MS. CYNDEN: I object, Your Honor.[39]

THE COURT: I think he has stated the bases which he just used in making his diagnosis, and I think that is sufficient now for him to go ahead and tell what his diagnosis is.

BY MS. TRILO:

Q. Doctor, would you tell us what your diagnosis is regarding the mental condition of Mr. Green? **A.** I take his primary diagnosis to be what is called in psychiatry an adolescent adjustment reaction which had primarily to do with identity diffusion. The secondary diagnosis, which is less clear and harder to document, but for which there is considerable evidence, is that Mr. Green might very possibly have minimal brain damage from birth trauma.

Q. Doctor, would you explain in a little more detail both parts of your diagnosis? What is the effect, for example, of possible brain damage? Will you explain again the first part of your diagnosis so that a mere layman might understand? **A.** How much detail do you want me to go into at this time? Would you like for me at this point to give specific clinical facts and specific information on which all of my clinical conclusions have basically been drawn?

MS. CYNDEN: May it please the Court: I think that we are beginning to get into just exactly the part of this matter that the Court has ruled is inadmissible. It is my understanding from the recent conference that he was to be asked if he had a diagnosis and then certain questions based on that.[40]

THE COURT: I think that was the understanding that he made a diagnosis and he has stated it. Now I think you get to the hypothetical question.

39. The objection is well taken. As indicated in the previous footnote, the judge made it clear in chambers that the specific data were to be excluded. Viewed in this light, is the defense acting improperly in asking this question? Does the defense have a right to show the jury that it is not intentionally concealing the information behind the diagnosis?

40. Again the prosecutor is correct, but in chambers neither the prosecutor nor the judge foresaw the need to explain medical terminology. If the defense counsel foresaw this need, did she have an obligation to mention it explicitly?

MS. TRILO: I will ask that, Your Honor. It is not perfectly clear to me what the testimony of the doctor means in layman's terms.

THE COURT: All I want him to do is explain these terms that he has used as his diagnosis. I think you can do that.[41]

MS. TRILO: I think I can question him this way.

BY MS. TRILO:

Q. Without going into the facts on which you based your opinion, can you explain what it is that you mean by the psychological terms that you have used in both the first and second parts of your diagnosis?[42] A. The term adolescent adjustment reaction is in essence a waste paper basket term – – –

MS. CYNDEN: I am sorry, but I didn't get that. A. It covers a broad category, a broad spectrum of emotional disorders that occur in adolescence. The reason why the category has been developed is that adolescence is basically a period of tremendous turmoil. Then the personality and character structure of a person is much more fluid, much more shifting, than it becomes as a person reaches full adulthood. Therefore, typically, what we find is that the adolescent patient who is having emotional problems will show fluid systems that can be classified sometimes as depression, sometimes as looking to be psychotic and sometimes as hysterical kinds of symptoms. Therefore, it is difficult because of the shifting nature of the character structure to pin on one particular label. Also, we don't like to do that without overwhelming evidence because it might lead to a certain kind of treatment process.

He has indications of depression and he has a lot of acting out. Adult patients who become depressed very often withdraw. Younger kids and adolescents, when they become depressed, act out as a way of avoiding the depressive feelings. He shows evidence of that. He shows evidence of having an intense vulnerability to other people's expectations; in other words, he adjusts himself particularly to the expectations of significant others like his parents, and as a consequence he has had a great deal of difficulty coming to terms with himself.

He has tried because he is so vulnerable to external influence. He has reacted to – – –

MS. CYNDEN: May it please the Court: I think we have gone far beyond anything – – –

THE COURT: Define the term adolescent adjustment reaction – – – there must be a – – – some definition of it. A. Well, O.K. This is emotional turmoil that occurs in adolescence and in a patient in whom no definitive diagnosis can be determined. This is the best diagnosis that I can

41. Note how the defense nudged the judge from ruling that the hypothetical question must be put immediately to tolerating more explanation. Is it possible that the doctor could have testified to a specific di-

agnosis without indicating some of the information upon which he relied?

42. Counsel rephrased the original question in an important way. Did you catch this? Do you think it was intentional?

give or the best definition of that diagnosis. The reason that I started to go into more detail is that I am not sure how much that diagnosis really helps you in understanding the dynamics of the character structure of Mr. Green. I will say however – – –

MS. CYNDEN: Is he going to bring Mr. Green's character into it, Your Honor?

MS. TRILO: We are not.

THE COURT: Well – – – **A.** O.K. I have explained adolescent adjustment reaction. Identity diffusion which, in essence, is where a person has no solid sense of self but his sense of self varies over time to such a degree that his conception of his own behavior is bluer than his own eyes [sic] and causes a great deal of confusion about who he is. A person like this generates many, many questions about internal questions as to "What am I?" "Who am I?" and "Where am I going?" Now the secondary diagnosis that I talked about was minimal brain damage, secondary to birth trauma, the kind of brain damage – – –

THE COURT: Counsel, does this last part relate to the question that we are trying to get at? **A.** I think for the purposes of being concise here the thing about the minimal brain damage, the reason it would be important from the medical standpoint, is that it can form a causative relationship for the first diagnosis. People who have minimal brain damage can have high I.Q.'s, but the problem they often have, and this shows up on clinical psychological tests, is that these people have trouble translating their I.Q.'s into actual performance.

On the psychological test on I.Q. there are two scores. There is a verbal score, and there is a performance score. Usually a person will have a parallel congruence between these two scores. With a person with minimal brain damage there is a divergence and a discrepancy such that the verbal is higher, quite a bit higher, than the performance. It would only have effect in this case as an explanation as to why identity diffusion took place, and if the Court is interested in how that particular diagnosis would be – – –

MS. TRILO: I have only two more questions, Your Honor. I would like to make one point about going into the details. The defense, of course, would preserve our continuing objections to the inability to go into details.

Is that enough to identify the objection?

THE COURT: Yes, now I understand when we had our conference awhile ago, that there were certain diagnoses – – –

MS. TRILO: Well, I am going to ask that question now.

BY MS. TRILO:

Q. Doctor Locket, I am going to ask you a hypothetical question. I assume that you know what a hypothetical question is. I would like to explain, if I may. I would like for you to assume something is true. I would like to ask, based on your diagnosis, assuming that this jury believes everything that the defendant Green said when he testified this afternoon, have you a medical opinion as to whether or not Green was conscious or unconscious at the time of the commission of the alleged offense which this case is about?

MS. CYNDEN: Object, Your Honor.

THE COURT: On what grounds?

MS. CYNDEN: On the grounds, Your Honor, it is not assumed that the jury believes what he said is true, it is assuming that it is true. What the jury believes is up to the jury and he is assuming that.

MS. TRILO: I would like to state the question again and state it that way. I was referring to what we had agreed on in chambers.

THE COURT: All right.

BY MS. TRILO:

Q. Let me state the question again. Based on your diagnosis of the defendant, assuming that everything he said on the witness stand this afternoon is the truth, have you an opinion, based on your medical expertise, as to whether or not he was conscious or unconscious at the time of the murder?
A. Let me get this clear now, do you want me to – – –

Q. Based on your – – – A. Let me just ask this question
– – –

MS. CYNDEN: May it please the Court: I think the witness should be required to answer whether or not he has an opinion; I think the question is clear.

THE COURT: Will you state the question?

BY MS. TRILO:

Q. Based on your diagnosis, your complete diagnosis – – – A. That is what I am confused about.

Q. Complete diagnosis of this defendant? A. Yes.

Q. Based on the entire diagnosis of this defendant as to his medical condition, I want to know whether or not you have a medical opinion, assuming the truth of everything that he said from the witness stand this afternoon, as to whether or not he was conscious or unconscious at the time of the murder about which this case is concerned. A. Yes, I have an opinion on that.

MS. TRILO: Will you state your opinion for the Court and the jury?
A. It is my opinion based on those facts that you mentioned that the defendant was unconscious at the time the murder took place.

* * *

[The remainder of the examination is omitted].

The memorandum of law which is referred to in the transcript cited cases involving expert witnesses generally and psychiatrists in particular. It made the following argument:

This is a difficult case in which to do justice because the defendant finds himself charged with a murder that no one saw committed. There is, of course, no doubt that Molly Glick was murdered, nor is there any question but that the defendant was at the scene of the murder. But two great questions remain to be determined. Did the defendant commit the crime? If so, what was his state of mind at the time, i.e., what crime did he commit?

Both of these questions can best be answered by the defendant himself, since there are no other eyewitnesses. As the court well knows, the defendant has a right under the fifth amendment to the United States Constitution to remain silent and to refuse to assist the court in any way that might result in conviction. But the accused does not seek to avail himself of that right. Rather the accused seeks to aid the court in the search for truth. Indeed, the accused asks the court, implores it really, to let him be heard.

The problem for the accused is that he has virtually no recollection of the events that transpired on the night of the murder. He has a basic recollection of a few fragmentary facts, but they are of no help. Yet, with the aid of hypnosis conducted by a qualified psychiatrist, Dr. Locket, he is able to recall the night in question and to relate the events as he actually experienced them. What he remembers under hypnosis is absolutely crucial for the defense, as his more complete recollection raises the distinct possibility that the crime was not committed by him and that the defendant was unconscious at the time of the crime, irrespective of who committed it.

Now it is unusual for the courts to accept testimony made in a hypnotic trance. But the unusual is needed in this case. It is more than needed; in fact, it is constitutionally required, as we shall demonstrate.

* * *

Overriding state law on evidentiary points is not something that is lightly urged. On the contrary, it is something that is urged because the defendant has the right to be acquitted of a given offense as long as the state cannot prove him guilty BEYOND A REASONABLE DOUBT. The only evidence available to the accused is his own testimony, and he can only adduce that with the aid of psychiatric help and the specific tool of hypnosis. The only way that the truth can be learned and the jury can decide whether there is a reasonable doubt about the commission of the act generally or about a given state of mind is to have the testimony of the accused that is bottled in his subconscious.

* * *

More recently there is the very important decision of the Supreme Court in Chambers v. Mississippi [discussed in Chapter Seven, supra] * * *

Chambers is deliberately written as a narrow opinion; it does not sweep under the rug any state evidentiary rules. Rather, it analyzes the specific facts of the case before the court. We submit that a similar analysis can leave no doubt that the testimony given under hypnosis by the accused, either in the form of testimony by Dr. Locket about his interviews or testimony by the accused while hypnotized on the stand, is necessary to a fair trial in this case.

As indicated above, it is all the evidence there is. Moreover, such evidence, when obtained under controlled conditions of an expert medical hypnotist, is within certain limits quite reliable.

* * *

Let us be clear then that we are not asking for a ruling that hypnotism is a preferred technique to ordinary testimony. Nor are we asking the court to rule that testimony given in a hypnotic trance can be used to support the testimony of a witness who has no memory problem. Our point is much narrower. We urge that under the facts of this case, where there are no eyewitnesses and where the accused is the key to the truth, and where the memory locked in the subconscious of the accused is the only means of his defending himself, then a fair trial requires that testimony be admitted even though the accused is hypnotized while testifying, or that at least the psychiatrist be permitted to relate what the accused said to him as part of his expert opinion.

If the court accepts, as we believe that it must, the arguments made thus far, the question arises as to whether to limit the defense to the testimony of the psychiatrist or to put the accused on the stand with the aid of hypnosis. In many ways the former is the position that is theoretically most favorable to the defense. This is because the prosecution would never have an opportunity to ask the accused questions. But the defense seeks no such cowardly route; it does not seek to ask the court to reach for the truth and then attempt to hide much of the truth behind the fifth amendment.

What the defense asks is simple. We ask to have the defendant hypnotized in the presence of the court and jury. We propose to have Dr. Locket ask him questions about the night of the murder and to have the Doctor ask proper questions that the court and prosecutor think are relevant, as well as those deemed relevant by the defense. In this way we believe justice can be done.

* * *

Ending where we began, it is true that the procedure advocated herein is unique in the annals of state criminal practice. But that does not mean that it is improper. Indeed, as Professor Wigmore pointed out some time ago, courts too frequently forget that evidentiary rules are designed to produce truth in many different kinds of cases. They should be interpreted in light of the peculiar necessities of the case before the court. See 1 J. Wigmore, Evidence, § 8a, at 245 (3rd ed. 1940): "[T]he infinite variety of justice is forgotten. A precedent is built up narrowly by [courts] out of a few elements; the really new and special elements of the present case are not allowed to have any effect."

Let the court recognize that justice is not inflexible. To reach the truth in the myriad of difficult circumstances presented by the multifarious forms in which criminal cases are presented, courts must tailor procedures to individual cases.

* * *

Are you persuaded? The appellate court which heard the defendant's appeal from a conviction for second degree murder was not:

"GREEN v. STATE"

Despite defendant's argument to the contrary, the record discloses that Dr. Locket was permitted to state, within the proper rules of evidence, the basis of his opinion that defendant was unconscious at the time the homicide was committed. He told the jury that the nature of his diagnosis, the nature of the diagnostic tools used, and the extent of his examination of the defendant.

A detailed statement of what the members of defendant's family told Dr. Locket would have been hearsay and could have confused the jury with evidence that had no probative value. The same is true of defendant's school and medical records.

* * *

From all the data, Dr. Locket, an expert had obtained relating to defendant's state of mind, including what was excluded by the trial court, he was unable to determine the cause of the unconsciousness. Hence, a more detailed statement of the data obtained by Dr. Locket would not have aided a jury of laymen in determining whether the unconsciousness was induced voluntarily or involuntarily.

Moreover, there is nothing in the record disclosing what additional admissible data could have been shown as a basis for Dr. Locket's opinion that the defendant was unconscious at the time of the homicide. There was no proffer of such evidence. Thus, the exclusion of the more detailed testimony was not error.

The second part of defendant's argument under his first assignment of error is that the trial court should have permitted Dr. Locket to state what he learned from the defendant while he was under hypnosis. Defendant concedes that there is no law in this [state] to support his argument, but he says several other states have admitted hypnotic evidence under limited circumstances. He argues that the hypnotic evidence should have been admitted in the present case in order to fully develop his defense because there were no eyewitnesses to the crime, he had no memory of having committed the crime, and he was not identified as the man seen running from the scene of the crime.

It is true, as defendant says, that a few jurisdictions have permitted hypnotic evidence to be admitted under limited circumstances. In those jurisdictions where such evidence has been admitted, its admissibility has rested in the sound discretion of the trial judge. But even in those jurisdictions, the trial judge in exercising his discretion must weigh the probative value of defendant's statements under hypnosis as part of the expert's opinion against the risk of the jury considering it "as independent proof of the facts recited." See People v. Modesto, 59 Cal.2d 722, 31 Cal.Rptr. 225, 382 P.2d 33 (1963); People v. Hiser, 267 Cal.App.2d 47, 72 Cal.Rptr. 906, 41 A.L.R.3d 1353 (1968); State v. Harris, 241 Or. 224, 405 P.2d 492 (1965).

In Harding v. State, 5 Md.App. 230, 246 A.2d 302, cert. denied, 395 U.S. 949 (1968), relied on by the defendant, the prosecuting witness in a rape case was put under hypnosis sometime before trial for the purpose of restoring her memory. In allowing her testimony, the court emphasized the fact that her testimony was substantially corroborated by other evidence.

Most experts agree that hypnotic evidence is unreliable because a person under hypnosis can manufacture or invent false statements. See 3A Wigmore, Evidence, § 998 at 943, Chadbourn (rev. 1970); "Hypnosis as a Defense Tactic," 1 Toledo L.Rev. 691, 700 (1969); Note: "Hypnotism and the Law," 14 Vand.L.Rev. 1509, 1518 (1961); Herman, "The Use of Hypno-Induced Statements in Criminal Cases," 25 Ohio St.L.J. 1, 27 (1964). A person under a hypnotic trance is also subject to heightened suggestibility. McCormick, Law of Evidence, § 208 at 510 (2d ed. 1972). There it is said:

> "Declarations made under hypnosis have been treated judicially in a manner similar to drug-induced statements. The hypnotized person is ultrasuggestible, and this manifestly endangers the reliability of his statements. The courts have recognized to some extent the usefulness of hypnosis, as an investigative technique and in diagnosis and therapy. However, they have rejected confessions induced thereby, statements made under hypnosis when offered by the subject in his own behalf, and opinion as to mental state based on hypnotic examination." (Footnotes omitted.)

See also Note: "Hypnotism, Suggestibility and the Law," 31 Neb.L.Rev. 575, 576 (1952).

In fact, we have held that "truth serum" test results were properly excluded by the trial court because they were unreliable and led to self-serving answers. * * *

We agree with the vast majority of authorities which have concluded that hypnotic evidence, whether in the form of the subject testifying in court under hypnosis or through another's revelation of what the subject said while under a hypnotic trance, is not admissible.

* * *

Do you agree that the defendant's expert was permitted to explain effectively the nature of his diagnosis? Defendant argued at trial and on appeal that medical records, school records and other similar records were official or business records and as such within a hearsay exception. Both the trial and appellate courts rejected this argument without discussion. Why? Contrary to what the appellate court states, Dr. Locket had an opinion as to whether the unconsciousness in this case was attributable to drugs. In the final discussion in chambers between counsel and the court, the court barred such an opinion. Is the appellate court correct when it says that because Dr. Locket could not specify the cause of the unconsciousness, he could not have aided the jury in determining whether or not it was induced voluntarily or involuntarily? Should the lack of a proffer of additional evidence from the doctor have the significance which the ap-

pellate court affords it? Remember that defense counsel asked for an opportunity to make an offer of proof, but the opportunity was temporarily denied. In fact, the appellate court was informed that the defense informed the trial judge that the expert could not remain for an extended period of time after trial to make a record. What more did the appellate court need to know other than that the details of the psychiatric examination were excluded? Was there any ambiguity in the defense's attempt to have the expert relate the patient's history? Is it permissible for a trial court to deny an opportunity for an offer of proof at the time a witness testifies, at least where the judge is informed of the possibility that the expert will be unavailable later?

Green was litigated in a jurisdiction that did not and does not now have a version of the Federal Rules of Evidence to guide trial judges. Assume that the case were litigated under the Federal Rules. What rulings would change?

Would the out-of-court statements made under hypnosis be admissible? Would the statements by Green's family to the psychiatrist be admissible? What about the school records? When you think about how Green would be tried under the Federal Rules, you may want to reconsider some of the expanded hearsay exceptions found in those rules. What effects do these have in a case like *Green*? Are these effects likely to produce a fairer trial or one that is less fair?

Would you let Green testify under hypnosis before the jury? Would you, as judge, first want to view a hypnotic session? Would you want that session videotaped?

If you would not permit hypnosis in court, would you permit the psychiatrist to make reference to the out-of-court hypnosis? In thinking about this, note that FRE 703 permits an expert to rely on data not independently admissible in evidence. Thus, even if a judge would not accept statements made under hypnosis as evidence generally, an expert may rely on them if similar experts in the field do and the court decides that this is reasonable reliance. But how much of the evidence that is not independently admissible would

you permit the expert to relate as an explanation for any opinion that is offered?

At the time *Green* was decided, some courts and commentators advocated a more receptive approach to hypnotic evidence. In recent years, the reliability of hypnosis as a technique has been questioned. Some courts are now insisting on special safeguards before hypnosis is used even to refresh the memory of a witness.[43] What guarantees of reliability, if any, would you require before permitting hypnosis to be used to assist in the production of evidence? Would you be more or less likely to permit hypnosis to be used in a case like *Green* where there are no eyewitnesses than in a case in which people claim to have seen what happened?

The cases cited by the *Green* appellate court include California decisions suggesting that the trial judge has discretion in deciding whether to receive evidence obtained as a result of using hypnosis. Ironically, a decade later the California Supreme Court would rely on *Green* to hold that a witness who is hypnotized prior to trial may never be permitted to testify.

A substantial portion of the California decision follows. It involves a government witness, a rape complainant, who was hypnotized before trial. The opinion recites the conflicts in the testimony as well as the procedure used to hypnotize the witness.

PEOPLE v. SHIRLEY

Supreme Court of California, 1982.
31 Cal.3d 18, 181 Cal.Rptr. 243, 641 P.2d 775, cert. denied
— U.S. —, — S.Ct. —, — L.Ed.2d —.

MOSK, J.

* * *

The record discloses a classic case of conflicting stories. There were only two witnesses to the principal events: the complaining witness, Cath-

43. For a discussion of recent cases and an explanation of the dangers of hypnotic evidence, see Note, The Admissibility of Testimony Influenced by Hypnosis, 67 Va.L.Rev. 1203 (1981). See also Alderman & Barrette, Hypnosis on Trial: A Practical Perspective on the Application of Forensic Hypnosis in Criminal Cases, 18 Cr.L.Bull. 5 (1982); Annot., Admissibility of Hypnotic Evidence at Criminal Trial, 92 A.L.R.3d 442 (1979).

erine C., told the jury that defendant compelled her by threat and force to submit to sexual intercourse and to orally copulate him; defendant testified, however, that Catherine willingly participated in the act of intercourse, and there was no oral copulation. The jury believed part of Catherine's story, as it convicted defendant of rape; but it also apparently found that she was lying when she described in detail the alleged act of oral copulation, as it acquitted defendant of that charge. The jury doubtless had a difficult task, since Catherine's performance as a witness was far from exemplary: the record is replete with instances in which her testimony was vague, changeable, self-contradictory, or prone to unexplained lapses of memory. Indeed, on occasion she professed to be unable to remember assertions that she had herself made on the witness stand only the previous day.

* * *

Catherine was a 32-year-old bartender at a saloon named Bud's Cove, not far from the Camp Pendleton Marine base. The first prosecution witness, Marine Sergeant Charles Lockskin, testified that at 8:50 p. m. on January 25, 1979, he entered Bud's Cove and approached Catherine, whom he had known for several months. She was off duty, and "looked like she was feeling kind of bad." She had a half-consumed martini in front of her, was under the influence of alcohol, and staggered when she walked.

After talking with her for some 15 minutes, Lockskin offered to get her something to eat and take her home. They drove in his car to a take-out restaurant, purchased some food, and arrived at Catherine's apartment house at 9:30 p. m. She vomited when she got out of the car; as this was happening, defendant came up to Lockskin and addressed him by name; Lockskin asked him to leave, and defendant did so. Lockskin then helped Catherine into the apartment and went into the kitchen to prepare some drinks. When he returned to the living room, however, she had passed out on the couch and was fast asleep. After failing to rouse her by shaking her, he covered her with a blanket, turned out the lights, locked the front door, and departed. It was shortly before 10 p. m.

The next witness was Catherine. She testified that on the evening in question she went off duty at Bud's Cove at 6:30 p. m., ordered two martinis, and sat "relaxing" until Lockskin came in. Her testimony as to her activities with Lockskin generally corroborated his, and she admitted she could "feel" the alcohol she had consumed.

Catherine's version of the events occurring after she fell asleep was as follows: she testified that she awoke some time later, still lying on the couch fully clothed, and found defendant standing naked by the coffee table holding a butcher knife. Defendant assertedly took her into the bedroom, ordered her to remove her clothes, and compelled her to orally copulate him for several minutes. The witness admitted that she felt "like I was in a dream" and events were moving in "slow motion."

Catherine then stated that defendant made her get on her knees, tied her hands behind her back and gagged her with nylon stockings, put her head down on the bed, and had intercourse with her in that position for up to half an hour. When she tried to turn her head to see who he was, he struck her with his hand and ordered her not to look at him; later he put a pillow over her head for the same purpose, and struck her on the hip. She claimed the latter blow sobered her so that she no longer felt the effects of her prior drinking.

Until this point the apartment had remained totally dark, and she could see the intruder only as "a shadow." According to Catherine, however, defendant abruptly desisted from further intercourse, removed her bonds and gag, took her back into the living room, and turned on the lights. For the next half hour the two sat naked on the couch, she on his lap, and chatted. Finally he asked her if she liked beer, and she replied that she did; he volunteered to get some from his apartment, and told her where he lived. He dressed and left on this errand; on his return with the beer he took his clothes off again, she got back on his lap, and the conversation resumed.

After another quarter of an hour, defendant suggested they take a shower together, and she agreed. As they entered the bathroom, however, the telephone rang. The caller was assertedly a "girlfriend" of Catherine named Mickie, who announced she was coming over to the apartment. Catherine relayed this fact to defendant, and told him that he could return at another time and she would cook dinner for him. According to Catherine, defendant then got dressed, wrapped the knife and screwdriver in an extra T-shirt he had brought, thrust them down the front of his pants, and left when Mickie arrived. Catherine testified she told Mickie she had been raped by a Marine, and Mickie gave her a strong sedative—a 100-milligram dose of a drug called Mellaril. Mickie stayed for half an hour, and immediately after she left Catherine called the police. According to Catherine, it was 10 minutes before 1 a. m.

On cross-examination Catherine admitted that during their long conversation in the living room defendant told her numerous personal details about himself, e.g., that he lived in the next apartment building, that his name was Don, that he was 22 years old, that he was married and had a child, that he was a Marine but was not happy in the service, and that the next morning he had to go to Bridgeport, California, for cold-weather training. She claimed that she engaged defendant in the foregoing conversation only because she was afraid he would do her further harm; yet she conceded that when defendant went to get the beer he left the knife and screwdriver on her living room floor but that she did nothing about them, and that while he was gone she remained sitting naked on the couch. Although she had a telephone she did not call the police or anyone else for help, nor did she dress and go to the nearby apartment of the building manager who was admittedly "a big guy," nor did she even lock the front door. She also acknowledged that she did not know Mickie's last name, address, or telephone number, or where she was at the time of trial, and indeed had never seen her since the night in question.

On redirect examination Catherine testified that until defendant turned on the lights in the apartment, she thought the person having intercourse with her was an older man who resembled defendant and had flirted with her at the bar where she worked.

Police Officer Russell Lane testified that the telephone call reporting the rape came at 1:45 a. m., an hour later than Catherine claimed. He went immediately to her apartment and found her under the influence of alcohol: her breath had the smell of someone who "had been drinking quite heavily," her speech was slow and at times difficult to understand, and her walk was unsteady. She told the officer she had been brought home "very drunk" from Bud's Cove at midnight, that she fell asleep on the couch, and that she awoke in her bed at 12:30 a. m. She gave the officer a physical description of defendant, and repeated the personal information defendant had disclosed to her during their conversation. She then complained that her buttocks hurt, and the officer took her to a local hospital.

At the hospital she was examined by a physician. He testified that he found a bruise on her right hip and "crease marks" on her wrists. But although the latter were consistent with her hands having been tied by a fabric, he could not tell their cause and described them as the kind of marks one receives from sleeping on wrinkles in the bed linen. She reported to the physician that she used "occasional Mellaril and alcohol frequently." He testified that Mellaril is "a major tranquilizer," and that in doses of 100 milligrams or more per day it is prescribed primarily for psychotic states, schizophrenia, and manic-depressive cases.

After the physical examination, Police Officer Leonard Goodwin took a statement of the evening's events from Catherine. The next morning Officer Lane went to defendant's apartment and arrested him as he was leaving to report for duty. When the officer announced the charges were burglary and rape, defendant became angry and said he had "picked up a drunk bitch at Bud's Cove and took her home and fucked her," and "now she wants to report that he raped her" and "that is all a bunch of bullshit."

Defendant took the stand in his own defense. He testified that a few days before these events Catherine had waited on him at Bud's Cove. On the evening in question he entered the bar and saw her sitting with Sergeant Lockskin, whom he recognized. When Lockskin went to the men's room, defendant approached her and asked how she was feeling. They had a brief conversation; according to defendant, she told him her name was Cathy, identified the apartment house in which she lived, and invited him to "grab a six-pack sometime and come over." When Lockskin returned, defendant left the bar and bought some beer at a liquor store. After failing to locate a friend of his, defendant walked to Catherine's apartment house. As he approached, Catherine and Lockskin drove up and defendant spoke briefly with the latter. Defendant then returned to his own apartment for a while, drank some beer, and went back to Catherine's building. When asked why he did so, he explained, "Well, my wife was back home in Indiana. I was by myself. Kind of lonely. And I had an invitation to come to her apartment."

On his arrival, defendant knocked twice on Catherine's door; there was no response, but he thought he heard someone inside who was moaning as if ill. When no one answered further knocking, he called her name through the window and lifted off the screen. He testified that he believed someone inside was sick.

At that point Catherine opened the front door and defendant asked, "Are you okay?" He handed her the screen; she put it next to the front door, went back to the living room, and lay down on the couch. Defendant sat next to her and repeated his question, "Are you okay?" Her reply was to put her arms around his neck and begin kissing him. He responded, and at his suggestion they soon moved to the bedroom. There she cooperated in helping him remove her clothes; defendant returned briefly to the living room for his cigarettes, stripped down, and rejoined her on the bed. They proceeded to have intercourse in the "missionary position," then turned so that he entered her vaginally from behind. She abruptly asked defendant to stop and he did so. He inquired what was wrong, and she replied that she "couldn't be emotionally turned on by men."

Defendant's testimony as to the ensuing events was substantially the same as Catherine's.   *   *   *

We relate next the evidence bearing on the issue of hypnosis. Prior to trial, counsel for defendant moved to exclude all testimony of the complaining witness that was the result of her having been hypnotized. He offered to prove that the case was originally set for trial on May 1, 1979, but was trailed because of the unavailability of an adequate jury pool; that in the evening of April 30, 1979, i.e., more than three months after the events in question, the deputy district attorney assigned to the case, Richard Fulton, had Catherine hypnotized by another deputy district attorney, Richard Farnell, at the courthouse and in the presence of Mr. Fulton and one Terry Moore; and that Catherine made certain statements under hypnosis which would cause her testimony at trial to be significantly different from her testimony at the preliminary hearing. Counsel then identified one such discrepancy, and argued that "this is an improper use of hypnosis" because "it is not in fact refreshing a witness's recollection" but "it is in fact manufactured evidence." He distinguished those cases in which hypnosis has been used for such purposes as helping an eyewitness to remember a license plate number. He denied that any court in this state had ruled the use of hypnosis permissible in all cases, and charged that here the People were attempting "to expand hypnosis into an area [in] which they cannot lay adequate foundation for its reliability" as a tool for refreshing recollection.

The trial court denied the motion, ruling that prior hypnosis of a witness affects the weight but not the admissibility of the testimony. Accordingly, the court directed that if Catherine gave evidence that she could not remember—or did not exist—before she was hypnotized, the fact and circumstances of that hypnosis should be put before the jury.

Pursuant to this ruling, Catherine was allowed to testify to a number of matters that she assertedly had been unable to recall on two occasions prior to hypnosis, i.e., when she gave statements to the police on the night of the events in question, and when she testified at the preliminary hearing. For example, on those occasions she stated that after falling asleep in her clothes on the couch in her living room, she awoke in her bedroom and found herself lying naked on the bed, gagged and bound. At trial, as noted above, she testified instead that when she awoke she was still on the couch and fully clothed, and defendant then forced her to go into the bedroom and get undressed. Again, prior to hypnosis she stated that defendant had sexual intercourse with her before as well as after the alleged act of oral copulation, while at trial she testified that the oral copulation preceded any intercourse whatever.   Prior to hypnosis she stated that her hands were tied during the oral copulation, while at trial she denied this claim.   Finally, prior to hypnosis she stated that the first time she saw the knife in defendant's hand was when they returned to the living room after the sexual intercourse, while at trial she testified she saw it when she awoke on the couch before entering the bedroom.

Both counsel explored the nature and effect of Catherine's hypnotic experience.   According to Catherine, before being hypnotized she recalled the events of the evening in question only "vaguely."   She discussed the gap in her recollection with Deputy District Attorney Fulton, and consented to be hypnotized "for the purpose of going back over what occurred that night." She verified that she was hypnotized on April 30, 1979, in the courthouse, by Mr. Farnell;   although the latter had "some training," he was not a psychiatrist or even a physician.   She had not been hypnotized before, but she "just knew" that it enables a person to "remember more than normal."

Apparently she was not disappointed in that expectation.   She agreed that the hypnosis at least partly "cured" her recollection as to "this sort of dreamlike period that we're talking about."   She credited the hypnosis with causing her to "fill in the gap" in her memory, and also to recall that certain events took place in a different sequence.   In particular, she specifically ascribed to the effect of hypnosis each of the above-listed changes between her testimony at trial and her pretrial statements to the police and testimony at the preliminary hearing.

The defense called Dr. Donald W. Schafer as an expert witness to testify on the subject of hypnosis.   Dr. Schafer is a board-certified psychiatrist with 16 years of private practice and 10 years on the staff of the University of California at Irvine, where he is a clinical professor of psychiatry.   He has had extensive training in hypnosis, and has used it in his practice for two decades.   Dr. Schafer acknowledged that hypnosis has certain valid medical uses, such as pain control and relief from various psychosomatic symptoms. In appropriate cases it can also be used for the treatment of neuroses, e.g., by assisting a patient to recover repressed memories of traumatic events, including rape.

Dr. Schafer warned, however, that there are grave risks in relying for other purposes on the accuracy of memories recalled under hypnosis.   He explained that while no one knows exactly how the human mind stores information, it does *not* act like a videotape recorder, i.e., a machine capable of "playing back" the exact images or impressions it has received.   Rather, "there are many things that alter the storage of exact memory."   There is therefore no assurance, the doctor testified, that a memory recalled in hypnosis is correct.   On the contrary, a person under hypnosis can be mistaken in his recollection, or can hallucinate, or can "confabulate," i.e., create a false or pseudomemory, or can even deliberately lie.   Indeed, it may be easier to lie under hypnosis, because from the viewpoint of the person in the trance "the hypnosis would put the responsibility on the shoulders of the hypnotist."

Dr. Schafer made four additional important points.   First, when a person is put under hypnosis and asked to recount an event, no one is able to determine whether he is telling the truth.   Second, when a person has a subconscious motive to distort the truth, e.g., in order to make himself look better in the eyes of others, that motive will usually operate even under hypnosis; indeed, "hypnosis would in a sense give [him] permission" to engage in such distortion. Third, the effect of hypnosis on a preexisting memory is usually additive, i.e., it may permit the recall of additional details; if instead the person remembers the event differently under hypnosis, the discrepancy implies either that his statement describing the preexisting memory was a lie or that the memory under hypnosis was a confabulation. Fourth, when a person has been asked to recall an event while under hypnosis, and after hypnosis is asked to remember the same event, the effect of the prior hypnosis is to remove all doubt he may have had about the event; such persons would be "convinced that what they had said in hypnosis was the truth."

On cross-examination Dr. Schafer testified that although the hypnotic induction in the case at bar was excellent from the viewpoint of technique, the hypnotist did not take into consideration Catherine's possible motivation to distort the truth under hypnosis; one of the factors leading Dr. Schafer to question that motivation was the above-discussed discrepancies in her testimony.

Summing up, Dr. Schafer had no doubt as to the unreliability of hypnosis for discovering the truth of a particular matter. He warned that "hypnosis in no way is a truth serum-like experience," and concluded "there is no way of assessing the reliability of something produced in hypnosis, as such."

* * *

[The court discusses authorities permitting the use of a previously hypnotized witness where safeguards are employed.]

After careful consideration, we decline to join in the foregoing effort to develop a set of "safeguards" sufficient to avoid the risks inherent in admitting hypnotically induced testimony. To begin with, we are not persuaded that the requirements * * * will in fact forestall each of the dangers at which they are directed. Next, we observe that certain dangers of hypnosis are not even addressed by the * * * requirements: virtually all of those rules are designed to prevent the hypnotist from exploiting the suggestibility of the subject; none will directly avoid the additional risks * * * that the subject (1) will lose his critical judgment and begin to credit "memories" that were formerly viewed as unreliable, (2) will confuse actual recall with confabulation and will be unable to distinguish between the two, and (3) will exhibit an unwarranted confidence in the validity of his ensuing recollection. * * * The Attorney General proposes no "safeguards" to deal with these knotty problems.

Lastly, even if requirements could be devised that were adequate in theory, we have grave doubts that they could be administered in practice without injecting undue delay and confusion into the judicial process. To be sure, it would usually be easy to determine if the hypnotist was an appropriately trained psychiatrist or psychologist. It might be harder to establish that he was sufficiently independent of the prosecution or defense to avoid subconscious bias. And it would certainly be far more difficult to prove strict compliance—* * * with each of the remaining "safeguards." It strains credulity, for example, to believe that a conscientious defense counsel would meekly agree that the prosecution had recorded every bit of relevant information conveyed to the hypnotist prior to the session, or that the hypnotist had conveyed absolutely none of that information to the subject either while extracting the latter's prehypnotic version of the facts or while questioning him both during and after hypnosis, or that every single contact between the hypnotist and the subject, no matter how innocuous, had been preserved on videotape.

On the other hand, it takes little prescience to foresee that these and related issues would provide a fertile new field for litigation. There would first be elaborate demands for discovery, parades of expert witnesses, and special pretrial hearings, all with concomitant delays and expense. Among the questions our trial courts would then be expected to answer are scientific issues so subtle as to confound the experts. * * * Their resolution would in turn generate a panoply of new claims that could be raised on appeal, including difficult questions of compliance with the "clear and convincing" standard of proof. And because the hypnotized subject would frequently be the victim, the eyewitness, or a similar source of crucial testimony against the defendant, any errors in ruling on the admissibility of such testimony could easily jeopardize otherwise unimpeachable judgments of conviction. In our opinion, the game is not worth the candle.

For all these reasons, we join instead a growing number of courts that have abandoned any pretense of devising workable "safeguards" and have simply held that hypnotically induced testimony is so widely viewed as unreliable that it is inadmissible under the *Frye* test. This disposition, of course, is consistent with the above-discussed case law uniformly excluding evidence of the truth of statements made under hypnosis. * * * And both rules, as we shall see, are supported by the overwhelming consensus of contemporary scientific opinion on hypnosis.

* * *

The *Frye* rule is deeply ingrained in the law of this state. * * *

The Attorney General contends the *Frye* rule is inapplicable in the present context, making in essence the following argument: The rule is assertedly limited to cases in which (1) an expert witness gives his opinion (2) interpreting the results of a new technique for scientifically testing or analyzing physical evidence, and (3) that opinion goes directly to the existence or nonexistence of a disputed fact, which is often the ultimate issue in the litigation. By contrast, in cases such as the present it is not the expert (i.e., the hypnotist) who ordinarily testifies; the process involved (i.e., the hypnotizing of a potential witness to improve his recall) has nothing to do with testing physical evidence; if the expert does testify, he should not be asked to interpret the results of the technique (i.e., to give his opinion on whether the revived memories of the hypnotized subject are true) but simply to discuss its methodology (i.e., to explain how the hypnotic session was conducted); and the latter testimony evidently does not go to the disputed fact or ultimate issue (e.g., the identity of the culprit). Rather, in the typical case the witness is the person who actually perceived the event that is the subject of the litigation, and his testimony is the same as that of any other lay witness, i.e., he states his present recollection of that event to the best of his ability. It is true that his recollection has been refreshed by hypnosis, and that hypnosis does not guarantee truthful or accurate recall. But neither does any other method of reviving memory. That guarantee, as with all witnesses, comes from cross-examination, which permits the trier of fact to determine the truth and accuracy of the hypnotically refreshed testimony.

The argument is unpersuasive for a number of reasons. First, it proceeds from an unduly narrow reading of the opinions invoking the *Frye* rule * * *. Nor are those techniques necessarily limited to manipulation of physical evidence: we do not doubt that if testimony based on a new scientific process operating on purely psychological evidence were to be offered in our courts, it would likewise be subjected to the *Frye* standard of admissibility. In either case, the rule serves its salutary purpose of preventing the jury from being misled by unproven and ultimately unsound scientific methods. * * *

Moreover, from the unchallenged expert testimony in the case at bar and the uniform findings of the jurisdictions that have inquired into the matter, it appears that hypnotizing a witness to improve his memory is not in fact like "any other method" of refreshing a witness' recollection. These sources reveal that the hypnotic process does more than permit the witness to retrieve real but repressed memories; it actively contributes to the formation of pseudomemories, to the witness' abiding belief in their veracity, and to the inability of the witness (or anyone else) to distinguish between the two. In these circumstances, as noted above, the resulting recall of the witness "is dependent upon, and cannot be disassociated from" the underlying hypnosis. * * * And if the testimony is thus only as reliable as the hypnotic process itself, it must be judged by the same standards of admissibility.

* * *

It is the proponent of such testimony, of course, who has the burden of making the necessary showing of compliance with *Frye*, i.e., of demonstrating by means of qualified and disinterested experts that the new technique is generally accepted as reliable in the relevant scientific community. * * *

* * *

Accordingly, for this limited purpose scientists have long been permitted to speak to the courts through their published writings in scholarly treatises and journals. * * * The courts view such writings as "evidence," not of the actual reliability of the new scientific technique, but of its acceptance *vel non* in the scientific community. Nor do the courts "pick and choose" among the writings for this purpose. On many topics—including hypnosis—the scientific literature is so vast that no court could possibly absorb it all. But there is no need to do so, because the burden is on the proponent of the new technique to show a scientific consensus supporting its use; if a fair overview of the literature discloses that scientists significant either in number or expertise publicly oppose that use of hypnosis as unreliable, the court may safely conclude there is no such consensus at the present time.

That is the case before us. On the topic of hypnotically aided recall we have reviewed numerous scientific treatises and articles in scholarly journals. From this review it clearly appears that major voices in the scientific community oppose the use of hypnosis to restore the memory of potential witnesses, with or without procedural safeguards, on the ground of its intrinsic unreliability. This unreliability is due both to certain properties of human memory and to factors inherent in the nature of hypnosis. We begin with the former, which have been little mentioned in the cases.

The principal proponent of hypnotically aided recall is a police department psychologist, Martin Reiser, Ed.D. According to his published writings, Dr. Reiser operates on the belief that human memory is like a videotape machine that (1) faithfully records, as if on film, every perception experienced by the witness, (2) permanently stores such recorded perceptions in the brain at a subconscious level, and (3) accurately "replays" them in their original form when the witness is placed under hypnosis and asked to remember them. * * *

The professional literature, however, rejects this belief: the scientists who work in the field generally agree that, as Dr. Schafer testified at trial, the memory does *not* act like a videotape recorder, but rather is subject to numerous influences that continuously alter its content. * * *

* * *

We have dwelt on the reports of current research into the operation of human memory for two reasons. First, as we have seen, that research convincingly undermines the "videotape recorder" theory on which most law enforcement hypnosis of potential witnesses is premised. Second, each of the phenomena found by such research to contribute to the unreliability of normal memory reappears in a more extreme form when the witness is hypnotized for the purpose of improving his recollection.

We turn, then, to the professional literature on the latter topic. For present purposes we need not add to this already lengthy discussion by analyzing that literature in detail; it will be enough if we simply set forth its principal relevant conclusions, with citations to a representative sample of supporting studies. The conclusions will necessarily be oversimplified, but full explanations of each point can be found in the cited authorities and similar works.

1. Hypnosis is by its nature a process of suggestion, and one of its primary effects is that the person hypnotized becomes extremely receptive to suggestions that he perceives as emanating from the hypnotist. The effect is intensified by another characteristic of the hypnotic state, to wit, that the attention of the subject is wholly focused on and directed by the hypnotist. The suggestions may take the form of explicit requests or predictions by the hypnotist; or they may be inferred by the subject from information he acquired prior to or during the hypnotic session, or from such cues as the known purpose of that session, the form of questions asked or comments made by the hypnotist, or the hypnotist's demeanor and other nonverbal conduct. The suggestions can be entirely unintended—indeed, unperceived—by the hypnotist himself.

2. The person under hypnosis experiences a compelling desire to please the hypnotist by reacting positively to these suggestions, and hence to produce the particular responses he believes are expected of him. Because of this compulsion, when asked to recall an event either while in "age regression" or under direct suggestion of heightened memory ("hypermnesia"), he is unwilling to admit that he cannot do so or that his recollection is uncertain or incomplete. Instead, he will produce a "memory" of the event that may be compounded of (1) relevant actual facts, (2) irrelevant actual facts taken from an unrelated prior experience of the subject, (3) fantasized material ("confabulations") unconsciously invented to fill gaps in the story, and (4) conscious lies—all formulated in as realistic a fashion as he can. The likelihood of such self-deception is increased by another effect of hypnosis, i.e., that it significantly impairs the subject's critical judgment and causes him to give credence to memories so vague and fragmentary that he would not have relied on them before being hypnotized.

3. During the hypnotic session, neither the subject nor the hypnotist can distinguish between true memories and pseudomemories of various kinds in the reported recall; and when the subject repeats that recall in the waking state (e.g., in a trial), neither an expert witness nor a lay observer (e.g., the judge or jury) can make a similar distinction. In each instance, if the claimed memory is not or cannot be verified by wholly independent means, no one can reliably tell whether it is an accurate recollection or mere confabulation. Because of the foregoing pressures on the subject to present the hypnotist with a logically complete and satisfying memory of the prior event, neither the detail, coherence, nor plausibility of the resulting recall is any guarantee of its veracity.

4. Nor is such guarantee furnished by the confidence with which the memory is initially reported or subsequently related: a witness who is uncertain of his recollections before being hypotized will become convinced by that process that the story he told under hypnosis is true and correct in every respect. This effect is enhanced by two techniques commonly used by lay hypnotists: before being hypnotized the subject is told (or believes) that hypnosis will help him to "remember very clearly everything that happened" in the prior event, and/or during the trance he is given the suggestion that after he awakes he will "be able to remember" that event equally clearly and comprehensively. Further enhancement of this effect often occurs when, after he returns to the waking state, the subject remembers the content of his new "memory" but forgets its source, i.e., forgets that he acquired it during the hypnotic session ("posthypnotic source amnesia"); this phenomenon can arise spontaneously from the subject's expectations as to the nature and effects of hypnosis, or can be unwittingly suggested by the hypnotist's instructions. Finally, the effect not only persists, but the witness' conviction of the absolute truth of his hypnotically induced recollection grows stronger each time he is asked to repeat the story; by the time of trial, the resulting "memory" may be so fixed in his mind that traditional legal techniques such as cross-examination may be largely ineffective to expose its unreliability.

The professional literature thus fully supports the testimony of Dr. Schafer. * * * It also demonstrates beyond any doubt that at the present time the use of hypnosis to restore the memory of a potential witness is *not* generally accepted as reliable by the relevant scientific community. Indeed, representative groups within that community are on record as expressly opposing this technique for many of the foregoing reasons, particularly when it is employed by law enforcement hypnotists. In these circumstances it is obvious that the *Frye* test of admissibility has not been satisfied. We therefore hold * * * that the testimony of a witness who has undergone hypnosis for the purpose of restoring his memory of the events in issue is inadmissible as to all matters relating to those events, from the time of the hypnotic session forward. It follows that the trial court erred in denying defendant's motion to exclude Catherine's testimony.

* * *

RICHARDSON, Justice, concurring.

I concur in the judgment. Under the circumstances in this case, the prosecutrix' testimony was subject to objection because it was the product of a hypnotic session conducted by a deputy district attorney rather than by a trained professional who was wholly unaffiliated with law enforcement.

I am unable, however, to support an absolute rule rendering inadmissible *all* hypnotically induced testimony without regard to the safeguards under which the hypnosis occurred. Consistent with recent authority and critical commentary, such testimony should be admissible if elicited under adequate safeguards including requiring that, (1) the hypnosis is conducted by a trained, independent psychiatrist or psychologist who in writing is supplied with only sufficient factual background necessary to conduct the session; (2) the hypnosis is videotaped or otherwise recorded for purposes of subsequent review; (3) no persons other than the hypnotist and his subject are present; and (4) the hypnotist obtains a written description of the subject's prior description of the event for comparison purposes. (See *State v. Hurd* (1981) 86 N.J. 525, 432 A.2d 86, 96–97; Note, *The Admissibility of Testimony Influenced by Hypnosis* (1981) 67 Va.L.Rev. 1203, 1230–1232.) If the procedures used are free of suggestion and, in the discretion of the trial court, the probative value of the testimony is not outweighed by its potential for prejudice, I would admit it.

As stated by the New Jersey Supreme Court in *Hurd*, "we believe that a rule of per se inadmissibility is unnecessarily broad and will result in the exclusion of evidence that is as trustworthy as other eyewitness testimony." (432 A.2d p. 94; accord, Note, supra, at p. 1233.) I share that belief.

KAUS, Justice, concurring and dissenting.

I concur in the reversal of the judgment, but feel compelled to dissent from several conclusions of the majority unnecessary to decide this appeal.

On the record before us, this is a relatively simple case. At the outset of the trial, defense counsel objected that a portion of the testimony Catherine was about to give—concerning a period of time during which she had previously testified that she had been asleep—was the result of the improper use of hypnosis, that "it is not in fact refreshing a witness' recollection

* * * but that it is * * * *manufactured evidence*." (My emphasis.) The trial court overruled the objection on the basis that the hypnosis only went to the weight of Catherine's testimony.

That ruling was patently wrong, even if there may have been some out-of-state case law to support it. Section 702 of the Evidence Code demands that the testimony of any witness, except an expert, be based on personal knowledge and provides that "[a]gainst the objection of a party, such personal knowledge must be shown before the witness may testify concerning the matter." Defendant clearly objected that the witness was about to testify from other than personal knowledge—that she was about to give "manufactured evidence." This placed the burden of showing that the witness would testify from personal knowledge on the prosecutor, who did nothing except argue that *People v. Colligan* (1979) 91 Cal.App.3d 846, 154 Cal.Rptr. 389 "indicated that hypnosis did not as a matter of law render inadmissible the subsequent identification of a defendant by the witness." Obviously the citation of a case is not a showing that a particular witness is about to testify from personal knowledge, and, in fact, the *Colligan* decision does not purport to relieve a prosecutor of the burden of demonstrating the personal knowledge of a previously hypnotized witness in response to a proper objection.

Thus, on this state of the record, the trial court should not have admitted Catherine's challenged testimony. Given the ambiguities and inconsistencies of Catherine's additional testimony, and the substantial evidence presented by the defense, the error was clearly prejudicial and requires reversal of the judgment. This is all we need to decide in this case.

I recognize, of course, that we have about a dozen additional hypnosis cases pending before us, and that the majority has chosen to use this appeal as a vehicle for deciding the broader issues presented by some of the others. In my view, however, it is a mistake to adopt at this point the sweeping, "per se" rule that the majority proposes—excluding virtually all testimony of a witness who has undergone pretrial hypnosis—without more carefully considering the varied contexts in which hypnosis may take place and the many factors which may affect both the potential danger and the potential utility of hypnosis in a particular instance.

This is the first time we have been called upon to consider the admissibility of a witness' post-hypnosis testimony, and it is by no means clear to me that the facts of this case are typical of hypnosis cases in general. There are obviously a number of factors that render Catherine's post-hypnosis testimony particularly suspect. Because she was at least somewhat intoxicated at the time of the alleged offense, there is a good possibility that she has no clear memory to be refreshed by hypnosis, and instead that she has simply constructed or "confabulated" a "memory" while under hypnosis. * * * In addition, at the time she was hypnotized she had already given a number of somewhat different accounts of the evening in question, and the academic literature suggests that under such circumstances there is a particularly strong danger that hypnosis will simply serve to fix one particular version—not necessarily the historically accurate one—in the subject's mind and render the witness impervious to cross-examination. (See Orne, *The Use and Misuse* *of Hypnosis in Court* (1972) 27 Internat.J.Clinical & Experimental Hypnosis 311, 332–334.)   Finally, of course, the hypnosis in this case was not performed by an impartial hypnotist in a setting calculated to minimize potential suggestiveness, but by a deputy district attorney in the presence of the investigating police officers.   Given all these facts, I can agree with the majority that, if this case is retried, Catherine should not be permitted to testify.

I think, however, that we should be very wary about establishing a broad, generally applicable exclusionary rule for all post-hypnosis testimony on the basis of the rather egregious facts of this case alone.   In other instances, hypnosis may arise in a completely different setting, as, for example, when a victim or a witness to a crime is hypnotized shortly after the offense to aid a police artist compose a sketch of the suspect.   In such a case, none of the participants to the hypnosis may have any preconceived bias which would pose a special danger of suggestiveness, and in some cases the witness' post-hypnosis statements may not differ at all from his or her pre-hypnosis statements, or the suspect may be later caught with incriminating evidence corroborating the reliability of at least some of the witness' post-hypnosis memory.   If, in such a case, an adequate record of the hypnosis session exists and demonstrates the session's basic fairness, it is not clear to me that the mere fact that the victim or witness has at one time been hypnotized necessarily mandates the total exclusion of the potentially crucial testimony at a later trial.

Contrary to the majority's conclusion, I do not believe that faithful adherence to the *Frye* standard compels the all-encompassing *per se* exclusionary rule adopted in its opinion.   Just last year, in *State v. Hurd* (1981) 86 N.J. 525, 432 A.2d 86, the New Jersey Supreme Court, in a thoughtful and scholarly opinion by Justice Pashman, applied the *Frye* standard to post-hypnosis testimony and concluded that "a rule of *per se* inadmissibility is unnecessarily broad and will result in the exclusion of evidence that is as trustworthy as other eyewitness testimony."   * * *   In *Hurd*, a number of preeminent authorities in the field of hypnosis—including Dr. Orne—testified in person at a pretrial evidentiary hearing.   On appeal, the New Jersey court, after reviewing both this testimony and much of the same academic literature discussed by the majority in this case, pointed out that while the experts had made it clear that hypnosis is not a tool which can in any way guarantee the accuracy or historical "truth" of a subject's recall, they had at the same time indicated "that *in appropriate cases* and *where properly conducted* the use of hypnosis to refresh memory is comparable in reliability to ordinary recall."   * * *

Although keenly aware of the potential problems of "confabulation" and possible interference with cross-examination posed by hypnosis, the *Hurd* court recognized that recent psychological research has demonstrated that similar problems inhere in eyewitness testimony in general, particularly when—as is very often the case—a witness has been repeatedly interrogated and has recounted his proposed testimony several times before trial.   * * * Indeed, given the majority's own rendering of modern views concerning the nature and fallibility of unhypnotized human memory,   * * *   it may not be entirely facetious to suggest that if we are to exclude eyewitness testimony unless shown to be scientifically reliable, we may have little choice but to return to trial by combat or ordeal.

Observing that courts have never required "historical accuracy as a condition for admitting eyewitness testimony," the *Hurd* court concluded that, under *Frye*, hypnotically aided testimony should properly be admitted in a criminal trial if the party proffering the evidence demonstrates "by clear and convincing evidence" * * * "that the use of hypnosis in the particular case was reasonably likely to result in recall comparable in accuracy to normal human memory." * * * The court then went on to discuss in some detail various factors—e.g., the kind of memory loss encountered, the apparent motivations of the hypnotized witness, and the procedural safeguards under which the hypnosis session was conducted—that are likely to affect the reliability of post-hypnosis testimony in a given case. * * *

In my view, if we are to reach the broad question of the general admissibility of post-hypnosis testimony at this time, we should adopt the more cautious approach of the *Hurd* decision, rather than pronounce a general rule excluding virtually all post-hypnosis testimony regardless of the facts of a particular case. Perhaps in the future, as we gain more experience in this area, we will find that post-hypnosis testimony is so often unreliable that "the game is not worth the candle" * * * and that a broad, prophylactic exclusionary rule is warranted. At this point, however, I think such a judgment is premature.

* * *

———

This decision, together with *Green*, raises questions about how a trial judge should proceed in considering scientific evidence never before relied upon in a jurisdiction. Should a trial judge await some appellate signal before relying on scientific evidence that, for the judge at least, is novel? Can there be appellate consideration of new scientific techniques without some willingness by trial judges to experiment? Does the fact that a technique might be viewed with increasing alarm as it is employed by courts suggest that judges should be wary of experimenting? Is there a justifiable distinction between a defendant's offer of evidence based on a new technique and an offer by the government? Should the nature of the other evidence in a case affect the decision on whether or not to permit reliance on novel scientific evidence?

Which approach would you choose in *Green* and *Shirley*? To admit evidence based on hypnosis and to leave credibility decisions to juries? To exclude all evidence based on hypnotic techniques? To admit some evidence based on hypnosis where certain procedures are employed or independent guarantees of reliability are present? To permit one party to offer evidence but not another? Some other approach?

E. CROSS-EXAMINING THE EXPERT

In dealing with expert testimony, courts often appear unconcerned with the opposing attorney's ability to question the expert on cross-examination. Nevertheless, we suspect that such concern exists. It may in part explain the lack of enthusiasm with which courts at times greet expert testimony. Certainly there are special problems in cross-examining expert witnesses. Usually experts are chosen and paid by the party calling them. This may give rise to feelings of loyalty, and experts may have a long term financial interest in the success of those for whom they are testifying. Often, experts are experienced witnesses, not easy to pin down. Some take delight in exposing the examiner's ignorance or in otherwise generating laughter at the examiner's expense. Above all, experts are usually masters of technical material. The attorney cannot hope to match their expertise, but he must develop considerable sophistication about the particular matter in issue if he is to maximize his chances for a successful cross-examination.

The following transcript, drawn from a trial demonstration, presents two distinguished attorneys cross-examining the same expert. The basic facts of the underlying hypothetical case are as follows:[44] In the course of a routine physical examination, Virginia Lemmon's physician, a general practitioner named Clayburn, discovered a condition which he diagnosed as diabetes mellitus. To control the diabetes, Dr. Clayburn prescribed LowShug, a sulfonylurea compound. After her condition appeared to stabilize, Mrs. Lemmon became pregnant. Because she seemed to be getting along well, Dr. Clayburn continued her on LowShug. Mrs. Lemmon gave birth to a baby girl, who died the next day. Six days after delivery, Dr. Clayburn discontinued the LowShug and placed Mrs. Lemmon on insulin treatment.

In the aftermath of the birth and death of her child, Mrs. Lemmon has felt tired and weak. She has suffered depression and leg discomforts. Her marriage has become less stable.

Both Mr. and Mrs. Lemmon sue Dr. Clayburn for malpractice, alleging that he was negligent in failing to keep Mrs. Lemmon's diabetes under control. They further allege that the doctor's negligence caused the death of the child; caused permanent physical and emotional injury to Mrs. Lemmon and emotional injury to her husband; caused the family to face substantial medical costs that will continue to increase; and caused each of them to be deprived of the comfort and companionship of the other. Judgment in the amount of $150,000 is demanded. Dr. Clayburn denies negligence, denies the claimed injuries and damages, and claims that any injury or damage was not caused by his actions. Among the defense witnesses called to testify at the trial is a psychiatrist who examined Mrs. Lemmon for the defense. As you read the transcript, ask yourself which of the two cross-examinations is more effective. Why?

DIRECT EXAMINATION

JUDGE KAVANAGH: You may proceed.

BY DEFENSE COUNSEL: State your name please. **A.** John Paul Winters.

[The witness was then qualified as a psychiatrist.]

Q. Doctor, have you, at the request of my partner, Mr. Brandeis, examined a Mrs. Virginia Lemmon? **A.** I have.

---

44. The hypothetical trial is more fully set forth in the Legal-Medical Library of the Michigan Institute of Continuing Legal Education, Volume 2, Examining the Medical Expert: Lectures and Trial Demonstrations (1969).

Q. And did you report that examination by transmittal letter, enclosing a copy of the report that you have made on her? **A.** I did.

Q. On what date did you see her? **A.** On the first of February, 1968.

Q. Where was the examination conducted? **A.** Within my office.

Q. What were the complaints of mental problems that Mrs. Lemmon related? **A.** Well, she complained of having chronic depression. She was fatigued all the time, wasn't able to work; general problems of depression.

Q. Did she relate to you the date of the onset of these symptoms? **A.** Yes, she did. This problem she related to the death of her baby after she was discharged from the hospital following the delivery of that baby on September 15, 1967, and she left the hospital 12 days after that. But there was a short period of time before the onset of her symptoms; about three weeks after the delivery.

Q. Then actually, Doctor, the beginning of the symptoms did not coincide with either the birth or death of the child. Is that correct? **A.** That is correct.

Q. What was her attitude with regard to the examination, Doctor? Was she cooperative? **A.** Well, she was, but on the other hand, she didn't particularly go out of her way to respond to me. This is not completely unusual. She was somewhat reluctant. I had to try very hard to get information from her. She didn't ever volunteer very much.

Q. And I believe she did give a history of the child having died approximately 24 hours after birth? **A.** Yes, she did.

Q. To what extent did she indicate a depression, Doctor? How serious a depression did she describe? **A.** Well, she told me she had had a great deal of difficulty. Actually, the onset of these symptoms seemed to be related to the departure of her mother. Her mother stayed with her about three weeks after she came home. Her mother then left. At this point she began to have the symptoms she complained of. She had great difficulty in sleeping, she would wake up, on and off during the night, she felt very tired in the morning, had great difficulty in starting her housework. There was loss of appetite; she lost about ten pounds below her ordinary weight before pregnancy. She also mentioned that she became irritable, with her family, with her husband, and she said she was ill-tempered. In short, she cries very easily, and doesn't see very much future for herself. She – – – the expression she used, as a matter of fact, was she felt as if she were at the bottom of a dark, black pit. And I might add that it seemed to me that as I talked to her about these symptoms that they had been more profound somewhat earlier, that they were diminishing when I talked to her.

Q. In other words, there had been an improvement over her earlier state? **A.** That is correct.

* * *

Q. Now what about her personal history? I assume that a personal history in a case such as this is very important? **A.** Yes it is. There were everal upsetting events in Mrs. Lemmon's background; the first of these was the death of her father when she was about six years old.   By the way, she doesn't remember this very well.   She blocks it out of her memory.   She doesn't remember whether she was sad when this happened or not.   That's probably a significant fact.   Her mother remarried about six years after the father's death, just about the time of the onset of her puberty.   She doesn't particularly feel fondness toward her mother.   She feels that her mother didn't really pay much attention to her, didn't teach her the things that a woman should know—sewing, cooking, and things of that sort.   She feels that her stepfather did not like her.   She didn't particularly get along with him.   She attended high school, and then went to a university, Eastern Michigan University.   After that she took graduate courses in social work, and had been very active in this profession until her marriage.   She was fairly active in the community, such as with the League of Women Voters. I might say that she is also a very devout Catholic.   She participated in the usual church affairs.   In her childhood years, one gets the picture that she was somewhat slow to begin to involve herself in normal social life for a young girl.   She didn't begin to date, for example, until a couple of years after most of her friends.   She was only an average student, but she was very fond of things athletic.   She played on all the girls' athletic teams in her high school.   She did other things outside of school such as horseback riding, skiing, tennis, and so forth.[45]

Q.   Sort of a tomboy type?   **A.**   Yes, I think you could characterize her so, much more interested in that sort of thing than boy-girl type things.

Q.   Having problems with adjustment even in that period, I assume.

PLAINTIFF'S COUNSEL: Now, I object to that, if the Court please. I don't know what my friends' daughters are like, but I think normal girls are this way.   In any event, I object to it.

JUDGE KAVANAGH: The objection will be sustained.[46]

BY DEFENSE COUNSEL: Excuse me, Your Honor.   Go ahead, Doctor, I'm sorry I interrupted you.   **A.**   Similarly, as she grew older, and in college she made considerable point of the fact that she had had no active sexual life at all until she got married, I had the impression that she stayed away from heavy petting and things that are not too uncommon in people of that age.   She doesn't smoke or drink; occasionally she'll take a drink at something like a New Year's party or something of that sort.   And as she told about these things I had a feeling that she was being quite moralistic about it, and could not really see these things in the proper social perspective.   She met her husband while she was in college.   He's an accountant, considerably older than herself, nine years, as a matter of fact.   They courted for 18 months and then got married.   And again she made the point that she would have preferred to have the courtship last quite a bit longer.   In discussing her marital relations, she made quite a point of the fact that she and

45. Would the *Green* court have refused to accept this evidence on hearsay grounds? Does it make a difference that it is offered by the defense, not by Mrs. Lemmon?

46. What is the legal basis for the objection?

her husband do not enjoy their sexual relationship. For example, she does not often achieve climax, and this has been a problem for them. But she said they have been working on this for some time. She made a point of this in regard to this incident. She said that recently her sexual relationship has deteriorated. She's even been less interested, and quite, I would say, hostile toward her husband in his sexual interest in her.

Q. Recently? Did she mean since the pregnancy and the delivery? **A.** That's right, since she's had this depression.

Q. Now, did you make an examination of her mental status as you were able to observe and test it in your office? **A.** Yes, I did. Of course I observed her general demeanor throughout. I observed that she was very responsive to my questions, very logical, she took each of them in very appropriate frames of reference. She was completely oriented as to time, place, and person. She had a very good memory of the past, except for these significant areas which were her conflicts, of course. But she could tell me everything else accurately, apparently. She seemed to be at least average intelligence. I gave her the opportunity to demonstrate her memory. The serial sevens test she was able to do very accurately, repeating eight digits forward and six in reverse, which indicates a good memory. She had excellent judgment about her life and the situation in relationship to it. In discussing proverbs, which is one of the things we always do, she could always account for the proverb very accurately and she didn't get her own sensations mixed up with them as disturbed people do. She had no delusions or hallucinations of any sort, no distortions of her body image. She could see herself completely accurately. No depersonalization at all. However, I did see considerable evidence of guilt. I have already mentioned that she was a very rigid kind of person; she has a very sharp notion of what is right and wrong and any threat of deviation makes her feel very badly. I thought that she had lots of guilt sensations about some of her feelings about her family. She talks as though some of her current difficulties were brought on by herself, which is a typical kind of guilt response. She couldn't tell me why she thought this. This was just a sensation. There was no evidence of any difficulty in body motions or physical activity of any sort that was apparent to me during the examination.

Q. Doctor, did you make every test and elicit all of the history that you felt was necessary in order for you to reach an opinion concerning the mental health or status of the patient? **A.** Yes, I did. I took it to be my task to see how she had responded to this loss of the baby. I was aware of the fact, of course, that she was going to be involved in a legal action, and I wanted to find out whether or not in fact her problem had related to this episode.

Q. Well, did you arrive at an opinion, to a reasonable degree of medical certainty, as to the status of her mental health and the causes of it? **A.** Yes, I think I did.

Q. If you would, please state that conclusion in your opinion, Doctor. **A.** I would say that this woman came into her adult life, came into the episode of her pregnancy, with a great deal of confusion about her feminine role. In other words, she was quite uncomfortable about how to be an adequate, normal woman. She had this tremendous tendency to feel guilty about her behavior if it didn't come up to her own, very high, standards that she had learned. When she lost the baby, therefore, she was already in a condition which I would believe would make it very likely that she would have had one of these postpartum psychosis syndromes which we see very commonly in women of this sort after they deliver the baby, even when the baby lives.

Q. In other words the post partum depression syndrome is not related to the health of the child, but the mere fact of the delivery, is that correct? **A.** Yes.

CROSS-EXAMINATION I

Q. Doctor, the one thing I didn't hear when you were qualifying yourself as a psychiatrist, was the length of time that you'd practiced psychiatry here in Ann Arbor. How long has it been? **A.** Approximately 10 years.

Q. And when attorney Brandeis got in touch with you and asked you to make this examination, he told you, did he not, that Mrs. Lemmon was claiming depression? **A.** Yes. Yes, he did.

Q. And he told you that she had made a claim and was involved in a lawsuit? **A.** Yes. I knew that.

Q. And he told you, didn't he, that Dr. Clayburn was the defendant in the lawsuit? **A.** I believe he did.

Q. And he told you that she was making her claim and basing it on the idea that Dr. Clayburn's treatment of her had been negligent. **A.** Yes.

Q. And when you heard that, and knew it was a malpractice suit, you didn't like that, did you? **A.** Well, I don't know, I – – –

Q. You didn't like that, did you? **A.** I would say that it was largely irrelevant to me.

Q. Did you like it? The idea of that suit or not? **A.** I believe that things properly brought before a court should be brought before a court, so I didn't mind.

Q. You didn't mind? **A.** No, why should I?

Q. All right. Well, I'll come to that. You knew Doctor Clayburn was a practicing physician here in Ann Arbor, didn't you? **A.** Yes, I've heard of him.

Q. You knew him before you were retained in this case, didn't you? **A.** Well, only as somebody I'd say hello to, that's all. We're not friends.

Q. You knew him, didn't you? **A.** I know his name. I've seen him like you've seen all the lawyers that walk through the courthouse.

Q. Doctor, can't you understand my question? **A.** Well, can't you understand my answer? I told you I know him. But I don't know him beyond that.

Q. Doctor, please. Let's get along here. Did you know Dr. Clayburn before you made this examination? A. I know not a thing about him; I know that he practices medicine in Ann Arbor. That's all I know.

Q. Well, Doctor, there are only 98 doctors and specialists and surgeons altogether in Ann Arbor. Isn't that so? A. I've never counted them, but there are – – –

Q. Would you take my word for it that in the yellow pages there are listed exactly 98 doctors who practice in Ann Arbor? A. Well, I won't, because if you look in there, you'll find that my name is not listed. There are probably another 500 of us who are not listed in the phone book.

Q. All right. In the hundred that are listed, are you saying that you only had a hello-good-bye acquaintance with Dr. Clayburn in the 10 years that you've practiced here in Ann Arbor? A. That is totally correct.[47]

Q. Well, you examined her when she came to your office, didn't you? A. Yes.

Q. That took you about an hour and a half? A. An hour and three quarters, I believe.

Q. Well, I think that it said someplace an hour and thirty-five minutes, Doctor. A. You are correct. An hour and thirty-five minutes.

Q. Thank you. And then after you examined her, you sat down and put the facts together and made up a report, Doctor? A. I wrote my report after I'd examined her. Correct.

Q. And you spent what, a half-hour, or an hour on your report? A. Well, I think I spent quite a bit more time than that, because I dictated a draft and then I went over the draft. I suppose I spent in all perhaps another hour and a half.

Q. Another hour and a half? A. Correct.

Q. So that your involvement with her by way of examination and the report, a matter of three hours of your time? A. That would be approximately correct.

Q. And I suppose you submitted the usual fifty dollar bill, Doctor?[48] A. No, I submitted the bill that I – – –

Q. No, Doctor, did you – – – did you submit a bill for fifty dollars? A. No.

Q. You mean that you charged more than that? A. I believe that – – –

Q. Wait a minute, Doctor. Don't you understand me? A. I understand very well that you are trying to make something out of nothing.

47. Do you see what the examiner is trying to suggest? Is he succeeding? Can you think of better questions to make this point? Could the defense counsel have done any-thing to protect the psychiatrist from this attack? Would he want to?

48. Is this question objectionable? Should the defense counsel object?

Q. Doctor, did you submit a bill for more than fifty dollars? **A.** I submitted a bill to cover my examination, my report, and my appearance in court, to the sum of four hundred dollars. Is that what you want me to say?

Q. I don't want you to say anything that isn't true, Doctor. Now, did you say that you submitted a bill for four hundred dollars to cover your examination, your report, and your appearance in court? **A.** Yes. I noticed the bill says – – –

Q. Doctor, you've answered me. Let's go on to the next question. You submitted the bill with the report, didn't you? **A.** Yes.

Q. And did you anticipate and charge in advance for your testimony in court? **A.** I only wanted to submit a single bill. I don't suppose you know psychiatrists do not maintain large office staffs. We do our own bookkeeping. We try to – – –

Q. Doctor, please. If you can answer me without a long lecture, I'd appreciate it. **A.** I want you to understand the facts of this case.

Q. Doctor, did you send a letter with your bill? **A.** Yes, a covering letter and the report.

Q. And is this the letter? [Exhibit omitted]. **A.** That's correct.

Q. And did you write in that letter that went with the bill, "I deeply appreciate your having referred the case to me. If I may be of help to you with regard to the trial itself, should there be one, I hope you will feel free to call on me." Did you say that? **A.** It looks as though I did, doesn't it?

Q. And I suppose if you charged the four hundred dollars for the examination, report and your appearance in court, if there was to be no trial, then how much refund were you going to give him? **A.** I suspect that the way that I have to explain this last paragraph is that I wasn't thinking very carefully. I knew this was coming to trial. I'd already been told that, and obviously I don't have a lawyer's precision.

Q. Were you thinking this carefully when you wrote the letter, and when you made the bill, as when you made your report? **A.** No, I didn't. I was very casual when I dictated the letter, because this was just a letter to counsel.

Q. Doctor, pay attention to me. Were you just as casual when you made up your report? **A.** I was very careful when I made up my report.

Q. All right. Thank you. Now one of the last things I heard you say in direct examination was that you thought Dr. Clayburn had done a fine job in handling Mrs. Lemmon, particularly in view of the type of person she was. **A.** Yes, I did.

Q. Now, did you ever find a single fact in anything reported by Dr. Clayburn to indicate that she was anything but a perfectly normal patient during all the time he took care of her, before she lost her baby? **A.** Dr. Clayburn's records are like most doctor's records – – –

Q. Now, Doctor, please. Can't you answer the question? **A.** Not and have you understand what I'm trying to say, if I don't explain it.

Q. Doctor, please, do you understand my question? **A.** I guess I don't.

Q. All right. My question is did you ever learn from any record of Dr. Clayburn's that while he had treated her up to the time she delivered and lost her baby that there was anything abnormal with her except, let me put it this way, abnormal in a psychic or mental way? **A.** He didn't say anything that would tell me what his impression of her psyche was.

Q. I see. So that when you say that he did a fine job, considering what kind of a person she was, you got no idea of what kind of person she was from him, did you? **A.** No, I – – –

Q. All right. **A.** – – – I formed that largely from my impressions of her and what she told me about her medical experiences.

Q. I see, in the hour and thirty-five minutes you spent on her, right? **A.** Yes.

Q. Well, let's go on, Doctor. Now, I've read your report, you've testified to your report, and can we agree that when you described factors in the report and have recorded them, they were important to you? **A.** Yes.

Q. And the very first one of importance that I see here concerning her appearance when she appeared, you said she was slightly disheveled, right? **A.** Correct.

A. And that was on February 26, 1968. Right? **A.** No, this was on February 1, 1968.

Q. Do you remember on that day that we had a storm and it was windy? [49] **A.** Well, I don't think I can remember what the day was like, but I can tell you that my reaction to her appearance, whatever the day was like, was considering all those factors in my estimate of her.

Q. All right, you said that she was slightly disheveled, right? **A.** Right.

Q. And that she had used little makeup, right? That was an important factor, right? **A.** Yes.

Q. It struck you as being an unusual thing, right? **A.** Well, it told me something about how she felt about herself as a woman, yes.

Q. You haven't the slightest idea whether she had ever in her life used more than a little makeup? **A.** Not explicitly, but I have some general hunches about it.

Q. And there are millions of women in this country who use little makeup, and who are perfectly normal. Isn't that so? **A.** Well, I wasn't

49. If the lawyer does not know this to be the case, but is asking about a storm to test the doctor's recollection and to suggest a reason for his client's disheveled appearance, is the question permissible? Is it ethical to ask such a question for either or both of these purposes?

talking about normality, abnormality. I was talking about how she saw herself as a woman.

Q. Well, this is how you saw her, wasn't it? **A.** Well, certainly.

Q. Let's go on, Doctor. Now you said she appeared to be defensive, or she was defensive, she was guarded and a bit hostile. Right? **A.** Correct.

Q. Doctor, you practice this specialty of taking care of adult patients in psychiatric matters, isn't that so? **A.** Correct.

Q. And even with people who seek your help, who come to you for treatment, you frequently find, do you not, that they're defensive? **A.** Oh, sure.

Q. And that they're guarded, and sometimes even a little hostile? **A.** Of course.

Q. And it takes you a visit, certainly more than a visit, a number of visits, before you've drawn them out and established a rapport between you and the patient. **A.** Sure. It's one of the variables I observe.

Q. So that there was nothing unusual about that, was there? **A.** Yes, there was. This woman has these characteristics which differentiate her from I don't know what percentage of a large number of others.

Q. These are characteristics of a woman with a depression? **A.** That's right.

Q. All right. Let's go further. Another of the things you said this morning was that she told you that she became depressed three weeks after her mother went home. Now she didn't tell you that, did she? **A.** No, she told me when she got depressed. She told me when her mother left. I put together the fact that she got depressed at about the same time that her mother left her household. That's a deduction that I made.

Q. All right. So that would have been about three weeks after she lost the baby. **A.** About three weeks after she returned home. Let me just check my notes here.

Q. She was 12 days in the hospital. **A.** Correct.

Q. Right? **A.** Yes.

Q. She told you she got along fairly well the first two or three weeks after she lost the baby, right? **A.** Correct.

Q. And then her mother stayed with her, and it was after her mother's departure that she showed the – – – or complained of the signs of depression, right? **A.** That's correct.

Q. Well, in the 12 days she was in the hospital she was not alone, was she? **A.** Well, she was with other patients. She was in a semi-private room, doctor, nurses – – –

Q. Usual activity. **A.** Correct.

Q. Then her mother stayed with her, right? **A.** Correct.

Q. And so that at the end of three weeks when her mother went home, then she was alone, was she not? **A.** Correct.

Q. And then she showed or felt the effects of the depression. **A.** Correct.

Q. The impact then had hit her, hadn't it? **A.** The impact of what?

Q. Of her experience in her baby's dying. **A.** Well, the experience of having a baby, delivering it, dying—all these things together she experienced.

Q. Don't drop your voice. The dying. The experience of having the baby, having delivered it, AND the baby dying – – – **A.** All of these were her experience. Correct.

Q. And that's when it really hit her hard—when she was alone. Right? **A.** Well, she began to have these depressive symptoms when her mother departed.

Q. Which is three weeks afterwards! **A.** Correct.

Q. All right. **A.** The usual time when postpartum psychosis – – –

Q. Please, Doctor, had I asked you anything more? **A.** I presume you want to understand the circumstances as I see them.

Q. Please, you just presume that you understand me one question at a time, and we'll get along just fine. She said she was irritable? **A.** Correct.

Q. Symptom of depression? **A.** Correct.

Q. She said her husband says she's ill-tempered now. **A.** Correct.

Q. And assuming she is, for a woman who was previously normal so far as her temper was concerned, this is a symptom of depression? **A.** Correct.

Q. When she told you she had difficulty completing her housework and that she was lethargic continuously and tired, and that she cries easily and she can see no bright future ahead—when she told you those things did you believe her? **A.** Yes, this is how she felt about herself.

Q. And in each of these things we start to have more and more factors that indicate that this woman was in a depression, isn't that right? **A.** Correct.

Q. Now you went into some personal history with her, right? **A.** Right.

Q. She said she was rather, that's the one place you've used the quotation, "a moody person." I suppose those were her exact words. Right? **A.** Yes.

Q. You don't often find a person's self-analysis terribly reliable, do you? **A.** Well, this woman, you must remember, is a social worker and she's rather given to using the language, and indeed she's had a lot of training experiences, that would permit her to be – – –

Q. Except that now, Doctor, she was describing herself. Right? **A.** It's part of her training to gain skill in describing herself.

Q. All right. Normal for any normal person to have moods? **A.** Well, when she's – – –

Q. No, please, won't you answer me, Doctor? **A.** What do you mean by moods?

Q. I mean times when you feel happy, times when you feel sad. That's normal, isn't it? **A.** Right, but that's not how this patient used the word moody.

Q. I'm not talking about – – – Please listen to my question. It's perfectly normal for a normal person to have moods, isn't that so? **A.** If you use mood to mean shifts of emotion, yes.

Q. And isn't it true that when you're talking about these next few lines where she says she's had periods of happiness and exuberance and other periods of relative sadness and loneliness, that the only way you can make up your mind as a psychiatrist, Doctor, whether that's usual and normal or not usual and normal, is to know whether these things happen under appropriate circumstances? **A.** Yes.

Q. And did you ever mention in your report where you recorded the important things that these things happened under anything but appropriate circumstances? **A.** Well, I said here that these happened all through her life, obviously – – –

Q. No – – – **A.** – – – obviously this doesn't contain every word – – –

Q. Doctor! **A.** – – – that I elicited from her. I'm making a relative judgment here – – –

Q. Doctor, both of us can't talk. When you've finished your answer, please stop, and I'll go on. Doctor, did you ever get any set of circumstances that you deemed were not appropriate for her feelings, times when she was happy and exuberant, or other times when she was moody and depressed? **A.** Sure, she told me for example about her social life in college, and she very often felt very very depressed, sad, because she didn't feel she was having the kind of experiences that her friends were having. There were other times when she, looking back, describing her reactions to incidents, felt that she, in fact, had responded with happiness that wasn't appropriate to the circumstance. Is that what you mean?

Q. Well, if that's what she told you, that's what I mean. **A.** It is what she told me. I told you not everything she told me is in this record.

Q. Now when she talked about the times she felt sad in college—a girl in college, that's not unusual, is it? **A.** Her behavior was unusual, yes.

Q. I see. For her it was unusual. **A.** No. She, compared with her group, experienced an unusual response.

Q. One of the things that you thought was unusual in her experience as against her group, was that she started to date a couple of years after her chums did. **A.** That's right.

Q. You made mention of that. **A.** Right.

Q. You thought that was unusual. **A.** Yes.

Q. You know from her background that she's a girl of conscience and discrimination, don't you? **A.** Yes.

Q. Would it be unusual if she were a little bit more discriminatory than her chums? **A.** No, it wouldn't, I would expect her to be – – –

Q. All right, thank you, let's – – – **A.** – – – but that's not what I'm alluding to here. I'm not talking about her being discriminating, I'm talking – – – in effect that she was afraid to date at the time when her friends did.

Q. Not one place in this report did you ever put down a statement from her that she was afraid to date. **A.** That's correct. That isn't in there. I should have put it in if you – – –

Q. I'm sure now you realize you should have. Now, she got into social work after college, right? **A.** Correct.

Q. And you make mention of the fact that she's been active in that field both before and after she was married. **A.** Right.

Q. Anything wrong in that? **A.** No.

Q. All right. Now you also said she's an active member of the League of Women Voters; that was an important factor you put down. Anything wrong in that? **A.** No.

Q. And certainly you don't say there's anything wrong that because, like her mother, she was a devout, practicing Catholic? **A.** No.

Q. But these are important factors that you put here. **A.** Right.

Q. All right. Now, she was interested in athletics, anything wrong in that? **A.** No.

Q. She engaged in no premarital sexual intercourse. I'm afraid to ask this one, Doctor. **A.** That's your problem.

Q. Anything wrong in that – – – **A.** That may be your problem.

Q. Well, I have no problem with it. Anything wrong in that? **A.** No, not at all.

Q. All right. Let me ask you this, Doctor, do you say that a woman who carries a child nearly full term and delivers normally and then learns that the child has lived for about twenty-four hours and has died, do you say that that is a matter of emotional shock to the average, normal young woman? **A.** Certainly. Certainly it is.

Q. All right. And are you saying to this judge and this jury that in your opinion, that is not – – – that emotional shock is not an adequate cause – – – to cause her to go into this depression? **A.** That is exactly what I am saying.

Q. I see. We have this girl you've described here, which you say I think someplace in the report, put her in a position where she was liable to go into a depression, right? **A.** Correct.

Q. We know she had this experience concerning the child, right? **A.** Correct.

Q. We know it affected her by way of an emotional shock, right? **A.** Yes.

Q. And you say that has nothing whatever to do with the depression she went into? **A.** Correct.

Q. And you mean that. **A.** Correct.

Q. I haven't a single other question, Doctor.

Before reading the next examination, analyze the strengths and weaknesses of this one. Is this examination an attack on the witness, or on the evidence supplied by the witness? Exactly what does the examiner do in his attempt to make the jury discount the psychiatrist's testimony? By the end of the examination has the force of the witness' testimony been dissipated to a significant extent? What do you think the psychiatrist thought of the attorney after the examination had been concluded?

CROSS-EXAMINATION II

Q. I represent Mr. and Mrs. Lemmon, and I would like to ask you a few questions, if I may, on the things that we would undoubtedly agree on, then get to a point where perhaps you and I will have some disagreement. May I do that? First of all, as to some definitions. You have used the word, and I'm sure that everyone does, as to predisposition, and this is a word ordinarily used to try to describe what Mrs. Lemmon was like before she had her pregnancy or before she had diabetes, but what she brought in all of her mature life and her childhood to the problem that we're now dealing with today. Is that a fair word, sir? **A.** That's correct.

Q. And then there is another word that is used all of the time and it is called stress and that's the situation that brought about, in combination with her predisposition, either something that was a bad result or a mild result, or something. But this is a word normally used, is it not, sir, in psychiatric language? **A.** Yes.

Q. And here we are also dealing with the last word, which is a depression. And I believe that you have described that Mrs. Lemmon in your opinion does have a depression, and that this is something that is chronic in her case. It is something that you feel, however, is very real to her. It is in fact a psychosis, but it has been described by you as a depression. Is that true, sir? **A.** Yes. It's not a psychosis, but it is a depression, right.

Q. Now, each of these, I assume, can be mild, or they can be moderate, or they can be severe. And that's used normally in medical terminology, is it not? **A.** Correct.

A. All right, so now, in this lady's case, if I understand what you've told us on direct examination, is that this lady's predisposition of her personality was such that she had some problems, when she got into a pregnancy, of feminine identification, of some sexual development, and so forth, and a little strong superego, but that her personality here very definitely contributed to bringing about the depression. Am I correct in that? **A.** Correct.

Q. Would you describe it as mild, moderate, or severe—her predisposition in relation to our problem here? **A.** Well, I would say that she had a moderate to strong predisposition.

Q. Now we all, all people that grow up, have a predisposition. No one is perfect. We all have things that under certain stress would bring about certain results, do we not, sir? **A.** Correct.

Q. We all, as we're walking around at age 29 as she was, we all have these things. Since the last nearly 2,000 years we haven't had anybody born perfectly here, is that right? **A.** Correct.

Q. So you understand, do you not, that the courtrooms of America are open to people who are not the strongest Charles Atlases in the world. You understand, do you not, that the courtrooms are for weak people as well as for so-called strong people. You understand that, do you not, sir? [50] **A.** Yes.

Q. And you have told us, in your opinion, from what came about, that the stress in this situation was her pregnancy alone, and her mother leaving her afterwards, after three weeks—that that stress brought about the depression which you have described. Is that correct? **A.** That is correct.

Q. And this depression, would you call it mild, moderate, or severe? **A.** Oh, moderate; I think it is down to about mild at this point.

Q. And so that I understand you completely, sir, is it your position that even if this child had lived, that she, with this predisposition that she had here, which you class as moderate to severe, she would have still had this depression? **A.** That is very well put. That is exactly what I think.

Q. And it is your position, sir, as I understand it, that the death of this baby did not contribute to this depression? That it did not, in the three weeks, activate, accelerate, or aggravate it! That it did not contribute to it! And that it did not precipitate it! That is your position, isn't it, sir? **A.**

---

50. Is this a proper question to ask a psychiatrist? Is it a proper question to ask any witness? Why is it asked?

Yes, I suppose I would have to say that it might have made her a bit more vulnerable to what happened before. You know, these predispositional factors, I wouldn't say that it had no effect on her. Well, oh, I guess that is what I wanted to say, that it is true that it had some effect on her, but it was not the major cause of the illness.

Q. The death of the baby? **A.** Right.

Q. All right, sir, are you then saying, not as you said in your report, and let me read your report to you, sir; on the last page of your report, your last sentence, "There is no clear indication that psychological status is a consequence of, or is necessarily related to, the death of her child," and I use your words, "in any way." You don't believe that here today, do you? **A.** I guess I do, but you see the problem is, as you've quite accurately put it, everything that happens to a human being affects him.

Q. But I'm asking you about a predisposition, sir. I'm asking you— this last sentence, in your language, signed by you, in your report, that we go by that today. Or do you want to say that you believe that the death of Jennifer had something to do with her depression over here? **A.** I guess that the way that I could put it most accurately is that if Jennifer had not died, she would look to me, as nearly as I can tell, exactly as she looks now. She might have some sadness about Jennifer in addition. In other words, the symptomatology that I described would have been there, regardless, just as you said earlier.

Q. You don't go along with, I assume, the school that might think a lot of women have postpartum depression, but they get over it and replace it with the natural maternal love that comes because they have a baby? And that they can love that baby? And that overcomes that postpartum. You don't agree with that in this case, do you? **A.** Well, I don't know that that is exactly how they overcome the depression, from the baby.

Q. Then you wouldn't agree with it? **A.** No, I guess I wouldn't.

Q. All right, sir. Now may I turn and ask this. Since you don't feel, in your words, that it in any way contributed, then may I also assume, logically from that, that if instead, if I could through some magic wand, bring to Mrs. Lemmon over here, Jennifer, through that door, who is now four and a half, five months old, and put that child in her arms, and let that child be in her mother's arms instead of being out today, three miles out in a grave, under the snow, in the cold ground, do you feel that would not help in this case, sir? **A.** No, I don't think it would.

Q. It has no effect on her whatsoever? **A.** That is not the same thing.

Q. It's more important to you that her mother left her than having her child taken away from her by the possible negligence of a doctor. Is that true, sir? **A.** Well, you put two or three things in there that I don't know if I want to respond to at all. I'm saying that the issue about whether or not she would be, whether her mental health would change if she had the baby back—in my opinion, it would not change, because I don't think that was the cause of the depressive response. It would have an effect on her. She would be glad of it, you know, obviously, she would have all kinds of positive feelings, but she would still be depressed. That is my opinion.

Q. Well, she is a sick lady. I'm not asking you if she wouldn't still be depressed with what she had. But don't you think it would help her to get over her depression? A. No. In fact the baby doesn't help get over the depression. The baby causes the depression in the first place.

Q. Well, as a matter of fact, you took the position that because of lack of feminine identification, she gets pregnant, she gets depressed afterwards; why, if she has the baby, doesn't that remove the problem of having to assume a maternal role? A. I don't understand what you're saying here.

Q. Well, I'll come at you in another way. Why is it, if you feel that the pregnancy and her lack of feminine identification caused her to be stressfully [sic] in a situation that resulted in – – – why was it she was asymptomatic during her pregnancy? Why didn't she have any problem of depression then, sir? A. Because these things happen this way. They don't have depressions during pregnancy. It is only after delivery that these symptoms erupt.[51]

Q. Doctor, I have a great deal of respect for the field of psychiatry and I want to ask you just a couple of questions about your qualifications. You, sir, when you graduated, of course, from medical school, did not consider yourself a psychiatrist until you went and did some additional work, is that right, sir? A. That is correct.

Q. And since that time, so we can understand it, you did your residency, you went immediately into private practice. Now, have you, sir, ever studied or practiced in the field of psychoanalysis? A. No.

Q. You are not and do not term yourself to be a psychoanalyst, do you, sir? A. That is correct. I read some of the psychoanalytic materials, but I'm not a psychoanalyst.

Q. You, sir, have never yourself been through psychoanalysis, have you? A. No.

Q. To be a psychoanalyst you have to go to medical school, you have to take an internship, you have to take a residency, you are then a psychiatrist. But then you must also go through analysis yourself, must you not, sir? A. That is part of their training, yes.

Q. And one of the reasons for that is – – – when a doctor passes opinions and judgments on other people, he can make sure that he is not reacting to his own prejudices or his own problems of his own unconsciousness, that he is not reacting to a red tie like a bull to red. You've got to learn about yourself to make sure you don't react wrongly, and that you do everything professionally, isn't that true? A. That is correct. That is their theory.

---

51. The examiner changes his approach at this point? The subsequent questions have a different objective than the preceding ones?

Why might the examiner choose this point to change direction? Why does he embark on the line of questioning that follows?

Q. Now, in your situation, you have arrived at a judgment where you yourself have not been through psychoanalysis, and you are not a psychoanalyst. And I assume that you can assure this jury that you are not motivated hereby any subconscious problems of your own here, such as the fact that a fellow doctor is getting sued. That doesn't bother you, does it, sir? **A.** No, I don't think so.

Q. I'm sure. The fact that you − − − I assume that you can assure us that the fact that this defense lawyer over here sent this patient and got this appointment for you, that doesn't bother you at all, does it? You can overlook that in your subconscious? **A.** Well, I, it's just a conscious issue as far as I'm concerned. I don't think it bothers me.

Q. We can assume − − − you can assure us that the fact that you are being paid here, you can overlook that and that has nothing to do with it, right? **A.** I don't suppose that it bothers me any more than it bothers you. To be a good lawyer you get paid.

Q. It helps me tremendously to be motivated by money. I'm asking you − − − you have made judgments about, on your direct examination, about this lady, being a Roman Catholic as a child, and a devout one, that she was a rigid personality. You are not a Roman Catholic, are you? **A.** No.

Q. And that, we can assume, assures that that doesn't have any motivation to you whatsoever? **A.** I don't think so.

Q. And I assume, sir, that you can assure us that there is no motivation here about the fact, respectfully, that you have not had any children of your own, or a teenage daughter who grew up under these circumstances. You can assure us of that, can't you, Doctor? **A.** I don't believe it does.

Q. And you did not, in this case, take advantage of or use any psychometric testing with this lady before coming here and passing these judgments on her, did you? **A.** No. This is just a clinical psychiatric examination.

Q. And psychometric testing is something we've heard of as inkblot tests, the Brenner Gestalt test, the I.Q. test, all these things that are available either at the Medical School over at the University of Michigan, or with a good clinical psycholgist; that is a very standard professional way of testing, is it not, sir? **A.** Yes, it is, but we don't often use them.

Q. You don't use them yourself, I understand that, but − − − **A.** I think most psychiatrists don't use them often. I guess we really only use them if we're going to try to prove something in court, and we didn't really have time here to get them.

Q. But you knew that you were coming here, to court, didn't you, sir? **A.** Pardon me?

Q. I said that you knew you were coming here to court, didn't you, sir? **A.** Oh, yes.

Q. And – – – but you didn't take advantage of that. Now my client has cooperated and done everything that you asked her to do. You told her to do things and she did them. Is that right? **A.** That is right.

Q. Now, Doctor, in this predisposition, you wrote down in your report things that you thought significant. You thought some things were significant enough that you wrote that this lady wasn't taught to cook and sew—items about her dating—such things as that. You put down the things that you thought were significant, that we all ought to know about before we try to arrive at a judgment. I'm concerned about the things here that you've said about this lady, because of the fact that she did have these problems—that her mother didn't teach her to cook and sew, and that she had had trouble with her menstrual periods when she started, and so forth, and her father died at six. You mentioned these things. Now I want to ask you if any of these 15 things that I'm going to read to you are such that this should have been avoided, because I have a 13-year-old daughter myself, you know, who plays tennis and is pretty good, and I want to make sure that she goes through a normal pregnancy. Now, will you help me, and tell me why you feel that there is a moderately severe predisposition here with this lady who has done this?

(1) High school grad;

(2) College grad;

(3) Done graduate work in social work;

(4) Joined the League of Women Voters;

(5) Been a devout Catholic;

(6) An average student;

(7) Learned to ski and ride and play tennis;

(8) She doesn't smoke;

(9) She doesn't drink;

(10) She married an accountant;

(11) She's had no premarital intercourse;

(12) She was engaged for eighteen months;

(13) She's of strong character;

(14) She had a brother;

(15) She did greatly attest she felt above average and she was well-oriented and she was healthy except for diabetes.

Now were any of those things in your opinion, sir, such that you can arrive at a diagnosis that she had moderate to severe predisposition to a depression merely by getting pregnant? **A.** Well, you obviously know a great deal about our theories, * * * and you know that all of these things together give an image of the kind of person she is. She is the kind of person who is more comfortable with physical, active-type things, which in our culture tends to make a person feel, possibly feel, conflicts about whether they're a good woman or a good man and that sort of thing. All of these things must be taken together. You can't take one of them out of context.

It's just simply a, you might call it a tendency, to things which cause a conflict in individuals in our society.

Q. Now, we've got a bunch of hippies in the United States today who don't do any of these things. And they do have premarital intercourse, and they're not devoutly religious, and they don't go through college, and they don't graduate, and they don't help out society, and they don't marry accountants. Now do you think that that type of person, who doesn't wash well, wouldn't have had this type of reaction? Is that what you are saying? A. Not at all. I'm not sure that I know exactly what would happen to them.

Q. Now, Doctor, I want to ask you, sir, I noticed in your direct examination that you stated the predisposition, the stress, and the resulting depression, but you never told us the reasons that you based getting there. Just so that our – – – I'm not asking you about the use, you made no mention here about any castration problems that are in the subconscious of some women when they lose a child that may cause conflict – – – you made no mention of that. You have no belief of that, do you, sir? A. Well, that's psychoanalytic type language – – –

Q. And you don't like that – – – A. Well, I don't dislike that; it's just a different kind of language.

Q. All right, sir. You made no mention of a central authority figure here. She'd lost her father at age six, now comes along and has a doctor whom she believes prescribe medicine to her and doesn't even read this, an authority figure who is taking care of her, and doesn't even read the simple literature that comes with it, which says, don't give it to a woman that might get pregnant, don't give it to her. And if you do prescribe this at all, you should test them every day and test them every week. Then that person comes along after she gets pregnant and he still gives it to her after he finds it out. She ends up with a dead baby. And another very important figure in her life disappoints her. That has no symbolic meaning to you, does it, sir? A. Well, I don't know that I thought about it in terms of symbolic – – – sure, she was involved with this doctor, yes.

Q. Doctor, the type of symptoms she has in this depression, you know these symptoms and I won't go over them, but the lack of appetite, waking up at night, the loss of weight, the burning sensations, those are the type of symptoms that very definitely still could be caused by a depression and could have been created by this stress technically, could it not, sir? A. Oh, technically, yes. Any stress could have done it technically, yes.

Q. Thank you, sir. Doctor, you charged four hundred dollars to handle a one and a half hour examination for this lady, on February 1, 1968. Is that the same rate you charge your private patients, sir? A. No, I guess when I have a problem like this, I anticipate the fact that I'm going to have to spend much more time thinking about the report that I write, because I know very well that when I come into the courtroom, you lawyers are going to be very meticulous about what words I use, and don't use.

Q. So you charged more than you charge your own patients for Mrs. Lemmon's examination in this case, even though a fellow doctor was being sued. Is this correct? **A.** I suppose in the last analysis I don't charge more, because I'm spending more time worrying and thinking about it, so that in fact, if I worked it out on an hourly basis, it probably isn't really any more.

Q. One last question, Doctor. If you can believe me in that this lady, when she saw you last month, one month ago today, nearly 29 years of age, if she has lived for two hundred and seventy-one thousand, five hundred and sixty hours in her life, you've seen her one and a half hours of that quarter of a million plus hours, and you arrived at all of these judgments on that, didn't you, sir? **A.** Yes, I did.

Q. That will be all. Thank you, sir.

Recall the direct examination of Dr. Winters. What effect would it have had on the jury had there been no cross-examination? Rethink both cross-examinations. What, if anything did one accomplish that the other did not? Did the accomplishments of either or both examiners go beyond the discrediting of the psychiatrist's testimony? Should more emphasis have been placed on the fact that the doctor's report was made directly to defense counsel? Should the first examiner have engaged in more questioning about psychological theories? Should the second examiner have done more to emphasize the closeness of the Ann Arbor community and the general attitude which doctors have toward malpractice cases? Would either of these examinations have been effective if the attorneys had not had access to the psychiatrist's medical report?

F. REVIEW PROBLEMS

Problem X–8. Earl Gardey stands charged with mail fraud. Gardey is a federal employee who secured health insurance coverage through the government. Thereafter he applied for additional insurance policies providing hospitalization and disability coverage. According to the government, he misrepresented facts in applying for the policies. In particular, the government charges that Gardey answered questions about his other insurance by falsely denying he had any. Gardey calls a professor of finance at the state university who will testify that the questions on the policies concerning other insurance could reasonably have been taken as referring only to life insurance. The expert would in essence explain the language ordinarily found in insurance contracts to the jury. The government objects, claiming that the language speaks for itself and that the question of what a policy means is a question of law for the judge to decide. **Should the witness be permitted to testify?**

Problem X–9. Marie Malloy brought an action for damages against defendant claiming permanent injuries arising out of an automobile accident. A dispute arose as to whether the plaintiff's injuries manifested themselves a full month prior to the accident, negating her causation theory or whether certain injuries, admittedly suffered before the accident, were unrelated to the post-accident suffering. Dr. Ballard, plaintiff's expert, testified that, in his opinion, the accident damaged Malloy's cervical arteries leading to a spasm or thrombosis which cut off blood from the brain. He also testified that Malloy's earlier hospitalization, a month before the accident, was unrelated to her later injuries and arose from a salt deficiency. On cross-examination the doctor conceded that previously he had stated that the proper explanation for the pre-accident treatment was that Malloy had suffered a stroke. This view the doctor now repudiated. The doctor indicated that to arrive at his opinion he relied upon his own observations, hospital records and statements by other doctors. On cross-examination the defendant offered into evidence a report by a Dr. Orr stating that Malloy had told him that she had suffered three small strokes one month before the date of the accident. Although Dr. Ballard had seen the report, he did not accept its conclusions. Dr. Orr was not available to testify. **Should the report be admitted? If so, for what purpose?**

Problem X–10. A son is attempting to have his father committed to a mental institution. He presents witnesses who testify that his father has been acting strangely in that he has frequently been seen walking around the house naked, he seems impatient with his son, he constantly watches television, especially horror and detective and police shows, he has been buying a collection of "girlie" magazines, and he has an increasing tendency to go off by himself. The defendant father introduces the testimony of neighbors who have known him for years and who state that his mind is quick, that he has always been pleasant, that his interest in television is shared by them, that he has always liked "girlie" magazines, and that his impatience with his son is understandable because the son is a very irritating person. On rebuttal, the son introduces the testimony of two witnesses. The first, a salesman testifies that the father commented while attempting to buy a handgun, "if Sergeant Friday were in this town, I might not need the gun." The second, a psychiatrist, is asked, "Based on everything that you have heard so far, and you have been here for all the testimony, have you an opinion as to whether the defendant is a danger to himself or to the community?" The defendant objects to the question. **Should the objection be sustained?**

Problem X–11. Paul Kettle is charged with robbing a grocery store. The theory of the prosecution's case is that Kettle is a narcotics addict who needed money to sustain his habit. To bolster the state's case, the prosecution seeks to introduce the testimony of a federal agent from the Bureau of Narcotics and Dangerous Drugs. The agent would testify that he has been working with the Bureau for 10 years, that he has investigated over 1,000 narcotics cases, that he has investigated and interviewed thousands of addicts, and that he considers himself to be an expert on narcotics addiction. In response to the question, "With respect to narcotics addicts, is there any generalization that you can make concerning their propensity to commit economic crimes," the witness would answer, "Yes, narcotics addicts have a difficult time holding jobs. Therefore, they have tremendous difficulty in securing sufficient funds to sustain their habit. This often results in their seeking money illegally. I personally have been involved in investigating hundreds of cases in which addicts have committed robberies, burglaries, and other crimes for the purpose of obtaining funds to purchase drugs." **Should this testimony be admitted?**

SECTION III. SPECIFIC EXAMPLES OF EXPERT AND SCIENTIFIC EVIDENCE

There are as many kinds of expert evidence as there are people with special skills and training. Given the diversity of human experience and the creativity of trial lawyers, sooner or later one might expect that almost every type of expert will be presented to a court. Not all will be welcomed, however. As we note briefly at the end of section I of this chapter, some scientific evidence is rejected on the ground that it lacks the required scientific acceptance among appropriate authorities. While the word "scientific" could be read narrowly, any expert evidence may be evaluated on the basis of its acceptability to those of acknowledged expertise in the relevant area.

In Chapter Three we pointed out that evidence may be relevant, and at times very helpful to the trier of fact, despite imperfections or ambiguity. Evidence from ordinary witnesses is admitted as long as a minimal test of relevance is satisfied. Yet expert evidence, which might be of enormous value in resolving a controversy, is sometimes excluded without any explicit attempt to balance its probative value against potential prejudice. Why?

To assist you in dealing with this question, we discuss briefly several examples of scientific evidence and the ways that courts have reacted to them.

A. PSYCHIATRIC EVIDENCE [52]

We begin with a relatively familiar example, psychiatric evidence. The two transcripts presented in Section II are examples of such evidence.

One common use of psychiatric evidence is to establish the defense of insanity in criminal cases. Whatever the test used (knowledge of right and wrong, irresistible impulse, product of a mental disease, etc.), psychiatric evidence is accepted to establish the defense, or to counter it. Indeed, the court may require expert evidence, or an adequate substitute, as a precondition for an instruction on the insanity defense. All American jurisdictions recognize the defense, but they differ considerably on the proper test of insanity. The tests vary in the ways they make psy-

chiatric testimony relevant. In 1954, in the famous case of Durham v. United States,[53] the United States Court of Appeals for the District of Columbia abandoned the traditional test which defined exculpatory insanity in terms of knowledge of right and wrong and the ability to resist impulses. Instead it adopted a test which focused on whether forbidden acts were the product of a mental disease or defect. One of the court's goals in *Durham* was to develop a rule which would allow experts to communicate their findings in ways they deemed helpful.[54] "However, the pristine statement of the *Durham* rule opened the door to 'trial by label' "[55] by failing to explain when an abnormality of the mind amounted to a disease or defect. After some experience with *Durham*, the court

---

52. Though we shall speak of "psychiatric evidence" our discussion applies to testimony by psychologists, particularly clinical psychologists, as well as to testimony by psychiatrists.

53. 94 U.S.App.D.C. 228, 214 F.2d 862 (1954).

54. It is not clear that the traditional M'Naghten test necessarily prevented such communication. See, e.g., A. Goldstein, The Insanity Defense 54 (1967); Livermore and Meehl, The Virtues of M'Naghten, 51 Minn.L.Rev. 789, 800–08 (1967).

55. United States v. Brawner, 153 U.S. App.D.C. 1, 471 F.2d 969, 977 (1972).

of appeals became concerned that medical terminology might be controlling legal outcomes, and in 1962 it defined mental disease or defect.[56] In 1967 the court of appeals gave trial judges the following advice:

The trial judge should limit the psychiatrists' use of medical labels—schizophrenia, neurosis, etc. It would be undesirable, as well as difficult, to eliminate completely all medical labels, since they sometimes provide a convenient and meaningful method of communication. But the trial judge should ensure that their meaning is explained to the jury and, as much as possible, that they are explained in a way which relates their meaning to the defendant.

The problem with labels, such as "product" and "mental disease or defect," is even more difficult. Because these labels are employed in the legal test for responsibility, there is a danger that the psychiatric witness will view them as a legal-moral rather than a medical matter. There are two possible solutions. We could simply prohibit testimony in terms of "product" and "mental disease or defect." Or we could clearly instruct the expert to stick to medical

judgments and leave legal-moral judgments to the jury.

A strong minority of this court has consistently advocated that psychiatrists be prohibited from testifying whether the alleged offense was the "product" of mental illness, since this is part of the ultimate issue to be decided by the jury. We now adopt that view. The term "product" has no clinical significance for psychiatrists. Thus there is no justification for permitting psychiatrists to testify on the ultimate issue. Psychiatrists should explain how defendant's disease or defect relates to his alleged offense, that is, how the development, adaptation and functioning of defendant's behavioral processes may have influenced his conduct. But psychiatrists should not speak directly in terms of "product," or even "result" or "cause."

It can be argued that psychiatrists should also be prohibited from testifying whether the defendant suffered from a "mental disease or defect," since this too is part of the ultimate issue. But unlike the term "product," the term "mental disease or defect" may have some clinical significance to the psychiatrist. Moreover, prohibition of testi-

---

56. McDonald v. United States, 114 U.S.App.D.C. 120, 312 F.2d 847 (D.C.Cir. 1962).

The Court stated:

Our eight-year experience under *Durham* suggests a judicial definition, however broad and general, of what is included in the terms "disease" and "defect." In *Durham*, rather than define either term we simply sought to distinguish disease from defect. Our purpose now is to make it very clear that neither the court nor the jury is bound by ad hoc definitions or conclusions as to what experts state is a disease or defect. What psychiatrists may consider a "mental disease or defect" for clinical purposes, where their concern is treatment, may or may not be the same as mental disease or defect for the jury's purpose in determining criminal responsibility. Consequently, for that purpose the jury should

be told that a mental disease or defect includes any abnormal condition of the mind which substantially affects mental or emotional processes and substantially impairs behavior controls. Thus the jury would consider testimony concerning the development, adaptation and functioning of these processes and controls.

We emphasize that, since the question of whether the defendant has a disease or defect is ultimately for the triers of fact, obviously its resolution cannot be controlled by expert opinion. The jury must determine for itself, from all the testimony, lay and expert, whether the nature and degree of the disability are sufficient to establish a mental disease or defect as we have now defined those terms. What we have said, however, should in no way be construed to limit the latitude of expert testimony. Id. at 850–51.

mony about "mental disease or defect" would not be a panacea. Other words and other concepts may similarly be transformed into labels. For example, in *McDonald* we spoke about "abnormal" conditions of the mind, about impairment of mental and emotional processes, and about control mechanisms. The transcript of this trial illustrates how easily these concepts can become slogans, hiding facts and representing nothing more than the witness's own conclusion about the defendant's criminal responsibility.

At least for now, rather than prohibit testimony on "mental disease or defect," we shall try to help the psychiatrists understand their role in court, and thus eliminate a fundamental cause of unsatisfactory expert testimony. A copy of the explanatory instruction to psychiatrists which we have set out in the Appendix should accompany all orders requiring mental examinations so that the psychiatrists will be advised of the kind of information they are expected to provide. To ensure that counsel and the jury are also so advised, the trial judge should give the explanatory instruction in open court to the first psychiatric witness immediately after he is qualified as an expert. It need not be repeated to later witnesses. * * *

* * *

APPENDIX

Court's Instruction to Expert Witness in Cases Involving the "Insanity Defense."

Dr. _____ , this instruction is being given to you in advance of your testimony as an expert witness, in order to avoid confusion or misunderstanding. The instruction is not only for your guidance, but also for the guidance of counsel and the jury.

Because you have qualified as an expert witness your testimony is governed by special rules. Under ordinary rules, witnesses are allowed to testify about what they have seen and heard, but are not always allowed to express opinions and conclusions based on these observations. Due to your training and experience, you are allowed to draw conclusions and give opinions in the area of your special qualifications. However, you may not state conclusions or opinions as an expert unless you also tell the jury what investigations, observations, reasoning and medical theory led to your opinion.

As an expert witness, you may, if you wish and if you feel you can, give your opinion about whether the defendant suffered from a mental disease or defect. You may then explain how defendant's disease or defect relates to his alleged offense, that is, how the development, adaptation and functioning of defendant's behavioral processes may have influenced his conduct. This explanation should be so complete that the jury will have a basis for an informed judgment on whether the alleged crime was a "product" of his mental disease or defect. But it will not be necessary for you to express an opinion on whether the alleged crime was a "product" of a mental disease or defect and you will not be asked to do so.

It must be emphasized that you are to give your expert diagnosis of the defendant's mental condition. This word of caution is especially important if you give an opinion as to whether or not the defendant suffered from a "mental disease or defect" because the clinical diagnostic meaning of this term may be different from its legal meaning. You should not be concerned with its legal meaning. Neither should you consider whether you think this defendant should be found guilty or responsible for the alleged crime. These are questions for the court and jury. Further, there are considerations which may be relevant in other proceedings or in other contexts which are not relevant here; for example, how the defendant's condition might change, or whether he needs treatment, or is treatable, or dangerous, or whether there are adequate hospital facilities, or whether commitment would be best for him, or best for society. What is desired in this case is the kind of opinion you would give to a family which brought one of its members to your clinic and asked for your diagnosis of his mental condition and a description of how his condition would be likely to influence his conduct. Insofar as counsel's questions permit, you should testify in this manner.

When you are asked questions which fall within the scope of your special training and experience, you may answer them if you feel competent to do so; otherwise you should not answer them. If the answer depends upon knowledge and experience generally possessed by ordinary citizens, for example questions of morality as distinguished from medical knowledge, you should not answer. You should try to separate expert medical judgments from what we may call "lay judgments." If you cannot make a separation and if you do answer the question nonetheless, you should state clearly that your answer is not based solely upon your special knowledge. It would be misleading for the jury to think that your testimony is based on your special knowledge concerning the nature and diagnosis of mental conditions if in fact it is not.[57]

———————

Are you satisfied with the rationality of the court's distinction between testimony that an act is a product of a disease and testimony that the defendant is suffering from a mental disease or defect? Do psychiatrists have less to offer the jury on one issue than on the other? Do you think instructions like those prepared by the court for psychiatrists should be prepared for experts in all areas?

In 1972 a new test, that of the American Law Institute (ALI), was adopted by the D.C. Circuit in United States v. Brawner.[58] Referring to the problem of presenting the jury with all relevant evidence, the Court stated:

A principal reason for our decision to depart from the *Durham* rule is the undesirable characteristic, surviving even the *McDonald* modification, of undue dominance by the experts giving testimony. * * * The difficulty is rooted in the circumstance that there is no generally accepted understanding, either in the jury or the community it represents, of the concept requiring that the crime be the "product" of the mental disease.

When the court used the term "product" in *Durham* it likely assumed that this was a serviceable, and indeed a natural, term for a rule defining criminal responsibility—a legal reciprocal, as it

———————

57. Washington v. United States, 129 U.S.App.D.C. 29, 390 F.2d 444, 454–58 (1967).

58. 153 U.S.App.D.C. 1, 471 F.2d 969 (1972). The ALI test found in § 4.01(1) of the Model Penal Code is, "A person is not responsible for criminal conduct if at the time of such conduct as a result of mental disease or defect he lacks substantial capacity either to appreciate the criminality [wrongfulness] of his conduct or to conform his conduct to the requirements of the law." There is also a "caveat paragraph" which the Brawner court adopted "as a rule for application by the judge, to avoid miscarriage of justice, but not for inclusion in instructions to the jury" 471 F.2d at 994. This paragraph, 4.01(2) provides, " * * * the terms mental disease or defect do not include an abnormality manifested only by repeated criminal or otherwise anti-social conduct." The definition of "mental disease or defect" found in McDonald v. United States, set forth in note 56 supra, was retained as part of the ALI test.

were, for the familiar term "proximate cause," used to define civil responsibility. But if concepts like "product" are, upon refinement, reasonably understood, or at least appreciated, by judges and lawyers, and perhaps philosophers, difficulties developed when it emerged that the "product" concept did not signify a reasonably identifiable common ground that was also shared by the non-legal experts, and the laymen serving on the jury as the representatives of the community.

The doctrine of criminal responsibility is such that there can be no doubt "of the complicated nature of the decision to be made—intertwining moral, legal, and medical judgments." * * * The "moral" elements of the decision are not defined exclusively by religious considerations but by the totality of underlying conceptions of ethics and justice shared by the community, as expressed by its jury surrogate. The essential feature of a jury "lies in the interposition between the accused and his accuser of the commonsense judgment of a group of laymen, and in the community participation and shared responsibility that results from that group's determination of guilt or innocence."

The expert witnesses—psychiatrists and psychologists—are called to adduce relevant information concerning what may for convenience be referred to as the "medical" component of the responsibility issue. But the difficulty—as emphasized in *Washington*—is that the medical expert comes, by testimony given in terms of a non-medical construct ("product"), to express conclusions that in essence embody ethical and legal conclusions. There is, indeed, irony in a situation under which the *Durham* rule, which was adopted in large part to permit experts to testify in their own terms concerning matters within their domain

which the jury should know, resulted in testimony by the experts in terms not their own to reflect unexpressed judgments in a domain that is properly not theirs but the jury's. The irony is heightened when the jurymen, instructed under the esoteric "product" standard, are influenced significantly by "product" testimony of expert witnesses really reflecting ethical and legal judgments rather than a conclusion within the witnesses' particular expertise.

It is easier to identify and spotlight the irony than to eradicate the mischief. The objective of *Durham* is still sound—to put before the jury the information that is within the expert's domain to aid the jury in making a broad and comprehensive judgment. But when the instructions and appellate decisions define the "product" inquiry as the ultimate issue, it is like stopping the tides to try to halt the emergence of this term in the language of those with a central role in the trial—the lawyers who naturally seek to present testimony that will influence the jury who will be charged under the ultimate "product" standard, and the expert witnesses who have an awareness, gained from forensic psychiatry and related disciplines, of the ultimate "product" standard that dominates the proceeding.

The experts have meaningful information to impart, not only on the existence of mental illness or not, but also on its relationship to the incident charged as an offense. In the interest of justice this valued information should be available, and should not be lost or blocked by requirements that unnaturally restrict communication between the experts and the jury. The more we have pondered the problem the more convinced we have become that the sound solution lies not in further shaping of the *Durham* "product" approach in more refined molds, but in adopting the ALI's formulation as the linchpin of our jurisprudence.

Our adoption of the ALI rule does not depart from the doctrines this court has built up over the past twenty years to assure a broad presentation to the jury concerning the condition of defendant's mind and its consequences. Thus we adhere to our rulings admitting expert testimony of psychologists, as well as psychiatrists, and to our many decisions contemplating that expert testimony on this subject will be accompanied by presentation of the facts and premises underlying the opinions and conclusions of the experts, and that the Government and defense may present, in Judge Blackmun's words, "all possibly relevant evidence" bearing on cognition, volition and capacity. We agree with the amicus submission of the National District Attorneys Association that the law cannot "distinguish between physiological, emotional, social and cultural sources of the impairment"—assuming, of course, requisite testimony establishing exculpation under the pertinent standard—and all such causes may be both referred to by the expert and considered by the trier of fact.

Breadth of input under the insanity defense is not to be confused with breadth of the doctrines establishing the defense. As the National District Attorneys Association brief points out, the latitude for salient evidence of e.g., social and cultural factors pertinent to an abnormal condition of the mind significantly affecting capacity and controls, does not mean that such factors may be taken as establishing a separate defense for persons whose mental condition is such that blame can be imposed. We have rejected a broad "injustice" approach that would have opened the door to expositions of e.g., cultural deprivation, unrelated to any abnormal condition of the mind.

We have recognized that "Many criminologists point out that even normal human behavior is influenced by such factors as training, environment, poverty and the like, which may limit the understanding and options of the individual." Determinists may contend that every man's fate is ultimately sealed by his genes and environment, over which he has no control. Our jurisprudence, however, while not oblivious to deterministic components, ultimately rests on a premise of freedom of will. This is not to be viewed as an exercise in philosophic discourse, but as a governmental fusion of ethics and necessity, which takes into account that a system of rewards and punishments is itself part of the environment that influences and shapes human conduct. Our recognition of an insanity defense for those who lack the essential, threshold free will possessed by those in the normal range is not to be twisted, directly or indirectly, into a device for exculpation of those without an abnormal condition of the mind.

Finally, we have not accepted suggestions to adopt a rule that disentangles the insanity defense from a medical model, and announces a standard exculpating anyone whose capacity for control is insubstantial, for whatever cause or reason. There may be logic in these submissions, but we are not sufficiently certain of the nature, range and implications of the conduct involved to attempt an all-embracing unified field theory. The applicable rule can be discerned as the cases arise in regard to other conditions—somnambulism or other automatism; blackouts due, e.g. to overdose of insulin; drug addiction. Whether these somatic conditions should be governed by a rule comparable to that herein set forth for mental disease would require, at a minimum, a judicial determination, which takes medical opinion into account, finding convincing evidence of an ascertainable condition characterized by "a broad consensus that free will does not exist."

* * *

The goal of avoiding undue dominance of the jury by expert testimony does not require ostrich disregard of the key issue of causality. That issue, however, is focused more meaningfully, for both expert and jury, by asking whether the mental disease or defect resulted in lack of substantial capacity to control the behavior in question (or appreciate its wrongfulness). The question is differently put under *Durham* and the difference has proved to be both confusing and significant. The issue today is not whether this confusion could or should have been foreseen, but whether it shall be corrected. The rule contemplating expert testimony as to the existence and consequence of a mental disease or defect is not to be construed as permission to testify solely in terms of expert conclusions. Our jurisprudence to the contrary is not undone, it is rather underscored. It is the responsibility of all concerned—expert, counsel and judge—to see to it that the jury in an insanity case is informed of the expert's underlying reasons and approach, and is not confronted with ultimate opinions on a take-it-or-leave-it basis. * * *

The Appendix to *Washington* still stands in effect, although we do not retain *Washington* insofar as it reflects the product rule, and we permit testimony by the expert, and cross-examination, on the causal relationship between the mental disease and the existence of substantial capacity for control (and knowledge) at the time of the act. The jury will consider this testimony under the instruction on need to acquit if as a result of mental disease or defect there is a lack of substantial capacity to control the behavior in question (or appreciate its wrongfulness). We think this sufficiently communicates to the jury the kind of hard question it is called upon to decide, and the instructions will make clear that the jury is not foreclosed by opinions of experts. The experts add to perspective, without governing decision. The law looks to the experts for input, and to the jury for outcome.[59]

* * *

[In a separate opinion, concurring in part and dissenting in part, Judge Bazelon joined the majority in repudiating the *Durham* test. But he could not agree that the adoption of the ALI test solved the problems of *Durham*:]

* * *

Durham was designed to throw open the windows of the defense and ventilate a musty doctrine with all of the information acquired during a century's

---

59. 153 U.S.App.D.C. 1, 471 F.2d 969, at 981–83, 994–95, 1006 (1972). Four years later, The District of Columbia Court of Appeals was asked to follow Brawner in criminal cases tried in the District's local courts. The court traced the problems that the District of Columbia Circuit had encountered over the years, but ultimately followed *Brawner* and adopted the ALI test in substantial part. Bethea v. United States, 365 A.2d 64 (D.C.App. 1976), certiorari denied, 433 U.S. 911 (1977). The court rejected any form instruction for experts and suggested that "the witnesses should be free to testify directly in an unrestricted manner concerning all relevant matters to which their competence extends, including their conclusions as to the existence of a mental impairment and its relationship to the condemned behavior." Id. at 82. The court emphasized, however, that the trial judge could control the testimony provided by experts and endorsed jury instructions that explain to jurors their role in deciding an insanity question. California also adopted the ALI test, abandoning 100 years of exclusive reliance on *M'Naghten*. People v. Drew, 22 Cal. 3d 333, 149 Cal.Rptr. 275, 583 P.2d 1318 (1978). Ironically, one justification for the court's decision in *Drew* is that it provides more flexibility for experts asked to provide juries with opinions.

study of the intricacies of human behavior. It fueled a long and instructive debate which uncovered a vast range of perplexing and previously hidden questions. And the decision helped to move the question of responsibility from the realm of esoterica into the forefront of the critical issues of the criminal law.

* * *

Plainly, we did not fail for want of trying. *Durham* reformulated the responsibility test in the hope that new and more useful information would be presented to the jury. We acted largely in response to the plea of behavioral scientists that they did not want to decide ultimate questions of law and morality, but wanted only an opportunity to report their findings as scientific investigators without the need to force those findings through the prism of M'Naghten. * * * By removing the obstacles to the presentation of those findings, *Durham* challenged the experts to provide the information they had long promised. We expected, perhaps naively, that the presentation of this new information would permit—indeed, require—the jury to undertake a much broader inquiry and to rely less on the ultimate conclusions of the experts. But it quickly became apparent that while our decision produced some expansion of the inquiry, it did not do nearly enough to eliminate the experts' stranglehold on the process. Even after *Durham* counsel for both sides often sought to present the issue to the jury in "simplified" form by eliciting from the experts little more than conclusory yes-or-no answers to the questions, "Was the accused suffering from a mental disease or defect?" "Was his act the product of that disease or defect?" And so the experts continued, on the whole, to speak in conclusory terms which inevitably included but concealed their underlying value judgments, and their own views as

to the appropriate legal outcome. The use of conclusory psychiatric labels often provided an aura of certainty which made it difficult to discern the inadequacies of the examination on which the expert testimony was based, and the limitations of psychiatric knowledge generally.
* * *

* * *

The Court today asserts that it has rejected "suggestions to adopt a rule that disentangles the insanity defense from a medical model," and adds that a successful responsibility defense must be predicated on the existence of an "ascertainable condition characterized by 'a broad consensus that free will does not exist.'" I fear that counsel, the experts, and the trial courts will view that requirement as a delegation of sweeping new authority to the medical experts.

Of course, the Court does point out that a defendant can make a broad presentation to the jury, offering all of the evidence, even if not strictly medical, which is pertinent to an abnormal condition of the mind. But that broad presentation is already guaranteed by the traditional rules of evidence. The real impact of the Court's decision is to establish a barrier which will prevent some defendants from taking any evidence at all to the jury on the issue of responsibility. The power to open and close that barrier is effectively delegated to the psychiatric experts.

We can only speculate on the impact of this requirement, but it seems likely to produce very substantial distortions of the process. First, it focuses attention on an entirely irrelevant issue. If a defendant is prepared to present evidence that his mental or emotional processes and behavior controls were in fact impaired, it is not clear why anything should turn on the experts' view of his condition in the abstract.

Second, the requirement obliges the defendant to make a vastly greater showing to have the issue of responsibility submitted to the jury than to have any other issue submitted. We held many years ago that "sanity is an 'essential' issue which, if actually litigated—that is, if 'some proof is adduced' tending to support the defense—must be submitted to the jury under the guidance of instructions." Conceding "that any attempt to formulate a quantitative measure of the amount of evidence necessary to raise an issue can produce no more than an illusory definiteness," we pointed out that "so long as there was *some evidence relevant to the issue* * * * the credibility and force of such evidence must be for the jury, and cannot be [a] matter of law for the decision of the court." As I read the Court's opinion, a defendant who can introduce "some evidence" that his capacity to control his behavior was in fact impaired cannot take the responsibility issue to the jury unless he can also offer, should the question be put in issue, "convincing evidence" that he is suffering from a medically-recognized condition characterized by a broad consensus that free will does not exist.

Still, the greatest difficulty is not that the requirement shifts attention onto an extraneous issue or that it imposes an unwarranted obstacle to the presentation of an affirmative defense. Those difficulties could be tolerated if the requirement of a "broad consensus that free will does not exist" reflected the Court's effort to achieve some important purpose of the responsibility defense. At no point in its opinion does the Court explain why the boundary of a legal concept—criminal responsibility—should be marked by medical concepts, especially when the validity of the "medical model" is seriously questioned by some eminent psychiatrists. Nor does the Court explain what it means by "convincing evidence" of the existence of a "broad consensus." If five psychiatrists are prepared to assert that a particular condition *does* tend to impair free will, how many psychiatrists must be willing to testify that it *does not* have such an effect before we can preclude a responsibility defense on the ground that there is no "broad consensus" that the defendant's condition tends to impair free will? How many psychiatrists must be convinced that a particular condition is "medical" in nature before a defendant will be permitted, within the confines of the "medical model," to predicate a responsibility defense on such a condition?[60]

* * *

———

Clearly the debate in *Brawner* between Judge Bazelon and the majority recognizes the defects of psychiatric evidence. Much of the struggle for an appropriate test is an effort to control the experts. Yet few propose that expert testimony be banned, or that the general accuracy of psychiatric judgments be proved before any specific psychiatric evaluations are accepted.[61]

60. Id. at 1010–11, 1028–29.

61. Recently, a few commentators have seriously questioned the extent of psychiatric expertise and the appropriateness of at least some uses of psychiatrists as courtroom experts. A recent task force report of the American Psychiatric Association acknowledged that psychiatric expertise does not enable a person to predict with any accuracy the future dangerousness of a given individual: "Neither psychiatrists nor anyone else have reliably demonstrated an ability to predict future violence or 'dangerousness.' Neither has any special psychiatric 'expertise' in this area been established." American Psychiatric Association Task Force Report No. 8: Clinical Aspects of the Violent Individual 28 (July 1974). Yet dangerousness to self or others is often the crucial issue in involuntary commitment hearings. In an article generally

What explains the welcome the law extends to psychiatric experts? Is it that the legal standard for insanity embraces a technical or scientific concept? Is there a difference between offering a psychiatrist to testify about the general mental health of a defendant in order to demonstrate that the defendant is more likely than most individuals (or less likely) to commit a particular act, such as homicide, and offering a psychiatrist to testify that the defendant is or is not mentally responsible for his actions?[62]

Do you believe that insanity today is a concept misunderstood by laypersons, one which can only be appreciated with expert help? If so, do you subscribe to the following portion of the model instruction provided in Appendix B to *Brawner?*

There was also testimony of lay witnesses, with respect to their observa-

---

critical of psychiatric testimony, Ennis, a lawyer, and Litwack, a lawyer and psychologist, cite studies indicating that psychiatrists accurately predict dangerousness less than fifty percent of the time. Psychiatry and the Presumption of Expertise: Flipping Coins in the Courtroom, 62 Calif.L.R. 693, 711–16 (1974). Ennis and Litwack argue, "It is inconceivable that a judgment could be considered an 'expert' judgment when it is less accurate than the flip of a coin. Accordingly, psychiatrists should not be permitted to testify as expert witnesses until they can prove through empirical studies that their judgments are reliable and valid." Id. at 737–38.

Another problem with psychiatric evidence is that psychiatrists vary widely both in the diagnostic labels they assign to various groups of symptoms and in their perceptions of given symptoms in particular individuals. Because there is no general agreement on diagnoses and because judges and jurors are likely to be overwhelmed by psychiatric jargon, Ennis and Litwack suggest that, at least as to civil commitment hearings, psychiatrists' "testimony be limited to descriptive statements which would exclude diagnoses, opinions, and predictions." Id. at 742. This would arguably increase the factfinder's ability to assess conflicting testimony, and, by decreasing the experts' role in deciding ultimate issues, would reduce the likelihood that the verdicts of judges and juries will merely "rubber stamp" those reached by psychiatrists.

A few critics express even greater skepticism about psychiatric expertise. Rosenhan argues that psychiatric diagnoses are largely contextual. He cites his own research in which sane individuals voluntarily committed themselves to various mental hospitals, claiming they heard voices which said "thud," "empty," and "hollow." Once admitted, the pseudopatients tried to act normally, yet none were detected as sane by any of the hospital staffs (although a few genuine patients suspected that the experimenters were not mentally ill). Rosenhan, On Being Sane in Insane Places, 13 Santa Clara Lawyer 379 (1973).

Thomas Szasz maintains that there is no such thing as mental illness (as differentiated from brain disease) and that so-called mental illness is really a label attached to those who find it difficult to cope with the problems of everyday life. He feels that psychiatry serves a function in helping people deal with (or avoid) the stresses of life, but that psychiatry should not usurp the function of determining moral (or legal) responsibility by disguising sociopsychological problems of living as diseases. The Myth of Mental Illness in T. Szasz, Ideology and Insanity 12 (1970).

For an optimistic view of the assistance that psychiatrists and mental health professionals who understand what help courts want and need can offer, see Bonnie & Slobogin, The Role of Mental Health Professionals in the Criminal Process: The Case for Informed Speculation, 66 Va.L. Rev. 427 (1980).

The acquittal in 1982 of John Hinckley, who was charged with attempting to assassinate the President, caused some legislators to question the way insanity defenses are now tried. See Kiernan, Family Pledges No Try for Early Release, Wash. Post, June 23, 1982 at A1. Some reports indicate that the judge's charge was particularly important to the jury in the Hinckley case. See Pianin, Experts Believe Judge's Charge Swayed Jurors, Wash. Post, June 23, 1982, at A10. See also Robinson, The Hinckley Decision: Psychiatry in Court, Wall St. J., June 23, 1982, at 26.

62. See generally Korn, Law, Fact and Science in the Courts, 66 Colum.L.Rev. 1080, 1095–97 (1966).

tions of defendant's appearance, behavior, speech, and actions. Such persons are permitted to testify as to their own observations and other facts known to them and may express an opinion based upon those observations and facts known to them. In weighing the testimony of such lay witnesses, you may consider the circumstances of each witness, his opportunity to observe the defendant and to know the facts to which he has testified, his willingness and capacity to expound freely as to his observations and knowledge, the basis for his opinion and conclusions and the nearness or remoteness of his observations of the defendant in point of time to the commission of the offense charged.

You may also consider whether the witness observed extraordinary or bizarre acts performed by the defendant, or whether the witness observed the defendant's conduct to be free of such extraordinary or bizarre acts. In evaluating such testimony, you should take into account the extent of the witness's observation of the defendant and the nature and length of time of the witness's contact with the defendant. You should bear in mind that an untrained person may not be readily able to detect mental disease [or defect] and that the failure of a lay witness to observe abnormal acts by the defendant may be significant only if the witness had prolonged and intimate contact with the defendant.

You are not bound by the opinions of either expert or lay witnesses. You should not arbitrarily or capriciously reject the testimony of any witness, but you should consider the testimony of each witness in connection with the other evidence in the case and give it such weight as you believe it is fairly entitled to receive.[63]

Could a system allowing an insanity defense work if it rejected expert testimony and required the parties to provide the jury with the raw data necessary for a decision on the insanity claim? How might this be done? If a need for expert evidence is inherent in the insanity defense, may the jury reject expert testimony uncontradicted by similar evidence? Does this depend on which side offers the expert? How is the need for expert testimony on the insanity issue affected by reports of the defendant's actions introduced by ordinary witnesses?

Consider the following procedure which Judge Bazelon favored in *Brawner*. Do you prefer it to the majority's test? What role would experts play if this test prevailed?

Our instruction to the jury should provide that a defendant is not responsible *if at the time of his unlawful conduct his mental or emotional processes or behavior controls were impaired to such an extent that he cannot justly be held responsible for his act.* This test would ask the psychiatrist a single question: what is the nature of the impairment of the defendant's mental and emotional processes and behavior controls? It would leave for the jury the question whether that impairment is sufficient to relieve the defendant of responsibility for the particular act charged.

The purpose of this proposed instruction is to focus the jury's attention on the legal and moral aspects of criminal responsibility, and to make clear why the determination of responsibility is entrusted to the jury and not the expert witnesses. That, plainly, is not to say that the jury should be cast adrift to acquit or convict the defendant according to caprice. The jury would not be instructed to find a defendant responsible if that seems just, and to find him not

---

63. United States v. Brawner, 153 U.S.
App.D.C. 1, 471 F.2d 969, 1009 (1972).

responsible if that seems just. On the contrary, the instruction would incorporate the very requirements—impairment of mental or emotional processes and behavior controls—that *McDonald* established as prerequisites of the responsibility defense.

The proposed instruction has the additional advantage of avoiding any explicit reference to "mental disease" or "abnormal condition of the mind." As used in our prior tests, these terms were never intended to exclude disabilities that originate in diseases of the body, but simply reflect the fact that the defense of non-responsibility has traditionally been associated with mental illness, or in the language of an earlier day, "insanity." [64]

Do you believe that jurors can properly evaluate psychiatric testimony stating conclusions or involving complex diagnoses and detailed opinions? Do you believe that lay jurors are aided by psychiatric testimony when expert opinions conflict? How, if at all, may a lawyer on cross-examination assist the jury in coping with technical psychiatric testimony? Is the cross-examiner's goal to help the jury cope? Reconsider the two transcript cases. Would you, as a juror, have felt comfortable relying upon the psychiatric evidence offered in those cases? How does thinking about the evidentiary aspects of proving insanity affect your attitude toward the substantive defense?

Problem X–12. **Which of the following offers of psychiatric evidence do you think a court should be willing to accept? Which do you think a court should be unwilling to accept? Why?**

1. In a rape case, psychiatric testimony that the alleged victim was a nymphomaniac, where the opinion is based on the psychiatrist's observations while sitting in the courtroom during the testimony of the victim.

2. Psychiatric testimony, based on an in-depth interview, that at the time a husband shot his wife the condition of the husband's mind was such that he was more likely than the average person to respond to a certain kind of provocation and to kill in the heat of passion.

3. Evidence that a defendant possessed XYY chromosomes; that the normal human cell has 22 pairs of autosomal chromosomes (each pair having an X and a Y) plus two more chromosomes which are either X or Y; that XX is female and XY is male; and that if an extra Y chromosome is present in a male, some theorists predict anti-social behavior, although it is difficult to obtain proof to support or negate the theory because of an inadequate sample of people with XYY chromosomes in the general population.

4. Psychiatric testimony based upon interviews with those who knew that a homicide victim possessed aggressive tendencies and was far more likely than the average person to react violently to situations of stress. The testimony is offered by the defendant who claims to have killed in self-defense.

5. Psychiatric testimony based upon the results of a court ordered psychiatric examination that the victim of a crime is suffering from a mental disease or defect that casts doubt on the veracity of his testimony.

64. Id. at 1032.

6. Psychiatric testimony based upon facts reported by witnesses with firsthand knowledge offered to prove the incompetency of a decedent to make a will.

7. On the same issue as in number six, testimony to the same effect based on the observations of the decedent's personal psychotherapist.

Problem X–13. Stan Tucker is accused of murder. He admits killing the victim but pleads not guilty by reason of insanity. He introduces three psychiatrists who have examined him with the aid of numerous diagnostic tests and extensive interviews. They testify that he is a psychotic and that he has been suffering from psychotic episodes since his return from Vietnam seven years before the killing. They testify that at the time of the killing he was deluded, that he did not know right from wrong, and that he could not have resisted the impulse to kill. The prosecution counters the psychiatrists' testimony with the testimony of Tucker's former wife, who had been married to him for ten years and who had lived with him until a week before the killing. She testifies that Tucker's behavior did not change at all following his year of service in Vietnam, that he always seemed normal to her, and that he was a very moral man with a firm sense of right and wrong. Indeed, she testifies that she finally decided to get a divorce because he thought it was immoral for her to drink, smoke, or play church Bingo. At the end of the spouse's rebuttal testimony the prosecutor rests her case and the defendant moves for a directed verdict, claiming that on the evidence the jury must acquit him by reason of insanity. **How should a court rule?**

B. THE POLYGRAPH (LIE DETECTOR)

The polygraph, or lie detector, which we mentioned in our discussion of the *Frye* case, continues to be controversial. In recent years, the case for admitting polygraph evidence has been forcefully argued. Some judges have been convinced.[65]

Moenssens, Moses, and Inbau describe the operation of the polygraph in their

65. **As one Court noted concerning *Frye*:**

The instrument employed for the detection of deception in *Frye* was a systolic blood pressure device, essentially consisting of a sphygmomanometer, an instrument used by physicians in determining a patient's blood pressure, by means of which periodic discontinuous blood pressure readings were obtained. This was a crude instrument compared to the modern polygraph, which by definition records more than a single parameter such as blood pressure. The machine used in the defendant's examination, a Stoelting polygraph, records changes in five different parameters including blood pressure, pulse rate, respiration rate, diaphragmatic area of the body, and the resistance of the skin to electrical current.

United States v. Zeiger, 350 F.Supp. 685, 686, n. 3 (D.D.C.), reversed 155 U.S.App. D.C. 11, 475 F.2d 1280 (1972). The same court also made the following point:

Part of the holding in *Frye* was phrased in terms of "recognition among physiological and psychological authorities" but the general rule established by the case called for "general acceptance in the particular field in which [the polygraph] belongs." Although polygraphy at one time may have been dependent on physiological and psychological authorities for certification of its reliability, it is no longer appropriate to confine consideration solely to those disciplines. Certainly any individuals who have had experience in the specialized area of the polygraph, whether they are medical doctors, scientists, or polygraph examiners, can contribute to

book Scientific Evidence in Criminal Cases §§ 14.03, 14.06–14.07, at 540–41, 543–45, 549–50 (1973):

§ 14.03   The Instrument

The two principal features of a Polygraph are (a) a pneumatically operated recorder of changes in respiration and (b) a similar recorder of changes in blood pressure and pulse. The records of these two physiological changes are the most valuable of any that are presently obtainable.

There is also a unit for recording what is known as the galvanic skin reflex, or electrodermal response. It is presumably the result of changes in the activity of the sweat pores in a person's hands. An additional unit is available for recording muscular movements and pressures.

Any instrument that consists of only one of the aforementioned units is inadequate for actual case testing.

The body attachments by which respiration, pulse, blood pressure, and galvanic skin reflex recordings are obtained are as follows:

1. A "pneumograph tube", which with the aid of a beaded chain is fastened around the chest or abdomen of the person being tested.

2. A blood pressure cuff, of the type used by physicians, which is fastened around the subject's upper arm.

3. Electrodes, fastened to the hand or fingers, through which an imperceptible amount of electrical current is passed for the purpose of obtaining the galvanic skin reflex.

No body attachments are required for recording body movements and pres-

sures. They are obtained by means of metal bellows or inflated bladders located under the arms, seat, or back of the chair occupied by the subject.

* * *

§ 14.06   Pretest Interview

Before administering a Polygraph examination, a competent examiner will explain to the subject the purpose and nature of the examination and something about the instrument itself. Also during the pretest interview, the examiner will seek to condition the subject for the test by relieving the apprehensions of the truthful subject as well as satisfying the lying subject of the effectiveness of the technique. Another reason for the pretest interview is the opportunity it affords for the formulation of the test questions, particularly the ones which will serve as "controls."

During the pretest interview the examiner must remain completely objective with regard to the subject's truthfulness or deception. Under no circumstance should he indulge in an interrogation at that time. To do so then would seriously impair the validity of the technique, because of the incompatibility of any accusation or insinuation of lying and a subsequent scientific test avowedly designed to determine the very fact of truthfulness or deception. Interrogation is appropriate only *after* the results of the Polygraph examination have indicated deception.

§ 14.07   Test Questions

1.   CONTROL QUESTIONS

Indispensable to a proper Polygraph examination is the development and use of control questions. A control question is unrelated to the matter under in-

the Court's inquiry into the matters of acceptance and reliability. For this reason, testimony by any qualified expert in the field of polygraphy concerning stud-

ies and experiences with the machine is relevant to questions which are before the Court.

350 F.Supp. at 689.

vestigation but is of a similar, though less serious, nature. In all probability, the subject will lie in answering it both before and during the test, or at least his answer will give him some concern with respect to either its truthfulness or its accuracy. For instance, in a burglary case the control question might be: "Have you ever stolen anything?" or, "Since you were 21 years old, have you ever stolen anything?" The recorded physiological response or lack of response to the control question (in respiration, blood pressure-pulse, etc.) is then compared with what appears in the tracings when the subject was asked questions pertaining to the matter under investigation.

2. RELEVANT QUESTIONS

Questions relating to the particular matter under investigation are known as "relevant" questions.

3. IRRELEVANT QUESTIONS

In order to ascertain the subject's "norm" under the test conditions, he is asked several question that have no bearing on the case investigation. These are known as "irrelevant" questions. An example of such a question is one regarding the place where the test is being conducted—for instance, "Are you in Chicago now?".

Prior to the test the subject is told precisely what the questions will be, and he is also assured that no questions will be asked about any other offense or matter than that which has been discussed with him by the examiner. *Surprise has no part in a properly conducted basic test.*

4. CONSTRUCTION AND NUMBER OF QUESTIONS

The following is a list of the kinds and arrangement of questions which are asked during a typical Polygraph test and to which the subject is to answer with a "yes" or a "no". They are based on a hypothetical robbery-murder case in which the victim is John Jones and the suspect is Joe "Red" Blake.

1. Do they call you "Red"? (The pretest interview has disclosed that he is generally called "Red".)

2. Are you over 21 years of age? (Or reference is made to some other age unquestionably but reasonably, and not ridiculously, below that of the subject.)

3. Did you steal John Jones' watch last Saturday night?

4. Are you in Chicago now?

5. Did you shoot John Jones last Saturday night?

6. Besides what you told about, did you ever steal anything else?

7. Did you ever go to school?

8. Were those your footprints near John Jones' body?

9. Do you know who shot John Jones?

10. Did you ever steal anything from a place where you worked?

The time interval between each question is fifteen or twenty seconds.

One such test does not constitute a Polygraph examination. There must be at least three and usually more tests of a similar nature before a diagnosis can be attempted. The entire examination may take approximately one hour.

5. THE DIAGNOSIS

At the risk of oversimplification, it may be said that if the subject responds more to the control questions than to the relevant questions, he is considered to be telling the truth with regard to the matter under investigation. On the other hand, a greater response to the relevant questions is suggestive of deception.

* * *

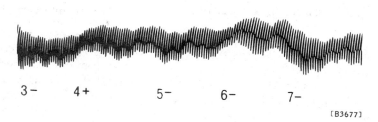

3 −   4 +   5 −   6 −   7 −

[B3677]

Fig. 93. Record of truth-telling embezzlement suspect. Indications of truthfulness in both respiration and blood pressure-pulse.

Questions 3 and 5 pertained to the embezzlement of a large sum of money, 3 being "Do you know who stole the missing money?" and 5 being "Did you steal the missing money?". Questions 4 and 7 were irrelevant. Observe the suppression in respiration and the blood pressure rise at control question 6, when the subject was asked: "Did you ever steal anything?" His answer was a lie, according to the subject's later admission.

On the basis of the above control question test record, the examiner was able to report that the subject was telling the truth about the missing money. The conclusion was later confirmed.

* * *

Effect of Nervousness Upon Diagnosis

One of the most frequently asked questions about the Polygraph Technique is the effect of extreme nervousness. First of all, the pretest interview lessens the apprehension of a truthful, tense or nervous subject. Secondly, a subject whose nervousness persists will reveal that factor by the uniformly irregular nature of his Polygraph tracings; in other words, physiological changes or disturbances induced only by nervousness usually appear on the Polygraph

record without relationship to any particular question or questions. They are usually of no greater magnitude—or, in any event, not consistently so—when relevant questions are asked than when irrelevant or control questions are asked. Finally, and most importantly, the employment of control questions offers great security against a misinterpretation of reactions caused by nervousness.

6. SUPPLEMENTARY "PEAK OF TENSION" TESTS

When a person who is to undergo a Polygraph examination has not been informed of all the important details of the offense under investigation, the examiner can conduct as part of his examination what is known as a "peak of tension" test. It consists of the asking of a series of questions in which only one refers to some detail of the offense, such as the amount of money stolen or the kind of object taken or the implement used to commit the offense—something that would be unknown to the subject unless he himself committed the crime or unless he had been told about it by someone else. For instance, if a suspected thief has not been told about the exact amount of money involved, he may be asked a series of questions which refer to various amounts, one of which will be the actual amount stolen. The theory behind the peak of tension test is that if the person tested is the one who took the money, for instance, he will be apprehensive about the question referring to that amount, whereas an innocent person would not have such a particularized concern.

Before conducting a peak of tension test, the examiner prepares a list of about seven questions, among which, near the middle, is the question pertaining to the actual detail. The list is then read off to the subject, and he is informed that during the test those questions, and no others, will be asked, in that precise order. A truth-telling subject, unaware of the accuracy of any one question, will not ordinarily be concerned about one more than any of the others. On the other hand, a lying subject will have that question in mind as the test is being conducted and, in anticipation of it, he is apt to experience a buildup of tension that will climax at the crucial question—in other words, at that point he will reach a "peak of tension."

————

* * *

One District Court took extensive evidence on the attributes of the polygraph and summarized it as follows:

The Court received testimony from several experts during the course of the hearings verifying the reliability of the polygraph. John E. Reid, one of the leading authorities in the field, testified that in studies he had recently conducted in collaboration with Frank S. Horvath, an accuracy of better than 91 per cent among experienced examiners was found. He also asserted that in the 1966 edition of his text, Truth and Deception, coauthored with Fred E. Inbau, a professor of law at Northwestern University, the authors reversed the position on the admissibility of polygraph evidence which they adopted in an earlier work because of significant advances in the field. In their recent text the authors explain:

The Polygraph technique which we have described, when properly used by competent, experienced examiners, possesses a high degree of accuracy. This we can conscientiously report from our experience in the examinations, personally, or in the supervision of the Polygraph examinations, of over 35,000 subjects.

Lynn P. Marcy, a polygraph examiner with 15 years of experience, testified that of the 30 per cent of the 8,000 examinations which he conducted and which were subjected to verifications through supporting admissions, confessions, or additional evidence, only six known errors were noted. The accuracy of his diagnoses was estimated in excess of 90 per cent.

David C. Raskin, a psychologist who performed research in the areas of psychophysiology, stated that his laboratory studies in simulated field situations showed an agreement among examiners of 95.5 per cent and a rate of correct decisions of almost 82 per cent, which was considered "quite good" for a laboratory situation. He concluded:

I feel strongly that (polygraph technique) is a highly accurate, extremely useful technique for detecting deception.

This is based on my experience both in our laboratory study and experiences we have had based upon live cases * * *.

Martin T. Orne, a respected polygraph authority and a professor of psychiatry and psychology at the University of Pennsylvania, testified for the Government that the true accuracy of the polygraph is not known but that there is agreement in the scientific community that the polygraph works "far better than chance" and that he would place its accuracy at 85 per cent or perhaps higher.

The testimony of the experts and the studies appearing in the exhibits lead the Court to believe that the polygraph is an effective instrument for detecting deception. The failure of the Government to demonstrate significant disagreement with this basic proposition, the absence of statistical data pointing to any other conclusions, and the accepted and widespread absorption of the polygraph into the operations of many government agencies, all confirm the Court's conclusion that the polygraph has been accepted by authorities in the field as being capable of producing highly probative evidence in a court of law when properly used by competent, experienced examiners.[66]

But another federal judge was less sanguine about the use of the polygraph:

A study of the theory and process of the polygraphy examination reveals complexities not present in the fields of fingerprint, handwriting, voiceprint, ballistics and neutron activation analysis, all of which are based on the identity or behavior of physical phenomena. The experts and studies differ as to the capability of the polygraph industry to cope with these complexities, but none would dispute their existence. The distinction is that polygraphy, albeit based on a scientific theory, remains an art with *unusual responsibility* placed on the examiner. The acquainting of the examiner with the subject matter is often a source of improper suggestion, conscious or subconscious. The prepara-

tion of the test and discussion with the examinee of the polygraph procedure furnishes additional opportunity for improper subjective evaluation.

The experts are in accord that the examiner must carefully watch for signs of psychosis, extreme neurosis, psychopathology, drunkenness and drugs, any of which might preclude a successful examination. While the "control" question is a built-in check on the subject's reactability, speculation survives that a portion of the population, sometimes called "pathological liars," can "beat" the machine. Since reactability is a matter of degree, it would appear that the danger of prejudice from subtle, undetected psychological conditions is not imaginary.

The construction of the examination further proliferates controversy. Experts disagree on the effectiveness of an examination which lacks a galvanic component. The formulation of test questions, the pacing, the interspersing of relevant with irrelevant and "control" questions, the making of mechanical adjustments, and the number of charts taken—all add to the responsibility of the examiner. * * *

The subjective nature of the examination extends to the test itself. The failure of a subject to react to a relevant question may be attributable to a yoga-like abstraction of the mind or perhaps even unusually low blood pressure, coupled with control of breathing. Alternatively, the subject may attempt to react artificially to irrelevant questions by hidden muscle contractions or self-infliction of pain, and by artificial con-

---

66. Id. at 689–90. Several clinical studies provide evidence of the reliability of the polygraph, but each is slightly flawed. The most common flaw is the inability to prove that the examination in fact separated truth from falsity. Often the most that can be proved is that subsequent jury verdicts or admissions accord well with the judgments of poly-

graph experts. See Lykken, Guilty Knowledge Test: The Right Way to Use a Lie Detector, Psychology Today 57–60 (March 1975). See also Tarlow, Admissibility of Polygraph Evidence in 1975: An Aid in Determining Credibility in a Perjury-Plagued System, 26 Hast.L.J. 917, 931–34 (1975).

juring of exciting images. At the opposite end of the spectrum, a reaction to a relevant question may be imputable to external physical stimuli or subtle psychological stress factors not necessarily associated with deception.

The proponents of polygraphy stress that a good examiner will exclude subjective factors, carefully note external stimuli, and seek out possible psychological characteristics which impair the effectiveness of the examination. For example, it is the duty of the examiner to ask the examinee to explain his *reactions* to relevant questions. The Court does not gainsay the usefulness of examinations conducted by leading experts in an investigative setting. But even the *experts* admit to varying degrees of error, compounded when one considers the proficiency of less qualified examiners.

The subtleties of physiological and psychological reaction also result in divergence in interpretation of the polygraph charts and the consistency of reaction necessary to reach a definite conclusion. * * * The absence of national standards for the education of polygraph examiners causes still more concern. Even among the schools considered to have adequate programs, the curriculum and admissions standards vary substantially. Despite the efforts of the American Polygraph Association, it is admitted that there exist numerous incompetent examiners. A majority of states have enacted licensing programs; Maryland has no such program. Thus, the admissibility of polygraph examination results would open a pandora's box.

The proponents of admissibility suggest that a jury can properly assess the competence and merit of the testimony of an examiner subjected to cross-examination. This contention is of dubious validity, as a rule. The cross-examination of an expert poses a formidable task; it is the rare attorney who knows as much as the expert. Given the numerous subtleties of interpretation inherent in modern polygraphy and the mysteriousness of the technique to the citizen, the danger of confusion of the jury is great. The jury may be misled, and may give undue weight to the testimony.

The danger level rises geometrically because of the disproportionate influence the polygraph examination evidence inevitably will exercise, both because [it is] germane to credibility on the ultimate finding and because of the consumption of time necessarily involved in examination, cross-examination and battle of experts. The specter of "trial by polygraph" replacing trial by jury is more than a felicitous slogan. The prospect of the admission of polygraph examinations taken by a non-party witness accentuates this troublesome proposition.

It is argued that eyewitness testimony is fallible, yet admitted. But eyewitness testimony is virtually indispensable. In addition, the jury of twelve men is designed to evaluate such testimony based on common sense and ordinary experience. This historic function should not be lightly exposed to drastic revision. Evaluation of the testimony of polygraph experts is indeed beyond the realm of ordinary experience.

It is argued in addition that polygraphy is as reliable as fingerprinting, handwriting, ballistics, neutron activation analysis, medical analysis (bloodtesting, toxicology), and other forms of scientific evidence which courts have admitted. Like polygraphy, the physical sciences often rely on non-physical intellectual models. For example, the theory which underlies neutron activation analysis and bloodtesting involves *conceptual* models which explain and predict observable phenomena. But like fingerprints and handwriting, *these pro-*

cesses are much more susceptible to controlled experimental verification. The Court may take judicial notice that the physical sciences exceed the social sciences, including clinical psychology, in terms of experimental quantification and verifiability. Indeed, the uniqueness of the human psyche still provokes debate as to whether the study of human behavior can approach scientific standards as understood in the physical disciplines. The fundamentally psychological component of the examination, the subjectivity of interpretation, and the incipient stage of experimental research, preclude the finding of a *particular* degree of probability of accuracy of a polygraph examination. Thus, it is impossible at this time to assess the substantiality of the degree of error in the polygraph process. This is not to deny absolutely the probative value of the technique, but to underline the analytical difficulties which remain unsolved.

It is finally argued that psychiatric testimony is admissible on important issues, such as the criminal defense of insanity. Judicial experience with psychiatric testimony has been less than satisfactory, reflected in the various attempts to reformulate the insanity defense and reform laws relating to civil commitment. Granting however, that such testimony is admissible, it is *indispensable* to the resolution of the particular legal issues. Such is not the case with polygraphy. It is also noteworthy that the educational prerequisites for a

degree in psychiatry are uniformly higher than for completion of training in polygraphy.[67]

———

These criticisms of the polygraph warrant analysis. First, the suggestion is made that the test may not be accurate when a pathological liar, a yoga-devotee, or one bent on beating the machine is being examined. Yet research suggests that psychopathic liars are easily detectable, that one cannot use yoga techniques to avoid detection, and that the greater the desire to beat the machine the more accurate the test results.[68] The research, however, is not conclusive, and there is a dispute as to whether one can affect results by focusing on exciting images.[69] But no one has claimed that lie detectors are perfect, only that they possess a high degree of accuracy.

Second, there is concern that different polygraph examiners will interpret results differently. Yet the evidence shows a high degree of uniformity in the interpretation of skilled examiners.[70]

Third, the heavy reliance on the ability of the examiner, is a drawback. It has been noted that:

Because the Polygraph Technique involves a diagnostic procedure rather than a mere mechanical operation, a prime requisite to its effectiveness and reliability is examiner competence. An examiner must be a person of intelligence, with a good educational background—

67. United States v. Wilson, 361 F.Supp. 510, 512–514 (D.Md.1973).

68. See, e.g., Tarlow, supra note 66, at 965; Lykken, The Validity of the Guilty Knowledge Technique: The Effect of Faking, 44 J. Applied Psych. 258 (1960); Gustafson & Orne, Effects of Heightened Motivation on the Detection of Deception, 47 J. Applied Psych. 408 (1963).

69. See Tarlow, supra note 66, at 964.

70. Id. at 960–61. However, what is, as we write, the most recent systematic research casts doubt on these propositions. Kleinmutz and Szucko presented six professional polygraph examiners with the charts of 100 subjects, half of whom had confessed to a theft, and half of whom had been cleared by another's confession. Agreement among examiners was low and the six examiners classified an average of 37% of the innocent subjects as guilty. Kleinmetz and Szucko, On the Fallibility of Lie Detection, 17 Law & Society Review (in press, 1982).

preferably a college degree. And since he will be dealing with persons in delicate situations, he must also possess suitable personality characteristics, which might be categorized as the ability "to get along" well with others and to be persuasive in his dealings with them.

The training must have been received on an internship basis under the guidance of a competent, experienced examiner who has a sufficient volume of actual cases to permit the trainee to make frequent observations of Polygraph examinations and to conduct his own examinations under the instructor's personal supervision. Along with this the trainee should have read, and received instruction in, the pertinent phases of psychology and physiology. Attention must also have been given to the detailed study and analysis of a considerable number of Polygraph test records in actual cases in which the true facts of truthfulness or deception were later established by independent evidence. The time required for this individualized training is approximately six months.[71]

———————

Not many examiners have these qualifications. But does this mean no polygraph evidence should be admitted? Should courts exclude testimony from qualified examiners because many examiners are not qualified? Expert testimony in other fields is not conditioned on the absence of quacks and incompetents. One judge has suggested the following solution:

* * * Although the profession of polygraph experts is becoming standardized and professionalized, it has not yet developed adequate ways and means to police itself. Although the profession has adopted a code of ethics and

machinery exists in the professional organization to discipline the unqualified and unethical, the chance of serious impropriety on the part of polygraph examiners must be considered. Further controls over the admissibility of evidence are needed. In this case it is not sufficient for a person to testify that he has the minimum qualifications of an expert and thus be allowed to testify. The chance of fraud or mistake coupled with the great weight the opinions may have with the jury have given Courts pause in connection with the use of the test, and were there not other ways to provide balance and a check on the evidence, this Court would have serious doubts about whether the evidence should be admitted. Of course a stipulation of the parties should provide a way. But in these matters, in the absence of a rule permitting use otherwise, parties are not likely to agree.

The hurdle can be overcome, however, by the use of the Court's power to appoint experts. Federal Rules of Criminal Procedure, Rule 28; Proposed Rules of Evidence for U. S. District Courts, Rule 706. Because it may not be easy for the Court to determine the quality of the polygraph experts tendered by the defendant, it seems proper in such cases to cause polygraph experts of the Court's own choosing to be appointed who should be directed to test the defendant. The purpose of such test will be to provide an independent check on the opinion of the defendant's expert and to make certain that the subject is testable. In the event that the expert concludes positively that the subject is or is not telling the truth, the expert of the defendant and the expert of the Court may be produced and give testimony. In such a case, the Court's experts and the defendant's experts both agree that the sub-

———————

71. A. Moenssens, R. Moses, F. Inbau, Scientific Evidence in Criminal Cases ¶ 14.04, at 541 (1973).

ject is a person who can be tested appropriately and the testimony of each should be admitted, even though it might disagree on the ultimate issue. If, on the other hand, the Court's expert believes that it cannot be determined whether or not the subject is telling the truth, the opinion of both experts should be rejected. This result could be caused by the defendant's failure to cooperate with the Court's appointed expert or because the defendant is not a person who can be tested. In either event, doubt is cast upon the validity of the testimony offered by the defendant, and it should be rejected.

The use of the Court appointed expert, whether or not he agrees with the expert tendered by the defendant, is a practical solution to the problem presented by the fact that only minimal standards exist for polygraph experts. It will in most cases permit the jury to hear the evidence.[72]

———

Finally, there are the related arguments that if polygraphs are recognized at trial, trials will become trial by machine rather than by jury, and that because the polygraph is not necessary for fair trials it should not be used. One judge has responded to the first argument this way:

The trial process very likely will be substantially affected in a number of respects by the use of polygraph opinion in Courts.

It seems likely that fewer cases will reach trial once the use of the polygraph is fully developed by the prosecution and the defense. The validity of polygraph opinions is clearly established and when a method has been developed to assure the check on the defendant's clearance by the examiners, it

is likely that more cases will be dismissed. In the same way when procedures have been opened to permit government use of the polygraph opinion under the checks suggested herein, it appears that the probability of pleas will be increased. In either case, the result is likely to be a benefit both to the innocent and society and will eliminate many cases from the Courts.

The argument that the jury will be displaced by a machine or by a polygraph examiner lacks merit. The jury will make the final determination of guilt or innocence. In this connection it is important to understand how different juries are today than they were when the restrictive rules of evidence were first developed. On the whole they read widely. Largely because of television they know generally what is going on in the world. Their educational background is extensive. They think. They reason. They are really very good at sorting out good evidence from bad, at separating the credible witness from the incredible, and at disregarding experts who attempt to inject their opinions into areas of which they have little knowledge. They would welcome all evidence having a bearing on the problem they are deciding and the give and take of deliberation would expose weaknesses in any witness or evidence. A modern jury, that must deliberate, and must agree, is the ideal body to evaluate opinions of this kind. The search for truth should be enhanced, eliminating some cases in which both sides agree there is no real issue, and in other cases assisting the jury to reach a just result.[73]

———

As for the second argument, that because polygraph evidence is not necessary for a fair trial it should not be used, doesn't

72. United States v. Ridling, 350 F.Supp. 90, 96, 97 (E.D.Mich.1972).

73. Id. at 98.

that assume the conclusion? No one would seriously urge that assessing the credibility of witnesses is not very important in judging a case. If the polygraph aids substantially in correctly assessing credibility, is it not necessary to a fair trial? Indeed, might the argument be better turned around? If the polygraph is accurate, it may be especially necessary to help assess witnesses' credibility because human beings are very fallible.

Both sides of the polygraph controversy are presented above. We suggest that there are seven principal reasons why the same courts that gladly receive psychiatric experts shun polygraph evidence. We offer these reasons together with questions that must be answered if the decision on whether to admit polygraph evidence is to be a sound one.

(1) Jurors will have difficulty understanding that a polygraph does not measure absolute truth, but instead tests whether a person believes what he is saying to be true. Is this fear a realistic one? Can any danger be eliminated by suitable jury instructions or careful examination of the polygraph expert?

(2) Although the polygraph is not perfect, it is likely to be treated by the jury as though it were 100% accurate. Assuming the polygraph is 70–90% accurate, but is followed on issues of credibility as if it were perfect, are the overall results likely to be less satisfactory than the results when juries assess credibility? Is there a difference between the present system, which cannot prevent all errors but presumes that all decisions are accurate, and a system that by definition will err 10–30% of the time?

(3) Our system depends upon the public's confidence that the jury is an accurate fact finder. Since many kinds of evidence—documents, hearsay statements, exhibits—do not lend themselves to polygraph analysis, acceptance of the lie detector to assess the credibility of witnesses may suggest a dissatisfaction with the jury, thereby undermining public confidence in the jury's capacity to decide factual questions without mechanical aids. Is the modern jury regarded as an accurate fact finder? Would acceptance of the polygraph undermine the public's confidence in juries if the public understood that a jury could reject lie detector results?

(4) Many trial judges may not be as careful as they should be in judging the qualifications of an examiner. Are these same judges likely to be any more careful in screening potential jurors? In qualifying other experts? Suppose they are not. Is this an argument for admitting polygraph evidence?

(5) It is uncomfortable and offensive for witnesses to face a polygraph, and it may discourage citizens from voluntarily cooperating with the courts. Is it any less uncomfortable or offensive to be subpoenaed to testify in court? Is there a legitimate privacy concern here?

(6) If lie detector evidence were admissible, there would be enormous pressure on all parties to have all witnesses tested, since jurors would be aware that polygraph evidence can be offered and might presume that those who do not use it have something to hide. The problem is exacerbated when one witness in a case is tested and the jury learns of the test but is asked to treat this witness like all other witnesses. Is there a substantial danger of unfair prejudice if any party can use the polygraph to bolster or to impeach credibility? If no mention of the machine is made, is one side hurt more than another? Are there fifth amendment problems here?

(7) Once polygraph results are accepted as evidence, the polygraph will be used in many other contexts, e.g., to screen jurors and judges for bias and to test political candidates and government officers. This will reduce the human element in decision making, creating a machine dominated atmosphere that makes life less humane. But are human values necessarily

threatened by testing for the truth and promoted by ignoring a mechanical means to minimize error? Is it more or less humane to seek perfection in things that matter? If the worry is that businesses will use the polygraph to screen employees and investigate white collar crime, this is happening today. Is a change in the judicial attitude toward the polygraph likely to enhance reliance on the polygraph in the private sphere?

The authors of this book are cautious defenders of gradually opening the door to polygraph evidence. We believe there are situations in which polygraph evidence should be received, but we are reluctant to see polygraph evidence admitted routinely in all cases. In our view the problem of expertise is a major one. The expert is crucial in lie detection. Moenssens and his colleagues comment:

> In the examination of approximately twenty-five percent of the subjects presented to a competent Polygraph examiner truthfulness or deception may be so clearly disclosed by the nature of the reactions to relevant or control questions that the examiner will be able to point them out to any layman and satisfy him of their significance. In approximately sixty-five percent of the cases, however, the indications are not that clear; they are sufficiently subtle in appearance and significance as to defy explanation to nonexperts. In about ten percent of the cases, the examiner may be unable to make any diagnosis at all because of a subject's physiological or psychological characteristics or because of other inhibiting factors.[74]

A prima facie showing of expertise is usually sufficient to qualify a witness as an expert. We can expect judges to allow expert testimony from almost any polygraph examiner who possesses formal credentials and apparent experience. Indeed, it is not clear how judges could do otherwise, since they are not experts themselves. While some polygraph examiners have reputations beyond reproach, the best in the field cannot be appointed in every case. Every field has individuals with the proper credentials and experience who do shoddy work or who consciously or unconsciously shape their opinions to accord with the desires of those who pay their fees. If a battle of experts should develop, and this may happen in a surprising number of cases, the jury may be without any rational way of resolving the dispute. There is no point in exchanging a swearing contest between witnesses for one between polygraph examiners.

The question of accuracy is also more complicated than it may appear. Depending on the population tested and the costs of mistaken decisions, a 90% accuracy rate may or may not be impressive. Suppose for example, 1100 criminal suspects were tested on the polygraph, 1000 of whom were innocent truth-tellers and 100 of whom were guilty liars. The polygraph would identify 900 of the innocents as telling the truth and 100 as lying, and it would identify 10 of the guilty as telling the truth and 90 as lying. Within each group it would have achieved 90% accuracy. However, if instead of asking how accurate the machine is within each group one asks how helpful its results are in determining who is innocent and who is guilty, the answer is quite different. The machine made very few errors among those it labeled truthful and hence innocent, only 10 of the 910 individuals so labeled, or about 1% of the total, were mistakenly exonerated. However, 100 out of 190 individuals whom the machine labeled as liars and hence guilty, or more than 50% of this group, would be mistakenly convicted if the machine evidence were dispositive. Of course, if the proportion of guilty and in-

---

74. Moenssens et al., supra note 71, ¶ 14.08, at 552.

nocent among the original examinees were reversed, the success rates in identifying the innocent and guilty would also be reversed. We do not know what the proportion of innocent truth-tellers and guilty liars is in tested populations, but if polygraph evidence were routinely admissible the polygraph would probably be more widely used as a screening device, and the proportion of innocent truth-tellers among those tested would rise in consequence. This would lead to an increase in the proportion of mistakes among those labeled as liars (and hence guilty) by the polygraph.[75]

Also very important are the human values which are very hard to articulate and the influence which the testing of only some witnesses will have on the jury's evaluation of all witnesses. These matters are suggested by the questions asked above and will not be discussed further.

Despite these reservations, we do not conclude that polygraph evidence should be excluded completely. It still may be by far the most probative evidence in a particular case. We think it appropriate to admit such evidence as an aid in deciding preliminary evidentiary questions, particularly those with constitutional overtones, by stipulation in any case, and in situations where a case hinges on the credibility of witnesses telling conflicting stories.

The polygraph seems to hold particular promise as an economical and relatively reliable way of determining conflicts between witnesses as to whether *Miranda* warnings were given or whether proper procedures were followed in the course of a search or seizure. These issues are decided by the judge in the absence of the jury, so there is no danger that the jury will misestimate the accuracy of the polygraph or be influenced by the fact that only some witnesses have undergone testing.

At this time there are relatively few courts willing to admit polygraph evidence absent a stipulation, but, despite judicial skepticism, the polygraph plays an important role in the criminal justice system. In many areas it is common for prosecutors and defendants to agree that if the defendant passes a polygraph examination charges shall be dropped, but if he fails a plea of guilty shall be entered. Police also have been known to use the mystique of the polygraph to encourage confessions. There is no general privilege or rule of evidence which protects admissions made to a polygraph operator. Also a few lawyers have clients or prospective clients tested so that they can better evaluate the credibility of their stories.

Whatever your conclusion as to the desirability of using the polygraph in jury trials, are you satisfied that polygraph evidence is distinguishable from psychiatric evidence generally? If you are inclined to reject the evidence, on what grounds does this inclination rest, the *Frye* test, a relevance analysis, or values not related to the

---

75. For an article which makes the point of this paragraph well and presents a general case against polygraph evidence, see Skolnick, Scientific Theory and Scientific Evidence: An Analysis of Lie Detection, 70 Yale L.J. 694 (1961).

Commonwealth v. Vitello, 376 Mass. 426, 381 N.E.2d 582 (1978), offers a useful summary of recent cases involving polygraph results. It adopts a view that neither the prosecution nor the defense may offer polygraph evidence to prove guilt or innocence, but that polygraph evidence may be introduced to impeach or corroborate the defen-

dant's testimony. The court indicated that an examination could only be conducted at the defendant's request and it required certain safeguards to ensure reliable results.

Recent federal cases are annotated at 43 A.L.R. Fed. 68 (1979).

A few cases have rejected polygraph evidence even where the parties have stipulated to its admissibility. Such decisions represent a judgment that polygraph evidence is unreliable and cannot be made reliable by stipulation. See, e.g., Akonom v. State, 40 Md.App. 676, 394 A.2d 1213 Md. (1978).

accuracy of the machine? Would you admit polygraph evidence if the parties stipulate that the results of a polygraph test will be accepted? What would you do if one party attempts to withdraw the stipulation after learning the results of the test? Would you admit the results of a polygraph test if the defendant in a criminal case wishes to introduce them?

C. VOICEPRINTS

One of the most controversial scientific advances now being offered in courts is the voiceprint:

> What is the "voiceprint" technique? The theory of voice identification by the "voiceprint" technique is that people differ anatomically in the size, shape, and structure of the oral and nasal cavities and the larynx. In addition, it is claimed that people have different, but stable speech patterns in the way they use the articulators (teeth, tongue and lips) and the other parts of the vocal apparatus. Proponents of the technique state that the combination of so many factors uniquely characterizes a particular speaker and sets him apart from all others.
>
> Identification is attempted by both aural and visual means. The operator compares the voices by listening to recordings of the known and unknown voices, and by visually analyzing high-speed sound spectrograms of the voices. The sound spectrogram is a graphic display of some of the factors claimed to uniquely characterize a particular speaker: frequency and intensity of sound as a function of the time period over which the word is spoken. The "voiceprint" operator examines the two spectrograms of the same spoken word (produced from recordings of the known and unknown voices), seeking points of similarity. If he finds sufficient points of similarity, he says the two voice samples were made by the same person. If he cannot find enough points of similarity, he is unable to make a "match" and cannot say whether the two voices were the same or not. In some cases, the spectrograms may be so dissimilar that he will state that the two recordings were *not* made by the same person.[76]

Under the ordinary test of relevance, voiceprint evidence seems clearly admissible. Yet some courts have excluded it under the *Frye* test.[77]

In 1966 the Acoustical Society of America's Technical Committee of the Speech Communications Section asked some of its members to examine voiceprints. The members concluded in their 1970 report:

> Experimental studies of voice identification using visual interpretation of spectrograms by human observers indicate false identification rates ranging from zero to as high as 63%, depending on the type of task set for the observer, the observer's training, and other factors. Reliable machine methods for voice identification have not yet been established.
>
> Experience in applying spectrographic voice identification in law enforcement has led proponents of the method to express confidence in its reliability. The basis for this confidence is not, however, accessible to objective assessment.

*   *   *

---

76. Jones, Danger—Voiceprints Ahead, 11 Am.Crim.L.Rev. 549, 550 (1973). See also Comment, Voiceprints—The Admissibility Question: What Evidentiary Standard Should Apply? 19 St. Louis L.J. 509 (1975).

77. See, e.g., United States v. Addison, 162 U.S.App.D.C. 199, 498 F.2d 741 (1974). Other courts do not mention the *Frye* case. E.g., Worley v. State, 263 So.2d 613 (Fla.1972).

* * * [A]vailable results are inadequate to establish the reliability of voice identification by spectrograms. We believe this conclusion is shared by most scientists who are knowledgeable about speech; hence, many of them are deeply concerned about the use of spectrographic evidence in courts.[78]

One critic states:

Other scientists have expressed grave doubt that enough is presently known about speech patterns themselves to allow development of a technique for reliable voice matching. The opinion has been expressed that in time, perhaps in the next decade, techniques might be developed by which it would be possible to identify a person by voice alone. But first, we must learn much more than we presently know about speech, and secondly, it is not likely to be done through use of the high-speed sound spectrograph. According to Bolt, "the root of the voice identification problem lies in the nature of speech itself. This may not be immediately apparent, because speech is so familiar and so seemingly simple, but intensive research, especially over the past 20 years, has shown it to be a very complex process that is only partially understood even now." Speech consists of numerous different messages which have been blended by the speaker into a single acoustical stream; these messages, though different, lose their distinct character and cease to be represented by single acoustical elements of speech. In addition, two factors exist which limit the value of comparing voice samples for similarities and differences. The need to communicate intelligibly in a standard dialect operates to limit broad differences which

might otherwise be found in speech patterns; similarities between two voices, speaking the same dialect, will frequently be the product of the standard pattern of the dialect, rather than of the possible identity of the voices. Equally, such dialects are not rigid; within the dialect, there exist numerous variations adopted at will by the individual speaker and differences in spectrographic patterns may indicate either two different speakers or a single speaker freely varying a single sound feature. Thus, neither similarities nor differences in spectrographic patterns provide unambiguous evidence as to the identity of a speaker.

[t]he primary objective in developing the spectrograph was to find a way of recording speech that would emphasize the similarities and differences among *words*. It follows that other differences, and in particular the differences *between speakers,* have been subordinated to this primary objective. Clearly, we need * * * but do not know how to build * * * an instrument that would give good graphic patterns that emphasize the distinctive characteristics of speakers. It may be that, when we have learned much more about sound features that characterize individual speakers, it will be possible to design an instrument that can be a powerful aid to the eye in voice identification, or even one that can operate automatically in a completely objective manner.[79]

If an expert in speech acoustics testifies to her personal experiments with voiceprint identification and her conclusion that voiceprints are 92% accurate, and if no

78. Bolt, Cooper, David, Denes, Stevens & Pickett, Speaker Identification by Speech Spectrograms: A Scientist's View of its Reliability for Legal Purposes, 47 J.Acoust. Soc.Am. 597, 603 (1970).

79. Jones, supra note 76, at 569–70, quoting at length from Bolt, supra note 78, at 603.

But see Black et al., Reply to "Speaker Identification by Speech Spectrograms: Some Further Observations," 54 J. Acoust. Soc. Am. 535 (1973) and Nash & Tosi, Identification of Suspects by the Voiceprint Technique, 38 Police Chief 49 (Dec. 1971).

contradictory evidence is offered, should a trial judge admit a voiceprint identification, or should the judge take judicial notice of the criticisms of the technique and exclude it? When does a technique become acceptable for use in court? When evidence is not generally approved by the appropriate scientific community because there is insufficient validation although there is no demonstrated failure, is it wiser to admit the evidence and inform the jury about the scholarly criticism or to exclude it altogether? Are you more willing to admit voiceprint evidence offered *by* rather than *against* a defendant? If there are relatively few voiceprint experts in the world, is it fair to permit voiceprint evidence to be offered if the objecting party cannot locate and produce one of the critics as a witness? To the extent that lawyers need to prepare with their own experts in order to cross-examine other experts, should the limited supply of experts be taken into account in ruling on the admissibility of scientific evidence? Are you satisfied that psychiatric evidence

and handwriting analysis should be treated differently from polygraph evidence and voiceprints? Why? How do these kinds of evidence differ? Is an advantage of the *Frye* rule saving time at trials, since one appellate ruling can establish that a type of evidence is not generally accepted? Or can it? If appellate courts mandate the exclusion of certain kinds of evidence or strongly suggest that trial judges use their discretion to exclude, are lawyers likely to continue offering such evidence in all cases? Where such evidence is offered, is it not likely to be offered on new issues or in ways that shed increased light on the scientific technique? Is a principal disadvantage of the *Frye* rule that it unduly hampers change?[80] Assuming that time is saved by a special rule for scientific evidence, does this factor alone justify the rule? How should one balance time saved against the costs of rejecting relevant evidence? These are the kinds of questions that one must face in deciding whether to admit the evidence made available by innovative scientific techniques.

D. NEUTRON ACTIVATION ANALYSIS

One recently developed technique that has attracted the attention of some courts is neutron activation analysis. The following excerpt describes the way in which it works:

At its best, NAA is simply a method of quantitative chemical analysis. It measures the elemental composition of materials, that is, the amount of each chemical element in a given sample of material. * * *

The detection of elements by activation analysis is possible because most elements can be made artifically radioactive. The resulting radioactive products can be identified by observation of the ways in which they undergo radioactive decay. * * *

* * *

* * * [T]he result of subjecting a piece of material to neutron activation

80. It may be useful to remember that virtually all scientific evidence was suspect at one time or another. Consider, e.g., People v. Berkman, 307 Ill. 492, 500–01, 139 N.E. 91, 94–5 (1923), which termed "preposterous" reliance on ballistics evidence.

It also may be important to remember that a breakthrough in admissibility may not be permanent. Voiceprints are a good example. When the influential United States Court of Appeals for the Second Circuit approved the use of voiceprints in United States

v. Williams, 583 F.2d 1194 (1978), certiorari denied, 439 U.S. 1117 (1979), many thought that voiceprints would be more readily accepted throughout the federal system. However, a report by the National Academy of Sciences was released after the decision warning against too much reliance on voiceprints. On the Theory and Practice of Voice Identification (1979). No clear trend has emerged since, but it appears that the evidentiary use of voiceprints is today more suspect than it was but a few years ago.

analysis is that the material is found to contain certain elements in the measured concentrations, within experimental error. The next step is to determine the relevance this result has to the legal issues in the case at hand. Broadly speaking, NAA can have significance in two ways. Sometimes the legal issue depends directly on the *amount* of a selected element in the material. For example, if the question is whether a particular death was due to arsenic poisoning, the activation analyst might measure the amount of arsenic in the victim's hair or in other tissues, and if the amount exceeds the normal amount by a considerable value, then death by arsenic poisoning has a high probability. In other cases the legal issue is whether a given piece of evidence came from a particular source—the *identification* problem. For example, a hair found on the body of a murder victim might be compared in its trace element concentrations to the hairs of a suspect. Then the crucial question is the degree to which the comparison singles out the suspect as the guilty party.

In neither of these cases is the NAA evidence sufficient in itself; additional data are needed to evaluate the significance of the chemical analyses done by neutron activation techniques. In the first case it is necessary to know the normal amount of arsenic in the tissue or hair measured. More precisely, knowledge of the distribution of arsenic concentrations in hairs of the living general population is required so that one can calculate the probability that a person chosen at random would have an arsenic concentration equal to what was measured in the tissue or hair of the deceased. In the second case more information is needed to determine how much more likely the hair found on the victim is to have come from the suspect than from a person chosen at random from the general population.

Although the detailed considerations are quite different in the different types of cases, the analysis in each instance depends on the existence of sufficient background information with which the evidence at hand can be compared; only then can the evidence be properly interpreted. * * *

AN EXAMPLE

People v. Woodward provides an example illustrating many of the considerations necessary to the proper use of NAA evidence.

The Fact Situation and the Trial

In response to a silent burglar alarm, the police arrived at the scene of an attempted burglary about 1 a.m. and found the suspect Woodward not far from the door which a burglar attempted to open. Woodward said he had just happened by and was on the way to his car which was parked nearby. A tool used for changing tires was found several feet from the doorway. Upon inspection of Woodward's car it was discovered that the tire tool was missing from the jack in his trunk and that the tool found near the doorway fit the jack; however, Woodward denied that the tool was his.

Some specks of brown paint were found on the wedge end of the tire tool and a few specks of light-blue paint were found adhering to the shaft. Visual comparison of the paints indicated that the brown specks resembled the paint on the doorway and the light-blue specks resembled that of Woodward's car. Other specks of light-blue paint were found on the floor of the car trunk and because of the very small amounts of paint on the tire tool NAA appeared to be the best method of chemical analysis. The brown paint on the tool was found to match the brown paint of the door in seven elements; no element was found in one that was not found in the other and the concentrations were the same wtihin small statistical limits. The light-blue paint on the tool similarly matched specks found in the trunk of Woodward's car, except that only five elements were detected in each.

Earlier studies in the same laboratory that performed the analysis on the evidence specks had indicated that two similar-type paints of similar color but of different brands would contain a given element in concentrations within 10 percent of each other only about one time in five. If one assumes that the chance of finding a given amount of one element is independent of the amounts of any other elements present, then the chance that two similar-type paints of similar color but of different brands will match concentrations within 10 percent in each of five elements is $(\frac{1}{5})^5$—one chance in 3,125 or 0.03 percent. Similarly, the chance of matching in seven elements is about one in 100,000 or 0.001 percent. This evidence was presented at trial and the defendant was convicted.

Interpreting the Evidence

Postponing discussion of the difficulties in making a probability calculation of the type used in *Woodward,* we here assume that the probabilities stated are valid and ask what they mean. Since in the actual case the defendant denied that the tire tool was his, discussion can be simplified by assuming that the tool was, in fact, used by the actual burglar, thereby eliminating the need to evaluate the brown paint comparison.

The light-blue paint comparison indicates that if 10,000 light-blue cars which are painted with a brand of paint *different* from that of the defendant's car are chosen at random, then only three of them will be found to match the paint on defendant's car within 10 percent in all five elements. If this were the only consideration, and if it could be shown that far fewer than 10,000 light-blue cars, all painted with brands of paint different

from that used on defendant's car, could conceivably have been the supplier of the tire tool, then the evidence against the defendant is quite powerful. On the other hand, if more than 10,000 light-blue cars might have been involved, there are three in each 10,000 that would give the same activation analysis results when compared with the specks on the tire tool as the defendant's car did.

There is a much more important consideration, however. Even if the activation analysis could *positively* identify the brand of paint, that is, even if it were 100 percent certain that the specks of paint on the tire tool were of the same brand as the paint on defendant's car, the NAA evidence in itself still does no more than reduce the number of possible culprits to those owning or somehow associated with light-blue cars painted with that brand of paint. Therefore, the NAA evidence only points up the defendant as being a member of a restricted subclass of the general population. That the defendant is singled out only as a member of a restricted subclass is a *typical result* of NAA evidence, although the *size* of the subclass varies greatly with the type of thing being compared. Before the NAA evidence can be meaningfully evaluated, it is necessary in each case to determine the size of the subclass. If, for simplicity, it is assumed in the actual Woodward case that the car which supplied the guilty tire tool came from the metropolitan area where the crime occurred, then the number of cars in the subclass of which Woodward's car was a member (those cars whose paint match the specks found on the tire tool in the way his car's paint did) is the number of light-blue cars in the metropolitan area which were painted with the same brand of light-blue paint plus 0.03 percent of the total number of other light-blue cars in the area. This number could be moderately large if the manufacturer of Woodward's car used the same brand of light-blue paint on many models, especially if the same brand were used for a period of years, or if the other manufacturers used the same brand of paint, or simply if there were many light-blue cars in the area.[81]

———

Do you think the jury in a case like Woodward can be trusted to use properly data generated by NAA? Remember, even the assumption that the blue paint came from an auto might be disputed. The author of the above commentary suggests the following way of helping the jury. Do you approve?

[The jury] should consider the other evidence against defendant in the light of a restricted number of possible suspects; the guilty party is assumed to come from the restricted subclass. Thus, in Woodward, the jury could have been told that there were, say, 100 cars in the San Francisco Bay area which could have supplied the tire tool, and that the defendant's car was one of them. They can be reminded that the only significance of the NAA evidence is its indication that the defendant owns a car in this group of 100 cars, any one of which could have been used in the crime. The nonstatistical evidence should then be considered as singling out, if it is sufficiently persuasive, the defendant from the people associated with the other 99 cars. In a case like Woodward, where the other evidence against the defendant is so strong, the jury should not have much trouble finding him guilty. On the other hand, the prosecution's case would be quite weak if, for example, Woodward had been picked up the next day at his home and the only evidence against him were that provided by NAA and perhaps his failure to produce a verifiable alibi.

Here, the defense attorney could point out to the jury that anyone who lives alone and who was sleeping at the time of the crime might well not be able to verify that fact, so that the evidence against the defendant is little stronger than against any other member of the subclass (those who had access to cars with paint similar to defendant's) chosen at random. When the strength of the other evidence is somewhere in between, assistance can still be given to the members of the jury by discussion of these two polar examples.[82]

———

The author describes the function of the expert testifying about NAA as follows:

Objection Versus Subjective Opinion

A leading commentator has stated that expert opinion is appropriate "when the facts can be interpreted and conclusions be drawn only by a person having technical qualifications or special opportunities for knowledge not possessed by the average layman." Some cases involve questions that are capable of reasonably precise definition and to which the expert can give firm, objective answers, including most particularly the limitations on his conclusions. In other types of cases, the expert may have to rely mainly on the depth of his general background in the subject, and he may not be able to articulate the precise foundations for his conclusions or the limitations thereon. Evidence derived from activation analysis provides a good example of the former type of expert opinion, and it is useful to compare this type of evidence with that produced by experts in such areas as fingerprints, handwriting, and firearms identification, all of which are examples of the latter.

81. This quotation is taken from Karjala, The Evidentiary Uses of Neutron Activation Analysis, 59 Cal. L. Rev. 997, 998–1000, 1013–

17, 1020–24 (1971). See also Moenssens et al., supra, note 71 at 389–408.

82. Karjala, supra, note 81, at 1014–20.

Identification by trace element characterization rests on the hypothesis that materials of similar type but which derive from different sources (for example, two hairs, two pieces of glass, two blood samples) will usually be sufficiently different in their minute concentrations of trace elements that they can be distinguished, at least to some extent. Thus, a "match" by NAA may tend to show that they come from a common source. Similar considerations are involved in the other types of identification procedures. For example, the fingerprint expert compares types of characteristics, such as ridge endings and bifurcations, and their locations, and depending on the number of points of agreement he draws conclusions as to whether identification has been established. Similarly, the handwriting expert compares peculiarities of letter formation and the firearms expert compares such things as the rifling marks on the bullets fired by a given gun. Yet these latter procedures differ in a fundamental way from a comparison of the results of an NAA measurement: the characteristics which are compared are not amenable to what has been called a total-ordering.

Basically, totally-orderable data is simply that which can be catalogued in a systematic manner. If the results of measurements on a true random sample are thus catalogued, it is easy to calculate the probability that a particular measurement will "match" from a random choice by finding the number of measurements on the random sample which gave the same results and taking the ratio to the total number of measurements in the sample. Comparison techniques which are not amenable to total-ordering are necessarily somewhat subjective, at least in the sense that adequate criteria do not exist which would permit the expert to articulate the precise foundations for his conclusion that a "match" exists or that there is a cer-

tain probability of identity. Thus, one expert may feel that a positive result is established while another feels equally strongly that the same evidence does not warrant such a conclusion. These identifications thus depend on the "intuitive ability" and "common sense" of the expert. Numerous authors have called for more recognition and investigation of the logical processes which lie behind these methods, but it is not the purpose of this Comment to weight the conflicting factors involved in the evidentiary use of such subjective procedures. The different considerations involved in the use of NAA evidence, however, are crucial. In the first place, the quantitative values of element concentrations and their respective experimental errors determined by activation analysis do lend themselves well to total-ordering. Therefore, it is always possible, at least in principle, to build up the background data required to evaluate definitely the significance of the analysis. Equally important, if practical problems make the necessary data collection difficult, or if insufficient background data are simply not yet available in a particular case, the expert can nevertheless state clearly and precisely what inferences his measurements warrant and how these conclusions must be limited. Thus, a subjective approach to the interpretation and presentation of NAA results is unnecessary.

Second, the subjective approach can claim much less validity in the interpretation of NAA results than it can in, say, fingerprint analysis. There is no group of activation analysis experts, comparable to fingerprint analysts, who can claim to possess valuable funds of experience comparing objects in general and finding that they can identify two objects with a common origin. On the contrary, the NAA expert's ability to trace an object's origin stems not from his background experience and intuition, but solely from the statistical analysis of the trace element compositions of similar objects. Ideally, the background information required for the statistical analysis should be performed by analysts other than the expert testifying at trial, but, in any event, the testifying expert's knowledge does not extend beyond its statistical foundation. Any claim that he has a subjective or intuitive ability to identify objects with a common origin is unfounded and misleading.

Third, the risks involved in employing a subjective approach to neutron activation analysis are extremely great. The jury may give undue weight to the expert's opinion simply because of his scientific reputation or because his field is so esoteric. Furthermore, the meanings of terms such as "common origin" or "same batch," which must be precisely defined in an objective analysis, become hazy and confused under the subjective approach, rendering it even more difficult for the trier of fact to understand how the evidence should be interpreted. Finally, subjective testimony is much more easily colored by the natural self-interest that government laboratory scientists have in obtaining convictions than is objective testimony based on scientifically-accepted background information and well-established statistical interpretation procedures.

These considerations distinguish NAA evidence from fingerprint data and other more or less subjective identification techniques. They make it extremely important that experts present their NAA conclusions as carefully and precisely as possible. A general feeling that two pieces of material came from a common source—based, for example, on an examination of their gamma-ray spectra—contains little or no probative value and can be seriously misleading.

Nevertheless, few experts have used appropriate care in limiting their testimony, and the courts have not been diligent in requiring them to be objective.[83]

E. PROBLEMS

Problem X–14.   In your view, can courts guarantee that NAA experts exercise the requisite care in offering opinions to lay juries? Can courts distinguish neutron activation analysis from the polygraph on the question whether juries can understand what the evidence does and does not prove? Is there something about NAA that makes it more acceptable than the polygraph as scientific evidence?

Problem X–15.   Carter was convicted of burglarizing a government facility. He complained on appeal about the trial court's ruling that "doodles" which Carter made during the trial be provided the court and admitted into evidence for comparison with a photo of a doodle found at the scene of the crime. An FBI agent testified at the trial that there was insufficient time to make a comparison of the handwriting and that more experienced agents had concluded that there were insufficient points of comparison to warrant a conclusion as to whether the same "doodler" did all drawings. Citing FRE 401, the appellate court concluded that without expert evidence to support the comparison, "the exhibits, as offered, were not possessed of probative

---

83. Id. at 1020–24.

value." Thus, the convictions for stealing government property were reversed. **Do you agree with this ruling?**

Problem X–16. In a murder case, the prosecution contended that the victim died as a result of a toxic dose of succinylocholine chloride, which, prior to this case, scientists believed to be undetectable in human tissue. A toxicologist testified that certain tests conducted on the tissue of the body of the deceased revealed unusual amounts of the toxic substance. The tests were described by one appellate judge as novel and devised specially for this case. Yet the trial judge admitted the evidence and was affirmed on appeal. **Do you agree that the decision of the trial judge was a proper exercise of judicial discretion?**

Problem X–17. In an obscenity prosecution the state desires to offer expert evidence to prove the obscenity of a movie "The Porno-History of the Law of Evidence," which was seized from a theater run by Salacious Saltzburg and Libidinous Lempert. The prosecution is brought in Los Angeles, California. **Which, if any, of the following persons is an appropriate expert, assuming that local community standards provide the relevant guidelines, and that the relevant criteria are whether the movie appeals to a prurient interest in sex, whether it is patently offensive, and whether it is a serious work of art?**

    a.   The librarian at the city library.

    b.   A rabbi and a priest whose synagogue and church are located in Los Angeles.

    c.   The deputy chief probation officer for the Los Angeles County Adult Probation Department.

    d.   A movie buff living in Los Angeles and holding a 1970 master's degree in English from UCLA.

Salacious and Libidinous wish to offer their own experts: the owner of an adult bookstore, the proprietor of a chain of massage parlors who numbers most of the city's prominent politicians among her customers, and a sociologist who has surveyed the reading, movie-going and private sex habits of people living in the Los Angeles area. **Will any of these individuals be allowed to testify as experts?**

Problem X–18. A stock broker, who is being sued for damages arising out of the sale of unregistered stock in violation of federal law, offers the testimony of another broker that he would have been able to sell the same stock at the same price even if a proper registration statement had been filed. **Should the district court reject the evidence on the ground that no one is sufficiently expert to predict the activities of the stock market?**

Problem X–19. The State of Rhode Island condemns Bob Harris' land for a new elementary school. Harris and the state disagree on the value of the land and a condemnation suit is filed. To establish the value of the land Harris calls Sarah Burns, a local realtor who for twenty years has been selling property in the same area as the land in controversy. Before Burns testifies, the State questions her on voir dire concerning the basis of the testimony. She replies that she arrived at her opinion as to the value of

Harris' property by relying on the prices at which land in the area similar to the land in question has sold recently, and on her knowledge of offers to buy or sell similar land. Since land is unique, no previous sale or offer is precisely analogous, so the realtor has reached a final opinion by estimating the value of particular features characterizing Harris' property and not the comparison properties, and vice versa. **Is the realtor a qualified expert? Should the court exclude the realtor's testimony but give evidence of the sale prices directly to the jury? What about evidence of the offers?**

Problem X–20. Een sued Dulski for injuries resulting when Een's car collided with Dulski's truck. Dulski claimed that Een's car crossed the middle of the highway and caused the accident. To support this theory of causation, Dulski offered the testimony of a deputy sheriff and former city police officer with 17 years experience in investigating accidents. The officer arrived at the scene approximately 80 minutes after the accident occurred and before the damaged vehicles were moved. Dulski asked the officer for an opinion concerning the place of the impact. **Is this opinion admissible? What more would you want to know before you answer this question?** The Advisory Committee Note to FRE 703, states that "[t]he language would not warrant admitting in evidence the opinion of an 'accidentologist' as to the point of impact in an automobile collision based on statements of bystanders * * *" **Are you convinced that the language of FRE 703 is not this broad? Why should such evidence be objectionable? Should the existence of eyewitness testimony support, impair, or have no effect on a claim that an accidentologist has useful information to convey to a jury?**

Problem X–21. Juliet and Herbert Pren were badly injured in an automobile accident; both will be confined to wheelchairs for the rest of their lives. Juliet and Herbert sue for damages. One element of their damage claim relates to their inability to do housework after the accident. **May the Prens introduce an economist to testify to the value of various household services—e.g., cooking, cleaning, washing clothes, serving meals and caring for children?**

SECTION IV. MECHANICS OF OBTAINING EXPERT TESTIMONY

A. COURT APPOINTED EXPERTS

McCormick suggests that one of the most objectionable aspects of expert testimony is its partisan presentation and argues that the remedy "lies simply in using the trial judge's common law power to call experts."[84]

FRE 706 responds to the argument by codifying the judge's power:

(a) Appointment.—The court may on its own motion or on the motion of any party enter an order to show cause why expert witnesses should not be ap-

---

84. McCormick § 17, at 38.

pointed, and may request the parties to submit nominations. The court may appoint any expert witnesses agreed upon by the parties, and may appoint expert witnesses of its own selection. An expert witness shall not be appointed by the court unless he consents to act. A witness so appointed shall be informed of his duties by the court in writing, a copy of which shall be filed with the clerk, or at a conference in which the parties shall have opportunity to participate. A witness so appointed shall advise the parties of his findings, if any; his deposition may be taken by any party; and he may be called to testify by the court or any party. He shall be subject to cross-examination by each party, including a party calling him as a witness.

(b) Compensation.—Expert witnesses so appointed are entitled to reasonable compensation in whatever sum the court may allow. The compensation thus fixed is payable from funds which may be provided by law in criminal cases and civil actions and proceedings involving just compensation under the fifth amendment. In other civil actions and proceedings the compensation shall be paid by the parties in such proportion and at such time as the court directs, and thereafter charged in like manner as other costs.

(c) Disclosure of appointment.—In the exercise of its discretion, the court may authorize disclosure to the jury of the fact that the court appointed the expert witness.

(d) Parties' experts of own selection.—Nothing in this rule limits the parties in calling expert witnesses of their own selection.

But, is there such a person as a nonpartisan expert? Some judges have expressed doubts,[85] as have some commentators.

DIAMOND, THE FALLACY OF THE IMPARTIAL EXPERT

3 Archives of Crim. Psychodynamics 221 (1959).

It is quite generally assumed that the battle of the experts, that always disconcerting and often sensational disagreement of psychiatrists in testifying on issues of legal insanity and criminal responsibility, could be eliminated through the device of the neutral or impartial expert.

Such a neutral expert witness is supposedly entirely outside the traditional adversary system of the courts. Not in the employment of either the defense or the prosecution, but acting in the name of the court, such a witness presumedly can remain detached and objective. Disagreement between expert witnesses is supposed to be greatly reduced; thereby aiding the court in reaching a higher level of fair, just, and impartial decisions.

* * *

I would guess that, today, nine-tenths of the psychiatrists in this country would unhesitatingly agree to the desirability of removing the psychiatric expert from the legal adversary system. It is the purpose of this editorial to challenge this wide-spread agreement. It is proper that this discussion take the form of an editorial, rather than that of a scientific paper. For opinions pro and con this matter can hardly be considered as objective facts to be solemnly presented as a scientific advance. Quite properly they are to be considered as personal opinions of the author and nothing more.

It is a fiction of the law that only the immediate parties to a legal action—the defendant and the plaintiff or prosecutor and

85. E.g., Scott v. Spanjer Bros., Inc., 298 F.2d 928, 932 (2d Cir. 1962) (Hincks, J., dissenting in part).

their counsel—are adversaries. All else: the judge, the jury, and the witnesses, are not to be partisans. All witnesses, both expert and lay witnesses of fact, are sworn to tell the truth, the whole truth, and nothing but the truth. This truth, as revealed in the testimony of the witness, may favor one or the other side, but the witness may not. That this is a fiction, not a reality, is evidenced by the customary manner of labeling witnesses as *for* the defendant or *for* the prosecution.

I will thus concede at the outset that the expert witness called by either adversary is likely to be biased to some degree, that his opinions are not truly impartial, and that he, himself, as a party to the adversary system, becomes to a certain degree an advocate. I concede this with full awareness that both legal and medical codes of ethics demand the impartiality of the expert witness, irrespective of the side that calls him. The desirability of such an ethical ideal must not blind us to the reality fact that the ideal is seldom, if ever, achieved.

The crude charge is sometimes asserted that under the adversary system the expert witness sells his opinion. Because he is paid by one or the other side, he is accused of prostituting his medical knowledge in providing untruthful testimony in return for the money he is paid. This charge is too base to defend by more than just a simple statement: I do not believe that this happens.

Undoubtedly what does happen is that the expert witness, through his close operational identification with one side of the conflict, does become an advocate. Because his testimony does in fact support one side of the legal battle, he, if he is at all human, must necessarily identify himself with his own opinion, and subjectively desire that "his side" win. This can vary all the way from a deliberate, conscious participation in the planning of the legal strategy with the lawyers who call upon him

for expert advice and opinion, to a more aloof, detached facsimile of impartiality that masks his secret hope for victory of his own opinion. Such a detached witness may be totally unconscious of the innumerable subtle distortions and biases in his testimony that spring from this wish to triumph.

* * *

Because both the impartial, court appointed, independent witness as well as the adversary witness are required to submit to cross examination and defend their opinions, it is here asserted that there is no such thing as a truly impartial expert; that all witnesses, regardless of who engaged them, identify closely with their own opinions, and unintentionally introduce, as a result, a certain degree of bias and deviation from their oath to tell the truth, the whole truth, and nothing but the truth.

Certain other factors also contribute to the lack of impartiality of the court appointed expert. However, let us first place these issues within the framework of a specific case. I deliberately chose a trial in which all elements are greatly exaggerated. I do not mean that the description of the trial to be given below is exaggerated, for the description is entirely accurate of what actually occurred. But the facts of the case, itself, and the circumstances of the expert examinations and testimony are far more extreme than is usual.

A certain California multi-millionaire was charged with perverse sexual acts on two adolescent boys. It was a matter of common public knowledge that the defendant had overtly and unashamedly practiced homosexuality for many years, but he had never previously been accused of seducing children. He pleaded not guilty by reason of insanity. The defendant had no insight into his mental illness, nor did he consider himself insane in any sense of the word. However, he consented to the plea on the insistence of his attorneys and his family. Practically unlimited sums of money were available for purposes of his defense. An exceptionally high powered battery of attorneys, headed by the most outstanding criminal lawyer in the area, represented him. He was quickly convicted of the acts charged in the indictment, for the evidence was conclusive. Then he was tried on the question of his insanity, as is required by the peculiar split-trial system used in California. A jury trial had been waived.

Two court appointed psychiatrists had examined him, and submitted reports to the court stating that he was sane under the M'Naghten rules; that he was a sociopath, manifesting a sexual deviation which made him a menace to society; hence he came under the California sexual psychopathy law permitting indefinite confinement.

Two other psychiatrists, who had been engaged by the defense, testified that they had examined the defendant, and found him to be suffering from a major psychosis; that he was insane under the M'Naghten rules; that his long standing homosexuality as well as the specific perverse sexual acts with the children were symptoms of his psychosis; and that he was not a sociopath or a sexual psychopath.

The court appointed psychiatrists received the usual fee for their examinations and time spent in court, probably not over fifty or one hundred dollars each. The two defense psychiatrists each were paid several thousand dollars for their examinations and time in court.

Here we have an extreme instance of the battle of the experts. How to explain the disparate testimony of the experts? Would the verdict of the judge have been more just if all four psychiatrists had been neutral? What role did the sharp discrepancy in fees paid to the witnesses play?

The differences in the diagnoses reached by the court appointed witnesses and the defense witnesses hinged largely upon the question as to whether certain statements asserted by the defendant were actually delusions or whether they were either true, or possible exaggerations, or perhaps even deliberate lies. The neutral experts had only the usual hour or so of examination time, and no sources of information outside the defendant's statements, to formulate their opinion on this very difficult question. The defendant had no intention of admitting even the possibility that he might be suffering from a psychotic thinking disorder. He went to great lengths to rationalize his peculiar thoughts and to justify his conduct, both past and present, as the actions of a sane person who chose voluntarily to lead an eccentric life. He concealed from the court appointed psychiatrists the details of his past history, which included hospitalization in private sanitariums in England and in France on nine previous occasions.

It was certainly no reflection upon the clinical abilities of the two neutral experts that they reached the conclusions they did. Under the limited circumstances of their examination and with the restricted information that they had access to, it is difficult to imagine how they could have reached any other conclusions.

On the other hand, the defense psychiatrists were paid to spend practically unlimited time and to use all possible clinical facilities in their study of the defendant. Batteries of psychological tests were administered. An exhaustive neurological investigation was done, including spinal puncture and an EEG (certain symptoms suggested general paresis). An attorney was dispatched to Europe to obtain copies of the previous hospital records and to take depositions from all of the European physicians who had previously treated him over a period of some thirty years. The aged mother of the defendant was brought to California from her home in Europe and made available for a social history. When the clinical evidence was all in, the conclusion was inescapable that this man was psychotic and not responsible for his actions. The judge agreed and found him not guilty by reason of insanity, and he was committed to a state hospital.

Beyond doubt the verdict was just. The great wealth of the defendant was not used to purchase biased and untruthful testimony from dubious experts. Rather it was used to make certain that every scrap of evidence, every clinical possibility was exhaustively investigated, and that nothing was overlooked. The injustice inherent in this extreme example is, of course, the fact that if this defendant had been a poor man he would have probably been found to be sane, and would have been imprisoned.

The assumption is often made that the elimination of the adversary expert witness will lead to testimony of greater objectivity, thoroughness, and accuracy. Corollary to this assumption is the implication that examinations performed by adversary witnesses are neither objective, thorough, nor accurate. In our case of the millionaire sex offender, just the opposite was true. But how about in ordinary cases? It is very difficult to give a definite answer to this question without having some basis of statistical information. However, I believe there are logical reasons to infer that quite generally psychiatric investigations done for the defense are likely to be more thorough than those done by the ordinary court appointed psychiatrist. The latter is apt to approach the examination situation in a routine manner, a job to be done, so to speak, and to restrict his time, energy, and thought on the case to a level determined by the habitual fees paid for this work. The public funds available to the court appointed psychiatrist are very limited, the courts taking it for granted that he should be able to perform an adequate examination and reach a conclusion in one or two hours. Rarely is money available for auxiliary examinations, such as projective techniques. The fact that there are a few notable exceptions

to this situation does not alter the general inference. * * *

* * *

In short, I think it is possible to make the generalization that court appointments tend to be handled by psychiatrists as a kind of routine job, in which, despite totally unreasonable time restrictions, there nevertheless results a fairly medium level of clinical competence. The psychiatrist called by the defense, on the other hand, is much more apt to regard the examination situation as a highly challenging task, to which he devotes considerable time and effort, with or without adequate remuneration. * * *

Does the fact that a psychiatrist is called as a witness for the court, that he is neither directly involved with the prosecution nor the defense make it more likely that his opinion is less biased and more truthful and objective than that of the adversary witness? I concede that the defense psychiatrist is apt to be biased in favor of the side which has engaged him. It is my editorial opinion that court appointed experts are consistently biased in favor of the prosecution. The selection of court appointed psychiatrists is seldom made from the random universe of the psychiatric population. Certain psychiatrists tend to be appointed over and over again. These are generally men who have an active interest in forensic psychiatry. More than not they tend to be Kraepelinian and less dynamic in their approach to their cases. They are often drawn from the ranks of administrative psychiatry, an area deficient in psychoanalytically oriented therapists. They are less inclined to probe deeply, more inclined to uncritically accept surface manifestations, and are prone to interpret the legal criteria for insanity in a narrowly restricted way. (Many of my forensic psychiatrist friends will take me to task for making these assertions—I will merely tell them that they are the exceptions who prove the rule.)

A second reason for this biased selection of court appointed experts is the unfortunate fact that dynamically oriented psychotherapists with liberal, enlightened, and non-moralistic attitudes towards mental illness and criminal behavior, shamefully avoid their social responsibility to participate in the administration of justice. They make it clearly known that they would not accept appointment as expert witness, and they ensure that they will not even be asked by having an abysmal ignorance of even the basic principles of forensic psychiatry.

Thirdly, in many communities, the District Attorney has an undue influence over the courts in the selection of the panels from which the court appointed expert is drawn. Psychiatrists who have more liberal views which have been revealed through their testimony in previous cases may be systematically excluded from appointment by the court. * * *

*   *   *

Everyone would concede, I think, that the ideal solution would be to provide each and every defendant with the extensive type of clinical investigation which was afforded to the millionaire defendant of our example above. Unlimited funds would be available for investigational purposes and only the most competent and experienced witnesses, well skilled in the presentation of technical clinical data to lay audiences, would be utilized in the courtroom. Obviously this is not going to be the case in the foreseeable future. The average defendant is going to be examined and evaluated in a highly abbreviated procedure by experts with varying degrees of skill, experience, bias, and partiality.

The traditional adversary system of calling witnesses for each side and then examining the witness by direct and cross-examination has been evolved for just the purpose of exposing these shortcomings and biases. The court and jury are then free to take them into consideration in allotting the weight which it will attach to the testimony of each witness. To utilize a system in which the expert witness is labeled as "impartial" in no way eliminates the shortcomings; it merely conceals them from the jury and creates the illusion of psychiatric omniscience. Such illusions may be good for the public relations of psychiatry, but they are not good for the administration of justice.

———

Are there more likely to be neutral experts in fields other than psychiatry? Assuming Diamond is right and there are no "neutral experts," are there, nonetheless, good reasons for courts to appoint experts? What would they be? Will there ever be situations where a judge should reject an expert agreed to by the parties?

———

Problem X–22. In Chapter Two we suggest that an indigent criminal defendant may have a constitutional right to investigative or expert assistance under the fifth and fourteenth amendments. **If there is a right to expert assistance, is it satisfied by the appointment of an expert who is expected to provide the court as well as the defendant with her findings? If an appointed defense counsel asks for the appointment of a psychiatrist on the ground that insanity might be a defense, should the defendant have a right to choose the psychiatric expert or should he be required to take whomever the court appoints? Does the answer turn on whether**

the prosecution will present its own expert? When an expert is appointed, should her findings be made available to the court or prosecution regardless of the defendant's litigation strategy?

Problem X–23. FRE 706(c) provides that the court may disclose to the jury the fact that an expert is judicially appointed. There was some dispute among the members of the Advisory Committee about the wisdom of allowing disclosure. The fear of those opposed is that the mantle of court appointment will cause the jury to give unjustified weight to the opinions of appointed experts. Indeed, some scholars have argued that parties who hire their own experts are wasting their money if the jury is going to be informed that one expert is court-appointed. **What is your reaction to this?** [86]

Problem X–24. In many jurisdictions, legislation requires that a plaintiff bringing a malpractice claim against a doctor to appear first before a committee that examines the claim. In Virginia, for example, the Medical Malpractice Review Panel is composed of "three impartial attorneys and three impartial health care providers, licensed and actively practicing their professions in this State, and one active judge of a circuit court who shall serve as chairman of the panel." Either party can request a hearing before the panel, which has subpoena power. Strict rules of evidence need not be observed. At the conclusion of its hearing the panel deliberates and renders a decision. The decision of the panel by majority vote is admissible as evidence, but is not conclusive, and any party can call any member of the panel as a witness. **Do you think this kind of a system is preferable to a system of court-appointed experts? Should comparable systems be instituted in areas other than medical malpractice? How might this be done?**

B. COMPELLING AN EXPERT TO TESTIFY

FRE 706(a) states in part that "[a]n expert witness shall not be appointed by the court unless he consents to act." Some states have similar rules. One study concludes that "[t]he majority of states hold that the expert may be subpoenaed to give a professional opinion based upon facts observed and opinions arrived at *prior* to being ordered to testify, even though he is not to be compensated with an expert witness fee." [87] Apparently the expert cannot be required to engage in any additional study or preparation, but if special preparation is not required or an opinion has already been formed, the expert is treated like any lay witness.

In support of the federal rule one commentator states that "[a]s a practical matter, a reluctant expert presents too great a haz-

---

86. For an argument that trial judges should be generally reluctant to call witnesses and to examine them or to disclose that they are court-appointed see Saltzburg, The Unnecessarily Expanding Role of the American Trial Judge, 64 Va.L.Rev. 1 (1978).

87. Moenssens et al., supra note 71, at 9 (emphasis in original). Other states' views are either narrow—that the expert cannot be

compelled to testify except as to facts personally observed, or very broad—that the expert can be forced to testify to facts and opinions in all circumstances. See Tyree, The Opinion Rule, 10 Rutgers L.Rev. 601, 616–17 (1956); Annot., 77 A.L.R.2d 1182 (1961). If an expert is forced to testify, should she receive more than an ordinary witness fee? Should the nature of the testimony control?

ard to justice."[88] Is this a judgment that should be codified, or should the parties (they may request an independent expert) and the court be free to make their own judgments in a particular case? What will happen in federal court if no expert con-

sents to assist a criminal defendant who needs expert assistance to present an effective defense? What will happen in malpractice cases if no doctor will voluntarily aid an injured plaintiff?

Problem X–25. Herman Rancourt sues defendant Urban Renewal Authority for undervaluing property taken from him by eminent domain. Rancourt calls Ted St. Pierre as a witness in order to rebut the Authority's expert testimony concerning the value of the condemned property. Objection is made by the Authority on the ground that St. Pierre's appraisal was made under a contract with the Authority which provided that the information gathered as a result of the appraisal was to be held strictly confidential unless the Authority gave its consent to disclosure. **What is the proper ruling? Does your answer depend on the public nature of the Authority?**

Problem X–26. Would you permit a plaintiff in a medical malpractice case to ask a defendant doctor for an opinion of the qualifications of plaintiff's medical expert?

Problem X–27. Shari Jackson wants to sue her psychiatrist for malpractice. Her claim is that the doctor had sexual relations with her, abusing his position of trust and fiduciary responsibility. Shari is having trouble finding expert witnesses to testify on her behalf. She has little money and her lawyer is working on a contingency fee basis. She finally locates a psychiatrist who will testify if he is guaranteed a fee of one-third of any recovery. **Should Shari be able to retain the expert on this basis?**

C. DISCOVERY

Fed.R.Civ.P. 26(b)(4)(A) provides for broad discovery of the evidence of expert witnesses who will testify at trial. But Rule 26(b)(4)(B) restricts discovery if the expert will not be called to testify.

(4) *Trial Preparation: Experts.* Discovery of facts known and opinions held by experts, otherwise discoverable under the provisions of subdivision (b)(1) of this rule and acquired or developed in anticipation of litigation or for trial, may be obtained only as follows:

(A)(i) A party may through interrogatories require any other party to identify each person whom the other party expects to call as an expert witness at trial, to state the subject matter on which the expert is expected to testify, and to state the substance of the facts and opinions to which the expert is expected to testify and a summary of the grounds for each opinion. (ii) Upon motion, the court may order further discovery by other means, subject to such restrictions as to scope and such provisions pursuant to

---

88. 3 Weinstein's Evidence ¶ 706[02], at 706–15.

subdivision (b)(4)(C) of this rule, concerning fees and expenses as the court may deem appropriate.

(B) A party may discover facts known or opinions held by an expert who has been retained or specially employed by another party in anticipation of litigation or preparation for trial and who is not expected to be called as a witness at trial, only as provided in Rule 35(b)[89] or upon a showing of exceptional circumstances under which it is impracticable for the party seeking discovery to obtain facts or opinions on the same subject by other means.

(C) Unless manifest injustice would result, (i) the court shall require that the party seeking discovery pay the expert a reasonable fee for time spent in responding to discovery under subdivisions (b)(4)(A)(ii) and (b)(4)(B) of this rule; and (ii) with respect to discovery obtained under subdivision (b)(4)(A)(ii) of this rule the court may require, and with respect to discovery obtained under subdivision (b)(4)(B) of this rule the court shall require, the party seeking discovery to pay the other party a fair portion of the fees and expenses reasonably incurred by the latter party in obtaining facts and opinions from the expert.

Why should this rule exist? Does it make sense to distinguish for discovery purposes experts who will testify from those who will not? Is anything we discussed in Chapter Eight on privileges relevant to this issue? FRE 706, in its provision for much broader discovery, conflicts with Fed.R.Civ.P. 26 and also with Fed. R.Crim.P. 15.

Since the courts must see that experts retained by the parties are compensated for time spent giving depositions, why should there be greater discovery of court-appointed experts than other experts? If the idea of FRE 706 is to ensure against surprise, is not the same assurance needed with respect to retained experts? Indeed, if experts can be independent, is it not likely that surprise is less important with appointed experts than with experts of the parties' own choosing?[90]

BIBLIOGRAPHY

McCormick §§ 13–17, 69, 202–211.

Moenssens, Moses & Inbau, Scientific Evidence in Criminal Cases (1972).

3 Weinstein's Evidence ¶¶ 702–706.

2 Wigmore §§ 445–460, 563; 7 Wigmore §§ 1923, 1925.

Beuscher, The Use of Experts by the Courts, 54 Harv.L.Rev. 1105 (1941).

Diamond, The Fallacy of the Impartial Expert, 3 Archives of Crim. Psychodynamics 221 (1959).

Diamond & Louisell, The Psychiatrist As An Expert Witness, 63 Mich.L.Rev. 1335 (1965).

Greene, Voiceprint Identification: The Case in Favor of Admissibility, 13 Am.Crim.L.Rev. 171 (1975).

Haines, Future of Court Psychiatry, 2 J.For.Sci. 59 (1957).

89. Fed.R.Civ.P. 35(b) governs reports of physical or mental examinations ordered by the court after a showing of good cause.

90. Lawyers understand the need to depose experts. In fact, there is much more sharing of information about experts and many more agreements to permit depositions than one would expect from reading Fed.R.Civ.P. 26(b)(4). See generally, Graham, Discovery of Experts Under Rule 26(b)(4) of the Federal Rules of Civil Procedure: Part One, Part Two, 1976 U.Ill.L.For. 895; 1977 U.Ill.L.For. 169.

Jones, Danger—Voiceprints Ahead, 11 Am.Crim.L.Rev. 549 (1973).

Karjala, The Evidentiary Uses of Neutron Activation Analysis, 59 Cal.L.Rev. 997 (1971).

Korn, Law, Fact and Science in the Courts, 66 Colum.L.Rev. 1080 (1966).

Maguire & Hahesy, Requisite Proof of Basis for Expert Opinion, 5 Vand.L.Rev. 432 (1952).

Marshall, Evidence, Psychology, and the Trial: Some Challenges to Law, 63 Colum.L.Rev. 197 (1963).

McElhaney, Expert Witnesses and the Federal Rules of Evidence, 28 Mercer L.Rev. 463 (1977).

Mitchell, The Proposed Federal Rules of Evidence: How They Affect Product Liability Practice, 12 Duquesne L.Rev. 551 (1974).

Morgan, Suggested Remedy for Obstructions to Expert Testimony by Rules of Evidence, 10 U.Chi.L.Rev. 284 (1943).

Parker, Automobile Accident Analysis By Expert Witnesses, 44 Va.L.Rev. 789 (1958).

Rose, The Social Scientist As An Expert Witness, 40 Minn.L.Rev. 205 (1956).

Rheingold, The Basis of Medical Testimony, 15 Vand.L.Rev. 473 (1962).

Saltzburg, The Unnecessarily Expanding Role of the American Trial Judge, 64 Va.L.Rev. 1 (1978).

Shuck, Techniques for Proof of Complicated Scientific and Economic Facts, 40 F.R.D. 33 (1967).

Seidelson, Medical Malpractice Cases, 16 Cath.U.L.Rev. 158 (1966).

Spector & Foster, Admissibility of Hypnotic Statements: Is the Law of Evidence Susceptible? 38 Ohio St.L.J. 567 (1977).

Tarlow, Admissibility of Polygraph Evidence in 1975: An Aid in Determining Credibility in a Perjury-Plagued System, 26 Hast.L.Rev. 917 (1975).

Tyree, The Opinion Rule, 10 Rutgers L.Rev. 601 (1956).

Weihofen, An Alternative to the Battle of Experts: Hospital Examination of Criminal Defendants Before Trial, 2 Law & Contemp.Prob. 419 (1935).

Note, The Admissibility of Bite Mark Evidence, 51 So.Cal.L.Rev. 309 (1979).

Note, The Admissibility of Testimony Influenced by Hypnosis, 67 Va.L.Rev. 1203 (1981).

Note, Contingent Fees for Expert Witnesses in Civil Litigation, 86 Yale L.J. 1680 (1977).

Chapter Eleven

REAL AND DEMONSTRATIVE EVIDENCE

SECTION I.   INTRODUCTION

This chapter discusses real evidence and demonstrative evidence. These terms refer to things which convey firsthand sense impressions to triers of fact in ways that testimonial evidence cannot. Some courts and commentators do not distinguish between real and demonstrative evidence since the same general evidentiary principles apply when either real or demonstrative evidence is offered. For other courts and commentators real evidence refers to tangible objects that played some role in the matter giving rise to the litigation while demonstrative evidence refers to tangible materials that illustrate matters of importance to the litigation. A gun used in a crime, counterfeit money that was passed, and a defective cotter pin that caused a safety device to fail are examples of real evidence. Diagrams, scale models and filmed reenactments of an event are examples of demonstrative evidence. Although the same general principles apply to the admission of each, the fundamental question with respect to real evidence is whether it is in fact the object that played a role in the matter giving rise to litigation while the fundamental question with respect to demonstrative evidence is whether it portrays the matter it is offered to illustrate in a way that is likely to aid and not mislead the jury. This difference has given rise to specific rules that are more often invoked with respect to one kind of evidence than with respect to the other. For example, one must often show a chain of custody in the case of real evidence, such as the can of marihuana in the Whale case, but this is rarely, if ever, required when evidence is demonstrative.[1]

Testimonial evidence reports a witness' sense impressions; its influence depends on the witness' perceived credibility. Real or demonstrative evidence is available for the fact finder's own sensing, be it by sight, hearing, taste, smell, touch or some combination of these.

Consider, for example, a homicide trial which turns on whether the defendant's use of a gun was a reasonable response to the deceased's movement for a knife. Any testimonial description of the knife would have to be evaluated in light of the witness' apparent biases and opportunity to observe. If, however, the knife itself were introduced, the jurors could see with their own eyes whether it was a pen-knife or a machete. The knife would be introduced as real evidence in the case. Or consider a witness' description of an auto accident. If the witness testified that he saw the defendant's car run a red light, that would be direct testimonial evidence of the defendant's negligence. If the witness testified that he did not see the light when the defendant entered the intersection but noticed it was red very shortly thereafter, that

---

1. You may also find real evidence referred to in legal scholarship or appellate opinions as "autoptic proference." This awkward phrase is Wigmore's. He believes it precisely defines the quality of the evidence involved. Wigmore feels that "this [term] avoids the fallacy of attributing an evidential quality to that which is in fact nothing more nor less than the thing itself." 1 Wigmore § 24, at 397. He comments, "No logical process is employed; only an act of sensible apprehension occurs, apprehension of the existence or non-existence of the thing as alleged." See also 4 Wigmore § 1150. Does this oversimplify the way in which real evidence is perceived and used? We think so.

would be circumstantial testimonial evidence of the defendant's negligence. In either case the value of the witness' testimony would depend on his credibility. If, however, the witness were taking home movies at the time of the accident and happened to photograph the intersection, the movies would be real or demonstrative evidence of what had occurred.[2] They might be direct evidence of the defendant's negligence, circumstantial evidence of negligence or no evidence at all, depending on what the camera captured. The value of the film would not depend upon credibility in the ordinary sense of the term, for film is not credible or incredible in the way that a witness is. Instead its value would depend on the film being what it purported to be—a film of the accident at issue—and on the way in which the film was shot and processed.

The basic evidentiary requirement that all witnesses speak from personal knowledge recognizes that testimonial evidence begins as real evidence; i.e., what the witnesses see, feel, hear or otherwise sense firsthand would be real evidence if the jurors were present at the event and able to share the witnesses' sense perceptions. It becomes testimonial because a need to assess credibility is interposed between the occurrence and the jury's assessment of its meaning.[3]

Testimonial evidence in its simplest form is a statement of one witness' observations; for example, a statement by W that the defendant's car ran a red light. When a witness reports the statements of another (for example, W's statement that X said that the defendant's car ran a red light) we speak of compound testimonial evidence if the other's statement is offered for its truth. In the latter case, the jury must assess the credibility of two individuals before reaching a conclusion about the fact in issue.[4] Statements offered for their truth are testimonial in nature even if reduced to writing.

When an out-of-court statement is offered to prove something other than the truth of what is therein asserted, the evidence can be either real or testimonial. For example, a police officer's oral or written report that the plaintiff spoke to him after an accident would be testimonial evidence that the witness was conscious at that time. A statement written by the plaintiff immediately after an accident would be real evidence that the witness was conscious at that time.

We have indicated a basic distinction between real and testimonial evidence, but there is no bright line to mark the difference. Indeed, to the extent that demeanor is important in judging credibility, real and testimonial evidence merge, since

---

2. Note here how the distinction between real and demonstrative evidence breaks down. The movie does more than just illustrate the accident, yet it was in no way involved with the event. In situations like this the primary concerns with both kinds of evidence would have to be met. The party offering the film would have to show that it was the actual film taken of the accident or an accurate copy and he would have to show that it fairly depicted the event. If for example, the film was taken through a lens that substantially foreshortened distant objects, it might be excluded as misleading even if it was a film of the accident in issue.

3. **In one sense testimonial evidence remains real, since it must be perceived by a jury in some sensate manner, usually through the sense of hearing. But, all evidence must be perceived through the senses, so there is no point in focusing on the way testimonial evidence is real if we are looking for a way to distinguish testimonial evidence from other forms of evidence. Analytically, however, one may argue that there is really only one form of evidence, although there may be different forms of proof. Michael and Adler make this point in a perceptive and sophisticated article. Real Proof: I, 5 Vand.L.Rev. 344, 356 (1952).**

4. FRE 806, which provides for the impeachment of hearsay declarants, implicitly recognizes the testimonial nature of reported hearsay.

demeanor evidence is real evidence.[5] The two kinds of evidence also merge whenever the probative value of real evidence depends upon the foundation laid for the evidence by the testimony of a witness.

The previous chapters have focused almost entirely on testimonial evidence. A number of the evidence rules you have learned, such as the relevance rules, apply to real or demonstrative evidence in much the same way as they apply to testimonial evidence. Others, such as the opinion and hearsay rules, do not apply to real or demonstrative evidence per se, although they may apply to statements contained in such evidence. In this chapter we shall discuss special rules that apply only to real or demonstrative evidence.

Because real and demonstrative evidence appeal directly to the jurors' senses and because such evidence may create impressions more vivid than any words, real and demonstrative evidence have the potential to be particularly persuasive. However, real and demonstrative evidence may also be as weak or as questionable as the weakest testimonial evidence. It depends on how the evidence was developed and on what it purports to be.

In thinking about the persuasive power of evidence, whether testimonial or non-testimonial, it is important to keep two different aspects in mind: First, a jury must believe that certain evidence is credible before it will use the evidence to decide a case. Second, a jury must decide how to use what it finds credible.

Consider, for example, the prosecution for selling heroin of someone we shall call Howard Smith. A witness testifies, "I called a telephone number listed as belonging to Howard Smith. The person who answered said he was Howard Smith. He said he had gotten hold of some heroin, so we arranged for a sale, and the heroin was delivered as arranged." When this evidence is offered against Smith, the jury must decide whether it believes that the witness is testifying truthfully. If it does not, the evidence will be dismissed as unhelpful. If it believes the witness, the jury's next step is to decide whether the defendant Howard Smith is the person who identified himself as the Howard Smith on the phone. The evidence may suggest that this is likely but it may leave room for doubt, just as the credibility of the witness who testified about the conversation may be doubted. If the jury believes the witness and believes that the defendant is the Smith who agreed to sell the heroin, it will convict.

Now consider the situation where the witness has tape recorded the conversation with Smith. The jury must make the same two inferences. First, it must decide whether a conversation took place. The tape recording is likely to be particularly persuasive on this issue. Second, it must decide whether the defendant is the person who identified himself as Smith on the tape. Unless the recording is clear enough to allow an unequivocal identification of Smith's voice there will be some degree of uncertainty. If the jury resolves the uncertainty by concluding that Smith is the voice on the tape, it will again convict. Otherwise it will not.

In this example, real evidence is likely to lead the jurors to accept more quickly

---

5. **Demeanor evidence is an exception to the general rule that before something can become an item of evidence it must be offered by a litigant and admitted by a judge. Michael and Adler argue that this is the only exception. Real Proof, supra note 1, at 365–66 and n. 65. Another possible exception is when a jury takes "judicial" notice of common experience, a phe-** nomenon explored in several problems in Chapter Nine. **Should a judge or a jury be permitted to consider the demeanor of a person sitting in the courtroom? See e.g. Morrison v. People of State of California, 291 U.S. 82, 94 (1934); United States v. Schipani, 293 F.Supp. 156, 163 (E.D.N.Y. 1968), affirmed, 414 F.2d 1262, 1268 (2d Cir. 1969), certiorari denied, 397 U.S. 922 (1970).**

certain facts as true;–i.e., that the witness in fact conversed with someone who identified himself as Howard Smith. But it is also possible that testimonial evidence might be more persuasive evidence of certain facts. If the prosecution produced an apparently credible witness who had been with Howard Smith when he arranged the deal, that witness' testimony that the defendant was the person talking on the phone is likely to be more persuasive than a voice identification based on a tape that is full of interference and hard to hear.

One might ask why special attention should be given to non-testimonial evidence if a jury is expected to use it in what is logically the same way as testimonial evidence? There are several reasons. First, neither lawyers nor judges can question exhibits that are offered in evidence. This makes the testimony of witnesses who set exhibits in context critically important. The Smith drug case is an illustration. The tape recording is only helpful if a jury can relate it to the charge made against Smith. In the usual case, a witness should testify to information such as how he placed the call and when the call was made, and he would then go on to say that the tape was an accurate recording of the ensuing conversation. If this witness is not believed, the tape is not likely to be useful. The foundation is vital. Neither real nor demonstrative evidence is assumed to be helpful until its connection to the case is shown. Thus, many of the rules that relate to real and demonstrative evidence are concerned with the requisite foundation for admissibility. These rules are designed to ensure that such evidence meets some minimal standards of reliability and that the jury can reasonably find that the evidence is what it purports to be.

Other rules that relate specifically to real and demonstrative evidence are concerned with the possibility that a jury may place special emphasis on evidence that it experiences firsthand. The particularly vivid or dramatic quality of some such evidence, the impossibility of cross-examining pictures or other objects, and the fact that intermediaries do not filter the information contained in real and demonstrative evidence suggest a likelihood that such evidence will receive special, perhaps undue, emphasis in the jury's deliberations. Thus, special restrictions may be placed on real or demonstrative evidence when it is feared that such evidence might receive undue weight.

In what follows we examine the evidentiary restrictions that are placed on real and demonstrative evidence.

SECTION II. THE FOUNDATION REQUIREMENTS

A. AUTHENTICATION: BASIC RELEVANCE

FRE 901(a) provides that "[t]he requirement of authentication or identification as a condition precedent to admissibility is satisfied by evidence sufficient to support a finding that the matter in question is what its proponent claims." It has been said that "[a]uthentication and identification of evidence are merely aspects of relevancy which are a necessary condition precedent to admissibility."[6] Michael and Adler called authentication the logical condition of the admissibility of real proof and noted that "the satisfaction of this condition depends upon the identification of the offered thing or event with one of the litigants in some way."[7] Wigmore agrees:

In short, when a claim or offer involves impliedly or expressly any element of *personal connection with a corporal ob-*

---

6. 5 Weinstein's Evidence ¶ 901(a)[02].

7. Real Proof, supra note 3, at 362.

ject, that connection must be made to appear, like the other elements, else the whole fails in effect.[8]

It is true of both testimonial and non-testimonial evidence that before it is accepted there must be a sufficient basis for a rational fact finder to use the evidence for the purpose for which it is offered. Thus, in dealing with the testimony of ordinary witnesses, some showing of firsthand knowledge is crucial. FRE 901 states the general principle and illustrates ways of establishing the necessary basis for certain kinds of testimonial evidence and for real and demonstrative evidence as well.

Rule 901. Requirement of Authentication or Identification

(a) *General provision.*—The requirement of authentication or identification as a condition precedent to admissibility is satisfied by evidence sufficient to support a finding that the matter in question is what its proponent claims.

(b) *Illustrations.*—By way of illustration only, and not by way of limitation, the following are examples of authentication or identification conforming with the requirements of this rule:

(1) Testimony of witness with knowledge.—Testimony that a matter is what it is claimed to be.

(2) Nonexpert opinion on handwriting.—Nonexpert opinion as to the genuineness of handwriting, based upon familiarity not acquired for purposes of the litigation.

(3) Comparison by trier or expert witness.—Comparison by the trier of fact or by expert witnesses with specimens which have been authenticated.

(4) Distinctive characteristics and the like.—Appearance, contents, substance, internal patterns, or other distinctive characteristics, taken in conjunction with circumstances.

(5) Voice identification.—Identification of a voice, whether heard firsthand or through mechanical or electronic transmission or recording, by opinion based upon hearing the voice at any time under circumstances connecting it with the alleged speaker.

(6) Telephone conversations.—Telephone conversations, by evidence that a call was made to the number assigned at the time by the telephone company to a particular person or business, if (A) in the case of a person, circumstances, including self-identification show the person answering to be the one called, or (B) in the case of a business, the call was made to a place of business and the conversation related to business reasonably transacted over the telephone.

(7) Public records or reports.—Evidence that a writing authorized by law to be recorded or filed and in fact recorded or filed in a public office, or a purported public record, report, statement, or data compilation, in any form, is from the public office where items of this nature are kept.

(8) Ancient documents or data compilation.—Evidence that a document or data compilation, in any form, (A) is in such condition as to create no suspicion concerning its authenticity, (B) was in a place where it, if authentic, would likely be, and (C) has been in existence 20 years or more at the time it is offered.

(9) Process or system.—Evidence describing a process or system used to produce a result and showing that the process or system produces an accurate result.

(10) Methods provided by statute or rule.—Any method of authentication or identification provided by Act of Con-

---

8.   7 Wigmore § 2129, at 564 (emphasis in original).

gress or by other rules prescribed by the Supreme Court pursuant to statutory authority.

Saltzburg and Redden describe some problems with Rule 901 and discuss the examples set forth in subsection (b) of the rule:

Rule 901 establishes a general provision that the requirement of authentication or identification as a condition precedent to admissibility is satisfied by evidence sufficient to support a finding that the matter in question is what its proponents claim. If this Rule is read literally, it makes tremendous inroads into common law doctrine, and it greatly simplifies the task of getting evidence before the jury. But as this Comment indicates below, it is by no means clear that the changes in the common law that the text of the Rule seems to make are intended by either the Advisory Committee or the Congress.

To understand the problem presented by the general provision of Rule 901(a), consider the case of a psychologist called to testify in support of an insanity defense raised by a criminal defendant. Through the witness, defendant wishes to introduce the results of certain psychological tests. In common law jurisdictions, the first thing that defense counsel will do is establish the qualifications of the expert. The expert will identify the tests and establish their reliability. If he cannot do this to the satisfaction of the Judge, the tests will be excluded. Rule 901(a) may change this. The second sentence of section (a) of the Rule states that the requirement of authentication of the evidence is satisfied if counsel can introduce evidence sufficient to support a finding. Thus, if a reasonable jury can find the tests to be reliable psychological tools, which is that the expert claims, it would seem that the evidence should be admitted. The problem is that nothing in the Ad-

visory Committee's Note indicates that this radical change is intended. There are indications that the Rule is designed to simplify the authentication process. But it would be odd if the preexisting process of authenticating tests, experiments, research methods, etc., is completely changed by a Rule that does not squarely address the point and which emerges from a history that fails to indicate that this matter was given sufficient thought. Rule 702 (Testimony By Experts) offers little assistance on this point. Nor does Rule 703.

Another example may help to illustrate the problem with the Rule. Because of the tape recordings made at the White House under former President Nixon, many lawyers, Judges, and scholars have turned their attention to the requirements of authenticating a tape recording. Before the new Federal Rules, it was clear that the Judge had to make a finding that the tapes were sufficiently accurate and reliable to be admitted into evidence. Apparently, Rule 901(a) only requires that the Judge insure that there is enough evidence so that a reasonable jury could find that the tapes are accurate. * * * Was this intended by the drafters? There is no certain way of knowing. * * *

One more example should remove all doubts that there is a problem here. In a typical narcotics case—one, for example, where the defendant is charged with possession of heroin—before the prosecutor is permitted to introduce the narcotics in common law jurisdictions, he is required to demonstrate a chain of custody. Rule 901(b)(1) provides that one of the ways of authenticating evidence is to introduce the testimony of a witness with knowledge. The Advisory Committee's Note states that this subsection contemplates a broad spectrum of evidence including the traditional chain of custody evidence. The problem, however, is that Rule 901(a) can easily be read as doing away with any chain of custody requirement. In pointing this out, we do not intend to suggest that some modification of the traditional requirement would be unwise. We point this out for the purpose of demonstrating that there is a problem in interpretation. Whenever these Rules are applied in a criminal case involving narcotics, the Judge may be called upon to determine whether any chain of custody must be demonstrated. If he interprets Rule 901(a) to permit a loose presentation with gaps that ordinarily would not be allowed, he runs the risk of reversal. The Advisory Committee and the Congress have failed to provide definitive guidance to the Judge in determining what the Rule really means.

* * *

Section (b) of Rule 901 contains ten illustrations of ways of authenticating evidence. It is plain that these are only illustrative; they are not limitations on the ways authentication can be accomplished. These examples are considered seriatim below.

(1) Testimony of a witness who has personal knowledge as to a piece of evidence is a classic way of authenticating the evidence. Someone who is an eyewitness to the signing of a document may testify to that fact, for example.

(2) A lay person can identify handwriting based upon familiarity with the handwriting, as long as the familiarity was not acquired solely for purposes of the litigation in which the testimony is offered. Such testimony is reserved for an expert.

(3) Handwriting, fingerprints, blood, hair, clothing fibers, and numerous other things can be authenticated by comparison with specimens that have been authenticated. Sometimes the comparison can be done by the trier of fact; at other times an expert witness will be required, especially when scientific knowledge is needed to make a valid examination of the samples. The Advisory Committee's Note makes clear its intent to allow specimens to be used if the jury could find them to be genuine. The Judge need not make a factual finding, but must insure that enough evidence exists to support a jury finding.

(4) Sometimes the characteristics of an item will themselves serve to authenticate the item. A letter may be authenticated, for example, by content and the circumstances indicating it was a reply to a duly authenticated letter.

(5) One who is familiar with the voice of another may authenticate a conversation or identify the speaker on a tape or other recording. However, if the tape or recording is offered for its truth, hearsay problems still will exist and must be solved following the satisfaction of the authentication requirement. Best evidence problems may likewise exist, and they too must be addressed. Authentication is thus just one hurdle among many to admissibility. Note that the person making the identification may have become familiar with the voice for purposes of litigation, something not allowed in connection with handwriting.

(6) When a voice identification cannot be made because the person wishing to introduce evidence of a conversation cannot testify as to familiarity with the voice of the person to whom he allegedly spoke, authentication may be established in other ways. For example, a telephone conversation might be authenticated in the case of a business by showing that a call was made to the number assigned to a business by the telephone company, that someone answered the phone purporting to represent the business, and that the conversation related to business reasonably transacted over the telephone. In the

case of an individual, the fact that the number was assigned to the individual and that the person talking on the phone identified himself as being a certain person may be enough to authenticate the conversation.

(7) Public records are usually authenticated by proof of custody. This illustration extends the traditional thinking to cover data stored in computers.

(8) This is the traditional authentication by showing an ancient document. If evidence is presented that a document or data compilation (apparently including data stored in computers) is in such condition as to create no suspicion concerning its authenticity, is in a place where it would likely be if it were authentic, and has been in existence 20 years or more at the time it is offered, this is sufficient authentication. (Common law required 30 years.)

(9) Authentication may be accomplished by showing that a process or system produces an accurate result when it is employed. In order to introduce an X-ray, for instance, it may be necessary to demonstrate that the X-ray machine is accurate. Judicial notice may sometimes solve the problem here. Judges must be careful to differentiate, however, between authentication of a process generally and a showing that a particular machine works as intended.

(10) Any method of authentication or identification provided by an Act of Congress or by Rules prescribed by the Supreme Court shall be valid to authenticate. This is included to insure that no one interprets the Rules of Evidence as superseding the established Civil and Criminal Rules of Procedure or Bankruptcy Rules.

*   *   *

Because (b) offers illustrations, it is arguable that some of the limitations —e.g., that the person identifying handwriting have been familiar with the writing prior to the litigation—are hortatory only and need not be honored. Whether they are binding or not most Courts are following the limitations and seem to appreciate the guidance provided by the Rule.[9]

———

Sometimes no witness is needed to lay the foundation for real evidence because the material one seeks to admit is treated as self-authenticating under FRE 902. These include: foreign and domestic public documents, copies of public records,[10] commercial paper and related documents, documents made self-authenticating by Act of Congress, official publications, trade inscriptions and the like, and newspapers and periodicals. In some states the class of self-authenticating documents is considerably more restricted. The idea behind self-authentication is that the nature of the documents or things makes it so unlikely that they are not what they appear to be that a decision maker needs no additional testimonial basis for accepting the evidence at face value. This is not an exception from the logical basis requirement; it is a recognition that the logical basis is supplied by the appearance of the object and by past experience which suggests that such objects may be assumed to be what they apparently are. A party who questions this may dispute it before the jury, but the evidence will be received.

In addition to these modes of authentication, one may ask the opposite party to stipulate that materials to be introduced are what they purport to be, or if a stipulation

---

9. S. Saltzburg & K. Redden, Federal Rules of Evidence Manual 697–98, 701–02 (3d ed. 1982).

10. In the case of foreign documents, domestic documents not under seal and copies of public records, there are special certification requirements before the documents will be treated as self-authenticating.

appears unlikely, one may seek a formal admission of authenticity under Fed.R.Civ.P. 36. An unreasonable failure to admit may make the opposing party liable for the expenses of proving authenticity. Similarly, if both sides agree on the relationship evidence has to a case, the jury may be told of their agreement and the presentation of background evidence becomes unnecessary.

At common law, before any attested writing could be introduced the attesters had to be called or their absence explained.[11] According to Professor Morgan, "[t]his requirement which had its origin in the ancient Germanic transaction or business witness doctrine never had any basis in reason after the use of witnesses in open court became established in the common law."[12] At one time whenever a writing was attested the execution of that writing could only be proved through the attesters, unless they were shown to be unavailable. This rule was applied regardless of whether the writing was of a kind required by law to be attested. To-

day, attesters do not have to be called unless the writing is one required by law to be attested. The modern view is embodied in FRE 903 which provides that "[t]he testimony of a subscribing witness is not necessary to authenticate a writing unless required by the laws of the jurisdiction whose laws govern the validity of the writing."[13] In many jurisdictions, existing attestation requirements are softened by various exceptions. One of the most common waives the requirement of authentication by attesting witnesses for writings that are only collaterally involved in the case being tried. Rules softening the requirement that attesting witnesses be called do not signify a lowering of the basic relevance standard for evidence. Rather, they recognize that relevance can be demonstrated without calling specific witnesses. When a jurisdiction adopts a rule requiring the testimony of a subscribing witness, it is signifying that it seeks a stronger guarantee of reliability as to certain documents than that which the normal rules of authentication ensure.

B. ADDITIONAL REQUIREMENTS

As we noted in our introduction to FRE 901, the rule is not restricted to real evidence. A witness who describes a telephone conversation such as the one we

hypothesized earlier in our Howard Smith example must give the jury a basis for concluding that it really was the defendant, Howard Smith, on the phone arranging the

---

11. These requirements were waived if the opposing party admitted the genuineness of the writing. The general rule was that an admission of authenticity was valid only if found in the pleadings or in a stipulation. Wigmore, however, argued for authentication by extrajudicial admissions. 4 Wigmore § 1300. See also FRE 1007, discussed infra.

12. E. Morgan, Basic Problems of Evidence 378 (1963).

13. **Weinstein and Berger suggest that "[t]he rule, as it should be applied in the federal courts, only limits proof of execution to show the jural effect of the document * * *." 5 Weinstein's Evidence ¶ 903[03]. While this view is in accord with Wigmore's approach, 4 Wigmore § 1293, and**

has much to commend it as matter of policy, we find it somewhat difficult to interpret the words "unless required by the laws of the jurisdiction" in the manner suggested. The Advisory Committee's Note is not helpful. If a state were misguided enough to have a rule that "no will may be introduced into evidence for any purpose unless the attesting witnesses are first called to authenticate it," FRE 903 might well require the federal courts to follow the state rule unless the final clause of the rule— "whose laws govern the validity of the writing"—is read as if it were qualified by the phrase "and only where the validity of the writing is material." When Congress has not qualified the rule with this phrase, is it appropriate for a court to do so?

drug deal. If a tape is offered, the offeror must give the jury some basis for assuming that it is Smith's voice on the tape.

When a witness testifies on such topics as a conversation he heard or an accident he saw, courts use a simple relevance analysis to decide whether the jury has a basis for using the evidence. The requirement of personal knowledge plus ordinary relevance principles screen out testimony when the fact finder has no logical basis for accepting it as reliable and helpful.

When real or demonstrative evidence is offered in the form of an exhibit, courts sometimes speak of the authentication requirement as if it were different in kind from that imposed on testimony. But the basic requirement that the decision maker have sufficient information to treat the evidence as the offeror intends is really no different for testimony than it is for exhibits. It is an elementary requirement that there be a logical nexus between the evidence and the point on which it is offered.

Given the required nexus, the question arises as to whether this is the only preliminary requirement for the introduction of real evidence. Some courts have adopted special rules governing the way certain evidence must be handled. These rules are especially important in the case of evidence that has played a part in the activity that is the subject matter of the litigation. Suppose, for example, that a police officer arrests Jennie Jones and takes from her a substance that he believes, based on his experience or training, to be cocaine. Would the officer be permitted to testify that the substance was cocaine? Given his expertise, the officer probably would be permitted to identify the substance as cocaine since the jury has a reasonable basis for accepting his characterization. Often, however, as in the Whale case in the first chapter, the prosecution chemically analyzes substances seized in

order to remove any doubts about their nature. Before a chemist could testify about the results of tests run on a substance, it is necessary for the state to show that the substance it has offered in evidence is not only that which was tested but also that which was seized from the defendant. In our example, the state would have to show that the powder that tested out as 90% pure cocaine is the powder that was taken from Jones.

Suppose that a chemist testifies that the labels fell off two packets sent to him for analysis and that a powder he can identify as cocaine might have been seized from either Jones or Smith. The evidence would be excluded as lacking the nexus needed to attribute its possession to Jones. This is so even though the chemist's testimony is logically relevant, for knowing that a substance taken from either Jones or Smith was cocaine makes the conclusion that Jones possessed cocaine more likely than it would be without the evidence or if the substance taken from either Jones or Smith had been identified as sugar. Thus, the decision to exclude the chemist's testimony must be based on more than a concern for logical relevance. In this case it would reflect a judicial judgment that the jury could only guess whether the substance was taken from Jones and that such guessing was impermissible when the narcotic quality of the substance was a matter that had to be proven beyond a reasonable doubt.

Now suppose the chemist identifies the substance offered in court as that which he tested but says he does not know from whom the substance was taken. If the arresting officer testifies that the substance is that which he took from Jones and that he kept careful control over it before giving it to the chemist for testing, the evidence will be admitted. What many courts call a chain of custody has been established. For a material like cocaine that has no distinctive markings, a chain of custody requires some system of identification, such as inserting the substance in a sealed envelope and having each person who handles the substance sign the envelope as evidence that he returned what he took.

Thus, a chain of custody requirement involves more than mere relevance. It specifies a degree of care that is required in the handling of evidence. Although tampering with evidence is probably not a great problem, the more sloppily evidence is handled, the greater the chances of tampering and the greater the likelihood it will go undetected. Fear of tampering has also led some courts to adopt rules requiring special care in the handling of tape recordings.[14] They think that the possibility of alteration is great enough and alterations are difficult enough to detect that special rules are justified.

Although there are holdings suggesting that a chain of custody must be shown in civil as well as in criminal cases, problems with the handling of evidence arise most often in the criminal context. This is probably because careful handling requirements are thought to be most appropriate when litigation is clearly anticipated and when one side is in possession of important evidence. The requirement is also more manageable when an institution, such as a police department, can be expected to implement chain of custody rules as a matter of course. In many civil cases it is unclear that an item will be used as evidence until it has been handled for a considerable period of time, and the people first possessing the evidence may know nothing about what the law requires.

With respect to some evidence, tampering or alteration is not likely to be a problem, so a chain of custody or a showing of careful handling is less important and unlikely to be required. Consider, for example, a .45 caliber pistol seized from a suspect in a murder case. If the officer who seized it carves his initials into the base of the pistol, it is unlikely that he will have any trouble identifying the weapon in court, even if it has been in a place accessible to others between the time of seizure and the time of trial. The difference between the pistol and the cocaine is the difference between an object that is unique or can be made so and one that is not.

In some situations one person has the exclusive possession of evidence from the time of its seizure to the time of the trial and the foundation for admissibility is easily established. In other cases, where the evidence changes hands, several witnesses may be required. This was the situation in *Whale*. Norton received the can of marihauna allegedly from Whale and took it to Barrott, who gave it to Wall. All three witnesses testified. To better meet chain of custody requirements many police departments have established property departments that store evidence in a secure place until it is examined by the state's experts and then retain custody in that same secure place after the experts have finished their analyses.

Once there is a gap or a break in the handling of an object that cannot be ac-

---

14. See, e.g., United States v. McMillan, 508 F.2d 101 (8th Cir. 1974), certiorari denied, 421 U.S. 916 (1975), where the court listed seven foundation requirements:

(1) That the recording device was capable of taking the conversation now offered in evidence.

(2) That the operator of the device was competent to operate the device.

(3) That the recording is authentic and correct.

(4) That changes, additions or deletions have not been made in the recording.

(5) That the recording has been preserved in a manner that is shown to the court.

(6) That the speakers are identified.

(7) That the conversation elicited was made voluntarily and in good faith, without any kind of inducement.

counted for, the question is whether the gap or break is serious enough to warrant exclusion. As a matter of relevancy only, some courts today say that absent a showing of actual tampering a break goes to weight, not admissibility. Those that adhere to a greater care-in-handling requirement typically require more than just a small break before excluding—e.g., no court would exclude evidence if an officer left it on a desk for a few moments while using the restroom. Reasonable care and a reasonable showing that there was no realistic opportunity for tampering are all a court is likely to require.[15]

Similarly, when the condition of an object is important, it is not necessary to show that there is absolutely no possibility that its condition is unchanged. Showing that there is no reasonable possibility that the object is changed is, except in the courtrooms of rather idiosyncratic judges, enough.

There are situations in which an object is offered in evidence even though its condition at the time of the trial is very different from its condition at an earlier time. In some cases the changed condition is irrelevant and can be disregarded—for example, a gun has been dropped and dented but the dent is clearly not relevant. Even if the change is important, the evidence may be admitted. This is permissible as long as the decision maker is able to understand, with the assistance of testimonial evidence, how the evidence has been changed and can appreciate how the evidence appeared when the relevant event took place. For example, a machine that caused an injury may have been repaired before suit was filed. At the trial, the machine may be offered as evidence along with a description of how it appeared when the accident occurred. The exhibit may, however, be excluded under FRE 403 if the changes made in it are such that the jury is likely to be confused by seeing it or if the probative value of the evidence is likely to be outweighed by prejudice to the opposing party.

C. GENERAL OBJECTIONS

Problems relating to the handling of evidence generally arise only with real evidence; i.e., evidence that has been involved in the events giving rise to trial. They almost never exist when parties present demonstrative evidence, i.e., exhibits

15. Where evidence relating to an essential element in a case lacks distinctive characteristics that make for ready identification the authors agree with those courts that impose a chain of custody restriction on possible modes of authentication. The courts that admit evidence where a chain of custody has been in some substantial way broken and juries that evaluate such evidence may misassess its probative value by not noticing what we call the "negative" aspects of relevance. If police typically follow a routine and know that courts prefer or require them to follow that routine, the question arises as to why the routine was not followed on a particular occasion. If no convincing explanation can be offered, the probability of tampering may be considerably greater than it would be if the routine had never been established in the first instance. By moving away from rigid chain of custody requirements courts are also lowering the probative value of the fact that a chain of custody was broken. A good compromise between a rigid rule and a rule that relegates a break in the chain to weight only, would be a rule that requires that either a chain of custody be shown or that a good reason for the break be given. For discussions of the probative value of what is not introduced into evidence see Lempert, Modeling Relevance, 75 Mich.L.Rev. 1021, 1047–48 (1977) and Saltzburg, A Special Aspect of Relevance: Countering Negative Inferences Associated with the Absence of Evidence, 66 Calif.L.Rev. 1011 (1978). One of the authors also believes that abandonment of any chain of custody rule is an invitation to tampering and that one reason why tampering has been unusual in American courts is that, at least until the adoption of the Federal Rules of Evidence, courts have demanded care in the handling of evidence, typically through a chain of custody rule.

prepared for illustrative or explanatory purposes. No claim is made that demonstrative evidence is in the same condition as it was at the time of the event giving rise to the litigation since demonstrative evidence will almost never have been in existence at that time. But other concerns take their place.

When a party creates an exhibit for illustrative or explanatory purposes, there is always some danger that the party will take unfair advantage. Courts are well aware of this. They require that the exhibit be relevant, just as any other evidence is relevant. Moreover, the usual protections against unfair prejudice and confusion of the issues provided by FRE 403 are available to exclude exhibits that do more harm than good.

There is no requirement that evidence created for illustrative purposes be essential to the jury's understanding of testimony. If the evidence is of any help in understanding testimony it should satisfy the basic test of relevance, and unless there is some countervailing consideration, the evidence will be admitted. One factor that will be considered is the time required to explain the exhibit. The objection that evidence is merely cumulative often arises with exhibits prepared for illustrative purposes. These objections are not necessarily stronger or weaker than objections directed at pure testimony. A case-by-case approach to the evidence is required.

Objections (other than to the handling of evidence) are more likely to be successful when demonstrative evidence has been constructed to illustrate a point than when real evidence records some aspect of the matter being litigated (for example, a tape recording of an oral contract) or is otherwise directly involved in that matter (for example, a gun allegedly used by a defendant charged with armed robbery). The reason for the distinction is easy to understand. There is little that the parties can do to make evidence that is di-

rectly involved in the case more presentable and less prejudicial. The form of the evidence is important and cannot be changed without distorting it. This does not mean that real evidence must be admitted, but it does mean that its chances of surviving an objection are greater than the chances of evidence created to illustrate a point in a case.

There are, however, situations in which courts prefer illustrative evidence to proof that comes from the actual events giving rise to the litigation. A good example is a homicide or wrongful death case in which the cause of death is disputed. It might be possible to preserve the relevant portion of a corpse as evidence of how the deceased died. Yet, the prejudicial aspects of doing so lead the courts to prefer models or diagrams. If the real thing is so dramatic or emotional that will be excessively prejudicial, illustrative evidence may be required.

Objections that an exhibit distorts the facts, exaggerates an injury, or is misleading are more likely to be made to demonstrative evidence than to real evidence because the former is subject to manipulation while the latter should be faithful to the condition it was in. You can see the difference if you compare a reenactment of an accident with a videotape of the accident itself. The reenactment may emphasize what a party wants emphasized. The videotape may suffer from problems of camera angle and the like, but there is nothing that a party can do, other than edit the film—which would produce problems under the authentication rules—to change it once it is made.

Whether a lawyer seeks to admit real or demonstrative evidence, certain steps should be followed. Professor Cady has made the following suggestions:

Procedurally, counsel would do well to review the "five steps" ordinarily necessary in verifying demonstrative evidence. Scott summarizes these in connection with photographs and [a] similar procedure is customarily employed with other demonstrative evidence as well.

1. Call the verifying witness to the stand. Set the background for the witness' testimony. That is, let the judge and jury know why the witness is in court. Is he the photographer? Is he the technician who took the x-rays? Was he at the scene? Is he familiar with Blank's medical charts? Does he use these charts in teaching his own classes? The answer to this basic "why?" inquiry should be further developed by like queries.

2. Hand the picture to the court reporter and request that it be marked as an exhibit for identification.   *   *   *

3. Show the photograph to the opposing counsel and the court.[16] It is at this stage that opposing counsel should analyze carefully the evidence in light of the strategy of the case and determine if there are objections that should be advanced.

4. Lay the Foundation by testimony that the picture is a fair representation of the subject.

5. Offer the exhibit in evidence.[17]

_____

Professor Cady also describes a number of objections that are commonly made to demonstrative evidence in the following excerpt.

16. In many jurisdictions, as a theoretical matter, the party does not have a duty to show an item to opposing counsel until it is offered as evidence. If this is the rule, counsel may show the object to the witness and only later move its admission. As a practical matter, opposing counsel will be able to see any item when it is shown to the witness, and the party using the item is unlikely to object to an opponent's seeing it since the judge or jury may respond adversely to such tactics.

One reason why some courts insist that the object be shown to opposing counsel immediately is that they want any objections to be made before the only possible remedy is to strike testimony that should not have been admitted in the first place.

17. Cady objections to demonstrative evidence, 32 Mo.L.Rev. 333, 339–40 (1967). Often it is said that exhibits should be offered on direct or redirect examination, rather than on cross-examination. Nothing in the Federal Rules of Evidence requires this. Any exhibit that can usefully be employed while the witness is on the stand may be used subject to the judge's discretion to maintain an orderly trial. See FRE 611(a).

In some jurisdictions exhibits will go to the jury room, unless for some reason the judge chooses to use a different procedure. In other jurisdictions the evidence actually involved in the case may go to the jury room but not the evidence prepared for explanatory or illustrative purposes. Some judges will not send exhibits to the jury room unless the parties agree to this. There are few hard and fast rules. You can see the conflicting policies. On the one hand, the jury might learn more from the evidence if it has it during deliberations. On the other hand, the jury without a transcript of the testimony may give the exhibits disproportionate weight. One author thinks that the reason why exhibits are sometimes, and should sometimes be, sent to the jury room is that each juror does not always get sufficient time to examine an exhibit during the trial, whereas each juror hears the complete testimony of witnesses. When lawyers offer real or demonstrative evidence, they often want the jurors to use their own powers of observation to evaluate the evidence. This requires that jurors have an adequate opportunity to examine such evidence. The other author thinks the distinction is a vestige of history. Documents (e.g., contracts, wills and deeds) used to be at the core of most lawsuits and were given to the jury for examination. Transcripts were for centuries not made, and even when cases started to be transcribed, transcripts were not available at the time the deliberations began. Thus, we developed a tradition of sending real but not testimonial evidence to the jury room. Though they differ in how they explain the practice of sending exhibits to the jury room, both authors believe it wise to vest judges with discretion to send exhibits to the jury room when they think the situation calls for it.

CADY, OBJECTIONS TO DEMONSTRATIVE EVIDENCE

32 Mo.L.Rev. 333, 336–353 (1967).

I.   "GROUNDLESS" OBJECTIONS

A.   Not Instructive

Although a line of Massachusetts cases established as a criterion of admission the "practical instructiveness" of an exhibit it is suggested that this is merely a cliché and so misses the mark.   The preferable test asks whether the matter is offered "for the purpose of enabling the jury to better understand and apply the evidence."   Considerations of materiality and relevancy hold the key to admissibility rather than considerations of "instructiveness."

B.   Not "Best Evidence"

This objection to demonstrative evidence—as contrasted to the narrower "documentary evidence"—is not in point, for " * * *   only documents or things bearing writing can be within the purview of this rule."   Thus, a Texas trial judge who forbade the use of a skeleton because it did not comprise the very bones of the plaintiff seated at counsel table on a "best evidence" theory was not following orthodox rules of evidence!

C.   "Hearsay!"

* * *   In reply to the argument that one "cannot cross-examine a picture (or other object)," it should be noted that the material offered is part of, and is used in conjunction with, testimony of a witness who is subject to cross-examination.

II.   VERITY OR CORRECTNESS

* * *

B.   Incorrect Representation

A protest that an exhibit is not a fair representation is probably the strongest objection to be leveled at demonstrative evidence.   Because of the risks of a general objection, counsel should normally follow up by pointing out particular inaccuracies. The following objections are variations on this central theme.

1.   *Distortion.*   When a proponent offers an exhibit as a true and correct representation and in fact it is not, the court has discretionary power to refuse its admission.   On the other hand, courts have shown a disposition to hold that such objection goes merely to the weight of the evidence and not to its admissibility. Consequently, the objection may be overruled and the complaining party then be entitled to a precautionary instruction.   He can, of course, expose the distortion on cross-examination or as part of his affirmative case.

2.   *Injury exaggerated.*   In an unreported Texas case, "The defendant being indicted for aggravated assault by biting off a piece of the complainant's ear, the complainant was permitted to exhibit the maimed ear to the jury."   In exhibiting such a "gaping wound of Caesar" or photographs of such a wound, how far can the proponent go in emphasizing the character of the wound?

* * *

4.   *Exhibit Retouched or Marked.*   The fact that a photograph is retouched is not enough to justify its exclusion.   Emphasizing marks placed on an exhibit do not necessarily render it inadmissible.

* * *

5.   *Misleading, Confusing, or Too Suggestive.*   This language is often incorporated in objections dealing with many forms of demonstrative evidence.   There are three situations, however, in which this tenor of objection is especially important.

First, an objection to a scale model offered in evidence has been sustained on this ground.   "While models may frequently be of great assistance to a court and jury, it is common knowledge that, even when constructed to scale, they may frequently, because of the great disparity in size between the model and the original, also be very misleading * * *."

Second are objections to posed photographs or movie re-enactments. The dangers of deception are substantial enough to result in a split of authority among different jurisdictions. A leading authority is Richardson v. Missouri-K. T. R. Co. of Texas, a F.E.L.A. case in which the jury found damages of $6,000 but cut it in half on account of plaintiff's own negligence. To establish plaintiff's negligence, defendant introduced a color motion picture that showed the shop foreman demonstrating how the plaintiff's hand "could be caught and run through the blades" of a shaping machine. The foreman testified, however, that "he did not know how the fingers of appellant were caught in the machine and therefore his experiments did not undertake to show how appellant was operating it at the time." The court thrust aside plaintiff's objections and his plea that by the use of such skillfully technical picture, the appellee took from the appellant the sum of $3,000. "In the final analysis, the increased danger of fraud peculiar to posed photographs must be weighed against their communicative value. Only the additional danger of fraud or suggestion separates this question from that of the admissibility of ordinary photographs." This danger of fraud and suggestion is no doubt at work when judges have excluded "certain photographs which were taken during the period when plaintiff was being treated for his injuries and which showed his face distorted with pain."

The third category comprises comparison exhibits. This not only involves comparison of bodily parts of an injured party with a witness with similar injuries, but also brings into the arena comparison photographs and x-rays. Although it is a common and approved practice to introduce "normal" x-rays for comparison with x-rays of the injured party, there is authority that

though such x-rays were "proper subject matter for jury consideration," exclusion by the trial court was not an abuse of discretion.

Other cases deciding whether an exhibit is "misleading," serves as "an agent of confusion," or "injects * * * an issue foreign to the matter under inquiry" are also best listed under this general heading.

III. UNDUE PREJUDICE

Even though proffered demonstrative evidence passes the test of verity with flying colors, still a large hurdle remains—judicial discretion. Even though an exhibit be perfectly accurate, the trial judge has discretion to exclude demonstrative evidence that may create undue prejudice in the minds of the tribunal—such "sympathy," "distraction," "resentment," "repulsion," or "indignation" that overcomes the rational processes of the trier of fact. The ambit of judicial discretion here tends to be narrow; "[W]hen the balance wavers the court should lean toward admission." Wigmore compares criminal and civil cases and concludes that the risks of unfair prejudice are of greater frequency in personal injury cases and so implies that the trial court should exercise discretion to exclude more firmly in civil than in criminal cases. In any event, the court's discretion is to "prevent abuse" of demonstrative evidence.

A. *Inflammatory*

Perhaps the most common objection directed toward exercise of judicial discretion to exclude is that the matter offered is inflammatory. Photographs of corpses in criminal and wrongful death cases are most often considered in the reports. * * *

* * *

B. *Unnecessary*

Some opinions exclude demonstrative evidence by holding that the particular exhibit is "unnecessary." Analysis suggests that this is not appropriate terminology. Conceding that the offered evidence is both material and relevant, and so not "unnecessary" in either of those senses, the nature of the objection in contest seems to be that the evidence is inflammatory or cumulative. For example, a landmark case in food law concerned a commercial orange drink which was lacking in vitamin C, according to Food and Drug Administration laboratory studies. Comparative photographs of healthy guinea pigs regularly fed orange juice and those which had apparently died in agony after being fed the beverage in question during controlled tests were held "neither necessary nor proper." But the court, in discussing admissibility, stated that "[i]t is impossible to calculate the effect of such testimony in *creating prejudice* rather than objective conviction in the minds of the jurors."

* * *

It is submitted that counsel should phrase his objections in terms of the evidence being inflammatory and cumulative rather than in terms of its being unnecessary.

C. *Cumulative*

Trial courts have discretion to exclude testimony that is merely cumulative and, since demonstrative evidence is usually intertwined with testimony, the court should be able to exclude cumulative exhibits. On the other hand, it is established that no reversible error occurs if cumulative exhibits are admitted.

D. *Gruesome*

Although "[o]ne favorite ground for objection to the admissibility of photographs in evidence is that it is too gruesome," the general rule is that gruesomeness per se does not render a photo inadmissible. * * *

When confronted with gruesome exhibits, the advocate is advised to phrase his objection in other terms. * * *

E. *Indecent*

An objection that an exhibit is indecent often raises similar problems to those concerned with the inflammatory or gruesome quality of the demonstrative evidence. The primary issue under this head, however, is the basic scope limits to be established in public trials. When the exhibition is otherwise proper, it should be allowed despite the fact that it borders on the lewd or obscene. To quote Wigmore:

When justice and discovery of truth are at stake, the ordinary canons of modesty and delicacy of feelings cannot be allowed to impose prohibition upon necessary measures. Where it is a question of what would otherwise be an *indecency,* two limitations seem appropriate; (a) there should be a fair necessity for the jury's inspection, the trial Court to determine; (b) the inspection should take place apart from the public court-room, in the sole presence of the tribunal and the parties. Such seems to be the inclination of the Courts.

D. GENERAL PROBLEMS

Problem XI–1. Gary Let was suspected by federal narcotics agents of smuggling narcotics. The agents secured a warrant to wiretap the telephone in Let's home to "obtain evidence of the participation of Let and others unnamed in a conspiracy to smuggle heroin and other narcotic drugs into the United States in violation of federal law." Several of Let's conversations with unidentified persons discussed "importation of the material," but no mention of drugs was made. **At Let's trial for smuggling, are the taped**

conversations admissible?   What steps should the government attorney take in an attempt to lay a foundation?

Problem XI–2.   Pringle and Stangle share a two-bedroom apartment in the East Side of New York.   After an extensive investigation, the New York police have probable cause to believe that the two are selling heroin.   The police obtain a warrant and search the apartment.   In both bedrooms they find vials containing a white powdery substance that looks like heroin.   To protect the evidence, the police place the vials in a sack and label it.   Unfortunately, all the vials are placed in the same sack.   When they learn of this, each defendant moves to suppress the use of the evidence against her. **Should the motions be granted?   If not, what method of authentication would you suggest?   Would there be any possibility of introducing this evidence if analysis revealed that some vials contained heroin and others did not?**   Assume that instead of searching for and finding drugs, the police had suspected the two women of receiving stolen property, had searched both bedrooms and had found jewelry, some of which was stolen, in each bedroom. **If the police had commingled all the jewelry, would the problem be the same?   Would any jewelry be admissible at a joint trial?   At separate trials?   At a trial for conspiring to receive stolen property?**

Problem XI–3.   Defendant is charged with conducting an illegal gambling business.   The Government offers evidence at trial that two sheets of paper were found during a search of a location in which telephones had been tapped by the Government.   Each sheet bore a notation reflecting the payment of $100 for "service," but neither identified to whom the $100 had been paid.   The Government's evidence indicates that other persons, in addition to the defendant, reported race results over the telephone lines that the Government had tapped.   The Government wants to introduce the sheets against the defendant for what they are worth, but defendant claims that they cannot be introduced because they cannot be identified as belonging or relating to him rather than to others. **What is the proper ruling?**

Problem XI–4.   Sofa is accused of kidnapping the young daughter of a wealthy industrialist.   Shortly after Sofa's arrest the police searched his car and found red threads, which looked like wool, in the trunk of the car.   The girl had been wearing a red woolen sweater at the time she was kidnapped. When the prosecution offers the threads as evidence at Sofa's trial, the defense counsel asks whether any tests have been made comparing the girl's sweater and the threads.   Receiving a negative answer, counsel moves to suppress the evidence. **Should the motion be granted?   If the sweater was removed from the girl by the kidnapper and never found, could the threads be admitted?   What foundation would you require?**

Problem XI–5.   FRE 901(b)(2) permits nonexpert opinion on handwriting as long as the witness' knowledge has not been acquired for the purpose of testifying. **In criminal cases where a writer's identity is crucial, should the prosecution be able to take advantage of this rule to call lay witnesses rather than handwriting experts?   In a forgery prosecution, for example, should the government be permitted to introduce nonexpert testimony that**

one signature is a forgery or that an exemplar in the possession of the government is a true signature?

Problem XI–6.   Section (6) of FRE 902 makes newspapers self-authenticating.   Thus in federal court in litigation arising out of an automobile accident there would be no need to authenticate an account of the accident in a local newspaper.   Yet the account would remain inadmissible.   **Why?**

Problem XI–7.   Someone enters the Big Seller department store and charges $100 to the account of John B. Jones, presenting Jones' credit card and signing Jones' name.   When the bill is sent to Jones, he refuses to pay, stating in a letter that his credit card was apparently stolen and that he never bought the charged merchandise.   Big Seller sues Jones, who demands and receives a jury trial.   At the outset of its case, Big Seller opens by offering as evidence the charge slip containing the signature "John B. Jones."   The letter by Jones referred to above is offered as a handwriting exemplar.   Jones objects and urges that before either document can be displayed to the jury, the judge must determine that Jones signed the charge slip.   **Is Jones correct?   Would Jones fare better if he argued that before the letter could be introduced it must be authenticated?   How might the department store go about doing this?**

Problem XI–8.   Assume that Jones never wrote the letter referred to in the previous problem.   Instead, Big Seller seeks to introduce as a handwriting exemplar a signature on another charge slip, for which Jones had been billed.   The charges on this bill had been paid by check after a bill was sent to Jones' house.   **Could Jones successfully object to its introduction?**

Problem XI–9.   **Specify what authentication problems exist and how they might be resolved for each of the following items of evidence:**

A.   A movie of plaintiff changing a tire on his car, introduced by defendant to show that plaintiff had not been crippled in an automobile accident.

B.   An X-ray of plaintiff's knee, introduced by him to show the damage done to his knee in an automobile accident.

C.   A can of peas, bearing the label Green Midget Company, introduced to show that the defendant, Green Midget Company, was responsible for the presence in the can of a stone on which the plaintiff broke a tooth.

D.   Testimony that a voice on a recorded phone conversation demanded that the witness pay $100,000 to the defendant, X, introduced to show that X was guilty of attempted extortion.

E.   A bill, prepared by computer, introduced to show that the defendant owed the plaintiff oil company $900 for purchases charged to his credit card.

F.   A copy of the defendant's birth certificate introduced to show she was not a deportable alien.

G.   A telegram reading, "Accept your offer of 8 a. m. this morning—stop—will buy 10,000 bushels at $4.69—stop—Grant Grain Company," introduced to show that the Grant Grain Company had contracted to buy the plaintiff's wheat.

H. An attested will, offered to prove the contents of the will, when one attesting witness is outside the jurisdiction and the other is in a state mental hospital.

I. Testimony that a voice on a phone had answered, "Police Headquarters," had taken the defendant's oral account of an accident and had stated that there was no need for the defendant to file a written report, introduced to show that the defendant had not failed to report an accident.

J. Testimony by company employees, who had attempted to organize a union, that they had received telephone calls threatening their families, introduced at an unfair labor practice hearing in which the company denies responsibility for the calls.

SECTION III.   KINDS OF REAL EVIDENCE

A.   RECORDED COMMUNICATIONS

1.   THE BEST EVIDENCE RULE

The best evidence rule is found by many to be among the most confusing of the evidence doctrines. McCormick states the rule succinctly:

> The rule is this: in proving the terms of a writing, where the terms are material, the original writing must be produced unless it is shown to be unavailable for some reason other than the serious fault of the proponent.[18]

Another commentator has said:

> The Best Evidence Rule of the common law is a misnomer. It is merely "a convenient short description of the rule as to proving the contents of a writing," i.e., it aims at securing, not the best but primary evidence. The rule is one of exclusion, arising from the fear that juries and judges will be misled into ren-

dering unjust judgments, because of fraud or perjury upon the part of litigants, unless the evidence which they are permitted to consider is limited to primary, or first-hand, proof.[19]

According to most modern writers, the primary purpose of the rule is to ensure that the exact contents of a writing are brought before the trier of fact. Commentators point to the distortion that may occur in duplicating writings or in orally recounting the contents of a writing. Production of an original writing is also seen as insurance against fraud. McCormick notes a third purpose for the rule: to protect against misleading inferences resulting from the intentional or unintentional introduction of selected portions of a larger set of writings.[20]

---

18. McCormick § 230, at 560. See also Cleary and Strong, The Best Evidence Rule: An Evaluation in Context, 51 Iowa L.Rev. 825 (1966).

19. Rogers, The Best Evidence Rule, 1945 Wis.L.Rev. 278.

20. McCormick § 231, at 561. Wigmore traces the evolution of the rule from "the primitive medieval conception [of] *a document* directly affecting rights of property or contract" where "[i]ts physical, material existence was what counted, and nothing else," through a more rational period when the rule

It is important to remember that the best evidence rule only applies to writings or equivalent recorded communications; there is no requirement that parties introduce the best available evidence bearing on matters they seek to prove in court. Thus, in applying the best evidence rule it is crucial to know what recorded communications are regarded as the equivalent of writings. Before extensive revisions generally conforming the Uniform Rules of Evidence to the Federal Rules of Evidence, Uniform Rule 1(13) defined "writing" to include "handwriting, typewriting, printing, photostating, photographing, and every other means of recording upon any tangible thing, any form of communication or representation, including letters, words, pictures, sounds, or symbols, or combinations thereof."[21] FRE 1001 is not quite as broad; it focuses on "letters, words, or numbers, or their equivalent" rather than on any form of communication.[22]

FRE 1002 presents the federal version of the best evidence principle:

> To prove the content of a writing, recording, or photograph, the original writing, recording, or photograph is required, except as otherwise provided in these rules or by Act of Congress.

FRE 1003 provides special treatment for duplicates of the original:

A duplicate is admissible to the same extent as an original unless (1) a genuine question is raised as to the authenticity of the original or (2) in the circumstances it would be unfair to admit the duplicate in lieu of the original.

FRE 1001(3) defines "original" in the following manner:

> An "original" of a writing or recording is the writing or recording itself or any counterpart intended to have the same effect by a person executing or issuing it. An "original" of a photograph includes the negative or any print therefrom. If data are stored in a computer or similar device, any printout or other output readable by sight, shown to reflect the data accurately, is an "original."

A "duplicate" is defined by FRE 1001 (4) to include all copies produced by processes that are very likely to result in accurate reproduction:

> A "duplicate" is a counterpart produced by the same impression as the original, or from the same matrix, or by means of photography, including enlargements and miniatures, or by mechanical or electronic re-recording, or by chemical reproduction, or by other equivalent techniques which accurately reproduces [sic] the original.

---

began to have more of a procedural than substantive effect. 4 Wigmore § 1177, at 406 (emphasis in original). Also traced in Wigmore is the separation of the best evidence rule from the pleading rule of profert which "required that a certain *allegation be made in the written pleading*, namely, after the statement of title by document, the allegation that the document was hereby prolatum in curiam." Id. at 410 (emphasis in original). The rule of profert applied in civil cases only to documents under seal and judicial records.

21. Wigmore concluded that it was "impossible to say that any settled doctrine has found favor respecting the application of the rule to *material objects, not paper, bearing inscriptions* in words." 4 Wigmore § 1182, at 421 (emphasis in original).

22.   FRE 1001 provides:
For purposes of this article the following definitions are applicable:
(1) Writings and recordings.—"Writings" and "recordings" consist of letters, words, or numbers, or their equivalent, set down by handwriting, typewriting, printing, photostating, photographing, magnetic impulse, mechanical or electronic recording, or other form of data compilation.
(2) Photographs.—"Photographs" include still photographs, X-ray films, video tapes, and motion pictures.

In order to understand better the difference between an original writing and a writing not considered original, consider a carbon copy. If parties to a contract embody their contract in a written instrument with four carbon copies, they can make all four copies originals by executing the copies and treating them as originals. What is crucial is the intent that each carbon be an independent legally binding document rather than a copy of such a document. If, however, they only execute the typed copy, the four carbon copies might be treated as secondary evidence—i.e., as something other than an original.

Even if the carbon copies are not executed, some common law courts would admit them as duplicate originals. In these courts, carbon copies are often treated more favorably than xerox or other photocopies. The former are treated as originals, and the latter as secondary evidence. The theory is that the carbon was made with the same stroke of the key as the original, while the photocopy was made after the original. But a person bent on creating a false copy can do so with carbon paper almost as easily as with a Xerox machine. Most jurisdictions have a statute, modeled on the Uniform Photographic Copies of Business and Public Records as Evidence Act, providing that regularly kept photographic copies of business and public records are admissible without accounting for the original. Other reproductions which some courts deem to be duplicate originals are letterpress, printed, and multilith copies.

FRE 1003, reproduced above, eliminates special treatment for carbon copies, making all duplicates as defined in FRE 1001(4), presumptively admissible. Thus in federal court it is often unnecessary to puzzle over the question of what is an original. Handwritten copies do not benefit from the Rule 1003 presumption. The idea behind the federal rule is to eliminate best evidence objections to copies made in clearly reliable ways, except where the objecting party can offer a good reason to support the production of the original.

The best evidence rule applies only when a writing (broadly defined) is introduced *for the purpose of proving the contents thereof.* Often, the limitation we have set off in italics is not fully appreciated. Even though a written record is made of an event, there is no requirement that the event be proved by the writing. Consider a case in which there is a dispute about payment on a credit account. The debtor could introduce a receipt to prove payment. If so, the best evidence rule would apply and an original receipt would be needed if one were available because the debtor would be trying to prove that the receipt contained an acknowledgment of payment in order to prove that payment was made. Unless he could account for the unavailability of the original receipt, the debtor could not testify that *the receipt said,* "Paid in Full." However the *fact of payment* is not contained in the writing even if an acknowledgment of that fact is, and there is ordinarily no legal requirement that payment be proved by written acknowledgment.

So the debtor might simply testify that payment was made and permit the trier of fact to rule on the credibility of his testimony. Naturally, in cases in which the applicable substantive legal rules make a writing indispensable—e.g., cases involving deeds or contracts—the best evidence rule usually applies, since the contents of the writing are usually in dispute. There has been criticism of the distinction drawn between cases involving deeds, judgments or contracts and cases where the fact that a writing has been made has no independent legal significance.[23] Critics of the rule

23. See McCormick § 233, at 564–65.

ask why a contract, which is nothing more than a written expression of the agreement of the parties, should be treated differently from a receipt, which is a written record of a transaction between the parties. McCormick suggests that the distinction should be abandoned in favor of a rule that permits the trial judge to exercise discretion in applying the best evidence rule. The exercise of discretion would turn on such factors as the importance of the writing to the litigation and the reliability of the secondary evidence.[24]

The best evidence rule does not require that a writing be produced when its existence rather than its contents is at issue. If, for example, the question arises whether a particular report was written and filed, a witness could testify that the report was made without accounting for the original. Of course, if it were important to one party to show that the report existed, good trial tactics usually would require the party to produce the report or account for its absence.

Some courts invoke the best evidence principle where there seems to be compelling reason for the production of an original writing although the contents of the writing is not technically at issue. One such situation is a dispute about the authenticity of a particular document. If, for example, there is testimony that the alleged author of a questioned document would never write in purple ink, some courts would require that the document be produced or accounted for before they would allow a witness to testify that the document was written in purple ink. Questions like this rarely arise because a sense of trial tactics leads counsel to pro-

duce or account for such documents. The best evidence principle has also been invoked by some courts to require that past testimony be proved by transcript, if a transcript is available. The leading federal case is to the contrary.[25]

There are also situations where the contents of a writing are to be proved but the best evidence rule is not invoked. This is the case where the writing is so tangentially relevant to the litigation that an attempt to produce the original is not deemed to be worth the effort. Here the writing is held to relate to a "collateral matter." One may also stipulate to the contents of a writing, enter an admission as to contents, or waive a best evidence claim either explicitly or by failing to object to an offer of secondary evidence.

Inability to produce an original or duplicate of a document, the contents of which are at issue, does not ordinarily prevent proof of contents by other means. The best evidence rule is a rule of preference. Original documents are preferred, but if there is a good reason why the original cannot be produced, secondary evidence, such as written copies or oral testimony, will be admitted. FRE 1004 sets forth those situations in which secondary evidence is commonly admitted:

The original is not required, and other evidence of the contents of a writing, recording, or photograph is admissible if—

(1) *Originals lost or destroyed.* All originals are lost or have been destroyed, unless the proponent lost or destroyed them in bad faith;[26] or

(2) *Original not obtainable.* No original can be obtained by any available judicial process or procedure;[27] or

---

24. Id. at 565.

25. Meyers v. United States, 84 U.S. App.D.C. 101, 171 F.2d 800, (1948) certiorari denied, 336 U.S. 912 (1949).

26. **What search should be required? Wigmore concluded that "there is not and cannot be any universal or fixed rule to test the sufficiency of the search for a docu-** ment alleged to be lost." **4 Wigmore § 1194, at 440. The burden of proving the loss is on the proponent of the evidence, but the weight of the burden is unclear. More than a possibility of loss is required, but how much more depends on the jurisdiction.**

27. A deposition combined with a subpoena duces tecum may be used to obtain a

(3) Original in possession of opponent. At a time when an original was under the control of the party against whom offered, he was put on notice, by the pleadings or otherwise, that the contents would be a subject of proof at the hearing, and he does not produce the original at the hearing;[28] or

(4) Collateral matters. The writing, recording, or photograph is not closely related to a controlling issue.[29]

Another common exception to the best evidence rule is found in FRE 1005, which provides that the contents of an official record or of a document authorized to be recorded and filed, which is actually recorded and filed, may be proved by a copy. It is felt that such copies are particularly reliable and that the original records should not be removed from their usual place of keeping.[30]

Since the purpose of the best evidence rule is to get the best possible evidence before the court, at one time most American jurisdictions required that the "next

best" evidence be submitted when an original writing, recording or photograph is not available. Thus, distinctions were drawn between kinds of secondary evidence. A certified or sworn copy was always preferred to other kinds of secondary evidence. The next most reliable copy usually was a mechanical reproduction. Other kinds of copies—such as a firsthand copy made while looking at the original came next on the hierarchy and were preferred to oral testimony. The federal rules follow the minority position in recognizing no degrees of secondary evidence, and most jurisdictions that have adopted rules have taken the same position. The Advisory Committee note accompanying FRE 1004 states:

> While strict logic might call for extending the principle of preference beyond simply preferring the original, the formulation of a hierarchy of preferences and a procedure for making it effective is believed to involve unwarranted complexities. Most, if not all, that

writing from an absent non-party. It is unclear under the federal rule whether a claim of great expense or difficulty is enough to establish that the original is not obtainable.

28. The Advisory Committee's Note states that:

The notice procedure here provided is not to be confused with orders to produce or other discovery procedures, as the purpose of the procedure under this rule is to afford the opposite party an opportunity to produce the original, not to compel him to do so.

29. The word "collateral" is as difficult to interpret and as susceptible to misuse in FRE 1004(4) as it is when used to limit the impeachment of witnesses, as discussed in Chapter Five. While the word may have "an exasperating indefiniteness about it" (Morgan, Basic Problems of Evidence 387 (1963)), it softens the rule and "precludes hypertechnical insistence [upon it] * * * when production * * * would be impractical and [the writing's] contents are not closely related to any important issue in the case." Calif. Evid. Code § 1504, comment. To avoid misuse, judges should examine the importance of the document to the issue in

the case and not treat labeling as an end in itself.

Notice that this subsection is different from the first three. They require some attempt to get the original while this subsection requires nothing more than a finding that an issue is not controlling.

30. FRE 1005 provides:

The contents of an official record, or of a document authorized to be recorded or filed and actually recorded or filed, including data compilations in any form, if otherwise admissible, may be proved by copy, certified as correct in accordance with rule 902 or testified to be correct by a witness who has compared it with the original. If a copy which complies with the foregoing cannot be obtained by the exercise of reasonable diligence, then other evidence of the contents may be given.

Note that this rule establishes a preference for two specific kinds of proof. Compare it with FRE 1004 which establishes no preference, the drafters felt that the preferences were easily satisfied and guaranteed reliability.

would be accomplished by an extended scheme of preferences will, in any event, be achieved through the normal motivation of a party to present the most convincing evidence possible and the arguments and procedures available to his opponent if he does not.

It is normal practice in most courts to permit summaries to be introduced where original writings are voluminous. It is required, however, that the originals or duplicates of the originals be made available to the opposing party for examination or copying. FRE 1006 codifies this procedure. The best practice is to provide an opportunity for inspection and examination of both the original and the summaries prior to trial. This saves time, prevents surprise and allows disputes about the evidence to be resolved before trial.

Under FRE 1007[31] and in many jurisdictions, the testimony, deposition or written admission of an opposing party may be offered to prove the contents of a writing without accounting for the nonproduction of the original. In some states ordinary oral admissions also may be used this way.

FRE 1008 specifies the roles of judge and jury when best evidence questions arise:

> When the admissibility of other evidence of contents of writings, recordings, or photographs under these rules depends upon the fulfillment of a condition of fact, the question whether the condition has been fulfilled is ordinarily for the court to determine in accordance with the provisions of rule 104. However, when an issue is raised (a) whether the asserted writing ever existed, or (b) whether another writing, recording, or photograph produced at the trial is the original, or (c) whether other evidence of contents correctly reflects the contents, the issue is for the trier of fact to determine as in the case of other issues of fact.

Saltzburg and Redden specify nine questions that the judge must decide:

> Prior to permitting evidence of the contents of a writing, recording, or photograph to go to the jury, the Judge must insure that the technical requirements of the Best Evidence Rule have been sat-

---

31. FRE 1007 reads as follows:

Contents of writings, recordings, or photographs may be proved by the testimony or deposition of the party against whom offered or by his written admission, without accounting for the nonproduction of the original.

Saltzburg & Redden, supra note 9, at 753 explain the rule as follows:

Although some cases have taken a different view, most American decisions have held that if the secondary evidence offered consists of an admission of the contents by the opponent of the evidence, no showing is required of why the original is not produced. Prior to the enactment of the Federal Rules, it was not altogether clear whether all admissions would serve to prove the contents of an item otherwise covered by the Best Evidence Rule. Rule 1007 provides that the contents of writings and recordings may be proved only by admissions made in the course of giving testimony under oath or by written admissions. Since one of the

strong policies underlying the Best Evidence Rule is obtaining an accurate version of the contents of writings and the other items covered by the Rule, if all oral admissions sufficed to prove the contents of writings, accuracy would be jeopardized. The Advisory Committee accepted the argument that the possibility of error was reduced if this Rule was confined to written admissions or admissions under oath, since the possibility of mistransmission of information was practically eliminated.

It is important to note that this Rule does not mean that an oral admission can never be used to prove the contents of a writing. If A sues B for breach of contract, for example, and A satisfies Rule 1004 by showing that the original of the contract was destroyed and that there was no bad faith on his part, A can then offer into evidence admissions made by B concerning the contents of the contract. The difference between Rule 1004 and the instant Rule is that the former requires an accounting for the original, while the instant Rule does not.

isfied.   Hence, the Judge must determine the following questions:

(1) whether a given item of evidence is an "original";

(2) whether a given item of evidence qualifies as a duplicate and is thus presumptively admissible;

(3) whether a genuine question is raised as to the authenticity of the original for purposes of Rule 1003;

(4) whether it would be unfair to admit a duplicate in lieu of an original as provided for in Rule 1003;

(5) whether an original is lost or destroyed;

(6) whether the proponent lost or destroyed evidence in bad faith;

(7) whether an original can be obtained by any available judicial process;

(8) whether proper notice was given a party in control of evidence;

(9) whether evidence goes to a collateral matter or to a controlling issue.

If an issue is raised as to: (a) whether the asserted writing ever existed, (b) whether another writing, recording, or photograph produced at the trial is the original, or (c) whether other evidence of contents correctly reflects the contents, the issue is for the jury to determine. . . .[32]

Problem XI–10.   A man charged with murder is taken into custody and given the requisite warnings.   Under questioning, he describes in detail how the killing occurred.   A stenographer takes shorthand notes of the interview and later types a written transcript.   The accused is never shown a copy of the transcript.   At trial, a police officer takes the stand and testifies to the statements made by the defendant.   The defendant objects, arguing that the stenographer's notes are the best evidence of what he said.   **Is the best evidence rule applicable?   If so, must the stenographic notes be introduced, or is the typed transcript the best evidence?   If the notes and transcript have been destroyed, will the officer's testimony be allowed?**

Problem XI–11.   The plaintiff brings an action for libel against Joanne Mulvey and the Charlottesville Times.   The complaint alleges that Mulvey was the author of a statement, in the form of a letter, accusing the plaintiff of bribery and corruption in office, that Mulvey handed the letter to a reporter for the paper, and that it thereafter appeared in the paper.   Without any preliminary proof, the plaintiff offers in evidence the issue of the paper containing the allegedly libelous letter.   Mulvey and the Times both object on the basis of the best evidence rule.   They argue that the original letter to the paper should be produced.   **Would you sustain either objection?**

Problem XI–12.   Heavy brings an action against Stiles to set aside a mechanic's lien that Stiles has recorded for unpaid wages.   Heavy claims that Stiles has been paid in full for his services.   As part of his case, Heavy introduces evidence tending to prove that Stiles had prepared time sheets for work performed and that Stiles had been paid in accordance with the time sheets.   Heavy offers the time sheets in evidence and they are admitted over Stiles' hearsay objection.   [To review the hearsay point, they are prob-

32.   Saltzburg & Redden, supra note 9, at 755.

ably admissible either as admissions by Stiles or as business records.] Stiles then testifies that he has actually spent more time working for Heavy than is shown on the sheets. Heavy objects, claiming that Stiles' testimony is not admissible since the time sheets are the best evidence of the hours Stiles has worked. **What is the proper ruling on the objection?**

Problem XI–13. Stubbs is charged with auto theft. The prosecution seeks to introduce a witness, Cole, to testify that she saw Stubbs break into a white Chevrolet and drive away. During the course of Cole's testimony, the prosecution offers a photo of a Chevrolet automobile and asks whether or not Cole can identify the picture. Cole replies that she can and says that it is a picture of the automobile she saw Stubbs take. Stubbs objects on the ground that the photo is not the best evidence of the automobile. **Is there substance to the objection?**

Problem XI–14. During the Vietnam war, Bleriot Leparre and Benny Morgan formed a corporation to produce parts used in army helicopters. When the war ended, the United States Senate decided to investigate whether there had been instances of fraud, corruption, mismanagement, excessive profits or inefficiency in the nation's war effort. It created a special committee to conduct the investigation. Morgan testified before that committee. Morgan's testimony was given in executive session. Only several Senators; their counsel, Henry Adams; the clerk; the reporter; and Morgan were present. As a result of his testimony, the government charged him with perjury. When Morgan was indicted he requested a transcript of his testimony. The court denied his request, however, sustaining the government's claim of privilege to protect military secrets. At trial, the principal witness for the government was Adams. Over Morgan's objection he testified to the substance of Morgan's testimony to the committee. The government offered other evidence to prove that what Morgan said was untruthful. Morgan claimed that the court was obliged under the best evidence rule to require the government to produce and to offer the transcript of his testimony as evidence, and that Adams should not be permitted to testify in lieu of a transcript. **Would you sustain his claim? Is there any other claim that you would make if you were Morgan's attorney?** Assume that Adams had been out of the room during a portion of Morgan's testimony and had read the transcript of that portion. **Would Morgan's best evidence claim then be stronger? If the government ultimately decided not to resist Morgan's claim and provided the defense with a transcript of Morgan's testimony just before the defense began its case, would Morgan have any claim left to raise?**

Problem XI–15. Findlay wished to accept Malcolm's offer to sell him a 1982 Mercedes Benz automobile, one year old at the time of sale, for $20,000. The offer was made on January 2, 1983, to expire on January 10, 1983. Findlay sent his acceptance via Western Union on January 9, 1983, but the telegram was not delivered until January 12, two days after the offer expired. Findlay sues the telegraph company for damages and wishes to introduce evidence of the acceptance sent to Malcolm. **What is the best evidence?**

Problem XI–16. Sergeant Friday, a Los Angeles policeman, was placed in charge of an investigation into the identity of an armed robber terrorizing Hollywood families. He xeroxed for each officer under his command a composite description of the robber and distributed it to them. Officer Monday possessed a copy when he encountered a suspect fitting the description. Aware that the description contained the notation that "suspect is believed to be armed and extremely dangerous", Monday panicked when the suspect reached into his pocket. He shot the suspect, seriously wounding him. It turned out that the injured man was innocent of any wrongdoing and was reaching for identification. Pursuant to state tort law and federal civil rights statutes, the injured "suspect" sues for damages. Monday claims a defense of good faith and seeks to introduce the description given him by Sergeant Friday. **If you were a lawyer in a jurisdiction that interpreted the best evidence rule strictly, would you offer the original description prepared by Friday, the xerox copy sent to Monday, one of the other xerox copies that had been distributed to the officers by Friday, or a xerox prepared from the original a week before the trial? Even in a strict jurisdiction, do you think it would matter which you offered?**

Problem XI–17. Saltzer, an undercover agent for the United States Department of the Treasury, was wired for sound before a scheduled meeting with a suspected counterfeiter. After the suspect made several incriminating statements and produced some counterfeit bills, Saltzer arrested her. At trial, the government offers as evidence a re-recorded tape of the meeting, and a best evidence objection is raised. The government explains that the original recording is difficult to hear and somewhat garbled. By editing, some material has been deleted and some noise suppressed. **Should the re-recording be admitted? What if a portion of the conversation recorded on the original was so garbled as to be beyond comprehension? Should the re-recording still be admitted?** Suppose the original recording was perfectly clear, but instead of offering it, the government chose to have Saltzer testify to what was said. **Would there be any best evidence problem? Would there be best evidence problems if the government wanted to introduce a witness who had listened to the tape to testify to what had been said?**

Problem XI–18. Alex is charged with stealing a United States Treasury check from the mail. At trial the government seeks to introduce a thermofax copy of the check with the payee's name and address typed in because the machine failed to reproduce them. The prosecutor supports the offer with this statement: "We wish to offer this evidence to identify the stolen check and to illustrate what it looked like." The defense objects on best evidence grounds. **Should the objection be sustained?**

---

2. THE PAROL EVIDENCE RULE

Like the best evidence rule, the parol evidence rule has many facets, too many in fact. Thayer commented that "[f]ew things are darker than this, or fuller of subtle difficulties." [33] Wigmore agreed, complaining that "the so-called Parol Evidence rule is attended with a confusion and an obscurity which make it the most discouraging subject in the whole field of Evidence." [34]

What exactly is the rule? [35] One legal encyclopedia states it in the following manner.

The well-established general rule is that where the parties to [an instrument] have deliberately put their engagement in writing in such terms as import a legal obligation without any uncertainty as to the object or extent of such engagement, it is conclusively presumed that the entire engagement of the parties, and the extent and manner of their undertaking, have been reduced to writing, and all parol evidence of prior or contemporaneous conversations or declarations tending to substitute a new and different contract for the one evidenced by the writing is incompetent. Stated otherwise, the intention of the parties as evidenced by the legal import of the language of a valid written [instrument] cannot ordinarily be varied by parol proof of a different intention. [36]

Corbin's definition is similar:

When two parties have made a contract and have expressed it in a writing to which they have both assented as the complete and accurate integration of that contract, evidence, whether parol or otherwise, of antecedent understandings and negotiations will not be admitted for the purpose of varying or contradicting the writing. [37]

As is Williston's:

Briefly stated, this rule requires, in the absence of fraud, duress, mutual mistake, or something of the kind, the exclusion of extrinsic evidence, oral or written, where the parties have reduced their agreement to an integrated writing. [38]

If the parol evidence rule is really a rule of contract law rather than an evidence rule, why is it mentioned here? Our answer is that despite its substantive nature, the policy of the rule is similar to the policies of true evidence rules previously examined. It is related, for example, to best evidence problems and hearsay concerns. But even more important for our purposes, and too often overlooked, is the relationship of the rule to the allocation of fact-finding functions to the jury.

[The rule establishes a] reservation in the trial judge of a special and added authority over the question: Was this writing intended by the parties to displace this asserted oral term or agreement, if there was any such oral expression? Thayer was entirely aware that the parol evidence doctrine had been used by the judges to serve this purpose, but his main preoccupation was with the pioneer job of driving the parol evidence rule out of the "evidence" fold. Wigmore explicitly recognizes this special allocation of authority to the trial judge, but he cites no decisions to the point and apparently treats it as a minor and incidental feature of the subject. Williston, in his lucid and realistic treatment of the matter, follows, in the main, the lines laid down

---

33. J. Thayer, A Preliminary Treatise on Evidence at the Common Law 390 (1898).

34. 9 Wigmore § 2400, at 3.

35. See generally McCormick & Ray, Texas Law of Evidence § 725, at 947–48 (1937):

The Parol Evidence Rule is the rule which, upon the establishment of the existence of a writing intended as a completed memorial of a legal transaction, denies

efficacy to any prior or contemporary expressions of the parties relating to the same subject-matter as that to which the written memorial relates.

36. 30 Am.Jur.2d Evidence § 1016, at 149–50.

37. 3 Corbin, Contracts § 573, at 357 (1960).

38. 4 Williston, Contracts § 631 at 948–49 (3d ed. 1957).

by Thayer and Wigmore. Like them, he touches but casually this question of "Who decides whether the document was intended to supersede that alleged oral agreement?"—a question which will be decisive of the result in most actual cases of competition between an alleged oral agreement and a written document. By couching his discussion of "collateral" oral agreements in terms of "admissibility," however, he reverts to the earlier "rule-of-evidence" phraseology.[39]

Elsewhere the same author joins another to develop the argument further:

One of the chief motives in the development and preservation of the nexus of doctrines called the Parol Evidence Rule has been the belief on the part of judges that the needs of the business world demand that contracts as written be guarded against claims of inconsistent oral agreements. But the extension of such protection has been none too easy in a legal system where disputed fact questions are usually left to the decision of untrained juries. In a contest involving choice between a writing and an alleged oral agreement the average juror's sympathy will ordinarily be with the one setting up the spoken against the written word. He will seldom take sufficient account of the high probability of error in the narrative of a witness (even disinterested, which is usually not the case) as to the purported substance of words, spoken months or even years before. The trial judge, on the other hand, is equipped by training and experience to take a long view and make proper allowance for such factors.[40]

Many, cases still turn on the parol evidence rule. Naturally most of them are state cases. If you examine the evidence headnotes in the advance sheets, you may be surprised at how often the rule is in issue.

Having discussed the rule briefly, we leave it. In the first edition of this book we treated the parol evidence rule at greater length because of the relationship it has to other rules of evidence and to issues involving the proper allocation of responsibility between judge and jury. Those who want to study the doctrine further should examine the sources cited in the first edition.

---

39. McCormick, The Parol Evidence Rule As a Procedural Device for Control of the Jury, 41 Yale L.J. 365, 374–75 (1932).

40. McCormick & Ray, supra note 35, § 727, at 951.

Writing alone, McCormick makes the same point in a slightly different way.

That the parol evidence rule chiefly stems from an anxiety to protect written bargains from rewriting by juries is confirmed by the comparative freedom which was allowed in chancery in respect to reformation, and in regard to oral variations asserted as a ground for denying specific performance. * * * It is true that other doors for jury intervention in support of oral variations have not been closed, as in the case of oral agreements that the writing shall not go into effect until the happening of a condition, and likewise oral agreements modifying the written terms after the execution of the document. Each of these escapes from the writing presents difficulties to the one who attempts it, and, in any event, the fact that protection in some situations has not been perfect, does not disprove the desire to furnish it generally.
The Parol Evidence Rule As A Procedural Device for Controlling the Jury, supra note 39, at 368, n. 6.

It is not intended to suggest that these doctrinal devices were newly invented by the judges, consciously, to meet this need, in modern times. Thayer and Wigmore have traced too clearly the origin of the parol evidence formula against "varying the writing," to a primitive formalism which attached a mystical and ceremonial effectiveness to the carta and the seal. (5 Wigmore, Evidence § 2426 (2d ed. 1923). The writer merely ventures to submit that this formalism, abandoned elsewhere in so many areas of modern law, had here a special survival value— the escape from the jury—which led the judges to retain for writings the conception that they had a sort of magical effect of erasing all prior oral agreements.
Id. at 369, n. 8.

B. VIEWS

Information that cannot be effectively captured by evidence that can be brought to the courtroom or faithfully conveyed by testimony presents an obvious problem. To deal with this problem, the judge or jury may leave the courtroom to observe places or objects. We call such excursions "views." The decision to grant a view is usually within the discretion of the trial judge, who will analyze the importance of the information to be gained in relation to issues in dispute and will consider the extent to which such information can be secured from maps, photographs, diagrams and the like. The fact that perfect information may not be available through secondary sources is not dispositive. The trial judge will also be influenced by the inconvenience of the excursion and by the extent to which the place or object to be viewed may have changed since the controversy arose.

In civil cases the trial judge's presence at the view is usually not required, and it is not uncommon for the jury to be conducted to the scene by someone specially commissioned to show the jury the view.[41] In criminal cases however, statutes usually require that the judge be present. The constitutional right to confrontation may give the accused the right to be present at a view.[42] There may also be a constitutional right to the judge's presence because confrontation is significant only if the accused is able to raise and preserve all objections. This may be difficult to do in the trial judge's absence.[43] Even if the trial judge is not required to be present, the judge's presence is in our opinion advisable. It helps ensure that no unauthorized comments are made to the jury during the view, that nothing improper is viewed, and that jurors instructed not to talk about the case do not do so.

Most jurisdictions hold that a view is not evidence; its purpose is assisting the trier of fact to understand and to evaluate the evidence. This rule reflects some recognition of the impossibility of embodying the facts garnered from a view in a written transcript. If views were deemed to be evidence, appellate courts would have difficulty reviewing the weight or sufficiency of evidence in trials including a view. It is easier to say that a view is not evidence than to explain what this really means. It is questionable whether jurors instructed to treat a view as an aid in deciding a case but not as evidence treat the view differently than they treat other facts brought to their attention.[44] A view presents problems similar to those presented by demeanor evidence: appellate courts cannot know what the jurors perceived, yet the jurors may have been influenced significantly by their perceptions.

Problem XI–19. "Red" Zinger, a pedestrian, was injured when struck by Gossip's automobile at a main intersection in Middletown. Zinger sues to recover damages for the negligence of Gossip. Gossip contends that Zinger emerged from the sidewalk into the street from a position where he was

---

41. See 4 Wigmore §§ 1162–1169. Certain statutes—e.g., in eminent domain cases—require a view upon request of a party. See McCormick § 216, at 537.

42. But compare Snyder v. Commonwealth of Massachusetts, 291 U.S. 97 (1934) with State v. Garden, 261 Minn. 97, 125 N.W.2d 591 (1963), and People v. De Lucia, 20 N.Y.2d 275, 282 N.Y.S.2d 526, 229 N.E.2d 211 (1967). See also Note, Confrontation, Cross-Examination, and the Right to Prepare a Defense, 56 Geo.L.J. 939, 959–60 (1968). If the view is not evidence (a possibility discussed in the next paragraph of the text), do confrontation problems exist?

43. See 47 A.L.R.2d 1227 (1956) (necessity of judge's presence).

44. See Wendorf, Some Views on Jury Views, 15 Baylor L.Rev. 379 (1963).

invisible to Gossip, and that Zinger should have seen the moving automobile from the sidewalk. Zinger contends that Gossip should have seen him and that he did not see Gossip's car. The case is tried to a judge. **Should the judge be able to visit the accident scene alone to inspect the features of this intersection? Does it matter if she knows the intersection well? Should she be barred from going to the intersection unless counsel and the parties are also present? May the judge decide on her own motion that there should be a view? If a view is to be held, should the view take place before, during, or after the presentation of the parties' cases? Does it depend in part on the extent of discovery allowed? If the case had been tried to a jury and there had been no view, would it have been improper for one juror who knew the intersection well to tell the other jurors during their deliberations what the intersection was like? How might such communications be prevented?**

C. DEMONSTRATIONS AND EXPERIMENTS

McCormick writes:

The exhibition of the wound or physical injury, e.g., the injury sustained by a plaintiff in a personal injury action, will frequently be the best and most direct evidence of a material fact. Not surprisingly, therefore, exhibitions of physical injuries to the jury are commonly allowed.[45]

In general, the trial judge has broad discretion to permit injuries to be displayed, even though the injuries may produce an emotional reaction on the part of the jury. Courts have been more reluctant to allow litigants to demonstrate the ways in which they are affected by their injuries. The fear is that the injury will be made to appear more debilitating than it in fact is: the limp will be exaggerated or tolerable pain made to appear excruciating. Nevertheless, the trial judge has discretion to allow such demonstrations where they promise to be more helpful than harmful.

The judge also has discretion to admit experimental evidence. Experiments in the presence of the jury may be excluded if they involve considerable confusion and delay, but simple experiments by witnesses are usually permitted and more complicated experiments may be allowed. Courtroom experiments may be strikingly effective and, for this reason, should not be attempted unless one is sure the results will be favorable. Witnesses may also report the results of experiments conducted before trial. This is the more common kind of experimental evidence. It allows the rigorous testing of conflicting hypotheses in a controlled fashion.

Regardless of whether an in-court or an out-of-court experiment is involved, the judge's decision on admissibility will turn on answers to questions like the following: How reliable is the experiment? How similar are the conditions under which the experiment was conducted to the conditions surrounding the event the experiment is designed to elucidate? How helpful will the experimental evidence be to the jury? What is the likelihood that the jury will give the experimental evidence undue weight?[46]

---

45. McCormick § 215, at 535.

46. In some cases similarity of conditions is not important—e.g., a test to disprove an assertion that a given result is *impossible* under *any* set of circumstances. Should a jury be permitted to duplicate experiments in the jury room or to examine real evidence in ways not attempted by the parties? See Annot., 95 A.L.R.2d 351 (1964).

Problem XI–20. Louie Lampa sued the defendant for injuries to his right sacral region and sacroiliac joint, his sciatic nerve, and his back. During the trial the following occurred:

Q. Will you demonstrate this man up here before this jury, Doctor? **Dr. A.** Demonstrate him?

MR. NORBLAD: Just a minute; are you going to demonstrate that he couldn't bend over?

MR. GREEN: No, have the doctor explain what he did.

A. Is it all right?

COURT: Go ahead.

A. (To plaintiff) First thing stand with your heels in a military position, and you do as I do, stoop forward with your hands up, stoop over as far as you can.

MR. LAMPA: I can't stoop at all.

A. Try it.

MR. LAMPA: It hurts so bad I can't stoop.

A. Just try it.

MR. NORBLAD: I submit, Your Honor, that this is not proper; I can do the same thing; I submit it is improper.

COURT: No, objection overruled.

A. I am doing my best.

MR. NORBLAD: Please understand you are making no comments here: I am making my objection to the court, not you.

COURT: Both of you keep still.

A. Put you hands down and try stooping forward; I will measure how far you can stoop down.

MR. LAMPA: It hurts me right now like dickens: it hurt me right now.

A. Thirty inches this time; the first time I examined him was within 17 inches; that was in February; on my second examination he acted about like he did now; he couldn't stoop forward very well.

Q. Go ahead and tell the result of your examination.

A. This is just one; try to stoop backwards like this.

MR. LAMPA: It is impossible.

MR. NORBLAD: This is certainly improper; there are comments being made by this man all the time; I would like to have the record show that the plaintiff is making statements here constantly that is [sic] absolutely improper.

COURT: Objection overruled.

A. Let us see what happens when you try to do this. (Bends backwards).

MR. LAMPA: I can't do it at all, Doctor; just like that, oh, oh, it hurts. Uh.

A. What side does that hurt?

MR. LAMPA: Right here; right here.

A. Try this motion (sideways bending). Now the other side as far as you can.

MR. LAMPA: It still hurts.

At the conclusion of the trial the defendant moved for a new trial because this demonstration was allowed. **Would you grant a new trial?**

Problem XI–21. In a personal injury action in which the plaintiff claims that he suffered severe injuries to his hands as a result of being burned, the plaintiff moves before trial for permission to have each juror touch his burned hands in order to feel their hardness. The defendant objects. **Should the motion be granted? If the judge is concerned with juror sensibilities, should he consider having only those jurors who want to touch the hands do so?**

Problem XI–22. Driving in their new passenger car, Tom and Flora Hackley suddenly found themselves colliding with a tractor-trailer. They have sued the driver's employer, alleging that the truck failed to stop at a stop sign. Although they themselves did not see whether the trucked stopped, a physicist they have hired as an expert testifies that it would have been impossible for the truck to have stopped based on his estimate of the speed it was travelling at the time of the collision. The physicist bases his opinion on the testimony of a police officer who arrived at the scene shortly after the collision. The officer has previously testified that the truck left approximately 20 feet of skid marks, travelled from the point of impact some sixty feet along the road and then went into a ditch where it moved 126 feet further up an incline. In response to this evidence the employer offers the testimony of a metallurgist and his assistant who conducted an experiment. They took a similar truck and had a driver start at the stop sign after coming to a complete stop, accelerate, and follow the approximate path of the accident vehicle. The driver accelerated from the stop sign to the point where the defendant's experts estimated the collision took place, whereupon he lifted his foot from the accelerator and steered the truck along the road past the point where the accident vehicle had overturned in the ditch. According to the employer, this evidence supports the driver's claim that he stopped by showing that had he stopped he still could have ended up at the same point in the ditch where he actually overturned. Plaintiffs object to this testimony for three reasons: (1) the test vehicle was unloaded while the accident vehicle was fully loaded and weighed 37,000 pounds more than the test vehicle; (2) the test vehicle had an 8 cylinder engine while the accident vehicle had a 6 cylinder engine; and (3) the test produced no skid marks and permitted the test vehicle to travel on the roadway while the accident vehicle produced skid marks and went 126 feet up a ditch. The defendant's experts respond by saying that these differences go to the weight of the evidence rather than to its admissibility. **Should the trial judge permit them to testify?**

Problem XI–23. Harry Torres was driving a Volkswagen Van when it "rolled over" on a North Carolina highway as he was making a turn. Torres was thrown from the van through the front windshield, as was a passenger. Torres was injured and the passenger was killed. Torres and the estate of the passenger sue the manufacturer, claiming that the van's glass retention system was negligently designed. Plaintiffs offer into evidence statistical data compiled by the National Highway Traffic and Safety Administration's Fatal Accident Reporting System, which show that there is a greater likelihood of ejection from a VW van than from competitive vehicles. VW objects to the evidence on the ground that the government data do not indicate at what speed the accidents occurred, whether the other accidents were single or multi-car accidents, how the other accidents occurred, and in what manner the ejections occurred. VW claims that this data is like a "bad experiment" with no variables held constant. **Should the evidence be admitted?**

Problem XI–24. Joan petitioned the family court for an adjudication of paternity against Harvey, for the reimbursement of expenses incurred because of the pregnancy, and for an order to pay child support. Joan was married at the time the child was conceived, but she was not living with her husband. Harvey is not Joan's husband.

Joan won her case, perhaps because of the following occurrence. Prior to the close of Joan's case-in-chief and over Harvey's objection, the court permitted Joan to display her nine-month-old baby to the jury for about 30 seconds. Harvey objected to the exhibition for the following reasons: (1) the presence of the child would create sympathy in favor of Joan, (2) the exhibition of the child for the purpose of showing some physical resemblance to the defendant is "contrary to the facts of life", and (3) the exhibition "does not and would not add to the probative evidence in the case." The court ruled that the reasons for permitting the exhibition were two-fold: "to let the jurors see that there is a live baby and to generally appraise the physical characteristics of the baby." **How should a court rule on appeal? If blood tests aid considerably in determining paternity, should they be required and exhibition barred?** American jurisdictions have divided on the issue of exhibiting a child in a paternity action. Some courts permit the exhibition in any case in which paternity is an issue. Other courts only permit exhibition if a child has "settled features." Still other courts bar altogether exhibition evidence offered to show a physical resemblance of the child to the putative father. Most courts permit exhibition of a child for the purpose of showing racial characteristics where they are relevant. **What rule would you select for paternity proceedings? Would you distinguish between showing a child for the purpose of establishing that the child is or is not** of the father's race and showing the child to establish a physical resemblance with the father?[47]

Problem XI-25. Claude Kagan is charged with murdering his wife. There were no eyewitnesses to the shooting. The defendant testifies that he and his wife were alone in their house when he heard a shot from her bedroom. He ran into the room and found her sitting on the bed with his .22 calibre pistol in her hand. A chemist employed by the government testifies that he examined the nightgown that the wife was wearing at the time of her death. He found no gun powder residue on the gown, although the material of the gown generally would produce residue if a shot were fired from between 18 and 24 inches away. The expert had also run certain tests. He had fired the defendant's pistol at various distances into a test gown made of similar material and of a similar weave pattern as the gown worn by the deceased wife. Before doing this, he had fired into the wife's gown, which had been given him by the police, in order to determine if the residue patterns on both materials were the same. His experiments supported his conclusion that residue would be found if the gun were fired at close range. The defendant objects to evidence of the experiment, claiming that the conditions of the experiment and the murder scene were not identical. **Should the expert be permitted to testify if there is no chain of custody established and the gown is not introduced? Should the expert be permitted to testify about the experiment?**

D. MAPS, DIAGRAMS, DUPLICATES, SUMMARIES

Evidence offered not because it tends to prove a given fact but because it illustrates important facts and makes other proof more meaningful does not require the same sort of authentication as other demonstrative evidence.[48] Illustrative evidence may be admitted for its value in understanding relevant testimony in the case. Maps and diagrams are often used to convey a complete picture of a scene or area to the

47. For a discussion of blood tests to prove paternity, see Johnson, Proof of Paternity— The New Test, Va.B.News, June 1978, at 17.

48. **Some foundation is necessary, however.** Wigmore writes:

We are to remember, then, that a document purporting to be a map or diagram is, for evidential purposes simply nothing, except so far as it has a human being's credit to support it. It is mere waste paper,—testimonial nonentity. It speaks to us no more than a stick or a stone. It can of itself tell us no more as to the existence of the thing protrayed upon it than can a tree or an ox. We must somehow put a testimonial human being behind it (as it were) before it can be treated as having any testimonial standing in court. It is somebody's testimony, or it is nothing. It may, sometimes, to be sure, not be offered as a source of evidence, but only as a document whose existence and tenor are material in the substantive law applicable to the case,—as where, on a prosecution for stealing a map or in ejectment of land conveyed by deed containing a map, the map is to be used irrespective of the correctness of the drawing; here we do not believe anything because the map represents it. But whenever such a document is offered as proving a thing to be as therein represented, then it is offered testimonially, and it must be associated with a testifier.

3 Wigmore § 790, at 218 (emphasis in original deleted).

factfinder. Duplicates of objects may also illustrate important points. For example, if the prosecution knows the kind of gun that was used in a slaying but has been unable to find the murder weapon, it may wish to introduce a gun of the same make and model to show how the murder weapon was held or concealed.

One use of charts that is increasingly popular is to summarize aspects of trial testimony on a chalkboard or other large display that is highly visible to the jury. For example, in a prosecution against a store clerk for embezzlement, the prosecutor might note on a chart the dates that money was found missing from the store and the dates large deposits of cash were made by the clerk in order to show that the deposits followed closely after the thefts. Such a chart might assist the jury in remembering a series of dates and amounts and their interrelationships.

In some instances a chart does little more than repeat testimony in a way that might give one party an unfair advantage. For example, if the prosecutor in a bank robbery case presents testimony of three bank employees who identify the defendant, the prosecutor adds nothing to his case by writing on a large chalkboard a summary of the testimony like the following: "Employee 1 said, 'The defendant is the man.' Employee 2 said, 'He's the one.' Employee 3 said, 'I'll never forget him.'"

The trial judge has considerable control over the way in which evidence is presented. See FRE 611(a). Summaries that help the jury understand testimony should be welcome. But those that are used to simply repeat evidence without adding to it are suspect.

The lawyer who uses a chart usually may refer to it during closing argument. Some judges will admit the chart as evidence, and if other exhibits are sent to the jury room, the chart will also be sent. Because of the size of some charts and summaries, the trial judge may be cautious about sending all of them to the jury room, even when they are admitted as evidence. The judge must decide how much help the chart will be and weigh its value against the unfair advantage that its form may confer upon the party who prepared it. If the judge determines that a chart should not be sent, it may be possible to send a picture of the chart instead.

Problem XI–26. Allen is charged with willfully attempting to evade federal income taxes for the years 1967 and 1968. The government tries the case on a "net worth" theory. The government's evidence tends to prove that Allen and his wife, in joint tax returns, reported a taxable income of slightly over $11,000 for 1967 and about $16,500 for 1968, but their net worth increased approximately $18,000 during 1967 and an additional $35,000 the following year. According to the evidence, Allen was employed prior to 1967 by various magazine subscription companies, supervising activities of magazine salesmen. Late in 1966 Allen started his own business, acting as a middle man in the selling of magazine subscriptions. At the trial, the government offers the testimony of persons who allegedly made payments to Allen not reflected in his income records. To conclude the government's case, an Internal Revenue Agent is called and asked to identify a chart which summarizes the testimony of all the government's witnesses concerning the unreported income of the defendant. Allen objects to the introduction of the chart. **Is there any valid ground for objection?**

Problem XI–27. Paul Fix, Judy Miller, and Frank Miller are accused of conspiring to help Martha Fix escape from a state penitentiary. The government's theory is that Paul Fix parked his car near the prison, leaving his keys under the seat and then drove with the Millers to the airport where the three intended to rent a helicopter, fly it over the prison, and spray tear gas while Martha Fix escaped in the confusion. The plot was aborted when a police officer who had stopped Miller for speeding a quarter mile from the airport noted tear gas cannisters partially hidden under the back seat. Even if the cannisters had not been spotted, the stop would have effectively thwarted the plan for that day because there was only one fifteen minute period when the conspirators could count on Martha's being in the prison yard with the rope ladder she had made. The government wishes to introduce a map showing the airport where the helicopter the conspirators had arranged to rent was located, the place where Fix's car was found, and the spot where the three defendants were arrested. The defendants object that the map is not drawn to scale, does not include many of the existing streets and roadways and shows the three particular locations with large red marks to unduly emphasize them. The government admits that its map is neither drawn to scale nor complete, but urges that it should be admitted for background purposes. **Who wins?**

E. PHOTOS, MOVIES AND SOUND RECORDINGS

Like maps and diagrams, photographs are also demonstrative evidence. They are admissible whenever a witness can testify from personal knowledge that they accurately portray relevant facts. Assume, for example, that a witness is present at the scene of a riot, and that while he is present photographs are taken. At a trial for crimes committed during the riot, relevant photographs of the riot will be admissible if the witness can state that they accurately represent what he saw while he was on the scene. The photographs need not have been taken by the witness who authenticates them, although they might have been. Color photographs and enlargements are normally admissible on the same foundation—i.e., the testimony of a witness that they accurately represent what he saw.[49]

Photographs that are unduly prejudicial may be excluded.[50]

Suppose no picture was taken during the riot, but the prosecution seeks to introduce a posed picture portraying what happened according to the testimony of the prosecution's witnesses. Should the picture be allowed? Such pictures of artificially reconstructed scenes are almost always admitted when the positions of the persons and objects reflect undisputed testimony.[51] Thus, if there is no dispute that the defendants were at the scene at the spots indicated in the photograph and that all the other people and things in the photograph were accurately represented, the photograph will be admitted. When facts are disputed, posed photographs may be

49. Of course, the mere fact that the witness so testifies does not guarantee that the jury will believe him. See M. Houts, From Evidence to Proof 173–87 (1956).

50. See Rosen, Admission into Evidence of Prejudicial Photographs, 31 J.Crim.L. &

Criminology 604 (1941). Sometimes a color photo may be more prejudicial than a black and white photo but no more probative.

51. See 19 A.L.R.2d 877 (1951).

admitted to illustrate one side of the case.[52] The judge must balance prejudicial effect against probative value.

At one time courts were reluctant to admit motion pictures into evidence.[53] Now it is generally recognized that motion pictures may be treated like other photographs. The trial judge has more discretion to exclude motion pictures than still pictures, since they require considerable time and trouble in some cases. Yet, motion pictures of actual events may be accurate, reliable, and persuasive evidence. Often the court must view the film to determine whether it should be admitted in whole or in part. The impact of motion pictures may be substantially greater than that of still photographs, and in some cases it is feared that the jury might treat a filmed reproduction of one party's version of the facts as if it were a film of what actually happened. For this reason, when a film depicts only part of an event or when a simulated film depicts disputed facts, the trial judge will want to be convinced that the film is important and not misleading before allowing the jury to see it.

We pointed out earlier that some courts have been very strict in dealing with sound recordings. McCormick suggests that the treatment of sound recordings and motion pictures should be similar, and that sound recordings should be admitted if a witness testifies that the recording played for the court is an accurate reproduction of rele-

vant sounds previously heard by the witness.[54] Whether you accept his suggestion will depend on whether you want to impose careful handling rules as a condition to admitting evidence. If you do, you could impose them for film as well as for audiotapes.

Sometimes surveillance results in recordings while no one is listening to or watching what is being recorded. A tape may be left running in connection with a wiretap, for example. Or, when bank surveillance film is used, no one may be watching exactly what the machine captures. When no one can testify to the accuracy of what has been captured on film or tape, courts insist on a foundation that shows how the machine was employed. This includes showing that the recording was continuous and uninterrupted, or if that is not the case, showing how irregular the recording was and identifying any control devices that might have affected what the machine picked up. Those courts that apply a special standard of care require the same showing of freedom from editing or tampering that they require for other recordings. It may also be necessary to show that the machine was in good working order, although some courts will presume this if the recording appears to be adequate. Plainly such evidence is not offered solely for illustrative purposes. It may be the most powerful evidence of what happened on an occasion. In fact, the recording may be the only "witness" to the events.

Problem XI–28. Stryker is charged with selling heroin to an undercover federal agent. Stryker raises a defense of entrapment, claiming that the idea for the sale had originated not with him but with the government agent, that he (Stryker) had been reluctant to become involved, that only

---

52. See McCormick § 214, at 533. Some jurisdictions may exclude such pictures regardless.

53. See id. § 214, at 533 and n. 69. Some courts have established more rigorous authentication requirements for films than for

photographs. See, e.g., Balian v. General Motors, 121 N.J.Super. 118, 296 A.2d 317 (1972). See generally Paradis, The Celluloid Witness, 37 Colo.L.Rev. 235 (1965).

54. McCormick, § 214, at 534.

after tremendous pressure had been put on him by the agent was the sale made, and that he had had no propensity to commit such a crime. The government attempts to overcome the defense of entrapment by introducing a tape recording made by the agent at the time of the sale. The recording contained the following conversation:

Agent: Where did you get the stuff?

Stryker: From a friend. What do you care?

Agent: I don't care. Just curious.

Stryker: All right. Where's the money?

Agent: Here it is.

Stryker: Thanks.

Agent: You're welcome, and thank you. I'll be in touch.

Stryker: Great.

Stryker's contention is that the tape recording is likely to be misused by the jury because it is a tape recording only of the actual sale and not of any previous meetings. He also argues that the tape could be misinterpreted by a jury as signifying more agreement and less pressure than actually existed. **Should the court accept Stryker's argument and exclude the tape?**

Problem XI–29. Sylvia Post was a student at the University of Stanton. One night, while studying at home, Sylvia was kidnapped by an underground revolutionary group. Later, Sylvia participated with members of the group in a bank robbery. Sylvia's parents and friends believe that she was coerced into participating, but one week after the bank robbery a tape recording was received by a Stanton radio station containing statements by Sylvia asserting that she voluntarily participated in the bank robbery and that she repudiated the capitalistic ideas and ideals for which her parents and friends stood. Subsequently Sylvia is arrested and charged with bank robbery. Sylvia's defense is that she was coerced and "brainwashed" into participating in the bank robbery. To negate this defense and to establish knowing participation, the government wishes to introduce the tape recording received by the radio station. **Should the tape be admitted if the only authentication of the tape is that it is Sylvia speaking? What might Sylvia demand by way of further authentication?**

F. COMPUTER RECORDS

The use of computers to collect and sort data is increasingly common. Because of their peculiar characteristics, computers present some difficult questions for judges and lawyers.[55] William A. Fenwick and Richard M. McGonigal have created a "mock

----

55. See generally Jenkins, Computer-Generated Evidence Specially Prepared for Use at Trial, 52 Chi.-Kent L.Rev. 600 (1976); Roberts, A Practitioner's Primer on Computer-Generated Evidence, 41 U.Chi.L.Rev. 254 (1974), and Tapper, Evidence From Computers, 8 Ga.L.Rev. 562 (1974); Comment, A Reconsideration of Computer-Generated

trial" to illustrate the problems of establishing a proper foundation for computer records. We reproduce substantial excerpts from their helpful article:[56]

MOCK TRIAL

Plaintiff, a privately owned corporation which manufactures exclusive widgets, is suing defendant, a Euphoria corporation, in Euphoria state court, for lost profits resulting from lost sales due to defendant's refusal to perform a written contract with plaintiff to supply an important component used in plaintiff's widget. Plaintiff ran out of the components in November of 1973 and had its production facilities closed for four months. Starting in March 1974 plaintiff was forced to use an inferior component. The issue of liability was resolved in plaintiff's favor on a summary judgment motion and the only remaining issue at this trial is damages.

Plaintiff is a small company which uses a data processing service bureau by the name of Acme Computer Service Bureau ("Service Bureau"), to process and keep its sales and accounts receivable records. Service Bureau prepares the picking lists, bills of lading and invoices from the order information received from plaintiff. Service Bureau also prepares periodical sales reports for use in plaintiff's financial statement preparation. For some years, plaintiff has employed Service Bureau to process its sales orders and do the necessary record keeping for the accounts receivable. Because of costs, however, other accounting, inventory controls, production scheduling, and all other record-keeping is still done manually by plaintiff. Service Bureau operates a time-sharing computer system with several users, including plaintiff.

*   *   *

Plaintiff seeks to enter into evidence a computer prepared summary of its sales of widgets for the past four years and a set of tables and other information prepared by the computer to show relative profitability of plaintiff at various levels of gross sales. The summary was specially prepared for this litigation from processing information stored on magnetic tapes which are created and kept by Service Bureau. The tables and other information were prepared from cost and sales projection information given to Service Bureau by plaintiff. Service Bureau wrote a special program which exploded the cost information and correlated the data to produce the tables. Neither of the special programs written to prepare the summary and tables were documented in the manner required by Service Bureau's documentation standards because they were not permanent programs.

Plaintiff has the following items in court:

(i) the eight magnetic tapes used to produce the summary;

(ii) a tape print showing the information contained in the first few records on one of the magnetic tapes;

Evidence, 126 U.Pa.L.Rev. 425 (1977), and authorities cited therein.

56. Admissibility of Computerized Business Records, 15 Jurimetrics Journal 206, at 210–11, 224–46 (Spring 1975).

(iii) a listing of the source and object code for the special programs which were written solely for producing the summary and tables; and

(iv) a record format which explains the content of the records contained on the magnetic tapes.

* * *

TESTIMONY

1. Identity and Qualification of Authenticating Witness

Q. Would you state your name and address, please? **A.** Corebite Jones. (States address).

Q. Are you presently employed? **A.** Yes.

Q. By whom are you employed? **A.** Acme Computer Service Bureau.

Q. Is it acceptable to you if we simply refer to your employer as Service Bureau? **A.** Yes.

Q. Could you tell us what position you have with Service Bureau? **A.** I'm a vice president.

Q. Could you tell us the nature of Service Bureau's business? **A.** It's a data processing bureau that performs data processing for business organizations for a fee.

Q. Could you tell us what your responsibilities are at Service Bureau? **A.** I have responsibility for all systems development, testing, and for operations. I also have responsibility for systems design, system programming and I have primary responsibility for certain specified customers.

Q. Are you familiar with the Wigmore Widget Company? **A.** Yes, I am.

Q. What is the basis of your familiarity with the Wigmore Widget Company? **A.** I have responsibility for that account.

[Counsel then proceeds to elicit Jones' work history and educational background, emphasizing Jones' extensive experience in working with computers.]

2. Maintenance of Wigmore's Records by Service Bureau

Q. You indicate that you have responsibility for the Wigmore Widget Company account, is that correct? **A.** Yes.

Q. How long have you worked on that account? **A.** As long as the account has been with Service Bureau.

Q. What is the nature of the work that you perform on the account? **A.** I handle all problems dealing with the customer. In addition I handle or supervise the programming, scheduling and operating of all applications having to do with the customer's account.

Q. Can you describe the nature of the work performed on the account? **A.** We do keypunching and data processing for the account in connection with Wigmore's accounts receivable.

Q. What is your responsibility with regard to Wigmore? **A.** I have responsibility for all of the processing, systems design and problem resolution for that client.

Q. How long have you had responsibility for the Wigmore account? **A.** During the entire period they have used Service Bureau.

Q. Would you describe, again, what Service Bureau does for Wigmore? **A.** Service Bureau provides the data processing necessary for Wigmore's accounts receivable.

Q. What does that mean? **A.** We get information from Wigmore about orders, returns and payments. We process the information producing invoices, picking lists and shipping documents. We also provide the sales data for preparation of financials and we maintain their accounts receivable records for all their customers.

Q. How does the processing arrangement with Wigmore work? **A.** We receive information from Wigmore in two forms; one form is source documents. These consist of customer orders and return authorizations. When a customer sends in an order to Wigmore, a copy of that order is forwarded to us. When Wigmore authorizes return of goods, Wigmore sends us a copy of the return authorization. The second form of information is teletyped data that goes directly into our computer. The information received via teletype terminal is all payment information and all information for processing what Wigmore calls "expedited orders."

Q. Where is the teletype terminal located? **A.** At Wigmore's place of business.

Q. Who operates the teletype terminal? **A.** Employees of Wigmore, I don't know their names.[57]

Q. Once Service Bureau has received source documents from Wigmore what is done with them? **A.** The source documents go to our keypunching department at Service Bureau. The keypunch operator punches cards containing information from the orders or the return authorizations in a predetermined format. The source documents, that is the orders and the return authorizations, along with the punched cards, are then sent to our verifying department. The verifying department has machines which are very similar to keypunch machines except that the machines do not punch any cards. The punched cards and the source documents are given to the operator. The operator takes the punched cards, puts them into the verifying machine, takes each source document and again proceeds to enter the information from the source document in the same sequence as the key punch operator. The machine verifies that the information the second operator is entering agrees with the information entered by the first operator. This is called verification.

---

57. Does the fact that both Wigmore and Service Bureau employees must cooperate to produce records affect their potential admissibility?

The punched cards are then given to computer operations for processing. An operator will take the punched cards, load the appropriate programs for processing the cards, read the cards into the computer and the computer processes the information, updating the records which we maintain for Wigmore on magnetic disks. The computer also prints out invoices, picking lists and shipping documents for each order.[58]

Q. What records do you maintain for Wigmore on the magnetic disks? **A.** We maintain all the information in connection with their accounts receivables.

Q. Is the information from the cards the only information processed by you? **A.** No.

Q. What other information is processed? **A.** Wigmore has the on-line hook-up for its teletype machine, which permits Wigmore to dial up our computer and enter information directly into the computer through the teletype terminal. That information is stored on a disk pack and, periodically throughout the day, that information will be processed by the computer using the programs necessary to process Wigmore's data. Whenever the information is processed during the day the computer generates information for the picking lists and shipping instructions which are in turn transmitted back to Wigmore and printed via the teletype terminal. Those runs also generate invoice information which is combined with the invoice information generated from the daily processing of the cards and each night invoices are generated for Wigmore customers. The next day those invoices are sent out by Service Bureau to Wigmore customers.[59]

Q. Is any other information transmitted to Service Bureau by Wigmore via the teletype? **A.** Yes.

Q. And what information is that? **A.** Information regarding payments on account by Wigmore customers.

Q. And what happens to that information? **A.** It is stored on a disk pack and each night it is processed as a part of the processing done for Wigmore. The balances due from the customer are up-dated along with the payment record for the customer to reflect the payments received via the teletype the previous day.

Q. Are there any other outputs produced by Service Bureau for Wigmore on a daily basis? **A.** Yes.

Q. What are they? **A.** From each night's processing there is generated the picking lists which are to be used by Wigmore in filling orders received the previous day. There is also generated the necessary shipping documents for the shipment of the order to the Wigmore customer. The

58. Exactly what is being verified, the accuracy of the order and return forms or the accurate reproduction of the order and return forms on punched cards?

59. Are you concerned about the amount of material transmitted directly from Wig-more to Service Bureau's computer rather than transmitted on "order and return" forms? Are additional possibilities of error present here?

picking lists and shipping documents are delivered by messenger to Wigmore first thing every day. At night the same messenger returns to Wigmore to pick up the source documents which are to be keypunched and processed that night.

3. Procedures Employed to Assure Accuracy, Reliability and Freedom from Tampering

Q. Are all the records that you keep for Wigmore maintained solely on a disk pack? [60] **A.** No.

Q. How else are they maintained? **A.** All the cards that are keypunched and processed by Service Bureau on a daily basis are stored in card files at Service Bureau and retained for a specified period of time. In addition all of the information received via teletype is at some point during the processing punched into cards and these cards are stored along with cards punched by Service Bureau keypunchers as a part of the backup for the processing done. In addition, periodically, every six or eight months, the inactive data on the disk packs is dumped onto magnetic tapes for permanent storage.

Q. When you say inactive data, what do you mean? **A.** The data relating to the details of any orders which have already been processed and paid for will be removed from the disk pack and dumped onto magnetic tapes.

Q. Is there any other information dumped on the tape? **A.** Yes, there is.

Q. What other information? **A.** All of the information contained on the disk pack at the time of the dump will be put onto the magnetic tape. However, only the active data will remain on the disk pack. This is a process we call purging. It simply means that we take the inactive data off of the disk pack after it is stored on the tape.

Q. Does Service Bureau keep the disk packs and the tapes? **A.** Yes. One other point I forgot to mention with regard to the records kept for Wigmore is that, on a daily basis, Service Bureau dumps all of its disk packs onto tape for back-up use should information on the disk packs be accidentally destroyed.

Q. Is this the same dump you spoke of previously with respect to Wigmore data? **A.** No, this is a general dump, on a daily basis, of all disk packs for all customers that are active in on-line systems at Service Bureau. [61]

Q. You indicated that the tape dumps which you prepared for Wigmore data were also used as back-up. Can you explain what you meant? **A.** Yes. If information on a disk pack is accidentally destroyed, the first back-

---

60. Do you believe that the words "disk pack," used once previously by the witness, are clear to the jury? Should the jury be told disk packs are packs of ten or so disks, and that they are portable or that different disk packs may serve different purposes?

61. Shouldn't the words "on-line" be explained? In preparing for trial, you would want to know that the words can be used several different ways. They can stand for information that is kept in the computer at all times or for situations in which people who operate terminals are connected up with the computer. How are the words used here?

up will be the daily dumps onto magnetic tape which Service Bureau maintains for all information contained in files that are on-line. Should this first back-up tape contain an error or for some reason be unavailable or incapable of being processed, it would be necessary to recreate all customers' files. To recreate Wigmore's files, we would take the last tape dump of the Wigmore data, reload it on the disk pack and process all of the punched cards reflecting transactions that have occurred subsequent to the tape dump. This would recreate the file in the form in which it existed immediately before the information was destroyed.

Q. So then, if I understand what you are saying, the tape dumps of the Wigmore files contain only the information regarding Wigmore and is used only as a second back-up to the disk packs? **A.** That is correct.

Q. What happens to the disk packs and the tapes with the Wigmore information on them? **A.** When the Wigmore disk packs are not on-line they are stored in our tape library. When the tapes are prepared they are likewise stored in our tape library.

Q. Can you explain what a tape library is? **A.** Yes, it is a specially prepared room which is fireproof and furnished with special environmental equipment to control humidity and maintain appropriate temperatures. It is equipped with racks in which tapes and disk packs are stored. When a tape or disk pack is sent to the library, it is logged in; that is, the library log sheets for that particular customer are up-dated to reflect the status of the file. If it is a new file, a new entry is made. If it is an old file, an indication is made that it has now been returned to the library. The disk pack or the tape is then placed in the library in a predetermined location specified by the log sheet. When the tapes or the disk packs are taken out of the library, an indication is made on the log sheet that they have been removed, who removed them and where they are presently located.

Q. Can you tell us where the library is located at Service Bureau? **A.** The entryway to the tape library is right off the lobby of our reception area.

Q. Is the tape library equipped with a lock? **A.** The tape library is equipped with a vault door which contains a combination lock.

Q. To whom is the combination for the lock given? **A.** To all employees of Service Bureau.

Q. You indicate that the keypunching done by Service Bureau is verified, is that one hundred percent verification? **A.** Yes.

Q. Is there any verification of the transmitted input by Service Bureau? **A.** No, there is not verification as such. The computer programs which are used to process Wigmore data have certain editing procedures which are employed on all data. The transmitted information is subjected to these edit procedures.

Q. And what function do the edit procedures perform? **A.** The edit procedures assure that input data conforms to certain specified conditions. For instance, the procedures make sure that the right number of digits are present in a particular field of information. In some cases, they verify that the information does not exceed certain maximum and minimum limits. They

also check information to make sure that where it is numerical or alphabetical, all information entered is correspondingly numerical or alphabetical.
The edit procedure also makes sure that the account numbers are valid, existing account numbers.   This is done by checking the account master against
each entry to verify that there is an account number in the account master
for that particular transaction.[62]

Q.   Mr. Jones, I show you a document that has been marked as plaintiff's Exhibit "A" and ask you if you can identify that document.   **A.**   Yes.

Exhibit "A"
Page One
WIGMORE WIDGET COMPANY
Monthly Sales—1971

Month	Gross Sales Quantity	Gross Sales Dollars	Returns (Units)	Payments ($)	Total Sales ($)
JANUARY	340,000	170,000	10,000	165,000	165,000
FEBRUARY	330,000	165,000	4,000	163,000	163,000
MARCH	344,000	172,000	0	172,000	172,000
APRIL	350,000	175,000	5,000	172,500	172,500
MAY	340,000	170,000	0	170,000	170,000
JUNE	315,000	157,500	0	157,500	157,500
JULY	300,000	150,000	0	150,000	150,000
AUGUST	300,000	150,000	0	150,000	150,000
SEPTEMBER	405,000	202,500	5,000	200,000	200,000
OCTOBER	375,000	187,500	0	187,500	187,500
NOVEMBER	375,000	187,500	0	187,500	187,500
DECEMBER	260,000	130,000	10,000	125,000	125,000
TOTAL	4,034,000	2,017,000	34,000	2,000,000	2,000,000

[similar sheets for the years 1972–74 deleted]

Q.   Would you tell us what that document is?   **A.**   The document is
the monthly sales for Wigmore Widget Company for the years 1971, '72, '73,
and '74.

Q.   Do you know who prepared Exhibit "A"?   **A.**   Service Bureau.

Q.   Do you know how Exhibit "A" was prepared?   **A.**   Yes, I do.

Q.   How do you know?   **A.**   I was in charge of preparing it.

Q.   Would you tell us how it was prepared?   **A.**   Exhibit "A" is a computer print-out which contains all of the sales information for the Wigmore
Widget Company for the last four years.   It was generated by the computer
utilizing a program which I wrote for the purpose of preparing Exhibit "A."
The program processed the order detail information contained on the tape
dumps of Wigmore files for the last four years.

---

62. Compare the procedure discussed
here with the verification procedure discussed in the text accompanying note 58
supra.   What check is employed here?

Q. You say you wrote the program to prepare Exhibit "A"? **A.** Yes, I did.

Q. Did someone request you to write the program? **A.** Yes.

Q. Who? **A.** Wigmore's president.

Q. Can you tell us what the program does? **A.** Yes. The program reads the tapes which contain the details of all the orders received by Wigmore. The program then selects from the detailed information the quantity of widgets ordered and the dollar amount for each order. It also selects information regarding any return of widgets, and information regarding payments. It then totals all of this information to produce the gross sales, both the quantity and the dollar amounts, the number of returned units, the total payments made for orders received in each of the months, and it computes the total sales by subtracting returns from gross sales.

Q. Can you tell us how you went about writing the program? **A.** I took programming code sheets and wrote the various instructions necessary for locating and manipulating the required data. The code sheet contents were then keypunched and sent to the computer for a process called assembling. When the computer assembles a program it takes the instructions written by the programmer and converts them into symbols which are understood by the computer. The assembly process results in what is commonly called an object deck. The object deck is normally a group of punched cards prepared by the computer which contain the symbols necessary for the computer to perform various operations. At the same time as the assembly, a listing is prepared of the source deck, that is, the deck containing the instructions written by the programmer, as well as the object deck, that is, the deck prepared by the computer.

Q. Now once the program was assembled, what happened? **A.** Well, I had selected a series of transactions from the tapes containing the Wigmore files to prepare what is known as test data. I created the test data by taking samples of various records contained on the Wigmore tape dumps. At the time I selected these records I performed the calculations necessary to get the results manually. My manual calculations were rechecked by another person to verify their accuracy. I then took the test data and processed it with the computer program to generate a test output. I then compared the totals on the test output to the totals that had been achieved manually to verify that they were identical. Once this was done I determined that the program functioned accurately. I then instructed the computer room to process all the Wigmore tape dumps for the years 1971, '72, '73 and '74 using the program I had written. The operator took the tapes and my program, processed the tapes using my program and generated Exhibit "A."[63]

Q. Now, am I correct, Mr. Jones, in believing that there is no way a human being can visually review a magnetic tape and determine the information contained on it? **A.** That is correct.

---

63. Should the fact that this is specially prepared for litigation matter? See, e.g., Transport Indemnity Co. v. Seib, 178 Neb. 253, 132 N.W.2d 871 (1965).

Q. Is there some way of determining what information is contained on a tape? **A.** Yes, there is.

Q. How is that? **A.** There is a program which is provided by the computer company that is called TAPEPRINT. Using that program and running the tape through the computer, the computer prints out all of the information that is contained on the tape.

Q. I show you a document which has been marked as plaintiff's Exhibit "C" and ask you if you can tell me what that is.[64] **A.** That is a tapeprint of one of the records contained on the Wigmore tape dumps.

Q. Now, is there some way you can determine by looking at this tapeprint what information is contained on the magnetic tape regarding Wigmore's accounts receivable? **A.** Yes, there is.

Q. And how is that done? **A.** In the documentation of the accounts receivable programs used for Wigmore there is prepared a document entitled a Record Format. The Record Format is a narrative of the information contained on the tape and specifies not only the type of information contained on the tape but where it is contained within any specified record. Exhibit "C" is a series of records which is in fact contained in a single block of records which are written on one of the Wigmore tape dumps.

Q. I show you plaintiff's Exhibit "F" and ask you if you can identify that? **A.** It's the Record Format for the Wigmore accounts receivable records.

Q. Do you know who prepared it? **A.** Yes, I prepared it.

Q. When was it prepared? **A.** It was prepared when I documented the accounts receivable programs which process the Wigmore accounts.

Q. I show you plaintiff's Exhibit "D" and ask you if you can identify that document? **A.** Yes.

Q. What is it? **A.** That's a Record Layout of the Wigmore accounts receivable record.

Q. What is a Record Layout? **A.** It is a graphic illustration of the information contained on the record.

Q. Now, can you take the information there and translate the blob of numerical and alphabetical information contained in Exhibit "C"? **A.** Yes, you can. If you will note in Exhibit "D" the type of information is identified for each section of the record. A Record Overlay can be prepared which, when laid on a tapeprint, clearly identifies the information.

Q. I show you plaintiff's Exhibit "E" and ask you if you can identify that document? **A.** Yes, that's a Record Overlay.[65]

Q. Do you know who prepared it? **A.** I did.

Q. Would you take the Overlay and go through the first record on the tapeprint telling us the subject matter of the information as well as what the

---

64. **What is the significance of this step?**   65. **Exhibits, C, D, E and F are not reproduced.**

information says? **A.** Yes. (Goes through the first and second line of the first record.)

5. Other Uses Made of the Tapes Which Were Used As Inputs to the Special Programs

Q. To your knowledge, are the Wigmore tape dumps used for any other purpose other than those which you have described? **A.** Yes. From time to time we generate miscellaneous reports requested by Wigmore. These normally have something to do with sales or payments or things of that nature. In addition, we generate a report annually which contains the sales figures for the year. This is done by processing the tape dumps. Those reports also contain various other statistics such as the number of orders as well as a breakdown of the number of orders by customer. And, as I indicated before, the tape dumps are also prepared as a second back-up to the disk packs. To my knowledge they have never been used for that. The tapes are also kept for Internal Revenue purposes.[66]

Q. Now, you indicate that you wrote the special program to prepare Exhibit "A," is that correct? **A.** Yes.

Q. Did you employ the normal procedures of the Service Bureau in writing the special program? **A.** Yes, I followed normal procedures for writing any program. The only departure from normal procedures is that the programs that I wrote to prepare both Exhibits "A" and "B" are not as extensively documented as they would be if they became permanent programs because they are special programs to be used only one time.

Q. Can you tell us how you prepared Exhibit "B"?

Exhibit "B"
WIGMORE WIDGET COMPANY
TABLE OF PROFITABILITY

Sales In Units (000)	Direct Labor Cost	Indirect Labor Cost	Material Cost	Admin. and Overhead Cost	Sales Cost	Profit
1400	$112,000	$ 28,000	$140,000	$400,000	$ 70,000	$ (50,000)
1800	144,000	36,000	180,000	400,000	90,000	50,000
2200	176,000	44,000	220,000	400,000	110,000	150,000
2400	192,000	48,000	240,000	400,000	120,000	200,000
2800	224,000	56,000	280,000	400,000	140,000	300,000
3200	256,000	64,000	320,000	400,000	160,000	400,000
3600	288,000	72,000	360,000	400,000	180,000	500,000
4000	320,000	80,000	400,000	400,000	200,000	600,000
4400	352,000	88,000	440,000	400,000	220,000	700,000
4800	384,000	96,000	480,000	450,000	240,000	750,000
5200	416,000	104,000	520,000	450,000	260,000	850,000
5600	448,000	112,000	560,000	450,000	280,000	950,000
6000	480,000	120,000	600,000	500,000	300,000	1,000,000

66. **Is reliance on the tapes for other purposes important? Why or why not?**

A. Yes. I received from Wigmore the direct labor cost incurred by Wigmore in the manufacturing of a widget, as well as the indirect labor cost, the material cost and the sales cost. Wigmore also gave me the administrative and overhead costs for producing widgets at various levels of production. I then prepared a program which took that information as well as the information regarding pricing of Wigmore widgets which was already contained in our files and wrote a program which produced Exhibit "B."

Q. Did you utilize any of the information contained on the Wigmore tape dumps in the production of Exhibit "B"? **A.** No. The only information I used from any of the files we maintain for Wigmore was the pricing information which I took from Wigmore customer invoices. The program did nothing more than make the calculations for the various quantities of output and print out the information, as well as computing the profit or loss based on the total costs subtracted from the total sales.

BY MR. FENWICK

Your Honor, I move the admission of Exhibits A & B.

CROSS-EXAMINATION

Your Honor, I object on the grounds that the Exhibits are hearsay and violate the Best Evidentiary Rule. I would like to cross-examine Mr. Jones to establish further the factual basis for objection.

THE COURT: Proceed.

Q. Mr. Jones, what information do you have regarding Wigmore's accounting practices? **A.** I don't have any information other than the processing that we provide for them.

Q. Have you ever seen any of Wigmore's books and records? **A.** No. Other than the copies of the orders we receive and the records we generate.

Q. Do you ever communicate with any of Wigmore's customers regarding their orders? **A.** No.

Q. Do you ever receive any documents from Wigmore's customers? **A.** Do you mean other than copies of the orders which are sent over by Wigmore?

Q. Yes. **A.** No.

Q. Do you have any relationship with Wigmore other than as Service Bureau's account manager? **A.** No.

Q. Then the only knowledge you have regards the keypunching and processing of the order information and returning the results of that processing to Wigmore, is that correct? **A.** Yes.

Q. Isn't it true that you never see any documents regarding payments by Wigmore customers? **A.** That is correct.

Q. Do you ever receive any documents or have any other source of knowledge that in fact the goods reflected in the orders you process are sent?

A.　There is information transmitted via the teletype regarding payments received by Wigmore.

Q.　Do you see that information?　**A.**　No.

Q.　Do you see any documents from Wigmore customers indicating they have paid their accounts?　**A.**　No.

Q.　With regard to expedited orders do you see any documents from Wigmore or Wigmore's customers concerning those orders?　**A.**　No.

Q.　In fact there is no verification by Service Bureau of the expedited order information, is that correct?　**A.**　We do not verify the expedited order information other than the edits that are performed by the computer programs.

Q.　Do you see any information with regard to expedited orders from any source?　**A.**　We generate invoices for expedited orders.

Q.　But are those identified in any way so that you can determine that the invoices relate to expedited orders?　**A.**　No.

Q.　In fact, you do not even see the picking lists and shipping instructions for expedited orders, is that correct?　**A.**　That's correct.

Q.　Have there ever been errors in processing the Wigmore accounts receivable?　**A.**　Yes, I am sure there have been.

Q.　Do you have any recollection of specific errors made in the processing of Wigmore accounts receivables?　**A.**　Yes, there have been seven or eight occasions when we have had to reprocess a day's orders in order to correct errors.

Q.　How did you discover the errors?　**A.**　With the exception of one occasion in which an operator, while removing invoices from the printer, noticed the control totals appeared unrealistic, we were notified by Wigmore of problems which eventually resulted in reprocessing.

Q.　You indicate there are control totals on the invoice runs.　Do you do anything with those control totals?　**A.**　No, other than sending them to Wigmore along with the picking lists and shipping documents.

Q.　With regard to the special programs that you have written that produced Exhibits "A" and "B", is it correct that reports similar to Exhibits "A" and "B" are not produced normally for Wigmore?　**A.**　That is correct.

Q.　You indicated that you did not follow your standard documentation procedure in documenting the programs that prepared Exhibits "A" and "B". Is that correct?　**A.**　Yes.

Q.　What is the function of the documentation of a program?　**A.**　The documentation provides an explanation of what the program does and how it does it.　It makes it much easier to modify the program.　It is also used extensively in correcting bugs in the program.

Q.　What is a bug?　**A.**　That is where the program has not functioned properly.

Q. Regarding the testing of the special program you wrote, would it be accurate to say that your test data did not include examples of all types of input that were contained on the Wigmore tape dumps? **A.** What do you mean by examples of input?

Q. I mean that they did not contain all of the input conditions that would be encountered when the programs processed the Wigmore tape dumps. **A.** I think that is probably accurate. However, an attempt was made to include examples of all input conditions which it can be anticipated will cause a problem or will have a different impact on the processing. That is a part of the designing of the test data.

Q. Do you have any doubt that there were input conditions that existed in the Wigmore tape dump which were not included in the test data? **A.** I do not know whether there were or not.

Q. In your experience, does the test data normally contain all of the conditions which exist in the information to be processed? **A.** No.

Q. When were these exhibits prepared? **A.** They were prepared on the date contained on the top of each exhibit, which is February 4, 1975.

Q. When were the magnetic tapes prepared? **A.** The dates the tapes were prepared are contained on the labels. They vary.

Q. Now, you indicated that the dumps are made every six or eight months. Is that correct?[67] **A.** Yes.

Q. Therefore, in the case of some of the information being dumped it is being written on the tape eight or nine months after the orders for widgets were received? **A.** That would probably be correct for some of the information.

Q. Now, regarding the tape library, is it not true that all Service Bureau employees have access to the tape library? **A.** That is correct.

Q. Do all of the employees of Service Bureau perform some function related to Wigmore? **A.** No.

Q. How many employees does Service Bureau have? **A.** Approximately eighty.

Q. How many employees of Service Bureau perform any function relating to Wigmore? **A.** Including keypunch operators, I would say twelve to fourteen.

Q. Now, regarding the other exhibits that have been marked here, the tape print, the Record Layout, the Record Format and the Overlay, were they prepared specifically for this litigation? **A.** No.

Q. When were they prepared? **A.** I am not sure of the exact date but they would have been prepared as part of the documentation of the accounts receivable programs for Wigmore.

67. How is this fact significant?

Q. Are those kept at Service Bureau? **A.** Yes, they are. They are also made available to employees of Wigmore.

Q. Are those documents made available to all employees of Service Bureau? **A.** Yes, they are.

Q. Does Service Bureau employ any security system to insure that only employees are on the premises? **A.** Well, an attempt is made to make sure people who are not employees of Service Bureau or clients of Service Bureau do not go into the computer room. However, Service Bureau is a business and the reception area of Service Bureau is of course open to the public.

Q. Does Service Bureau employ any means of special identification of persons having access to the computer room? **A.** If by special identification you mean are there identification cards or that sort of thing, the answer is no. There is a door that separates the computer room from the rest of Service Bureau's facilities, and it contains a sign that specifies that only authorized personnel are permitted in the computer room. Other than that we rely on personal recognition by employees.

Q. Where is the tape library located with regard to the reception area? **A.** The door to the tape library is on the side of the reception room.

Q. Is that door kept locked at all times? **A.** No.

Q. Is there a security guard on the tape library? **A.** No.

Q. Do you maintain a log of people coming in and out of the computer room? **A.** No.

Q. What about the tape library? **A.** No.

Q. Does Service Bureau perform any types of security checks on its employees? **A.** Not to my knowledge.

Q. Now, regarding the programs that generate the original records on the disk packs for the Wigmore accounts receivable processing, do you have listings of those programs in Court today? **A.** No, I do not.

Q. Do you know who wrote those programs? **A.** Yes, I did.

Q. Do you know if any changes have been made in those programs since they were written? **A.** Yes.

Q. Have any changes been made? **A.** Yes.

Q. Do you know who made those changes? **A.** Yes.

Q. And who made them? **A.** I did.

Q. The testimony you gave today as to the testing of programs and the specific functions performed by programs, did that relate only to the programs for the preparation of Exhibits "A" and "B"? **A.** That is correct.

Q. Would it be accurate to say that the records contained on the magnetic tapes are copies of the records contained on the disk packs? **A.** Yes.

Q. And is it not true that it is the records on the disk packs which are used in the accounts payable processing? **A.** That is correct.

Q. Now, when these records are dumped from the disk pack onto the tapes, is any attempt made to verify that the dumps are accurate? **A.** No. Not any other than hardware checks.

Q. What are hardware checks? **A.** The tape drives have built into them the ability to sense that a tape is damaged and should not be written on.

Q. Is there a method by which you could verify that the dumps are accurate duplicates of the information on the disk? **A.** Yes, there is a computer program which will verify that.

Q. And do you use that program when the dumps are made? **A.** No, we do not.

Q. And why is that? **A.** It would simply add to the cost of processing and the tapes are not used for the accounts receivable processing except in a situation where they might be used as a back-up. Basically, it's a cost trade-off.

Q. Did you write the programs that dump the disk packs onto the tapes? **A.** I did not.

Q. Do you know who did? **A.** Those programs come with the computer and are written by, I assume, employees of the computer manufacturer. I don't know.

Q. Do you have listings of the programs that dump the records onto the tapes? **A.** I do not. I assume I could get them if I wanted them, but the programs are not very complicated.

Q. Did you have anything to do with the design of that program? **A.** I did not.

Q. Have you ever had occasion to compare the dumps with the information on the disk? **A.** I have not.

Q. Did you run the programs that originally put the accounts receivable information on the disk pack for Wigmore's accounts receivable? **A.** No, I do not operate the computers under normal circumstances.[68]

Q. Do you know who did operate the computers? **A.** It would have been one of our operators.

Q. Do you know which operator? **A.** I do not personally know. I believe from a review of the log sheets we could determine, but it might be any one of fifteen people.

Q. Do you know whether or not any processing errors were incurred during the processing? **A.** I assume that none occurred that weren't corrected.

68. How significant is this fact?

Q. But do you know whether any occurred that weren't corrected? **A.** I do not know for sure.

Q. Do you know who operated the programs that dumped the information onto the tapes? **A.** I do not.

Q. Do you know if they incurred any processing errors? **A.** I do not, but we have a procedure where, if processing errors are incurred, certain steps are to be taken.

Q. But you don't have personal knowledge of whether any processing errors occurred? **A.** That is correct.

Q. Now, Mr. Jones, would it be possible to print out all the information on the magnetic tapes that were used to produce Exhibits "A" and "B"? **A.** Yes, it would be.

Q. Do you have any idea of what size the print-out would be? **A.** I couldn't be sure, but I would imagine that since seven of those tapes are completely occupied the print-out would be quite huge.

Q. How huge? **A.** It might be thirty or forty feet high.[69]

Q. Getting back to the security of Service Bureau's premises, have you ever had any break-ins? **A.** Yes, we have had.

Q. How many? **A.** One that I can recall.

Q. When was that? **A.** Approximately two years ago.

Q. Was anything taken? **A.** We were unable to determine if anything was in fact taken.

Q. Was any damage done? **A.** Yes.

Q. What was done? **A.** A number of the reels of tape that were in the library were taken from the library and unwound, strewing the tape throughout the reception area.

Q. Were any of Wigmore's tapes unwound? **A.** No, they were not.

Q. What did you do to replace the tapes? **A.** In the case of the tapes that were active customer files, various procedures were followed to re-create them.

Q. Did you recreate all of the tapes? **A.** We did not.

Q. Why not? **A.** With regard to some of the tapes there was no need to recreate them because they did not contain active data or data that was required for processing. In the case of two or three files all of the grandfather tapes of those files were destroyed and therefore they could not be recreated without tremendous expense. We recreated only those files that were absolutely essential for processing.

69. Should this matter? See, e.g., City of Seattle v. Heath, 10 Wash.App. 949, 520 P.2d 1392 (1974).

Q. Now regarding Exhibit "B" is it correct to say that none of the information contained in any of the Wigmore files was used in the preparation of Exhibit "B"? **A.** That is not correct.

Q. What information was used? **A.** We got the price information from the Wigmore invoices.

Q. Other than the price information, did you use any information from the Wigmore files? **A.** We did not.

Q. Do you have any information regarding Wigmore costs of production? **A.** We have the information that they gave us and I used in preparing the exhibit.

Q. Other than the information they gave you, do you have any other information? **A.** No, we do not.

Q. Did you verify the cost information provided you by Wigmore in any way? **A.** I did not.

Q. Could you have verified it? **A.** I do not know because I do not know what records Wigmore keeps regarding the cost.

Q. Thank you.

What portions, if any, of the offered evidence would you exclude? Why?

G. VIDEOTAPE

In recent years there has been a wealth of literature concerning the current and the predicted future use of videotape in litigation.[70] From most of the writing, one gets a sense that videotapes are viewed as the wave of the future, and that nothing can stem the tide. In 1974, retired Supreme Court Justice Tom C. Clark wrote:

We in the law have learned the hard way that other disciplines offer much in the adjudication of the great economic, social, and political issues that are thrust upon the courts. Witness the economic, financial, and social testimony that is now commonplace in our trials. But, unfortunately, we have not been as ready and willing to rely on these kindred disciplines in the internal management of

the legal system itself. It appears to me, however, that the legal profession is becoming increasingly more willing and anxious not only to accept the guidance of the social and technical scientists but also to enlist their active support. This is itself a milestone in judicial management. * * *

* * *

I am told that there have been well over 4,000 depositions taken on videotape and that there have been several hundred trials in which videotape testimony has been used. These figures are small when measured against the total number of cases tried in the state and federal courts, but they seem a sig-

70. Most of the authorities are cited in Doret, Trial By Videotape—Can Justice Be Seen To Be Done? 47 Temp.L.Q. 228 (1974) and Bermant, Critique—Data in Search of Theory in Search of Policy: Behavioral Re-

sponses to Videotape in the Courtroom, 1975 Brig.Y.U.L.Rev. 467. The latter article appears as part of an interesting Symposium: The Use of Videotape in the Courtroom, 1975 Brig.Y.U.L.Rev. 327.

nificant number to me when one considers the remarkable change they represent in traditional procedures and the short time since the initial experiments began.

Lawyers and judges, we often have been told, are very much in favor of progress but sit on their hands when someone suggests change! Instead of doing this, the lawyers must not only support progress but welcome change, for they go hand in hand.   *   *   *

Thus far, as Judge McCrystal reminds us, experience with the videotape trial "has attracted the attention of the scientist to a far greater degree than that of the judge and lawyer." But, knowing the judges and the Bar, we can count on them to correct this imbalance. I predict the universal use of videotape in personal injury cases, especially as to medical testimony, and its expansion to other litigation as the Bar and the court become satisfied as to its adaptability. Perhaps not in my day, but I truly believe not too far in the future, we will be "videoing" the entire case.[71]

A more cautious observer, citing one important experimental effort,[72] makes the following comment:

[The experimenters] concluded quite unequivocally that "[o]n the basis of the results of this study and the impressions we gleaned while conducting the research, we find the videotaped trial format *not guilty* of any charges of detri-

mental effects [on] juror responses." Here is the opinion of the social scientist nicely phrased to catch the lawyer's ear. In sum, all the lights appear green, and there seems no reason to delay realization of the obvious benefits of videotaped trial presentations.

Or almost no reason. In the rush to pick the legal fruits of videotape technology it is possible that the unintended consequences of videotape utilization may be overlooked. Those persons advocating or responding to the use of videotape have been so close to the issue as, perhaps, to have lost sight of its potentially broader ramifications. Lest this sound like a plea by modern-day legal Luddites, we hasten to say that we do not know whether a widely increased use of PRVTT [prerecorded videotape testimony] would have deleterious socio-legal consequences—but neither does anyone else.[73]

It is important to distinguish the various situations in which videotape evidence might be used. We shall discuss three such situations, all of which have received attention in the recent literature: 1) where videotape is used to record routine extra-judicial activities, especially the activities of government officials who know that their behavior is likely to be scrutinized by courts; 2) where information is recorded extra-judicially in case it proves impossible to otherwise present the information to the trier of fact; and 3) where videotape testimony is substituted for the "live" testimony of available witnesses because the use of videotape is more convenient for the witnesses or the court.

---

71. Introduction to Symposium, supra note 90, at 327, 328–30. The internal quote is from McCrystal, The Videotape Trial Comes of Age, 57 Judicature 446, 449 (1974).

72. Miller, Bender, Florence & Nicholson, Real Versus Reel: What's the Verdict? 24 J. Communication 99 (1974).

73. Bermant & Jacoubovitch, Fish Out of Water: A Brief Overview of Social and Psychological Concerns About Videotaped Trials, 26 Hastings L.J. 999, 999–1000 (1975), quoting Miller, supra note 72.

1. Extra Judicial Government Activities

The first situation is related to a recommendation of the Model Code of Pre-Arraignment Procedure, §§ 130.4(1) & (3):

(1) *Obligation to Make Records Relating to Periods of Custody.* In accordance with regulations, * * * law enforcement agencies shall make the full written and sound records required by Subsections (2) and (3) of this Section and, where identification procedures pursuant to Article 160 are employed, shall make the records required by Section 160.4.

* * *

(3) *Sound Recordings.* The regulations relating to sound recordings shall establish procedures to provide a sound recording of [various warnings, questioning of suspects, and statements made in response to questions]. Such recordings shall include an indication of the time of the beginning and ending thereof. The arrested person shall be informed that the sound recording required hereby is being made and the statement so informing him shall be included in the sound recording. The station officer shall be responsible for insuring that such a sound recording is made.

In lieu of the required sound recording, it would be possible to provide videotape evidence. Since identification procedures and police interrogation take place outside the courtroom, those who feel that effective judicial control over the police requires an accurate record of what happens in the stationhouse might favor recording devices that can provide a relatively complete record of what occurs. Assuming that government officials are willing to cooperate in an effort to provide recordings of maximum accuracy, is there any reason not to require that such out-of-court activities be videotaped? Unless there is some indication that suspects will be adversely influenced by the use of videotape in place of sound recordings, it would appear that videotape evidence should be received. In many situations the videotape evidence will never reach the jury. It will only be used to allow the trial judge to rule on the preliminary issues of whether statements were voluntarily made, whether warnings were properly given, and whether identification techniques were unduly suggestive. However, in some situations the jury will be asked to view the tape, perhaps as demonstrative evidence bearing on a defendant's guilt or as evidence that undermines the credibility of a government witness.

Whether the tape is used by the judge, the jury, or both, it will be necessary to examine the conditions under which the tape was made. It is easy to make the mental leap from need to the assumption that "the use of the [videotape] medium represents a simple substitution in the means of transmitting information."[74] This leap is particularly easy when videotape records an event, because the videotape medium appears to be more reliable than the subsequent testimony of a witness concerning what occurred. But Bermant and Jacoubovitch suggest cogent reasons why a more cautious attitude might be appropriate. Do the reasons offered apply to the videotaping of stationhouse procedures?

There are three ways in which the assumption [quoted above] may be inaccurate. First, *technical differences* between forms of presentation will sometimes result in differences in the saliency of details. For example, in the Liggons v. Hanisko[75] trial, Mrs. Liggons's

74. Bermant & Jacoubovitch, supra note 73, at 1000.

75. Civil No. 637–707 (Super.Ct. San Francisco Co., Cal., Sept. 19, 1973) discussed

poorly set, misshapen shin bone did not have as much visual impact on videotape as it did in person. This was due, in part, to a relatively low degree of visual contrast between the color of Mrs. Liggon's [sic] leg and the background against which the leg was videotaped during her testimony. With higher contrast, it is conceivable that the close-up shot of the leg would have more forcefully impressed the jury, perhaps to the point of returning a verdict in her favor. * * *[76]

The second level of potential non-substitutability resides in the *inevitable editorial process* involved in translating from one medium to another, particularly when a change of scope is unavoidable. * * * Because the camera becomes the juror's eye on the participants, it locks the juror's perspective in important ways: the jurors are no longer free to look around the setting of the trial and determine their own priorities, for assessing what is relevant and what is not. Videotaping is, therefore, an unavoidably inscoping, manipulative translation of the live confrontational situation. * * *

* * *

The third level at which the substitutability of PRVTT for live trials needs to be examined involves the question whether properties inherent in the video medium,[77] when combined with our cultural history and expectations in regard to it, may produce undesirable unintended consequences in PRVTT.

In some situations a record must be made. Any record is going to suffer from defects that are avoided by live trials. Yet, it is possible that a videotaped record will have certain strengths not shared by live testimony. What are they likely to be? If a record is to be made of a police interrogation, what are the options? One is to have a stenographer present, but a stenographer can record only what is said, not what is done. Furthermore, what is said will be captured in a transcript that does not reflect tones of voice, certain kinds of hesitation and demeanor. A tape recording could be made, but it would not capture gestures that accompany words, the physical condition of the person being interrogated, or the quality of the interrogation room. An observer could be placed in the interrogation room, but human memory is not perfect and the observer's account may be colored by personal interests. Videotape can probably capture more of what goes on at a police interrogation than any of the available alternatives, but it presents the problems discussed above. If there is any distortion, intentional or unintentional, it might be particularly prejudicial because of people's feelings that cameras do not lie.

If you were a legislator or a judge, which form of recording would you prefer? What, if anything, would you do to combat the potential defects of the form you have selected? If the idea of videotaping is attractive, would you as a judge wish to control the way the videotape equipment is set up in the police station, or should this be left to the police?

---

in Bermant, Chappell, Crockett, Jacoubovitch & McGuire, Juror Responses to Prerecorded Videotape Trial Presentations in California and Ohio, 26 Hastings L.J. 975 (1975). This entire quote is drawn from Bermant and Jacoubovitch supra note 73, at 1001, 1003–04 (emphasis in original).

76. Will lineups and other identification procedures be accurately recorded on videotape? Is there a viable alternative?

77. The author suggests examples in a footnote: "impoverishment of the live field of observation * * *; interposition of at least one observer necessarily exercising an editorial function between the field of observation and the final audience; and temporal juxtapositions via editing that create implications not apparent in the live setting." Bermant and Jacoubovitch, supra note 73 at 1003 n. 13.

2. DEPOSITIONS

The second use to which videotape can be put is the recording of out-of-court actions that might have to be reproduced in court if certain contingencies occur. The most familiar example is the deposition. In Chapter Two we discussed the use of depositions in the Federal Rules of Civil Procedure. Fed.R.Civ.P. 30(b)(4) provides that:

The court may upon motion order that the testimony at a deposition be recorded by other than stenographic means, in which event the order shall designate the manner of recording, preserving, and filing the deposition, and may include other provisions to assure that the recorded testimony will be accurate and trustworthy. If the order is made, a party may nevertheless arrange to have a stenographic transcription made at his own expense.

The Advisory Committee's Note accompanying this Rule reads as follows:

In order to facilitate less expensive procedures, provision is made for the recording of testimony by other than stenographic means—e.g., by mechanical, electronic or photographic means. Because these methods give rise to problems of accuracy and trustworthiness, the party taking the deposition is required to apply for a court order. The order is to specify how the testimony is to be recorded, preserved, and filed, and it may contain whatever additional safeguards the court deems necessary.

As discussed in Chapter Two, the wise lawyer tries to assess the likelihood that a given witness will be unavailable at the trial. Naturally it is impossible for the lawyer to know with certainty what will happen some months or years in the future, but there are times at which the lawyer has notice that a given witness may become unavailable. In such circumstances, a lawyer may seek a deposition to perpetuate testimony under Fed.R.Civ.P. 27 or a similar state rule. Alternatively the lawyer may seek to advance the time for taking a regular deposition pursuant to Fed.R.Civ.P. 30(b)(2). The Advisory Committee considering the Federal Rules of Civil Procedure apparently was opposed to the general use of videotape and other recording techniques for taking depositions on the ground that they tended to be less accurate than stenographic recording. Do you agree? Somewhat surprisingly, a factor influencing the committee to approve modern forms of recording was that they promise to be less costly than stenographic transcriptions. Clearly this is the case with sound recording. Once capital costs are absorbed, it is probably true of videotape as well. If videotape depositions were permitted as a general rule, would this provide an edge to firms that can afford to set up elaborate videotape systems in their offices? What problems do you see with encouraging the use of videotape for depositions? Are these the same problems that you saw with respect to recording police station activities?

3. THE VIDEOTAPED TRIAL

The most ambitious of the suggested applications of videotape techniques is the videotaping of entire trials, done on a piecemeal basis, with the jury being shown a final compilation. One commentator, building on the work of another, suggested that a videotape trial might proceed along the following lines:

All witnesses [would testify] under oath in mutually agreed upon settings in the presence of the lawyers and a court officer other than the trial judge. The order of taping the testimony [would] not [be] stipulated, nor [would] it [be] binding on the subsequent order of presentation. All objections [would be] formally noted, but questioning [would] not [be] curtailed. The master tape, containing the entirety of the testimony, [would be] reviewed subsequently in chambers in the presence of the attorneys. At this time, the trial judge [would pass] and [rule] on all objections. Both the formal objections and the objectionable statements [would be] deleted on a second tape. Thus, this edited version of the trial tape [would be] prepared without destroying the continuity of the admissible testimony. The trial tape [would] then [be] further spliced so that the witnesses could be presented in the agreed upon order. The master tape [would remain] intact for appeal purposes.

The jurors [would] not [be] impaneled until the completion of the trial tapes. After the attorneys [deliver] their opening statements in the courtroom, the trial tape [would be] shown to the jurors on monitors. Neither lawyers nor trial judge [would remain] in the courtroom [during] the presentation, although an officer of the court [would be] in attendance at all times. * * * [L]awyers [might give] their closing statements live, but judges [would render] instructions to jurors on tape.[78]

The advantages of videotaped trials have been described as follows:

The trial proceeding has traditionally required that parties, counsel, witnesses, judge, jury and interested observers from the community convene at a single time, in a single place (and a special one at that—the courtroom), to conduct the trial's business. For this reason, it may be said that the conduct of the trial is bound by time and space restrictions. Videotape, as an electronic recording medium, has the capacity to preserve audio and video data for later replay, allowing a viewer-listener to experience an event, in something approximating its original form, at a delayed time and in a place different from the event's occurrence. Moreover, videotape equipment is widely available at reasonable cost, is simple to operate, and may be used in ordinary rooms without special lighting equipment or electrical facilities. As a result of these properties, videotape permits the taking of testimony in segments, at different times and places, with less than all of the necessary participants present at the time taping is done. It thus relieves the adjudicatory process from some of the spatial and temporal restrictions hitherto imposed upon it. Further, videotape permits deletions without impairing any matter which is to be preserved. From these characteristics derive the advantages, efficiencies and economies which videotape offers the trial process.[79]

Another commentator has noted the following advantages of videotaping trials:

Perhaps one of the principal advantages would be increased availability of expert witnesses, resulting from at least two characteristics of videotaped evidence. First, by obviating the need for the expert to be physically present where the trial takes place, either at the time of the trial or at any other time, it will be possible to bring the testimony of truly eminent experts to virtually any part of the country. Second, the fact that the expert will not have to remain "on tap" for a period of several days during the pendency of the trial will mean greater convenience for the experts and reduced costs to the parties.[80]

78. Doret, supra note 70, at 232, building upon Comment, Videotape Trials: Legal and Practice Implications, 9 Col.J.L. & S.Prob. 363, 365–66 (1973). (brackets in original)

79. Doret, supra note 70, at 231.

80. One poll of judges and lawyers rated this as the greatest advantage of videotape trials. See Comment, Opening Pandora's Box: Asking Judges and Attorneys to React to the Videotape Trial, 1975 Brig.Y.U. L.Rev. 487, 494–500.

The arguments that videotape trials would save court time are severalfold. First, by videotaping the evidence and then previewing this record in advance, the lawyers could probably agree on some disputed evidentiary points. The attention of the judge, who need not be present during the taping of the evidence, could be turned directly to those portions of the tape that raise evidentiary questions. The judge would not have to be present during the presentation of the evidence to the jury. Jury time is also saved, principally by the elimination of delays while the court and counsel resolve evidentiary and procedural matters.[81]

Let us consider the advantages of videotaping testimony and then editing the videotapes to make a trial "record." If witnesses need not appear at the time of trial but can be deposed at the convenience of the parties, it may be that the parties can save money and that the courts will save time. However, concern has been expressed by some lawyers and judges that the absence of the judge during taping sessions may affect the manner in which lawyers question witnesses, the tone of the proceedings, and perhaps even the capacity of the judge to make evidentiary rulings. One commentator suggests the following problems:

> Several problems, however, probably make the judge's presence, during testimony-taking, in all but mildly contested cases, essential. First, in the absence of a judge, it is necessary to rely on the self-supervision and joint cooperation by counsel to maintain the decorum and dignity that attaches to testimony taken in courtroom surroundings. Second, a judge must be present to make immediate rulings on disputed points of relevance, prejudice, admissibility, competence and the like because subsequent examination of the witness could depend on the resolution of the dispute. For example, if question one of a long series of questions is ruled out, the tactics of the examiner in succeeding questions might be considerably different. It would seem that bench rulings are inextricable from the testimony-taking process itself, and that ex post [facto] rulings, contemplated by using videotape without the judge's presence, would be an unsatisfactory solution. At best such rulings could only delete material, and not reconstruct a line of questioning ultimately held improper as taped. Unfortunately, total retaping of the testimony might then become necessary, or, in the interest of avoiding duplication of efforts, a judge might be inclined to permit tainted material to remain. Third, judicial presence would act to discourage any feeling that "retakes" could be made if the examination did not go well.
>
> The fact that testimony is recorded prior to the time the jury views it may create the feeling on the part of counsel that retakes might be possible. Such "do-overs" or second chances do not exist in the conventional courtroom proceeding and should not exist in the videotape medium. The reasons are clear. The jury must continue to be able to see, in its spontaneous form, the surprise or embarrassment of a witness when the unexpected occurs. Such spontaneity is clearly an aid to truthfinding. In addition, unless retakes were prohibited lawyers might feel that they need not present their best effort on the first taping.[82]

Another argument made in favor of videotaping trials is that by careful editing

81. Williams, Farmer, Lee, Cundick, Howell & Rooker, Juror Perceptions of Trial Testimony as a Function of the Method of Presentation: A Comparison of Live, Color Video, Black-and-White Video, Audio, and Transcript Presentations, 1975 Brig.Y.U. L.Rev. 375, 380–81 nn. 23 & 24.

82. Doret, supra note 70, at 238–39.

the jurors will not hear inadmissible evidence or objectionable questions which they are later instructed to disregard. Nor will jurors have their time "wasted" when bench conferences, client conferences, and sessions in the judge's chambers force the jury to return to the jury room to await the continuation of the trial. Since we cannot be certain about the capacity of instructions to correct mistakes of counsel or the court, this argument for videotaping seems quite powerful. On the other hand, is it a good thing that the jury will not see fully the demeanor of counsel and of clients during the taking of testimony? If objectionable questions during the course of videotaping upset a witness, does a party gain from exclusion? If the upsetting influence persists, the jury might attribute the witness' shaky demeanor to the unobjectionable questions it does see. Should a jury be aware of the entire course of counsel's questioning or is it more important to screen the jury from improper questions and evidence? Our questions suggest our concerns; we have no satisfactory answers. The following excerpt raises similar concerns:

In regard to objectionable testimony there are two issues to consider. First is the content of the testimony. There is good reason to believe that people remember what they are told to forget or ignore; however, there is no direct evidence that actual juries regularly use the content of objectionable testimony in their deliberations. Nevertheless, the "cleansing" of the trial by prior videotape editing does seem a real advantage. The second issue, however, concerns the wider effect of objections on the jury and spectators. Objections and the striking of inadmissible evidence engender an appreciation by jury and spectators that not all information is legitimate for purposes of legal fact-finding, and that the judge presides to insure that the rules of fair play are followed. The sustaining of an objection, the reprimand of a witness or an attorney by the judge, and in general all the procedural work that PRVTT proponents would put backstage, instruct the laymen on the differences between everyday resolution of disputes and the formal procedures by which trial proceedings are governed. The metamessage—"Not everything goes here—we have a set of rules that prescribe proper conduct and they will be followed,"—may be lost in a seamlessly edited videotape shown in a courtroom from which the judge, attorneys, plaintiff, defendant, and witnesses are absent. Observation of confrontations stemming from errors may be an important instructional device for those unfamiliar with the judicial process.

A similar point may apply in the case of interruptions and delays of various sorts that would be eliminated or minimized by PRVTT. While aggravating and wasteful of precious court time, they nevertheless carry the metamessage: "We will not cut our procedures short for the sake of efficiency or expediency. This is the most deliberate process in our social structure, and we will not betray it—we have time to be fair." Of course this may be only one of many implicit messages in protracted proceedings. But the value of this metamessage and the costs of foregoing it for a presentation that is pre-timed to the split second have yet to be ascertained.

Perhaps this line of thought seems only a curious variant on the concern that the "dignity of the court" is lost in PRVTT. To the extent, however, that some of the procedural weaknesses of live trials carry valuable educational, socializing metamessages for laymen, strong reason exists to maintain them in spite of, indeed because of, their technical inefficiency, at least to some degree.[83]

83. Bermant & Jacoubovitch, supra note 73, at 1008-09.

The most recent studies suggest that too much editing may detract from the credibility of the persons taped. It appears that the greater the amount of distraction caused by editing that is associated with a party, the lower the jury assesses the credibility of that party.[84]

Two sets of arguments in favor of videotape—the efficiency and cleansing-of-the-process arguments—may run into constitutional problems in criminal cases. It is quite possible that the sixth amendment's right of confrontation, discussed in Chapter Seven, will be interpreted to give defendants the right to be present whenever witnesses are examined in videotaped proceedings intended to substitute for testimony at trial. A contrary interpretation seems unlikely, for adequate cross-examination at times requires consultation between the defendant and defense counsel. In addition, there may be value in forcing witnesses to physically confront those they are testifying against. Similar arguments apply to civil litigants, although the constitutional question is controlled by the due process clause rather than the sixth amendment. To the extent that parties must be allowed to be present, the flexibility of the videotape procedure is reduced, but some efficiencies remain. Constitutional questions may also be raised by the excising of improper remarks or the absence of the judge while testimony is taken. The absence of the judge might interfere with the tone of what occurs and, as we have noted, a change of demeanor due to a question excised as improper might appear to be caused by a subsequent proper question.

Perhaps the greatest hurdle to the use of videotape in lieu of a live trial is the absence of conclusive evidence that videotapes do not affect the outcome of cases by distorting the jurors' perceptions.

There is evidence that the type of videotape used is important, because "jurors not only retain more trial-related information when the presentation is in black-and-white rather than color, but they are also more emotionally aroused by a black-and-white."[85] There is also evidence that all witnesses do not fare the same. For example, one study "noted rather consistently that the color format enhances the credibility of witnesses, particular witnesses with strong presentational skills," and that "color may maximally enhance the impact of a skilled presentation of information."[86] Another study made the following observations:

First, the results of this study indicated that the biasing effects of media presentations do not affect everyone alike. Rather, juror perceptions of trial testimony were found to be related both to the characteristics of the witness and to the medium used. * * * In addition, the effects of a media presentation upon juror perceptions of any given individual are difficult, if not impossible, to predict in advance. Thus, given the present state of information, the parties to a trial could not knowledgeably assess whether they would be injured or benefited by selecting a video trial.

Second, analysis of the relative impact of the trial participants * * * indicated that substantial shifts occurred between the live and media trials [with respect to the jurors' preferred dollar awards in a condemnation case]. For example, the preferred dollar awards demonstrated strong correlations with the jurors' perceptions of the expert witness in the live trial, but in the media trials the awards were more strongly correlated with the jurors' perceptions of the landowner. This question of impact is central to the purpose of a trial, since

84. Miller & Fontes, The Effects of Videotaped Court Materials on Juror Response (Final Report 1978).

85. Miller et al., supra note 72, at 372.

86. Id.

both parties are attempting to persuade the jurors to accept their point of view. If media trials substantially change one participant's impact on the jurors relative to the other trial participants, videotape trials may produce results substantially different from live trials in terms of juror perceptions and decisions.[87] More recent studies confirm that there is a danger that the characteristics of different individuals may affect a jury's response to a tape. Also, it appears that if one party uses tape while the other uses live witnesses, the party using tape is likely to be disadvantaged.[88]

––––––––

One commentator, Doret, eloquently states what for us is a most important problem with videotapes:

The symbolism and ceremony of the trial process—the complex pattern of gestures comprising its ritualistic aspect—helps contribute to the sense of solemnity and dignity attached to the judicial process. This in turn contributes to the respect of the community toward that process and, ultimately, acceptance of its decisions. The court room, the judicial robe, the practice of standing upon the judge's entrance and exit, the oath taken by witnesses and, in general, the formalism attached to trial procedure are all part of the ceremony and drama—as Maitland said, the "picturesque garb"—of the process by which justice is rendered. These practices have symbolic value which transmutes their abstract nature into a more dramatic and easily understood form. Through the religious overtones in these symbols, the judicial process associates itself with the reverence ascribed to religion. In general, ritual and formality give the law authority, visibility and symbolic power. By severing testimony-taking from the courtroom, and by fragmenting the unitary trial proceeding into a series of mere "assembly line" inputs, videotape may undermine the trial's complex pattern of symbols and ceremonies and thus vitiate the support which the ritual power of the trial lends to acceptance of its decisions by the community.

The trial is more than an apparatus for rendering decisions in individual cases based upon an objective search for historical truth. It is also a means by which the judicial process communicates with the community at large, and vice versa:

1. The trial is an outlet, in criminal cases, for community condemnation of the defendant; through the trial, the community expresses its disapproval of the defendant's conduct.

2. The trial, through its decision-making, formulates rules to regulate the out-of-court-behavior of those members of the community not party to the instant controversy.

3. The trial serves as a reminder to the community of the substantive principles that it holds important. Further, the trial is a ritual whose repetition expresses to the community the notions of justice, fairness and, in criminal cases, the respect for the rights of the accused which are embodied in its adjudicatory procedure.

4. As demonstrated in a number of recent and notable "political" trials, the trial can be a forum for the expression of ideological positions to the community, and the direction of community attention to political issues.

Any evaluation on the effect of videotape on the communication role of the trial is elusive. The capacity of the trial to deliver outcomes remains unim-

––––––––

87. Williams et al., supra note 81, at 411–12.

88. Doret, supra note 70, at 256–58.

paired, and to the extent that the trial's communication function derives from this capacity, its communication role should similarly remain unimpaired. However, it must be stressed that much of the power of the trial as a medium of social communication derives from the visibility of the different participants at a single, centralized forum, rather than at several, fragmented forums. It is ironic that for the very reason adjudication is convenienced by videotape that same adjudication becomes less visible and its communications easier to overlook.

_____

Bermant and Jacoubovitch add these thoughts:

These arguments against technical innovations based on esthetic, symbolic, or ritualistic grounds are difficult to sustain—time runs against them. Progress means modernity, and conservative positions are often portrayed as fustiness. Thus, Judge McCrystal makes effective rhetorical use of the positive connotations of modern technology when he contrasts the slow evolution of courtroom practice with the rapid progress in the hardware and practice of medicine. Doret makes a similar point in his concluding paragraph:

One need only recall the curious phenomenon of trial by ordeal in a former age to appreciate that future ages might regard our live judicial assemblies in a similar way.

He reminds us, however, that

[t]he task for the present—after considering the compatibility of video-

tape with the "essential elements" of our judicial institutions—is to determine if its use comports with the deeply-felt values of *our* time and place.

In sum, the primary concern is that, *even if* all the technical and editorial problems could be solved to general satisfaction, there may be further objections on normative grounds. * * *

Essentially this concern rests on grounds apart from the efficacy of videotape. No matter how well it works, implementation must not be based on technical considerations alone. * * * Current empirical techniques, while of some assistance, have yet to address the problem of changes in the socializing or educative functions of courts and trials. Jurors report positively on PRVTT and experiments show the absence of differences between PRVTT and a live trial; yet the metamessages for all parties may still be quite different in the two contexts. Of course the message may be a salutary one in the case of PRVTT, but without specifications of exactly what the message is and what it ought to be, we cannot make that judgment.

The advent of PRVTT is not an isolated event in a technologically static societal milieu. On the contrary, the legal system has been relatively slow to adopt technology already widely used in other contexts. Nontechnical arguments against its widespread implementation must therefore be based on a demonstration that a loss attending transition to videotape warrants foregoing the technical advantages the medium provides.[89]

89. Bermant & Jacoubovitch, supra note 73, at 1006–07, quoting Doret, supra note 70, at 268.

Time and further experiments may help to explain why California jurors taking part in a videotape trial indicated with virtual unanimity that they would oppose video- **taped criminal trials. One juror is quoted as saying:**

It is strictly a gut reaction on my part because I simply feel that because of the seriousness of a criminal trial, absolutely every word that is spoken and absolutely every emotion should be ob-

If both parties consented, would you allow trials to be presented to the jury on videotape? Would you allow this over the objection of one party in a civil case? In a criminal action?

BIBLIOGRAPHY

McCormick, Ch. 21.

Miller & Fontes, The Effects of Videotaped Court Materials on Juror Response (Final Report 1978).

National Center for State Courts, Video Support in the Criminal Courts, Executive Summary (May, 1974).

Scott, Photographic Evidence (2d ed. 1969).

5 Weinstein's Evidence ¶¶ 1001, 1003, 1007.

4 Wigmore §§ 1150–1169.

Beyers, Microfilming of Business Records, 6 Drake L.Rev. 74 (1953).

Busch, Photographic Evidence, 4 DePaul L.Rev. 195 (1954).

Cady, Objections to Demonstrative Evidence, 32 Mo.L.Rev. 333 (1967).

Cleary, Evidence—Best Evidence—Admissibility of a Carbon Copy as Primary Evidence, 3 Vill.L.Rev. 219 (1958).

Cleary & Strong, The Best Evidence Rule: An Evaluation in Context, 51 Iowa L.Rev. 825 (1966).

Conrad, Magnetic Recordings in the Court, 40 Va.L.Rev. 23 (1954).

Lanhan, The Propriety of Demonstrative Evidence When Exploited by Trial Lawyers, 18 Ala.L.Rev. 447 (1966).

Michael & Adler, Real Proof: I, 5 Vand.L.Rev. 344 (1952).

Paradis, The Celluloid Witness, 37 Colo.L.Rev. 235 (1965).

Rogers, The Best Evidence Rule, 1945 Wis.L.Rev. 278.

Shaffer, Judges, Repulsive Evidence and the Ability to Respond, 43 Notre Dame Law. 563 (1968).

Tracy, The Introduction of Documentary Evidence, 24 Iowa L.Rev. 436 (1939).

Wendorf, Some Views on Jury Views, 15 Baylor L.Rev. 379 (1963).

served personally. If I thought about that for awhile, I know it doesn't jive with what I'm saying about a civil trial—but * * *?

Bermant et al., supra note 75, at 994.

We have not addressed the separate question of electronically transmitting testimony to the courtroom. Similar problems of logistics, presence of parties and effects on the jury would be raised. We believe we have put to the reader the hardest questions.

Chapter Twelve

THE ROLES OF JUDGE AND JURY

SECTION I. THE ORTHODOX DIVISION OF LABOR

The allocation of questions of law to the court and questions of fact to the jury is now well established. In practice this usually means that the judge is responsible for determining what evidence the jury may receive and whether sufficient evidence has been introduced to justify a jury verdict. The judge also specifies the legal questions that the jury is to resolve, and he may influence the jury's deliberations by summarizing the evidence and (in some jurisdictions) commenting on the weight of the evidence. In this subsection we shall first examine the roles played by the judge and jury in deciding whether evidence is admissible and then discuss briefly other ways in which the judge may control or influence jury decision making.

A. DETERMINING ADMISSIBILITY

1. ISSUES OF LAW

When evidence is offered and objected to, the decision on admissibility may turn on an interpretation of law or on a finding of fact. When the decision turns on an interpretation of law, courts have no difficulty allocating responsibility; only the judge is responsible. Suppose that a person, *P,* turns to another, *O,* for confidential legal advice. *O* is a recent law school graduate but has not taken a bar examination. Later, at a trial, *O* is placed on the stand and asked to reveal *P's* confidences. *P* claims the attorney-client privilege. The party seeking *O's* testimony responds that the privilege does not apply because *O* was not a member of the bar at the time *P* confided in her. Whether one must be a member of the bar to qualify for the protection of the attorney-client privilege is purely a question of law which the judge would decide without in any way involving the jury.

2. MOST ISSUES OF FACT

Matters are only slightly more difficult when the admissibility of evidence turns on findings of fact. FRE 104(a) states the general rule and FRE 104(b) denotes a common exception:

(a) *Questions of admissibility generally.*—Preliminary questions concerning the qualification of a person to be a witness, the existence of a privilege, or the admissibility of evidence shall be determined by the court, subject to the provisions of subdivision (b). In making its determination it is not bound by the rules of evidence except those with respect to privileges.

(b) *Relevancy conditioned on fact.*— When the relevancy of evidence depends upon the fulfillment of a condition of fact, the court shall admit it upon, or subject to, the introduction of evidence sufficient to support a finding of the fulfillment of the condition.

The general rule is that the judge determines all questions of admissibility. If the admissibility of evidence turns in whole or in part on some matter of fact, the judge is usually responsible for determining whether that fact or state of facts exists. Ordinarily, allocating this fact-finding responsibility to the judge maximizes six goals first identified by Maguire and Epstein:[1] minimizing the complexity of the jury's task, enhancing the predictability of results, preserving with precision issues for appeal, keeping prejudicial material from the jury, vindicating the policies of the privileges and other exclusionary rules, and saving time at the trial.

Let us vary our earlier example so that P's right to claim the attorney-client privilege turns on an issue of fact. Assume that P claims he reasonably believed that O was an attorney and that under the laws of the forum state a reasonable belief that a confidant is an attorney will justify a claim of privilege. If the judge must determine whether P believed O was an attorney and, if so, whether this belief was reasonable, this determination may be made out of the presence of the jury. The hearing is likely to be relatively brief. The judge is likely to have had experience in deciding cases of this kind, he may know how other courts have dealt with similar cases, and he may, through his own questioning, be able to pinpoint those aspects of the matter which he thinks crucial to a resolution of the issue. If the judge relies on evidence which is inadmissible under the ordinary rules of evidence, as he is generally allowed to do, the jury will not learn of it. The jury will also not learn of information relevant to the preliminary question, but irrelevant and perhaps prejudicial on the main issue. If, as sometimes happens, the possible privilege must be breached slightly to determine whether any privilege exists, this may occur in chambers so that the dissemination of privileged information is kept to a minimum. Finally, if the judge decides that the privilege applies and the testi-

mony should be excluded, care may be taken that the jury does not learn of the kind of information that has been kept from them.

If the decision on the availability of the privilege were given to the jury, this might be done in one of two ways. First, the trial might be interrupted and the jury asked for an interlocutory judgment on the issue of whether P reasonably believed O to be a lawyer. This would be time-consuming, if for no other reason than the jury's need to deliberate. The jury's concentration on the main issues in the case would be interrupted. Problems of inadmissible or prejudicial evidence might also exist. Finally, the jury would learn of the kind of evidence one party was seeking to keep from them, and its decision on the facts might be influenced by a desire to receive the evidence in question. The other approach would be to present the jury with the privileged testimony as well as the evidence pertaining to the availability of the privilege. The jurors would be instructed that they were not to consider O's testimony if they found that P's statements to O were privileged. This has many of the disadvantages of the interlocutory verdict and some additional ones. One obvious disadvantage is that, regardless of whether the privilege was found applicable, the privileged material would be revealed, thus destroying a principal value of the privilege. A second disadvantage is the possibility that the jurors would not be able to dismiss O's testimony from their minds even if they found that it should not be admitted. Finally, a general verdict would not reveal whether O's testimony was found to be admissible. This might hamper an appellate court in

---

1. Preliminary Questions of Fact in Determining the Admissibility of Evidence, 40 Harv.L.Rev. 392, 393–95, 412 (1927). We do not necessarily agree with all the arguments made in favor of the division of responsibility. See, e.g., Saltzburg, Standards of Proof and Preliminary Questions of Fact, 27 Stan.L.Rev. 271, 272 n. 2 (1975). See also Morgan, Functions of Judge and Jury in the Determination of Preliminary Questions of Fact, 43 Harv.L.Rev. 165, 169 (1943). But these arguments have been accepted in many jurisdictions.

reviewing the sufficiency of the evidence below, because a court determining that the privilege should have applied would not know whether it was in fact applied by the jury.

3. RELEVANCY CONDITIONED ON FACT

When disputes about admissibility relate to the competency of evidence (i.e., whether the evidence is barred by some rule that assumes relevance but applies an extra test to meet special dangers or to promote special policies), the above are usually compelling reasons for placing fact-finding responsibility on the judge. But when the only objection to proffered evidence is that it is not logically relevant unless certain other facts exist, the advantages of giving the judge responsibility for finding preliminary facts are substantially diminished and are counterbalanced by the possibility that the judge's findings will deprive the jury of the opportunity to pass on the central issues in a case. This situation, where the relevance of certain facts is conditioned on the existence of certain other facts, is known as the situation of conditional relevance. McCormick comments:

> When the conditioning fact determines merely the relevancy of the offered fact there is no need for any special safeguarding procedure, for relevancy is a mere matter of probative pertinence which the jury understands and is willing to observe. Accordingly, where the fact conditions relevancy merely, the judge will not permit the adversary to raise a preliminary dispute upon it, but will merely require the proponent to bring forward evidence from which the jury could find it to be true, after which the conditionally relevant fact will be admitted. At his next stage of proof, the adversary may bring disputing evidence, and the dispute will in the end be for the jury, not the judge, to resolve.[2]

Suppose, for example, that the plaintiff, who had borrowed the defendant's car, was injured when a tire blew out while she was driving at seventy miles per hour. The defense is assumption of the risk, and the defendant wishes to testify that he shouted to the plaintiff before she pulled out of the driveway, "Keep it under fifty! One tire is bad." A defense witness will testify that the plaintiff acknowledged the shout. The plaintiff objects to the defendant's testimony, claiming that she never heard the warning and that the warning is therefore irrelevant. The plaintiff's argument is correct. If she never heard the defendant's warning, the fact that it was made has no bearing on whether she assumed any risks. Who should determine what the plaintiff heard? This is the kind of question that the jury is clearly able to decide. No interlocutory procedures are necessary or desirable. So long as the jury understands what must be shown to establish assumption of the risk, an assessment of what the plaintiff heard is a natural step in reaching a general verdict. If the judge were responsible for finding the preliminary fact, it is possible that his best judgment would be that the weight of the evidence suggests that the plaintiff did not hear the warning. If on the basis of this the judge excluded the defendant's testimony, his action might destroy the defendant's case in a situation where reasonable people might well have disagreed with the judge's assessment of who was telling the truth. Presumably the parties chose a jury trial rather than a bench trial to get the judgment of twelve lay people on these issues. If the rule made the judge responsible for finding all the facts on which proffered evidence was conditionally relevant, jury trials might often be aborted by the bench. Cases are commonly built around specific theories, and evidence

2. McCormick § 53, at 125.

offered at one stage of a trial is often relevant only if some fact that the party attempted to prove at some other stage is taken as established.[3]

The judge does not avoid all responsibility when the jury is assigned the task of finding facts on which the relevance of other evidence is conditioned. The judge must determine whether the evidence bearing on the preliminary fact is such that reasonable people could find that it exists. If not, evidence conditioned on a finding of that fact must be excluded.[4] What the judge avoids is the need to decide, by some standard, whether he believes the preliminary fact exists. In most cases the judge will also, upon request, charge the jurors that if they do not find that the preliminary fact existed, they must ignore the evidence conditioned on it. In some circumstances no instruction will be necessary,

---

3. Professor Vaughn Ball, in an insightful and original article, has called the idea of a conditional relevancy a "myth". Professor Ball's basic point is that in situations where the relevance of fact A (e.g. in a case where assumption of the risk is in issue, the fact that the defendant warned the plaintiff of the risk) has been assumed by legal scholars to be conditional on the existence of fact B (e.g. that the plaintiff heard the warning), fact A is by itself logically relevant. At the time evidence of fact A is offered this must be true, for evidence of fact A makes the existence of the conjunction of facts A and B more likely than it would be if there were no evidence of A. In our parenthetical example what the court is really saying is that fact A is material to the case only in conjunction with fact B and no matter how strong the evidence of A is, unless there is evidence of B the fact finder will not be allowed to conclude that both facts exist. If the jury might nevertheless conclude that B exists from the presence of A and if A is not sufficiently probative of B to justify the conclusion, its inadequacy will be made clear by striking the evidence of A from the record and instructing the jury to disregard it.

It does not seem that the same analysis should be applied to all the situations that are commonly cited as examples of conditional relevance. To say, as courts have, that an expert's answer to a hypothetical question is conditionally relevant on the introduction of evidence sufficient to support all facts mentioned in the hypothetical seems to be a special rule of relevance like the chain of custody requirement, for the expert's opinion would probably have probative value on the matter in issue even if some facts on which it rested had not been shown by other evidence. The notion that the relevance of a witness' testimony depends on his having firsthand knowledge of the facts to which he testifies is probably an example of true conditional relevance,

for if a witness knows nothing about the facts to which he testifies, his views tend in no way to prove or disprove the existence of those facts. The overall topic is too complicated and Professor Ball's analysis too rich to be sufficiently treated in the space we could allot it. In the text, we present the traditional analysis, both because this is the way courts will deal with such matters and because, contrary to Professor Ball, we believe it provides a sensible scheme for dealing with a number of complicated but related issues. For Professor Ball's treatment see, The Myth of Conditional Relevance, 14 Ga.L.Rev. 435 (1980). He has specifically disavowed an article by the same title to which his name is attached which appeared in the Arizona State Law Journal.

4. The comment taken from McCormick, note 3, supra, suggests that evidence of the preliminary fact must be introduced before conditionally relevant evidence will be admitted. FRE 104(a) and general practice are to the contrary. Conditionally relevant evidence may be offered subject to "connecting up," i.e., the later introduction of evidence tending to prove facts which make the earlier evidence logically relevant. Where evidence proving preliminary facts has not been introduced before conditionally relevant evidence is offered, the judge may require the party to specify the evidence pertaining to the preliminary fact. More commonly, the conditionally relevant evidence is admitted on the attorney's assurance that it will be connected up. If connecting evidence is not forthcoming, the opposing party must usually call the judge's attention to this lapse by making a motion to strike. If the motion is not made the evidence will stay in the record and the jurors will not be informed that they are to ignore it. For another example of the need to connect up, see Saltzburg, supra note 1, at 272 n. 3.

because it will be obvious that if a particular fact is not found certain other evidence has no probative value.

There are specific rules of evidence that are little more than special guarantees of logical relevance. Where the question is whether evidence is admissible under the standards set by such a rule, the task of finding facts pertaining to admissibility is on some issues and in some jurisdictions given to the judge and on other issues and in other jurisdictions assigned to the jury. Perhaps the best example of such a rule is the rule requiring authentication. Suppose, for example, that Jones sues Smith for failure to deliver 100,000 widgets by the date specified in their contract. Jones introduces a document that he says is his current contract with Smith. The authentication requirement means that Jones must introduce some evidence that the document is what he claims it to be. If the document is not his contract with Smith, its terms are irrelevant to their litigation. If Smith claims the document is not his current contract with Jones, who is to decide the factual dispute? Does the fact that Jones seeks to qualify the document under a specific rule of evidence mean that preliminary factual matters are for the judge under FRE 104(a), or does the fact that authentication rules exist primarily to ensure that evidence is relevant mean that the jury should determine the genuineness of the document under FRE 104(b)? Because the authentication requirement is a special guarantee of logical relevance, and because issues of authentication may go to the heart of a case, material requiring authentication may generally be introduced so long as there is evidence sufficient to support a jury finding that the material is what it purports to be. If you are in federal court, you do not have to puzzle over FRE 104 to decide how fact-finding responsibility is allocated in this area. FRE 901(a) provides specifically for the general rule:

General provision.—The requirement of authentication or identification as a condition precedent to admissibility is satisfied by evidence sufficient to support a finding that the matter in question is what its proponent claims.

Another evidence rule that relates to considerations of relevance is the rule requiring special qualifications for expert witnesses. If a witness does not have the special qualifications of an expert, the witness' opinion on a technical issue is unlikely to aid the trier of fact. The task of determining whether a witness qualifies as an expert is entrusted to the judge. However, it is not clear that the judge intrudes on the fact-finding process any more when determining expertise than he does when finding facts related to authentication. It takes so little to qualify as an expert that a judicial finding that a witness is not an expert might be equivalent to a judgment that no reasonable jury could conclude that the witness has expertise. If the judge allows a witness to testify as an expert, the opposing side may attack the witness' qualifications in front of the jury in order to convince the jury that the witness' opinions are worthless.

4. QUESTIONS OF COMPETENCY AND "ULTIMATE" ISSUES

The allocation of fact-finding responsibility is most difficult when the factual determination on which a question of competency rests coincides with a fundamental factual determination that the jury is expected to make. Here the orthodox rule is that the determination is for the judge. But there are numerous decisions allocating responsibility to the jury since, if the judge finds the evidence incompetent, he may, in effect, be taking a central issue from the jury.

Consider a case in which the plaintiff, suing on a contract, offers a copy of the contract, claiming that the defendant holds the original. The defendant states that he never entered into a contract with the plaintiff and so never had the original of the contract that the plaintiff offers. The defendant then argues that the plaintiff's copy of the alleged contract is not the "best evidence" since, if he did not have the original, the plaintiff has not accounted for it. In this example, the decision on the best evidence question turns on essentially the same factual question that the jury must decide: was there ever a contract between the plaintiff and the defendant?[5] If the judge decides that the defendant never possessed the original of the alleged contract and then applies the best evidence rule to exclude the plaintiff's copy, the plaintiff may be unable to prove his case. Yet the judge may base his belief that no contract was made on evidence from which a reasonable jury might reach the opposite conclusion. Jurisdictions vary in the way they allocate fact-finding responsibility when problems are of this type. FRE 1008 provides:

> When the admissibility of other evidence of contents of writings, recordings, or photographs under these rules depends upon the fulfillment of a condition of fact, the question whether the condition has been fulfilled is ordinarily for the court to determine in accordance with the provisions of rule 104. However, when an issue is raised (a) whether the asserted writing ever existed, or (b) whether another writing, recording, or photograph produced at the trial is the original, or (c) whether other evidence of contents correctly reflects the contents, the issue is for the trier of fact to determine as in the case of other issues of fact.

Consider another situation where a question of competency coincides with an ultimate issue. A man is charged with raping a woman in a jurisdiction where the crime is defined so that a man cannot rape his wife. The man defends on the ground that he is married to his alleged victim. When the prosecutor puts the victim on the stand to testify to both the alleged assault and the fact that she is not married to the assailant, the man objects, claiming spousal immunity. If the judge believes that the woman is married to the man (even though a reasonable jury might conclude otherwise), he will allow the claim of privilege (assuming the jurisdiction does not follow Trammel v. United States and the privilege otherwise applies), and the jury will be deprived of what may be the most probative evidence available, both on the details of the assault and on the fact of the alleged marriage.

In these circumstances some jurisdictions would have the judge decide the fact of marriage, some would give it to the jury, and others would have the judge make a preliminary determination, barring the victim's testimony if the judge thought she was married to the man or, if the judge believed there was no marriage, admitting the testimony with an instruction that it should be disregarded if the jury believed that the man and woman were married. There are difficulties with all three solutions. Giving the decision to the judge means that the most probative evidence available may be kept from the jury. Giving the decision to the jury ensures that if a marriage exists the harm that the spousal immunity is supposed to prevent—the setting of spouse against spouse—will occur.[6] Moreover it is doubtful whether the jury will be able to ignore the woman's testimony simply because they find that she was

---

5. The best evidence question also requires the fact finder to determine whether the defendant ever possessed the original of any contract made with the plaintiff. It seems almost certain that a fact finder who disbelieved the defendant's claim that there was no contract would also disbelieve his claim that he never possessed the original.

6. In the specific case posed it would seem that spouse has been set against spouse. But rules apply generally, and the state, in theory, wants to prevent this in the general case. Of course, many states will not allow the privilege when one spouse assaults another. The rape example may not be realistic, but it points up the problems and issues quite

married to the defendant. The third alternative has the deficiencies of the other two, depending on how the judge resolves the initial question.

Under the federal rules, it appears that where competency issues coincide with ultimate issues the judge is to determine admissibility unless a specific rule, such as FRE 1008, provides otherwise. In state courts decisions vary. In some cases of coincidence, issues that the federal rules assign to the judge will go to the jury.[7] Where the overlap of preliminary and ultimate issue is complete, courts should be wary of keeping from the jury evidence that might reasonably be found competent when that evidence may be the best available on a matter the jury is expected to resolve.[8]

Furthermore, when the coincidence of issues is complete the danger of confusing the jurors may be minimal, since there is often no need to instruct them on the competency issue. In the rape example offered above, the jury does not have to be told that if it finds the victim is married to the defendant it must disregard the victim's testimony. It need only be instructed that if it finds the two are married, it must return a verdict of acquittal.[9]

There are some competency issues which many states give to the jury either in the first instance or after a preliminary determination by the judge, even though they do not coincide with ultimate issues. This allocation of responsibility has been most common with questions pertaining to the

clearly. For a discussion of the general problem and the specific concern in conspiracy prosecutions, see Saltzburg, supra note 1, at 302–04 and our discussion in Chapter Six of the procedures used to determine the admissibility of one conspirator's statements against another.

7. See the cases cited in McCormick § 53, at 124 n. 97.

8. Some would disagree with this judgment and argue that the matter should still be for the judge. The strongest case for retaining judicial responsibility in this situation probably exists with respect to privileges, since giving the jury responsibility means that either an interlocutory verdict will be necessary or the privilege will be breached regardless of the ultimate decision on admissibility. In certain cases of privilege, we agree that the judge should make the preliminary determination. Other cases that the judge should decide are those where the jury might not understand the competency rule, and the evidence governed by it is of questionable value. See, e.g., Saltzburg, supra note 1, at 302–04 (conspirators' statements). In the hypothetical rape case that is posed in the text we would give the matter to the jury, because even if the woman is married to the man the values that lie behind the spousal immunity will almost certainly not be served by barring the woman's testimony. Of course, a proper definition of privilege should avoid the problem. Often privileges are inapplicable in circumstances where the determination of whether a priv-

ileged relationship exists coincides with what is likely to be an ultimate issue. For example, if an attorney sues a client for her fee, the client might claim both that no attorney-client relationship existed, and that the attorney cannot reveal the client's statements to prove the relationship because if the attorney's claim is correct, the client's statements are privileged. The judge need not resolve this dilemma because the attorney-client privilege does not prevent the disclosure of information pertaining to disputes over fees.

9. Problems associated with instructions to disregard will exist if a decision on an ultimate issue will not resolve all matters facing the fact finder. For example, if a simple assault charge, to which marriage was not a defense, were linked to the rape charge, the jury should be instructed that if they found that the victim and the assailant were married they should acquit the defendant on the rape charge and ignore the victim's testimony in deciding the charge of simple assault. The hypothetical problem assumes, of course, that the marriage between the man and woman was not terminated after the alleged rape and before the trial. It also assumes that the jurisdiction does not abrogate the privilege where one spouse assaults the other and does not vest the privilege in the witness rather than the defendant spouse. Deciding whether or not to instruct a jury to disregard evidence may involve some consideration of the standard of proof used in making the preliminary decision. See, e.g., Saltzburg, supra note 1, at 302–04.

admissibility of dying declarations and allegedly involuntary confessions. Jurors informed of a dying declaration are in some jurisdictions instructed that if they find that the declaration was not made in contemplation of death, they are to ignore it, and jurors offered confessions might be told that if they find the confession involuntary, they are not to consider it against the accused. Many believe that these instructions do not protect effectively against inadmissible evidence. They feel that when jurors learn of such evidence, they are unable to ignore it regardless of how they view the preliminary facts.

In 1964, in the case of Jackson v. Denno,[10] the Supreme Court held that due process requires the trial judge to find a confession voluntary before it is given to the jury. The Court's decision was motivated in part by the fear that a jury could not completely disregard inculpatory statements it found involuntary. The Court did not rule on the so-called Massachusetts procedure. In states that follow this procedure the judge makes a preliminary determination of voluntariness, excluding any confessions found involuntary. Confessions found voluntary are admitted, but the jurors are told that if they believe the confession was involuntary they should ignore it in their deliberations. This procedure has been called the "humane rule" because it appears to give defendants two chances to establish involuntariness. Critics contend that this humanity is illusory. They believe the rule encourages judges to resolve all doubts against the accused in making preliminary determinations on voluntariness.

5. PROCEDURE AND STANDARDS

When the judge acts as fact finder to determine the admissibility of evidence, he must allow the parties to be heard on the issue. FRE 104(c) and FRE 104(d) specify the procedures that apply in federal court:

(c) *Hearing of jury.*—Hearings on the admissibility of confessions shall in all cases be conducted out of the hearing of the jury. Hearings on other preliminary matters shall be so conducted when the interests of justice require or, when an accused is a witness, if he so requests.

(d) *Testimony by accused.*—The accused does not, by testifying upon a preliminary matter, subject himself to cross-examination as to other issues in the case.

Except when the admissibility of a confession is in issue or when an accused intending to testify so requests, the judge has discretion to hear facts relating to admissibility either in front of or away from the jury. Sometimes hearings on the competency of evidence will be brief and the evidence offered innocuous. In these circumstances there is little reason to send the jury out. In some situations, such as the qualification of an expert witness, the jury's presence may be desirable, for it eliminates a need to repeat the same testimony. If allegedly objectionable evidence will have to be presented during the competency hearing or if evidence relevant to the competency issue is irrelevant to the main issues of the case and possibly prejudicial, the better procedure is to determine competency outside the hearing of the jury.

Under FRE 104(d) a defendant may testify on issues relating to the admissibility of evidence without waiving his right to remain silent at the trial. If the jurors could see the defendant testify on certain issues, they might be particularly suspicious of the defendant's refusal to testify on the substantive issues in the case. So as not to burden the defendant's right to testify on preliminary issues, FRE 104(c) gives the defendant the right to testify on

10. 378 U.S. 368 (1964).

preliminary issues outside the presence of the jury.[11] The defendant in testifying to preliminary facts does not subject himself to cross-examination on other issues in the case. However, if the defendant's testimony on direct examination extends beyond the preliminary matter in dispute, the defendant may find that he has opened the door to cross-examination on the new issues he has raised. Although the jury may not be present during the cross-examination, the prosecution might later be allowed to introduce the defendant's testimony on issues not relating to the preliminary matter and his responses when cross-examined. If the defendant's testimony is confined to the preliminary matter, it cannot subsequently be introduced as an admission tending to show guilt, but it might be admissible for impeachment purposes if the defendant later testifies.[12] Thus defense counsel must be very careful in questioning a client on a preliminary matter, even if the jury is absent.

A final situation in which courts should determine preliminary matters out of the hearing of the jury is where the factual issue on which admissibility turns coincides when an issue that is given to the jury. If the jury is present at the hearing and the judge decides the evidence is inadmissible, the jurors are likely to have heard the inadmissible evidence. If the judge decides the evidence is admissible, the jurors will know the judge's view on a factual matter that is given to them to resolve.

The judge in making factual determinations under FRE 104(a) is not bound by rules of evidence other than rules of privilege. Some states give the judge similar freedom, while others purport to apply the ordinary rules of evidence to determinations of preliminary facts. However, even in the latter states, the rules of evidence are likely to be quite relaxed in practice. Rules of evidence are ordinarily somewhat relaxed when trial is to a judge, and there is less reason to adhere to the rules when only a preliminary fact is in issue.

The federal rules say nothing about the standard that the judge is to apply in deciding whether there is sufficient proof of some fact that must be shown to justify admissibility. For a long time courts were split. Some held that the preponderance of the evidence standard was always appropriate, while others held that the standard should vary depending upon whether the case was criminal or civil and upon the particular issue involved. There were a number of cases holding that before a confession could be introduced in a criminal case voluntariness had to be proved beyond a reasonable doubt. In 1972, in Lego v. Twomey,[13] the Supreme Court decided that due process was not offended when the trial judge determined whether a confession was voluntary by the preponderance of the evidence. The Court also suggested by way of dictum that the Federal Courts of Appeals should not require a higher standard in the exercise of their supervisory power.[14] Since the case for deciding preliminary questions by some stricter standard than the preponderance of the evidence is probably strongest when

---

11. On its face FRE 104(c) gives an accused only the right to have his testimony taken outside the hearing of the jury. In certain circumstances the court may be able to listen to testimony and arguments concerning the admissibility of evidence in the presence of the jury but out of their hearing. If the issue is simple and the evidence slight, a conference at the bench may be all that is needed to resolve the matter. However, the defendant's right under FRE 104(c) should be interpreted as a right not to be seen giving testimony. This requires that the defendant's testimony be taken out of the presence of the jury when the defendant so demands.

12. See Walder v. United States, 347 U.S. 62 (1954); Simmons v. United States, 390 U.S. 377, 389–94 (1968); United States v. Havens, 446 U.S. 620 (1980); cf. Harris v. New York, 401 U.S. 222 (1971).

13. 404 U.S. 477 (1972).

14. Id. at 488 n. 16.

the voluntariness of a confession is at issue, *Lego* almost certainly means that as a matter of constitutional law no higher standard will ever be required.[15]

When the judge refuses to admit certain evidence, the party offering that evidence is not precluded from offering other evidence that tends to prove his case. When the judge chooses to admit evidence over objection, the objecting party is not precluded from attacking the admitted evidence by any permissible means. FRE 104(e) emphasizes this right:

> *Weight and credibility.*—This rule does not limit the right of a party to introduce before the jury evidence relevant to weight or credibility.

However, facts that bear on the competency of an opponent's evidence do not always go to the weight or credibility of that evidence. When they do not, they are not admissible simply because the opponent's evidence is allowed. For example, if a party was overruled on a claim of attorney-client privilege, he could not attack the testimony of his alleged attorney by showing that his statements to the attorney were made in confidence for the purpose of securing legal advice. Where decisions on admissibility turn on factors which go to reliability or relevancy, evidence that did not persuade the judge that the oppo-

nent's proof was unreliable may be offered to the jury. If the judge determines that a witness' credentials are sufficient to qualify her as an expert, the opponent is not thereby precluded from attacking those credentials in front of the jury. Similarly, if the judge finds that a statement was sufficiently against interest when made to qualify for that hearsay exception, the opponent is not precluded from showing the jury the ways in which the statement was self serving.

FRE 104 does not require the judge to state for the record the reasons that underlie his decisions on those preliminary questions of fact that determine the admissibility of evidence. Nevertheless, an increasing number of appellate opinions say that it is good practice to do so. Indeed, in the case of some rules which explicitly require that a balance be struck [e.g. FRE 609 (a) and (b)] a few courts have found reversible error where a judge has not indicated that he has done the requisite balancing. More often than not, however, particularly where balancing under FRE 403 is in issue, the court will assume from the decision to admit or exclude evidence that an appropriate balance has been struck. Whether appellate courts will continue to assume this if trial judges continue to ignore the hints they are given remains to be seen.

Problem XII–1. You are in a jurisdiction where prior inconsistent statements are admissible for substantive purposes. Clem Byer has told the police that he bought a stolen tape recorder from Fred Filch. At the trial a year later, Byer is asked to name the person who sold him the stolen tape recorder. He replies, "I forget." At this point the prosecution seeks to have the police officer testify to Byer's earlier identification of Filch. Filch objects, claiming that Byer's statement from the stand is not inconsistent with his earlier statement of identification. **Should the judge or the jury de-**

---

15. For a time some thought *Lego* vulnerable to reversal because it was a 4–3 decision, but the preponderance standard was later applied by six Justices in a case where

consent to a search was in issue. See, United States v. Matlock, 415 U.S. 164 (1974); for an article criticizing *Lego* see Saltzburg, supra note 1.

termine whether Byer's earlier statement is sufficiently inconsistent with his courtroom testimony to qualify as a prior inconsistent statement?

Problem XII-2. The state highway department has condemned a vacant parcel of land owned by Lynn Franklin. Franklin does not believe that she has been offered the fair market value of the land and a trial is held on this issue. The Highway Department wishes to introduce an expert appraiser to give an opinion on the fair market value of the land. The expert's opinion is based largely on the prices at which four neighboring parcels of vacant land have sold during the preceding year. Franklin argues that the appraiser should not be allowed to testify as an expert because the sales on which the appraiser relies did not involve land sufficiently similar to the condemned land to justify an expert opinion. **Should the judge or the jury determine whether the sales involved land sufficiently similar to Franklin's as to justify an expert opinion?**

Problem XII-3. In the same situation as the preceding problem, Franklin has a report prepared for her by a geologist which states that the soil conditions on her land are such that one could construct a high-rise apartment building or a heavy industrial plant without the need for any special reinforcement. The report also states that because of soil conditions and the presence of subsurface water it would be considerably more expensive to construct such buildings on any of the four parcels that the appraiser relied upon for his opinion. **May this report be presented to the judge if the judge is responsible for determining whether the other parcels are sufficiently similar to Franklin's to justify an expert opinion? May they be given to the jury if it is given the responsibility for finding this preliminary fact? If the judge has the responsibility for finding the preliminary fact and determines that the appraiser's opinion is admissible, may Franklin offer the jury evidence tending to show that the sales on which the appraiser relies involved land that is not similar to hers? May she introduce the report of the geologist in her effort to prove dissimilarity?**

Problem XII-4. Polly Peck sues the estate of Henry Jacobs as the assignee of a debt which Jacobs owed her brother Phil. Polly wishes to put Phil on the stand to testify that he loaned Jacobs $3000, of which only $400 had been repaid at the time of Jacobs' death. The estate claims that Phil may not testify to this transaction because of the Dead Man's Statute. Under state law, the Dead Man's Statute bars only parties in interest from testifying to transactions with the deceased. The rule in cases of assignment is that if an assignment has been made in good faith, the assignor may testify to transactions with the deceased. If the assignment has been made to circumvent the Dead Man's Statute, the assignor is barred from testifying. **Should the judge or the jury determine whether Phil's assignment of the debt to Polly was made in good faith?**

Assume that the matter is held to be for the judge and that the judge determines that Phil may testify because the assignment was made in good faith. **May the estate introduce evidence before the jury that tends to show the assignment was made to circumvent the Dead Man's Statute?**

Problem XII-5. Mack Lee has murdered James Williams and fled the jurisdiction. Eight years later a man calling himself Guy Fenner is arrested and identified as Mack Lee. He is tried for murdering Williams and the case turns entirely on whether he is Mack Lee. At the time of this case, spouses were not competent to testify for or against each other in the jurisdiction in question. Fenner puts Mack Lee's wife on the stand to testify that he is not Mack Lee. The prosecution objects, citing the spousal incompetency rule. **Should the judge or the jury determine whether Mrs. Lee is the defendant's wife and thus not competent to testify on his behalf? If the judge refuses to decide the competency issue and allows Mrs. Lee to testify, what should the jury be told about the competency issue?**

Problem XII–6. Eric Kent is charged with bigamy. The prosecution wishes to introduce Eric's second wife, Marcy, to testify against him. Eric, in a jurisdiction that does not follow Trammel v. United States, claims spousal immunity to keep Marcy from testifying. The prosecution claims that Eric's marriage to Marcy was invalid since he was married at the time, so Eric may not claim the spousal privilege. **Eric claims Marcy is the only woman he has ever married. How should this dispute be resolved? Should the judge or the jury decide whether Eric is legally married to Marcy?** Suppose Eric admits that Marcy is his second wife, but he argues that this marriage is not bigamous since he had divorced his first wife before marrying Marcy. The prosecution alleges that the first marriage has never been validly terminated and wishes to introduce the testimony of Eric's first wife to establish this fact. Eric claims spousal immunity to keep this woman (whom he says he has divorced) off the stand. The prosecutor (who has alleged that Eric's first wife is still his spouse) argues that Eric, because of his allegation of divorce, cannot invoke spousal immunity. **How should this tangle be resolved? What are the proper roles for judge and jury?**

Problem XII–7. Rocky Rhodes is charged with conspiring with Jane Stone to rob a bank. The prosecutor wishes to introduce Stone's out-of-court statements as the admissions of a coconspirator. Rhodes objects, denying that he ever conspired with Stone and arguing that the government should not be allowed to introduce the admissions of an alleged coconspirator in a trial where the existence of the alleged conspiracy is in issue. **Should the admissions of a coconspirator be admissible in a trial where conspiracy is charged? Assuming that they are, who should decide whether there is sufficient proof of conspiracy to justify a finding that the admissions are those of a coconspirator? If the decision is given to the judge and she decides to admit the testimony, should the jurors be given any special instructions about how they are to treat the statement? In deciding the preliminary question of whether Rhodes conspired with Stone and is thus responsible for her admissions, by what standard should the prosecution be required to prove the conspiracy? By what standard should the prosecution be required to prove the conspiracy in order to convict Rhodes of having conspired with Stone?**

Problem XII–8. Harrison is accused of arson. The state's theory is that Harrison intentionally set fire to the building next to the county jail so that three prisoners could escape during the confusion. Harrison claims that the fire started accidentally when he threw a cigarette he thought was out into a pile of oily rags that had been discarded by some painters. When the state attempts to introduce evidence of the jailbreak, Harrison argues that the evidence is not relevant on the issue of arson unless the state can prove that Harrison knew that a jailbreak was planned at the time the fire was started.   The state has evidence tending to show that Harrison did know of the planned break.   **To whom should the evidence be presented, the judge, the jury, or both?   What decisions, if any, must the judge reach on this issue?   What decisions, if any, must the jury reach?**

Problem XII–9.   In the same situation as the preceding problem, the state wishes to introduce evidence that Harrison has books in his home library entitled: Lives of the Great Arsonists, How to Set a Fire in the Rain, and A Theory of Combustion.   Harrison objects to the introduction of this evidence, claiming that since he has six hundred books in his library that have nothing to do with fire, the prejudicial impact of introducing these books is likely to outweigh their probative value.   **Should the judge or the jury decide this issue?**

Problem XII–10.   Ginger Pickles runs a small grocery.   Often she extends credit.   When she does, she sometimes says to the customer, "Don't forget," and does nothing else.   On other occasions she notes the transaction in a record book.   On still other occasions she doesn't note the transaction at the time of the sale, but, if she remembers, she marks it down in the book before closing the shop in the evening.   After numerous unsuccessful attempts to collect on a two hundred twelve dollar debt that Samuel Whiskers has run up, Pickles brings suit against Whiskers.   To prove the amount of the debt, Pickles seeks to introduce her account book either as a business record or under the shopbook rule.   Whiskers objects, claiming that the records in the account book do not qualify as business records because they are not regularly kept.   He also claims that the records are not admissible under the ancient version of the shopbook rule that is still available in the jurisdiction because Pickles employs a clerk, Sally Penny.   Pickles responds that Penny is a friend, not a clerk.   She comes to chat for three or four hours every day and, while there, naturally helps out.   For this Pickles gives her free groceries.   **Should the judge or the jury decide whether Pickles' books are regularly kept or whether Pickles employs a clerk?   Are these questions of fact or questions of law?**

B.   CONTROLLING THE JURY

There are many ways in which the trial judge may influence or even control jury behavior.   At one extreme, the judge who believes the evidence will support only one result may direct a verdict for either party in a civil case or for the defendant in a criminal case.   The same belief, arrived at after the jury has completed its deliberations, justifies the entry of judgment notwithstanding the verdict.   At the other extreme, the judge may influence the jury, intentionally or unintentionally, by the manner in which the trial is conducted.   The attention paid to different witnesses, the kinds of questions asked, the manner in which rulings are made on objections and tones of voice when instructing the jury are just some of the ways that judges convey to juries their feelings about the case.[16] No one really knows how much subtle cues like this influence juries, but they are probably quite important in some cases. A colleague of one of the authors reports having overheard two jurors conversing at the end of their term of service. One said with obvious pride, "I think we've done very well this past month. I honestly believe we've managed to decide every case the way the judge wanted us to." A single anecdote proves little, but the attitude that this comment reveals should not be surprising. In the courtroom the judge is a figure of high prestige and great authority. Individuals regularly defer to others with these characteristics. The judge has great experience in the trial of cases, while the jurors are often acutely aware of their own ignorance. Because the jurors must look to the judge for guidance on many matters, it is natural that some should seek judicial guidance on the fundamental issue in the case.

One of the most difficult problems an attorney can face is the problem of the judge who does not appear neutral. Tones of voice and variations in attention do not appear on the record, and the attorney who remarks on subtle biases of demeanor does so at the risk of further alienating the judge in the current and future cases.

We have discussed in some detail one important way in which judges exercise control over juries—the decision to admit or exclude evidence. In this section we will discuss two other ways in which judges may influence jury behavior: giving instructions and summarizing and commenting on the evidence. Some of this material is briefly covered in prior chapters, but here we have an opportunity to examine judge-jury relationships at greater length.

1. INSTRUCTING THE JURY

a. Types of Instructions

Jury instructions may be classified in many different ways. We will break them down into four categories. First, there are instructions that inform the jury of the substantive law applicable to the case. Instructions defining negligence or specifying the elements of a crime are of this type. Instructions on substantive points of law may be phrased generally; e.g., an instruction which defines negligence as "a failure to exercise ordinary care * * *," and then directs the jury to determine whether, according to this definition, the defendant was negligent. Instructions may also be phrased in terms of the specific facts of the case; e.g., an instruction which reads, "If you find that when Jane Doe turned from Main Street into Monroe Street she was not exercising ordinary care, either because she did not look to her left before turning or because * * *, and if you further find * * * then you shall find that Jane Doe was acting negligently at the time of the accident." Instructions at intermediate levels of abstraction are also possible. In some jurisdictions and on some issues courts prefer relatively abstract instructions; in other jurisdictions or on other issues courts prefer instructions linked specifically to the facts of the case. It has been suggested that the more complicated the case the greater the desirability of instructions incorporating the contested facts.

Second, there are limiting instructions that tell the jury to consider certain evidence on only certain issues. A typical limiting instruction is given when a criminal defendant is impeached by evidence of prior crimes. The jury is instructed that they may consider the criminal record only

---

16. See the fine student note, Judges' Nonverbal Behavior in Jury Trials: A Threat to Judicial Impartiality, 61 Va.L.Rev. 1266 (1975).

as it bears on the defendant's credibility as a witness; they may not treat it as evidence that the defendant is guilty of the crime charged. Whenever evidence is admissible for only certain of the inferences it supports, the party opposing the evidence has the right to have the jurors instructed that they should consider the evidence for only the permissible purposes. Many attorneys feel that limiting instructions do little good, and some shun them, fearing that they will remind the jurors of evidence that would not otherwise command their attention or call attention to inferences that might otherwise have been overlooked. In a joint trial in which the confrontation clause prevents the confession of one defendant from being improperly used against another the Supreme Court has held that limiting instructions do not provide constitutionally sufficient protection.[17]

A third type of instruction calls the jurors' attention to the quality of particular evidence and suggests how they should deal with it. An example of this is the missing witness instruction that may be given on certain occasions when a party fails to call a knowledgeable available witness. The instruction informs the jurors that they may infer from the party's failure to call the witness that had he been called his testimony would have been contrary to the interests of that party. We saw a variant of this instruction requested in the *Whale* case with respect to the missing witness Earl Stible.

Perhaps the most common kind of instruction that falls within this third type is called the "cautionary instruction". As its name implies, this kind of instruction directs the jury to regard certain types of evidence with particular caution. Cautionary instructions are often given with reference to admissions, dying declarations, and the testimony of accomplices and informers. For example, a court might tell a jury:

The government's principle witness in this case, Mr. Martin, has admitted he is a drug addict and was addicted to heroin at the time he was serving as an informant. You should weigh the uncorroborated testimony of an addict-informer with extreme caution because of the possibility of the addict's special interest and motive to fabricate.

Finally, the jury may be instructed on how it is to conduct itself, both during the deliberations and at other times. For example, the jurors will be told not to discuss the case, even among themselves, until they begin their deliberations, and they may be instructed on such details as how to go about electing a foreperson. The most controversial jury instruction of this type is the supplementary instruction,[18] known as the "dynamite" or "*Allen*" charge, that is used to encourage deadlocked juries to return verdicts.[19] When a jury reports itself as hopelessly deadlocked, it may be instructed in more or less the following words:

In a large proportion of cases absolute certainty cannot be expected. Although your verdict must be the verdict of each of you individually and not a mere acquiescence in the conclusion of your fellows, yet you should examine the question submitted with candor and with a proper regard for and deference to the opinions of each other. It is your duty

---

17. See, e.g., Bruton v. United States, 391 U.S. 123 (1968); but c.f. Harrington v. California, 395 U.S. 250 (1969) and Parker v. Randolph, 442 U.S. 62 (1979). These cases are discussed in Chapter Seven in the text following note 25.

18. A supplementary instruction is an instruction given when a jury returns to the courtroom after beginning deliberations because it has reached an impasse or some point of confusion, or because the judge wishes to correct an erroneous instruction or instruct on a matter not previously covered.

19. For a good discussion of the general problem, see Note, On Instructing Deadlocked Juries, 78 Yale L.J. 100 (1968).

to decide the case if you can conscientiously do so. You should listen, with a disposition to be convinced, to each other's arguments. If much the larger number are for conviction, a dissenting juror should consider whether his doubts are reasonable ones when they make no impression upon the minds of so many others, equally honest and equally intelligent. If, upon the other hand, the majority is for acquittal, the minority ought to ask themselves whether they might not reasonably doubt the correctness of a judgment which was not concurred in by the majority.[20]

This instruction, a paraphrase of an instruction approved by the Supreme Court in 1896 in the case of Allen v. United States, has engendered considerable criticism. Many feel that it is too coercive to be tolerated in our system of criminal justice. Judge John Brown of the Fifth Circuit has said of the Allen charge, "The time has come * * * to forbid this practice. Like the silver platter, this is too dear to keep."[21]   Going to the heart of the issue, Judge Brown argues, "This is an intrusion by the Judge into the exclusive domain of fact-finding by the jury. It is nonetheless so merely because the Judge does not indicate which of two decisions must be reached. * * * I think a mistrial from

a hung jury is a safeguard to liberty. In many areas it is the sole means by which one or a few may stand out against an overwhelming contemporary public sentiment. Nothing should interfere with its exercise."[22]

While the Allen charge is still generally tolerated, judges giving the charge must be careful because of the controversy surrounding it. Any substantial deviation from the language approved by the Supreme Court may, particularly if it tends to be more coercive, result in reversal.

Except for a few instructions like the Allen charge, many lawyers and commentators believe that the judge's instructions have little influence on the jury. This may be generally true of limiting or cautionary instructions, but we believe that the jury tries to be faithful to the law and that the instructions given the jury on points of law are often quite important. Jurors certainly act as if the instructions are important, for they often ask to have them reread or clarified.[23]   Even if jury instructions have little to do with jury verdicts, they still merit counsel's close attention, for it has been said that "[e]rrors in instructing the jury have become the single most common ground for appellate reversal in the Anglo-American legal tradition."[24]

20.   Cf. Allen v. United States, 164 U.S. 492 (1896). In several jurisdictions a modified version of the charge is used. The modification asks all jurors, whether they are in the majority or minority, to reconsider their verdict.

21.   Huffman v. United States, 297 F.2d 754, 759 (5th Cir.) (dissenting opinion), certiorari denied, 370 U.S. 955 (1962).

22.   Id.

23.   See Meyer & Rosenberg, Questions Juries Ask: Untapped Springs of Insight, 55 Judicature 105 (1971). There has been little controlled research on the impact of jury instructions. The results in the most elaborate study to date are equivocal. Instructions on insanity seem to have affected the jury verdicts on one experimental trial and not another. R. Simon, The Jury and the De-

fense of Insanity 66–77 (1967). Another study reports clear effects associated with different instructions on the meaning of criminal intent. Sanders and Colasanto, The Use of Responsibility Rules in Jury Decision Making: Morissette Revisited, Paper Presented at the 1976 Meetings of the American Sociological Association.

It is also clear that many jury instructions are not well understood, but they can be rewritten so as to be substantially more comprehensible. See, e.g.,—Charrow and Charrow, Making Legal Language Understandable: A Psycholinguistic Study of Jury Instructions, 79 Colum.L.Rev. 1306 (1979); Elwork, Sales & Alfini, Making Jury Instructions Understandable (1982).

24.   Robinson, A Proposal for Limiting the Duty of the Trial Judge to Instruct the Jury Sua Sponte, 11 San Diego L.Rev. 325 (1974).

b. Procedural Matters

Instructions may be given at any time during the trial. The jury may be instructed on some of the legal issues in the case before any evidence is received. Limiting instructions are often given at the time the evidence to which they apply is received. They may be repeated at the close of the case. Most instructions on the substantive law and most cautionary instructions are given at the close of the case. In some jurisdictions the instructions are given before counsel's final argument to the jury, but the usual practice is to give them after the final arguments, immediately before the jury begins to deliberate. A jury that has begun to deliberate may ask to have certain instructions reread or it may seek supplementary instructions on matters that are causing confusion. Instructions given during the course of the trial are given orally. Those given at the close of the case may be given orally or in writing, depending upon the jurisdiction and the exercise of judicial discretion.

A party has a right to have the jury instructed on all points of law applicable to the case. The party may also have a right to certain cautionary or limiting instructions. In criminal cases, at least in felonies, the judge has the obligation to ensure that the jury is instructed on all applicable points of law whether or not the parties request particular instructions. In federal court, the judge's duty to instruct without request extends to civil cases as well,[25] but in many states the right to a particular instruction in a civil case is waived if the instruction is not specifically requested. The right may also be waived if the request is in some way in error.[26]

Instructions are commonly prepared by counsel and submitted to the judge with the request that the jury be charged in the terms of the proposed instructions. Often the instructions offered by opposing counsel will conflict in tone, if not in substance. The judge may resolve any conflict on his own, or he may confer with both counsel in an attempt to devise instructions that each can accept. The judge may also reject the submissions of counsel and prepare his own instructions on some or all of the issues. Each party's right is to have the jury instructed on the legal issues in the case. So long as the jury is correctly instructed on every legal issue, a party cannot complain because his preferred instructions were not given.

In writing instructions, lawyers and judges draw on many sources. The more experienced often have accumulated a variety of favorite instructions that easily can be adapted to the facts of particular cases. Model instructions may be found in unofficial form books or in compilations prepared by bar associations or under the authority of the state judiciary. Original instructions may also be offered. Some courts charge in the language of statutes or look to instructions that have been upheld in appellate opinions. Although instructions drawn from these sources are likely to be upheld on appeal, usually the better practice is to avoid them. The fact that an instruction has been upheld on appeal does not mean that it is a good instruction; it simply means that its use in the case in question did not constitute reversible error. Statutory language may convey the legislature's meaning precisely, but it may convey it in language that the jury will not understand. Instructions should be impartial and easy to understand, since they do no good if the jury cannot follow them. Too often jury in-

25. 9 C. Wright & A. Miller, Federal Practice & Procedure § 2556, at 654–55 (1971).

26. A common way to request an instruction is to submit a proposed instruction for the judge's use. Some Alabama cases suggest that a spelling error in a proposed instruction may be sufficient to justify the judge's re-

fusal to give that instruction. Watkins v. Potts, 219 Ala. 427, 430, 122 So. 416, 418 (1929); cf. Milford v. Tidwell, 276 Ala. 110, 114, 159 So.2d 621, 624 (1963). This position is extreme. It is unlikely that any jurisdiction today would hold that such a trivial error waives a right to a requested instruction.

structions are long, complicated and written in language that even lawyers have trouble understanding. Bench and bar share the blame.

Counsel do not cease being advocates when they suggest instructions for the court's use. The art of writing instructions is to state the law correctly while subtly favoring the conclusion that one wants the jury to reach. The liberties that lawyers take with instructions depend in part upon whom they represent. If a criminal defendant is acquitted because the jury has received an unduly defense-oriented instruction, the verdict will not be reversed on appeal. The prosecutor, on the other hand, must be wary of getting more than he is entitled to at the instruction stage, for the price may be a later reversal. For similar reasons, the large institutional defendant that can easily afford a retrial can be more venturesome in seeking favorable instructions than the individual plaintiff with limited resources. Some see an even more subtle game at the instruction stage. Lawyers who think that instructions matter little may not offer instructions in situations where they perceive technical deficiencies in the instructions prepared by the court or opposing counsel. They make the minimum objection needed to preserve the point, hoping that they will be overruled, so that if the verdict goes against them they will have valid grounds for appeal. Such tactics are ethically questionable and, if an appellate court perceived counsel's motivation it would, no doubt, hold that error had not been preserved.

Instructions are supposed to aid juries in deciding cases according to the law. They are not intended as a final stage in the adversary process. In order to avoid the deficiencies of partisan instructions,

many jurisdictions have attempted to develop model or pattern instructions that provide jurors with a clear explanation of the law while not advancing (however subtly) the case of one side or the other. In most jurisdictions these pattern instructions are only models. The judge has discretion to insist on their use, to prepare his own instructions, or to use instructions prepared by counsel. However, in some jurisdictions the court in civil cases must offer a pattern instruction if one is on point and correctly states the law.[27] Pattern instructions are often praised for removing partisanship from the instruction phase of the trial and for decreasing reversible error, but the mandatory use of pattern instructions is not without some difficulty. Claims have been made that these theoretically neutral instructions are not impartial, but tend to favor systematically one side[28] or the other. Pattern instructions have also been justly criticized for falling far short of the ideals of brevity and clarity.

When deficiencies exist in mandatory pattern instructions, they must be corrected by a rule-making procedure, for the case-by-case growth of law has been hampered. Occasionally, courts have exacerbated the problems of mandatory instructions by rigidly restricting any variation. In Houston v. Northup[29] the plaintiffs submitted their case on two different theories of negligence. Two of the instructions that the jury received appeared to conflict. A confused jury asked for clarification, and the trial judge gave an additional instruction, not an approved pattern instruction, which clarified the matter by explaining that the plaintiff's two theories were independent of each other and that there was no conflict of instructions because one applied only to the plaintiff's first theory and

27. An A.L.R. annotation lists six jurisdictions where the use of pattern instructions is mandatory in civil cases. 49 A.L.R.3d 128 (1973) and 1975 Supp.

28. Compare Dooley, Jury Instructions: An Appraisal by a Plaintiff's Attorney, 1963

Ill.L.F. 586, with Fowler, Jury Instructions: An Appraisal by a Defendant's Attorney, Id. at 612, and Hannah, Jury Instructions: An Appraisal by a Trial Judge, Id. at 627.

29. 460 S.W.2d 572 (Mo.1970).

the other applied only to the second. The Missouri Supreme Court held that the clarifying instruction was erroneously given and suggested that the court should simply have reread the apparently contradictory instructions and told the jury that both were proper.[30] How a second reading of these instructions would have helped the jury is unclear, and how the appellant was prejudiced by the clarifying instruction is also a mystery. If pattern instructions are applied as rigidly as they were in this case, they will probably do more harm than good in the long run. Our view is that the better practice is to make the use of pattern instructions advisory but not mandatory. Where pattern instructions are mandatory, the judge should certainly have the discretion to supplement the instructions if they cause confusion.

When a faulty instruction has been given, a party must raise his objection immediately or else the matter will not be preserved for appeal.[31] Courts differ as to the specificity with which objections must be made. In some jurisdictions an advantage of submitting instructions is that a general objection to a refusal to give the submitted instruction preserves for appeal all arguments that might have been made in support of the instruction. Other jurisdictions and the federal courts require objections specific enough so that the judge is alerted to error and has a chance to correct it before the jury begins to deliberate. Usually counsel will be informed of the court's proposed instructions before final argument. This allows the attorneys to frame their arguments to the jury in the light of what the judge will later tell them.

Even where pattern instructions are used, attorneys must be alert to preserve their clients' rights. There are certain instructions, such as cautionary instructions, which will almost certainly be given if requested, but which the judge may fail to give if not requested to do so. In addition, counsel may not want the jury to receive certain instructions to which his client has a right. For example, counsel may feel that an instruction to ignore the defendant's failure to take the stand serves only to draw the jury's attention to this failure. If the court volunteers this protection, counsel will want to tell the court that it is not desired.

Problem XII–11. Sam Carter is leaving a cocktail party after drinking three double martinis in the preceding hour and a half. He notices a large cardboard box on the edge of the driveway. Several children are standing near it. Instead of taking the trouble to drive around the box, Carter swerves only slightly, hitting a corner of the box with the car's fender and injuring a child who was playing inside. The child sues Carter for negligence. Below are the pattern instructions used to define negligence in the states of New York and Michigan. **If you were defending Carter, in which jurisdiction would you rather be?**

New York Pattern Jury Instructions:

>   **PJI 2:10. Common Law Standard of Care—Negligence Defined—
>   Generally**

>   Negligence is lack of ordinary care. It is a failure to exercise that
>   degree of care which a reasonably prudent person would have exercised under

---

30. Id. at 575.

31. In extreme cases, courts will recognize "plain error" even if an objection has not been made.

the same circumstances. It may arise from doing an act which a reasonably prudent person would not have done under the same circumstances, or, on the other hand, from failing to do an act which a reasonably prudent person would have done under the same circumstances.

PJI 2:12.   Common Law Standard of Care—Foreseeability—Generally

Negligence require [sic] both a foreseeable danger of injury to another and conduct unreasonable in proportion to the danger. A person is not responsible for the consequences of his conduct unless the risk of injury was reasonably foreseeable. The exact occurrence or precise injury need not have been foreseeable; but injury as a result of negligent conduct must have been not merely possible but probable.

If a reasonably prudent person could not foresee any injury as a result of his conduct, or if his conduct was reasonable in the light of what he could foresee, there is no negligence. Conversely, there is negligence if a reasonably prudent person could foresee injury as a result of his conduct, and his conduct was unreasonable in the light of what he could foresee.

[*The charge should be related to the particular facts of the case.*]

Michigan Standard Jury Instructions—Civil:

10.01   Negligence of Adult Defendant—Definition

Instruction

When I use the word "negligence," with respect to defendant's conduct, I mean the failure to do something which a reasonably careful person would do or the doing of something which a reasonably careful person would not do, under the circumstances which you find existed in this case. It is for you to decide what a reasonably careful person would do or not do under such circumstances.

10.02   Ordinary Care—Adult—Definition

Instruction

When I use the words "ordinary care," I mean the care a reasonably careful (person) would use under the circumstances which you find existed in this case. The law does not say what a reasonably careful (person) would do or would not do under such circumstances. That is for you to decide.

10.04   Duty to Use Ordinary Care—Adult—Defendant

Instruction

It was the duty of (the defendant), in connection with this occurrence, to use ordinary care for the safety of (the plaintiff) (and) (plaintiff's property).

If you knew the jury was going to receive the New York instruction, would your final argument vary from what it would be if you knew the jury was going to receive the Michigan instruction? How?

Assume that you are in a jurisdiction without pattern instructions. Prepare the instruction on negligence which you would offer the court if you were the attorney for Carter's insurance company. Prepare the instruction which you would offer the court if you were the plaintiff's attorney. In both instructions, incorporate the facts of the case.

Problem XII–12. Presented below are two pattern jury instructions. Each notes the existence of the presumption of innocence and each explains what it means to be convinced that the defendant is guilty beyond a reasonable doubt. One is from California and the other is from Michigan. **If you were a prosecutor, which instruction would you prefer? If the judge were to ask you to submit an instruction covering these matters, what would you submit as prosecutor? What would you submit as defense counsel?**

California:

A defendant in a criminal action is presumed to be innocent until the contrary is proved, and in case of a reasonable doubt whether his guilt is satisfactorily shown, he is entitled to an acquittal. This presumption places upon the State the burden of proving him guilty beyond a reasonable doubt. Reasonable doubt is defined as follows: It is not a mere possible doubt; because everything relating to human affairs, and depending on moral evidence, is open to some possible or imaginary doubt. It is that state of the case which, after the entire comparison and consideration of all the evidence, leaves the minds of the jurors in that condition that they cannot say they feel an abiding conviction, to a moral certainty, of the truth of the charge. [CALJIC 2.90]

Michigan:

Basic to our system of criminal justice is the principle that a person accused of a crime is presumed to be innocent. This presumption of innocence starts at the very beginning of this case and continues throughout the trial and during your deliberations. Each and every one of you must be satisfied beyond a reasonable doubt, after deliberating, that the defendant is guilty, or you must find him not guilty. You must begin your deliberations with the presumption of innocence foremost in your minds.

The fact that the defendant was arrested and is on trial is no evidence against him. There must be evidence introduced in this trial that convinces you of the defendant's guilt beyond a reasonable doubt. The law does not require a defendant to prove his innocence or to produce any evidence whatsoever.

The burden of proving guilt is upon the prosecution throughout the entire course of the trial and at no time does the burden of proof shift to the defendant. This burden of proof means that every element of the offense charged must be proven by evidence beyond a reasonable doubt.

By stating that the prosecution must prove guilt beyond a reasonable doubt I mean that there must be such evidence as causes you to have a firm conviction amounting to a moral certainty of the defendant's guilt.

If, after considering all of the evidence, you do not have such a certainty, then that is a reasonable doubt. A reasonable doubt is a state of mind which would cause you to hesitate to make an important decision in your own life. It can arise from the evidence, the lack of evidence, or from the unsatisfactory nature of the evidence.   [Mich.Crim.Jury Instructions, Vol. I, 72–74.]

Problem XII–13.   You are the defense attorney in a criminal case.   When the judge charges the jury on the elements of the offense, she speaks slowly and distinctly.   When the judge charges the jury on the presumption of innocence and the requirement of proof beyond a reasonable doubt, she mumbles and rushes through the charge.   **What can you do?   What will you do?**

Problem XII–14.   Recall the case of Nelson Whale in Chapter One. Whale was accused of selling marihuana.   He denied the sale.   At the close of the trial Whale requested that an instruction on entrapment be given.   **Did the judge err by refusing to give this instruction?   Why or why not?**

Problem XII–15.   Ted Murphy is charged with selling narcotics.   The prosecution's case is built on the testimony of three accomplices.   Murphy's attorney, in her cross-examination of these witnesses and in her oral argument, tries to convince the jury that the accomplices turned state's evidence in the hope they would be treated leniently.   The court instructs the jury: "I want to say that the power of sentence in this court is reposed in the judges, and only in the judges, and the United States Attorney and Assistant United States Attorneys have no power whatever with respect to the sentence.   In saying this, however, I do not wish to suggest what weight should be given to the defense argument that a human being may color his testimony in the hope that some judge may give him recognition for such cooperation, if such it can be called.   You should consider this matter in your assessment of the credibility of these witnesses.   As you did with other witnesses, you must ask yourselves, 'Is he telling the truth?'   In the case of the witnesses I am talking about, 'Have they colored their testimony in the unwarranted hope that they can secure more favorable treatment?'   This is for you and you only to decide."   **Is this instruction proper?**

Problem XII–16.   On the same facts as the preceding problem, the trial judge gives an instruction to the jury that all witnesses are presumed to speak the truth.   Murphy objects.   **Should the objection be sustained?**

Problem XII–17.   Marilyn Cool was charged with possessing and concealing counterfeit money with the intent to defraud the United States. Another person, who admitted participation in the crime, testified for the defendant and said that the defendant had no idea that criminal activity was taking place.   Over the objection of the defendant, the trial judge defined the word accomplice and warned the jury that an accomplice's testimony is "open to suspicion."   Then the judge made the following statement: "However, I charge you that the testimony of an accomplice is competent evidence and it is for you to pass upon the credibility thereof.   If the testimony carries conviction and you are convinced it is true beyond a reasonable doubt, the jury should give it the same effect as you would to a witness not in any respect implicated in the alleged crime and you are not only justified, but it is your duty, not to throw this testimony out because it comes from a tainted source."   **Should the objection have been sustained?**

Problem XII–18. Sandra Beal is charged with robbery. She requests the trial judge to instruct the jury that where there are two possible inferences from the evidence—one of guilt, and one of innocence—the jury must find the defendant not guilty. In other words, the jury must choose the inference of innocence if it is available. **Should the trial judge give this instruction?**

Problem XII–19. You are representing a client in each of the following circumstances. **To what instructions are you entitled? When are you entitled to receive such instructions? What instructions would you request?**

a. Your client is charged with robbing a grocery store by holding up a stick of dynamite and threatening to blow up the whole place, herself included, unless the money was handed over. Evidence that your client robbed a liquor store using the same *modus operandi* is offered on the issue of identity.

b. Your client, the defendant in an automobile negligence case, is impeached by evidence that he once pled guilty to vehicular homicide.

c. Your client in a criminal case has decided not to testify in her own defense.

d. Your client is charged with bank robbery and the prosecution's chief witness is a participant in the bank robbery who, in return for his testimony, has been allowed to plead guilty to a misdemeanor.

e. You are the prosecutor, and the defendant's chief alibi witness is his wife.

f. The state has introduced a codefendant's confession, portions of which implicate your client, against the codefendant. The codefendant has indicated that he will testify in his own defense.

g. The same as the preceding situation except the codefendant has indicated he will not testify.

h. In a tort suit, the fact that your client had paid for the insurance on a car driven by a messenger is introduced to show that the messenger was his agent.

i. The general manager of your client who testifies that your client's procedures were the safest possible is impeached by evidence that after the accident giving rise to the litigation your client changed the procedures.

j. Your client, a high school teacher, is on trial for the statutory rape of a fourteen year old student, who admits to having had a serious crush on him and during the six month period surrounding the alleged event to smoking marihuana daily. There is physical evidence that the girl is not a virgin, but it is not conclusive and the identification of your client as her lover turns entirely on her testimony.

---

2. SUMMARY AND COMMENT

At common law the judge had the power both to summarize the evidence and to comment on it. This power is retained by the federal judiciary and by the judiciary in a minority of states, but in the majority of states the power to comment on the evidence has been taken from the judge. The movement to eliminate the judge's common law power of comment began in the late eighteenth century in North Carolina.[32] New states joining the union often adopted constitutional provisions to this effect.[33] Other states curbed the judge's power by statute or court rule.[34] The fear was that the power to comment on the evidence gave the judge undue influence over the resolution of factual questions that were reserved for the judgment of the jury.

There is no hard and fast line between summary and comment. The judge in summarizing the evidence cannot repeat everything that was said at trial. Any summary will to some extent indicate which evidence the judge thought important. Nevertheless, many jurisdictions which prevent the judge from commenting on the evidence allow the judge to sum up. Indeed, in some jurisdictions the judge has not only the power to sum up but also the duty. A refusal to give a fair and impartial summary of the evidence covering the parties' basic theories may be reversible error.

In summing up, the judge is expected to marshal for the jury the evidence that has been presented without suggesting what weight the evidence should be given. It is error to unduly emphasize the evidence of one party or to ignore evidence bearing on important issues in the case.[35] Summaries may be organized in a number of different ways. The judge may review the evidence in the order in which it was presented at the trial or in the order in which the events allegedly occurred. A summary may be organized around the parties' theories of the case or integrated into the jury instructions on the law. In multiple party cases it may be important to summarize the evidence as it relates to each party, since some evidence may have been admitted against one party but not against another. There is no one correct way to organize a summary. This depends on the facts of the case.[36]

When the judge comments on the evidence there is one general requirement. The judge must instruct the jurors that they are to determine for themselves the weight of the evidence and the credibility of the witnesses and that they are in no way bound by the judge's comments.[37]

Comment on the evidence may take many forms.[38] The judge may give an opinion on the evidence without in any way suggesting who should prevail. For example, the judge may point to the evidence on each side which he finds most persu-

---

32. Johnson, Province of the Judge in Jury Trials, 12 J.Am.Jud.Soc'y 76, 78 (1928).

33. Id. at 80.

34. See Annot. 10 A.L.R. 1112 (1921).

35. As with other parts of the jury charge, counsel may point out deficiencies in a summary or comment and may suggest improvements. A failure to object at the trial may be held to waive objection on appeal.

36. See 1 Weinstein's Evidence ¶ 107 (1975).

37. Congress chose not to include PFRE 107 as part of the Federal Rules of Evidence, but acknowledged that this rule stated the common law as it has been applied in the federal courts. PFRE 107 provided:

After the close of the evidence and arguments of counsel, the judge may fairly and impartially sum up the evidence and comment to the jury upon the weight of the evidence and the credibility of the witnesses, if he also instructs the jury that they are to determine for themselves the weight of the evidence and the credit to be given to the witnesses and that they are not bound by the judge's summation or comment.

An argument against judicial comment and summary in cases in which one or both parties object to it is found in Saltzburg, The Unnecessarily Expanding Role of the American Trial Judge, 64 Va.L.Rev. 1 (1978).

38. Judge Wyzanski has suggested that the judge should be more restrained when commenting in some kinds of trials (e.g., criminal trials and suits for defamation) than in others (e.g., complex civil litigation). A Trial Judge's Freedom and Responsibility, 65 Harv.L.Rev. 1281 (1952).

asive, he may point to defects in the evidence offered by both parties, or he may call the jury's attention to a crucial conflict in the testimony offered by the parties and suggest that the resolution of the case should turn on whose testimony is believed. Where the judge does nothing to suggest that one party's case is stronger than the other's, reversal on appeal will not occur in a jurisdiction allowing comment so long as the judge's assessment of what is important is reasonable.

The judge may also comment on the weight of the evidence or the credibility of the witnesses. In doing so the judge must always be wary of crossing the thin line between permissible comment and prejudicial error. The basic rule is that the judge, in commenting on the evidence, must remain a judge and not become an advocate. The judge cannot base his comments on evidence not in the record or on assumptions that indicate partisanship, such as the assumption that the defendant is guilty. Emotional harangues are out of order as are any comments that suggest the judge believes a rational decision must reflect his opinion. Comments that

touch upon the ultimate issues are also highly suspect.

It appears that judges often choose not to exercise their powers of summary and comment. Kalven and Zeisel found that in states allowing only summary, judges summarized the evidence in just thirty-two percent of the reported trials.[39] In states allowing comment and summary, judges commented or commented and summarized in thirty-two percent of the trials, and summarized only in twenty-one percent.[40] Of those judges who reported on more than one case, seventy-eight percent of the judges in jurisdictions allowing only summaries never summarized, while forty-two percent of the judges in jurisdictions allowing comment and summary never did either.[41] It would appear from these data that one of the most important effects of granting judges the power to comment on the evidence is to encourage them at least to summarize it. This may be because judges with the power to comment on the evidence are not afraid that they will be reversed on appeal if they inadvertently cross the line between summary and comment.[42]

Problem XII–20. Mike Ferris is charged with armed robbery. The government's evidence includes testimony from the arresting officers, from a ballistics expert, from three eyewitnesses and from two of Ferris' alleged accomplices. Ferris offers no evidence in his own behalf, but vigorously cross-examines each of the government's witnesses. The jurisdiction is one in which the judge is permitted to sum up the evidence but not to comment on it. The judge spends thirty minutes summarizing the government's evidence and no time summarizing the defendant's evidence. The judge does instruct the jury on the government's burden of proof and the fact that a defendant in a criminal case need not present any evidence. **Has the judge committed reversible error? Would the judge have been better advised**

39. H. Kalven & H. Zeisel, The American Jury 421 (1966).

40. Id. at 422.

41. Id. at 424.

42. Weinstein and Berger suggest that the primary significance of the power to comment on the evidence is that it enables an appellate court to uphold a jury verdict where the trial judge did not intend to express an opinion on the evidence but the jurors probably inferred it from the wording of his charge or the manner of his delivery. 1 Weinstein's Evidence ¶ 107 (1975).

to have inferred from the defendant's cross-examination the defendant's theory of the case and then to have specified that theory for the jury, noting any testimony in support of that theory which was elicited on cross-examination?

Problem XII–21. Gary Altman is charged with evading the draft. The government's evidence tends to show that Altman received an order to report for induction and never reported. Altman testifies on his own behalf. He does not deny receiving an order to report for induction. He claims to have ripped up everything the draft board sent him without opening it because he believed the draft was immoral. He further testifies that he feels he should not be convicted of a failure to report for induction, because had he reported it is likely that he would have been sent to Vietnam to fight in an illegal war. At the close of the evidence the judge charges the jury: "So far as the facts are concerned in this case, members of the jury, I want to instruct you that whatever the court may say as to the facts, is only the court's view. You are at liberty to entirely disregard it. The court feels from the evidence in this case that the government has sustained the burden cast upon it by the law and has proved that this defendant is guilty in manner and form as charged beyond a reasonable doubt." The jury returns a guilty verdict after only fifteen minutes of deliberation. **Should an appellate court reverse because of the judge's instructions? Would your answer be different if the jury had deliberated for seven hours before returning a guilty verdict?**

Problem XII–22. In a criminal trial, the judge charges the jury: "Now I am going to tell you what I think of the defendant's testimony. You may have noticed that he wiped his hands during his testimony. It is a rather curious thing, but that is almost always an indication of lying. Why it should be so, we don't know, but that is the fact. I think that every single word that man said, except when he agreed with the government's testimony, was a lie. Now, that opinion is an opinion of evidence and is not binding on you, and if you don't agree with it, it is your duty to find the defendant not guilty. If, on the other hand, you believe the government agents, where their statements contradict those of the witness, the evidence is sufficient to justify a verdict of guilty." The defendant objects to this charge. **If the jury returns a verdict of guilty, should the appellate court reverse?**

Problem XII–23. Hillman and Burton are charged with organizing a complicated scheme to defraud widows and orphans. The trial takes four days. About half the government's case is devoted to laying out the details of the scheme to defraud and about eighty-five percent of the government's remaining evidence implicates only Hillman. Burton testifies extensively in his own defense, but Hillman chooses not to take the stand. At the close of the trial Burton asks the judge to summarize the evidence for the jury as part of his final charge to them. The judge refuses, saying that she doesn't want to "color the jury's deliberations." **Has the judge committed reversible error? Would there be reversible error if Burton had never requested a summary?**

SECTION II. THE JURY AND QUESTIONS OF LAW

A. HISTORICAL BACKGROUND: THE CRIMINAL JURY [43]

The jury takes its name from the Latin word "iurare," meaning "to swear". It is a body of persons sworn to speak the truth on some legal matter. Jury-like bodies were known in ancient Greece and Rome, but the English jury is more directly traceable to the oath-taking practices of the early Germanic societies. Jury-information-on-oath probably goes back as far as the Anglo-Saxon conquest of England and was certainly known during the later Anglo-Saxon period.

The Normans also contributed to the development of the jury. Continental monarchs, from at least the ninth century, had utilized a procedure in which royal officials, acting under royal orders, chose and put on oath a number of persons in order to obtain information about a particular matter. This procedure was known as the *inquisitio* or royal inquest. Most historians believe that the *inquisitio* was brought to England in 1066. By 1170 an institution had developed—we call it jury trial—that combined features of the *inquisitio* and the verdict-rendering jury. These early jury trials, beginning or becoming common during the reign of Henry II (1154–1189), dealt primarily with civil matters relating to land.

On the criminal side, Henry II's reign saw the development of the jury of accusation, the forerunner of the grand jury. This jury in Henry's time was composed of freemen from each hundred [44] sworn to "present" all those in the hundred who were suspected of having committed crimes. All persons named in these "presentments" were taken by the sheriff to be tried before royal justices or local officials.

Trial in cases begun by presentment was usually by ordeal, an attempt to place the accused's fate in the hands of the Divine. A typical ordeal required the accused to grasp a hot iron or stones from the bottom of a pot of boiling water. If the subsequent burn healed, the accused was thought innocent; if it festered and did not heal, God had found him guilty.

In 1215 the Fourth Lateran Council removed the religious sanction from ordeals by forbidding clerical participation. In England, King John responded to the Papal action by ending the ordeal in trials begun by presentment. In 1219 John's successor, Henry III, ordered the royal justices to exhort criminal defendants to put themselves "on the country," that is, to the test of trial by their countrymen. [45] Exhorta-

---

43. This history discusses only the criminal jury, for it is in the context of the criminal trial that questions regarding the jury's right to decide issues of law are most commonly raised. After the thirteenth century the history of the civil jury differs markedly from that of the criminal jury, in large part because of the complicated system of pleading that developed on the civil side. We would like to thank Professors John Langbein, William Nelson and especially Thomas Green for the aid that they gave us in writing this section. For other materials on the history of jury trial, see W. Holdsworth, 1 A History of English Law, 312–350 (7th ed. rev. 1956), T. F. T. Plucknett, A Concise History of the Common Law 106–138 (5th ed. 1956), J. Thayer, A Prelim-

inary Treatise on Evidence at the Common Law 47–262 (1898).

44. The "hundred" was a division of a county created for administrative purposes and coextensive with the local community.

45. From the late twelfth century, in cases of appeal (prosecutions arising from private accusation rather than presentment) the accused could avail himself of the writ de odio et atia, in which he claimed he was being falsely accused "out of hatred and malice" and being forced into a trial by battle. A jury trial could be granted on the issue of whether the appeal was the result of hatred. By 1215 this right had been generalized to include other defenses, such as self-defense. Therefore the use of jur-

tion was necessary because defendants could not be tried by the "country" unless they consented to the new mode of trial by entering a plea. Ultimately those who refused to put themselves on the country were coerced by the *peine forte et dure,* the piling of stones on the accused's chest until he either consented or was crushed to death.[46] Thus by 1225 almost all criminal cases in the royal courts were decided by juries.

Throughout the medieval period the most important feature of the criminal jury was its self-informing character. The jurors came to court to deliver a verdict, not to listen to evidence. Because of this, a court could hold as many as several dozen felony trials in a single day. The jurors were chosen from the hundred in which the crime had occurred. They were not required to be witnesses in the strict sense, but they were responsible for gathering evidence in the community where the crime occurred and for assessing the credibility of that evidence. The jurors were conceived of as representatives of the community who, on the basis of any information available to them, spoke what they thought to be the "truth."

The jury's verdict (truth-saying) was a conclusory statement finding the defendant guilty or not guilty and, if the defendant was found to have committed the act charged, stating whether the act was done with some justification. Verdicts could also be accompanied by statements of fact. Findings of justification and factual statements accompanying verdicts were important because they might entitle defendants found to have committed capital offenses to pardons or acquittals. There is evidence that from a very early time jurors would shape their findings of fact to se-

cure results which they perceived as just.[47] The medieval jury, by virtue of its fact-finding power, could choose what law was to be applied to each case.

So long as the jury remained self-informing, there was little that the judge could do to contest the jury's version of the facts. In extreme cases a different jury could be empaneled and its verdict received, but this was very rare. The judge could also question jurors about specific findings, particularly those offered by way of justification, but if the jurors affirmed their findings that was the end of the matter. The verdict was final.

The character of the criminal trial changed dramatically between the middle of the fifteenth and the middle of the sixteenth centuries. Justices of the peace (J.P.'s), county-based officials empowered to hear grand jury presentments and to try certain kinds of cases, had turned the presenting process around. In about 1350 the J.P.'s had begun to take responsibility for the initiation of criminal actions. They took the complaints of accusers, perhaps corroborated them, and then put the information to the grand jury in the form of a bill. Gradually the grand jury became not a presenting body but an indicting one, a body that responded to the J.P.'s bills with the verdicts of *billa vera* (true bill) or *ignoramus* (we know nothing) more regularly than it sought out crime on its own.

By the middle of the fifteenth century some of those whom the J.P.'s—acting now as prosecutors—called upon to corroborate complaints may have appeared at trial as witnesses for the prosecution.[48] By the middle of the next century, the use of witnesses was well-established. Trial rolls make it clear that witnesses appeared to

---

ies in criminal cases was not a complete novelty in 1219.

46. The incentive for preferring death to a trial is that the property of a convicted felon was forfeited. If one died without pleading, one's property passed to one's heirs.

47. Green, Societal Concepts of Criminal Liability for Homicide in Mediaeval England, 47 Speculum 669 (1972).

48. For a cautious account emphasizing how small a role such witnesses probably played, see Thayer, supra note 43, at 130–32.

give testimony under oath for the prosecution, and there was a statute requiring J.P.'s to take the depositions of witnesses and bind them over for appearance at trial.[49]

The replacement of the self-informing jury with trial by witnesses was a gradual process. In 1550 verdicts based on what the jurors knew personally rather than on what transpired in the courtroom were still permissible, but in most cases jury verdicts were a response to what occurred in court. The case against the defendant was based largely on the sworn testimony of witnesses. The defendant's case was based largely on his own unsworn statement. The judge often attempted to illuminate matters by closely questioning the defendant. The defendant could not, as a rule, introduce witnesses to support his case. His right was to have a group of neighbors judge his word against that of his accusers. The principal rule of evidence was that all testimony had to be oral.[50] This was fundamental, for it allowed the jurors to assess the credibility of the defendant and his accusers by hearing their voices and observing their demeanor. On this assessment verdicts were expected to turn.

As the jury came to rely increasingly on the evidence presented at trial, the bench came to treat the jury as if it were bound by the evidence presented.[51] The recorded evidence is sparse, but it appears that the use of prosecution witnesses was increasingly accompanied by detailed judicial charges on the proper verdicts for

given sets of facts. Often the judges summarized the evidence and told the jurors how they viewed it. Threats to fine or imprison jurors for deciding against the weight of the evidence occurred with some frequency, although they were seldom carried out, except in cases where the Crown's political interest was paramount.[52]

The practice in the sixteenth and seventeenth centuries of threatening jurors with fines or imprisonment for returning verdicts with which the bench disagreed was a departure from tradition that threatened to undermine one of the fundamental aspects of jury trial, the finality of verdicts of acquittal. If this practice engendered protest in the sixteenth century, that protest is lost to history. But in the seventeenth century it became the subject of stirring debate.

By the time of Sir Edward Coke (1552–1634) it was settled doctrine—so far as the bench was concerned—that the jury was the sole judge of the facts and the judge was the sole judge of the law. However, in the middle of the seventeenth century sociopolitical opponents of Cromwell's government (some of the so-called "Levellers") argued strenuously for the jury's right to decide issues of law.[53] For some of the more radical "Levellers", the true law was scripturally based and accessible to men of "conscience." They believed that the jury had not only the right but the duty to acquit defendants indicted for acts which the jury, in its conscience, believed not to be criminal. Lilburne, the most famous of

49. For an account of the role of justices of the peace in criminal prosecutions, see J. Langbein, Prosecuting Crime in the Renaissance, Part I (1974).

50. For a contemporary description of a sixteenth century felony trial, see T. Smith, De Republica Anglorum, (1583) (Alston ed. 1906) at 94–104. An exception to the orality rule was made for the depositions of those who died before trial.

51. For a discussion of the effect of the transformation of trial on jury behavior see

Green, The Jury and the English Law of Homicide, 1200–1600, 74 Mich.L.Rev. 413, 487–97 (1976).

52. See, e.g., Proceedings Against Sir Nicholas Throckmorton's Jury (1554) 1 State Trials 902 (T. Howell ed. 1816).

53. The discussion which follows of the jury's right to decide questions of law (1640–1800) is based largely on the research of Professor Thomas A. Green, who is preparing a history of the Anglo-American criminal jury for publication.

Cromwell's opponents, made that claim in both his 1649 and 1653 trials.[54] This position went well beyond the claim that the jury's decision was final with respect to the facts.

Though the Leveller movement was crushed, its conception of the criminal trial jury never entirely died out. In the years after the demise of Cromwell and the restoration of the monarchy (1660), some confused the claim that the jury could decide the law with the claim that jury verdicts were final on the facts. The finality issue was soon decided; the jury's role in determining questions of law took longer to resolve. Some argue that it remains open today.

In 1667 Justice Kelyng was censured by Parliament for badgering juries in run-of-the-mill (as opposed to "political") trials. This action was generally interpreted as reflecting Parliamentary recognition that jury verdicts were final on the facts. Three years later, William Penn and William Mead were tried for disturbing the peace by preaching Quaker doctrine. Penn (as had Lilburne before him) exhorted the jury to acquit on the ground that he had not been charged with an activity that was criminal under the common law. The jury did acquit Penn, but several of its members were heavily fined and then imprisoned for their failure to pay the fines. The jury foreman, Edward Bushell, sought a writ of *habeas corpus,* arguing that jurors could not be fined for refusing to return verdicts ordered by the bench. The Court of Common Pleas granted the writ, holding that jurors could not be fined or threatened on account of their verdicts. Chief Justice Vaughan gave two reasons for the court's decision: 1) since the jurors might be basing their decision on information they

knew privately, it was impossible for a judge to evaluate the reasonableness of their decision; 2) even if the verdict was based solely on information given in court, the jurors must "hear with their own ears," and reach a verdict according to *their* sense of the evidence.[55] The latter argument was a powerful statement of the position that the verdict of a jury trying a criminal case should be the judgment of twelve laymen and not that of one professional judge.

Vaughan's opinion represents the most significant statement on the finality of jury verdicts in English law. Nothing in it suggests that the jury may reject the bench's view of the law, but the opinion brought an end to the litigation arising out of Penn's trial, a trial in which the jury almost certainly rejected the indictment because they believed it was not in accordance with the law. Against this background, several important contemporary jury tracts used Vaughan's opinion as support for the argument that the jury had the right to decide questions of law as well as those of fact.[56]

During the next twenty years, even the Whigs, establishment opponents of the Stuart regime, appeared to embrace the concept of the law-deciding jury as they struggled against the Stuart regime. Only after attaining power in 1688–89 did they discard the concept. The later Whig view correctly interpreted Vaughan's opinion in Bushell's Case, conceding the finality of jury verdicts on issues of fact but insisting that the jury take the law from the bench. The issue nevertheless remained a live one, especially in the context of trials for seditious libel. In these cases the bench put to the jury only the questions of publication and innuendo (e.g., when the author wrote "K — — —," was he referring to the

54. See P. Gregg, Free-Born John: A Biography of John Lilburne (1961).

55. Bushell's Case, 124 Eng.Rep. 1006, 1012–13 (1670).

56. See, e.g., H. Care, English Liberties (1680); Hawles, The Englishman's Right (1680).

king). The seditious nature of the pamphlet was treated by the courts as a question of law reserved for the judges. Opponents of this practice made three arguments: that seditiousness was a question of fact and hence for the jury; that the jury could decide questions of law including seditious nature; and that the special verdict procedure, by not resolving the issue of guilt, undermined the finality of the jury's verdict and prevented the extension of jury mercy, an extension that some judges had allowed without question in non-political cases.

The seditious libel matter was settled twice: first in the Court of King's Bench and then in the legislature. In 1783, in the case of Rex v. Shipley, Chief Justice Mansfield upheld the bench's position on judgments of law. He conceded that jurors could not be punished for acquitting a defendant, but denied that this proved they had the right to decide questions of law. The jurors' duty was obeisance to the rules, and if the jurors flouted them, they were acting wrongly and in bad conscience. Mansfield's view was that verdict "according to conscience" implied a duty to obey the law as set forth by the court. On the specific issue in question, Mansfield held that seditious nature was a matter of law and hence not for the jury.

Fox's Libel Act (1792) "reversed" Mansfield's decision, giving juries the issue of seditious nature (some thought *qua* law, others *qua* fact) and restoring the general verdict in seditious libel cases.[57] However, on the more fundamental issue Mansfield prevailed. His conception of the jury's role became the English position on the duty of the jury in criminal cases: the jury may not be second-guessed as to the facts when it acquits; it ought not to acquit against the law, except perhaps in rare cases where mercy requires this; it has the duty to accept the judicial charge on the law; and it is not to second-guess the bench on the legality of the indictment. This position, which was more or less achieved in England by 1800, only gradually took hold in the United States.[58]

The right to jury trial was one of the fundamental liberties that the English brought with them to America. Modes of jury trial varied among the colonies, and within each colony there was often variation from county to county. It is likely that in many areas the jury was thought to have law-deciding power, but the issue was not the focus of popular attention until 1735 when John Peter Zenger was tried for the crime of seditious libel.[59] The defense, drawing on the English experience, argued for both the general verdict and the jury's right to decide questions of law. Zenger's acquittal is often thought to have established both of these rights and to have provided the framers of the constitution with a specific theory of trial by jury. However, it is hard to extract from Zenger's trial the exact scope of any jury right to decide questions of law. Read narrowly, the case stands as precedent only for the proposition that the jury could return a general verdict of "not guilty" which would be final.

57. Even with these powers juries often convicted in cases of seditious libel, occasionally going against the opinion of the court or the apparent weight of the evidence. See L. Levy, Legacy of Suppression 252–54 (1960).

58. This account neglects one element that certainly played a role in diminishing the discretion accorded jurors. This is the development of rules of evidence and other procedural means of controlling jury behavior. On the criminal side, the rules of evidence are largely a product of the late eighteenth and nineteenth centuries. A good history of evidentiary rules in criminal cases has not been written.

59. See J. Alexander, A Brief Narrative of the Case and Trial of John Peter Zenger (1963). For an earlier case raising the same issue, see the discussion in Brown, The Case of William Bradford, 1 The Forum 272 (1956). This case and any others that may have occurred did not receive the widespread publicity among all the colonies that was given Zenger's case.

At the time of the Constitutional Convention, the criminal jury was generally viewed as having the power to decide questions of law as well as fact. As with Zenger's trial, this clearly meant that the general verdict was sacrosanct, but beyond this little is clear. Juries no doubt applied the law where questions of law and fact were inextricably interlinked and they were probably thought to have the right to exercise mercy or to reflect the community's opposition to a specific prosecution. Whether a jury was supposed to pass on the legality of the indictment or the correctness of the judge's charge or on the judge's interpretation of statutes remains in doubt. Attitudes may have varied among the states. One view is that the jury was generally thought to have only a residual right to decide the law, a right to be scrupulously exercised after carefully considering the bench's instructions. The jury's law deciding power was probably thought greatest where general legal rules were subject to more than one interpretation and where laws such as sedition statutes penalized what was essentially political activity. Jurors were probably not supposed to judge the constitutionality of statutes or of common law precedent (although some later commentators argue that this was done), and it does not appear that juries passed on the admissibility of evidence.

Whatever the law-deciding powers of the early American jury, the concept of a law-deciding jury came under attack early in the national period. The Jacksonian celebration of the legislature as the predominant democratic institution undermined claims that the jury was the ultimate democratic check. Expanded suffrage, the codification movement and an optimistic belief that society could be shaped through law contributed to a climate in which the wisdom of allowing the jury to nullify legislation on

an ad hoc basis was increasingly questioned. Legislation, like the jury verdict, was seen as a community-based decision process. It is likely that instructions to juries became more specific as the judges adhered more closely to the letter of statutes, particularly in criminal cases. Also the rise of state appellate courts and reporter systems increased the feeling that the law on many issues was settled. If law-deciding meant anything more than the right to extend mercy to those technically guilty, it could be viewed as introducing uncertainty in the law to the extent of negating due process. This concern with due process was noted by a number of courts deciding against the law-deciding jury.[60]

The increased technicality of the trial and of the law also had an impact on conceptions of the jury's role. Rules of evidence and notions of relevance were built around the idea of the jury as fact finder. The shift from a natural law theory to a positivistic conception of law meant that laypeople could no longer, even in theory, be expected to have access to fundamental legal principles. However, natural law conceptions continued to prevail where moral issues were overriding. Thus, in the decade preceding the Civil War, efforts to circumvent the Fugitive Slave Act gave temporary vitality to the claims for a law-deciding jury. Arguments for jury nullification were based on the jury's alleged right to decide the constitutional and moral validity of the Act and of prosecutions under it.

By the late nineteenth century, criticism of the intelligence of the average juror, insistence on the scientific nature of law (which made intelligence crucial to the understanding of law) and the affirmation of the principle of legal certainty meant that even the jury's role as fact finder came under attack.

60. E.g., Commonwealth v. Porter, 51 Mass. (10 Metc.) 263 (1845), Sparf and Hansen v. United States, 156 U.S. 51 (1895).

Today it is clear in almost every American jurisdiction that the court alone decides questions of law. Maryland and Indiana preserve the jury's law-deciding role in their constitutions, but even in these states jurors are expected to follow the law as given to them by the court. Current attacks on the jury are generally on the jury as fact finder. However, the idea of the jury as law-decider has not died. It is a conception that throughout history has found favor among those whose moral authority was greater than their political power. Individuals who seek morally to justify "illegal" action continue to argue for the jury's right to decide questions of law. (The most recent stimuli to claims of this sort were the protests against the Vietnam war.[61]) The jury, with the power of the general verdict, may continue to do just that.

B. A BRIEF FOR THE LAW-DECIDING JURY

As we have seen, the general assumption that questions of law are for the judge and those of fact for the jury is, in this country, of relatively recent origin. In the article that follows, Professor Jon Van Dyke discusses some of the important cases that mark the rise of this assumption and argues for a return to the earlier view.

VAN DYKE, THE JURY AS A POLITICAL INSTITUTION

The Center Magazine, 17–26 (March 1970).

* * *

Although the American jury is still praised as a bastion of democracy, standing between oppressive governments and the people, most of today's American judges in fact do everything they can to emasculate the jury until the only role left for jurors is to review the facts and then rubber-stamp the application of the law for the government.

In every criminal case in California, for instance, the jury is given the following instruction on the limitations of its power:

Ladies and Gentlemen of the Jury:

It becomes my duty as judge to instruct you concerning the law applicable to this case, and it is your duty as jurors to follow the law as I shall state it to you.

The function of the jury is to try the issues of fact that are presented by the allegations in the information filed in this court and the defendant's plea of "not guilty."

This duty you should perform uninfluenced by pity for the defendant or by passion or prejudice against him. * * *

You are to be governed solely by the evidence introduced in this trial and the law as stated to you by me. The law forbids you to be governed by mere sentiment, conjecture, sympathy, passion, public opinion, or public feeling. Both the People and the defendant have a right to demand, and they do demand and expect, that you will conscientiously and dispassionately consider and weigh the evidence and apply the law of the case, and that you will reach a just verdict, regardless of what the consequences may be. * * *

Appellate judges typically justify such restrictive instructions by saying that if jurors were given greater leeway they would be more likely to follow their prejudices than their consciences. If jurors were permitted to pass upon the appropriateness of a law, appellate judges say, then the

---

61. See, e.g., Sax, Conscience and Anarchy: The Prosecution of War Resisters, 42 Yale Review 483 (1968).

rule of law would be replaced by the rule of lawlessness.

* * *

The most forceful American advocate of limiting the jury's function to finding the facts was Supreme Court Justice Joseph Story in the early nineteenth century. While sitting as a trial judge in a case involving the transportation of slaves along the coast of Africa, Story was presented with the argument that the jury can judge the law as well as the facts. Story conceded that the jurors have the "physical power to disregard the law, as laid down to them by the court," but, he continued, they do not have the "moral right to decide the law according to their own notions or pleasures."

He went on to say: "On the contrary, I hold it the most sacred constitutional right of every party accused of a crime that the jury should respond as to the facts, and the court as to the law. It is the duty of the court to instruct the jury as to the law and it is the duty of the jury to follow the law as it is laid down by the court. This is the right of every citizen, and it is his only protection. If the jury were at liberty to settle the law for themselves, the effect would be not only that the law itself would be most uncertain, from the different views which different juries might take of it, but in case of error there would be no remedy or redress by the injured party, for the court would not have any right to review the law as it had been settled by the jury. Every person accused as a criminal has a right to be tried according to the law of the land, the fixed law of the land, and not by the law as a jury may understand it, or choose, from wantonness or ignorance or accidental mistake, to interpret it. If I thought that the jury were the proper

judges of the law in criminal cases, I should hold it my duty to abstain from the responsibility of stating the law to them upon any such trial. But believing as I do, that every citizen has a right to be tried by the law and according to the law, [and] that it is my privilege and truest shield against oppression and wrong, I feel it my duty to state my views fully and openly on the present occasion."[62]

* * *

Story's successor in leading the judicial campaign to limit jury freedom was Supreme Court Justice Benjamin R. Curtis. In 1851, Curtis was sitting as trial judge in a case involving a violation of the Fugitive Slave Act. The lawyer for the defendant began his summation to the jury by arguing, "This being a criminal case, the jury were rightfully the judges of the law as well as of the fact." If, he continued, any of the jurors believed the statute "to be unconstitutional, they were bound by their oaths to disregard any direction to the contrary which the court might give them.[63] Curtis interrupted the argument at this point and rendered a lengthy opinion rejecting the assertion. * * * If, Curtis said, the jurors were permitted to decide questions of law, then they could overturn decisions of the Supreme Court, the purpose of the statute would be subverted, and uniform interpretations of the law would not be possible.

In making this argument, Curtis was raising a straw man even within the context of this case, and the argument is certainly inapplicable to the contentions raised by lawyers in * * * [modern] cases of conscience and protest. No lawyer is asking that juries be allowed to reverse a decision of the Supreme Court or even that any jury's decision should have effect be-

62. United States v. Battiste, 24 F.Cas. 1042, 1043 (No. 14,545) (C.C.D.Mass.1835). This footnote and others are taken from an expanded version of this article in 16 Cath.Law. 244 (1970).

63. United States v. Morris, 26 F.Cas. 1323, 1331 (No. 15,815) (C.C.D.Mass.1851).

yond the confines of the specific case being tried. The contention is simply that within one courtroom and with regard to one set of facts the impaneled jurors should have the discretion to refuse to apply the law to one defendant.

The rulings of Justices Story and Curtis had wide impact throughout the country, but each was only the decision of an individual judge and hence was only as influential as it was persuasive. In 1895, the full Supreme Court finally considered the question and, quoting extensively from the decisions of Story and Curtis, agreed with the conclusion of the individual judges by a vote of seven to two. The case, Sparf and Hansen vs. United States,[64] involved two sailors accused of having thrown overboard a third on an American vessel near Tahiti. The sailors were charged with the crime of murder; their defense was that what they did was the less serious offense of manslaughter. The defendants asked the judge to tell the jurors that it was within their power to return a verdict of either murder or manslaughter. The judge refused, saying there was no evidence that would support a verdict of manslaughter. Though he conceded it was within the power of the jury to return a verdict of manslaughter, he maintained that such a conclusion would not be legally defensible.

The majority opinion of the Supreme Court spends forty-two pages reviewing the earlier decisions and comes to the conclusion that because we cannot tolerate allowing jurors to increase the penalties or create laws on their own, we cannot tolerate allowing them to reduce the penalties or nullify laws. The reasoning parallels that of Justices Story and Curtis and suffers from the same inability to distinguish between the two directions a jury can move. Even though no one in the case before the Court argued that the jury should

be allowed to create its own crimes or to render stiffer punishment than the law allows, the Court was haunted by that specter. Because the Supreme Court could not distinguish between lowering and raising the punishment, it deprived the jurors of the power to do either.

In the Court's words: "* * * If it be the function of the jury to decide the law as well as the facts—if the function of the Court be only advisory as to the law—why should the Court interfere for the protection of the accused against what it deems an error of the jury in matter of law?"[65]

* * * Modern courts must stop relying on the inapplicable reasoning of Sparf and Hansen,[66] however, because it is clear that the distinction the Supreme Court was unable to make in 1895 can be made today.

One example of a system in which the jury is given the power of mercy but not of vengeance is found in Maryland. The Maryland constitution reads: "In the trial of all criminal cases the jury shall be the judge of the law as well as the facts," and under this provision the following instruction is given to the jury in every criminal case:

Members of the jury, this is a criminal case and under the Constitution and the laws of the State of Maryland in a criminal case the jury are the judges of the law as well as of the facts in the case. So that whatever I tell you about the law, while it is intended to be helpful to you in reaching a just and proper verdict in the case, it is not binding upon you as members of the jury and you may accept the law as you apprehend it to be in the case.

* * * Even critics of jury freedom concede that in Maryland criminal trials are conducted with fair success and justice. To protect the accused against a jury that might be tempted to act improperly, a

---

64. 156 U.S. 51 (1895).
65. Id. at 101.

66. See, e.g., United States v. Moylan, 417 F.2d 1002, 1005–07 (4th Cir. 1969).

number of safeguards have been built into the trial process. The judge decides all questions of the admissibility of evidence. If either party requests the judge to do so, he must give the jury an advisory instruction on the law. If the trial judge thinks there is insufficient evidence to support a jury verdict of guilty, he is empowered to direct a verdict of acquittal. If the jury has misapplied the law to the prejudice of the accused, the trial judge can set the verdict aside and order a new trial. Similarly, the Maryland Supreme Court can review the sufficiency of the evidence to sustain a conviction if the defendant argues on appeal that the jury has convicted improperly. The defendant, therefore, has the benefit of a jury determination on the applicability of the law, but is protected from a jury that might use its power to his detriment.

* * * If we are not going to give the jury the right to nullify the law, is the institution of the jury worth preserving? Are jurors good enough fact finders that we should maintain the institution with its huge expense and aggravation solely to decide facts? Are juries essential to insure fundamental fairness in the determination of facts?

* * *

"[T]he average man, it is said, reacts favorably neither to the notion that matters he knows to be complex are being decided by other average men, nor to the way the jury system distorts the process of adjudication." [67]

* * *

It has not been shown that jurors are better fact finders than judges; quite probably they are worse. Why then do we impanel a million jurors in eighty thousand criminal trials and an untold addi-

tional number in civil trials each year? Are we throwing away our money because of some unfounded illusion? Or do we preserve the jury because, though we will not admit it, we really want the jury to do more than find facts?

Striking examples of the difference between the rhetoric applied to juries and the real goals that lie behind our continuing adherence to the jury system can be found in two cases decided by the Supreme Court in the spring of 1968. In Duncan v. Louisiana,[68] the Supreme Court ruled that the Sixth Amendment right to a jury trial applied to the states through the Fourteenth Amendment. The Court in its introductory remarks speaks of a jury's value in insuring a "fair trial," and discusses the jury as being "fundamental to the American scheme of justice." But as the opinion progresses, it becomes clear that the real importance of the jury is not its fact-finding but its political role. Writing for the majority, Justice White gives the following justification for the jury:

"The guaranties of jury trial in the federal and state constitutions reflect a profound judgment about the way in which law should be enforced and justice administered. A right to jury trial is granted to criminal defendants in order to prevent oppression by the government. Those who wrote our constitutions knew from history and experience that it was necessary to protect against unfounded criminal charges brought to eliminate enemies and against judges too responsive to the voice of higher authority. * * * Beyond this, the jury trial provisions in the federal and state constitutions reflect a fundamental decision about the exercise of official power—a reluctance to entrust plenary powers over the life and liberty of the citizen to one judge or to a group of judges. Fear of unchecked power, so typical of our

67. Duncan v. Louisiana, 391 U.S. 145, 188–89 (1968) (Harlan, J., joined by Stewart, J., dissenting).

68. 391 U.S. 145 (1968).

state and federal government in other respects, found expression in the criminal law in this insistence upon community participation in the determination of guilt or innocence. The deep commitment of the nation to the right of jury trial in serious criminal cases as a defense against arbitrary law enforcement qualifies for protection under the due process clause of the Fourteenth Amendment, and must therefore be respected by the states." [69]

* * *

America's founding fathers argued repeatedly and forcefully for the principle of jury nullification. * * * Perhaps more significantly, the first Chief Justice of the United States, John Jay, recognized the need to tell a jury it had the power to ignore judicial instructions. In a jury trial before the full Supreme Court, Jay told the jurors:

"It may not be amiss, here, gentlemen, to remind you of the good old rule that on questions of fact, it is the province of the jury, on questions of law it is the province of the court to decide. But it must be observed that by the same law, which recognizes this reasonable distribution of jurisdiction, you have, nevertheless, a right to take upon yourself the judge of both, and to determine the law as well as the fact in controversy. On this, and on every other occasion, however, we have no doubt, you will pay that respect which is due to the opinion of the court: for as, on the one hand, it is presumed that juries are the best judges of facts; it is, on the other hand, presumable that the courts are the best judges of law. But still, both objects are lawfully within your power of decision." [70]

* * *

A second decision of the Supreme Court, Witherspoon v. State of Illinois,[71] rendered two weeks after *Duncan,* confirmed the

view that the Supreme Court is conscious of the jury's political role and is willing to strengthen that role. Witherspoon was sentenced to death by a jury from which all persons who had any doubts whether they could impose the death penalty were excluded. This procedure followed an Illinois statute that said the judge should excuse every juror who states that "he has conscientious scruples against capital punishment or that he is opposed to the same." * * *

The Supreme Court's refusal to allow this result is ostensibly based on the need for a fair and impartial jury. * * *

The most telling clue to the Supreme Court's view of the jury's role is found in a footnote to the *Witherspoon* decision: "One of the most important functions any jury can perform in making a selection [between life and death] is to maintain a link between contemporary community values and the penal system—a link without which the determination of punishment could hardly reflect 'the evolving standards of decency that mark the progress of a maturing society.' " [72]

If the jury is to maintain this link, then it must be given the authority to reject judicial instructions when they conflict with the values of the community.

* * *

One other event took place in 1968, this time in the Congress, that appears to be a small blow in the favor of recognizing the jury's political role. Congress passed the Jury Selection and Service Act of 1968 to insure that juries in federal courts are a true cross-section of the community. This parallels the thinking of the founding fathers, who specified in the Sixth Amendment to the Constitution that in all criminal cases the jury must be drawn from "the state and district wherein the crime shall

---

69. Id. at 155–56.

70. State of Georgia v. Brailsford, 3 U.S. (3 Dall.) 1, 4 (1794).

71. 391 U.S. 510 (1968).

72. Id. at 519 n. 15, quoting Trop v. Dulles, 356 U.S. 86, 101 (1958).

have been committed, which district shall have been previously ascertained by law. * * * "

* * *

[A]t least one court, the U. S. Court of Appeals for the First Circuit, seems to have moved in the direction of acknowledging and respecting, if not directly encouraging, the jury's power to nullify laws. In the proceedings against Dr. Spock and his co-defendants, the trial judge put to the jury, in addition to the general issue of guilty or not guilty, ten special questions to be answered "Yes" or "No" in arriving at their decision. The Court of Appeals criticized this action in strong language: "In a criminal case a court may not order the jury to return a verdict of guilty, no matter how overwhelming the evidence of guilt. * * * Put simply, the right to be tried by a jury of one's peers finally exacted from the king would be meaningless if the king's judges could call the turn." * * * A little farther on, the Court of Appeals adds: " – – – the jury, as the conscience of the community, must be permitted to look at more than logic – – –. If it were otherwise, there would be no more reason why a verdict should not be directed against a defendant in a criminal case than in a civil one. The constitutional guaranties of due process and trial by jury require that a criminal defendant be afforded the full protection of a jury unfettered, directly or indirectly." [73]

* * *

One problem is whether the jury's power to nullify should extend equally to crimes of violence as to crimes of conscience. Certainly the need for the power seems more evident in crimes of conscience, and it is in the realm of crimes of conscience that most of the debate over jury nullification has taken place. In a case of conscience, the defendant is being prose-cuted because he has protested against a policy of the state. The victims of the crime are the persons who are in power at the time and who are making policy for the government. Cases of seditious libel and draft-card burning are obvious examples of situations in which the government is the victim of the crime. The jury stands between the policymakers and the defendant and can repudiate the state's policy with a verdict of acquittal.

Some commentators, worried about Southern juries who have acquitted white defendants despite strong evidence that the defendants killed blacks, have argued that juries should not be told they have the power to nullify in a trial involving a violent crime. * * * [T]he solution to the problem of Southern juries is not to deprive them of their power to nullify but to make them more representative of the community, i.e. to have more black citizens on the jury rolls.

In a non-Southern context, juries will ordinarily not even be tempted to exercise their power to nullify the law in a crime of violence. The jury is unlikely to ignore the law and the judge's instructions, because the people—and the jurors as representatives of the people—are the victims of these crimes. There are times, however, when the power to nullify becomes important even with regard to a crime of violence. Juries have recurringly nullified the law by acquitting a defendant charged with murder when the evidence shows that he ended the life of a relative or patient whose suffering from an incurable illness had become unendurable. Most appellate courts have therefore recognized that the concept of jury nullification should apply to crimes of violence if it applies at all, as is evidenced by the cases of *Sparf and Hansen, Duncan,* and *Witherspoon,* all involving acts of violence.

* * *

73. United States v. Spock, 416 F.2d 165, 180–182 (1st Cir. 1969).

There are three types of situations when the added safeguard of jury discretion is particularly important: (1) the prosecutor may be overzealous in bringing a prosecution because a particularly prominent or controversial person is involved or because of some personal relationship he has to one of the parties; (2) the trial judge may not be able to view the case objectively because of some personal eccentricity or deep-seated bias; and (3) the government may be the victim of the crime in a way that makes it impossible for the prosecutor not to prosecute or for the judge to dismiss the matter.

In each of these three situations, but most particularly in the third, the jury can act mercifully when the policeman, the prosecutor, and judge are unable to be merciful, because the jury will not be called to answer for its acts.

As Judge Learned Hand once put it: "The institution of trial by jury—especially in criminal cases—has its hold upon public favor chiefly for two reasons. The individual can forfeit his liberty—to say nothing of his life—only at the hands of those who, unlike any official, are in no wise accountable, directly or indirectly, for what they do, and who at once separate and melt anonymously in the community from which they came. Moreover, since if they acquit their verdict is final, no one is likely to suffer whose conduct they do not morally disapprove; and this introduces a slack into the enforcement of law, tempering its rigor by the mollifying influence of current ethical conventions. A trial by any jury, however small, preserves both these fundamental elements and a trial by a judge preserves neither, at least to anything like the same degree."

* * *

Jurors should not therefore be told by the trial judge, as they are told in California and in almost every other jurisdiction, that "it is your duty as jurors to follow the law as I shall state it to you." Jurors should be told instead that although they are a public body bound to give respectful attention to the laws, they have the final authority to decide whether or not to apply a given law to the acts of the defendant on trial before them. More explicitly, jurors should be told that they represent their communities and that it is appropriate to bring into their deliberations the feelings of the community and their own feelings based on conscience. Finally, they should be told that, despite their respect for the law, nothing would bar them from acquitting the defendant if they feel that the law as applied to the factual situation before them would produce an inequitable or unjust result.

Problem XII–24. A legislator in your state has proposed a bill which would give juries trying criminal cases the power to decide certain questions of law and would require judges to inform juries of the existence of this power. The bill specifically provides that the jury may pass judgment on the following questions:

A. Whether the defendant's behavior is in fact prohibited by the statute the defendant is alleged to have violated.

B. Whether the defendant's behavior should be punished as criminal, regardless of what statutes appear to apply.

C. Whether the statute the defendant is alleged to have violated is constitutional, both as enacted and as applied.

D. Whether evidence should be admitted or excluded under applicable evidence law.

The bill also allows counsel to argue any issue of law to the jury that the jury has authority to decide.

Do you support the general concept of this bill? Do you support the bill in all its aspects? Why or why not? What aspects of this bill do you think Van Dyke would support? What aspects would he not support? Would you support all or part of a similar bill applying to civil cases? Why or why not?

Problem XII–25. In a portion of his article omitted above Van Dyke writes:

> One cannot help but feel * * * that the Supreme Court [in Duncan v. Louisiana] thought that a fairly constituted jury passing on Duncan's alleged crime would have exercised its political power of nullification as advocated by the country's early leaders. Gary Duncan, a black nineteen-year-old, was given a sixty-day jail sentence because he jostled a white youth after a discussion in which Duncan was apparently trying to make peace between whites and blacks. A representative jury, numbering black as well as white citizens, might well have refused to send Duncan to jail for this act. [at 23]

Did the Duncan jury need the power to decide questions of law to decide the case in the manner that Van Dyke suggests is appropriate? Did they need to be told that they had such power? Had they been told that they had law-deciding power, do you think the result in Duncan would have been different?

Problem XII–26. Professor Van Dyke notes that some commentators fear that if juries were given law-deciding power and told of that power they might exercise it to treat unpopular defendants more harshly than they can be treated under enacted law, and they might use that power to acquit defendants whose actions against unpopular victims are supported in the community. One response that Van Dyke makes to these arguments in a portion of his article omitted above is that juries act in these ways today, although they do not have law-deciding power and are not told that they do. Thus Van Dyke does not think his suggested changes will make the unpopular worse off or the harasser of the unpopular better off than they are under the current system. **Do you accept this argument? Do you believe that informing the jury that they have the power to decide questions of law would not change the incidence of "undesirable" jury law-making? May the basic argument be turned against Van Dyke? Under the current system, have there not been trials where juries acquitted defendants who, under technical legal rules, were guilty of crimes? If so, why do we need the change Van Dyke suggests? Could you draft a law, allowing juries to nullify the law only where defendants acted from conscience, which would allow the jury to acquit someone who had burned draft records in clear violation of the law, but would not allow the jury to acquit someone who had burned the home that a black family had bought in a white neighborhood?**

Problem XII–27. Dougherty is charged with trespass to property and vandalism. The charges arise out of an anti-war protest directed at Dow

Chemical Company. Dougherty asks the trial judge to give the jury an instruction on jury nullification to the effect that even though the jury may find the defendant technically guilty, it has the power to return a not guilty verdict if it finds that, under the circumstances of the particular case, justice and morality require that an exception be created to the law. **Should the requested instruction be given?**

SECTION III. THE RULES OF EVIDENCE IN BENCH TRIALS

When the right to jury trial, which exists in criminal cases and most civil actions, is waived by the parties, both factual and legal issues are resolved by a single judge. Although the rules of evidence in bench trials are, in theory, the same as they are in jury trials, there must be practical differences in the way they operate. This is because the judge usually must hear disputed evidence in order to decide whether to admit it. Thus the judge, unlike the jury, knows the contents of evidence ruled inadmissible. This knowledge may color the judge's general view of the facts even if the judge does not consciously rely on it.

This is the only necessary difference between the way the rules of evidence operate in bench trials and the way they operate in jury trials.[74] Trial judges could treat issues of admissibility in bench trials in the same way that they treat them in jury trials, and appellate courts could review errors of admission and exclusion in the same way no matter who found the facts. Often, however, the identity of the fact finder is crucial to the way in which evidentiary questions are resolved. Devices used by the trial and appellate courts make appellate reversal for the erroneous admission of evidence considerably less likely when trial has been to a judge than it is when trial has been to a jury. In the article that follows, A. Leo Levin and Harold Cohen discuss these devices and present their views on how the rules of evidence should operate in nonjury criminal cases.

LEVIN & COHEN, THE EXCLUSIONARY RULES IN NONJURY CRIMINAL CASES

119 U.Pa.L.Rev. 905–932 (1971).

It should occasion no surprise that the vast welter of doctrine which has become our law of evidence is not applied with equal rigor when a judge rather than a jury

74. In theory, even this is not necessary, for a second judge could be made available to pass on the admissibility of evidence. However, except for matters which might be disposed of before a second judge at a preliminary hearing, this procedure is too expensive to be practical.

Although expressions of concern are rare some judges have noted their uneasiness about their ability to disregard evidence they exclude at bench trials. Recently a few have tried to do something about this. For example, three judges in the United States District Court for the Northern District of Illinois have established a procedure whereby in any case in which a jury waiver appears likely, pretrial rulings on evidentiary issues are referred from the judge who would try the case to another judge. Thus, if the evidence is excluded the judge trying the case never learns of it. Judge Prentice Marshall, who has described the process in several talks, believes that it has worked well and reports that he and the other judges are happy with it.

sits as trier of the fact. At least two major policy considerations support the prevailing practice under which the exclusionary rules are applied with far less stringency if there is no jury. First, our law of evidence has long been viewed as a product of the jury system, of the need to shelter untrained citizens from the temptation to accept uncritically that which may be unreliable and of doubtful credibility. Stated differently, the judge, a professional experienced in evaluating evidence, may more readily be relied upon to sift and to weigh critically evidence which we fear to entrust to a jury.

Secondly, there has been, for some decades at least, a basic dissatisfaction with the "lush exuberance of doctrines which bloom in the digests," with the plethora of rules and exceptions which deter the progress of a trial and multiply the risk of reversal at every turn. * * * "It might have been more expedient," Professor McCormick has suggested, "if these rules had been, at least in the main, discarded in trials before judges."

This has not, however, been the course of the law in most jurisdictions. The point of departure, the prevailing theory at least, applies basically the same governing doctrine in trials before judges as before juries. True, the same strictness in application will not be demanded; the sharp edges of the exclusionary rules will be blunted and their impact softened. Yet, by and large, as a matter of formal doctrine no separate rules permit admission in the nonjury case where the same evidence would be proscribed before a jury.

To limit the inquiry to formal doctrine, however, is to take too narrow a view, for the law has countenanced techniques for avoiding formal doctrine altogether by allowing the trial judge to hear objections to evidence without ruling on them. Even if he should choose to rule, and rules erroneously, he may be saved from reversal because a different set of rules govern appellate review of evidence questions in the nonjury case. The net result is that, insofar as the admissibility of evidence is concerned, the law in operation differs substantially from that in the hornbooks. * * *

Where evidentiary questions are concerned, reviewing courts invoke new and interesting principles. Presumptions of propriety govern, ascribing to the trial judge—so long as he sits without a jury—the wisdom to have disregarded the inadmissible and to have relied solely on the evidence which he later adjudged competent. At times the presumption may appear a bit tenuous, for the very judge who has been found to have erred in favor of admissibility is presumed to have gained new wisdom, if not a measure of sheer omniscience, by the end of the case when he is obliged to weigh and assess the evidence and is presumed to have disregarded that which he earlier erroneously admitted. The earlier error is thus rendered harmless by power of presumption. However one may view the reasoning or the decision, such holdings do not affect formal evidence law. In theory, the rules of admissibility which should be applied in subsequent cases have not changed. To hold error harmless is, after all, to concede that there was error. In practical terms, however, there is no sanction for failure to follow the applicable "law." The formal rules must ultimately ring hollow.

The courts appear persistent in refusing either to apply formal evidence doctrine or to change it. This very persistence, an almost stubborn adherence to formal rules which are denied substance and reality, suggests the need to re-evaluate the situations in which the problems arise, to examine the exclusionary rules involved, and to inquire whether there are not some which should be applied in the nonjury case and others which should not. The former deserve to be enforced at the appellate level; the latter require change.

THE ROLES OF JUDGE AND JURY   Ch. 12

Candid recognition of their inapplicability would be preferable to the present pattern of fiction and unreality.

We consider next the other device, that of avoiding erroneous rulings by simply not ruling, the technique of avoiding difficult decisions by deciding not to decide. Patently, this is not an available alternative when a jury sits as trier of the fact and the judge must determine what they shall and shall not hear. The problem in the non-jury case, however, is different, for here the judge screens the evidence to determine what he himself shall consider. The alternative of not ruling becomes practicable and has in fact been sanctioned by usage. Admitting hearsay for what it is worth and hearing evidence subject to a later ruling which is never made have become acceptable means of avoiding decisions concerning the evidence. * * *

Inherent in this procedure, it must be obvious, is the risk of convictions based on improper evidence and immune from meaningful appellate review. Indeed, it renders evidence doctrine irrelevant, for there is little point to delineating the finer points of the applicable law if the trial judge is encouraged not to rule even in the face of timely objection by defense counsel. In the criminal trial, particularly, there are significant risks, operating primarily against the defendant, and in such cases we seek with some effort, to minimize those risks. We espouse a willingness to free many guilty in the effort to avoid convicting even a few innocent. This is a tradition which runs deep, and, however far from the mark we may come in the implementation, the oft-repeated articulation of the values which we hold is in itself significant.

This does not yet argue for applying the full panoply of the rules of exclusion with force and vigor to the nonjury criminal case, but it does argue for the need for critical analysis, and if such analysis bespeaks the drawing of lines or the fixing of guidelines we may, perhaps, avoid the incidence

of injustice which unfettered discretion tends to spawn.

It has been wisely observed that "judges, being flesh and blood, are subject to the same emotions and human frailties as affect other members of the species." If all the rules of evidence amounted to no more than prophylactic devices to guard against the lack of experience and supposed lack of sophistication of the average jury in assessing the credibility of evidence and in fixing its probative weight, there might be little need for invoking them in the jury-waived case. We might then free the judge, not by permitting him to hide his rulings or presuming him error-less, but by accommodating doctrine to reality. Presumptively, we should then impose no more onerous restrictions on the judge than on a trial examiner in an administrative hearing.

But the exclusionary rules in criminal cases have, in significant measure, a different focus. Many are designed to minimize the risk of conviction because defendant has been shown a bad man; they deal with the potential for prejudice, with emotional impact, rather than with the risk of intellectual error in tracing a chain of inferences or in recognizing the pitfalls of double hearsay. Other rules, such as that barring an involuntary confession however reliable it may be, are designed to serve extrinsic policies even at the cost of quality in the trial process, a less rational resolution of an issue of fact. In situations involving such rules it would be wrong to assume a priori that a judge would be immune from prejudice * * *.

We propose to consider the problem of rules of evidence in nonjury criminal cases in three selected areas. First, that presented by evidence of a defendant's prior criminal record. These cases present in sharp outline the potential for prejudice. Moreover, in the normal course, there is no reason for the judge to rule the evidence admissible, to "receive the evidence for what it is worth," or to defer decision. For the judge to do any of these should constitute error.

Closely related is the offer of evidence of other crimes. These cases present a similar potential for prejudice. However, they also demand serious concern for an important countervailing consideration, the need to assure at least a minimum level of administrative convenience, to avoid the unmanageable trial or interminable series of trials and retrials which, in the long run, cannot possibly serve the needs of society.

We suggest that the judge be required to rule, to recognize explicitly the impropriety of considering inadmissible evidence of this type in the process of decision. However, we also recognize the need for an added measure of flexibility and suggest that he be afforded greater latitude in the nonjury trial than in the jury trial. Certainly, it would be folly to call for a mistrial where the prosecution has in good faith made an offer of proof concerning evidence of other crimes which the judge promptly rejects.

Secondly, we consider problems of the involuntary confession and related exclusionary rules of constitutional dimension. Here again the prejudice potential is sharp and clear, certainly undiminished and perhaps having even greater force. Problems of administrative convenience are also present, but with the relevant exclusionary rules of constitutional dimension these require fresh analysis and a somewhat different resolution. The importance of the underlying policies together with the risk of prejudice are, in our view, sufficient reason for imposing some measure of added administrative burdens, even to the point of requiring, where feasible, that one judge rule on admissibility of confessions at preliminary hearings and a different judge sit to determine guilt or innocence. And if the safeguards of the process make

for more jury waivers, where such waivers are permitted, the added administrative cost will have been amply recompensed.

Finally, we turn to cases of hearsay evidence. Here we have the analogy of the administrative experience and the classic case of judicial experience at the task of discrimination in the effort to measure probative weight. The process would, in basic terms, be one of distinguishing credible evidence from that unworthy of belief, not through categorization in terms of artificial exceptions to the hearsay rule, but in terms of the circumstances of the individual case. New procedural safeguards, a broader scope of appellate review on the issue of sufficiency would be necessary, but both the quality of the result and the added efficiency of the process argue for this much-needed liberalization.

We begin with evidence of prior convictions and other crimes.

I. PRIOR CONVICTIONS AND OTHER CRIMES

Commonwealth v. Oglesby,[a] recently decided by the Pennsylvania Supreme Court, illustrates in dramatic fashion the risk of informing a trial judge of a defendant's prior record. Moreover, it underscores, at least by implication, the potential for prejudice inherent in anything less than a clear-cut ruling on the part of the trial court should the issue be presented. Defendant had been charged with carrying a concealed deadly weapon. Trial was to the judge who, at the conclusion of the case, sought as further evidence, "any additional investigation on [defendant] at all that would be relevant to the case." None was forthcoming, for the request was explicitly limited to admissible evidence and all sides appear to have conceded that the exclusionary rule should be obeyed. The weapon defendant had in his possession was a straight razor, but he testified that he was a barber going to shave a cus-

a. 438 Pa. 91, 263 A.2d 419 (1970).

tomer—circumstances which, if believed, were sufficient defense under substantive law. The judge, with a candor as refreshing as it appears atypical, continued to speculate for the record on defendant's motive for carrying his razor and concluded by announcing, "I'm going to adjudge him guilty. Let me see his record."

Had the record of the case lapsed at this juncture, one might be tempted to speculate concerning the mental processes of the trial judge as he went about resolving the issue of reasonable doubt against defendant barber. The trial judge, however, without going off the record, announced in unambiguous terms precisely what he had done: "I had a little feeling on this and it turns out he has a record a mile long." And turning to defendant, "If I found that you had no record, that your story was unquestionably true, then I could have reconsidered my judgment and found you not guilty * * *."

The Pennsylvania Supreme Court reversed. No ruling on evidence had tainted the trial, and the holding goes to the issue of a conditional finding of guilt, of the lower court's application of an erroneous standard of "beyond a reasonable doubt." But the opinion is nonetheless instructive. It suggests, if it does not demonstrate, that judges are vulnerable to the prejudice of a prior record. Moreover, in the ordinary course of a criminal trial there should be no occasion for disclosing the substance of any prior record to the court. If a ruling is necessary, it should, in the normal case, be possible without the court learning any of the details of the record.

Judicial attitudes differ, however, and the cases are divided. Consider State v. Garcia.[b] Defendant, charged with illegal possession of marijuana, was in trouble enough. Some thirty years earlier he had been found guilty on a marijuana charge,

which was alleged as a prior conviction in the amended complaint upon which he was tried. The trial court, over objection, admitted evidence that a stolen gasoline credit card was in defendant's possession at the time of his arrest, which fact served to connect defendant with a burglary for which he was scheduled to stand trial separately. In addition, again over objection, evidence was introduced that defendant was wanted for burglary elsewhere and that he was in this country illegally. The Arizona Supreme Court had no difficulty finding it was error to admit any of this evidence. Nevertheless, it affirmed the conviction.

The holding is a troublesome one on a number of counts. First is the standard of review. "We cannot say," the opinion reads, "that it clearly appears that the finding would have been different if the evidence of other crimes had not been admitted." At best this is an unhappy standard, imposing undue burdens on a defendant who has concededly been subjected to error below. We return, however, to the more basic problem: the attitude which a reviewing court should take toward the risk of prejudice inherent in evidence of other crimes. It can, of course, be asserted that a judge is disciplined enough not to consider the forbidden evidence or, having considered it, to exclude it from the calculus of decision when he weighs the proof. This appears highly doubtful, indeed fictional, in the face of erroneous rulings in the course of the trial. Moreover, Wigmore's conclusion concerning prior crimes appears far preferable as a basis for decision:

The natural and inevitable tendency of the tribunal—whether judge or jury—is to give excessive weight to the vicious record of crime thus exhibited, and either to allow it to bear too strongly on the present charge, or to take the proof

b. 97 Ariz. 102, 397 P.2d 214 (1964); cf. People v. Guzanich, 13 Mich.App. 634, 164 N.W.2d 749 (1968).

of it as justifying a condemnation irrespective of guilt of the present charge. Moreover, the use of alleged particular acts ranging over the entire period of the defendant's life makes it impossible for him to be prepared to refute the charge, any or all of which may be mere fabrications.

*   *   *

We need not, however, limit ourselves to speculation concerning the impact on a judge of evidence of other crimes. Empirical data is available. In their classic study, *The American Jury,* Professors Kalven and Zeisel devote a full chapter to disagreements between judge and jury where additional facts are available to the judge which, generally by application of the exclusionary rules, are kept from the jury. Some are cases in which the judge alone knew defendant personally, or was aware that a guilty plea had been withdrawn or that a blood test had been refused or suppressed. But by far the most significant category to account for the judge's willingness to convict where the jury ultimately acquits is the situation where the judge alone knew of defendant's prior record. * * * No definitive conclusions can be drawn, however, primarily because the data regarding instances where similar additional facts were available to the judge and no disagreement resulted are not available. What is instructive, though, is the authors' analysis and conclusion. They assume that, of course, judges will decide the cases differently because they are privy to such additional, albeit inadmissible, information. Further, the data are cited in support of the exclusionary rules and the policy considerations which lie behind them. "The disagreements that are the subject of this chapter offer an interesting commentary on the merits of the exclusionary rules. Some of these cases represent the price—in 'unjustified' acquittals—which the system is willing to pay for avoiding prejudice in other cases, where

the shared information could lead to an unjust conviction." *   *   *

We have focused on the risk of prejudicing the defendant—one which, in our view, is serious enough. In general, the cases point to the desirability of avoiding difficult rulings on "insignificant" questions of evidence. But such countervailing advantages are in this situation tenuous enough, if not totally non-existent, and a trial court should not be permitted to avoid the issue by accepting the evidence "to be considered if subsequently found admissible." The evil inheres in the information being imparted to the court; absent a clear and unequivocal ruling of exclusion there is certainly no basis for indulging in a presumption of propriety on the part of the trial judge and assuming that he considered only that which should have been considered.

*   *   *

Closer questions can arise, particularly with respect to evidence of other crimes. Such evidence, tending to show defendant has committed criminal acts of which he has never been convicted and for which he is not now on trial, has a prejudice potential which, for our purposes, is no less potent than knowledge of a prior record. Standard doctrine excludes such evidence from jury consideration except in a relatively narrow range of cases where admissibility is predicated on some theory of relevance other than one merely showing defendant to be a "bad man," as in those cases where the other crimes are "so nearly identical in method as to earmark them as the handiwork of the accused." Here, too, the judge should not in the normal case be allowed to learn of such added prejudice-laden information. As a simple principle, this should suffice, but the problems, as they arise in the courtroom, are not simple and the problems of administration which emerge are significant.

The difficulty is that there are many theories of relevance under which the prosecution can seek to admit evidence of other crimes and the rules of exclusion are far from precise. Even in a jury case a great deal of testimony focused on proving other offenses may be admitted. * * * It is hard to argue that the rule of admissibility in the nonjury case should be precisely identical with what will be allowed before a jury. Feats of discrimination are expected of the jurors and it is not unreasonable to allow an added measure of tolerance where it is the judge who will be weighing the evidence.

In addition there is need to consider the realities of the trial situation. It would certainly be improper for the trial judge, sitting without a jury, summarily to exclude other-crime evidence where it is properly offered by the prosecution. But the question of admissibility may be a difficult one, and the judge may find it necessary to learn more of the prosecution's theory and of the nature of the proffered proof in order to rule. At this point a countervailing consideration enters into the equation: the value of efficient and speedy administration, the need for the trial judge to screen as well as to weigh and evaluate.

Appellate law can afford to be less rigorous and more flexible. It may be appropriate then to inquire into the subsequent course of the trial, and the acceptance or rejection of the tainted testimony by the trial judge at a later point. Suffice it here to suggest that a rule of rigorous exclusion of a defendant's prior criminal record does not preclude a more flexible view of analogous, but distinguishable, testimony concerning other crimes.

II. COERCED CONFESSIONS: THE CONSTITUTIONAL DILEMMA

Coerced confessions are constitutionally prohibited without regard to credibility or reliability. As Mr. Justice White has long since reminded us, if a court, in admitting a confession, has employed "a standard infected by the inclusion of references to probable reliability," the resultant conviction is constitutionally tainted. Such a confession is no more permissible as evidence in a jury-waived case, and if erroneously admitted and followed by conviction, that conviction is similarly tainted. This much may be taken as conceded premise; the difficult problems concern procedures.

From the point of view of a trial judge who wishes to avoid an erroneous ruling on the admissibility of a confession and who is nevertheless hesitant to deprive himself of knowledge of its contents, either of two expedients might appear attractive. The first is not to rule at all, taking the matter under advisement and never announcing a decision; the other is to postpone ruling, hold the evidence inadmissible at the end of the trial, and announce that it will not be considered in the determination of guilt or innocence. The latter course might be particularly appealing where there is other evidence sufficient to convict. In the event of review, there would not even be the need for the appellate court to resort to presumptions of propriety below. The trial judge has excluded the impermissible and the record is explicit in its statement that the tainted evidence played no role in the decision. As a matter of formal logic the record must be viewed as impeccably correct.

Neither solution commends itself as a norm for the nonjury criminal case. At some point defendant should receive a clear-cut finding on the issues presented by his challenge to the confession. * * *

For the trial judge to postpone decision presents a somewhat more difficult question, although in our view it represents a practice fraught with unnecessary risk of prejudice and one which, absent significant countervailing considerations, should be disapproved. Is there a risk that the trial judge will dissemble, ruling formally one way but allowing himself to consider "just a little bit," the fact of confession, particularly when he has learned that the confession is sufficiently rich in detail to preclude any doubt concerning its reliability?   In the case of some judges, perhaps the answer should be in the affirmative, but for us this is not the central question.   A more fundamental inquiry concerns the desirability, and perhaps ultimately the legal propriety, of having one judge rule on both the voluntariness of a confession and the ultimate issue of guilt.   This question appears in sharpest focus in cases in which there was a preliminary hearing to determine voluntariness.   * * *

Perhaps the simplest situation is that of the judge who finds a confession involuntary.   It is ruled inadmissible in evidence, but if that very judge becomes the trier of the fact on the issue of guilt, the question arises whether the judge is likely to succeed in clearing his mind of the tainted evidence.   If our analysis of proof of a defendant's prior record is correct, a negative answer is compelled a fortiori. A preliminary hearing does involve a certain amount of administrative inconvenience, but in the normal case assignment of different judges to the hearing and to the trial would not add a significant burden. Certainly, the burden would not, in most courts, be serious enough to prevail over the interest of the defendant in obtaining a trial free of that "admixture of reliability and voluntariness" against which the Supreme Court has warned us.

A subtler question, perhaps, concerns the influence of evidence of guilt on a judge's ability to rule impartially on the issue of voluntariness.   * * *

* * *

Lines should be drawn.   In the first instance it is desirable so to organize the calendar that the judge who has presided over the preliminary hearing will not be assigned to try the case if a jury has been waived.   Where a confession or an incul-patory statement has been ruled admissible, it would seem unobjectionable for the same judge to sit as trier of the fact when guilt or innocence is adjudicated.   After all, the statement will in any event be introduced into evidence and the circumstances of the making of the statement are admissible on the issue of credibility. When the trial judge, hearing the evidence concerning the circumstances surrounding the challenged interrogation, determines that the statement in question should not have been ruled admissible, we have a more difficult question.   * * * A new trial before a third judge is certainly a possibility.   * * *   It is difficult to quarrel with this further measure of solicitude for defendant, particularly if we assume that the trial judge may in fact have been influenced by inadmissible, tainted testimony.   Yet, there has been an adjudication of admissibility, and the judge whose findings are the subject of review has evidenced a particular sensitivity to the inadmissible evidence.   He has identified it and recorded his determination not to consider it in the final adjudication. Countervailing considerations of administrative convenience, not merely in the assignment of judges, but in avoiding retrials on the merits, enter.   Absent unusual circumstances, it is difficult to find a retrial required.

* * *

It is quite another matter when the issue of the voluntariness of a proffered statement has not been considered at a preliminary hearing and arises for the first time at the trial itself.   Assuming the availability of another judge, it would be highly desirable to have a "preliminary" hearing, out of the presence of the trier of the fact, to determine the admissibility of the challenged statement.   * * *   A ruling finding the evidence unobjectionable would allow the trial to proceed with the defendant accorded no less protection than in the analogous cases considered above.   If

the statement were held inadmissible, the trial could proceed without further consideration of the challenged statement. True, the trial judge would be aware of the existence of such a statement. In theory, at least, if a jury had been sitting, the very existence of a damaging statement would have been kept from them. Yet, the precise content of the statement—the extent of the damage, and the details which tend to create credibility and which so often also create the prejudice—are kept from the trier. There are, after all, countervailing considerations in a world of backlogs and interminable, insufferable delays. And there are risks in inviting and rewarding defense tactics which would necessitate new trials after investment of substantial time and judicial manpower in the trial itself.
* * *

It is of course simplistic to talk of administrative convenience in black and white terms. As a first step in the analysis we have found it useful to speak in terms of another judge being available or unavailable, but it is hardly adequate, in many cases, to stop at this point. Another judge may in fact be available, even in a one-judge judicial district, by assignment of a higher court. Conversely, in a metropolitan court with many judges, assignment of another judge for the hearing on voluntariness may, in fact, force a recess which would seriously inconvenience prosecution witnesses, occasion undesirable delays in the orderly progress of the trial, or force a mistrial if the trial judge has conflicting commitments once the trial had been delayed. These considerations are appropriately considered first at the trial level and subsequently on appeal. The nature of the offense which is the subject of the prosecution, the precise nature of the constitutional infirmity alleged, the extent of trial disruption, and the justification for first raising the objection to the evidence in mid-trial, are all relevant in considering whether in the first instance a different judge should hold the "preliminary" hearing and, separately, whether failure to do so is reversible error.

* * *

III. HEARSAY EVIDENCE

Much of the controversy concerning reform of the law of evidence has centered on the hearsay rule. * * * But, for all the difference of opinion concerning the path which reform ought to follow, there is substantial agreement on a number of significant propositions which are relevant to our inquiry and which define and sharply delimit the alternatives realistically available in proposing rules to govern the nonjury criminal trial. First is the dissatisfaction, so widespread as to approach unanimity, with the present state of the law. Nevertheless, no one seriously contends for the exclusion of all hearsay. Our courts would be deprived of too much which is too valuable. * * * By the same token, there is no significant support for the opposite alternative, to admit all hearsay. So much that is dross would be included that every serious proposal includes at least minimal safeguards, guidelines for exclusion.

If, then, we are to retain a hearsay rule but provide for exceptions, the nub of the problem must be the nature of the exceptions and their content. It is precisely at this point that the anomaly of the present system obtrudes. The purpose of a hearsay exception is to provide the trier of the fact with trustworthy evidence, absent direct evidence which is more probative. Necessity and reliability, these are the two great principles which are said to govern. The present system, however, operating by category and by class, fails too often in the attempt. The exceptions regularly exclude evidence that has a higher probative force than the evidence they admit. This unhappy result might almost be a fair price to pay for simplicity and efficiency in the trial process. Ease of administration should be a significant factor, but it has been neither achieved nor approached. Instead, complexity compounded appears to be the rule. * * *

These points bear elaboration if we are to gain a realistic appreciation of the pressures which have developed to relieve the trial judge sitting without a jury of the obligation to apply the full panoply of the law of hearsay in all its pristine rigor. * * * [T]he emphasis on category invites the creation of subcategories; the rules spawn sub-rules. Admissions of a party opponent gain entry when he himself is the declarant. But this is not the end to the matter. There are authorized admissions, adoptive admissions and vicarious admissions. Dying declarations are admissible, but only in prosecutions for homicide. Thus, the identical out-of-court statement is admissible when offered by the prosecution if the offense is murder, but not at the instance of the plaintiff who seeks a money recovery. * * * Finally, distinctions are drawn in terms of the use to which admissible evidence may be put. It is familiar law that prior inconsistent statements may be offered to "neutralize," or to impeach, but not as substantive evidence of the matter stated. Whatever may be said for preserving these distinctions in the jury trial, with only the judge learning the purport of the challenged testimony as he screens the permissible from the impermissible, keeping the latter from the triers of the fact, though not from himself, by way of preliminary rulings, it hardly seems the way of wisdom to require rigid adherence to doctrine where the judge himself tries the fact. Trial judges have sought, and appellate courts have condoned, a more direct approach to that evidence which, although hearsay, is considered both reliable and trustworthy.

The law has allowed the trial judge freedom from the fetters of the rules, the categories and subcategories. In the main, however, it has not done so by promulgating a different standard for the nonjury

case, but by allowing the judge not to rule and by indulging in presumptions when he has ruled erroneously. Reasoned arguments for changing this approach and recognizing the desirability of a different approach in the nonjury case have not been lacking: the ability of the judge, by reason of training and experience, to assess the probative weight of out-of-court declarations and to separate and to disregard the dross is certainly a significant factor. The added flexibility in the ordering of a trial which the absence of a jury permits, thus allowing a litigant to combat unfair surprise, has also been pointed out.

Certainly, not all hearsay need be admitted, even in a nonjury case. Standards, however, are not lacking: "the kind of evidence on which responsible persons are accustomed to rely in serious affairs," has the twin advantages of flexibility and ease of administration. Candid recognition of a rule allowing such hearsay to be admissible in the nonjury criminal case would be a substantial advance. Certainly, it would contribute to simplicity and efficiency in the trial process, obviating the need for the judge constantly to be concerned with the latest version of the exceptions and their technicalities. It would not do so at the expense of reliability and trustworthiness, but rather by means of making these the tests and pursuing directly that which has always been viewed as the ultimate goal.

Adoption of such a proposal, one which has been recommended and which we endorse, would not effect radical change in the nature of criminal prosecutions. True, it would obviate the need for fictive presumptions and buried rulings. It would not, however, obviate the need for compliance with the constitutional requirement that a defendant be afforded his right of confrontation. The limits of the right have yet to be defined with precision, but at the least the prosecution would find it necessary to obtain the presence of witnesses who, with diligence, can be produced. A realistic opportunity for cross-examination would be assured defendants, and the Supreme Court has given ample notice that no redefinition of hearsay doctrine will be permitted to subvert that right. But the Court has made it at least equally clear that the Constitution will not be read so as to import all of the finer distinctions of the hearsay rule under the rubric confrontation. So long as the basic policies of the right of confrontation are adequately served, the states remain free to bring a fresh approach to the hearsay rule. In short, the right of confrontation clearly limits what a court may do, even in the nonjury case, but the constraints are not those of present doctrine nor is the path of change limited to revising and refining the categories which currently obtain. And, of no lesser significance, the right of confrontation operates on behalf of the defendant. No similar constraints operate against him, allowing for a flexibility in development already in evidence in more than one jurisdiction.

Adoption of a rule which allows the trial judge to admit hearsay simply because it is "the kind of evidence on which responsible persons are accustomed to rely in serious affairs" could permit founding a conviction entirely on evidence inadmissible both under present rules and under the rules which would then, as now, obtain in jury cases within the same jurisdiction. * * * Thus, the possibility of such a conviction must be faced and seriously considered. It need not, however, be viewed as a disadvantage or a reason for rejecting the basic rule. The central problem is one of sufficiency of the evidence to convict. True, the willingness to relax the rules of admissibility should imply an added willingness on the part of appellate courts to consider afresh, and free from artificialities which often obtain under the present system, whether in fact the evidence viewed as a whole is sufficient to convict. The standard remains unaltered:

beyond a reasonable doubt. * * * If the standard has in fact been met, it seems purposeless to inquire whether inapplicable rules governing jury-trial admissibility have also been met. In the normal case, the trial judge, certainly in cases of serious crime, may aid the appellate court by recording the factors which led to his conclusion, giving evidence of the seriousness of his pursuit of the facts and his awareness of the need for careful assessment of the hearsay on which he relied. In an analogous situation, Israel has developed the requirement that the judge give evidence that he has "warned himself" of the need for care. We would not recommend any requirement which could be met by insertion of a talismanic phrase, and, indeed, alternatives which go to the reality of the judge's concern rather than the phrasing of his opinion have been recommended in that jurisdiction. But the result on appellate review need not turn, as it does now, on whether the trial judge has lapsed and allowed himself to demonstrate reliance on technically inadmissible hearsay, or on whether there is in the record a "residuum" of evidence admissible in a jury-tried case. It should turn, rather, on the quality of the evidence as revealed by the entire record, examined by an appellate court which takes seriously the obligation to be increasingly sensitive to problems of sufficiency as the technical rules of admissibility are relaxed.

CONCLUSION

We have considered three different types of problems with respect to admission and exclusion of evidence in the jury-waived case. We seek neither to relax all the rules nor to be more stringent in their application. For us, what emerges from the analysis is the need to treat differently different problems. * * *

———————

Do you agree with the analysis of Levin and Cohen? Do you think that the procedures for ruling on the admissibility of evidence in bench trials should vary depending upon the type of evidence at issue? Do you think this will cause any problems? Do you think that some rules of evidence, such as the hearsay rule, should be different in bench trials than in jury trials? How would such variation affect decisions to choose bench trials? Is the system of evidence law for which Levin and Cohen argue superior to the system which would exist today if the appel-late courts reversed trial courts whenever they heard evidence without passing on admissibility or whenever errors in admitting evidence would necessitate reversal if the case were tried to a jury? If the appellate courts did reverse for these reasons, how would you expect trial judges to behave in admitting evidence? How would you expect trial judges to behave in finding facts? Would the costs of this kind of policy outweigh the benefits? Do they in jury cases? Consider the following problems.

Problem XII–28. Harold Barber is charged with sodomy and with contributing to the delinquency of a minor. Trial is to a judge. During a recess in the trial, the prosecutor shows the judge, at the judge's request, photographs of Barber, his wife, and his children posing in the nude and simulating various sexual acts. The pictures are never introduced into evidence; in fact, they are not even offered. After Barber is convicted, he discovers that the judge saw these photographs. He appeals on the ground that these photos may have affected the judge's verdict. **Should Barber prevail? Does it matter whether the photographs would have been admissible had they been offered into evidence? What weight should the appellate court give to an affidavit of the trial judge stating that he was not influenced in his decision by the fact that he saw the photos?**

Problem XII–29. An automobile driven by Carl Jackson hits Tina Sanchez, a pedestrian. Sanchez sues Jackson, claiming that he ran a red light. Jackson says that he had a green light. He also alleges contributory negligence, claiming that Sanchez rushed into the intersection where the accident occurred without looking. At the trial Sanchez calls Shirley Abzug, the police officer who investigated the accident. Abzug testifies that in the course of her investigation she took the statements of three witnesses. The three agreed that Jackson's automobile had run a red light. Jackson moves to strike Abzug's testimony on the ground that it is hearsay. The judge, who is hearing the case without a jury, reserves decision on the matter. On cross-examination Abzug states that when she interviewed them the three witnesses were standing in front of a tavern located at one corner of the intersection. When asked whether she knows whether they were drinking, Abzug says that she does not. On redirect examination Abzug testifies that she thought the witnesses were all absolutely sober when she talked to them and that their stories were consistent with each other. She also says that she has since tried to locate the witnesses, but they have all left the jurisdiction. Sanchez testifies that she suffered amnesia during the accident and remembers nothing about the way in which the accident occurred. Jackson testifies that he never ran a red light and that Sanchez jumped out in front of him so that he did not have time to stop without hitting her. Jackson also introduces a witness who corroborates his version of the accident.

Without ever making a final judgment on the hearsay objection to Abzug's testimony, the trial judge finds that Jackson was negligent and that Sanchez was free from contributory negligence. Jackson appeals. **How should the appellate court rule?**

Problem XII–30. Ellen Dannin is charged with armed robbery. Dannin allegedly entered a grocery store with a red bandana over her face, forced the owner at gunpoint to open the safe, and took $1400. Three weeks after the robbery, the storeowner testifies before the grand jury as follows:

Q. Did you recognize the person who shot you? **A.** Yes, her name is Ellen Dannin. She lives a block up the street from my place and never seems to work.

Q. How do you know it was Dannin if the robber was wearing a bandana over her face? **A.** I could tell by her walk and her mannerisms. It is hard to say what makes me so sure, but I am positive of my identification.

Q. Have you any doubt that it was Dannin? **A.** No.

Q. How much money was taken? **A.** About $1400.

The storeowner dies of a heart attack before the trial, and the prosecution attempts to introduce this grand jury testimony. The trial judge admits this testimony, overruling a hearsay objection. The only other evidence for the prosecution is testimony by a friend of Dannin's that at the time of the robbery Dannin owned a handgun, and testimony by another witness that the day after the robbery Dannin paid off a loan of $1100 which the witness had been pressuring Dannin to pay off for some time before that. **If the trial judge, hearing the case without a jury, convicts Dannin on this evidence, should the appellate court sustain the conviction? Should the conviction be sustained if the trial judge had stricken the grand jury testimony as hearsay after it had been presented? Would your answer be different if the trial judge had not allowed the grand jury testimony to be read because he had decided it was hearsay without knowing what it contained? Should the conviction be sustained if the storeowner had not died and had testified in court exactly as he did before the grand jury?**

Problem XII–31. On the same facts as the preceding problem, the prosecution introduces a confession signed by Dannin which the defense moves to strike as involuntary. The judge rules that the motion to strike is not timely and admits the confession. In addition to the testimony about the gun and the debt, the wife of the storeowner corroborates the confession by testifying that she was present at the robbery and that she is sure that the robber was Dannin because of the way the robber walked and her other mannerisms. The judge finds Dannin guilty, but the appellate court remands the case for a determination of whether the confession was voluntary. Dannin asks that the voluntariness question be given to a judge other than the judge to whom the case was tried. **Should this be done? Must it be done?**

Problem XII–32. Player sues Denver for damages resulting from an automobile accident. Trial is to a judge. When Denver takes the stand,

Player's counsel asks her if she is insured and if so for how much. Over objection by Denver's counsel, the judge orders her to answer, commenting, "I'd like to find out what the pot is here." **Is this error? Is it reversible error? Had the judge simply ordered Denver to answer and not made any comment, would it be reversible error? If the appellate court decides that the judge's order was reversible error, should it remand the case for a retrial on the merits or only for a retrial on the issue of damages? If the case is to be retried, may Denver demand that the retrial be before a different judge?**

BIBLIOGRAPHY

1 Holdsworth, A History of English Law 312–350 (7th ed. rev. 1956).

1 Louisell & Mueller, Federal Evidence.

McCormick §§ 53, 58–60.

Plucknett, A Concise History of the Common Law 106–138 (5th ed. 1956).

Thayer, A Preliminary Treatise on Evidence at the Common Law 47–262 (1898).

1 Weinstein's Evidence ¶¶ 102[02], 104, 105[5], 107.

9 Wigmore §§ 2549–2559.

2 Wright, Federal Practice and Procedure-Criminal §§ 481–502 (1969).

9 Wright & Miller, Federal Practice and Procedure-Civil §§ 2551–2558 (1971).

Ball, The Myth of Conditional Relevance, 14 Ga.L.Rev. 435 (1980).

Davis, Hearsay in Nonjury Cases, 83 Harv.L.Rev. 1362 (1970).

James, Sufficiency of the Evidence and Jury-Control Devices Available Before Verdict, 47 Va.L.Rev. 218 (1961).

Laughlin, Preliminary Questions of Fact: A New Theory, 31 Wash. & Lee L.Rev. 285 (1974).

Maguire & Epstein, Preliminary Questions of Fact in Determining the Admissibility of Evidence, 40 Harv.L.Rev. 392 (1927).

Morgan, Function of the Judge and Jury in the Determination of Preliminary Questions of Fact, 43 Harv.L.Rev. 165 (1929).

Note, On Instructing Deadlocked Juries, 78 Yale L.J. 100 (1968).

Saltzburg, Standards of Proof and Preliminary Questions of Fact, 27 Stan.L.Rev. 271 (1975).

Saltzburg, The Unnecessarily Expanding Role of the Federal Trial Judge, 64 Va.L.Rev. 1 (1978).

Sax, Conscience and Anarchy: The Prosecution of War Resisters, 42 Yale Review 483 (1968).

Winslow, The Instruction Ritual, 13 Hast.L.J. 456 (1962).

Wyzanski, A Trial Judge's Freedom and Responsibility, 65 Harv.L.Rev. 1281 (1952).

Chapter Thirteen

USING THE BASIC EVIDENCE RULES

SECTION I.   INTRODUCTION

In litigation a lawyer is concerned not only with victory at trial, but also with the way in which a completed case will look to an appellate court. A trial court victory places the burden of appeal on the opposing party, it often carries great weight with the appellate court, and it may allow remedies, such as injunctive relief, that are effective pending an appellate decision. Only one side can win at trial. The loser must rely on appellate review or concede defeat. On appeal, the record made below will be crucial.

We have already examined some of the ways in which a lawyer creates a record for appeal. We have discussed objections, offers of proof, tactics and ethics. Up to this point we have emphasized particular rules and particular applications of rules to problems. When you read the *Whale* transcript in Chapter One you were at the beginning of the course, just learning what the rules of evidence are all about. Now you have the opportunity for a more sophisticated examination of the way in which a party's theory of a case is established, the application of the rules of evidence in the context of an entire case, and the problem of developing a record for appeal while attempting to prevail at trial.

With the emphasis in law schools on the case method of study, students rarely have an opportunity to study how the record in a case is made. This is unfortunate, since creating a record that serves the client's interest is one of the most important aspects of the art of litigation. It is from the record that an appellate court learns what has happened below. The loser at trial often stakes his appeal on defects in the record, while the winner needs a favorable record to defend against the other's case. Moreover, as you learned in Chapter Six, recorded testimony may be presented to the trier of fact in a subsequent trial if witnesses are unavailable or if they have forgotten the incidents described.

The most important goal in making a record is protecting all of one's points and objections so that the appellate court will see them in their best light. Appellate courts are acutely sensitive to the costs, both financial and otherwise, of retrying cases. Except where the mistakes at trial are fundamental and egregious, appellate courts rarely consider any evidentiary objections not made below by the loser or any points of law not presented to the trial judge. The theory is that the trial judge would have corrected any erroneous rulings had objection been made and the error explained. So, if the trial judge has not been made aware of the error in his rulings and presented with an adequate explanation of why the rulings are in error, the party failing to object or failing to present a valid reason for objecting is held partly responsible for the perpetuation of error and is not allowed to benefit from the error on appeal. The situation of the party prevailing below is more favorable in this respect. On appeal, to support the trial judge's ruling, the prevailing party may make arguments not previously made. The theory is that if the decision at trial was correct, on any ground, there is no sense in remanding the case for a new trial.

We have often emphasized how important it is for trial lawyers to have a firm grasp of substantive law. Knowledge of relevant law and the ability to extract information from witnesses are necessary to success in litigation. But it is not the need to know law or master facts which makes litigation an art. The art of litigation lies in the lawyer's ability to deal simultaneously with the problems of making a record and persuading the judge or jury. How a lawyer does something may be as important as what is done. Facts may be elicited from a witness so as to appear credible or incredible. A good sense for tactics is also important, particularly where the tasks of record-making and persuasion conflict. Consider, for example, a simple matter like entering an objection to an obviously improper line of questioning. If the objection is not entered and the case is lost, counsel will not be able to argue the error on appeal. If the objection is entered and sustained, the jury may feel that the objecting side has something to hide and, in its deliberations, may count the objection against the party that made it. A conflict also exists where the judge has overruled a series of similar objections, indicating impatience with the objecting attorney. If the next objectionable question goes to a crucial matter, how may the attorney ensure that the issue is preserved for appeal without further alienating the judge and jury?[1] Many of the problems faced by lawyers attempting to make favorable records are evident in the transcript which comprises the heart of this chapter.

The case, Brooks v. State, is one of the many death penalty cases disposed of by the United States Supreme Court in con-

nection with Furman v. Georgia.[2] *Furman* held that the death penalty as imposed in that case and its two companion cases was precluded by the eighth amendment's prohibition of cruel and unusual punishment. The Court vacated and remanded for resentencing several hundred cases following *Furman*. As with *Whale, Brooks* is not the true name of the case presented. The transcript is authentic, however.

Whale was a routine criminal case, not likely to inflame jurors' passions or play on their prejudices. We thought it a suitable vehicle to present the basic rules which govern trial procedure. Now we choose a different kind of transcript to illustrate the intense pressures operating in some cases and their impact on the application of rules of evidence and litigation strategy. *Brooks* involves the violent rape of a sixty-five year old woman, a crime then punishable by penalties ranging from five years imprisonment to death. The victim was white and the alleged rapist black. The jury, after hearing the evidence, has to determine both guilt and punishment. This is a case where the defense attorney is fighting two battles. First, he wants to see his client acquitted. Failing that, he wishes to save his client's life. The two goals do not always call for the same tactics. The prosecutor also faces a dual responsibility: to seek the conviction of a man he believes guilty and to seek an appropriate penalty.

In this case the participants seem to believe that race has been eliminated as a

---

1. If a judge's attitude toward a party is clear, some jurors are likely to reflect this attitude. For an interesting discussion of this phenomenon see Note, Judges' Nonverbal Behavior in Jury Trials: A Threat to Judicial Impartiality, 61 Va.L.Rev. 1266 (1975).

2. 408 U.S. 238 (1972). More recent death penalty cases upholding state statutes authorizing capital punishment with criteria to guide the sentencing decision and invalidating mandatory punishment statutes are Gregg v. Georgia, Jurek v. Texas, Profitt v. Flor-

ida, Woodson v. North Carolina, and Roberts v. Louisiana, which are found at 428 U.S. 153–363 (1976). Coker v. Georgia, 433 U.S. 584 (1977), indicates that the death penalty for rape is unconstitutional where no death results, although cases of particularly brutal rape might be distinguished from the rape charged to Coker. See also Eddings v. Oklahoma, 102 S.Ct. 869 (1982); Lockett v. Ohio, 438 U.S. 586 (1978); Enmund v. Florida, 102 S.Ct. 3368 (1982).

factor, but racial overtones are clearly present. At times the racial tension is palpable; one can only guess if, or to what extent, it operates to the detriment of the defendant. Some may be offended by the trial. We offer it not to provoke, but to show what too often happens, even today.

Finally, this is an odd case, for the defense disputes the legality of a search and seizure more earnestly that it disputes the identification of the defendant as the assailant. Yet the latter issue, central to the prosecution's case, is by no means clear. In most jurisdictions the search and seizure issue would have been decided by the judge alone, but in this jurisdiction at the time of *Brooks* it was given to the jury for an independent determination of legality. Much of the transcript relates to the search and seizure, affording an excellent opportunity to evaluate the wisdom of the defense counsel's strategy.

The defense counsel relies on both the state and federal constitutions in arguing the search and seizure issue. For our purposes the state constitutional provisions regulating searches and seizures are almost identical to the fourth amendment and need not be separately discussed. The only difference worth noting is that state law apparently requires police to obtain a warrant whenever there is time to do so, while federal law does not require that a warrant be obtained for the purpose of making an arrest. In this case the real issue is whether there was probable cause to arrest the particular suspect, Brooks. If there was, the arrest was valid under state law since there was no time to acquire a warrant. We mention this difference only because, as you will see in the transcript, the defendant's lawyer appears at times to be more concerned with the failure to obtain a warrant than with the fundamental issue of probable cause.

In the commentary following this case, you will see the jury instruction that was given on the fourth amendment issue. The instruction suggests that counsel in this case lost sight of the main point, which is that, as a general rule, police officers may not make warrantless arrests for felonies and searches incident thereto unless they have probable cause to believe that the person they seek to arrest has committed the felony in question. This rule implements the fourth amendment and is binding on the states through the fourteenth amendment.

If evidence is obtained in violation of the fourth amendment, it may not be introduced as part of the prosecution's case-in-chief. Any evidence which is in some way derived from illegally seized evidence will also be suppressed. For example, if shoes are illegally seized from an individual and compared with footprints found at the scene of the crime, testimony reporting the comparison should be excluded at trial.

Probable cause, a term found in the fourth amendment, is not easily defined. Justice Harlan wrote that "[p]robable cause to arrest means evidence that would warrant a prudent and reasonable man * * * in believing that a particular person has committed or is committing a crime."[3] Probable cause under this and similar definitions does not require a police officer to determine that it is "more probable than not" that the suspect has committed a crime.

In Terry v. State of Ohio,[4] the Supreme Court held that "where a police officer observes unusual conduct which leads him reasonably to conclude in light of his experience that criminal activity may be afoot and that the persons with whom he is dealing may be armed and presently dangerous, where in the course of investigating this behavior he identifies himself as a policeman and makes reasonable inquir-

3. Sibron v. State of New York, 392 U.S. 40, 75 (1968) (concurring in the result). The exclusion of evidence seized without probable cause is mandated by Mapp v. Ohio, 367 U.S. 643 (1961).

4. 392 U.S. 1 (1968).

ies, and where nothing in the initial stages of the encounter serves to dispel his reasonable fear for his own or others' safety, he is entitled for the protection of himself and others in the area to conduct a carefully limited search of the outer clothing of such persons in an attempt to discover weapons which might be used to assault him."[5] While the stop-and-frisk technique approved by *Terry* is governed by the fourth amendment, the fact that this technique is less of an intrusion into personal privacy than a full-scale search permits a less demanding standard than probable cause.

When reading the transcript in *Brooks*, assume that the lawyers and the court were familiar with applicable fourth amendment law. Note, however, that *Terry* was not decided until after Brooks was tried and convicted. Think about the defense counsel's responsibility for anticipating such a decision. At the time of Brooks' trial, state law on stop-and-frisk was not clear. Some cases could be read to disapprove the technique.[6] Yet stop-and-frisk was a subject of great controversy.[7] Stop-and-frisk was approved by the Uniform Arrest Act.[8] It was also approved by the first draft of the ALI Model Code of Pre-Arraignment Procedure (1966). Furthermore, the United States Court of Appeals for the relevant circuit had already indicated some acceptance of a police officer's right to stop and question citizens,[9] suggesting that relief by habeas corpus would not be likely if Brooks were convicted.

Other exceptions to the warrant requirement also must be kept in mind. First, there is the "plain view" doctrine, holding that it is not an improper search to observe that which is open to view from a place where the officer has a right to be, nor is it improper to seize evidence of criminal activity found in such a place. A plurality of the Supreme Court has noted that

> What the "plain view" cases have in common is that the police officer in each of them had a prior justification for an intrusion in the course of which he came *inadvertently* across a piece of evidence incriminating the accused.[10] (emphasis added)

We have emphasized the word "inadvertently" since a majority of the Court has not yet accepted this limitation on the exception, and its precise meaning is unclear.[11] It is sufficient for our purposes to assume that a police officer who properly intrudes upon the person or property of a citizen may seize items of an incriminating character. For purposes of this chapter, assume that the plain view exception was valid when Brooks was tried and when he appealed.[12] Second, there is the hot pursuit doctrine recognized in Warden, Maryland Penitentiary v. Hayden[13] before Brooks was tried. In *Hayden,* police officers, after being informed that an armed robber had gone into a particular house, entered the house, searched for the robber and found him. The Court held that a warrant was not needed in this situation.

---

5. Id. at 30. See also Adams v. Williams, 407 U.S. 143 (1972).

6. See, e.g., Timberlake v. State, 150 Tex.Cr. 375, 201 S.W.2d 647 (1947); cf., Pruitt v. State, 389 S.W.2d 475 (Tex. Cr.App.1965).

7. See Remington, The Law Relating to "On the Street" Detention, Questioning, and Frisking of Suspected Persons and Police Arrest Privileges in General, 51 J.Crim.L.C. & P.S. 386 (1960); Schwartz, Stop and Frisk, 58 J.Crim.L.C. & P.S. 433 (1967).

8. See Warner, The Uniform Arrest Act, 28 Va.L.Rev. 315 (1942).

9. See Nicholson v. United States, 355 F.2d 80, 83–84 (5th Cir. 1966).

10. Coolidge v. New Hampshire, 403 U.S. 443, 466 (1971).

11. See The Supreme Court, 1970 Term, 85 Harv.L.Rev. 3, 244–46 (1971).

12. But see Katz v. United States, 389 U.S. 347 (1967).

13. 387 U.S. 294 (1967).

As you read the transcript, consider the following questions: What is the defense counsel's basic strategy? What other strategies are available? Does the defense counsel adequately develop the record so that he may take maximum advantage of it if an appeal is necessary? How adequately does he use fourth amendment law? What are the facts, as you see them, regarding the search and seizure and the arrest? At the end of the transcript, think back over the facts developed by the defense counsel. Are you satisfied that the record is as clear as it should be? Following the transcript is the opinion of the state appellate court. Does it accurately describe the record?

Ask yourself whether the defense counsel utilized a strategy likely to save the life of his client. Even a cursory reading of his closing argument will convince you that he tried, and he tried hard. But you must decide whether his wits matched his efforts. Keep in mind the fact that Brooks ultimately prevailed in the Supreme Court and that the cryptic opinions of the five members of the majority in *Furman* show concern for the possibility that the defendant's race is associated with the imposition of the death penalty. Does this mean that the defense counsel in *Brooks* adopted a wise strategy? What would you have done?

Also watch the prosecutor's strategy. Do you approve of his methods? Following the transcript we present the opinion of the state appellate court affirming Brooks' conviction. We then go on to raise a number of questions concerning the performance of both counsel. Reading the transcript should also help you review what you have learned in previous chapters. Footnotes to the transcript raise review questions.

SECTION II.   THE TRIAL: STATE v. BROOKS

In the transcript that follows we have corrected a few confusing grammatical errors and some obvious mistranscriptions. We have also changed the names of people and places and deleted some redundant testimony. These are the only changes we have made. At times the participants use words in ways that seem strange. There is often ambiguity resulting from the way in which questions are asked and answered. These things happen at trials. As you read the transcript you should ask yourself whether you could have phrased questions and objections more effectively than the attorneys in this case. Because there are numerous witnesses and references to people, we have prepared a "cast of characters" to help you follow the roles played by the different participants in this case.

PARTICIPANTS

State v. Elmer Brooks

The Honorable Tom Batus Presiding Judge.

Mr. Tom Robin	Prosecuting Attorney.
Mr. Curtis Stilp	Defense Attorney.

Witnesses for the State

Mrs. Ethel Hill	The Victim.
Mr. P. H. (Phil) Hill	The Victim's Son.

Mr. Jim Gant	Sandle City Police Officer.
Mr. P. G. Henly &	
Mr. Rex V. Wende	Orange County Deputies.
Mr. Lyle Stack	Sheriff of Orange County.
Mr. Charles V. Endle	Desk Sergeant at the time of the incident.
Mr. Joe Ratlif	"Rubbernecker" who was at Mrs. Hill's home when the police were taking pictures.

Witnesses for the Defense

Mr. Arnold Tolot	Elmer Brooks' Parole Officer
Mr. Ira Hens	Institutional Parole Officer at Hardy Prison
Mr. James Wood	Employee of the State Department of Corrections
Mrs. Helen Allen	Mother of Elmer Brooks
Mrs. May Anna Block	Grandmother of Elmer Brooks
Mr. L. W. Wile	School Teacher and Former Principal of Booker T. Washington Elementary School

Not at the Trial

| Mr. Jackie Michael | Sandle City Police Officer on duty with Jim Gant at the time of the incident. |
| Hal Blaine's Wrecking Yard (sometimes called "Hal Blaine's") | A landmark in this case. |

THE STATE
vs
ELMER BROOKS

TRANSCRIPT OF EVIDENCE FROM THE 46th DISTRICT COURT
OF ORANGE COUNTY, AT SANDLE, STATE OF _____ .
HON. TOM BATUS, JUDGE PRESIDING

MRS. ETHEL HILL, after having been first duly sworn, testified as follows, to wit:

DIRECT EXAMINATION

BY MR. ROBIN:

Q. Mrs. Hill, you name is Mrs. Ethel Hill? A. Yes.

MR. STILP: Your Honor, I would like to ask if she does not have another name.

THE COURT: I beg your pardon?

MR. STILP: I would like to inquire if she doesn't go by another name besides Mrs. Ethel Hill.

WITNESS: Well, my given name is Pearl.

Q. (By Mr. Robin) Mrs. Hill, please talk toward the jurors, and talk loud enough that this last gentleman over here can hear your testimony. It's very important that they hear every word you say. Mrs. Hill, where do you live? **A.** I live twelve miles north of Sandle.

Q. That is on the east side of the highway, or the other side, other side of Northside? **A.** Yes.

Q. Mrs. Hill, is your husband deceased? **A.** Yes, he passed away last October, 1966.[14]

Q. 1966? **A.** October 8.

Q. Since that time you have been living out there by yourself? **A.** Yes.

Q. Mrs. Hill, on or about the 9th day of May, 1967, did or not someone enter your house? **A.** Yes.

Q. Were you or not assaulted?[15] **A.** Yes, I was assaulted.

Q. Approximately what time of the night was that? **A.** Well, it must have been a little before 2:00 o'clock.[16]

Q. Mrs. Hill, is the person who made that assault upon you in this courtroom? **A.** That is he right there (indicating Defendant).

Q. Sitting behind Mr. Stilp here? **A.** That colored man.

Q. Are you positive of that? **A.** Yes, I am positive.

Q. Now, Mrs. Hill, will you start out from the beginning, from the time that you discovered the Defendant in your presence? Will you describe to the jury what all happened in your own words? **A.** Yes.

Q. Please do so. **A.** Well, I wear a hearing aid, and when I take it off, I can't hear any noise much, and so I was asleep, in bed asleep, and I was lying on my left side, and the first thing I knew the cover was being jerked off of me. Well, my son has a key to my house, and I never thought about him being an intruder. I thought perhaps it was my little granddaughter; they had come in to wake me up or something, and so I turned over and I said, "What is it? What has happened?" and I threw my arms up like this, and I said "What do you want?" and this colored man grabbed my arms in a steel grasp, just grabbed them, and said, "I'll show you what I want." And so I thought "oh, my God, a colored man", and I began to struggle and struggle and try to get loose, and I couldn't break his grasp on my arms at all. It was just like a steel grasp on my arm, just holding me, and I struggled and struggled, and I was lying, to start with, I was lying with my head to the west and my feet to the east, and finally he got me across the bed and I scooted and scooted back away from him and hollered and tried to scream and hollered and hollered, and my bed was out just about that far from the wall, and he slid me back. He kept sliding me back until

14. Is this relevant? Is it harmless?

15. Is this leading? Will you object?

16. Is this improper speculation? Should the prosecutor be required to ask her how she knew what time it was?

he got my head hanging off the bed, butting it back against the wall, and then when he got me back in the corner, pinned in a corner like that, he was hurting me so, pushing my head against the wall, and he folded my arm over like this, and then he put his right arm—he held this arm, and put his right arm right across my throat like that and my head was already hanging off the bed, and pressed down on it just as hard, and every time I hollered he pressed that much harder and told me to shut up, he wasn't going to have any of that, and I kept trying to holler and he would just press harder every time and harder, and he held me with this one over here this way, and this one over here with his right arm, you see, right against my throat and I was hanging off the bed, you know, and it hurt right here, and he taken his left hand and stripped off my bottom part of my pajamas, and I was kicking and trying to keep my legs crossed and he kept on scratching and clawing until he got my legs apart, and then he assaulted, and I couldn't get away from him.   There wasn't anything I could do.   He just was so strong.   I had never seen a man with that kind of power in his hands, and then he told me— He got up after the act was over.   He got up and just stood there beside the bed and told me to get up, and I got up and sat on the side of the bed, and he said, "How much money you got?"   And I said—I was crying and screaming and taking on, and I said, "I don't have any money," and I said, "I don't keep any change out here at this time of year."   I said, "I give checks for everything," and he said, "Well, give me what you got," and I said, "Well, you will have to move."   He was standing right over me.   He said, "Where is it?" I said, "It's in my purse," so he moved back just a little, and I said, "I will get it for you. You can have it, if you will just go and leave me alone," [17] and I went in and turned around and reached in the closet and got my purse and took out this coin purse.   I have got the coin purse with me that I had.   I took it out, and he held out his hand.   You see, there was a light in the bathroom, right next to my room and that shone right down the hall, and I could see him.   In semi-darkness all the time I could see him, and there was a light in the back bedroom too.   I always have left one burning ever since my husband passed away, and I could see his hand out there, and I just turned it up and poured it in his hand, and I said "That's all I have got."   I said, "I'll give you a check, if you will just go on and leave me alone.   I will give you a check."   He said, "No, I won't take a check.   No, no checks," just like that.   I said, "I will give you any amount of money, put it in an envelope and drop it anywhere you say tomorrow, if you will just go on and leave me alone," and he said, "No.   No, that won't do."   Then he just backed up and stood over there, pushed me back and stood against my dresser, which is lined up like that is there, folded his arms, and I started to get up and he pushed me back again, a time or two, and I was crying and taking on, and he told me—he was mumbling.   I said, "What did you say?" He said, "I am going to keep you here until 12:00 o'clock tomorrow, and we are going to do this every hour—" He said a nasty word.   I am not going to say it, but he said, "I am going to use you every hour on the hour until 12:00 o'clock tomorrow."   And I told him, "You won't either."   I said, "My son is going to come down here in the morning.   He always comes and checks

17. Are these statements hearsay?

on me every morning, and I am going to have a hired hand at 7:00 o'clock to go to work." So he just kept shoving me back, mumbling and talking, and I couldn't understand him because I didn't have on my hearing aid, and I begin to pray. I said "Oh, God. Oh, God. Please be merciful. Please be merciful." Just like that, and I was crying and I didn't know what to do but pray. I knew he was so strong I couldn't do nothing, so after I prayed a little bit, why, he bellowed at me "Shut that up. Shut that up. We don't need him." Just like that, so I shut up, but I kept on praying in my mind. I prayed in my mind all through it. And finally I began to plead and beg him to let me get my hearing aid on. He kept talking and I couldn't understand anything he said, and I said, "Please let me get my hearing aid. I wear a hearing aid on my glasses. I can't hear a word you are saying,"[18] just like that, and I prayed and prayed, and I begged and begged "Please let me get my hearing aid," and finally he said, "Where is it?" And I said, "It's right on the dresser behind where you are standing." He said, "Well, get it then." Just like that. Well, I got up and got my hearing aid and put it on, and then I sat down in a chair that was over there about three feet, three or four feet from the bed, and I said, "Why? Why did you come out here and molest a woman my age? I am sixty-five years old, when there are plenty of nice pretty girls in town?" I said, "Why did you come out here and do a thing like this to me?" and he said, "I wanted to see how you felt about colored people." And that is the only excuse he ever gave me for doing that, and I told him, I said, "Well, if we hadn't felt all right about colored people, we wouldn't have used them on the farm for forty-five years." My husband always brought colored people out there and gave them the work, because he always said they needed the work. He always worked colored people, and I had worked a lot of colored kids in my cantaloupes and my produce and things like that, and I never did have any trouble with any of them. I gave kids, colored kids, work that would never get to work anywhere else. I tried to help them out as much as I could, and in picking my cantaloupes and things like that, you know. Of course, it would just be a little while in the morning, but it helped them.[19]

So we talked there for a while, and I told him, I said, "I have got a colored man that I have had for thirty years. He has worked for us ever since 1936, and he has been respectable, nice, long and true to us," and I said, "My husband used him all these years, and he come to me after my husband died and said, 'I can't get a job anywhere else. Are you going to let me work for you?' He said, 'At my age—I am sixty-three years old—I can't get a job anywhere else. Would you let me continue working for you?' He said, 'I know all about the farm, and I can carry it on just like Mr. Hill had me carry it on,' and I said, 'Yeah, you can go ahead and work for me.'" So I was telling him all this. I said "I loaned him money all this winter. He has got a big bunch of children and I loaned him money when he couldn't work, so he could go ahead and support his family, and even last Sunday morning he came by the house and wanted to borrow ten dollars because he was sick. He said he had to go to the doctor at Chiclet, and I loaned him

18. If this is true, why is the witness permitted to relate what the assailant said prior to her using the hearing aid?

19. What purpose does this testimony serve? Is it prejudicial?

the ten dollars to go to the doctor at Chiclet, and then by Tuesday he was able to come back to work." So I was telling this boy all this, you know, about how we had worked these colored people and how we had been good to them all these years, and I couldn't understand why he would come out there and molest me.[20]

Well, I was coughing and crying, and telling him all this, and I begged him to let me go to the bathroom, and finally—He kept me hostage, I would say, thirty to forty-five minutes, and I was coughing and choking. He had hurt my throat and I was hurting all over really. My throat was hurting and I couldn't hardly get my breath, and I asked him to let me go to the bathroom. I told him I needed a drink of water. And so he finally said, "Well, I will let you go to the bathroom if you won't go anywhere else," but he was standing in the door facing to see that I didn't go anywhere else, and of course the bathroom was lit up, and the hall light was shining down the— The bathroom light was shining down the hall, and so I went to the bathroom and got me a drink, and I was barefooted, of course, and didn't have on the bottom of my pajamas. I had tried to put them on, but he had jerked them away from me and wouldn't let me put them on, and so when I came out of the bathroom door, I just stepped back, oh, about as far as from here to there, and switched on the hall light. I switched on the hall light, and he yelled at me, "Cut that light off." And when I didn't shut it off—I just stood there a second, because I was going to try to make it to the backdoor and get out the backdoor. When I didn't shut the hall light off, he just come striding down and got me by the shoulders and he shook me, and said, "You shouldn't have done that." It scared me, of course, again, and I said, "Oh please, please don't hurt me any more," just like that. I looked right straight up in his face and begged him not to hurt me any more. I said, "Well, I'll shut the light off." And I did. I reached to shut it off. So he throwed me around and shoved me down the hall, shoved me on clear on back and made me sit on the bed again, and I was still crying and taking on, and— well, I didn't know what was going to happen to me, and finally he stood around, you know, and I knew not to pray out loud, but I was praying in the back of my mind all the time, and I asked him during the conversation if he had ever worked for me, and he said no, he hadn't ever worked for me, but he had seen me in '64, and I asked him how he knew I was out there by myself, that I lived by myself, and he said he had information, like that, and finally he decided to go. I was begging him all the time, "Please go on and leave me alone. Please don't hurt me any more." Just begging and beg- ging and begging and pleading with him to go on and leave me alone, not hurt me any more. Finally, he decided to go. He pitched me my pajamas, and he told me to put them on. Before that, though, he mentioned he was going out and talk with some man in the car, but then he decided to leave. He pitched me my pajamas and told me to put them on and get in bed and cover up and not to move until I heard his car start. I still had my glasses and my hearing aid on, you see, and I told him, "Go on and I will," and I did. I put them on and got in bed and covered up, and he walked to the

20. What objection(s) would you make to this testimony? How might the testi- mony be justified?

telephone and he jerked the receiver off, jerked the wire off the receiver, and laid the receiver back on the telephone, and then he turned around to me and he said, "Now, I will be back, and if you tell this, I will kill you the next time I come back." That is what he said. And I said, "Well, go on and leave me alone. Please go on and leave me alone. Go out the front door." So he went up and unlocked the front door and went out, and when I heard the screen hit the front door, I jumped up out of bed and run to the back door and unlocked it and let the screen to real easy, because I was afraid he would hear it, and I run, just as hard as I could run. I run straight east, around the car shed and down through the alfalfa patch, the grass burs sticking my feet and everything else, but I run through them, and I run down to my son's house, which is about, oh, I would say two blocks from my house, a block and a half, I don't know, about a block and a half or two blocks. I run on down there and beat on his back bedroom window crying and screaming and told him what happened, and of course he was out in just a minute, and I told him what happened, and he went right in and called the police, and I was so shook up I just went and fell on the bed.

Q. Mrs. Hill, while you were looking at him in the hall and he was standing over you there in the bedroom, did you have an occasion or chance to see how he was dressed? A. I seen how he was dressed in my bedroom.

Q. Well, can you tell this jury how? A. He had on tennis shoes and dark trousers, and I thought it was a grey shirt until I saw him in the hall, and I saw it was kind of a greenish, kind of a greyish-green T-shirt.

Q. Those tennis shoes, what color were the tennis shoes? A. White.

Q. They were white tennis shoes? A. They were white tennis shoes.

Q. Dark colored trousers? A. Dark colored trousers, and kind of a greyish-green shirt, T-shirt, but I thought it was grey in there in the bedroom, but when I seen him in the light, out in the hall light, I could see that it had more green in it.

Q. Did you tell your son—That is P. H., isn't it? A. Yeah.

Q. Did you tell him how he was dressed? A. Yes, I described him just exactly how he was dressed and I told him, I said, "He has got a pointed chin and a high cheekbone," and I said, "He is some taller than me, because I kind of looked up under his face."

Q. Now, Mrs. Hill, you said a while ago that he said a word that you couldn't repeat. When he said he was going to do this every hour. Was that distinct?

MR. STILP: Your Honor, I object to that.

THE COURT: Just withhold your answer, please, ma'am, and go ahead and ask the question, and I will rule on it.

Q. You said that the word he said was too vulgar to tell the jury? A. It is.

Q. I will ask you whether or not the word he expressed to you was commonly used to denote— A. Sexual intercourse.

MR. STILP: No objection.

Q. Is that what the word used meant? **A.** That is the word he said.

Q. And you did tell this jury he did complete the act of intercourse? **A.** Yes, he did.

Q. With you on that first occasion when he had you across the bed? **A.** Yes, he did. I couldn't get away from him. I was pinned back in the corner.

Q. Were you present in your son's house when he called the police department? **A.** Yes.

Q. Did you hear the description he gave the police department? **A.** Yes, I could hear it.

Q. And you heard him call the Sheriff, Lyle Stack? **A.** It was the same thing I told him.

Q. Mrs. Hill, do you know how he made his entry to your house? **A.** Yes, through my kitchen window. Came out in the paper my bathroom window, but it wasn't. It was the kitchen window. That is the dark side of the house. You see, I have those big lights on the south side. I have a light now on that side, but at that time that was the dark side of the house, and every other window in the house was latched, locked and that window, for some reason, some painter had taken the back catch off of that kitchen window, and the window wasn't locked, but the screen was latched and the window was down. He just taken ahold of it with his bare hands, I guess, and the screen was just broke into, you know, where it's joined on the side.[21] It was just broke there. He just taken hold of it and jerked it, because we didn't find any tools or anything around there he had used, and there was an old car wheel that we had had there for fifteen years, you see, that is the kitchen sink there, and the drain is there and the faucet is there on that side of the house, and we used to put sacks in half a bushel baskets, you know, and put it up over the drain, the faucet to keep it from freezing up in the winter time, and this car wheel, my husband had taken that around there fifteen years ago and put it up against that basket to keep the water from freezing up, and so he had stood up on that car wheel and crawled in the kitchen window, because, you know, kitchen windows are up high.

Q. Now, Mrs. Hill, the Defendant here had worked, had he not, for your husband in prior years? **A.** Yes. I found some checks. I went through all my checks. It must have been some colored kid that worked for me that had a grudge against me is all I could think, and I found—But he never worked for me. I found four checks here. Three cotton picking checks in December, and they were given 28th, 29th, 30th.

Q. What year? **A.** Sixty-one.

Q. Sixty-one. **A.** And on August 7th, '61, he was given a $4.10 check, and I asked this colored man that worked for me if he was out there that summer.[22] He said, "Yes, he helped me with some hay one day, about half

---

21. **What objection could be raised here? Tactically, should it be raised?**

22. **Is this hearsay? Should defense counsel object?**

a day, in the barn," that he brought him out and he helped him put some hay in the barn. That was in August. These are all signed by my husband, but I was keeping books in the field in '61 for my husband, and I wrote— This is my writing here, the check is, but my husband's signature on it, because I always helped him settle up with the cotton pickers, you know.

Q. Did you see the person to whom the checks were delivered? **A.** What?

Q. Did you see the person to whom those checks were delivered, or did your husband deliver the checks? **A.** These were in my husband's checks.

Q. I see. **A.** I went back through all my checks that I had given for any labor that I had ever had anybody to do for me, clear back through '60, and I never did find a check that I had given, but he did work for my husband. I guess he was out of school. He was just about fourteen then, if he is twenty now. I guess he was out of school and worked the 28th, 29th and 30th picking cotton, pulling cotton, because he got all these checks pulling cotton. Do you want to see them?

Q. No thank you. Mrs. Hill, did you or not use all resistance in your power to resist him when he made his attack upon you? **A.** Did I do what?

Q. Did you use all the power and resistance that you could with your body to keep him from making his attack upon you? **A.** I didn't understand you.

Q. I said, did you use all the resistance that you could— **A.** Yes.

Q. —at the time that he made his attack? **A.** Yes, I tried to fight him. I tried to get away from him, but he is as strong as an ox. I couldn't even break his grasp on me.

MR. ROBIN: Pass the witness.

THE COURT: Let's take about a five minute recess at this time.[23] Gentlemen of the Jury, if you will, retire to the jury room.

(At this time a recess was taken.)

(After recess.)

Q. (By Mr. Robin) Mrs. Hill, I must ask you two more questions, and they are very necessary. Did this attack happen in Orange County? **A.** Yes. Twelve miles north of Sandle.

Q. Now, one more question, Mrs. Hill. Did the Defendant put his private parts in your private parts? **A.** He certainly did.

MR. ROBIN: That is all.

CROSS-EXAMINATION

BY MR. STILP:

Q. Ethel Hill, is that correct? **A.** Yes.

23. Why does the judge call a recess at this time? Should the prosecutor have passed the witness?

Q. You have testified under oath, is that correct? **A.** Yes.

Q. You do not wish to change or withdraw anything that you have testified to? **A.** I do not.

Q. Thank you, Mrs. Hill.

MR. STILP: That is all.[24]

(Counsel approached the bench.)

THE COURT: Gentlemen of the Jury, at this time there are questions of law which have to be gone into out of your presence. I think we will take our mid-morning recess at this time. I am going to allow you fifteen minutes. Please do not come into the courtroom. If you desire to go across the street and get a cup of coffee, that is perfectly all right, but please bear in mind the Court's instructions not to discuss this case among yourselves, nor with anyone else, nor are you to permit anyone to discuss it with you. If you want to go get coffee, as I say, it's all right to leave, but please go promptly from the jury room to wherever you are going to coffee, and then report back directly to the jury room when you come back.

(Reporter's note: The following proceedings were had outside the presence of the jury.)

[Several witnesses testified. Most of their testimony is repeated before the jury and so is deleted here. A few significant portions of the testimony are retained.]

MR. JIM GANT, after having been first duly sworn, testified as follows, to-wit:

DIRECT EXAMINATION

BY MR. ROBIN:

Q. Mr. Gant, on the morning of May 9, 1967, did you receive instructions to apprehend anyone coming from the north, a colored man coming from the north in a car? **A.** I did.

Q. Who, if anyone, was with you? **A.** Jackie Michael.

* * *

Q. Did you and Mr. Michael then proceed down North Main Street? **A.** Yes.

Q. Tell just where you went and what happened. **A.** Well, we went down Main and the expressway, and we stopped one car or attempted to stop it and found out just before we stopped it, it was a white man, so we turned around and went back across the expressway, and just as we pulled up to the stop sign on the west side, well, there was a car that approached from the north, and he hesitated just right there at the driveway and we started backing up there, and he turned into the service station. So we pulled in behind him, and by the time we got in there, he had ordered some gas.

24. Is this limited cross-examination better than no cross-examination at all? Are there matters not raised by defense counsel which you would have raised on cross-examination?

Q. Was that this Defendant here?　**A.** Yes, sir.

* * *

CROSS-EXAMINATION

BY MR. STILP:

Q. Mr. Gant, did you testify that you received information to stop any Negro?　**A.** Yeah.

Q. That is your testimony?　**A.** Yes.

Q. It didn't make any difference who he was, what he was doing or anything else.　You were to stop and arrest the man, is that correct?　**A.** Detain him.

Q. Detain him.　That means arrest, does it not?　**A.** Yes.

Q. If you are going to detain a man, he can't walk off, can he?　**A.** Well, I could check his car.

Q. Mr. Gant, be honest with the Court and me.　Your orders were to detain any Negro.　That meant that you were to hold him there, is that correct? [25]　**A.** Yes, sir.

* * *

Q. You are familiar with the daily notes of the Sandle Police Department?　**A.** That is right.

Q. I show you a copy here of the daily notes for approximately 2:45 a. m., May 9, 1967.　Would you read the section there, starting at that point right there, please, sir?　**A.** Right here?

Q. Yes.　**A.** "Stop every car that has colored subjects".

Q. Stop every car?　**A.** Yes.

Q. Containing colored subjects.

MR. STILP: Your Honor, we introduce the daily notes in evidence in support of our objection to the testimony.[26]

THE COURT: All right.　Only that portion?

MR. STILP: Only that portion, yes.

* * *

LYLE STACK, after having been first duly sworn, testified as follows, to wit:

BY MR. ROBIN:

Q. Your name is Lyle Stack, Sheriff of Orange County?　**A.** Yes, sir.

---

25. The questions are beginning to get repetitious. Is this repetition wise?

26. Are these notes hearsay? Are they properly authenticated?

Q. On or about the 9th of May of this year, did you have an occasion, along about 2:45 in the morning to call the desk, to radio the desk over at the City Hall? **A.** Yes, I did.

Q. What request or orders did you give at that time? **A.** I asked Officer Endle to have his cars stop all cars coming from the north.[27]

Q. That had colored subjects in them? **A.** Yes. I briefly told him what happened.

Q. You did tell him that Phil Hill had called him and said that his mother had just been raped by a Negro? **A.** Yes, and he was headed towards Sandle.

Q. And he was headed towards Sandle? **A.** Yes.

Q. Where were you, Mr. Stack, at the time you called that order in? **A.** At home.

* * *

CROSS-EXAMINATION

BY MR. STILP:

Q. Mr. Stack, you didn't see a felony occur? **A.** No.

Q. You were just going on what had been telephoned in to you? **A.** Just information on the telephone.

Q. And you didn't have any description or anything else of the colored male? **A.** That is all.

Q. Or what he was driving? **A.** (Nodded no)

Q. And it was your order to stop any automobile containing Negro males so they could be investigated, is that correct? **A.** Yes.

CHARLES ENDLE, after having been first duly sworn, testified as follows, to wit:

DIRECT EXAMINATION

BY MR. ROBIN:

Q. Mr. Endle, on May 9, 1967, at 2:45 in the morning, were you or not on the radio desk at the City Hall acting as Desk Sergeant at that time? **A.** Yes, sir.

Q. Did you or not at that time receive the information in this paragraph here from Lyle Stack? **A.** I did.

Q. Are those the notes? **A.** Yes, sir.

Q. That you took on the conversation which you had relayed to Mr. Henly and Mr. Wende? **A.** Yes, sir.

---

27. **Is this hearsay? Is it relevant?**

Q. And you also relayed that to Car 6 in which Jim Gant and Mr. Michael were riding? **A.** Yes, sir.

MR. ROBIN: If the Court please, we would like to introduce that entire paragraph from the notes.

* * *

P. G. HENLY, after having been first duly sworn, testified as follows, to wit:

DIRECT EXAMINATION

BY MR. ROBIN:

Q. Mr. Henly, you are Deputy Sheriff, Orange County, are you not? **A.** Yes.

Q. Mr. Rex Wende is also a deputy sheriff? **A.** Yes, sir.

Q. State whether or not you and Mr. Wende were together around 2:45 on the morning of the 9th of May of this year? **A.** Yes, sir, we got together at Jones' Texaco Station.

Q. Had you received a call from the city desk? **A.** I received a call from the Sheriff.

Q. Sheriff over the telephone? **A.** Yes, sir.

Q. Over the telephone? **A.** Yes, sir.

Q. And what was the message that the Sheriff gave you and Mr. Wende over the telephone? **A.** He told me to get in the car as soon as I could and head north. He called Wende and had him also head north, and that Mrs. Hill had been raped by a colored subject; to get out there on the road.

* * *

MR. STILP: I have no further question of this witness.

THE COURT: Any further witnesses?

MR. ROBIN: Judge, Mr. Wende's testimony will be the same. I don't see any use to put that on there.

THE COURT: All right. And you are going to proffer into evidence the clothing the Defendant was wearing, is that right?

MR. ROBIN: That is right.

THE COURT: Your objection is it's the fruit of an illegal arrest, right?

MR. STILP: Yes, Your Honor. We have submitted to you this brief based first upon the Constitution of the State, then upon Article 3823 of the State Code of Criminal Procedure, and Article 106. I have cited for you approximately fifteen cases of which four are rape cases wherein the facts and circumstances are paralleled fairly closely to the facts and circumstances in question in this case.

I wish to point out to the Court that the cases have all held that it is what preceded the arrest and not the fruits, what the fruits developed, and that is what the testimony has been, in my opinion, whether they matched tracks out there or whether they did not. Because the shoes that were taken from this Defendant, if they matched, were subsequent to his illegal arrest.

Your Honor, 38.23 is relied upon by the Defendant. "No evidence obtained by an officer or other person in violation of any provisions of the Constitution or laws of the State, or of the Constitution or laws of the United States of America, shall be admitted in evidence against the accused on the trial of any criminal case."

Section 9 of the Constitution, Article 1: "The people shall be secure in their persons."

Now, Your Honor, it's regrettable that the arrest had to be made on such an open accusation of "stop every person of the Negro race". That would mean if it had been a preacher, if it had been a pregnant woman, they would have been subject to a stop and a search.

THE COURT: Counsel, pardon me just a moment. One of the instructions there, and I looked at it hastily, did it say coming from the north or on that highway?

MR. ROBIN: Yes; and males, not females.

MR. STILP: Your Honor, I believe that is incorrect. "If we would stop every car that had colored subjects in them and hold them until they could get there." There is no mention thereof only cars coming from the north.

THE COURT: All right.

MR. STILP: The reference to north is the address of the complaining witness in this case.

Furthermore, Your Honor, we would rely upon 1.06. "The people shall be secure in their persons, houses, papers and possessions from all unreasonable seizures or searches. No warrant to search any place or to seize any person or thing shall issue without describing them as near as may be, nor without probable cause supported by oath or affirmation." Certainly, there was not the least intimation here a felony was committed. Now, based upon our Supreme Court decision in Ray v. Boyd, Supreme Court, 1943, I call the Court's attention to the only circumstances there that an arrest may be made without a warrant are probable cause.

THE COURT: Counsel, let me have an opportunity to study this over just about five minutes here. I think the Court will then be in a position to make a ruling on it.

Did you have anything in particular you wanted to submit, Mr. Robin?

MR. ROBIN: Nothing except probable cause.[28]

28. Do you find Stilp's argument clear? Was it based at all on the Fourth Amendment? Does it matter?

Notice that counsel has prepared a brief for the court. Presumably the brief discusses the relevant law and applies the rel-

THE COURT: All right.

(Mr. Lyle Stack was again placed on the stand, and testified further, to wit:)

Q. (By Mr. Robin) Mr. Stack, when you directed Mr. Henly and Mr. Wende to stop the cars coming in from the north—

MR. STILP: Your Honor, I object to that. He is trying to discredit his own witness here.

THE COURT: He can testify to whatever he did.

MR. STILP: He has already testified once, Your Honor.

THE COURT: Well, he can put him back on the stand, Counsel.[29]

Q. (By Mr. Robin) Did you or not direct them to any specific location? A. Highway north of town, and I told Wende to go to the cutoff that went from the highway towards Avon to 825 toward Chiclet. There is a cutoff out there, and I told him to get on that cutoff that leads to 825 in case traffic went through there.

Q. Now, had you received a call from Phil Hill? A. Yes.

Q. What information did he convey to you? A. Wanted to know if I could come out there; said a Negro broke in the house and raped his mother. He said, "I have already called the City Police." I knew they was out in the car. Then I said, "I will be right on out." Then I called the deputies, then I called back and talked to Endle at the Police Station, because I knew Phil had already called him.

Q. Did Mr. Hill say anything about which way the car was directed? A. Coming towards Sandle.[30]

Q. En route to Sandle? A. Yes.

* * *

MR. P. H. HILL, after having been first duly sworn, testified as follows, to wit:

DIRECT EXAMINATION

BY MR. ROBIN:

Q. Mr. Hill, what your initials? A. P. H. Hill.

evant statutory and case law to the facts of this particular case. The record that will be transmitted to the appellate court usually will include every piece of paper filed during the course of litigation, although some jurisdictions exclude briefs and certain non-essential papers. In Chapter Nine we discuss the role of pleadings and their relationship to problems of proof. In most jurisdictions the appellate court will be able to see the briefs and the memoranda of points and authorities that are filed in support of trial motions. Orders entered by the court will also become part of the record. It should be obvious that a lawyer does not

have to state everything orally in order to preserve all points for appeal. Instead, lawyers can take advantage of preparation before trial and compile written statements of positions. Not only does this save court time, but a written statement is often a more careful outline of an argument than that which the lawyer is prepared to make during the rush of trial.

29. Is this proper procedure? Does defense counsel make an adequate response?

30. How could Mr. Hill possibly have known this?

Q. P. H. You are commonly known as Phil Hill? **A.** Yes, sir.

Q. Mr. Hill, on the morning of the 9th of May, 1967, did you by telephone call the Sheriff, Lyle Stack? **A.** I did.

Q. What if anything did you tell him at that time? **A.** I told him my mother had been raped, and that she thought the car went south; to stop everybody coming in from the north of town.

Q. You did tell him that the car was going south? **A.** Going south, yes, sir.

Q. Did you also call the city desk? **A.** I did.

Q. And give them the same information? **A.** I did.

Q. And how long after your mother got to your house did you call that information in? **A.** Well, I would say within five minutes. Soon as I got her tamed down and got all the details, I went right in the house and called.

Q. You didn't, of course, know who did the raping at all? **A.** No, I didn't.

Q. You knew somebody had raped your mother, and he was fleeing from the scene? **A.** I knew it was a Negro.

* * *

THE COURT: Mr. Stilp, the Court understands you have objected to all of this testimony with respect to the arrest, the clothes taken from the Defendant. If you desire to do so, the Court will afford you a running objection on this without the necessity of your having to object.[31]

MR. STILP: Thank you, Your Honor. We even wish to make it more explicit. We object to any mention of the automobile, any mention of tire tracks for the same reason, that they are fruits of the illegal arrest.

THE COURT: The Court understands that you have objection to all of this line of testimony without the necessity of having to object.

Let's bring the Jury in, please.

(At this time the Jury returned to the courtroom and the following proceedings were had, to wit:)

MR. LYLE STACK, having been previously sworn, testified as follows, to wit:

DIRECT EXAMINATION

BY MR. ROBIN:

[Most of the witness' testimony is similar to that given when the jury was absent. Note, however, how the defense raises new evidence issues.]

Q. Mr. Stack, on or about the 9th day of May, 1967, in the early hours of the morning, did you or did you not receive a call? **A.** Yes, I did.

---

31. What advantage is the trial judge conferring upon defense counsel?

Q. Who was the call from? **A.** From Phil Hill.

Q. What information, if any, did he convey to you?

MR. STILP: Your Honor, I am going to object to that on the basis it's hearsay. The witness is available to testify as to what he told the Sheriff. It would be admissible from him and not from the Sheriff as hearsay.

THE COURT: If he can identify his voice, I am going to allow him to testify.[32]

Q. (By Mr. Robin) Could you identify Phil's voice? **A.** Yes.

MR. STILP: Note our exception.

Q. As a matter of fact, he is a brother-in-law of yours? **A.** Yes.

MR. STILP: Now, Your Honor, that is uncalled for.

THE COURT: Sustain your objection. Gentlemen of the Jury, you are not to consider it for any purpose.

MR. ROBIN: He knew his voice.

THE COURT: All right, for that limited purpose only.[33]

MR. STILP: May I ask the Court to instruct the jury to disregard that completely for any purpose.

THE COURT: So far as the relationship of the Sheriff with P. H. (Phil) Hill, you will disregard any relationship and not consider it for any purpose whatsoever, other than the limited purpose for which it was admitted.

Q. (By Mr. Robin) Do you know or not the voice of Phil Hill? **A.** Yes, I know his voice. I talk to him on the phone quite a lot.

Q. And as a result of that call, what if anything did you do? **A.** I directed two deputies to go north of Sandle on the highway to stop any colored subject in a car.

Q. Do you know what happened, if anything, after that? **A.** After I called them?

Q. Yes. **A.** I called the City Police Station.

Q. What information did you give them? **A.** I told them to have their cars stop anything coming from the north with colored subjects in it.[34]

Q. Did you later receive any radio messages from either of the city cars or your own? **A.** As soon as I got in my car, I started talking to my deputies in their car, and at that time they had Elmer Brooks in the car with them.

Q. And where were they at that time? **A.** About a mile north of Blaine's Salvage on the Avon Highway, north of Sandle.

32. Is this the proper ruling?

33. What is the problem with this evidence? Is it relevant? Too prejudicial?

34. Is this the same testimony the witness gave outside the hearing of the jury?

Q. Did you or not then go to them? **A.** Yes.

Q. What if anything did you see at that time? **A.** I talked to them and talked to Elmer Brooks and observed his shoes and his clothing. We also stopped one truck there at a roadblock, and then I went on out to where the crime happened.

Q. Did you have any further conversation with the Sheriff's car? **A.** Yes. A little later I called them by radio from the location where the crime happened.

Q. What did you instruct them to do? **A.** I told them to place him in jail and bring his shoes back to the scene of the crime.

Q. Mr. Stack, would you be able to identify his shoes and trousers and shirt? **A.** Yes.

MR. STILP: Your Honor, we are going to object to the introduction of any shoes until custody has been shown and proven.

Q. (By Mr. Robin) Sheriff, have you had the custody of those shoes, pants and shirt ever since the night of May 9, 1967? **A.** I have had those shoes.

MR. STILP: "Those shoes", Your Honor, is incomplete. I would like to ask him to describe the shoes. "Those shoes" is meaningless to this Court and Jury.[35]

THE COURT: All right, you may answer the question. Describe the shoes. **A.** White tennis shoes.

Q. (By Mr. Robin) Are they the same shoes that you saw on the Defendant? **A.** Yes.

MR. STILP: We have a running objection on the introduction of all this testimony?

THE COURT: Yes, sir.

Q. (By Mr. Robin) Is that the shoes there? **A.** Yes, sir. These shoes have been in my vault ever since then.[36]

Q. Are there any distinguishing marks on the bottom of those shoes? **A.** There is some worn places and a crack on one of the heels.

Q. Is this the crack you refer to right here? **A.** Yes, sir.

Q. Mr. Stack, did you later see those shoes over there at Mrs. Hill's house? **A.** Yes, sir.

Q. Did you see any tracks? **A.** Yes, sir.

Q. Did you see those shoes compared to the tracks? **A.** Yes, sir.

Q. State whether or not they did fit the tracks. **A.** Identical.

---

35. Is the defense counsel helping his case by forcing the witness to become specific?

36. Had the Sheriff failed to lock up the shoes and left them in a desk drawer, would they be admissible?

Q. They were identical? **A.** Yes.

Q. State whether or not the split in the lefthand shoe was plain in the tracks in the sand? **A.** Yes, sir.

A. Did you observe where the tracks led to and led from out there at Hill's house that night? **A.** This track that I observed out there was in the driveway near her bedroom window on the south side of the house.

Q. That is the only place that you saw it? **A.** Yes.

Q. Now, I will ask you whether or not that is the shirt—

MR. STILP: Your Honor, we are going to object to dragging things out of this without setting a predicate or without proof by this witness he can identify them.

THE COURT: All right, Counsel, you will have to prove up your custody.

Q. (By Mr. Robin) Did you observe the shirt and trousers the Defendant was wearing? **A.** Yes, sir.

Q. Have you had them in your custody since that night? **A.** Not all the time.

Q. Where were they at the time when they were not in your custody? **A.** In the lab in Aldertown.

Q. They are the identical clothes you sent? **A.** Yes, sir.

Q. And when they were returned, they are still the identical clothes? **A.** Yes, sir.

MR. STILP: We object to their introduction, Your Honor. There has been a break in the custody of these clothes. We feel they have not been properly identified. There have been no identifying marks presented for which this witness can testify that that green shirt is the green shirt.

THE COURT: I don't believe the chain is complete there. I sustain your objection.[37]

MR. STILP: Thank you, Your Honor.

MR. ROBIN: If the Court please, now, I am asking if those were the identical clothes he sent down there, and were those the identical clothes again that come back to them, if he could swear to them, and he said he could.

THE COURT: Sustain the objection, Counsel.

Q. (By Mr. Robin) The shoes have been in your custody all the time? **A.** Yes.

MR. ROBIN: I believe that is all, Mr. Stack.

THE COURT: Cross-examination, Counsel?

---

37. **Why is the attempt at authentication ruled incomplete?**

CROSS-EXAMINATION

BY MR. STILP:

[The examination adds little to the testimony.]

* * *

Q. Were those good, solid footprints that you saw out there, complete footprints? **A.** They were pretty good footprints.

Q. Mr. Stack, what was the ground out there in that driveway? **A.** It's got a little sand in it. It's not too sandy. It's graveled.

Q. A lot of gravel? **A.** Yes.

MR. STILP: No further questions.

MR. ROBIN: That is all, Mr. Stack, at this time.

THE COURT: Your were sworn a few minutes ago?

MR. HENLY: Yes, sir.

MR. P. G. HENLY, having been previously sworn, testified as follows, to wit:

Q. Your name is P. G. Henly? **A.** Yes, sir.

Q. Deputy Sheriff, Orange County? **A.** Yes, sir.

Q. Mr. Henly on the morning of the 9th day of May, 1967, did you receive a call from anyone? **A.** Yes, sir, from Sheriff Stack; called me about 2:45.

Q. And what, if anything, did he order you to do? **A.** Told me to get in the car and get on the Avon Highway; that Phil's mother had been raped by a Negro male, to try to apprehend the subject coming from that direction.

Q. Was any other officer with you? **A.** Not at that time. He told me he would call Rex Wende, and I got in the car and started north and I was notified, when I went into service, I was notified by the city unit that they were at the intersection of the expressway and the Avon Highway at Jones' Texaco Station with the subject stopped there.

Q. Did you and Mr. Wende then proceed to that location? **A.** Yes, sir.

Q. Or did you meet Wende there at that location? **A.** Yes, sir.[38]

Q. At that time did you take the Defendant here into custody? **A.** Yes, sir.

Q. And then what, if anything, did you do with him? **A.** We started out the Avon Highway towards the Hills' to see if we could get him identified as being the subject that was out there, and in the process or on the way

38. **Does this witness seem more likely than the average witness to follow the lead** of the examiner? How would such an observation be helpful to the cross-examiner?

the Sheriff called and told us to hold up.   He wanted to talk to us before we went out there.   So he came and got with us at the intersection of Farm Road 531 and the Avon Highway, which I believe is 625, north of Sandle.

Q.   What happened there, if anything?   A.   He told us, after looking at the shoes and the clothes Brooks had on, to remain there and he would go on out to the scene and call us back, which he did.

Q.   When he called you back, what instructions did he give you?   A. He said that that was the subject and to put him in jail, bring his tennis shoes—

MR. STILP: Your Honor, I am going to object to any testimony about what the Sheriff said.   The Sheriff has been on the stand.[39]

THE COURT: Overrule your objection.

MR. STILP: Note our exception.

Q.   (By Mr. Robin) What did you all do?   A.   We turned around and started back to jail with him, and he threw a fit, blew up, and said he wasn't going to jail; no way we could take him there.   We would have to kill him first.   So I was driving, and I grabbed a set of handcuffs and stopped the car and handed the cuffs to Wende and we started to put the handcuffs on him.[40]

Q.   Did anyone come to your assistance?   A.   Yes.   I called for some assistance, because we didn't have enough room and couldn't manage to handcuff him in the car.

Q.   Who if anyone came to your assistance?   A.   Jim Gant and Jackie Michael.

Q.   Did you at that time put the cuffs on him?   A.   Yes, sir.

Q.   And what, if anything, did you do then?   A.   We carried him to jail and took his shoes off of him, put him in a cell, and took the shoes back to the Hills' residence and met the Sheriff out there.

Q.   All right.   Now, Mr. Henly, did you know the shoes that the Defendant had on?   A.   Yes, sir.

Q.   Do you know whether they have been in the custody of the Sheriff's Department ever since they were taken?[41]   A.   Yes, sir, they have.

Q.   I will ask you whether or not these are the shoes of the Defendant? A.   Yes, sir, those are the shoes that I took off of him at the jail, and the ones we have had in the vault every since.

Q.   Now, was that split there on that heel at the time?   A.   Yes, sir, it was just like that.

39.   **What is the basis of the objection? Is the ruling proper?**

40.   **Would you object to this evidence? On what ground?   As prosecutor how would you justify this testimony?**

41.   **Given the Sheriff's testimony, is this question objectionable?   Is this ruling correct?**

Q. Mr. Henly, did you later take those shoes out to the Hills? **A.** Yes, sir.

Q. What if anything did you do then? **A.** I laid them down beside the track that was made there at the scene and took a photograph of them.

MR. STILP: Your Honor, I have a running objection to all this testimony.

THE COURT: Yes, sir, I understand.

Q. (By Mr. Robin) Will you state whether or not in comparing the shoes to the tracks, whether or not in your opinion those shoes made those tracks? **A.** Yes, sir, in my opinion they were the ones that made them. They were identical to the tracks.

MR. STILP: Your Honor, I am going to object. He has not been classified and proved to be an expert.

THE COURT: Overrule your objection.[42]

MR. STILP: Note our exception.

Q. (By Mr. Robin) Mr. Henly, there is a split heel on one of those shoes on the lefthand shoe, is that right? **A.** Yes, sir the lefthand heel.

Q. State whether or not that marking showed up in those tracks perfectly. **A.** It did.

Q. Was it perfect? **A.** Yes, sir.

Q. Have you got those pictures with you that you took? **A.** Yes, sir.

Q. May I have them, please?
(Handed to Mr. Robin.)

THE COURT: Do you want to see them, Counsel?
(Handed to Mr. Stilp.)

MR. STILP: We object to the introduction of them, Your Honor.

THE COURT: What is the basis?

MR. STILP: There hasn't been an adequate predicate laid.

THE COURT: The Court is going to afford Counsel an opportunity to lay a predicate and then rule on your objection.

MR. STILP: Thank you, Your Honor.

Q. (By Mr. Robin) I believe you stated that you placed the shoes down beside the tracks out there and took the photograph?

MR. STILP: Your Honor, he is testifying for the witness. **A.** Yes, sir.

42. **Do you understand the basis of the objection?**

USING THE BASIC EVIDENCE RULES

THE COURT: I believe that testimony has been given. That is repetition.

Q. And are these the pictures that you took? A. Yes, sir. This was taken in the driveway south of the house, and so was this one, a picture of the left shoe and a ruler and the track between them. This one is a picture of the same track taken north of the house at the road leading down to an irrigation well. Those tracks led from that location to the house and back to this location.

Q. I see.

MR. ROBIN: I would like to introduce all three of these photographs.

THE COURT: Counsel, unless it shows that they correctly portray what he saw out there, the predicate hasn't been laid.[43]

Q. (By Mr. Robin) Mr. Henly, are those the pictures that you took? A. Yes, sir.

Q. And of the impressions made by these shoes? A. Yes, sir.

Q. Do they correctly portray the tracks there? A. Yes, sir. In my opinion, they do.

THE COURT: All right, the Court is going to admit them into evidence.

MR. STILP: Note our exception thereto.[44]

Q. (By Mr. Robin) Mr. Henly, did you have an occasion out there to examine the hallway in the home of Mrs. Hill? A. Yes, sir.

Q. Did you have an occasion to observe the telephone? A. Yes, sir.

Q. What condition, if any, was that phone in? A. The receiver wire was jerked off the telephone.

Q. Did you or not take a picture of that telephone and the condition it was in when you got out there? A. Yes, sir.

THE COURT: Counsel, one qualification the Court is going to make on any picture admitted into evidence is that any writing on the back is going to have to be obliterated before they are displayed to the jury, either by pasting on or some means.

MR. STILP: This is a new set of pictures, Your Honor. I would like to see them, if I may.

THE COURT: They haven't yet been admitted into evidence, Counsel.

Q. (By Mr. Robin) Is this the picture you took of the telephone? A. Yes, sir, it is.

Q. I believe the wire shows to be jerked off the receiver? A. Yes, sir, jerked loose from the receiver. That is in the hallway on the north side of the hall, right across the hall from her bedroom door.

43. **Should the Court suggest the predicate to the prosecutor?**

44. **Why is counsel still objecting?**

Q. Mr. Henly, did you or not take any picture of the kitchen window? **A.** Yes, sir. I believe I took two of those.

MR. ROBIN: I would like to introduce this picture of the telephone.

THE COURT: Counsel, until you show that it correctly portrays what he saw out there, I can't admit it into evidence.

Q. (By Mr. Robin) Is that a picture of what you saw? **A.** Yes, sir.

Q. Does it correctly show the kitchen window and its being open and all the details of it? **A.** Yes, sir. The picture of the telephone shows the cord hanging down there where it was jerked loose, and the picture of the window shows that the window was standing open and in the position it was when I got out there.

Q. All right.

THE COURT: All right.

MR. STILP: We object to the pictures of the window as superfluous in this case.[45]

THE COURT: Overruled.

MR. STILP: Note our exception.

MR. ROBIN: I believe that is all at this time.

CROSS-EXAMINATION

BY MR. STILP:

Q. Mr. Henly, have you ever seen any other tennis shoes that looked like those? **A.** No, sir, not just like those.

Q. You wouldn't testify whether or not they are a common pair or an odd pair or anything else, would you? **A.** They are pretty odd with the markings they have on them.

Q. Pretty well worn, aren't they? **A.** Yes, sir.

Q. Would you say that any tennis shoes that had the appearance those have would be well worn on the bottom?[46] **A.** Probably, but not in the exact places those are.

Q. Mr. Henly, how long have you been in law enforcement? **A.** Since January, 1956.

Q. All right. Since you have been in law enforcement, have you had the occasion to investigate many crimes? **A.** Quite a few, yes, sir.

Q. You take quite a few of the pictures for the Sheriff's Department? **A.** That is right.

Q. You do the fingerprinting? **A.** Some of it.

45. What does counsel mean by superfluous?

46. What is the point the defense counsel is trying to make? Is this witness the best person to use to attempt to make this point?

Q. Where are the fingerprints that were made at the Hill residence on May 9, 1967? **A.** I beg your pardon?

Q. Where are those fingerprints that were made at the Hill residence on May 9, 1967? **A.** I didn't obtain any fingerprints.[47]

Q. You didn't obtain any? **A.** No, sir.

Q. Did you try? **A.** Tried to.

Q. Where did you try? **A.** Oh, around the window where the entrance was gained.

Q. All right. **A.** But nothing but smudges there.

Q. Where else? **A.** That is all.

Q. Mr. Henly, you have testified that this picture portrays the true and exact circumstances of the telephone, is that correct? **A.** That is right.

Q. Did you check that telephone for fingerprints? **A.** No, sir.

Q. Why didn't you? **A.** Because it had been handled by too many people. You can't take fingerprints off those things.

THE COURT: Counsel, just a minute before any picture is displayed to the jury. Any writing that is on the back of those pictures is not admitted into evidence. I don't know unless it's just a name or something to identify it on there. I haven't seen what the writing is.

MR. STILP: I don't think it's any problem. You might instruct the jury not to look at the back of them. I am sure they wouldn't.

THE COURT: If it's just merely identification. I didn't know what was written on the back of the picture, and obviously any extraneous writing—

MR. STILP: I would like for the jury to see the telephone.

THE COURT: All right.

MR. STILP: Pass that around.

(Handed to the jury).

Q. (By Mr. Stilp) Mr. Henly, you say the telephone had been handled by a lot of people, is that right? The reason you didn't try to take any fingerprints on it? **A.** It probably had. They all usually do. In these circumstances it was Mrs. Hill's home, and I don't know how many times she handled it since it had been cleaned and so forth. You just don't pick up fingerprints off objects like that.[48]

Q. Mr. Henly, you knew, and you took the picture of the telephone, and you knew that the wire had been jerked off. **A.** Yes, sir.

47. Would an objection be sustained on the ground that this is outside the scope of the direct examination?

48. Do you believe the witness' explanation of why no attempt was made to take fingerprints?

Q. And you knew that it had been handled by the Defendant? **A.** The telephone necessarily hadn't been. You can jerk a wire without grabbing ahold of the telephone. You could grab the wire.

Q. How would you guess that he jerked—that whoever it was jerked the wire off that telephone? **A.** Well, that is hard to say. It would just be a guess on my part or anyone else's with the exception of him.

Q. Your guess would be as good as anybody else's, wouldn't it? **A.** With the exception of the one that jerked it off, yes, sir.

Q. But isn't it very likely that he put one hand on the telephone and one hand on the wire and jerked it? **A.** It's possible.

Q. Where did you find the telephone? **A.** On the stand.

Q. Right there just like it is? **A.** In the picture, yes.

Q. All right. Mr. Henly, if the individual that jerked that wire loose had not held the telephone, he would have jerked the telephone off the stand, wouldn't he? **A.** Possibly.

Q. And there is a good reason to believe there had to be some fingerprints on that telephone? **A.** Not necessarily.

Q. Okay. Now, where else did you try to find some fingerprints? **A.** That is all.

Q. You didn't try the front door? **A.** (Witness nodded no).

Q. Were you not told that the party left by the front door? **A.** Yes.

Q. And you didn't dust the— **A.** No, sir. That is another surface you cannot obtain fingerprints from.

Q. You have obtained fingerprints from doorknobs? **A.** No, sir.

Q. You never have? **A.** No, sir. I don't know of very many that have.[49]

Q. Okay. **A.** Those surfaces are too rough.

Q. Now, on the ground under the window at the Hill's residence there, what did you find besides that old tire there, tire rim or whatever that is? **A.** That is a tire wheel and the screen that came off the window.

Q. Okay. Did you find anything else there, Mr. Henly? **A.** Not that I recall. There was—Let's see. There was possibly some more items there, but I don't recall what they were.

Q. Did you find a flower pot about the size of this drinking glass? **A.** Yes, there was a flower pot there, since you mentioned it. I forgot about that.

Q. Was it standing upright, just like this? **A.** No, I believe it was lying on the ground.

49. Is this line of questioning likely to be effective absent the production of an ex-   pert witness to contradict the Deputy Sheriff regarding proper procedures?

Q. You are not sure about that, though? **A.** No, sir.

Q. That flower pot have a smooth or rough surface? **A.** It's rough.

Q. Did you dust it for fingerprints? **A.** No, sir, for the same reason I didn't dust the other.

Q. How long is the hallway, Mr. Henly, in the house that has been referred to by the District Attorney in this case, approximately? **A.** Exactly, I couldn't say. It's probably twelve feet, something like that. I would say roughly that, ten or twelve feet. There is, I believe four doors into it, I believe.

Q. Actually, isn't the hallway about as long from you to the other end of that blackboard there? Wouldn't that be about right? **A.** I didn't think it was quite that long. It could be. I didn't pay that much attention to it. I didn't measure it either.

Q. Did you notice the light in the hallway? **A.** Yes, sir.

Q. In your estimation, what was the size of that light bulb? **A.** I didn't look at it, but I would assume it's either a sixty or seventy-five watt bulb.

Q. A small one? **A.** Yes.

Q. Did you ever see a search warrant or a warrant of arrest for anyone on the night of May 9, 1967? **A.** Saw the warrant that day, that morning after we—

Q. I am talking about the night, from 2:45 until approximately 9:00 o'clock, we will say, on the morning of May 9th. Did you see a search warrant or a warrant of arrest? **A.** No.

Q. You did place Elmer Brooks in custody? **A.** Yes, sir.

Q. And you arrested him? **A.** Yes, sir.

Q. And he resisted arrest? **A.** Yes.

Q. And yet you went ahead and forcibly put the handcuffs on him and took him to jail? **A.** Yes.

Q. Yet you did not have a warrant of arrest? **A.** Had enough information I thought I didn't need one.

Q. Had anyone told you that night to arrest Elmer Brooks before you received a call from Sheriff Stack? **A.** From the Sheriff?

Q. Yes. **A.** No.

Q. Mr. Henly, after you left your home in the early hours of the morning, did you have radio contact—Was the car at your home? **A.** Yes.

Q. Did you have the car? **A.** I had one of them, yes, sir.

Q. Unit what? Nine? Ten? **A.** Nine.

Q. Did you receive any information by radio that night describing either the automobile that you were to apprehend or the individual? **A.** Not so far as an actual description of the automobile.   It was an automobile in route toward Sandle on that highway with a colored male in it.

Q.   Male or males?   A.   Colored male is all I had.

Q.   You just had male?   A.   Just male.   Colored subject is all I had there.

Q.   Colored subject or subjects?   A.   Subject.   I didn't know how many was in the car.   I had no way to know.

Q.   You had been in the courtroom when Sheriff Stack testified? [50]   A. Yes.

Q.   Do you remember that he testified "stop every car that had colored subjects?"   A.   Well, I would refer to that as not necessarily not being more than one in a car.

Q.   Or if there had been ten, you would have stopped them anyway, wouldn't you?   A.   Yes, sir, probably.

Q.   You didn't see any felony committed on the night of May 9, 1967? A.   No, sir, I didn't see.

Q.   When you arrived at the Texaco Station on the expressway, did you see a felony committed?   A.   No, sir.

Q.   Did you see a breach of the peace?   A.   No, sir.

Q.   All right.

MR. STILP: No further questions of this witness.

MR. ROBIN: That is all for the time being.

MR. REX WENDE, after having been first duly sworn, testified as follows, to wit:
BY MR. ROBIN:

Q.   Your name is Rex Wende?

MR. STILP: Your Honor, to expedite matters, we will stipulate that he will testify exactly as Officer Henly did.

MR. ROBIN: That is fine and dandy.

THE COURT: That stipulation is entered into by Defendant and counsel for Defendant?

MR. STILP: That is correct.

THE COURT: Does the Defendant so stipulate?

MR. STILP: Yes, Your Honor.

THE COURT: He will have to speak.

MR. STILP: We withdraw the stipulation.

50.   **Did the defense counsel make a mistake in not requesting that the witnesses be sequestered?**

THE COURT: All right. I am not going to admit the stipulation, unless it's entered into by the Defendant and counsel for Defendant. Only counsel for Defendant has entered into the stipulation.

MR. ROBIN: I understand, but I thought he did.

MR. STILP: Your Honor, I feel that I can enter the stipulation for the Defendant, but I would prefer the Defendant not enter into it.

THE COURT: All right. I am not going to admit your stipulation.[51]

Q. (By Mr. Robin) Your name is Rex Wende? A. Yes, sir.

Q. Deputy Sheriff of Orange County? A. Yes, sir.

[A portion of Deputy Sheriff Wende's testimony that repeats points made by prior witnesses is omitted.]

Q. Now, Mr. Wende, did you on that night see the shoes that the Defendant here was wearing? A. Yes, sir.

Q. Did you see them after they were taken off of him? A. Yes, sir.

Q. Did you or not go back out to the Hills' with the shoes in your custody? A. Yes, sir.

Q. State whether or not you compared out there yourself the shoes to the tracks at the Hills' residence? A. I did.

Q. Did they correctly portray the markings in the tracks as coming from those shoes?

MR. STILP: Your Honor, I object to leading the witness.

THE COURT: Overruled.

A. Exactly.

MR. STILP: Note our exception.

Q. Mr. Wende, did you or not go inside the Hills' residence? A. Yes, sir, I did.

Q. Did you or not see the telephone? A. Yes, sir, I did.

Q. State whether or not the telephone was in order or if anything had been done to it. A. Wire that goes to the receiver was broken off or cut off.

Q. Was the receiver back in the cradle? A. Right.

Q. Mr. Wende, are you acquainted with party line telephones? A. Yes, sir.

Q. Are you acquainted with the fact that if you leave a telephone off on a party line—

MR. STILP: Your Honor, that is leading.

---

51. **What reason might there be for defense counsel's unwillingness to permit the defendant to enter the stipulation?**

THE COURT: I believe you are getting into a leading question.

Q. (By Mr. Robin) Are you acquainted with the operation of those? **A.** Yes, sir.

Q. State what would happen if on that party line a receiver is left off the hook. **A.** There would be a busy signal. No one else on that line would be—On a party line, from four to eight on the party line, and I believe it would be four direct on that line, and if you pick up the receiver it would be a busy signal and you could not call out there.

Q. So what did that, if anything, indicate to you? **A.** Well, I don't know exactly what you mean by that.

Q. Would that receiver had to have been back on the cradle before her son—[52]

MR. STILP: Oh, Your Honor, please.

Q. —could have called in?

MR. STILP: Your Honor, that has no relevancy and no bearing whatsoever on any issue in this case.

THE COURT: What would be the relevancy?

MR. ROBIN: I want to show that he is bound to have been the one that put the receiver back in the cradle, because she went to her son's house, who is on the same line.

MR. STILP: Approach the bench?

THE COURT: Approach the bench.

(Counsel approached the bench.)

Q. (By Mr. Robin) Mr. Wende, did you observe anything about the kitchen or any of the windows or doors of the house? **A.** The kitchen window. The screen was torn off of it, and I believe there was a flower pot there which it looked like had just been pitched outside, and the window was up.

Q. The window was up? **A.** Yes, sir.

Q. And that was before daylight? **A.** That is right.

Q. That was in the early hours of the morning? **A.** Yes, sir.

Q. Of the 9th of May? **A.** Yes.

MR. ROBIN: I believe that is all.

CROSS-EXAMINATION

BY MR. STILP:

Q. Mr. Wende, can you truthfully say that I didn't take that screen off that window? **A.** Well, I wouldn't think you would.

---

52. Do you follow the prosecutor's line of questions? Are they relevant?

Q. Answer my question. You couldn't say that I didn't do it, could you? **A.** No.

Q. Mr. Wende, this case has been awfully hard on you because those are life-long friends out there? **A.** That is right.

Q. You have had to restrain yourself pretty heavy, haven't you? **A.** Right.[53]

Q. Just one or two questions, Mr. Wende. Did you see Elmer Brooks commit any felony or breach of the peace on the night of May 9, 1967? **A.** No.

Q. All right. When you arrived at the Texaco station, he was in custody of two officers, is that right? **A.** He was standing beside the car there when we drove up.

Q. And you and Officer Henly then in turn took him in your car? **A.** Right.

Q. He could not have left, is that right? **A.** We didn't intend for him to.

Q. Furthermore, when you told him you were going to take him to jail, he attempted to resist? **A.** Right.

Q He told you he was guilty of no crime, did he not? **A.** I don't remember him saying he wasn't guilty of any crime.

Q. Well, you are bound to have given him some reason for taking him to jail, wouldn't you? **A.** Well, I figured he knew what he had done is the reason he resisted arrest.

Q. Well, Mr. Wende, you are not trying to tell this jury or me that you are a mind reader? **A.** Well, no, I am not a mind reader.

Q. As I say, you are pretty emotional on this case?

MR. STILP: I don't think I have any further questions. Thank you.

MR. JOE RATLIF, after having been first duly sworn, testified as follows, to wit:

DIRECT EXAMINATION

BY MR. ROBIN:

Q. Your name is Joe Ratlif? **A.** Joe Ratlif.

Q. Mr. Ratlif, on the morning of May 9, 1967, did you or not go to the home of Mrs. Ethel Hill? **A.** I did.

Q. Would you state approximately what time it was when you went over there? **A.** It must have been around 3:00 o'clock, maybe a little after.

Q. In the morning? **A.** Yes, sir.

53. **How can these questions possibly help the defendant?**

Q. Mr. Ratlif, did you see any tracks around the Hill house? **A.** Yes, sir.

Q. Did you see any comparisons being made with the shoes and those tracks? **A.** Yes, sir.

Q. Of white tennis shoes? **A.** Yes, sir.

Q. Would you know those tennis shoes, if you should see them? **A.** I think so.

MR. STILP: Your Honor, we have objected to this entire line of testimony. May we have a running objection to this entire line of testimony?

THE COURT: What is the basis of your objection?

MR. STILP: The basis, Your Honor, is predicated back upon the original proposition that the entire arrest was illegal, and any evidence adduced from that arrest would be inadmissible.[54]

THE COURT: I am going to overrule your objection.

MR. STILP: Note our exception thereto. May I have a bill on that later?

THE COURT: Yes, sir, you may.

Q. (By Mr. Robin) Mr. Ratlif, can you identify those shoes as being the ones compared to the tracks? **A.** Yes, sir, that is the ones.

Q. Did those shoes or not fit the tracks? **A.** Yes, sir, they did.

Q. Was the markings perfect or obliterated or what? **A.** They looked real plain.

[The remaining testimony of Mr. Ratlif describes the condition of Mrs. Hills' telephone. It is omitted, as is a brief cross-examination by defense counsel.]

MR. JIM GANT, having been previously sworn, testified as follows, to wit:

[His testimony is largely redundant and therefore is omitted.]

* * *

MR. STILP: No further questions.

MR. LYLE STACK, recalled by the State, took the stand and testified further, to wit:

RE-DIRECT EXAMINATION

BY MR. ROBIN:

Q. Mr. Stack, the testimony shows that you called back to Mr. Wende and Mr. Henly to take the Defendant to jail and bring his shoes. Had you been given a description of the Defendant at that time?

---

54. Counsel was told by the judge that he did not have to make repeated objections. Yet he does. Why? Is there a danger that his tactics will backfire and that the defendant's case will be harmed?

MR. STILP: Your Honor, he is testifying.

A. Yes.

MR. STILP: I object to that.

Q. Who if anyone gave you that description?

THE COURT: Overrule your objection. Go ahead and answer the question.

MR. STILP: Note our exception thereto.

A. I stopped at Phil Hill's house and Mrs. Hill was there, and she described the clothing and the shoes that the Negro that raped her had on. I didn't tell her that we had him stopped at that time, but after she gave me the description of what he was wearing, and I had already seen before I went out there, then I went up to her house and looked at the shoe tracks, then knowing them in my own mind I thought we had the right Negro, and that is when I called in.

Q. That is when you called? A. The car that had him in their car, yes.

MR. ROBIN: That is all.

BY MR. STILP:

Q. Mr. Stack, do you know the mandates of the Code of Criminal Procedure that any man arrested without a warrant will be immediately taken before a magistrate? A. That is right.

Q. You did not take Elmer Brooks before a magistrate until 9:00 or 10:00 o'clock the next morning? A. We didn't right then, no.

MR. STILP: No further questions.

MR. ROBIN: That is all.

If the Court please, I think we need to approach the bench out of the presence of the jury.

(Counsel approached the bench.)

THE COURT: Gentlemen of the Jury, we are going to stand aside until 1:15. Bear in mind the Court's instructions heretofore given you not to discuss the case among yourselves or with anyone else, nor are you to permit anyone to discuss the case with you. You are not to listen to any report on the radio or television or read any account that there might be in the newspaper concerning this case.

When you return at 1:15, reassemble in the jury room where you assembled this morning.

Thank you very much. See you at 1:15.

(Reporter's note: The following proceedings were had outside the Jury's presence:)

THE COURT: All right. Now, have you got any preliminary matters to take up out of the jury's presence?

MR. ROBIN:　The State at this juncture rests.

MR. STILP:　Your Honor, we would like to make a Motion for Instructed Verdict, please.

Now comes the Defendant, Elmer Brooks—

THE COURT:　Now, let me suggest this, Counsel.　After the jury comes back in, maybe you better announce that you rest in their presence, Counsel, but for the purpose of this Motion, let the record reflect that he has already rested, so we won't have to get the jury back out again.

MR. STILP:　Now comes the Defendant, Elmer Brooks, and makes this his Motion for Instructed Verdict based upon the following facts:　First, that the State has not proved beyond a reasonable doubt that the Defendant is the party that committed the alleged crime for which he has been tried;　second, that the State has failed to sustain its burden, and that the evidence adduced at this point has been insufficient.　Furthermore, the Defendant would ask leave of this Court to file additional basis for the Instructed Verdict at such time as the State closes.

THE COURT:　Motion for Instructed Verdict is overruled.

MR. STILP:　Note our exception thereto.

(At this time a recess was taken.)

(At 1:15 the Jury returned to the courtroom and the following proceedings occurred in its presence:)

THE COURT:　All right, gentlemen, if you are ready to proceed.

MR. ROBIN:　The State rests.

* * *

THE COURT:　This is your first witness, Mr. Stilp?

MR. STILP:　Yes, Your Honor.

MR. ARNOLD TOLOT, after having been first duly sworn, testified as follows, to wit:

DIRECT EXAMINATION

BY MR. STILP:

Q.　Will you state your full name for the Court and jury, please, sir?　A.　Arnold Tolot.

Q.　Where do you live, Mr. Tolot?　A.　Wichita.

Q.　All right, sir.　What is your occupation, sir?　A.　I am a parole officer for the State.

Q.　Do you have a particular area that is assigned to you or that you work?　A.　I do.

Q.　What is that area, please, sir?　A.　It consists of ten counties of which Orange is one.

Q. Orange is one? **A.** Yes.

Q. Mr. Tolot, do you know the Defendant in this case, Elmer Brooks? **A.** I do.

Q. Have you had the occasion to handle him, so to speak, in your official capacity? **A.** Yes, sir.

Q. You have been his parole officer, is that correct? **A.** That is right.

Q. Do you remember when he was first given to you or assigned to you? **A.** He was paroled on the 30th of March of this year.

Q. Have you had the occasion to personally visit with Elmer Brooks? **A.** Yes, sir, I visited with him the day after he was paroled at his home, and subsequent to that, approximately two weeks later I again visited Elmer Brooks at his home, and then I again visited with him in the Orange County Jail.

Q. Do you remember when that visit was in the County Jail? **A.** I believe it was on the 17th of May.

Q. Mr. Tolot, in the course of your work, are you given certain reports by the various governmental agencies that handle prisoners or parolees? **A.** Yes, sir.

Q. Is one of them an admission report? **A.** Yes, sir, an admission summary.

Q. Do you have an admission summary in your possession that was sent to you by the Texas Department of Corrections? **A.** Yes, sir.

Q. Do you also have a parole summary, or do you get a summary from the State Parole Board? [55] **A.** Yes, sir.

Q. Is that called a parole summary? **A.** Yes, sir, there is a parole summary, a parole placement request and another document which is known as the parole summary.

Q. All right. Parole placement, parole summary, and what is the other? **A.** The parole placement request and the parole summary.

Q. The two items. The parole summary, which you have in your possession, by whom is that signed? **A.** It's signed by Mr. Willis, the Supervisor, but it was prepared by Ira Hens, the Institutional Parole Officer.

Q. May I have the parole summary, please, sir?
(Handed to Mr. Stilp.)

Q. Mr. Tolot, you are an employee of the State? **A.** I am.

Q. And you are here in answer to a summons issued by me in behalf of the Defendant in this case? **A.** I am.

---

55. Note that no objection is made that these reports are hearsay. Why not?

Q. You were also summoned to bring these reports with you? **A.** That is right.

Q. They have been in your official custody since you received them from the State Agency? **A.** That is right.

Q. They are not available to anyone except by this procedure? **A.** That is right.

Q. You are paid to come here by the State if you get any additional pay, is that correct? **A.** Yes, sir.

Q. You do not accept any pay from the Defendant in this case? **A.** No, sir.[56]

MR. STILP: We would like to offer the parole summary into evidence, your Honor, as Defendant's Exhibit 1.[57]

Q. (By Mr. Stilp) Mr. Tolot, in order to qualify for your job as a parole supervisor, do you have to possess certain educational qualifications?

A. Yes, sir.

Q. And what are those, please, sir? **A.** The law states that a person needs to be a graduate of an accredited college or to have two years of college with the equivalent being in experience, the other two years.

Q. Have you had training in the field of sociology? **A.** Yes, sir.

Q. Are you a sociologist? **A.** No, sir.

Q. Are you a psychologist? **A.** My major field of study in college was psychology.

Q. Could you give us any estimate of about how many parolees you have handled in your tenure in office? **A.** Possibly between eight and nine hundred.

Q. All right. Have you been able to form any opinion from your visits, association with the various parolees as to their mental capacities? **A.** I think that everyone is inclined to judge the mental capabilities of those persons with whom they come in contact.

Q. Have you seen and talked with Elmer Brooks enough to form an opinion as to his mental capabilities? **A.** The opinion that I have of his mental capabilities is not in variance with the indicated or the tested record of his intelligence as furnished me in the material you have there.

Q. All right, sir, I will read to you from the parole report. "Psychological: Appears of dull intelligence and institutional testing would tend to verify this. Seems to express himself and get along with others on a level

---

56. **Why are these questions asked? Are they premature?**

57. **If an objection were made on the grounds that the parole summary is hear-** say and not properly authenticated, would the objection be sustained?

about equal with people considered of dull intelligence, while his plans for the future seem realistic only to the extent he can project them and with his attitude toward acceptance of parole conditions seeming good only insofar as he understands them." Then would you go along with the State's evaluation, psychological evaluation of this Defendant?[58] **A.** Yes, sir.

Q. That he is of dull intelligence? **A.** Yes, sir.

Q. Now, do you have with you other reports, the admission summary? (Handed to Mr. Stilp.)

For the benefit of the jury, Mr. Tolot, could you tell them how this admission report is prepared, if you know? **A.** To my knowledge, it is prepared at the time the man initially arrives at the State Department of Corrections. It is compiled from information which is obtained from the inmate by personal interview, and also, I believe, that certain information is verified by certain records, documents and letters.

Q. They are given tests? I.Q. tests? **A.** It is my understanding they are, yes, sir.

Q. Is this the only summary that you have? **A.** I have a record of his test scores which is separate from that.

Q. May I see that, please, sir? (Handed to Mr. Stilp.)

Q. Mr. Tolot, I can't find the name of the party that prepared the admission summary. **A.** I don't believe that that is signed, sir. This is a combined effort at the institution.

Q. I see.

MR. STILP: Your Honor, I believe that is all I have of this witness at this time. I would like for him to be available for recall.

CROSS-EXAMINATION

BY MR. ROBIN:

Q. Mr. Tolot, at this time the parole has been revoked upon this Defendant, has it not? **A.** Yes, sir, it has.

Q. Upon a charge of three years for theft from a person of Orange County?[59] **A.** Yes, sir.

Q. I believe that was in 1965, is that correct? **A.** I believe that is correct, sir.

MR. ROBIN: No further questions.

MR. IRA B. HENS, after having been first duly sworn, testified as follows, to wit:

58. Is it proper to read from this document? Is the witness qualified to give an opinion? Why is there no objection?

59. Is this beyond the scope of direct? Is this impermissible evidence of "other crimes?" Why is there no objection?

DIRECT EXAMINATION

BY MR. STILP:

Q. Will you state your full name for the Court and jury, please, sir? **A.** Ira B. Hens.

Q. Where do you live, Mr. Hens? **A.** In Hardy.

Q. And where are you employed? **A.** I am employed as an institutional parole officer by the Division of Parole Supervision. Our office is in Richmond. I am assigned certain units for the compilation of parole reports for parole consideration.

Q. Mr. Hens, are there certain educational requirements you must possess before you can maintain that position? **A.** Yes, sir. They are the same as for the District Parole Officer, actually.

Q. And are you a graduate of a university or college? **A.** Yes, sir, I have a Bachelor Degree from the University of Hardy.

Q. In what field? **A.** Sociology.

Q. All right. That field of sociology deals with what? **A.** As I understand it, sociology deals with the factors going into—leading to the behavior of individuals.

Q. Mr. Hens, you are here because of a subpoena? **A.** I am.

Q. You were asked to bring, if you had any, records pertaining to the Defendant in this case, Elmer Brooks, is that not correct? **A.** I was so ordered.

Q. And you don't expect to receive any pay from the Defendant in this case, having been subpoenaed? **A.** No, sir.

Q. Being a State employee? **A.** That is correct.

Q. Is there a normal or accepted procedure whereby inmates are interviewed or processed before granted parole from the State Department of Corrections? **A.** Yes, sir.

Q. Is that the division that you are in? **A.** That is correct.

Q. All right. Do you remember having prepared the parole summary for Elmer Brooks? **A.** Actually, the name Elmer Brooks rings a bell, but the actual preparation of the summary, I couldn't testify definitely.

Q. If I show you a parole summary and ask you to examine that, please, sir. **A.** I believe this to be my report.

Q. All right, Mr. Hens, let me ask you if the information contained therein was derived through investigation by yourself or by subordinates, or both? **A.** I would say not subordinates. I would say associates.

Q. Excuse me. Associates. **A.** In as much as other documents were available to me, of which you have a sample here—

Q. Are you referring to the admission summary? **A.** That is correct.

Q. Which is prepared by the State Department of Corrections? **A.** Yes, sir.

Q. Mr. Hens, can you tell from that report what the I.Q. level or intelligence quotient is for Elmer Brooks? **A.** The psychological section of the report does not give an I.Q. level as such.

Q. Would the admission summary show that? **A.** Yes, sir, if you look in the education section.

Q. Would you examine the education portion and see if you can give us the figure shown for Elmer Brooks? **A.** This says his intelligence quotient is 67, according to the Gray-Votaw-Rogers General Achievement Test and the Otis-Form A Test.[60]

Q. Are you familiar with both of those tests, or those three tests, Mr. Hens? **A.** Not too familiar.

Q. Have you ever administered those tests, or any of them? **A.** No, sir.

Q. They are administered in the Department of Corrections by a qualified and competent person, is that correct? **A.** Yes, sir.

Q. All right. The figure 67, would you consider that high, low, average or what on the scale of human intelligence? **A.** I would consider it low.

Q. All right. I will ask you if you would consider it even mentally deficient? **A.** Borderline, if I may use that term.[61]

Q. Mr. Hens, I will ask you to examine the admission summary, please, sir, and tell me whether or not there is a grade level for the Defendant? **A.** This summary shows an educational achievement of 5.5. This is as of the time of his admission to the institution.

Q. What is that date, please, sir? **A.** February 25, 1966.

Q. All right, sir. 1966? **A.** Yes, sir.

Q. For the benefit of myself and the jury, could you tell me a little bit about that grade level of 5.5? Explain just exactly what that means, and if you can, how it was arrived at. **A.** Periodically, tests are given to determine educational achievement, and the grading on this test is measured against achievement on the part of people who have completed various periods of schooling. This would indicate a completion or achievement equal to someone who completed five and a half years of schooling.

Q. Five and a half years. Actually, Mr. Hens, is there any information in that report as to what grade Elmer Brooks did complete in school? Would you try and locate that for us, please sir? I hate to put you to the trouble, but I am not familiar with those reports, and I am sure you could find them a lot quicker than I could. **A.** He reported completion of the

---

60. Is this hearsay?   61. **Is the witness qualified to give this opinion?**

Eighth Grade in the Booker T. Washington Elementary School in Sandle, which he attended from 1955 until 1960. This was not verified.

Q. Which was not verified. All right, sir. As a practicing Psychologist, would you have an opinion, based upon the information that you have compiled there and what you have re-examined today, would you have an opinion as to the mental ability of this individual, the Defendant in this case, Elmer Brooks? **A.** I would describe it as limited.

Q. With the I.Q. of 67, the grade level of 5.5, would you feel that this type of individual could cope with society as a whole at this time? [62] **A.** Under appropriate direction.

Q. May I ask you to explain that a little further by way of clarifying it for me? **A.** A situation in which stresses and demands are not particularly great would be such in which a person of that intelligence level could adjust adequately, with the higher level decisions made for him by a competent person.

Q. Then you feel that a person of that intelligence level should be constantly supervised practically? **A.** Not necessarily constantly supervised as much as constantly assisted.

Q. Do you feel that constant assistance, help from any source would be beneficial, is that correct? **A.** Would you rephrase that question?

Q. Help from any source would be beneficial to any person of that grade level and intelligence level? **A.** I would say so, yes, sir.

Q. Mr. Hens, would you glance at the summary again, and tell this jury something of Elmer Brooks' family history, background there that you feel would be of benefit to them? [63] **A.** If I may be allowed to read my report concerning his family history. We use the letter "S" to stand for the subject in question.

"Subject is a twenty year old Negro male who was born in Sandle, of an illicit relationship between his natural parents, claiming one older and ten half-siblings by his mother's other relationships. Subject claims his half-brother, Robert Landers, has spent six months in SJTS for an unknown offense, claiming no other delinquency in his half-sibling group than his own. Subject reports separation of his natural parents when subject was about four years of age, indicating no contact with his father, and saying 'I wouldn't know him if I saw him.' Subject claims ceremonious marriage of his mother when he was about six years of age. Subject says his stepfather was always a farmer, while his mother was always a housewife. Subject says he feels closest to and feels himself most influenced by his mother's teachings, indicating his present situation does not reflect conformity to her example. Subject says he was raised by his mother and his maternal grandmother, receiving support from his stepfather's earnings as well as his mother's sometime work in the field. Subject claims child care was supplied by his grandmother, indicating departure from the family environment at age of

---

62. Is the witness qualified to answer this question?

63. Is this question proper? Why is no objection raised?

fourteen in order to go to SJTS, returning home thereafter until about age seventeen.   Subject claims at this time he moved out of the house to go to work and live with a female acquaintance.   Residence immediately prior to the instant offense is explained by subject as having been with his mother for about one year.   Subject claims life time State residence except for several months residence in another state in 1965, saying 'I went there to visit with my girlfriend.'   Subject claims a compatible relationship with all family members."

MR. STILP: No further questions.

THE COURT: Cross-examination?

CROSS-EXAMINATION

BY MR. ROBIN:

Q. Mr. Hens, it isn't your purpose in testimony to tell this jury that this Defendant didn't know the difference between right and wrong? **A.** No, sir.

Q. Having completed the Eighth Grade in school.   For my life, I can't see the purpose of the testimony.

MR. STILP: Your Honor, Mr. Robin certainly is not conducting—

THE COURT: If you have an objection to make, Counsel, make it and the Court will rule on it.

MR. ROBIN: I don't have an objection, and I am not asking any more questions.

THE COURT: All right.

MR. STILP: I ask the witness be excused, subject to recall.

THE COURT: All right.

MR. JAMES W. WOOD, after having been first duly sworn, testified as follows, to wit:

DIRECT EXAMINATION

BY MR. STILP:

Q. Will you state your full name for the Court and jury please, sir? **A.** James W. Wood.

Q. Where do you live, Mr. Wood? **A.** Hardy.

Q. Where are you employed? **A.** State Department of Corrections.

Q. How long have you been with them, sir? **A.** Since June of 1958.

Q. All right.   Mr. Wood, in your employment, do you prepare admission summaries for new prisoners coming into the penitentiary system? **A.** I did.

Q. I will show you an admission summary prepared for Elmer Brooks, and ask you if that was prepared either under your direction or if you are aware of the contents therein? **A.** I would like to say this, that a part of it I prepared. The balance of it is an accumulation of information from other departments in the Department of Corrections, part of it is.

Q. That is the formal and standard procedure, though, followed by the system, is that correct? **A.** Correct.

Q. Mr. Wood, I have never been down to Hardy, and I don't know whether the members of the jury have or not. Would you explain, if you would, please, how an inmate is treated when he first gets there, and say possibly through your report there. I hate to burden you, but I feel it would be important in this case. **A.** Well, when an inmate is received, he now is assigned to the diagnostic center for approximately three weeks prior to being assigned to his farm unit. During this period of time he is interviewed by the Sociologist, given I.Q. tests, E.A. tests; he is given a medical examination, something similar to a military reception center processing. After he has completed all this, he is then assigned with the qualification committee to a unit.

Q. About how long a period of time does that take? **A.** It ranges from two weeks to four weeks. Approximately three weeks would be average, I would say.

Q. The purpose for that is what? The basic purpose of that. **A.** In order to assign a man to the unit where he could best serve his time.

Q. Now, if you will examine the report there, Mr. Wood, do you find the results of an I.Q. test or intelligence quotient test? **A.** Yes, sir.

Q. And what is that figure? **A.** Subject's E.A. is 5.5, and his I.Q. is 67, according to Gray-Votaw-Rogers Achievement Test and Otis-Form A Test.

Q. Are you familiar with those tests? **A.** Not directly.

Q. Are they used constantly there in the system? **A.** Well, we use a test in sometimes assigning a man to the unit. We would like to know what his educational achievement is to assign him to the job he can properly do.

Q. Now, your educational achievement there was what? **A.** 5.5.

Q. And in your opinion, from having prepared—Have you prepared numerous reports of that type? **A.** Yes.

Q. And from your experience, having prepared those reports, what would you say the condition of a person be that has that 5.5? **A.** Well, it's slightly below the normal for the prison population.

Q. Where would it be on a scale for the average person of nineteen years of age, which is what he was at the time he was there? **A.** It would be below that.

Q. Would you even put it as far down as mentally deficient? **A.** Well, I am not qualified to say.

Q. Does the report in any way place it in the scale? Where does the report place it, or does it? **A.** It doesn't.

Q. Now, who does the evaluation, then, based upon that report? Do you do that in placement? **A.** With the committee, the classification committee.

Q. You are one of the members? **A.** Yes.

Q. What type of work, then, would you place an individual in that has that mental age? **A.** We assigned him to farm work.

Q. Farm work. Feeling that that would be the best place for him? **A.** Yes.

Q. Now, how about your I.Q. level? I believe you say that was 67 there? **A.** Right.

Q. Where would that fall in the average, the scale of average people? **A.** It would be below normal.

Q. Below the normal. Normal would be what? **A.** Well, for the prison population, the average, it averages approximately 80.

Q. And even for the prison population it was quite low? **A.** It was below normal.

Q. Do you have them as low as 25? **A.** I don't remember seeing any that low. If it was that low, usually they are not capable of testing.

Q. Do you remember about what figure your tests usually run? **A.** I beg your pardon?

Q. What is the lowest figure that your tests have shown? **A.** I couldn't tell you.

Q. I notice one of your sheets there say "No results". What does that sheet mean? I am sorry. It's on the parole summary. Are you familiar at all with these parole summaries? **A.** I know something about them. I am not familiar with the test, but to the best of my knowledge, this indicates what specific fields that the man might have an aptitude for, and it didn't indicate anything.

Q. Mr. Wood, you are here because you were summoned? **A.** Yes, sir.

Q. And you do not expect to be paid anything for your services by the Defendant? **A.** No, sir.

Q. You are a State employee? **A.** Yes.

MR. STILP: No further questions at this time.

CROSS-EXAMINATION

BY MR. ROBIN:

Q. Mr. Wood, I believe the Board of Corrections or the Board of Pardons and Paroles paroled this Defendant here sometime in March of this year. Have you got the date of that? **A.** He was released on parole on March 30, 1967.

Q. Now, Mr. Wood, does the Board of Pardons and Paroles, when they give a parole, consider the subject is qualified to go back to society, to normal life? **A.** I don't know, sir. I assume that they parole them with the hopes they can make adjustments of life. I am not a member of the Parole Board, and I don't know, sir.

Q. You don't know, then, whether there is any effort made to ascertain from all the prisoners before they are paroled whether or not they are due to be turned loose back on society to make the normal way with normal people? **A.** Well, the prison recommends an inmate for parole on the basis of his adjustment in prison, if he has. In other words, if he hasn't caused any undue trouble to the prison system, then we recommend him to the Parole Board for parole. It's then their decision as to who they will parole and who they will not parole.

Q. There is no intimation in your testimony in this case, is there, Mr. Wood, that this Defendant here didn't know the difference between right and wrong? **A.** Well, I haven't said that, no, sir. I don't know.

Q. I say, that isn't your thought as a member of the Corrections, the Board of Corrections? **A.** Well, in my personal opinion, sir, I just don't know.

MR. ROBIN: That is all.

MR. STILP: No further questions.[64]

MR. ARNOLD TOLOT, having been recalled, testified further, to wit:

RE-DIRECT EXAMINATION

BY MR. STILP:

Q. Mr. Tolot, did you have an occasion to investigate the home life and environment of Elmer Brooks when he was assigned to you? **A.** Yes, sir.

Q. Would you tell the jury what you found in that regard? **A.** Well, I found that he was living with his grandmother, Mrs. Block, and the home seemed to be adequate, possibly on par with other parolees' homes I have supervised.

Q. Would you read to the jury the offense there for which he was confined to the penitentiary? **A.** "He was sentenced to a three year term

64. Would you assess this witness' testimony as helpful to the defense, harmful to the defense, or helpful to no one?

on February 3, 1966, from Orange County for theft from person.   Orange County DA reports 'On or about the 27th day of February, 1965, a purse was taken from a person leaving the Tuxedo Cafe.' Subject reports this offense was committed in the company of his cousin, Raymond A. Stubbs, professing this offense occurred in Sandle, with the probated sentence received therefore being revoked due to his leaving the county without permission and issuing a worthless check."

Q.   And did you visit the Defendant, your parolee, in the County Jail here? **A.**   I did.

Q.   Did he deny the charges against him? **A.**   He did.

Q.   All right.   Has his parole been revoked? **A.**   It has.

Q.   And what basis was used to revoke it? **A.**   I can't say.   It was revoked by the Parole Board.

Q.   By the Parole Board.   I see.[65]

MR. STILP: I believe that is all the questions I have.

MR. ROBIN: No questions.

MRS. HELEN ALLEN, after having been first duly sworn, testified as follows, to wit:

DIRECT EXAMINATION

BY MR. STILP:

Q.   Will you state your full name for the Court and jury, please? **A.**   Helen Allen.

Q.   Helen, you are going to have to talk up, because the jury will have to hear you.   Will you speak just a little louder, please.

Where do you live, Helen? **A.**   704 Bacon.

Q.   And are you related to Elmer Brooks, the Defendant in this case? **A.**   He is my son.

Q.   He is your son.   Has he been living with you for the past two or three months? **A.**   My mother.

Q.   What is her name? **A.**   May Anna Block.

Q.   Where did you live before you moved to Sandle? **A.**   Out at Mr. Obenhaus's.

Q.   Where is that? **A.**   Out by Hackett is Mr. Obenhaus's.

Q.   And you lived there how many years? Do you know? **A.**   Oh, seven or eight years.

Q.   Was that where the Defendant was born? **A.**   No, sir, he wasn't born there.

65. **Why does defense counsel choose to elicit this information?**

Q. Where was Elmer born? **A.** Right here in Sandle.

Q. How old is he? **A.** He is twenty.

Q. Twenty years old. Did he attend school? **A.** Yes.

Q. Where? **A.** Sandle.

Q. In Sandle. How did he do in school? **A.** He was just slow a little bit.

Q. Do you know what grade he completed in school? **A.** Eighth Grade.

Q. Do you know if he passed or failed the Eighth Grade? **A.** He passed the Eighth Grade.

Q. What did he do after the Eighth Grade? **A.** He didn't go to school any more.

Q. Pardon? **A.** He wasn't in school any more.

Q. Did he live with you? **A.** Yeah, during that time he did.

Q. After he left school, did he live with you? **A.** With my mother.

Q. Now, you heard the parole officers testify that he had been in trouble for theft, is that correct? **A.** Yes.

Q. Did he ever give you any trouble of any serious nature while he was living with you? **A.** No.

Q. Now, you have some other children? **A.** Yes, sure do.

Q. How many all told? **A.** Twelve.

Q. Do you have some older than he is? **A.** One.

Q. One. How would you describe Elmer's mentality? **A.** I wouldn't know.

Q. Would you say slow, average? **A.** Yeah, he was always slow.

Q. Could he learn in school? **A.** Some years, and some he didn't.

MR. STILP: Pass the witness.

MR. ROBIN: No questions.

MR. STILP: No further questions.

MRS. MAY ANNA BLOCK, after having been first duly sworn, testified as follows, to wit:

DIRECT EXAMINATION

BY MR. STILP:

Q. Will you state your full name for the record and for the jury, please? **A.** May Anna Block.

Q. May Block? **A.** Mrs. Block.

Q. Are you related to the Defendant, Elmer Brooks? A. I am.

Q. And what is that relationship? A. Grandmother.

Q. All right, you are his grandmother. Until recently, has he been living with you? A. Well, a long he did, sometimes.

Q. You have taken care of Elmer most of his life, is that correct? A. Uh-huh, I have.

Q. Did he attend school while he was living with you? A. Well, part time.

Q. How did he do in school? A. Well, he didn't do too good. He was always slow.

Q. How would you describe Elmer, mentally? A. I beg your pardon?

Q. How would you describe him mentally? A. Well, didn't ever seem like he was real bright or something. I could tell he didn't understand.

Q. You know that he has been in the penitentiary? A. Oh, yes.

Q. Do you remember what that was for? A. Well, no, I really don't, the last time.

Q. Did he steal a purse from some woman? A. Yeah. Yeah.

Q. So far as you know, has he ever been in any trouble with any women at all? A. Well, no. No.

Q. Of your own knowledge, did he go with girls? A. Yes.

MR. STILP: No further questions.

MR. ROBIN: No questions.

MR. L. W. WILE, after having been first duly sworn, testified as follows, to wit:

DIRECT EXAMINATION

BY MR. STILP:

Q. Will you state your name for the benefit of the record and the jury, please, sir? A. I am L. W. Wile.

Q. Where do you live, Mr. Wile? A. I live at 2230 Dawson Street, Sandle.

Q. Do you follow some profession? A. I am a school teacher.

Q. All right. Have you been a principal? A. I was principal for Booker T. Washington for sixteen years.

Q. Do you know the Defendant, Elmer Brooks? A. Yes, I know Elmer Brooks.

Q. Was he one of your students? A. Yes, he was.

Q. Do you remember his school work? **A.** Yes, sir, I remember his school work.

Q. Would you tell the jury the best of your recollection as to how he performed his school work, his conduct and so forth? **A.** Well, Elmer attended school and at the time he was enrolled he came from the Hackett District, was transferred in from the Hackett School District, and his attendance wasn't always real regular. He attended school, but sometimes he had to be out some, and then naturally that made him a slow student. His work was passing at times, but he was slow, I believe, because of the attendance, and he attended school there for several years, and while he was there, the only problem we had was in him attending. He never gave us any problem otherwise.

Q. Did you have occasion to examine his grades and talk with his teachers? **A.** Oh, yes.

Q. Did you form any opinion or do you have an opinion at this time as to his mentality level, as to whether it's good, bad, slow, medium? **A.** He was a slow student. That was our findings from test results.

Q. He was just a slow learner? **A.** That is right.

Q. Was he at the top, medium, bottom level of his class? **A.** He was in the lower four percentile of the class.

Q. You are here in answer to subpoena? I subpoenaed you up here? **A.** Yes, sir.

Q. I asked you to bring his records, but they are locked up in the school and you couldn't get them? **A.** That is right.

MR. STILP: Pass the witness.

MR. ROBIN: No questions.

MR. STILP: Defense rests, Your Honor.[66]

MR. ROBIN: The State rests.

THE COURT: You both rest and close, gentlemen?

MR. STILP: Defense rests and closes.

MR. ROBIN: Right.

THE COURT: All right.

Gentlemen of the Jury, we have reached this stage in the trial of this case: All the testimony is in. The next phase is the preparation of the Court's Charge. That is done without your presence. I anticipate we can probably conclude that this afternoon or possibly early tonight, and then in the morning I am going to ask you to come back at 9:00 o'clock. Once the

---

66. If you were defense counsel would you rest your case at this point? What has defense counsel tried to show? What more would you want to show, if anything?

Why was the defendant not placed upon the stand? Has the defendant's "guilt in fact" been conceded? Is the prosecution's case so strong that it should be?

Charge is read to you, then your communication with the outside world comes to an end, so to speak, until the trial is over. You will not be permitted to separate, to make any telephone calls or have any outside communication. You will have to stay together from then on until such time as a verdict is reached. I would remind you again that you must not discuss the case among yourselves or with anyone else, nor permit anyone to discuss it with you. You are not to read any account that there might be of this trial in the newspaper, nor listen to any account that there might be on radio or TV.

We will see you in the morning at 9:00 o'clock, at which time you will please reassemble in the jury room.

Thank you very much, gentlemen. We will see you in the morning.

(At this juncture the Jury retired from the courtroom for the day.)

(Wednesday, July 26, 1967.)

(The Jury returned to the courtroom, and the following proceedings were had, to wit:)

THE COURT: Mr. Court Reporter, you will note that after both sides have rested and closed that the Court is affording the State an opportunity to proffer an item of evidence in this cause.

MR. LYLE STACK, having been previously sworn, was recalled and testified further, to wit:

RE-DIRECT EXAMINATION

BY MR. ROBIN:

Q. Mr. Stack, you were sworn yesterday and you testified on this stand? A. Yes, sir.

Q. Are these the shoes here that you testified to yesterday as being in your custody since the 9th day of May, 1967, and taken from the Defendant? A. Yes, sir, they are.

Q. Are those the same shoes that were identified by various witnesses in here on that stand yesterday? A. Yes, sir.

Q. As being the same shoes that were compared with the tracks at Mrs. Hill's house? A. Yes, sir.

MR. ROBIN: With that, Your Honor, I would like to introduce those shoes into evidence.

MR. STILP: We wish to object to the introduction of the shoes, Your Honor. First, that they are the fruits, the results of an illegal arrest made upon this Defendant without just cause in violation of his constitutional rights under the United States Constitution, the Constitution of the State, in complete derogation of the mandates, provisions, sections of the Code of Criminal Procedure. We feel that to allow these shoes to come into evidence, Your Honor, would be to allow this Defendant—or to force this Defendant to testify against himself, and we object to their introduction.

Also, we object further on the basis that the entire transaction from his illegal arrest until the time of his preliminary hearing or his appearance before a magistrate, which was not done immediately, was all attended only by a law enforcement officer; there was no one present or available who was not a law enforcement officer. We feel this would further substantiate the illegality by admitting these in evidence.[67]

THE COURT: Note the objection is overruled.

MR. STILP: Note our exception thereto.

THE COURT: Now, with that, Mr. District Attorney, do you again close?

MR. ROBIN: I again close.

THE COURT: Mr. Stilp?

MR. STILP: Close, Your Honor.

THE COURT: All right.

Gentlemen of the Jury, the Court will immediately read the Charge in this case, and you are instructed that once the Charge is read that you will have no further communication with anyone, except the fellow members of your jury, and to express any needs that you might have, while you are in the jury room, to the officer who is in attendance outside the jury room. You are not to make any telephone calls. You are not to permit anyone to talk to you. You are not to communicate with anyone, other than your fellow jurors, until such time as this case is completed.

All right, Gentlemen of the Jury, the Charge of the Court in this case reads as follows:

(At this time the Court's Charge was read to the Jury.)[68]

THE COURT: Gentlemen, you may address the Jury.

First Argument of Mr. Robin

MR. ROBIN: If it please the Court, Mr. Stilp, Gentlemen of the Jury: I am going to start out by saying, and I am not going to take much of your time on the opening argument. I will reserve most of my time for closing, but let me assure you gentlemen that if I hadn't called each and every one of you gentlemen—and each of you gentlemen have as much sense or more than I do—you wouldn't be on this jury, because I would have exercised a peremptory challenge, which I didn't do. Also, I hope you won't hold it against me since you were questioned on voir dire examination of what you considered an elderly person, what happened to be an elderly person, because I happen to be over sixty-five.[69]

I am not in this case to make any kind of a reputation. I have been in this game for thirty-five years, too long for me to be trying to do something

---

67. Why has the prosecutor recalled the witness? Why does defense counsel choose to reiterate his objection to the evidence?

68. Note that in this state the jury is charged before it hears closing arguments. Are there advantages in such a procedure? Disadvantages?

69. It is generally impermissible to indicate to a juror or jurors that peremptory challenges could have been used but were not? Why?

to make a reputation. My reputation, good or bad, has been established a good while.[70]

Gentlemen, I am going to tell you from the depths of my heart that I have always dreaded the day ever coming when a crime of this kind is committed. I have had a horror of it ever since I have been practicing law, and ever since I have been prosecuting attorney, which started back in 1933.

Now, let's examine this charge here. It's very simple. The testimony in this case is very simple. It isn't long. It isn't complicated. I don't think there is any question in the minds of anyone of you gentlemen but what this Defendant, Elmer Brooks, did on the 9th day of May, 1967, break into the home of Mrs. Ethel Hill, a widow, there by herself, and in a brutal, as almost as brutal a way as could have been done, raped her. You have her clear-cut testimony from that stand, of the details of that sordid affair. You have the telephone call from Phil Hill to our Sheriff telling him that his mother had just been raped by a Negro who was in route towards Sandle at that time.

All the defense has made up, played loud and long, is that this was an illegal arrest. May I submit to you gentlemen that the law provides and this Charge tells you the law provides that if a felony has been committed, any reliable citizen has called that the crime has been committed, and that the one who perpetrated the crime is in flight, they don't know who the party is at that time, that an arrest without warrant is perfectly legal. Otherwise, gentlemen, you could never arrest a bank robber leaving from the scene of the crime or any kind of a highjacker where the head was cov-

---

70. Is it proper for the prosecutor to rely upon his past reputation? Is it proper to suggest, as defense counsel fears the prosecutor is doing, that the defense counsel is using a case to make a reputation? Is the prosecutor improperly seeking to have the jury rely on his opinion? The ABA Standards for Criminal Justice, The Prosecution Function and The Defense Function, Standard 5.8(b), The Prosecution Function (App.Draft 1971) contain this standard: It is unprofessional conduct for the prosecutor to express his personal belief or opinion as to the truth or falsity of any testimony or evidence or the guilt of the defendant.

The following commentary explains the standard.

Commentary

Such expressions by the prosecutor are a form of unsworn, unchecked testimony and tend to exploit the influence of his office and undermine the objective detachment which should separate a lawyer from the cause for which he argues. Such argument is expressly forbidden. ABA Code DR 7–106(C)(4); Drinker, Legal Ethics 147 (1953). Many courts have recognized the impropriety of such statements. Annot.,

50 A.L.R.2d 766 (1956). This kind of argument is easily avoided by insisting that lawyers restrict themselves to statements which take the form, "The evidence shows * * *" or some similar form. The experienced American and British advocate will say, for example, "I leave it to you whether this evidence does not suggest * * *" etc. Harris v. United States, 131 U.S.App.D.C. 105, 402 F.2d 656, 657–59 (1968).

The line between permissible and impermissible argument is a thin one. Neither advocate may express his personal opinion as to the justice of his cause or the veracity of witnesses. Credibility is solely for the triers, but an advocate may point to the fact that circumstances or independent witnesses give support to one witness or cast doubt on another. The prohibition goes to the advocate's personally endorsing or vouching for or giving his opinion: the cause should turn on the evidence, not on the standing of the advocate, and the witnesses must stand on their own.

The ABA Standard is unchanged in the Second Approved Draft (3–5.8(b)), adopted in 1979.

ered up, because you wouldn't know who to charge while they were fleeing. Now, gentlemen, an arrest in that condition is perfectly legal, legitimate in every way, and is the only way that your homes and mine, your businesses and mine, your lives and mine can be protected. If we couldn't do that, you would have no protection in this state to your liberties.[71]

We still haven't reached the point—although sometimes I think we are getting close to it—to where the ninety-three per cent of good citizens are at the mercy of the seven per cent criminal law violators in our country, and that is what our statistics show at this time.[72]

Gentlemen, we have a man coming to Mrs. Hill's house at night. He has worked out there for her husband prior to his death. He knows that she is there by herself, that she is a widow. He rips the screen off the kitchen and crawls through; comes in and rips the cover off the bed, grabs the arms of Mrs. Hill. She is lying in the right direction on the bed, head to foot. Gets her around crosswise of the bed with her head down between the bed and the wall, and finally forces himself between her legs, forces his private parts into her's, and completes the act of intercourse. Then he has the temerity, the depravity to tell her he is going to do that on the hour every hour. She asked him "Why did you come to a person of my age?" His answer, "I wanted to see how you liked a colored man."

Now, gentlemen, I have tried to keep races out of this case. Whether you believe it or whether you don't, I prosecuted a man for raping a Negro woman here. I have forgotten now what the penalty was, but I prosecuted him just as hard as I am prosecuting that boy there, and I say to you as long as I am District Attorney, if it comes to my attention that a white man has gone down there and raped a Negro woman, I will prosecute him just as hard as I am prosecuting that boy here today.[73] Don't you think I won't. We

71. Should the prosecutor tell the jury the law regarding search and seizure in a jurisdiction that permits the jury to decide for itself the constitutionality of an arrest and search incident thereto, or should this task be left entirely to the court? Does the prosecutor correctly explain the law?

72. Are these facts in evidence? Could they ever be placed in evidence? Is this proper argument? Consider the American Bar Association's recommended standard for Criminal Cases and its commentary on the standard:

The prosecutor should refrain from argument which would divert the jury from its duty to decide the case on the evidence, by injecting issues broader than the guilt or innocence of the accused under the controlling law, or by making predictions of the consequences of the jury's verdict.

Commentary

References to the likelihood of other authorities, such as the governor or the appellate courts, correcting an erroneous conviction are impermissible efforts to lead the jury to shirk responsibility for its decision. Annot., 3 A.L.R.2d 1488 (1965). Predictions as to the consequence of an acquittal on lawlessness in the community also go beyond the scope of the issues in the trial and are to be avoided. Some courts have reversed convictions where such arguments were made. See, e.g., Cooper v. State, supra; see People v. Sawhill, 299 Ill. 393, 132 N.E. 477, 484 (1921); Note, 54 Colum.L.Rev. 946 (1954); Annot., 44 A.L.R.2d 978 (1955). Of course, the restriction must be reciprocal; a prosecutor may be justified in making a reply to an argument of defense counsel which may not have been proper if made without provocation. The better solution to this problem lies in having advocates adequately instructed as to the limits of proper argument and trial judges willing to enforce fair rules as to such limits.

ABA Standards, supra note 70, § 5.8(d). The standard is unchanged in the Second Approved Draft (3–5.8(d)).

73. Is this relevant? Is it likely to inject improper issues into the case? The

have got no place for that in this country. It's here. I know it's here, and in certain places they are having hell, but I still tell you we have no place for that in our society, but I tell you that any man that breaks into a widow's house where she has no protection, and rapes her by force should be sent to the electric chair to tell the whole world and anyone who is inclined to want to go and do likewise that if you do and we catch you, we will kill you.[74]

MR. STILP: Your Honor, I object to that. I don't believe that is proper argument. I believe it's highly prejudicial, as to "tell the whole world".[75]

THE COURT: Overruled. Go ahead.

MR. STILP: Note our exception thereto.

MR. ROBIN: That is what this trial is for and what the—

THE COURT: Continue your argument, Counsel. The Court has ruled on it.

MR. ROBIN: Sir?

THE COURT: The Court has ruled. Continue your argument.

MR. ROBIN: If the Court please, I am. I wasn't commenting on your ruling.

Now, gentlemen, we have got plenty of corroboration of Mrs. Hill's testimony that she ran down through the field to her son's house, excited and

American Bar Association proposes that "[t]he prosecutor should not use arguments calculated to influence the passions or prejudices of the jury." ABA Standards, note 70 supra, § 5.8. The commentary accompanying the standard provides:

Arguments which rely upon racial, religious, ethnic, political, economic or other prejudices of the jurors introduce elements of irrelevance and irrationality into the trial which cannot be tolerated in a society based upon the equality of all citizens before the law. Of course, the mere mention of the status of the accused as shown by the record may not be improper if it has some legitimate bearing upon some issue in the case, such as identification by color. But where the jury's predisposition against some particular segment of society is exploited to stigmatize the accused or his witnesses, such argument has clearly trespassed the bounds of reasonable inference or fair comment on the evidence. Accordingly, many courts have denounced such appeals to prejudice as inconsistent with the requirement that the defendant be judged only upon the evidence. See e.g., Tannehill v. State, 159 Ala. 51, 48 So. 662 (1909); Cooper v. State, 136 Fla. 23, 186 So. 230 (1930); Annot., 45 A.L.R.2d 303, 322–68 (1956).

74. Would you call this fair argument? See the ABA standards discussed in notes 70, 72, & 73 supra. As a general commentary to § 5.8, the ABA said:

As the culmination of his efforts in the case, the prosecutor's argument is likely to have significant persuasive force with the jury. Accordingly, the scope of argument must be consistent with the evidence and marked by the fairness which should characterize all of the prosecutor's conduct. Prosecutorial conduct in argument is a matter of special concern because of the possibility that the jury will give special weight to the prosecutor's arguments, not only because of the prestige associated with his office, but also because of the fact-finding facilities presumably available to him. * * * To attempt to spell out in detail what can and cannot be said in argument is impossible, since it will depend largely on the facts of the particular case. Nevertheless, certain broad guidelines based on the function of argument and the experience of courts in typical situations can be established.

75. Can you conceive of any reason why defense counsel would make this objection when so many others were available?

crying, stickers in her feet, told her son what had happened. The only thing that I regret is at that time she did, before she come to town, was that she cleaned herself up thoroughly.

MR. STILP: Your Honor, I am going to object. There is no evidence whatsoever of that.

THE COURT: Sustained.

MR. STILP: It's highly prejudicial.

THE COURT: Sustained.

MR. ROBIN: If the Court please—

THE COURT: I sustained the objection, Counsel.

MR. ROBIN: May I have the record read back, Judge?

THE COURT: Sustain the objection.

MR. ROBIN: May I tell this jury that she did take a bath?

THE COURT: No, sir. No, sir. It's not in evidence.

MR. STILP: I move for a mistrial, Your Honor.

THE COURT: Overruled.[76]

MR. STILP: Note our exception.

THE COURT: You will not consider the statement of the District Attorney for any purpose whatsoever.

Continue your argument.

MR. ROBIN: We have the son, Phil Hill, calling the Sheriff, also calling the Police Department, and giving an alarm. You have the testimony of the city officers that they immediately went on North Main Street, and after stopping one car and releasing it, they went across the intersection to this

76. The prosecution's statement is clearly error. Should a mistrial have been granted if the error is inadvertent? If it is deliberate?

The ABA provides:

It is unprofessional conduct for the prosecutor intentionally to refer to or argue on the basis of facts outside the record whether at trial or on appeal, unless such facts are matters of common public knowledge based on ordinary human experience or matters of which the court may take judicial notice.

ABA Standards, note 70 supra, § 5.9. Its commentary explains the provision:

The problem of digression from the record can arise at both the trial and appellate levels. It is beyond question that at the trial level it is highly improper for a lawyer to refer in colloquy, argument or other context to factual matter beyond the scope of the evidence or the range of judicial notice. This is true whether the case is being tried to a court or to a jury, but it is particularly offensive in a jury trial. It can involve the risk of serious prejudice with a mistrial as a possible remedy. Ordinarily a trial court should summarily exclude any reference in argument or otherwise to factual matter which is beyond the scope of the evidence in any significant way. The broad discretion a trial court has in such matters enables it to deal with them as they arise by allowing a party to reopen his case or take other appropriate steps to enlarge the record so as to provide an evidentiary basis for the matter he wishes to argue but has for some reason failed to establish.

The ABA Standard is unchanged in the Second Approved Draft (3–5.9).

Texaco station—I have forgotten the name of the party that runs it—in time to see this Defendant drive up in a car, stop in the street, hesitate, as if to make up his mind which way he was going, then he turned into the filling station. They closed in and told him that the deputy sheriff would like to talk to him. Then we have the two deputy sheriffs coming to join them, taking the Defendant over on the other side of Blaine's Junk Yard. In the meantime, the sheriff comes out there, observes the type clothing the Defendant has on, immediately goes over to Mrs. Hill's and gets her description of what the man wore and looked like. Then he calls back and tells them "that is the man we are after. Hold him. Take him to the jail and take his shoes and bring them out here." At that time the testimony is that the Defendant went haywire, cursed them and said, "You will never take me to jail." You have got the testimony of the police officers that when he drove in there that his pants were still unzipped. Why? Because he left the scene of his crime so fast that he didn't realize that he hadn't zipped his pants up. Then, as soon as the Defendant saw that he was going to be charged, that he was the man they wanted—he could hear that radio in the car the same as the officers could.—he went haywire and he said, "You can't take me to jail." They had to call for help. It took four of them to put a handcuff on him and take him to jail. If that isn't corroboration of Mrs. Hill's testimony, then I don't know anything about the practice of law, criminal law especially.

Now, gentlemen, please bear this in mind. This is not my case. Under the law, when the District Attorney has submitted all the testimony at his command to you gentlemen, and when my closing argument comes and I sit down, I will have discharged my duty to the State. My responsibility will then be at an end, and the responsibility of this case solely then rests upon the shoulders of you twelve men, and you wouldn't have it any other way. That is our way of life. That is our bulwark of justice, both for the State, the suppression of crime and the protection of those who are charged with the crime.

Now, gentlemen, I am going to let the Defense make their talk and I will close as soon as he finishes.

Thank you very much.

Closing Argument of Mr. Stilp

May it please the Honorable Court, Mr. District Attorney, Gentlemen of the Jury: First, I want to thank you for your attention, the time that you have been forced to take from your jobs and your home. Elmer Brooks thanks you. I thank you as an officer of this Court. We want to thank Judge Batus for his kind considerate handling of this case, his thorough attention to everything that has transpired. We want to thank these law enforcement officers who have given their time who have been here, have seen that this trial progresses smoothly.

Now, gentlemen, the evidence is in. As I told you before on voir dire examination, and as you well know, you now have your evidence. What Mr. Robin says and what I say is not evidence in this case. All that we can try to do is maybe point out some of the highlights, point out some of the factors of this case.   Certainly, I represent the Defendant, and I am going to try and show you evidence that was presented to you favorably to the Defendant, if any.[77]   The District Attorney is certainly going to try and substantiate his side.   The Code of Criminal Procedure lists among the duties of the District Attorney, "shall be the primary duty of all prosecuting attorneys, including any special prosecutors, not to convict, but to see that justice is done."   And that is all any of us want.

I wish that I were smart enough to get up here and be able to sway you with eloquence, with fancy talks with quotations from the Bible or books, great men, but I am not.   All I can do is to try and go over the facts of this case with you, which is my right and my privilege, and maybe, in some way, clarify that hard road that you have.

Gentlemen, I was appointed to represent the Defendant in this case on the 9th day of May, 1967, and I have had his life on my shoulders since that day.   As that clock ticks, that time grows shorter, then that will be handed to you.   We have no finer system in the world than the jury system.   I hope that we always have it.   Not that a judge is not a good system.   In this case, if this Defendant was guilty, pleaded guilty, and wanted to plead guilty before the Court, he could not do it.   In a capital case he cannot do it.   This Defendant wants a trial by jury, and that is what he has.[78]

Now, gentlemen, the District Attorney alluded to making a reputation and I presume he was alluding to me.   I will say this, gentlemen.   I took an oath when I completed my education to become an attorney, and I intend to abide by that oath, and I was appointed by this Court to represent this Defendant whether I wanted to or not, and nothing is going to keep me from doing that, if I felt I was obligated to do it and this Court saw fit to appoint me.   If I was trying to build a reputation, gentlemen, I believe that all of you would understand that I might possibly choose my cases, rather than hard ones, and this is a hard case.   Let's face it.   No one in that jury or myself would ever say that that lady lied.   She had never been on the witness stand before in her life, and she went through a horrible experience, and I don't think anyone in this jury would doubt that every word she says is true.   She was raped by a Negro.   The question is, was it this Defendant?   Now, there is a lot of evidence that points towards him.   Let's don't be naive and try to say that there isn't, and I am not going to try to tell you there isn't any evidence, because there is, and it's strong evidence.   We have a capable law enforcement agency in this community.   The City Police worked on it;   the Sheriff's Office worked on it, and the Sheriff's Office worked on it under a handicap, because there was extremely close feelings.   One of the officers was born and raised out there.   He knew this lady all his life just like I have, and I assure you there was feelings there that had to be overcome, and yet they maintained their position, they abided by the law as much as they could.   They didn't abuse, harass or harm this Defendant.   We also have the same proposition with the Sheriff.   I doubt that

77.   The words "if any" are used by many lawyers to avoid objections to leading questions.   Do they have any place in a closing argument?

78.   What, if anything, has defense counsel accomplished by his argument up to this point?

he will ever have a case that will more personally involve him, but I want to commend him at this time to you for treating Elmer Brooks as he would treat anyone.

Now, gentlemen, the question in my mind is whether or not Elmer Brooks was the Negro, the colored person, that raped Mrs. Hill. Now, if I made anyone mad on this jury, please be mad at me, not Elmer Brooks. I objected, yes, sir, strenuously, many times. I even objected in the course of the District Attorney's argument, and if I get out of line, he will object to something I may say. I want Elmer Brooks, or any man sitting next to me in that chair, to have a fair and impartial trial, and if I possibly can, I am going to see that he gets it, and I am going to object, and I am going to try to keep out evidence that I do not feel should be in the case. If it appeared at times I was hostile towards members of the law enforcement force, and I did ask you on voir dire if they took the stand and testified, would you give more weight to their testimony than you would any other individual, and each and every one of you assured me the fact they were wearing a uniform made no difference whatsoever, and I appreciate that and I am sure that is exactly the way you have considered their testimony. Well, I consider it the same. They are my personal friends. I see them every day, many, many times each day. We work on cases. I have been on the other side of cases; I have been on the same side they have been on, and I consider each and every one of these officers my personal friends. I would not hesitate one minute of accusing them or getting right in the middle of them if I thought they were out of line, because I feel like that is the only way the proper administration of the law can be had.[79]

Now, we will go back over an area that to me is of prime importance, and it's very important right now, gentlemen, because each of you has stated to me on voir dire under oath that you are well aware of riots and demonstrations all over the country. Law enforcement is having its problems, has its hands full. Now, paramount and above everything, though, is the right of the individual. If we ever lose that right, then, gentlemen, we are in trouble. You have heard me mention the Constitution of the United States of America, the Constitution of the State, and all of the laws pertaining thereto insofar as they are applicable in any area in this case. I maintain above all, gentlemen, that the individual must be protected, and in this case I have presented that problem, a problem in that area several times.

Now, gentlemen, we may have the right man. Elmer Brooks may have committed the rape, and he may not, but that is for you to say. That is your job, but I have maintained strenuously that his original arrest was illegal.

Gentlemen, the Charge which this Court charges you, and this is the law which you have sworn under oath to go by. "In this case the issue has been raised as to whether there was a legal arrest of the Defendant. In the event the arrest was not legal, the evidence relating to the shoes and foot prints

79. At this point do you sense confusion or ambivalence in the approach of defense counsel to his theory of the case? Is a trial which simultaneously presents the issues of verdict and sentence a wise procedure? Are counsel's statements about his relations with the police proper?

at or about the scene of the crime is not admissible." The fruit of an illegal arrest. "I instruct you that the only circumstances under which one may lawfully be arrested without warrant is where a peace officer is informed by a credible person that a felony offender is about to escape and there is no time to secure a warrant." Now, gentlemen, I don't want to bore you above all, but I do not believe that over one or two of you will ever be presented with this again for your consideration, but it directly affects each and every one of you, because the minute you drive down the street in your automobile, you are placed in the position of being treated as this Defendant was. Now, what can you do? The notes at the City of Sandle Police Department state that any officer listening to the radio message to "stop every car that had colored subjects in them and hold them until they could get there".

Now, gentlemen, I don't want to go far afield and bring in hypothetical cases that would be out of reason, but we must tie what happened in with the constitutional provisions which we have, thank God. That is, the right against an unreasonable search and seizure. I know that these officers were doing what they thought they could, in any way they could, that they wanted to try and apprehend the felon, but I maintain and will maintain that they exceeded their authority when they said "stop any colored subjects". You cannot do that, and any evidence that is secured after an illegal arrest is inadmissible.

Now, gentlemen, I don't know what weight you are going to give to the tennis shoes. Personally, I think you have heard enough testimony that you would be justified, in all probability, and I am not invading the province of the jury one way or the other, possibly you would say from the testimony that you have, and I have it verbatim, that they matched foot prints out there. That tends to put this Defendant at the scene of the crime. That is all you have.

Gentlemen, what worries most of you is, today, if you can take the shoes off of a man and use it in evidence against him, where will it stop? When will they be able to reach into your mouth and down your throat and jerk parts of your body out and use it in evidence against you? You have heard the facts and the testimony, and you have the job. Was a felon trying to escape? A Negro drives into a filling station. They have no description. They didn't know who he was. They didn't know if he was driving a car or if he wasn't. The testimony was by the prosecuting witness that the subject left in an automobile and made a statement that he had an automobile, and yet each and every colored person, and I believe on the second or third try the Sheriff finally said that his instructions were only the cars coming from the north. There are a number of Negro families living north of the expressway. Had anyone else come up, it matters not who he was, preacher, citizen, dish washer, whoever he might be, that man would be arrested, and as the officers told you, no, he couldn't leave. "If he had tried to have left, we would have forcibly detained him."

Now, the District Attorney has made much of the fact that when this Defendant was told he was going to jail he put up resistance. The law is that you have the right. I have the right, and I would use it, gentlemen. If I am ever illegally detained, I have the right to use whatever force is necessary to extricate myself, and I will do it. This man tried to extricate himself. You have the right. The District Attorney cannot tell you that that is not the law. Be that as it may, gentlemen, there is Elmer Brooks, nineteen or twenty year old boy. He is not a man. The District Attorney would like for you to believe he is a man, but he is not. He is either nineteen or twenty years old. I don't know whether he is even that. There has been no proof as to his age.[80]

There is a pair of shoes that very few people would wear. Now, I presume they are the ones that were taken from the Defendant, but I think if you will look at them you will see there is Elmer Brooks. Now, gentlemen, these shoes may match the prints out there. Maybe they do. That is for you to say. Where is the plaster cast of the foot prints found there? Where is the scientific sand analysis of soil found on those shoes with the analysis of dirt and sand found at the prosecuting witness' residence? Where are the finger prints? Gentlemen, we are not living in horse and buggy days any more. We are modern today. We are travelling so fast now you can't even comprehend the speed. Law enforcement has all the money in the world available to them. They have the most scientific of all crime detection. Laboratories. Nothing. Maybe that is enough. You are the ones that are going to decide that.[81]

Gentlemen, on voir dire examination I questioned each of you as much as I felt necessary. I did that for two reasons. Of course, one was to try to attempt to rapport with you or maybe know you a little bit. Of course, another basis was that I had to try and look into your mind to determine what kind of a person you are, and evaluate whether or not I felt that you should serve on the jury to determine whether or not Elmer Brooks is guilty or whether he is innocent, and if either way, what type of punishment you might render. Gentlemen, I didn't do that blindly. I have had extensive training in psychology and sociology myself. I feel I can evaluate an individual, and I would be telling you a falsehood if I didn't also tell you that I knew a lot more about you before you came in here than you think I did. I investigated practically the entire panel ahead of time. I think I knew the answer to practically every question I asked you before you answered. I wasn't deceiving you. I wanted to find out what kind of person you were, and I think I know, and whichever way you decide in this case, I know you will do it from your heart, and I know you will do it because you feel it's right, and I believe you will do it because whatever punishment, if any, and you find him guilty is applicable.[82]

Gentlemen, on voir dire examination I asked you if you would accept testimony from that stand by psychologist, sociologist, medical doctors, whoever they might be, and every one of you assured me that you would. I think one or two of you said you weren't too familiar with that type of

80. Defense counsel did not ask the Court to so instruct the jury. Would it have been wise to have done so?

81. Could this argument have been made more powerfully? Is there any evidence which defense counsel might have presented to strengthen the claim that Brooks was not in fact the rapist? Why wasn't such evidence presented?

82. Are these admissions strategically sound?

practice or that endeavor, but that you would give it whatever weight you thought it should have. Now, gentlemen, I subpoenaed three men, employees of the State, the same as the District Attorney. They draw their checks out of the same place, out of our contributions. You heard these men testify that they didn't expect a penny from this Defendant, because they came up here under subpoena, and they had to be here or else Mr. Stack would have gone and gotten them and brought them down here, I will assure you.

Now, why did I bring these men here? I believe each of you know now. We had Mr. Wood from the State Department of Corrections who presented his report. Now, they are all stapled here together, and you have the right to take these to the jury room with you. I am not going to read them to you, because you have heard excerpts from these reports. Now, these are the combination reports. They are the parole summary from the Board of Pardons and Paroles, and the admission summary is from the State Department of Corrections. Now, Mr. Wood is with the State Department of Corrections, and his report is here based upon findings, by psychology, sociology, and other qualified personnel when Elmer Brooks went to Hardy to start serving time on a three year sentence for theft. Gentlemen, you were told by Mr. Wood that Elmer Brooks has the mental age of a 5.5 individual; that he has an I.Q. of 67, which if I am correct, I believe he stated was low, and I believe that I am correct. You remember, I hope. I am not trying to confuse you, but I believe, if I remember correctly, that he stated that Elmer Brooks, in his opinion, was dull; that he needed—No, that was Mr. Hens. But I believe that he got his point over to you that from his analysis, his report that he submitted that Elmer Brooks has the mental age of a 5.5 year old individual and has the I.Q. of a 67 rating. Gentlemen, that was substantiated by Mr. Hens who is with the Board of Pardon and Paroles. His opinion was that this boy needed supervision, needed somebody to follow him around and tell him what to do.

Mr. Tolot, his probation officer, had the benefit of both reports, and he visited and counseled with the Defendant until such time as he was arrested and charged in this case. Then he visited him in jail, and what did he testify to from that stand that Elmer Brooks told him in jail? "I didn't do it."

Gentlemen of this jury, I am not going to try in any way to influence you or to invade your sole job. The province is yours, what you do in this case, but I don't believe, if you find this Defendant guilty, that you will send a boy to the electric chair.

Now, gentlemen, the indictment was read to you that (leaving out the formal parts) on or about the 9th day of May, 1967, before the presentment of this indictment in the county and state aforesaid Elmer Brooks did then and there unlawfully and in and upon Mrs. Ethel Hill make an assault and did then and there by force, threats and fraud.

Gentlemen, you will notice in the charge to you, you will remember the evidence, that the only instructions you have is "to constitute rape by force." The State had to abandon and leave threats and fraud out. I told you before we came in here, I told each of you on voir dire, the District Attorney would know a lot more about the case after it was over than he did then, and he does. If this Defendant is guilty of raping Mrs. Hill, it is only by force, and how much force? You heard it. Thank God you didn't miss a word, and that is what I wanted. You paid strict attention to every word that Mrs. Hill told you, and I think you know the amount of force, enough force to overcome her resistance, if he did. Some Negro did. There is no doubt. I have known this family all my life, and I will probably lose them as friends over this case, because I am representing this Defendant. Sometimes things work out that way.

Now, gentlemen, I point that out to you for this reason. I am entitled to, first. Secondly, we read in the papers and we are told, those of us who practice law, and for instance in this case, I have probably read a hundred rape cases in the last three days. I point out that the original indictment, as brought, alleged things that wasn't there, alleged threats and fraud, and there wasn't any proof. The State had to abandon it. I point out to you further in the charge the punishment, and that again is an element that I went over with you in voir dire examination. "The penalty prescribed by the statute of the State for the offense of rape is death, or confinement in the penitentiary for life or for any term of years not less than five." At this point I ask you and each of you, please, does it say a white man, does it say a colored man, does it say a Japanese, a German, a Jew or anyone? The punishment is the same for anyone.

Now, gentlemen, on voir dire I asked you individually, after the State had qualified you on the death penalty, and each of you answered affirmatively, that you could render a death penalty, if the law authorized it, and the facts and circumstances so warranted it. Now, that question wasn't asked just because Mr. Robin wanted to hear himself talk, or I didn't reiterate it two or three times to you because I wanted to hear myself talk. We had a purpose and reason in that, and I sure had one. Mr. Robin's was could you award the death penalty. His job is not to convict, but to see that justice is done. My job is to represent, to present Elmer Brooks' case to you, and I am not being presumptuous, gentlemen. A 5.5 mental age individual cannot present a case to you. Now, why, again I ask you, why does the law give those extremes in a rape case? A maximum of death; a minimum of five years? And I received an answer from one man on the jury panel, which I appreciated, "I won't give five years, if I think he is guilty." That was directly, bluntly to the point, and that is the way he felt, and he is on that jury. He is one of you. That is the way he felt. All of you may feel that way. Well, that is fine. That is up to you individually.

As I say, I'm trying to point these out to you. It's not evidence in this case. You don't even have to consider what I say, but I want to impress upon you. Why did our legislature see fit to vary the punishment in a rape case? My interpretation of that is this. As I mentioned a moment ago, I have read over a hundred rape cases in the last few days researching the law. The reason, in my opinion, and it's only my opinion, which I am allowed to give you, I am qualified, I believe, as a practicing attorney, my opinion is that the severity, the brutality, the animosity, the cruelty of the act determines the punishment, and thank God, all of us do, except for the act of sexual intercourse, Mrs. Hill is not harmed. She is embarrassed to no end, gentlemen. We are embarrased for her, but there is not one bit of testimony in this case that she was harmed.　Now, the threats and fraud part of the indictment were thrown out.　She wasn't threatened before the act was committed on her, either by this Defendant or whoever the individual was that assaulted her.　She was held and forcibly assaulted, but she was not stabbed with a knife, thank God.　She was not hammered over the head with a blunt instrument, thank God.　She was not shot with a gun. She was not kicked.　She was not stomped.　No brutality, other than the act of intercourse.　What transpired after the act, gentlemen, doesn't come in.　I think you should consider it as a basis and as a factor in your punishment.[83]

As I say, I didn't cross-examine Mrs. Hill on the stand, because I feel like that what she said was the truth, other than possibly the identification. I don't know, gentlemen, if you find the death penalty, whether Mrs. Hill could sleep at nights.　I am not positive that she knows that this is the individual.　Let's face it, gentlemen.　Negro males of this age and size look alike.[84]

This was a traumatic experience.　This undoubtedly was the most horrible thing she has ever gone through in her life, and we are all thankful she was a strong woman and had presence of mind, and only her conduct, only her—I am going to say—tenacity of self preservation there made the crime what it was.　No, she didn't voluntarily submit, and I think she put up a resistance to the utmost of her strength, and I think that whoever assaulted her, "I never saw a man with that kind of power in his hands."　Those are her words.　Gentlemen, that is the reason the legislature saw fit to give you, the jury, that latitude and that leeway and those extremes in punishment.　If Mrs. Hill had been nine or ten years old, she had been brutally stabbed in the back and rendered paralyzed for life, if she was mentally incompetent and out of a state hospital and had no control over her will—these are all cases that have happened—I think those are factors that you would consider, and I think that they would tend to move you up the ladder, if you find this Defendant guilty beyond a reasonable doubt, but you have the leeway, and whatever you find, that is for you to decide.

Ironically enough, alibis are hard to have at 2:00 or 3:00 o'clock in the morning.　No alibi was presented to you.　Let's face it.[85]　But the unrefuted testimony from that stand, the mother of Elmer Brooks substantiated his mental condition, his slowness, his level;　his grandmother the same. These are factors, gentlemen, which I know you will consider.　No father. Poverty.　I don't know how many nights the boy went to bed without any supper.　What chance did he have?　If he had a chance, he didn't have anything to do it with.　You are to weigh the testimony of Mr. Wood, Mr. Hens and Mr. Tolot.　It is unrefuted.　I ask that you give whatever weight you feel that it should have.

83.　Does this argument, together with counsel's report of having read a hundred rape cases in the last three days, help the defense or the prosecution?

84.　Is this in evidence?　Is this the best counsel could do for the defendant—forego cross-examination of the victim, concede her truthfulness, and advance a stereotype of Negroes?

85.　What purpose does this serve other than to remind the jury of the silence of the defendant?

Gentlemen, before I close, I do want to tell you that the District Attorney, as is the procedure in criminal cases, has the right to open, which he has already done, and I have the right to make my argument, which I have just about concluded, then the District Attorney gets a chance to come back in rebuttal. That gives him a pretty good edge on me, because he can take a little advantage of me in what he can say, and I cannot refute it in any way. I ask that you consider whatever else Mr. Robin tells you in that light, and again I hope that I have not made any of you mad at this Defendant. I hope that I have not caused any of you to feel bitter towards me. If you have, please towards me and not this Defendant.

Remember, if the arrest was illegal, the shoes and the fact that the tracks are purported to have matched is not to be considered. If you feel that Mrs. Hill's testimony convinces you beyond a reasonable doubt, as clear as light, that Elmer Brooks committed the offense of rape, then and only then will you find him guilty. I ask that you and each of you weigh all of these circumstances, please. If you find him guilty, the supreme penalty only if you can find the facts warrant it.

Thank you.

Concluding Argument of Mr. Robin

If it please the Court, Mr. Stilp, Gentlemen of the Jury: I am not going to take too much time in closing argument. You have been patient. As I said before, the evidence is short. It isn't too involved, but I want to make this clear. He mentioned the fact that I abandoned threats and fraud. Gentlemen, you all are not attorneys. He understands that. There are numerous indictments that carry four or five counts. The State has the privilege when the evidence is brought in to elect upon which count the State relies, and that was done in this case. It could be a rape, all right, by threats alone, of putting a person in fear of life, serious bodily injury, where they give in and still there is rape and carries a death penalty as the maximum penalty, and the same thing is true for fraud, but be that as it may, if that indictment wasn't good, the Court would already have thrown it out.

Now, when he first started making his argument, he made the remark that all we had was the shoes. If all we had was the shoes in this case, I would be shaking in my boots so far as a verdict was concerned. We have Mrs. Hill's testimony that the light always stayed on in the bathroom; that she sat on the side of the bed, she could see the Defendant. He asked her for what money she had. She finally got him to step aside where she could get her purse. She poured the money into his hand, and she started begging to go to the bathroom to get her a drink of water, which he finally gave in and let her do, but as she come out of the bathroom, she flipped the hall light on, and he asked her, "What did you want to do that for?" She got a good look at his face, and now the defense attorney says Negro boys or all young men look alike. If he doesn't have a distinctive look, then turn him loose. There is not a man on this jury, if you had to come in close contact with him under heat of passion or excitement but what you would remember his face as long as you live. He has a distinctive look. Lyle Stack testified she told him he had a sharp chin and high cheek bones, had on certain type clothes, and he had on those white tennis shoes.

Talking about not having probable cause for arrest without warrant. When he called in and told them to take the man to jail, that he was the man they wanted, she had already told him and he so testified what the Defendant looked like, and I submit to you again—

MR. STILP: Your Honor, we are going to object to that. The arrest in question is not when the Sheriff placed the Defendant in the County Jail, but the moment that the City Police apprehended him at the service station.

THE COURT: The law you will receive from the Court's Charge, and from that source alone, Gentlemen of the Jury.

MR. ROBIN: Now, we go back to the call that came into town from Mr. Hill. His mother had run over there in just a few minutes time from the time as soon as she got loose from the Defendant, as soon as he took off in his car. She tells you that he went south. As soon as Phil could get the information from his mother, he called it in. He didn't know who the Negro was. She didn't know who the Negro was. Told the desk sergeant over at the city and on another call told the Sheriff, said, "Mother has been raped by a Negro, and is in a car and headed south toward town." "Stop all cars with colored subjects in them and check them out." Harping about it being an unlawful arrest. Gentlemen, how many times have you all heard of roadblocks put up? Just last Sunday we had roadblocks all over Ford County.

MR. STILP: Your Honor, I am going to object to that. That is extraneous evidence from another case and has no bearing on it whatsoever.

THE COURT: Sustained.

MR. STILP: Thank you, Your Honor.

It's an attempt to bring in prejudice into this case; I ask for a mistrial.

THE COURT: Overruled.

MR. STILP: Note our exception.

MR. ROBIN: Now, let's get back to the evidence and go over it briefly again. He says, the defense says, she wasn't hurt, she wasn't maimed for life. She told you right there that he had his arm down against her throat and her head over the back of the edge of the bed and pressing down and it hurt, and he finally pressed down enough and he wiggled around enough until he finally got between her legs, and gentlemen, I still don't know what the State men were doing up here, and I don't know whether you do or not, except to try to impress you that someone with a lower mentality than you have got is licensed to do anything he wants to and go free. And you gentlemen remember I asked one of them—I forget which one it was, that is the only question I asked—"Are you trying to tell this jury that he didn't know right from wrong?" He said, "No, I am sure not. I am not telling that."

Now, gentlemen, if the test is because someone, if he doesn't have a high I.Q. is licensed to go over the country and rape your wives or your widows if anything happens to you, then we have come to a poor pass in our way of life.

You have got at least five men that testified proving these were the Defendant's shoes taken off of him. They showed you that mark there, that break in those shoes. They said that it was perfect in the track; it fitted in. The worn places and everything on that particular heel, together with the track. You may take those into the jury room, if you want to, and examine them. You can take those pictures into the jury room, if you want to, and examine those. I want you to take this into the jury room with you. That shows a record of the call from Mr. Hill to the City Police, as soon as his mother told what had happened. It also reflects the call to the Sheriff. It also reflects what was done, and this was introduced by the Defendant. It wasn't introduced by me. It was marked and introduced by the defense, and if that doesn't confirm that that arrest was legal, then I don't know how to convince you that it was an arrest made with a felon escaping or trying to elude the officers, and at such time when they did not have time to get a warrant. No one at the time she called in, that Phil Hill called in, knew who the Defendant was. We had to go by the description that she gave to try and make a case and go from there, and if this jury should see fit to turn this Defendant loose because an officer had gone out with that procedure, then you don't need any officers, you don't need any law enforcement.

Let me tell you something else, gentlemen. The responsibility lies with me and solely with me for you being qualified on the death penalty. The State allows me, the law allows me, as State's Attorney, to waive the death penalty, but it also directs me, in a case I am going to insist on the death penalty, that I give written notice to the Defendant within a certain length of time, which has been done in this case, that I am going to qualify the jury and ask for the death penalty. I don't know how much confidence you folks have in me as your District Attorney, but I am telling you, gentlemen, that had I not thought that this was a case that justified the supreme penalty, I would have waived the death penalty in this case,[86] but I think and I believe that the evidence all ties in, the shoes tie in, the fact that he was so excited and in flight that he forgot to zip his pants up. The play the defense attorney made about the Sheriff—"Do you arrest every man that has his pants unzipped?"—is silly, but that evidence is not silly in this case, because that is one thing that clinches this thing, the shoes, the testimony of Mrs. Hill that he is the Negro. She pointed him out. She didn't make any hesitancy about it at all. She said, "That is the man." The fact he came into that filling station in a state of excitement running in there from the north with his pants unzipped is just another piece of evidence showing that he is as guilty as sin.

Now, gentlemen, it's up to you. You have got a responsibility. I had a responsibility when I asked you to qualify yourselves on the death penalty, and I could have left it off, but the State feels that this is a case that requires and justifies the death penalty.

I have said all that I can, presented all the evidence that is at my command. Now, when I sit down there, as I told you before, my responsibility

86. Is this proper argument?

in this case seizes.[87]   It is now, or will be in just a minute, your case, your responsibility to show the world, if need be, that that cannot happen in this county, in this district, without the death penalty being assessed against you if you are caught.

MR. STILP: Your Honor, that is improper argument.   I object to it, because it is global; no reference to what it will stop.   There has been no testimony that it would.

THE COURT: Overrule.   Continue.

MR. STILP: Note our exception.

MR. ROBIN: Thank you, gentlemen.   The case is yours.

SECTION III.   THE APPEAL

The following opinion was written affirming the conviction and sentence. See whether it is in accord with the facts as you understand them from the transcript.

BROOKS v. STATE

The offense is rape by force; the punishment, death.

The record reflects that the victim, a widow, lived alone some twelve miles north of Sandle and a distance of about two blocks from the home of her son.   Testifying at the trial she positively identified appellant as the Negro man who, about 2 A.M., after gaining entrance into her house through a window, by force ravished and had sexual intercourse with her, and after demanding and taking money she had in her coin purse and threatening to repeat his act, finally drove away.   She immediately ran to her son's home and reported the matter.   She described her assailant as being a young Negro man, wearing dark trousers and tennis shoes.   Her son relayed the information to the sheriff by telephone and told the sheriff that the suspect was believed to be in an automobile headed toward Sandle.

The sheriff immediately alerted all officers in the area by radio, requesting them to stop any car containing colored subjects coming into Sandle from the north.   Within minutes a vehicle driven by appellant pulled into a service station on the north side of Sandle.   Police officers of the City of Sandle observed that he was wearing tennis shoes and dark trousers which were unzipped, and detained him until other officers arrived.

The tennis shoes worn by appellant were compared with the footprints found near the house in which the offense was committed and they matched.

* * *

87. The word should obviously be "ceases".   The transcription process is not perfect.   Since the appellate court bases its decision on what is in the record, mistakes or a failure to transcribe could be important.   What may an attorney do if he is worried about errors in the preparation of the transcript?

The arrest claimed to be illegal was the detention and subsequent arrest of appellant. The evidence claimed to have been unlawfully seized is the tennis shoes appellant was wearing.

The officer had no warrant and no time to obtain a warrant. The identity of the suspect was not known. The officer who detained appellant some 15 minutes after he left his victim did so at the request of the sheriff who had information that the suspect, a Negro man wearing tennis shoes, was in a car believed to be headed toward Sandle.

Art. 14.04 of the State Code reads as follows:

> "Where it is shown by satisfactory proof to a peace officer, upon the representation of a credible person, that a felony has been committed, and that the offender is about to escape, so that there is no time to procure a warrant, such peace officer may, without warrant, pursue and arrest the accused."

Appellant points up the fact that the arresting officers did not have a description of the suspect or his vehicle, and therefore, he contends that the officers did not have sufficient probable cause to make the arrest.

The officer receiving the report of the rape observed appellant as he stepped from his car and noticed that his trousers were unzipped.

If the requesting officer is in possession of sufficient knowledge to constitute probable cause, he need not detail such knowledge to the arresting officer.

In the light of these circumstances, the officers had probable cause to arrest the suspect.

The arrest without warrant under the circumstances was not unlawful and the court did not err in overruling the motion to suppress the evidence.

We note, further, that having found the arrest legal and having admitted the evidence, the court at appellant's request submitted the question as a fact issue to the jury and instructed that in the event the jury found the arrest was illegal, or had reasonable doubt that it was legal, not to consider for any purpose any testimony relating to the tennis shoes and the comparison of same to the footprints at or about the scene of the crime.

* * *

SECTION IV. A REVIEW OF THE CASE

A. THE ARREST, SEARCH AND SEIZURE

When you review the performance of counsel for both sides, are you impressed with their grasp of the essential issues, their knowledge of the law, their familiarity with the facts, and their control over the course and pace of the trial? Or do you see problems with the basic approach of one or both sides?

Consider first the defense. What stands out is counsel's emphasis on the search and seizure claim. Do you believe that such a claim had any chance of success with the jury? If you don't believe that it had much chance of prevailing, does this mean that there were no reasons for emphasizing the argument in the way that the defense counsel did? As we point out in the introduction to this chapter, in most jurisdictions the judge decides the legality of a search and seizure and the jury does not make an independent judgment on the constitutionality of police conduct. However, in the state where this trial occurred the jury had the duty of independently determining the constitutionality of the police efforts. But the jury had no lawyers, law students, law teachers, or judges among its members. Hence, the only law the jury knew was the law provided by the judge in his instructions and the nuances argued by counsel in closing argument. If the search and seizure point was the essence of your defense, what sort of instruction would you have wanted? As defense counsel would you have wanted the judge to explain to the jury the purpose of suppressing evidence seized in violation of the fourth amendment?

Should Brooks' counsel have settled, without objection, for the following instruction, the sole search and seizure instruction given in *Brooks*?

In this case the issue has been raised as to whether there was a legal arrest of Defendant. In the event the arrest was not legal, the evidence relating to the shoes taken from the Defendant and the comparison of the shoes and the footprints at or about the scene of the crime is not admissible. I instruct you that the only circumstances under which one may lawfully be arrested without warrant is where a peace officer is informed by a credible person that a felony offender is about to escape and there is not time to secure a warrant.

In the event you find the arrest illegal, or if you have a reasonable doubt that the arrest was legal, you are instructed not to consider for any purpose any testimony relating to the shoes of Defendant in comparison of the same to the

footprints at or about the scene of the crime.

It is also interesting to note that this state apparently requires its prosecutors to prove the validity of a warrantless search beyond a reasonable doubt. This is a higher burden than most jurisdictions place on the prosecutor.[88] Is the advantage conferred upon the defendant by this unusually high burden utilized to maximum advantage in *Brooks*? If not, how might the defense have obtained more mileage from the prosecutor's burden?

Given the prosecutor's theoretically onerous task of justifying Brooks' arrest and the ensuing search and seizure and assuming that the jury would follow instructions, consider the arguments and strategies not used by the defense. For example, take the testimony of Officer Gant who, together with Officer Michael, stopped another car prior to stopping Brooks. One disputed issue bearing on the legality of the search and seizure was whether information concerning the direction in which the assailant had fled was given to the sheriff and relayed to the other officers. Officer Gant states that he and Officer Michael "went down Main and the expressway, and we stopped one car or attempted to stop it and found out just before we stopped it, it was a white man, *so we turned around and went back across the expressway and* * * *." (Emphasis added). Isn't this fairly persuasive evidence that the officers were stopping cars traveling in both directions, at least if the cars had Negro occupants? Isn't the obvious inference that the sheriff must have ordered officers to stop cars regardless of the direction in which they were moving? Why does the defense counsel fail to raise this point with the court or the jury? He is clearly aware of the importance of establishing what the police knew when they stopped Brooks initially, yet a significant fact is apparently not no-

---

88. See Saltzburg, Standards of Proof and Preliminary Questions of Fact, 27 Stan.L.Rev. 271 (1975). The burden is made clear in the jury instructions in this case.

ticed by counsel. Can the jury be expected to pick out such facts if the attorney does not emphasize them? Does this testimony suggest that the defense counsel should have moved to sequester the witnesses? Would this have prevented the officers' stories from congealing as they did? Can you think of any reasons why sequestration was not requested?

Any failure to recognize relevant information may have costs which extend beyond the lost impact of the unrecognized item. Information important to a case may often lead to other information that is even more helpful. Had counsel focused on the fact that attempts were made to stop cars traveling in both directions, perhaps this would have suggested a vitally important question: how could the sheriff possibly know in what direction the suspect was

heading, given the fact that no one else seemed to know? The victim testified that she ran from the house as soon as her assailant left by the front door. Did she have personal knowledge that the assailant had a car? Or did she assume the existence of a car from a comment made by the assailant? Assuming she had some reason to think there was a car, how could she know in what direction it was going? This question will remain unanswered because it was not asked. Yet there is a statement by Lyle Stack that Mr. Hill stated that the car was going toward Sandle. This is alluded to by the prosecutor in the first part of his closing argument. The prosecutor says that Mrs. Hill said the car was going south. She never said this in her testimony and it is unclear how she could have known it.

B. THE JURY AS FACT FINDER

Brooks, after moving to suppress evidence outside the hearing of the jury, chose to take advantage of his right to argue the legality of his arrest to the jury. This right, which is not found in most jurisdictions, is, in theory, an added protection. But the difficulty of winning a search and seizure point before a jury unschooled in constitutional law and previously unaware of the language and history of the fourth amendment is apparent. Furthermore, a jury is likely to see an implicit concession of substantive guilt when a defense is based largely on procedural issues.

If, as Brooks' lawyer, you could preserve the suppression issue for appeal without again raising it before the jury, would you have wanted to do so? The problem is similar to that faced by defense counsel who move to suppress confessions on *Miranda* or other "technical" grounds that juries might regard as unrelated to true guilt or innocence. Even in the majority of jurisdictions that do not allow the jury to reconsider the issue of the admissibil-

ity, a defendant has the right, codified in FRE 104(e), to challenge the weight to be given admitted evidence. Thus, in the confession area a defendant might argue that because he was not given *Miranda* warnings he did not take an interrogation seriously, and so his responses to police questions should be given little weight. A danger with such an argument is that if the jury finds it implausible, it may regard a defendant's focus on the technical deficiencies of the evidence as an implicit admission of substantive significance. Knowing when to raise issues before juries and when to forego them requires experience. Skilled counsel learn that they need not use all available opportunities to challenge opposing evidence.

If, however, as Brooks' lawyer, you knew that in order to preserve the search and seizure issue for appeal you were required under state law to raise your search and seizure issue in front of the jury and to request an instruction on the point, what would you have done? Would you have given up the search and seizure claim entirely once the judge indicated that he was not persuaded, or would you have tried it to the jury?   If you did try it to the jury, how would you have treated it?

C. THE IMPORTANCE OF THE SEARCH AND SEIZURE ISSUE AND THE OTHER EVIDENCE

Much of the testimony in *Brooks* was devoted to the legality of the arrest and to the admissibility of its fruits.   How important do you think each of the following was to the state's case?

1.   The victim's eyewitness identification.

2.   Brooks' presence at the gas station at an early morning hour.

3.   The description given by the victim to the police on the night of the rape.

4.   The cancelled checks showing that Brooks had worked for the victim and her husband.

5.   The clothes Brooks was wearing when he was arrested.

6.   The observation that Brooks' zipper was open when he stepped from his car.

7.   Brooks' attempt to resist being taken to the police station.

8.   The tire tracks and the match with Brooks' car.

9.   Brooks' shoes and the match with footprints in the gravel.

10.   Brooks' failure to explain what he was doing on the night in question.

11.   The fact that Brooks was black.

12.   Brooks' criminal record.

How did the defense counsel deal with the items that you found most damaging? Could you have done better?

Which of the following was, in your opinion, likely to have had a substantial impact on the jury's sentencing decision?

1.   The overall strength of the state's case?

2.   The way in which the crime was committed.

3.   Mrs. Hill's age.

4.   The particular vulnerability of Mrs. Hill.

5.   Brooks' prior criminal record.

6.   Brooks' educational history.

7.   Brooks' intellectual development.

8.   Brooks' family background.

9.   The racial difference between Brooks and Mrs. Hill.

10.   The southern, rural setting of the trial.

Which of these items, if any, does the prosecutor emphasize?   How does the defense counsel meet the prosecutor's arguments?   Which of these items does the defense emphasize?   Why did the defense counsel present the evidence he did?

D. THE STRENGTH OF THE CASE

Notice that the defense counsel did not engage in extensive cross-examination of the victim, probably because he was afraid of alienating the jury.   However, he did argue mistaken identification to the jury. Could the jury be expected to take this argument seriously when Mrs. Hill's ability to observe and her actual observations went unchallenged?   Mrs. Hill testified not only that she gave her son a description of the height and physical appearance of the assailant, but also that she heard the son call the sheriff and tell the sheriff "the same thing I [Mrs. Hill] told him [the son]?"   If Mrs. Hill is correct, everyone else must be incorrect, because the son and the sheriff testified that, at most, the sheriff knew only that a Negro suspect was traveling by auto in a particular direction. Probably Mrs. Hill was mistaken. Mrs. Hill's accuracy on this point is important in deciding whether Brooks was actually guilty.

Consider the following scenario. After Brooks was stopped and detained by the police, the sheriff came to look at him. Then the sheriff went to see Mrs. Hill, told her that someone had been arrested for the crime, and described Brooks to her. Mrs. Hill may have indicated that the description sounded like the assailant. Later, Mrs. Hill thought she had given an accurate description to the sheriff, whereas in truth her description was based largely on what the sheriff said about Brooks' appearance. If this happened, no witness who testified at trial would necessarily have committed perjury. The defense counsel's task would have been to convince the jury that the passage of time leads people to assimilate information and to assemble perceptions in a logical order that may be far removed from what was actually perceived. Why did he not do this? Was it not possible to examine Mrs. Hill about the events subsequent to the rape without suggesting that she was a liar? How would you have conducted such an examination? Is it asking too much to expect a jury to understand that confusion, fear and anger can lead to mistakes of memory and perception? How might you have tried to convince a jury of this?

Is there support for the above scenario in the sheriff's apparent failure to ask for a description of the fleeing assailant? Is it likely that the sheriff, upon being awakened by a call reporting a rape, would simply ask about the race of the assailant and the direction in which he was driving? Wouldn't a more complete description of the assailant be requested? If it could be shown that Mrs. Hill (through her son) did not initially provide the sheriff with even a brief description of the rapist, would her

allegedly independent description of Brooks become suspect? At the very least, shouldn't counsel, who was resting so heavily on a search and seizure theory, attempt to show how easily the police could have obtained a description (assuming Mrs. Hill could give one), thereby obtaining probable cause for arrest and avoiding any need to stop drivers simply because of their race?

Perhaps you are thinking at this point what the defense counsel apparently thought, i.e., the case against Brooks was so strong that none of these things would have mattered. But was the case that strong? What evidence was offered against the defendant?

First, there was the eyewitness evidence of the victim. There is considerable evidence that eyewitness testimony is often unreliable. The prosecutor's statement in final argument that "there is not a man on this jury, if you had come in close contact with him under heat of passion or excitement but what you would remember his face as long as you live," conflicts with the findings of modern psychology. Passion and excitement interfere substantially with the capacity to observe and remember. It is quite possible that Mrs. Hill will always be haunted by an image of the man who attacked her, but it is not unlikely that the image would be mistaken in many respects and that she would find it impossible to pick out her assailant from a group of similar individuals.

From the cold transcript the eyewitness testimony appears to be routine and undramatic. It is given before the attack was described, at a time that the jury was not wondering who committed the atrocious assault. The prosecutor makes no claim that Mrs. Hill was especially confident in her identification, nor is there evidence describing when or how the defendant was first presented to Mrs. Hill or what her first reaction was. The force which the eyewitness testimony has in this case may result largely from its going unchallenged. Counsel for the defendant might have emphasized the poor lighting, Mrs. Hill's excitement, the period of time Mrs. Hill was without her glasses, Mrs. Hill's age and the way age probably affected her eyesight, and the fact that Mrs. Hill did not recognize the defendant even though he had once worked for her family. Counsel might have requested a lineup, even a courtroom lineup, to test the perception of the victim. Of course, challenging Mrs. Hill's identification testimony carried some risk, but was it as great as the risk of failing to test the key prosecution witness?

The most convincing incriminating evidence was the testimony that the shoe prints found outside Mrs. Hill's house matched the shoe prints of the defendant. A possible way of accounting for this is to assume that the police took the defendant's shoes to the scene of the crime and made their own prints, confident that they had the guilty party or anxious to "clear" the case immediately regardless of who was arrested. The first rationale seems particularly inappropriate here, since at the time the prints were compared there was little evidence connecting the defendant to this crime. The second rationale may appeal to those who are generally suspicious of police integrity, but there is nothing to support it in this case. If you were a defense counsel arguing before a state jury in a rural area would you expect either theory of police misconduct to be believed? If your client's life were at stake, would the risk of alienating the jury with such an argument be sufficient reason not to advance it?

There is no evidence of police misconduct in the transcript, but one wishes the shoe prints had been photographed or plaster casts had been made before the shoes were brought to the scene. A difficulty with the print evidence is that the prints were not found near the window by which the assailant supposedly entered the house, nor by the door the assailant used to leave the house. They were found instead by a bedroom window. Can this be explained on the theory that the house was being "cased"? Perhaps, but why weren't prints found elsewhere? Does Sheriff Stack's testimony that the ground was full of gravel make the finding of only one footprint reasonable, or does it make the finding of even one footprint suspect? Not seeing the footprint photographs, you cannot know how powerful the evidence was, and not having the shoes before you, you are unable to judge whether the print was distinctive enough to be significant. But you still can wonder. Would you have been helped had the defense counsel experimentally tested the ground to see if it yielded footprints? Perhaps he did.

Was there any evidence in the record favorable to the defendant? One is hard pressed to find mention of any in the defense counsel's closing argument, but that does not mean that there was none. Are you convinced that someone as mentally slow as Brooks allegedly was could plan things sufficiently to commit this crime? Would a borderline mentally deficient person case the house, hide the car, refuse a check, respond as the assailant did when a light was turned on, remember to disconnect the phone, find the open window in the house, etc.? Would someone who took such care to commit the crime casually pull into a gas station with his zipper open? Since the defendant's mental, social, and criminal history is brought out at trial, you know that he had a girl friend, that he had never been arrested for any sex crime before, and that no examination had ever shown him to be abnormal in any way except in intelligence. Are these things important?

Reconsidering the evidence, how strong is it? Do you find yourself thinking that even if it is not as strong as you thought at first the fact that the defendant's presence in the area at an early hour was unexplained is important? If so, what about the fifth amendment? The trial judge instructed the jury as follows:

In a criminal case the law permits the defendant to testify in his own behalf; but the same law provides his failure to testify shall not be considered as a circumstance against him. You will, therefore, not consider the failure of the defendant to testify as a circumstance against him; and you will not in your deliberation of your verdict consider or allude to, comment on, or in any manner refer to the fact that the defendant has not testified.

Would you, as defense counsel, have wanted this instruction or would you have preferred that nothing be said about the defendant's failure to take the stand? Was it likely that the jury would follow this instruction? Would you, as a juror, follow this rule without any explanation as to why it should apply? Is there any explanation which should satisfy a jury that the defendant's silence has no bearing on his guilt or innocence? Indeed, isn't this a case where there is greater than average reason to conclude that the defendant's silence was indicative of guilt? Where innocent defendants choose not to testify, the choice is often due to the desire to keep a prior criminal record from being revealed to the jury under the guise of impeachment. Here this motive is absent. The defense reveals the defendant's record as part of its case-in-chief. Are there reasons other than guilt why counsel might have decided not to put the defendant on the stand? Was counsel worried that a slow witness might be tricked by the prosecutor? If so, was this sufficient reason in a capital case to risk the adverse inference the jury might draw from silence? Recall the discussion in Chapter Five of the impact of the defendant's silence.

The state where this case was tried no longer requires that questions relating to both guilt and punishment be presented simultaneously to the jury, but this was the procedure with which counsel had to cope in trying Brooks' case. What dilemmas are posed by this procedure? How successful was defense counsel in dealing with these problems? Are you satisfied that the jury understood defense counsel's purpose in calling his witnesses? Are you persuaded that counsel used the testimony of these witnesses to best advantage in arguing to the jury? In what ways, if any, would you have argued differently? What would you expect to influence a jury in its choice of penalties ranging from five years imprisonment to death?

The defense is not the only side with an interest in clarifying ambiguous testimony. If there were gaps in proof concerning the search and seizure, shouldn't a careful prosecutor have filled those gaps to avoid the possibility of appellate reversal? Should the prosecutor have clarified Officer Gant's testimony about stopping individuals traveling in both directions on the highway? Should the prosecutor have made clear the source or sources from which the arresting officers learned about the car and its direction of travel?

Assuming that these gaps could not be filled or could only be filled by calling into further question the legality of the search, does the prosecutor have a duty to bring these gaps to the attention of the judge and the jury? Section 1.1(a), ABA Standards for Criminal Justice, The Prosecution Function and the Defense Function, The Prosecution Function (App. Draft 1971) begins with this definition of the function of the prosecutor:

The office of the prosecutor is an agency of the executive branch of government which is charged with the duty to see that the laws are faithfully executed and enforced in order to maintain the rule of law.

Subsection (c) of the same section provides:

The duty of the prosecutor is to seek justice, not merely to convict.

Is it proper for the prosecutor to obfuscate the facts where obfuscation is helpful to his case? Does it matter whether the prosecutor believes the defendant is guilty? Should it make a difference that the gaps referred to here related to the legality of a search and seizure rather than the identity of the assailant? Does the situation differ when it is the defense counsel who engages in obfuscation?

Knowing he might well ask for the death penalty, should the prosecutor have asked the police to check the telephone, the doorknob and the window by which the suspect supposedly entered the house for fingerprints in order to ensure that there was no evidence available that might cast doubt on the guilt of Brooks? Should the prosecutor have been more careful in supervising the handling of the clothing taken from Brooks? Should he have been prepared for the chain of custody problem and offered witnesses from the laboratory?

Perhaps the most troublesome aspect of the prosecutor's conduct is the quality of his closing argument. Was he concerned about fairness to the defendant? Did he want the jury to have a correct understanding of the law of search and seizure? In footnotes we have pointed out some of the problems with his argument. Yet, even where the argument is most questionable, the defense rarely objects. Does this in any way excuse what the prosecutor did? When a society entrusts a prosecutor with

discretion to seek a capital penalty or any severe penalty, but requires that a jury choose the sentence, should the prosecutor explain to the jury his view of appropriate sentencing criteria, or should the prosecutor play upon the emotions of lay jurors, hoping to persuade them to accede to his judgment on the penalty issue? What did the prosecutor do in this case? What did the defense counsel do?

When a case is over, it is easy to be very critical of the way the case was handled. Perhaps it is impossible for those outside of Orange County, or Sandle, to ever appreciate what was going on in *Brooks*. Surely the most vigilant defense advocates and the most sensitive prosecutors sometimes forget to touch every base in every case. But in this case life and death apparently hung in the balance. If ever care must be required and error condemned, it is in cases like this. In one sense every trial is a test of a system of justice as well as a contest among litigants. If care cannot realistically be demanded because it is impossible for busy lawyers and judges to provide it, if gaps are endemic to litigation, and if prosecutors cannot seek justice and convictions simultaneously, what does this say about the kinds of punishment a judicial system should be permitted to impose? How does this affect your confidence in the adversary system? Are the problems visible in *Brooks* indeed endemic? Are there obvious ways in which some problems could be eliminated?

E. RECONCILING SUBSTANCE AND SENTENCE

You might think that the problems presented in this transcript are unique or are unlikely to arise in the future, either because the death penalty is impermissible for rape unaccompanied by murder or because when capital punishment is imposed most jurisdictions now use a bifurcated proceeding—i.e., the jury first determines guilt or innocence and then decides whether or not to recommend death. However, juries in some jurisdictions rec-

ommend sentences when death is not an option, and even where trials are bifurcated an attorney must be concerned with the way in which his substantive case might influence a later sentencing decision. If procedures are more traditional, with the judge solely responsible for the sentence, the lawyer's tactics might change somewhat, but he must still be aware of the possibility that the way he approaches the guilt-innocence determination may affect the judge's sentencing decision following a conviction.

Thinking about how to try guilt and sentence simultaneously is difficult, but similar difficulties confront lawyers in civil litigation where issues of liability and damages often are handled in one proceeding. In both criminal and civil cases lawyers must carefully assess how their approach to one issue will affect the resolution of others. Knowing the rules of evidence is a prerequisite to success at trial, but it is no guarantee of it. Careful lawyers must pay at least as much attention to the *gestalt* of the trial as they do to any of the evidentiary pieces.

Trial lawyers are the artists of the profession. They take the evidence that comes into their possession and decide how to present it to a tribunal. What happens in litigation is what they make happen. Their tapestries are filled with words and exhibits that they put together. The value of their work turns on how it measures up to the tests of logic, experience, and common sense. Only if lawyers perform well will justice in the long run be served.

BIBLIOGRAPHY

ABA Standards, The Prosecution Function and the Defense Function (App. Drafts, 1971, 1979).

Appleman, Successful Jury Trials, A Symposium (1952).

Belli, Modern Trials (1954).

Busch, Law and Tactics in Jury Trials (1949).

Goldstein & Lane, Trial Technique (1966).

Keeton, Trial Tactics and Methods (1954).

Wellman, The Art of Cross-Examination (4th ed. 1944).

Appendix I

A BRIEF HISTORY OF CODIFICATION

Because this book has paid considerable attention to the Federal Rules of Evidence, we think it desirable to briefly describe the background of these rules. We believe that the student will appreciate the labor pains preceding the adoption of this new code, and that the student will also appreciate the continuing vitality of some common law concepts, even in code jurisdictions.

The following excerpt describes the general background of the codification movement and traces the developments leading to the drafting of the Model Code of Evidence in 1942:

The background of the codification movement in the United States is indeed a curious one; there appears to have been and still to be a fairly constant demand among some lawyers for evidentiary codes. But it also appears exceedingly difficult to build up sufficient momentum to enact codes into law. Ambivalent is probably the best description of the attitude of lawyers towards legislation in the evidentiary domain.

There is apparently some appreciation of the benefits of uniformity and ease of ascertainment of the rules when a statute is enacted. At the same time there is some fear that legislation produces wooden rules and some concern that case by case adjudication is a superior means of doing justice. Lurking in the background also is a sense on the part of most lawyers that some evidentiary rules are of questionable value and that some may even approach the realm of the absurd. But the problem has been to find the appropriate means to change the rules without impairing the functioning of those that are justifiable and that are presently working well.

Legislation offers a nice clean solution. One swing of the legislative (or rulemaking) axe and the umbilical cord tying present to past is cut and legislation emerges that solves the problems of the past and serves the needs of the future. But when it is remembered that not all lawyers agree on which are the silly rules and which the wise, that too radical a departure from tradition makes it difficult to enact legislation, that the problem of too much rigidity is a real one, and that there are many possible solutions, not simply one, the difficulties of enacting legislation become readily apparent.

Common law courts, on the other hand, can examine the facts of particular cases and seek to mold rules to fit those facts. They are also somewhat free to modify past rules to meet present needs. However, the mere mention of the term *stare decisis* should serve to explain one of the "problems" of common law courts, i.e., precedent is important. Moreover, while molding rules to fit particular facts may do justice in individual cases, it makes practicing law ever so much more difficult because the lawyer has difficulty predicting precisely what the court will say about the rules of evidence in any given case. Finally, there is the feeling on the part of many Judges that once a rule has stood over time, even if it is of questionable value, legislative intervention is a more appropriate response than judicial overruling.

More could be said on the relative advantages and disadvantages of legislation and adjudication. It is sufficient for the purposes of this brief background, however, to note that the demand for codification has never come unanimously from the lips of the members of the bar. Codification has had its opponents as well as its adherents. It is, in fact, difficult to review the history of the last 30 years and derive any firm conclusion as to whether feelings about codification of evidentiary rules differ greatly from the feelings of most lawyers about the relative merits of legislation versus adjudication generally.

* * *

Not surprisingly, much of the impetus toward legislation arose from enactment of the Federal Rules of Civil Procedure in the late 1930's. When the original Advisory Committee on Civil Rules issued its report in 1937, it suggested that evidentiary rules be largely excluded, since at that time there was no ready reference for codification and there was apparently insufficient time for the task. It is also likely that inclusion of evidentiary rules with the Rules of Civil Procedure would have provoked much of the same controversy that surrounded the 1970's attempt at codification and thus diverted attention from the much needed Rules of Civil Procedure. The Chairman of the Advisory Committee, William D. Mitchell, said:

> "There was tremendous pressure brought on the advisory committee by those familiar with the subject of evidence insisting that there was a need for reform which we did not meet, and some advisory committee should tackle the task of revising the rules of evidence and composing them into a new set of rules to be promulgated by the Supreme Court."

The final product of the Advisory Committee included two rules relating to the admissibility of evidence. Rule 44 was relatively narrow, covering only the manner in which an official record should be proved. Much more significant was Rule 43, which was an evidentiary rule providing in relevant part that evidence should be received if admissible under (1) a federal statute or (2) federal equity practice or (3) practice of the state where the Federal Court sat, with the statute or rule favoring admissibility to govern.

On the face of it, the rule seemed both straightforward and simple. The main problems which developed thereafter were in determining what federal equity practice was and what state law was. There has been considerable dispute among scholars and Judges as to whether Rule 43 worked in practice.

Although it is somewhat outside the chronological sequence, it is useful at this point to consider Rule 26 of the Rules of Criminal Procedure, which was enacted in 1946 and was designed quite differently from Rule 43 of the Civil Rules. Prior to the Criminal Rules, there was some disagreement as to the source of rules of evidence in criminal cases. Federal Criminal Rule 26 provided that Federal Courts should use common law rules of evidence as interpreted in the light of reason and experience. Since the Criminal Rules were not tied in any way to State Rules, uniformity seemed to be more likely in criminal than in civil cases. But even in criminal cases, uniformity was elusive. The Supreme Court did not review many evidence cases, and the Circuit Courts took different approaches in various areas.

Following the suggestion of William D. Mitchell that some Advisory Committee should tackle the task of revising the rules of evidence and composing them into a new set of rules to be promulgated by the Supreme Court, other prominent members of the legal profession made similar proposals.

These clarion calls did not go unheeded. In 1939, the American Law Institute turned to the subject of evidence, and with Professor Edmund Morgan of

Harvard as its Reporter, promulgated the Model Code of Evidence in 1942. Despite the "tremendous pressure" of which the Advisory Committee Chairman had spoken, no jurisdiction ever adopted the Model Code of Evidence.[1]

Those state bar associations or law revision groups that did not wholly ignore the Model Code rejected it in language ranging in tone from vehement rejection of the basic concept to approval of the concept but rejection of the specific code proposed. California is an example of a jurisdiction that vigorously opposed the basic concept of the Code. The California Committee to the Governors of the State Bar charged that:

[T]he Code seeks to destroy the foundation upon which our structure for the administration of justice is founded and substitute an entirely new theory.

* * * The Code proceeds upon the theory that all the wisdom and learning of the past is to be discarded; that the rights of the parties are no longer to depend upon settled rules of law or evidence but upon the view of each individual judge, and that the life, liberty and property rights of any person within the state may be taken from him not by testimony of facts within the knowledge of the witnesses, but upon the conclusions of witnesses with or without foundation, and upon neighborhood gossip. Be-

tween the philosophy of the Code and the philosophy of our present system there should be no question as to the choice of bench and bar.[2]

The Massachusetts Bar Association had similar objections, noting that "the Code gives too much power to the trial judge. * * * Furthermore, the unlimited discretion which in many instances is given to the court gives the bar practically no standard to go by."[3]

The attitude of a majority of a Pennsylvania State Bar Committee evidenced a more sympathetic view of the Code. In 1945 a majority of the Committee recommended preparation of a Code adhering as closely as possible to the structure of the Model Code. But even in Pennsylvania, a minority was opposed to any code of evidence or comprehensive statute "because it believes that the law of evidence, by reason of its broad, diverse and relative character, is not the proper subject of a code or comprehensive statutory enactment.[4]

Those jurisdictions that expressed some appreciation for the advantages of the Code found it difficult, if not impossible, to amend the Code to include more particularized rules, to adequately control the discretion of the trial judge, and to clarify confusing parts.[5] In 1953, for example, the Arizona Committee on the Model Code of Evidence reported to the Governors of the State Bar that there was no demand among the bar for a Code of Evidence like the Model Code. They suggested that the preparation and recommendation of "a few

1. S. Saltzburg & K. Redden, Federal Rules of Evidence Manual 1–2 (3d ed.1982).

2. 29B, West.Ann.Cal.Evid.Code XXVII. Among the Rules referred to was Rule 306 which permitted character evidence to be admitted in civil cases to prove conduct on a particular occasion, but not the quality of conduct. Opinion evidence was also permitted.

3. 18 Mass.L.Q. 28 (April, 1942). This is a common criticism of codes, and an ironic one, since one goal of codes is to promote uniform decisionmaking.

4. See Report of the Special Committee to Consider Drafting Code of Evidence, 20 Pa.B.A.Q. 283–85 (1949), cited in Note on Code as Means of Promoting Nation-Wide Reform, in Selected Writings on the Law of Evidence and Trial 1160, 1162–63 (1957) [hereinafter cited as Note].

5. Many complaints of confusion were undoubtedly well taken. Rule 11 is an outstanding example of drafting which has retained its original capacity to confuse over time.

specific statutory changes in the law of evidence would be preferable to recommendation of a Code."[6] In 1948, a Subcommittee on the Model Code of Evidence to the Michigan Bar Committee on Civil Procedure noted that because the Code was an integrated whole containing many cross-references, one rule depended upon many others and it did not seem feasible to pick out any substantial number of rules and write them into the existing law. "[T]he Code must be considered and dealt with as a whole * * *."[7] Michigan was not ready to substitute the Code for its body of evidence law. It may well be that a similar feeling ultimately prevented Pennsylvania from drafting a new Code.

Perhaps the most substantial effort at redrafting took place in Missouri. Missouri attempted to remedy what it viewed as the chief defects in the Model Code: (1) the "unbridled discretion [given] to the trial judge to admit or exclude evidence—even direct material evidence—and to comment on the weight of the evidence and the credibility of witnesses * * *"; (2) the paring-down of the hearsay exclusion rule; (3) and the abstractions of the Model Code which made it deficient as a practical guide "to the introduction of competent evidence."[8] But even the supposedly superior Missouri Code was not adopted.

The ultimate failure of efforts to promulgate the Model Code was foreseen by some critics. Dean Wigmore is perhaps the most notable. Originally the chief consultant on the project, he disassociated himself from the final product because of what he saw as defects in draftsmanship. He enumerated these defects in an important article.[9]

Wigmore charged that "the number of novel changes, towards an ideal code, is so great that the Bars of our States, when made aware of them beforehand, would not accept them."[10] He noted as an example the Code's enlargement of judicial "discretion" without appropriate definitional limitations of that term. He also listed many large areas of evidence law not treated by the Model Code, which in his view amounted to "a large proportion of everyday practice * * * apparently either abrogated altogether, or handed over to the discretion of each and every one of some 5,000 trial judges to administer as their momentary wisdom moves them."[11] Wigmore also quarreled with "the frequent use of novel terms and the constant use of long sentences with involved syntax,"[12] which impede efficient use of the rules during the heat of trial.

But these were subsidiary criticisms for Wigmore. The chief defect of the Code in his view was its failure to deal with all the concrete rules passed upon in a majority of jurisdictions, and its failure to give concrete examples of the applications of the proposed rules:

The Draft Code has thrown overboard scores of these detailed rules of guidance, substituting some broad abstractions, potent only to reduce to guesswork the practitioner's preparation for trial, and to breed argument and dispute in the conduct of the case.[13]

In summary, the Model Code was viewed as "an academic composition * * * not meriting legislative favor, first because its advanced proposals are far too radical at the present time, and secondly because its imperfections in the formulation of the

6.   Report of Arizona Committee on Model Code of Evidence to Governors of State Bar (1953), quoted in Note, at 1162 n. 9.

7.   27 Mich.S.B.J. 24 (1948), cited in Note, at 1162 n. 10.

8.   Carr, The Proposed Missouri Evidence Code, 29 Tex.L.Rev. 627, 638–41 (1951).

9.   The American Law Institute Code of Evidence Rules: A Dissent, 28 A.B.A.J. 23 (1942).

10.   Id. at 23.

11.   Id. at 25.

12.   Id.

13.   Id. at 27.

rules render it quite unfit for practical use." [14]

Although the Model Code was viewed with disfavor, the enterprise was not entirely in vain:

While unadopted, the Model Code was not entirely disregarded. In 1943 the American Bar Association took action. Its House of Delegates directed a study of uniform evidentiary rules, and the following year specifically provided that the Model Code should serve as the basis of the study.

In the interim, the Advisory Committee had an opportunity once again to consider whether or not it should undertake to compile rules of evidence. It concluded:

"While consideration of a comprehensive and detailed set of rules of evidence seems very desirable, it has not been feasible for the Committee so far to undertake this important task."

Since the American Bar Association recognized that the Model Code as drafted would not receive support from the various states, it enlisted the National Conference of Commissioners on Uniform State Laws in a program of revision in the hope that acceptable rules could be promulgated.

The actual drafting by the Commissioners began in 1950 and culminated in the Uniform Rules of Evidence, in 1953. [15]

The Uniform Rules were based upon the Model Code, but were modified to avoid what appeared to be the major objections to the Code. The goal was to achieve "sensible change without shock." [16] When proposals in drafts of the Uniform Rules seemed to be great departures from the traditional and generally prevailing common law and statutory rules of evidence and

seemed too far-reaching and drastic for acceptance by the Bar, modifications were made. Such modifications included limiting the general scheme to deal primarily with the basic problem of admissibility of evidence and omitting rules that were viewed as more "procedural" than "evidentiary" and thus outside the proper scope of evidence rules. Thus, the controversial Model Code provisions allowing the judge to comment on the evidence and control the trial procedure were avoided. [17] A second important departure from the Model Code was in terminology. The Commissioners freely reworded the rules and cut down the volume of words wherever possible to effect greater simplicity and to make the Uniform Rules more palatable to bench and bar than their predecessor.

Only a handful of jurisdictions adopted comprehensive evidence codes based in large part on the Uniform Rules. The California and New Jersey experiences may help to explain why substantial reworking of the Rules was thought to be necessary. The Report of the California Law Revision Committee explained the reasons for the substantial modification of the Uniform Rules in the drafting of the California Evidence Code in the mid-1960's. [18]

First, it was felt that the Uniform Rules would change the existing law of California to an undesirable extent. For example, the Rules would allow admission of a hearsay statement of a person present and subject to cross-examination without requiring a showing of loss of memory or inconsistency. Second, the rules did not include some existing California statutes that "had served the state well and should be continued * * *." [19] Because of the contradictory formats of the Rules and the state statutes, integration of the two bodies of law was thought impossible without

---

14.   Id. at 28.
15.   Saltzburg & Redden, supra note 1, at 3.
16.   Gard, 31 Tulane L.Rev. 19, 23 (1956).

17.   Model Code, Rule 8 covered this subject.
18.   29B West.Ann.Cal.Evid.Code XXIII.
19.   Id. at XXVIII.

substantially reworking the Rules. Third, the Commission criticized the drafting of some of the Rules. Fourth, the limitation of the Rules to procedural aspects of evidence made the need for uniformity nationwide less pressing a goal. Since the Rules were viewed as having little substantive significance insofar as the law of other states was concerned, California questioned the need for uniformity and felt free to change provisions in any way it deemed desirable.

The evidence code actually passed by California is based on the Uniform Rules, but the bulk of it conforms to the previous body of state evidence law, reorganized and redrafted so as to be easier to find and to understand.

The New Jersey Commission to Study the Improvement of the Law of Evidence also considerably modified the Uniform Rules. Most of the changes that were made were changes in form designed to produce greater clarity or to make the rules more concise. It is somewhat ironic that among the changes in substance made in New Jersey, some were intended to provide more discretionary power for the trial judge than was provided in the Uniform Rules.[20]

The fact that most states ignored the Uniform Rules is perhaps more instructive than the specific changes made by those states that accepted them. Professor Edmund Morgan suggested possible reasons for the hesitancy of most jurisdictions to move towards a code. He declared that when the need for change is not overwhelming, lawyers feel it is "better to endure present injustices than to take a chance of inviting others that we fear even though experience elsewhere has shown the fear

to be groundless."[21] Morgan cited Judge Learned Hand's protest against "this continuous conjuring of disaster which seems to pervade every effort of this sort. * * *."[22] Morgan also noted the absence of an organized group able or willing to spend the time or money required to secure the enactment of changes in the established system. Morgan sounded an optimistic note, however:

When the need for a change becomes imperative, the far-seeing leader appears and succeeds in making marked progress toward the goal before the force of reaction or inertia becomes dominant. The next champion begins where his predecessor was checked. Finally, the goal is reached.[23]

Another perceptive observer remarked that the Uniform Rules, like the Model Code, "strike down certain landmarks of evidence as to which we have made a fetish during our entire legal careers."[24] Noting, inter alia, the addition of new exceptions to the hearsay rule, this commentator foresaw that the states would be more receptive to the Uniform Rules if they were first accepted by the federal courts, just as the Federal Rules of Civil Procedure were first promulgated by the Supreme Court of the United States and then copied by many states.

Thus the advocates of evidentiary reform came to look to the federal courts. The following excerpt describes the history of the adoption of the Federal Rules of Evidence:

* * * In 1958, the House of Delegates of the American Bar Association urged the Judicial Conference of the

20. See Report of the New Jersey Commission to Study the Improvement of the Law of Evidence (1956).

21. Morgan, Practical Difficulties Impeding Reform in the Law of Evidence, 14 Vand.L.Rev. 725, 732 (1961).

22. 18 ALI Proceedings 191 (1940–41), cited in Morgan, supra note 21, at 732.

23. Morgan, supra note 21, at 739.

24. Nordbye, Proposed Rules to Cover the Field of Evidence, in Civil and Criminal Procedures Reviewed, 26 Hennepin Lawyer 131, 135 (1958).

United States to appoint a special committee to adapt the Uniform Rules for use in Federal Courts in order to clarify and improve the evidentiary rules and to provide a means of uniformity and conformity.

In March, 1961, in special session, the Judicial Conference of the United States approved a proposal of the Standing Committee on Rules of Practice and Procedure that called for a project devoted to Federal Rules of Evidence. The Chief Justice implemented the proposal by naming a Special Committee under the chairmanship of the distinguished Yale Professor James William Moore. The Committee's mandate was to inquire into the feasibility and advisability of Federal Rules of Evidence. In 1961, its report (A Preliminary Report on the Advisability and Feasibility of Developing Uniform Rules of Evidence for the United States District Courts) was written. This report concluded that uniform Rules of Evidence were both advisable and feasible. On February 12, 1962, the report was circulated to members of the bar and to Judges. After considering their comments, the Standing Committee and the Judicial Conference confirmed the recommendation of the Special Committee. On March 8, 1965, Chief Justice Warren appointed an Advisory Committee on Rules of Evidence.

The Advisory Committee transmitted to the Standing Committee a "Preliminary Draft of Proposed Rules of Evidence for the United States District Courts and Magistrates" on January 30, 1969. On March 31, 1969, the Standing Committee circulated the preliminary draft to the Bar and Bench for consideration. It was not until October, 1970, that the Standing Committee presented to the Judicial Conference its revised draft of evidentiary rules which substantially modified the preliminary draft. The revised draft was approved by the Judicial Confer-

ence and referred to the Supreme Court. The Supreme Court concluded that the revised draft should be submitted for comments to lawyers and Judges in the same manner as the preliminary draft. This was done in March, 1971.

Many comments and criticisms were made with respect to both drafts, and revisions were made in the revised draft, just as they had been made in the previous draft. After the Advisory Committee had reworked its product, it submitted it to the Standing Committee, which made some revisions before approving the draft and submitting it to the Judicial Conference. The Judicial Conference also approved the draft and then forwarded it to the Supreme Court in October, 1971. Although the Court did not promulgate this revision of the revised draft, it did receive further comments and suggestions, including some from the Department of Justice. Upon receipt of these comments, the Court requested the Advisory Committee and the Standing Committee to evaluate them. Early in 1972 the Advisory Committee and the Standing Committee met again and made further modifications. On November 20, 1972, the Supreme Court approved a final draft.

* * *

Had the same procedure that was used in adopting the Federal Rules of Civil Procedure and the Federal Rules of Criminal Procedure been used with respect to the evidentiary Rules (a procedure that would also have applied absent any contrary Congressional action), the Supreme Court draft would have become effective automatically after the passage of 90 days. It would have taken objections by both Houses of Congress to stop the Rules. Because Congress recognized the importance of the evidentiary Rules and because the label "substantive" was persistently applied to several of the Rules, Congress enacted Public Law 93–12 in early 1973 which provided that the Rules should not be effective until expressly approved by the Congress.

Two days after receiving the proposed Rules from Chief Justice Burger on February 5, 1973, the Subcommittee on Criminal Justice of the Committee on the Judiciary of the House of Representatives (formerly designated as Special Subcommittee on Reform of Federal Criminal Laws) opened hearings on the desirability of the uniform code of evidence and the merits of the Rules approved by the Supreme Court. After six days of hearings, and receipt of numerous written communications, the Subcommittee circulated a draft on June 28, 1973. Following extensive comments from the public, the Subcommittee revised its draft and on October 10, 1973, reported its revised draft to the full Judiciary Committee. On October 16 and 18, and on November 6, 1973, the full Committee debated the bill and amended it in several respects before reporting it to the full House. Several additional amendments were made by the full House before the Rules were passed on February 6, 1974. A Senate version of the Rules was passed on November 22, 1974, following hearings on July 4th and 5th, 1974, before the full Senate Committee on the Judiciary. As a result of compromises by House and Senate conferees, the final bill was approved by the House on December 16, and the Senate on December 18. It was sent to President Ford who approved it on January 2, 1975, whereupon it became Public Law 93–595, 88 Stat. 1926 et seq.[25]

More than twenty states, Puerto Rico, and the military courts now use evidence codes that are based largely on the Federal Rules of Evidence. Although some states have changed specific rules, most have chosen to make few departures from the federal model. Other states have drafting committees at work. In the near future a majority of states, perhaps a substantial majority, may be operating under rules that closely resemble those used in federal courts.

25. Saltzburg & Redden, supra note 1, at 3-5.

Appendix II

EVIDENCE OUTLINE

———

We offer the following outline as a quick review of many of the principles discussed in the course. To conserve space, we use shorthand expressions that may easily be misunderstood or misused by those lacking a full understanding of the course material. Thus, the outline is a convenient tool for reviewing or refreshing recollection; it is not a substitute for the text. For your convenience, we cite the federal rules relevant to the various portions of the outline and the chapters in which the subjects mentioned in the outline are discussed.

I. **Different Kinds of Evidence.** [Chapters One, Three and Eleven]

A. *Testimonial Evidence v. Real Evidence (or Demonstrative Evidence).*

1. Testimonial—A witness provides assertive answers in the courtroom to questions put by counsel. The trier of fact is dependent on the witness for an interpretation of sensory data.

2. Real and Demonstrative—An exhibit, report, book, experiment or some other evidence from which the trier can glean its own sensory data is offered, often in connection with testimonial evidence. Real evidence is directly involved in the events giving rise to the litigation. Demonstrative evidence is prepared for use in litigation.

B. *Direct Evidence v. Circumstantial Evidence.*

1. Direct—If the witness is believed or if the real evidence is regarded as authentic, the proposition that the evidence is offered to prove is established.

2. Circumstantial—Testimonial or real evidence that indirectly—i.e., through inference—aids the trier in resolving a disputed issue.

3. Probative Value—Direct evidence is not necessarily more probative than circumstantial evidence bearing on the same issue.

C. *Material Evidence v. Immaterial Evidence*

1. Material evidence—Real or testimonial evidence that bears on an issue contested by the parties.

2. Immaterial—Evidence that does not bear on an issue that is in dispute.

3. General Rule—Only material evidence is admitted. (FRE 401)

D. *Relevant Evidence v. Irrelevant Evidence.*

1. Relevant—Evidence having any tendency to make the existence of any material fact more probable or less probable. (FRE 401)

2. Irrelevant—Evidence that has no tendency to help the trier determine any fact in dispute. (FRE 401)

3. General Rule—Only relevant evidence is admitted. (FRE 402) But the trial judge may exclude relevant evidence if its probative value is outweighed by its prejudicial effect, including its potential for confusion,

or if the time and costs involved in presenting the evidence are not warranted by the assistance it offers the trier of fact.   (FRE 403)

4.   Federal Rule—FRE 401 combines materiality and relevance but abandons the term "materiality."

II.   The Basic Conditions for Offering and Excluding Evidence.   [Chapters One, Three, Ten, Eleven, and Thirteen]

A.   *Offering Evidence.*

1.   Testimonial Evidence.

a.   The lay witness (i.e., non-expert) must speak from personal knowledge.   (FRE 602)

b.   All witnesses must swear or affirm that testimony will be truthful. (FRE 603)

c.   In a common law jurisdiction the witness must be competent.   (But see FRE 601: "Every person [but a judge or juror, see FRE 605–606] is competent   *   *   *   "   except where state law governs the decision of all or part of a case).

d.   A lay witness in a common law jurisdiction must relate facts, not opinions, in most instances.   FRE 701 permits a witness to give helpful opinions.   An expert may give an opinion and may sometimes base the opinion on information supplied by others.   In a common law jurisdiction, this latter opinion is usually elicited through a hypothetical question.   FRE 703 expands the use of such opinions.   A common law jurisdiction may bar opinions on ultimate issues, but not FRE 704.

e.   Any expert witness must be qualified by knowledge, skill, experience, training, or education.

2.   Real Evidence.

a.   Procedure for Admitting Evidence.

i.   Evidence must be marked for identification by the clerk.

ii.   Evidence must be authenticated (FRE 901) or be self-authenticating (FRE 902) so that the court knows it is what it is supposed to be.

iii.   Opposing counsel must have a chance to examine the evidence.

b.   Special Foundations for Some Evidence.

i.   Especially in criminal cases, a chain of custody must be laid if the item is not somehow unique and is subject to tampering.

ii.   Tape recordings and other evidence that is easily "manufactured" may be subject to special requirements.

iii.   Scientific evidence may have to be accepted as reliable by experts in the relevant fields (*Frye* test).

iv.   Experiments often must be made under conditions similar to those that characterized the event giving rise to the litigation.

v.   The best evidence rule, which might more properly be named the better evidence rule since it provides that secondary evidence of the contents of a writing or recording (FRE 1001(1)) is inadmissible in the absence of an explanation for failure to introduce the original, may restrict the choice of real evidence. (FRE 1001–1008)

- *a.* Collateral writings are not included.
- *b.* Certified copies of public or recorded writings are usually admissible.
- *c.* If an original is lost, destroyed without bad intention, or if it is not reasonably available, secondary evidence is admissible.   (FRE 1004)
- *d.* If the original is in control of the opponent and if notice is given to produce it, the opponent must either produce it or accept secondary evidence.   (FRE 1004)
- *e.* The English rule is that there are no degrees of secondary evidence, but common law American jurisdictions tended to favor copies over oral testimony.   FRE 1004 does not recognize degrees of secondary evidence.
- *f.* FRE 1003 provides that a duplicate is admissible unless there is some question as to authenticity or as to the fairness of accepting a duplicate.

3. Offers of Proof—If the trial judge sustains an objection, the offering counsel must make the substance of the excluded evidence part of the record to preserve a claim of error.

B. *Objecting to Evidence.*

1. General Rules.

- a. An objection is required to exclude evidence and to preserve a point for appeal.   (FRE 103)
- b. An objection must be made immediately after a question is asked or tangible evidence is offered.   (FRE 103)
- c. A motion to strike will be entertained if an objection was not possible or available when the question was asked or the evidence was first offered.
- d. An objection should state specific reasons for exclusion.   A general objection that is overruled will receive little appellate consideration. If a general objection is sustained, counsel offering the evidence should seek to ascertain the specific reason or face a similarly unsympathetic appellate court.
- e. An *available* objection need *not* be made.

2. Specific Objections.

- a. One or more of the basic evidence rules is violated—e.g., the hearsay rule, the privilege rules, the character evidence rules, the limitations on impeachment, the relevance rules.
- b. One or more of the conditions of admissibility is not satisfied.
- c. A question is misleading (e.g., when did you stop beating your spouse?).

    d.   Two questions are phrased as if they were one; a compound question is improper (e.g., did you live on Oak Drive and sell narcotics there?).

    e.   Facts not in evidence are assumed (e.g., when did you stop beating your spouse?). Note the overlap between the more general objection "misleading" and this more specific objection.

    f.   A question has previously been asked and answered.

C. *Functions of Judge and Jury.*

  1. Preliminary Questions of Competency—Such questions involve evidence that would be deemed relevant, but that might be excluded despite its probative value. (FRE 104)

    a.   Examples of factual questions:

       i.   Whether a witness is qualified as an expert.

      ii.   Whether a statement in a homicide case made by the deceased was made with a sense of impending death.

     iii.   Whether an admission of liability was made during compromise negotiations.

     iv.   Whether a statement made by a client to a lawyer was made in confidence.

      v.   Whether a party destroyed the original of a writing in bad faith.

    b.   The judge decides factual questions surrounding evidence rules.

    c.   Usually a preponderance of the evidence standard is used. (Lego v. Twomey)

  2. Conditional Relevancy—Fact A is only relevant if Fact B is also proved.

    a.   Evidence of both facts must be presented—i.e., they must be connected up.

    b.   The judge determines whether there is enough evidence for a reasonable jury to find both facts. If there is, evidence of both goes to the jury. If not, the jury is instructed to disregard evidence of both.

    c.   The jury decides whether both facts have been proved.

    d.   Example: A spoken statement is relied upon to prove notice to X. Jury must find both Fact (A) that statement was made and Fact (B) that it was heard to have relevant evidence.

  3. When a question of fact relating to a competency rule is identical with an ultimate issue, judges will sometimes leave the issue for the jury.

    a.   FRE 1008 specifically provides that certain issues will be decided by the jury.

    b.   In ruling on the admissibility of conspirators' statements under FRE 801(d)(2)(E), judges now tend to make their own independent decision whether a conspiracy has been proved.

III. **The Course of the Trial.**   (Chapters One and Five)

A. *Opening Argument.*

1. The party with the burden of proof will have an initial opportunity to outline the case, not to argue the merits.

2. The other party may open before any evidence is presented or, in some courts, may reserve the right to open until after the other side ends its case.

B. *Order of Presentation.*

1. Generally the party with the burden of proof will proceed first, calling witnesses and presenting real evidence, until that party rests.

2. Next the opposing party will have an opportunity to call witnesses and to offer real evidence until resting.

3. Both parties will have a chance to present additional rebuttal evidence, limited in theory to meeting the adversary's presentation.

C. *Direct Examination.*

1. Witnesses, except those who are adverse or hostile, must be examined by direct examination.

2. Leading questions are generally barred.   (FRE 611(c))

3. In a common law jurisdiction, the direct examiner may not impeach a non-hostile witness.

   a.   But see Chambers v. Mississippi.   (Chapter Seven)

   b.   The vouching rule has been rejected in many jurisdictions.

4. Under FRE 607, any party may impeach any witness.

   a.   This rule does not generally permit leading questions, but they may be permitted under FRE 611.

   b.   Courts place more limits on the use of prior inconsistent statements to impeach than on other forms of impeachment.

D. *Cross-Examination.*

1. Cross-examination is part of the right to confront accusers protected by the sixth and fourteenth amendments in criminal cases.   It is generally regarded as an equally important right in civil trials.

2. Leading questions may be asked.

3. The cross-examiner may impeach a witness.

4. Most American jurisdictions limit cross-examination to the scope of the direct.   (FRE 611(b))   The English rule and the minority American rule allow for a "wide-open" cross-examination that elicits all relevant evidence.   When the cross-examination goes beyond the scope of the direct, leading questions should not be permitted.

E. *Other Examinations.*

1. Re-direct and re-cross examination will generally be permitted, limited in theory to clarifying evidence elicited by the immediately preceding examination.

2.   The court may call witnesses and interrogate any witnesses regardless of who called them.   (FRE 614)

F. *Closing Argument.*

1.   The party with the burden of proof speaks first at the close of the evidence and in most courts again after the other party has argued.

2.   A closing argument addresses the merits of the case and argues for the drawing of inferences from the facts presented.

G. *Instructions.*

1.   The judge instructs the jury on the law.

2.   Attorneys generally have the opportunity to submit proposed instructions.

IV.   Otherwise Relevant Evidence Excluded for Policy Reasons.   (Chapter Four)

A. *Character Evidence* is often excluded because of its low probative value or its tendency to be unduly prejudicial.

1.   Character evidence can be offered for several reasons.

a.   Character may be in issue—e.g., libel case.

b.   Character evidence may be circumstantial evidence of specific acts.

c.   Character evidence may be used to impeach or bolster credibility. This is discussed in the next section of the outline dealing with impeachment.

2.   Restrictions on Character Evidence.

a.   Civil Cases.

i.   If a character trait is an issue in the case, it must be proved and so character evidence is allowed.

ii.   Character evidence is generally excluded as circumstantial evidence of how someone acted on a particular occasion.   (FRE 404(a))

iii.   Where a civil case involves assault and a dispute as to who was the aggressor, character evidence may be allowed.   Some jurisdictions allow such evidence in other civil cases where the defendant's alleged conduct is a crime as well as a tort.

b.   Criminal Cases.

i.   The prosecution cannot initiate an inquiry into the defendant's character if its only purpose is to show a propensity toward crime.

ii.   A defendant may introduce evidence of his character traits that are relevant to the crime charged.   (FRE 404(a)(1))

iii.   The prosecution may rebut the defendant's evidence.

iv.   Usually, only the defendant can initiate an inquiry into the victim's character, but in some places self-defense claims are considered to put the character of the victim in issue.   (FRE

404(a)(2)) Victims of rape and other sex offenses may receive special protection. (FRE 412)

3. Mode of Presentation.

    a. Common law jurisdictions generally require that character, when it is not in issue, be proved by reputation evidence. Reputation in the community where the person lives is preferred, but reputation in the community where the person works, goes to school, etc. may be satisfactory in many jurisdictions today.

    b. FRE 405(a) permits opinion evidence as well as reputation evidence.

    c. Where character is in issue, the range of inquiry is broader. Specific acts may be inquired into (FRE 405(b)), and such inquiry may be required in many jurisdictions.

B. *Other Crimes*—Evidence is generally excluded if offered to show a propensity to commit crimes. (FRE 404(b))

1. It may be admissible to show modus operandi, intent, etc.

2. A careful balance between probative value and prejudicial effect must be struck.

C. *Evidence of Custom and Habit*—Such evidence is more likely to be admitted than general character evidence. (FRE 406)

1. Habit is narrower than character; it may be only one component of a broader character trait. It may be used to show conduct in many jurisdictions that reject character evidence.

    a. E.g.,—that a driver is careful may be inadmissible character evidence; that a driver stops at a specific stop sign may be admissible as habit.

    b. Some states exclude habit evidence totally; others reject it when there are eyewitnesses.

2. Evidence of a business custom is even more likely to be admitted than habit evidence to prove that an act was or was not accomplished on a particular occasion.

D. *Offers to Compromise*—Such offers are generally not admissible to prove the strength or weakness of a case.

1. Civil Cases.

    a. Offers to settle a claim disputed as to validity or amount are generally not admitted to show a weak case; nor is refusal to settle or refusal to accept an offer admissible to show a strong case. (FRE 408)

    b. In common law jurisdictions factual admissions unnecessary to a settlement offer may be used as evidence; FRE 408 bars the use of conduct or statements made in settlement negotiations.

2. Criminal Cases.

    a. Offers to plead guilty or to accept a guilty plea are generally not admissible. (FRE 410)

     b.   Withdrawn pleas or statements made in connection with pleas later withdrawn are generally not admissible.

     c.   Voluntary, but unnecessary, admissions in the course of offering to plead may be admissible in a common law jurisdiction, but not under FRE 410.

E.   *Offers to Pay or Payment of Medical Expenses*—This evidence is usually inadmissible.   (FRE 409)

    1.   Conduct or statements made in connection with these offers or payments are admissible.

    2.   There is no requirement that the offer or payment relate to a claim disputed as to validity or amount.

F.   *Subsequent Repairs*—Evidence of subsequent remedial measures is usually excluded if offered to show negligence or absence thereof.   (FRE 407)

    1.   Such evidence is not excluded if offered to show something other than culpable conduct or freedom therefrom; e.g., if offered to prove control over an object or to show feasibility of better precautions.

    2.   Such evidence is admissible in some jurisdictions in products liability cases to show culpable conduct.

G.   *Insurance*—Evidence of insurance is generally excluded if offered to prove negligence or lack of negligence.   (FRE 411)

    1.   Evidence of insurance may be discovered, however.

    2.   It may be admitted for other purposes; e.g., to prove bias or to prove ownership.

H.   *Similar Circumstance Evidence*—Some Courts invoke the doctrine of *res inter alios acta* to exclude evidence of events similar to, but not directly related to, events giving rise to litigation.

    1.   No absolute rule is really involved.

    2.   A general probative value versus prejudicial effect balance should provide satisfactory answers in most instances.

V.   Grounds for Impeachment.   (Chapter Five)

A.   *Bias or Interest in Outcome.*

    1.   A foundation must be laid in a majority of states; but there is a substantial minority.   The Federal Rules are silent on the point.   (But cf., FRE 613—witness must be given an opportunity to explain or deny an inconsistent statement).

    2.   A criminal defendant, under the sixth and fourteenth amendments, has a constitutional right to show substantial biases of prosecution witnesses. (Davis v. Alaska)

B.   *Character for Honesty or Veracity*—Generally witnesses can be impeached by showing their reputation for dishonesty.

    1.   Common law jurisdictions require reputation evidence; FRE 608 permits opinion evidence or reputation evidence.

    2.   Rehabilitative character evidence is only admissible after an attack on character has been made.

C. *Specific Instances of Conduct.*

    1. Criminal convictions.

        a. Many American jurisdictions allow impeachment by any felony or crime evincing dishonesty and provide a right to impeach any witness, including a criminal defendant.

        b. FRE 609 provides for a right of impeachment by showing a conviction for dishonesty or false statement, but opts for a balancing approach in the case of other convictions with special concern for the plight of the criminal defendant.

    2. Other bad acts.

        a. English rule—permits cross-examination on any bad act that discredits. This was the rule in most American jurisdictions, but was not the predominant federal rule prior to the adoption of FRE 608.

        b. FRE 608 adopts the English rule but emphasizes that the evidence must be probative of truthfulness or untruthfulness.

        c. With this form of impeachment, no extrinsic evidence of bad acts is allowed; the examiner may ask about the acts, but is bound by the witness' answer.

D. *Prior Inconsistent Statements.*

    1. In common law jurisdictions, a foundation must be laid before an inconsistent statement is introduced. FRE 613(b) abandons the requirement of a prior foundation but provides that at some point the witness should have an opportunity to explain the inconsistency.

    2. At common law (The Queen's Case) the witness had to be shown a written statement before being asked about it. FRE 613(a) abandons the rule but provides that opposing counsel may see or be told the statement upon request.

E. *Other Forms of Impeachment.*

    1. Mental or physical defects or incapacities may be shown.

    2. Defects in knowledge may be explored.

        a. E.g., *Michelson* type cross-examination of character witnesses regarding specific acts of person whose character is tested (FRE 404(a)(3) and 608(b)(2)).

        b. E.g., an expert opinion may be probed, the factual bases explored, and the gaps in knowledge highlighted. (FRE 703)

        c. Leading questions may be useful. See Section III, c.4.a., supra.

F. *Collateral Matters.*

    1. The generally stated common law rule is that there can be no impeachment on a collateral matter, which usually means that the impeaching evidence is not relevant in the case for any purpose other than impeachment. No similar rule is contained in the Federal Rules.

    2. In lieu of any bright line rule, federal courts use the same probative value versus prejudicial effect balancing approach to so-called collateral matters that they use for all relevance questions. (FRE 403)

G. *Rehabilitation.*

   1. Generally a witness cannot be rehabilitated until attacked, and the rehabilitation must meet as closely as possible the focus of the attack.

   2. Some examples:

      a. A prior consistent statement can come in to rebut a charge of recent fabrication; in some jurisdictions it can come in after any inconsistent statement.

      b. Bias may be rebutted by showing lack of bias.

      c. Evidence of good character may rebut evidence of bad character.

      d. Usually where a prior inconsistent statement is introduced, evidence of good character for truth and veracity can be used.

VI. The Basic Hearsay Rule—An out-of-court statement introduced for the truth of the matter stated is hearsay and excluded unless it comes within an exception. (FRE 802) (Remember that under the federal rules some out-of-court statements of witnesses present at trial and available for cross-examination may not be hearsay). (FRE 801) (Chapter Six)

A. *Reasons for Excluding*—Cross-examination of the declarant is impossible and the following problems cannot be explored:

   1. Sincerity.

   2. Ambiguity or narration.

   3. Perception.

   4. Memory.

B. *Non-assertive Conduct*—At common law, hearsay includes non-assertive conduct. The federal rules exclude non-assertive conduct from their definition of hearsay.

   1. E.g., ship captain sails to sea with family. At common law his conduct is not admissible to show the seaworthiness of the ship.

   2. E.g., evidence that a person was placed in a hospital's burn ward is hearsay at common law if offered to show that the person was burned.

C. *Non-hearsay*—If introduced for a purpose other than to prove the truth of the matter asserted, a statement may come in because for this purpose it is not hearsay.

   1. E.g., notice of defective condition in tort case.

   2. E.g., verbal act (oral contract, for instance).

D. *Prior Statements of Witness Available for Cross-Examination*—These are deemed non-hearsay in three circumstances. (FRE 801(d)(1))

   1. An inconsistent statement was made under oath, subject to penalty of perjury in some proceeding (including grand jury).

   2. A consistent statement is offered to rebut a charge of recent fabrication.

   3. A prior identification is offered.

VII. Exceptions to Hearsay Rule. (Chapter Six)

A. *Availability of Declarant Immaterial*—Proponents of hearsay evidence falling within these exceptions need not show that the declarant is unavailable at trial. (FRE 801, 803)

1. Admissions (FRE 801 classifies admissions as non-hearsay)—Assertions or non-assertive conduct by a party that are hearsay if offered against the party at trial. The theory is that the party can explain, not necessarily that there is any guarantee of trustworthiness in the statements.

   a. Basic admissions are statements by an actual party. Lack of personal knowledge is not a disqualification. In most places, the opinion rule will not operate to bar an admission. (FRE 801(d)(2)(A))

      i. E.g., a pleading or affidavit signed by a party.

      ii. E.g., flight from scene of crime (if considered to be hearsay).

      iii. Other rules may come into play such as FRE 410, covering withdrawn pleas in criminal cases, FRE 407, covering subsequent remedial measures and FRE 408 covering settlement negotiations in civil cases.

   b. Statements adopted by a party become that party's admissions, including adoptions by silent acquiescence. (FRE 801 (d)(2)(B))

   c. Authorized admissions are as useful as personal admissions by the party. (FRE 801(d)(2)(c))

   d. Agent's admissions are admissible against the principal at common law only if the agent is authorized to speak. FRE 801 (d)(2)(D) expands the admissibility of such statements, using a scope of employment test.

   e. One coconspirator's statements made during and in furtherance of a conspiracy are admissible against all conspirators. (FRE 801(d)(2)(E))

   f. One partner's statements made on behalf of the partnership are admitted against other partners. (FRE 801(d)(2)(C))

   g. At common law statements by a predecessor in interest can be binding on a successor to a property interest. The Federal Rules have no such exception.

2. Present Sense Impression—Spontaneity is the key to reliability.

   a. The statement must describe or explain an event or condition.

   b. It must be made while perceiving it or immediately thereafter.

3. Excited Utterance—Absence of time to fabricate and honesty prompted by excitement justifies the exception. (FRE 803(a)2)

   a. The statement must be made under the stress of excitement.

   b. The statement need only relate to the event or condition producing the excitement.

4. Mental, Emotional or Physical Condition. (FRE 803(3), (4))

   a. Statements of existing physical or mental conditions are admissible on the theory that they are related to present sense impressions and are spontaneous.

      i. The statements can be made to anyone.

      ii. When made to a doctor, some common law courts require that the doctor be treating as well as diagnosing.

iii. FRE 803(4) expands the common law exception by permitting medical history (i.e., statements of past, as well as present, condition) to qualify if made to a physician who is either treating or diagnosing.

iv. In will cases, many common law courts allow statements regarding past mental or emotional conditions made to anyone.

b. Statements of design or plan to do something (*Hillmon*) are admissible as states of mind on the theory that cross-examination at the time of the statement would not be especially useful (no memory or perception problems since act has not yet occurred). Backward looking statements are not admissible as states of mind unless they relate in certain ways to the declarant's will. (Shephard v. United States). (Rule 803(3)) Most courts allow one declarant's stated intention to do something with another to be used against the other in some circumstances (*Alcalde*); FRE 803(3) does not explicitly state whether it adopts the majority view or the opposing view favored by the House Committee on the Judiciary.

5. Recorded Recollection—The rationale is that the witness who made the declaration is present for some cross-examination and that a statement close in time to an event is likely to be reliable. (FRE 803(5))

a. A witness' current memory must be impaired. At common law it may have to be completely gone; the federal rule offers more flexibility.

b. A witness must be able to swear that the statement was accurate when made and that it was made while the event described was fresh in mind.

c. The witness need not be the person who recorded the statement, but the recorder will have to be present if the declarant did not review the transcription and adopt it.

6. Business Records—If the business can rely on them while competing in the marketplace, a court, it is argued, is justified in doing so. (FRE 803(6))

a. Records must be kept in the ordinary course of the business.

b. The entrant must have a business duty. (Johnson v. Lutz)

c. Self-serving entries may be excluded. (Palmer v. Hoffman)

d. The absence of entries, if hearsay, may be shown. (FRE 803(7))

e. Computers present special problems, especially because of the ordinary course of business requirement.

f. Opinions are allowed as part of records, but courts will reject some speculation.

7. Public Records and Reports—If a public agency prepares a record or report, there is a presumption of regularity that warrants admission. (FRE 803(8))

a. FRE 803(8) covers records and reports of public agencies, matters observed and recorded by public officers, and factual findings arising from investigations by public agencies. At common law only agency records and data were likely to be admitted.

b. Public records and reports under FRE 803(8)(A) are most likely to be admitted in any case.

c. Matters observed by law enforcement officers are excluded in criminal cases by FRE 803(8)(B), although some courts will admit reports containing such matters when offered by a defendant.

d. Factual findings may be used against the government in a criminal case but not against a criminal defendant. (FRE 803(8)(C)).

e. Public records need not be made in the routine course of business; they may be compiled for a special purpose.

f. No custodian need be called to authenticate public records, although the records will have to be authenticated.

g. Evaluative reports may be considered to be the same as factual findings by many courts.

h. When the information upon which evaluations or findings rest is unreliable, courts are likely to exclude the evaluations or findings.

i. A public record may be excluded because the circumstances in which it was prepared suggest a lack of trustworthiness.

8. Learned Treatises—These may be used in connection with expert testimony under FRE 803(18). At common law the treatises were usually regarded as inadmissible hearsay.

a. The proponent of the treatise must show that it is reliable.

b. An expert can read from the treatise on direct examination as long as he has relied on the treatise.

c. The cross-examiner may read to the expert from the treatise, once he has called the expert's attention to it.

9. Other Exceptions.

a. Records of vital statistics. (FRE 803(9))

b. Absence of public record or entry. (FRE 803(10))

c. Records of religious organizations. (FRE 803(11))

d. Marriage, baptismal, and similar certificates. (FRE 803(12))

e. Family records. (FRE 803(13))

f. Records of documents affecting an interest in property. (FRE 803(14))

g. Statements in documents affecting an interest in property. (FRE 803(15))

h. Statements in ancient documents. (FRE 803(16))

i. Market reports, commercial publications. (FRE 803(17))

j. Reputation concerning personal or family history. (FRE 803(19))

k. Reputation concerning boundaries or general history. (FRE 803(20))

l. Reputation as to character. (FRE 803(21))

    m.   Judgment of previous conviction. (FRE 803(22))

    n.   Judgment as to personal, family, or general history, or boundaries. (FRE 803(23))

B. *Unavailability of Declarant Required*—The proponent of these exceptions must show that the hearsay declarant is unavailable to testify. (FRE 804)

1. Former Testimony—It has already been offered in a forum where there has been an opportunity to test it. (FRE 804(b)(1)).

    a.   There must be a substantial identity of issues, and the party against whom the statement is offered must have had an opportunity to examine the witness. Under the federal rule, it is sufficient if a predecessor in interest had an opportunity to test the statement.

    b.   The prior opportunity to examine may have been on direct, rather than on cross-examination.

2. Dying Declaration—The justification is predominantly a religious or moral one; one will not meet his maker with a lie on his lips.

    a.   Common law courts limited the exception to homicide cases; FRE 804(b)(2) allows it in civil cases also.

    b.   The statement must be made under a sense of impending death and generally the declarant must die (not under the federal rule).

3. Declaration against Interest—The rationale is that people don't make statements that are damaging to themselves unless they are true.

    a.   Common law courts limited the exception to statements against pecuniary or proprietary interests. FRE 804(b)(3) recognizes statements against penal interest, but requires corroboration if used to exculpate a defendant in a criminal case. Some courts have read a corroboration requirement into the federal rule when the government offers declarations against penal interest against someone other than the declarant.

    b.   Some courts recognize statements that are against "social interest," i.e., the kind that might subject the declarant to ridicule.

4. Personal or Family History—The reliability comes from the knowledge possessed by the sources close to the person or family.

    a.   Statements by a declarant or blood relative concerning the declarant's family history were admissible at common law if made before a dispute arose.

    b.   FRE 804(b)(4) expands the common law by allowing close friends of families to qualify and by allowing statements made after a dispute arose to be admitted.

C. *Residual Exceptions*—FRE 803(24) and 804(b)(5) permit hearsay to be admitted that does not qualify under specific exceptions.

1. Notice must be given before this hearsay is used.
2. The hearsay must be reliable.
3. The evidence will be excluded if better evidence is available.

VIII. Privileges. (Chapters Two and Eight)

A. *General Rules.* (PFRE 501)

   1. The holder, as defined by statute or common law, can claim a privilege, as can someone authorized to do so by the holder.

   2. There is a waiver by a failure to claim the privilege.

   3. One joint holder does not waive for another.

   4. If holder discloses to third party, the privilege is waived unless communication to third party is also privileged or it is reasonably necessary to effectuate the purposes of the privilege.

   5. Eavesdroppers could usually testify at common law, but a trend away from this has developed.

   6. In most jurisdictions, comment on the exercise of a privilege is not permitted.

B. *Lawyer-Client Privilege.* (PFRE 503)

   1. Holder—Client.

   2. Requirements:

       a. Professional relationship.

       b. Client belief that person to whom statement is made is a lawyer.

       c. Confidential communication for the purpose of obtaining legal advice.

   3. The privilege includes written documents prepared during litigation and communicated to a lawyer by a client. But, documents prepared by the lawyer are generally protected only by the work product doctrine (Hickman v. Taylor, Fed.R.Civ.P. 26(b)(3)), not this privilege. Work product doctrine does not require strict confidentiality.

   4. The privilege applies to those who assist the lawyer.

   5. In some situations, the privilege does not apply:

       a. Advice sought in furtherance of crime or fraud.

       b. Issue between parties all claiming through same client—e.g., will contest.

       c. Malpractice suit or suit for fees.

       d. Lawyer is attesting witness.

       e. Litigation between joint holders.

   6. The privilege applies in all jurisdictions.

   7. Corporations can claim privilege to some extent. The federal privilege is not confined to members of a "control group." (Upjohn Co. v. United States)

C. *Physician-Patient Privilege.*

   1. Holder—Patient.

   2. Requirements.

       a. Consultation for treatment (or diagnosis in minority jurisdictions).

    b. Communication to one believed to be a physician in course of a professional relationship.

  3. Examples of extensive exceptions:

    a. If patient tenders condition in suit—e.g., plaintiff in negligence case.

    b. Criminal proceedings.

    c. Tort action for conduct of patient that amounts to crime.

    d. Advice sought in furtherance of crime or tort.

    e. Malpractice suits.

    f. When two parties claim through same deceased patient.

    g. Commitment proceedings.

    h. Proceedings to establish patient's competence.

    i. Requirements of public records.

    j. Disciplinary proceedings against doctor.

  4. Recognized in most, but not all, states.

D. *Privilege Not to Testify Against Spouse*—This is not the confidential marital communications privilege (see Subsection *E* infra). (PFRE 505)

  1. In some jurisdictions, both the spouse who is called to testify in a criminal case and the spouse against whom the testimony is directed have a privilege. Most states that have the privilege have not given it to the testifying spouse—only to the accused in a criminal case. The federal courts now give the privilege only to the testifying spouse. (Trammel v. United States)

  2. Requirements.

    a. Valid marriage.

    b. Marriage in effect when privilege is asserted.

  3. Waiver—Any testimony by spouse is a waiver of the privilege in that proceeding.

  4. Typical exceptions:

    a. Proceedings between spouses.

    b. Commitment proceedings against spouse.

    c. Crimes against the spouse or child.

    d. Bigamy or adultery (some jurisdictions).

E. *Confidential Marital Communications Privilege.*

  1. Held by communicating spouse, or both spouses.

  2. Requirements.

    a. Communications made during marriage.

    b. Some jurisdictions take a broad view of what one spouse communicates to other.

    c. Marriage must have been valid, but need not be in effect when privilege is invoked.

3. Typical exceptions—Same as D.4., supra, and communications made in furtherance of crime or fraud, or a criminal case where defendant wants the testimony.

F. *Psychotherapist—Patient Privilege.* (PFRE 504)

1. Holder—Patient.

2. Same requirements as doctor—Patient above.

3. Fewer exceptions—Privilege applies in all proceedings except when defendant tenders the mental condition in criminal case or commitment proceedings when patient is dangerous.

4. This privilege is becoming more widely adopted.

G. *Clergyman—Penitent.* (PFRE 506)

1. Holder—Penitent generally.

2. Requirements.

   a. Confidential communication.

   b. Made by penitent to spiritual adviser.

   c. Some jurisdictions limit the privilege to a confession mandated by a religion.

H. *Government Privilege and Identity of Informer.* (PFRE 509 and PFRE 510)

1. A governmental body has a privilege to prevent disclosure of confidential and official information that might endanger national security or private citizens who cooperate with their government.

2. An informer's identity can be secreted if not necessary to defense of a case on the merits.

3. Both of these privileges can be made absolute by statute.

4. If privileged information is material to a criminal case, the prosecution may have to be dropped. In civil cases there are a variety of options available when a privilege claim is sustained.

I. *News Reporter's Privilege.*

1. None under Constitution (Branzburg v. Hayes). Many lower courts have provided protection even after *Branzburg*.

2. Many states provide a privilege.

3. Pending legislation in Congress has been dormant for years.

4. Holder—Source, but the privilege is generally exercised by the reporter to protect the source's identity.

J. *Privilege Against Self-Incrimination*—5th Amendment to United States Constitution made binding on states through 14th Amendment and Malloy v. Hogan.

1. A natural person has privilege not to be compelled to be witness against himself in criminal proceeding.

   a. Anytime that legal process is used to compel a person to speak— criminal or civil trial, grand jury proceeding, etc.—he can protect himself against potential incrimination.

   b.   The privilege is applicable in all stages of an actual criminal pro-
        ceeding.

2.   To be a witness against himself, a person must be called upon to give
     "testimonial" evidence.

   a.   Lineups (*Wade, Gilbert, Kirby*), are not testimonial statements;
        nor is a blood sample (*Schmerber*).

   b.   Lie detectors may present problems.

   c.   Implicit authentication of documents may be tantamount to testi-
        monial incrimination, and a person may have a right to refuse to
        produce subpoenaed records (*Fisher*).

3.   Waiver by the accused in a criminal case.

   a.   There is a waiver by taking the stand—At least to the point that
        there may be cross-examination of the testimony on direct exami-
        nation.   With regard to preliminary matters, usually there is no
        waiver by testifying (e.g., motion to suppress evidence).

   b.   Taking the stand at preliminary hearing is not a waiver at trial.

   c.   Taking the stand at a first trial is not a waiver at a second trial.

   d.   Disagreement exists whether "voluntary" testimony before a grand
        jury is a waiver at trial also.   (Jenkins v. Anderson)

4.   "Tendency to incriminate"—This is enough to warrant invocation of
     privilege—a link in a chain of evidence that could eventually lead to
     prosecution.

   a.   Malloy v. Hogan gives virtual carte blanche to defendants to invoke
        the privilege, because the judge must determine propriety of priv-
        ilege without destroying it.

   b.   Privilege applies even where potential prosecution is under another
        sovereignty.   (Murphy v. Waterfront Comm'n.)

   c.   If prosecution is impossible, as where immunity is given, the pro-
        tection of the privilege ceases.

   d.   Use immunity is all that is constitutionally required.   (Kastigar v.
        United States)

IX.   **Shortcuts to Proof.**   (Chapter Nine)

A.   *Judicial Notice.*

1.   Judicial Notice of Adjudicative Facts.   (FRE 201)

   a.   A court may notice facts that are generally known in its jurisdiction
        or that are easily determinable from reliable sources.

   b.   Notice may be taken sua sponte or at the request of a party, and
        at any stage of a case.

   c.   All parties should have a chance to be heard on the propriety of
        the notice.

   d.   In civil cases some courts instruct the jury that judicial notice is
        conclusive, while others permit contradictory evidence to be intro-
        duced.   In criminal cases whether a judge can instruct a jury, over

a defendant's objection, that it must treat a noticed fact as true is unclear.

2. Judicial Notice of Legislative Facts.

    a. Virtually everyone agrees that courts must look beyond admitted evidence if the law is to grow and if courts are to develop sensible principles to guide citizens as to the range of permissible and impermissible, or protected and unprotected, conduct. Disagreement centers on which legislative facts should be consulted in particular cases.

    b. Few rules now govern the use of legislative facts, although there is a substantial argument that the parties should have a chance to address themselves to outside sources deemed important by courts.

3. Judicial Notice of Law.

    a. Domestic law of a state is noticed by state courts, as is federal law.

    b. Federal courts take notice of federal law and most state law.

    c. In some states, municipal laws, laws of sister states, and laws of foreign countries must be pleaded and proved.

B. *Rebuttable Presumptions.*

1. Civil Cases.

    a. Bursting Bubble Theory—After proof of one fact, if the fact to be presumed is rebutted, the presumption disappears and what remains, if anything, is any inference that the trier of fact may draw from proof of the basic fact (Thayer view). (FRE 301)

    b. Shifting the Burden of Proof—McCormick argues that a presumption should shift the burden of proof to the party against whom the presumption operates. Morgan advocated this also.

2. Criminal Cases.

    a. General Rule—Rebuttable presumptions, whether created by the legislature or the courts, may be employed in criminal cases as well as civil cases. Leary v. United States; Barnes v. United States.

    b. If the presumption is explained as announcing that the jury may, if it wishes, draw an inference from one fact about another fact, the presumption will be upheld if there is a rational basis for drawing the inference. (County Court v. Allen)

    c. Limitation—If a presumption suggests that the jury must or should draw an inference form one fact about another fact, courts insist that it can be said with substantial assurance that the presumed fact is more likely than not to flow from the proved fact on which it is made to depend. The Supreme Court has left open the question whether a strong presumption must satisfy an even more demanding standard.

Appendix III

PROBLEM ON THE FEDERAL RULES OF EVIDENCE

In 1976 one of the authors prepared a problem on the Federal Rules of Evidence for use by the Federal Judicial Center in training judges and magistrates faced with the new evidence code. With the permission of the Center, we reproduce the problem below. It affords users of the book an opportunity to review almost all aspects of evidence law discussed in the book.

A CRIMINAL ANTITRUST CASE

In 1976, George and Martha Washington contracted to buy a home in Mount Vernon, Virginia. The financing agency required them to secure title insurance. This required a title examination, and only a member of the Virginia State Bar could legally perform that service. George and Martha therefore contacted a lawyer (Dolley Madison) who quoted them a fee of one percent of the value of the property involved. The Washingtons then tried to find a lawyer who would examine the title for less. All the law firms and sole practitioners they contacted quoted the same fee.

A lawyer friend in another area of the state advised the Washingtons that the absence of competition suggested price-fixing or price-setting, conduct that would violate Section 1 of the Sherman Act, 15 U.S.C. Sec. 1, which was applied to bar associations and lawyers' organizations in the landmark decision of the United States Supreme Court in Goldfarb v. Virginia State Bar, 421 U.S. 773, 95 S.Ct. 2004, 44 L.Ed.2d 572 (1975). The Washingtons contacted the United States Department of Justice, which sent an investigative team into the area. Subsequently, the Department obtained a criminal indictment against the Mount Vernon Bar Association and all of

the lawyers and firms contacted by the Washingtons who quoted the one percent fee.

Set forth below are certain events that happen at trial. Our problem is to decide what the proper ruling is in each of the situations described.

THE GOVERNMENT'S CASE

1. The United States seeks to offer a minimum fee schedule report published by the State Bar, which report clearly recommended the adoption of a fee schedule by local bar associations but did not require adoption. The report was published in 1962. The government also wishes to offer a second report published in 1969 containing a similar schedule with higher fees. This report also stated that no local bar association was bound by its recommendation for adoption of a minimum fee schedule. The defendants object on four grounds: that the evidence is irrelevant; that the reports are hearsay; that they are not properly authenticated, and that the originals are required, not copies obtained by grand jury subpoenas to several defendants.

2. The government calls Martha Washington to testify about the contact that she and her husband had with the lawyer Dolley Madison, one of the named defendants. Mrs. Washington is asked: "What happened when you spoke to Ms. Madison?" Her answer is: "She told me, 'One percent is the standard fee.'" All of the defendants object to the introduction of this evidence.

3. On cross-examination, the defense lawyer asks: "Didn't you tell your husband that you were shocked at his inviting Ms. Madison out to dinner, and didn't you

tell him that you couldn't stand Ms. Madison and that you wanted to see her pay for her improper conduct?" The government objects on the ground that the question calls for privileged information. Defense counsel also asks the following question: "Mrs. Washington, I show you a statement purporting to be written by you and to describe your conversation with Ms. Madison, which statement you made to my investigator. Is this your statement?" The answer is affirmative, and the lawyer asks: "In that statement, where the one percent fee that Ms. Madison indicated would be charged is described by you, is there any indication that the word 'standard' was used in connection with it?" The answer is "No, I must have forgotten to put it in." The defense lawyer now offers the written statement into evidence, and the government objects. If the defense lawyer had not asked Mrs. Washington about the statement on cross-examination, but instead had called the investigator who took the statement to testify about it as part of the defense case, would the statement be admissible?

4. Assuming that Mrs. Washington was contradicted by a prior inconsistent statement, can the government introduce evidence that Mrs. Washington has a good reputation in the community for truth and veracity? Could the government offer evidence of neighbors of Mrs. Washington who have known her for years and who hold the opinion that Mrs. Washington's character for truth telling is beyond question? What about evidence of her regular attendance at church and of her disciplining her children for telling lies? Evidence of her husband's renowned reputation as a truth teller, including a famous cherry tree incident? If character witnesses are permitted to testify as to Mrs. Washington's good character for truth-telling, can they be asked on cross-examination whether they have heard that Mrs. Washington was expelled from college for violating the honor system?

5. The government now wishes to call J. Hoover, the investigator who did most of the work in preparing the facts for trial. Mr. Hoover, if permitted, will relate a conversation with B. Arnold, an employee of the defendant firm, Burr & Hamilton, who said to Mr. Hoover: "Sure, we were involved in the price-fixing. It was the only way to get a decent living in the area. I know that my firm was willing to go along, as were all the firms." B. Arnold is head of the stenographic pool. An objection is made to this on the ground that it is hearsay. Should the testimony be allowed? Would it make any difference if B. Arnold is a senior partner in the law firm?

6. The government offers into evidence the complete investigative report compiled by J. Hoover. The report contains basic information concerning the local lawyers and their uniform one percent rate, a record of certain statements made by local lawyers to the investigator, opinions of the investigator concerning the common intent of the members of the bar, and finally findings of the investigator that price-fixing was indeed taking place in Mount Vernon. An objection is made that the report is hearsay, conclusory, opinion, and inadmissible.

7. In order to show the uniform nature of the charges for real estate work, the government seeks to introduce into evidence the billing records of the three law firms named as defendants. The records are offered in the form of a computer printout, since all three firms utilize a computer for billing purposes. It so happens that the three law firms share a computer, which is owned and run by "Computer International." The law firms send to the computer center a statement of hours worked and the rate per hour to be charged, or any percentage fee arrangement to be employed in a particular case. The computer center then codes the material and records it on keypunch cards, which are eventually processed on to

a tape. The documents offered at trial are printouts of the real estate transactions handled by each of the firms, which printouts were prepared for this litigation. An objection is made that these printouts are inadmissible hearsay. Should this objection be sustained? Could the court order a defendant to prepare a printout of real estate transactions without violating the constitutional rights of the defendant?

8. John Marshall, one of the defendants, engaged in negotiations with the government concerning his participation in price-fixing almost immediately upon learning that the government was considering filing an action against him and others. Unaware of whether the government intended to file a criminal or civil suit, Marshall made the following statement in one of the negotiating sessions: "I know I was wrong in agreeing to participate in the conspiracy. I'd like to do something to make up for my wrongdoing. If you agree not to prosecute me, I will agree to a consent order prohibiting price-fixing in the future, and I will testify for you in any action civil or criminal against any other defendant." The government accepted this offer. A consent agreement was entered. At trial, Marshall is called to testify for the government. During cross-examination, the defense wishes to inquire into the settlement between Marshall and the government. The government objects on the ground that settlement negotiations are protected against disclosure in court.

9. While Marshall is testifying, the government asks whether the defendants engaged in other price-fixing activities. Marshall responds that they did. In response to questioning by the government, Marshall explains that percentage fees of 30 percent in negligence cases and 40 percent in products liability cases, and flat fees of $150 in uncontested divorce actions and $50 for drafting a simple will were established at Bar Association meetings. The defense objects on the ground that the

complaint charges only price-fixing with respect to real estate. The government responds that the other crimes' evidence is admissible to show a modus operandi and to establish the illegal intent of the defendants.

10. To support Marshall's testimony, the government offers into evidence notes apparently written by Gov. Morris, an associate of the law firm of defendant Dolley Madison. The notes read as follows: "10/15/75—meeting of local bar. Dolley suggests that members be more careful in real estate transactions; suggests that they make sure that they get one percent of the selling price for their services. Discussion followed. James Monroe and Richard Lee support Dolley." Morris died before trial, and the defense objects to the introduction of the notes as hearsay. Morris had no official position with the Bar Association and did not record his notes for use by the Association. He recorded the notes at the direction of Dolley for her personal records. The government argues that the notes are business records, that they are past recollection recorded, that they are admissions, and that even if they are none of these things they are still admissible. What is the proper ruling?

11. The government also wishes to offer into evidence a typed summary of the events taking place during the 11/15/75 meeting of the local Bar Association. The government contends that the notes were made by Ben Franklin, an associate with Burr & Hamilton. Franklin is out of the country on business and will not return for a year. The government is unable to authenticate the typing on the note and to demonstrate that it came from Franklin's typewriter. But, the government tries another form of authentication. It asks Marshall, who is Franklin's best friend, whether Franklin was in the habit of typing out notes of Bar Association meetings. Marshall explains that he was, and that after every meeting of the Bar Association, Franklin

typed up the notes that he had taken during the meeting and placed them in the left hand bottom drawer of his office desk. The government offers six other typewritten summaries which were found in the same drawer as the summary of the 11/15/75 meeting to bolster the claim of regularity in the record-keeping. Should the evidence be admitted?

12. If the government had refused to enter into a consent agreement with Marshall, and had insisted instead upon Marshall's pleading guilty to a charge of conspiracy to fix prices, would any plea of guilty be admissible against Marshall if the Washingtons brought a separate civil suit against him for damages? What about a plea of nolo contendere? What about a judgment following a jury trial in which he was found guilty?

THE DEFENDANTS' CASE

13. The defendants wish to introduce into evidence character testimony to the effect that their character for honesty and law abidingness is excellent. Should this evidence be admitted?

14. Defendants ask the trial judge to take judicial notice of the fact that one percent of the selling price of a home is not an unreasonable charge for a real estate closing. Is this a proper subject for judicial notice? Could the Trial Judge, who practiced for 22 years in Mount Vernon before taking the bench eight years ago, take judicial notice of the fact that the bar has always shared information concerning prices?

15. One of the individual defendants, Richard Lee, testifies at trial that there was never any explicit or implicit agreement among the members of the Mount Vernon bar to fix prices. On cross-examination, this witness is asked: "In a meeting between you, your lawyer, and lawyers for the government, did you make the following statement, 'Nobody knew that the Goldfarb decision was going to come down. So we

fixed prices; no one intended to do anything wrong. Why don't we settle this matter for a reasonable sum or with a reasonable consent agreement?'" Objection is made that this statement, while possibly relevant, is barred because of a policy of encouraging settlement negotiations. Is this objection sound?

16. After testifying for the defense, Richard Lee is asked on cross-examination whether he previously had spoken to defense counsel about his upcoming testimony. The witness admits that he did speak with counsel in order to prepare for trial. The witness is then asked whether he reviewed any documents in order to sharpen his testimony at trial, and the witness indicates that he reviewed counsel's entire file in the case. The Assistant Attorney General trying the case then asks to see the file reviewed by the witness prior to taking the stand. An objection is made on the ground that the file is privileged. What is the proper ruling?

17. Lee is also asked whether he has ever been convicted of drunken driving, whether he has ever been charged with income tax evasion, whether he has ever been convicted of tax evasion, whether he has ever been suspended from the practice of law for commingling a client's money with his own. Objections are made to all these questions. Which, if any, are proper?

THE GOVERNMENT'S REBUTTAL

18. As part of the government's rebuttal case, it offers a tape recording made by Mr. Washington in one of his visits to the defendant James Monroe. Mr. Washington, it appears, secreted a tape recorder with him when he visited the lawyer. After recording the conversation, Mr. Washington kept the tape in his desk drawer until turning it over to the government about a month before trial. Numerous members of the Washington family, including seven children, had access to the drawer. A person employed to do cleaning duties also

had access to the drawer. Other guests may have had access as well. Mr. Washington is not an expert on tape recordings, and the machine that he used to record this particular conversation has been lost. Only the tape remains. The defense objects to the introduction of the evidence. Should it be admitted?

INDEX

References are to Pages

1221

DIRECT EVIDENCE
See also Relevance, Legal vs. logical relevance.
Definition, 150–151.

DIRECT EXAMINATION
Generally, 255–258.
Admissibility of evidence, 257.
Impeachment, 257–258.
Restrictions on, 255–256.
"Scope of direct rule", 256–257.

DIRECTED VERDICT
See also Burden of Persuasion; Burden of Producing Evidence; Judicial Notice; Presumptions.

DISCOVERY
See also Opinion Evidence, Expert opinion, Discovery of.
Generally, 114, 123–124.
Civil cases,
Depositions,
Generally, 115–119.
Motion to terminate or limit, 115.
Notice, 115.
Oral, 115–116.
Preserving testimony, 115–117.
Subpoena duces tecum, 114–115.
Written, 115–116.
Government reports, 112–113.
Interrogatories, 119–120.
Physical and mental examinations, 120–121.
Police reports, 112–113.
Requests for admissions, 121.
Requests for production, 120.
Scope of, generally, 114–115.
Work product, 121–122.
Criminal cases,
Generally, 124.
ABA standards, 126, 129–130, 133–134.
Arguments against, 124–125.
Arguments for, 125–126.
By grace, 127–128.
Depositions, 129–130.
To preserve testimony, 130.
Grand jury testimony, 130–131.
Interrogatories, 130.
Names and statements of witnesses, 128–129.
Physical and scientific evidence, 130.
Police reports, 112–113, 135–137.
Preliminary hearings, 131.
Prosecution's duty to disclose, 138–141.
Prosecution's right to discovery, 141–144, 882.
Notice of alibi rules, 142, 624.
Res gestae witness, 46.

DISCOVERY—Cont'd
Work product, 133–134, 143–144.
Ethical problems, 111–112.
Order compelling, 114–115.

DYING DECLARATIONS
See Hearsay, Exceptions, Dying declarations.

ERROR
See Appellate Review.

EXAMINATION OF WITNESSES
See also Cross-examination; Judge and Jury.
Form of question,
Leading, non-leading, 17–19, 52, 283–284, 326.
Form of testimony,
Narrative, 11–12.
Hostile witness, 18–19, 283–284, 620–621, 624–625.
Scope of examination, 52–53.

EXCITED UTTERANCES
See Hearsay, Exceptions, Excited utterances.

EXECUTIVE PRIVILEGE
See Privileges, Executive privilege.

EXPERT OPINION
See Opinion Evidence, Expert opinion.

EXPERT TESTIMONY
See also Opinion Evidence, Expert opinion.
Accused's right to, 132–133.

EYEWITNESS EVIDENCE
See also Relevance, Exclusionary rules, Habit and custom.
Generally, 167.
Experiments, 173–175.
Factors affecting perception and memory, 169–172.
Identification, generally, 167.
Lineups, 172–174.
Relationship to circumstantial evidence, 176.

FIRSTHAND KNOWLEDGE
See Witnesses, Firsthand knowledge.

FORMER TESTIMONY
See Confrontation Clause, Cross-examination, Prior judgments, Prior statements of witnesses; Hearsay, Exceptions, Former testimony.

†